Lecture Notes in Computer Science 9065

Commenced Publication in 1973
Founding and Former Series Editors:
Gerhard Goos, Juris Hartmanis, and Jan van Leeuwen

Editorial Board

More information about this series at http://www.springer.com/series/7410

Javier Lopez · Yongdong Wu (Eds.)

Information Security Practice and Experience

11th International Conference, ISPEC 2015
Beijing, China, May 5–8, 2015
Proceedings

 Springer

Editors
Javier Lopez
University of Malaga
Malaga
Spain

Yongdong Wu
Institute for Infocomm Research
Singapore
Singapore

ISSN 0302-9743   ISSN 1611-3349   (electronic)
Lecture Notes in Computer Science
ISBN 978-3-319-17532-4   ISBN 978-3-319-17533-1   (eBook)
DOI 10.1007/978-3-319-17533-1

Library of Congress Control Number: 2015935495

LNCS Sublibrary: SL4 – Security and Cryptology

Printed on acid-free paper

Springer International Publishing AG Switzerland is part of Springer Science+Business Media
(www.springer.com)

Preface

The 11th International Conference on Information Security Practice and Experience (ISPEC 2015) was held in Beijing, China, during May 5–8, 2015, and hosted by Beihang University, Beijing, China.

The ISPEC conference series is an established forum that brings together researchers and practitioners to provide a confluence of new information security technologies, including their applications and their integration with IT systems in various vertical sectors. In previous years, ISPEC has taken place in Singapore (2005), Hangzhou, China (2006), Hong Kong, China (2007), Sydney, Australia (2008), Xi'an, China (2009), Seoul, Korea (2010), Guangzhou, China (2011), Hangzhou, China (2012), Lanzhou, China (2013), and Fuzhou, China (2014). All the ISPEC papers were published by Springer in the Lecture Notes in Computer Science series.

Acceptance into the conference proceedings is very competitive. This year the conference received 117 anonymous submissions from 25 countries/regions. All the submissions were reviewed by experts in the relevant areas on the basis of their significance, novelty, technical quality, and practical impact. After careful reviews and intensive discussions by at least three reviewers, 38 papers were selected from 14 countries for presentation at the conference and inclusion in this Springer volume, with an acceptance rate of 32%. The accepted papers cover multiple topics in information security, from technologies to systems and applications. This state of affairs reflects the fact that the research areas covered by ISPEC are important to modern computing, where increased security, trust, safety, and reliability are required.

ISPEC 2015 was made possible by the joint effort of numerous people and organizations worldwide. There is a long list of people who volunteered their time and energy to put together the conference and who deserve special thanks. First and foremost, we are deeply grateful to all the PC members for their hard tasks of reading, commenting, debating, and finally selecting the papers. We are indebted to the PC's collective knowledge, wisdom, and effort, and we have learned a lot from the experience. The committee also used external reviewers to extend the expertise and ease the burden. We wish to thank all of them for assisting the PC in their particular areas of expertise. It was a truly nice experience to work with such talented and hard-working researchers. We also would like to express our appreciation to the keynote speakers: Prof. Robert Deng, Dr. Rene Peralta, and Prof. Kui Ren.

We are also very grateful to all the people whose work ensured a smooth organization process: Honorary Chairs Feng Bao and Weifeng Lv, General Chairs Qinghua Cao and Robert Deng, Organization Chair Zhoujun Li, Publication Chair Cristina Alcaraz, and Website designer Ying Qiu. Also, thanks to Ana Nieto for her help in the edition of the proceedings.

Last but certainly not least, our thanks go to all the authors, the attendees, and the sponsor Huawei International.

May 2015
Javier Lopez
Yongdong Wu

ISPEC 2015
11th Information Security Practice and Experience Conference

Beijing, China
May 5–8, 2015

Organized by
Beihang University, China

Honorary Chairs

Feng Bao	Huawei, Singapore
Weifeng LV	Beihang University, China

General Chairs

Qinghua Cao	Beihang University, China
Robert Deng	Singapore Management University, Singapore

Program Chairs

Javier Lopez	University of Málaga, Spain
Yongdong Wu	Institute for Infocomm Research, Singapore

Organization Chair

Zhoujun Li	Beihang University, China

Publicity Chair

Cristina Alcaraz	University of Málaga, Spain

Program Committee

Joonsang Baek	Khalifa University of Science, Technology and Research, UAE
David Chadwick	University of Kent, UK

Rei Safavi-Naini	University of Calgary, Canada
Kouichi Sakurai	Kyushu University, Japan
Pierangela Samarati	University of Milan, Italy
Wenchang Shi	Renmin University of China, China
Miguel Soriano	Universitat Politècnica de Catalunya, Spain
Chunhua Su	JAIST, Japan
Vivy Suhendra	Institute for Infocomm Research, Singapore
Hung-Min Sun	National Tsing Hua University, Taiwan
Shaohua Tang	South China University of Technology, China
Vrizlynn Thing	Institute for Infocomm Research, Singapore
Cong Wang	City University of Hong Kong, Hong Kong
Lingyu Wang	Concordia University, Canada
Guilin Wang	Huawei, Singapore
Huaxiong Wang	Nanyang Technological University, Singapore
Jian Weng	Jinan University, China
Zhuo Wei	Singapore Management University, Singapore
Qianhong Wu	Beihang University, China
Yang Xiang	Deakin University, Australia
Rui Xue	Chinese Academy of Sciences, China
Jeff Yan	Newcastle University, UK
Yanjiang Yang	Institute for Infocomm Research, Singapore
Moti Yung	Google, USA
Futai Zhang	Nanjing Normal University, China
Rui Zhang	Chinese Academy of Sciences, China
Yan Zhu	University of Science and Technology Beijing, China

External Reviewers

Ahmad Ahmad	Gurchetan Grewal
Sang-Yoon Chang	Haihua Gu
Jie Chen	Lei Hao
Zhigang Chen	Matt Henricksen
Yao Cheng	John Iliadis
Xingmin Cui	Ravi Jhawar
Jeroen Delvaux	Shaoquan Jiang
Hua Deng	Miltos Kandias
Michael Denzel	Xin Kang
Raushan Ara Dilruba	Li Ling Ko
Hiroshi Doi	Su Mon Kywe
Xinshu Dong	Hyung Tae Lee
Xiutao Feng	Juanru Li
Ivan Gazeau	Miya Liang
Maciej Gebala	Bei-Bei Liu
Jonathan Goh	Jia Liu

Jianghua Liu
Weiran Liu
Zhe Liu
Zhiqiang Liu
Hui Ma
Lianrong Ma
Suryadipta Majumdar
Xianping Mao
Antony Martin
Dan Martin
Shinichi Matsumoto
Lilian Mitrou
Andrzej Mizera
Seiichiro Mizoguchi
Dustin Moody
Daisuke Moriyama
Alexios Mylonas
Khoa Nguyen
Mihai Ordean
Jun Pang
Dimitrios Papamartzivanos
Sergio Pastrana

Baodong Qin
Elizabeth Quaglia
Evangelos Rekleitis
Panagiotis Rizomiliotis
Andrew Ruddick
Bagus Santoso
Hendra Saputra
Jae Hong Seo
Paria Shirani
Ben Smyth
George Stergiopoulos
Chunhua Su
Le Su
Guillermo Suarez-Tangil
Yang Sun
Gelareh Taban
Fei Tang
Aggeliki Tsohou
Nick Virvilis
Ding Wang
Grace Wang
Yujue Wang

Contents

System Security

Stream Cipher I

Analysis

Key Exchange Protocol

Elliptic Curve Cryptography

Stream Cipher II

Authentication

Attribute-Based Encryption

Mobile Security

Theory

Implementation

Privacy and Indistinguishability

System Security

Operating System Security Policy Hardening via Capability Dependency Graphs

Zhihui Han, Liang Cheng, Yang Zhang, and Dengguo Feng

Institute of Software, Chinese Academy of Sciences, Beijing, China
{hanzhihui,chengliang}@tca.iscas.ac.cn

Abstract. An operating system relies heavily on its access control mechanism to defend against various attacks. The complexities of modern access control mechanisms and the scale of possible configurations are often overwhelming to system administrators and software developers. Therefore, misconfigurations are very common and the security consequences are serious. It is very necessary to detect and eliminate these misconfigurations. We propose an automated and systematic approach to address how to correct the misconfigurations based on capability dependency graph generating and MaxSAT solving. Given the attacker's initial capabilities, we first automatically generate a capability dependency graph to describe attacker's potential capabilities and the dependency relationships among these capabilities. Based on the capability dependency graph, we then develop a solution to automate the task of hardening operating system security policy against multi-step attacks resulting from misconfigurations. In this solution, we first represent each capability obtained by an attacker as a propositional logic formula of initial conditions, and then transfer the policy hardening problem to a MaxSAT problem. Finally, we present a notation called normal capability loss to aid an administrator to select an optimal hardening solution leading to minimum system usability loss. We apply our approach to analyze misconfigurations in Ubuntu10.04 shipped with SELinux and study an attack case to evaluate the effectiveness of our approach.

Keywords: Operating System, Access Control, Security Policy Misconfigurations, Capability Dependency Graph, MaxSAT.

1 Introduction

Access control subsystem is the major mechanism to provide user isolation and protect operating systems against attacks from malicious users. Security policy is the set of access control configurations for security entities, including processes, file system, network ports, and user accounts. Security policy directly determines the security status of an operating system. A vulnerable security policy will make the access control mechanism to exist in name only and lead to serious security consequences. Therefore, it is important to analyze and detect vulnerabilities in security policy configurations. And more important, detected vulnerabilities should be well fixed to make the security policy more secure.

© Springer International Publishing Switzerland 2015
J. Lopez and Y. Wu (Eds.): ISPEC 2015, LNCS 9065, pp. 3–17, 2015.
DOI: 10.1007/978-3-319-17533-1_1

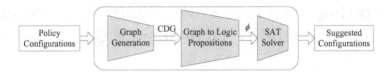

Fig. 1. Solution Overview

Existing approaches in operating system security policy analysis, such as Vul-SAN [2], WACCA [1], ACQE [7], can identify all possible attack paths leading to privilege escalation and output them in a graph structure or some patterns. However, while attack graphs or attack patterns reveal the security threats, they do not directly identify the root causes of attack paths and no systematic solutions exist to correct security policy to eliminate the detected attack paths. Since the number of attack paths is huge, it is impossible for an administrator to manually check and correct possible misconfigurations.

In this paper, we focus on solving security problems caused by access control misconfigurations and propose a systematic solution to aid administrators or root users in hardening their security policies, shown in Fig. 1. Since a major functionality of access control is to provide user isolation and privilege escalation is the precondition for most attacks, we target at privilege escalation attack. A privilege escalation attack is a multi-step attack, in which each step gains some additional capabilities and prepares for the next. Given the attacker's initial capabilities, our approach first generates a capability dependency graph (CDG), which describes all possible transitions of capabilities and intuitively illustrates all possible capabilities the attacker can obtain under the constraint of current (problematic) security policy configurations. Then, for each capability in the capability dependency graph, we compute a propositional logic formula, which describes the relationship between the capability and security policy configurations. Finally, we construct a Boolean formula ϕ in conjunctive form by adding negations of the logic formulas which represent privileged capabilities. The formula ϕ means disabling all privileged capabilities. And the security policy hardening problem is converted to finding a model of ϕ.

There may be multiple hardening options, and different option penalizes the system with different usability cost. We design an algorithm to generate an optimal solution leading to minimum capability loss. Our algorithm adds some additional constraints to the formula ϕ to guide a SAT solver to derive a satisfying solution with minimum usability loss. Our hardening solution is easy to enforce because the hardening options only require disabling some independent initial conditions. Our contributions are as follows:

- We propose the concept of capability dependency graph to intuitively describe all possible dependency relationships among user's potential capabilities. A capability dependency graph can reveal threats by enumerating possible alternate sequences of actions and capabilities.
- We present a logic-based process to automatically generate a capability dependency graph with specifying some capabilities and a set of atomic actions to obtain these capabilities.

- We design an algorithm to transfer each node in a capability dependency graph to a propositional logic formula of initial conditions. Based on these logic formulas, we give out a group MaxSAT-based approach to compute a solution leading to minimum capability loss, which hardens the security policy completely while decreasing minimum system usability.
- We implement a prototype based on our approach, and use the prototype to study the default configurations of Ubuntu 10.04 shipped with SELinux.

The rest of this paper is organized as follows. Section 2 provides the definition of capability dependency graph and presents the automatic process to generate a capability dependency graph. Section 3 states the security policy hardening problem and derives a solution with minimum capability cost based on SAT solving. Section 4 describes the implementation. Section 5 provides an experiment to illustrate the effectiveness and performance of our method. Section 6 is dedicated to related work. Finally, section 7 concludes the paper.

2   Capability Dependency Graph

Capability dependency graphs represent prior knowledge about capabilities and their dependencies. A capability dependency graph describes the pre-conditions required for each action and resulting post-conditions, illustrating all possible means how an attacker compromises the system. The misconfiguration detection and solution are conducted on the graph.

2.1   Definition

Definition 1. A **capability dependency graph** is a directed graph $G = (C_0 \cup C_d, A, E)$, where C_0 is the set of *initial vertices* which can be divided into initial condition nodes and initial capability nodes, C_d is the set of *intermediate vertices* indicating the reachable vertices from initial vertices, A is the set of *action vertices*, E is the set of directed edges, and $E \subseteq ((C_0 \cup C_d) \times A) \cup (A \times C_d)$, $(C_0 \cup C_d) \times A$ is a *require* relation and $A \times C_d$ is an *imply* relation.

There are two types of directed edges that inter-connect different types of vertices. First, an edge can point from an initial or intermediate vertex to an action vertex. Such an edge denotes the require relation, which means the action cannot be executed unless the pre-condition is satisfied. Second, an edge pointing from an action vertex to an intermediate vertex denotes the imply relation, which means executing the action will lead to the post-condition.

2.2   Generating a Capability Dependency Graph

To generate a capability dependency graph, we begin with specifying a set of capabilities that an attacker can get in a system. A capability is essentially a combination of its nature and the objects to which it applies. Since processes and files are mostly exploited to achieve privilege escalation attacks, we consider the following capabilities related to processes and files in our research:

1) control_process_code(proc(*Uid, Gid, Domain*)). The attacker controls a process with security context proc(*Uid, Gid, Domain*). This may happen because the attacker has a local account, or because the attacker exploits or launches a program to further control another process.
2) control_network_input(*Port*). The attacker can access the system remotely through the port *Port*. This is an initial capability for a remote attacker.
3) control_file_data(*FileName*). The attacker controls the data of a file.

In order to achieve attacks, an attacker begins with his initial capabilities, and tries to execute some actions to obtain new capabilities. We specify deriving rules to model attacker's atomic actions, which describe the transition relationship between different capabilities. Each atomic action takes the format of (*pre-conditions, action, new capability*), where *pre-conditions* define the pre-conditions of *action*, and they consist of capabilities and security configurations that must be satisfied, and *new capability* is the capability endowed by the access control mechanism after *action* is taken. The atomic actions considered in our research are listed in Table 1.

Table 1. Atomic Actions Overview

Action	Description
WaitExecute(Program)	The attacker waits a program executed in some process to be executed again with the same security context.
CompromiseRead(Process, FileName)	The attacker writes a file that a process is reading to compromise a process.
CompromiseNetwork(Process, Port)	The remote attacker sends malicious packets to compromise a network process.
HopeExecute(Program)	A program is hoped to be executed by privileged users.
Execute(Program)	The attacker executes a program.
WriteFile(FileName)	The attacker writes a file.

An important purpose of access control is to prevent against privilege escalation attack even if a vulnerable program is compromised. Therefore, we introduce "what if" analysis to the specifications of atomic actions, we assume that a program might be compromised and exploited to execute arbitrary code.

After specifying the atomic actions, we collect the meta configurations of the target operating system, and encode them into the form of logic predicates. In particular, we also need to formalize the access control mechanism of the target operating system with logic programming language, which is presented as some Horn clauses. Finally, based on the configurations, specifications of atomic actions and the formalized access control mechanism, we build a capability dependency graph through a multi-step process as follows:

1) Search the action specifications to find atomic actions that are enabled by current capabilities under the constraint of configurations.
2) If an atomic action is identified in step 1, calculate the new capability defined in the post-condition of this action, and then construct a record in the form of (*pre-conditions, action, new capability*). If the record has not been generated, log this record.
3) Add the calculated capability to current capabilities, and repeat step 1 and step 2 until no new log record is generated.

Finally, we can generate a capability dependency graph by adding edges pointing from each *pre-condition* to *action*, and from *action* to *new capability*.

However, there might be cycles in the graph, which introduces infinite loops into further analysis over the graph. Examining the graph, we find that it is the actions *Execute* and *WriteFile* that introduce cycles into the graph because these two actions allow a security context to transfer to the same security context, which is a secure transition and make none security threat. In order to avoid cycles, we add some additional restricts to filter such kind of transitions.

One important feature of capability dependency graphs is that the require relation is always conjunctive, whereas the imply relation is always disjunctive. More specifically, an action cannot be performed until all of its pre-conditions have been satisfied, whereas a capability is satisfied if any of executed actions implies the capability. However, an action may require different sets of conditions, whence the require relation for this action is disjunctive between these sets of conditions. We handle this case by constructing a separate vertex for each variant of the action so that the require relation for each variation is still strictly conjunctive. In particular, actions with different pre-conditions and post-conditions are always labeled as distinct vertices.

In the graph, vertices representing privileged capabilities are called *goal nodes*, such as control a process of root user. Attack paths from initial capabilities to goal nodes indicate how an unprivileged attacker obtains privileged capabilities. We hope to find a solution to disable these attack paths.

3   Deriving Solutions to Harden the Security Policy

Intuitively, we aim to find out the causality relationships between goal nodes and the current problematic configurations, and disable the goal nodes by changing associated configurations. The problem we are going to solve becomes *which initial conditions should be changed to disable attacker's goal nodes*. It is impossible and error-prone to manually deal with an actual capability dependency graph with hundreds of thousands vertices. We propose an automatic approach based on advanced SAT solving techniques to refine security policy configurations. Our approach can automatically suggest optimal configuration changes to address the security problem within the context of usability requirements.

3.1   Transforming Capability Dependency Graphs to Logic Propositions

We first extract causality relationships between intermediate vertices and initial vertices and express them as propositional logic formulas. In a capability dependency graph, the require relation can be expressed in conjunctive form, whereas the imply relation can be expressed in disjunctive form. Therefore, an action vertex can always be represented as a conjunctive form of all its predecessor condition vertices, and a condition vertex can always be represented as a disjunctive form of all its predecessor action vertices. Initializing initial condition vertices as atomic proposition variables, we search the capability dependency graph to generate propositional logic formulas for every action vertex and intermediate capability vertex with these variables. In particular, we do not use original configurations of access control directly as initial vertices, but use a one-to-one relationship to describe a single access ability that a subject can apply over an object, such as "*dac_can_access(Uid, Gid, FileName, FileType, write)*". This one-to-one relationship can help us to identify the configuration error more precisely. Algorithm 1 and Algorithm 2 describe the procedure to generate propositional logic formulas.

Algorithm 1. GenerateFormulas

Input: G {capability dependency graph}, $initCapaNodes$ {set of initial capability vertices}, $initCondNodes$ {set of initial condition vertices}
Output: $formulaMap$ {map of generated propositional logic formulas, ⟨vertex, formula⟩},
Uses: $queue$ {queue of graph vertices}
1. **for all** vertex $v \in initCapaNodes$ **do**
2. $G.removeVertex(v)$
3. **end for**
   //Initialize the initial conditions as Boolean variables
4. **for all** vertex $v \in initCondNodes$ **do**
5. $formulaMap.put(v, v)$
6. **end for**
7. **for all** vertex v encountered while breadth-first search **do**
8. $Process(v)$
9. **end for**
10. **while** $queue$ is not empty **do**
11.   Let $v = queue.removeFirst()$
12. $Process(v)$
13. **end while**

Algorithm 2. Process(v)

Input: G, $initCondNodes$, $formulaMap$, $queue$ (defined in Algorithm 1)
Output: $formulaMap$, $queue$
1. **if** v is a condition vertex and $v \notin initCondNodes$ **then**
2.   Let $S_a = \{a_1, a_2, ..., a_n\}$ be the action vertices pointing to v in G
3.   **if** $S_a \subseteq formulaMap.keyset()$ **then**
4.   Let $T = (a_1 \vee a_2 \vee ... \vee a_n)$
5. $formulaMap.put(v, T)$
6.   **else**
7. $queue.add(v)$
8.   **end if**
9. **end if**
10. **if** v is an action vertex **then**
11.   Let $S_c = \{c_1, c_2, ..., c_n\}$ be the condition vertices pointing to v in G
12.   **if** $S_c \subseteq formulaMap.keyset()$ **then**
13.   Let $T = (c_1 \wedge c_2 \wedge ... \wedge c_n)$
14. $formulaMap.put(v, T)$
15.   **else**
16. $queue.add(v)$
17.   **end if**
18. **end if**

In Algorithm 1, the first three lines remove initial capability vertices and their associated edges from a capability dependency graph because they are what we protect and should not be changed. The next three lines (lines 4-6) initialize every initial condition node as an atomic proposition variable. For the sake of clarity, we name every atomic proposition variable with the name of its associated vertex. The algorithm then traverses the capability dependency graph in a breadth-first manner to generate propositional logic formulas as many as possible (lines 7-9).

Each vertex reached during breadth-first search will be handled by Algorithm 2 (line 8). Lines 10-13 are used to iteratively generate formulas for the vertices whose formulas are not generated in the graph traversal.

Algorithm 2 is designed to generate formula for a vertex. The algorithm first determines the types of the vertex, lines 1-9 are used to deal with condition vertices and lines 10-18 are for action vertices. For each case, the formula for the vertex will be generated only if formulas of all its predecessor vertices have been generated. Otherwise, the vertex is stored in *queue* for further process.

Since there is no cycle in a capability dependency graph, the iterative process described in lines 10-13 of Algorithm 1 is converged and will stop stating that every vertex has associated with a formula.

3.2   The Security Policy Hardening Problem

Algorithm 1 and Algorithm 2 generate propositional logic formulas for all vertices, which also include the formulas for goal nodes. Assuming that the set of goal nodes in a capability dependency graph is C_g, $C_g = \{c_{g1}, c_{g2}, ..., c_{gn}\}$. The set of propositional logic formulas for goal nodes is P_g, $P_g = \{p_{g1}, p_{g2}, ..., p_{gn}\}$. We now can express the privilege escalation threats in the system by ψ, $\psi = p_{g1} \vee p_{g2} \vee ... \vee p_{gn}$. Our enhancing solution intends to eliminate all privilege escalation threats, so our aim can be expressed as $\phi = \neg\psi = \neg(p_{g1} \vee p_{g2} \vee ... \vee p_{gn}) = \neg p_{g1} \wedge \neg p_{g2} \wedge ... \wedge \neg p_{gn}$.

Therefore, the problem to harden security policy configurations can be converted to finding a model of ϕ. Seeking a satisfaction model of ϕ amounts to finding configuration settings that can prevent an attacker from gaining privileged capabilities. Every variable representing a configuration will be assigned T ("enabled") or F ("disabled"). If a variable is assigned F, it means that the corresponding configuration needs to be removed or disabled. There are multiple models for this formula, and we select an optimal one which not only disables all attack paths but also minimizes system usability loss.

3.3   A Minimum Cost Solution Based on SAT Solving

In order to select an optimal solution with minimum cost in multiple candidate models, we first need an approach to measure the cost of a solution which consists of multiple hardening measures.

In an operating system, it is a challenge for an administrator to assess the cost of an individual hardening measure, e.g., a configuration change. First, it is difficult to directly and separately assess the cost of a configuration change. Second, there are hundreds of thousands of configurations in a system and it is impossible for an administrator to manually assign a cost to each of them. Instead of assessing configuration changes individually, we propose a measurement method based on user's capabilities to automatically assess the cost of a hardening solution. Our method considers hardening measures not in isolation, but in combination. Some configuration changes may reduce system usability. In a given system, the usability can be described with user's capabilities.

We divide intermediate capability vertices into two types, normal capability nodes and privileged capability nodes. The intermediate capability vertices indicating goal nodes are called privileged capability nodes, and the rest of intermediate capability vertices are called normal capability nodes. A hardening solution must prevent privilege escalation attacks by disabling all privileged capability nodes, while it may have to disable some normal capability nodes, which we call *normal capability loss*.

Definition 2. Given a capability dependency graph G, the propositional logic formula to express the policy hardening problem is ϕ, S is a model of ϕ, the number of normal capability nodes in the graph is k and the set of associated formulas is $\{p_1, p_2, ..., p_k\}$, capability loss for ith capability node caused by S is denoted by $cost_i(S)$, and the normal capability loss resulting from S can be calculated with the following evaluation formula,

$$C = \sum_{i=1}^{k} cost_i(S), \ and \ cost_i(S) = \begin{cases} 1 & p_i(S) = false \\ 0 & p_i(S) = true \end{cases}$$

We expect such a model that minimizes the normal capability loss. It is impossible to iterate all models of ϕ to select the optimal model with minimum normal capability loss because resolving all models is NP-hard. For a real system, we could not get all models within acceptable time. Fortunately, our problem can benefit much from *Group MaxSAT* [8].

Group MaxSAT. A group MaxSAT formula is $\psi = \psi_H \cup G_S$ where ψ_H is a set of hard clauses and $G_S = \{(G_1, w_1), ..., (G_m, w_m)\}$ is a set of soft groups. Each group $(G_i, w_i) \in G_S$ is defined by a set of clauses $G_i = \{C_{i1}, ..., C_{ik}\}$ and a weight w_i. Any assignment that unsatisfies a subset of the clauses in a soft group (G_i, w_i) will be penalized with a unique cost of w_i. The objective of the group MaxSAT problem is to find an assignment that satisfies all hard clauses and minimizes the sum of weights of unsatisfied soft groups.

Our security policy hardening problem can be modeled as a group MaxSAT problem. Assuming that the security requirement is expressed as ϕ which is mentioned in section 3.2, and the set of propositional logic formulas for all normal capability nodes is P_s, $P_s = \{p_1, p_2, ..., p_k\}$. By applying De Morgan's law [11], we can convert the proposition ϕ and the propositional logic formulas in P_s to their conjunctive normal forms (CNF).

Given ϕ' representing the CNF of ϕ, $P_s' = \{p_1', p_2', ..., p_k'\}$ is the CNF set of P_s, policy hardening problem ψ can be represented as group MaxSAT, $\psi = \phi' \cup G_S$, where $G_S = \{(p_1', 1), (p_2', 1), ..., (p_k', 1)\}$. It can also be expressed intuitively with following formula, $\psi = (\phi', \infty) \land (p_1', 1) \land (p_2', 1) \land ... \land (p_k', 1)$, where the weight ∞ means ϕ' must be satisfied. A model of ψ is such an assignment that satisfies ϕ' and minimizes the number of unsatisfied CNFs in G_S.

Group MaxSAT has been thoroughly studied by the SAT solving community [20], [8]. Although the problem is NP-hard, modern SAT solvers have been very successful in practice, being able to handle Boolean formulas with millions of variables and clauses in seconds.

4   Implementation

Our prototype consists of three components: *Capability Dependency Graph Generator, Graph Translator* and *SAT Solver*.

The Capability Dependency Graph Generator first scans the host system and collects current system information and meta configurations of access control. All the collected information is encoded into Prolog fact. All specifications of atomic actions are encoded to Prolog deriving rules. Table 2 summarizes the deriving rules for Ubuntu with SELinux. In our implementation, we consider two types of privilege escalation attacks. The first type is that a local attacker with an unprivileged local account wants to control a privileged process, and his initial capability can be presented as *control_process_code(Proc)*, where *Proc* is the security context of an unprivileged local user. The second type is that a remote attacker who can access the targeted host through a network port wants to control a privileged process, and his capability is indicated with *control_network_input(Port)*. After initializing attacker's initial capabilities, we use the following Prolog rule to start the Capability Dependency Graph generation:

search :- control_process_code(_Proc), fail.

The Capability Dependency Graph Generator is implemented with 100 lines of bash scripts, 500 lines of Prolog code and 450 lines of Java code.

Table 2. Deriving Rules of Atomic Actions for SELinux

Capability	Pre-conditions	Action
control_process_code(proc(Uid, Gid, Domain))	process_running(Pid, Uid, Gid, Program, User, Role, Domain) control_file_data(Program)	WaitExecute(Program)
control_process_code(proc(Uid, Gid, Domain))	process_reading(Pid, FileName) control_file_data(FileName) process_running(Pid, Uid, Gid, Program, User, Role, Domain)	CompromiseRead(Program, FileName)
control_process_code(proc(Uid, Gid, Domain))	control_network_input(Port) receiving_data(Program, Port) process_running(Pid, Uid, Gid, Program, User, Role, Domain)	CompromiseNetwork (Program, Port)
control_process_code(*)	is_executable(Program) control_file_data(Program)	HopeExecute(Program)
control_process_code(proc(Uid, Gid, Domain))	user_info(TestUser, OldUid, OldGid) process_running(_, OldUid, OldGid, _, _, _, Old-Domain) is_executable(Program) dac_can_execute(OldUid, OldGid, Program) dac_execv(OldUid, OldGid, Uid, Gid, Program) se_can_execute(OldDomain, Program, Domain) privilege_enhancing(OldUid, OldGid, OldDomain, Uid, Gid, Domain)	Execute(Program)
control_file_data(FileName)	control_process_code(proc(Uid, Gid, Domain)) dac_can_access(Uid, Gid, FileName, FileType, write) se_can_access(Domain, FileName, write)	WriteFile(FileName)

The wildcard of * means that the value can be manipulated by the attacker.

The Graph Translator demands three inputs: a capability dependency graph, the initial capabilities and the goal nodes. All vertices whose in-degrees are 0 represent security configurations, which are declared as Boolean variables. The Graph

Translator traverses the capability dependency graph in a breadth-first manner to calculate propositional logic formulas for each vertex. The goal nodes are specified in an input file where an administrator declares the capabilities to be disabled. In our implementation, we focus on the privileged capabilities. The Graph Translator consists of about 1000 lines of Java code.

The SAT Solver is implemented on the top of Sat4j [12]. It first constructs the final group MaxSAT expression discussed in Section 3.3, and computes all the maximal satisfiable subsets (MSS). By computing the normal capability loss for each MSS, it selects the MSS with minimum capability loss. Then, it reconstructs a SAT expression with the formulas included in the selected MSS, which is satisfiable. Finally, it solves the new SAT expression and gets an optimal model. The SAT Solver is implemented with about 500 lines of Java code.

5   Experiment and Evaluation

To evaluate the effectiveness and performance, we applied our approach to a real operating system to enhance the security policy, including both DAC and MAC meta configurations. The operating system we selected is Ubuntu10.04 with the standard targeted SElinux policy enabled, where the version of the policy is *selinux-policy-ubuntu_0.2.20091117-0ubuntu1*. During the experiment, we install and run some common software in the system, namely openssh-server, apache-server, mysql-server, bind, filezilla, firefox and adobe reader, and use the default security policy configurations when the system is installed. In our experiment, the part of system information collection is conducted on a virtual machine running Ubuntu 10.04 Desktop with SELinux enabled, and the other parts of our experiment are conducted on a Windows machine with Intel(R) Core(TM) i7-4770 3.40 GHz 3.40 GHz CPU, with 8GB memory, and running Windows 7.

5.1   Experiment Results

In the experiment, the Graph Generator takes about 10 minutes to scan and collect relevant information, with most of the time spent on file system scanning, and it takes approximately 30 minutes to generate a capability dependency graph by Prolog's built-in interpretation engine.

The capability dependency graph consists of 815 graph nodes and 922 graph edges, including 207 action vertices, 117 capability vertices, 18 initial capability vertices and 8 goal nodes. The goal nodes can be represented as the control of a process such that (1)the security context is "*", or (2) the security context contains the SID of root user. We search the capability dependency graph to enumerate all attack paths, each of which is an alternate sequence of capabilities and actions starting from an initial node and ending with a goal node. We find 355 attack paths, where 34 are local attacks and 355 are remote attacks.

To block these attack paths, our prototype traverses the capability dependency graph to construct a group MaxSAT expression. Then it solves the expression with our SAT solver and gets a satisfaction model. Information of the group MaxSAT expression and the time consumed for the whole process from graph generating to SAT solving are list in Table 3.

Table 3. Group MaxSAT

# variables	# clauses	# T	# F	cost	time(sec)
343	644	192	151	16	<3

Although there are large numbers of initial conditions in the capability dependency graph, only 343 of them are related to privilege escalation attacks. From Table 3, we can see that our prototype gives 151 suggested configurations, which are indicated with F assignment. The 151 configurations involve 53 files, and all of these 53 files are executable files. Every one of them is somewhere on one or more attack paths. By disabling these configurations, none of the detected attack paths is enabled. Based on the involved privileges, all the 151 configurations can be divided into 6 groups listed in Table 4.

Table 4. Configuration Groups

5	receiving_data(Program, Port)
15	dac_can_access(Uid, Gid, FileName, FileType, write)
38	dac_can_execute(Uid, Gid, Program)
38	dac_execv(OldUid, OldGid, Uid, Gid, Program)
15	se_can_access(Domain, FileName, write)
40	se_can_execute(OldDomain, Program, Domain)

The recommended configurations are easy to be enforced by the administrator (root user). Configuration *receiving_data(Program, Port)* can be corrected by forbidding *program* to connect to network.

It is easy for the administrator to enforce the recommendations by modifying the security attributes of related files or programs. To correct *dac_can_access(Uid, Gid, FileName, FileType, write)*, the administrator just needs to remove the user's write permission, whose DAC context is *(Uid, Gid)*, from the file *FileName*'s ACL. *dac_can_execute(Uid, Gid, Program)* is the variant of *dac_can_access*, so its correction is similar with that of *dac_can_access* but to remove the execute permission. The configuration *dac_execv(OldUid, OldGid, Uid, Gid, Program)* is due to abuse of setuid or setgid, to correct this configuration, the administrator can disable the setuid flag or setgid flag. For example, if *Uid* is not equal to *OldUid*, the administrator should disable the setuid flag.

To correct the *se_can_access(Domain, FileName, write)*, the administrator has to modify the policy file to remove the write privilege over the type of *FileName* from *Domain*'s privilege list. *se_can_execute(OldDomain, Program, Domain)* indicates a domain transition. To disable this domain transition, the administrator can declare a Boolean to guard this transition and turn it off.

Disabling the 151 configurations will lose 16 normal capabilities for benign users whose initial capabilities are the same as the attackers. 15 of the 16 lost capabilities are *control_file_data* type, and the other one is *control_process_code* type. 15 files are involved in the 15 *control_file_data* configurations, where 12 of them are shell scripts used to collect system configurations in our experiment and another 3 files are executable files owned by other accounts. Fortunately, it seems that removing these capabilities is not harmful for normal users. The *control_process_code* configuration is *control_process_code(proc(33,33,unconfined_t))*, where *proc(33,33,unconfined_t)* is the security context of *apache2* process. Blocking this capability seems not harmful for a normal user since *apache2* is often launched by privileged users but not unprivileged users.

5.2   A Case Study

In this section, we present a case study to demonstrate how our computed recommendation prevents privilege escalation attacks. Figure 2 is a subgraph of the generated capability dependency graph, which presents a remote attack path related to mysql process. This path is a classic instance of Trojan attack. A remote attack is able to compromise mysql process to execute arbitrary code by exploiting the vulnerability indicated with CVE-2012-5611, and then the attacker is allowed to write to local executable file *traverse.sh*. If it is executed by a privileged user, the attacker achieves privilege escalation. In particular, the file *traverse.sh* is executed by root users to scan file system, which is more likely to be exploited by the attacker.

Our prototype identifies that the root reason of this attack is that write permission of this file is granted to other group. The recommended configuration is marked with big arrow, which should be disabled. After the marked configuration is disabled, the attacker is prevented from writing the file and the attack path is blocked.

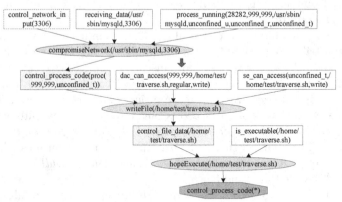

Fig. 2. A Subgraph of the Capability Dependency Graph

5.3   Discussion

In our approach, we adopt "what is" analysis to assume that a program might be compromised and exploited to execute arbitrary code. This is an extreme assumption, but it is an advantage to the system protection because no one can ensure that a program is free of vulnerabilities and an objective of the access control subsystem is to protect the system as good as possible even if some programs are compromised.

On another hand, if an involved program is checked with addition program analysis to ensure that it is hard to be compromised, the related recommended configurations could not be enforced. For example, in Figure 2, if we can check that the process running */usr/sbin/mysqld* is difficult to be compromised, the related attack path is hardly to be performed successfully, and the related two recommendations are not necessary for these attack paths.

However, it is hard to ensure none vulnerabilities in executable files. Considering that disabling 16 capabilities is not harmful for a normal user, we think that enforcing the recommendations is a better choice.

Further more, our recommendation is not only to enhance the security of operating systems before attacks happen, but also can mitigate damage even if some programs are compromised and no security patches are released.

6   Related Work

Research on operating system security policy focuses on analyzing and measuring the protection quality provided by access control mechanisms. Govindavajhala and Appel [5] proposed a logical model to study the security of access control mechanism on Windows XP. Host MulVAL [6], [17], [16] is a vulnerability analysis framework to detect privilege escalation attacks. NETRA [14] is a tool to detect information flow vulnerabilities. VulSAN [2] is a tool to analyze and compare the quality of protection offered by different MAC systems. WACCA [1] is an automated tool to systematically analyze Windows configurations. SEAL [13] is a logic programming language and tool to model and analyze dynamic access control systems. ACQE [7] and ACVAL [3] quantify and compare the protection quality offered by different operating systems.

Unfortunately, all previous works do not offer an automated approach to find a solution to enhance security policy configurations in operating systems. We proposed a systematic methodology to automatically conduct a solution with minimum cost to harden security policy configurations. Our approach generated a capability dependency graph to compute suggested configurations. Even more, our approach is scalable, attack graphs generated by other tools, including host MulVAL, NETRA, VulSAN and WACCA can be input to our prototype with some modifications. The computed solution consists of only initial configurations, and it is easy for administrators to enforce the suggestion.

There are some works to address the problem of how to use attack graphs to better manage the security of network. Wang *et al.* [18] improved one-pass algorithm in deriving a logic proposition for given critical resources. [4] presents the use of a Fuzzy Cognitive Map to find attack scenarios causing worst impact on network security. Wang *et al.* [19] developed an approach to bridge vulnerability analysis with risk assessment in cost-aware enterprise networks. Steven *et al.* [15] used an efficient exploit dependency graph to compute a configuration with minimum cost. Homer and Ou [9] proposed a context-aware enterprise network security management to balance security and usability adopting SAT solving. Huang *et al.* [10] provided an approach to shift out the most critical portion of an attack graph through minimum-cost SAT solving.

Our approach distinguishes itself from existing approaches in the following aspects: 1. Our problem space is different, as we consider control of processes under different access control restrictions, rather than control of network-connected hosts. 2. In network-systems, building attack graphs involves manual construction of attack models and attack scenarios, limiting their use in practice. Through specifying deriving rules to describe user atomic actions, our approach automates the construction of attack scenarios and the generation of capability dependency graphs. 3. Previous SAT-based approaches require administrator to manually assign cost values to network configurations individually. However, it is an impossible task in an operating system since there are hundreds of thousands configurations. We proposed the notation of normal capability loss to automatically and comprehensively assess the security impact of security configurations, which helps an administrator to understand the security importance of a configuration set without assigning cost value. 4. Considering the comprehensive security impact of a configuration set, we proposed a group MaxSAT method to compute a security policy hardening solution leading to minimum usability loss.

As far as we know, we are the first to propose a systematic methodology to harden security policy configurations with group MaxSAT. We focus on operating systems and apply our prototype to study the DAC and MAC configurations on Ubuntu 10.04 shipped with SELinux.

7 Conclusions

In this paper, we have proposed a methodology where operating system security policy hardening problem can be converted to a propositional logic formula. Then using SAT solving technique, one can quickly correct misconfigurations that lead to multi-step privilege escalation attacks. Our approach can account for both security and usability requirements, through the adoption of modern SAT solving techniques such as group MaxSAT. We applied our approach to harden a real system, Ubuntu10.04 with SELinux enabled. The results illustrate that our approach is scalable and powerful enough to handle a real-world system, and effective to help administrators or privileged users to reconfigure their systems.

Acknowledgement. This work was supported in part by NSFC grant No. 61471344, NSFC grant No.61100227 and National 863 Program of China under Grant 2011AA01A203.

References

1. Chen, H., Li, N., Gates, C.S., Mao, Z.: Towards analyzing complex operating system access control configurations. In: Proceedings of the 15th ACM Symposium on Access Control Models and Technologies, pp. 13–22 (June 2010)

2. Chen, H., Li, N., Mao, Z.: Analyzing and comparing the protection quality of security enhanced operating systems. In: Proceedings of the 16th Network and Distributed System Security Symposium, NDSS 2009 (February 2009)
3. Cheng, L., Zhang, Y., Han, Z.: Quantitatively measure access control mechanisms across different operating systems. In: 2013 IEEE 7th International Conference on Software Security and Reliability (SERE), pp. 50–59. IEEE (2013)
4. Diamah, A., Mohammadian, M., Balachandran, B.M.: Network security evaluation method via attack graphs and fuzzy cognitive maps. In: Intelligent Decision Technologies, pp. 433–440. Springer (2012)
5. Govindavajhala, S., Appel, A.W.: Windows access control demystified. Technical report, Technical Report TR-744-06, Department of Computer Science, Princeton University (January 2006)
6. Govindavajhala, S., Appel, A.W.: Automatic configuration vulnerability analysis. Technical report, Technical Report TR-773-07, Department of Computer Science, Princeton University (February 2007)
7. Han, Z., Cheng, L., Zhang, Y., Feng, D.: Measuring and comparing the protection quality in different operating systems. In: Network and System Security, pp. 642–648. Springer (2013)
8. Heras, F., Morgado, A., Marques-Silva, J.: An empirical study of encodings for group maxsat. In: Advances in Artificial Intelligence, pp. 85–96. Springer (2012)
9. Homer, J., Ou, X.: Sat-solving approaches to context-aware enterprise network security management. IEEE Journal on Selected Areas in Communications 27(3), 315–322 (2009)
10. Huang, H., Zhang, S., Ou, X., Prakash, A., Sakallah, K.: Distilling critical attack graph surface iteratively through minimum-cost sat solving. In: Proceedings of the 27th Annual Computer Security Applications Conference, pp. 31–40. ACM (2011)
11. Huth, M., Ryan, M.: Logic in Computer Science: Modelling and reasoning about systems, 2nd edn. Cambridge University Press (2007)
12. Le Berre, D., Parrain, A., et al.: The sat4j library, release 2.2, system description. Journal on Satisfiability, Boolean Modeling and Computation 7, 59–64 (2010)
13. Naldurg, P., Raghavendra, K.R.: Seal: a logic programming framework for specifying and verifying access control models. In: Proceedings of the 16th ACM Symposium on Access Control Models and Technologies, pp. 83–92 (June 2011)
14. Naldurg, P., Schwoon, S., Rajamani, S.K., Lambert, J., Lambert, J.: Netra:seeing through access control. In: Proceedings of the 4th ACM Workshop on Formal Methods in Security Engineering, pp. 55–66 (2006)
15. Noel, S., Jajodia, S., O'Berry, B., Jacobs, M.: Efficient minimum-cost network hardening via exploit dependency graphs. In: 2003 Proceedings of the 19th Annual Computer Security Applications Conference, pp. 86–95. IEEE (2003)
16. Ou, X., Appel, A.W.: A logic-programming approach to network security analysis. Phd, Princeton University Princeton (2005)
17. Ou, X., Govindavajhala, S., Appel, A.W.: Mulval: A logic-based network security analyzer. In: USENIX Security (2005)
18. Wang, L., Noel, S., Jajodia, S.: Minimum-cost network hardening using attack graphs. Computer Communications 29(18), 3812–3824 (2006)
19. Wang, S., Zhang, Z., Kadobayashi, Y.: Exploring attack graph for cost-benefit security hardening: A probabilistic approach. Computers and Security 32, 158–169 (2013)
20. Zhu, Z., Li, C.-M., Manyà, F., Argelich, J.: A new encoding from minSAT into maxSAT. In: Milano, M. (ed.) CP 2012. LNCS, vol. 7514, pp. 455–463. Springer, Heidelberg (2012)

Expanding an Operating System's Working Space with a New Mode to Support Trust Measurement

Chenglong Wei, Wenchang Shi, Bo Qin, and Bin Liang

School of Information, Renmin University of China, Beijing, China
chenglwei@163.com, {wenchang,bo.qin,liangb}@ruc.edu.cn

Abstract. Integrity measurement for Operating Systems (OS) is of practical significance. To make a measurement trustworthy, it is essential to protect the Integrity Measurement Mechanisms (IMM). However, much is still to be done to this end. This paper tries to take a step forward to shoot the target. Firstly, it puts forward the concept of trust mode, which expands the working space of an OS from two-mode, consisting of user mode and kernel mode, to tri-mode, consisting of user mode, kernel mode and trust mode. The trust mode is of the highest privilege level, in which the Core Measurement Mechanism (CMM) of an OS is executed. The CMM is in charge of measuring the IMM, which is running in kernel mode. Even if the OS kernel is compromised, the CMM would work normally without interference. Then, the paper proposes an approach to building the trust mode. It also develops a prototype to implement the trust mode by fully utilizing potentialities of modern hardware.

Keywords: Tri-mode Operating System, Trust Mode; Integrity Measurement Mechanism Protection, Hardware Virtualization, Code Measurement.

1 Introduction

Integrity measurement for Operating Systems (OS) is a hot research topic and there have been many achievements. Modern computer systems are constructed hierarchically, which means that a lower layer has control over a higher layer. An OS is always sitting at the lowest layer and has the highest privilege level. The whole system is controlled by the OS. To ensure the security of a computer system, the trust of an OS is very important. From different perspectives, much work [1-3] has been done in discussing the support of an OS in building trusted computer systems. It can be shown that an OS kernel has an indispensable role in this aspect [4-5].

The protection of an Integrity Measurement Mechanism (IMM) is involved in all topics related to integrity measurement. The measurement issue of a system can be stated briefly as that an object is to be measured by a measurement mechanism. The essential idea is that the mechanism determines whether the object meets security or trust requirements of the system. Obviously, the conclusion about the security or trustworthiness of the object is made by the mechanism. To protect the mechanism is paramount. Otherwise, the conclusion would be unconvincing.

Integrity measurement for an OS is a similar case, where the IMM corresponds to the measurement mechanism and the OS corresponds to object. To make the

© Springer International Publishing Switzerland 2015
J. Lopez and Y. Wu (Eds.): ISPEC 2015, LNCS 9065, pp. 18–32, 2015.
DOI: 10.1007/978-3-319-17533-1_2

measurement conclusion credible, it is essential to protect the IMM. The difficulty is that in current system architecture, an OS kernel has the highest privilege level and can gain access to all software layers. How to protect an IMM from interference of an OS kernel under the control of an attacker is a key problem.

There are many research results about protection of an IMM, but satisfactory methods are still hard to find. In work [6-7], an IMM is implanted into the OS kernel or applications. This kind of IMM will be compromised if the OS kernel is corrupted. Special hardware is utilized to isolate an IMM in some work [8-9]. Although security of the IMM is improved, compatibility and flexibility of the systems are lost. Some other efforts [10-11] implement an IMM based on existing Virtual Machine Monitors (VMM) [12]. Although risks from an OS kernel can be avoided and no special hardware is needed, complexity of these existing VMMs may induce security problems [13-14].

To protect an IMM from interference of an OS kernel, this paper puts forward the concept of trust mode. Compatible with current OS design, the working space of an OS will be expanded from two-mode, consisting of user and kernel mode, to tri-mode, with trust mode being the third mode. The user mode is the same as the original OS design. The kernel mode is almost the same except that when some specific instructions are executed, it will be trapped into the trust mode. This kind of traps is triggered by hardware and completely transparent to kernel mode code. The trust mode is dedicated to run a new mechanism, called Core Measurement Mechanism (CMM). The CMM is used to ensure that the kernel mode IMM is trustworthy. The trust mode is at the highest privilege level and catches traps from the kernel mode. After a trap being handled, the execution flow is returned to the kernel mode.

The development of software is always lagging far behind hardware in computer systems. This paper fully utilizes potentialities of modern hardware and proposes an approach to building the trust mode for an OS. The CMM is designed to run in the trust mode, which has the highest privilege level. Even if the OS kernel is compromised, the CMM in trust mode would work normally without interference.

The main contributions of the paper are as follows.

- It puts forward the concept of trust mode to expand the working space of an OS from two-mode to tri-mode. It designs a CMM to run in trust mode to ensure the trustworthiness of the IMM running in kernel mode.
- It proposes an approach to building the trust mode and develops a prototype to implement the new mode by utilizing potentialities of modern hardware.
- It introduces the private page table technology to protect the trust mode CMM by memory remapping. The CMM runs in a private memory region that cannot be accessed by the OS kernel. However, memory belonging to the IMM can be mapped for the CMM to measure the integrity of the IMM.

The rest of the paper is organized as follows. Section 2 outines the problem we face. Section 3 introduces the design of the tri-mode architecture. Section 4 presents the way to build the trust mode for an OS. Section 5 shows how to implement the trust mode prototype. Section 6 evaluates the prototype. Section 7 discusses related work. The conclusion and future work will be given in section 8.

2   Problem Definition

We describe the threats we face at first, and then state the goals of our design to confront those threats.

2.1   Threat Model

We consider an attacker who controls everything in a computer system but the CPU, the memory controller, the main memory, a Trusted Platform Module (TPM) [15] and the buses that interconnect them.

We assume that the attacker can execute arbitrary code in kernel mode or user mode. The attacker can also access the system's DMA-capable devices, such as Firewire interface. Thus, the attacker may be able to read or write secrets in memory without modifying the legacy OS.

The traditional privilege structure of an OS leaves the attacker a chance to tamper with executing code of the OS kernel. Common manifestations of the attacker's abilities are rootkits and Trojans.

2.2   Design Goals

We have four design goals for the trust mode: (1) small code size, (2) no kernel code change, (3) no special hardware, and (4) the highest privilege level.

Small code size implies that we may ensure the trustworthiness of the trust mode by formal verification and manual audit. No kernel change means that commodity kernels can work directly above the trust mode without any modification. The third goal indicates that we are to fully utilize potentialities of modern commodity hardware to implement the trust mode. The last goal means that the trust mode has the highest privilege level and can work normally even if the OS kernel is compromised.

3   Design of the Tri-mode Architecture

Presented in this section is the conceptual design of the trust mode that is independent of any CPU or OS kernel. Expanding the working space of an OS from two-mode to tri-mode is to protect the kernel mode IMM. The CMM, a new mechanism, is added to the OS, which is to run in trust mode to ensure that the kernel mode IMM is trusted. Even if the OS kernel is compromised, the trust mode CMM can work normally.

Our architecture of a tri-mode OS is given as Fig. 1. Applications are executed in user mode and the OS kernel is executed in kernel mode. As with current design, interaction between user mode and kernel mode is implemented by system calls and interrupts.

The CMM runs in trust mode and possesses the highest privilege level. Interaction between kernel mode and trust mode is enforced by specific instructions. Execution of specific instructions in kernel mode will be trapped into trust mode. This kind of traps is triggered by hardware and completely transparent to the kernel mode. Under the

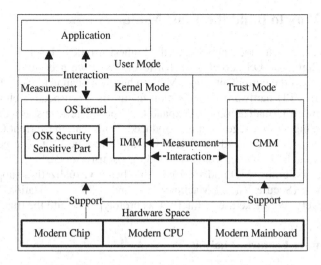

Fig. 1. Tri-mode OS Architecture

support of hardware, specific instructions executed in kernel mode are caught by the trust mode.

After a trap is handled, the execution flow will be returned to the kernel mode. Security sensitive parts of an OS kernel are measured by the IMM. The IMM is timely measured by the trust mode CMM. And problems are dealt with as soon as they are recognized. Even if an OS kernel is compromised, the CMM running at the highest privilege level can work normally without interference.

Our mission in this paper is to build the trust mode for an OS to protect the kernel mode IMM. To this end, the following objectives are to be reached.

- Fully utilize potentialities of modern hardware, hiding details of specific products and abstracting hardware features to support the trust mode.
- Based on hardware features, figure out a way to build the trust mode for the CMM to run separately from the OS kernel. The CMM has the ability to measure the IMM and avoid interference from the OS kernel and other software components.
- Enforce interaction between kernel- and trust-mode. Specific instructions cause kernel mode executions trapped into trust mode, in which the CMM measures the IMM. After that, the execution flow is sent back to kernel mode. Both the traps and the launch of the CMM are triggered by hardware.
- Carry out transfer of execution flows. Traps from user- into kernel-mode happen in way of system calls or interrupts. Transfer from kernel- to user mode occurs after relevant events. This is common transfer of execution flows. We focus on transfer between kernel- and trust-mode.

4   The Way to Build the Trust Mode

By definition, the trust mode must be of the highest privilege level. However, in the existing paradigm, the OS kernel is of that level. What we need to do is to create a new mode beyond the current situation. Modern hardware can help us to do that.

The modern CPU hardware virtualization feature is a prospective choice. The essence of hardware virtualization is to expand CPU privilege levels. Beyond the original ring 0-3, a higher privilege level is introduced. With that, the current OS paradigm with applications in ring 3 and the kernel in ring 0 may be kept. The new privilege level is in fact the highest one, which is sound for the trust mode.

Among others, both AMD and Intel have hardware virtualization supports, which are called SVM (Secure Virtual Machine) [16] and VT (Virtualization Technology) [17], respectively. We make use of Intel VT as prototype to build the trust mode.

4.1   Hardware Features Analysis

Intel VT includes VT-x, VT-D and VT-C that support virtualization of processor, chipset and network. We take VT-x as the fundamental to build the trust mode.

The basic idea of VT-x is to provide two kinds of processor operations, or VMX operations. One is called VMX root operation for running a VMM. The other is called VMX non-root operation for running guest software. Specific instructions executed in non-root operation state will be trapped into root operation state. After a trap is handled by root operations, code of non-root operations continues to run. VMCS (Virtual Machine Control Structure) is the core control unit of VT-x. It will be updated automatically by the CPU when transitions between non-root and root operations occur. When VMCS is initialized, configuration can be set for instructions to cause traps or not, so that guest software may be controlled by the VMM.

A set of instructions are introduced to manage VMX operations as shown in Table 1. Another 5 instructions are also introduced to manage and configure VMCS, which are VMREAD, VMWRITE, VMCLEAR, VMPTRLD and VMRTRST.

At a first glance, VT-x is designed to support processor virtualization architecture. It simplifies the design of a VMM and improves the performance of software-based virtualization. However, the essence of hardware virtualization is to expand privilege levels of CPU beyond the original ring 0-3 privilege levels.

In order for the CMM to ensure the trustworthiness of the IMM running in kernel mode, it is critical to run the CMM at a higher privilege level than the OS kernel.

Table 1. VMX management instructions

Instruction	Function
VMXON	Open VMX, put CPU in root operation
VMXOFF	Close VMX, CPU leaves VMX operation
VMCALL	Non-root operation guest calls VMM for service, transit to root operation
VMLAUNCH	Launch a VMM, transit to non-root operation
VMRESUME	Resume a VM, transit to non-root operation

A higher privilege level is introduced by Intel VT, which is a fundamental hardware support. With that privilege level is built the trust mode, in which the CMM is executed to avoid interference from an OS kernel. The CMM is in charge of checking the integrity of the IMM running in kernel mode.

Gaining insight into Intel VT, we found that it can be used to enhance the security of an OS in addition to supporting hardware virtualization. Creating a trust mode for an OS with the potential capabilities of modern hardware, we can execute the CMM in the highest privilege level to monitor the activities of security sensitive components running in kernel mode.

4.2   Building the Trust Mode

Based on the new operation state introduced by Intel VT, we can create a trust mode and give it the highest privilege level. It is a necessary mode to execute the CMM, whose responsibility is to check the kernel mode IMM. As being shown in Fig. 2, the working process of the prototype system includes building the trust mode and monitoring the kernel mode.

To build the trust mode, a trust mode module is loaded at a proper time during the launching of an OS. The first step is to enable hardware features (enter VMX operation). Then a specific structure (VMCS) is configured. There are two parameters in the structure that directly influence an execution flow. One is the return address (RIP_G) of the kernel mode and the other is the entrance address (RIP_H) of the trust mode. RIP_G is set to the next instruction right after loading the trust mode module. When hardware instruction VMLAUNCH is executed, the execution flow can be transferred to kernel mode to resume the execution of the OS from RIP_G.

When the kernel mode is being monitored, once specific instructions are executed, a trap into the trust mode will be triggered by the CPU. Then the execution flow will be transferred to the trust mode CMM at RIP_H. As a result, specific kernel mode instructions may be monitored by the CMM. After the trap caused by specific instructions is handled, the execution flow is returned to the kernel mode.

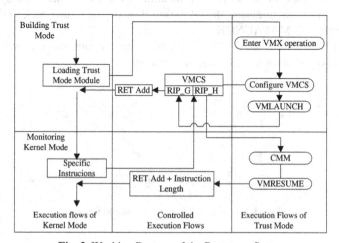

Fig. 2. Working Process of the Prototype System

5   Trust Mode Implementation

We developed a prototype to implement the trust mode concept in accordance with our approach. The prototype may carry out real-time monitoring of security sensitive parts of an OS kernel, including the IMM.

5.1   Interaction Between Kernel- and Trust-Mode

The higher privilege level introduced by Intel VT is the hardware fundamental for the creation of a trust mode. The first issue in utilizing the advanced hardware feature is to solve the problems of interaction between kernel mode and trust mode.

The advanced hardware feature to be utilized was originally designed to provide support for running a VMM. The life circle of a VMM and its guest software as well as interaction between them is illustrated in Fig. 3, which may be stated as follows.

a) A program enters the VMX operation state by executing the VMXON instruction. It then runs in the root operation state, or the trust mode.

b) When VMLAUNCH/VMRESUME is executed, the execution flow is transferred to a guest in non-root operation state, or the kernel mode.

c) Execution of specific instructions in a guest leads to trapping into the VMM in root operation state, or trust mode.

d) The VMM shuts down and leaves the VMX operation state by executing the VMXOFF instruction, which results in termination of the trust mode.

Interaction between root and non-root operation state is enforced through specific instructions. In the prototype, the first step the trust mode module takes is to enter the VMX root operation state, or trust mode, by executing VMXON. Then after VMCS having been configured, the execution flow is transferred to the non-root operation state, or kernel mode, as a result of VMLAUNCH being executed. The execution of specific kernel mode instructions will cause a trap into the trust mode. The integrity of security sensitive parts of an OS kernel, including the IMM, is measured by the trust mode CMM. After measurement, the execution flow can be turned back to the kernel mode as a result of VMALAUNCH.

In summary, it is by using VMX management instructions that the prototype enforces interaction between kernel mode and trust mode.

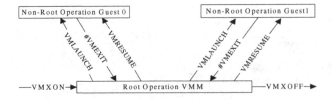

Fig. 3. Interaction between VMM and Guest

5.2   Handling Traps of Kernel Mode

Intel VT identifies two kinds of instructions that can cause traps into root operation state, or our trust mode. Some instructions cause traps unconditionally and others conditionally depending on the settings of VMCS. The way by which these instructions are handled is as follows.

a)   Handling instructions that cause traps unconditionally. Instruction CPUID and INVD are executed in trust mode. Other instructions, such as VMCLEAR, VMLAUNCH, VMPTRLD, VMPTRST, VMREAD, VMWRITE, VMRE-SUME, VMXOFF, VMXON, VMCALL, etc, are ignored and skipped directly.

b)   Handling instructions that cause traps conditionally. Instruction RDMSR, WRMSR and reading or writing of CR (Control Register) are executed in trust mode. Other instructions are ignored and skipped directly.

Taking instruction mov %eax, %cr3 as an example, machine code 0F 22 D8 is handled as follows.

a)   Get instruction address, i.e. RIP, from VMCS.
b)   Get instruction length, i.e. LEN, from VMCS, which is 3.
c)   Get Exit reason from VMCS, i.e. 0x0000001C, which means that traps are caused by reading or writing CR (Control Register).
d)   Get Exit Qualification from VMCS, where information such as writing CR is available. The number of CRs is 3. The source operand is stored in EAX.
e)   Execute mov %eax, %cr3 in trust mode.
f)   The return address in kernel mode is set to RIP + LEN, and then VMRE-SUME is executed to transfer control back to kernel mode.

Generally speaking, if a trapped instruction needs to be executed, it will be executed in trust mode. Otherwise, that instruction will be skipped. Finally, the original execution flow in kernel mode is restored.

5.3   Transfer of System Execution Flows

After the trust mode mechanism starts working, it is necessary to transfer back and forth between trust- and kernel-mode. The state of an OS, which is mainly related to general-purpose registers and flags register, must be saved before entering trust mode. The code for saving and restoring this state is shown as Fig. 4.

```
/* Store the state of OS */              /* Restore the state of OS */
asm volatile("pusha \n");                asm volatile("push GuestEFlags \n");
asm volatile("pop GuestEDI\n");          asm volatile("popf \n");
asm volatile("pop GuestESI \n");         asm volatile("push GuestEAX \n");
asm volatile("pop GuestEBP\n");          asm volatile("push GuestECX \n");
asm volatile("pop GuestESP\n");          asm volatile("push GuestEDX \n");
asm volatile("pop GuestEBX \n");         asm volatile("push GuestEBX \n");
asm volatile("pop GuestEDX \n");         asm volatile("push GuestESP \n");
asm volatile("pop GuestECX \n");         asm volatile("push GuestEBP \n");
asm volatile("pop GuestEAX\n");          asm volatile("push GuestESI \n");
asm volatile("pushf \n");                asm volatile("push GuestEDI \n");
asm volatile("pop GuestEFlags\n");       asm volatile("popa \n");
```

Fig. 4. Save and Restore the State of an OS

```
/* Code that sets stack frame */
push %ebp
mov %esp %ebp

/* Get return address for function with stack frame */
/* and return address is stored in ret_EIP */
push 0x4(%ebp);
pop ret_EIP;

/* Get return address for function without stack frame */
/* and return address is stored in ret_EIP */
pop ret_EIP;
push ret_EIP;
```

Fig. 5. Store return address in ret_EIP

The address of the instruction right after the one that invokes the trust mode module should be saved, so that the execution flow of the original OS can be restored after work in trust mode is finished. In our experiments, there exist two different cases. In one case, there is a stack frame before a function begins. In the other case, there is no stack frame. The code that gets return address is shown in Fig. 5.

After the trust mode is set up, the address for return to kernel mode, i.e. a field in VMCS, is set to ret_EIP. Therefore, the original execution flow will turn back to executing from the instruction right after the one that invokes the trust mode module when VMLAUNCH is executed.

In the process of monitoring kernel mode, when specific instructions are executed in kernel mode, a trap into trust mode, in which the CMM is executed, occurs. The CMM gets the address (RIP) and length (LEN) of the instruction that causes the trap. After the trap is handled, the address for return to kernel mode is set to RIP + LEN. So when VMRESUME is used to restore the execution in kernel mode, the execution flow goes on from the instruction next to the one that causes the trap.

5.4   Technology of Private Page Table

Memory is managed by the kernel in a legacy OS. The CMM is vulnerable if it can be accessed by the kernel. To protect CMM's memory from being tampered with by kernel mode code, a memory hiding mechanism is applied to conceal the trust mode CMM completely. On the contrary, the CMM must be able to measure the integrity of the kernel mode IMM. Therefore, memory belonging to the IMM has to be accessed by the CMM. The technology of private page table is used to fulfill these two goals.

The private page table technology, as shown in Fig. 6, patches the page table entries belonging to the CMM running in the OS kernel. It copies page tables of the CMM for private use in trust mode and then changes the page tables in kernel mode to refer to a spare physical memory. As a result, the OS kernel cannot access the memory area belonging to the CMM.

As to memory area allocated to the IMM, it is mapped for the CMM, because the integrity of the IMM must be measured by the CMM. As a result, the CMM is capable of accessing memory area of the IMM for the purpose of measurement.

Both trust mode and kernel mode have their own CR3 register, which points to the base address of their own page directory table. CR3 is stored in VMCS, it can

Page Tables of OS Kernel, CMM Memory is Hidden

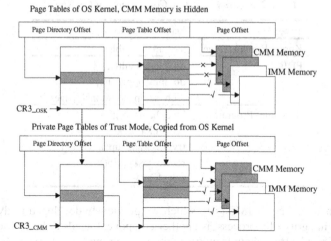

Fig. 6. Private Page Table Technology

be loaded automatically by the CPU when interaction between trust mode and kernel mode takes place.

6   Evaluation

The platform used for our prototype is a Thinkpad T400 with Intel Core2 Duo P8600 processor, 2GB RAM and a Trust Platform Mode (TPM). The operating system is Ubuntu 11.04. We evaluated the prototype with two metrics, i.e. effectiveness and performance, where the former stands for the ability of the trust mode CMM to measure the integrity of the kernel mode IMM.

To evaluate the effectiveness, we develop a kernel integrity measurement mechanism called OSKIM, which is an implementation of the IMM.

Here, we describe how to implement the OSKIM, introduce the protected function of the CMM, and demonstrate the performance cost of the prototype.

6.1   Design and Implementation of OSKIM

The OSKIM is responsible for measuring the integrity of security sensitive components of the OS kernel. In order for the OSKIM to get clear semantics of the OS kernel, it is implemented in kernel mode. The trustworthiness of the OSKIM, i.e. its integrity, is checked by the trust mode CMM at proper time.

Two design principles are set for the OSKIM, i.e. small code size and the least dependency on the OS kernel. As being implied by software engineering, small code size means fewer bugs. Less dependency on the OS kernel means that it is easier for the CMM to perform measurement. A TPM is fully used to help obtain the goals.

To implement the OSKIM, the following tasks should be undertaken.

1)   Extract security sensitive components from the OS kernel

Threat vectors should be taken into account. Kernel level rootkit is one of the most severe threats to an OS kernel. System call table is often tampered with by this kind of rootkits [18]. Consequently, it belongs to kernel security sensitive components.

Table 2. Security Sensitive Components of OS Kernel

Type	Data or functions
Kernel Rootkit Target	system call table

PDIMS	do_page_fault();
	do_mmap_pgoff();
	arch_setup_additional_pages();

Scheduler Program	load_balance();
	scheduler_tick();
	try_to_wake_up();
	recalc_task_prio():
	schedule():

A mechanism called PDIMS [19], which we previously developed to dynamically measure the integrity of a process, is another component needs to be considered. It is necessary to build a trust chain from trust mode to user mode as shown in Fig. 7.

The scheduler program in the OS kernel is of great importance to the OS, it is another component needs to be considered.

Listed in Table 2 are all presently considered security sensitive components of the OS kernel, which should be measured by the OSKIM. An interface is provided for users to dynamically add other security sensitive components as required.

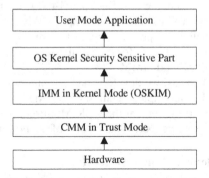

Fig. 7. Chain of trust from hardware to application

2)   Determine how to measure security sensitive components

The SHA-1 cryptographic hash function is used for measurement. To reduce code size and make hash function trustworthy, a hardware TPM is employed. Three TPM commands, i.e. TPM_SHA1Start, TPM_SHA1Update and TPM_SHA1Complete, are used to perform SHA-1 calculation. The first command starts an SHA-1 session. The second transfers data to the TPM. The third gets the result of the SHA-1 calculation.

3)   Get the start address and length of a security sensitive component

In a Linux-based prototype, kernel file System.map-xxx may be used to get the start address, or start_add, of a kernel component with the following commands.

```
cat /boot/System.map-xxx | grep security_sensitive_part
```

In the case of system call table, the length is a constant. Considering a kernel sensitive function, we can get the address next to its last instruction, or end_add, and take (end_add – start_add) as its length.

4)   Determine the time to run the OSKIM

The OSKIM is implemented as a kernel thread and runs at a proper time. For simplicity, the OSKIM may measure the security sensitive part of the OS kernel at a regular interval. Other policies may be used as well.

To enforce the measurement time policy, we need to get trustworthy time. As we presume that the kernel may be compromised, we have to get trustworthy time from other place. We use the hardware TPM to get a trusted time with the TPM_GetTicks command. A trusted time interval may be produced with the following code.

```
/* a kernel thread */
while(1) {
  measure integrity of kernel security sensitive part;
  startTicks = TPM_GetTicks();
  do {
      schedule();
      endTicks = TPM_GetTicks();
  } while(endTicks - startTicks < TIMEOUT);
}
```

6.2   Protected Functions of the CMM

Supported by the CPU, specific instructions may be caught by the trust mode CMM. Instructions caught by our prototype CMM include VMCLEAR, VMLAUNCH, VMPTRLD, VMPTRST, VMREAD, VMWRITE, VMRESUME, VMXOFF, VMXON, VMCALL, CPUID, INVD, RDMSR, WRMSR, reading or writing CR1, CR2, CR3, CR4, etc.

Experimental test shows that the trust mode mechanism we proposed can effectively monitor sensitive kernel mode operations and measure the integrity of the kernel mode IMM. Running in the highest privilege level and supported by memory protection mechanism, the CMM is of high security and reliability.

6.3   Performance Test Results

We used UnixBench version 5.1.3 to evaluate the performance cost of our prototype. As is shown in Fig. 8, the IMM has little influence on system performance. The overall performance degrades by 1.4% after the IMM is loaded. When the IMM and the CMM are both loaded, the Pipe-based Context Switching test is most heavily influenced by the prototype mechanism, with 51.5% of performance penalty, because the test contains lots of sensitive operations such as reading and writing CR3. Fortunately, with the IMM and the CMM in action, the overall system performance cost is about 8.9%, as shown by the last column in Fig. 8, which is acceptable.

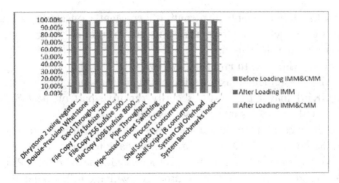

Fig. 8. UnixBench results

7   Related Work

To measure system integrity with hardware support is not a new idea. Dyad [20], BITS [21], AEGIS [22], IBM 4758 [8] and TPod [23] are representatives of earlier efforts that use hardware to support system integrity measurement. They focus on boot-time integrity measurement, not taking runtime integrity into consideration.

IMA [2] makes load-time integrity measurement for executable objects, which pushes a step forward from boot-time measurement. PRIMA [24] is an improvement on IMA. By introducing the CW-Lite access control model, it tries to dynamically measure system integrity with information flow being taken into account. Neither IMA nor PRIMA can provide effective way to protect measurement mechanisms.

Intel TXT [25], AMD SVM [16] and AMD TrustZone [26] are technologies that provide hardware support to system integrity measurement. Intel TXT is similar to AMD SVM. TrustZone is dedicated to embedded system platforms. These technologies may provide hardware features to be utilized by our work, which is on software mechanisms. We make use of Intel VT [17], which is a part of Intel TXT.

SecVisor [27] is a tiny hypervisor that ensures code integrity for OS kernels. It runs in the VMM privilege level that is higher than the kernel. It uses CPU-Based memory virtualization to implement isolation between monitor and OS kernel. To this point, our work is similar to SecVisor in some sense. However, SecVisor treats kernel code as a whole and does not identify security sensitive parts.

Flicker [28] is an architecture for isolating sensitive code execution with a minimal Trusted Computing Base. It utilizes hardware support of AMD SVM to create a completely isolated environment for security-sensitive code to run. It can provide attestation of the executed code to a remote party. It shows no concern on OS integrity, while OS kernel integrity monitoring is a key point of our work.

TrustVisor [29] is a special hypervisor that protects security sensitive code based on AMD SVM hardware features. It has three basic operating modes called Host mode, secure guest mode and legacy guest mode. Although our work is also involved with three modes, they are different from those of TrustVisor.

SIM [10] is a framework that monitor OS kernel based on Intel VT. It copes with a situation where a monitor and the OS kernel to be monitored coexist in the same guest VM. It implements isolation between a monitor and the OS kernel. The biggest problem of SIM is that it depends on VMM. Our work does not bother with VMM.

8   Conclusion and Future Work

Based on popular modern hardware features, this paper puts forward the concept of trust mode to expand the working space of an OS from two-mode, consisting of user mode and kernel mode, to tri-mode, with trust mode as the third newly added mode. It then proposes an approach to building the trust mode for an OS to monitor and protect the integrity measurement mechanism running in kernel mode. A prototype has been developed to implement the trust mode by fully utilizing potentialities of modern hardware, i.e. hardware-virtualization-enabled CPU and TPM. The effectiveness and performance of the trust mode are demonstrated with experiments.

To improve the performance of our prototype is one part of our future work. We are using multi-core technologies to enable measuring and measured entities to work in parallel so as to reduce performance cost. Since the code size of a trust mode mechanism (3500 lines of code) is small, we also want to use formal verification to prove the trustworthiness of the mechanism.

Acknowledgments. We would like to thank the anonymous reviewers for their insightful comments that helped improve the presentation of this paper. The work was supported in part by the National Natural Science Foundation of China under grant No. (61472429, 61070192, 91018008, 61303074, 61170240), Beijing Natural Science Foundation under grant No. 4122041, and National High-Tech Research Development Program of China under grant No. 2007AA01Z414.

References

1. Loscocco, P.A., Wilson, P.W., Pendergrass, J.A., et al.: Linux Kernel Integrity Measurement Using Contextual Inspection. In: 2007 ACM workshop on Scalable Trusted Computing, pp. 21–29. ACM Press, New York (2007)
2. Sailer, R., Zhang, X., Jaeger, T., et al.: Design and Implementation of a TCG-based Integrity Measurement Architecture. In: 13th USENIX Security Symposium, pp. 223–238 (2004)
3. Jaeger, T., Sailer, R., Shankar, U.: PRIMA: Policy-Reduced Integrity Measurement Architecture. In: 11th ACM Symposium on Access Control Models and Technologies, pp. 19–28. ACM Press, New York (2006)
4. Shi, W.: On Design of a Trusted Software Base with Support of TPCM. In: Chen, L., Yung, M. (eds.) INTRUST 2009. LNCS, vol. 6163, pp. 1–15. Springer, Heidelberg (2010)
5. Loscocco, P.A., Smalley, S.D., Muckelbauer, P.A., et al.: The Flawed Assumption of Security in Modern Computing Environments. In: 21st National Information Systems Security Conference, pp. 303–314 (1998)
6. Swift, M.M., Bershad, B.N., Levy, H.M.: Improving the Reliability of Commodity Operating Systems. ACM Transactions on Computer Systems 23(1), 77–110 (2005)
7. Venema, W.: Isolation Mechanisms for Commodity Applications and Platforms. IBM Technical Report, RC24725(W0901-048) (2009)
8. Dyer, J.G., Lindemann, M., Perez, R., et al.: Building the IBM 4758 Secure Coprocessor. IEEE Computer 34(10), 57–66 (2001)
9. Suh, G.E., Clarke, D., Gassend, B., et al.: AEGIS: Architecture for Tamper-Evident and Tamper-Resistant Processing. In: 17th Annual International Conference on Supercomputing (ICS 2003), pp. 160–171. ACM Press, New York (2003)

10. Sharif, M., Lee, W., Cui, W., et al.: Secure In-VM Monitoring Using Hardware Virtualiza-tion. In: 16th ACM Conference on Computer and Communications Security (CCS 2009), pp. 477–487. ACM Press, New York (2009)
11. Azab, A.M., Ning, P., Sezer, E.C., et al.: HIMA: A Hypervisor Based Integrity Measure-ment Agent. In: 25th Annual Computer Security Applications Conference (ACSAC 2009), pp. 461–470. IEEE Press (2009)
12. Rosenblum, M., Garfinkel, T.: Virtual Machine Monitors: Current Technology and Future Trends. IEEE Computer 38(5), 39–47 (2005)
13. Garfinkel, T., Rosenblum, M.: When Virtual is Harder than Real: Security Challenges in Virtual Machine Based Computing Environments. In: 10th USENIX Workshop on Hot Topics in Operating Systems. USENIX Press, Berkeley (2005)
14. Drepper, U.: The Cost of Virtualization. ACM QUEUE, 30–35 (January/February 2008)
15. TPM Main - Part 1 Design Principles - Specification Version 1.2. Trusted Computing Group (July 2007)
16. Advanced Micro Devices: AMD64 Virtualization: Secure Virtual Machine Architecture Reference Manual. AMD Publication, no.33047, rev. 3.01. (2005)
17. Neiger, G., Santoni, A., Leung, F.: Intel Virtualization Technology: Hardware Support for Efficient Processor Virtualization. Intel Technology Journal 10(03), 167–177 (2006)
18. Levine, J.F., Grizzard, J.B., Owen, H.L.: Detecting and Categorizing Kernel-Level Rootkits to Aid Future Detection. IEEE Security & Privacy 4(1), 24–32 (2006)
19. Wei, C., Song, S., Hua, W.: Operating Systems Support for Process Dynamic Integrity Measurement. In: IEEE Youth Conference on Information, Computing and Telecommuni-cation (YC-ICT 2009), pp. 339–342. IEEE Press (2009)
20. Tygar, J.D., Yee, B.: Dyad: A System for Using Physically Secure Coprocessors. Technic-al Report, CMU-CS-91-140R, Carnegie Mellon University (1991)
21. Clark, P.C., Hoffman, L.J.: BITS: A Smartcard Protected Operating System. Communica-tions of the ACM 37(11), 66–70, 94 (1994)
22. Arbaugh, W.A., Farber, D.J., Smith, J.M.: A Secure and Reliable Bootstrap Architecture. In: 1997 IEEE Symposium on Security and Privacy (S&P 1997), pp. 65–71 (1997)
23. Maruyama, H., Seliger, F., Nagaratnam, N., et al.: Trusted Platform on Demand. Technical Report, RT0564, IBM (2004)
24. Jaeger, T., Sailer, R., Shankar, U.: PRIMA: Policy-Reduced Integrity Measurement Archi-tecture. In: 11th ACM Symposium on Access Control Models and Technologies, pp. 19–28. ACM Press, New York (2006)
25. Intel Trusted Execution Technology - Software Development Guide - Measured Launched Environment Developer's Guide. Document Number: 315168-005, Intel (2008)
26. Alves, T., Felton, D.: TrustZone: Integrated Hardware and Software Security - Enabling Trusted Computing in Embedded Systems. Information Quarterly 3(4), 18–24 (2004)
27. Seshadri, A., Luk, M., Qu, N., et al.: SecVisor: A Tiny Hypervisor to Provide Lifetime Kernel Code Integrity for Commodity OSes. In: 21st ACM Symposium on Operating Sys-tems Principles (SOSP 2007), pp. 335–350. ACM Press, New York (2007)
28. McCune, J.M., Parno, B., Perrig, A.: Flicker: An Execution Infrastructure for TCB Mini-mization. In: ACM European Conference on Computer Systems, EuroSys 2008 (2008)
29. McCune, J.M., Li, Y., Qu, N., et al.: TrustVisor: Efficient TCB Reduction and Attestation. In: 2010 IEEE Symposium on Security and Privacy (SP 2010), pp. 143–158 (2010)

Stream Cipher I

Differential Fault Analysis of Streebog

Riham AlTawy and Amr M. Youssef

Concordia Institute for Information Systems Engineering,
Concordia University, Montréal, Québec, Canada

Abstract. In August 2012, the Streebog hash function was selected as
the new Russian federal hash function standard (GOST R 34.11-2012).
In this paper, we present a fault analysis attack on this new hashing
standard. In particular, our attack considers the compression function
in the secret key setting where both the input chaining value and the
message block are unknown. The fault model adopted is the one in which
an attacker is assumed to be able to cause a bit-flip at a random byte in
the internal state of the underlying cipher of the compression function.
We also consider the case where the position of the faulted byte can be
chosen by the attacker. In the sequel, we propose a two-stage approach
that recovers the two secret inputs of the compression function using
an average number of faults that varies between 338-1640, depending on
the assumptions of our employed fault model. Moreover, we show that
the attack can be extended to the iterated hash function using a feasible
pre-computation stage. Finally, we analyze Streebog in different MAC
settings and demonstrate how our attack can be used to recover the
secret key of HMAC/NMAC-GOST.

Keywords: Differential fault analysis, Hash functions, Cryptanalysis,
HMAC, NMAC, GOST R 34.11-2012, Streebog.

1 Introduction

Streebog is a Russian hash function that was originally proposed in 2010 [24]
as a replacement for the previous standard GOST R 34.11-94 which has been
theoretically broken in [26,25]. Later, in 2012, the Russian Federation Technical
Committee for Standardization (TC 26) announced Streebog as the new hash
standard GOST R 34.11-2012. The function supports digest sizes of 256 and 512
bits. The compression function employs a 12-round AES-like cipher with 8×8-
byte internal state. The compression function operates in Miyaguchi-Preneel
(MP) mode and is plugged in a modified Merkle-Damgård domain extender with
a modular checksum finalization step [1]. The new GOST is also standardized
by IETF as RFC 6896 [17].

Due to the significance of this standard, its security has been thoroughly investigated in a series of works appearing in a relatively short time. These works
include the analysis of the collision resistance of its compression function and
internal cipher by AlTawy et al. [2] and Wang et al. [30]. An integral analysis
of the compression function has been presented by AlTawy and Youssef where

© Springer International Publishing Switzerland 2015
J. Lopez and Y. Wu (Eds.): ISPEC 2015, LNCS 9065, pp. 35–49, 2015.
DOI: 10.1007/978-3-319-17533-1_3

integral distinguishers for the reduced compression function was proposed [3]. Moreover, preimage attacks on the reduced hash function have been independently proposed by Altawy and Youssef [4] and Zou *et al.* [31], and later the attacks were improved by Bingka *et al.* [23]. Also, Kazymyrov and Kazymyrova presented an analysis of the algebraic aspects of the function [19], and a long second preimage attack was proposed by Guo *et al.* [15]. Finally, a malicious version of the whole hash function was presented in [5].

In this work, we present a practical differential fault analysis attack (DFA) on Streebog. The attack considers the compression function when operating with secret inputs which is the default setting when the function is used in a message authentication code (MAC) scheme. In other words, we consider that both the input chaining value and message block are unknown and that we can only observe the output of the compression function. In the sequel, we propose a two-stage attack using the one-bit fault model where the attacker is able to cause a bit flip at a chosen or random byte in the internal state of the function. Employing a specific property of the Streebog Sbox and by observing several correct and faulty compression function outputs, the first stage of the attack bypasses the final feedforward and retrieves the state of the internal cipher. Since all inputs are unknown, the retrieved state does not allow us to invert the internal cipher of the compression function because its round keys are dependant on the input chaining value which is a secret. Accordingly, in the second stage of the attack, we recover one of the round keys which enables the recovery of both the chaining value and message block of the attacked compression function. To this end, we are restricted to the processing of the last compression function in the iterated hash function as it is the only one which we can observe both its correct and faulty outputs. For that, we employ two precomputed tables which allows us to extend the attack to the whole hash function. Finally, we analyze the GOST hash function in different MAC [7] settings and show how to use our attack to recover the secret MAC key of simple prefix and secret-IV MACs [27], HMAC, and NMAC [7].

The rest of the paper is organized as follows. In the next section, a brief overview on fault analysis attacks is given. The description of the Streebog hash function along with the notation used throughout the paper are provided in section 3. Afterwards, in section 4, we provide a detailed description of the used fault model, our two-stage approach, and show how to extend the attack from the compression function to the whole hash function. In section 5, we consider Streebog operating in different MAC settings and present the approaches used in the key recovery of simple prefix, secret-IV, HMAC, and NMAC. Simulation results and analysis of the number of required faults for different attack scenarios are given in section 6. Finally, the paper is concluded in section 7.

2 Fault Analysis

In mathematical attacks, such as differential and linear cryptanalysis, the attacker tries to exploit any weakness in the underlying mathematical structure of the cryptographic primitive. In fault analysis, which is an implementation dependant attack, the attacker faults the state of the primitive during its computation to deduce information about its secret material. In particular, the attacker applies some kind of physical intervention during the computation of the internal state of the primitive which corrupts random or known bits in the state. Consequently, the attacker observes the correct and the faulty outputs and performs differential fault analysis [9]. During this analysis, the attacker gains non negligible information about the secret material embedded in the hardware by comparing the correct and faulty outputs. Fault injection can be done in many ways which include power glitches, clock pulses, and laser radiation. The reader is referred to [28,12] for more details about the practical experimentation with different methods of fault injection.

Fault analysis was first introduced when Boneh *et al.* showed how the private key of the RSA-CRT-algorithm can be successfully recovered by observing the correct ciphertext and then injecting a fault and acquiring the faulty ciphertext [10]. Later on, Biham and Shamir combined fault analysis with differential cryptanalysis and presented differential fault analysis [9] against DES. Their attack works by observing the difference between the correct and faulty ciphertexts and exploiting this relation to recover the key of DES. DFA attacks have been used for the analysis of the hardware security of many ciphers (e.g., see [6,14,29]). In particular and due to its significance as a standard, AES has received a lot of attention with regards to DFA where some of the works used fault injection in the encryption process [29,14], and others attacked the key schedule [21]. DFA attacks vary in the number of required faults depending on the employed fault model. Generally, all models assume that the attacker has access to the physical device, and is able to reset the device to the same unknown initial settings as often as needed. Furthermore, different assumptions with respect to the amount of control the attacker has over the position and the Hamming weight of the induced faults are employed.

While most of the DFA work in the literature is targeted towards block and stream ciphers, only few researchers considered hash functions. This fact might seem logical at first glance because ciphers have a secret key input. On the other hand, hash functions are usually analyzed with known inputs. However, lately, DFA attacks have been considered on hash functions with secret inputs, which is the default setting for the hash function when used in a MAC scheme. In general, adapting DFA attacks against hash functions operating in the secret key setting is somewhat inherently more difficult than adapting it against stream and block ciphers. In fact, unlike block and stream ciphers where one assumes that only the input key material is unknown, when a hash compression function is used in a MAC setting, we consider all its inputs as secrets. Additionally, when a hash function is employed in a MAC scheme, there are usually several applications of the hash function and even a single application of the hash function uses a domain extender with occasionally a complex finalization stage.

Literature related to DFA attacks on hash functions include the analysis of SHACAL [22], which is the internal cipher of the SHA1 compression function. Later, the attack was adapted to deal with the feedforward which masks the output of the internal cipher and both the secret chaining value and message block were retrieved [16]. Afterwards, DFA was used to analyze HAS1-60 [18], and Grøstl [13]. In particular, in the analysis of Grøstl [13], the authors have used the one-bit fault model to invert the truncated output transformation, and to retrieve the input chaining value and message block of its permutation based compression function. In our attack on Streebog, we employ some of the concepts introduced in [13]. In the following section, we give the description of the Streebog hash function.

3   Specification of Streebog

Streebog outputs a 512 or 256-bit hash value, where half the last state is truncated when adopting the 256-bit output. The standard [1] specifies two different *IVs*, one for each output length. Streebog can process messages of length up to $2^{512} - 1$. The compression function iterates over 12 rounds of an AES-like cipher with an 8×8 byte internal state and a final round of key mixing. The compression function operates in Miyaguchi-Preneel mode and is plugged in Merkle-Damgård domain extender with a finalization step. The input message M is padded into a multiple of 512 bits by appending one followed by zeros. The message length for MD-strengthening is further included as an extra separate block, followed by a block of a checksum evaluated by the modulo 2^{512} addition of all message blocks as a finalization step. More precisely, let $n = \lfloor \frac{|M|}{512} \rfloor$ and the input message $M = x\|m_n\| \cdots \|m_1\|m_0$, where $|M|$ is length of M, and x is a non complete or an empty block. Let $m_{n+1} = 0^{511-|x|}\|1\|x$, then the padded message $M = m_{n+1}\|m_n\| \cdots \|m_1\|m_0$. As depicted in Figure 1, the compression function g_N is fed with three inputs: the chaining value h_{i-1}, a message block m_{i-1}, and the counter of bits hashed so far $N_{i-1} = 512 \times i$. Let h_i be a 512-bit

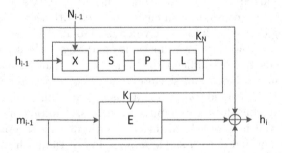

Fig. 1. Streebog's compression function g_N

chaining variable. The first state is loaded with the initial value IV and assigned to h_0. The hash value of M is computed as follows:

$$h_i \leftarrow g_N(h_{i-1}, m_{i-1}, N_{i-1}) \text{ for } i = 1, 2, .., n+2$$
$$h_{n+3} \leftarrow g_0(h_{n+2}, |M|, 0)$$
$$h(M) \leftarrow g_0(h_{n+3}, \Sigma, 0),$$

where $\Sigma = m_{n+1} + \cdots + m_1 + m_0$, $h(M)$ is the hash value of M, and g_0 is g_N with $N = 0$. As depicted in Figure 1, the compression function g_N consists of:

- K_N: a nonlinear whitening round of the chaining value. It takes a 512-bit chaining variable h_{i-1} and a counter of the bits hashed so far N_{i-1} and outputs a 512-bit key K.
- E: an AES-based cipher that iterates over the message for 12 rounds in addition to a finalization key mixing round. The cipher E takes a 512-bit key K and a 512-bit message block m as a plaintext. As shown in Figure 2, it consists of two similar parallel flows for the state update and the key scheduling.

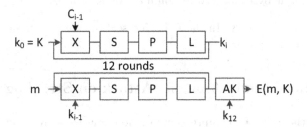

Fig. 2. The internal block cipher (E)

Both K_N and E operate on an 8×8 byte key state K. E updates an additional 8×8 byte message state M. In one round, a given state is updated by the following sequence of transformations:

- AddKey(X): XOR with either a round key, a constant, or the counter of bits hashed so far (N).
- SubBytes (S): A nonlinear byte bijective mapping.
- Transposition (P): Byte permutation.
- Linear Transformation (L): Row multiplication by an MDS matrix in GF(2).

Initially, state K is loaded with the chaining value h_{i-1} and updated by K_N as follows:

$$k_0 = L \circ P \circ S \circ X[N_{i-1}](K).$$

Now K contains the key k_0 to be used by the cipher E. The message state M is initially loaded with the message block m and $E(k_0, m)$ runs the key scheduling function on state K to generate 12 round keys, $k_1, k_2, .., k_{12}$, as follows:

$$k_i = L \circ P \circ S \circ X[C_{i-1}](k_{i-1}), \text{ for } i = 1, 2, .., 12,$$

where C_{i-1} is the ith round constant. The state M is updated as follows:

$$M_i = L \circ P \circ S \circ X[k_{i-1}](M_{i-1}), \text{ for } i = 1, 2, ..., 12.$$

The final round output is given by $E(k_0, m) = M_{12} \oplus k_{12}$. The output of g_N in the Miyaguchi-Preneel mode is $E(K_N(h_{i-1}, N_{i-1}), m_{i-1}) \oplus m_{i-1} \oplus h_{i-1}$ as shown in Figure 1. For further details, the reader is referred to [1].

Let M and K be (8×8)-byte states denoting the message and key state, respectively. The following notation is used throughout the paper:

- M_i: The message state at the beginning of round i.
- M_i^U: The message state after the U transformation at round i, where $U \in X, S, P, L$.
- $M_i[r, c]$: A byte at row r and column c of state M_i.
- $M_i[\text{row } r]$: Eight bytes located at row r of M_i state.
- $M_i[\text{col } c]$: Eight bytes located at column c of M_i state.

Same notation applies to K. In the following section, we give the details of our attack on Streebog.

4   Differential Fault Analysis Attack on Streebog

Our attack on the Streebog compression function aims to recover the secret input chaining value and message block. We proceed in a two-stage approach. In the first stage, given the compression function output, we recover the internal state of the last round of the internal cipher. Unlike the attack on the permutation based Grøstl, the knowledge of the internal state is not sufficient to recover the secret inputs since Streebog employs an internal cipher with secret round keys additions and not known constants. Hence, we adopt a second stage for the attack where we use the knowledge of the retrieved state from stage one to successfully recover one of the secret round keys, thus inverting the cipher and acquiring both the secret inputs of the compression function. In what follows, we give the definition of the used fault model and one of the Streebog Sbox properties that we are going to use in our attack.

Fault model: In our attack, we use the one-bit fault model which is used in [13,14]. For each fault injection, the attacker is assumed to be able to flip one bit in a given byte of the processed state whose position at row r and column c may be known or not. The practicality of this model has been demonstrated in [12], where the authors showed how tuning the laser injection parameters enables them to control with a 100% success rate the fault injection effect on a single bit: 0 to 1 or 1 to 0. Let M be a correctly computed state and M' a faulty state with a fault induced during its computation, then $M' = M \oplus \Delta$ where Δ is the error state with only one non-zero byte. Formally, the employed fault model is defined as follows:

$$\Delta[r,c] = \begin{cases} \delta \in E & \text{for only one byte position,} \\ 0 & \text{otherwise,} \end{cases}$$

where $\Delta[r,c]$ denotes the error at the byte in row r and column c, and the set $E = \{0x01, 0x02, 0x04, 0x08, 0x10, 0x20, 0x40, 0x80\}$.

For the Streebog Sbox, if x is a random input byte, $\delta x_i \in E$ for $i = 1, .., n$, $n \le 8$ is a randomly chosen but distinct one bit faults, and

$$\delta y_i = S(x) \oplus S(x \oplus \delta x_i),$$

then x is uniquely identified by the values of δy_i only. In other words, the value of the Sbox input byte x can be recovered by observing n output differences δy_i corresponding to n one-bit distinct input faults. According to our exhaustive simulation, depending on x, the average number of unique fault insertions which affect different bits δx_i required to identify x varies between 2.071418 - 4.86861, and the overall average is $\overline{n} \approx 2.635$ faults per byte. For the case when fault insertions δx_i are not uniquely selected, the overall average is $\overline{n} \approx 3.077$ faults per byte. Another observation is that, for all x, there always exist two unique δx_i that would identify x. In what follows, we give the details of the first stage of the attack.

4.1 Stage One

In this stage, we recover the message state of the internal cipher of the compression function $g_N(h_{i-1}, m)$. We first observe the value of the correct compression function output $h_i = g_N(h_{i-1}, m)$. Afterwards and as depicted in Figure 3, we induce one-bit fault in a given byte of M_{11}, which is the input to the last round of the cipher, such that, $M'_{11} = M_{11} \oplus \Delta$, and Δ has only one non zero byte at position $[r, c]$. This fault results in a faulty h'_i that differs from the correct h_i state in one row as shown in Figure 3.

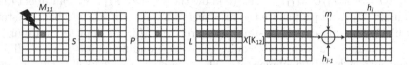

Fig. 3. Fault injection in the first stage of the attack

For a fault in a given byte position $M_{11}[r, c]$ we get the following two equations:

$$h_i = (X[k_{12}] \circ L \circ P \circ S(M_{11})) \oplus h_{i-1} \oplus m,$$
$$h'_i = (X[k_{12}] \circ L \circ P \circ S(M_{11} \oplus \Delta)) \oplus h_{i-1} \oplus m.$$

Since, $X, L,$ and P are bijective linear functions, we can propagate the difference at h_i backwards until the state after the Sbox as follows:

$$h_i \oplus h'_i = L \circ P \circ (S(M_{11}) \oplus S(M_{11} \oplus \Delta)),$$
$$P \circ L^{-1}(h_i \oplus h'_i) = S(M_{11}) \oplus S(M_{11} \oplus \Delta).$$

To this end, the difference state at the output of the Sbox of the last round of the internal cipher is given by $\Delta_{out} = S(M_{11}) \oplus S(M_{11} \oplus \Delta)$, where $\Delta_{out} = P \circ L^{-1}(h_i \oplus h'_i)$ and has only one non-zero value at row r and column c. Since, the substitution transformation operates on the state bytes independently, then the knowledge of the difference state Δ_{out} reveals the position $[r, c]$ of the induced fault. Accordingly, if we assume that we have enough faulty compression function outputs h'_i such that we know enough Δ_{out} states for each byte position in state M_{11}^S, then using the Sbox property presented in the previous section, we can recover the value of the entire state M_{11}.

4.2   Stage Two

Although in stage one, we are able to bypass the effect of the feedforward and recover state M_{11} of the internal cipher, we are still not able to invert the compression function and retrieve the secret input chaining value and message block. This is due to the fact that unlike other AES-based hash functions such as Grøstl which employs an internal permutation where known round constant additions are used, the Streebog internal cipher employs round key addition. These round keys are derived from the secret input chaining value and consequently they are not known to the attacker. For that reason, the knowledge of a round state of the compression function is not sufficient to invert it.

Our strategy in this stage is to recover the value of round key k_{11}, which is the key used in the round before the last one. Once we retrieve the value of k_{11}, we invert the key schedule to compute all previous round keys and finally, using the knowledge of the compression function counter N, the secret input chaining value is recovered. The employed approach depends on the knowledge of state M_{11} which we have recovered in the first stage of the attack. To recover the value of k_{11}, we first retrieve the value of state M_{10}, then evaluate $k_{11} = L \circ P \circ S(M_{10}) \oplus M_{11}$. Since, we know the value of M_{11}, we can inject one-bit faults in M_{10} and propagate the resulting differences in state h_i back to state M_{11} which is then used as h_i in stage one to recover M_{10}. As depicted in Figure 4, we inject one-faults in M_{10} and acquire the corresponding faulty h'_i which differs from the correct h_i in the whole state. The difference state $h_i \oplus h'_i$ is then propagated backward through the linear transformations until state M_{11}^S. Accordingly, the value of the faulty state M'_{11} is given by:

$$M'_{11} = S^{-1}(S(M_{11}) \oplus (P \circ L^{-1}(h_i \oplus h'_i))).$$

To this end, we get the difference at M_{11} which is then propagated backward to state M_{10}^S. The difference at M_{10}^S is the output difference of the Sbox at

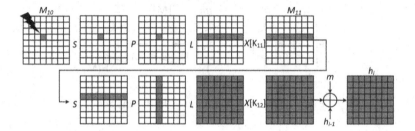

Fig. 4. Fault injection in the second stage of the attack

the eleventh round corresponding to the fault that we injected at state M_{10}. Consequently, this difference has only one active byte which reveals the byte position of the injected fault. The difference at state M_{10}^S is denoted by Δ_{out} and is given by:

$$\Delta_{out} = P \circ L^{-1}(M_{11} \oplus M_{11}').$$

Now, if we repeat stage two such that we get enough Δ_{out} values for each of the 64 positions in state M_{10}^S, we can recover the value of state M_{10}. Consequently, the value of k_{11} is computed by the following equation:

$$k_{11} = (L \circ P \circ S(M_{10})) \oplus M_{11}).$$

In the sequel, using k_{11} we invert the key schedule and acquire all the round keys. Then by utilizing the knowledge of the compression function counter N within the hash function, the input chaining value h_{i-1} is recovered. Since, we only observe the output of the last compression function call of the hash function, we always assume that we are processing $g_0(h_{i-1}, \Sigma)$ so that $N = 0$. However, the attack can work on any g_N within the hash function as described in the following subsection. Finally, with the knowledge of the round keys and state M_{10}, we invert the message encryption and recover the input message block m of $g_N(h_{i-1}, m)$.

4.3 Extending the Attack to the Hash Function

The two-stage attack presented in the previous section works on a compression function that one can observe the effect of the induced fault on its output. When Streebog is used in various MAC applications, full hash function application is used and, as depicted in Figure 5, one can only observe the output $H(M)$ of the last compression function call $g_0(h_{t+1}, \Sigma)$ of the hash function. Accordingly, to be able to retrieve the inputs of the previous compression function, we first launch the two-stage attack on $g_0(h_{t+1}, \Sigma)$. Because we observe both the correct and faulty values of $H(M)$, we can retrieve the values of Σ and h_{t+1}. To attack $g_0(h_t, |M|)$, the first stage of the attack requires the difference at h_{t+1} in addition to its value which cannot be deduced from observing the faulty $H'(M)$.

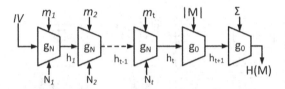

Fig. 5. The Streebog iterated hash function

This requirement can be fulfilled with a precomputed table T_1 for all the possible differences at h_{t+1} that result from injecting any fault at all the 64 byte positions of state M_{11} and their corresponding faulty $H'(M)$. Building this table is quite feasible for the fact that whatever the value of the induced fault at M_{11}, as depicted in Figure 3, each byte position at M_{11}^S may have up to 255 difference values which linearly maps to 255 one row differences Δh_{t+1} at state h_{t+1}. Accordingly, for each byte position in M_{11}^S, we linearly propagate the 255 possible differences forward to get Δh_{t+1}. Using our knowledge of the values of h_{t+1} and Σ, we evaluate the faulty $H'(M)$ corresponding to each difference. Finally, table T_1 will have 64×255 pairs of Δh_{t+1} and their corresponding $H'(M)$. Consequently, table T_1 enables us to complete the first stage of our attack because, when we inject a fault in M_{11}, the value of Δh_{t+1} corresponding to the resulting observed faulty $H'(M)$ is obtained from T_1. This step allows the recovery of the value of state M_{11} of $g_0(h_t, |M|)$.

The second stage of our attack requires the knowledge of the difference ΔM_{11} at state M_{11}. As depicted in Figure 4, a fault at a given position in M_{10} may have up to 255 difference after the Sbox which internally linearly map to 255 one row difference ΔM_{11} at state M_{11}. Since, we already know the value of state M_{11} from the previous step, we can get the corresponding 255 output differences after the Sbox at state M_{11}^S and linearly propagate them to get the full active state differences Δh_{t+1} at state h_{t+1}. Similar to the previous step, we build a second table, T_2 with all the 64×255 differences Δh_{t+1} and their corresponding $H'(M)$. This table allows us to finish stage two of our DFA and recover the values of h_t and $|M|$ of $g_0(h_t, |M|)$. The knowledge of $|M|$ reveals the number of the processed message blocks and accordingly the number of compression function calls and their corresponding counter values. Finally, we repeat the previous two-steps for each compression function and hence invert all of the compression function calls within the iterated hash function and retrieve all their secret inputs. Although we consider the 512-bit version of the hash function in our 2-stage attack, it also works on the 256-bit version where the last four rows of the last compression function are truncated. We only have to add an initial stage that deals with the truncation. We utilize the fact that the position and value of a single byte difference in a given row can be uniquely identified from the knowledge of the difference in any two bytes in the same row after the linear transformation (*cf.* Lemma 3 in [13]). In the added initial stage, we retrieve half of the state of the last round. Then, in stage one of our attack, we recover the whole state in the round before the last one with the knowledge of half of the difference state after the linear transformation, then continue with the rest of the attack.

5 DFA on Streebog in Different MAC Settings

One of the prospective applications of the new Russian standard is using it in MAC schemes. Despite the fact that both the simple prefix and the secret-IV MACs [27] are vulnerable to length extension attacks, Streebog is by design not vulnerable to length extension attacks due to its finalization stage. This property may tempt users to adopt one of the simpler MAC constructions. Indeed, the designers of the NIST SHA-3 hash function, Keccak [8,11] state on their website that since Keccak is not vulnerable to length extension attacks, it does not need HMAC and propose that MAC computation can be done by concatenating the key with the message [20]. Accordingly, in what follows, we consider Streebog in both the simple and standardized MAC settings, and show how our attack can be used to recover the secret MAC key.

Simple prefix/Secret-IV MACs: As depicted in Figure 6, in the simple prefix MAC, the secret key is used as the first message block of the processed message in the iterative construction of the hash function. More formally, $MAC(M) = H(K\|M)$. On the other hand, in the secret-IV MAC, the standard initial value is replaced by the secret key in the iterative construction of the hash function. More formally, $MAC(M) = H_K(M)$, where $H_K(M)$ is the keyed hash value of the message M using the secret key K as the IV. The knowledge of the authenticated message reveals its corresponding message blocks and accordingly their modular sum. We can retrieve the secret key of the simple prefix MAC using the two-stage DFA on the last compression function call. The attack recovers Σ which is the modular summation of all processed message blocks including the secret key. Accordingly, to recover the key, we simply subtract the summation of the known message blocks of the authenticated message from the retrieved Σ. As for secret-IV MAC, we use our DFA and invert the compression function calls until the first one with $N = 0$, the retrived chaining value is the secret key. In both schemes, if we do not know the authenticate message, we can easily retrieve the number of message blocks from $|M|$ and iterate the attack backwards until the compression function with $N = 0$ to recover the key.

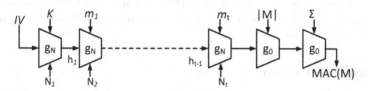

Fig. 6. Simple prefix MAC using Streebog

HMAC/NMAC: HMAC [7] is defined as:

$$HMAC(M) = H((K \oplus opad)\|H((K \oplus ipad)\|M)),$$

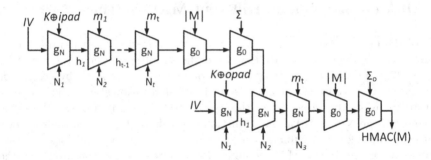

Fig. 7. HMAC using Streebog

where *opad* and *ipad* are known padding constants and H denotes a hash function call. The algorithm is standardized by ANSI, IETF, ISO and NIST, and is widely deployed in many Internet security protocols (e.g. SSL, SSH, IPSec). As depicted in Figure 7, the Streebog hash function is called twice. Our analysis works on the outer hash function call where $K \oplus opad$ is used as the first message block. Accordingly, our DFA is applied on the outer hash function and using the observed HMAC(M), we iterate the attack backwards to invert five compression function calls. The retrieved message block of the fifth backward compression function reveals the key value after xoring it with *opad*.

NMAC [7] employs two keys and is defined as:

$$NMAC(M) = H_{K_2}(H_{K_1}(M)),$$

where the keys are used as the initial values in the outer and inner hash function calls. The algorithm has a similar structure to HMAC but differs in that the first compression function call in both hash function calls in HMAC is omitted, and K_1 and K_2 are used as the IV for the following compression function call. Accordingly, if Figure 7 is to describe NMAC, we omit $g_N(IV, K \oplus ipad)$ and replace the resulting h_1 by K_1, and remove $g_N(IV, K \oplus opad)$ and use K_2 as the IV for the following compression function call. In the sequel, our attack works first to recover K_2 by iterating the two-stage attack backwards for four compression function calls. Afterwards, the retrieved message block corresponding to the output of the inner hash function is used to further recover K_1 from the inner hash function application.

6 Simulation Results

Since the attack has a very low complexity, we have simulated three scenarios of the attack on the compression function on an 8-core Intel i7 CPU running at 2.67GHz and the secret inputs were recovered in less than one minute. The scenarios vary in the assumptions of whether the attacker can control the injection of distinct faults and if the faulted byte position can be chosen or not. The provided average fault requirements are the result of running our simulation using

1000 different inputs to the compression function. As shown by our simulations, the number of required faults to retrieve 128 bytes in both stages depends on the assumptions used during fault injections. In what follows, we give the results of our simulation:

1. When the faults are selected distinctly and the byte position $[r, c]$ is chosen by the attacker, then one needs an average of 338 faults which is equivalent to an average of 2.635 faults per byte.
2. If we randomly induce non distinct one-bit faults and select the byte positions, then the attack requires an average of 394 fault injections in total with an average of 3.077 faults per byte.
3. In the case where both the byte position and the induced one-bit faults are randomly chosen, the attack requires an average of 1640 fault injections in total, and accordingly an average 12.807 fault per byte.

7   Conclusion

In this paper, we have investigated the security of the new Russian hash function standard GOST R 34.11-2012 with respect to differential fault analysis. In particular, we have proposed a two-stage approach that considers the compression function operating with secret inputs. Accordingly, using one-bit faults, the first stage of our attack bypasses the final feedforward and retrieves the internal state of the cipher used in the compression function. The second stage retrieves one of the round keys used in the cipher which enables the generation of the rest of the round keys and consequently, the input chaining value and message block are recovered. We have simulated the attack on the compression function with different assumptions regarding the control of the attacker over the induced faults and the faulted position. The results show that our two-stage attack requires between 338 and 1640 faults on average, depending on what are the assumptions of the employed fault model. Moreover, we have proposed a feasible precomputation step where we require two tables of size 2^{14} state each to enable the extension of the attack to the whole hash function. Finally, we have shown how our proposed approach is used to recover the secret MAC key when Streebog is used in simple prefix, secret-IV, HMAC, and NMAC settings. A naive approach to prevent our attack is to use spatial/temporal algorithm level redundancy and to disable the device output if the two produced MAC tags do not match. Another approach is to add parity bits to detect corruptions of the inner state registers and disable the device output if any of these parity checks is violated. Efficient fault analysis resistant implementations for Streebog, as well as for other hash functions deployed in MAC schemes, need to be addressed in future research.

Acknowledgment. The authors would like to thank the anonymous reviewers for their valuable comments and suggestions that helped improve the quality of the paper. This work is supported by the Natural Sciences and Engineering Research Council of Canada (NSERC).

References

1. The National Hash Standard of the Russian Federation GOST R 34.11-2012. Russian Federal Agency on Technical Regulation and Metrology report (2012), https://www.tc26.ru/en/GOSTR34112012/GOST_R_34_112012_eng.pdf
2. AlTawy, R., Kircanski, A., Youssef, A.M.: Rebound attacks on stribog. In: Lee, H.-S., Han, D.-G. (eds.) ICISC 2013. LNCS, vol. 8565, pp. 175–188. Springer, Heidelberg (2014)
3. AlTawy, R., Youssef, A.M.: Integral distinguishers for reduced-round Stribog. Information Processing Letters 114(8), 426 (2014)
4. AlTawy, R., Youssef, A.M.: Preimage attacks on reduced-round stribog. In: Pointcheval, D., Vergnaud, D. (eds.) AFRICACRYPT. LNCS, vol. 8469, pp. 109–125. Springer, Heidelberg (2014), http://dx.doi.org/10.1007/978-3-319-06734-6_7
5. AlTawy, R., Youssef, A.M.: Watch your Constants: Malicious Streebog. IET Information Security (2015) (to appear)
6. Banik, S., Maitra, S., Sarkar, S.: A differential fault attack on the Grain family of stream ciphers. In: Prouff, E., Schaumont, P. (eds.) CHES 2012. LNCS, vol. 7428, pp. 122–139. Springer, Heidelberg (2012)
7. Bellare, M., Canetti, R., Krawczyk, H.: Keying hash functions for message authentication. In: Koblitz, N. (ed.) CRYPTO 1996. LNCS, vol. 1109, pp. 1–15. Springer, Heidelberg (1996)
8. Bertoni, G., Daemen, J., Peeters, M., Van Assche, G.: Keccak sponge function family main document. Submission to NIST, Round 2 (2009)
9. Biham, E., Shamir, A.: Differential fault analysis of secret key cryptosystems. In: Kaliski Jr., B.S. (ed.) CRYPTO 1997. LNCS, vol. 1294, pp. 513–525. Springer, Heidelberg (1997)
10. Boneh, D., DeMillo, R.A., Lipton, R.J.: On the importance of checking cryptographic protocols for faults. In: Fumy, W. (ed.) EUROCRYPT 1997. LNCS, vol. 1233, pp. 37–51. Springer, Heidelberg (1997), http://dx.doi.org/10.1007/3-540-69053-0_4
11. Chang, S.-J., Perlner, R., Burr, W.E., Turan, M.S., Kelsey, J.M., Paul, S., Bassham, L.E.: Third-round report of the SHA-3 cryptographic hash algorithm competition (2012)
12. Courbon, F., Loubet-Moundi, P., Fournier, J.J.A., Tria, A.: Adjusting laser injections for fully controlled faults. In: Prouff, E. (ed.) COSADE 2014. LNCS, vol. 8622, pp. 229–242. Springer, Heidelberg (2014)
13. Fischer, W., Reuter, C.A.: Differential fault analysis on Grøstl. In: IEEE Workshop on Fault Diagnosis and Tolerance in Cryptography, pp. 44–54 (2012)
14. Giraud, C.: DFA on AES. In: Dobbertin, H., Rijmen, V., Sowa, A. (eds.) AES 2005. LNCS, vol. 3373, pp. 27–41. Springer, Heidelberg (2005)
15. Guo, J., Jean, J., Leurent, G., Peyrin, T., Wang, L.: The usage of counter revisited: Second-preimage attack on new russian standardized hash function. In: Joux, A., Youssef, A. (eds.) SAC 2014. LNCS, vol. 8781, pp. 195–211. Springer, Heidelberg (2014)
16. Hemme, L., Hoffmann, L.: Differential fault analysis on the SHA1 compression function. In: IEEE Workshop on Fault Diagnosis and Tolerance in Cryptography, pp. 54–62 (2011)
17. IETF. GOST R 34.11-2012: Hash Function, RFC6896 (2013)

18. Zou, J., Wu, W., Wu, S.: Cryptanalysis of the round-reduced GOST hash function. In: Lin, D., Xu, S., Yung, M. (eds.) Inscrypt 2013. LNCS, vol. 8567, pp. 307–320. Springer, Heidelberg (2014)

19. Kazymyrov, O., Kazymyrova, V.: Algebraic aspects of the russian hash standard GOST R 34.11-2012. In: CTCrypt, pp. 160–176 (2013), http://eprint.iacr.org/2013/556

20. Keccak team. Strengths of Keccak - Design and security, http://keccak.noekeon.org/ (last accessed: December 2, 2014)

21. Kim, C.H., Quisquater, J.-J.: New differential fault analysis on AES key schedule: Two faults are enough. In: Grimaud, G., Standaert, F.-X. (eds.) CARDIS 2008. LNCS, vol. 5189, pp. 48–60. Springer, Heidelberg (2008)

22. Li, R., Li, C., Gong, C.: Differential fault analysis on SHACAL-1. In: IEEE Workshop on Fault Diagnosis and Tolerance in Cryptography, pp. 120–126 (2009)

23. Ma, B., Li, B., Hao, R., Li, X.: Improved cryptanalysis on reduced-round GOST and Whirlpool hash function. In: Boureanu, I., Owesarski, P., Vaudenay, S. (eds.) ACNS 2014. LNCS, vol. 8479, pp. 289–307. Springer, Heidelberg (2014)

24. Matyukhin, D., Rudskoy, V., and Shishkin, V. A perspective hashing algorithm. In: RusCrypto (2010) (in Russian)

25. Mendel, F., Pramstaller, N., Rechberger, C.: A (Second) preimage attack on the GOST hash function. In: Nyberg, K. (ed.) FSE 2008. LNCS, vol. 5086, pp. 224–234. Springer, Heidelberg (2008)

26. Mendel, F., Pramstaller, N., Rechberger, C., Kontak, M., Szmidt, J.: Cryptanalysis of the GOST hash function. In: Wagner, D. (ed.) CRYPTO 2008. LNCS, vol. 5157, pp. 162–178. Springer, Heidelberg (2008)

27. Preneel, B., van Oorschot, P.C.: On the security of iterated message authentication codes. IEEE Transactions on Information Theory 45(1), 188–199 (1999)

28. Skorobogatov, S., Anderson, R.: Optical fault induction attacks. In: Kaliski Jr., B.S., Koç, Ç.K., Paar, C. (eds.) CHES 2002. LNCS, vol. 2523, pp. 2–12. Springer, Heidelberg (2003)

29. Tunstall, M., Mukhopadhyay, D., Ali, S.: Differential fault analysis of the Advanced Encryption Standard using a single fault. In: Ardagna, C.A., Zhou, J. (eds.) WISTP 2011. LNCS, vol. 6633, pp. 224–233. Springer, Heidelberg (2011)

30. Wang, Z., Yu, H., Wang, X.: Cryptanalysis of GOST R hash function. Information Processing Letters 114(12), 655–662 (2014)

31. Zou, J., Wu, W., Wu, S.: Cryptanalysis of the round-reduced GOST hash function. In: Lin, D., Xu, S., Yung, M. (eds.) Inscrypt 2013. LNCS, vol. 8567, pp. 307–320. Springer, Heidelberg (2014)

Fault Attacks on Stream Cipher Scream

Shaoyu Du[1,4,*], Bin Zhang[1,2], Zhenqi Li[1], and Dongdai Lin[3]

[1] Trusted Computing and Information Assurance Laboratory,
Institute of Software, Chinese Academy of Sciences, Beijing, China
[2] State Key Laboratory of Computer Science, Institute of Software,
Chinese Academy of Sciences, Beijing, China
[3] State Key Laboratory of Information Security, Institute of Information Engineering,
Chinese Academy of Sciences, Beijing, China
[4] University of Chinese Academy of Sciences, Beijing, China
du_shaoyu@163.com

Abstract. In this paper we present a differential fault attack (DFA) on the stream cipher Scream which is designed by the IBM researchers Coppersmith, Halevi, and Jutla in 2002. The known linear distinguishing attack on Scream takes 2^{120} output words and there is no key recovery attack on it, since the S-box used by Scream is key-dependent and complex. Under the assumption that we can inject random byte faults in the same location multiple number of times, the 128-bit key can be recovered with 2^{94} computations and 2^{72} bytes memory by injecting around 2000 faults. Then combined with the assumption of related key attacks, we can retrieve the key with 2^{44} computations and 2^{40} bytes memory. The result is verified by experiments. To the best of the our knowledge this is the first DFA and key recovery attack on Scream.

Keywords: Fault Attacks, Scream, Key-dependent S-box, Stream Cipher.

1 Introduction

The stream cipher Scream was developed by the IBM researchers Coppersmith, Halevi, and Jutla in 2002[1]. In the proposal, several versions of Scream are given. The so-called "toy cipher" denoted as $Scream_0$ uses the AES S-box whereas the Scream cipher uses secret S-boxes, generated by the 128-bit key and the AES S-box. In the security analysis of the Scream family, two distinguishing attacks on $Scream_0$ were proposed[1,3], with the best complexity around 2^{80}. For Scream, Alexander Maximov and Thomas Johansson[2] proposed a linear distinguishing attack using around 2^{120} output words. The use of secret S-boxes makes the attack complicated. Until now, there are no key recovery attacks on Scream.

Since the work of [4] by Hoch and Shamir, fault attacks have been employed to test the strengths and weaknesses of stream ciphers. It is known to be very efficient against stream ciphers and has received a lot of attention in recent cryptographic literature[5,6,7,8,9,10]. Under the differential fault attacks scenario in

---

* Corresponding author.

© Springer International Publishing Switzerland 2015
J. Lopez and Y. Wu (Eds.): ISPEC 2015, LNCS 9065, pp. 50–64, 2015.
DOI: 10.1007/978-3-319-17533-1_4

stream cipher, the attacker is allowed to inject faults in the internal state. Then by analyzing the difference between the faulty and right keystreams, the attacker can deduce some information about the internal state and secret key. There are multiple techniques like glitches in the clock input line, laser beam, or under-powering the device to induce the faults to the hardware design of a cipher. A typical fault attack involves the random injection of faults in a device which changes one or more bits of its internal state. In order to perform the attack, certain privileges are required like the ability to re-key the device, control the timing of the faults etc. The attack becomes impractical and unrealistic if the adversary is granted too many privileges.

In this paper, we assume that the attacker have the following abilities, in which the first two privileges are generally acceptable and the last one is similar to that in the published works [7,11,12]:

1. The attacker can induce random single byte faults at any position of the internal states of Scream at any time during the keystream generating phase.
2. The attacker does not know the position and value of the faults. Obtaining the fault's position and value by comparison of the fault-free and faulty key-streams is one of the challenges while mounting the fault attack.
3. The attacker can re-key the cipher multiple times and reproduce multiple faults in the same (but unknown) position at the same clock.

Under these assumptions, we give several differential fault attacks on Scream to recover the 128-bit key. The novel idea of our fault attack is based on certain specific observations related to the key-dependent S-box of the cipher. And the different update frequencies of the internal states in the cipher's "mainloop" make us easy to derive the input and output differences of the secret 8-bit S-box $S_1[\cdot]$ from the faulty and fault-free keystreams. The differences have the forms as $(\delta, S_1[x \oplus \delta] \oplus S_1[x])$, where x and $S_1[\cdot]$ are unknown and δ is exactly the value of the effective fault injected. Then from the differences the adversary can restore all the 128 key bits in the following ways.

If the random faults can be injected multiple times on the same but random location, then the adversary can get a sequence as $\Delta_0[i] = S_1[m \oplus i] \oplus n$ ($i = 0, \ldots, 255$) where m, n are unknown but $n = S_1[m]$. The key will be recovered through precomputing 8 bytes of the key and then exhausting m, n and the other 8 bytes key. The attack takes about 2^{94} computations with 2^{72} bytes memory and about 2000 random faults. Furthermore, under the assumptions of related key attacks, we get another attack which can reveal the key with 2^{40} bytes memory and 2^{44} computations. The attack mainly utilizes the structure of the secret S-box, which uses modula addition of key bytes and the AES S-box iteratively 16 times. In fact if we get two S-boxes $S[\cdot]$ and $S'[\cdot]$ satisfy

$$S[x] = S'[x \boxplus key_0] \boxplus key_{15},$$

then the unknown key bytes key_0 and key_{15} can be revealed trivially. Therefore, the attacker can utilize the S-boxes generated by two related keys which are different in only two bytes to restore the distinct bytes. Experiments show that five related keys are enough to regain the outmost 8-byte key $(key_0, \ldots, key_3)$, $(key_{12}, \ldots, key_{15})$ in one day. And then the rest 8-byte key can be revealed by means of precomputing 4 bytes and exhausting the other 4 bytes.

The paper is organized as follows. In Section 2, we present a short description of the Scream cipher, where we also present some notations that will be used in this paper. Section 3 shows how to obtain the effective fault's value and position and derive the input and output differences of the S-box generated by the key we need to recover. The attacks assuming that the adversary is able to induce multiple faults in the same location with single and related keys are described in Section 4. Finally, Section 5 concludes this paper.

2   Description of Scream

In this paper variables denoted by a capital letter X will usually mean a 16-byte block, unless otherwise stated. It can also be expressed as $X = (x_0, x_1, \ldots, x_{15})$, where x_i ($i \in [0, 15]$) stands a byte. Moreover, x_i^t denotes the byte in clock t.

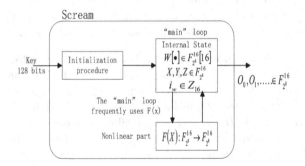

Fig. 1. Scream functionality

The stream cipher Scream, whose functionality is presented in Figure 1, takes as an input a 128-bit key and a nonce value and produces an arbitrary long keystream sequence, denoted by $\mathbf{O} = O_0, O_1, O_2, \ldots$, where $O_i \in \mathbb{F}_{2^8}^{16}$. In the initialization stage, Scream initializes a number of internal state variables (X, Y, Z) and tables (W - and S - box tables), see [1] for details. Then Scream enters the main loop, where in each iteration ($i = 1, 2, \ldots$) in the main loop the state variables and tables are updated and one output word O_i is generated.

The calculations in the main loop of Scream are based on a certain function $F(X) : \mathbb{F}_{2^8}^{16} \to \mathbb{F}_{2^8}^{16}$ called the round function. The detailed structure of $F(X)$ is illustrated in Figure 2. This round function is quite similar to a round function in block ciphers and uses S-boxes $S_1[\cdot]$ and $S_2[\cdot]$ with mixing operations and it is the only nonlinear component of Scream. The mixing matrices are respectively $M_1 = \begin{pmatrix} 1 & \alpha \\ \alpha & 1 \end{pmatrix}, M_2 = \begin{pmatrix} 1 & \alpha+1 \\ \alpha+1 & 1 \end{pmatrix}$, where α is a primary element in $\mathbb{F}_{2^8}$. An

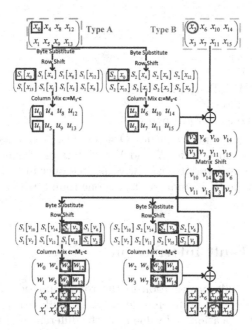

Fig. 2. Scream round function in details. Variables in '□' indicate the difference propagations path.a and variables in '○' indicate path.b for the attack.

important fact is that Scream uses secret (keyed) S-boxes derived from the key (but independent of the nonce) using the AES S-box, as follows:

$$S_1[x] := SR[\ldots SR[SR[x \boxplus key_0] \boxplus key_1] \ldots \boxplus key_{15}],$$

for all $x \in [0 \ldots 255]$, where $SR[\cdot]$ is the AES S-box, and $key_0, \ldots, key_{15}$ are 16 bytes of the secret key K, $\boxplus$ denotes integer addition modulo 256. Furthermore, the inverse of $SR[\cdot]$ is denoted as $SR^{-1}[\cdot]$ and $\boxminus$ denotes integer minus modulo 256, the second S-box is defined as $S_2[x] = S_1[x \oplus 00010101]$ where $\oplus$ stands the XOR operation. Finally, a pseudocode of the main loop of Scream is as follows:

Require: X, Y, Z–three 16-byte blocks, W–a table of sixteen 16-byte blocks, i_w–an index into W (initially $i_w = 0$)

1: **repeat**
2:     **for** $i = 0$ to 15 **do**
3:         $X := F(X \oplus Y)$
4:         $X := X \oplus Z$
5:         output $X \oplus W[i \bmod 16]$
6:         **if** $i = 0$ or $2 \bmod 4$ **then**
7:             rotate Y by 8 bytes, $Y := Y_{8..15,0..7}$
8:         **else if** $i = 1 \bmod 4$ **then**
9:             rotate each half of Y by 4 bytes, $Y := Y_{4..7,0..3,12..15,8..11}$
10:         **else if** $i < 15$ **then**
11:             rotate each half of Y by 3 bytes to the right, $Y := Y_{5..7,0..4,13..15,8..12}$

12:        **end if**
13:        **end for**
14:    $Y := F(Y \oplus Z)$
15:    $Z := F(Z \oplus Y)$
16:    $W[i_w] := F(W[i_w])$
17:    $i_w := i_w + 1 \mod 16$
18: **until** you get enough output bytes

In line 5 above the output sequence $\mathbf{O} = O_0, O_1, O_2, \ldots$, is generated, one word at a time. In summary, the X and Y variables are frequently updated in the inner loop, whereas Z variable is slowly updated once in each round. One 16-byte vector of the table W is updated during one round, whereas the remaining entries are unchanged.

3   Derive the Fault Information

In this section, the fault propagation in the round function $F(x)$ and in the cipher when it was injected in different locations is analyzed. We also show how to derive some fault's location and value from the differences of the key-streams. Then we give the method to extract the input and output differences of the key-dependent S-box from the effective fault. And we present how to count the number of faults we need to conduct the key recovery attack.

For the sake of simplicity, hereafter "innerloop" denotes the inner iteration when the index i is updated in a main loop and "round" denotes a whole round when the index i_w is updated. Obviously, each round contains 16 innerloops and there is an output word O_i in each innerloop.

3.1   Fault Propagation in Round Function F(x)

Review the structure of function $F(x)$. There are two types of input variables, x_i ($i = 0$ or $1 \mod 4$) belong to Type A and the other 8 bytes belong to Type B as shown in Figure 2. Due to the symmetry of $F(x)$ in its input and output bytes, here and hereafter we only analyze the propagation of the fault injected in the bytes x_0 (stands for Type A) and x_2 (stands for Type B).

- **Type A.** When a fault is injected in x_0, it propagates in $F(x)$ as path.a, which shows that the output bytes $x'_2, x'_3, x'_8, x'_9, x'_{10}, x'_{11}, x'_{12}, x'_{13}, x'_{14}, x'_{15}$ will be changed.
- **Type B.** When a fault is injected in x_2 it propagates as path.b, only the output bytes $x'_8, x'_9, x'_{10}, x'_{11}$ of $F(x)$ have differences.

Moreover, if the fault of Type A continues to propagating through $F(x)$ a second time, then all the output variables will be different. And if the Type B fault passes through $F(x)$ a second time, then all the output bytes except x'_{12} and x'_{13} will have differences.

3.2   Fault Propagation in Cipher

Based on the analysis above, we continue to focus on the fault's propagation in cipher. The internal states of Scream which are classified by X, Y, Z and W-table update in different ways and have different affects to the output word. Therefore, the faults injected in different internal states have different propagations which will be specialized in this section. For simplicity, only x_0 and x_2 of the states are considered as stated above and the unknown fault value is denoted as e. Actually faults injected in the rest 14 bytes have similar propagations.

When the Fault Is Injected in Y. Assume that the attacker injects a fault e in Y after line 5 (see the pseudocode of main loop) of the t innerloop and before line 5 of the $t + 1$ innerloop. Moreover, the t and $t + 1$ innerloops are in the same round. Afterwards in line 3 of the $t + 1$ innerloop, the fault propogates to X from Y and changes the output word in line 5. The difference between the right and faulty output word of the $t + 1$ innerloop has the pattern as that showed in path.a if e is in x_0 (or path.b if e is in x_2). Furthermore, the differences propagates through a second $F(x)$ lead to that all the bytes of the $t+2$ output word have differences (or only x'_{12} and x'_{13} have no difference). Table 1[1] demonstrates the differences the attacker can observe. Since in this case the

Table 1. Differences in the cipher after a fault is injected to some byte of Y

byte	t	$t + 1$	$t + 2$
x_0	all zero	2,3,8,9,10,11,12,13,14,15	[0,15]
x_2	all zero	8,9,10,11	[0,15]/{12,13}

output difference of the $t+1$ innerloop is the result of the fault 'e' after one $F(x)$ operation and the attacker is unaware of the internal states, it is impossible to derive any information about the fault.

When the Fault Is Injected in Z. If the fault occurs in Z at the time stated above, it is directly XORed to X in line 4 of the $t + 1$ innerloop and then affects the output words of the $t + 1$ and $t + 2$ innerloop as showed in Table 2. It is notable that the fault is directly XORed to the output of the $t+1$ innerloop which means the difference in it reveals the fault's value e. Moreover, the fault only propagates through one $F(x)$ function in the $t + 2$ innerloop and the corresponding differences are as the output of path.a (or path.b) added e itself, since Z has been changed.

---

[1] The number in Table 1 expresses that the attacker can observe differences in the corresponding byte. For example, "2, 3, 8, 9, 10, 11, 12, 13, 14, 15" means the differences have the pattern "00??0000????????", where '0' and '?' both stand for one byte. So as to the following Table 2,3,4,5.

Table 2. Differences in the cipher after a fault is injected to some byte of Z

byte	t	$t+1$	$t+2$
x_0	all zero	0	0,2,3,8,9,10,11,12,13,14,15
x_2	all zero	2	2,8,9,10,11

When the Fault Is Injected in W-table. Under this case, we declare that the fault injecting time is just in the innerloop before the one that we can observe a changed output word as a primary. Actually the fault can occur in some earlier time because the update and use frequency of W-table is very slow. For accordance, the fault is still injected at the time as above. Due to its unique role of linearly masking the output word, W-table has no influence to other internal states. In addition, a different entry is used to mask the output word in the next innerloop. Consequently, there will be no difference in the output after the $t+1$ innerloop for at least one word. Then we can derive Table 3.

Table 3. Differences in the cipher after a fault is injected to some byte of W-table

byte	t	$t+1$	$t+2$
x_0	all zero	0	all zero
x_2	all zero	2	all zero

When the Fault Is Injected in X. Finally we assume the fault is injected to the internal state X between line 4 of the t and $t+1$ innerloop. Owing to X's most frequent updating, this situation is classified into two cases.

Case 1: the fault occurs before line 3 (included) of the $t+1$ innerloop. In this case it results in the same difference as Table 1 shows.

Case 2: the fault occurs after line 3 (not included) of the $t+1$ innerloop. Here the result is similar to that of the fault injected in state Z. The only difference is that there is no effect of the initial fault in the output word of the $t+2$ innerloop. Table 4 shows the new distribution of the difference.

Table 4. Differences in the cipher after a fault is injected to some byte of X-Case2

byte	t	$t+1$	$t+2$
x_0	all zero	0	2,3,8,9,10,11,12,13,14,15
x_2	all zero	2	8,9,10,11

3.3 Extract Differences of the S-Box from Effective Faults

For faults injected in some other bytes of state X and state Z, the attacker can pick them up by a similar manner as that in Table 2 and Table 4. These faults are called *effective faults* in our attacks and their values, locations and output differences are summarized in Table 5.

Table 5. Faults which can be picked up and their differences in the output words

fault locations	t	$t+1$	$t+2$
x_0 of Z	all zero	0	0,2,3,8,9,10,11,12,13,14,15
x_0 of X	all zero	0	2,3,8,9,10,11,12,13,14,15
x_4 of Z	all zero	4	0,1,2,3,4,6,7,12,13,14,15
x_4 of X	all zero	4	0,1,2,3,6,7,12,13,14,15
x_8 of Z	all zero	8	0,1,2,3,4,5,6,7,8,10,11
x_8 of X	all zero	8	0,1,2,3,4,5,6,7,10,11
x_{12} of Z	all zero	12	4,5,6,7,8,9,10,11,12,14,15
x_{12} of X	all zero	12	4,5,6,7,8,9,10,11,14,15
x_2 of Z	all zero	2	2,8,9,10,11
x_2 of X	all zero	2	8,9,10,11
x_{15} of Z	all zero	15	8,9,10,11,15
x_{15} of X	all zero	15	8,9,10,11
x_3 of Z	all zero	3	3,12,13,14,15
x_3 of X	all zero	3	12,13,14,15
x_6 of Z	all zero	6	6,12,13,14,15
x_6 of X	all zero	6	12,13,14,15
x_7 of Z	all zero	7	0,1,2,3,7
x_7 of X	all zero	7	0,1,2,3
x_{10} of Z	all zero	10	0,1,2,3,10
x_{10} of X	all zero	10	0,1,2,3
x_{11} of Z	all zero	11	4,5,6,7,11
x_{11} of X	all zero	11	4,5,6,7
x_{14} of Z	all zero	14	4,5,6,7,14
x_{14} of X	all zero	14	4,5,6,7

Suppose there are two key-streams with their difference sequences as the pattern in the first row of Table 5. The difference in x_0^{t+1}, which denotes the x_0 byte of the $t+1$ innerloop's output word, is exactly the fault's value e. Then from the $t+2$ innerloop's output, we can reveal $S_1[x_0^{t+1}] \oplus S_1[x_0^{t+1} \oplus e]$. Since

$$
\begin{aligned}
x_2^{t+2} &= u_0^{t+2} \oplus w_2^{t+2} \\
&= S_1[x_0^{t+1}] \oplus \alpha \cdot S_1[x_{13}^{t+1}] \oplus S_2[v_{10}^{t+2}] \oplus (1+\alpha) \cdot S_2[v_7^{t+2}] \\
&= S_1[x_0^{t+1}] \oplus \alpha \cdot S_1[x_{13}^{t+1}] \oplus S_2[(x_{10}^{t+1} \oplus S_2[x_8^{t+1}] \\
&\quad \oplus (1+\alpha) \cdot S_2[x_5^{t+1}])] \oplus (1+\alpha) \cdot S_2[(x_7^{t+1} \oplus S_2[x_1^{t+1}] \\
&\quad \oplus (1+\alpha) \cdot S_2[x_4^{t+1}])],
\end{aligned}
$$

where $\cdot$ denotes multiplication in $\mathbb{F}_{2^8}$ and there are no differences in other bytes x_i^{t+1} $(i = 1,2,3,\ldots,15)$, then

$$
\Delta x_2^{t+2} = S_1[x_0^{t+1}] \oplus S_1[x_0^{t+1} \oplus e].
$$

It illustrates that though we do not know the value of x_0 and $S_1[x_0]$, we can get the output difference of $S_1[\cdot]$ when its input pair is $(x_0, x_0 \oplus e)$.

3.4 Strategy of Counting the Faults

In Section 4, we will conduct the key recovery process assuming we know a series of input and output differences of $S_1[\cdot]$, whose inputs walk through $x \oplus 0$ to $x \oplus 255$ (x denotes an unknown byte). It is notable that only the effective faults can be used to derive the differences and their values must take 1 to 255 at least once to reveal the key.

In order to pick up the effective faults, the attacker can repeat the process of injecting random faults in random positions of the cipher and searching for a match between the difference-patterns in Table 5 and the difference of the keystreams (the faulty and fault-free ones) until he gets one match, which means the corresponding fault is an effective fault. Since the picking-up phase is relative simple, we omit the number of faults needed before we find an effective one.

Recall the assumptions stated in the introduction, the adversary has the ability of re-keying the cipher and injecting multiple faults with random values into the same but unknown location at the same clock multiple times. Then, the attacker can inject random faults to the same location at the same clock as the effective fault he picked up continuously until he gets all the 255 fault values. Assume that there are N faults injected, then the probability that all the 255 value is contained can be calculated from inclusion-exclusion principle as

$$p = \sum_{i=0}^{254} (-1)^i C_{255}^i \left(\frac{255-i}{255}\right)^N, \tag{1}$$

where C_m^n stands for the combination number of choosing n from m. The relation between N and p is depicted in Table 6, which shows that about $N = 2^{11} = 2048$ faults are enough to get a relative high success probability $p \approx 0.93$.

Table 6. The relation of faults' number N and the success probability p

N	1024	1500	2000	2048
p	0.01	0.5	0.91	0.93
N	2500	3000	3500	4096
p	0.98	0.998	0.9997	0.99998

4   Recovering the Key from the Differences of the Key-dependent S-box

The key recovery attack on Scream can be transformed to *Problem 1* using 255 pairs of input and output differences of the key-dependent S-box $S_1[\cdot]$, where the input differences walk along 1 to 255.

Problem 1. Given a key-dependent S-box which is constructed as $S_1[\cdot]$ of Scream and fixed but unknown values m_0, $n_0 = S_1[m_0]$. If the attacker knows the sequence of $\Delta_0[0], \Delta_0[1], \ldots, \Delta_0[255]$ where $\Delta_0[i] = S_1[m_0 \oplus i] \oplus n_0$, $i \in \{0, \ldots 255\}$, how to recover the 16 bytes of the secret key $key_0, \ldots, key_{15}$?

4.1   Basic Attacks

Despite $S_1[\cdot]$ is constructed based on the famous AES S-box $SR[\cdot]$ that has a mass of study in its properties, the sufficient large iteration rounds make it difficult to recover the 128-bit key. An essential idea is to use pre-computations.

In the precomputing phase, a table T with 2^{64} entries is established as the steps below.

Step 1. For all the values of $key_0, \ldots, key_7$, evaluate the corresponding S-boxes:
$S'[x] = SR[\ldots SR[SR[x \boxplus key_0] \boxplus key_1] \ldots \boxplus key_7]$, for all $x \in \{0 \ldots 255\}$.

Step 2. Store the values of $S'[x]$ in order of $x = 0, \ldots 255$ to the table T as an entry with $key_0, \ldots, key_7$ as its index.

Step 3. Sort the table T based on the order of the sequence $S'[x]$ $x \in \{0 \ldots 255\}$.

During the online phase, the attacker can firstly exhaust all the 2^{16} values of two bytes $\overline{m_0}$ and $\overline{n_0}$. For each choice of $\overline{m_0}$ and $\overline{n_0}$, a determined S-box $S[\overline{m_0}, \overline{n_0}][i] = \Delta_0[i \oplus \overline{m_0}] \oplus \overline{n_0}$ ($i \in \mathbb{F}_2^8$) is computed. Obviously, $S[m_0, n_0][\cdot]$ equals $S_1[\cdot]$.

Next every $S[\overline{m_0}, \overline{n_0}][\cdot]$ can be decrypted using the rest 8-byte key key_8 to key_{15} and generates the corresponding S-box

$$S'[\overline{m_0}, \overline{n_0}][i] = SR^{-1}(SR^{-1}(\ldots (SR^{-1}(S_1[\overline{m_0}, \overline{n_0}][i]) \boxminus key_{15}) \ldots) \boxminus key_9) \boxminus key_8.$$

If $key_8, \ldots, key_{15}$ and m_0, n_0 are correct, then

$$S'[m_0, n_0][i] = SR[\ldots SR[SR[i \boxplus key_0] \boxplus key_1] \ldots \boxplus key_7].$$

Hence, each time a new $S'[\overline{m_0}, \overline{n_0}][\cdot]$ is produced, use the sequence $S'[\overline{m_0}, \overline{n_0}][x]$ $x \in \{0 \ldots 255\}$ to search table T and if there is a match, then return the key bytes $key_8, \ldots, key_{15}$ and the matching entry's index which is $key_0, \ldots, key_7$.

Complexity. In this paper, the complexity of sorting a table with 2^n entries is $O(n \cdot 2^n)$ computations and searching the ranked table takes $O(n)$ computations. In the offline phase, the table T is established and sorted which employs $2^{64} \cdot (2^8 + 8)$ bytes memory and $2^{64} \cdot 2^8 + 2^{64} \cdot 64$ computations, that indicates the memory and computation complexity of the offline phase are about $O(2^{72})$, respectively. For the online phase, the bytes $\overline{m_0}, \overline{n_0}, key_8, \ldots, key_{15}$ and i are exhausted, which leads to a computation complexity of $O(2^{16} \cdot 2^{64} \cdot 2^8 \cdot 64) = O(2^{94})$. And as stated in Section 3.4, the number of faults needed is about 2000.

4.2 Related Key Attacks

In order to recover the 128-bit key in reality, the attacker can take use of some related keys to the one he wants to restore. The main idea comes from that the S-box $S_1[\cdot]$ utilizes module adding 8-bit key and $SR[\cdot]$ iteratively.

Preparations. In order to strip the bytes of the key iteratively, a series of $S_1[\cdot]$ boxes keyed by the related keys are necessary. Therefore, we assume that the attacker knows the keystreams which are encrypted by keys related to the one he focuses on and some unknown IVs (can be different). Denote the secret key he wants to recover as $k0$.

$$k0 := key_0, key_1, key_2, key_3, key_4, key_5, key_6, key_7, key_8,$$
$$key_9, key_{10}, key_{11}, key_{12}, key_{13}, key_{14}, key_{15}.$$

Then the four related keys have the forms as follows, where some bytes of the keys are set to zero.

$$k1 := 0, key_1, key_2, key_3, key_4, key_5, key_6, key_7, key_8,$$
$$key_9, key_{10}, key_{11}, key_{12}, key_{13}, key_{14}, 0;$$
$$k2 := 0, 0, key_2, key_3, key_4, key_5, key_6, key_7, key_8,$$
$$key_9, key_{10}, key_{11}, key_{12}, key_{13}, 0, 0;$$
$$k3 := 0, 0, 0, key_3, key_4, key_5, key_6, key_7, key_8, key_9, key_{10}, key_{11}, key_{12}, 0, 0, 0;$$
$$k4 := 0, 0, 0, 0, key_4, key_5, key_6, key_7, key_8, key_9, key_{10}, key_{11}, 0, 0, 0, 0.$$

Each time the new keystream is generated from a related key, we can derive a new sequence $\Delta_j[0], \Delta_j[1], \ldots, \Delta_j[255]$ ($j = 0, \ldots, 4$) similar as that in problem 1, i.e., $\Delta_j[i] = S_1[m_j \oplus i] \oplus n_j$ $i \in \{0, \ldots 255\}$, with unknown m_j and $n_j = S_{1,kj}[m_j]$.

Procedure. Then the key recovery procedure is as follows, where Step 0 stands for the precomputing phase and other Steps constitute the online phase.

Step 0

For the key bytes $key_4, key_5, key_6, key_7$, precompute a 2^{32}-entry table T' similarly to the table T above to store $S''[x]$ and sort it, where

$$S''[x] = SR[\ldots SR[SR[x \boxplus key_4] \boxplus key_5] \ldots \boxplus key_7], \text{ for all } x \in \{0 \ldots 255\}.$$

Step 1

1. For 2^{16} (m_1, n_1) pairs, compute

$$S_{m_1 n_1}[x] = SR^{-1}(SR^{-1}(\Delta_1[SR^{-1}(x) \oplus m_1] \oplus n_1))$$

using the sequence $\Delta_1[i]$. Store $S_{m_1 n_1}[x]$ in turn of $x = 0, \ldots, 255$ as an entry to the table T1 with the index (m_1, n_1). Sort T1. Note that if m_1 and n_1 are correct, then

$$S_{m_1 n_1}[x] = SR(\ldots SR(x \boxplus key_1) \ldots) \boxplus key_{14}.$$

2. Similarly, for 2^{16} (m_3, n_3) pairs, compute

$$S_{m_3 n_3}[x] = SR^{-1}(SR^{-1}(SR^{-1}(SR^{-1}(\Delta_3[$$
$$SR^{-1}(SR^{-1}(SR^{-1}(x))) \oplus m_3] \oplus n_3))))$$

using the sequence $\Delta_3[i]$. Store $S_{m_3 n_3}[x]$ in turn of $x = 0, \ldots, 255$ as an entry to the table T3 with the index (m_3, n_3). Sort T3. Similarly if m_3 and n_3 are correct, then the corresponding

$$S_{m_3 n_3}[x] = SR(\ldots SR(x \boxplus key_3) \ldots) \boxplus key_{12}.$$

Step 2

1. For 2^{16} (m_0, n_0) pairs, compute

$$S_{m_0 n_0}[x] = SR^{-1}(\Delta_0[x \oplus m_0] \oplus n_0)$$

in turn of $x = 0, \ldots, 255$ which will be

$$SR(\ldots SR(x \boxplus key_0) \ldots) \boxplus key_{15}$$

if m_0 and n_0 are correct.

2. For each sequence $S_{m_0 n_0}[x]$, exhaust key_0 and key_{15}, compute $T0[i]$ in turn of $i \in \{0, \ldots 255\}$,

$$T0[i] = SR^{-1}(S_{m_0 n_0}[SR^{-1}(i) \boxminus key_0] \boxminus key_{15}).$$

3. Every time a new sequence $T0$ is generated, use it to search the entries in T1. If there is a match, return the current $key_0, key_{15}, m_0, n_0$ and the table's index m_1, n_1, i.e. a six bytes tuple

$$(m_0, n_0, m_1, n_1, key_0, key_{15}).$$

Step 3

1. For 2^{16} (m_2, n_2) pairs, compute

$$S_{m_2 n_2}[x] = SR^{-1}(SR^{-1}(SR^{-1}(\Delta_2[SR^{-1}(SR^{-1}(x)) \oplus m_2] \oplus n_2)))$$

in turn of $x = 0, \ldots, 255$. If m_2, n_2 are correct,

$$S_{m_2 n_2}[x] = SR(\ldots SR(x \boxplus key_2) \ldots) \boxplus key_{13}.$$

2. For each sequence $S_{m_2 n_2}[x]$, exhaust key_1 and key_{14}, compute two sequences $T2^1[i]$ and $T2^3[i]$ in turn of $i \in \{0, \ldots 255\}$,

$$T2_1[i] = SR(S_{m_2 n_2}[SR(i \boxplus key_1)]) \boxplus key_{14},$$

$$T2_3[i] = SR^{-1}(S_{m_2 n_2}[SR^{-1}(i) \boxminus key_1] \oplus key_{14}).$$

3. Every time a new sequence $T2_1$ is generated, use it to search the table T1. If there is a match in T1, return the current six bytes

$$(m_1, n_1, m_2, n_2, key_1, key_{14}).$$

And every time a new sequence $T2_3$ is generated, use it to search the table T3. If there is a match in T3, return the corresponding six bytes

$$(m_2, n_2, m_3, n_3, key_2, key_{13}),$$

where $key_2 = key_1, key_{13} = key_{14}$.

Step 4

1. For 2^{16} (m_4, n_4) pairs, compute

$$S_{m_4 n_4}[x] = SR^{-1}(SR^{-1}(SR^{-1}(SR^{-1}(SR^{-1}(\Delta_4$$
$$[SR^{-1}(SR^{-1}(SR^{-1}(SR^{-1}(x)))) \oplus m_4] \oplus n_4)))))$$

   in turn of $x = 0, \ldots, 255$. The correct m_4 and n_4 will lead to that

$$S_{m_4 n_4}[x] = SR(\ldots SR(x \boxplus key_4) \ldots) \boxplus key_{11}.$$

2. For each sequence $S_{m_4 n_4}[x]$, exhaust key_3 and key_{12}, compute $T4[i]$ in turn of $i \in \{0, \ldots 255\}$,

$$T4[i] = SR(S_{m_4 n_4}[SR(i \boxplus key_3)]) \boxplus key_{12}.$$

3. Every time a new sequence $T4$ is generated, use it to search the table T3. If there is a match, return the current

$$(m_3, n_3, m_4, n_4, key_3, key_{12}).$$

Step 5

1. Use the revealed m_4 and n_4, which is determined by the overlap of (m_i, n_i), $(i = 1, 2, 3)$ in the last steps to compute

$$S_4[x] = S_{m_4 n_4}[x]$$

   in turn of $x = 0, \ldots, 255$. As mentioned above, the right one equals to that

$$SR(\ldots SR(x \boxplus key_4) \ldots) \boxplus key_{11}.$$

2. Exhaust the key bytes $key_8, key_9, key_{10}, key_{11}$, for each choice compute

$$T5[i] = SR^{-1}(SR^{-1}(SR^{-1}(S_4[i] \boxminus key_{11}) \boxminus$$
$$key_{10}) \boxminus key_9) \boxminus key_8, \text{ for all } i \in \{0 \ldots 255\}.$$

3. Search the entries of T' which is established in Step 0 for a match with the sequence $T5$. If there is a match, return $key_4, \ldots, key_{11}$.

Until now we have get all the candidates for the sixteen bytes of the key by leaving only the key bytes together with the coincided m_j, n_j.

Validity of the Attack. For 10 random keys, we have simulated the process of revealing the outmost 8 bytes' key $key_0, \ldots, key_3, key_{12}, \ldots, key_{15}$. For each key we simulate $\Delta_j[0], \Delta_j[1], \ldots, \Delta_j[255]$ $(j = 0, \ldots, 4)$ by random chosen m_j. For example, one testing random key is

$$k0 := 0x38, BA, 52, DE, 33, 79, 45, BB, BC, BD, 1F, 74, F2, 36, A5, 52$$

and the corresponding random ms are

$$m_0, m_1, m_2, m_3, m_4 := 0xD8, A0, 21, F9, 38, 4B, 43.$$

Then we search the key bytes as Step 1 to Step 4. Experiments show that we only need one day to restore the 8-byte key in one computer when the codes are not optimized. But there is a fact we need to mention.

Fact. If $key_0, \ldots, key_3, key_{12}, \ldots, key_{15}$ are all zero, then the revealed (m_4, n_4) pairs in Step 5 are not unique, which will lead Step 5 to be impractical.

The fact is caused by that if $key_3 = key_{12} = 0$, then $\Delta_4[i] = \Delta_3[i \oplus x] \oplus y$, where $x, y \in \mathbb{F}_2^8$ are fixed but unknown. Therefore, totally 2^{16} m_4, n_4, m_3, n_3 satisfy that $m_4 \oplus m_3 = x$ and $n_4 \oplus n_3 = y$ can lead to a match in Step 4. Moreover, situations are similar to the other 6 bytes of key. Consequently, in order to conduct Step 5 successfully $key_0, \ldots, key_3$ and $key_{12}, \ldots, key_{15}$ must not be all zero together. Since if they are all zero, the candidates for m_4 and n_4 are too many which result in about $O(2^{40+16}) = O(2^{56})$ computation complexity.

Complexity. The procedure occupies small complexity, which can be practical. The table T' stores $2^{32} \cdot (256 + 4) \approx 2^{40}$ bytes data, and the table T1 and T3 only employ $2^{16} \cdot (256 + 2) \approx 2^{24}$ bytes. Then the memory complexity is about 2^{40} bytes. In aspect of computing complexity, Step 0 establishes table T' and sorts it, which totally consumes $2^{32} \cdot 2^8 + 2^{32} \cdot 32 \approx 2^{40}$ computations. Step 1 has two table-establishing computations and requires $2 \cdot (2^{16} \cdot 2^8 + 2^{16} \cdot 16) \approx 2^{25}$ complexity. Step 2 to 4 have the same computation complexity of $O(2^{16} \cdot 2^{16} \cdot 2^8 \cdot 16) = O(2^{44})$. Finally, Step 5 takes $O(2^{40})$ operations. For the reason that step 2 to 4 can be conducted in parallel, the total computing complexity is about $O(2^{44})$. Finally the number of required faults is about $5 \times 2^{11} \approx 2^{13}$ from Table 6 and formula (1) to get a high success probability.

5   Conclusion

This is the first reported differential fault attack and key recovery attack on the stream cipher Scream. The proposed cipher poses challenges to a traditional attack due to its complex internal states and key-dependent S-boxes. The paper shows how to detect and derive the key-dependent S-boxes' input and output differences from injecting random faults in some random internal states of the cipher. Various methods to retrieve the key directly from the key-dependent S-boxes are given, which means ignoring the complex initializing and updating steps the key can be detected if differences of the S-box are leaked since the S-box depends on the 128-bit key. The assumptions and results of the attacks are summarized in Table 7. Moreover, attacks under more related keys will take less memory complexity meanwhile more faults injected, which means there is a tradeoff between the memory complexity and the number of faults.

It is worth noting that though the secret S-box keyed by 16-byte key leads to high traditional attacks' complexity, it really gives a method to recover the key without concerning the structure of the cipher by side-channel attacks. This means that for cipher using key-dependent S-boxes there is a potentially danger that if the differences of the S-box is exposed, the key will be revealed directly. Similar attacks using the differences of the key-dependent S-boxes are conducted

Table 7. Summary of the attacks in this paper

Assumption	Keys	Faults	Memory (byte)	Computation	Precomputation
Injecting random byte	1	2^{11}	2^{72}	2^{94}	2^{72}
fault multiple times	5	2^{13}	2^{40}	2^{44}	2^{40}

in other ciphers such as Mir-1[13,14] and Twofish[15]. In the further works, the employment of key-dependent S-boxes must be masked and hidden meticulously to avoid the capacity of fault attacks.

Acknowledgments. This work was supported by the National Grand Fundamental Research 973 Programs of China(Grant No. 2013CB338002, 2011CB302400), the programs of the National Natural Science Foundation of China (Grant No. 61303258, 60833008, 60603018, 61173134, 91118006, 61272476).

References

1. Halevi, S., Coppersmith, D., Jutla, C.S.: Scream: A Software-Efficient Stream Cipher. In: Daemen, J., Rijmen, V. (eds.) FSE 2002. LNCS, vol. 2365, pp. 195–209. Springer, Heidelberg (2002)
2. Alexander, M., Thomas, J.: A Linear Distinguishing Attack on Scream. IEEE Transaction on Information Theory 53(9) (2007)
3. Coppersmith, D., Halevi, S., Jutla, C.S.: Cryptanalysis of Stream Ciphers with Linear Masking. In: Yung, M. (ed.) CRYPTO 2002. LNCS, vol. 2442, pp. 515–532. Springer, Heidelberg (2002)
4. Hoch, J.J., Shamir, A.: Fault Analysis of Stream Ciphers. In: Joye, M., Quisquater, J.-J. (eds.) CHES 2004. LNCS, vol. 3156, pp. 240–253. Springer, Heidelberg (2004)
5. Berzati, A., Canovas-Dumas, C., Goubin, L.: Fault Analysis of Rabbit: Toward a Secret Key Leakage. In: Roy, B., Sendrier, N. (eds.) INDOCRYPT 2009. LNCS, vol. 5922, pp. 72–87. Springer, Heidelberg (2009)
6. Hojsík, M., Rudolf, B.: Differential Fault Analysis of Trivium. In: Nyberg, K. (ed.) FSE 2008. LNCS, vol. 5086, pp. 158–172. Springer, Heidelberg (2008)
7. Banik, S., Maitra, S., Sarkar, S.: A Differential Fault Attack on the Grain Family of Stream Ciphers. In: Prouff, E., Schaumont, P. (eds.) CHES 2012. LNCS, vol. 7428, pp. 122–139. Springer, Heidelberg (2012)
8. Banik, S., Maitra, S.: A Differential Fault Attack on MICKEY 2.0. In: Bertoni, G., Coron, J.-S. (eds.) CHES 2013. LNCS, vol. 8086, pp. 215–232. Springer, Heidelberg (2013)
9. Yupu, H., Juntao, G., Qing, L., Yiwei, Z.: Fault Analysis of Trivium. Designs, Codes and Cryptography 62(3), 289–311 (2012)
10. Kircanski, A., Youssef, A.M.: Differential Fault Analysis of Rabbit. In: Jacobson Jr., M.J., Rijmen, V., Safavi-Naini, R. (eds.) SAC 2009. LNCS, vol. 5867, pp. 197–214. Springer, Heidelberg (2009)
11. Berzati, A., Canovas, C., Castagnos, G., Debraize, B., Goubin, L., Gouget, A., Paillier, P., Salgado, S.: Fault Analysis of Grain-128. In: IEEE International Workshop on Hardware-Oriented Security and Trust, pp. 7–14 (2009)
12. Karmakar, S., Roy Chowdhury, D.: Fault analysis of Grain-128 by targeting NFSR. In: Nitaj, A., Pointcheval, D. (eds.) AFRICACRYPT 2011. LNCS, vol. 6737, pp. 298–315. Springer, Heidelberg (2011)
13. Tsunoo, Y., Saito, T., Kubo, H., Suzaki, T.: Cryptanalysis of Mir-1: A T-Function-Based Stream Cipher. IEEE Transaction on Information Theory 53(11) (2007)
14. Tsunoo, Y., Saito, T., Kubo, H., Suzaki, T.: Key Recovery Attack on Stream Cipher Mir-1 Using a Key-Dependent S-Box. In: Chen, L., Ryan, M.D., Wang, G. (eds.) ICICS 2008. LNCS, vol. 5308, pp. 128–140. Springer, Heidelberg (2008)
15. Ali, S.S., Mukhopadhyay, D.: Differential Fault Analysis of Twofish. In: Kutyłowski, M., Yung, M. (eds.) Inscrypt 2012. LNCS, vol. 7763, pp. 10–28. Springer, Heidelberg (2013)

New Related Key Attacks on the RAKAPOSHI Stream Cipher*

Lin Ding[1], Chenhui Jin[1], Jie Guan[1], Shaowu Zhang[1],
Ting Cui[1], and Wei Zhao[2]

[1] Information Science and Technology Institute, 450000 Zhengzhou, China
[2] Science and Technology on Communication Security Laboratory,
610041 Chengdu, China
{dinglin_cipher,guanjie007}@163.com, jinchenhui@126.com

Abstract. RAKAPOSHI is a hardware oriented stream cipher designed by Cid et al. in 2009. It is based on Dynamic Linear Feedback Shift Registers, with a simple and potentially scalable design, and is particularly suitable for hardware applications with restricted resources. The RAKAPOSHI stream cipher offers 128-bit security. In this paper, we point out some mistakes existing in the related key attack on RAKAPOSHI by Isobe et al., and propose a new related key attack on RAKAPOSHI, which recovers the 128-bit secret key with a time complexity of 2^{56}, requiring one related key and 2^{55} chosen IVs. Furthermore, an improved key recovery attack on RAKAPOSHI in the multiple related key setting is proposed with a time complexity of 2^{33}, requiring $2^{12.58}$ chosen IVs. As confirmed by the experimental results, our new attack can recover all 128 key bits of RAKAPOSHI in less than 1.5 hours on a PC.

Keywords: Cryptanalysis, Related key attack, RAKAPOSHI, Stream cipher.

1 Introduction

Stream ciphers are symmetric encryption algorithms based on the concept of pseudorandom keystream generator. Although it seems rather difficult to construct a very fast and secure stream cipher, some efforts to achieve this have recently been deployed. The NESSIE project [1] launched in 1999 by the European Union did not succeed in selecting a secure enough stream cipher. In 2005, the European project ECRYPT decided to launch a competition to identify new stream ciphers that might be suitable for widespread adoption. This project is called eSTREAM [2] and received 35 submissions. Those candidates are divided into software oriented and hardware oriented stream ciphers. Hardware

* This work is supported in part by the National Natural Science Foundation of China (Grant No. 61202491, 61272041, 61272488, 61402523), the Foundation of Science and Technology on Information Assurance Laboratory (Grant No. KJ-13-007), and the Science and Technology on Communication Security Laboratory Foundation of China under Grant No. 9140C110203140C11049.

© Springer International Publishing Switzerland 2015
J. Lopez and Y. Wu (Eds.): ISPEC 2015, LNCS 9065, pp. 65–75, 2015.
DOI: 10.1007/978-3-319-17533-1_5

oriented stream ciphers should be suitable for deployment on passive RFID tags or low-cost devices such as might be used in sensor networks. Such devices are exceptionally constrained in computing potential because of the number of logic gates available or the amount of power that might realistically be available.

In 2009, Cid et al. [3] proposed a new stream cipher called RAKAPOSHI, which aims to complement the current eSTREAM portfolio of hardware oriented stream ciphers. RAKAPOSHI is based on Dynamic Linear Feedback Shift Registers (DLFSR), with a simple and potentially scalable design, and is particularly suitable for hardware applications with restricted resources. A Dynamic Linear Feedback Shift Register scheme is a general construction consisting usually of two registers: the first subregister A, is clocked regularly and updated using a fixed mapping. Subregister B, is updated using a linear mapping, which varies with time and depends of the state in register A. The design can be seem as a generalization of constructions found in early designs, including the stop-and-go generator [4], LILI [5], dynamic feedback polynomial switch [6], and K2 [7]. In fact, the RAKAPOSHI stream cipher is in fact a successor of the K2 stream cipher, but aiming at low-cost hardware implementations.

The RAKAPOSHI stream cipher offers 128-bit security. The designers claimed that the cipher design and security evaluation incorporates lessons learned during the several years of extensive analysis in the eSTREAM process, and thus RAKAPOSHI is less likely to be susceptible to more recent attacks, such as initialization attacks. However, three similar initialization attacks on RAKAPOSHI that were done independently have been reported recently. In [8], Isobe et al. analyzed the slide property of RAKAPOSHI stream cipher. They gave a related key attack which recovers the 128-bit key with time complexity of 2^{41} and 2^{38} chosen IVs. Orumiehchiha et al. [9] reported a related key attack on RAKAPOSHI with a time complexity of 2^9. However, their attack requires 32 related keys. It is difficult even impossible for the attacker to obtain so many related keys. In December 2012, our preliminary cryptanalysis result [10], which was done independently of two similar works (i.e., [8] and [9]), was announced on the IACR ePrint. The attack has a time complexity of 2^{37}, requiring 47 related keys and 2^8 chosen IVs. No attack on RAKAPOSHI stream cipher has been published except these three attacks.

In this paper, we make a deep security evaluation of RAKAPOSHI against related key attack. Firstly, we examine the related key attack on RAKAPOSHI proposed by Isobe et al., and show that their correct time complexity is 2^{84}, instead of 2^{41} claimed by them. Secondly, we present a new related key attack on RAKAPOSHI, which recovers the 128-bit secret key with a time complexity of 2^{56}, requiring 2^{55} chosen IVs. The attack is 'minimal' in the sense that it only requires one related key. Furthermore, we explore a related key attack on RAKAPOSHI with low complexities using less related keys than the attack by Orumiehchiha et al., which uses 32 related keys. Our attack has a time complexity of 2^{33}, requiring only 12 related keys and $2^{12.58}$ chosen IVs. The attack is an improvement of the cryptanalysis results of [9,10] . As confirmed by the experimental results, our attack can recover all 128 key bits of RAKAPOSHI in less than 1.5 hours on a PC.

This paper is organized as follows. In Section 2, we briefly describe RAKA-POSHI stream cipher. Section 3 proposes new related key attacks on RAKA-POSHI. Section 4 concludes this paper.

2   Brief Description of RAKAPOSHI Stream Cipher

The RAKAPOSHI stream cipher consists of three main building blocks, namely a 128-bit Non-Linear Feedback Shift Register (denoted as register A), a 192-bit Linear Feedback Shift Register (denoted as register B), and a non-linear filter function over $GF(2^8)$. It uses two bits from the state of the NLFSR to select and dynamically modify the linear feedback function of the LFSR. The keystream is produced by combining the output of both registers with the output of the non-linear filter function. An overview of its structure can be found in Figure 1.

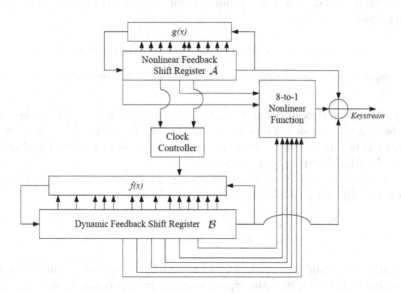

Fig. 1. The structure of RAKAPOSHI stream cipher

We denote by $A_t = (a_t, a_{t+1}, \cdots, a_{t+127})$ the contents of the LFSR at time t. Similarly, the content of the NFSR is denoted by $B_t = (b_t, b_{t+1}, \cdots, b_{t+191})$ at time t.

Non-Linear Feedback Shift Register A. The register A is a 128-bit NLSFR, defined using the following recurrence relation.

$$a_{t+128} = g(a_t, a_{t+6}, a_{t+7}, a_{t+11}, a_{t+16}, a_{t+28}, a_{t+36}, a_{t+45}, a_{t+55}, a_{t+62}) = 1 \oplus$$
$$a_t \oplus a_{t+6} \oplus a_{t+7} \oplus a_{t+11} \oplus a_{t+16} \oplus a_{t+28} \oplus a_{t+36} \oplus a_{t+45} \oplus a_{t+55} \oplus a_{t+62} \oplus a_{t+7}a_{t+45} \oplus$$
$$a_{t+11}a_{t+55} \oplus a_{t+7}a_{t+28} \oplus a_{t+28}a_{t+55} \oplus a_{t+6}a_{t+45}a_{t+62} \oplus a_{t+6}a_{t+11}a_{t+62}$$

Linear Feedback Shift Register B. The register B is a 192-bit dynamic LFSR. Register A is used to select and dynamically modify the feedback function of LFSR B using two bits from the state of register A, and as a result, Register B, which can use four different linear recursive functions, presents an irregular updating mechanism. Let c_0 and c_1 be the 42nd and 90th bits of register A at time t, respectively (that is, $c_0 = a_{t+41}$ and $c_1 = a_{t+89}$). Then LFSR B at time t is defined by the following recurrence relation. Here, $\overline{c_i} = c_i \oplus 1$ represents the negation of c_i.

$$b_{t+192} = f(c_0, c_1, b_t, b_{t+14}, b_{t+37}, b_{t+41}, b_{t+49}, b_{t+51}, b_{t+93}, b_{t+107}, b_{t+120}, b_{t+134},$$
$$b_{t+136}, b_{t+155}, b_{t+158}, b_{t+176}) = b_t \oplus b_{t+14} \oplus b_{t+37} \oplus b_{t+41} \oplus b_{t+49} \oplus b_{t+51} \oplus b_{t+93} \oplus \overline{c_0} \cdot$$
$$\overline{c_1} \cdot b_{t+107} \oplus \overline{c_0} \cdot c_1 \cdot b_{t+120} \oplus c_0 \cdot \overline{c_1} \cdot b_{t+134} \oplus c_0 \cdot c_1 \cdot b_{t+136} \oplus \overline{c_0} \cdot b_{t+155} \oplus c_0 \cdot b_{t+158} \oplus b_{t+176}$$

Non-Linear Filter. The 8-to-1 non-linear filter function is the same function used as the non-affine component of the AES S-Box. This function is a balanced Boolean function, with polynomial representation (ANF) of degree 7. In the RAKAPOSHI stream cipher, the input bits for this function are extracted from both registers A and B, as

$$s_t = v(a_{t+67}, a_{t+127}, b_{t+23}, b_{t+53}, b_{t+77}, b_{t+81}, b_{t+103}, b_{t+128})$$

The explicit polynomial expression of the function is given in the [3].

Initialization Process. The RAKAPOSHI stream cipher supports key size of 128 bits and IV size of 192 bits. Before the generation of the cipher keystream, the cipher is initialized with the secret key and a selected IV. The initialization process of RAKAPOSHI is done as follows.

Firstly, the secret key $K = (k_0, \cdots, k_{127})$ and $IV = (iv_0, \cdots, iv_{191})$ are loaded into the NLFSR and DLFSR, respectively, as follows.

$$(a_0, \cdots, a_{127}) \leftarrow (k_0, \cdots, k_{127})$$
$$(b_0, \cdots, b_{191}) \leftarrow (iv_0, \cdots, iv_{191})$$

Secondly, the cipher then clocks 448 times with the output of the filter function (i.e., s_t) being fed back into the cipher state. This process is divided into two stages.

- In the first stage of the initialization, the cipher runs for 320 cycles, with the output of the non-linear filter function being fed back into the register B.
- In the second stage of the initialization, the cipher runs for further 128 cycles, with the output of the non-linear filter function being fed back into the register A.
- At the end of the initialization, the cipher internal state is $S_{448} = (A_{448}, B_{448})$, and it is ready to produce the first keystream bit z_0.

Keystream Generation. The cipher outputs one keystream bit at each cycle. Given the cipher state $S_t = (A_t, B_t)$ at time t, the cipher operates as follows.

- The keystream bit z_t is computed as $z_t = a_t \oplus b_t \oplus s_t$.
- $c_0, c_1 \in A_t$ are used to update the register B.
- Registers A and B are updated to obtain A_{t+1} and B_{t+1}, respectively.

3   New Related Key Attacks on RAKAPOSHI Stream Cipher

In this Section, we will propose new related key attacks on RAKAPOSHI stream cipher. The basic related key attack relies on an assumption, i.e., encryption is performed using two different keys with a linear or nonlinear relationship which is known to the attacker, while the values of these keys are unknown, and the attacker is allowed to get enough keystream bits generated by each related key. As we know, this assumption is reasonable in the related key setting [33].

Let (K, IV) and (K', IV') be two different Key-IV pairs, and their corresponding internal states at time t are denoted as $S_t = (a_t, a_{t+1}, \cdots, a_{t+127};$ $b_t, b_{t+1}, \cdots, b_{t+191})$ and $S'_t = (a'_t, a'_{t+1}, \cdots, a'_{t+127}; b'_t, b'_{t+1}, \cdots, b'_{t+191})$, respectively. For convenience, we give a definition as follows.

Definition 1. Two different Key-IV pairs (K, IV) and (K', IV') are called an **i-bit slide** of RAKAPOSHI, if $S_i = S'_0$ holds for a certain positive integer i satisfying $1 \leqslant i < 448$.

In the following Subsection, we will introduce a simple related key attack on RAKAPOSHI stream cipher based on 1-bit slide property.

3.1   Related Key Attack on RAKAPOSHI Based on 1-bit Slide Property

The attack on RAKAPOSHI is done by assuming that the relation of (K, IV) and (K', IV') is defined as follows.

$$K = (k_0, \cdots, k_{127}) \Rightarrow K' = (k_1, \cdots, k_{127}, k'_0)$$
$$IV = (iv_0, \cdots, iv_{191}) \Rightarrow IV' = (iv_1, \cdots, iv_{191}, 0)$$

where $k'_0 = g(k_0, k_6, k_7, k_{11}, k_{16}, k_{28}, k_{36}, k_{45}, k_{55}, k_{62})$.

Let Z and Z' be keystream sequences generated from (K, IV) and (K', IV'). According to the initialization process of RAKAPOSHI, we can get two properties as follows.

Property 1. $S_1 = S'_0$ holds when the following two conditions are simultaneously satisfied.
  a) $g(A_0) = k'_0$
  b) $f(B_0) \oplus s_0 = 0$.

Property 2. If $S_1 = S'_0$ holds, the system $S_{i+1} = S'_i$ holds for $i \geqslant 1$ when the following two conditions are simultaneously satisfied.

   c) $s_{320} = 0$;

   d) $s_{448} = 0$.

Since the conditions c) and d) are obtained in different clocks, and then are assumed to be independent to facilitate calculation of probability $\Pr(c \cap d) = \Pr(c) \cdot \Pr(d) = 2^{-2}$. It is easy to see that if the system $S_{449} = S'_{448}$ holds, there exists a clear relation between Z and Z', i.e., $z_{i+1} = z'_i$ for $i \geqslant 0$. The discovered weakness allows the adversary to distinguish the cipher from a random bit generator easily.

In the Subsection 5.1 of [8], Isobe et al. presented a simple algorithm to recover four key bits, and then explored a related key attack, which recovers a 128-bit secret key with time complexity of 2^{124}, 2^6 chosen IVs and one related key. As showed in Subsection 3.3 of [9], the number of chosen IVs required can be reduced to 2^5 by choosing appropriate bits for IVs. We give a detailed related key attack on RAKAPOSHI stream cipher based on the 1-bit slide property in Appendix, which is omitted in [9].

3.2   Related Key Attacks on RAKAPOSHI Based on n-bit Slide Property

There are much more Key-IV slides for longer shifts, but the equations making $S_n = S'_0$ to be satisfied would be much more complicated. As pointed out in [8,9], a useful property is introduced as follows.

Property 3. [8,9] For an n-bit slide, (K', IV') produces n-bit shifted keystream with respect to (K, IV) with probability of 2^{-2n}.

As showed in [8], Isobe et al. presented related key attack on RAKAPOSHI based on 4-bit and 11-bit slides. Unfortunately, they made mistakes in their attacks, which lead to wrong complexities. Take 4-bit slide as an example. As claimed in Subsection 5.2 of [8], '$\{y_0, \cdots, y_3\}$ *includes 4, 13, 13 and 13 key bits, respectively, and in total these involve independent 41 key bits. If 13 independent equations regarding each y are obtained (For y_0, 4 independent equations are enough), we can determine key bits included in each equation*'. In their paper, $y_i = f(B_i) \oplus s_i$ is defined. In fact, for $i = 1, 2, 3$, the a_{127+i} appears as a variable in the expression of y_i. The value of a_{127+i} is fixed, since its expression only involves key bits. Though different IVs are used in their attack, only the values of $\{a_{128}, a_{129}, a_{130}\}$ can be recovered, the key bits involved in their expressions (i.e., the figures between parentheses in lines 3-5 of Table 1) can not be recovered. Thus, the attacker can not recover 41 key bits. The correct way is to recover 13 key bits and obtain 3 equations, and then guess 112 key bits to recover 3 key bits using the obtained 3 equations. Thus, their attack recovers the key with a time complexity of 2^{112}, rather than 2^{87}.

Table 1. Included key bits in each y_t

y_t	Included key bits
y_0	41, 67, 89, 127
y_1	42, 68, 90, (0, 6, 7, 11, 16, 28, 36, 45, 55, 62)
y_2	43, 69, 91, (1, 7, 8, 12, 17, 29, 37, 46, 56, 63)
y_3	44, 70, 92, (2, 8, 9, 13, 18, 30, 38, 47, 57, 64)
y_4	45, 71, 93, (3, 9, 10, 14, 19, 31, 39, 48, 58, 65)
y_5	46, 72, 94, (4, 10, 11, 15, 20, 32, 40, 49, 59, 66)
y_6	47, 73, 95, (5, 11, 12, 16, 21, 33, 41, 50, 60, 67)
y_7	48, 74, 96, (6, 12, 13, 17, 22, 34, 42, 51, 61, 68)
y_8	49, 75, 97, (7, 13, 14, 18, 23, 35, 43, 52, 62, 69)
y_9	50, 76, 98, (8, 14, 15, 19, 24, 36, 44, 53, 63, 70)
y_{10}	51, 77, 99, (9, 15, 16, 20, 25, 37, 45, 54, 64, 71)

Furthermore, their attack requires 2^{17} chosen IVs, which can be reduced to 2^9. As showed in Subsection 3.1, the attacker can simplify the equation $f(B_i) \oplus s_i = 0$ $(i = 0, 1, 2, 3)$ by fixing some IV bits and then recover the key bits involved in the simplified equations. According to Property 3, the expected number of (IV, IV') pairs used in the attack is 2^8. Thus, our attack requires 2^9 chosen IVs on average to recover 13 key bits and obtain 3 equations, which leads to a time complexity of 2^9. Then we have to make an exhaustive search of 112 bits of the key to recover all 128 key bits, which leads to a time complexity of 2^{112}. Thus, the correct related key attack based on 4-bit slide property recovers the 128-bit key with a time complexity of $2^{112} + 2^9 \approx 2^{112}$, requiring 2^9 chosen IVs and one related key.

Similarly, the related key attack on RAKAPOSHI based on 11-bit slide presented by [8] is also wrong. In fact, their attack can only recover 44 key bits, rather than 88 key bits claimed by them. Thus, the correct time complexity of of their attack is $2^{128-44} = 2^{84}$, rather then 2^{41}. Their attack requires 2^{38} chosen IVs, which can also be reduced, similar to the attack based on 4-bit slide property.

For a general case, i.e., n-bit slide of RAKAPOSHI stream cipher, we can apply the related key attack on it similarly. The related key attack based on n-bit slide property recovers the 128-bit key with a time complexity of $2^{128-4n} + 2^{3n+1}$, requiring 2^{3n+1} chosen IVs and one related key. Table 2 shows the complexities of our attack on RAKAPOSHI for parameter n.

Table 2. Our results on RAKAPOSHI for parameter n

n	Time complexity	Chosen IVs
12	2^{80}	2^{37}
14	2^{72}	2^{43}
16	2^{64}	2^{49}
18	2^{56}	2^{55}

Clearly, the choice of $n = 18$ is reasonable. Thus, we can recover the 128-bit secret key of RAKAPOSHI with a time complexity of 2^{56}, requiring one related key and 2^{55} chosen IVs.

3.3 New Related Key Attack on RAKAPOSHI in the Multiple Related Key Setting

In the Subsection 3.2, we present a related key attack on RAKAPOSHI with a time complexity of 2^{56}, which is still high and makes the attack impractical. In [9], the authors showed that the 128-bit secret key of RAKAPOSHI can be recovered with a time complexity of 2^9. However, their attack requires 32 related keys. It is difficult even impossible for the attacker to obtain so many related keys. Obviously, there exists a trade-off relationship between the complexities and the number of related keys. In this Subsection, we aim to present a new related key attack on RAKAPOSHI with low complexities using less related keys. This attack is based on 4-bit slide property of RAKAPOSHI. In this attack, we use m related keys, which are showed as follows.

For $0 \leqslant j \leqslant m - 1$,

$$K_j = (k_0, \cdots, k_{127}) \Rightarrow K_{j+1} = (k_4, \cdots, k_{127}, k'_0, k'_1, k'_2, k'_3)$$
$$IV_j = (iv_0, \cdots, iv_{191}) \Rightarrow IV_{j+1} = (iv_4, \cdots, iv_{191}, 0, 0, 0, 0)$$

Note that $K_0 = K$. For each (K_j, K_{j+1}) pair, we run a related key attack based on 4-bit slide property of RAKAPOSHI. As showed in the Subsection 3.2, we can recover 13 key bits and obtain 3 equations, with a time complexity of 2^9, requiring 2^9 chosen IVs. Given 12 related keys, we can recover 95 key bits directly, i.e., $k_0, \cdots k_8, k_{41}, \cdots, k_{127}$. Simultaneously, we can obtain 36 equations. Then we can make an exhaustive search of the remaining 33 key bits, and recover them utilizing these 36 equations. Thus, we can recover the 128-bit secret key of RAKAPOSHI with a time complexity of $2^9 \times 12 + 2^{33} \approx 2^{33}$, requiring 12 related keys and $2^9 \times 12 = 2^{12.58}$ chosen IVs.

We validate our result by simulating the related key attack above. The result shows that we can recover the 95 key bits within one second. By simulating RAKAPOSHI stream cipher, the remaining 33 can be recovered within 1.44 hours on average. The simulation was implemented on AMD Athlon(tm) 64 X2 Dual Core Processor 4400+, CPU 2.31GHz, 768 Gb RAM, OS Windows XP Pro SP3. The experimental result corroborates our assertion.

4   Conclusions

RAKAPOSHI is a hardware oriented stream cipher designed by Carlos Cid et al. in 2009. The RAKAPOSHI stream cipher offers 128-bit security. In this paper, we make a deep security evaluation of RAKAPOSHI against related key attack. A new related key attack on RAKAPOSHI is proposed, which recovers the 128-bit secret key with a time complexity of 2^{56}, requiring 2^{55} chosen IVs. The attack is 'minimal' in the sense that it only requires one related key. Furthermore, we aim to improve the existing related key attacks in the multiple related key setting. As confirmed by the experimental results, our attack recovers all 128 key bits of RAKAPOSHI in less than 1.5 hours on a PC. The comparisons of our attack with all known related key attacks on RAKAPOSHI are showed in Table 3.

Table 3. Comparison of our attack with all known related key attacks on RAKAPOSHI

Attacks	Related keys	Time complexity	Chosen IVs
[8]	1	Claimed: 2^{41} (Corrected: 2^{84})	2^{38}
Out attack	1	2^{56}	2^{55}
[9]	32	2^{9}	2^{9}
[10]	47	2^{37}	2^{8}
Out attack	12	2^{33}	$2^{12.58}$

References

1. New European Schemes for Signatures, Integrity, and Encryption, http://www.cryptonessie.org (accessed August 18, 2003)
2. ECRYPT. eSTREAM: ECRYPT Stream Cipher Project, IST-2002-507932, http://www.ecrypt.eu.org/stream/ (accessed September 29, 2005)
3. Cid, C., Kiyomoto, S., Kurihara, J.: The RAKAPOSHI Stream Cipher. In: Qing, S., Mitchell, C.J., Wang, G. (eds.) ICICS 2009. LNCS, vol. 5927, pp. 32–46. Springer, Heidelberg (2009)
4. Beth, T., Piper, F.: The Stop-and-Go Generator. In: Beth, T., Cot, N., Ingemarsson, I. (eds.) EUROCRYPT 1984. LNCS, vol. 209, pp. 88–92. Springer, Heidelberg (1985)
5. Simpson, L.R., Dawson, E., Golić, J.D., Millan, W.L.: LILI Keystream Generator. In: Stinson, D.R., Tavares, S. (eds.) SAC 2000. LNCS, vol. 2012, pp. 248–261. Springer, Heidelberg (2001)
6. Horan, D., Guinee, R.: A Novel Keystream Generator using Pseudo Random Binary Sequences for Cryptographic Applications. In: Proceedings of Irish Signals and Systems Conference, pp. 451–456. IEEE (2006)
7. Kiyomoto, S., Tanaka, T., Sakurai, K.: K2: A Stream Cipher Algorithm Using Dynamic Feedback Control. In: Proceedings of SECRYPT 2007, pp. 204–213 (2007)
8. Isobe, T., Ohigashi, T., Morii, M.: Slide cryptanalysis of lightweight stream cipher RAKAPOSHI. In: Hanaoka, G., Yamauchi, T. (eds.) IWSEC 2012. LNCS, vol. 7631, pp. 138–155. Springer, Heidelberg (2012)
9. Orumiehchiha, M.A., Pieprzyk, J., Shakour, E., Steinfeld, R.: Security Evaluation of Rakaposhi Stream Cipher. In: Deng, R.H., Feng, T. (eds.) ISPEC 2013. LNCS, vol. 7863, pp. 361–371. Springer, Heidelberg (2013)
10. Ding, L., Guan, J.: Cryptanalysis of RAKAPOSHI Stream Cipher, Cryptology ePrint Archive Report 2012/696, http://eprint.iacr.org/

Appendix

In Appendix, We will give a detailed related key attack on RAKAPOSHI stream cipher based on the 1-bit slide property, which is omitted in [9].

Firstly, we give two useful simplified equations of $f(B_0) \oplus s_0 = 0$ by fixing some IV bits.

- If we choose $iv_{107} = iv_{120} = iv_{134} = iv_{136} = iv_{155} = 0$ and $iv_{158} = 1$, the equation $f(B_0) \oplus s_0 = 0$ can be simplified to equation (1) as
$f(B_0) \oplus s_0 = iv_0 \oplus iv_{14} \oplus iv_{37} \oplus iv_{41} \oplus iv_{49} \oplus iv_{51} \oplus iv_{93} \oplus c_0 \cdot iv_{158} \oplus iv_{176} \oplus s_0 =$
$iv_0 \oplus iv_{14} \oplus iv_{37} \oplus iv_{41} \oplus iv_{49} \oplus iv_{51} \oplus iv_{93} \oplus k_{41} \oplus iv_{176} \oplus s_0 = 0$
Where $s_0 = v(a_{67}, a_{127}, b_{23}, b_{53}, b_{77}, b_{81}, b_{103}, b_{128}) = v(k_{67}, k_{127}, iv_{23}, iv_{53}, iv_{77}, iv_{81}, iv_{103}, iv_{128})$.

- If we choose $iv_{107} = iv_{136} = iv_{158} = iv_{155} = 0$ and $iv_{120} = iv_{134} = 1$, the equation $f(B_0) \oplus s_0 = 0$ can be simplified to equation (2) as
$f(B_0) \oplus s_0 = iv_0 \oplus iv_{14} \oplus iv_{37} \oplus iv_{41} \oplus iv_{49} \oplus iv_{51} \oplus iv_{93} \oplus \overline{c_0} \cdot c_1 \cdot iv_{120} \oplus c_0 \cdot \overline{c_1} \cdot iv_{134} \oplus iv_{176} \oplus s_0 = iv_0 \oplus iv_{14} \oplus iv_{37} \oplus iv_{41} \oplus iv_{49} \oplus iv_{51} \oplus iv_{93} \oplus k_{41} \oplus k_{89} \oplus iv_{176} \oplus s_0 = 0$

Recall the non-linear filter function. Three functions, denoted as (3-5), can be obtained as follows.

If $iv_{23} = iv_{53} = iv_{77} = iv_{81} = iv_{128} = 0$ and $iv_{103} = 1$,

$$s_0 = v(k_{67}, k_{127}, iv_{23}, iv_{53}, iv_{77}, iv_{81}, iv_{103}, iv_{128}) = 1$$

If $iv_{23} = iv_{53} = iv_{77} = iv_{103} = iv_{128} = 0$ and $iv_{81} = 1$,

$$s_0 = v(k_{67}, k_{127}, iv_{23}, iv_{53}, iv_{77}, iv_{81}, iv_{103}, iv_{128}) = k_{67} \oplus 1$$

If $iv_{77} = iv_{81} = iv_{103} = iv_{128} = 0$ and $iv_{23} = iv_{53} = 1$,

$$s_0 = v(k_{67}, k_{127}, iv_{23}, iv_{53}, iv_{77}, iv_{81}, iv_{103}, iv_{128}) = k_{127}$$

Now, we will introduce a method to recover four key bits, named Algorithm 1.

Algorithm 1

1. Under the related keys K and K', do the followings.

a) For each of chosen IVs satisfying $iv_{107} = iv_{120} = iv_{134} = iv_{136} = iv_{155} = iv_{23} = iv_{53} = iv_{77} = iv_{81} = iv_{128} = 0$ and $iv_{158} = iv_{103} = 1$, generate two keystream sequences using (K, IV) and (K', IV') respectively, and then check if (K', IV') produces 1-bit shifted keystream with respect to (K, IV). If these two keystream sequences pass the check, then a 1-bit slide is found. It means that the equations (1) and (3) are simultaneously satisfied, and then the key bit k_{41} can be easily recovered. Otherwise go back to try other chosen IVs.

b) For each of chosen IVs satisfying $iv_{107} = iv_{136} = iv_{155} = iv_{158} = iv_{23} = iv_{53} = iv_{77} = iv_{81} = iv_{128} = 0$ and $iv_{120} = iv_{134} = iv_{103} = 1$, generate two keystream sequences using (K, IV) and (K', IV')respectively, and then check if(K', IV') produces 1-bit shifted keystream with respect to (K, IV). If these two keystream sequences pass the check, then a 1-bit slide is found. It means that the equations (2) and (3) are simultaneously satisfied, and then the key bit k_{89} can be easily recovered, since the key bit k_{41} has been recovered above. Otherwise go back to try other chosen IVs.

c) For each of chosen IVs satisfying $iv_{107} = iv_{120} = iv_{134} = iv_{136} = iv_{155} = iv_{23} = iv_{53} = iv_{77} = iv_{103} = iv_{128} = 0$ and $iv_{158} = iv_{81} = 1$, generate two keystream sequences using (K, IV) and (K', IV') respectively, and then check if(K', IV') produces 1-bit shifted keystream with respect to (K, IV). If these two keystream sequences pass the check, then a 1-bit slide is found. It means that the equations (1) and (4) are simultaneously satisfied, and then the key bit k_{67} can be easily recovered, since the key bit k_{41} has been recovered above. Otherwise go back to try other chosen IVs.

d) For each of chosen IVs satisfying $iv_{107} = iv_{120} = iv_{134} = iv_{136} = iv_{155} = iv_{77} = iv_{81} = iv_{103} = iv_{128} = 0$ and $iv_{158} = iv_{23} = iv_{53} = 1$, generate two keystream sequences using (K, IV) and (K', IV') respectively, and then check if (K', IV') produces 1-bit shifted keystream with respect to (K, IV). If these two keystream sequences pass the check, then a 1-bit slide is found. It means that the equations (1) and (5) are simultaneously satisfied, and then the key bit k_{127} can be easily recovered, since the key bitk_{41} has been recovered above. Otherwise go back to try other chosen IVs.

Since the probability that the conditions c) and d) are simultaneously satisfied is 2^{-2}, the expected number of (IV, IV') pairs used in each step of Algorithm 1 is 4. Thus, Algorithm 1 requires $4 \times 4 \times 2 = 2^5$ chosen IVs on average to recover four key bits, which leads to a time complexity of 2^5. Then we have to make an exhaustive search of $124(= 128 - 4)$ bits of the key to recover all 128 key bits, which leads to a time complexity of 2^{124}. Thus, the related key attack based on 1-slide property recovers the 128-bit key with a time complexity of $2^{124} + 2^5 \approx 2^{124}$, requiring 2^5 chosen IVs and one related key.

Analysis

Cramer-Shoup Like Chosen Ciphertext Security from LPN*

Xiaochao Sun[1,2,3], Bao Li[1,2], and Xianhui Lu[1,2]

[1] Data Assurance and Communication Security Research Center,
Chinese Academy of Sciences, Beijing, 100093, China
[2] State Key Laboratory of Information Security, Institute of Information Engineering,
Chinese Academy of Sciences, Beijing, 100093, China
[3] University of Chinese Academy of Sciences, Beijing, China
{xchsun,lb,xhlu}@is.ac.cn

Abstract. We propose two chosen ciphertext secure public key encryption schemes from the learning parity with noise problem. Currently, all existing chosen ciphertext secure public key encryption schemes from the hard learning problems are constructed based on the All-But-One technique, while our schemes are based on the Cramer-Shoup technique.

Keywords: Public key encryption, chosen-ciphertext security, LPN.

1 Introduction

Indistinguishability against adaptive chosen ciphertext security (IND-CCA2) is the most widely studied security notion in the public key encryption (PKE) area and there are many constructions, among which Cramer and Shoup [11] proposed hybrid encryption. The hybrid encryption [11, 29, 43] includes a key encapsulation mechanism (KEM) part to encapsulate a session key and a data encapsulation mechanism (DEM) part to encrypt the actual message with this session key. Basically, there are two efficient and practical approaches for a PKE (KEM) scheme to achieve IND-CCA2 security, one is through the All-But-One technique [14, 25], the other is through the *hash proof system* (HPS) approach [10, 21, 28], which is a generalization of Cramer and Shoup's PKE scheme based on the Diffie-Hellman (DDH) problem in [9].

The *learning with errors* (LWE) problem, a generalization of the *learning parity with noise* (LPN) problem, has been applied in many cryptographic scenarios in the last decade, including chosen-plaintext (IND-CPA) secure PKE [19,24,37, 40], IND-CCA2 secure PKE [32,36,38], *identity-based encryption* (IBE) [1,8,32] and *fully homomorphic encryption* (FHE) [17, 18]. Formally, for a dimension $n \in \mathbb{Z}$, a modulus $q \in \mathbb{Z}$ and an error distribution χ over $\mathbb{Z}_q$, it asks to distinguish

---

* This work is supported by the National Basic Research Program of China (973 project)(No.2013CB338002), the National Nature Science Foundation of China (No.61379137, No.61272040) and the State Key Laboratory of Information Security IIEs Research Project on Cryptography (No.Y4Z0061403).

J. Lopez and Y. Wu (Eds.): ISPEC 2015, LNCS 9065, pp. 79–95, 2015.
DOI: 10.1007/978-3-319-17533-1_6

the distribution $D_{\mathrm{LWE}(n,m,\chi)} = ((\mathbf{A}, \mathbf{b} = \mathbf{A}\mathbf{s} + \mathbf{e})|\mathbf{A} \leftarrow \mathbb{Z}_q^{m \times n}, \mathbf{s} \leftarrow \mathbb{Z}_q^n, \mathbf{e} \leftarrow \chi^m)$ from the uniform. LPN is the special case where $q = 2$.

CCA FROM LWE. LWE based PKE was first proposed by Regev in [40], where χ is the discrete Gaussian distribution and $q = poly(n)$ is a prime. Peikert and Waters proposed a new framework to construct IND-CCA2 secure PKE schemes based on a newly introduced primitive named as lossy trapdoor function (LTDF), and showed that LTDF can be realized from the LWE problem [38]. Peikert observed that the LWE problem can be used to construct correlated products trapdoor function [36], which can be used to construct IND-CCA2 secure PKE schemes [42]. Using the generic conversion technique in [6], one can obtain IND-CCA2 secure PKE schemes from IBE schemes based on the LWE problem [1, 8]. Micciancio and Peikert proposed a new method to generate trapdoors for the LWE problem [32]. Based on their new technique, an efficient IND-CCA2 secure PKE scheme was proposed. In fact, they constructed an *adaptive trapdoor function* (ATDF) based on the LWE problem by using their new technique and achieved IND-CCA2 security according to the technique in [27].

CCA FROM LPN. The LPN problem seems quite different from the LWE problem. In the standard LPN problem, the noise rate p is constant (typically, $p = \frac{1}{10}$). The approaches to PKE based on LWE cannot be used to construct PKE based on LPN directly. For LPN based PKE, Alekhnovich introduced a low-noise variant of the LPN problem by lowering the number of samples and the noise rate simultaneously [2]. In the variant, the noise rate is $p = \Theta(1/\sqrt{n})$ rather than a constant in the standard LPN problem, and the number of samples is $m = O(n)$ rather than $poly(n)$. After lowering the noise rate and the number of samples, the classical algorithms to solve the variant still requires $2^{O(\sqrt{n})}$ time [4,5,44]. It seems that no quantum algorithm performs better than classical algorithms.

Döttling et al. developed a PKE scheme based on Alekhnovich's variant [15]. They gave a new IND-CPA secure PKE scheme, which can be viewed as the LPN analog of Regev's PKE scheme from the LWE problem [40]. The main idea is to handle the errors produced in decryption by using *error-correcting code*. To achieve IND-CCA2 security, the generic All-But-One technique is used [14, 42]. As a result, the size of both the public key and the secret key are large. Kiltz et al. proposed a more compact and efficient IND-CCA2 secure PKE scheme with *double-trapdoor mechanism* and a computational variant of leftover hash lemma [26].

1.1   Motivation

Currently, all IND-CCA2 secure PKE schemes from hard learning problems are based on the All-But-One technique [14]. Whether an IND-CCA2 secure PKE scheme can be constructed from hard learning problems under the technique of HPS is an interesting open problem theoretically.

1.2 Our Contribution and Techniques

We propose two IND-CCA2 secure hybrid encryption schemes under the LPN assumption. In our schemes, we employ randomness extraction based on LPN assumption to obtain a uniform session key in KEM part [28], and encrypt message using one-time authenticated encryption with the session key in DEM part.

Compared with the previous PKE schemes based on the Cramer-Shoup technique from subset membership problems [7, 9, 21, 25], the main difficulty in the construction of LPN based schemes is how to deal with the noise in the simulation of the challenge ciphertext. Concretely, the ciphertext generated by the encryption algorithm is $(\mathbf{A}_1\mathbf{s} + \mathbf{e}_1, \mathbf{A}_2\mathbf{s} + \mathbf{e}_2, \mathbf{H}\mathbf{s} + \mathbf{T}'_1\mathbf{e}_1 + \mathbf{T}'_2\mathbf{e}_2 + \mathbf{G}\mathbf{r}, \mathsf{AE}.\mathsf{E}(\mathbf{k}, \mathbf{m}))$, where $\mathsf{AE}.\mathsf{E}(\cdot, \cdot)$ the encryption algorithm of an authenticated encryption scheme $\mathsf{AE} = (\mathsf{AE}.\mathsf{E}, \mathsf{AE}.\mathsf{D})$. However, in the security reduction, when the LPN problem is embedded into the first two elements of the challenge ciphertext, the simulator does not possess the random coins $\mathbf{s}$ and the noise $\mathbf{e}_1, \mathbf{e}_2$. Hence, the third element of the challenge ciphertext generated directly by using the secret key $(\mathbf{T}_1, \mathbf{T}_2)$ is $\mathbf{H}\mathbf{s} + \mathbf{T}_1\mathbf{e}_1 + \mathbf{T}_2\mathbf{e}_2 + \mathbf{G}\mathbf{r}$. Similar problem also occurs in the security reduction of Kiltz et al.'s scheme [26]. They settle this problem by using the double trapdoor mechanism. However, this technique increases the size of the ciphertext. To solve this problem without increasing the size of the ciphertext, we prove that $\mathbf{H}\mathbf{s} + \mathbf{T}'_1\mathbf{e}_1 + \mathbf{T}'_2\mathbf{e}_2$ and $\mathbf{H}\mathbf{s} + \mathbf{T}_1\mathbf{e}_1 + \mathbf{T}_2\mathbf{e}_2$ are indistinguishable based on the EKLPN problem and the KLPN problem (actually a new problem based on EKLPN and KLPN), even if given an access of decryption oracle. Intuitively, we embed the basic EKLPN into the ciphertext. In the security reduction the simulator possesses all rows of $(\mathbf{T}_1, \mathbf{T}_2)$ except one row where the EKLPN is embedded. Thanks to the error-correcting codes, the simulator can answer the decryption query successfully in this case.

2 Preliminaries

Let $\mathbb{Z}_q$ be the q-ary finite field for a prime $q \geq 2$. If $\mathbf{x}$ is a vector over $\mathbb{Z}_2^n$, then $|\mathbf{x}|$ denotes the hamming weight of $\mathbf{x}$. If $\mathcal{A}$ is an algorithm, then $y \leftarrow \mathcal{A}(x)$ denotes that $\mathcal{A}$ outputs y with input x, no matter $\mathcal{A}$ is deterministic or probabilistic. Specially, we denote by $y \leftarrow \mathcal{A}^{\mathcal{O}}(x)$ that when $\mathcal{A}$ has access to an oracle $\mathcal{O}$, $\mathcal{A}$ outputs y with input x. Assuming that there is an efficient algorithm that samples from a distribution D, $e \leftarrow D$ denotes that the random variable e is output from the algorithm. If S is a finite set, then $s \leftarrow S$ denotes sampling s from S uniformly at random. We write $\mathcal{B}_p$ to denote the Bernoulli distribution with parameter $0 < p < \frac{1}{2}$, i.e. $\mathrm{Pr}_{X \sim \mathcal{B}_p}[X = 1] = p$.

2.1 Information Theory and Code

The q-ary entropy function $H_q : [0, 1] \rightarrow \mathbb{R}$ is defined as $H_q(x) \triangleq x \log_q(q - 1) - x \log_q x - (1 - x) \log_q(1 - x)$. Particularly in binary case, $H(x) \triangleq -x \log x - (1 - x) \log(1 - x)$. In finite field $\mathbb{Z}_q$, a linear code $\mathcal{C}$ is a linear subspace of the linear space $\mathbb{Z}_q^n$. If the dimension of $\mathcal{C}$ is k, $\mathcal{C}$ is called an $[n, k]$-code. The ratio $R \triangleq \frac{k}{n}$ is called the information rate of $\mathcal{C}$. A linear code $\mathcal{C} \subset \mathbb{Z}_2^n$ is specified by a generator matrix $\mathbf{G} \in \mathbb{Z}_2^{n \times k}$. We denote that $\mathcal{C}(\mathbf{G}) = \{\mathbf{c} = \mathbf{Gs} : \mathbf{s} \in \mathbb{Z}_q^k\}$ and $R_{\mathbf{G}}$ is the information rate of $\mathcal{C}(\mathbf{G})$. The minimum distance d of $\mathcal{C}$ is $d = d(\mathcal{C}) = \min_{\mathbf{x} \neq \mathbf{y} \in \mathcal{C}} |\mathbf{x} - \mathbf{y}| = \min_{\mathbf{c} \in \mathcal{C} \setminus \{\mathbf{0}\}} |\mathbf{c}|$. $\mathcal{C}$ is a $[n, k, d]$-code when the minimum distance d is emphasized. For a code $\mathcal{C}$, the n-dimension hamming ball centered at $\mathbf{c}$ with radius r is defined as $\mathsf{B}_q(n, r, \mathbf{c}) \triangleq \{\mathbf{e} \in \mathbb{Z}_q^n : |\mathbf{e} - \mathbf{c}| \leq r\}$ and $N_w(\mathcal{C}) \triangleq |\mathsf{B}_q(n, w) \cap \mathcal{C}|$. Both the index $q = 2$ and the center $\mathbf{c} = \mathbf{0}$ are omitted. We concern the estimation of N_w, it relates to a definition of *relative Gilbert-Varshamov distance*. Let $0 < R < 1$. The relative Gilbert-Varshamov distance $D_{\mathsf{GV}} \in \mathbb{R}$ is the unique solution in $0 \leq x \leq 1 - \frac{1}{q}$ of the equation $H_q(x) = 1 - R$. Then there are some results about linear codes.

Lemma 1 ([30]). *For almost all linear codes $\mathcal{C}$ of rate R it holds that $d(\mathcal{C}) \geq \lfloor D_{\mathsf{GV}}(R)n \rfloor$ and*

$$N_w = \begin{cases} q^{n(H_q(\omega/n) - (1-R)) + o(n)}, & D_{\mathsf{GV}}(R)n < \omega < (1 - 1/q)n \\ q^{nR - o(n)}, & (1 - 1/q)n \leq \omega \leq n. \end{cases}$$

Lemma 2 ([23, 26]). *For any rate $0 < R_{\mathbf{G}} < 1$, there exists a binary linear error-correcting code family $\{\mathcal{C}_n\}$, which is a $[n, R_{\mathbf{G}}n, \delta n]$-code, polynomial time constructible, encodable and decodable and can decode from up to $\lfloor \frac{\delta n}{2} \rfloor$ errors where $\delta \approx \frac{1}{2}(1 - R_{\mathbf{G}})$.*

We denote the rate of correctable errors by $\mathbf{Decode_G}$ as a constant $\alpha \in (0, 1)$, i.e. $\mathbf{Decode_G}$ corrects up to $\alpha n = \lfloor \frac{\delta n}{2} \rfloor$ errors. Moreover, for sufficiently large n, $\alpha \approx \frac{\delta}{2}$ and $R_{\mathbf{G}} \approx 1 - 4\alpha$. In our schemes, we let $\alpha = \frac{1}{5}$, $R_{\mathbf{G}} \approx 1 - 4\alpha = \frac{1}{5}$.

2.2 Public Key Encryption

A public key encryption scheme $\mathbf{PKE} = (\mathbf{KeyGen}, \mathbf{Enc}, \mathbf{Dec})$ consists of three (either probabilistic or deterministic) polynomial time algorithms. For security parameter $k \in \mathbb{Z}$, the pair of public and secret key is generated using $\mathbf{KeyGen}(1^k) \to (\mathsf{PK}, \mathsf{SK})$. Given a public key PK, a message μ is encrypted using $\mathbf{Enc}(\mathsf{PK}, \mu) \to \mathsf{CT}$. Given a secret key SK, a ciphertext CT is decrypted using $\mathbf{Dec}(\mathsf{SK}, \mathsf{CT}) \to \bar{\mu}/\bot$, where $\bot$ denotes that the ciphertext is invalid.

The correctness of the scheme $\mathbf{PKE}$ requires that

$$\Pr[\mathbf{Dec}(\mathsf{SK}, \mathbf{Enc}(\mathsf{PK}, \mu)) \neq \mu : (\mathsf{PK}, \mathsf{SK}) \leftarrow \mathbf{KeyGen}(1^k)] < negl(k).$$

IND-CCA2 Security. Let $\mathcal{A} = (\mathcal{A}_1, \mathcal{A}_2)$ be a two-stage adversary. The advantage of $\mathcal{A}$ in IND-CCA2 experiment against a public key encryption scheme $\mathbf{PKE} = (\mathbf{KeyGen}, \mathbf{Enc}, \mathbf{Dec})$ is defined as

$$\mathbf{Adv}_{\mathbf{PKE}}^{cca2, \mathcal{A}}(k) \triangleq \left| \Pr \left[b = b' : \begin{array}{l} (\mathsf{PK}, \mathsf{SK}) \leftarrow \mathbf{KeyGen}(1^k), \\ (\mu_0, \mu_1, St) \leftarrow \mathcal{A}_1^{\mathbf{Dec}(\mathsf{SK}, \cdot)}(\mathsf{PK}), \\ b \leftarrow \{0, 1\}, \mathsf{CT}^* \leftarrow \mathbf{Enc}(\mathsf{PK}, \mu_b), \\ b' \leftarrow \mathcal{A}_2^{\mathbf{Dec}(\mathsf{SK}, \cdot)}(\mathsf{PK}, \mathsf{CT}^*, St) \end{array} \right] - \frac{1}{2} \right|,$$

where $\mathcal{A}_1$ and $\mathcal{A}_2$ both have access to a decryption oracle $\mathbf{Dec}(\mathsf{SK}, \cdot)$, but $\mathcal{A}_2$ is not allowed to ask the decryption oracle on CT^*. And $\mathbf{Adv}^{cca2}_{\mathbf{PKE},t,Q}(k) = \max_{\mathcal{A}} \mathbf{Adv}^{cca2,\mathcal{A}}_{\mathbf{PKE}}(k)$, where the equation is taken over all the adversaries $\mathcal{A}$ that run in time t and make Q decryption queries at most. $\mathbf{PKE}$ is said to be indistinguishable against adaptive chosen-ciphertext attacks (IND-CCA2 secure in short) if $\mathbf{Adv}^{cca2}_{\mathbf{PKE},t,Q}(k) < negl(k)$ for all $t = poly(k)$ and $Q = poly(k)$.

2.3   Authenticated Encryption

A symmetric key encryption scheme consists of two polynomial time algorithms: $\mathsf{SE} = (\mathsf{E}, \mathsf{D})$. Let $\mathcal{K}$ be the key space. The encryption algorithm E takes as input a message m and a secret key K and outputs a ciphertext $\sigma \leftarrow \mathsf{E}(K, m)$; the decryption algorithm D takes as input a secret key K and the ciphertext σ and outputs a message m or $\bot$, $m/\bot \leftarrow \mathsf{D}(K, \sigma)$. For correctness, it requires that $\mathsf{D}(K, \mathsf{E}(K, m)) = m$.

Ciphertext Indistinguishability. For a symmetric key encryption scheme $\mathsf{SE} = (\mathsf{E}, \mathsf{D})$, the advantage of an adversary $\mathcal{A}$ in breaking the ciphertext indistinguishability (IND-OT) of SE is defined as:

$$\mathbf{Adv}^{ind\text{-}ot,\mathcal{A}}_{\mathsf{SE}}(k) \triangleq \left| \Pr\left[b = b' : \begin{array}{l} K^* \leftarrow \mathcal{K}(k), (m_0, m_1) \leftarrow \mathcal{A}, \\ b \leftarrow \{0,1\}, \sigma^* \leftarrow \mathsf{E}(K^*, m_b), b' \leftarrow \mathcal{A}(\sigma^*) \end{array} \right] - \frac{1}{2} \right|.$$

The symmetric encryption scheme SE is one-time secure in the sense of indistinguishability (IND-OT) if $\mathbf{Adv}^{ind\text{-}ot}_{\mathsf{SE},t}(k) \triangleq \max_{\mathcal{A}} \mathbf{Adv}^{ind\text{-}ot,\mathcal{A}}_{\mathsf{SE}}(k) \leq negl(k)$, where the equation is taken over all the adversaries $\mathcal{A}$ that run in time t and $t = poly(k)$.

Ciphertext Integrity. For a symmetric key encryption scheme $\mathsf{SE} = (\mathsf{E}, \mathsf{D})$, the advantage of an adversary $\mathcal{A}$ in breaking the ciphertext integrity (INT-OT) of SE is defined as:

$$\mathbf{Adv}^{int\text{-}ot,\mathcal{A}}_{\mathsf{SE}}(k) \triangleq \Pr\left[\sigma \neq \sigma^* \wedge \mathsf{D}(K^*, \sigma) \neq \bot : \begin{array}{l} K^* \leftarrow \mathcal{K}(k), (m) \leftarrow \mathcal{A}, \\ \sigma^* \leftarrow \mathsf{E}(K^*, m), \sigma \leftarrow \mathcal{A}(\sigma^*) \end{array} \right].$$

The symmetric encryption scheme SE is one-time secure in the sense of integrity (INT-OT) if $\mathbf{Adv}^{int\text{-}ot}_{\mathsf{SE},t}(k) \triangleq \max_{\mathcal{A}} \mathbf{Adv}^{int\text{-}ot,\mathcal{A}}_{\mathsf{SE}}(k) \leq negl(k)$, where the equation is taken over all the adversaries $\mathcal{A}$ that run in time t and $t = poly(k)$.

Authenticated Encryption. A symmetric key encryption scheme SE is secure in the sense of one-time authenticated encryption (AE-OT) iff it is IND-OT and INT-OT secure.

2.4   Randomness Extraction

Let $\mathcal{HS} = \{\mathcal{H}_\kappa : \mathcal{X} \to \mathcal{Y}\}$ be a family of hash functions. Let $k > 1$ be an integer. $\mathcal{HS}$ is k-wise independent if for any $\{x_i\}^k_{i=1} \in \mathcal{X}$ with $x_i \neq x_j, i \neq j$

and $\mathcal{H}_\kappa \leftarrow \mathcal{HS}$, $\mathcal{H}_\kappa(x_i)$ are uniformly random. Let X be a random variable over a finite support $\mathcal{X}$. The *min-entropy* of X is $H_\infty(X) \triangleq -\log(\max_{x\in\mathcal{X}}(\Pr[X = x]))$. Given a random variable Y (possibly correlated with X), the *conditional min-entropy* of X is $H_\infty(X|Y) = -\log(\mathbb{E}_{y\leftarrow Y}[\max_{x\in\mathcal{X}}]\Pr[X = x|Y = y])$ [13].

Lemma 3 (Generalized leftover hash lemma [28]). *Let X_1, X_2 be two random variables over the identical support $\mathcal{X}$ with $H_\infty(X_1) \geq \sigma$, $H_\infty(X_2) \geq \sigma$ and $\Pr[X_1 = X_2] \leq \delta$. Let $\mathcal{HS} = \{\mathcal{H}_\kappa : \mathcal{X} \to \mathbb{Z}_2^k\}$ be a family of 4-wise independent hash functions. Then*

$$\Delta((\mathcal{H}_\kappa, \mathcal{H}_\kappa(X_1), \mathcal{H}_\kappa(X_2)), (\mathcal{H}_\kappa, U_{2k})) \leq \sqrt{1 + \delta} \cdot 2^{k-\sigma/2} + \delta,$$

where $\mathcal{H}_\kappa \leftarrow \mathcal{HS}$ and $U_{2k} \leftarrow \mathbb{Z}_2^{2k}$. Particularly, if $\delta \leq 2^{-k}$ and $\sigma \geq 4k + 1$, then

$$\Delta((\mathcal{H}_\kappa, \mathcal{H}_\kappa(X_1), \mathcal{H}_\kappa(X_2)), (\mathcal{H}_\kappa, U_{2k})) \leq \sqrt{1 + 2^{-k}} \cdot 2^{-k-\frac{1}{2}} + 2^{-k} \leq 2^{-k+1}.$$

3   Learning Parity with Noise

Let $n \in \mathbb{Z}^*$ be the size of the secret vector, $m > n$ be the number of the given equations and $0 < p < \frac{1}{2}$ be the parameter of the noise distribution.

Definition 1 (LPN and Knapsack LPN). *The LPN and knapsack LPN (KLPN) distributions are defined as*

$$D_{\mathrm{LPN}(n,m,p)} \triangleq ((\mathbf{A}, \mathbf{As} + \mathbf{e})|\mathbf{A} \leftarrow \mathbb{Z}_2^{m\times n}, \mathbf{s} \leftarrow \mathbb{Z}_2^n, \mathbf{e} \leftarrow \mathcal{B}_p^m),$$

$$D_{\mathrm{KLPN}(m-n,m,p)} \triangleq ((\mathbf{A}, \mathbf{A}^\mathsf{T}\mathbf{e})|\mathbf{A} \leftarrow \mathbb{Z}_2^{m\times n}, \mathbf{e} \leftarrow \mathcal{B}_p^m).$$

The advantage of a distinguisher $\mathcal{D}_1$ in distinguishing $D_{\mathrm{LPN}(n,m,p)}$ from uniform distribution is defined as

$$\mathbf{Adv}_{\mathrm{LPN}(n,m,p)}^{\mathcal{D}_1} \triangleq \left| \Pr_{\mathbf{A},\mathbf{s},\mathbf{e}} [\mathcal{D}_1(\mathbf{A}, \mathbf{As} + \mathbf{e}) = 1] - \Pr_{\mathbf{A},\mathbf{u}} [\mathcal{D}_1(\mathbf{A}, \mathbf{u}) = 1] \right|,$$

where $(\mathbf{A}, \mathbf{As} + \mathbf{e}) \leftarrow D_{\mathrm{LPN}(n,m,p)}$, $\mathbf{u} \leftarrow \mathbb{Z}_2^m$. The advantage of a distinguisher $\mathcal{D}_2$ in distinguishing $D_{\mathrm{KLPN}(m-n,m,p)}$ from uniform distribution is defined as

$$\mathbf{Adv}_{\mathrm{KLPN}(m-n,m,p)}^{\mathcal{D}_2} \triangleq \left| \Pr_{\mathbf{A},\mathbf{e}} [\mathcal{D}_2(\mathbf{A}, \mathbf{A}^\mathsf{T}\mathbf{e}) = 1] - \Pr_{\mathbf{A},\mathbf{b}} [\mathcal{D}_2(\mathbf{A}, \mathbf{b}) = 1] \right|,$$

where $(\mathbf{A}, \mathbf{A}^\mathsf{T}\mathbf{e}) \leftarrow D_{\mathrm{KLPN}(m-n,m,p)}$, $\mathbf{b} \leftarrow \mathbb{Z}_2^n$. Also define $\mathbf{Adv}_{\mathrm{LPN}(n,m,p),t} \triangleq \max_{\mathcal{D}_1} \mathbf{Adv}_{\mathrm{LPN}(n,m,p)}^{\mathcal{D}_1}$, and $\mathbf{Adv}_{\mathrm{KLPN}(m-n,m,p),t} \triangleq \max_{\mathcal{D}_2} \mathbf{Adv}_{\mathrm{KLPN}(m-n,m,p)}^{\mathcal{D}_2}$, where the equations are taken over all $\mathcal{D}_1$ and $\mathcal{D}_2$ that run in $t = poly(n)$ time.

As in the LWE problem, the equivalence between LPN and KLPN was shown in [26,31]. With a standard hybrid argument technique, we have results on the ℓ-fold LPN and ℓ-fold KLPN that

$$\mathbf{Adv}_{\mathrm{LPN}^\ell(n,m,p),t}$$

$$\triangleq \max_{\mathcal{D}_1} |\Pr[\mathcal{D}_1(\mathbf{A}, \mathbf{AS} + \mathbf{X}) = 1] - \Pr[\mathcal{D}_1(\mathbf{A}, \mathbf{B}_1) = 1]| \leq \ell \cdot \mathbf{Adv}_{\mathrm{LPN}(n,m,p),t},$$

$$(1)$$

$$\mathbf{Adv}_{\mathrm{KLPN}^\ell(m-n,m,p),t}$$
$$\triangleq \max_{\mathcal{D}_2} \left| \Pr\left[\mathcal{D}_2(\mathbf{A}, \mathbf{T}^\mathsf{T}\mathbf{A}) = 1\right] - \Pr\left[\mathcal{D}_2(\mathbf{A}, \mathbf{B}_2) = 1\right]\right| \leq \ell \cdot \mathbf{Adv}_{\mathrm{KLPN}(m-n,m,p),t},$$
$$(2)$$

where $\mathbf{A} \leftarrow \mathbb{Z}_2^{m\times n}$, $\mathbf{S} \leftarrow \mathbb{Z}_2^{n\times\ell}$, $\mathbf{X}, \mathbf{T} \leftarrow \mathcal{B}_p^{m\times\ell}$, $\mathbf{B}_1 \leftarrow \mathbb{Z}_2^{m\times\ell}$, $\mathbf{B}_2 \leftarrow \mathbb{Z}_2^{\ell\times m}$ and the maximums are taken over all algorithm $\mathcal{D}_1$ and $\mathcal{D}_2$ that run in $t = poly(n)$ time.

The *extended LPN* problem and *extended knapsack LPN* problem defined below state that the LPN problem and KLPN problem remain hard even if the information of errors is leaked to the adversary partially [3, 26, 35].

Definition 2 (Extended LPN and Extended Knapsack LPN). *The extended LPN (ELPN) and extended knapsack LPN (EKLPN) distributions are defined as*

$$D_{\mathrm{ELPN}(n,m,p)} \triangleq \left((\mathbf{A}, \mathbf{As} + \mathbf{x}, \mathbf{e}, \mathbf{x}^\mathsf{T}\mathbf{e}) \,|\, \mathbf{A} \leftarrow \mathbb{Z}_2^{m\times n}, \mathbf{s} \leftarrow \mathbb{Z}_2^n, \mathbf{x}, \mathbf{e} \leftarrow \mathcal{B}_p^m\right),$$

$$D_{\mathrm{EKLPN}(m-n,m,p)} \triangleq \left((\mathbf{A}, \mathbf{A}^\mathsf{T}\mathbf{t}, \mathbf{e}, \mathbf{t}^\mathsf{T}\mathbf{e}) \,|\, \mathbf{A} \leftarrow \mathbb{Z}_2^{m\times n}, \mathbf{t}, \mathbf{e} \leftarrow \mathcal{B}_p^m\right).$$

The advantage of a distinguisher $\mathcal{D}_1$ is defined as

$$\mathbf{Adv}_{\mathrm{ELPN}(n,m,p)}^{\mathcal{D}_1} \triangleq \left|\Pr\left[\mathcal{D}_1\left(\mathbf{A}, \mathbf{As} + \mathbf{x}, \mathbf{e}, \mathbf{x}^\mathsf{T}\mathbf{e}\right) = 1\right] - \Pr\left[\mathcal{D}_1\left(\mathbf{A}, \mathbf{b}, \mathbf{e}, \mathbf{x}^\mathsf{T}\mathbf{e}\right) = 1\right]\right|,$$

where $\left(\mathbf{A}, \mathbf{As} + \mathbf{x}, \mathbf{t}, \mathbf{x}^\mathsf{T}\mathbf{t}\right) \leftarrow D_{\mathrm{ELPN}(n,m,p)}$*,* $\mathbf{b} \leftarrow \mathbb{Z}_2^n$*, and* $\mathbf{e}, \mathbf{x} \leftarrow \mathcal{B}_p^m$*. The advantage of a distinguisher $\mathcal{D}_2$ is defined as*

$$\mathbf{Adv}_{\mathrm{EKLPN}(m-n,m,p)}^{\mathcal{D}_2} \triangleq \left|\Pr\left[\mathcal{D}_2\left(\mathbf{A}, \mathbf{A}^\mathsf{T}\mathbf{t}, \mathbf{e}, \mathbf{t}^\mathsf{T}\mathbf{e}\right) = 1\right] - \Pr\left[\mathcal{D}_2\left(\mathbf{A}, \mathbf{b}, \mathbf{e}, \mathbf{t}^\mathsf{T}\mathbf{e}\right) = 1\right]\right|,$$

where $\left(\mathbf{A}, \mathbf{A}^\mathsf{T}\mathbf{t}, \mathbf{e}, \mathbf{t}^\mathsf{T}\mathbf{e}\right) \leftarrow D_{\mathrm{EKLPN}(m-n,m,p)}$*,* $\mathbf{b} \leftarrow \mathbb{Z}_2^n$*,* $\mathbf{t}, \mathbf{e} \leftarrow \mathcal{B}_p^m$*. Also define* $\mathbf{Adv}_{\mathrm{ELPN}(n,m,p),t} \triangleq \max_{\mathcal{D}_1} \mathbf{Adv}_{\mathrm{ELPN}(n,m,p)}^{\mathcal{D}_1}$*, and* $\mathbf{Adv}_{\mathrm{EKLPN}(m-n,m,p),t} \triangleq \max_{\mathcal{D}_2} \mathbf{Adv}_{\mathrm{EKLPN}(m-n,m,p)}^{\mathcal{D}_2}$*, where the equations are taken over all $\mathcal{D}_1$ and $\mathcal{D}_2$ that run in $t = poly(n)$ time.*

Define some intermediate distributions

$$G_2 \triangleq \left((\mathbf{A}, \mathbf{As} + \mathbf{x}', \mathbf{e}, \mathbf{x}^\mathsf{T}\mathbf{e}) \,|\, \mathbf{A} \leftarrow \mathbb{Z}_2^{m\times n}, \mathbf{s} \leftarrow \mathbb{Z}_2^n, \mathbf{x}, \mathbf{x}', \mathbf{e} \leftarrow \mathcal{B}_p^m\right),$$

$$L_2 \triangleq \left((\mathbf{A}, \mathbf{A}^\mathsf{T}\mathbf{t}', \mathbf{e}, \mathbf{t}^\mathsf{T}\mathbf{e}) \,|\, \mathbf{A} \leftarrow \mathbb{Z}_2^{m\times n}, \mathbf{t}, \mathbf{t}', \mathbf{e} \leftarrow \mathcal{B}_p^m\right).$$

We will have the following results which are crucial in the proof of our schemes.

Lemma 4. *For any distinguishers $\mathcal{D}_1$ and $\mathcal{D}_2$ that run in $t = poly(n)$ time, it has that*

$$\left|\Pr\left[\mathcal{D}_1(D_{\mathrm{ELPN}(n,m,p)}) = 1\right] - \Pr\left[\mathcal{D}_1(G_2) = 1\right]\right|$$
$$\leq \mathbf{Adv}_{\mathrm{ELPN}(n,m,p),t} + \mathbf{Adv}_{\mathrm{LPN}(n,m,p),t},$$
$$(3)$$

$$\left|\Pr\left[\mathcal{D}_2(D_{\mathrm{EKLPN}(n,m,p)}) = 1\right] - \Pr\left[\mathcal{D}_2(L_2) = 1\right]\right|$$
$$\leq \mathbf{Adv}_{\mathrm{EKLPN}(m-n,m,p),t} + \mathbf{Adv}_{\mathrm{KLPN}(m-n,m,p),t}.$$
$$(4)$$

The proof will be given in full verison. In our dual-Regev type scheme, we introduce a variant of LPN problem, *twin LPN*.

Definition 3 (Twin LPN). *The twin LPN (TLPN) distribution is defined as*

$$D_{\text{TLPN}(n,2m,p)} \triangleq \left((\mathbf{A}_1, \mathbf{A}_2, \mathbf{A}_1\mathbf{s}_1 + \mathbf{e}_1, \mathbf{A}_2\mathbf{s}_2 + \mathbf{e}_2) \,\middle|\, \begin{array}{l} \mathbf{A}_1, \mathbf{A}_2 \leftarrow \mathbb{Z}_2^{m\times n}, \\ \mathbf{e}_1, \mathbf{e}_2 \leftarrow \mathcal{B}_p^m, \\ \mathbf{s}_1, \mathbf{s}_2 \leftarrow \mathbb{Z}_2^n, \mathbf{s}_1 \neq \mathbf{s}_2, \end{array} \right).$$

The advantage of a distinguisher $\mathcal{A}$ is defined as

$$\mathbf{Adv}_{\text{TLPN}(n,2m,p)}^{\mathcal{A}} \triangleq |\Pr[\mathcal{A}(\mathbf{A}_1, \mathbf{A}_2, \mathbf{A}_1\mathbf{s} + \mathbf{e}_1, \mathbf{A}_2\mathbf{s} + \mathbf{e}_2) = 1]$$
$$- \Pr[\mathcal{A}(\mathbf{A}_1, \mathbf{A}_2, \mathbf{A}_1\mathbf{s}_1 + \mathbf{e}_1, \mathbf{A}_2\mathbf{s}_2 + \mathbf{e}_2) = 1]|,$$

where $(\mathbf{A}_1, \mathbf{A}_2, \mathbf{A}_1\mathbf{s} + \mathbf{e}_1, \mathbf{A}_2\mathbf{s} + \mathbf{e}_2) \leftarrow D_{\text{LPN}(n,2m,p)}$ and $(\mathbf{A}_1, \mathbf{A}_2, \mathbf{A}_1\mathbf{s}_1 + \mathbf{e}_1, \mathbf{A}_2\mathbf{s}_2 + \mathbf{e}_2) \leftarrow D_{\text{TLPN}(n,2m,p)}$. And $\mathbf{Adv}_{\text{TLPN}(n,2m,p),t} \triangleq \max_{\mathcal{A}} \mathbf{Adv}_{\text{TLPN}(n,2m,p)}^{\mathcal{A}}$, where the equation is taken over all $\mathcal{A}$ that run in $t = poly(n)$ time.

In the following lemma, we show that the hardness of TLPN is based on the LPN problem, and we will give the proof in full version due to space limitation.

Lemma 5.

$$\mathbf{Adv}_{\text{TLPN}(n,2m,p),t} \leq 2 \cdot \mathbf{Adv}_{\text{LPN}(n,m,p),t} + \mathbf{Adv}_{\text{LPN}(n,2m,p),t} + 2^{-n}.$$

4   The Proposed Schemes

4.1   Dual-Regev Type Scheme

Here we present dual-Regev type scheme, which is IND-CCA2 secure.

4.1.1   Description of the Scheme

The following parameters and public settings are involved in the scheme.

- The security parameter k, $n = \Theta(k^2) \in \mathbb{Z}$, $m \in \mathbb{Z}$ such that $0.0487m \geq 4k+1$ and $m \geq 10n$. Noise rate $p = \sqrt{c/m}$ for a constant $c \leq -\frac{1}{2}\ln(1 - \frac{1}{5}\alpha)$.
- A generator-matrix $\mathbf{G} \in \mathbb{Z}_2^{m\times\ell}$ of a binary linear error-correcting code $\mathcal{C} = \mathcal{C}(\mathbf{G})$ as in Lemma 2 which is $[m, \ell = R_{\mathbf{G}}m, \delta m]$-code and has an efficient decoder algorithm $\mathbf{Decode}_{\mathbf{G}}$ correcting up to αm errors, where $\alpha \approx \frac{1}{5}$ and $R_{\mathbf{G}} \approx 1 - 4\alpha = \frac{1}{5}$.
- A family of 4-wise independent hash functions $\mathcal{HS} = \{\mathcal{H}_\kappa : \{0,1\}^* \rightarrow \mathbb{Z}_2^k\}$.
- An authenticated encryption scheme $\mathsf{AE} = (\mathsf{AE.E}, \mathsf{AE.D})$ with the key space $\mathbb{Z}_2^k$ and the ciphertext space $\mathbb{Z}_2^d$.

KeyGen(1^k) $\rightarrow$ (PK, SK): The algorithm runs as follows:

$$\mathbf{A}_1, \mathbf{A}_2 \leftarrow \mathbb{Z}_2^{m\times n}, \mathbf{T}_1, \mathbf{T}_2 \leftarrow \mathcal{B}_p^{m\times m}, \mathcal{H}_\kappa \leftarrow \mathcal{HS}, \mathbf{H} \leftarrow \mathbf{T}_1\mathbf{A}_1 + \mathbf{T}_2\mathbf{A}_2.$$

$\mathsf{SK} \leftarrow (\mathbf{T}_1, \mathbf{T}_2) \in (\mathbb{Z}_2^{m\times m})^2$, $\mathsf{PK} \leftarrow (\mathbf{A}_1, \mathbf{A}_2, \mathbf{H}, \mathcal{H}_\kappa) \in (\mathbb{Z}_2^{m\times n})^2 \times \mathbb{Z}_2^{m\times n} \times \mathcal{HS}$.

Enc(PK, m) $\rightarrow$ **CT**: The algorithm runs as follows:

$$\mathbf{s} \leftarrow \mathbb{Z}_2^n, \mathbf{e}_1, \mathbf{e}_2 \leftarrow \mathcal{B}_p^m, \mathbf{T}_1', \mathbf{T}_2' \leftarrow \mathcal{B}_p^{m \times m}, \mathbf{r} \leftarrow \mathbb{Z}_2^\ell,$$
$$\mathbf{c}_1 \leftarrow \mathbf{A}_1\mathbf{s} + \mathbf{e}_1, \mathbf{c}_2 \leftarrow \mathbf{A}_2\mathbf{s} + \mathbf{e}_2, \mathbf{c}_3 \leftarrow \mathbf{Hs} + \mathbf{T}_1'\mathbf{e}_1 + \mathbf{T}_2'\mathbf{e}_2 + \mathbf{Gr}$$
$$\mathbf{k} \leftarrow \mathcal{H}_\kappa(\mathbf{c}_1, \mathbf{c}_2, \mathbf{c}_3, \mathbf{r}), \mathbf{c}_4 \leftarrow \mathsf{AE.E}(\mathbf{k}, \mathbf{m}),$$
$$\mathsf{CT} \leftarrow (\mathbf{c}_1, \mathbf{c}_2, \mathbf{c}_3, \mathbf{c}_4) \in \mathbb{Z}_2^m \times \mathbb{Z}_2^m \times \mathbb{Z}_2^m \times \mathbb{Z}_2^d.$$

Dec(SK, CT) $\rightarrow (\perp/\bar{\mathbf{m}})$: The algorithm computes

$$\bar{\mathbf{y}} \leftarrow \mathbf{c}_3 - \mathbf{T}_1\mathbf{c}_1 - \mathbf{T}_2\mathbf{c}_2, \perp/\bar{\mathbf{r}} \leftarrow \mathbf{Decode}_\mathbf{G}(\bar{\mathbf{y}}).$$

If $\mathbf{Decode}_\mathbf{G}(\bar{\mathbf{y}}) = \perp$, then the algorithm outputs $\perp$. Otherwise, it computes $\bar{\mathbf{k}} \leftarrow \mathcal{H}_\kappa(\mathbf{c}_1, \mathbf{c}_2, \mathbf{c}_3, \bar{\mathbf{r}})$ and outputs $\mathsf{AE.D}(\bar{\mathbf{k}}, \mathbf{c}_4)$.

4.1.2 Correctness

We now prove the correctness of the dual-Regev type scheme. Some properties on Bernoulli distributions are required.

Lemma 6 (Chernoff bound). *Let* $X_1, \cdots, X_d$ *be independent 0-1 random variables according to* $\mathcal{B}_p$, *and* $X = \sum_{i=1}^d X_i$. *It holds that, for all* $0 \leq \delta \leq 1$,

$$\Pr[X > (1 + \delta)pd] < 2e^{-\frac{\delta^2}{3}pd}.$$

Lemma 7 ([12]). *Let* $V_1, \cdots, V_m$ *be the binary independent random variables,* $V_i \sim \mathcal{B}_\tau$, *for* $i = 1, \cdots, m$, *and set the binary random variable* $W \triangleq \sum_{i=1}^m V_i \bmod 2$. *Then* $\Pr_{V_i \leftarrow \mathcal{B}_\tau}[W = 1] = \frac{1}{2} - \frac{1}{2}(1 - 2\tau)^m$.

Lemma 8. *Assume* $\mathbf{x} = (x_1, \cdots, x_m)^\mathsf{T} \sim \mathcal{B}_{p_1}^m$ *and* $\mathbf{e} = (e_1, \cdots, e_m)^\mathsf{T} \sim \mathcal{B}_{p_2}^m$. *Then* $\Pr[\mathbf{x}^\mathsf{T}\mathbf{e} = 1] = \frac{1}{2} - \frac{1}{2}(1 - 2p_1p_2)^m$.

Theorem 1 (Correctness). *In the above scheme with the choice of the public settings, for* $(\mathsf{PK}, \mathsf{SK}) \leftarrow \mathbf{KeyGen}(1^k)$, $\mathbf{Dec}(\mathsf{SK}, \mathsf{CT})$ *outputs* $\mathbf{m}$ *with overwhelming probability, where* $\mathsf{CT} \leftarrow \mathbf{Enc}(\mathsf{PK}, \mathbf{m})$.

Proof. Since $\bar{\mathbf{y}} = \mathbf{c}_3 - \mathbf{T}_1\mathbf{c}_1 - \mathbf{T}_2\mathbf{c}_2 = \mathbf{T}_1'\mathbf{e}_1 + \mathbf{T}_2'\mathbf{e}_2 - \mathbf{T}_1\mathbf{e}_1 - \mathbf{T}_2\mathbf{e}_2 + \mathbf{Gr}$, the decryption algorithm must bound the weight of error-term. For $\mathbf{e} \leftarrow \mathcal{B}_p^m$ and $\mathbf{T} = (\mathbf{t}_1, \cdots, \mathbf{t}_m)^\mathsf{T} \leftarrow \mathcal{B}_p^{m \times m}$ with $p = \sqrt{c/m}$, it follows that

$$\bar{p} \triangleq \Pr[\mathbf{t}_i^\mathsf{T}\mathbf{e} = 1] = \frac{1}{2} - \frac{1}{2}(1 - 2p^2)^m = \frac{1}{2} - \frac{1}{2}(1 + \frac{1}{\frac{-m}{2c}})^{\frac{-m}{2c}(-2c)} < \frac{1}{2} - \frac{1}{2}e^{-2c} \triangleq \epsilon, \tag{5}$$

is a constant and $\epsilon > \bar{p}$, where the approximation $\lim_{m \to \infty}(1 + \frac{1}{\frac{-m}{2c}})^{\frac{-m}{2c}} = e$. From the independence of the rows of $\mathbf{T}$ and $c \leq -\frac{1}{2}\ln(1 - \frac{1}{5}\alpha)$, it has that $\frac{1}{5}\alpha m \geq 2\epsilon m \geq 2\bar{p}m$, then Chernoff bound implies $\Pr[|\mathbf{Te}| > \frac{1}{5}\alpha m] \leq \Pr[|\mathbf{Te}| > 2\epsilon m] \leq \Pr[|\mathbf{Te}| > 2\bar{p}m] < 2e^{-\frac{1}{3}\bar{p}m} = 2^{-\Theta(m)} = negl(m) = negl(k)$. Then

$$|\mathbf{T}_1\mathbf{e}_1 + \mathbf{T}_2\mathbf{e}_2 + \mathbf{T}_1'\mathbf{e}_1 + \mathbf{T}_2'\mathbf{e}_2| \leq |\mathbf{T}_1\mathbf{e}_1| + |\mathbf{T}_2\mathbf{e}_2| + |\mathbf{T}_1'\mathbf{e}_1| + |\mathbf{T}_2'\mathbf{e}_2| \leq \frac{4}{5}\alpha m \tag{6}$$

holds with overwhelming probability $1 - negl(m)$. Hence $\mathbf{Decode_G}(\bar{\mathbf{y}}) = \bar{\mathbf{r}} = \mathbf{r}$ and $\mathcal{H}_\kappa(\mathbf{c}_1, \mathbf{c}_2, \mathbf{c}_3, \bar{\mathbf{r}}) = \bar{\mathbf{k}} = \mathbf{k} = \mathcal{H}_\kappa(\mathbf{c}_1, \mathbf{c}_2, \mathbf{c}_3, \mathbf{r})$. Finally, the correctness of AE ensures that $\bar{\mathbf{m}} = \mathsf{AE.D}(\bar{\mathbf{k}}, \mathbf{c}_4) = \mathsf{AE.D}(\mathbf{k}, \mathbf{c}_4) = \mathbf{m}$. We complete the proof of correctness.

□

4.1.3   Proof of Security

Theorem 2 (IND-CCA2 Security). *If the LPN problem is hard, then the scheme is secure against IND-CCA2 adversary. In particular, for any PPT adversary $\mathcal{A}$ that runs in time t and makes Q decryption queries, it has*

$$\mathbf{Adv}_{\mathsf{PKE}}^{cca2,\mathcal{A}}(k) \leq 2m \cdot (\mathbf{Adv}_{\mathrm{EKLPN}(m-n,m,p),t} + \mathbf{Adv}_{\mathrm{KLPN}(m-n,m,p),t})$$
$$+ \mathbf{Adv}_{\mathrm{TLPN}(n,2m,p),t} + m \cdot \mathbf{Adv}_{\mathrm{KLPN}(m-n,m,p/2),t} \qquad (7)$$
$$+ 2Q \cdot \mathbf{Adv}_{\mathsf{AE},t}^{int\text{-}ot}(k) + (4Q+1) \cdot 2^{-k} + \mathbf{Adv}_{\mathsf{AE},t}^{ind\text{-}ot}(k).$$

Proof. $\mathsf{CT}^* = (\mathbf{c}_1^*, \mathbf{c}_2^*, \mathbf{c}_3^*, \mathbf{c}_4^*)$ denotes the challenge ciphertext, and $\mathsf{CT} = (\mathbf{c}_1, \mathbf{c}_2, \mathbf{c}_3, \mathbf{c}_4)$ denotes one of $Q = poly(n)$ decryption queries. We assume that the adversary $\mathcal{A}$ makes Q decryption queries. $\mathcal{A}(\mathbf{Game}_i) = 1$ denotes the event that $\mathcal{A}$'s output b' equals to the $\mathcal{S}$'s random choice b in **Game i**. We define

$$\mathbf{T}_1 = \begin{pmatrix} \mathbf{t}_{1,1}^\mathsf{T} \\ \vdots \\ \mathbf{t}_{1,m}^\mathsf{T} \end{pmatrix}, \mathbf{T}_2 = \begin{pmatrix} \mathbf{t}_{2,1}^\mathsf{T} \\ \vdots \\ \mathbf{t}_{2,m}^\mathsf{T} \end{pmatrix}, \mathbf{T}_1' = \begin{pmatrix} \mathbf{t}_{1,1}'^\mathsf{T} \\ \vdots \\ \mathbf{t}_{1,m}'^\mathsf{T} \end{pmatrix}, \mathbf{T}_2' = \begin{pmatrix} \mathbf{t}_{2,1}'^\mathsf{T} \\ \vdots \\ \mathbf{t}_{2,m}'^\mathsf{T} \end{pmatrix}.$$

Game 0. This is the IND-CCA2 game between the adversary $\mathcal{A}$ and the challenger. We have $\mathbf{Adv}_{\mathsf{PKE}}^{cca2,\mathcal{A}}(k) = |\Pr[\mathcal{A}(\mathbf{Game}_0) = 1] - \frac{1}{2}|$.

Next, we give two sequences of games $\{\mathbf{Game\ 1\text{-}[1,i]}\}_{i=1}^m$ to replace $\mathbf{T}_1'$ with $\mathbf{T}_1$ and $\{\mathbf{Game\ 1\text{-}[2,i]}\}_{i=1}^m$ to replace $\mathbf{T}_2'$ with $\mathbf{T}_2$ in the $\mathbf{c}_3^*$ row by row.

$\{\mathbf{Game\ 1\text{-}[1,i]}\}_{i=1}^m$. **Game 1-[1,i]** is identical to **Game 1-[1,i-1]** for any $i \in \{1, \cdots, m\}$ except that the challenger replaces $\mathbf{t}_{1,i}'^\mathsf{T}$ with $\mathbf{t}_{1,i}^\mathsf{T}$. Without loss of generality, let **Game 1-[1,0]** be **Game 0**.

We will show that the hardness of the EKLPN problem ensures that the adversary $\mathcal{A}$ can not distinguish **Game 1-[1,i]** from **Game 1-[1,i-1]** with non-negligible probability. Indeed, if $\mathcal{A}$ is able to distinguish **Game 1-[1,i]** from **Game 1-[1,i-1]** with non-negligible probability, then we construct an algorithm $\mathcal{A}_1$ to solve EKLPN problem. $\mathcal{A}_1$ is given a quadruple $(\mathbf{A}_1, (\bar{\mathbf{t}}_{1,i}^\mathsf{T} \mathbf{A}_1)^\mathsf{T}, \mathbf{e}_1, \bar{z}_{1,i})$, where $\bar{z}_{1,i}$ either is $\bar{\mathbf{t}}_{1,i}^\mathsf{T} \mathbf{e}_1$ and the quadruple from the distribution $D_{\mathrm{EKLPN}(n,m,p)}$, or $\bar{\mathbf{t}}_{1,i}'^\mathsf{T} \mathbf{e}_1$ and the quadruple from the distribution L_2. Recall that $D_{\mathrm{EKLPN}(n,m,p)}$ and L_2 are given in Lemma 4. $\mathcal{A}_1$ sets

$$\mathbf{H} \leftarrow \begin{pmatrix} \mathbf{t}_{1,1}^{\mathsf{T}}\mathbf{A}_1 \\ \vdots \\ \mathbf{t}_{1,i-1}^{\mathsf{T}}\mathbf{A}_1 \\ \boxed{\bar{\mathbf{t}}_{1,i}^{\mathsf{T}}\mathbf{A}_1} \\ \mathbf{t}_{1,i+1}^{\mathsf{T}}\mathbf{A}_1 \\ \vdots \\ \mathbf{t}_{1,m}^{\mathsf{T}}\mathbf{A}_1 \end{pmatrix} + \mathbf{T}_2\mathbf{A}_2, \quad \mathbf{c}_3^* \leftarrow \mathbf{H}\mathbf{s} + \begin{pmatrix} \mathbf{t}_{1,1}^{\mathsf{T}}\mathbf{e}_1 \\ \vdots \\ \mathbf{t}_{1,i-1}^{\mathsf{T}}\mathbf{e}_1 \\ \boxed{\bar{z}_{1,i}} \\ \mathbf{t}_{1,i+1}^{\mathsf{T}}\mathbf{e}_1 \\ \vdots \\ \mathbf{t'}_{1,m}^{\mathsf{T}}\mathbf{e}_1 \end{pmatrix} + \mathbf{T}_2'\mathbf{e}_2 + \mathbf{G}\mathbf{r}^*,$$

and the rest is the same as before except that $\mathcal{A}_1$ simulates decryption oracle without $\bar{\mathbf{t}}_{1,i}^{\mathsf{T}}$. We will show that the output of decryption oracle is not changed even if $\mathcal{A}_1$ has no knowledge of $\bar{\mathbf{t}}_{1,i}^{\mathsf{T}}$ at the end of this game.

If $\bar{z}_i = \bar{\mathbf{t}}_i'^{\mathsf{T}}\mathbf{e}_1$, then $\mathcal{A}_1$ simulates the behavior of the challenger in **Game 1-[1,i-1]** exactly. Hence,

$$\Pr\left[\mathcal{A}(\mathbf{Game}_{1-[1,i-1]}) = 1\right] = \Pr\left[\mathcal{A}_1(\mathbf{A}_1, (\bar{\mathbf{t}}_{1,i}^{\mathsf{T}}\mathbf{A}_1)^{\mathsf{T}}, \mathbf{e}_1, \bar{\mathbf{t}}_{1,i}'^{\mathsf{T}}\mathbf{e}_1) = 1\right].$$

If $\bar{z}_i = \bar{\mathbf{t}}_i^{\mathsf{T}}\mathbf{e}_1$, then $\mathcal{A}_1$ simulates the behavior of the challenger in **Game 1-[1,i]** exactly. Hence,

$$\Pr\left[\mathcal{A}(\mathbf{Game}_{1-[1,i]}) = 1\right] = \Pr\left[\mathcal{A}_1(\mathbf{A}_1, (\bar{\mathbf{t}}_{1,i}^{\mathsf{T}}\mathbf{A}_1)^{\mathsf{T}}, \mathbf{e}_1, \bar{\mathbf{t}}_{1,i}^{\mathsf{T}}\mathbf{e}_1) = 1\right].$$

Therefore, for $i \in \{1, \cdots, m\}$, we have

$$\begin{aligned} |\Pr[\mathcal{A}(\mathbf{Game}_{1-[1,i-1]}) = 1] &- \Pr\left[\mathcal{A}(\mathbf{Game}_{1-[1,i]}) = 1\right]| \\ &\leq \mathbf{Adv}_{\mathrm{EKLPN}(m-n,m,p),t} + \mathbf{Adv}_{\mathrm{KLPN}(m-n,m,p),t}. \end{aligned} \quad (8)$$

Since the challenger has no knowledge about $\bar{\mathbf{t}}_{1,i}^{\mathsf{T}}$ in **Game 1-[1,i]**, which comes from the instance of the hard problem, it has to simulate decryption oracle without $\bar{\mathbf{t}}_{1,i}^{\mathsf{T}}$. More precisely, it runs the decryption algorithm with a new secret key $(\mathbf{T}_{1,[1,i]}, \mathbf{T}_2)$, where $\mathbf{T}_{1,[1,i]}$ is $\mathbf{T}_1$ except replacing the ith row with a uniform random $\mathbf{u}_{1,i}^{\mathsf{T}}$, i.e. $\mathbf{T}_{1,[1,i]} \triangleq (\mathbf{t}_{1,1}, \cdots, \mathbf{t}_{1,i-1}, \mathbf{u}_{1,i}, \mathbf{t}_{1,i+1}, \cdots, \mathbf{t}_{1,m})^{\mathsf{T}}$. In **Game 1-[1,i]**, the **Dec** computes $\mathbf{y}_{1,i} = \mathbf{c}_3 - \mathbf{T}_{1,[1,i]}\mathbf{c}_1 - \mathbf{T}_2\mathbf{c}_2$, and $\mathbf{r}_{1,i} = \mathbf{Decode}_{\mathbf{G}}(\mathbf{y}_{1,i})$. And let $\mathbf{y}_{1,i} = \mathbf{G}\mathbf{r}_{1,i} + \mathbf{\Delta}_{1,i}$, where $|\mathbf{\Delta}_{1,i}| \leq \frac{4}{5}\alpha m \leq \alpha m$ from **Eq.(6)**. Since the hamming weight of $\Delta\mathbf{y}_{1,i} \triangleq \mathbf{y}_{1,i} - \mathbf{y}_{1,i-1} = (\mathbf{T}_{1,[1,i]} - \mathbf{T}_{1,[1,i-1]})\mathbf{c}_1$ is 2 at most and $\mathbf{G}\mathbf{r}_{1,i} + \mathbf{\Delta}_{1,i} = \mathbf{y}_{1,i} = \mathbf{y}_{1,i-1} + \Delta\mathbf{y}_{1,i} = \mathbf{G}\mathbf{r}_{1,i-1} + \mathbf{\Delta}_{1,i-1} + \Delta\mathbf{y}_{1,i}$, with $|\mathbf{\Delta}_{1,i} = \mathbf{\Delta}_{1,i-1} + \Delta\mathbf{y}_{1,i}| \leq \frac{4}{5}\alpha m + 2$ and $\mathbf{Decode}_{\mathbf{G}}$ also can handle correct $\mathbf{r}_{1,i} = \mathbf{r}_{1,i-1}$ from $\mathbf{y}_{1,i}$ Therefore, the decryption oracle behaves identically in **Game 1-[1,i-1]** and **Game 1-[1,i]**.

Note that the error-term in the game sequence cannot be accumulated since that for any $i \neq j \in [m]$, $\mathbf{T}_{1,[1,i]}$ and $\mathbf{T}_{1,[1,j]}$ are only different in i^{th} and j^{th} rows. In **Game 1-[1,j]**, $\mathbf{t}_{1,i}^{\mathsf{T}}$ can be used as a rows of secret key to answer the query of decryption.

After the game sequence of $\{\textbf{Game 1-[1,i]}\}_{i=1}^{m}$, we have

$$
\begin{aligned}
|\Pr\left[\mathcal{A}(\textbf{Game}_0) = 1\right] - \Pr\left[\mathcal{A}(\textbf{Game}_{1-[1,m]}) = 1\right]| \\
\leq m \cdot (\textbf{Adv}_{\text{EKLPN}(m-n,m,p),t} + \textbf{Adv}_{\text{KLPN}(m-n,m,p),t}).
\end{aligned}
\tag{9}
$$

$\{\textbf{Game 1-[2,i]}\}_{i=1}^{m}$. Similarly, $\textbf{Game 1-[2,i]}$ is identical to $\textbf{Game 1-[2,i-1]}$ for any $i \in \{1, 2, \cdots, m\}$ except that the challenger replaces $\textbf{t}_{2,i}'^{\text{T}}$ with $\textbf{t}_{2,i}^{\text{T}}$. Without loss of generality, let $\textbf{Game 1-[2,0]}$ be $\textbf{Game 1-[1,m]}$ exactly. With the same analysis in $\{\textbf{Game 1-[1,i]}\}_{i=1}^{m}$, we have

$$
\begin{aligned}
|\Pr[\mathcal{A}(\textbf{Game}_{1-[1,m]}) = 1] - \Pr\left[\mathcal{A}(\textbf{Game}_{1-[2,m]}) = 1\right]| \\
\leq m \cdot (\textbf{Adv}_{\text{EKLPN}(m-n,m,p),t} + \textbf{Adv}_{\text{KLPN}(m-n,m,p),t}).
\end{aligned}
\tag{10}
$$

Game 2. In this game, the challenger answers the decryption queries with the secret key $(\textbf{T}_1, \textbf{T}_2)$ and sets $\textbf{c}_3^* \leftarrow \textbf{T}_1\textbf{c}_1^* + \textbf{T}_2\textbf{c}_2^* + \textbf{Gr}^*$. The decryption oracle behaves identically in $\textbf{Game 1-[2,m]}$ and $\textbf{Game 2}$. Since $\textbf{c}_3^* = \textbf{T}_1\textbf{c}_1^* + \textbf{T}_2\textbf{c}_2^* + \textbf{Gr}^* = \textbf{Hs} + \textbf{T}_1\textbf{e}_1 + \textbf{T}_2\textbf{e}_2 + \textbf{Gr}^*$, which is identical to $\textbf{c}_3^*$ in $\textbf{Game 1-[2,m]}$, we have $\Pr\left[\mathcal{A}(\textbf{Game}_{1-[2,m]}) = 1\right] = \Pr\left[\mathcal{A}(\textbf{Game}_2) = 1\right]$.

Game 3. The challenger changes the generation of $\textbf{c}_1^*$ and $\textbf{c}_2^*$. More precisely, it selects $\textbf{s}_1 \neq \textbf{s}_2 \leftarrow \mathbb{Z}_2^n$, $\textbf{e}_1, \textbf{e}_2 \leftarrow \mathcal{B}_p^m$ and sets $\textbf{c}_1^* \leftarrow \textbf{A}_1\textbf{s}_1 + \textbf{e}_1, \textbf{c}_2^* \leftarrow \textbf{A}_2\textbf{s}_2 + \textbf{e}_2$. The rest is identical to $\textbf{Game 2}$. Assuming that $\mathcal{A}$ distinguishes $\textbf{Game 3}$ from $\textbf{Game 2}$, we construct an algorithm $\mathcal{A}_1$ to solve TLPN problem. $\mathcal{A}_1$ is given a quadruple $(\textbf{A}_1, \textbf{A}_2, \textbf{z}_1, \textbf{z}_2)$, where either $(\textbf{z}_1, \textbf{z}_2) = (\textbf{A}_1\textbf{s} + \textbf{e}_1, \textbf{A}_2\textbf{s} + \textbf{e}_2)$ or $(\textbf{z}_1, \textbf{z}_2) = (\textbf{A}_1\textbf{s}_1 + \textbf{e}_1, \textbf{A}_2\textbf{s}_2 + \textbf{e}_2)$. $\mathcal{A}_1$ sets $\textbf{c}_1^* \leftarrow \textbf{z}_1$, $\textbf{c}_2^* \leftarrow \textbf{z}_2$. It sends $(\textbf{c}_1^*, \textbf{c}_2^*, \textbf{c}_3^*, \textbf{c}_4^*)$ to $\mathcal{A}$ and outputs whaterver $\mathcal{A}$ outputs. If $(\textbf{z}_1, \textbf{z}_2) = (\textbf{A}_1\textbf{s} + \textbf{e}_1, \textbf{A}_2\textbf{s} + \textbf{e}_2)$, then $\mathcal{A}_1$ simulates the behavior of the challenger in $\textbf{Game 2}$. Hence,

$$
\Pr\left[\mathcal{A}(\textbf{Game}_2) = 1\right] = \Pr\left[\mathcal{A}_1\left(\textbf{A}_1, \textbf{A}_2, \textbf{A}_1\textbf{s} + \textbf{e}_1, \textbf{A}_2\textbf{s} + \textbf{e}_2\right) = 1\right].
$$

If $(\textbf{z}_1, \textbf{z}_2) = (\textbf{A}_1\textbf{s}_1 + \textbf{e}_1, \textbf{A}_2\textbf{s}_2 + \textbf{e}_2)$, then $\mathcal{A}_1$ simulates the behavior of the challenger in $\textbf{Game 3}$. Hence,

$$
\Pr\left[\mathcal{A}(\textbf{Game}_3) = 1\right] = \Pr\left[\mathcal{A}\left(\textbf{A}_1, \textbf{A}_2, \textbf{A}_1\textbf{s}_1 + \textbf{e}_1, \textbf{A}_2\textbf{s}_2 + \textbf{e}_2\right) = 1\right].
$$

Therefore, it implies that

$$
|\Pr\left[\mathcal{A}(\textbf{Game}_2) = 1\right] - \Pr\left[\mathcal{A}(\textbf{Game}_3) = 1\right]| \leq \textbf{Adv}_{\text{TLPN}(n,2m,p),t}.
\tag{11}
$$

Game 4. The challenger sets $\textbf{A}_2 \leftarrow \textbf{TA}_1$ with $\textbf{T} \leftarrow \mathcal{B}_{p/2}^{m \times m}$ and $\textbf{T}_1, \textbf{T}_2 \leftarrow \mathcal{B}_{p/2}^{m \times m}$. The rest is identical to $\textbf{Game 3}$. $\mathcal{A}$ can not distinguish $\textbf{Game 4}$ from $\textbf{Game 3}$ for the hardness of KLPN problem. More specifically, assuming that $\mathcal{A}$ distinguishes $\textbf{Game 4}$ from $\textbf{Game 3}$, we construct an algorithm $\mathcal{A}_1$ to solve KLPN problem. Given a tuple $(\textbf{A}_1', \textbf{A}_2')$, where $\textbf{A}_2'$ is either $\textbf{TA}_1'$ or uniformly random, $\mathcal{A}_1$ sets $\textbf{A}_1 \leftarrow \textbf{A}_1'$ and $\textbf{A}_2 \leftarrow \textbf{A}_2'$. The rest is identical in $\textbf{Game 3}$. $\mathcal{A}_1$ outputs whatever $\mathcal{A}$ outputs. If $\textbf{A}_2' = \textbf{TA}_1'$, then $\mathcal{A}_1$ simulates the behavior of the challenger $\mathcal{C}$ in **Game 4**. If $\mathbf{A}_2'$ is uniformly random, then $\mathcal{A}_1$ simulates the behavior of the challenger $\mathcal{C}$ in **Game 3**. Therefore, we immediately have

$$| \Pr[\mathcal{A}(\mathbf{Game}_3) = 1] - \Pr[\mathcal{A}(\mathbf{Game}_4) = 1] |$$
$$\leq \mathbf{Adv}_{\mathrm{KLPN}^m(m-n,m,p/2),t} \leq m \cdot \mathbf{Adv}_{\mathrm{KLPN}(m-n,m,p/2),t}. \tag{12}$$

Moreover, $\mathbf{H} = \mathbf{T}_1\mathbf{A}_1 + \mathbf{T}_2\mathbf{A}_2 = (\mathbf{T}_1 + \Delta\mathbf{T}_1)\mathbf{A}_1 + (\mathbf{T}_2 + \Delta\mathbf{T}_2)\mathbf{A}_2$, where $\Delta\mathbf{T}_2 \in \mathcal{T}(m) \triangleq \{\mathbf{P} \in \mathbb{Z}_2^{m \times m} : \mathbf{P} \text{ has one 1 in every row and column at most}\}$ and $\Delta\mathbf{T}_1 = \Delta\mathbf{T}_2\mathbf{T}$. We will show that $(\bar{\mathbf{T}}_1 = \mathbf{T}_1 + \Delta\mathbf{T}_2\mathbf{T}, \bar{\mathbf{T}}_2 = \mathbf{T}_2 + \Delta\mathbf{T}_2)$ is a valid secret key in full version.

Game 5. The challenger changes the running of decryption oracle as follows.

- Case 1: If $(\mathbf{c}_1, \mathbf{c}_2, \mathbf{c}_3) \approx (\mathbf{c}_1^*, \mathbf{c}_2^*, \mathbf{c}_3^*)$, then the challenger decrypts $\mathbf{c}_4$ (not equals to $\mathbf{c}_4^*$) and outputs $\mathsf{AE.D}(\mathbf{k}, \mathbf{c}_4) = \perp/\bar{\mathbf{m}}$ under the key $\mathbf{k} = \mathcal{H}_\kappa(\mathbf{c}_1, \mathbf{c}_2, \mathbf{c}_3, \mathbf{r} = \mathbf{Decode_G}(\mathbf{c}_3 - \mathbf{T}_1\mathbf{c}_1 - \mathbf{T}_2\mathbf{c}_2))$.
- Case 2: If $(\mathbf{c}_1, \mathbf{c}_2, \mathbf{c}_3)$ does not approximates $(\mathbf{c}_1^*, \mathbf{c}_2^*, \mathbf{c}_3^*)$, then the challenger checks whether $|\mathbf{T}\mathbf{c}_1 + \mathbf{c}_2| > \frac{1}{5}\alpha m$. If it holds, then the challenger rejects. Otherwise, it decrypts CT as normal.

Note that in case 1, the challenger responses the decryption queries as in **Game 4**. More precisely, there is the following lemma.

Lemma 9.

$$| \Pr[\mathcal{A}(\mathbf{Game}_4) = 1] - \Pr[\mathcal{A}(\mathbf{Game}_5) = 1] |$$
$$\leq Q \cdot \Pr[E(\mathsf{CT})] = Q \cdot (\mathbf{Adv}_{\mathsf{AE},t}^{int\text{-}ot}(k) + 2^{-k+2}). \tag{13}$$

The proof will be given in full version.

Game 6. The challenger changes the generation of $\mathbf{c}_4^*$. It sets $\mathbf{c}_4^* \leftarrow \mathsf{AE.E}(\tilde{\mathbf{k}}^*, \mathbf{m}_b)$ under a uniformly random $\tilde{\mathbf{k}}^* \leftarrow \mathbb{Z}_2^k$ rather than $\mathbf{k}^* = \mathcal{H}_\kappa(\mathbf{c}_1^*, \mathbf{c}_2^*, \mathbf{c}_3^*, \mathbf{r}^*)$. The rest is identical to **Game 5**. We define the random variable

$$\bar{\mathbf{r}}^* \triangleq \mathbf{Decode_G}(\mathbf{c}_3^* - \bar{\mathbf{T}}_1\mathbf{c}_1^* - \bar{\mathbf{T}}_2\mathbf{c}_2^*) = \mathbf{Decode_G}(\mathbf{Gr}^* + \Delta\mathbf{T}_2(\mathbf{A}_2\Delta\mathbf{s} + \mathbf{Te}_1 + \mathbf{e}_2)).$$

From the proof of Lemma 9, we have $H_\infty(\bar{\mathbf{r}}^* | \mathbf{H}) \geq 4k + 1 \geq 3k$. Lemma 3 gives us $\Delta((\mathbf{H}, \mathcal{H}_\kappa, \bar{\mathbf{k}}^* \triangleq \mathcal{H}_\kappa(\mathbf{c}_1^*, \mathbf{c}_2^*, \mathbf{c}_3^*, \bar{\mathbf{r}}^*)), (\mathbf{H}, \mathcal{H}_\kappa, \tilde{\mathbf{k}}^*)) \leq 2^{-k}$. Then it has

$$|\Pr[\mathcal{A}(\mathbf{Game}_6) = 1] - \Pr[\mathcal{A}(\mathbf{Game}_5) = 1]| \leq 2^{-k}. \tag{14}$$

Game 7. In this game, the challenger rejects all decryption $\mathsf{CT} = (\mathbf{c}_1 = \mathbf{c}_1^*, \mathbf{c}_2 = \mathbf{c}_2^*, \mathbf{c}_3 = \mathbf{c}_3^*, \mathbf{c}_4 \neq \mathbf{c}_4^*)$. The one-time integrity of AE implies that

$$|\Pr[\mathcal{A}(\mathbf{Game}_7) = 1] - \Pr[\mathcal{A}(\mathbf{Game}_6) = 1]| \leq Q \cdot \mathbf{Adv}_{\mathsf{AE},t}^{int\text{-}ot}(k). \tag{15}$$

Finally, from one-time indistinguishability of AE, it has

$$\left|\Pr[\mathcal{A}(\mathbf{Game}_7) = 1] - \frac{1}{2}\right| \leq \mathbf{Adv}_{\mathsf{AE},t}^{ind\text{-}ot}(k). \tag{16}$$

We complete the proof after summing up all the probabilities.

$\square$

4.2   Regev-Type Scheme

4.2.1   Description of the Scheme

The following parameters and public settings are involved in the scheme.

- The security parameter $k, n = \Theta(k^2) \in \mathbb{Z}$, $m \in \mathbb{Z}$ such that $(H(\frac{1}{4}) - \frac{4}{5})n \geq 4k + 1$ and $m \geq 4n$. Noise rate $p = \sqrt{c/m}$ for a constant $c \leq -\frac{1}{2}\ln(1 - \frac{1}{3}\alpha)$
- A generator-matrix $\mathbf{G} \in \mathbb{Z}_2^{n \times \ell}$ of a binary linear error-correcting code $\mathcal{C} = \mathcal{C}(\mathbf{G})$ as in Lemma 2 which is $[n, \ell = R_{\mathbf{G}}n, \delta n]$-code and has an efficient decoder algorithm $\mathbf{Decode_G}$ correcting up to αn errors, where $\alpha \approx \frac{1}{5}$ and $R_{\mathbf{G}} = 1 - 4\alpha \approx \frac{1}{5}$.
- A family of 4-wise independent hash functions $\mathcal{HS} = \{\mathcal{H}_\kappa : \{0,1\}^* \to \mathbb{Z}_2^k\}$.
- An authenticated encryption scheme $\mathsf{AE} = (\mathsf{AE.E}, \mathsf{AE.D})$ with the key space $\mathbb{Z}_2^k$ and the ciphertext space is $\mathbb{Z}_2^d$.

Our scheme is described as follows:

$\mathbf{KeyGen}(1^k) \to (\mathsf{PK}, \mathsf{SK})$: The algorithm runs as follows:

$$\mathbf{A}_1, \mathbf{A}_2 \leftarrow \mathbb{Z}_2^{m \times n}, \mathbf{S}_1, \mathbf{S}_2 \leftarrow \mathbb{Z}_2^{n \times n}, \mathbf{X} \leftarrow \mathcal{B}_p^{m \times n},$$
$$\mathcal{H}_\kappa \leftarrow \mathcal{HS}, \mathbf{H} \leftarrow \mathbf{A}_1\mathbf{S}_1 + \mathbf{A}_2\mathbf{S}_2 + \mathbf{X}.$$

$\mathsf{SK} \leftarrow (\mathbf{S}_1, \mathbf{S}_2) \in (\mathbb{Z}_2^{n \times n})^2$, $\mathsf{PK} \leftarrow (\mathbf{A}_1, \mathbf{A}_2, \mathbf{H}, \mathcal{H}_\kappa) \in (\mathbb{Z}_2^{m \times n})^2 \times \mathbb{Z}_2^{m \times n} \times \mathcal{HS}$.

$\mathbf{Enc}(\mathsf{PK}, \mathbf{m}) \to \mathsf{CT}$: The algorithm runs as follows:

$$\mathbf{e} \leftarrow \mathcal{B}_p^m, \mathbf{X}' \leftarrow \mathcal{B}_p^{m \times n}, \mathbf{r} \leftarrow \mathbb{Z}_2^\ell,$$
$$\mathbf{c}_1 \leftarrow \mathbf{A}_1^\mathsf{T}\mathbf{e}, \mathbf{c}_2 \leftarrow \mathbf{A}_2^\mathsf{T}\mathbf{e}, \mathbf{c}_3 \leftarrow \mathbf{H}^\mathsf{T}\mathbf{e} + \mathbf{X}'^\mathsf{T}\mathbf{e} + \mathbf{Gr},$$
$$\mathbf{k} \leftarrow \mathcal{H}_\kappa(\mathbf{c}_1, \mathbf{c}_2, \mathbf{c}_3, \mathbf{r}), \mathbf{c}_4 \leftarrow \mathsf{AE.E}(\mathbf{k}, \mathbf{m}),$$
$$\mathsf{CT} \leftarrow (\mathbf{c}_1, \mathbf{c}_2, \mathbf{c}_3, \mathbf{c}_4) \in \mathbb{Z}_2^n \times \mathbb{Z}_2^n \times \mathbb{Z}_2^n \times \mathbb{Z}_2^d.$$

$\mathbf{Dec}(\mathsf{SK}, \mathsf{CT}) \to (\perp/\bar{\mathbf{m}})$: The algorithm computes

$$\bar{\mathbf{y}} \leftarrow \mathbf{c}_3 - \mathbf{S}_1^\mathsf{T}\mathbf{c}_1 - \mathbf{S}_2^\mathsf{T}\mathbf{c}_2, \perp/\bar{\mathbf{r}} \leftarrow \mathbf{Decode_G}(\bar{\mathbf{y}}).$$

If $\mathbf{Decode_G}(\bar{\mathbf{y}}) = \perp$, then the algorithm outputs $\perp$. Otherwise, it computes $\bar{\mathbf{k}} \leftarrow \mathcal{H}_\kappa(\mathbf{c}_1, \mathbf{c}_2, \mathbf{c}_3, \bar{\mathbf{r}})$ and outputs $\mathsf{AE.D}(\bar{\mathbf{k}}, \mathbf{c}_4)$.

5   Conclusion

In this work we constructed two IND-CCA2 secure public key encryption schemes from LPN problem via Cramer-Shoup technique rather than the All-But-One technique which are used in all the LWE/LPN-based IND-CCA2 secure schemes. Our two schemes are dual-Regev type and Regev-type. All existing schemes are dual-Regev type.

Acknowledgments. We are very grateful to anonymous reviewers for their helpful comments. We also thank Yamin Liu and Dingding Jia for helpful discussions.

References

1. Agrawal, S., Boneh, D., Boyen, X.: Efficient Lattice (H)IBE in the Standard Model. In: Gilbert, H. (ed.) EUROCRYPT 2010. LNCS, vol. 6110, pp. 553–572. Springer, Heidelberg (2010)
2. Alekhnovich, M.: More on Average Case vs Approximation Complexity. In: FOCS, pp. 298–307 (2003)
3. Alperin-Sheriff, J., Peikert, C.: Circular and KDM Security for Identity-Based Encryption. In: Fischlin, M., Buchmann, J., Manulis, M. (eds.) PKC 2012. LNCS, vol. 7293, pp. 334–352. Springer, Heidelberg (2012)
4. Becker, A., Joux, A., May, A., Meurer, A.: Decoding Random Binary Linear Codes in 2 n/20: How 1 + 1 = 0 Improves Information Set Decoding. In: Pointcheval, Johansson (eds.) [39], pp. 520–536
5. Bernstein, D.J., Lange, T., Peters, C.: Smaller Decoding Exponents: Ball-Collision Decoding. In: Rogaway (ed.) [41], pp. 743–760
6. Boneh, D., Canetti, R., Halevi, S., Katz, J.: Chosen-Ciphertext Security from Identity-Based Encryption. SIAM J. Comput. 36(5), 1301–1328 (2007)
7. Camenisch, J.L., Shoup, V.: Practical Verifiable Encryption and Decryption of Discrete Logarithms. In: Boneh, D. (ed.) CRYPTO 2003. LNCS, vol. 2729, pp. 126–144. Springer, Heidelberg (2003)
8. Cash, D., Hofheinz, D., Kiltz, E., Peikert, C.: Bonsai Trees, or How to Delegate a Lattice Basis. In: Gilbert (ed.) [20], pp. 523–552
9. Cramer, R., Shoup, V.: A Practical Public Key Cryptosystem Provably Secure Against Adaptive Chosen Ciphertext Attack. In: Krawczyk, H. (ed.) CRYPTO 1998. LNCS, vol. 1462, pp. 13–25. Springer, Heidelberg (1998)
10. Cramer, R., Shoup, V.: Universal Hash Proofs and a Paradigm for Adaptive Chosen Ciphertext Secure Public-Key Encryption. In: Knudsen, L.R. (ed.) EUROCRYPT 2002. LNCS, vol. 2332, pp. 45–64. Springer, Heidelberg (2002)
11. Cramer, R., Shoup, V.: Design and Analysis of Practical Public-Key Encryption Schemes Secure against Adaptive Chosen Ciphertext Attack. SIAM J. Comput. 33(1), 167–226 (2003)
12. Damgård, I., Park, S.: How Practical is Public-Key Encryption Based on LPN and Ring-LPN? Cryptology ePrint Archive, Report 2012/699 (2012), http://eprint.iacr.org/
13. Dodis, Y., Ostrovsky, R., Reyzin, L., Smith, A.: Fuzzy Extractors: How to Generate Strong Keys from Biometrics and Other Noisy Data. SIAM J. Comput. 38(1), 97–139 (2008)
14. Dolev, D., Dwork, C., Naor, M.: Nonmalleable Cryptography. SIAM J. Comput. 30(2), 391–437 (2000)
15. Döttling, N., Müller-Quade, J., Nascimento, A.C.A.: IND-CCA secure cryptography based on a variant of the LPN problem. In: Wang, X., Sako, K. (eds.) ASIACRYPT 2012. LNCS, vol. 7658, pp. 485–503. Springer, Heidelberg (2012)
16. Dwork, C. (ed.): Proceedings of the 40th Annual ACM Symposium on Theory of Computing, Victoria, British Columbia, Canada, May 17-20. ACM (2008)
17. Gentry, C.: A Fully Homomorphic Encryption Scheme. Ph.D. thesis, Stanford University (2009), http://crypto.stanford.edu/craig

18. Gentry, C.: Fully homomorphic encryption using ideal lattices. In: Mitzenmacher (ed.) [33], pp. 169–178
19. Gentry, C., Peikert, C., Vaikuntanathan, V.: Trapdoors for hard lattices and new cryptographic constructions. In: Dwork (ed.) [16], pp. 197–206
20. Gilbert, H. (ed.): EUROCRYPT 2010. LNCS, vol. 6110. Springer, Heidelberg (2010)
21. Hofheinz, D., Kiltz, E.: Practical Chosen Ciphertext Secure Encryption from Factoring. In: Joux (ed.) [22], pp. 313–332
22. Joux, A. (ed.): EUROCRYPT 2009. LNCS, vol. 5479. Springer, Heidelberg (2009)
23. Justesen, J.: Class of constructive asymptotically good algebraic codes. IEEE Transactions on Information Theory 18(5), 652–656 (1972)
24. Kawachi, A., Tanaka, K., Xagawa, K.: Multi-bit Cryptosystems Based on Lattice Problems. In: Okamoto, Wang (eds.) [34], pp. 315–329
25. Kiltz, E.: Chosen-Ciphertext Secure Key-Encapsulation Based on Gap Hashed Diffie-Hellman. In: Okamoto, Wang (eds.) [34], pp. 282–297
26. Kiltz, E., Masny, D., Pietrzak, K.: Simple Chosen-Ciphertext Security from Low-Noise LPN. In: Krawczyk, H. (ed.) PKC 2014. LNCS, vol. 8383, pp. 1–18. Springer, Heidelberg (2014)
27. Kiltz, E., Mohassel, P., O'Neill, A.: Adaptive trapdoor functions and chosen-ciphertext security. In: Gilbert (ed.) [20], pp. 673–692
28. Kiltz, E., Pietrzak, K., Stam, M., Yung, M.: A new randomness extraction paradigm for hybrid encryption. In: Joux (ed.) [22], pp. 590–609
29. Kurosawa, K., Desmedt, Y.G.: A New Paradigm of Hybrid Encryption Scheme. In: Franklin, M. (ed.) CRYPTO 2004. LNCS, vol. 3152, pp. 426–442. Springer, Heidelberg (2004)
30. Meurer, A.: A Coding-Theoretic Approach to Cryptanalysis (2012)
31. Micciancio, D., Mol, P.: Pseudorandom Knapsacks and the Sample Complexity of LWE Search-to-Decision Reductions. In: Rogaway (ed.) [41], pp. 465–484
32. Micciancio, D., Peikert, C.: Trapdoors for Lattices: Simpler, Tighter, Faster, Smaller. In: Pointcheval, Johansson (eds.) [39], pp. 700–718
33. Mitzenmacher, M. (ed.): Proceedings of the 41st Annual ACM Symposium on Theory of Computing, STOC 2009, Bethesda, MD, USA, May 31-June 2. ACM (2009)
34. Okamoto, T., Wang, X. (eds.): PKC 2007. LNCS, vol. 4450. Springer, Heidelberg (2007)
35. O'Neill, A., Peikert, C., Waters, B.: Bi-Deniable Public-Key Encryption. In: Rogaway (ed.) [41], pp. 525–542
36. Peikert, C.: Public-Key Cryptosystems from the Worst-Case Shortest Vector Problem: Extended Abstract. In: Mitzenmacher (ed.) [33], pp. 333–342
37. Peikert, C., Vaikuntanathan, V., Waters, B.: A Framework for Efficient and Composable Oblivious Transfer. In: Wagner, D. (ed.) CRYPTO 2008. LNCS, vol. 5157, pp. 554–571. Springer, Heidelberg (2008)
38. Peikert, C., Waters, B.: Lossy trapdoor functions and their applications. In: Dwork (ed.) [16], pp. 187–196
39. Pointcheval, D., Johansson, T. (eds.): EUROCRYPT 2012. LNCS, vol. 7237. Springer, Heidelberg (2012)

40. Regev, O.: On Lattices, Learning with Errors, Random Linear Codes, and Cryptography. In: STOC, pp. 84–93 (2005)
41. Rogaway, P. (ed.): CRYPTO 2011. LNCS, vol. 6841. Springer, Heidelberg (2011)
42. Rosen, A., Segev, G.: Chosen-Ciphertext Security via Correlated Products. In: Reingold, O. (ed.) TCC 2009. LNCS, vol. 5444, pp. 419–436. Springer, Heidelberg (2009)
43. Shoup, V.: Using Hash Functions as a Hedge against Chosen Ciphertext Attack. In: Preneel, B. (ed.) EUROCRYPT 2000. LNCS, vol. 1807, pp. 275–288. Springer, Heidelberg (2000)
44. Stern, J.: A method for finding codewords of small weight. In: Wolfmann, J., Cohen, G. (eds.) Coding Theory 1988. LNCS, vol. 388, pp. 106–113. Springer, Heidelberg (1989)

Partial Prime Factor Exposure Attacks on RSA and Its Takagi's Variant

Liqiang Peng[1,2,3], Lei Hu[1,2,*], Zhangjie Huang[1,2], and Jun Xu[1,2]

[1] State Key Laboratory of Information Security, Institute of Information Engineering,
Chinese Academy of Sciences, Beijing, China
[2] Data Assurance and Communication Security Research Center,
Chinese Academy of Sciences, Beijing, China
[3] University of Chinese Academy of Sciences, Beijing, China
{pengliqiang,hulei,huangzhangjie,xujun}@iie.ac.cn

Abstract. There are many partial key exposure attacks on RSA or its variants under the assumption that a portion of the bits of the decryption exponent d is exposed. Sarkar and Maitra presented a further attack when some bits of the private prime factor q in the modulus $N = pq$ are simultaneously revealed and the total number of bits of q and d required to be known is reduced compared to previous partial key exposure attacks. In this paper, for both the standard RSA with moduli $N = pq$ and the Takagi's variant of RSA with moduli $N = p^2q$, we propose partial key exposure attacks when most significant bits (MSBs) or least significant bits of q are exposed. Compared with previous results, our theoretical analysis and experimental results show a substantial improvement in reducing the number of known bits of the private key to factor N.

Keywords: RSA, partial key exposure attack, lattice, Coppersmith's method.

1 Introduction

Since its invention, the RSA public key scheme [13] has been widely used in practical cryptographic systems due to its security and effective encryption and decryption implementation. For obtaining higher implementation efficiency, RSA with specific parameters were adopted in practical applications, including RSA with small encryption exponents aiming to achieve a very fast encryption operation and those with small decryption exponents for a speedup of decryption. Meanwhile, many variants of RSA have also been proposed, for instance, for gaining a fast decryption implementation, Takagi proposed in [16] a variant of RSA with moduli of the form $N = p^rq$, where $r \geq 2$ is a small integer. The polynomial-time equivalence between factoring such a modulus and recovering the private exponent for the Takagi scheme can be proved.

However, the RSA scheme and its variants will not be secure if the encryption or decryption exponent is not properly chosen or is produced by a pseudorandom

---

* Corresponding author.

© Springer International Publishing Switzerland 2015
J. Lopez and Y. Wu (Eds.): ISPEC 2015, LNCS 9065, pp. 96–108, 2015.
DOI: 10.1007/978-3-319-17533-1_7

number generator with bad randomness. Along this direction, many researchers have paid much attentions to factoring RSA moduli under some conditions like small decryption exponents or exposition of partial bits of the private key.

Small Decryption Exponent Attack. For standard RSA with moduli $N = pq$, Wiener [17] firstly proved that when the secret decryption exponent $d \leq N^{0.25}$, one can factor the modulus N in polynomial time by a continued fraction method. Later, by utilizing a seminal method of Coppersmith for finding small roots of univariate or bivariate integral polynomial equations by lattice basis reduction [4] and the extension method of Jochemsz and May [10], many attacks on RSA have been proposed, for instance, [4,2], and moreover, the size of d which can be broken has been improved. Boneh and Durfee obtained the same bound $N^{0.25}$ as Wiener's by constructing a lattice and solving a modular polynomial equation, and they further improved the bound to $N^{0.284}$ by deriving extra polynomial equations and adding the corresponding vectors of these polynomials to the lattice [2]. By using a sublattice of the previous lattice, they finally improved the bound to $N^{0.292}$. In 2010, Herrmann and May proved that the bound $N^{0.292}$ can be obtained by a simpler and more effective method [6]. For the Takagi's variant of RSA with moduli $N = p^r q$, Itoh et al. [9] can factor the modulus under the condition that $d \leq \frac{2-\sqrt{2}}{r+1}$ by applying Coppersmith's method.

Partial Key Exposure Attacks on RSA. Motivated by side-channel attack which may find a portion of the bits of the private key in practical implementation, partial key exposure attacks on RSA are worth studying. In 1998, Boneh et al. [3] firstly proposed a partial key exposure attack on RSA provided the encryption exponent e satisfies $e < N^{0.5}$ and portion bits of the decryption exponent d are exposed. Then, Ernst et al. [5] gave an extended analysis with respect to the full size encryption exponents e. Note that, all these attacks assume that one may obtain some bits of d. Shortly later, Sarkar and Maitra [14] improved partial key exposure attacks under an extra assumption that one can guess some bits of the prime factor q, especially, they proved that for factoring the RSA modulus, the total number of bits of q and d which are required to be known is fewer than the number of bits of d required to be known in the Ernst et al. attack [5]. Such an extra assumption on private prime factors q sometimes holds in practical cryptographic applications, for example, distinct but slightly different prime factors were used by different users in the Taiwan Citizen Digital Certificate [1].

For Takagi's variant of RSA, Huang et al. [8] gave partial key exposure attacks when most significant bits (MSBs), least significant bits (LSBs) or middle bits of d are known.

The following propositions are a brief review on the results of the above partial key exposure attacks on RSA and its Takagi's variant.

Proposition 1. (*Ernst et al. [5]*) *Given a balanced RSA modulus $N = pq$, $e \simeq N$ and $d = N^\delta$. Assume that $|d - d_0| \leq N^\gamma$, where d_0 is known, then the modulus N can be factored in polynomial time when*

$$\gamma \le \frac{5}{6} - \frac{1}{3}\sqrt{1 + 6\delta}, \quad \text{or}$$

$$\gamma \le \frac{1}{3}\lambda + \frac{1}{2} - \frac{1}{3}\sqrt{4\lambda^2 + 6\lambda}, \text{where } \lambda = \max\{\gamma, \delta - \frac{1}{2}\}.$$

Proposition 2. *(Sarkar-Maitra [14]) Given a balanced RSA modulus $N = pq$, $e \sim N$ and $d = N^\delta$. Assume that $|d - d_0| \le N^\gamma$ and $|q - q_0| \le N^\beta$, where d_0 and q_0 are known, then the modulus N can be factored in polynomial time when*

$$\gamma \le 1 - \frac{\beta + 2\sqrt{\beta(\beta + 3\delta)}}{3}, \quad \text{or}$$

$$\gamma \le 1 + \frac{1}{3}\lambda - \beta - \frac{2}{3}\sqrt{\lambda(\lambda + 3\beta)}, \text{where } \lambda = \max\{\gamma, \delta - \frac{1}{2}\}.$$

Proposition 3. *(Huang et al. [8]) Given a modulus $N = p^2q$ where p and q are primes with same bit-length. Let $e = N^\alpha$ and $d = N^\delta$ be integers satisfying $ed \equiv 1 \,(mod\,(p-1)(q-1))$ and $\gcd(e, p) = 1$. Assume that $|d - d_0| \le N^\gamma$ where d_0 is known, the modulus N can be factored in polynomial time when*

$$\gamma \le \frac{7 - \sqrt{72(\delta + \alpha) - 39}}{12}.$$

Proposition 4. *(Sarkar et al. [15]) Given a modulus $N = pq$ where p and q are primes with same bit-length. Let $e \sim N$ and $d = N^\delta$ be integers satisfying $ed \equiv 1 \,(mod\,(p-1)(q-1))$. Assume that $|q - q_0| \le N^\beta$, where q_0 are known, then the modulus N can be factored in polynomial time when*

$$\delta < 1 - \sqrt{\beta}.$$

Note that, in [15] Sarkar et al. considered the case that only partial bits of q are exposed. Then based on the idea of [2], Sarkar et al. utilized geometrically progressive matrix to gave the analysis. In this paper, we follow the line of [14,15] and give key exposure attacks on RSA with modulus $N = pq$ and its variant with $N = p^2q$ under the circumstance that partial bits of q are known. More specifically, when a certain number of MSBs of q with $N = pq$ are exposed, we utilize the technique proposed in [6] which is more acceptable to derive a bound on d to let N be factorable in polynomial time and obtain the same bound with Sarkar et al. in [15]. This attack was verified by our experiments. For the variant with $N = p^2q$, we use the construction of lattice in [9] and obtain a bound on d to let $N = p^2q$ be factorable with known MSBs of q. Especially, for large e, our method needs fewer known bits of the private key q to factor N.

The rest of this paper is organized as follows. Preliminaries on lattices and L^3 lattice basis reduction are given in Section 2. In Section 3, we give theoretical analyse and experimental results of key exposure attacks on RSA with $N = pq$ when MSBs of q are known. Section 4 is theoretical analysis and experimental results on key exposure attacks on the RSA variant with $N = p^2q$. For the replacements in the lattice construction which do not produce new variables, similar analysis can be proposed when LSBs of the prime factor q are exposed. Section 5 is the conclusion.

2 Preliminaries

Let $w_1, w_2, \cdots, w_k$ be k linearly independent vectors in $\mathbb{R}^n$. A lattice L spanned by $(w_1, \cdots, w_k)$ is a discrete additive subgroup of $\mathbb{R}^n$, namely k-dimensional lattice L is the set of all integer linear combinations, $c_1 w_1 + \cdots + c_k w_k$, of $w_1, \cdots, w_k$, where $c_1, \cdots, c_k \in \mathbb{Z}$. The set of vectors $(w_1, \cdots, w_k)$ is called as a basis of the lattice L. The lattice basis is not unique, one can obtain another basis by multiplying any matrix with determinant ± 1, it means that any lattice of dimension larger than 1 has infinitely many bases [12]. Hence, how to find a lattice basis with good properties has been a hot problem.

In 1982, Lenstra et al. [11] introduced the famous L^3 lattice basis reduction algorithm which can find out a relatively short and nearly orthogonal lattice basis in polynomial time. Instead of finding shortest vectors in a lattice, L^3 reduced basis also has some useful properties.

Lemma 1. $(L^3, [12,11])$ *Let L be a lattice of dimension k. Applying the L^3 algorithm to L, the outputted reduced basis vectors $v_1, \cdots, v_k$ satisfy that*

$$\|v_1\| \leq \|v_2\| \leq \cdots \leq \|v_i\| \leq 2^{\frac{k(k-i)}{4(k+1-i)}} det(L)^{\frac{1}{k+1-i}}, \text{for any } 1 \leq i \leq k.$$

Since the first appearance of L^3 lattice basis reduction algorithm, the application of lattice in cryptanalysis is more and more widespread. In one significant application, lattices are used to find small roots of univariate modular equations and bivariate equations [4] and this strategy is now usually called Coppersmith's technique. Then Jochemsz and May extended this technique and gave a general result to find roots of multivariate polynomials [10].

The following lemma due to Howgrave-Graham [7] gives a sufficient condition under which roots of a modular equation also satisfy a integer equation. Note that, for a given polynomial $g(x_1, \cdots, x_k) = \sum\limits_{(i_1, \cdots, i_k)} a_{i_1, \cdots, i_k} x_1^{i_1} \cdots x_k^{i_k}$, we define the norm of g as

$$\|g(x_1, \cdots, x_k)\| = \left(\sum\limits_{(i_1, \cdots, i_k)} a_{i_1, \cdots, i_k}^2 \right)^{\frac{1}{2}}.$$

Lemma 2. *(Howgrave-Graham, [7]) Let $g(x_1, \cdots, x_k) \in \mathbb{Z}[x_1, \cdots, x_k]$ be a integer polynomial with at most w monomials. Suppose that*

$$g(y_1, \cdots, y_k) \equiv 0 \pmod{p^m} \text{ for } |y_1| \leq X_1, \cdots, |y_k| \leq X_k, \text{ and}$$

$$\|g(x_1 X_1, \cdots, x_k X_k)\| < \frac{p^m}{\sqrt{w}}.$$

Then $g(y_1, \cdots, y_k) = 0$ holds over the integers.

Once we obtain the polynomials $g_1(y_1, \cdots, y_k) = 0, \cdots, g_k(y_1, \cdots, y_k) = 0$, we can solve out the roots over integers by calculating resultant or Gröbner basis based on the following heuristic assumption and note that in practical experiments, the following heuristic assumption is always founded.

Assumption 1. *The common roots of the polynomials yielded by lattice based constructions can be efficiently computed by using numerical method, symbolic method or exploiting the special structure of these polynomials.*

3   Attack for $N = pq$ When MSBs of q Known

In this section, we follow the technique proposed in [6] to analyze the bound of d when a certain number of MSBs of q with $N = pq$ are exposed and obtain the following result.

Theorem 1. *Given a balanced RSA moduli $N = pq$, $e \simeq N$ and $d \simeq N^\delta$. Assume that a certain number of MSBs of q are exposed, namely $|q - q_0| < N^\beta$, where q_0 is known and $\frac{1}{4} < \beta \leq \frac{1}{2}$, then one can factor N in polynomial time when*

$$\delta \leq 1 - \sqrt{\beta}.$$

Proof. Let $q = q_0 + q_1$, where $|q_1| \leq N^\beta$. Then we calculate $p_0 = \lfloor \frac{N}{q_0} \rfloor$. It can be verified that $|p - p_0| \leq N^\beta$. Assume that $p = p_0 + p_1$, where $|p_1| \leq N^\beta$. Hence, from the equality $ed = 1 + k(N - p - q + 1)$, we obtain the following equation

$$f(x, y) = 1 + x(N - p_0 - q_0 + 1 + y) \mod e. \tag{1}$$

By letting $u = xy + 1$ and $A = N - p_0 - q_0 + 1$, equation (1) can be rewritten as

$$f(x, u) = u + Ax \mod e. \tag{2}$$

It is obviously that $(k, -k(p_1 + q_1) + 1)$ is a solution of modular equation (2) and the size of the desired solution can be estimated as $|k| \leq X = N^\delta$, $|p_1 + q_1| \leq Y \simeq N^\beta$ and $|-k(p_1 + q_1) + 1| \leq U \simeq N^{\delta+\beta}$.

Based on the idea of [6], we collect the following polynomials

$$g_{i,k}(x, y, u) = x^i f^k(x, u) e^{m-k},$$
$$\text{for } k = 0, \cdots, m, \ i = 0, \cdots, m - k;$$
$$g'_{i,j}(x, y, u) = y^j f^k(x, u) e^{m-k},$$
$$\text{for } j = 1, \cdots, t, \ k = \lfloor \frac{m}{t} \rfloor j, \cdots, m,$$

where m and t are integers. Each occurrence of xy in above polynomials is replaced by $u - 1$.

Note that $g_{i,k}(k, -(p_1 + q_1), -k(p_1 + q_1) + 1) \equiv 0 \pmod{e^m}$ and $g'_{j,k}(k, -(p_1 + q_1), -k(p_1 + q_1) + 1) \equiv 0 \pmod{e^m}$. Then we construct a triangular matrix corresponding to lattice L which is composed by the coefficients of $g_{i,k}(xX, yY, uU)$ and $g'_{j,k}(xX, yY, uU)$ and the diagonal entries are

$$X^i U^k e^{m-k}, \text{ for } k = 0, \cdots, m, \ i = 0, \cdots, m - k;$$
$$Y^j U^k e^{m-k}, \text{ for } j = 1, \cdots, t, \ k = \lfloor \frac{m}{t} \rfloor j, \cdots, m.$$

Similarly, as the calculations in [6] we can calculate the determinant of L,

$$\det(L) = (\prod_{k=0}^{m} \prod_{i=0}^{m-k} X^i U^k e^{m-k})(\prod_{j=1}^{t} \prod_{k=\lfloor \frac{m}{t} \rfloor j}^{m} Y^j U^k e^{m-k})$$

$$= X^{\frac{1}{6}m^3 + o(m^3)} Y^{\frac{\tau^2}{6}m^3 + o(m^3)} U^{(\frac{1}{6}+\frac{\tau}{3})m^3 + o(m^3)} e^{(\frac{1}{3}+\frac{\tau}{6})m^3 + o(m^3)}$$

where $t = \tau m$. On the other hand, we have that $\dim(L) = \frac{1+\tau}{2}m^2 + o(m^2)$. Neglecting the lower terms $o(m^3)$, from Lemma 1 and Lemma 2 one can obtain equations $h_i(k, -(p_1+q_1), -k(p_1+q_1)+1) = 0$, for $i = 1, 2, 3$, which holds over integers when $\det(L)^{\frac{1}{\dim(L)}} < e^m$, or equivalently,

$$\frac{1}{6}\delta + \frac{\tau^2}{6}\beta + (\frac{1}{6}+\frac{\tau}{3})(\delta+\beta) + \frac{1}{3} + \frac{\tau}{6} \le \frac{1}{2} + \frac{\tau}{2}.$$

Letting $\tau = \frac{1}{\sqrt{\beta}} - 1$, we have that

$$\delta \le 1 - \sqrt{\beta},$$

where $\frac{1}{4} < \beta \le \frac{1}{2}$. Then under Assumption 1, we can collect the roots successfully, this concludes the proof of Theorem 1.   □

Comparison with Previous Works. From Theorem 1, we can obtain following bound $\beta \le (1-\delta)^2$. Since the constraint on β, the value of δ is bounded as $0.292 \le \delta < \frac{1}{2}$. We make a comparison on the required known bits of private key to factor N with specific d between our method and previous works. Based on Proposition 1 and Proposition 2, we obtain following table by straightforward calculations. Note that when $\beta = \frac{1}{2}$, namely there is no known MSBs of q in Proposition 2, we obtain the same bound as Proposition 1 on δ.

Table 1. Required fraction of private key to factor N with specific d

δ	known fraction of the MSBs of q in our method and [15]'s work	known fraction of the MSBs of d in [14]		
		no known MSBs of q	known $N^{0.01}$ MSBs of q	known $N^{0.03}$ MSBs of q
0.3	0.010	0.024	0.014	0.000
0.35	0.077	0.134	0.092	0.070
0.4	0.140	0.181	0.179	0.147

Remark. Note that, the column of no known MSBs of q can be considered as that only partial bits of d are exposed and the column of known $N^{0.01}$ MSBs of q can be considered as that the total exposed private keys include $N^{0.01}$ MSBs of q and some bits of d. As it is shown in the Table 1, the required known fraction of private key in our method is just as the result in [15] and less than result in [14]. For example, in order to reveal $d \simeq N^{0.35}$, we need known $N^{0.077}$ MSBs of q, however, for the same d the requirement is $N^{0.03}$ MSBs of q and $N^{0.070}$ MSBs of d in [14]. However since [15] didn't provide experimental results, we give a comparison on experiments between our results and existing results in [14].

Experimental Results. We have implemented the experiments in Magma 2.11 computer algebra system on a PC with Intel(R) Core(TM) Duo CPU(2.53GHz, 1.9GB RAM Windows 7). For 1024-bits balanced modulus $N = pq$, we choose small lattice dimension $\dim(L) = 11$, the experimental results are listed in Table 2 and all the experiments are done within one minute.

Table 2. Required fraction of private key to factor 1024-N with specific d in small dimensions

bits of d	known MSBs of q in our method	known MSBs of d and q in [14]	
		known MSBs of d	known MSBs of q
308	70	80	21
359	160	150	55

As it is shown, known 70 MSBs of q are sufficient to factor 1024-bits N with 308-bits d by a 11-dimensional lattice, however the requirement in [14] is 80 MSBs of d and 21 MSBs of q by using a lattice with 16 dimension. Namely, for 308-bits d we need know fewer bits of private keys to factor 1024-bits N in a 16-dimensional lattice. And the same is true for 359-bits d.

We also use lattices with lager dimension to implement our experiments. Table 3 shows our results.

Table 3. Known MSBs of q for 1024-bits N with larger lattice

d (bits)	known MSBs of q (bits)	m	t	$\dim(L)$	time(L^3)
295	20	9	3	67	562.883s
305	30	9	4	75	956.255s
311	40	9	4	75	1016.705s

For 1000-bit N with $\delta = 0.300$, we needed to know 38 bits of q to successfully factor N with 48-dimensional lattice in 139 seconds of L^3 algorithm and 212 seconds of calculating Gröbner basis, this experimental result is same with Sarkar et al in [15] and seems better in running time.

4   Attack for Takagi's Variant of RSA when MSBs of q Known

In this section we consider that a certain number of MSBs of prime q with the modulus $N = p^2q$ are exposed. We will study to this method following the work of [9] and start with the following result.

Theorem 2. *Given RSA modulus $N = p^2q$ which p and q are of same bit size, consider that certain MSBs of prime q are exposed, namely $|q - q_0| < N^\beta$, where*

q_0 *is known. Let* $e \simeq N^\alpha$ *and* $d \simeq N^\delta$, *then one can factor* N *in polynomial time when*

$$\delta < \frac{4 + 9\beta - \sqrt{2\beta(1 + 36\alpha + 12\beta + 54\alpha\beta + 9\beta^2)}}{6 + 9\beta}.$$

Proof. Let $q = q_0 + q_1$, where q_0 is known and $|q_1| \leq N^\beta$. For Takagi's variant of RSA, we have the following equation,

$$ed = 1 + k(p-1)(q-1) = 1 + k(p-1)(q_0 + q_1 - 1) \tag{3}$$

where $p \simeq q \simeq q_0 \simeq N^{\frac{1}{3}}$.

Since $e \simeq N^\alpha$ and $d \simeq N^\delta$, the unknown k can be estimated as

$$k = \frac{ed - 1}{(p-1)(q-1)} \simeq N^{\alpha + \delta - \frac{2}{3}}.$$

Based on (3), we have that (k, p, q_1) is a solution of the following modular equation

$$f(x, y, z) = 1 + x(y-1)(z + q_0 - 1) \pmod{e}$$

and the upper bounds of desired solution can be estimated as $|k| \leq X = N^{\alpha + \delta - \frac{2}{3}}$, $|p| \leq Y = 2N^{\frac{1}{3}}$ and $|q_1| \leq Z = N^\beta$.

In order to solve out the desired solution, we follow the idea of [9] to construct the lattice. For a integer m we collect polynomials as following,

$$x^{u-i}f^i(x,y,z)e^{m-i}, x^{u-i}yf^i(x,y,z)e^{m-i}, x^{u-i}yzf^i(x,y,z)e^{m-i},$$
$$\text{for } u = 0, \cdots, m, i = 0, \cdots, u-1;$$
$$y^j f^u(x,y,z)e^{m-u},$$
$$\text{for } u = 0, \cdots, m, j = 0, \cdots, s; \tag{4}$$
$$yz^k f^u(x,y,z)e^{m-u}, z^k f^u(x,y,z)e^{m-u},$$
$$\text{for } u = 0, \cdots, m, k = 1, \cdots, t,$$

where s, t are integers.

Obviously, all the above polynomials have the same roots (k, p, q_1) modulo e^m and each occurrence of monomials $y^2 z$ is replaced by $N - q_0 y^2$ because of $p^2(q_0 + q_1) = N$.

Note that, the expansion of $f^n(x, y, z)$ can be represented as following,

$$(1 + x(y-1)(z + q_0 - 1))^n$$
$$= x^n(a_1 y^n + a_2 y^{n-1} + \cdots + a_n y + b_1 yz^n + b_2 yz^{n-1} + \cdots + b_n yz + c_1 z^n + c_2 z^{n-1}$$
$$+ \cdots + c_n z + c_{n+1}) + x^{n-1}(\cdots\cdots) + \cdots\cdots + x(\cdots\cdots) + 1$$

where $a_1, \cdots, a_n, b_1, \cdots, b_n, c_1, \cdots, c_{n+1}$ are integers and $y^2 z$ is replaced by $N - q_0 y^2$.

Since the monomial $x^n y^n$ can be obtained from $x^n y^n z^l$, for $l = 0, 1, \cdots, n$, namely the monomial $x^n y^n z^l$ provides $(-q_0)^l x^n y^n$. On the other hand, the coefficient of $x^n y^n z^l$ is $\binom{n}{l}(q_0 - 1)^{n-l}$, hence the coefficient a_1 of $x^n y^n$ in $f^n(x, y, z)$ can be determined as

$$a_1 = \sum_{l=0}^{n} (-q_0)^l * \binom{n}{l} (q_0 - 1)^{n-l} = (q_0 - 1 - q_0)^n = (-1)^n.$$

Similarly, the coefficient c_1 of $x^n z^n$ can also be determined as $c_1 = (-1)^n$.

Putting the upper bounds (X, Y, Z) of desired solution into polynomials of (4), we obtain the polynomials with form of $g_{ijk}(xX, yY, zZ)$. Then we build a triangular matrix corresponding to the lattice L which is composed by the coefficients of $g_{ijk}(xX, yY, zZ)$. The monomial appeared in the diagonal of each polynomial is selected as $x^n y^n$ or $x^n z^n$ in $f^n(x, y, z)$, then the diagonal entries are

$$X^u Z^i e^{m-i}, \ X^u Y^{i+1} e^{m-i}, \ X^u Y Z^{i+1} e^{m-i},$$
$$\text{for } u = 0, \cdots, m, \ i = 0, \cdots, u - 1;$$
$$X^u Y^{u+j} e^{m-u},$$
$$\text{for } u = 0, \cdots, m, \ j = 0, \cdots, s;$$
$$X^u Y Z^{k+u} e^{m-u}, \ X^u Z^{k+u} e^{m-u},$$
$$\text{for } u = 0, \cdots, m, \ k = 1, \cdots, t.$$

We follow the similar computations as in [9], thus one can calculate the determinant of L as

$$\det(L) = (\prod_{u=0}^{m} \prod_{i=0}^{u-1} X^u Z^i e^{m-i}) * (\prod_{u=0}^{m} \prod_{i=0}^{u-1} X^u Y^{i+1} e^{m-i})$$
$$* (\prod_{u=0}^{m} \prod_{i=0}^{u-1} X^u Y Z^{i+1} e^{m-i}) * (\prod_{u=0}^{m} \prod_{j=0}^{s} X^u Y^{u+j} e^{m-u})$$
$$* (\prod_{u=0}^{m} \prod_{k=1}^{t} X^u Y Z^{k+u} e^{m-u}) * (\prod_{u=0}^{m} \prod_{k=1}^{t} X^u Z^{k+u} e^{m-u})$$
$$= X^{S_x} Y^{S_y} Z^{S_z} e^{S_e},$$

where

$$\begin{cases} S_x = (1 + \tau + \dfrac{\sigma}{2})m^3 + o(m^3), \\[2mm] S_y = (\dfrac{1}{6} + \dfrac{\sigma}{2} + \dfrac{\sigma^2}{2})m^3 + o(m^3), \\[2mm] S_z = (\dfrac{1}{3} + \tau + \tau^2)m^3 + o(m^3), \\[2mm] S_e = (1 + \tau + \dfrac{\sigma}{2})m^3 + o(m^3), \end{cases}$$

where $t = \tau m$ and $s = \sigma m$.

On the other hand, the dimension of L is

$$w = \sum_{u=0}^{m}\sum_{i=0}^{u-1} 3 + \sum_{u=0}^{m}\sum_{j=0}^{s} 1 + \sum_{u=0}^{m}\sum_{k=1}^{t} 2 = (\frac{3}{2} + 2\tau + \sigma)m^2 + o(m^2).$$

From Lemma 1 and Lemma 2, one can obtain equations $h_1(x,y,z), h_2(x,y,z),$ $h_3(x,y,z)$ which share the roots (k,p,q_1) over integers, when

$$\det(L)^{\frac{1}{w}} < \gamma e^m,$$

where γ is a small term. Now, for large N and e, the required condition can be reduced as $\det(L)^{\frac{1}{w}} < e^m$, namely $X^{S_x}Y^{S_y}Z^{S_z}e^{S_e} < e^{mw}$.

Putting the bounds $X = N^{\alpha+\delta-\frac{2}{3}}, Y \simeq N^{\frac{1}{3}}, Z = N^{\beta}, e = N^{\alpha}$ into the inequation, we obtain that

$$(\alpha + \delta - \frac{2}{3})((1 + \tau + \frac{\sigma}{2})m^3 + o(m^3)) + \frac{1}{3}((\frac{1}{6} + \frac{\sigma}{2} + \frac{\sigma^2}{2})m^3 + o(m^3)) +$$
$$\beta((\frac{1}{3} + \tau + \tau^2)m^3 + o(m^3)) + \alpha((1 + \tau + \frac{\sigma}{2})m^3 + o(m^3)) \tag{5}$$
$$< \alpha((\frac{3}{2} + 2\tau + \sigma)m^3 + o(m^3)).$$

Neglecting lower terms $o(m^3)$ in (5), we get that

$$\frac{\sigma^2}{6} - \sigma(\frac{1-3\delta}{6}) + \beta\tau^2 - \tau(\frac{2}{3} - \beta - \delta) + \frac{\beta}{3} + \delta - \frac{11}{18} + \frac{\alpha}{2} < 0.$$

By setting $\sigma = \frac{1-3\delta}{2}$ and $\tau = \frac{2-3\beta-3\delta}{6\beta}$, we obtain the following inequality

$$\delta^2(18 + 27\beta) - \delta(24 + 54\beta) + 8 + 23\beta - 36\alpha\beta - 6\beta^2 > 0.$$

Hence we get the required bound for δ as follows,

$$\delta < \frac{4 + 9\beta - \sqrt{2\beta(1 + 36\alpha + 12\beta + 54\alpha\beta + 9\beta^2)}}{6 + 9\beta}.$$

Then under Assumption 1, we can collect the roots successfully, this concludes the proof of Theorem 2.   □

Note that. in [9] Itoh et al. used geometrically progressive matrices to improved the bound on d, here we only achieved the general bound which is used full rank matrix.

Comparison with Previous Work. From Proposition 3, we know that given a certain number of MSBs of d can be used to factor larger d than original bound in [9]. Now for fixed d, we make a comparison between the number of the MSBs of d and the number of the MSBs of q are needed to know to factor $N = p^2q$.

By straight forward calculations from equations of Proposition 3 and Theorem 2, we obtain following bounds on δ when a certain number bits of q and d are exposed respectively,

$$\delta_{(our\ bound)} < \frac{7 - 9\lambda - \sqrt{2(1 - 3\lambda)(2 + 18\alpha - 6(1 + 3\alpha)\lambda + 3\lambda^2)}}{9(1 - \lambda)}, \quad \lambda \in \{0, \tfrac{1}{3}\},$$

$$\delta_{(Huang\ et\ al's\ bound)} < \frac{5}{6} + \lambda - \frac{1}{2}\sqrt{\frac{1}{3} + 2\lambda + 2\alpha}, \quad \lambda \in \{0, \delta\},$$

where N^λ denotes the number of known bits of q in our work and d in [8] respectively.

Comparing this two bounds, we can get the following Figure 1.

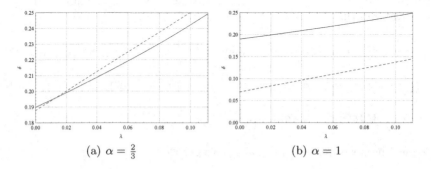

(a) $\alpha = \frac{2}{3}$ (b) $\alpha = 1$

Fig. 1. Comparison with previous ranges on δ with respect to λ. Here the dotted line denotes the upper bound on δ in [8], and the thin solid line denotes that in this paper.

Remark. In order to make an explicit comparison between our work and Huang et al.'s work in [8], we use the the known bits to denote the horizontal axis of Fig. 1. As it is shown, for $\alpha = \frac{2}{3}$ our method is more efficient when known bits of private key is smaller than $N^{0.012}$, and our method is always more powerful than Huang et al. [8] for $\alpha = 1$ in theory. Moreover for LSB case, we need to take care of the coefficients of the leading monomials of the polynomials in the selected polynomials and keep the determinant of lattice constant.

Experimental Results. We have implemented the experiments in Magma 2.11 computer algebra system on a PC with Intel(R) Core(TM) Duo CPU(2.53GHz, 1.9GB RAM Windows 7). We list our experimental results in Table 4.

We make a comparison between our work and Huang et al.'s work [8] in practical experiments. For the case 1000-bit N and 100-bits d, correctly guessing 20-MSBs of q is enough to factor N in less than 15 minutes. On the other hand, for same size of N and d, one needs to know 70-MSBs of decryption exponent d and 36 hours to factor N in [8].

Table 4. Known MSBs of q with modulus $N = p^2q$

	N (bits)	δ	λ	$\dim(L)$	$\text{time}(L^3)$
	1000	0.10	0.02	105	797.680s
$\alpha = \frac{2}{3}$	1000	0.13	0.07	117	1981.181s
	1000	0.15	0.10	117	2539.072s
	1000	0.03	0.02	123	1280.597s
$\alpha = \frac{3}{4}$	1000	0.05	0.07	135	1983.428s
	1000	0.08	0.10	129	2634.326s

5   Conclusion

In this paper, we presented partial key attacks on standard RSA with moduli $N = pq$ and its Takagi's variant with moduli $N = p^2q$ provided some most significant bits of the prime factor q are exposed. Compared with previous results, for RSA with modulus $N = pq$, the required known bits of private key is reduced in our method and the experiments also showed our result. For the RSA variant with modulus $N = p^2q$, the fewer known bits of private key are needed to factor N under the conditions that both encryption and decryption exponents are small and that the encryption exponents are large.

Acknowledgements. The authors would like to thank anonymous reviewers for their helpful comments and suggestions. The work of this paper was supported by the National Key Basic Research Program of China (2013CB834203), the National Natural Science Foundation of China (Grants 61472417 and 61402469), the Strategic Priority Research Program of Chinese Academy of Sciences under Grant XDA06010702, and the State Key Laboratory of Information Security, Chinese Academy of Sciences.

References

1. Bernstein, D.J., Chang, Y.-A., Cheng, C.-M., Chou, L.-P., Heninger, N., Lange, T., van Someren, N.: Factoring RSA keys from certified smart cards: Coppersmith in the wild. In: Sako, K., Sarkar, P. (eds.) ASIACRYPT 2013, Part II. LNCS, vol. 8270, pp. 341–360. Springer, Heidelberg (2013)
2. Boneh, D., Durfee, G.: Cryptanalysis of RSA with private key d less than $N^{0.292}$. IEEE Transactions on Information Theory 46(4), 1339–1349 (2000)
3. Boneh, D., Durfee, G., Frankel, Y.: An attack on RSA given a small fraction of the private key bits. In: Ohta, K., Pei, D. (eds.) ASIACRYPT 1998. LNCS, vol. 1514, pp. 25–34. Springer, Heidelberg (1998)
4. Coppersmith, D.: Small solutions to polynomial equations, and low exponent RSA vulnerabilities. Journal of Cryptology 10(4), 233–260 (1997)
5. Ernst, M., Jochemsz, E., May, A., De Weger, B.: Partial key exposure attacks on RSA up to full size exponents. In: Cramer, R. (ed.) EUROCRYPT 2005. LNCS, vol. 3494, pp. 371–386. Springer, Heidelberg (2005)

6. Herrmann, M., May, A.: Maximizing small root bounds by linearization and applications to small secret exponent rsa. In: Nguyen, P.Q., Pointcheval, D. (eds.) PKC 2010. LNCS, vol. 6056, pp. 53–69. Springer, Heidelberg (2010)
7. Howgrave-Graham, N.: Finding small roots of univariate modular equations revisited. In: Darnell, M.J. (ed.) Cryptography and Coding 1997. LNCS, vol. 1355, pp. 131–142. Springer, Heidelberg (1997)
8. Huang, Z., Hu, L., Xu, J., Peng, L., Xie, Y.: Partial key exposure attacks on Takagi's variant of RSA. In: Boureanu, I., Owesarski, P., Vaudenay, S. (eds.) ACNS 2014. LNCS, vol. 8479, pp. 134–150. Springer, Heidelberg (2014)
9. Itoh, K., Kunihiro, N., Kurosawa, K.: Small secret key attack on a variant of RSA (due to Takagi). In: Malkin, T. (ed.) CT-RSA 2008. LNCS, vol. 4964, pp. 387–406. Springer, Heidelberg (2008)
10. Jochemsz, E., May, A.: A strategy for finding roots of multivariate polynomials with new applications in attacking RSA variants. In: Lai, X., Chen, K. (eds.) ASIACRYPT 2006. LNCS, vol. 4284, pp. 267–282. Springer, Heidelberg (2006)
11. Lenstra, A.K., Lenstra, H.W., Lovász, L.: Factoring polynomials with rational coefficients. Mathematische Annalen 261(4), 515–534 (1982)
12. Nguyen, P.Q., Valle, B.: The LLL algorithm: survey and applications. Springer Publishing Company, Incorporated (2009)
13. Rivest, R.L., Shamir, A., Adleman, L.: A method for obtaining digital signatures and public-key cryptosystems. Communications of the ACM 26(1), 96–99 (1983)
14. Sarkar, S., Maitra, S.: Improved partial key exposure attacks on RSA by guessing a few bits of one of the prime factors. In: Lee, P.J., Cheon, J.H. (eds.) ICISC 2008. LNCS, vol. 5461, pp. 37–51. Springer, Heidelberg (2009)
15. Sarkar, S., Maitra, S., Sarkar, S.: Rsa cryptanalysis with increased bounds on the secret exponent using less lattice dimension. Cryptology ePrint Archive, Report 2008/315 (2008), http://eprint.iacr.org/
16. Takagi, T.: Fast RSA-type cryptosystem modulo $p^k q$. In: Krawczyk, H. (ed.) CRYPTO 1998. LNCS, vol. 1462, pp. 318–326. Springer, Heidelberg (1998)
17. Wiener, M.J.: Cryptanalysis of short RSA secret exponents. IEEE Transactions on Information Theory 36(3), 553–558 (1990)

Analysis of Fractional ωmbNAF
for Scalar Multiplication*

Weixuan Li[1,2,3], Wei Yu[1,2,**], and Kunpeng Wang[1,2]

[1] State Key Laboratory of Information Security,
Institute of Information Engineering,
Chinese Academy of Sciences, Beijing, China
wxli13@is.ac.cn
[2] Data Assurance and Communication Security Research Center,
Chinese Academy of Sciences, Beijing, China
yuwei_1_yw@163.com
[3] University of Chinese Academy of Sciences, Beijing, China

Abstract. In the current work we analyze the average Hamming weight of recoded sequence obtained by fractional ωmbNAF algorithm using Markov theory. Cost comparison between fractional ωmbNAF and different scalar recoding methods is given. Regardless of memory restraint, it is shown that $\{2,3,5\}\mathrm{NAF}_{3+\frac{3}{4}}$ improves tree-based double base chain by a factor of 6.8% and 13.2% is Jacobian curves(with efficiency-orient selected parameter $a = 3$) and inverted Edwards curves respectively.

Keywords: Elliptic curve cryptosystem, scalar multiplication, Hamming weight, multi-base non-adjacent form, fractional window.

1   Introduction

Proposed by Koblitz [7] and Miller [12] independently as a new form of public key cryptography, elliptic curve cryptosystem(ECC) has draw a lot of attention in decades due to its shorter key requirement as well as higher implementation performance compared with RSA scheme and other discrete-logarithm-based cryptosystems. Since scalar multiplication [2, Chapter 13] is the most time-consuming operation in practical application of ECC, how to promote it's efficiency in resource-scarce systems or devices like smart cards or hand-held equipments is intensively studied. To our knowledge, many countermeasures have been proposed successively in the past years to enhance the performance of scalar multiplication algorithm from three computational levels: scalar recoding algorithm, point arithmetic, field arithmetic. In this work, we mainly focus on the first kind.

* This work is supported in part by National Research Foundation of China under Grant No. 61272040, 61379137, and in part by National Basic Research Program of China (973) under Grant No. 2013CB338001.
** Corresponding author.

J. Lopez and Y. Wu (Eds.): ISPEC 2015, LNCS 9065, pp. 109–120, 2015.
DOI: 10.1007/978-3-319-17533-1_8

Traditional 2-radix methods, like Window-ω Non Adjacent Form(ωNAF) [8] and Window-ω Mutual Opposite Form(ωMOF) [15], translate scalars into representations with smaller Hamming weight to reduce the amount of required addition at the expense of more pre-stored points. To avoid this trade-off between time costs and memory requirements, Double-Base(Multi-Base) [3,6,5,16] Number System was introduced to fulfill shorter representation length with less precomputed points or even without precomputations. Then, Longa applied this idea to Multi-base Non Adjacent Form(mbNAF) [10]. When the same amount of points are stored before evaluation stage, NAF can be considerably optimized by its multi-base version.

However, a common drawback of NAF, ωNAF, mbNAF, ωmbNAF recoding scenarios is the limitation of possible window size for precomputation table, namely, only exactly 2^ω points are allowed to store in advance regardless of in which device ECC is embedded, providing that $\omega \in N^+$. Therefore, there is inevitable memory waste in the case of no table size fitting exactly the available storage in practice. Möller put forward fractional window technique [13] based on ωNAF to satisfy arbitrary table sizes without losing its efficiency, then its variant—fractional ωmbNAF was presented in PKC–09 by Longa and Gebotys [11]. Nevertheless, there is a small flaw in their analysis.

Our contributions can be summarized as follows: we revise the original flaw and obtain the average Hamming weight of the achieved digit sequence using Markov theory; we analyze fractional ωmbNAF from a universal aspect, that is, with general bases $\mathscr{A} = \{2, a_2, \ldots, a_J\}$, contrasting with [11] that only $\mathscr{A} = \{2, 3\}$ and $\mathscr{A} = \{2, 3, 5\}$ are discussed; moreover, the average amount of operations corresponding to each base is given, so that total time complexity of fractional ωmbNAF can be theoretically confirmed.

As principle mathematic tool in this work, Markov theory is of great help for modeling randomized algorithm. If the execution of an algorithm can be regarded as a Markov process with aperiodic and irreducible transition matrix, we view its stationary distribution as the asymptotic condition that each state happens at fixed probability. The algorithm's asymptotic behavior is consequently inferred.

This paper is organized as follows. We briefly review some essential backgrounds of ECC in section 2. In the next section, a comprehensive analysis of ωmbNAF with generalized bases $\mathscr{A} = \{2, a_2, \ldots, a_J\}$ is given. Then we exploit its relation with fractional ωNAF and ωmbNAF. In section 4, we compare ωmbNAF with other scenarios in Jacobian and inverted Edwards curves by extensive tests. Finally, we summarize this article in section 5.

2   Preliminary

An elliptic curve E over prime field $\mathbb{F}_p$ defined by Weierstrass equation is written as:

$$E : y^2 = x^3 + ax + b$$

where $\text{char}(\mathbb{F}_p) \neq 2, 3$; $a, b \in \mathbb{F}_p$.

The rational points on E together with the identity element at infinity $\mathcal{O}$ compose an abelian group under the chord-and-tangent law. Elliptic curve cryptosystem is designed on this group under the hypothesis of discrete logarithm problem. Given P, P_1, P_2 on E in affine coordinates, the negative element of $P = (x, y)$ is given by $-P = (x, -y)$; the group addition $P_1(x_1, y_1) + P_2(x_2, y_2) = P_3(x_3, y_3)$ is determined by the following equations:

$$x_3 = \begin{cases} (\frac{y_2 - y_1}{x_2 - x_1})^2 - x_1 - x_2, & \text{if } P_1 \neq P_2, \\ (\frac{3x_1^2 + a}{2y_1})^2 - 2x_1, & \text{if } P_1 = P_2, \end{cases}$$

$$y_3 = \begin{cases} (\frac{y_2 - y_1}{x_2 - x_1})(x_1 - x_3) - y_1, & \text{if } P_1 \neq P_2, \\ (\frac{3x_1^2 + a}{2y_1})(x_1 - x_3) - y_1, & \text{if } P_1 = P_2. \end{cases}$$

Scalar multiplication kP in elliptic curve group is the k times addition of the point P, as a counterpart of exponentiation in number field.

In what follows we briefly describe fractional ωNAF and ωmbNAF.

2.1 Fractional ωNAF

As a generalization of sliding window and ωNAF techniques, fractional ωNAF is remarkably distinguish by the flexibility of pre-stored table sizes. Roughly speaking, by fractional ωNAF, an integer k is reformed as the following sequence

$$k = (k_l, k_{l-1}, \ldots, k_2, k_1)_2$$

with properties:

- each $k_i \in B = \{0, \pm 1, \pm 3, \ldots, \pm(2^{\omega_0 - 1} + m)\}$, m is an odd integer and $1 \leq m \leq 2^{\omega_0 - 1} - 1$. B is called digit set which restricts the possible values of digits.
- among successive ω_0 digits there is at most one nonzero bit.

For brevity, we denote $\frac{m+1}{2^{\omega_0 - 1}}$ as ω_1, then the digit set B can be equivalently written as $B = \{0, \pm 1, \pm 3, \ldots, \pm((1 + \omega_1)2^{\omega_0 - 1} - 1)\}$. The notion $\omega = \omega_0 + \omega_1$ extends the definition of window width, suggests that B consists of $(1 + \omega_1)2^{\omega_0 - 1}$ points and exact $(1 + \omega_1)2^{\omega_0 - 2} - 1$ points require precomputation in inversion-free coordinates of elliptic curves that $-P = (x, -y)$ can be immediately concluded by $P = (x, y)$.

The rules of recoding is defined as map $digit: \{0, 1, 2, \ldots, 2^{\omega_0 + 1} - 1\} \rightarrow B$, where:

Case 0. If x is even, $digit(x) = 0$.

Case 1. Elseif $0 < x \leq (1 + \omega_1)2^{\omega_0 - 1} - 1$, $digit(x) = x$.

Case 2. Elseif $(1 + \omega_1)2^{\omega_0 - 1} - 1 < m < (3 - \omega_1)2^{\omega_0 - 1} + 1$, $digit(x) = x - 2^{\omega_0}$.

Case 3. Elseif $(3 - \omega_1)2^{\omega_0 - 1} + 1 \leq x < 2^{\omega_0 + 1}$, $digit(x) = x - 2^{\omega_0 + 1}$.

Obviously, if x is not even, $x - digit(x) \in \{0, 2^{\omega_0}, 2^{\omega_0 + 1}\}$. Hence for random odd integer x, $X \triangleq x \bmod 2^{\omega_0 + 1}$ is a uniformly distributed random variable valued at odd points in the interval $[0, 2^{\omega_0 + 1}]$. After straight forward calculation, it can be concluded that case 1 happens at probability $\frac{1+\omega_1}{4}$, so that $x - digit(x) = 0$; case 2 happens at probability $\frac{1-\omega_1}{2}$, so that $x - digit(x) = 2^{\omega_0}$; case 3 happens at probability $\frac{1+\omega_1}{4}$, so that $x - digit(x) = 2^{\omega_0+1}$. Fractional window multi-base NAF algorithm is derived by inserting aforementioned map $digit$ in map mod of standard window method. See Alg.1.

Algorithm 1. Frac-window Algorithm

Input: an integer k; window width $\omega = \omega_0 + \omega_1$, $\omega_0 \in N^+$, $0 < \omega_1 < 1$
Output: signed digit representation of k
 1: $i \leftarrow 1$
 2: **while** $k > 0$ **do**
 3:     $k_i \leftarrow digit(k \mod 2^{\omega_0+1})$
 4:     $k \leftarrow \frac{k-k_i}{2}$
 5:     $i \leftarrow i + 1$
 6: **end while**
 7: Return$(k_l, \ldots, k_2, k_1)$

The window width parameter ω is inversely proportional to asymptotic nonzero density of representation returned by fractional ωNAF algorithm. The reader is referred to [15] for a detailed survey.

2.2 ωmbNAF

Recall from [11] that by ωmbNAF, an integer k is represented in the following form:

$$k = \sum_{i=1}^{m} k_i \prod_{j=1}^{J} a_j^{c_j(i)} \qquad (1)$$

where $\{c_j(i)\}_i$ is a decreasing exponentiation chain of base a_j for $2 \leq j \leq J$; for the main base a_1, $\{c_1(i)\}$ is a decreasing chain with window width ω_0, that is to say, $c_1(i) \geq c_1(i+1) + \omega_0$, for $1 \leq i \leq m - 1$.

Alg.2 presents an efficient method to calculate ωmbNAF representation of input k given bases $\mathscr{A} = \{a_1, \ldots, a_J\}$, window size ω_0 and digit set $B = \{0, \pm 1, \pm 2, \ldots, \pm \lfloor \frac{a_1^{\omega_0-1}-1}{2} \rfloor\} \setminus \{\pm 1a_1, \pm 2a_1, \ldots, \pm \lfloor \frac{a_1^{\omega_0-1}-1}{2} \rfloor a_1\}$.

Notice that the consequential digit sequence $(\ldots, k_2^{(a_j)}, k_1^{(a_j)})$ achieved by Alg.2 can be translated into (1) from left-to-right using Horner's method. The relevance between each digit and operation with base a_j is indicated by its superscript. [9] presents a theoretical analysis of ωmbNAF.

3   Fractional Window Multi-base NAF

In [13] Möller offered a new methodology on how to select window width flexibly and map integers into digit set appropriately. Then his idea was utilized

---

Algorithm 2. ωmbNAF Algorithm

Input: an integer k; a set of bases $\mathscr{A} = \{a_1, \ldots, a_J\}$; window width $\omega_0 \in Z^+$
Output: ωmbNAF representation of k
1: $i \leftarrow 1$
2: **while** $k > 0$ **do**
3:     **if** $k \mod a_1 = 0$ **then** $k_i = 0^{(a_1)}$, $k \leftarrow \frac{k}{a_1}$
4:     **else if** $k \mod a_2 = 0$ **then** $k_i = 0^{(a_2)}$, $k \leftarrow \frac{k}{a_2}$

5:         $\vdots$
6:     **else if** $k \mod a_J = 0$ **then** $k_i = 0^{(a_J)}$, $k \leftarrow \frac{k}{a_J}$
7:     **else** $k_i = (k \mod a_1^{\omega_0})^{(a_1)}$
8:         $k \leftarrow \frac{k-k_i}{a_1}$
9:     **end if**
10:     $i \leftarrow i + 1$
11: **end while**
12: Return $(\ldots, k_2^{(a_j)}, k_1^{(a_j)})$

---

to improve window multi-base non-adjacent form by Longa and Gebotys [11]. According to Alg.3 with bases $\mathscr{A} = \{2, a_2, \ldots, a_J\}$ of fractional ωmbNAF, an integer k is translated into a sequence of digits $(\ldots, k_2^{(a_j)}, k_1^{(a_j)})$ from right-to-left as well, where each bit k_i is either in a set of zeros $A^* = \{0^{(2)}, 0^{(a_2)}, \ldots, 0^{(a_J)}\}$ or a set of nonzero coefficients $B^* = \{\pm 1, \pm 3, \ldots, \pm((1+\omega_1)2^{\omega_0-1}-1)\}$, $\omega_0 \in Z^+$, $0 < \omega_1 < 1$.

Algorithm 3. Fractional ωmbNAF with main base $a_1 = 2$

Input: an integer k; a set of bases $\mathscr{A} = \{2, a_2, \ldots, a_J\}$; window width $\omega = \omega_0 + \omega_1$,
    $\omega_0 \in N^+$, $0 < \omega_1 < 1$
Output: fractional ωmbNAF representation of k
1: $i \leftarrow 1$
2: **while** $k > 0$ **do**
3:     **if** k is even **then** $k_i = 0^{(2)}$, $k \leftarrow \frac{k}{2}$
4:     **else if** $k \mod a_2 = 0$ **then** $k_i = 0^{(a_2)}$, $k \leftarrow \frac{k}{a_2}$

5:         $\vdots$
6:     **else if** $k \mod a_J = 0$ **then** $k_i = 0^{(a_J)}$, $k \leftarrow \frac{k}{a_J}$
7:     **else** $k_i = digit(k \mod 2^{\omega_0+1})$
8:         $k \leftarrow \frac{k-k_i}{2}$
9:     **end if**
10:     $i \leftarrow i + 1$
11: **end while**
12: Return $(\ldots, k_2^{(a_j)}, k_1^{(a_j)})$

In this context, we analyze the average Hamming weight and the average number of operations based on a_j of achieved form returned by Alg.3 using

Markov theory. We do not include details, yet in compensation the reader is referred to [14] for elementary Markov theory.

3.1 Analysis of Fractional ωmbNAF

Lemma 1. *Let $a_1, a_2, \cdots, a_j$ be distinct primes, then for randomly chosen integer n we have $P\left((a_1 \nmid n) \wedge (a_2 \nmid n) \wedge \cdots \wedge (a_{j-1} \nmid n) \wedge (a_j \mid n)\right) = (1 - \frac{1}{a_1})(1 - \frac{1}{a_2})\cdots(1 - \frac{1}{a_{j-1}})\frac{1}{a_j}$.*

Proof. Since n is coprime to $a_1, a_2, \cdots, a_{j-1}$ and divisible by a_j, there are integers $n_1 \neq 0, n_2 \neq 0, \cdots, n_{j-1} \neq 0$, s.t,

$$\begin{cases} n \equiv n_1 \mod a_1 \\ n \equiv n_2 \mod a_2 \\ \vdots \\ n \equiv n_{j-1} \mod a_{j-1} \\ n \equiv 0 \mod a_j. \end{cases} \tag{2}$$

Because $a_1, a_2, \ldots, a_j$ are coprime, for every $n_1 \in \{1, 2, \cdots, a_1 - 1\}$, $n_2 \in \{1, 2, \cdots, a_2 - 1\}$, $\cdots$, $n_{j-1} \in \{1, 2, \cdots, a_{j-1} - 1\}$, there is a unique solution of (2) in the residue ring $Z_{a_1 \times a_2 \times \cdots \times a_j}$ by Chinese remainder theorem(CRT). So (2) is equivalent to $(a_1 - 1)(a_2 - 1)\cdots(a_{j-1} - 1)$ systems of linear congruence equations with different solutions in $Z_{a_1 \times a_2 \times \cdots \times a_j}$. Therefore for arbitrary integer n, $P(a_i \nmid n, \text{for } 1 \leq i \leq j - 1, a_j \mid n) = \frac{(a_1 - 1)(a_2 - 1)\cdots(a_{j-1} - 1)}{a_1 a_2 \cdots a_j} = (1 - \frac{1}{a_1})(1 - \frac{1}{a_2})\cdots(1 - \frac{1}{a_{j-1}})\frac{1}{a_j}$. □

For the reminder, the main base a_1 is set to be 2 from three aspects of consideration: fractional window technique is supposed to be an efficient improvement of radix-2 representation; the operation with $a_1 = 2$ refers to be a doubling, which is experimentally shown superior to other point operations; an efficiently computable table of pre-stored points is guaranteed.

Lemma 2. *Let $2, a_2, a_3, \cdots, a_J$ be distinct primes, window width $\omega \in N^+$, and n is an integer that coprime to $2a_2a_3 \cdots a_J$. Then the random variable $X = n$ mod 2^ω is uniformly distributing on odd integers in the interval $[0, 2^\omega - 1]$.*

Proof. Above conditions indicate the system of equations:

$$\begin{cases} n \equiv 1 \mod 2 \\ n \equiv n_2 \mod a_2 \\ \vdots \\ n \equiv n_{J-1} \mod a_{J-1} \\ n \equiv n_J \mod a_J, \end{cases} \tag{3}$$

where $n_2 \neq 0, \cdots, n_J \neq 0$. By CRT, fixed $n_2, n_3, \cdots, n_J$ then there is a unique solution in the residue ring $Z_{2 \times a_2 \times \cdots \times a_J}$. Thus all solutions of (3) in Z can be denoted as $n = 2a_2 \cdots a_J m + l$, where $m \in Z$, l is an odd integer that relevant to the specific valuations of $n_2, n_3, \cdots, n_J$.

Obviously, the operation $mod\ 2^\omega$ maps $2a_2 \cdots a_J m + l$ into an odd number in $[0, 2^\omega - 1]$. For arbitrary odd number k in $[0, 2^\omega - 1]$, suppose we have

$$2a_2 \cdots a_J m + l \equiv k \quad mod\ 2^\omega.$$

Thus,

$$a_2 \cdots a_J m \equiv \frac{k - l}{2} \quad mod\ 2^{\omega-1}.$$

$$m \equiv (a_2 \cdots a_J)^{-1} \frac{k - l}{2} \quad mod\ 2^{\omega-1}$$

is permitted by existence of the unique inverse of $a_2 \cdots a_J$ in $Z_{2^{\omega-1}}$, resulting from $\gcd(a_2 \cdots a_J, 2^{\omega-1}) = 1$. From the arbitrariness of k, for each $k' \in Z_{2^{\omega-1}}$, there is a unique $m \in B = \{a, a+1, \cdots, a+2^{\omega-1}-1\}$ of any $2^{\omega-1}$ successive integers, such that $a_2 \cdots a_J m \equiv k' \mod 2^{\omega-1}$. The map φ between $Z_{2^{\omega-1}}$ and B defined by

$$\varphi : B \to Z_{2^{\omega-1}}$$

$$m \to k'$$

$$\varphi(m) \equiv a_2 \cdots a_J m \quad mod\ 2^{\omega-1}$$

is an epimorphism. Since the cardinality of A and B is identical, φ is isomorphic. Equivalently, for fixed l, $X = 2a_2 \cdots a_J m + l \mod 2^\omega$ uniformly values at every odd points in Z_{2^ω} when m varies in Z.

The above result is obtained by fixing the values of $n_2, n_3, \cdots, n_j$ to get corresponding certain odd l. Meanwhile generalizing $n_2, n_3, \cdots, n_j$ to all possible valuations, Lemma 2 holds true.   □

In consideration of practical use, random or pseudorandom numbers are widely used in ECC-based cryptographic primitives like key agreement, encryption or decryption, digit signature, etc. Therefore, it's important to exploit the asymptotic feature of fractional ωmbNAF scalar representation method on condition that the scalars are arbitrary. Lem.1, Lem.2 reveal some intrinsic properties of integers, which are of great value to us when studying the asymptotic behavior of fractional ωmbNAF algorithm.

Theorem 1. *Let $\omega = \omega_0 + \omega_1$ be the window width of fractional ωmbNAF with bases $\mathscr{A} = \{2, a_2, \ldots, a_J\}$ and digit set $B = \{0, \pm 1, \pm 3, \cdots, \pm((1 + \omega_1)2^{\omega_0 - 1} - 1)\}$. Then Alg.3 exports a sequence of average nonzero density $\frac{1}{\omega + C}$, moreover the average number of digits based on 2 and a_j are $\frac{\omega + 1}{\omega + C}$ and $\frac{1}{a_j - 1} \frac{1}{\omega + C}$, where $C = \frac{1}{2 - 1} + \sum_{j=2}^{J} \frac{1}{a_j - 1}$. More precisely, importing random scalar k of bitlength n, the average densities of addition, doubling and point operation with base a_j*

are approximately $\#A = n\theta$, $\#D = n(1+\omega)\theta$ and $\#a_jP = \frac{n}{a_j-1}\theta$, where
$\theta = \frac{1}{(1+\omega+\frac{1}{a_2-1}\log_2 a_2+\cdots+\frac{1}{a_J-1}\log_2 a_J)}$.

Proof. Considering scalar k as an infinitely long sequence that randomly distributes at each bit, the procedure of fractional ωmbNAF algorithm is a Markov chain with the following states:

S_0: $k \mod 2 = 0$, output $0^{(2)}$ and $k \leftarrow \frac{k}{2}$.

S_1: $k \mod a_2 = 0$, output $0^{(a_2)}$ and $k \leftarrow \frac{k}{a_2}$.

S_2: $k \mod a_3 = 0$, output $0^{(a_3)}$ and $k \leftarrow \frac{k}{a_3}$.

$\vdots$

S_{J-1}: $k \mod a_J = 0$, output $0^{(a_J)}$ and $k \leftarrow \frac{k}{a_J}$.

S_J: k is coprime to $2a_2a_3\cdots a_J$ and $|k \mod 2^{\omega_0+1}| \leq (1+\omega_1)2^{\omega_0-1} - 1$, then Alg.3 output a block of $\overbrace{0\ldots0}^{\omega_0 \text{ zeros}} k_i$, and $k \leftarrow \frac{k-k_i}{2^{\omega_0+1}}$.

S_{J+1}: k is coprime to $2a_2a_3\cdots a_J$ and $|k \mod 2^{\omega_0+1}| \geq (1+\omega_1)2^{\omega_0-1} + 1$, then Alg.3 output a block of $\overbrace{0\ldots0}^{\omega_0-1 \text{ zeros}} k_i$, and $k \leftarrow \frac{k-k_i}{2^{\omega_0}}$.

Let π_{ij} denotes the probability that the algorithm turns S_i into S_j. The transition matrix $H = (\pi_{ij})_{i,j=0}^{J+1}$ of this Markov chain is a $(J+2) \times (J+2)$ matrix. From Lem.1, Lem.2 and the comments in Sect.2.1, the transition matrix H is:

$$\begin{pmatrix} \frac{1}{2} & \frac{1}{2}\frac{1}{a_2} & \frac{1}{2}(1-\frac{1}{a_2})\frac{1}{a_3} & \cdots & \frac{1}{2}(1-\frac{1}{a_2})\cdots\frac{1}{a_J} & \frac{1}{2}(1-\frac{1}{a_2})\cdots(1-\frac{1}{a_J})\frac{1+\omega_1}{2} & \frac{1}{2}(1-\frac{1}{a_2})\cdots(1-\frac{1}{a_J})\frac{1-\omega_1}{2} \\ 0 & \frac{1}{a_2} & (1-\frac{1}{a_2})\frac{1}{a_3} & \cdots & (1-\frac{1}{a_2})\cdots\frac{1}{a_J} & (1-\frac{1}{a_2})\cdots(1-\frac{1}{a_J})\frac{1+\omega_1}{2} & (1-\frac{1}{a_2})\cdots(1-\frac{1}{a_J})\frac{1-\omega_1}{2} \\ 0 & 0 & \frac{1}{a_3} & \cdots & (1-\frac{1}{a_3})\cdots\frac{1}{a_J} & (1-\frac{1}{a_3})\cdots(1-\frac{1}{a_J})\frac{1+\omega_1}{2} & (1-\frac{1}{a_3})\cdots(1-\frac{1}{a_J})\frac{1-\omega_1}{2} \\ \vdots & \vdots & \vdots & \vdots & & \vdots & \vdots \\ 0 & 0 & 0 & \cdots & \frac{1}{a_J} & (1-\frac{1}{a_J})\frac{1+\omega_1}{2} & (1-\frac{1}{a_J})\frac{1-\omega_1}{2} \\ \frac{1}{2} & \frac{1}{2}\frac{1}{a_2} & \frac{1}{2}(1-\frac{1}{a_2})\frac{1}{a_3} & \cdots & \frac{1}{2}(1-\frac{1}{a_2})\cdots\frac{1}{a_J} & \frac{1}{2}(1-\frac{1}{a_2})\cdots(1-\frac{1}{a_J})\frac{1+\omega_1}{2} & \frac{1}{2}(1-\frac{1}{a_2})\cdots(1-\frac{1}{a_J})\frac{1-\omega_1}{2} \\ 0 & \frac{1}{a_2} & (1-\frac{1}{a_2})\frac{1}{a_3} & \cdots & (1-\frac{1}{a_2})\cdots\frac{1}{a_J} & (1-\frac{1}{a_2})\cdots(1-\frac{1}{a_J})\frac{1+\omega_1}{2} & (1-\frac{1}{a_2})\cdots(1-\frac{1}{a_J})\frac{1-\omega_1}{2} \end{pmatrix}$$

To demonstrate the $(J+2)$-th row of H, suppose the current state X_n is S_{J+1}, then line 7, 8 in Alg.3 are executed and $|(k \mod 2^{\omega_0+1}) - k_i| = 2^{\omega_0}$. The block of the lowest $\omega_0 + 1$ bits of k is reshaped by sliding lower ω_0 bits into k_i at the position of the least significant bit(that is, the last bit), the $(\omega_0 + 1)$-th bit is therefore settled to be 1. After generating a sequence of $\overbrace{0\ldots0}^{\omega_0-1 \text{ zeros}} k_i$, $k \leftarrow \frac{k-k_i}{2^{\omega_0}}$ is a random odd integer, $P(X_{n+1} = S_0 \mid X_n = S_{J+1}) = 0$ consequently.

The transition matrix is irreducible and aperiodic since $0 < \omega_1 < 1$, its stationary distribution σ is:

$$\sigma = (\sigma_0, \sigma_1, \cdots, \sigma_{J+1})$$
$$= ((1+\omega_1)\eta, \frac{2}{a_2-1}\eta, \frac{2}{a_3-1}\eta, \cdots, \frac{2}{a_J-1}\eta, (1+\omega_1)\eta, (1-\omega_1)\eta),$$

where $\eta = \frac{1}{2C+1+\omega_1}$, $C = \frac{1}{2-1} + \sum_{j=2}^{J}\frac{1}{a_j-1}$. A nonzero bit is merely generated during either state S_J or S_{J+1}, thus the average nonzero density of achieved sequence is $\frac{\sigma_J+\sigma_{J+1}}{(\sigma_0+\cdots+\sigma_{J-1})+\sigma_J(\omega_0+1)+\sigma_{J+1}\omega_0} = \frac{1}{\omega_0+\omega_1+C}$. Similarly, the average density of digits with main base 2 is $\frac{\sigma_0 + \sigma_J(\omega_0+1) + \sigma_{J+1}\omega_0}{(\sigma_0 + \cdots + \sigma_{J-1}) + \sigma_J(\omega_0+1) + \sigma_{J+1}\omega_0} = \frac{\omega+1}{\omega+C}$, the average density of digits with base a_j is $\frac{\sigma_{j-1}}{(\sigma_0 + \cdots + \sigma_{J-1}) + \sigma_J(\omega_0+1) + \sigma_{J+1}\omega_0} = \frac{1}{a_j-1} \frac{1}{\omega+C}$.

In addition, suppose Alg.3 stops after λ state transitions to represent a n-bit integer k. Hence the returned value satisfies $2^{\sigma_0\lambda} \cdot a_2^{\sigma_1\lambda} \cdots a_J^{\sigma_{J-1}\lambda} \cdot 2^{(1+\omega_0)\sigma_J\lambda} \cdot 2^{\omega_0\sigma_{J+1}\lambda} \le 2^n$. Let $\theta = \frac{1}{(1 + \omega + \frac{1}{a_2-1}\log_2 a_2 + \cdots + \frac{1}{a_J-1}\log_2 a_J)}$, then $\lambda \le \frac{n}{2\eta}\theta$. Therefore, the average Hamming weight is approximately $\lambda(\sigma_J + \sigma_{J+1}) = n\theta$, as the same amount of required additions in evaluation stage; the number of doubling is $\lambda(\sigma_0 + \sigma_J(\omega_0+1) + \sigma_{J+1}\omega_0) = n\theta(1+\omega)$; the number of point operation with base a_j is $\lambda\sigma_{j-1} = \frac{n}{a_j-1}\theta$, for every $2 \le j \le J$. $\square$

For the correctness of the above results, we observe that if we restrict the content of $\mathscr{A}$ to be a single base $\mathscr{A} = \{2\}$, fractional ωmbNAF is accordingly degenerated into fractional ωNAF. As a direct corollary of Theorem 1, in this case the average density of nonzeros is $\frac{1}{\omega+1}$, which is proven correct in [15]. In the same way, when the fractional part ω_1 of window width is confined to be 0, fractional ωmbNAF is therefore degenerated into ωmbNAF. As a direct corollary of Theorem 1, in this case the average density of nonzeros is $\frac{1}{\omega_0+C}$, $C = \sum_{j=1}^{J} \frac{1}{a_j-1}$, corresponding to the resultant analysis of ωmbNAF in [9].

Theorem 1 convinces that fractional ωNAF and ωmbNAF are special instances of fractional ωmbNAF, in other words, fractional ωmbNAF generalizes fractional ωNAF and ωmbNAF both in algorithmic form and theoretic outcomes. We believe fractional ωmbNAF is no less efficient than fractional ωNAF or ωmbNAF. As a matter of fact, as a joint improvement of these two methods, fractional ωmbNAF scalar-recoding scheme can make full use of memory resources thanks to its fractional window nature, meanwhile realize efficient implementation performance in practice due to its multi-base property.

4   Performance Comparison

In this section, we present the efficiency of fractional ωmbNAF by testing extensive random 160-bit scalars on Weierstrass and Edwards curves, and compare the total computational consumption with scenarios.

The result from [11,1] shows the costs of addition(A), *mixed* addition(mA), doubling(D), doubling-addition(DA), *mixed* doubling-addition(mDA), tripling(T), quintupling(Q), septupling(S) on Weierstrass curves($a = -3$) using Jacobian($\mathcal{J}$) coordinates and Edwards curves in inverted Edwards($\mathcal{IE}$) coordinates, see Table 1. Since no efficient explicit formulae are presented to date for quintupling and septupling in $\mathcal{IE}$, we count these two operations by $2D+A$, $T+D+A$ respectively. Point operations are expressed in terms of multiplication(M) and squaring(S) on prime fields, for their overwhelming influence on implementation speed. Without lose of practical supports, we disregard the cost of addition and multiplication by small constant on prime fields for simplification purposes. Besides we assume $1S = 0.8M$ as generally suggested.

Table 1. Costs of operations in Jacobian coordinates($a = -3$)

Operations	Cost/Total Cost	
	Jacobian	InvEdw
A	11M+5S/15M	9M+1S/9.8M
mA	7M+4S/10.2M	8M+1S/8.8M
D	3M+5S/7M	3M+4S/6.2M
DA	14M+9S/21.2M	-
mDA	11M+7S/16.6M	-
T	7M+7S/12.6M	9M+4S/12.2M
Q	10M+12S/19.6M	15M+9S/22.2M
S	14M+15S/26M	21M+9S/28.2M

What can be observed in the evaluation stage based on radix-2 window method is that an addition is always followed by a doubling. Benefiting from a doubling-addition formula requires less field operations than the sum of a doubling with an addition, replacing addition by doubling-addition and modifying the amount of required doubling will reduce the total costs even further. Similarly, if the precomputation points are saved in their affine forms, mixed addition($\mathcal{J} + \mathcal{A} \to \mathcal{J}$) is more preferred than addition($2\mathcal{J} \to \mathcal{J}$) operation.

Then we study the trade-off between the number of precomputation points and the total costs of $\{2,3\}$NAF using different window widths. Theorem 1 shows that a conspicuous vantage of enlarged precomputation table is converting (costly) additions, triplings to (cheap) doublings, by means of increasing the proportion of $0^{(2)}$ in the achieved sequence. As experimental data reveal in Table 2, it can be concluded that in $\mathcal{J}$, $\{2,3\}$NAF with window width $\omega = 3 + \frac{3}{4}$ is approximately 8.9% faster than $\{2,3\}$NAF at the cost of six extra precomputation points, and its efficiency is superior to $\{2,3\}$NAF$_3$ for about a ratio of 3.2%, providing additional three points are allowed to store. Furthermore, in $\mathcal{IE}$, the ratios rise to 9.5% and 3.4%.

Finally, we compare fractional ωmbNAF with various methods for integer representing, *cf* Table 2. We include the results in [5] to estimate the complexity of double-base chain, based on greedy-search and tree-search respectively. As for NAF family, we select several double-base or multi-base methods with various window size. Precomputation cost is excluded in Table 2, resulting from their fixed timing consumption can be neglected compared with the enormous cost of intensive scalar testings. If storage resources are abundant, fractional ωmbNAF with six extra precomputation points achieves the best performance using $\{2,3,5\}$-bases in both Jacobian and inverted Edwards coordinates, as indicated by the data(highlighted in **bold**) in Table 2. Precisely speaking, in Jacobian coordinates, $\{2,3,5\}$NAF$_{3+\frac{3}{4}}$ is roughly 20.9% faster than NAF, 5.4% faster than $\{2,3,7\}$NAF$_{3+\frac{3}{4}}$, 6.8% faster than double-base chain with tree-search approach. To our surprise, comparing with Jacobian coordinates, in inverted Edwards curves $\{2,3,5\}$NAF$_{3+\frac{3}{4}}$ is even more optimized than tree-based double-base chain by a factor of 13.2%. The advantage in $\mathcal{IE}$ is conceived to be existed because of two mutually promotional reasons: the cost ratio of doubling out of tripling in $\mathcal{IE}$ is smaller than that in $\mathcal{J}$, which implies a relatively cheaper doubling in $\mathcal{IE}$; the proportion of $0^{(2)}$ in the digit sequence returned by $\{2,3,5\}\text{NAF}_{3+\frac{3}{4}}$ is higher whereas tripling operations are more required in double-base chain method.

Table 2. Performance comparison of different schemes, $n = 160$ bits

Methods	#Pts	Jacobian		InvEdw	
		Operation Count	Total Costs	Operation Count	Total Costs
NAF	0	53.3mDA+106.7D	1631.68M	53.3mA+160D	1461.04M
$\{2,3\}$NAF	0	42.2mDA+84.4D+21.1T	1557.18M	42.2mA+126.6D+21.1T	1413.7M
$\{2,3\}$NAF$_3$	3	33.4mDA+100.1D+16.7T	1465.56M	33.4mA+133.5D+16.7T	1325.36M
$\{2,3\}$NAF$_{3+\frac{1}{4}}$	4	31.7mDA+103.1D+15.9T	1448.26M	31.7mA+134.8D+15.9T	1308.7M
$\{2,3\}$NAF$_{3+\frac{1}{2}}$	5	30.2mDA+105.8D+15.1T	1432.18M	30.2mA+136D+15.1T	1293.18M
$\{2,3\}$NAF$_{3+\frac{3}{4}}$	6	28.9mDA+108.3D+14.4T	1419.28M	28.9mA+137.1D+14.4T	1280.02M
$\{2,3,5\}$NAF$_3$	3	29.8mDA+89.3D+14.9T+7.4Q	1452.56M	29.8mA+119.1D+14.9T+7.4Q	1346.72M
$\{2,3,5\}$NAF$_{3+\frac{3}{4}}$	6	26.1mDA+98D+13.1T+3.3Q	**1349M**	26.1mA+124.1D+13.1T+3.3Q	**1232.18M**
$\{2,3,7\}$NAF$_3$	3	30.4mDA+91.3D+15.2T+5.1T	1467.86M	30.4mA+121.7D+15.2T+5.1S	1351.32M
$\{2,3,7\}$NAF$_{3+\frac{3}{4}}$	6	26.6mDA+99.8D+13.3T+4.4T	1422.14M	26.6mA+126.4D+13.3T+4.4S	1304.1M
Greedy DB-chain[4]	0	36.3mDA+57.9D+40.9T	1472.12M	36.3mA+94.2D+40.9T	1421.3M
Tree-based DB-chain[5]	0	32.8mDA+58.3D+42.9T	1440.98M	32.8mA+91.1D+42.9T	1395.06M

5 Conclusion

In this paper, we present an exhaustive analysis of fractional ωmbNAF scheme from a general aspect, i.e., given bases set $\mathscr{A} = \{2, a_2, \cdots, a_J\}$. Next we figure out its relevance with fractional ωNAF and ωmbNAF by specific restricted conditions. Ultimately we compare the performance of fractional ωmbNAF with other scalar-recoding scenarios in the article. The analysis suggests that among all the discussed approaches, $\{2,3,5\}\text{NAF}_{3+\frac{3}{4}}$ is the most optimized method in both Jacobian curves and inverted Edwards curves.

References

1. Bernstein, D.J., Lange, T.: Explicit-formulas database (2007)
2. Cohen, H., Frey, G., Avanzi, R., Doche, C., Lange, T., Nguyen, K., Vercauteren, F.: Handbook of elliptic and hyperelliptic curve cryptography. CRC Press (2010)
3. Dimitrov, V., Imbert, L., Mishra, P.: The double-base number system and its application to elliptic curve cryptography. Mathematics of Computation 77(262), 1075–1104 (2008)
4. Dimitrov, V., Imbert, L., Mishra, P.K.: Efficient and secure elliptic curve point multiplication using double-base chains. In: Roy, B. (ed.) ASIACRYPT 2005. LNCS, vol. 3788, pp. 59–78. Springer, Heidelberg (2005)
5. Doche, C., Habsieger, L.: A tree-based approach for computing double-base chains. In: Mu, Y., Susilo, W., Seberry, J. (eds.) ACISP 2008. LNCS, vol. 5107, pp. 433–446. Springer, Heidelberg (2008)
6. Doche, C., Imbert, L.: Extended double-base number system with applications to elliptic curve cryptography. In: Barua, R., Lange, T. (eds.) INDOCRYPT 2006. LNCS, vol. 4329, pp. 335–348. Springer, Heidelberg (2006)

7. Koblitz, N.: Elliptic curve cryptosystems. Mathematics of Computation 48(177), 203–209 (1987)
8. Koyama, K., Tsuruoka, Y.: Speeding up elliptic cryptosystems by using a signed binary window method. In: Brickell, E.F. (ed.) CRYPTO 1992. LNCS, vol. 740, pp. 345–357. Springer, Heidelberg (1993)
9. Li, M., Miri, A., Zhu, D.: Analysis of the hamming weight of the extended wmbnaf. IACR Cryptology ePrint Archive, pp. 569–569 (2011)
10. Longa, P.: Accelerating the scalar multiplication on elliptic curve cryptosystems over prime fields. PhD thesis, University of Ottawa (2007)
11. Longa, P., Gebotys, C.: Fast multibase methods and other several optimizations for elliptic curve scalar multiplication. In: Jarecki, S., Tsudik, G. (eds.) PKC 2009. LNCS, vol. 5443, pp. 443–462. Springer, Heidelberg (2009)
12. Miller, V.S.: Use of elliptic curves in cryptography. In: Williams, H.C. (ed.) CRYPTO 1985. LNCS, vol. 218, pp. 417–426. Springer, Heidelberg (1986)
13. Möller, B.: Improved techniques for fast exponentiation. In: Lee, P.J., Lim, C.H. (eds.) ICISC 2002. LNCS, vol. 2587, pp. 298–312. Springer, Heidelberg (2003)
14. Norris, J.R.: Markov chains. Number 2008. Cambridge University Press (1998)
15. Schmidt-Samoa, K., Semay, O., Takagi, T.: Analysis of fractional window recoding methods and their application to elliptic curve cryptosystems. IEEE Transactions on Computers 55(1), 48–57 (2006)
16. Yu, W., Wang, K., Li, B., Tian, S.: Triple-base number system for scalar multiplication. In: Youssef, A., Nitaj, A., Hassanien, A.E. (eds.) AFRICACRYPT 2013. LNCS, vol. 7918, pp. 433–451. Springer, Heidelberg (2013)

On the Effectiveness of Different Botnet Detection Approaches

Fariba Haddadi, Duc Le Cong, Laura Porter, and A. Nur Zincir-Heywood

Faculty of Computer Science
Dalhousie University
Halifax, NS, Canada
{haddadi,lporter,zincir}@cs.dal.ca, duc.le@dal.ca

Abstract. Botnets represent one of the most significant threats against cyber security. They employ different techniques, topologies and communication protocols in different stages of their lifecycle. Hence, identifying botnets have become very challenging specifically given that they can upgrade their methodology at any time. In this work, we investigate four different botnet detection approaches based on the technique used and type of data employed. Two of them are public rule based systems (BotHunter and Snort) and the other two are data mining based techniques with different feature extraction methods (packet payload based and traffic flow based). The performance of these systems range from 0% to 100% on the five publicly available botnet data sets employed in this work. We discuss the evaluation results for these different systems, their features and the models learned by the data mining based techniques.

Keywords: Feature extraction, traffic analysis, botnet detection.

1 Introduction

A network of compromised hosts (aka bots) that are remotely controlled by a master (aka botmaster) is called a botnet. These infected bots perform various malicious tasks such as spreading spam, conducting Distributed Denial of Service (DDOS) attacks or identity thefts to name a few. Hence, with the high reported infection rate, the vast range of illegal activities and powerful comebacks, botnets are one of the main threats against the cyber security.

Given that botnets use automatic update mechanisms, automatic pattern discovery could potentially enable security systems to adapt to such changes in the botnet evolution. The clustering and classification techniques that are used for traffic analysis require the network traffic to be represented in a meaningful way to enable pattern recognition. Thus, an important component for such systems is extracting the features (attributes) from the network traffic. These features can be extracted per packet (or in some cases specific packets) or per flow[1] basis.

---

[1] Flow is defined as a logical equivalent for a call or a connection in association with a user specified group of elements [13]. The most common way to identify a traffic flow is to use a combination of five properties (aka 5-tuple) from the packet header, namely source/destination IP addresses and port numbers as well as the protocol.

© Springer International Publishing Switzerland 2015
J. Lopez and Y. Wu (Eds.): ISPEC 2015, LNCS 9065, pp. 121–135, 2015.
DOI: 10.1007/978-3-319-17533-1_9

Network packets include two main parts: (i) Packet header, which includes the control information of the protocols used on the network, and (ii) Packet payload, which includes the application information used on the network. The per-packet analysis can use any of these two parts while per-flow analysis only utilize network packet headers. Hence, in this work, we evaluate both: Packet payload based and Flow based approaches. Since recent botnets tend to use encryption to hide their information and methodology from the detection systems, clearly the flow-based detection systems have advantage over the packet-based systems given that they can be applied to encrypted traffic (where the payload is opaque). However, we aim to understand how much could be gained (loss) in terms of performance when a system employs payload analysis (flow analysis). To this end, we employ not only data mining techniques but also publicly available intrusion/botnet detection systems to measure performance for both the payload and the traffic flow analysis.

In this case, we evaluate Snort and BotHunter as the rule based detection systems. Snort is a popular intrusion detection and prevention system (IDS/IPS). It is open source and therefore its rule set can be customized easily. BotHunter, which is another publicly available system, utilizes the Snort sensors and customizes Snort rule set to specifically detect botnets. In summary, in this work, we have evaluated Snort, BotHunter, a data mining based packet header/payload analysis system and a data mining based traffic flow analysis system as the four different approaches for botnet detection. In the case of data mining based approaches, we have employed four different machine learning algorithms, namely C4.5 decision trees, Support Vector Machines (SVM), K- Nearest Neighbour (KNN) and Bayesian Networks, for analyzing (i) traffic flows only and (ii) all the packets including the payload. Last but not the least, we have evaluated all of the approaches on five different publicly available botnet data sets coming from different resources to evaluate how well these different approaches could generalize.

The rest of the paper is structured as follows: Related works on botnet traffic analysis are summarized in section 2. The evaluated approaches and the methodology are discussed in Section 3. Evaluation and results are provided in section 4. Finally, conclusions are drawn and the future work is discussed in section 5.

2   Background and Related Work

Unlike first botnets that had a list of exploits to launch on targets where all the commands were set at the time of infection, today a typical advanced bot uses five stages to create and maintain a botnet [10]. The first stage is the initial infection stage. In this stage, attacker infects the victim using several exploitation techniques to find its existing vulnerabilities. In the second stage, secondary injection, the shell-code is executed on the infected victim to fetch the image of the bot binary. Bot binary then installs itself on the victim. At this time, the infected machine is completely converted into a bot. The next stage is the connection stage. In this stage, the bot binary establishes the C&C

channel to be used by the bot master. Once the connection is established then the malicious C&C stage, the fourth stage, starts. This is when the master sends the commands to the botnet, short for bot network. Finally, when the master needs to update the bots for one reason or another, the update and the maintenance stage starts.

Since botnets have employed different protocols, topologies and techniques to implement the stages of their lifecycle while avoiding detection, naturally an arms race has started between the botnets and the detection systems. Thus, detection methods can be categorized based on the data being analyzed and the approach employed. From the data perspective, while some techniques focus on malware source/binary analysis, others use host and/or network based data. On the other hand, rule (signature) based traffic analysis and anomaly detection are some of the highly employed data analysis approaches. For the rule based as well as anomaly based approaches, the rules or anomalies can be obtained via data analysis performed by a human expert or can be automatically generated via a support system using data mining algorithms to assist the human expert.

Gu et al. [8] developed a system called BotHunter, which correlates Snort IDS alerts to detect botnets. The correlation process is based on the fact that all botnets share a common set of actions as a part of their lifecycle. This technique works the best when an infected bot has passed all the phases of its lifecycle when being monitored by BotHunter. Payload analysis is a part of the detection procedure in this system. Wurzinger et al. proposed an approach to detect botnets based on the correlation of commands and responses in the monitored network traces [18]. To identify traffic responses, they located the corresponding commands in the preceding traffic. Then, using these command and response pairs, the detection model was built focusing on IRC, HTTP and P2P botnets. Traffic features such as the number of non-ASCII bytes in the payload were analyzed to characterize bot behavior. Perdisci et al. proposed a network-level malware clustering system focusing on HTTP-based malwares [12]. The similarity metrics among HTTP traffic traces were defined and used to develop the malware clustering system where the clusters resulted in the signatures. Specifically, to decrease the computational cost and obtain high quality clusters, multi-level clustering was employed. Celik et al. proposed a flow-based botnet C&C activity detection system using only headers of traffic packets [7]. They investigated the effect of calibration of time-based flow features. They employed techniques such as C4.5, Naive-Bayes and logistic regression. Wang et al. proposed a fuzzy pattern recognition approach to detect HTTP and IRC botnets' behavioral patterns [16]. It is known that botnets query several domain names in a given period of time to identify their C&C server, and then form a TCP connection with the C&C server. So, Wang analyzed the features of DNS queries (such as the number of failed DNS responses) and TCP flows to detect malicious domain names and IP addresses. Zhao et al. investigated a botnet detection system based on flow intervals [20]. Flow features of traffic packets were utilized with several ML algorithms focusing on P2P botnets such as Waledac.

In our previous work, we proposed a flow based botnet detection system [10]. We evaluated five different feature sets extracted by open source flow exporters (Maji, YAF, Softflowd, Netmate and Tranalyzer) and investigated the effect of those flow features in botnet detection. Since botnets employ various protocols as their communication carrier, we also investigated the effect of protocol filters. In this work, we will follow on the results of these evaluations.

3   Methodology

As discussed in section 2, network traffic has been analyzed in various ways to detect botnets. However, the differences between these methods are not only based on the analysis method or technique used but also are based on the specific parts of the network traffic traces being analyzed and moreover the features extracted. Some systems/approaches [8,18] require both the payload and the header section of the packets to extract the necessary features while others [7,20,10] only need the header of the packets. Between these two categories, the systems that can detect botnet communication only based on the packet header do have privilege over the other category given that they can be employed on encrypted traffic where the packet payload is opaque. The importance of such systems can be better understood knowing that the most recent aggressive botnets employ encryption to better hide themselves and their information from the detection systems. As discussed earlier, to explore the effectiveness of such systems, we aim to evaluate and analyze the following systems for botnet detection: (i) Packet payload based system; (ii) Flow based system; (iii) Snort intrusion detection system and (iv) BotHunter botnet detection system.

3.1   Systems Employed

Packet Payload Based System: Some of the works in the literature proposed specific packet analysis methods to detect botnet behaviour [9,16]. These systems have focused on specific packets and features from the header and/or payload sections of these packets to identify the type of malware they are interested in. For example, Haddadi et al. [9] extracted the domain name from the DNS packets to detect automatically generated malicious domain names while Mohaisen et al. [11] introduced a set of features focusing on the Zeus botnet. We employ the features introduced by Mohaisen et al. in our evaluations for packet payload based system. Table 1 presents the selected features for this approach.

Since some of the data mining techniques employed in this work can only be applied to numeric features, string to numeric feature conversions are performed and the quartile object sizes are calculated for each of the data sets. Detailed information of the features can be found in [11]. Once the features are extracted from each data set, four classifiers (C4.5, SVM, KNN, Bayesian Networks) are used for botnet detection.

Table 1. Packet-based approach– network features

Feature set	
Port	Source and destination port numbers
Connections	TCP, UDP, RAW
Request type	GET, HEAD, POST
Response type	Response code 200–599
Object Size	Categorised quartiles (1–4)
DNS	MX, NS, A records, PTR, SOA, CNAME

Flow Based System: Among the approaches that use the information of packet headers only, flow based feature extraction methods are highly employed in the recent literature [7][10][16]. In such approaches, communication packets are aggregated into flows and then statistics are calculated. Given that botnets employ encryption techniques to avoid the detection systems that analyze the communication information embedded in the packet payload, flow based approaches can be very effective since they use only network packet headers. Hence, we develop a flow based botnet detection system based on the results obtained from our previous work [10]. The critical phase of such a system is the flow exporting. Our previous work on the effect of such exporters reported Tranalyzer as the best performing flow exporter among the five tools (Maji, YAF, Softflowd, Tranalyzer and Netmate) that we have evaluated under multiple scenarios. Hence, in this work, we employ Tranalyzer to export the flows. After extracting the flow features, the aforementioned classifiers are employed to detect the botnet behaviour as an early warning system. It should be noted here that we employ all of the features exported by Tranalyzer as inputs to the data mining techniques except the IP addresses, port numbers and any non-numeric features. The reasons behind this are two folds: IP addresses can be spoofed whereas port numbers can be assigned dynamically. Thus, employing such features may decrease the generalization abilities of the detection system for unseen behaviours. On the other hand, the presentation of non-numeric features may introduce other biases to the detection system so it is left to the future work to introduce such features.

Tranalyzer: Flow exporters summarize network traffic utilizing the network packet headers only. These tools collect packet information with common characteristics such as IP addresses and port numbers, aggregate them into flows and then calculate some statistics such as the number of packets per flow etc. Tranalyzer is a light weight uni-directional flow exporter that employs an extended version of NetFlow feature set. This tool exports both the binary and the ASCII formats and therefore, does not require any collector. This makes it very easy to use. Tranalyzer supports 93 flow features that can be categorized into Time, Inter-arrival, Packets&Bytes and Flags groups. More detailed information on the tool and its feature set can be found in [4,10].

Snort Intrusion Detection System: Snort is an intrusion detection and prevention system that analyzes packet payload as well as packet header data to detect any evidence of harmful actions that match predefined signatures (rule sets) [1].

Some of these pre-defined rules/signatures take advantage of payload information while the others require only the header features to be analyzed. Snort has been supported by two rule sets: VRT (Vulnerability Research Team), which is the official rule set for Snort, and ET (Emerging Threat), which is published by emergingthreats.com. In our evaluations, we used the VRT rule set. We discuss this in more detail in section 4.3. These two main rule sets have come with many rules that aim to cover all possible network conditions. Hence, users should carefully enable the rules that fit their network conditions and alert priority settings and disable the others. Since 1998, Snort has been known and used in network security area given that it is a cross-platform open source IDS/IPS that can be modified to fit the network security challenges and needs as shown by the BotHunter research.

BotHunter botnet Detection System: Gu et al. introduced BotHunter as a botnet detection system and made it publicly available. This tool uses the combination of Snort and a clustering approach to detect botnet infections. BotHunter is based on the idea of all botnet infection processes are similar and can be illustrated by a lifecycle model explained in section 2. Hence, it uses a modified version of Snort with its plugins to detect specific bot actions of the lifecycle and then correlates the Snort alerts to detect the botnets' behaviour and infected machines. The developers have modified and selected the botnet related Snort rules, developed many additional rules and inserted the IP address checking to Snort rules to make BotHunter's Snort sensors work more efficiently. The initial version of BotHunter used two plugins: *SLADE* and *SCADE*, which are designed for the anomalous traffic pattern and payload detection. Recently, these plugins are replaced by three new plugins: (i) *bhDNS* for malicious DNS analysis, (ii) *bhSD* for scanning detection; and (iii) *Con-P2P* for Conficker-C P2P detection and ethernet tracking. All new plugins use existing information like DNS lists, IP lists, port lists and so on to detect malicious (botnet) behaviour. It should be noted here that to be able to detect new botnets, BotHunter relies on Snort signature updates of new malicious behaviours where the signatures use header and payload information.

3.2 Data Mining Techniques Employed

As discussed in section 3, the first two systems evaluated employ various data mining techniques for botnet detection. These include: C4.5 decision tree, SVM, KNN and Bayesian Networks. These are the four well-known machine learning algorithms that are widely used in the literature for network traffic classification [11,16,20,10].

C4.5 is an extension to ID3 algorithm that aims to find the small decision trees (using pruning) and then convert the trained tree into an if-then rule set. The algorithm employs a normalized information gain criterion to select attributes from a given set of attributes to determine the splitting point of the decision tree. *SVM* is a binary learning algorithm that can easily be extended to K-class classification by constructing k two-class (binary) classifiers. The goal of this classification algorithm is to build an N- dimensional hyperplane that optimally separates the samples of data into classes with maximal margin. *KNN* stores the training samples and uses Euclidean distance to compute the distance of the test instances from the K nearest neighbour of n-dimensional training feature space. The classifier then assigns a class label to the test instance using a majority voting mechanism. *Bayesian Networks* are graphical representations for probabilistic relationships among the variables given a set of discrete features. The learning process aims to find a Bayesian Network structure that describes the training data in the best possible way. Detailed descriptions of all the algorithms can be found in [5].

3.3   Traffic Employed

All four aforementioned systems require botnet traffic data while the first two systems (Packet payload based and Flow based) also require legitimate traffic given that they employ classification algorithms. In this work, several Zeus botnet traffic captures available at NETRESEC [3] and Snort[2] [2] web sites are employed. Hereafter, we refer to these two data sets as Zeus (Snort) and Zeus (NETRESEC). Moreover, since many researchers in the literature [18,12,16] employed generated botnet traffic in a sandbox environment using the public botnet binaries and toolkits, we also did the same using a public Zeus toolkit version 1.2.7.19. This toolkit is also analyzed and employed in [6]. We set up 12 Zeus bots (infected machines with Zeus botnet) and two C&C servers (one Windows server and one Linux server) in the test bed. Hereafter, we will refer to this data set as Zeus-2 (NIMS)[3]. Since the aforementioned three data sets are purely malicious and the systems based on various data mining techniques require legitimate traffic for training purposes, we employed a data set[3] representing normal behaviour used in [10].

Furthermore, University of Victoria also made a data set publicly available in 2013 [14]. This data set has combined two separate data sets of botnet malicious traffic from the French chapter of honeynet project on Strom and Waledac botnets. This combination represents the malicious side of the data set. On the other hand, their legitimate traffic is represented by two data sets: one data set from the Traffic Lab at Ericsson Research in Hungary and another data set from the Lawrence Berkeley National Laboratory (LBNL) in USA. Hereafter, we will refer to this data set as ISOT-UVic. This data set not only introduces different botnet traffic for our experiments but also introduces different normal traffic than the above.

Finally, CAIDA organization has also captured and made publicly available a Conficker botnet data set [15]. This three day captured traffic is collected by the CAIDA UCSD network telescope when the Conficker botnet was active. The first and the second day covers the Conficker-A botnet infection while during the

---

[2] "Sample_1" Zeus traffic file is used in this work.

[3] These data sets can be found at
http://web.cs.dal.ca/~haddadi/data-analysis.htm

third day Conficker-A and B were active. This data set has been anonymized, the payload has been removed from the packets and the CAIDA network addresses have been masked (destination IP addresses). A more detailed description of the CAIDA Conficker data set can be found in [15]. We included this data set in our evaluations, since it provides different botnet traffic for our evaluations. Hereafter, we will refer to this data set as the Conficker (CAIDA).

4   Evaluations and Results

As discussed earlier, our goal in this work is to evaluate different botnet detection systems where each uses specific parts of the traffic. To achieve this, we chose four different detection systems which are highly employed in academia and industry. These four systems are: packet payload based, flow based, BotHunter and Snort. For evaluation purposes, we have employed five different traffic traces for the botnets: Zeus (Snort), Zeus (NETRESEC), Zeus-2 (NIMS), ISOT-UVic and Conficker (CAIDA); and three different traffic traces for the legitimate traffic: Alexa, Ericsson and LNBL. Last but not the least, we have employed four different data mining techniques, namely C4.5, SVM, KNN and Bayesian Networks, for both the packet payload and the flow based systems.

4.1   Data Sets

Snort web site [2] officially has provided a description of the sample files and also has given information to use as the groundtruth for the data set. On the other hand, we analyzed the employed protocols, domain names and the communication patterns of Zeus (NETRESEC) traffic and compared them against the published characteristics of Zeus botnet to extract the malicious IP addresses. Regarding the Zeus-2 (NIMS) data set, since we set up the data generation environment in the laboratory, we had all the necessary information of the servers and the infected machines in this data set. Moreover, the information about the IP address mapping and the scenarios which were used to combine all four traffic traces from the ISOT-UVic data set can be found at [14]. Last but not the least, since UCSD telescope carries no legitimate traffic and given that there are other malicious background traffic than the Conficker infections in their captures, we used the information provided by CAIDA as the groundtruth for this data set.

For the data mining based systems, uniform sampling was used to create balanced (in terms of malicious vs non-malicious traffic) data sets for training purposes. For Conficker (CAIDA) data set specifically, we ensured that the training data set included data samples of each day so that behavioural examples of every version of Conficker traffic is represented in the data set. Having said this, there are no training samples (zero) for the Conficker (CAIDA) data set for the packet payload based approach. That is because this approach requires information from the packet payload while such information is not provided by CAIDA in this data set. It should be noted here that the traffic files that are used in the sampling process for the first two systems, are also employed for BotHunter and Snort. This provides consistency for our evaluations.

4.2   Performance Metrics

In traffic classification, two metrics are typically used in order to quantify the performance of the classifiers: Detection Rate (DR) and False Positive Rate (FPR). DR reflects the number of the correctly classified specific botnet samples in a given data set using $DR = \frac{TP}{TP+FN}$ where TP (True Positive) is the number of botnet traffic samples that are classified correctly, and FN (False Negative) is the number of botnet samples that are classified incorrectly (as legitimate samples). On the other hand, FPR shows the number of legitimate samples that are classified incorrectly as the botnet samples using $FPR = \frac{FP}{FP+TN}$ where TN (True Negative) is the number of legitimate traffic samples that are classified correctly.

4.3   Results

Packet Payload Based and Flow Based Systems: We employed the four data mining techniques (classifiers) using an open source tool called Weka [17] for the packet payload based and flow based systems. Our previous study on flow based botnet detection systems showed that C4.5 and Bayesian Networks are the best performed classifiers compared to Artificial Neural Networks, SVM and Naive Bayes [10]. Moreover, in this work, we added KNN to our evaluations since it was reported to give high performance in [11,19]. To evaluate these classifiers on the aforementioned data sets, we run them on each dataset using 10-fold cross-validation to further avoid any dataset biases that might affect the results. Table 2 and Table 3 shows the classification performances of these two systems on the five data sets. Considering the DR and FPR of the classifiers, C4.5 seems to be the best performing classifier that resulted in the detection rate of up to 100% for all five data sets. This classifier's output is in the form of rules that makes it easier to be used by a human expert to understand what this technique models on a given data set. For the packet payload based system, the size of the decision tree output is 5 for ISOT-UVic dataset and 7 for all other datasets. On the other hand, the size of the decision tree is 9, 21, 25, 7 and 525 for the Zeus (Snort), Zeus (NETRESEC), Zeus-2 (NIMS), Conficker (CAIDA) and ISOT-UVic, respectively, for the traffic flow based system. The results indicate that the flow based system solutions are bigger in size, even though the difference is not much in 4 of the 5 data sets. However, for the ISOT-UVic dataset, the complexity difference is significant. This can be caused by the fact that ISOT-UVic dataset is a combination of multiple botnet and legitimate datasets.

BotHunter: This tool provides Snort installation with a customized malware rule set from ET (Emerging Threats rule set and DNS/IP blacklist). Running BotHunter with a traffic pcap file (Batch mode) creates two types of results: BotHunter's Snort alerts (used as input for BotHunter correlator), and bot profiles. Moreover, to run BotHunter on any data set, the user needs to specify the trusted network or the monitored network. Indeed, such a requirement necessitates the users to have information about the data set or the monitored network (if using BotHunter in live mode).

Table 2. Classification results of the packet payload based system

Data Set		DR	Botnet		Legitimate	
			TPR	FPR	TNR	FNR
C4.5	Zeus (Snort)	100%	100%	0%	100%	0%
	Zeus (NETRESEC)	100%	100%	0%	100%	0%
	Zeus-2 (NIMS)	99.44%	98.9%	0%	100%	1.1%
	Conficker (CAIDA)	-	-	-	-	-
	ISOT-UVic	99.77%	99.7%	0.1%	99.9%	0.3%
KNN	Zeus (Snort)	100%	100%	0%	100%	0%
	Zeus (NETRESEC)	100%	100%	0%	100%	0%
	Zeus-2 (NIMS)	100%	100%	0%	100%	0%
	Conficker (CAIDA)	-	-	-	-	-
	ISOT-UVic	99.72%	99.7%	0.3%	99.7%	0.3%
SVM	Zeus (Snort)	99.52%	99%	0%	100%	1.0%
	Zeus (NETRESEC)	100%	100%	0%	100%	0%
	Zeus-2 (NIMS)	99.72%	99.4%	0%	100%	0.6%
	Conficker (CAIDA)	-	-	-	-	-
	ISOT-UVic	99.79%	99.7%	0.1%	99.9%	0.3%
Bayesian Networks	Zeus (Snort)	100%	100%	0%	100%	0%
	Zeus (NETRESEC)	100%	100%	0%	100%	0%
	Zeus-2 (NIMS)	93.82%	98.9%	11.2%	88.8%	1.1%
	Conficker (CAIDA)	-	-	-	-	-
	ISOT-UVic	99.79%	99.7%	0.1%	99.9%	0.3%

Table 4 shows the results of BotHunter on the five data sets. The "# infected hosts" column in the table shows the number of infected machines with the bot program. The "# remote hosts" shows the malicious remote machines that the infected hosts communicate with in the captured data sets. Although finding the infected host in the network is important, it is only one phase of the detection. However, finding the source of the attacks or at least the remote hosts that are utilized by the C&C server is another important phase of detection. Hence, in this work, we also analyzed the remote host information. These remote machines can be the malicious C&C servers or new targets of the botnet that the infected machine aims to infect. BotHunter correlates the Snort alerts (shown in the second column) and finally generates the bot profiles revealing the malicious hosts. In the cells of the Table 4 where two numbers are separated by "/", the first number is the count of IP addresses detected and the second number is the total number of IP addresses in that category. In each cell, the DR for each category is included. However, the overall detection rate of the BotHunter including the infected hosts and the remote hosts is shown in Table 6.

In short, based on the performance of BotHunter presented in Tables 4 and 6, we make the following observations: (1) No alert or bot profile was raised for Conficker (CAIDA) data set. That is because the payload part of the traffic was not provided by CAIDA. Given that BotHunter and its Snort sensors use payload of the traffic (packets) for detecting the botnets, they could not perform

Table 3. Classification results for the traffic flow based system

	Data Set	DR	Botnet		Legitimate	
			TPR	FPR	TNR	FNR
C4.5	Zeus (Snort)	98.9%	97.2%	1.4%	98.6%	2.8%
	Zeus (NETRESEC)	98.25%	98.5%	2%	98%	1.5%
	Zeus-2 (NIMS)	99.67%	99.8%	0.5%	99.5%	0.2%
	Conficker (CAIDA)	99.95%	100%	0.1%	99.9%	0%
	ISOT-UVic	99.9%	99.9%	0.1%	99.9%	0.1%
KNN	Zeus (Snort)	98.6%	99.3%	2.1%	97.9%	0.7%
	Zeus (NETRESEC)	96.75%	97.0%	3.5%	96.5%	3.0%
	Zeus-2 (NIMS)	99.74%	99.8%	0.3%	99.7%	0.2%
	Conficker (CAIDA)	99.95%	99.9%	0%	100%	0.1%
	ISOT-UVic	99.91%	99.8%	0%	100%	0.2%
SVM	Zeus (Snort)	99.3%	100%	1.4%	98.6%	0%
	Zeus (NETRESEC)	91.01%	89.3%	7.3%	92.8%	10.7%
	Zeus-2 (NIMS)	99.90%	99.6%	1.8%	98.2%	0.4%
	Conficker (CAIDA)	99.89%	99.9%	0.1%	99.9%	0.1%
	ISOT-UVic	99.82%	99.8%	0.2%	99.8%	0.2%
Bayesian Networks	Zeus (Snort)	97.21%	100%	5.6%	94.4%	0%
	Zeus (NETRESEC)	83.89%	76.8%	9.0%	91.0%	23.2%
	Zeus-2 (NIMS)	99.61%	99.6%	0.4%	99.6%	0.4%
	Conficker (CAIDA)	98.47%	99.9%	3.0%	97.0%	0.1%
	ISOT-UVic	99.86%	99.9%	0.2%	99.8%	0.1%

well on this data set. (2) BotHunter could successfully detect all the infected machines and remote hosts of the Zeus-2 (NIMS) data set. That is because payload is provided and all the phases of the botnet lifecycle are present in this data set. (3) Although Snort did create serious alarms on Zeus (Snort) (such as "E4[rb] TROJAN Zeus POST Request to CnC"), BotHunter did not report any bot profile. This could be because a combination of different types of alerts (representing different phases of lifecycle) is required by BotHunter to form a bot profile. (4) For ISOT-UVic data set, BotHunter could successfully detect four infected hosts out of five known ones. However, from almost 15000 remote hosts with which these infected machines communicate, only 40 of them were identified in the generated bot profiles. Again, we think that this was because BotHunter: (i) requires all the phases of the botnet lifecycle for all the machines; and (ii) depends on Snort sensor rule set.

Snort: To run Snort, the first thing required is to set the rule set that will be used. Two main rule sets for Snort are VRT and ET. In our evaluations, we used the VRT rule set because it is the official rule set of Snort that gets updated frequently. Furthermore,the other rule set, ET, is the one used by BotHunter in our evaluations. In our analysis of Snort, we found that many rules of the VRT rule set are disabled and specifically all pre-processor and shared-object rules are disabled by default. Based on the information Snort has provided on botnet detection, we enabled all of the rules such as (*sid= 16460 and 11192*) that are

Table 4. BotHunter detailed detection results

Data Set	Snort alerts	# infected hosts	# remote hosts
Zeus (Snort)	26	0/1 (0%)	0/14 (0%))
Zeus (NETRESEC)	23	1/1 (100%)	7/11 (63.6%)
Zeus-2 (NIMS)	486	12/12 (100%)	2/2 (100%)
Conficker (CAIDA)	0	0 (0%)	0 (0%)
ISOT-UVic	831	4/5 (80%)	40/15000 (0.3%)

Table 5. Snort detailed detection results

Data Set	Snort alerts	# infected hosts	# remote hosts
Zeus (Snort)	11	1/1 (100%)	7/14 (50%)
Zeus (NETRESEC)	58	1/1 (100%)	7/11 (63.6%)
Zeus-2 (NIMS)	401	12/12 (100%)	2/2(100%)
Conficker (CAIDA)	7244	6457/360191 (1.8%)	430/80380 (0.5%)
ISOT-UVic	102755	2/5 (40%)	2326/15000 (15.5%)

Table 6. BotHunter and Snort overall performances

	Data Set	DR	TPR	FNR
BotHunter	Zeus (Snort)	0%	0%	0%
	Zeus (NETRESEC)	66.6%	66.6%	0%
	Zeus-2 (NIMS)	100%	100%	0%
	Conficker (CAIDA)	0%	0%	0%
	ISOT-UVic	2.9%	2.9%	0%
Snort	Zeus (Snort)	53.3%	53.3%	0%
	Zeus (NETRESEC)	66.6%	66.6%	0%
	Zeus-2 (NIMS)	100%	100%	0%
	Conficker (CAIDA)	1.6%	1.6%	0%
	ISOT-UVic	15.5%	15.5%	0%(6/23140)

related to Zeus botnet. Tables 5 and 6 show the performance of Snort on our five data sets. For big data sets that contain considerable number of malicious traffic, Snort raises a lot of alerts. This makes it complicated to process the results (such as for Conficker CAIDA and ISOT-UVic data sets shown in Table 5). Thus, in this work, any alert with high priority that was raised on botnet IP addresses (such as alerts indicating "Win.Trojan.Zeus") is considered as TP, and any such alert triggered on legitimate IP addresses is considered as FP.

Table 7 shows detailed information on the type of rules that Snort and BotHunter employed for all of the five data sets. The "Header+payload based" column shows the rules that require both the header and the payload of the packet traces whereas the "Header based" rules are the ones that use only the packet header information. The first number in each category shows the number of rules triggered and the second number in parenthesis shows the number of alerts

Table 7. The number and the type of Snort and BotHunter Rules

Data Set	Snort		BotHunter	
	Header based	Header+payload based	Header	Header+payload based
Zeus (Snort)	2 (9)	1 (2)	0 (0)	2 (26)
Zeus (NETRESEC)	3 (38)	8 (20)	0 (0)	4 (23)
Zeus-2 (NIMS)	2 (202)	1 (199)	0 (0)	4 (486)
Conficker (CAIDA)	1 (7244)	0 (0)	0 (0)	0 (0)
ISOT-UVic	3 (102755)	0 (0)	0 (0)	9 (831)

generated in that category. As indicated in the table, BotHunter only used the Snort rules (ET) that are based on both the header and the payload information while Snort utilized more of the header based rules from the VRT rule set. In the "Header+payload" category the "MALWARE-CNC" type rules and in the "Header" category the "CONTENT-LENGTH" type rules are frequently used by Snort. On the other hand, BotHunter employed the "E4[rb] " and "E4[rb]" type rules more frequently. The results also shows that when almost all phases of communication are available in the data set (as for the Zeus-2 (NIMS)), the number of alerts being triggered is increased as well as the DR.

Finally, it should be noted that all the tools and the data sets are publically available and the experiments can be repeated to be compared against other approaches.

4.4   Discussion and Highlights

The main advantage of the first two systems based on data mining (packet payload based and flow based) is the ability to automatically discover patterns in big traffic data sets. This also provides the capability of detecting malicious communications at any stage of the botnet lifecycle without focusing on one side of the network (as BotHunter does). The performances of these two systems indicate that both feature extraction techniques can be used to build botnet detection models with high performances. However, given that the packet payload based approach requires the payload information of the packets for analysis and this information may not be available due to encryption or simply not captured, we believe that the flow based detection system is the winner among the two. As demonstrated in our evaluations, the performance of the flow based system is higher or similar to the results reported in the literature (with detection rate of up to 100%, up to 79%, 88% and 99% in [8], [12], [18] and [20], respectively.

On the other hand, BotHunter focuses on finding the Snort alerts corresponding to the botnet lifecycle and correlating them to create a bot profile. Our evaluations show that it cannot detect the botnet related malicious communications on the network if it cannot find the necessary phases of the botnet lifecycle in the traffic. However, BotHunter seems to be successful when a specific network is under constant monitoring and the goal is to detect the infected machines of a trusted network. Constant monitoring helps the Snort sensors to detect all the phases of a botnet lifecycle. Having said this, it uses the pre-defined customized Snort rule set so it cannot correlate different behaviours if they are not detected by Snort.

Unlike BotHunter, Snort does not just focus on detecting the infected hosts based on tracing the existence of the botnet lifecycle. Instead, it monitors all the network communications (the default HOME_NET is "any") and flags any suspicious communication that matches its pre-defined rules if using the VRT rule set. The performance of Snort depends on the quality of the rules. Since Snort is a well-known IDS/IPS, its rule set gets updated frequently. This makes it one of the more popular detection systems available today. However, as we observed in our evaluations, it generates a lot of alerts.

5   Conclusions

In this work, four botnet detection systems are investigated. Each one of these uses specific features from network traffic with different levels of human involvement. The first system is a packet payload based system, which employs classifiers using the features extracted from the header and the payload of a packet. The second system is a traffic flow based system where features are extracted on a per flow basis instead of packets. Since the features used by this system are extracted from only the header section of the packets, this approach can be applied to encrypted traffic as well. In addition to these two systems, Snort and BotHunter are also evaluated as publicly available botnet detection systems. These two systems represent rule based detection systems where both the packet headers and the packet payloads are analyzed. The evaluation of all four systems on five public data sets show that the first two systems performed better than the last two systems with detection rates approaching up to 100% on some of the data sets. Comparing the payload based and flow based systems, neither of them significantly out-performed the other and they both achieve very similar detection performances (highest when C4.5 was used in both cases). Having said this, the packet payload based system results in much lower false positive rates. This makes it very desirable on all data sets except the ones that do not have any payload. In those cases, this system cannot perform at all. However, the flow based system can still perform. This gives the flow based method an important advantage.

Acknowledgments. This research is supported by the Canadian Safety and Security Program(CSSP) E-Security grant. The CSSP is led by the Defense Research and Development Canada, Centre for Security Science (CSS) on behalf of the Government of Canada and its partners across all levels of government, response and emergency management organizations, nongovernmental agencies, industry and academia.

References

1. https://www.snort.org/
2. https://labs.snort.org/papers/zeus.html
3. NETRESEC repository: publicly available pcap files, http://www.netresec.com/?page=PcapFiles.
4. Tranalyzer, http://tranalyzer.com/
5. Alpaydin, E.: Introduction to Machine Learning. MIT Press (2004)
6. Binsalleeh, H., Ormerod, T., Boukhtouta, A., Sinha, P., Youssef, A., Debbabi, M., Wang, L.: On the analysis of the zeus botnet crimeware toolkit. In: PST (2010)
7. Celik, Z.B., Raghuram, J., Kesidis, G., Miller, D.J.: Salting public traces with attack traffic to test flow classifiers. In: CSET (2011)
8. Gu, G., Porras, P., Yegneswaran, V., Fong, M., Lee, W.: Bothunter: detecting malware infection through ids-driven dialog correlation. In: 16th USENIX Security Symposium (2007)
9. Haddadi, F., Kayacik, H.G., Zincir-Heywood, A.N., Heywood, M.I.: Malicious automatically generated domain name detection using stateful-SBB. In: Esparcia-Alcázar, A.I. (ed.) EvoApplications 2013. LNCS, vol. 7835, pp. 529–539. Springer, Heidelberg (2013)
10. Haddadi, F., Zincir-Heywood, A.N.: Benchmarking the effect of flow exporters and protocol filters on botnet traffic classification. IEEE Systems Journal, 1–12 (2014)
11. Mohaisen, A., Alrawi, O.: Unveiling Zeus. In: IW3C2 (2013)
12. Perdisci, R., Corona, I., Dagon, D., Lee, W.: Detecting malicious flux service networks through passive analysis of recursive DNS traces. In: ACSAC (2009)
13. RFC 2722 (October 1999), http://tools.ietf.org/html/rfc2722
14. Saad, S., Traore, I., Ghorbani, A., Sayed, B., Zhao, D., Lu, W., Fleix, J., Hakimian, P.: Detecting P2P botnets through network behavior analysis and machine learning. In: PST (2011)
15. The CAIDA USCD Network Telescope- 'Three Days of Conficker', http://www.caida.org/data/passive/telescope-3days-conficker_dataset.xml
16. Wang, K., Huang, C., Lin, S., Lin, Y.: A fuzzy pattern-based filtering algorithm for botnet detection. Computer Networks 55, 3275–3286 (2011)
17. weka, http://www.cs.waikato.ac.nz/ml/weka/
18. Wurzinger, P., Bilge, L., Holz, T., Goebel, J., Kruegel, C., Kirda, E.: Automatically generating models for botnet detection. In: Backes, M., Ning, P. (eds.) ESORICS 2009. LNCS, vol. 5789, pp. 232–249. Springer, Heidelberg (2009)
19. Zhang, J., Chen, C., Xiang, Y., Zhou, W., Vasilakos, A.: An effective network classification method with unknown flow detection. IEEE Transactions on Network and Service Management 10 (2013)
20. Zhao, D., Traore, I., Sayed, B., Lu, W., Saad, S., Ghorbani, A., Garant, D.: Botnet detection based on traffic behavior analysis and flow intervals. Computers and Security 39 (2013)

Key Exchange Protocol

Strongly Secure Key Exchange Protocol with Minimal KEM

Baoping Tian, Fushan Wei, and Chuangui Ma

State Key Laboratory of Mathematical Engineering and Advanced Computing,
Zhengzhou Information Science and Technology Institute, Zhengzhou 450001, China
{baoping_tian@163.com}

Abstract. In this paper, we give a generic construction of two-pass authenticated key exchange (AKE) protocol from key encapsulation mechanism (KEM). Our construction is provably secure without random oracles in the CK^+ model which is stronger than CK model and eCK model. Compared with similar KEM-based AKE protocols, our generic construction achieves CK^+ security with the minimal KEM (namely, one CCA-secure KEM and one CPA-secure KEM).

Keywords: pubic key cryptography, KEM, twisted PRF, CK^+ model, standard model.

1 Introduction

Authenticated key exchange (AKE) protocol enables two entities over the public network to establish a shared session key and at the same time authenticates mutually, while the established session key can later be used to communicate privately or construct MACs etc. Currently, most of AKE protocols are provably secure only in the random oracles [1, 2, 3, 4]. However, the security of these protocols rely on the random oracle assumption which cannot be achieved in the real world. In practice, when the random oracles are replaced by specific functions, there may be security flaws [5]. Thus, constructing AKE protocol without random oracles is also one field of interest in cryptography.

One way to accomplish AKE without random oracles is by using key encapsulation mechanism (KEM) as the building block. Generally speaking, KEM is a kind of asymmetric encryption technique which enables a sender and a receiver to share a common session key. Two important notions of security related to KEM are chosen-plaintext-attack (CPA) security and chosen-ciphertext-attack (CCA) security, while the latter offers a decryption oracle to the adversary. Due to the simplicity and flexibility of KEM, it's very convenient to adopt this modular approach to construct AKE protocol.

Boyd et al. [6] presented two one-round key exchange protocols from CCA-secure identity-based KEM (IB-KEM) in the CK model [7], one without weak perfect forward secrecy (wPFS) and the other with wPFS but needs to run an extra ephemeral Diffie-Hellman. Based on the work of Boyd et al. [6], in PKC

© Springer International Publishing Switzerland 2015
J. Lopez and Y. Wu (Eds.): ISPEC 2015, LNCS 9065, pp. 139–153, 2015.
DOI: 10.1007/978-3-319-17533-1_10

2012 Fujioka et al. [8] proposed a strongly secure generic construction of two-pass AKE protocol in the CK^+ model [8]. In order to resist maximal exposure (MEX) attack , especially the exposure of ephemeral keys of both users, they introduced the twisted PRF trick. Their construction employs the CCA-secure KEM and the session-specific CPA-secure KEM which can make it to achieve wPFS. Recently, in the conference of CT-RSA 2014 Kurosawa et al. [9] presents three generic constructions(2-PASS-CK, 2-PASS-ECK and 2-PASS-BOTH) of two-pass key exchange protocols with wPFS from CPA-secure KEM. Meanwhile, they formulate the notion of twisted PRF (tPRF) and give correct construction of tPRF. Their three constructions all use tPRF trick to resist MEX attacks. 2-PASS-CK, the mainly one, is secure in the CK model [7], while 2-PASS-ECK is eCK-secure [3], 2-PASS-BOTH is secure in both CK model and eCK model.

In this paper, we mainly focus on the KEM-based protocol. In practice, since KEM is not that highly efficient as data encapsulation mechanism (e.g. AES)[10], hence the number of KEM (required times of running KEM) in the KEM-based protocol will effect the performance. Therefore, it's a desirable thing to use KEM as few as possible in the KEM-based protocol. Boyd et al. [6] use two CCA-secure KEMs [1], Fujioka et al. [8] employ two CCA-secure KEMs and one CPA-secure KEM, Kurosawa et al. [9] only apply one CPA-secure KEM in their construction.

Table 1. Number of KEM Comprison

Protocol	CCA-KEM	CPA-KEM	total of KEM
Boyd et al. [6]	2	0	2
Fujioka et al. [8]	2	1	3
Kurosawa et al. [9]	0	1	1

From table 1, we can see that Kurosawa et al. [9] use the minimal KEM. However, for the three generic constructions of Kurosawa et al. [9], if secret key of KEM is compromised, then the adversary can reply the message of session initiator to impersonate the initiator. And the session key is completely computed by the session responder without the session initiator's any contribution, i.e. the key control security in their schemes are absent.

In this paper, we present a generic construction of two-pass key exchange protocol from KEM. Our construction achieves CK^+ security with only one CCA-secure IB-KEM and one CPA-secure KEM. Compared with existing KEM-based AKE protocols, our construction employs the minimal KEM to achieve strong security. In our generic construction, the main reason of employing IB-KEM is that identity-based setting can get rid of troubles with the certificates. If PKI-based setting is really needed, then we can just replace the IB-KEM with a PKI-based KEM. Therefore, it's very convenient for our construction to switch between identity-based setting and PKI-based setting.

---

[1] When considering the number of KEM in a scheme, we don't distinguish CCA-secure IB-KEM from CCA-secure KEM.

In a word, our contributions in this paper are listed as below

1. We present a generic construction of two-pass AKE protocol without random oracles.
2. Comparison shows that our construction achieves CK^+ security with the minimal KEM namely one CCA-secure IB-KEM and one CPA-secure KEM.
3. Our construction can switch between identity-based setting and PKI-based setting easily.

ORGANIZATION. The rest of this paper is organized as follows : In section 2, we introduce some related preliminaries. Section 3 outlines the CK^+ model. Then, we propose our generic construction in section 4 and prove the security in section 5. We compare our protocol with other KEM-based protocols in section 6. In the final section, we draw a conclusion on this paper.

2 Preliminaries

Notations. Let k be the security parameter. By $\mathcal{A}(x, y, ...)$, we denote a PPT algorithm $\mathcal{A}$ with $(x, y, ...)$ as inputs. We denote by $z \leftarrow \mathcal{A}(x, y, ...)$ running $\mathcal{A}$ with inputs $(x, y, ...)$ outputs z. We use the symbol " $\in_R$ " to denote "choosing uniformly at random".

Definition 1 (Min-Entropy). *Let X be a probability distribution over K, the minimum entropy of X over K is defined as follows*

$$H_{\min}(X) = \min\{-\log_2(Pr_X[x]) : x \in K, Pr_X[x] \neq 0\}$$

If $H_{\min}(X) = t$, it means that for all $x \in K$, we have $Pr_X[x] \leq 2^{-t}$.

Definition 2 (Strong Randomness Extractor). *Let $Exct : \mathcal{S} \times \mathcal{X} \to \mathcal{Y}$ be a function family with seed space $\mathcal{S}$, finite domain $\mathcal{X}$ and finite range $\mathcal{Y}$. $Exct$ is called (m, ϵ)-strong randomness extractor if for any random variable X over $\mathcal{X}$ with $H_{\min}(X) = m$ and for any seed $s \in_R \mathcal{S}$, the two distributions $\langle s, Exct(s, X) \rangle$ and $\langle s, R \rangle$ where $R \in_R \mathcal{Y}$ have statistical distance ϵ, i.e.*

$$\frac{1}{2} \sum_{x \in \mathcal{Y}} |Pr[Exct(s, X) = x] - Pr[R = x]| = \varepsilon$$

Definition 3 (Pseudorandom Function Family (PRF) [6]). *Let $\mathcal{F} = \{f_s\}_{s \in S}$ be a family of functions where $S = S(k)$. For a PPT distinguisher $\mathcal{D}$, and it has an access to oracle $\mathcal{O}$ which is $F_s(\cdot)$ or a truly random function $RF(\cdot)$ with the domain and range of $\mathcal{F}$, the advantage of which is defined as*

$$Adv_{\mathcal{D}}^{PRF}(k) = |Pr[1 \leftarrow \mathcal{D}^{F_s(\cdot)}(1^k)] - Pr[1 \leftarrow \mathcal{D}^{RF(\cdot)}(1^k)]|$$

If the advantage $Adv_{\mathcal{D}}^{PRF}(k)$ is negligible in k for all distinguisher $\mathcal{D}$, then $\mathcal{F}$ is said to be pseudorandom.

2.1   Key Encapsulation Mechanisms (KEM)

A KEM includes three ploynomial-time algorithms (Gen, Enc, Dec) which are defined as below

- $(pk, sk) \leftarrow Gen(1^k)$: key generation algorithm Gen takes the security parameter k as the input, returns public/private key pairs (pk, sk).
- $(C, K) \leftarrow Enc(pk)$: encryption algorithm Enc takes as the input pk(encapsulation key) outputs a key $K \in \mathcal{K}$ and a ciphertext $C \in \mathcal{C}$.
- $K \leftarrow Dec(sk, C)$: decryption algorithm Dec takes as inputs sk and C, outputs the session key K.

Definition 4 (CPA-secure KEM). *For a PPT adversary $\mathcal{A}$, the security of KEM against which is defined via the following security experiment*

$$\text{EXPERIMENT } Exp_{KEM,\mathcal{A}}^{CPA}(k)$$
$$(pk, sk) \leftarrow Gen(1^k)$$
$$(C^*, K_0) \leftarrow Enc(pk), K_1 \in_R \mathcal{K}$$
$$b \in_R \{0, 1\}, b' \leftarrow \mathcal{A}(pk, C^*, K_b)$$
$$If \ b = b' \ return \ 1; otherwise \ 0$$

the advantage of $\mathcal{A}$ is defined as $Adv_{KEM,\mathcal{A}}^{CPA}(k) = |Pr[1 \leftarrow Exp_{KEM,\mathcal{A}}^{CPA}(k)] - \frac{1}{2}|$. A KEM is said to be CPA-secure if for all PPT adversary $\mathcal{A}$, $Adv_{KEM,\mathcal{A}}^{CPA}(k)$ is negligible.

2.2   Identity-Based Key Encapsulation Mechanisms (IB-KEM)

An identity-based key encapsulation mechanism (IB-KEM) is made up of four PPT algorithms $(KeyGen, KeyDer, IBEnc, IBDec)$ which are defined in the following

- $(msk, MPK) \leftarrow KeyGen(1^k)$: this algorithm takes the security parameter k as the input, returns the master key msk and master public key MPK.
- $d_{ID} \leftarrow KeyDer(msk, MPK, ID)$: this algorithm takes as inputs master key, master public key and the user's identity ID, outputs a private key d_{ID} corresponding to ID.
- $(C, K) \leftarrow IBEnc(MPK, ID)$: encryption algorithm takes as inputs master public key and the user's identity ID, outputs the session key $K \in \mathcal{K}$ and a ciphertext C with respect to the user's identity ID.
- $K \leftarrow IBDec(d_{ID}, C)$: decryption algorithm takes as inputs ciphertext C and the user's private key d_{ID}, outputs the session key K.

Definition 5 (CCA-secure IB-KEM). *For a PPT adversary $\mathcal{A}$, the security of IB-KEM against which is defined using the following security experiment*

$$\text{EXPERIMENT } Exp^{CCA}_{IB-KEM,\mathcal{A}}(k)$$

$$(msk, MPK) \leftarrow KeyGen(1^k)$$

$$(ID^*, state) \leftarrow \mathcal{A}^{\mathcal{O}_{KeyDer}(\cdot),\mathcal{O}_{Dec}(\cdot,\cdot)}(find, MPK)$$

$$(C^*, K_0) \leftarrow IBEnc(MPK, ID^*), K_1 \in_R \mathcal{K}$$

$$b \in_R \{0,1\}, b' \leftarrow \mathcal{A}^{\mathcal{O}_{KeyDer}(\cdot),\mathcal{O}_{Dec}(\cdot,\cdot)}(state, MPK, C^*, K_b)$$

$$If\ b = b'\ return\ 1; otherwise\ 0$$

where $\mathcal{O}_{Dec}(\cdot,\cdot)$ is the decryption oracle that on inputs $(ID, C) \neq (ID^*, C^*)$, outputs the session key with respect to ID, and $\mathcal{O}_{KeyDer}(\cdot)$ takes $ID \neq ID^*$ as the input returns the corresponding private key. The advantage of $\mathcal{A}$ is defined as $Adv^{CCA}_{IB-KEM,\mathcal{A}}(k) = |Pr[1 \leftarrow Exp^{CCA}_{IB-KEM,\mathcal{A}}(k)] - \frac{1}{2}|$. An IB-KEM is said to be CCA-secure if for all PPT adversary $\mathcal{A}$, $Adv^{CCA}_{IB-KEM,\mathcal{A}}(k)$ is negligible.

2.3   Improved Twisted PRF

In the conference of PKC 2012, Fujioka et al. [8] proposed a trick named twisted PRF to resist the exposure of ephemeral secret keys. However, they didn't use it rightly. Although, they use the correct form in the full version [11] on the ePrint; a formal definition wasn't presented by them. Untill recently, in the CT-RSA 2014 Kurosawa et al. [9] formulate the notion of twisted PRF (tPRF) and also carry on related proof. In the following, we will review the definition of tPRF formulated by Kurosawa et al.

Definition 6 (Improved tPRF [9]). *Let F be a function such that $F : \{0,1\}^{k_1} \times \{0,1\}^{k_2} \to \{0,1\}^{k_2}$, F is called tPRF if the following two conditions hold*

1. *For any polynomial time queries q, $[(x_1, F(K, x_1)), \ldots, (x_q, F(K, x_q))]$ is indistinguishable with $[(x_1, R_1), \ldots, (x_q, R_q)]$ where $K, x_1, \ldots, x_q, R_1, \ldots, R_q$ are selected randomly.*
2. *$[K, F(K, x)]$ is indistinguishable with $[K, R]$, where K, x, R are chosen randomly.*

3   Security Model

Since Bellare and Rogaway [12] proposed the first security model for AKE protocol, many security models are presented one after another. Two of the most famous among them are CK model proposed by Canetti and Krawczyk [7] in 2001 and eCK model by LaMacchia, Lauter and Mityagin [3] in 2007. Although eCK model covers key compromise impersonation attacks, MEX attacks and wPFS etc, it disallows the adversary to reveal the session state. Thus, eCK model is no stronger than CK model [13]. In 2012, Fujioka et al. [8] presented CK$^+$ model. Essentially, CK$^+$ model is based on eCK model but adds the query to the user's internal session state. Therefore, CK$^+$ model is one of the strongest security models.

In this section, we give a short review of the id-CK$^+$ model, for details the readers may refer to this paper [11] which is the full version of Fujioka et al. [8].

There are n users to participate in the protocol, and each user with an unique identifier ID_i(e.g. a binary string related to their actual name) is modeled as a probabilistic polynomial Turing machine(PPT). The user obtains the static private key corresponding to her/his identity from the KGC through a secure channel.

Session. An instance of a protocol is called a session which can be activated by an incoming message of the form (ID_i, ID_j) or (ID_i, ID_j, Y). If it's activated by the first form, then ID_i is called the *session initiator*, otherwise the *session responder*. A session can be uniquely identified by the *session identifier* with the form $sid = (ID_i, ID_j, X, Y)$ where X and Y are generated by ID_i and ID_j respectively. A session is called *completed* if it outputs the session key. We denote by $\Pi_{i,j}^s$ the sth session executed by the owner ID_i with intended peer ID_j.

Adversary. The PPT adversary owns the competence of controlling all the communications between users(e.g. intercept, modify, delay, inject its own messages, schedule sessions etc) except that between users and KGC. The adversary can capture the leakage of private information of users via the following queries

1. $Send(\Pi_{i,j}^s, m)$: The adversary sends a message m to the session $\Pi_{i,j}^s$ and obtains a response according to the description of the protocol.
2. $SessionKeyReveal(\Pi_{i,j}^s)$: The adversary learns the session key of $\Pi_{i,j}^s$ if it holds one.
3. $SessionStateReveal(\Pi_{i,j}^s)$: The adversary learns the session state related to the owner of $\Pi_{i,j}^s$ if it is uncompleted. Session state consists of all the ephemeral information and the intermediate results without being erased timely. But the static private key is not included in the session state.
4. $EphemeralKeyReveal(\Pi_{i,j}^s)$: The adversary learns the ephemeral secret key of $\Pi_{i,j}^s$. Exposure of ephemeral secret keys may happen if they are pre-computed or stored in insecure storage.
5. $Corrupt(ID_i)$: By this query, the adversary learns all the information of ID_i and controls ID_i completely. Users who are not revealed by this query are called *honest*, otherwise *dishonest*.
6. $MasterKeyReveal()$: The adversary learns the master key of KGC.
7. $Test(\Pi_{i,j}^s)$: On this query, the simulator flips a coin, and returns the session key of $\Pi_{i,j}^s$ to the adversary if it's 0, otherwise a random string under the distribution of the session key. This query can only be asked once. The goal of adversary is to distinguish the session key from a random string. If the adversary guesses the coin correctly and the test session is still *fresh*, then the adversary *wins*.

Definition 7 (Matching Session). *Let $\Pi_{i,j}^s$ be a completed session with $sid = (ID_i, ID_j, X, Y)$ where X, Y are the messages prepared by ID_i and ID_j respectively. $\Pi_{j,i}^t$ is called the **matching session** of $\Pi_{i,j}^s$ if it's completed and $sid = (ID_j, ID_i, X, Y)$. Similarly, $\Pi_{i,j}^s$ is the **matching session** of $\Pi_{j,i}^t$.*

Definition 8 (Freshness). *Let $\Pi_{i,j}^s$ be a completed session executed between two honest users ID_i and ID_j. Let $\Pi_{j,i}^t$ be the matching session of $\Pi_{i,j}^s$ if it exists. $\Pi_{i,j}^s$ is fresh if none of the following happens:*

1. *The adversary issues **SessionKeyReveal**($\Pi_{i,j}^s$ or $\Pi_{j,i}^t$) (if $\Pi_{j,i}^t$ exists)*
2. *$\Pi_{j,i}^t$ exists and the adversary issues **SessionStateReveal**($\Pi_{i,j}^s$) or **SessionStateReveal**($\Pi_{j,i}^t$)*
3. *$\Pi_{j,i}^t$ does not exist and the adversary issues **SessionStateReveal**($\Pi_{i,j}^s$)*

Definition 9 (id-CK$^+$ Security). *The advantage of the adversary $\mathcal{M}$ is defined as*

$$Adv_{\mathcal{M}}^{AKE}(k) = Pr[\mathcal{M}\,wins] - \frac{1}{2}$$

An AKE protocol is said to be secure if the following conditions hold:

1. *If two honest users complete matching sessions then they compute the same session key.*
2. *For all PPT adversary $\mathcal{M}$, $Adv_{\mathcal{M}}^{AKE}(k)$ in the following cases is negligible*
   (a) *The matching session of test session doesn't exist, and the adversary obtains the static private key of the test session owner.*
   (b) *The matching session of test session doesn't exist, and the adversary obtains the ephemeral private key of the test session.*
   (c) *The matching session of test session exists, and the adversary obtains the test session owner's static private key and its peer's ephemeral private key.*
   (d) *The matching session of test session exists, and the adversary obtains the test session owner's ephemeral private key and its peer's static private key.*
   (e) *The matching session of test session exists, and the adversary obtains static private keys of the test session owner and its peer.*
   (f) *The matching session of test session exists, and the adversary obtains ephemeral private keys of the test session owner and its peer.*
   (g) *The adversary obtains the master key of KGC.*

4 Our Construction

4.1 Design Principle

Our principle of construction is that achieving a strongly secure AKE protocol from KEM, and it should be used as few as possible. In order to resist the MEX attacks, we employ the improved twisted PRF (tPRF) [9]. In the MEX attack, the exposure of ephemeral keys is the most dangerous case, while tPRF trick guarantees that without getting the static private key and the ephemeral key of a user simultaneously, there is no way to get the value of tPRF provided it's erased immediately. To achieve wPFS, we use a CPA-secure KEM, but we don't use it alone, we combine tPRF trick with it,i.e. we replace the random string used in CPA-secure KEM with the value of tPRF. The merits of doing in this way are that we can not only achieve wPFS, but also at the same time protect the private key of CPA-secure KEM from being compromised.

However, it's not enough to use CPA-secure KEM and tPRF trick. Because the adversary can substitute the value of tPRF with a random value chosen by itself without being detected. Therefore, we employ CCA-secure IB-KEM and signature scheme additionally. We use one CCA-secure IB-KEM in our construction and CCA security is necessary. Because in the the process of simulation, there is a case that the challenge ciphertext C^* is embedded; in which case the static private key to decrypt C^* is unknown. However, in order to simulate the sessions owned by the same user(unknown static private key), the decryption oracle is needed. At last, without signature to the outgoing message the adversary can impersonate the session initiator to the responder.

4.2   Protocol Description

System Set Up. Let k be the security parameter. Let $F : \{0,1\}^{k_1} \times \{0,1\}^{k_2} \rightarrow \{0,1\}^{k_2}$ be a tPRF, $Exct : \mathcal{S} \times \mathcal{X} \rightarrow \mathcal{Y}$ be a strong randomness extractor and $G : \{0,1\}^* \times \mathcal{Y} \rightarrow \{0,1\}^k$ be a pseudorandom function. And IB-KEM= $(KeyGen, KeyDer, IBEnc, IBDec)$, KEM=$(Gen, Enc, Dec)$ and SIG=$(SigGen, Sign, Verify)$.

Static Private Key Derivation. The KGC first runs the algorithm $(msk, MPK) \leftarrow KeyGen(1^k)$ to get master public and secret key. For the user U with identifier ID_U, KGC chooses $s_U \in \{0,1\}^{k_1}$ randomly, then runs the algorithms $KeyDer$ and $SigGen$ to generate d_U and k_U respectively. The static private key of ID_U is (k_U, d_U, s_U).

Key Agreement. Let's assume that two users A and B with identifier ID_A and ID_B respectively want to establish a shared session key. Without loss of generality, supposing A is the session initiator and B the responder. The static private keys of A and B are (k_A, d_A, s_A) and (k_B, d_B, s_B) respectively.

Step1 : A chooses $r_A \in_R \{0,1\}^{k_2}$ and computes $R_A = F(s_A, r_A)$. Then, A runs $(epk, esk) \leftarrow Gen(1^k, R_A)$ and $(C_1, K_1) \leftarrow IBEnc(MPK, ID_B)$. Afterwards A sets $X = (ID_A, epk, C_1)$ and calculates the signature of which as $\sigma_X = Sign(k_A, X)$. At last, A sends (X, σ_X) to B.

Step2 : On receiving the communication from A, B verifies the signature σ_X; if it passes the verification, B chooses $r_B \in_R \{0,1\}^{k_2}$ and computes $R_B = F(s_B, r_B)$. Later, B runs $(C_2, K_2) \leftarrow Enc(epk, R_B)$ and sets $Y = (ID_B, C_2)$. After B computes the signature $\sigma_{YX} = Sign(k_B, (Y, X))$, B sends $((Y, X), \sigma_{YX})$ to A. Afterwards, B computes $K_1 \leftarrow IBDec(d_B, C_1)$, $K_2' = Exct(s, K_2)$ and $K_1' = Exct(s, K_1)$. Finally, B sets the session key as $K = G_{K_2'}(sid) \oplus G_{K_1'}(sid)$ where $sid = (X, Y, \sigma_X, \sigma_{YX})$.

Step3 : Similarly, after receiving the communication from B, A verifies the signature σ_{YX}; if the verification passes, A computes $K_2 \leftarrow Dec(esk, C_2)$, $K_1' = Exct(s, K_1)$ and $K_2' = Exct(s, K_2)$. At last, A sets $sid = (X, Y, \sigma_X, \sigma_{YX})$ and the session key $K = G_{K_2'}(sid) \oplus G_{K_1'}(sid)$.

Remark 1. At the side of user A, session state includes r_A and K_1. One thing to be noted is that esk is not counted as session state, whenever esk is needed, it's computed as $R_A \leftarrow F(s_A, r_A), (epk, esk) \leftarrow Gen(1^\lambda, R_A)$. After receiving the communication from B, other information computed for A can be erased as soon as the session key is calculated. while for B, r_B and K_2 are included in the session state.

A		B
(k_A, d_A, s_A)		(k_B, d_B, s_B)
$r_A \in_R \{0,1\}^{k_2}, R_A \leftarrow F(s_A, r_A)$		
$(epk, esk) \leftarrow Gen(1^\lambda, R_A)$		
$(C_1, K_1) \leftarrow IBEnc(MPK, ID_B)$		
$X \leftarrow (ID_A, epk, C_1)$		
$\sigma_X \leftarrow Sign(k_A, X)$		
	$\xrightarrow{X, \sigma_X}$	
		$Verify\ \sigma_X$
		$r_B \in_R \{0,1\}^{k_2}, R_B = F(s_B, r_B)$
		$(C_2, K_2) \leftarrow Enc(epk, R_B)$
		$Y \leftarrow (ID_B, C_2)$
		$\sigma_{YX} \leftarrow Sign(k_B, (Y, X))$
	$\xleftarrow{(Y,X), \sigma_{YX}}$	
$Verify\ \sigma_{YX}$		
$K_2 \leftarrow Dec(esk, C_2)$		$K_1 \leftarrow IBDec(d_B, C_1)$
$K_1' = Exct(s, K_1); K_2' = Exct(s, K_2)$		$K_2' = Exct(s, K_2); K_1' = Exct(s, K_1)$
$K = G_{K_1'}(sid) \oplus G_{K_2'}(sid)$		$K = G_{K_2'}(sid) \oplus G_{K_1'}(sid)$

Fig. 1. A Strongly Secure Key Exchange Protocol

5 Security Proof

In this section, we present a formal security proof of our construction in the id-CK$^+$ model.

Theorem 1. *If IB-KEM=(KeyGen, KeyDer, IBEnc, IBDec) is CCA-secure, KEM=(Gen, Enc, Dec) is CPA-secure, F is a tPRF, SIG=(SigGen, Sign, Verify) is unforgeable against chosen message attack, Exct is a strong randomness extractor and function G is pseudorandom; then our generic construction of two-pass AKE protocol is secure in the id-CK$^+$ model.*

PROOF. We assume that the adversary $\mathcal{M}$ activates at most $n(k)$ honest users and $s(k)$ sessions within each user where k is the security parameter. Let $\Pi_{i,j}^s$ be the test session and $\Pi_{j,i}^t$ be its matching session if it exists. Without loss of generality, we assume that the owner of $\Pi_{i,j}^s$ and its peer are A and B respectively. Let M be the event that the adversary $\mathcal{M}$ wins the distinguishing game. Considering the following two complementary cases

$E1$. the test session has no matching session.
$E2$. the test session has a matching session.

When the the test session has no matching session, this case can be divided into the following four sub-cases

$E1.1$. $E1$ occurs, user A is session initiator and the adversary obtains the static private key of A.

$E1.2$. $E1$ occurs, user A is session initiator and the adversary obtains the ephemeral private key of A.

$E1.3$. $E1$ occurs, user A is session responder and the adversary obtains the static private key of A.

$E1.4$. $E1$ occurs, user A is session responder and the adversary obtains the ephemeral private key of A.

5.1   Analysis of $E1.1$

Assuming that $M \wedge E1.1$ happens, in the following we will demonstrate via a series of game that the advantage of M in this case is negligible. Let S_i be the event that M wins the test game in $Gamei$. The advantage of M in $Gamei$ is defined as $Adv_i = Pr[S_i] - \frac{1}{2}$.

Game0. This game is the original game, thus the advantage of M in this game is identical to that in the real experiment. i.e.

$$Adv_0 = Adv_M^{AKE}(k)$$

Game1. This game is almost the same with $Game0$ except that two sessions output the same session identifier. This can be seen as chosing two numbers randomly from a random space such that they are equal, obviously this happens with negligible probability. i.e.

$$|Adv_0 - Adv_1| \leq negl$$

Game2. This game is the same with the previous one except that before attack, simulator selects s^{th} session of A. If M doesn't choose the sth session of A as the test session, then aborts. Since the probability that abortion doesn't happen is $\frac{1}{n(k)^2 s(k)}$, therefore

$$Adv_2 \geq \frac{Adv_1}{n(k)^2 s(k)}$$

Game3. $Game3$ is the same with $Game2$ except that the adversary forges signature of B to the outgoing message. However, without the static private key of B there is no way for M to forge due to the unforgeability of signature. Thus,

$$|Adv_3 - Adv_2| \leq negl$$

Game4. *Game*4 is the same with *Game*3 except that simulator substitutes $F(s_A, r_A)$ with a random value R. According to the definition of tPRF, $(s_A, F(s_A, r_A))$ and (s_A, R) are indistinguishable. As a result,

$$|Adv_4 - Adv_3| \leq negl$$

Game5. In this game, K_1 in $(C_1, K_1) \leftarrow IBEnc(MPK, ID_B)$ is replaced by a random value K^*. $C^* = C_1$ is challenge ciphertext. Next, we will construct a CCA adversary $\mathcal{M}'$ from $\mathcal{M}$, if $\mathcal{M}$ can distinguish *Game*4 from *Game*5; then $\mathcal{M}'$ can break CCA-security of IB-KEM.

Set up. The simulator chooses pseudorandom function G and strong randomnes extractor *Exct*. The simulator first runs the algorithm $(msk, MPK) \leftarrow KeyGen(1^k)$ to get master public and secret key. For the user except B, simulator chooses $s_{ID_i} \in \{0, 1\}^{k_1}$ randomly, then runs the algorithms $KeyDer$ and $SigGen$ to generate d_{ID_i} and k_{ID_i} respectively, at last it sets $(k_{ID_i}, d_{ID_i}, s_{ID_i})$ as the static private key for the user. For B, simulator only sets the static private key partially. Namely, the simulator only randomly selects $s_B \in \{0, 1\}^{k_1}$ and runs $SigGen$ to get k_B for B. It's worth noting that d_B is unknown. When we simulate sessions related to B, although we don't know the static private key of B completely. But there is not any obstacle to simulate these sessions. Because when B is the session initiator, d_B is not used; if B is session responder, with the help of decryption oracle the ciphertext it receives can be decrypted successfully(from here, we can see that CCA-security is needed). This can also be seen as a designing trick of our scheme reflected in the proof.

Given the challenge identity ID_B^* and challenge ciphertext C^* the simulation goes as follows

1. $Send(\Pi_{i,j}^s, role, m)$: the simulator $\mathcal{S}$ maintains an initially empty list SK^{list} which contains queries and answers of $SessionKeyReveal$.
   $role \in \{initiator, responder\}$, if $role = initiator$, this means the adversary impersonates the session initiator to send message m to session $\Pi_{i,j}^s$. Otherwise, if $role = responder$ the adversary impersonates the responder.
   - if $\Pi_{i,j}^s$ is the test session, in event $E1.1$, $role = responder$. The simulator $\mathcal{S}$ chooses K^* randomly from the key space of $IBEnc(\cdot, \cdot)$. Instead of $(C^* = C_1, K_1) \leftarrow IBEnc(MPK, ID_B^*)$, $\mathcal{S}$ substitutes K_1 with K^*. Then $\mathcal{S}$ computes $(epk, esk) \leftarrow Gen(1^\lambda, R)$ and $\sigma_X \leftarrow Sign(k_A, X)$ where $R \in_R \{0, 1\}^{k_2}$ and $X = (ID_A, epk, C^*)$. Afterwards, $\mathcal{S}$ sends (X, σ_X) to the adversary. Finally, $\mathcal{S}$ uses K^* and K_2 to compute session key and stores it in SK^{list}.
   - if $\Pi_{i,j}^s$ is not the test session, without loss of generality we assume $ID_j = ID_C$, the simulation is as follows
     - if $ID_i = ID_B$ and $role = initiator$, B can generate the outgoing message successfully. But in order to decrypt the received ciphertext, it has to query the decryption oracle $\mathcal{O}(d_B, \cdot)$. At last, B computes session key and inserts it into SK^{list}.

- if $ID_i = ID_B$ and $role = responder$, B can generate the outgoing message successfully even d_B is unknown. At last, B computes session key and stores it in SK^{list}.
- if $ID_i \neq ID_B$, $\mathcal{S}$ obeys the description of protocol.

2. $SessionKeyReveal(\Pi_{i,j}^s)$: the simulator returns the corresponding value in SK^{list} to the adversary.
3. $SessionStateReveal(\Pi_{i,j}^s)$: the simulator returns the ephemeral key and intermediate results of $\Pi_{i,j}^s$ to the adversary.
4. $Corrupt(ID_i)$: the simulator returns the static private key of ID_i and all state information.
5. $Test(\Pi_{i,j}^s)$: the simulator answers as the definition.

Analysis. If (C^*, K_1) is used, then the simulation is the same with $Game4$; otherwise the simulation is the same as $Game5$. if $\mathcal{M}$ can distinguish $Game4$ from $Game5$ then we can distinguish K_1 from K^*. However, IB-KEM is CCA secure; so it only happens with negligible probability. i.e.

$$|Adv_5 - Adv_4| \leq negl$$

Game6. In this game, we replace $Exct(s, K^*)$ with a random value K_R from $\mathcal{Y}$. By the definition of strong randomness extractor, $(s, Exct(s, K^*))$ and (s, K_R) are indistinguishable. Thus,

$$|Adv_6 - Adv_5| \leq negl$$

Game7. This game is the same with the previous one except that the computation of session key $K = G_{K_R}(sid) \oplus G_{K_2'}(sid)$ is changed as $K = x \oplus G_{K_2'}(sid)$ where $x \in_R \mathcal{Y}$. By the definition of pseudorandom function, the advantage of distinguishing $G_{K_R}(sid)$ from x is negligible. Therefore

$$|Adv_7 - Adv_6| \leq negl$$

Whatever the coin is in the test session, the adversary will always receive a truly random value in this game, so $Adv_7 = 0$.

Overall Analysis. Combining all these games, we can derive easily that the advantage of original game is negligible, that's to say $Pr[M \wedge E1.1]$ happens with negligible probability.

5.2   Analysis of $E1.2$

In this case, the simulation is almost the same with event $E1.1$. The difference is that in the $Game4$ of this occasion $[(r_1, F(s_1, r_1)), \ldots, (r_q, F(s_q, r_q))]$ is replaced by $[(r_1, R_1), \ldots, (r_q, R_q)]$ where q is the times of query. By the definition of tPRF $[(r_1, F(s_1, r_1)), \ldots, (r_q, F(s_q, r_q))]$ and $[(r_1, R_1), \ldots, (r_q, R_q)]$ are indistinguishable.

5.3 Analysis of $E1.3$

The simulation of this case is similar to that in event $E1.1$ except for $Game5$. Next, we will mainly sketch the simulation of $Game5$.

Game5. In this game, when computing $(C_1, K_1) \leftarrow Enc(epk, R_B)$, K_1 is replaced by a random value K^* from the key space of $Enc()$. $C^* = C_1$ and $epk^* = epk$ are called challenge ciphertext and public key respectively. The simulator chooses pseudorandom function G and strong randomnes extractor $Exct$. The simulator first runs the algorithm $(msk, MPK) \leftarrow KeyGen(1^k)$ to get master public and secret key. For all the users, simulator generates the static private keys for them obeying the protocol. Because $\mathcal{S}$ knows all users' static private keys, it's easy for it to simulate the whole procedure (due to the limited space, we leave it to readers).

5.4 Analysis of $E1.4$

In this case, $[(r_1, F(s_1, r_1)), \ldots, (r_q, F(s_q, r_q))]$ is replaced by $[(r_1, R_1), \ldots, (r_q, R_q)]$ where q is the times of query, apart from that the simulation is the same with event $E1.3$.

When the test session has a matching session i.e. $E2$ happens, this case can be analyzed similarly as event $E1$, due to the limited space we omit it here.

6 Performance Comparison

We compare our construction with some KEM-based protocols in terms of building blocks, total number of KEM, security model and whether the protocol has key control security or not. In the table, the number before CCA-KEM or CPA-KEM denotes the number of which is used in a protocol, KCS is short for key control security, Y stands for "Yes" and N is "No", PRF is pseudorandom function family, Exct refers to strong randomness extractor, tPRF denotes twisted PRF trick. We only distinguish CCA-KEM from CPA-KEM, i.e. CCA-secure IB-KEM is also denoted as CCA-KEM and we don't distinguish the improved tPRF from tPRF in the table[2].

Table 2. KEM-based Protocol Comprison

Protocol	Building Blocks	Total of KEM	Security Model	KCS
Boyd et al. [6]	2CCA-KEM,Exct,PRF	2	CK	Y
Fujioka et al. [8]	2CCA-KEM,1CPA-KEM, Exct,PRF,tPRF	3	CK^+	Y
Kurosawa et al. [9]	1CPA-KEM, signature, tPRF	1	CK	N
Our Construction	1CCA-KEM,1CPA-KEM, signature, Exct, PRF, tPRF	2	CK^+	Y

---

[2] No matter improved tPRF or tPRF, it achieves the same function, i.e. binding the ephemeral key with static key.

From the table above, we can see that our construction has the same total of KEM with the scheme of Boyd et al. [6]. However, as pointed out by Fujioka et al. [8], if the ephemeral key of both users are compromised in the scheme of Boyd et al. [6], then the adversary can compute the session key in other words the scheme of Boyd et al. [6] fails to achieve CK^+ security. Despite that this flaw in Boyd et al.'s construction can be fixed by arming with a Diffie-Hellman key exchange additionally, but in that case it's not generic anymore. From the viewpoint of security, both our construction and Fujioka et al. [8] are CK^+-secure. But the total of KEM in our scheme is lesser than that in Fujioka et al. [8]. Although the construction of Kurosawa et al. [9](we refer to the mainly one of their three constructions, i.e. 2-PASS-CK) has the minimal KEM in the table, but it doesn't achieve key control security and the exposure of secret key of KEM can lead to the reply attack.

Therefore, comparison shows that our generic construction achieves CK^+ security with the minimal KEM.

7   Conclusion

In this paper, we present a generic construction of two-pass key exchange protocol in the standard model. Our generic construction can be proved to be secure in the CK^+ model which is among the strongest security models. Comparison shows that our generic construction achieves strong(CK^+) security with the minimal KEM. Unfortunately, we find that the signature in our construction can not be removed, it's an interesting problem to construct a generic scheme without signature scheme in the strong security model(e.g. CK^+ model) by applying the minimal KEM.

Acknowledgments. The authors would like to thank the anonymous referees for their helpful comments. This work is supported by the National Natural Science Foundation of China (Nos. 61309016,61379150,61201220), Post-doctoral Science Foundation of China (No. 2014M562493), Post-doctoral Science Foundation of Shanxi Province and Key Scientific and Technological Project of Henan Province(No. 122102210126).

References

[1] Law, L., et al.: An efficient protocol for authenticated key agreement. Designs, Codes and Cryptography 28(2), 119–134 (2003)

[2] Krawczyk, H.: HMQV: A high-performance secure diffie-hellman protocol. In: Shoup, V. (ed.) CRYPTO 2005. LNCS, vol. 3621, pp. 546–566. Springer, Heidelberg (2005)

[3] LaMacchia, B.A., Lauter, K., Mityagin, A.: Stronger security of authenticated key exchange. In: Susilo, W., Liu, J.K., Mu, Y. (eds.) ProvSec 2007. LNCS, vol. 4784, pp. 1–16. Springer, Heidelberg (2007)

[4] Ustaoglu, B.: Obtaining a secure and efficient key agreement protocol from (H) MQV and NAXOS. Designs, Codes and Cryptography 46(3), 329–342 (2008)

[5] Dent, A.W.: Adapting the weaknesses of the random oracle model to the generic group model. In: Zheng, Y. (ed.) ASIACRYPT 2002. LNCS, vol. 2501, pp. 100–109. Springer, Heidelberg (2002)

[6] Boyd, C., Cliff, Y., Gonzalez Nieto, J.M., Paterson, K.G.: Efficient One-Round Key Exchange in the Standard Model. In: Mu, Y., Susilo, W., Seberry, J. (eds.) ACISP 2008. LNCS, vol. 5107, pp. 69–83. Springer, Heidelberg (2008)

[7] Canetti, R., Krawczyk, H.: Analysis of Key-Exchange Protocols and Their Use for Building Secure Channels. In: Pfitzmann, B. (ed.) EUROCRYPT 2001. LNCS, vol. 2045, pp. 453–474. Springer, Heidelberg (2001)

[8] Fujioka, A., Suzuki, K., Xagawa, K., Yoneyama, K.: Strongly secure authenticated key exchange from factoring, codes, and lattices. In: Fischlin, M., Buchmann, J., Manulis, M. (eds.) PKC 2012. LNCS, vol. 7293, pp. 467–484. Springer, Heidelberg (2012)

[9] Kurosawa, K., Furukawa, J.: 2-Pass Key Exchange Protocols from CPA-Secure KEM. In: Benaloh, J. (ed.) CT-RSA 2014. LNCS, vol. 8366, pp. 385–401. Springer, Heidelberg (2014)

[10] Kurosawa, K., Phong, L.T.: Kurosawa-Desmedt Key Encapsulation Mechanism, Revisited. In: IACR Cryptology ePrint Archive 2013, p. 765 (2013), http://eprint.iacr.org/2013/765

[11] Fujioka, A., et al.: Strongly Secure Authenticated Key Exchange from Factoring, Codes, and Lattices. In: IACR Cryptology ePrint Archive 2012, p. 211 (2012), http://eprint.iacr.org/2012/211

[12] Bellare, M., Rogaway, P.: Entity authentication and key distribution. In: Stinson, D.R. (ed.) CRYPTO 1993. LNCS, vol. 773, pp. 232–249. Springer, Heidelberg (1994)

[13] Cremers, C.J.: Formally and Practically Relating the CK, CK-HMQV, and eCK Security Models for Authenticated Key Exchange. In: IACR Cryptology ePrint Archive, p. 253 (2009)

sHMQV: An Efficient Key Exchange Protocol for Power-Limited Devices

Shijun Zhao and Qianying Zhang

Institute of Software Chinese Academy of Sciences,
ISCAS, Beijing, China
{zqyzsj,zsjzqy}@gmail.com

Abstract. In this paper we focus on designing authenticated key exchange protocols for practical scenarios where the party consists of a powerful but untrusted host (e.g., PC, mobile phone, etc) and a power-limited but trusted device (e.g., Trusted Platform Module, Mobile Trusted Module, Smart Card, etc). HMQV and (s,r)OAKE[1] protocols are the state-of-the-art in the integrity of security and efficiency. However, we find that they are not suitable for the above scenarios as all (or part) of the online exponentiation computations must be performed in the power-limited trusted devices, which makes them inefficient for the deployment in practice.

To overcome the above inefficiency, we propose a variant of HMQV protocol, denoted sHMQV, under some new design rationales which bring the following advantages: 1) eliminating the validation of the ephemeral public keys, which costs one exponentiation; 2) the power-limited trusted device only performs one exponentiation, which can be pre-computed offline; 3) all the online exponentiation computations can be performed in the powerful host. The above advantages make sHMQV enjoy better performance than HMQV and (s,r)OAKE, especially when deployed in the scenarios considered in this paper. We finally formally prove the security of sHMQV in the CK model.

Keywords: Authenticated Key Exchange, CK model, Security Analysis, Power-limited Devices.

1 Introduction

The authenticated key exchange (AKE) protocols aim to establish a shared secret session key between two parties via the public insecure communication while providing identity authentication. Based on the way they are authenticated, the AKE protocols can be categorized as the explicitly authenticated or the implicitly authenticated. The explicitly authenticated key exchange protocols use digital signatures or additional authenticating message flows to provide authentication and prevent replay attacks, and the typical protocol is SIGMA [4]. The

---

[1] Yao et al. give two versions of the OAKE protocol family [28,29], which use different terminologies to denote the protocol. In this paper, we adopt the terminologies of the full version [28], i.e., (s,r)OAKE.

© Springer International Publishing Switzerland 2015
J. Lopez and Y. Wu (Eds.): ISPEC 2015, LNCS 9065, pp. 154–167, 2015.
DOI: 10.1007/978-3-319-17533-1_11

implicitly authenticated key exchange protocols were first put forth by Matsumoto [18] which need only the basic Diffie-Hellman exchanges [7], yet they provide authentication by combining the ephemeral keys and long-term keys in the derivation of the session key. Due to the efficiency in both communication and computation, the implicitly authenticated key exchange protocols are widely studied and many protocols are proposed [20,23,17,11,13,16,15,26,8,27,5,6,28,29].

For authenticated key exchange protocols, it's a basic requirement to achieve the basic security property defined by security models for key exchange, such as the CK [3] or the eCK model [15]. Besides, it's desirable to achieve the following security properties: (1) the key-compromise impersonation (KCI) resistance property; that is, the knowledge of a party's long-term private key doesn't allow the adversary to impersonate *other, uncorrupted, parties* to the party; and (2) the Perfect Forward Secrecy (PFS) property; that is, the expired session keys established before the compromise of the long-term key cannot be recovered.

1.1 Motivation

We first introduce some preliminaries used in the protocols which will be described below. Let G' be a finite Abelian group of order N, $G \subseteq G'$ be a subgroup of prime order q. Denote by g a generator of G, by 1_G the identity element, by $G\backslash 1_G = G - \{1_G\}$ the set of elements of G except 1_G and by $h = N/q$ the cofactor. The party having A as its public key will be denoted by $\hat{A}$.

Up to now, many works have been done to design secure and efficient implicitly authenticated key exchange protocols. The MQV protocol was once the most efficient and most standardized [1,2,9,10,21]. Krawczyk gave a thorough analysis of MQV and found some weaknesses, then proposed a hashed variant of MQV, i.e., HMQV, which is seen as the milestone of the development of the implicitly

$\hat{A} : (a, g^a)$		$\hat{B} : (b, g^b)$
$X = g^x$	$\xrightarrow{\qquad\qquad X \qquad\qquad}$	$Y = g^y$
	$\xleftarrow{\qquad\qquad Y \qquad\qquad}$	

$$Z_A = (YB^e)^{s_A}, Z_B = (XA^d)^{s_B}, s_A = x + da, s_B = y + eb, K = H_2(Z_A) = H_2(Z_B)$$

MQV: $d = 2^l + (X \bmod 2^l), e = 2^l + (Y \bmod 2^l), l = |q|/2$

HMQV: $d = H_1(X, \hat{B}), e = H_1(Y, \hat{A}), l = |q|/2$

sHMQV: $d = H_1(X, \hat{B}, Y), e = H_1(Y, \hat{A}, X), l = |q|/2$

$$Z_A = B^{fa+dx}Y^{ca+ex}, Z_B = A^{fb+cy}X^{db+ey}, K = H_2(Z_A) = H_2(Z_B)$$

OAKE: $c = H_1(\hat{A}, A, Y), d = H_1(\hat{B}, B, X), e = H_1(X, Y), f = 0, l \approx q$

sOAKE: $c = d = 1, e = H_1(\hat{A}, A, \hat{B}, B, X, Y), f = 0, l \approx q$

rOAKE: $c = H_1(\hat{A}, A, Y), d = H_1(\hat{B}, B, X), e = H_1(X, Y), f = 1, l \approx q$

Fig. 1. (H)MQV, sHMQV, and (s,r)OAKE protocols

authenticated key exchange protocols because of its efficiency and the first formal analysis of such protocols. The MQV and HMQV protocols are described in Figure 1, where H_2 (resp., H_1) is a hash function of k-bit (resp., l-bit) output and l is set to be $|q|/2$.

Yao et al. [28] consider the deployment of key exchange protocols with power-limited devices, and find that HMQV has some disadvantages in such practical contexts. First, the protocol structure of HMQV makes it not support offline pre-computing parts of the shared DH-secret (Z_A or Z_B). Second, all the online computation of the shared DH-secret must be performed in the power-limited trusted devices. As the computing power of the trusted devices might be quite limited, for example, the Trusted Platform Module (TPM) 1.2 chip only operates at 33M Hz, the disadvantages of HMQV greatly limit its deployment in such scenarios.

In order to solve the disadvantages of HMQV and provide an efficient key exchange protocol for power-limited devices, Yao et al. proposed the (s,r)OAKE protocol family [28] under new design rationales. The protocol structure of (s,r)OAKE allows the value B^{fa+dx} (resp., A^{fb+cy}) can be offline pre-computed by party $\hat{A}$ (resp., $\hat{B}$), so the online computational complexity can be only one exponentiation, i.e., Y^{ca+ex} (resp., X^{db+ey}), at each party. So it seems that (s,r)OAKE achieves the online optimal efficiency for implicitly authenticated key exchange protocols.

Just as Yao et al. said, "due to the state-of-the-art nature and highly intensive study of (H)MQV, even slight efficiency improvement can be challenging", and it becomes more challenging after (s,r)OAKE improving the online efficiency of HMQV. However, we find that (s,r)OAKE still leaves some space to improve the efficiency.

1. Both HMQV and (s,r)OAKE only consider the case where the cofactor h is small. In this case, the validation of the ephemeral public key X (resp., Y) can be reduced significantly by the embedded public-key validation technology [17], i.e., require only that $\hat{B}$ (resp., $\hat{A}$) verify that $X \in G'$ (resp., $Y \in G'$) and that $Z_B^h \neq 1_G$ (resp., $Z_A^h \neq 1_G$) before computing the session key. However, if h is large, the validation of the ephemeral public key must be performed explicitly, i.e., verify $X^q = 1_G$ that costs one exponentiation, or the protocol would be vulnerable to small subgroup attacks [19] that let an attacker recover a victim's static private key. As the validation of the ephemeral public key must be performed online, it breaks the optimal online efficiency of (s,r)OAKE.

2. The trusted device still needs to perform one expensive exponentiation online. As the computing power of the trusted device might be quite limited, such as the TPM 1.2 chip, one exponentiation computation can cause a big decrease in the total efficiency. Yao et al. proposed an efficient deployment by adopting the split mechanism proposed by Kunz-Jacques and Pointcheval [14]. Here we only show the split of the online computation of (s,r)OAKE, and please consult [28] for the split of the whole protocol. With the computation of $\hat{B}$ as an example, the trusted device computes $s_B = db + ey$ and forwards

s_B to the powerful computing host, which computes $Z_B = A^{fb+cy}X^{s_B}$ and the session key. Although the split mechanism indeed improves the efficiency in practice, this deployment isn't in accordance with the formal security analysis of (s,r)OAKE: in the security analysis, the session state that is allowed to be exposed to the adversary is (y, Y, A^{cy}) but not s_B. So the security of (s,r)OAKE needs to be carefully and formally analyzed in such deployment.

The above disadvantages of HMQV and (s,r)OAKE make it inefficient for the scenario considered in this paper, i.e., the party consists of a power-limited trusted device and a powerful untrusted computing host. This leads to our motivations in the following:

1. Can we design a new protocol which doesn't need the validation of ephemeral public keys no matter how big the cofactor is, which can improve the total efficiency of the protocol by one exponentiation?
2. Can we leave all the expensive online exponentiation computations to the powerful host, which can greatly improve the online efficiency for deployment with power-limited devices in untrusted computing environment?

1.2   Our Contributions

In this paper, we propose a variant of HMQV, denoted sHMQV (the s stands for schnorr), which solves the above disadvantages of HMQV and (s,r)OAKE and thus provides good performance in both total and online computational complexity. We provide detailed comparisons in Section 4.2.

1. We provide a new design rationale for key exchange protocols which eliminates the validation of the public ephemeral keys no matter how big the cofactor is: protecting the ephemeral private keys in trusted devices and designing unforgeable interfaces for trusted devices. Another advantage of our design rationale is that we formally analyze that the adversary cannot mount small subgroup attacks if public ephemeral key validation is omitted.
2. Benefited from the new design rationale, sHMQV enjoys the best total efficiency of Diffie-Hellman based key exchange protocols: 2.5 exponentiations per party no matter the cofactor is small or big. Note that if the cofactor is big, the total efficiency of HMQV is 3.5 exponentiations, and (s,r)OAKE is 4 exponentiations.
3. The trusted device performs only one exponentiation which can be offline pre-computed, and all the 1.5 online exponentiations can be performed by the powerful host. This feature makes it more desirable for being deployed with power-limited devices in untrusted powerful computing environment.

1.3   Organization

The paper is organized as follows. Section 2 outlines the CK model on which all of our analysis is based. Section 3 describes details of the interfaces of the trusted device for sHMQV, formally proves the resistance to small subgroup attacks even if the validation of the ephemeral public keys is omitted, and then describes the details of the sHMQV protocol. Section 4 introduces the design rationales of sHMQV, and compares sHMQV with related protocols in details. Section 5 formally proves sHMQV, and resistant to KCI attacks and achieves the weak PFS property in the CK model. Section 6 concludes this work and gives our future work.

2   Security Model for AKE

We outline the CK model [3] for AKE protocols, and formally describe the attacker model which models the capabilities of the adversary by some queries.

In the CK model, AKE runs in a network of interconnected parties and each party has a long-term key and a certificate (issued by a certification authority (CA)) that binds the public key to the identity of that party. A party can be activated to run an instance of the protocol called a session. Within a session a party can be activated to initiate the session or to respond to an incoming message. As a result of these activations, the party creates and maintains a session state, generates outgoing messages, and eventually completes the session by outputting a session key and erasing the session state. A session can be associated with its holder or owner (the party at which the session exists), a peer (the party with which the session key is intended to be established), and a session identifier. The session identifier is a quadruple $(\hat{A}, \hat{B}, out, in)$ where $\hat{A}$ is the identity of the owner of the session, $\hat{B}$ the peer, out the outgoing messages from $\hat{A}$ in the session, and in the incoming messages from $\hat{B}$. In the case of the implicitly authenticated key exchange protocols, such as (s,r)OAKE and our sHMQV, this results in an identifier of the form $(\hat{A}, \hat{B}, X, Y)$ where X is the outgoing DH value and Y the incoming DH value. The session $(\hat{B}, \hat{A}, Y, X)$ (if it exists) is said to be **matching** to session $(\hat{A}, \hat{B}, X, Y)$.

2.1   Attack Model

The AKE experiment involves multiple honest parties and an adversary $\mathcal{M}$ connected via an unauthenticated network. The adversary is modeled as a probabilistic Turing machine and has full control of the communications between parties. $\mathcal{M}$ can intercept and modify messages sent over the network. $\mathcal{M}$ also schedules all session activations and session-message delivery. In addition, in order to model potential disclosure of secret information, the adversary is allowed to access secret information via the following queries:

- **SessionStateReveal(s)**: $\mathcal{M}$ queries directly at session s while still incomplete and learns the session state for s. In our analysis, the session state includes the values returned by interfaces of the trusted device and the intermediate information stored and computed in the host.
- **SessionKeyReveal(s)**: $\mathcal{M}$ obtains the session key for the session s.
- **Corruption($\hat{P}$)**: This query allows $\mathcal{M}$ to learn the long-term private key of the party $\hat{P}$.

– **Test(s)**: This query may be asked only once throughout the game. Pick $b \xleftarrow{R} 0, 1$. If $b = 1$, provide $\mathcal{M}$ the session key; otherwise provide $\mathcal{M}$ with a value r randomly chosen from the probability distribution of session keys. This query can only be issued to a session that is "clean". A completed session is "clean" if this session as well as its matching session (if it exists) is not subject to any of the first 3 queries above. A session is called *exposed* if $\mathcal{M}$ performs any one of the first 3 queries to this or the maching session.

The security is defined based on a game played by $\mathcal{M}$, in which $\mathcal{M}$ is allowed to activate sessions and perform Corruption, SessionStateReveal and Session-KeyReveal queries. At some time, $\mathcal{M}$ performs the Test query to a clean session of its choice and gets the value returned by Test. After that, $\mathcal{M}$ continues the experiment, but is not allowed to expose the test session nor any parties involved in the test session. Eventually $\mathcal{M}$ outputs a bit b' as its guess, then halts. $\mathcal{M}$ wins the game if $b' = b$. The adversary with the above capabilities is called a **KE-adversary**. The formal definition of security follows.

Definition 1. *An AKE protocol Π is called secure if the following properties hold for any KE-adversary $\mathcal{M}$ defined above:*

1. *When two uncorrupted parties complete matching sessions, they output the same session key, and*
2. *The probability that $\mathcal{M}$ guesses the bit b (i.e., outputs $b' = b$) from the Test query correctly is no more than $1/2$ plus a negligible fraction.*

3 Interfaces and Protocol Design

We introduce the interfaces of the trusted device which are a building block for the sHMQV protocol, and formally prove the unforgeability of the interfaces, then we formally prove that any protocols built on our interfaces can resist to small subgroup attacks. At last, we describe the details of the sHMQV protocol.

3.1 Interfaces Design and the Resistance to Small Subgroup Attacks

The trusted device stores the long-term private key of its owner, and it provides its owner two functionalities through the interfaces: 1) generating an ephemeral key, and 2) generating a Schnorr signature based on the long-term key and the ephemeral key. Figure 2 depicts the interfaces, and we give a detailed description in the following.

1. When party $\hat{A}$ wishes to establish a session key with party $\hat{B}$, its host calls the interface of its trusted device to get an ephemeral public key $X = g^x$. The ephemeral private key x is stored in the trusted device, and the public key X will be sent to $\hat{B}$.

2. After receiving the ephemeral key Y from party $\hat{B}$, $\hat{A}$ transmits $(\hat{B}, Y)$ to its trusted device through the interface, and the trusted device will perform the following steps:

   (a) Compute $d = H_1(X, \hat{B}, Y)$ and $s = x + da$ where H_1 is a hash function. d is of length $|q|/2$ where $|q|$ is the bit length of the group order.

   (b) Delete x, then return s to $\hat{A}$.

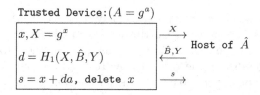

Fig. 2. The interfaces of Trusted Device

The two functionalities provided by the trusted device are actually a whole Schnorr signature (X, s) signed by the long-term key A on message $(\hat{B}, Y)$. The unforgeability of the interfaces of the trusted devices means that the adversary cannot create a legal interfaces return result which is not returned by the interfaces ever by invoking the interfaces of the trusted device at will. As it has been proven that the Schnorr signature is unforgeable against adaptive chosen message attacks in the random oracle model [22], we directly get Theorem 1. The unforgeability is based on the discrete logarithms (DL) assumption, which is explained in Appendix A.

Theorem 1. *The interfaces described above are unforgeable against adaptively chosen message attacks under the DL assumption.*

We then use the unforgeability of the interfaces to show that no adversary can successfully mount small subgroup attacks no matter whether the input ephemeral public key is validated.

Lemma 1. *If the interfaces of the trusted device are unforgeable, then the adversary cannot mount small subgroup attacks on protocols built on the interfaces.*

Proof. This lemma can be easily proved using proof by contradiction. Suppose the adversary successfully mount a small subgroup attack on some protocol, thus he obtains the long-term private key a of some party $\hat{A}$. After the adversary has obtained the long-term private key, he first computes an ephemeral key pairs $(x', X' = g^{x'})$, then computes $s' = x' + d'a$ where $d' = H_1(X', \hat{B}, Y)$. We can see that (X', s') is a legal interfaces return result on message $(\hat{B}, Y)$ forged by the adversary. This contradicts the unforgeability of the interfaces.   □

Lemma 1 shows that no matter how an attacker chooses Y, for example, Y is an element of some group with small order, he cannot learn the private key a of party $\hat{A}$.

3.2 The sHMQV Protocol

Figure 3 gives an informal description of sHMQV, and the computation performed by the trusted device is boxed by rectangles.

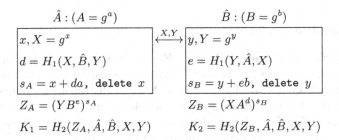

$$\hat{A} : (A = g^a) \qquad\qquad \hat{B} : (B = g^b)$$

$$
\begin{array}{ll}
x, X = g^x & y, Y = g^y \\
d = H_1(X, \hat{B}, Y) & e = H_1(Y, \hat{A}, X) \\
s_A = x + da,\ \texttt{delete}\ x & s_B = y + eb,\ \texttt{delete}\ y
\end{array}
$$

$$
\begin{array}{ll}
Z_A = (YB^e)^{s_A} & Z_B = (XA^d)^{s_B} \\
K_1 = H_2(Z_A, \hat{A}, \hat{B}, X, Y) & K_2 = H_2(Z_B, \hat{A}, \hat{B}, X, Y)
\end{array}
$$

Fig. 3. The sHMQV Protocol

We formally describe the sHMQV protocol by giving the following three session activations.

1. Initiate($\hat{A}, \hat{B}$): $\hat{A}$ calls the interface of its trusted device to generate an ephemeral key X, creates a local session of the protocol which it identifies as (the incomplete) session $(\hat{A}, \hat{B}, X)$, and outputs X as its outgoing message.
2. Respond($\hat{B}, \hat{A}, X$): After receiving X, $\hat{B}$ performs the following steps:
   (a) Verify that X is non-zero elements in the finite group (or points in a given elliptic curve).
   (b) Call the interface of its trusted device to get an ephemeral key Y, output Y as its outgoing message.
   (c) Transmit $(\hat{A}, X)$ to its trusted device and get $s_B = y + eb$ through the interface where y is the private part of Y and $e = H_1(Y, \hat{A}, X)$.
   (d) Compute $Z_B = (XA^d)^{s_B}$ where $d = H_1(X, \hat{B}, Y)$.
   (e) Compute the session key $K_2 = H_2(Z_B, \hat{A}, \hat{B}, X, Y)$ and complete the session with identifier $(\hat{B}, \hat{A}, Y, X)$
3. Complete($\hat{A}, \hat{B}, X, Y$): $\hat{A}$ checks that it has an open session with identifier $(\hat{A}, \hat{B}, X)$, then performs the following steps:
   (a) Verify that Y is non-zero elements in the finite group (or points in a given elliptic curve).
   (b) Transmit $(\hat{B}, Y)$ to its trusted device and get $s_A = x + da$ through the interface where x is the private part of X and $d = H_1(X, \hat{B}, Y)$.
   (c) Compute $Z_A = (YB^e)^{s_A}$.
   (d) Compute the session key $K_1 = H_2(Z_A, \hat{A}, \hat{B}, X, Y)$ and complete the session with identifier $(\hat{A}, \hat{B}, X, Y)$.

As d and e are of length $|q|/2$, B^e or A^d counts as "half exponentiation". Hence, the total computation of sHMQV is 2.5 exponentiations.

4   Design Rationales and Comparisons

We first describe the design rationales of sHMQV, then we make detailed comparisons between sHMQV, HMQV, (s,r)OAKE and the key exchange primitives in TPM 2.0 version [24].

4.1   Design Rationales

Protecting the Ephemeral Private Keys. As Menezes [19] has shown that if the ephemeral private key is allowed to be exposed to the adversary in the session state query, key exchange protocols are vulnerable to small subgroup attacks, which allow the adversary to recover long-term private keys. So in our design of sHMQV, the ephemeral keys are generated by the trusted devices and the ephemeral private keys are protected in the trusted device. The design of (s,r)OAKE allows the exposure of ephemeral keys as they think that "the offline pre-computed and stored DH-components are less protected in practice". However, it's practical to generate and protect ephemeral keys using a hardware crypto token. Take TPM 2.0 for example, it designs an efficient way to generate ephemeral keys with the following features:

- have the number of bits equal to the security strength of the signing key;
- not be known outside of the TPM; and
- only be used once.

Users can invoke the TPM2_EC_Ephemeral() [25] command to generate an ephemeral key. Note that the above features satisfy all the properties needed by sHMQV, so protecting the ephemeral private keys by trusted devices is practical.

Design Unforgeable Interfaces for Trusted Devices. Although protecting the ephemeral keys can resist small subgroup attacks to some extent, we cannot guarantee the resistance in a formal way. Then we provide a way to formally analyze the resistance to small group attacks. First, design unforgeable interfaces for trusted devices. Then use the proof by contradiction to formally prove the resistance to the small subgroup attacks. For more details, please see section 3.1.

Omitting Public Key Validation. Due to the above two design rationales, it's safe to omit the validation of the public keys in sHMQV, which can improve the total and online efficiency by one exponentiation.

Using Schnorr Signature. We choose the Schnorr signature as the functionality of the interfaces for two reasons: (1) it's computation ($s = x + da$) is negligible compared to the exponentiation computation, and it only costs one exponentiation if the ephemeral public key generation is considered as part of the signature, and (2) it is unforgeable and this feature is important for the security of sHMQV.

Hashing the Incoming Message. In HMQV, $d = H_1(X, \hat{B})$ and $e = H_1(Y, \hat{A})$. In sHMQV, the incoming message is included in the hash, i.e., $d = H_1(X, \hat{B}, Y)$ and $e = H_1(Y, \hat{A}, X)$. We show that if the incoming message is not included in the hash, sHMQV would be insecure. The adversary exposes one session, such as $(\hat{A}, \hat{B}, X, Y)$, and gets the Schnorr signature $s_A = x + da$ where $d = H_1(X, \hat{B})$. Then the adversary can always replay the message X to $\hat{B}$, and obtain the session key of $\hat{B}$ by computing $H_2(Z, \hat{A}, \hat{B}, X, Y')$ where $Z = (Y'B^e)^{s_A}$ and Y' is the ephemeral key generated by $\hat{B}$. Including the incoming message in computing d and e can resist to replay attacks. The resistance to replay attacks makes sHMQV secure even if the adversary gets the Schnorr signature, and that's why sHMQV can be deployed in such a way that the trusted device only computes the Schnorr signature and the host computes the expensive exponentiation computations while HMQV cannot. It seems that (s,r)OAKE protocol can also be deployed in such a way. However, their security analysis isn't in accordance with such deployment. We leave the formal analysis which allows the adversary to obtain $s_A = ca + ex$ and $s_B = db + ey$ as a future work.

Session Key Derivation. We include the identities in the key derivation to prevent the unknown key share (UKS) attacks [12]. Moreover, we include the session identifier in the session key derivation to simplify the argument that different sessions have different session keys in our proof.

Table 1. Protocols Comparisons

		sHMQV	HMQV	(s)OAKE	rOAKE	MQV	SM2²
Total efficiency with (without) public key validation		2.5(2.5)	3.5(2.5)	4(3)	4(3)	3.5(2.5)	2.5(2.5)
Online efficiency with public key validation	Trusted	0	1.5	1	1	-	1.5
	Host	1.5	1	1	1	-	1
	Total	1.5	2.5	2	2	-	2.5
Online efficiency without public key validation	Trusted	0	1.5	1	1	-	1.5
	Host	1.5	0	0	0	-	0
	Total	1.5	1.5	1	1	-	1.5
Allowed secrecy exposure		(s_B, Y, Z_B)	(y, Y)	(y, Y, A^{cy})	(y, Y)	-	(y, Y, Z_B)
Assumption		GDH	GDH, KEA	GDH, KEA	GDH	-	-
Require public key validation		No	Yes	Yes	Yes	Yes	No³
Require POP by CA		No	No	No	No	Yes	No

4.2 Comparisons

We first make comparisons between sHMQV and the state-of-the-art protocols, i.e., HMQV, and (s,r)OAKE. We also make comparisons with the key exchange protocols implemented in TPM 2.0, i.e., the MQV and SM2 key exchange protocols [27]. The comparisons show that sHMQV is particular suitable for scenarios

---

² Here we refer to a patched SM2 key exchange protocol which is briefly analyzed by Xu [27].

³ The SM2 key exchange protocol doesn't require public key validation is not because of the good design of the protocol but the restriction that it can only be used in elliptic curve groups whose cofactor is small.

where a party consists of a power-limited trusted device and a powerful computing host.

Our comparisons are summarized in Table 1. The numbers denote the exponentiations. For the item of "Assumptions", the GDH and KEA stand for the Gap Decisional Diffie-Hellman and Knowledge-of-Exponent assumptions respectively.

For total efficiency, we count all the exponentiation computations per party. The numbers in parentheses is the exponentiations in the case that public key validation is not required. For online efficiency, the Trusted row counts the exponentiations performed in trusted device, the Host row counts the exponentiations performed in host, and the Total row counts the online exponentiations in total. We count online efficiency in the two cases that whether public key validation is required. The item of "Allowed secrecy exposure" refers to the information that can be exposed to the adversary. The item of "Assumption" refers to the cryptographic assumptions used in the proof. The item of "Require public key validation" refers to whether the protocol needs to validate the ephemeral public keys. The item of "Require POP by CA" refers to whether the proof of possession (POP) of private key is required by the CA. To the best of our knowledge, no work has been done for the provable security of MQV, so we use the symbol "-" for the items that haven't been decided yet. Xu only gives a brief analysis of a patched SM2 key exchange protocol in [27], so the assumption of SM2 key exchange is unknown.

From Table 1, we can conclude that:

1. sHMQV enjoys the best performance no matter whether the public key validation is required or not.
2. sHMQV doesn't require trusted devices to perform any exponentiation computations, which makes it particular suitable for such applications that using TPMs to store keys. Even in general scenarios which don't consider the split of computation, sHMQV still performs very well: if public key validation is required, it enjoys the best online performance; if public validation isn't required, its online efficiency equals HMQV and is only 0.5 exponentiations more than (s,r)OAKE.
3. MQV is unpractical as the proof of possession of private key is required by the CA during public key registration.
4. Since the MQV and SM2 key exchange protocols have been adopted by the TPM 2.0 specification, which might be widely used in practice, their formal analysis work should be done as soon as possible.

5   Proof of the Protocol

In this section we analyze the security of sHMQV in the CK model. We show that it can achieve the basic security property in CK model, the weak PFS property and the resistance to KCI attacks. The security of sHMQV is based on the CDH (Computational Diffie-Hellman) and GDH (Gap Diffie-Hellman) assumptions, which are explained in Appendix A.

Session State. In order to simulate the protection of the ephemeral keys, we specify that a session state stores the results returned by the trusted devices and the information stored in the host, i.e., the Schnorr signature s and the shared secret Z before hashing.

Theorem 2. *Under the GDH assumption, the sHMQV protocol, with hash functions H_1 and H_2 modeled as random oracles, is a secure key exchange protocol and achieves the properties of weak PFS and resistance to the KCI attacks in the CK model.*

Due to the space limitation, we give the complete proof of theorem 2 in the full version [30].

6   Conclusions and Future Work

In this paper, we propose new design rationales for implicitly authenticated key exchange protocols, which can eliminate the public key validation and design protocols particular suitable for scenarios where the party consists of a power-limited trusted device and a powerful but untrusted computing host. Based on the new design rationales, we propose the sHMQV protocol, which performs the best total efficiency compared to the state-of-the-art protocols and leaves all the online exponentiation computations to the host.

As we have mentioned above, it seems that our design rationales can apply to the (s,r)OAKE protocol, so it's interesting to formally analyze (s,r)OAKE under our design rationales. Another work that should to be done is the security analysis of the MQV and SM2 key exchange protocols, which have been adopted by the TPM 2.0 specification.

References

1. American National Standard (ANSI) X9.42-2001. Public Key Cryptography for the Financial Services Industry: Agreement of Symmetric Keys Using Discrete Logarithm Cryptography
2. American National Standard (ANSI) X9.63. Public Key Cryptography for the Financial Services Industry: Key Agreement and Key Transport using Elliptic Curve Cryptography
3. Canetti, R., Krawczyk, H.: Analysis of key-exchange protocols and their use for building secure channels. In: Pfitzmann, B. (ed.) EUROCRYPT 2001. LNCS, vol. 2045, pp. 453–474. Springer, Heidelberg (2001)
4. Canetti, R., Krawczyk, H.: Security Analysis of IKE's Signature-Based Key-Exchange Protocol. In: Yung, M. (ed.) CRYPTO 2002. LNCS, vol. 2442, pp. 143–161. Springer, Heidelberg (2002)
5. Cremers, C., Feltz, M.: One-Round Strongly Secure Key Exchange with Perfect Forward Secrecy and Deniability. Eidgenössische Technische Hochschule Zürich, Department of Computer Science (2011)
6. Cremers, C., Feltz, M.: Beyond eCK: Perfect Forward Secrecy under Actor Compromise and Ephemeral-Key Reveal. In: Foresti, S., Yung, M., Martinelli, F. (eds.) ESORICS 2012. LNCS, vol. 7459, pp. 734–751. Springer, Heidelberg (2012)

7. Diffie, W., Hellman, M.: New Directions in Cryptography. IEEE Transactions on Information Theory 22(6), 644–654 (1976)
8. Gennaro, R., Krawczyk, H., Rabin, T.: Okamoto-tanaka revisited: Fully authenticated diffie-hellman with minimal overhead. In: Zhou, J., Yung, M. (eds.) ACNS 2010. LNCS, vol. 6123, pp. 309–328. Springer, Heidelberg (2010)
9. IEEE 1363-2000. Standard Specifications for Public Key Cryptography
10. ISO/IEC IS 15946-3. Information Technology - Security Techniques - Cryptographic Techniques Based on Elliptic Curves - Part 3: Key Establishment (2002)
11. Jeong, I.R., Katz, J., Lee, D.-H.: One-Round Protocols for Two-Party Authenticated Key Exchange. In: Jakobsson, M., Yung, M., Zhou, J. (eds.) ACNS 2004. LNCS, vol. 3089, pp. 220–232. Springer, Heidelberg (2004)
12. Kaliski Jr, B.S.: An unknown key-share attack on the MQV key agreement protocol. ACM Transactions on Information and System Security (TISSEC) 4(3), 275–288 (2001)
13. Krawczyk, H.: HMQV: A High-Performance Secure Diffie-Hellman Protocol. In: Shoup, V. (ed.) CRYPTO 2005. LNCS, vol. 3621, pp. 546–566. Springer, Heidelberg (2005)
14. Kunz-Jacques, S., Pointcheval, D.: A New Key Exchange Protocol Based on MQV Assuming Public Computations. In: De Prisco, R., Yung, M. (eds.) SCN 2006. LNCS, vol. 4116, pp. 186–200. Springer, Heidelberg (2006)
15. LaMacchia, B.A., Lauter, K., Mityagin, A.: Stronger Security of Authenticated Key Exchange. In: Susilo, W., Liu, J.K., Mu, Y. (eds.) ProvSec 2007. LNCS, vol. 4784, pp. 1–16. Springer, Heidelberg (2007)
16. Lauter, K., Mityagin, A.: Security Analysis of KEA Authenticated Key Exchange Protocol. In: Yung, M., Dodis, Y., Kiayias, A., Malkin, T. (eds.) PKC 2006. LNCS, vol. 3958, pp. 378–394. Springer, Heidelberg (2006)
17. Law, L., Menezes, A., Qu, M., Solinas, J., Vanstone, S.: An Efficient Protocol for Authenticated Key Agreement. Designs, Codes and Cryptography 28(2), 119–134 (2003)
18. Matsumoto, T., Takashima, Y.: On Seeking Smart Public-Key-Distribution Systems. IEICE Transactions (1976-1990) 69(2), 99–106 (1986)
19. Menezes, A.: Another look at HMQV. Mathematical Cryptology JMC 1(1), 47–64 (2007)
20. Menezes, A., Qu, M., Vanstone, S.: Some new key agreement protocols providing mutual implicit authentication. In: Second Workshop on Selected Areas in Cryptography, SAC 1995 (1995)
21. NIST Special Publication 800-56 (DRAFT). Recommendation on Key Establishment Schemes (January 2003)
22. Pointcheval, D., Stern, J.: Security proofs for signature schemes. In: Maurer, U.M. (ed.) EUROCRYPT 1996. LNCS, vol. 1070, pp. 387–398. Springer, Heidelberg (1996)
23. Skipjack and NIST. KEA algorithm specifications (1998)
24. TCG. Trusted Platform Module Library Part 1: Architecture, Family 2.0, Level 00 Revision 01.07 (2014)
25. TCG. Trusted Platform Module Library Part 3: Commands Family 2.0, Level 00 Revision 01.07 (2014)
26. Ustaoglu, B.: Obtaining a secure and efficient key agreement protocol from (H)MQV and NAXOS. Designs, Codes and Cryptography 46(3), 329–342 (2008)
27. Xu, J., Feng, D.: Comments on the SM2 key exchange protocol. In: Lin, D., Tsudik, G., Wang, X. (eds.) CANS 2011. LNCS, vol. 7092, pp. 160–171. Springer, Heidelberg (2011)

28. Yao, A.C., Zhao, Y.: A New Family of Implicitly Authenticated Diffie-Dellman Protocols. Technical report, Cryptology ePrint Archive, Report 2011/035 (2011) (Cited on pages 10 and 15), http://eprint.iacr.org/
29. Yao, A.C.-C., Zhao, Y.: OAKE: A New Family of Implicitly Authenticated Diffie-Dellman Protocols. In: Proceedings of the 2013 ACM SIGSAC Conference on Computer & Communications Security, pp. 1113–1128. ACM (2013)
30. Zhao, S., Zhang, Q.: sHMQV: An Efficient Key Exchange Protocol for Power-limited Devices. http://eprint.iacr.org/2015/110.pdf

A   Preliminaries

In this section we define the assumptions that are used in this paper.

Definition 2. *Let G be a cyclic group of order p with generator g. The DL assumption in G states that, given $A = g^a \in G$, it is computationally infeasible to compute the discrete logarithm a of A.*

Definition 3. *Let G be a cyclic group of order p with generator g. The CDH assumption in G states that, given two randomly chosen points $X = g^x$ and $Y = g^y$, it is computationally infeasible to compute $Z = g^{xy}$.*

Definition 4. *Let G be a cyclic group generated by an element g whose order is p. We say that a decision algorithm $\mathcal{O}$ is a Decisional Diffie-Hellman (DDH) Oracle for a group G and generator g if on input a triple (X, Y, Z), for $X, Y \in G$, oracle $\mathcal{O}$ outputs 1 if and only if $Z = CDH(X, Y)$. We say that G satisfies the GDH assumption if no feasible algorithm exists to solve the CDH problem, even when the algorithm is provided with a DDH-oracle for G.*

Elliptic Curve Cryptography

Models of Curves from GHS Attack in Odd Characteristic[*]

Song Tian[1,2,3], Wei Yu[1,**], Bao Li[1], and Kunpeng Wang[1]

[1] State Key Laboratory of Information Security, Institute of Information Engineering,
Chinese Academy of Sciences, Beijing, China
[2] Data Assurance and Communication Security Research Center,
Chinese Academy of Sciences, Beijing, China
szts1987@163.com
[3] University of Chinese Academy of Sciences, Beijing, China

Abstract. The idea behind the GHS attack is to transform the discrete logarithm problem(DLP) in the Jacobian of a (hyper-)elliptic curve over an extension field into DLPs in Jacobians of covering curves over the base field. Diem gives a condition under which explicit defining equations for some coverings are computed. In this paper, we show that his method works without that condition. We also give explicit map from the covering to the original curve if the covering is hyperelliptic. Our method is based on a formula for the embedding of rational subfield of the function field of (hyper)elliptic curve in that of the hyperelliptic covering.

Keywords: GHS Attack, Elliptic Curve, Hyperelliptic Curve.

1 Introduction

The GHS attack [4,1] aims to transform the discrete logarithm problem(DLP) in the Jacobian of a (hyper-)elliptic curve over an extension field into DLPs in Jacobians of specific curves of larger genera over the base field. The Galois theory of function fields is a useful tool for constructing coverings of the original (hyper)elliptic curves. If the targeted elliptic curve is defined over a binary field, then Artin-Schreier model of this elliptic curve defines an embedding of a rational function field over the base field in the function field of the elliptic curve. The Galois closure of this extension is the function field of a covering curve. This function field can be asked to be hyperelliptic with the unique rational subfield of index 2 an intermediate field of the Galois extension [4]. The situation is different in cases where the (hyper)elliptic curves are defined over fields of odd characteristics. The resulting function field constructed by Kummer extension may be non-hyperelliptic, or even if it is hyperelliptic, its rational subfield of

---

[*] This work is supported in part by National Research Foundation of China under Grant No. 61272040, 61379137, and in part by National Basic Research Program of China (973) under Grant No. 2013CB338001.
[**] Corresponding author: email: yuwei_1_yw@163.com

© Springer International Publishing Switzerland 2015
J. Lopez and Y. Wu (Eds.): ISPEC 2015, LNCS 9065, pp. 171–180, 2015.
DOI: 10.1007/978-3-319-17533-1_12

index 2 need not be an intermediate field of the corresponding Galois extension. The construction of explicit defining equations for these coverings is technical. Under a condition on the Galois group of the constructed Galois extension, Diem obtains equations of some coverings by calculating the minimal polynomials of primitive elements [1].

In this paper, we show that a primitive element can be constructed in general, hence Diem's condition is not necessary. We study necessary conditions for the covering to be hyperelliptic. For hyperelliptic covering, we see that the rational subfield of its function field of index 2 is always an intermediate field of some Galois extension. This leads us to represent the covering as a double covering of projective line by considering the fixed fields of Galois subgroups. We obtain a unified formula for the embedding of rational subfield of the function field of (hyper)elliptic curve in that of the hyperelliptic covering. By this formula one can easily get a standard equation of the hyperelliptic covering and an explicit covering map. The paper is organized as follows: first we recall in Section 2 how coverings are constructed by Kummer theory. In Section 3, we give a general method to compute an equation of the resulting curve. Then a different method is described in section 4 if it is hyperelliptic. Finally, in the last section, our work is summarized.

2   Construction of Covering

Diem's construction is also described in terms of function fields. General references are [1] and [10].

We first fix some notations that will be used throughout this article.

Let q be a power of odd prime and $k = \mathbb{F}_q$ the finite field of q elements. Let K be an extension of k of odd degree n and σ the Frobenius automorphism of K/k. Let E be a (hyper)elliptic curve given by $y^2 = f(x)$, where $f \in K[x]$ is a monic polynomial with only simple roots. We also assume that $f(x)$ is not defined over any proper intermediate fields of K/k.

Let $\bar{K}$ be a fixed algebraic closure of K and $K(E)$ the function field of E. Fix a separable closure $K(x)^{Sep}$ of $K(x)$ containing $\bar{K}(x)$ and $K(E)$. We also denote by σ the extension of σ to $K(x)$ which sends x to x. This σ can extend to an automorphism $\tilde{\sigma}$ of $K(x)^{sep}$. Then we have a composite field

$$L = K(E)\tilde{\sigma}(K(E)) \cdots \tilde{\sigma}^{n-1}(K(E)),$$

which is the Galois closure of extension $K(E)/k(x)$. Since the short exact sequence of Galois groups

$$1 \to \mathrm{Gal}(L/K(x)) \to \mathrm{Gal}(L/k(x)) \to \mathrm{Gal}(K(x)/k(x)) \to 1 \qquad (1)$$

splits(see [1, Lemma 2]), we can choose a $\tilde{\sigma}$ of order n. Let $L^{\tilde{\sigma}}$ be the fixed field of $\tilde{\sigma}$ in L. Then $L^{\tilde{\sigma}}$ determines an algebraic curve C over k which covers E.

Let y_0 be a root of the polynomial $y^2 - f(x) \in K(x)[y]$ in $K(E)$. That is, y_0 satisfies $y_0^2 = f(x)$. Then for $i = 1, 2, \cdots, n-1$, $y_i = \tilde{\sigma}(y_{i-1})$ satisfies $y_i^2 = \sigma^i(f)$.

Since the order of $\tilde{\sigma}$ is n, $\tilde{\sigma}(y_{n-1}) = y_0$. Let m be the integer defined by $[L : K(x)] = 2^m$. The Galois group G of $L/K(x)$, which is isomorphic to $(\mathbb{Z}/2\mathbb{Z})^{\oplus m}$, is generated by $e_0, e_1, \cdots, e_{m-1}$, where

$$e_i(y_i) = -y_i, \; e_i(y_j) = y_j \text{ for } 0 \le i \ne j \le m - 1. \tag{2}$$

The exact sequence (1) induces an operation of group $\mathrm{Gal}(K(x)/k(x))$ on group $\mathrm{Gal}(L/K(x))$ by taking preimages and conjugation inside $\mathrm{Gal}(L/k(x))$. If all elements $\xi \in \mathrm{Gal}(L/K(x))$ have norm 1 under this operation(i.e. they satisfy $\xi\sigma(\xi)\cdots\sigma^{n-1}(\xi) = \mathrm{id}$), then Diem derives explicit equations for the covering C [1, Section 7]. We will see in next section that this condition is not necessary for calculating the equations.

3   Equation of C

The method to compute an equation of C is based on the following proposition.

Proposition 1. *The fixed field $L^{\tilde{\sigma}}$ of $\tilde{\sigma}$ in L is $k(x, y_0 + y_1 + \cdots + y_{n-1})$.*

Proof. Let $[l]$ be the image of $l \in K(x)^*$ in group $K(x)^*/K(x)^{*2}$. Since $[L : K(x)] = 2^m$, by Abelian Kummer theory([9, VI, Theorem 8.2]), $[\sigma^m(f)] \in \langle[f], \cdots, [\sigma^{m-1}(f)]\rangle$, so

$$y_m = a(x)y_0 y_1^{r_1} \cdots y_{m-1}^{r_{m-1}}$$

for some $a(x) \in K(x)$ and $r_1, \cdots, r_{m-1} \in \{0, 1\}$. Hence for each $i \in \{0, 1, \cdots, n - m - 1\}$, $y_{m+i} = \sigma^i(y_m)$ is of form $a_i(x)y_0^{r_{i,0}} y_1^{r_{i,1}} \cdots y_{m-1}^{r_{i,m-1}}$ with $r_{i,0}, \cdots, r_{i,m-1} \in \{0, 1\}$. Note that none of $y_m, y_{m+1}, \cdots, y_{n-1}$ take form $b(x)y_j$ with $b(x) \in K(x)$ and $0 \le j \le m - 1$, since by assumption $f(x)$ is not defined over any proper intermediate fields of K/k.

Set $z = y_0 + y_1 + \cdots + y_{n-1}$. If $\tau(z) = z$ for some non-trivial $\tau \in G = \mathrm{Gal}(L/K(x))$, then we would get

$$0 = y_{i_1} + \cdots + y_{i_v} = \sum_{i_j < m} y_{i_j} + \sum_{i_j \ge m} y_{i_j},$$

where $\{i_1, \cdots, i_v\} = \{0 \le i \le n - 1 : \tau(y_i) = -y_i\}$. This is impossible since L is a vector space over $K(x)$ with a base $\{y_0^{\epsilon_0} y_1^{\epsilon_1} \cdots y_{m-1}^{\epsilon_{m-1}} : \epsilon_0, \cdots, \epsilon_{m-1} \in \{0, 1\}\}$ and $\sum_{i_j \ge m} y_{i_j}$ is a $K(x)$-combination of items $y_0^{\epsilon_0} y_1^{\epsilon_1} \cdots y_{m-1}^{\epsilon_{m-1}}$ which are different from $y_0, \cdots, y_{m-1}$. Hence we show that the 2^m elements $\tau(z)(\tau \in G)$ are distinct and the minimal polynomial of z over $K(x)$ is

$$h(y) = \prod_{\tau \in G} (y - \tau(z)). \tag{3}$$

Since $[L^{\tilde{\sigma}} : k(x)] = 2^m$ and $z \in L^{\tilde{\sigma}}$, we have $L^{\tilde{\sigma}} = k(x, z)$.

Note that $y_0 + y_1 + \cdots + y_{n-1}$ is integral over $K[x]$ since all y_i are integral over $K[x]$. Therefore $h(y)$ in (3) is a polynomial in $k[x, y]$ and C can be represented by irreducible affine plane curve $h(y) = h(x, y) = 0$. To calculate h, it suffices to find y_m. One can first represent $[\sigma^m(f)]$ by $[f], \cdots, [\sigma^{m-1}(f)]$, then choose $\tilde{y}_m \in \{\pm a(x) y_0 y_1^{r_1} \cdots y_{m-1}^{r_{m-1}}\}$, and check if $\tilde{\sigma}^{n-m}(\tilde{y}_m) = y_0$. If so, then $y_m = \tilde{y}_m$, otherwise $y_m = -\tilde{y}_m$.

Proposition 2. Let $e_0, e_1, \cdots, e_{m-1}$ be as in (2). If $L/K(x)$ contains a rational subfield of index 2, then the hyperelliptic involution is $e_0 e_1 \cdots e_{m-1}$.

Proof. For $i \in \{0, 1, \cdots, m-1\}$, let $G_i = \langle e_0 \rangle \times \cdots \times \langle \hat{e}_i \rangle \times \cdots \times \langle e_{m-1} \rangle$ be the maximal subgroup of G not containing e_i. If the hyperelliptic involution ι of L was not equal to $e_0 e_1 \cdots e_{m-1}$, then ι would be contained in some G_i. Hence $0 = g(K(C_K^\iota)) \geq g(\tilde{\sigma}^i(K(E))) = 1$, which is a contradiction.

If $m \geq 4$, then $L/K(x)$ contains no rational subfield of index 2[1]. In fact, we have

Proposition 3. If L is hyperelliptic, then $m \leq 3$.

Proof. We only need to consider the case that the rational subfield of index 2 is not an intermediate field of $L/K(x)$. Note that in this situation, the original curve E must be an elliptic curve. Let ι be the hyperelliptic involution of L. Then ι induces an involution on $K(E)$ with fixed field a rational field(see [8, p. 42, Lemma]). Hence the fixed field of ιe_0 in $K(E)$ has genus 1 and the fixed field of $\langle \iota, e_0 \rangle$ has genus 0(see [7, Theorem B]).

Let $K(u)$ be the fixed field of $\langle \iota, e_0 \rangle$ in $K(E)$. Then elements of $K(u)$ fixed by $\tilde{\sigma}$ form a rational field $k(s)$. In fact, it is the fixed field of $\langle \iota, e_0, \cdots, e_{m-1}, \tilde{\sigma} \rangle$ in L, which implies it is infinite and contained in a rational field. It is easy to see that $K(s) = K(u)$, hence we can assume that u is fixed by $\tilde{\sigma}$.

Let $K(E')$ be the fixed field of ιe_0 in $K(E)$, where E' is a curve of genus 1. Then we can choose $v_0 = u' y_0 \in K(E')$ such that $K(E') = K(u, v_0)$ and $v_0^2 = g_0(u)$ for some polynomial $g_0 \in K[u]$. Since $L/k(u)$ is Galois, the Galois closure $\tilde{L}$ of $K(E')/k(u)$ is contained in L. Note that $[\sigma^i(g_0)(u(x))] = [\sigma^i(f(x))]$ in $K(x)^*/K(x)^{*2}$, we see that $[\tilde{L} : K(u)]$ is equal to 2^m or 2^{m+1}. Since ι restricts to an involution of $\tilde{L}$ with fixed field an intermediate field of $\tilde{L}/K(u)$, we find that $m \leq 3$ or $m + 1 \leq 3$.

Corollary 4. If $m = 2$ and L is hyperelliptic, then there is a degree 2 map $E \to E'$ such that L is obtained by applying construction of Sect. 2 to quadratic extension $K(E')/K(u)$ and that the rational subfield of L of index 2 is an intermediate field of $L/K(u)$.

Proof. If $m = 2$, then $y_2 = a(x) y_0 y_1$, so $e_0 e_1(y_2) = y_2$. Note that $\tilde{\sigma}^2(v_0)^2 = \sigma^2(g_0)(u)$ and $\iota(\sigma^2(g_0)(u)) = \sigma^2(g_0)(u)$, we see that $\iota(\tilde{\sigma}^2(v_0)) = -\tilde{\sigma}^2(v_0)$, otherwise the fixed field $K(E)^\iota$ of ι in $K(E)$ contains $K(E')$, which is impossible since $K(E)^\iota$ has genus 0. Since $v_0 = u'(x) y_0$, we have $\tilde{\sigma}^2(v_0) = \tilde{\sigma}^2(u'(x)) y_2$. Hence

$e_0 e_1 \iota(\tilde{\sigma}^2(v_0)) = -\tilde{\sigma}^2(v_0)$. As $\iota e_0 e_1$ restricts to the identity map on $K(E')\tilde{\sigma}(K(E'))$, we find that

$$\tilde{L} \supseteq K(E')\tilde{\sigma}(K(E'))\tilde{\sigma}^2(K(E')) \supsetneq K(E')\tilde{\sigma}(K(E')),$$

so $\tilde{L} = L$.

Example 5. Let $\mathbb{F}_{101^3}$ be the finite field $\mathbb{F}_{101}[\alpha_0]/ < \alpha_0^3 + 3\alpha_0 + 99 >$, and let $E/\mathbb{F}_{101^3}$ be the elliptic curve defined by $y^2 = (x-\alpha_0)(x-\alpha_0^{101})(x-(80+74\alpha_0+10\alpha_0^2))(x-(80+74\alpha_0+10\alpha_0^2)^{101})$. Then $m = 2$, and C has a defining equation $y^4 + (95x^4 + 13x^3 + 24x^2 + 34x + 9)y^2 + (93x^6 + 26x^5 + 54x^4 + 65x^3 + 81x^2 + 60x + 58)y + 98x^8 + 13x^7 + 30x^6 + 46x^5 + 48x^4 + 27x^3 + 35x^2 + 78x + 70 = 0$. One can check that C is hyperelliptic(using Magma computer algebra package) and that there is a degree 2 map from E to the elliptic curve

$$E' : v^2 = (u^2 + 81u + 89)(u - \alpha_0)(u - \alpha_0^{101}),$$

which sends (x, y) to

$$\left(\frac{\alpha_0^{442917}x^2 + \alpha_0^{330565}x + \alpha_0^{603049}}{x^2 + \alpha_0^{714806}x + \alpha_0^{909561}}, y\frac{\alpha_0^{509885}x^2 + \alpha_0^{334734}x + \alpha_0^{314128}}{x^4 + \alpha_0^{725109}x^3 + \alpha_0^{794601}x^2 + \alpha_0^{604370}x + \alpha_0^{788822}} \right).$$

4 Equation of Hyperelliptic Curve C

We keep the notations of Sect. 2. For instance, the original (hyper)elliptic curve E is defined by $y^2 = f(x)$. There are some (hyper)elliptic curves of which one can obtain hyperelliptic coverings by Kummer theory. The equations of these (hyper)elliptic curves and their hyperelliptic coverings are given in [10], but the morphisms from the coverings to the original curves are not clear. In fact, each of these coverings corresponds to a commutative diagram

$$\begin{array}{ccc} C & \longrightarrow & E \\ \downarrow & & \downarrow {\scriptstyle x|_E} \\ \mathbb{P}^1 & \longrightarrow & \mathbb{P}^1. \end{array}$$

We will give a description of the induced map $\mathbb{P}^1 \to \mathbb{P}^1$, from which we can easily get the standard equation of C and the morphism from C to E.

Lemma 6. *Let $[K : k] = 3$. Let E be a (hyper)elliptic curve of genus g defined by*

$$y^2 = l(x)(x - \alpha)(x - \sigma(\alpha)),$$

where $\alpha \in K \setminus k, l(x) \in k[x], \deg l(x) = 2g$ or $2g - 1$. Then L is hyperelliptic and of genus $4g - 1$.

Proof. Let r be the number of ramified places of $\bar{K}(x)$ in $\bar{K}L$, then by Hurwitz genus formula, L has genus $2^{m-2}(r - 4) + 1$. As $m = 3$ and $r = 2g + 3$, L is of genus $4g - 1$. The fixed field of $e_0 e_1 e_2$ is $K(x, \frac{y_1}{y_0}, \frac{y_2}{y_0})$, which has genus 0 by Hurwitz genus formula. See also [10].

Lemma 7. *Let E be a (hyper)elliptic curve of genus g defined by*

$$y^2 = l(x)(x - \alpha),$$

where $\alpha \in K \setminus k, l(x) \in k[x], \deg l(x) = 2g$ or $2g + 1$. Then L is hyperelliptic and of genus $4g + 1$.

Proof. It can be similarly proved. See also [10]. ∎

We now represent C as a double covering of projective line. The idea is to find the rational subfield of $L^{\tilde{\sigma}}$ of index 2. We just do it for elliptic curves, then we see it works for hyperelliptic curve E as well.

Theorem 8. *Let $[K : k] = 3$, and E be an elliptic curve over K given by*

$$y^2 = f(x) = x(x - \alpha)(x - \sigma(\alpha)),$$

where $\alpha \in K \setminus k$, σ is the Frobenius automorphism of K/k. Then there exists a hyperelliptic curve C over k of genus 3 defined by

$$y^2 = (x - \alpha)(x - \sigma(\alpha))(x - \sigma^2(\alpha))U(x),$$

and a morphism $\pi = \pi_2 \circ \pi_1 : C \to E$ over K. Here

$$U(x) = [x^2 - (\alpha\sigma(\alpha) + \alpha\sigma^2(\alpha) + \sigma(\alpha)\sigma^2(\alpha))]^2$$
$$+ 4\alpha\sigma(\alpha)\sigma^2(\alpha)(2x - \alpha - \sigma(\alpha) - \sigma^2(\alpha)),$$
$$\pi_1(x, y) = (\frac{x^2 - (\alpha\sigma^2(\alpha) - \alpha\sigma(\alpha) + \sigma(\alpha)\sigma^2(\alpha))}{x - \sigma^2(\alpha)}, \frac{y}{(x - \sigma^2(\alpha))^2}),$$
$$\pi_2(x, y) = (\frac{x^2 - 4\alpha\sigma(\alpha)}{4(x - \alpha - \sigma(\alpha))}, y\frac{(x - 2\alpha)(x - 2\sigma(\alpha))}{8(x - \alpha - \sigma(\alpha))^2}).$$

Proof. Let L, y_0, y_1, y_2, e_0, e_1 and e_2 be as in Sect. 2. The fixed field of $e_0 e_1 e_2$ is $K(x, (y_0 + y_1 + y_2)^2) = K(x, \frac{y_1}{y_2}, \frac{y_0}{y_2})$, which is a rational subfield of L of index 2. Set $\tilde{s} = \frac{y_1}{y_2}$, then $\tilde{s}^2 = \frac{x - \sigma(\alpha)}{x - \alpha}$, $x = \frac{\alpha\tilde{s}^2 - \sigma(\alpha)}{\tilde{s}^2 - 1}$. Choose fractional linear transformation $\tilde{s} = \frac{-\frac{1}{2}s + \sigma(\alpha)}{-\frac{1}{2}s + \alpha}$, then we have $x = \frac{s^2 - 4\alpha\sigma(\alpha)}{4(s - \alpha - \sigma(\alpha))}$, and $K(x, \tilde{s}) = K(\tilde{s}) = K(s)$.

Since $y^2 = f(\frac{s^2 - 4\alpha\sigma(\alpha)}{4(s - \alpha - \sigma(\alpha))}) = \frac{(s^2 - 4\alpha\sigma(\alpha))(s - 2\alpha)^2(s - 2\sigma(\alpha))^2}{(4(s - \alpha - \sigma(\alpha)))^3}$, there is a 2-isogeny from

$$E_1 : Y^2 = (s - \alpha - \sigma(\alpha))(s^2 - 4\alpha\sigma(\alpha))$$

to E given by $(s, Y) \mapsto (\frac{s^2 - 4\alpha\sigma(\alpha)}{4(s - \alpha - \sigma(\alpha))}, Y\frac{(s - 2\alpha)(s - 2\sigma(\alpha))}{8(s - \alpha - \sigma(\alpha))^2})$.

Let $w = \frac{y_2(s - 2\sigma(\alpha))}{y_0}$. Then

$$(s - 2\sigma^2(\alpha) - w)(s - 2\sigma^2(\alpha) + w) = 4(\sigma^2(\alpha) - \alpha)(\sigma^2(\alpha) - \sigma(\alpha)). \quad (4)$$

Since $s = \alpha + \sigma^2(\alpha), w = \alpha - \sigma^2(\alpha)$ is a solution to this equation, set $w = \tilde{t}(s - \alpha - \sigma^2(\alpha)) + (\alpha - \sigma^2(\alpha))$ in (4), then we have

$$s = \frac{(\alpha + \sigma(\alpha))\tilde{t}^2 - 2(\alpha - \sigma(\alpha))\tilde{t} - 4\sigma^2(\alpha) + \alpha + \sigma(\alpha)}{\tilde{t}^2 - 1}.$$

Choose $\tilde{t} = \frac{t + \sigma(\alpha) - 2\sigma^2(\alpha)}{t - \sigma(\alpha)}$. Then $s = \frac{t^2 - (\alpha\sigma^2(\alpha) - \alpha\sigma(\alpha) + \sigma(\alpha)\sigma^2(\alpha))}{t - \sigma^2(\alpha)}$, $K(s, \frac{y_0}{y_2}) = K(s, w) = K(\tilde{t}) = K(t)$.

It follows that

$$Y^2 = (s - \alpha - \sigma(\alpha))(s^2 - 4\alpha\sigma(\alpha))$$
$$= \frac{(t - \alpha)(t - \sigma(\alpha))}{t - \sigma^2(\alpha)} \cdot \frac{U(t)}{(t - \sigma^2(\alpha))^2},$$

where $U(t) = [t^2 - (\alpha\sigma(\alpha) + \alpha\sigma^2(\alpha) + \sigma(\alpha)\sigma^2(\alpha))]^2 + 4\alpha\sigma(\alpha)\sigma^2(\alpha)(2t - \alpha - \sigma(\alpha) - \sigma^2(\alpha))$. It is easy to see that

$$Z^2 = (t - \alpha)(t - \sigma(\alpha))(t - \sigma^2(\alpha))U(t)$$

is a hyperelliptic curve of genus 3 over k with function field $L^{\tilde{\sigma}}$.

Remark 9. Let $C/\langle e_1 e_2 \rangle$ be the quotient of C by the automorphism induced by $e_1 e_2$. Here the morphism π is a composition of $C \to C/\langle e_1 e_2 \rangle$ and $C/\langle e_1 e_2 \rangle \to E$, which is exactly the same as [6]. We can also write it as $C \to C/\langle e_1 \rangle \to E$. For example, we have

$$C/\langle e_1 \rangle : y^2 = (x - \sigma(\alpha) - \sigma^2(\alpha))(x^2 - 4\sigma(\alpha)\sigma^2(\alpha))((x - 2\alpha)^2 - 4(\alpha - \sigma(\alpha))(\alpha - \sigma^2(\alpha)))$$

with a morphism from $C/\langle e_1 \rangle$ to E given by

$$(x, y) \mapsto (\frac{x^2 - 4\sigma(\alpha)\sigma^2(\alpha)}{4(x - \sigma(\alpha) - \sigma^2(\alpha))}, y\frac{x - 2\sigma(\alpha)}{8(x - \sigma(\alpha) - \sigma^2(\alpha))^2}),$$

and a morphism from C to $C/\langle e_1 \rangle$ by

$$(x, y) \mapsto (\frac{x^2 + \sigma(\alpha)\sigma^2(\alpha) - \alpha\sigma(\alpha) - \alpha\sigma^2(\alpha)}{x - \alpha}, y\frac{(x - \alpha)^2 - (\alpha - \sigma(\alpha))(\alpha - \sigma^2(\alpha))}{(x - \alpha)^3}).$$

An equation of genus 5 curve C is given in [10], we give it another form by our method.

Theorem 10. *Let $[K : k] = 3$, and E be an elliptic curve over K given by*

$$y^2 = (x - \alpha)p(x),$$

where $\alpha \in K \setminus k$, $p(x) = x^2 + ax + b \in k[x]$. Then there exists a hyperelliptic curve C over k of genus 5 defined by

$$y^2 = (x - \alpha)(x - \sigma(\alpha))(x - \sigma^2(\alpha))V(x),$$

and a morphism $\pi = \pi_2 \circ \pi_1 : C \to E$ *over* K, *where*

$$V(x) = U(x)^2 + 4aU(x)(x - \alpha)(x - \sigma(\alpha))(x - \sigma^2(\alpha))$$
$$+ 16b((x - \alpha)(x - \sigma(\alpha))(x - \sigma^2(\alpha)))^2,$$
$$U(x) = [x^2 - (a\sigma(\alpha) + a\sigma^2(\alpha) + \sigma(\alpha)\sigma^2(\alpha))]^2$$
$$+ 4a\sigma(\alpha)\sigma^2(\alpha)(2x - \alpha - \sigma(\alpha) - \sigma^2(\alpha)),$$
$$\pi_1(x, y) = (\frac{x^2 - a\sigma^2(\alpha) - a\sigma(\alpha) + \sigma(\alpha)\sigma^2(\alpha)}{x - \alpha}, y\frac{(x - \alpha)^2 - (\alpha - \sigma(\alpha))(\alpha - \sigma^2(\alpha))}{(x - \alpha)^4}),$$
$$\pi_2(x, y) = (\frac{x^2 - 4\sigma(\alpha)\sigma^2(\alpha)}{4(x - \sigma(\alpha) - \sigma^2(\alpha))}, \frac{y}{8(x - \sigma(\alpha) - \sigma^2(\alpha))^2}) \ .$$

Proof. We make explicit the second row of the following commutative diagram

$$\begin{array}{ccccc}
C & \longrightarrow & C/\langle e_1 e_2 \rangle & \longrightarrow & E \\
\downarrow & & \downarrow & & \downarrow \\
\mathbb{P}^1 & \longrightarrow & \mathbb{P}^1 & \longrightarrow & \mathbb{P}^1 \ .
\end{array}$$

First, $\tilde{s} = \frac{y_1}{y_2}$ satisfies $x = \frac{\sigma^2(\alpha)\tilde{s}^2 - \sigma(\alpha)}{\tilde{s}^2 - 1}$. By fractional linear transformation $\tilde{s} = \frac{-\frac{1}{2}s + \sigma(\alpha)}{-\frac{1}{2}s + \sigma^2(\alpha)}$, we get

$$x = \frac{s^2 - 4\sigma(\alpha)\sigma^2(\alpha)}{4(s - \sigma(\alpha) - \sigma^2(\alpha))} \ . \tag{5}$$

Second, $w = (s - 2\sigma^2(\alpha))\frac{y_0}{y_2}$ satisfies

$$(w - (s - 2\alpha))(w - (s - 2\alpha)) = -4(\alpha - \sigma(\alpha))(\alpha - \sigma^2(\alpha)) \ .$$

Let $w = \tilde{t}(s - \sigma(\alpha) - \sigma^2(\alpha)) + \sigma(\alpha) - \sigma^2(\alpha)$. Then we have

$$s = \frac{(\sigma(\alpha) + \sigma^2(\alpha))\tilde{t}^2 - 2(\sigma(\alpha) - \sigma^2(\alpha))\tilde{t} - 4\alpha + \sigma(\alpha) + \sigma^2(\alpha)}{\tilde{t}^2 - 1} \ .$$

After substituting $\tilde{t} = \frac{t + \sigma^2(\alpha) - 2\alpha}{t - \sigma^2(\alpha)}$, we have

$$s = \frac{t^2 - a\sigma^2(\alpha) - a\sigma(\alpha) + \sigma(\alpha)\sigma^2(\alpha)}{t - \alpha} \ . \tag{6}$$

Now (6) and (5) define the morphisms $\mathbb{P}^1 \to \mathbb{P}^1, t \mapsto s$, and $\mathbb{P}^1 \to \mathbb{P}^1, s \mapsto x$. The statement follows immediately from this.

Example 11. Let $\mathbb{F}_{19^3}$ be the finite field $\mathbb{F}_{19}[\beta_0]/ < \beta_0^3 + 5\beta_0^2 + 5\beta_0 + 5 >$, and let $E_0/\mathbb{F}_{19^3}$ be the elliptic curve defined by $y^2 = (x - \beta_0)(x^2 + 14x + 16)$. Then the hyperelliptic curve

$$H/\mathbb{F}_{19} : y^2 = x^{11} + 4x^{10} + 3x^9 + 11x^8 + 17x^7 + 9x^6 + 15x^5 + 17x^4 + 7x^3 + 14x^2 + 16x + 3$$

covers the elliptic curve E_0 by a morphism

$$\pi(x,y) = (\frac{5x^4 + 7x^2 + 9x + 5}{x^3 + 5x^2 + 5x + 5}, \frac{y(7x^2 + \beta_0^{3811}x + \beta_0^{2132})}{x^6 + 10x^5 + 16x^4 + 3x^3 + 18x^2 + 12x + 6}).$$

Using Magma computer algebra package, we find that the L-polynomial of H is $(6859T^6 - 46T^3 + 1)(361T^4 - 19T^3 + 28T^2 - T + 1)$, hence by Tate-Honda theorem [11] the Jacobian variety of H is isogenous to a product of abelian varieties $\mathcal{A}_2$ and $\mathcal{A}_3$ whose dimensions are 2 and 3. Moreover, $\mathcal{A}_3$ is isogenous to E_0^3 over $\mathbb{F}_{19^3}$.

Remark 12. The discrete logarithm problem in the group of rational points of $E/\mathbb{F}_{q^3}$ can be solved in an expected time of $\tilde{\mathcal{O}}(q^{3/2})$ by Pollard's rho algorithm. While for a genus 5 curve C over $\mathbb{F}_q$, the discrete logarithm problem in the Jacobian $\mathrm{Jac}(C)(\mathbb{F}_q)$ can be computed with complexity $\tilde{\mathcal{O}}(q^{8/5})$ by double large prime variation of index calculus proposed in [5]. Here we would like to stress that the unpublished result in [3] leads to a complexity of $\tilde{\mathcal{O}}(q^{4/3})$.

It is easy to see from the above proofs that for L in Lemma 5 and Lemma 6, $K(x)$ can be embedded in the rational subfield $K(t)$ of L of index 2 by $x = \{t^4 - 2(\alpha\sigma(\alpha) + \alpha\sigma^2(\alpha) + \sigma(\alpha)\sigma^2(\alpha))t^2 + 4\alpha\sigma(\alpha)\sigma^2(\alpha)(2t - \alpha - \sigma(\alpha) - \sigma^2(\alpha)) + (\alpha\sigma(\alpha) + \alpha\sigma^2(\alpha) + \sigma(\alpha)\sigma^2(\alpha))^2\}/\{4(t - \alpha)(t - \sigma(\alpha))(t - \sigma^2(\alpha))\}$. Since $(x - \alpha)(t - \alpha)(t - \sigma(\alpha))(t - \sigma^2(\alpha)), (x - \alpha)(x - \sigma(\alpha)) \in K(t)^2$, we have

$$(x - \alpha)l(x) = c_1(t)^2 S_1(t) \tag{7}$$

and

$$(x - \alpha)(x - \sigma(\alpha))l(x) = c_2(t)^2 S_2(t) \tag{8}$$

with $S_1(t), S_2(t) \in k[t]$. Therefore, we have the following theorem.

Theorem 13. *Let $S_1(t)$ and $S_2(t)$ be the polynomials in Equation (7) and Equation (8) respectively. Then $T^2 = S_1(t)$ and $T^2 = S_2(t)$ are equations of $L^{\tilde{\sigma}}$ for L in Lemma 5 and Lemma 6.*

5   Conclusion

In this paper, we have discussed the defining equations of covering curves C obtained from GHS attack in odd characteristic. We have shown that they can be obtained by computing minimal polynomials of some primitive elements. Once an equation of a curve C is given, one can always check whether it is hyperelliptic and find a nicer one [2].

That the magic number m should be less than 4 is necessary for a covering C to be hyperelliptic. For (hyper-)elliptic curves E given in [10], the hyperelliptic involution on C always induces $[-1]$ map(or hyperelliptic involution) on elliptic curve E(or hyperelliptic curve E). We have illustrated that a standard equation of C and a morphism from it to the original (hyper)elliptic curve can be obtained by considering the induced morphism between projective lines.

References

1. Diem, C.: The GHS attack in odd characteristic. J. Ramanujan Math. Soc. 18(1), 1–32 (2003)
2. Diem, C.: An index calculus algorithm for plane curves of small degree. In: Hess, F., Pauli, S., Pohst, M. (eds.) ANTS 2006. LNCS, vol. 4076, pp. 543–557. Springer, Heidelberg (2006)
3. Diem, C., Kochinke, S.: Computing discrete logarithms with special linear systems, available under
   http://www.math.uni-leipzig.de/MI/diem/preprints/
   dlp-linear-systems.pdf
4. Gaudry, P., Hess, F., Smart, N.P.: Constructive and destructive facets of Weil descent on elliptic curves. Journal of Cryptology 15(1), 19–46 (2002)
5. Gaudry, P., Thomé, E., Thériault, N., Diem, C.: A double large prime variation for small genus hyperelliptic index calculus. Mathematics of Computation 76(257), 475–492 (2007)
6. Joux, A., Vitse, V.: Cover and Decomposition Index Calculus on Elliptic Curves Made Practical. In: Pointcheval, D., Johansson, T. (eds.) EUROCRYPT 2012. LNCS, vol. 7237, pp. 9–26. Springer, Heidelberg (2012)
7. Kani, E., Rosen, M.: Idempotent relations and factors of Jacobians. Mathematische Annalen 284(2), 307–327 (1989)
8. Kuhn, R.M.: Curves of genus 2 with split Jacobian. Transactions of the American Mathematical Society 307(1), 41–49 (1988)
9. Lang, S.: Algebra, revised 3rd edn. Springer (2002)
10. Thériault, N.: Weil descent attack for Kummer extensions. J. Ramanujan Math. Soc. 18(3), 281–312 (2003)
11. Waterhouse, W.C., Milne, J.: Abelian varieties over finite fields. Ann. Sci. École Norm. Sup. 2(4), 521–560 (1969)

Some Elliptic Subcovers of Genus 3 Hyperelliptic Curves*

Song Tian[1,2,3], Wei Yu[1,**], Bao Li[1], and Kunpeng Wang[1]

[1] State Key Laboratory of Information Security, Institute of Information Engineering,
Chinese Academy of Sciences, Beijing, China
[2] Data Assurance and Communication Security Research Center,
Chinese Academy of Sciences, Beijing, China
szts1987@163.com
[3] University of Chinese Academy of Sciences, Beijing, China

Abstract. A morphism from an algebraic curve C to an elliptic curve is called an elliptic subcover of the curve C. Elliptic subcovers provide means of solving discrete logarithm problem in elliptic curves over extension fields. The GHS attack yields only degree 2 minimal elliptic subcovers of hyperelliptic curves of genus 3. In this paper, we study the properties of elliptic subcovers of genus 3 hyperelliptic curves. Using these properties, we find some minimal elliptic subcovers of degree 4, which can not be constructed by GHS attack.

Keywords: Elliptic Subcover, Hyperelliptic Curve, Discrete Logarithm Problem, GHS Attack.

1 Introduction

Let C be an algebraic curve and E an elliptic curve. We call a morphism $\phi : C \to E$ an elliptic subcover of C. The curves with elliptic subcovers all share the feature that their Jacobians are isogenous to products of elliptic curves and lower-dimensional abelian varieties. A curve whose Jacobian is isogenous to a product of elliptic curves is then said to have split Jacobian.

Curves with split Jacobians are of great interest. The Jacobians of those curves over the field of rational numbers can have large torsion subgroups [8]. Such curves over finite fields often have large number of rational points [1,11]. Split Jacobian curves also provide examples of nonisomorphic curves with isomorphic Jacobians[6,7]. Besides, split Jacobian curves are considered for cryptographic applications. To be sure to exclude weak curves in hyperelliptic curve cryptography, one should be able to count the rational points of Jacobian. In [13], Satoh gives an algorithm for computing the order of the Jacobian of a hyperelliptic

---

* This work is supported in part by National Research Foundation of China under Grant No. 61272040, 61379137, and in part by National Basic Research Program of China (973) under Grant No. 2013CB338001.
** Corresponding author: email: yuwei_1_yw@163.com

J. Lopez and Y. Wu (Eds.): ISPEC 2015, LNCS 9065, pp. 181–191, 2015.
DOI: 10.1007/978-3-319-17533-1_13

curve of genus 2 in certain form by considering the Zeta function over the extension field where the Jacobian splits. Split Jacobian curves and generally, elliptic subcovers, can also be used in a destructive way. It is well known that the first important step of Weil descent attack is to find a curve that covers an given elliptic curve. More precisely, for an elliptic curve defined over an extension field, if one can find a covering curve over the base field, then it might be possible that the discrete logarithm problem in the elliptic curve can be transformed into discrete logarithm problem in the Jacobian of the covering curve. The approaches to constructing coverings of elliptic curves are for the moment rather restricted. Indeed, there is only the GHS attack(see [3,5]). This motivates us to study the elliptic subcovers of hyperelliptic curves.

The theory of genus 2 curves with elliptic subcovers is developed in [4,10]. Since the Pollard methods on elliptic curves over quadratic extension fields are more efficient than index calculus on genus 2 curves over base fields there is no improvement to the complexity of solving discrete logarithm problems due to elliptic subcovers of genus 2 curves. In this paper, we confine ourselves to the study of the elliptic subcovers of a genus 3 hyperelliptic curve over a field of characteristic $p \neq 2$. Our aims here are (i) to determine the ramification patterns of the elliptic subcovers that hold "in general", and (ii) to give some elliptic subcovers that are different from those constructed by GHS attack.

We give a brief survey of this paper here. In section 2, we study the configuration of the Weierstrass points. As in the case of genus 2 curves, this configuration is complicated. An easier target is to derive the "generic" picture for minimal subcovers. In section 3, we consider some applications of degree 4 subcovers. An algorithm for finding such subcovers is given, and was tested on hyperelliptic curves. It turns out that there are some elliptic subcovers which can not be obtained by GHS attack.

2   The Ramification of Frey-Kani Map

Lemma 1. *Let H be a hyperelliptic curve of genus 3 with hyperelliptic involution τ. Let $\phi : H \to E$ be a map from H to a curve of genus 1. Then τ induce an involution on E with quotient curve of genus 0. The Weierstrass points of H lie over the fixed points of E under τ.*

Proof. Let P_0 be a Weierstrass point of H. Then we have maps of H and E into their Jacobians defined by points P_0 and $\phi(P_0)$. Since $(P) + (\tau(P)) - 2(P_0)$ is a principal divisor for all $P \in H$, $(\phi(P)) + (\phi(\tau(P))) - 2(\phi(P_0))$ is also a principal divisor, which means τ induces the involution $[-1]$ on the Jacobian of E under the above choice of embeddings. Hence there is an involution τ_E on E such that the quotient of E by τ_E is of genus 0 and that the following diagram

$$
\begin{array}{ccc}
H & \xrightarrow{\ \tau\ } & H \\
\phi \downarrow & & \downarrow \phi \\
E & \xrightarrow{\ \tau_E\ } & E
\end{array}
$$

is commutative.

One can take the image of one Weierstrass point of H under ϕ as the base point to make E into an elliptic curve. We will hereafter do this, so ϕ sends the Weierstrass points of H to the 2-torsion points of the elliptic curve E. Let H^τ and E^τ be the quotients of H and E by τ and τ_E. Let π_H and π_E be the natural projection maps. Then we have a map $\phi_1 : H^\tau \to E^\tau$ such that the following diagram

$$\begin{array}{ccc}
H & \xrightarrow{\ \pi_H\ } & H^\tau \\
{\scriptstyle \phi}\downarrow & & \downarrow{\scriptstyle \phi_1} \\
E & \xrightarrow{\ \pi_E\ } & E^\tau.
\end{array}$$

is commutative. The similar map for genus 2 curve has appeared in [10] and [4]. Following [14], we use the term Frey-Kani map to refer to the induced map ϕ_1.

Let $\{W_1, W_2, \cdots, W_8\}$ and $\{W_1', \cdots, W_4'\}$ be the sets of fixed points of τ and τ_E respectively. Let $w_i = \pi_H(W_i)$ and $w_i' = \pi_E(W_i')$. Then ϕ_1 induces a partition of the set $R = \{w_i : i = 1, \cdots, 8\}$:

$$R = R_1 \cup R_2 \cup R_3 \cup R_4,$$

where $R_i = R \cap \phi_1^{-1}(w_i')$ for $i = 1, 2, 3, 4$. If ϕ is unramified over the four points W_i', then the image of the set $(\cup_{i=1}^4 \phi^{-1}(W_i')) \setminus \{W_1, \cdots, W_8\}$ under π_H contains $2d - 4$ points, at which ϕ_1 is ramified with index 2, where d is the degree of ϕ. By Riemann-Hurwitz formula, the ramification divisor of ϕ_1 has degree $2d - 2$. Hence ϕ_1 is triply ramified at one more point or doubly ramified at two other points.

Definition 2. *If the induced map $\phi^*: Jac(E) \to Jac(H)$ of Jacobians is a closed embedding, then ϕ is said to be minimal or optimal.*

The map ϕ is optimal is equivalent to that ϕ does not factor over any cyclic étale coverings of E of degree $l \geq 2$(see [2, Proposition 11.4.3]). Since every ϕ factors into an optimal map followed by an étale covering of E, we focus on optimal maps. If ϕ is optimal, then we have an exact sequence of of abelian varieties:

$$0 \longrightarrow \mathcal{A} \longrightarrow Jac(H) \xrightarrow{\ \phi_*\ } E \longrightarrow 0.$$

It follows that $\#\mathrm{Ker}(\phi_*) \cap Jac(H)[2] = \#\mathcal{A}[2] = 2^4$. Hence, the image of the restriction of the group homomorphism ϕ_* to $Jac(H)[2]$ contains four points. This implies that there is at most one empty set among R_1, R_2, R_3, R_4. Assuming that ϕ is unramified over the W_i'(we call this the "generic" case), we now get the ramification configuration of the Frey-Kani map as stated in the following theorem.

Theorem 3. *If the map ϕ is unramified over the W_i', then for $i = 1, 2, 3, 4$, and any $w \in \phi_1^{-1}(w_i')$, the ramification index of ϕ_1 at w is 1 or 2, which depends on whether it is in R or not. There is either one more point of H^τ, at which ϕ_1 is triply ramified, or two more points at which ϕ_1 is doubly ramified. Furthermore, if ϕ is optimal, then the following two properties are true:*

- if ϕ has odd degree, then the multiset $\{\#R_1, \#R_2, \#R_3, \#R_4\}$ is $\{3, 3, 1, 1\}$ or $\{5, 1, 1, 1\}$.
- if ϕ has even degree. then the multiset $\{\#R_1, \#R_2, \#R_3, \#R_4\}$ is $\{2, 2, 2, 2\}$ or $\{4, 2, 2, 0\}$.

3 Application

In this section, we determine the hyperelliptic curves of genus 3 which admit degree 4 maps to elliptic curves. Then we give an algorithm to find such elliptic subcovers of hyperelliptic curves over finite fields, if they exist.

The algorithm was tested on hyperelliptic curves over finite fields of small size. A possible conclusion from the experiments is that hyperelliptic curves with degree 4 elliptic subcovers defined over cubic extension fields are very special. Using Theorem 3, it is also straightforward to compute elliptic subcovers of degrees 3 and 5, but we have not found elliptic subcovers of hyperelliptic curves whose Jacobians are simple.

3.1 Degree 4 Elliptic Subcover

Let H be a hyperelliptic curve of genus 3. Suppose that $\phi : H \to E$ satisfies the condition in Theorem 3 with multiset $\{2, 2, 2, 2\}$, and that ϕ is triply ramified at two points. We can illustrate these data with the following ramification picture for the Frey-Kani map ϕ_1. In this diagram, $\cdot$ represents an unramified point of ϕ_1 over one of the w_i', which is therefore one of the w_i. $\circ$ represents a doubly ramified point over one of the w_i', $*$ and $\triangle$ represent an unramified point and a triply ramified point of ϕ_1 over the point $-$ respectively.

$$\circ \quad \circ \quad \circ \quad \circ \quad \triangle$$
$$\cdot \quad \cdot \quad \cdot \quad \cdot$$
$$\cdot \quad \cdot \quad \cdot \quad \cdot \quad *$$
$$w_1' \ w_2' \ w_3' \ w_4' \ -$$

By linear fractional transformations on H^τ and E^τ, $\triangle$ and $*$ can be moved to 0 and ∞, w_1', w_2' and $-$ can be moved to 0, 1 and ∞. Hence we can assume that ϕ_1 is given by

$$\phi_1(x) = \frac{k(x^2 + ax + b)(x - c)^2}{x^3}.$$

Suppose that H and E are defined by

$$\begin{aligned} y^2 &= (x^2 + ax + b)(x^2 + e_0 x + f_0)(x^2 + e_1 x + f_1)(x^2 + e_2 x + f_2) \\ &= (x^2 + ax + b)(x^2 + e_0 x + f_0)(x^4 + a_3 x^3 + a_2 x^2 + a_1 x + a_0) \end{aligned}$$

and

$$t^2 = s(s - 1)(s - \lambda)(s - \mu).$$

Consider the following system of equations

$$\begin{cases} k(x^2 + ax + b)(x - c)^2 - x^3 = k(x - d_0)^2(x^2 + e_0 x + f_0), \\ k(x^2 + ax + b)(x - c)^2 - \lambda x^3 = k(x - d_1)^2(x^2 + e_1 x + f_1), \\ k(x^2 + ax + b)(x - c)^2 - \mu x^3 = k(x - d_2)^2(x^2 + e_2 x + f_2). \end{cases}$$

We have a system of 12 polynomial equations in variables a, b, c, d_0, d_1, d_2, e_0, e_1, e_2, f_0, f_1, f_2, k, λ, μ by comparing the coefficients of x. With the computer algebra system Maple, we find that H can be parametrized by a, c, d_0; namely,

$$k = \frac{d_0^2(3c - d_0)}{(c - d_0)^3(a + 2d_0)},$$

$$b = \frac{d_0(2ac + cd_0 + d_0^2)}{d_0 - 3c},$$

$$e_0 = \frac{c(ac^2 + (2c^2 - 3ac)d_0 - 2d_0^3)}{d_0^2(d_0 - 3c)},$$

$$f_0 = \frac{(2ac + cd + d^2)c^2}{d(d - 3c)},$$

$$a_3 = (c + d)(108a^2c^3 - 27ac^4 + (117ac^3 - 18c^4)d_0 + (12c^3 + 81ac^2)d_0^2 \\ + (46c^2 + 9ac)d_0^3 + 20cd_0^4 + 4d_0^5)/(-27c(2ac + cd + d^2)^2),$$

$$a_2 = (27a^2c^4 + 126a^2c^3d_0 + (27a^2c^2 + 132ac^3 - 9c^4)d_0^2 + (136ac^2 + 18c^3)d_0^3 \\ + (36ac + 58c^2)d_0^4 + 42cd_0^5 + 11d_0^6)/(27(2ac + cd_0 + d_0^2)^2),$$

$$a_1 = \frac{-2cd_0(c + d_0)(9ac + 3cd_0 + 5d_0^2)}{27(2ac + cd_0 + d_0^2)},$$

$$a_0 = \frac{1}{9}c^2d_0^2,$$

$$\lambda + \mu = d_0^2(3c - d_0)(216a^3c^3 - 540a^2c^4 - 27ac^5 + (108a^2c^3 - 558ac^4 - 18c^5)d_0 \\ + (216a^2c^2 - 612ac^3 - 168c^4)d_0^2 + (-18ac^2 - 320c^3)d_0^3 + (63ac - 204c^2)d_0^4 \\ - 30cd_0^5 + 4d_0^6)/(27c(c - d_0)^3(a + 2d_0)(2ac + cd_0 + d_0^2)^2),$$

$$\lambda\mu = \frac{4d^4(3ac + (2c - a)d_0 + 2d_0^2)(3ac + 3c^2 + 2cd_0 + d_0^2)^3(3c - d_0)}{27c(c - d_0)^6(a + 2d_0)^2(2ac + cd_0 + d_0^2)^2}.$$

3.2 Computational Aspects over Finite Fields

The following lemma indicates the definition fields of elliptic subcovers of a genus 3 curve over a finite field.

Lemma 4. *Let H be a genus 3 curve over finite field $\mathbb{F}_q$. Assume that its Jacobian $Jac(H)$ is ordinary and simple. If $Jac(H) \otimes \mathbb{F}_{q^n}$ is not simple, then $Jac(H) \otimes \mathbb{F}_{q^n}$ is isogenous to E^3 for some ordinary elliptic curve E over $\mathbb{F}_{q^n}$, and the minimal n is $3, 5, 7, 9$.*

Proof. Since $Jac(H)$ is simple, it is isotypic, so is $Jac(H) \otimes \mathbb{F}_{q^n}$. As $Jac(H) \otimes \mathbb{F}_{q^n}$ is not simple and of dimension 3, the only possibility is that $Jac(H) \otimes \mathbb{F}_{q^n}$ is isogenous to a power of an elliptic curve E. Since $\mathrm{Jac}(H) \otimes \mathbb{F}_{q^n}$ is ordinary, E is ordinary.

Now assume that n is minimal. Since $\mathrm{Jac}(H)$ is simple and ordinary, its characteristic polynomial h is irreducible over $\mathbb{Q}$(see [15]). Let α be a root of h. Then $\mathbb{Q}(\alpha)$ is quadratic extension of the totally real field $\mathbb{Q}(\alpha + q/\alpha)$. Since E is ordinary, $[\mathbb{Q}(\alpha^n) : \mathbb{Q}] = 2$, so $[\mathbb{Q}(\alpha + q/\alpha) : \mathbb{Q}] = 3$ implies that $\mathbb{Q}(\alpha) = \mathbb{Q}(\alpha + q/\alpha, \alpha^n)$.

Let α_1, α_2 be another two roots of h such that $\alpha_1^n = \alpha_2^n = \alpha^n$. Then $\alpha_1 = \zeta_1 \alpha$, $\alpha_2 = \zeta_2 \alpha$ for some n-th roots ζ_1, ζ_2 of unity. Since n is the minimal number such that $\alpha_1^n = \alpha_2^n = \alpha^n$, ζ_1, ζ_2 and ζ_1/ζ_2 are primitive. Let $\varphi(n)$ be the number of integers between 1 and n which are coprime to n. Then $\varphi(n) \geq 2$ because $\zeta_1 \neq \zeta_2$. Note that $\zeta_2 = \zeta_1^a$ for some a with $(a, n) = 1$, then we see that $(a - 1, n) = 1$ since $\zeta_2/\zeta_1 = \zeta_1^{a-1}$ is primitive. Therefore, n is odd.

If the extension $\mathbb{Q}(\alpha)/\mathbb{Q}$ is Galois, then $\mathbb{Q}(\zeta_1)$ is a subfield of $\mathbb{Q}(\alpha)$, which implies that $\varphi(n) = [\mathbb{Q}(\zeta_1) : \mathbb{Q}]$ is equal to 2 or 6. The possible values of n is 3, 7, 9.

If the extension $\mathbb{Q}(\alpha)/\mathbb{Q}$ is not Galois, then $\mathbb{Q}(\alpha + q/\alpha)/\mathbb{Q}$ is not Galois. Let L be the Galois closure of $\mathbb{Q}(\alpha + q/\alpha)/\mathbb{Q}$. Then $L(\alpha^n) = \mathbb{Q}(\alpha, \zeta_1)$ is Galois closure of $\mathbb{Q}(\alpha)/\mathbb{Q}$, and the Galois group $\mathrm{Gal}(\mathbb{Q}(\alpha, \zeta_1))/\mathbb{Q}$ is isomorphic to the product of symmetric group S_3 and cyclic group C_2. Note that $\mathbb{Q}(\zeta_1)/\mathbb{Q}$ is an abelian Galois extension of degree $\varphi(n)$, $\mathrm{Gal}(\mathbb{Q}(\alpha, \zeta_1)/\mathbb{Q}(\zeta_1))$ must be a normal subgroup of $\mathrm{Gal}(\mathbb{Q}(\alpha, \zeta_1)/\mathbb{Q})$. It is easy to check that

$$\{12/|T| : T \text{ is a normal subgroup of } S_3 \times C_2 \text{ with abelian quotient}\} = \{2, 4\}.$$

So the possible values of $\varphi(n)$ are 2 and 4, which implies that $n = 3$ or 5.

Remark 5. The Weil descent attack transforms discrete logarithm problem via the homomorphism $tr \circ \phi^* : \mathrm{Jac}(E)(\mathbb{F}_{q^n}) \to \mathrm{Jac}(H)(\mathbb{F}_{q^n}) \to \mathrm{Jac}(H)(\mathbb{F}_q)$. It is necessary that this homomorphism does not vanish on the large subgroup of prime order. Thus in the cryptological applications we have $\#\mathrm{Jac}(H)(\mathbb{F}_q) \geq \#\mathrm{Jac}(E)(\mathbb{F}_{q^n})$, which implies that $n \leq 3$.

Let H be a hyperelliptic curve of genus 3 defined by

$$y^2 = f(x), \ f(x) \in \mathbb{F}_q[x], \ \deg f = 8 \ .$$

Assume that the conditions of previous subsection are satisfied for the elliptic subcover $\phi : H \to E$. Then ϕ is defined over $\mathbb{F}_{q^n}$ for some $n \in \{3, 5, 7, 9\}$. Once Frey-Kani map ϕ_1 is given, one can easily obtain equation of E and an explicit map $\phi : H \to E$. Hence, we just have to compute polynomials $N(x) = N_4 x^4 + N_3 x^3 + N_2 x^2 + N_1 x + N_0$ and $D(x) = D_4 x^4 + D_3 x^3 + D_2 x^2 + D_1 x + D_0$ with $N(x), D(x) \in \mathbb{F}_{q^n}[x]$ such that $\phi_1(x) = N(x)/D(x)$.

Let R be the set of roots of f in $\bar{\mathbb{F}}_q$. Let $\mathbb{F}_{q^m}$ be the minimal field containing $\mathbb{F}_{q^n}$ and the splitting field of f. We construct a system of polynomial equations over $\mathbb{F}_{q^n}$ by restriction of scalars. Fix $\theta \in \mathbb{F}_{q^m}$ such that $\mathbb{F}_{q^m} = \mathbb{F}_{q^n}[\theta]$. For each possible partition $R = R_1 \cup R_2 \cup R_3 \cup R_4$, the elements of R_i are labelled with x_{2i-1}, x_{2i} for $i = 1, 2, 3, 4$. Suppose that $\phi_1(x_{2i-1}) = \phi_1(x_{2i})$, then we have

$$0 = N(x_{2i-1})D(x_{2i}) - N(x_{2i})D(x_{2i-1}) = \sum_{j=0}^{\frac{m}{n}-1} S_{i,j}^{(1)}\theta^j, i = 1,2,3,4$$

where $S_{i,j}^{(1)}$ are polynomials in $D_0, \cdots, D_4, N_0, \cdots, N_4$ with coefficients in $\mathbb{F}_{q^n}$.
    Let
$$U_i(x) = \frac{N(x)D(x_{2i}) - N(x_{2i})D(x)}{x - x_{2i}}.$$

Then we have polynomials $S_{i,j}^{(2)} \in \mathbb{F}_{q^n}[D_0, \cdots, D_4, N_0, \cdots, N_4]$ such that the discriminant of $\frac{U_i(x)-U_i(x_{2i-1})}{x-x_{2i-1}}$ is

$$\sum_{j=0}^{\frac{m}{n}-1} S_{i,j}^{(2)}\theta^j = 0, i = 1,2,3,4$$

So computing ϕ_1 is equivalent to calculating the $\mathbb{F}_{q^n}$-rational points of algebraic set defined by

$$\{S_{i,j}^{(1)}, S_{i,j}^{(2)} : i = 1,2,3,4; j = 0,1,\cdots,\frac{m}{n}-1\}.$$

One might fail to obtain rational points of this algebraic set since it is not zero-dimensional. To deal with this problem, one can assign values to $\phi_1(x_1)$, $\phi_1(x_3)$, $\phi_1(x_5)$, N_4, D_4 to get more equations. For the case that $m = n = 3$, we obtain the following algorithm.

Algorithm 1. Calculate Frey-Kani map

Input: The set R of roots of f in $\mathbb{F}_{q^3}$
Output: Frey-Kani map ϕ_1
1. Compute the set of partitions $R = \{z_1, z_2\} \cup \{z_3, z_4\} \cup \{z_5, z_6\} \cup \{z_7, z_8\}$
2. Set $\phi_1(x) \leftarrow 0$.
3. For each partition $R = \{z_1, z_2\} \cup \{z_3, z_4\} \cup \{z_5, z_6\} \cup \{z_7, z_8\}$:
4.   Set $N(Y) \leftarrow (Y - z_5)(Y - z_6)(Y - X_1)^2$.
5.   Set $D(Y) \leftarrow (Y - z_7)(Y - z_8)(Y - X_2)^2$.
6.   Set $s_1 \leftarrow ND(z_1) - DN(z_1) - (D(z_1) - N(z_1))(Y - z_1)(Y - z_2)(Y - X_3)^2$.
7.   Set $s_2 \leftarrow ND(z_3) - DN(z_3) - (D(z_3) - N(z_3))(Y - z_3)(Y - z_4)(Y - X_4)^2$.
8.   Set $sys \leftarrow \{$coefficients of s_1, s_2 with respect to variable $Y\}$.
9.   Set $\phi_1(x) \leftarrow \frac{(x-z_5)(x-z_6)(x-a_1)^2}{(x-z_7)(x-z_8)(x-a_2)^2}$ and break out of the loop if the algebraic set
10.   defined by sys has a rational point (a_1, a_2, a_3, a_4).
11. Return $\phi_1(x)$ if it is not equal to 0 and failure otherwise.

This algorithm is based on solving systems of quadratic equations. This kind of system consists of 8 quadratic polynomial equations in 4 variables. The resolution cost using Groebner base is heuristically polynomial in the degree of the corresponding zero-dimensional ideal.

3.3   Example

Applying the previous algorithm to hyperelliptic curves over finite fields $\mathbb{F}_p$ for primes $23 \le p \le 101$, we find some elliptic subcovers which are defined over $\mathbb{F}_{p^3}$ (see Appendix A). For example, let $H/\mathbb{F}_{101}$ be the hyperelliptic curve defined by

$$y^2 = f(x) = x^7 + 86x^6 + 17x^5 + 84x^4 + 24x^3 + 78x^2 + 16x + 98.$$

Let $\mathbb{F}_{101^3} = \mathbb{F}_{101}[\omega]/\langle \omega^3 + 3\omega + 99 \rangle$, and let $E/\mathbb{F}_{101^3}$ be the elliptic curve defined by $y^2 = x^3 + \omega^{463217} x^2 + \omega^{100810} x$. Then we have an elliptic subcover $\phi : H \to E$ given by

$$(x, y) \mapsto (\phi_1(x), y\, \frac{\omega^{751548} \phi_1'}{x^2 + \omega^{761536} x + \omega^{447943}}),$$

where ϕ_1' is the derivative of

$$\phi_1(x) = \frac{51x^4 + \omega^{121109} x^3 + \omega^{241216} x^2 + \omega^{209072} x + \omega^{208555}}{x^4 + \omega^{55351} x^3 + \omega^{945277} x^2 + \omega^{802233} x + \omega^{204872}}$$

with respect to x.

Now we show that the curve H can not be constructed by GHS attack. To see this, we just need to show that H has no hyperelliptic subcover(see Appendix B). If there was a map $\psi : H \to H'$ from H to a genus 2 curve H', then ψ would have degree 2 and send Weierstrass points to Weierstrass points. There would be a map $\psi_1 : \mathbb{P}^1 \to \mathbb{P}^1$ making the diagram

$$
\begin{array}{ccc}
H & \xrightarrow{\ \pi_H\ } & \mathbb{P}^1 \\
\downarrow{\scriptstyle \psi} & & \downarrow{\scriptstyle \psi_1} \\
H' & \xrightarrow{\ \pi_{H'}\ } & \mathbb{P}^1
\end{array}
$$

commutative(see Appendix B). Let $x_1, \cdots, x_7$ be distinct roots of f. One can apply linear fractional transformations on $\mathbb{P}^1$ and renumber those x_i so that ψ_1 can take a form

$$\psi_1(x) = \frac{(x - x_1)(x - x_2)}{x - x_3}$$

with $\psi_1(x_4) = \psi_1(x_5)$, $\psi_1(x_6) = \psi_1(x_7)$. It is easy to check this ψ_1 does not exist, so we get a contradiction.

We expect that degree 4 minimal elliptic subcovers can provide a new attack on discrete logarithm problem in elliptic curves, but we have no idea the general form of these subcovers over finite fields.

4   Conclusion and Perspectives

In this paper, we have given the "general" ramification structure of elliptic subcovers of genus three hyperelliptic curves. We have also shown that elliptic subcovers of a hyperelliptic curve over finite field $\mathbb{F}_q$ can be defined over an extension field of $\mathbb{F}_q$ of degree n with $n \in \{1, 3, 5, 7, 9\}$. These datum are helpful in finding elliptic subcovers over finite fields. In particular, some minimal elliptic subcovers of degree 4 over finite fields are found for the first time, as far as we know. This raises the following two questions: How to efficiently determine whether an given elliptic curve is the target of a degree 4 minimal elliptic subcover of some hyperelliptic curve and compute the subcover if so. Finally, it would be interesting to give examples of elliptic subcovers of hyperelliptic curves of larger degree or genus.

References

1. Auer, R., Top, J.: Some genus 3 curves with many points. In: Fieker, C., Kohel, D.R. (eds.) ANTS 2002. LNCS, vol. 2369, pp. 163–171. Springer, Heidelberg (2002)
2. Birkenhake, C., Lange, H.: Complex abelian varieties, vol. 302. Springer (2004)
3. Diem, C.: The GHS attack in odd characteristic. J. Ramanujan Math. Soc. 18(1), 1–32 (2003)
4. Frey, G., Kani, E.: Curves of genus 2 covering elliptic curves and an arithmetical application. Springer (1991)
5. Gaudry, P., Hess, F., Smart, N.P.: Constructive and destructive facets of weil descent on elliptic curves. Journal of Cryptology 15(1), 19–46 (2002)
6. Hayashida, T., Nishi, M., et al.: Existence of curves of genus two on a product of two elliptic curves. Journal of the Mathematical Society of Japan 17(1), 1–16 (1965)
7. Hayashida, T., et al.: A class number associated with the product of an elliptic curve with itself. Journal of the Mathematical Society of Japan 20(1-2), 26–43 (1968)
8. Howe, E.W., Leprévost, F., Poonen, B.: Large torsion subgroups of split jacobians of curves of genus two or three. Forum Mathematicum 12, 315–364 (2000)
9. Kani, E., Rosen, M.: Idempotent relations and factors of Jacobians. Mathematische Annalen 284(2), 307–327 (1989)
10. Kuhn, R.M.: Curves of genus 2 with split jacobian. Transactions of the American Mathematical Society 307(1), 41–49 (1988)
11. Lauter, K., Serre, J.-P.: The maximum or minimum number of rational points on genus three curves over finite fields. Compositio Mathematica 134(01), 87–111 (2002)
12. Momose, F., Chao, J.: Scholten forms and elliptic/hyperelliptic curves with weak Weil restrictions, cryptology ePrint Archive, Report 2005/277 (2005)
13. Satoh, T.: Generating genus two hyperelliptic curves over large characteristic finite fields. In: Joux, A. (ed.) EUROCRYPT 2009. LNCS, vol. 5479, pp. 536–553. Springer, Heidelberg (2009)
14. Shaska, T.: Curves of genus 2 with (n,n) decomposable jacobians. Journal of Symbolic Computation 31(5), 603–617 (2001)
15. Waterhouse, W.C., Milne, J.: Abelian varieties over finite fields. Ann. Sci. École Norm. Sup. 2(4), 521–560 (1969)

Appendix A: Examples of Elliptic Subcovers

Here we list some elliptic subcovers, one for each prime p with $23 \leq p \leq 101$. Let $H/\mathbb{F}_p$ be hyperelliptic curve of genus 3 defined by $y^2 = g(x)$ with g a polynomial of degree 8. The examples of elliptic subcovers $\phi : H \to E$ below share the following features:

1. The degrees of $\mathbb{F}_p$-irreducible factors of g are $1, 1, 3, 3$.
2. If $p \not\equiv 3 \mod 4$, then $\#E(\mathbb{F}_{p^3}) = 4l_1$, otherwise $\#E(\mathbb{F}_{p^3}) = 8l_2$, where l_1, l_2 are primes.

As mentioned previously, to obtain ϕ, we only need to know ϕ_1. For this, we write

$$g(x) = \delta_1 x(x-1)(x-\alpha)(x-\alpha^p)(x-\alpha^{p^2})(x-\beta)(x-\beta^p)(x-\beta^{p^2}) \quad (1)$$

and

$$\phi_1(x) = \frac{\delta(x-\alpha)(x-\alpha^p)(x-\gamma_1)^2}{(x-\beta)(x-\beta^p)(x-\gamma_2)^2}. \quad (2)$$

Then E has the form

$$y^2 = \delta_2 x(x-1)(x-\lambda). \quad (3)$$

Each row in Table 1 gives the field $\mathbb{F}_{p^3}$, and the values of δ_1, δ_2, λ, α, β, δ, γ_1, γ_2 in (1), (2), (3) in order.

Table 1. Examples of elliptic subcovers

$\mathbb{F}_{p^3}$	δ_1	δ_2	λ	α	β	δ	γ_1	γ_2
$\mathbb{F}_{23}[\omega]/\langle\omega^3+2\omega+18\rangle$	1	5	ω^{12130}	ω^{221}	ω^{12101}	ω^{2402}	ω^{475}	ω^{11191}
$\mathbb{F}_{29}[\omega]/\langle\omega^3+2\omega+27\rangle$	2	2	ω^{18416}	ω^{102}	ω^{22134}	ω^{9288}	ω^{11003}	ω^{2211}
$\mathbb{F}_{31}[\omega]/\langle\omega^3+\omega+28\rangle$	3	3	ω^{14304}	ω^{8}	ω^{22950}	ω^{2124}	ω^{13874}	ω^{20239}
$\mathbb{F}_{37}[\omega]/\langle\omega^3+6\omega+35\rangle$	1	2	ω^{24204}	ω^{9}	ω^{48015}	ω^{6704}	ω^{29879}	ω^{7527}
$\mathbb{F}_{41}[\omega]/\langle\omega^3+\omega+35\rangle$	1	3	ω^{66852}	ω^{943}	ω^{29899}	ω^{60566}	ω^{9790}	ω^{52277}
$\mathbb{F}_{43}[\omega]/\langle\omega^3+\omega+40\rangle$	1	2	ω^{32018}	ω^{174}	ω^{32801}	ω^{6992}	ω^{806}	ω^{41815}
$\mathbb{F}_{47}[\omega]/\langle\omega^3+3\omega+42\rangle$	5	5	ω^{64658}	ω^{109}	ω^{18824}	ω^{43470}	ω^{71377}	ω^{59240}
$\mathbb{F}_{53}[\omega]/\langle\omega^3+3\omega+51\rangle$	1	3	ω^{65216}	ω^{52}	ω^{103250}	ω^{102834}	ω^{133553}	ω^{3954}
$\mathbb{F}_{59}[\omega]/\langle\omega^3+5\omega+57\rangle$	2	2	ω^{76650}	ω^{8}	ω^{119246}	ω^{187722}	ω^{158081}	ω^{63539}
$\mathbb{F}_{61}[\omega]/\langle\omega^3+7\omega+59\rangle$	2	2	ω^{1512}	ω^{49}	ω^{153668}	ω^{224538}	ω^{68014}	ω^{184674}
$\mathbb{F}_{67}[\omega]/\langle\omega^3+6\omega+65\rangle$	1	2	ω^{239646}	ω^{34}	ω^{83528}	ω^{122226}	ω^{43523}	ω^{123079}
$\mathbb{F}_{71}[\omega]/\langle\omega^3+4\omega+64\rangle$	1	7	ω^{246146}	ω^{13}	ω^{264125}	ω^{33246}	ω^{25186}	ω^{197347}
$\mathbb{F}_{73}[\omega]/\langle\omega^3+2\omega+68\rangle$	1	5	ω^{71376}	ω^{192}	ω^{328091}	ω^{90566}	ω^{307528}	ω^{280044}
$\mathbb{F}_{79}[\omega]/\langle\omega^3+9\omega+76\rangle$	1	3	ω^{204028}	ω^{37446}	ω^{187933}	ω^{76636}	ω^{73589}	ω^{255402}
$\mathbb{F}_{83}[\omega]/\langle\omega^3+3\omega+81\rangle$	1	2	ω^{84318}	ω^{1245}	ω^{421102}	ω^{161542}	ω^{115074}	ω^{287217}
$\mathbb{F}_{89}[\omega]/\langle\omega^3+3\omega+86\rangle$	1	3	ω^{84388}	ω^{9}	ω^{660416}	ω^{592294}	ω^{42019}	ω^{580991}
$\mathbb{F}_{97}[\omega]/\langle\omega^3+9\omega+92\rangle$	1	5	ω^{865364}	ω^{3}	ω^{153368}	ω^{621504}	ω^{584858}	ω^{225765}
$\mathbb{F}_{101}[\omega]/\langle\omega^3+3\omega+99\rangle$	2	2	ω^{121416}	ω^{41}	ω^{642490}	ω^{13986}	ω^{918780}	ω^{615324}

Appendix B: Elliptic Subcovers from GHS Attack

Let $\mathbb{F}_q$ be a finite field of odd characteristic and $\mathbb{F}_{q^3}$ its cubic extension. Let $E/\mathbb{F}_{q^3}$ be an elliptic curve defined by $v^2 = u(x)$. The defining equation gives an embedding of rational function field $\mathbb{F}_{q^3}(x)$ in the function field $K(E)$ of E. Now the Galois closure $\mathbb{L}$ of $K(E)/\mathbb{F}_q(x)$ might be the function field of a curve C which can be defined over $\mathbb{F}_q$. If so, then one find a curve $C/\mathbb{F}_q$ with morphism $\phi : C \to E$ defined over $\mathbb{F}_{q^3}$.

We also ask the curve C to be of genus 3, which implies that E has form either

$$v^2 = (x - \mu)(x - \mu^q)u_1(x)$$

or

$$v^2 = (x - \mu_1)(x - \mu_1^q)(x - \mu_2)(x - \mu_2^q),$$

where $\mu \in \mathbb{F}_{q^3} \setminus \mathbb{F}_q$, $u_1(x) \in \mathbb{F}_q[x]$ of degree 1 or 2, $\mu_1, \mu_2 \in \mathbb{F}_{q^3} \setminus \mathbb{F}_q$ or $\mu_2 = \mu_1^{q^3}$ with $\mu_1 \in \mathbb{F}_{q^6} \setminus (\mathbb{F}_{q^2} \cup \mathbb{F}_{q^3})$(see [12, Section 4.1]). The map ϕ has degree 4 in the former case and 2 in the latter. Note that in the former case, $\phi : C \to E$ factors through a degree 2 map $\tilde{\phi} : C \to C'$ since the Galois group of $\mathbb{L}/K(E)$ is isomorphic to $\mathbb{Z}/2\mathbb{Z} \oplus \mathbb{Z}/2\mathbb{Z}$. By the next proposition, we see that C admits a degree 2 hyperelliptic subcover if C is hyperelliptic, and that the GHS attack only yields minimal elliptic subcovers of degree 2.

Proposition 6. *Let H be a hyperelliptic curve of genus 3. Then H has a degree 2 elliptic subcover if and only if H covers a genus 2 curve.*

Proof. If there is a degree 2 map from H to a curve, then H has an automorphism of order 2. Let σ be an automorphism of H of order 2 which is different from the hyperelliptic involution τ. Applying the Theorem B of [9] to the group with partition $\langle \sigma, \tau \rangle = \langle \sigma \rangle \cup \langle \tau \rangle \cup \langle \sigma\tau \rangle$, we obtain the statement. $\quad\square$

The following proposition says that the degree 2 hyperelliptic subcover sends Weierstrass points to Weierstrass points.

Proposition 7. *Let $\psi : H_1 \to H_2$ be a map of hyperelliptic curves. Let τ_i be the hyperelliptic involution on H_i for $i = 1, 2$. Then $\psi \circ \tau_1 = \tau_2 \circ \psi$.*

Proof. Let Q_0 be a fixed point of τ_1. Then $(Q) + (\tau_1(Q)) - 2(Q_0)$ is a principal divisor for all $Q \in H_1$, hence under ψ_* its image $(\psi(Q)) + (\psi(\tau_1(Q))) - 2(\psi(Q_0))$ is also a principal divisor. We can always choose Q such that the points $\psi(Q), \psi(\tau_1(Q))$ are different from $\psi(Q_0)$. Then we see that 2 is not a gap number of $\psi(Q_0)$, which implies that $\psi(Q_0)$ is a Weierstrass point. Therefore, for all $Q \in H_1$, we have

$$(\psi(Q)) + (\psi(\tau_1(Q))) - 2(\psi(Q_0)) \sim 0 \sim (\psi(Q)) + (\tau_2(\psi(Q))) - 2(\psi(Q_0)),$$

or in other words

$$\psi(\tau_1(Q)) \sim \tau_2(\psi(Q)),$$

which implies that $\psi(\tau_1(Q)) = \tau_2(\psi(Q))$ since the genus of H_2 is non-zero.

Batch Blind Signatures on Elliptic Curves

Yang Sun[1,2,3], Qianhong Wu[1,3], Bo Qin[4,2], Yujue Wang[5], and Jianwei Liu[6,1]

[1] School of Electronics and Information Engineering, Beihang University, China
[2] State Key Laboratory of Integrated Services Networks, Xidian University, China
[3] State Key Laboratory of Information Security, Institute of Information Engineering,
Chinese Academy of Sciences, Beijing, 100093, China
[4] Key Laboratory of Data Engineering and Knowledge Engineering (Renmin University of
China) Ministry of Education, School of Information, Renmin University of China, China
[5] School of Computer, Wuhan University, China
[6] The Academy of Satellite Application, Beijing, 100086, China

Abstract. Blind signature is a fundamental tool in electronic cash. In most existing blind signature schemes, both the signer and the verifier need to take expensive modular exponentiations. This situation is deteriorated in significant monetary transactions in which a large number of (multi-)exponentiations need to be calculated. This paper proposes batch blind signature to reduce the computation overheads at both the signer and the verifier sides in blind signatures on elliptical curves. To this end, we first propose a batch multi-exponentiation algorithm that allows a batch of multi-base exponentiations on elliptic curves to be processed simultaneously. We next apply our batch multi-exponentiation algorithm to speed up the Okamoto-Schnorr blind signature scheme in both the signing and the verification procedures. Specifically, the proposed algorithm is exploited for generating blind signatures so that multiple messages can be signed in a batch for sake of saving computation costs. The algorithm is further employed in the verification process, which gives a different batch signature verification approach from the existing batch verification algorithm. An attracting feature of our approach is that, unlike existing batch verification signature approach, our approach does distinguish all valid signatures from a batch purported signatures (of correct and erroneous ones). This is desirable in e-cash systems where a signature represents certain value of e-cash and any valid signature should not passed up. The experimental results show that, compared with acceleration with existing simultaneous exponentiation algorithm, our batch approach is about 55% and 45% more efficient in generating and verifying blind signatures, respectively.

Keywords: Modular exponentiation, Batch exponentiation, Batch signature, Blind signature.

1 Introduction

Blind signature is an interactive protocol which allows a user to get a message signed by a signer without revealing the message to the signer. Chaum [8] observed that it is an important tool for guaranteeing anonymity in electronic cash. When a user withdraws money from a bank, the bank returns electronic coins which have been blindly signed. The user is able to verify the validity of these electronic coins, i.e., blind signatures. For

© Springer International Publishing Switzerland 2015
J. Lopez and Y. Wu (Eds.): ISPEC 2015, LNCS 9065, pp. 192–206, 2015.
DOI: 10.1007/978-3-319-17533-1_14

real-world deployment, especially for large transactions, a larger number of electronic coins may be generated for and verified by a user. Hence, it is essential to speed up blind signatures when a large number of messages to be signed and many signatures need to be verified.

Blind signature has also other important applications such as vehicular ad hoc networks [20] where mobile vehicles need to anonymously access the services of roadside infrastructure. In fact, the blind signature technique has been confirmed to ensure non-linkability that prevents the signer from linking a blinded message he signed to an un-blinded message, and it can be useful in vehicular ad hoc networks for fulfilling the user's privacy requirement. In this scenario, the requirement of computation speed is strict due to the transient connections in vehicular networks.

Existing blind signature schemes require expensive modular exponentiations for generating and verifying blind signatures, which means that those schemes may be unsuitable for direct deployment in aforementioned applications. For example of electronic cash, the bank plays the role of the blind signer and may need to simultaneously provide instant signing services for many requesting users, while time-consuming modular exponentiations would significantly affect the overall performance and users' experience. It will be also a burden for the user when verifying a large amount of electronic coins signed by the bank in a short period to proceed to fulfill online purchases.

The existing approaches to accelerating modular exponentiations mainly fall into two categories. One is the batch exponentiation approach [10,26] that can reduce the time to compute multiple individual exponentiations with the same base, i.e., $g^{r_1}, g^{r_2}, \cdots, g^{r_n}$. The other is the fast multi-exponentiation approaches [3,5,11,30] for speeding up a multi-base exponentiation $g_1^{r_1} g_2^{r_2} \cdots g_m^{r_m}$. The performance strongly depends on the groups, e.g., Z/nZ and $GF(2^n)$, on which the exponentiations are computed. The exponentiations over $GF(2^n)$ have better performance because one square can be done cheaply with a single shift [1,31].

1.1 Our Work

Cryptosystems built on elliptic curves can have shorter key size and are more efficient than their counterparts on regular groups preserving the same level of security. Hence, we focus on accelerating blind signatures on elliptic curves [19,23], with an illustrative example of the Okamoto-Schnorr blind signature scheme [27]. Our contribution is twofold.

First, of independent interest, we propose an efficient algorithm to compute a number of multi-exponentiations $\{g_1^{r_{i,1}} g_2^{r_{i,2}} \cdots g_m^{r_{i,m}} : 1 \leq i \leq n\}$ over Elliptic curve in a batch, i.e., *signed-digit-recoding batch multi-exponentiations* (BME), which captures a very general case of multiple exponentiations. Compared with the existing *simultaneous exponentiation algorithm* [24], e.g., Shamir's trick [13], our algorithm is more efficient if m is not large.

Second, we propose a batch blind signature scheme and allow multiple messages to be signed in a batch as well as a number of signatures to be verified in a batch. Specifically, we employ our BME approach in two phases of a batch signature scheme, i.e., blind signature generation and signature verification of the Okamoto-Schnorr blind signature scheme, to reduce the computation costs. We provide thorough theoretical analysis and conduct extensive experiments on the proposed batch signature scheme. Our BME algorithm greatly accelerates the signature system, compared with Shamir's trick [13], by more than 55% in sign process and 45% in verification.

Although we only show the application of our batch multi-base exponentiation approach to accelerate the Okamoto-Schnorr blind signature scheme, we stress that it can also be applied to speed up other cryptographic systems if many multi-base exponentiations on elliptical curve are involved. Hence, our multi-base exponentiation algorithm is of independent interest and useful in practice.

1.2 Paper Organization

The rest of the paper is organized as follows. Section 2 reviews related work. We propose a batch multi-exponentiation algorithm and provide detailed complexity analyses and comparisons in Section 3. We present batch Okamoto-Schnorr blind signature by applying our batch multi-exponentiation technique in Section 4, followed with thorough theoretical performance analysis and extensive experimental results. Section 6 concludes the paper.

2 Related Work

Modular exponentiation is a basic component in many public-key cryptosystems. Accelerating exponentiations has received considerable research attentions. To compute g^r, the common way is the "square and multiply" [18] method (or binary method). This method takes the binary expansion of exponent r and then iteratively computes a multiplication or a square according to the current binary bit of r. If we do not discriminate between a multiplication and a square which is slightly more efficient, then the average computation complexity is $1.5l$ where l is the bit length of r. One way [22] to accelerate this process is to reduce the number of multiplications; another way is to cut down the time of multiplications [16,25]. Pre-computation [6,21,29] is also useful to accelerate fixed-base exponentiation, although it requires some additional spaces to store pre-computed intermediate results. A good survey of early efforts to speed up single-base modular exponentiations can be found in [15].

A straightforward way to compute a multi-exponentiation like $g_1^{r_1} g_2^{r_2} \cdots g_m^{r_m}$ is to compute the powers separately and then multiply them together. This approach needs $1.5lm$ multiplications on average. In order to reduce the computation time, the number of multiplications or squares should be cut down. Another way is to outsource the exponentiations to a third powerful party [32] but it requires extra communication and delay. The concise algorithm in [3] merges the process of squares, and based on which the Shamir's trick [13] improves multi-exponentiation computation by handling the identical bit of the exponents simultaneously, in such a way that the number of multiplications is reduced and the average computation complexity decreases from $3l$ to $1.75l$ multiplications for $m = 2$. The simultaneous 2^w-ary exponentiation method in [5] handles w bits of an exponent once, which further reduces the number of multiplications. The simultaneous sliding window exponentiation method due to Yen et al. [33] is an improvement of the 2^w-ary method, which cuts down the computation complexity to

$1.625l$ multiplications for $m = 2$ by setting the window size as 2. Both algorithms proposed by Dimitrov, Jullien and Miller [11] and Solinas [30] focus on the representation of exponents, which further reduce the computation complexity to $1.534l$ and $1.503l$ multiplications for $m = 2$, respectively.

Batch exponentiation is an acceleration approach to compute multiple modular exponentiations with a fixed base. M'Raïhi and Naccache [26] proposed the first batch exponentiation algorithm. Compared with the case of individually computing these exponentiations with the standard binary method, their batch fixed-base exponentiation approach can save $2/3$ computation costs. Chung et al. [10] improved this basic batch exponentiation by combining the M'Raïhi-Naccache algorithm with a decremental combination strategy. ippenger presented an almost optimal approach for fast computing batch multi-base exponentiations [28]. Their approach needs the knowledge of the shortest addition chain of the vector of the exponents. Unfortunately, to find such chain has been shown NP-complete [12].

The existing proposals mainly concentrate on computing single-base exponentiations, batch single-base exponentiations and multi-base exponentiations. Few efforts have been made to accelerate batch multi-exponentiations on elliptic curves. Therefore, these existing algorithms may only bring limited efficiency improvement if they are employed to speed up Okamoto-Schnorr like blind signature schemes for generating multiple blind signatures. The known algorithms for verifying multiple signatures are to calculate their product by using batch verification algorithms [4,7,9,14,34]. The public literatures on batch signature verification multiply the purported signatures by lifting each exponentiation to a small random power, instead calculate the results of all exponentiations. This implies that the verification may fail, even if only one signature of a large batch is incorrect. Clearly, this property is not desirable in e-cash: when some blind signatures do not pass the verification, they should not affect the verification of the rest signatures since one needs to identify all the valid signatures each of which represents certain value of money.

3   Batch Multi-exponentiation on Elliptic Curve

We investigate fast multiple multi-exponentiations over finite cyclic group G on Elliptic curves, i.e.,

$$c_i = g_1^{e_{i,1}} g_2^{e_{i,2}} \cdots g_m^{e_{i,m}} \in G, \quad \text{for } i \in [1, n]$$

where $e_{i,1}, e_{i,2}, \cdots, e_{i,m} \in Z_{ord(G)}$ are l-bit random exponents and $g_1, g_2, \cdots, g_m \in G$ are fixed bases. Since each exponent $e_{i,k}$ ($1 \leq i \leq n$ and $1 \leq k \leq m$) can be denoted by

$$e_{i,k} = \sum_{j=0}^{l-1} e_{i,k,j} 2^j$$

where $e_{i,k,j} \in \{0, 1\}$, the corresponding exponentiation can be written as

$$g_k^{e_{i,k}} = g_k^{\sum_{j=0}^{l-1} e_{i,k,j} 2^j} = \prod_{j=0}^{l-1} g_k^{e_{i,k,j} 2^j}.$$

For computing a tuple of multi-exponentiations

$$
\begin{cases}
c_1 = g_1{}^{e_{1,1}} g_2{}^{e_{1,2}} \cdots g_m{}^{e_{1,m}} \\
c_2 = g_1{}^{e_{2,1}} g_2{}^{e_{2,2}} \cdots g_m{}^{e_{2,m}} \\
\qquad\qquad \vdots \\
c_n = g_1{}^{e_{n,1}} g_2{}^{e_{n,2}} \cdots g_m{}^{e_{n,m}}
\end{cases},
\tag{1}
$$

a straightforward method is to employ Shamir's trick [13], which should calculate each c_i ($i \in [1, n]$) separately. We then show an algorithm to compute these multi-exponentiations in a batch, i.e., all c_i's can be computed simultaneously. Note that our batch multi-exponentiation covers M'Raïhi-Naccache batch single-base exponentiation [26] as a particular case.

3.1   Signed-Digit Recoding Batch Multi-exponentiation

We first give an overview of our *signed-digit recoding batch multi-exponentiation algorithm*, which concurrently computes a tuple of multi-exponentiations shown in Equations (1). On one hand, as we known, the number of multiplications is determined by the Hamming weight of exponents. We recode the exponents to reduce the number of multiplications. On the other hand, for a single exponentiation with base g_k, up to l squares with respect to g_k should be calculated and these squares can be shared in computing all c_i-es. We thus pre-compute these squares for all the bases g_k ($1 \le k \le m$) and online use them to calculate c_i for $i = 1, \cdots, m$. In this way, with some additional storage, the total number of square operations can be reduced significantly.

Our BME algorithm consists of two stages. In the first stage the algorithm does the preparation as in existing algorithms but with a different coding method to exploit the easiness in computing the inverse of an exponentiation on elliptic curves. The exponents are recoded as canonical-signed digits to reduce the Hamming weight of these exponents. For radix-2 signed-digit systems, where $\bar{1}$ denotes -1, the exponent recoding algorithm outputs the signed-digit vector representation $(e_{l-1} \cdots e_1 e_0)_{SD2}$ for element $e = \sum_0^{l-1} e_i \times 2^i$, where $e_i \in \{0, 1, \bar{1}\}$. The signed-digit recoding (SDR) is canonical if the outputted signed-digit representation contains no adjacent nonzero digits [17], and moreover, it is unique if the binary representation can be viewed as a padding with an initial zero. The details of SDR algorithm are reviewed in Algorithm 1 which converts a number into its canonical form.

The second stage is to calculate the multi-exponentiations in a batch with converted exponents, as shown in Algorithm 2. The algorithm starts from the first column exponents, scans from the least significant bit to the most significant bit and from the first row to the last row. If the current bit is 1 or $\bar{1}$ for row i, the algorithm multiplies the corresponding base to the result c_i. When approaching the last row, the algorithm squares the corresponding base. This process is repeated till the m-th column exponents are traversed. For each column, the base needs l times of squares on average. Therefore, all of m columns need in total lm squares shared by n rows during the computation, which reduces the total number of squares.

Algorithm 1. Signed-digit Recoding Algorithm

Input:

    the exponent $e = (e_{l+1}e_le_{l-1} \cdots e_1e_0)_2$ with $e_{l+1} = e_l = 0$

Output:

    the exponent $e' = (e'_le'_{l-1} \cdots e'_1e'_0)_{SD2}$, where $e'_i \in \{0, 1, \bar{1}\}$

1. BEGIN
2. $\alpha_0 = 0$
3. **for** $i = 0$ to l **do**
4. $\alpha_{i+1} = \lfloor (\alpha_i + e_i + e_{i+1})/2 \rfloor$
5. $e'_i = e_i + \alpha_i - 2\alpha_{i+1}$
6. **end for**
7. END

An Illustrative Example. We then illustrate the proposed BME algorithm with an illustrative example. Suppose that we compute the following multiple multi-exponentiations

$$c_1 = g_1{}^6 g_2{}^6, c_2 = g_1{}^7 g_2{}^{10}, c_3 = g_1{}^7 g_2{}^9.$$

By signed-digit recoding, we have

$$(10\bar{1}0) = SDR((0110)_2) = SDR((6)_{10}),$$
$$(100\bar{1}) = SDR((0111)_2) = SDR((7)_{10}),$$
$$(1001) = SDR((1001)_2) = SDR((9)_{10}),$$
$$(1010) = SDR((1010)_2) = SDR((10)_{10}).$$

Therefore,

$$c_1 = g_1{}^{10\bar{1}0} g_2{}^{10\bar{1}0} = g_1{}^{1 \cdot 0} g_2{}^{1 \cdot 0} g_1{}^{-2 \cdot 1} g_2{}^{-2 \cdot 1} g_1{}^{4 \cdot 0} g_2{}^{4 \cdot 0} g_1{}^{8 \cdot 1} g_2{}^{8 \cdot 1} = g_1{}^6 g_2{}^6,$$
$$c_2 = g_1{}^{100\bar{1}} g_2{}^{1010} = g_1{}^{-1 \cdot 1} g_2{}^{1 \cdot 0} g_1{}^{2 \cdot 0} g_2{}^{2 \cdot 1} g_1{}^{4 \cdot 0} g_2{}^{4 \cdot 0} g_1{}^{8 \cdot 1} g_2{}^{8 \cdot 1} = g_1{}^7 g_2{}^{10},$$
$$c_3 = g_1{}^{100\bar{1}} g_2{}^{1001} = g_1{}^{-1 \cdot 1} g_2{}^{1 \cdot 1} g_1{}^{2 \cdot 0} g_2{}^{2 \cdot 0} g_1{}^{4 \cdot 0} g_2{}^{4 \cdot 0} g_1{}^{8 \cdot 1} g_2{}^{8 \cdot 1} = g_1{}^7 g_2{}^9.$$

In finite cyclic groups on elliptic curves, the inverse of a point can be computed for free and g^{-i} can be seen as the inverse of g^i. This example shows that the bases $g_1{}^1, g_2{}^1$ can be shared in computing c_1, c_2 and c_3. Similarly, the squares of the bases $g_1{}^2, g_2{}^2$ can also be reused during the computations, so do $g_1{}^4, g_2{}^4$ and $g_1{}^8, g_2{}^8$. With BME algorithm, only 6 square operations are needed to fulfill this task, while 24 squares are if one repetitively invokes the Shamir's algorithm [13].

3.2 Complexity Analysis and Comparison

It is easy to see that for computing a batch of n multi-exponentiations

$$\{g_1{}^{e_{i,1}} g_2{}^{e_{i,2}} \cdots g_m{}^{e_{i,m}}\}_{i \in [1,n]}$$

the number of required squares is determined by the bit length l of the exponent $e_{i,k}$ and the number m of the bases. In contrast, the number of multiplications depends on

---

Algorithm 2. BME Algorithm

Input:
  the bases $g_1, g_2, \cdots g_m \in G$
  the exponents $e'_{i,k}$ for $i \in [1, n]$ and $k \in [1, m]$.
Output:
  $c_1, c_2, \cdots, c_n$
 1. BEGIN
 2. $c_i = 1$ for every $1 \le i \le n$
 3. **for** $j = 0$ to $l - 1$ **do**
 4. **for** $k = 1$ to m **do**
 5.   **for** $i = 1$ to n **do**
 6.   **if** $e'_{i,k,j} = 1$ **then**
 7. $c_i = c_i \times g_k$
 8.   **else if** $e'_{i,k,j} = -1$ **then**
 9. $c_i = c_i \times g_k^{-1}$
10.   **end if**
11.   **end for**
12. $g_k = g_k^2$
13. **end for**
14. **end for**
15. END
16. **return** $c_1, c_2, \cdots, c_n$

---

the Hamming weight of the exponents and the number of exponents. Therefore, the proposed BME algorithm not only merges the square processes of exponentiations in the same column to reduce the number of squares, but also reduces the Hamming weight of the exponents. Specifically, we have the following claim about the computation complexity of our BME algorithm.

Claim. For computing n multi-exponentiations $\{g_1^{e_{i,1}} g_2^{e_{i,2}} \cdots g_m^{e_{i,m}}\}_{i \in [1,n]}$, the proposed BME algorithm needs $l \cdot m$ squares and $l \cdot m \cdot n/3$ multiplications on average.

Proof. It has been proved that [2], at the end of the first stage of preparation, the appearance probability of the digit 0 is $2/3$, and the total occurrence probability of nonzero digits 1 and -1 is $1/3$ on average. That is, the Hamming weight of each exponent $e'_{i,k}$ on average is $l/3$, which means that the total Hamming weight of $m \cdot n$ exponents is $l/3 \cdot (mn) = l \cdot m \cdot n/3$. Hence $l \cdot m \cdot n/3$ multiplications on average are needed in the computations. On the other hand, with BME algorithm, each column of exponentiations take l squares. Therefore, the total number of square operations is $l \cdot m$.   □

Table 1. Computation complexity comparison between BME algorithm and Shamir's trick

	Number of multiplications	Number of squares
Shamir's trick [13]	$(1 - 2^{-m})ln$	ln
Our BME algorithm	$lmn/3$	lm

We proceed to compare the computation complexities of the proposed BME algorithm with existing Shamir's trick in terms of the number of required squares and multiplications. The results are summarized in Table 1 with respect to computing n multi-exponentiations $\{g_1{}^{e_{i,1}} g_2{}^{e_{i,2}} \cdots g_m{}^{e_{i,m}}\}_{i \in [1,n]}$. We have assumed that the square and multiplication take the same computation time. Therefore, as long as $m(n+3)/3 < 2n - n2^{-m}$, the BME algorithm consumes less time than Shamir's trick. As n increases which means that the batch size becomes larger, our algorithm is more efficient. This is because that the number of squares in our algorithm is only dependent on the number of bases, but independent of batch size n.

4   Batch Blind Signature

In this section, we consider batch blind signature scheme with an emphasis on the Okamoto-Schnorr blind signature scheme. A batch blind signature scheme has two phases, batch blind signature generation and batch blind signature verification. In the former stage, the signer signs multiple messages in a batch so that the total signing time can be saved. Notice that in many existing blind signature schemes such as Okamoto-Schnorr's scheme, the most time-consuming operations are multi-base exponentiations. We thereby employ our general batch multi-exponentiation algorithm to reduce the processing expenditures of the scheme. In the batch signature verification, one needs to verify a large number of received blind signatures. We show that the Okamoto-Schnorr blind signature scheme can support batch verification mechanism with our BME algorithm, without missing the valid signatures in a batch containing erroneous signatures.

4.1   Review of Okamoto-Schnorr Blind Signature Scheme

The Okamoto-Schnorr blind signature scheme consists of three components, including key generation, blind signature generation and verification. It is proven secure based on the difficulty of the discrete logarithm problem [27]. Suppose that $H : \{0,1\}^* \to Z_q^*$ is a collision-resistant hash function. The Okamoto-Schnorr blind signature is reviewed as follows.

Key Generation. The signer selects prime integers p and q such that $q|(p-1)$, $p \geq 2^{140}$ and $q \geq 2^{512}$. For a group Z_p^* with prime order q, pick random elements $g_1, g_2 \in_R Z_p^*$ and random numbers $s_1, s_2, t \in_R Z_q$. Calculate

$$v = g_1{}^{-s_1} g_2{}^{-s_2} \bmod p.$$

The public key is (g_1, g_2, p, q, t, v), and the secret key is (s_1, s_2).
Blind Signature Generation. This component comprises four steps.
  – **Step 1:** The blind signer selects random numbers $r_1, r_2 \in_R Z_q^*$ and computes

$$x = g_1{}^{r_1} g_2{}^{r_2} \bmod p.$$

Send x to the client.

- **Step 2:** For a message $m \in_R \{0,1\}^*$ to be signed, the client picks random numbers $d, u_1, u_2 \in_R Z_q^*$, and computes

$$x^* = g_1^{u_1} g_2^{u_2} v^d x \bmod p, \ e^* = H(x^*, m) \ and \ e = e^* + d \bmod q$$

Send e to the blind signer.
- **Step 3:** The blind signer computes

$$y_1 = r_1 + e s_1 \bmod q \ and \ y_2 = r_2 + e s_2 \bmod q,$$

and gives (y_1, y_2) to the client.
- **Step 4:** The client computes

$$y_1^* = y_1 + u_1 \bmod q, \ y_2^* = y_2 + u_2 \bmod q.$$

Therefore, the tuple (e^*, y_1^*, y_2^*) is the blind signature of message m.

Verification. Given a message m and a blind signature, a verifier is able to validate them by checking the following equality

$$e^* \stackrel{?}{=} H(g_1^{y_1^*} g_2^{y_2^*} v^{e^*}, m).$$

4.2 Batch Signature Generation

Consider the case in which multiple messages of some client need to be blindly signed. It can be seen from Section 4.1 that, the most resource-intensive parts of the blind signature generation is to compute x and x^*. We use our BME algorithm to offload these computations when generating n signatures in a batch. In detail, to sign on n messages, the blind signer computes

$$x_i = g_1^{r_{i,1}} g_2^{r_{i,2}} \bmod p$$

where $r_{i,1}, r_{i,2} \in_R Z_q^*$ for each $i \in [1, n]$. They can be simultaneously computed as follows

$$x = \begin{pmatrix} x_1 \\ x_2 \\ \vdots \\ x_n \end{pmatrix} = \begin{pmatrix} g_1^{r'_{1,1}} g_2^{r'_{1,2}} \\ g_1^{r'_{2,1}} g_2^{r'_{2,2}} \\ \vdots \\ g_1^{r'_{n,1}} g_2^{r'_{n,2}} \end{pmatrix} \leftarrow BME\Big(\{g_1, g_2\}; \{r'_{i,1}, r'_{i,2} : 1 \le i \le n\}\Big),$$

where $r'_{i,1} = SDR(r_{i,1})$ and $r'_{i,2} = SDR(r_{i,2})$ for each $1 \le i \le n$.

Similarly, to obtain these n blind signatures, the client computes

$$x_i^* = g_1^{u_{i,1}} g_2^{u_{i,2}} v^{d_i} x_i \bmod p$$

where $u_{i,1}, u_{i,2}, d_i \in_R Z_q^*$ for every $i \in [1, n]$. They can be simultaneously computed as follows

$$x^* = \begin{pmatrix} x_1^* \\ x_2^* \\ \vdots \\ x_n^* \end{pmatrix} = \begin{pmatrix} g_1^{u'_{1,1}} g_2^{u'_{1,2}} v^{d'_1} x_1 \\ g_1^{u'_{2,1}} g_2^{u'_{2,2}} v^{d'_2} x_2 \\ \vdots \\ g_1^{u'_{n,1}} g_2^{u'_{n,2}} v^{d'_n} x_n \end{pmatrix} \leftarrow BME^* \left(\begin{matrix} \{g_1, g_2, v\} \\ \{u'_{i,1}, u'_{i,2}, d'_i : 1 \le i \le n\} \end{matrix} \right),$$

where $u'_{i,1} = SDR(u_{i,1})$, $u'_{i,2} = SDR(u_{i,2})$ and $d'_i = SDR(d_i)$ for each $1 \leq i \leq n$. Note that the algorithm BME* is the same to BME except that all c_i are respectively initialized as x_i rather than 1.

4.3 Batch Verification

As shown in the Okamoto-Schnorr blind signature scheme, to validate n message-signature pairs $\{(m_i; e_i^*, y_{i,1}^*, y_{i,2}^*) : i \in [1, n]\}$ signed by using the same key, the verifier should repeatedly check whether the following equation holds

$$e_i^* \stackrel{?}{=} H(g_1{}^{y_{i,1}^*} g_2{}^{y_{i,2}^*} v^{e_i^*}, m_i)$$

for all $i \in [1, n]$.

To accelerate the verification process for multiple signatures, the most common way is to adopt the batch verification approach [4] by checking the equality of the product of different signature verification equations. However, it is not suitable in this situation because the values are hashed. Furthermore, in the traditional way, if the equation passes the verification, then all signatures are believed correct. If the verification fails, then at least one purported signature in the batch is invalid. In practice, either the batch is dropped or each of the signature in the batch is re-checked separately, which incurs even more computation cost. However, in e-cash systems, a valid blind signature represent a coin and must be found from the batch which may contain invalid ones. This implies the traditional batch signature verification cannot be applied to blind signatures. Therefore, we propose a new batch verification scheme by using the batch multi-exponentiation algorithm to get n intermediate values $g_1{}^{y_{i,1}^*} g_2{}^{y_{i,2}^*} v^{e_i^*}$ ($i \in [1, n]$) simultaneously. Specifically, the verifier first computes

$$\gamma = \begin{pmatrix} \gamma_1 \\ \gamma_2 \\ \vdots \\ \gamma_n \end{pmatrix} = \begin{pmatrix} g_1{}^{y'_{1,1}} g_2{}^{y'_{1,2}} v^{e'_1} \\ g_1{}^{y'_{2,1}} g_2{}^{y'_{2,2}} v^{e'_2} \\ \vdots \\ g_1{}^{y'_{n,1}} g_2{}^{y'_{n,2}} v^{e'_n} \end{pmatrix} \leftarrow BME\left(\{g_1, g_2, v\}; \{y'_{i,1}, y'_{i,2}, e'_i : 1 \leq i \leq n\}\right),$$

where $y'_{i,1} = SDR(y_{i,1}^*)$, $y'_{i,2} = SDR(y_{i,2}^*)$ and $e'_i = SDR(e_i^*)$ for each $1 \leq i \leq n$. Then, check if all the equalities $e_i^* \stackrel{?}{=} H(\gamma_i, m_i)$ hold.

5 Performance Evaluation

5.1 Theoretical Analysis

We give a theoretical analysis of the batch Okamoto-Schnorr blind signature scheme and compare it with the Shamir approach. Since the multiplication and the square are the basic operations inacceleration of the exponentiations, they are used as metrics to evaluate the efficiency of the optimized Okamoto-Schnorr blind signature schemes with BME and Shamir's trick, respectively. The comparison between them for batch generating and verifying n blind signatures are summarized in Table 2.

Table 2. Comparison of optimizing Okamoto-Schnorr blind signature scheme with BME and Shamir's trick

		With BME	With Shamir's trick [13]
Signing	Signer	$\frac{2ln}{3}$ + $2n$ multiplications + $2l$ squares	$\frac{3ln}{4}$ + $2n$ multiplications + ln squares
	Client	ln multiplications + $3l$ squares	$\frac{7ln}{8}$ multiplications + ln squares
Verification		ln multiplications + $3l$ squares	$\frac{7ln}{8}$ multiplications + ln squares

The signing process is an interactive protocol between the signer and the requesting client. We analyze the efficiency at both sides. Recall that in the signing process for many messages, the most complicated operations are to compute multi-exponentiations in x and x^*. Therefore, we measure the complexity in terms of required multiplications and squares to produce these vectors with the BME algorithm and Shamir's trick, respectively. Besides, in Step 3 of each signing process, the blind signer needs two additional multiplications for computing y_1 and y_2.

In computation of x that involves n multi-exponentiations for $m = 2$, the BME algorithm requires $2l$ squares, independent of n but linear with l; while Shamir's trick needs ln squares, dependent on both l and n. The number of required multiplications in BME algorithm is also less than that in Shamir's trick, i.e., $\frac{2ln}{3} < \frac{3ln}{4}$. Similarly, for computing x^* at the client side, our BME algorithm takes $ln/8$ multiplications on average, slightly more than that of Shamir's trick, but both algorithms need $3l$ and ln squares, respectively. As assumed that one square is equivalent to one multiplication, our BME algorithm can save nearly $\left(\frac{7ln}{8} + ln\right) - (ln + 3l) = \frac{7ln}{8} - 3l$ computations compared with Shamir's trick if $n > 4$. In fact, the larger of n, the more efficient our BME algorithm.

For batch verification of multiple blind signatures, the main computations are incurred by calculating the multi-exponentiations in γ. In fact, these multi-exponentiations satisfy $m = 3$, which is the same to the signing process at the client side. We omit the details for avoiding repetition. From the analysis, the proposed BME algorithm greatly saves the computation overheads of signing process and verification in batch Okamoto-Schnorr blind signature scheme, and shows advantages over existing Shamir's trick especially when n is large.

5.2   Experimental Analysis

We conducted a series of experiments to evaluate the practicality of batch Okamoto-Schnorr blind signature scheme and also compare it with the case where Shamir's trick is used. The experiments were run on a PC with a 2.80GHz CPU and 3GB RAM, by using C programming language in the GMP and PBC library. We set $|p| = 512$ and $l = |q| = 140$, that is, all the random exponents are 140-bits long, while g_1, g_2 and v are 512-bits long. At first, the Step 1 and 2 of signing process are executed for 100 times to remove any experimental noise. In the experiments, the number n is set as $100, 200, \cdots, 1000$ to see the performance improvements due to BME algorithm and Shamir's trick.

As we discussed that, during the signing process of multiple blind signatures, both the blind signer and the client should take n resource-intensive multi-exponentiations.

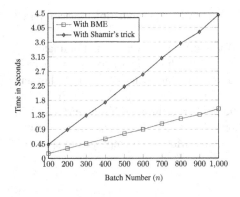

Fig. 1. The performance of blind signer for producing multiple signatures with BME/Shamir's trick

Fig. 2. The performance of the client for producing multiple signatures with BME/Shamir's trick

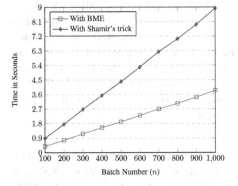

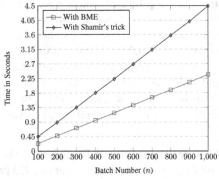

Fig. 3. The overall performance for producing multiple signatures with BME/Shamir's trick

Fig. 4. The performance for validating multiple signatures with BME/Shamir's trick

In our experiments, we thus evaluate the performance of these two parties separately in Figure 1 and Figure 2. That is, the simulation results in these two figures are dominated by computing vectors x and x^*, respectively. It can be seen that the performances at both sides for generating n blind signatures are linear with the number n of messages to be signed. Furthermore, computing n multi-exponentiations with $m = 2$, which are the main workloads of the blind signer when generating n signatures, by BME algorithm only requires roughly 40% computation time of that by Shamir's trick. Similarly, Figure 2 indicates that the main workloads of the client, i.e., calculating n multi-exponentiations with $m = 3$, takes roughly 55% computation time with BME algorithm of that with Shamir's trick. The overall performance of producing n blind signatures is shown in Figure 3, which takes into account the computation time at both sides of the blind signer and the client. Hence, it shows the similar trends as Figure 1 and Figure 2. One can also see from Figure 3 that, BME algorithm makes the whole signing process of generating n signatures save nearly 55% computation time compared to that with Shamir's trick.

For verifying n blind signatures, the performance of the verifier is dominated by computing n multi-exponentiations with $m = 3$ as shown in vector γ and n hash evaluations. When accelerating the computations by employing BME algorithm and Shamir's trick, the corresponding simulation results are shown in Figure 4. It demonstrates that BME algorithm makes the verification procedure more efficient than that accelerated by Shamir's trick with a rate about 45%. In all, these experimental results confirm that BME algorithm is superior to Shamir's trick when employed to speed up Okamoto-Schnorr blind signature scheme.

6   Conclusion

This paper proposed a batch multi-exponentiation algorithm to accelerate these computations. It shows better performance when compared with existing Shamir's trick. The algorithm was further used to speed up Okamoto-Schnorr blind signature scheme. In this way, multiple messages can be blindly signed simultaneously and many signatures for the same public key can also be efficiently validated in a batch. Both theoretical and experimental analyses show that our batch multi-exponentiation algorithm greatly improves the performance of the Okamoto-Schnorr blind signature scheme for generating and validating multiple signatures. This application also implies that our BME algorithm is useful to accelerate some other cryptographic schemes or protocols if many multi-exponentiations on elliptical curves are involved.

Acknowledgments and Disclaimer. The authors are supported by the Chinese National Key Basic Research Program (973 program) through project 2012CB315905, the Natural Science Foundation of China through projects 61370190, 61173154, 61472429, 61402029, 61272501, 61202465, 61321064 and 61003214, the Beijing Natural Science Foundation under project 4132056, the Fundamental Research Funds for the Central Universities, and the Research Funds (No. 14XNLF02) of Renmin University of China and the Open Research Fund of Beijing Key Laboratory of Trusted Computing.

References

1. Agnew, G.B., Mullin, R.C., Vanstone, S.A.: Fast Exponentiation in $GF(2^n)$. In: Günther, C.G. (ed.) EUROCRYPT 1988. LNCS, vol. 330, pp. 251–255. Springer, Heidelberg (1988)
2. Arno, S., Wheeler, F.S.: Signed Digit Representations of Minimal Hamming Weight. IEEE Transactions on Computers 42(8), 1007–1010 (1993)
3. Avanzi, R.M.: On multi-exponentiation in cryptography. Cryptology ePrint Archive, Report 2002/154 (2002)
4. Bellare, M., Garay, J.A., Rabin, T.: Fast batch verification for modular exponentiation and digital signatures. In: Nyberg, K. (ed.) EUROCRYPT 1998. LNCS, vol. 1403, pp. 236–250. Springer, Heidelberg (1998)
5. Bos, J.N.E., Coster, M.J.: Addition Chain Heuristics. In: Brassard, G. (ed.) Advances in Cryptology–CRYPTO 1989. LNCS, vol. 435, pp. 400–407. Springer, Heidelberg (1990)

6. Brickell, E.F., Gordon, D.M., McCurley, K.S., Wilson, D.B.: Fast Exponentiation with Precomputation (Extended Abstract). In: Rueppel, R.A. (ed.) Advances in Cryptology–EUROCRYPT 1992. LNCS, vol. 658, pp. 200–207. Springer, Heidelberg (1993)
7. Camenisch, J., Hohenberger, S., Pedersen, M.Ø.: Batch Verification of Short Signatures. Journal of Cryptology 25(4), 723–747 (2012)
8. Chaum, D.: Blind Signatures for Untraceable Payments. In: Chaum, D., Rivest, R.L., Sherman, A.T. (eds.) Advances in Cryptology–CRYPTO 1982, pp. 199–203. Springer US (1983)
9. Cheon, J.H., Kim, Y., Yoon, H.: A New ID-based Signature with Batch Verification. Cryptology ePrint Archive, Report 2004/131 (2004)
10. Chung, B., Hur, J., Kim, H., Hong, S.M., Yoon, H.: Improved batch exponentiation. Information Processing Letters 109(15), 832–837 (2009)
11. Dimitrov, V.S., Jullien, G.A., Miller, W.C.: Complexity and fast algorithms for multiexponentiations. IEEE Transactions on Computers 49(2), 141–147 (2000)
12. Downey, P., Leong, B., Sethi, R.: Computing sequences with addition chains. SIAM Journal on Computing 10(3), 638–646 (1981)
13. El Gamal, T.: A Public Key Cryptosystem and a Signature Scheme Based on Discrete Logarithms. In: Blakely, G.R., Chaum, D. (eds.) Advances in Cryptology–CRYPTO 1984. LNCS, vol. 196, pp. 10–18. Springer, Heidelberg (1985)
14. Ferrara, A.L., Green, M., Hohenberger, S., Pedersen, M.Ø.: Practical Short Signature Batch Verification. In: Fischlin, M. (ed.) CT-RSA 2009. LNCS, vol. 5473, pp. 309–324. Springer, Heidelberg (2009)
15. Gordon, D.M.: A survey of fast exponentiation methods. Journal of Algorithms 27(1), 129–146 (1998)
16. Hong, S.-M., Oh, S.-Y., Yoon, H.: New Modular Multiplication Algorithms for Fast Modular Exponentiation. In: Maurer, U.M. (ed.) Advances in Cryptology–EUROCRYPT 1996. LNCS, vol. 1070, pp. 166–177. Springer, Heidelberg (1996)
17. Joye, M., Yen, S.M.: Optimal left-to-right binary signed-digit recoding. IEEE Transactions on Computers 49(7), 740–748 (2000)
18. Knuth, D.E.: The Art of Computer Programming–Volume 2: Seminumerical Algorithms. Addison-Wesley Professional (2014)
19. Koblitz, N.: Elliptic curve cryptosystems. Mathematics of Computation 48(177), 203–209 (1987)
20. Li, C.T., Hwang, M.S., Chu, Y.P.: A secure and efficient communication scheme with authenticated key establishment and privacy preserving for vehicular ad hoc networks. Computer Communications 31(12), 2803–2814 (2008)
21. Lim, C.H., Lee, P.J.: More Flexible Exponentiation with Precomputation. In: Desmedt, Y.G. (ed.) Advances in Cryptology–CRYPTO 1994. LNCS, vol. 839, pp. 95–107. Springer, Heidelberg (1994)
22. Lou, D.C., Lai, J.C., Wu, C.L., Chang, T.J.: An efficient montgomery exponentiation algorithm by using signed-digit-recoding and folding techniques. Applied Mathematics and Computation 185(1), 31–44 (2007)
23. Menezes, A.J., Okamoto, T., Vanstone, S.A.: Reducing elliptic curve logarithms to logarithms in a finite field. IEEE Transactions on Information Theory 39(5), 1639–1646 (1993)
24. Möller, B.: Algorithms for multi-exponentiation. In: Vaudenay, S., Youssef, A.M. (eds.) SAC 2001. LNCS, vol. 2259, pp. 165–180. Springer, Heidelberg (2001)
25. Montgomery, P.L.: Modular multiplication without trial division. Mathematics of Computation 44(170), 519–521 (1985)
26. M'Raïhi, D., Naccache, D.: Batch Exponentiation: A Fast DLP-based Signature Generation Strategy. In: Proceedings of the 3rd ACM Conference on Computer and Communications Security, CCS 1996, pp. 58–61. ACM, New York (1996)

27. Okamoto, T.: Provably Secure and Practical Identification Schemes and Corresponding Signature Schemes. In: Brickell, E.F. (ed.) CRYPTO 1992. LNCS, vol. 740, pp. 31–53. Springer, Heidelberg (1993)
28. Pippenger, N.: On the evaluation of powers and monomials. SIAM Journal on Computing 9(2), 230–250 (1980)
29. de Rooij, P.: Efficient exponentiation using precomputation and vector addition chains. In: De Santis, A. (ed.) EUROCRYPT 1994. LNCS, vol. 950, pp. 389–399. Springer, Heidelberg (1995)
30. Solinas, J.: Low-weight binary representations for pairs of integers. Tech. rep., CORR 2001-41, Department of C&O, University of Waterloo (2001)
31. Stinson, D.R.: Some Observations on Parallel Algorithms for Fast Exponentiation in GF(2^n). SIAM Journal on Computing 19(4), 711–717 (1990)
32. Wang, Y., Wu, Q., Wong, D.S., Qin, B., Chow, S.S.M., Liu, Z., Tan, X.: Securely Outsourcing Exponentiations with Single Untrusted Program for Cloud Storage. In: Kutyłowski, M., Vaidya, J. (eds.) ESORICS 2014, Part I. LNCS, vol. 8712, pp. 326–343. Springer, Heidelberg (2014)
33. Yen, S.M., Laih, C.S., Lenstra, A.K.: Multi-exponentiation (cryptographic protocols). Computers and Digital Techniques 141(6), 325–326 (1994)
34. Zhang, C., Lu, R., Lin, X., Ho, P.-H., Shen, X.: An efficient identity-based batch verification scheme for vehicular sensor networks. In: The 27th Conference on Computer Communications on INFOCOM 2008, pp. 816–824. IEEE (April 2008)

Stream Cipher II

Improved Differential Analysis
of Block Cipher PRIDE

Qianqian Yang[1,2,3], Lei Hu[1,2,*], Siwei Sun[1,2], Kexin Qiao[1,2], Ling Song[1,2],
Jinyong Shan[1,2], and Xiaoshuang Ma[1,2]

[1] State Key Laboratory of Information Security, Institute of Information Engineering,
Chinese Academy of Sciences, Beijing 100093, China
[2] Data Assurance and Communication Security Research Center,
Chinese Academy of Sciences, Beijing 100093, China
[3] University of Chinese Academy of Sciences, Beijing 100049, China
{qqyang13,hu,swsun,kxqiao13,lsong,jyshan12,xsma13}@is.ac.cn

Abstract. In CRYPTO 2014 Albrecht *et al.* brought in a 20-round iterative lightweight block cipher PRIDE which is based on a good linear layer for achieving a tradeoff between security and efficiency. A recent analysis is presented by Zhao *et al.* Inspired by their work, we use an automatic search method to find out 56 iterative differential characteristics of PRIDE, containing 24 1-round iterative characteristics, based on three of them we construct a 15-round differential and perform a differential attack on the 19-round PRIDE, with data, time and memory complexity of 2^{62}, 2^{63} and 2^{71} respectively.

Keywords: Block Cipher, PRIDE, Differential attack, Active S-box, Automatic Method.

1 Introduction

In recent years, the field of lightweight cryptography has attracted a lot attention from the cryptographic community, due to the need of low-cost cryptosystems for several emerging applications. Because of the strong demand from industry, a lot of lightweight block ciphers are published, such as the ISO/IEC standards PRESENT [5] and CLEFIA [12], SIMON and SPECK [2], PRINCE [6], KLEIN [8], LED [9], TWINE [15] and LBlock [17]. In this context, it is important to estimate the security of block ciphers.

Proposed by Biham and Shamir, differential cryptanalysis [3] is one of the most well-known attacks in block cipher cryptanalysis today. Based on differential cryptanalysis a bunch of cryptanalytic techniques has been developed, such as impossible differential attack [4], truncated differential attack [10] and boomerang attack [16]. Those attacks are chosen plaintext attacks based on a differential distinguisher which uses pairs of plaintexts. The distinguisher exploits the fact that for the attacked cipher, the probability that an input difference

---

* Corresponding author.

© Springer International Publishing Switzerland 2015
J. Lopez and Y. Wu (Eds.): ISPEC 2015, LNCS 9065, pp. 209–219, 2015.
DOI: 10.1007/978-3-319-17533-1_15

results in an output difference is higher than that under a random permutation. For a differential attack, we should firstly find a high probability differential characteristic which is equal to trace a path of highly probable differences through the various stages of encryption. Since the number of differentially active S-boxes which are defined as those with non-zero input differences is used to evaluate the maximum differential probability of block ciphers, Mouha *et al.* [11] proposed a Mixed-Integer Linear Programming (MILP) based technique to automatically calculate a lower bound of the number of active S-boxes of block ciphers. Further more, Sun *et al.* extended MILP based method of Mouha *et al.* to bit-oriented model in [13,14].

PRIDE [1] is a 20-round iterative lightweight block cipher designed by Albrecht *et al.* in CRYPTO 2014, which is based on a good linear layer for achieving a tradeoff between security and efficiency and going to both software-friendly and hardware-friendly. A recent single-key differential analysis is presented by Zhao *et al.* [18]. They utilized the weaknesses of the S-box and the linear layer to find out 16 different 2-round iterative differential characteristics and construct several 15-round differentials. Based on one of the differential characteristics, they launched a single-key differential attack on the 18-round PRIDE with data, time and memory complexity of $2^{60}, 2^{66}$ and 2^{64}, respectively. For differential attack under related-key model, a stronger attack hypothesis than single-key model, very recently, a related-key differential analysis on the full-round PRIDE was presented by Dai *et al.* [7].

Our Contribution. In this paper, using the automatic methods based on Mixed-Integer Linear Programming presented in [13,14], we find out 24 1-round iterative differential characteristics and 32 2-round iterative characteristics, including the same 16 characteristics presented in [18]. With one of the 1-round iterative differential characteristics and inspired by the analysis of Zhao *et al.* [18] we construct a 15-round differential path of differential probability 2^{-60}, and based on which we perform an improved differential attack on the 19-round PRIDE, with data, time and memory complexity of 2^{62}, 2^{63} and 2^{71} respectively. At present, this analysis is the best one for single-key differential attack on PRIDE.

We organize this paper as follows: We give the notations and briefly describe the cipher PRIDE in Section 2. In Section 3 we show the differential characteristics of PRIDE and delineate differential attack on 19-round PRIDE. Finally, we summarize our results.

2   Description of Block Cipher PRIDE

2.1   Notations

The following notations are used in this paper:

I_r	the input of the r-th round
X_r	the state after the key addition layer of the r-th round
Y_r	the state after the Sbox layer of the r-th round input
Z_r	the state after the P permutation layer of the r-th round
W_r	the state after the matrix layer of the r-th round
O_r	the output of the r-th round
C	the ciphertext of block cipher PRIDE
ΔX	the XOR difference of X and X'
$\oplus$	bitwise exclusive OR (XOR)
$x\|y$	bit string concatenation of x and y
?	a bit with uncertain value
$X[n_1, n_2, ...]$	the n_1, n_2,...-th nibbles of state X, $1 \leq n_1 < n_2 < ... \leq 16$
$X\{b_1, b_2, ...\}$	the b_1, b_2,...-th bits of state X, $1 \leq b_1 < b_2 < ... \leq 64$, numbered from the left to right

2.2   Description of PRIDE

PRIDE is an FX-structure block cipher with 64-bit blocks and 128-bit keys. The 128-bit master key is composed of the subkey k_1 and the pre-whitening key k_0 which is equal to the post-whitening k_2, i.e.,

$$k = k_0\|k_1 \ with \ k_2 = k_0.$$

The cipher has an iterations of 20 rounds, of which the first 19 are identical. The structure of the cipher is depicted in Fig.1, which is redrawn from [1].

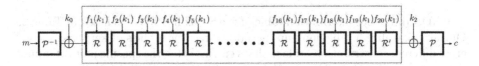

Fig. 1. Overall Structure of the PRIDE

The round function R of PRIDE is an SPN structure: The state is XORed with the round key, fed into 16 parallel 4-bit S-boxes and then permuted and processed by the linear layer, see Fig.2, which is also redrawn from [1].

The S-box of PRIDE is given in Table 1, and the linear layer is defined as

$$M := L_0 \times L_1 \times L_2 \times L_3$$

$$L := P^{-1} \circ M \circ P,$$

where detailed definitions of $L_i, i \in \{0, 1, 2, 3\}$ are given in Appendix A. The linear layer of the last round is omitted.

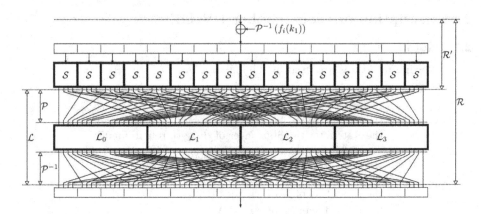

Fig. 2. Round Function R of PRIDE

Table 1. S-box of PRIDE

x	0x0 0x1 0x2 0x3 0x4 0x5 0x6 0x7 0x8 0x9 0xa 0xb 0xc 0xd 0xe 0xf
S(x)	0x0 0x4 0x8 0xf 0x1 0x5 0xe 0x9 0x2 0x7 0xa 0xc 0xb 0xd 0x6 0x3

3   Differential Attack on 19-Round PRIDE

In this section, we describe our differential attack on the 19-round PRIDE. We first give 24 1-round iterative characteristics, and then construct a 15-round distinguisher by concatenation. Finally we perform a key recovery procedure on the 19-round PRIDE.

3.1   Differential Characteristic of Block Cipher PRIDE

The XOR difference distribution table of the S-box in PRIDE is listed in Table 2. Our attack utilize a table look-up method to recover nibbles of key, thus a concrete difference distribution table with its entries being the specific pairs of input-output values is preferred.

We apply the automatic search methods of sun *et al* [13,14] to the block cipher PRIDE and find out 56 iterative differential characteristics, which includes 24 1-round characteristics with input(output) hamming weight 2, 16 2-round characteristics with input(output) hamming weight 3 and 16 same 2-round characteristics with input(output) hamming weight 1 as ones described in [18]. We only show the 24 1-round iterative characteristics in Table 3.

We choose the 4th differential characteristic in Table 3 to construct a 15-round differential characteristic with probability 2^{-60} to launch the differential attack on the 19-round PRIDE.

Table 2. XOR Difference Distribution Table for the S-box of PRIDE

	0x0	0x1	0x2	0x3	0x4	0x5	0x6	0x7	0x8	0x9	0xa	0xb	0xc	0xd	0xe	0xf
0x0	16	0	0	0	0	0	0	0	0	0	0	0	0	0	0	0
0x1	0	0	0	0	4	4	4	4	0	0	0	0	0	0	0	0
0x2	0	0	0	0	0	0	0	0	4	0	0	4	2	2	2	2
0x3	0	0	0	0	0	0	0	0	4	0	0	4	2	2	2	2
0x4	0	4	0	0	0	0	4	0	0	2	2	0	2	0	0	2
0x5	0	4	0	0	0	4	0	0	0	2	2	0	2	0	0	2
0x6	0	4	0	0	4	0	0	0	0	2	2	0	0	2	2	0
0x7	0	4	0	0	0	0	0	4	0	2	2	0	0	2	2	0
0x8	0	0	4	4	0	0	0	0	4	0	4	0	0	0	0	0
0x9	0	0	0	0	2	2	2	2	0	0	0	0	2	2	2	2
0xa	0	0	0	0	2	2	2	2	4	0	4	0	0	0	0	0
0xb	0	0	4	4	0	0	0	0	0	0	0	0	2	2	2	2
0xc	0	0	2	2	2	2	0	0	0	2	0	2	2	0	2	0
0xd	0	0	2	2	0	0	2	2	0	2	0	2	0	2	0	2
0xe	0	0	2	2	0	0	2	2	0	2	0	2	2	0	2	0
0xf	0	0	2	2	2	2	0	0	0	2	0	2	0	2	0	2

Table 3. 1-round iterative characteristics of PRIDE

1	1000 0000 0000 0000 1000 0000 0000 0000 0000 0000 0000 0000 0000 0000 0000 0000
2	1000 0000 0000 0000 0000 0000 0000 0000 1000 0000 0000 0000 0000 0000 0000 0000
3	1000 0000 0000 0000 0000 0000 0000 0000 0000 0000 0000 0000 1000 0000 0000 0000
4	0000 0000 0000 0000 1000 0000 0000 0000 1000 0000 0000 0000 0000 0000 0000 0000
5	0000 0000 0000 0000 1000 0000 0000 0000 0000 0000 0000 0000 1000 0000 0000 0000
6	0000 0000 0000 0000 0000 0000 0000 0000 1000 0000 0000 0000 1000 0000 0000 0000
7	0000 1000 0000 0000 0000 1000 0000 0000 0000 0000 0000 0000 0000 0000 0000 0000
8	0000 1000 0000 0000 0000 0000 0000 0000 0000 1000 0000 0000 0000 0000 0000 0000
9	0000 1000 0000 0000 0000 0000 0000 0000 0000 0000 0000 0000 0000 1000 0000 0000
10	0000 0000 0000 0000 0000 1000 0000 0000 0000 1000 0000 0000 0000 0000 0000 0000
11	0000 0000 0000 0000 0000 1000 0000 0000 0000 0000 0000 0000 0000 1000 0000 0000
12	0000 0000 0000 0000 0000 0000 0000 0000 0000 1000 0000 0000 0000 1000 0000 0000
13	0000 0000 1000 0000 0000 0000 1000 0000 0000 0000 0000 0000 0000 0000 0000 0000
14	0000 0000 1000 0000 0000 0000 0000 0000 0000 0000 1000 0000 0000 0000 0000 0000
15	0000 0000 1000 0000 0000 0000 0000 0000 0000 0000 0000 0000 0000 0000 1000 0000
16	0000 0000 0000 0000 0000 0000 1000 0000 0000 0000 1000 0000 0000 0000 0000 0000
17	0000 0000 0000 0000 0000 0000 1000 0000 0000 0000 0000 0000 0000 0000 1000 0000
18	0000 0000 0000 0000 0000 0000 0000 0000 0000 0000 1000 0000 0000 0000 1000 0000
19	0000 0000 0000 1000 0000 0000 0000 1000 0000 0000 0000 0000 0000 0000 0000 0000
20	0000 0000 0000 1000 0000 0000 0000 0000 0000 0000 0000 0000 1000 0000 0000 0000
21	0000 0000 0000 1000 0000 0000 0000 0000 0000 0000 0000 0000 0000 0000 0000 1000
22	0000 0000 0000 0000 0000 0000 0000 1000 0000 0000 0000 0000 1000 0000 0000 0000
23	0000 0000 0000 0000 0000 0000 0000 1000 0000 0000 0000 0000 0000 0000 0000 1000
24	0000 0000 0000 0000 0000 0000 0000 0000 0000 0000 0000 1000 0000 0000 0000 1000

Table 4. Differential Analysis on 19-round PRIDE

ΔI_1	???? ???? ???? 0000 ???? 0000 ???? 0000 ???? ???? 0000 0000 ???? ???? 0000 0000
ΔX_1	???? ???? ???? 0000 ???? 0000 ???? 0000 ???? ???? 0000 0000 ???? ???? 0000 0000
ΔY_1	?00? 00?0 00?0 0000 ?00? 0000 00?0 0000 ?0?? 00?0 0000 0000 ?00? 00?0 0000 0000
ΔZ_1	?000 ?000 ?000 ?000 0000 0000 0000 0000 0??0 00?0 ??00 0?00 ?000 ?000 ?000 ?000
ΔW_1	0000 ?000 ?000 0000 0000 0000 0000 0000 0000 ?000 ?000 0000 0000 ?000 ?000 0000
ΔI_2	0000 0000 0000 0000 ?0?? 0000 0000 0000 ?0?? 0000 0000 0000 0000 0000 0000 0000
ΔX_2	0000 0000 0000 0000 ?0?? 0000 0000 0000 ?0?? 0000 0000 0000 0000 0000 0000 0000
ΔY_2	0000 0000 0000 0000 1000 0000 0000 0000 1000 0000 0000 0000 0000 0000 0000 0000
ΔZ_2	0000 1000 1000 0000 0000 0000 0000 0000 0000 0000 0000 0000 0000 0000 0000 0000
ΔW_2	0000 1000 1000 0000 0000 0000 0000 0000 0000 0000 0000 0000 0000 0000 0000 0000
ΔI_3	0000 0000 0000 0000 1000 0000 0000 0000 1000 0000 0000 0000 0000 0000 0000 0000
ΔX_{18}	0000 0000 0000 0000 1000 0000 0000 0000 1000 0000 0000 0000 0000 0000 0000 0000
ΔY_{18}	0000 0000 0000 0000 ?0?? 0000 0000 0000 ?0?? 0000 0000 0000 0000 0000 0000 0000
ΔZ_{18}	0000 ?000 ?000 0000 0000 0000 0000 0000 0000 ?000 ?000 0000 0000 ?000 ?000 0000
ΔW_{18}	?000 ?000 ?000 ?000 0000 0000 0000 0000 ??00 000? ??00 0000 ?000 ?000 ?000 ?000
ΔI_{19}	?0?? 00?0 0000 0000 ?00? 0000 0000 00?0 ?0?? 00?0 0000 0000 ?00? 0000 0000 0000
ΔX_{19}	?0?? 00?0 0000 0000 ?00? 0000 0000 00?0 ?0?? 00?0 0000 0000 ?00? 0000 0000 0000
ΔY_{19}	???? ???? 0000 0000 ???? 0000 0000 ???? ???? ???? 0000 0000 ???? 0000 0000 0000
ΔO_{19}	???? ???? 0000 0000 ???? 0000 0000 ???? ???? ???? 0000 0000 ???? 0000 0000 0000

3.2 Differential Analysis on Block Cipher PRIDE

In this subsection, we put our 15-round differential characteristic from the 3rd to the 17th round of PRIDE, extending 2 rounds backward and forward respectively. The description is given in Table 4. We find that the hamming weight of ΔY_2 is one less than that of ΔY_1 in [18] and the hamming weight of ΔX_{18} is one less than that of ΔX_{17} in [18]. Additionally, we notice that when the input difference of the S-box is 1000, the output difference must be ?0??, and when the output difference is 1000, the input difference must be ?0??(the authors of [18] seemed to miss this point). Due to the above two rules, we can extend 2 rounds backward and forward respectively to achieve the differential attack on the 19-round PRIDE. Consequently the 1-round iterative characteristics are more appropriate than the 2-round iterative characteristics in [18].

-**Data Collection Phase.** Choose $2^{25.65}$ structures, in each of which, plaintexts fix in nibbles 4, 6, 8, 11, 12, 15, 16 and traverse in nibbles 1, 2, 3, 5, 7, 9, 10, 13, 14. There are 2^{36} plaintexts and their corresponding ciphertexts which consist of 2^{71} pairs. There are 16 possible values for ΔX_2 since only 4 different input differences of S-box can result in output difference 1000 and the probability is 2^{-2}. Thus, the probability that a pair of plaintexts in a structure can result in the expected input difference of the distinguisher is $16/2^{36} \times 2^{-4} = 2^{-36}$.

Observing from Table 2, we know that the output difference 1000 only has four different input differences. Thus, extending 2 rounds backward has 16 different cases. Similar to backward extending, the extending 2 rounds forward also has 16 different situations. In order to guarantee the bits of exhaustively searching less than 60, we choose the situations which the active S-boxes are more than 17 except for 21. There are 109 situations totally. Because of the 5th and the 6th differentials in Table 3 forming the same structures, we use the three differentials to recovery the information about the key. The expected number of right pairs is $2^{25.65+71} \times 2^{-36} \times 2^{-60} \times \frac{109}{16^2} \times 3 = 2$. The data complexity is $2^{25.65} \times 2^{36} \approx 2^{61.65}$.

After 19-round encryption, the ciphertext difference should satisfy $\Delta C[3,4,6, 7,11,12,14,15,16] = 0$, which makes only $2^{60.65}$ pairs left.

-Key Recovery Phase. For the appointed differential, we recover these bits of key, which correspond to $(k_0 \oplus P^{-1}(f_1(k_1)))[1,2,3,5,7,9,10,13,14]$ in the 1st round, $k_0[1,2,5,8,9,10,13]$ of the post-whitening, 8 bits $(M \circ P)^{-1}(f_{19}(k_1))[5,9]$ in the last 2nd round and 8 bits $P^{-1}(f_2(k_1))[5,9]$ in the 2nd round.

We choose one of the 109 situations that $\Delta Y_1 = 10000010001000000000100000$
$01000001011001000000001001001000000000$ and $\Delta X_{19} = 001000100000000010$
$0000000000001010000010000000000000000000000$. Since the 13th nibble of ΔX_{19} is 0000, there are $2^{60.65} \times 2^{-4} = 2^{56.65}$ pairs left. Through looking up the table we sieve the pairs with the probability of 4/16, 6/16, 6/16, 4/16, 6/16, 6/16, 6/16, 8/16, 6/16, 6/16, 6/16, 6/16, 4/16, 4/16, and 6/16. Thus there are $2^{56.65} \times (4/16)^4 \times (6/16)^{10} \times 8/16 \approx 2^{33.50}$ pairs left. Next we use the method of table look-up to recovery these bits of key.

- Step 1. Firstly, we recover the values of $(k_0 \oplus P^{-1}(f_1(k_1)))[1]$. For each remaining pair of plaintexts, look up the concrete difference distribution table by its input difference in the first nibble and output difference 1000, we get 4 candidates for $(k_0 \oplus P^{-1}(f_1(k_1)))[1]$ and then store the values in a table, say Table D. The time complexity is about $2^{33.50} \times \frac{1}{16} \times \frac{1}{19} \approx 2^{25.25}$.
- Step 2. For each pair of plaintexts associated with each of its corresponding candidates for $(k_0 \oplus P^{-1}(f_1(k_1)))[1]$, look up the concrete difference distribution table by its input difference in the 13th nibble and output difference 1001, we get 2 candidates for $(k_0 \oplus P^{-1}(f_1(k_1)))[13]$. Again we store the values in Table D. The time complexity is no more than $2^{33.50} \times 4 \times \frac{1}{16} \times \frac{1}{19} \approx 2^{27.25}$.
- Step 3. Similar to Step 2, for each pair of texts associated with each of its corresponding candidates for previously recovered key bits, look up the concrete difference table, we get the candidates for $(k_0 \oplus P^{-1}(f_1(k_1)))[2,3,5,7,9,10,14]$ and $k_0[1,2,8,9,10,5]$ successively. The time complexity is about $2^{54.65} \times \frac{1}{16} \times \frac{1}{19} \approx 2^{46.40}$.
- Step 4. Because the value of ΔX_2 and ΔY_{18} are fixed, in order to get the information of $(M \circ P)^{-1}(f_{19}(k_1))[5,9]$ and $P^{-1}(f_2(k_1))[5,9]$ we only need to look up four times for all pairs associated with their corresponding candidates for $(k_0 \oplus P^{-1}(f_1(k_1)))[1,2,3,5,7,9,10,13,14]$ and $k_0[1,2,5,8,9,10,13]$.
- Step 5. Repeating the same process 109×3 times for different characteristics, we get Table D containing $2^{56.65} \times 2^8 \times 27 \times 3 \approx 2^{70.99}$ candidates for at least 68 bits of key. The most frequently appeared candidate serves as the right one and it cost $2^{56.65} \times 2^8 \times 27 \times 3 \times \frac{1}{16} \times \frac{1}{19} \approx 2^{62.74}$ to find it by a common method.
- Step 6. For the rest of the no more than 60 bits, we perform an exhaustive search.

In summary, we achieve that the data, time and memory complexities are 2^{62}, 2^{63} and 2^{71}, respectively.

By observing and analysing, we find that the 56 iterative differential characteristics obtained by automatic search methods all utilize the two characteristics that the output difference and the input difference of S-box both are 0x8 with probability $1/4$ and L_0 is an involution. The two features maybe cause a weakness of PRIDE that produces some high probability iterative differential characteristics. If the designer revises the S-box or L_0, it perhaps avoids the attack.

4   Conclusion

In this paper, we proposed an improved differential attack on the 19-round PRIDE by utilizing new 1-round iterative differential characteristics which is found by automatic search methods. The differential characteristics we used are suitable for extending 4 rounds to launch the differential attack. The data, time and memory complexities of our attack are 2^{62}, 2^{63} and 2^{71} respectively. Moreover, if more differentials can be used at the same time, it may be possible to launch an attack on the full-round PRIDE.

Acknowledgements. The authors would like to thank anonymous reviewers for their helpful comments and suggestions. The work of this paper was supported by the National Key Basic Research Program of China (2013CB834203), the National Natural Science Foundation of China (Grants 61472417, 61402469 and 61472415), the Strategic Priority Research Program of Chinese Academy of Sciences under Grant XDA06010702, and the State Key Laboratory of Information Security, Chinese Academy of Sciences.

References

1. Albrecht, M.R., Driessen, B., Kavun, E.B., Leander, G., Paar, C., Yalçın, T.: Block Ciphers – Focus On The Linear Layer (feat. PRIDE). In: Garay, J.A., Gennaro, R. (eds.) CRYPTO 2014, Part I. LNCS, vol. 8616, pp. 57–76. Springer, Heidelberg (2014)
2. Beaulieu, R., Shors, D., Smith, J., Treatman-Clark, S., Weeks, B., Wingers, L.: The SIMON and SPECK Families of Lightweight Block Ciphers. Cryptology ePrint Archive (2013), https://eprint.iacr.org/2013/404
3. Biham, E., Shamir, A.: Differential cryptanalysis of DES-like cryptosystems. Journal of Cryptology 4(1), 3–72 (1991)
4. Biryukov, A.: Impossible Differential Attack. In: Encyclopedia of Cryptography and Security, pp. 597–597. Springer (2011)
5. Bogdanov, A.A., Knudsen, L.R., Leander, G., Paar, C., Poschmann, A., Robshaw, M., Seurin, Y., Vikkelsoe, C.: PRESENT: An Ultra-Lightweight Block Cipher. In: Paillier, P., Verbauwhede, I. (eds.) CHES 2007. LNCS, vol. 4727, pp. 450–466. Springer, Heidelberg (2007)

6. Borghoff, J., et al.: PRINCE – A Low-Latency Block Cipher for Pervasive Computing Applications. In: Wang, X., Sako, K. (eds.) ASIACRYPT 2012. LNCS, vol. 7658, pp. 208–225. Springer, Heidelberg (2012)

7. Dai, Y., Chen, S.: Cryptanalysis of Full PRIDE Block Cipher. Cryptology ePrint Archive (2014), http://eprint.iacr.org/2014/987

8. Gong, Z., Nikova, S., Law, Y.W.: KLEIN: A New Family of Lightweight Block Ciphers. In: Juels, A., Paar, C. (eds.) RFIDSec 2011. LNCS, vol. 7055, pp. 1–18. Springer, Heidelberg (2012)

9. Guo, J., Peyrin, T., Poschmann, A., Robshaw, M.: The LED Block Cipher. In: Preneel, B., Takagi, T. (eds.) CHES 2011. LNCS, vol. 6917, pp. 326–341. Springer, Heidelberg (2011)

10. Knudsen, L.R.: Truncated and higher order differentials. In: Preneel, B. (ed.) FSE 1994. LNCS, vol. 1008, pp. 196–211. Springer, Heidelberg (1995)

11. Mouha, N., Wang, Q., Gu, D., Preneel, B.: Differential and linear cryptanalysis using Mixed-Integer linear programming. In: Wu, C.-K., Yung, M., Lin, D. (eds.) Inscrypt 2011. LNCS, vol. 7537, pp. 57–76. Springer, Heidelberg (2012)

12. Shirai, T., Shibutani, K., Akishita, T., Moriai, S., Iwata, T.: The 128-Bit Blockcipher CLEFIA (Extended Abstract). In: Biryukov, A. (ed.) FSE 2007. LNCS, vol. 4593, pp. 181–195. Springer, Heidelberg (2007)

13. Sun, S., Hu, L., Wang, M., Wang, P., Qiao, K., Ma, X., Shi, D., Song, L.: Automatic Enumeration of (Related-key) Differential and Linear Characteristics with Predefined Properties and Its Applications. Cryptology ePrint Archive (2014), http://eprint.iacr.org/2014/747

14. Sun, S., Hu, L., Wang, P., Qiao, K., Ma, X., Song, L.: Automatic Security Evaluation and (Related-key) Differential Characteristic Search: Application to SIMON, PRESENT, LBlock, DES(L) and Other Bit-oriented Block Ciphers. In: Sarkar, P., Iwata, T. (eds.) ASIACRYPT 2014. LNCS, vol. 8873, pp. 158–178. Springer, Heidelberg (2014)

15. Suzaki, T., Minematsu, K., Morioka, S., Kobayashi, E.: TWINE: A Lightweight Block Cipher for Multiple Platforms. In: Knudsen, L.R., Wu, H. (eds.) SAC 2012. LNCS, vol. 7707, pp. 339–354. Springer, Heidelberg (2013)

16. Wagner, D.: The Boomerang Attack. In: Knudsen, L.R. (ed.) FSE 1999. LNCS, vol. 1636, pp. 156–170. Springer, Heidelberg (1999)

17. Wu, W., Zhang, L.: LBlock: A Lightweight Block Cipher. In: Lopez, J., Tsudik, G. (eds.) ACNS 2011. LNCS, vol. 6715, pp. 327–344. Springer, Heidelberg (2011)

18. Zhao, J., Wang, X., Wang, M., Dong, X.: Differential Analysis on Block Cipher PRIDE. Cryptology ePrint Archive (2014), http://eprint.iacr.org/2014/525

Appendix A

$$\mathcal{L}_0 = \mathcal{L}_0^{-1} = \begin{pmatrix} 0&0&0&0&1&0&0&0&1&0&0&0&1&0&0&0 \\ 0&0&0&0&0&1&0&0&0&1&0&0&0&1&0&0 \\ 0&0&0&0&0&0&1&0&0&0&1&0&0&0&1&0 \\ 0&0&0&0&0&0&0&1&0&0&0&1&0&0&0&1 \\ 1&0&0&0&0&0&0&0&1&0&0&0&1&0&0&0 \\ 0&1&0&0&0&0&0&0&0&1&0&0&0&1&0&0 \\ 0&0&1&0&0&0&0&0&0&0&1&0&0&0&1&0 \\ 0&0&0&1&0&0&0&0&0&0&0&1&0&0&0&1 \\ 1&0&0&0&1&0&0&0&0&0&0&0&1&0&0&0 \\ 0&1&0&0&0&1&0&0&0&0&0&0&0&1&0&0 \\ 0&0&1&0&0&0&1&0&0&0&0&0&0&0&1&0 \\ 0&0&0&1&0&0&0&1&0&0&0&0&0&0&0&1 \\ 1&0&0&0&1&0&0&0&1&0&0&0&0&0&0&0 \\ 0&1&0&0&0&1&0&0&0&1&0&0&0&0&0&0 \\ 0&0&1&0&0&0&1&0&0&0&1&0&0&0&0&0 \\ 0&0&0&1&0&0&0&1&0&0&0&1&0&0&0&0 \end{pmatrix}$$

$$\mathcal{L}_1 = \begin{pmatrix} 1&1&0&0&0&0&0&0&0&0&0&1&0&0&0&0 \\ 0&1&1&0&0&0&0&0&0&0&0&0&1&0&0&0 \\ 0&0&1&1&0&0&0&0&0&0&0&0&0&1&0&0 \\ 0&0&0&1&1&0&0&0&0&0&0&0&0&0&1&0 \\ 0&0&0&0&1&1&0&0&0&0&0&0&0&0&0&1 \\ 0&0&0&0&0&1&1&0&1&0&0&0&0&0&0&0 \\ 0&0&0&0&0&0&1&1&0&1&0&0&0&0&0&0 \\ 1&0&0&0&0&0&0&1&0&0&1&0&0&0&0&0 \\ 1&0&0&0&0&0&0&0&0&0&1&1&0&0&0&0 \\ 0&1&0&0&0&0&0&0&0&0&0&1&1&0&0&0 \\ 0&0&1&0&0&0&0&0&0&0&0&0&1&1&0&0 \\ 0&0&0&1&0&0&0&0&0&0&0&0&0&1&1&0 \\ 0&0&0&1&0&0&0&0&1&0&0&0&0&0&0&1 \\ 0&0&0&0&0&1&0&0&1&1&0&0&0&0&0&0 \\ 0&0&0&0&0&0&1&0&0&1&1&0&0&0&0&0 \\ 0&0&0&0&0&0&0&1&0&0&1&1&0&0&0&0 \end{pmatrix}$$

$$\mathcal{L}_2 = \begin{pmatrix} 0&0&0&0&1&1&0&0&0&0&0&0&0&0&0&1 \\ 0&0&0&0&0&1&1&0&1&0&0&0&0&0&0&0 \\ 0&0&0&0&0&0&1&1&0&1&0&0&0&0&0&0 \\ 1&0&0&0&0&0&0&1&0&0&1&0&0&0&0&0 \\ 1&1&0&0&0&0&0&0&0&0&0&1&0&0&0&0 \\ 0&1&1&0&0&0&0&0&0&0&0&0&1&0&0&0 \\ 0&0&1&1&0&0&0&0&0&0&0&0&0&1&0&0 \\ 0&0&0&1&1&0&0&0&0&0&0&0&0&0&1&0 \\ 0&0&0&0&1&0&0&0&1&0&0&0&0&0&0&1 \\ 0&0&0&0&0&1&0&0&1&1&0&0&0&0&0&0 \\ 0&0&0&0&0&0&1&0&0&1&1&0&0&0&0&0 \\ 0&0&0&0&0&0&0&1&0&0&1&1&0&0&0&0 \\ 1&0&0&0&0&0&0&0&0&0&0&1&1&0&0&0 \\ 0&1&0&0&0&0&0&0&0&0&0&0&1&1&0&0 \\ 0&0&1&0&0&0&0&0&0&0&0&0&0&1&1&0 \\ 0&0&0&1&0&0&0&0&0&0&0&0&0&0&1&1 \end{pmatrix}$$

$$\mathcal{L}_3 = \mathcal{L}_3^{-1} = \begin{pmatrix} 1&0&0&0&1&0&0&0&0&0&0&0&1&0&0&0 \\ 0&1&0&0&0&1&0&0&0&0&0&0&0&1&0&0 \\ 0&0&1&0&0&0&1&0&0&0&0&0&0&0&1&0 \\ 0&0&0&1&0&0&0&1&0&0&0&0&0&0&0&1 \\ 1&0&0&0&1&0&0&0&1&0&0&0&0&0&0&0 \\ 0&1&0&0&0&1&0&0&0&1&0&0&0&0&0&0 \\ 0&0&1&0&0&0&1&0&0&0&1&0&0&0&0&0 \\ 0&0&0&1&0&0&0&1&0&0&0&1&0&0&0&0 \\ 0&0&0&0&1&0&0&0&1&0&0&0&1&0&0&0 \\ 0&0&0&0&0&1&0&0&0&1&0&0&0&1&0&0 \\ 0&0&0&0&0&0&1&0&0&0&1&0&0&0&1&0 \\ 0&0&0&0&0&0&0&1&0&0&0&1&0&0&0&1 \\ 1&0&0&0&0&0&0&0&1&0&0&0&1&0&0&0 \\ 0&1&0&0&0&0&0&0&0&1&0&0&0&1&0&0 \\ 0&0&1&0&0&0&0&0&0&0&1&0&0&0&1&0 \\ 0&0&0&1&0&0&0&0&0&0&0&1&0&0&0&1 \end{pmatrix}$$

$$\mathcal{L}_1^{-1} = \begin{pmatrix} 0\,0\,0\,0\,0\,0\,1\,1\,0\,0\,0\,0\,0\,0\,1\,0 \\ 1\,0\,0\,0\,0\,0\,0\,1\,0\,0\,0\,0\,0\,0\,0\,1 \\ 1\,1\,0\,0\,0\,0\,0\,0\,1\,0\,0\,0\,0\,0\,0\,0 \\ 0\,1\,1\,0\,0\,0\,0\,0\,0\,1\,0\,0\,0\,0\,0\,0 \\ 0\,0\,1\,1\,0\,0\,0\,0\,0\,0\,1\,0\,0\,0\,0\,0 \\ 0\,0\,0\,1\,1\,0\,0\,0\,0\,0\,0\,1\,0\,0\,0\,0 \\ 0\,0\,0\,0\,1\,1\,0\,0\,0\,0\,0\,0\,1\,0\,0\,0 \\ 0\,0\,0\,0\,0\,1\,1\,0\,0\,0\,0\,0\,0\,1\,0\,0 \\ 0\,0\,0\,1\,0\,0\,0\,0\,0\,0\,0\,1\,1\,0\,0\,0 \\ 0\,0\,0\,0\,1\,0\,0\,0\,0\,0\,0\,0\,1\,1\,0\,0 \\ 0\,0\,0\,0\,0\,1\,0\,0\,0\,0\,0\,0\,0\,1\,1\,0 \\ 0\,0\,0\,0\,0\,0\,1\,0\,0\,0\,0\,0\,0\,0\,1\,1 \\ 0\,0\,0\,0\,0\,0\,0\,1\,1\,0\,0\,0\,0\,0\,0\,1 \\ 1\,0\,0\,0\,0\,0\,0\,0\,1\,1\,0\,0\,0\,0\,0\,0 \\ 0\,1\,0\,0\,0\,0\,0\,0\,0\,1\,1\,0\,0\,0\,0\,0 \\ 0\,0\,1\,0\,0\,0\,0\,0\,0\,0\,1\,1\,0\,0\,0\,0 \end{pmatrix} \qquad \mathcal{L}_2^{-1} = \begin{pmatrix} 0\,0\,1\,1\,0\,0\,0\,0\,0\,0\,1\,0\,0\,0\,0\,0 \\ 0\,0\,0\,1\,1\,0\,0\,0\,0\,0\,0\,1\,0\,0\,0\,0 \\ 0\,0\,0\,0\,1\,1\,0\,0\,0\,0\,0\,0\,1\,0\,0\,0 \\ 0\,0\,0\,0\,0\,1\,1\,0\,0\,0\,0\,0\,0\,1\,0\,0 \\ 0\,0\,0\,0\,0\,0\,1\,1\,0\,0\,0\,0\,0\,0\,1\,0 \\ 1\,0\,0\,0\,0\,0\,0\,1\,0\,0\,0\,0\,0\,0\,0\,1 \\ 1\,1\,0\,0\,0\,0\,0\,0\,1\,0\,0\,0\,0\,0\,0\,0 \\ 0\,1\,1\,0\,0\,0\,0\,0\,0\,1\,0\,0\,0\,0\,0\,0 \\ 0\,0\,0\,0\,0\,0\,0\,1\,1\,0\,0\,0\,0\,0\,0\,1 \\ 1\,0\,0\,0\,0\,0\,0\,0\,1\,1\,0\,0\,0\,0\,0\,0 \\ 0\,1\,0\,0\,0\,0\,0\,0\,0\,1\,1\,0\,0\,0\,0\,0 \\ 0\,0\,1\,0\,0\,0\,0\,0\,0\,0\,1\,1\,0\,0\,0\,0 \\ 0\,0\,0\,1\,0\,0\,0\,0\,0\,0\,0\,1\,1\,0\,0\,0 \\ 0\,0\,0\,0\,1\,0\,0\,0\,0\,0\,0\,0\,1\,1\,0\,0 \\ 0\,0\,0\,0\,0\,1\,0\,0\,0\,0\,0\,0\,0\,1\,1\,0 \\ 0\,0\,0\,0\,0\,0\,1\,0\,0\,0\,0\,0\,0\,0\,1\,1 \end{pmatrix}$$

Estimating Differential-Linear Distinguishers and Applications to CTC2

Chun Guo[1,2], Hailong Zhang[1,*], and Dongdai Lin[1]

[1] State Key Laboratory of Information Security, Institute of Information
Engineering, Chinese Academy of Sciences, Beijing 100093, China
[2] University of Chinese Academy of Sciences, China
{guochun,zhanghailong,ddlin}@iie.ac.cn

Abstract. At FSE 2014, Blondeau *et al.* proposed an exact expression of
the bias of differential-linear approximation and a multidimensional generalization of differential-linear distinguisher. In this paper, we study the
application of the theory to concrete designs. We first propose a meet-in-
the-middle style searching-and-estimating process. Then, we show that
the capacity of a multiple differential distinguisher using χ^2 statistical
test can be written as the summation of squared correlations of several differential-linear distinguishers. This link provides us with another
approach to estimating the theoretical capacity of multiple differential
distinguisher.

We apply the above methods to CTC2. CTC2 was designed by Courtois to show the strength of algebraic cryptanalysis on block ciphers. For
CTC2 with a 255-bit block size and key, we give a multiple differential
attack against 11-round version, which to our knowledge is the best with
respect to the number of attacked rounds. Experimental results firmly
verify the correctness of the proposed method. The attack itself, and its
potential to be further extended, reveals that the resistance of CTC2
against statistical attacks may be much weaker than expected before.

Keywords: block cipher, differential-linear cryptanalysis, truncated
differential, multiple differential cryptanalysis, CTC2.

1 Introduction

Statistical attacks consist of a set of powerful tools, which exploit non-uniformness
in the encryption data to recover the secret key. The two most prominent ones
among them are differential cryptanalysis introduced by Biham *et al.* [2] and linear cryptanalysis introduced by Matsui *et al.* [18]. They both lead to a plenty of
impressive results, e.g. [3,12,17,9].

Differential-Linear (DL) Cryptanalysis. With the two most prominent attacks
– differential attack, and linear attack – at hand, it is naturally wondered that
whether they two can be jointly applied to lead to better cryptanalysis results.

** Corresponding author.

© Springer International Publishing Switzerland 2015
J. Lopez and Y. Wu (Eds.): ISPEC 2015, LNCS 9065, pp. 220–234, 2015.
DOI: 10.1007/978-3-319-17533-1_16

The first such attempt was introduced in 1994 by Langford and Hellman [13], and named differential-linear (DL) cryptanalysis. DL cryptanalysis resulted in the best attack against 8-round DES at that time. The underlying idea of DL cryptanalysis is treating the block cipher as a cascade of two sub-ciphers such that there exists a strong (truncated) differential on the first one and a strongly biased linear approximation on the other, and then concatenating them to form a distinguisher on the entire cipher. Due to its success, many further discussions on DL cryptanalysis [1,14,15,16] have been made since then. Among them, the most recent one was made by Blondeau et al. [5], which complemented and unified the previous approaches. Starting from the observation that any DL relation can be regarded as a truncated differential (also pointed out in [7]), they derived a general expression of its bias based on the link between differential probabilities and linear correlations proposed in [8]. Their expression was in a closed form under the sole assumption that the two parts of the cipher are independent. Based on this expression, they shown how to approximate the bias efficiently under a clear assumption. They also proposed a multidimensional extension of DL distinguisher, named *"multidimensional" differential-linear distinguisher*.

Our Motivations. Despite the potential and generality of the framework of Blondeau et al., no new applications of DL cryptanalysis were presented in [5]. Therefore how to apply the framework in practical cases remains open. This paper tries to fill this gap. It aims at applying the theory of DL approximation to real ciphers to give better attacks, as well as further revealing the links between DL cryptanalysis and differential cryptanalysis, besides the sole observation that DL relations can be seen as truncated differentials.

Our Contributions. We explore the practical applications of the theory of DL cryptanalysis proposed in [5]. First, based on the theory, we propose a meet-in-the-middle style searching-and-estimating process. The process consists of simultaneously searching most of the "significant" differential trails forward from the input difference to the middle round and searching most of the "significant" linear trails backward from the output mask to the middle round, and then gathering all the results at the middle round to calculate the bias of the DL distinguisher. We apply the methodology to CTC2 with a 255-bit block size, and achieves noticeable improvements:

- revisiting the 8.5-round distinguisher in [15]: the bias should be $2^{-27.45}$ or even higher, instead of 2^{-68} estimated by Lu [15].
- the longest statistical distinguisher on CTC2: a 9.5-round DL distinguisher with bias $2^{-48.415}$.

Second, we show that the capacity of the multiple differential (MD) distinguishers using χ^2 statistical test can be expressed as the summation of squared correlations of several DL distinguishers. Such a link provides us with another approach to estimating the lower bound of the capacity of multiple differential distinguisher (hence upper bounding the attack complexity), that is, searching-and-estimating for all the relevant DL distinguishers and use the link to derive the capacity of the MD distinguishers. Since MD distinguishers are probably based on multiple truncated differential distinguishers, and truncated differential distinguishers are usually difficult to search and estimate in bit-based designs (consider PRESENT or CTC2), this method has its own advantage.

Based on the search results and the method for constructing MD distinguisher, we construct a 9.5-round MD distinguisher for CTC2. This distinguisher leads to a key recovery attack against 11-round CTC2, which is the best known attack with respect to the number of attacked rounds. For easy comparison, we list all known attacks against CTC2 in Table 1.

Table 1. Comparison of attacks against CTC2

Rounds	Attack	Data	Time	Memory	Source
6	Algebraic	4	2^{253}	not specified	[10]
4	Meet-in-the-Middle	4	4	not specified	[11]
10	DL	2^{142}	2^{207}	$2^{54.2}$ bytes	[15]
11	MD using χ^2	2^{101}	2^{207}	$\sim 2^{101}$	Sect. 5

Organization. Sect. 2 lists necessary notations and preliminaries. Sect. 3 contains our meet-in-the-middle style searching-and-estimating process. Sect. 4 presents the relationship between DL cryptanalysis and MD cryptanalysis using χ^2 statistical test and how to use it to construct MD distinguishers. Sect. 5 presents the results on CTC2. Finally, Sect. 6 concludes.

2   Preliminaries

Notations. The following notations will be used throughout this paper. First, denote by $\langle u, v \rangle$ the inner product of two bit vectors u and v; second, for an n-bit bit string $m = (m[n-1], m[n-2], \ldots, m[0])$, denote by $m[i]$ the i-th bit; third, denote by $Pr[e]$ the probability of event e; forth, denote by $Pr[\nabla \xrightarrow{\mathbb{T}} \Delta]$ the probability for a differential (∇, Δ) to hold on the transformation $\mathbb{T}$, i.e. $Pr[\nabla \xrightarrow{\mathbb{T}} \Delta] = 2^{-n} \sharp \{x \in F_2^n \mid T(x) \oplus T(x \oplus \nabla) = \Delta\}$; finally, denote by $c_{\mathbb{T}}(a, b)$ the correlation of a linear approximation (a, b) on $\mathbb{T}$, i.e. $c_{\mathbb{T}}(a, b) = 2^{-n}[\sharp \{x \in F_2^n \mid \langle a, x \rangle \oplus \langle b, T(x) \rangle = 0\} - \sharp \{\langle a, x \rangle \oplus \langle b, T(x) \rangle = 1\}]$.

For CTC2, we adopt the notation system used in [11] and [15]: for $0 \le j \le 254$, we denote by e_j a 255-bit value with zeros everywhere except for bit position j, and denote by $e_{i_0,\ldots,i_j}$ the 255-bit value equals to $e_{i_0} \oplus \ldots \oplus e_{i_j}$.

Theory of DL Cryptanalysis. As mentioned in [5], a DL distinguisher for a block cipher $\mathbb{E}$ with n-bit blocks can be characterized by an input difference $\nabla \in \{0,1\}^n$ and an output linear mask $M \in \{0,1\}^n$. More clearly, the DL distinguisher feeds $\mathbb{E}$ with the input difference ∇, and distinguishes according to the bias of the inner product of the output difference and the mask M:

$$\mathcal{E}_{\nabla,M} = Pr[\langle \mathbb{E}(x) \oplus \mathbb{E}(x \oplus \nabla), M \rangle = 0] - \frac{1}{2}. \tag{1}$$

For this, we denote by $DL\langle\nabla, M\rangle$ the DL distinguisher with input difference ∇ and output mask M. Furthermore, when we need to specify a distinguisher between round i and round j of some block ciphers, we use the notation $DL\langle\nabla^i, M^j\rangle$.

In [5], Blondeau *et al.* analyzed in more detail the intermediate layer of the DL approximation, and took into account not only more high-probability output differences from E_0 but also more linear approximations over E_1. Their main result was the concept *differential-linear hull*: if we treat the block cipher $\mathbb{E}$ as a cascade of two sub-ciphers $\mathbb{E} = \mathbb{E}_1 \circ \mathbb{E}_0$, then the bias of a DL distinguisher for $\mathbb{E}$ can be written as the sum of 2^n products, where each product consists of the bias of a DL distinguisher for $\mathbb{E}_0$ and the squared correlation of a linear distinguisher for $\mathbb{E}_1$:

Theorem 1 (Theorem 2 of [5]). *Assume that the parts $\mathbb{E}_0$ and $\mathbb{E}_1$ of the block cipher $\mathbb{E} = \mathbb{E}_1 \circ \mathbb{E}_0$ are independent, we have*

$$\mathcal{E}_{\nabla,M} = \sum_{v \in F_2^n} [Pr[\langle \mathbb{E}_0(x) \oplus \mathbb{E}_0(x \oplus \nabla), v\rangle = 0] - \frac{1}{2}]c_{\mathbb{E}_1}^2(v, M). \tag{2}$$

Estimating following Equation (2) requires estimating for 2^n shorter DL approximations and 2^n linear approximations, which is clearly infeasible in real cases where typical choice of block size n is 64 or 128 bits. To solve this, Blondeau *et al.* suggested decomposing Equation (2) into two sums with respect to a set $V \in F_2^n$ [5][1], that is, $\mathcal{E}_{\nabla,M} = \sum_{v \in V, v \neq 0}[Pr[\langle \mathbb{E}_0(x \oplus \nabla) \oplus \mathbb{E}_0(x), v\rangle = 0] - \frac{1}{2}]c_{\mathbb{E}_1}^2(v, M) + \sum_{v \notin V}[Pr[\langle \mathbb{E}_0(x \oplus \nabla) \oplus \mathbb{E}_0(x), v\rangle = 0] - \frac{1}{2}]c_{\mathbb{E}_1}^2(v, M)$ Then, under the following assumption, the bias of DL approximation can be approximated by only considering a subspace V of F_2^n.

Assumption 1 (Assumption 1 in [5]). Given a set V, we assume that

$$\left| \sum_{v \in V, v \neq 0} [Pr[\langle \mathbb{E}_0(x \oplus \nabla) \oplus \mathbb{E}_0(x), v\rangle = 0] - \frac{1}{2}]c_{\mathbb{E}_1}^2(v, M) \right| \leq |\mathcal{E}_{\nabla,M}|,$$

This assumption was verified to be valid on SMALL-PRESENT [5].

The correlation of a given DL distinguisher $DL\langle\nabla, M\rangle$ is defined as twice the bias. In the following sections, we denote by $\widetilde{c}_{\mathbb{E}}(DL\langle\nabla, M\rangle)$ the correlation of $DL\langle\nabla, M\rangle$ on block cipher $\mathbb{E}$, i.e. $\widetilde{c}_{\mathbb{E}}(DL\langle\nabla, M\rangle) = 2 \cdot \mathcal{E}_{\nabla,M}$.

MD Cryptanalysis Using χ^2 Statistical Test. Multiple differential cryptanalysis using χ^2 statistical test [4] is one of the latest improvements on differential cryptanalysis. Such an attack is based on multiple (truncated) differentials, and uses statistical tests to measure the score of the key guesses. To conduct MD attacks in real contexts, one is required to select suitable subsets of output differences or group them in a proper way. Two attack models were proposed in [4]: in the "unbalanced partitioning" one, a subspace of output differences

---

[1] How to choose V may depend on the concrete context.

is taken into consideration, with the probability distributions involving ordinary differential probabilities, while in the "balanced partitioning" one, attack is based on probability distributions of truncated differentials, allowing to take the information from the whole output space into consideration. We notice that there exists a clear relationship between the latter model and DL cryptanalysis, hence we focus on the "balanced partitioning" model in the following sections.

In the "balanced partitioning" model, partition functions induce a balanced partitioning of the difference space (the sets of differences that are projected to elements of V are all of equal cardinality) [4]. Such balanced partition functions have a particular structure linked to truncated differentials. It focuses on a subset of bits in the output difference. A support s to indicate this targeted difference bits subset is determined, with $s \in \{0, 1, \ldots, n-1\}$; then $|V| = 2^{|s|}$, and the partition function consists of considering only bits belonging to this support:

$$\pi_{bal}(\delta) = \delta|_s = \sum_{i=0}^{|s|} 2^i \cdot \delta[s(i)],$$

where $s(i)$ denotes the i-th bit that belong to the support. The MD cryptanalysis therefore functions by calculating the distribution of the values indicated by the $2^{|s|}$ difference bits, obtaining the distance between it and the uniform distribution, and then distinguishing/ranking key candidates by this statistics. χ^2 statistics is a choice that could be taken to measure this distance. Let $p = [p_v]_{v \in V}$ be the expected probability distribution vector, θ the uniform one and q^k the observed one for a key candidate k, then the capacity of the MD distribution is defined as the capacity of distribution p

$$Cap(p) = \sum_{v \in V} \frac{(p_v - \theta_v)^2}{\theta_v}, \tag{3}$$

and the χ^2 statistics is defined as $\chi^2(q^k, \theta) = N_S \sum_{v \in V} \frac{(q_v^k - \theta_v)^2}{\theta_v} = N_S \cdot Cap(q^k)$.

According to the theory of χ^2 test, the data complexity required by such multiple differential cryptanalysis is as follows.

Theorem 2 (Data Complexity in MDC [4]). *Let $Cap(p)$ be the capacity of the correct-candidate probability vector p. Then the number N_S of samples of the corresponding attack with success probability P_S and advantage a can be estimated by*

$$N_S = \frac{\sqrt{2|V|}b + 2t^2 + t(\sqrt{2|V|} + 2b)\sqrt{1 + 4\frac{t^2 - b^2}{(\sqrt{2|V|} + 2b)^2}}}{Cap(p)}, \tag{4}$$

where $b = \Phi_{0,1}^{-1}(1 - 2^{-a})$, $t = \Phi_{0,1}^{-1}(P_S)$. The notions advantage a and success probability P_S are defined as follows: assuming that the number of key guesses is 2^n, and the attack will take l among them as possible key candidates and use an exhaustive search to find the correct one, then the advantage of such attack *over pure exhaustive search is $a = n - log_2(l)$, and P_S is the probability that the correct key candidate is ranked among the l first guesses during the attack.*

By the discussions above, the balanced-partitioning MD distinguisher using χ^2 statistical tests can be characterized by an input difference ∇ and a projecting space V. Therefore, we denote such a distinguisher by $MD \langle \nabla, V \rangle$, and denote by $Cap_{\mathbb{E}}(MD \langle \nabla, V \rangle)$ the capacity of $MD \langle \nabla, V \rangle$ on block cipher $\mathbb{E}$. Similarly to the DL context, we also use the notation $MD \langle \nabla^i, V^j \rangle$ to denote a distinguisher between round i and round j (of some ciphers).

3   Applying the Theory: A MITM-Style Search-and-Estimate Strategy

Accurately estimating the bias following Equation (2) and its extensions still requires accurately estimating the linear approximations on $\mathbb{E}_1$ and the short DL approximations on $\mathbb{E}_0$. In real cases, both the number of rounds and the block size are large, and accurate theoretical estimation of the linear approximations and short DL approximations can not be obtained (especially the latter ones). Hence such approach is not practical yet. In these cases, cryptanalysts typically approximate the linear approximations with some dominant trails which brings in loss of precision, and the loss might accumulate to a high level during the summing process. Therefore to apply the theory to real ciphers, more discussions and verifications are necessary. Motivated by such intuitions, we investigate the possibility of using dominant trails to approximate the bias of DL distinguishers.

First, Theorem 1 yields to the following corollary:

Corollary 1. *Treating an n-bit block cipher $\mathbb{E}$ as a cascade of two sub-ciphers $\mathbb{E} = \mathbb{E}_1 \circ \mathbb{E}_0$ and assuming them to be independent, the correlation $\tilde{c}_{\mathbb{E}}(DL \langle \nabla, M \rangle)$ can be expressed as*

$$\tilde{c}_{\mathbb{E}}(DL \langle \nabla, M \rangle) = \sum_{v \in \mathbb{F}_2^n} \sum_{\delta \in \mathbb{F}_2^n} (-1)^{\langle \delta, v \rangle} Pr[\nabla \xrightarrow{\mathbb{E}_0} \delta] c_{\mathbb{E}_1}^2 (v, M). \qquad (5)$$

Proof. By Equation (2), we have:

$$\tilde{c}_{\mathbb{E}}(DL \langle \nabla, M \rangle) = 2 \cdot \mathcal{E}_{\nabla, M} = \sum_{v \in F_2^n} \tilde{c}_{\mathbb{E}_0}(DL \langle \nabla, v \rangle) c_{\mathbb{E}_1}^2 (v, M)$$

$$= \sum_{v \in F_2^n} [[\sum_{\delta \in F_2^n} (-1)^{\langle \delta, v \rangle} Pr[\nabla \xrightarrow{\mathbb{E}_0} \delta]] c_{\mathbb{E}_1}^2 (v, M)]$$

as claimed.   □

This corollary allows us to use a meet-in-the-middle style approach, i.e. simultaneously search forward from ∇ and backward from M and do a middle-calculating at a middle round. More clearly, the approach starts from the input difference ∇^0, and propagates it forward round by round. For every round, all the possible output differences $\nabla^0 \to \delta$ and the corresponding probabilities $Pr[\nabla^0 \to \delta]$

are collected as tuples $(\delta, Pr[\nabla^0 \to \delta])$ in a list, and they are used as the starting points for the next round in a width-first manner. This forward search process continues until it reaches the specified meet round $meet\_rnd$ and obtains all the tuples $(\delta_i^{meet\_rnd}, Pr[\nabla^0 \to \delta_i^{meet\_rnd}])$. Then, the approach starts from the output mask M^r, propagates it backward round by round (also in a width-first manner) until it reaches the meet round $meet\_rnd$ and obtains all the tuples $(M_j^{meet\_rnd}, c^2(M_j^{meet\_rnd}, M^r))$. Then the correlation of the DL approximation is calculated as the summation of $(-1)^{\langle \delta_i^{meet\_rnd}, M_j^{meet\_rnd} \rangle} \cdot Pr[\nabla^0 \to \delta_i^{meet\_rnd}] \cdot c^2(M_j^{meet\_rnd}, M^r)$ for each pair $(\delta_i^{meet\_rnd}, M_j^{meet\_rnd})$.

To reduce the time cost, the two searches are processed in a branch-and-bound manner. For S-box based designs, two bounds are introduced:

1. a bound d_bound is used to limit the number of active S-boxes in the differences processed during the forward searching phase;
2. another bound l_bound is used to limit the number of active S-boxes in the linear masks processed during the backward searching phase;

During the searching, at each round, if the number of active S-boxes in an obtained difference (linear mask, resp.) is more than d_bound (l_bound, resp.), then the difference (mask, resp.) will be immediately discarded and not taken into in the next step.

The time complexity of this process is exponential, because during the "matching" phase, we have to compute $(-1)^{\langle \delta_i^{meet\_rnd}, M_j^{meet\_rnd} \rangle} \cdot Pr[\nabla^0 \to \delta_i^{meet\_rnd}] \cdot c^2(M_j^{meet\_rnd}, M^r)$ for all pairs $(\delta_i^{meet\_rnd}, M_j^{meet\_rnd})$ derived by the two phases. Such a high complexity limits the use of this approach. Nevertheless, compared with the previous results, the process leads to better ones.

4   Constructing MD Distinguishers Using χ^2 Statistical Test from DL Distinguishers

In this section we show the links between the bias of DL distinguisher and the capacity of MD distinguisher using χ^2 statistical test, and we show how to construct MD distinguisher from the former.

4.1   Capacity of MD Distinguisher and Bias of DL Distinguisher

We now show the relationship between the capacity of the MD distinguisher defined in [4] with partitioning function $\pi_{bal}(\delta) = \delta \mid_s = \sum_{i=0}^{|s|} 2^i \cdot \delta[s(i)]$ and the bias/correlation of the one-dimensional DL distinguisher. *Wlog*, suppose that the set s of targeted difference bits used by the MD distinguisher consists of the most significant $d = |s|$ difference bits, i.e. the partition function is

$$\pi_{bal}(\delta) = (\delta[n-1], \delta[n-2], \ldots, \delta[n-d]) = \sum_{i=0}^{d} 2^i \cdot \delta[n-d+i].$$

In such cases, we provide the following lemma:

Lemma 1 (Truncated differential probability to DL correlation). *For any $v \in F_2^d$, it holds:*

$$Pr_{\mathbb{E}}[\pi_{bal}(\mathbb{E}(x) \oplus \mathbb{E}(x \oplus \nabla)) = v] = 2^{-d} \sum_{M \in F_2^d} (-1)^{\langle M, v \rangle} \widetilde{c}_{\mathbb{E}}(DL\langle \nabla, (M \mid 0^t)\rangle). \quad (6)$$

Proof. Let $t = n - d$, then

$$Pr[\nabla \xrightarrow{\mathbb{E}} (v \mid *)] = \sum_{\delta_t \in F_2^t} Pr[\nabla \xrightarrow{\mathbb{E}} (v \mid \delta_t)]$$

$$= \sum_{\delta_t \in F_2^t} \sum_{M \in F_2^n} \frac{1}{2^n} (-1)^{\langle M, (v \mid \delta_t) \rangle} \widetilde{c}_{\mathbb{E}}(DL\langle \nabla, M \rangle)$$

$$= \frac{1}{2^n} \sum_{M \in F_2^n} \left(\sum_{\delta_t \in F_2^t} (-1)^{\langle M, (v \mid \delta_t) \rangle} \widetilde{c}_{\mathbb{E}}(DL\langle \nabla, M \rangle) \right)$$

For $M \in \{(x \mid 0) \mid x \in F_2^d\}$, $\langle M, v \mid \delta_t \rangle = \langle x, v \rangle$. For these M, the partial summation is

$$\frac{1}{2^n} \sum_{x \in F_2^d} \left(\sum_{\delta_t \in F_2^t} (-1)^{\langle x, v \rangle} \widetilde{c}_{\mathbb{E}}(DL\langle \nabla, (x \mid 0^t)\rangle) \right) = \frac{1}{2^n} \cdot 2^t \sum_{x \in F_2^d} \widetilde{c}_{\mathbb{E}}(DL\langle \nabla, (x \mid 0^t)\rangle)$$

$$= 2^{-d} \sum_{M \in F_2^d} \widetilde{c}_{\mathbb{E}}(DL\langle \nabla, (M \mid 0^t)\rangle)$$

While for $M \notin \{(x \mid 0) \mid x \in F_2^d\}$, $\langle M, (v \mid \delta_t) \rangle$ is balanced. For these M, the partial summation will be

$$\frac{1}{2^n} \sum_{M \notin \{(x \mid 0) \mid x \in F_2^d\}} \left(\sum_{\delta_t \in F_2^t} (-1)^{\langle M, (v \mid \delta_t) \rangle} \widetilde{c}_{\mathbb{E}}(DL\langle \nabla, M \rangle) \right) = \frac{1}{2^n} \sum_{M \notin \{(x \mid 0) \mid x \in F_2^d\}} 0 = 0.$$

as claimed. □

Gathering Lemma 1 and Equation (3) yields the following theorem which writes the capacity of MD distinguisher as the summation of squared correlations of some one-dimensional DL distinguishers:

Theorem 3.

$$Cap_{\mathbb{E}}(MD\langle \nabla, V \rangle) = \sum_{M \in V, M \neq 0} (\widetilde{c}_{\mathbb{E}}(DL\langle \nabla, (M \mid 0)\rangle))^2. \quad (7)$$

Proof. Clearly $\widetilde{c}_{\mathbb{E}}(DL\langle\nabla,0\rangle) = 1$. Therefore

$$Cap_{\mathbb{E}}(MD\langle\nabla,V\rangle) = \sum_{v \in V} \frac{(p_v - \theta_v)^2}{\theta_v}$$

$$= 2^{-d}\Big[\sum_{\eta \in \mathbb{F}_2^d}\big[\sum_{b \in \mathbb{F}_2^d, b \neq 0}(-1)^{\langle b,\eta\rangle} \cdot \widetilde{c}_{\mathbb{E}}(DL\langle\nabla,(b\mid 0)\rangle) + 1 - 1\big]^2\Big]$$

$$= 2^{-d}\sum_{\eta \in \mathbb{F}_2^d}\big[\sum_{b \in \mathbb{F}_2^d, b \neq 0}(-1)^{\langle b,\eta\rangle} \cdot \widetilde{c}_{\mathbb{E}}(DL\langle\nabla,(b\mid 0)\rangle)\big]^2$$

$$= 2^{-d}\sum_{\eta \in \mathbb{F}_2^d}\big[\sum_{b \in \mathbb{F}_2^d, b \neq 0}\widetilde{c}_{\mathbb{E}}^2(DL\langle\nabla,(b\mid 0)\rangle)$$

$$+ \sum_{b_1,b_2 \in \mathbb{F}_2^d, b_1 \neq b_2}(-1)^{\langle b_1,\eta\rangle \oplus \langle b_2,\eta\rangle}\widetilde{c}_{\mathbb{E}}(\nabla,(b_1\mid 0)) \cdot \widetilde{c}_{\mathbb{E}}(\nabla,(b_2\mid 0))\big]$$

Since $\sum_{\eta \in \mathbb{F}_2^d}\sum_{b_1,b_2 \in \mathbb{F}_2^d, b_1 \neq b_2}(-1)^{\langle b_1,\eta\rangle \oplus \langle b_2,\eta\rangle}\widetilde{c}_{\mathbb{E}}(\nabla,(b_1\mid 0)) \cdot \widetilde{c}_{\mathbb{E}}(\nabla,(b_2\mid 0)) = 0$, we have

$$Cap_{\mathbb{E}}(MD\langle\nabla,V\rangle) = 2^{-d}\sum_{\eta \in \mathbb{F}_2^d}\sum_{b \in \mathbb{F}_2^d, b \neq 0}\widetilde{c}_{\mathbb{E}}^2(DL\langle\nabla,(b\mid 0)\rangle)$$

$$= \sum_{M \in V, M \neq 0}(\widetilde{c}_{\mathbb{E}}(DL\langle\nabla,M\rangle))^2$$

as claimed.   □

4.2   Constructing MD Distinguishers: The Methodology

By the discussions above, we can extend existent DL distinguishers to construct MD distinguishers. Suppose we have an r-round DL distinguisher $DL\langle\nabla^0, M^r\rangle$, then the constructing process follows 3 steps:

1. Choose a subspace V such that $M^r \in V$.
2. For each $M_i^r \in V$, use an "appropriate" method (probably the searching-and-estimating process given in Sect. 3) to obtain $\widetilde{c}(DL\langle\nabla^0, M_i^r\rangle)$.
3. Calculate the capacity of $MD\langle\nabla^0, V^r\rangle$ by Theorem 3: $Cap(MD\langle\nabla^0, V^r\rangle) = \sum_{i,M_i^r \neq 0}(\widetilde{c}(DL\langle\nabla^0, M_i^r\rangle))^2$. Then use Equation (4) to evaluate the data complexity.

Our theories provide us with another approach[2] to theoretically evaluate the capacity of MD distinguisher using χ^2 statistical test and launch MD attack on real ciphers.

---

[2] A similar work is [6]; however they focus on MD using LLR statistical test. Theoretically, following Lemma 6 to use accurate bias of DL distinguishers to compute truncated differential probabilities and build MD using LLR statistical test is possible; however the loss of precision of our results show that very accurately estimating requires unbearable complexity.

5   Application to CTC2

In order to make an easy comparison with previous results, we apply the above two methods to CTC2. The results are presented in this section.

Description of CTC2. CTC2 is a block cipher designed to show the strength of the algebraic analysis [10]. Its block size and key length are both variable. Here similarly to previous works [11,15], we only consider the version with a 255-bit block size and key.

CTC2 follows SPN structure, with the substitution layer $\mathbf{S}$ consists of applying the same 3×3-bit bijective S-box 85 times in parallel, and the linear diffusion layer $\mathbf{D}$ is defined as follows: $(Z_{254}, \ldots, Z_1, Z_0) = D((Y_{254}, \ldots, Y_1, Y_0))$, with $Z_{151} = Y_2 \oplus Y_{139} \oplus Y_{21}$ and $Z_{(i \times 202 + 2) \bmod 255} = Y_i \oplus Y_{(i+137) \bmod 255}, i = 0, 1, 3, 4, \ldots, 254$. Then during each round, the middle state will be xored with a round sub-key, then applied $\mathbf{S}$, and then $\mathbf{D}$. After the last round a whiten round sub-key will be xored with the middle state, leading to the cipher text.

As pointed out by Dunkelman and Keller (in [11]), CTC2 has the following two properties:

- for linear approximations, the diffusion of the linear transformation in the backward direction is extremely low;
- for differentials, the diffusion in the forward direction is very weak;

by this, the MITM-style search-and-estimate strategy will fit into CTC2 well.

Search Results: 9.5-round DL Distinguisher. We first revisit the 8.5-round DL distinguisher used in [15]. We search and estimate $\widetilde{c}(DL \langle e_0^0, e_{32,151}^r \rangle)$ [15] for r varies from 4.5 to 8.5. The results and all the parameters involved – d_bound, l_bound, and $meet\_rnd$ – are listed in Table 2. These results show that:

Table 2. Revisiting the DL distinguisher used in [15]. 1: Computed experimentally using 2^{22} plaintext pairs and averaged over 200 random key values; 2. It is well-known that the expected data complexity of DL attack is $\mathcal{O}(\frac{1}{corr^2})$, hence the expected complexity of the experiment on 8.5-round variant is $\mathcal{O}(2^{52.8})$.

r/Rounds Covered	Input Difference	Output Mask	Correlation (previous estimation)	Correlation (our estimation)	$meet\_rnd$	(d_bound, l_bound)	Correlation (experimental value[1])
4.5	e_0	$e_{32,151}$	-	$+2^{-4.94}$	2	$(\infty, 8)$	$+2^{-3.49}$
5.5	e_0	$e_{32,151}$	-	$+2^{-6.69}$	2	$(\infty, 8)$	$+2^{-6.11}$
6.5	e_0	$e_{32,151}$	-	$+2^{-15.37}$	2	$(\infty, 8)$	$+2^{-8.70}$
8.5	e_0	$e_{32,151}$	2^{-67} [15]	$+2^{-26.45}$	3	$(10, 7)$	$-^2$

- When the number of rounds turns large, the estimations suffer from loss of precision. However, they never overestimate when $r \leq 6.5$. Hence the lower bounds obtained by the search-and-estimate strategy are (probably) reliable.

- As shown in the last row of Table 2, our estimating process returns estimation much larger than that derived in [15]. This probably attributes to the large quantity of trails in CTC2: the more the trails are, the less precise the estimate approximated by a single trail (as done in [15]) is .
- The results on shorter rounds show that our estimation for 8.5-round are probably more accurate. Therefore, our strategy leads to significant improvement on the known results. Such improvement shows the effectiveness of the MITM-style search-and-estimate strategy.

We then estimate $\widetilde{c}(DL\langle e_0^0, e_{32}^r\rangle)$ for r varies from 4.5 to 9.5, because e_{32} has fewer active S-boxes than $e_{32,151}$, which might result in smaller search space, lower time cost, higher bias, and easier operation. We list the results and all the parameters in Table 3. For this difference-mask pair, even when $r = 9.5$, the searching-and-estimating process can return an estimation. Since $2^{-47.415} \gg 2^{-\frac{255}{2}}$, it seems like that we can further increase the value of r; however, we can not afford the search complexity.

Table 3. Several new DL distinguishers for CTC2. 1: Computed experimentally using 2^{18} plaintext pairs and averaged over 200 random key values

r/Rounds Covered	Input Difference	Output Mask	meet_rnd	Correlation (estimation)	(d_bound, l_bound)	Correlation (experimental[1])
4.5	e_0	e_{32}	2	$+2^{-2.36}$	(10,6)	$+2^{-1.88}$
5.5	e_0	e_{32}	2	$+2^{-8.81}$	(10,7)	$+2^{-3.84}$
6.5	e_0	e_{32}	3	$+2^{-8.52}$	(10,7)	$+2^{-7.15}$
9.5	e_0	e_{32}	5	$+2^{-47.415}$	(9,6)	-

9.5-round MD Distinguisher for CTC2. We follow the methodology in Sect. 4.2 to construct the 9.5-round MD distinguisher. There is only one active S-box in the output linear mask e_{32}, i.e. S_{10}. Consider all the masks in which the only active S-box is S_{10}: they are e_{30}, e_{31}, $e_{30,31}$, $e_{32,30}$, $e_{32,31}$, $e_{32,31,30}$ (and e_{32}). These seven output masks and the all-zero vector together form a subspace $V = \{e_{30}, e_{31}, e_{32}\}$. Then, taking V as the projecting subspace, we can estimate the capacity of $MD\langle e_0^0, V^{9.5}\rangle$ by estimating the correlations of all the above seven DL distinguishers and make a summation. We use the searching-and-estimating process (in Sect. 3) to estimate the parameters of them. The results are:

- $\widetilde{c}(\langle e_0^0, e_{30}^{9.5}\rangle) = \widetilde{c}(\langle e_0^0, e_{30,31}^{9.5}\rangle) = \widetilde{c}(\langle e_0^0, e_{31,32}^{9.5}\rangle) = +2^{-47.415}$
- $\widetilde{c}_{\mathbb{E}}(\langle e_0^0, e_{31}^{9.5}\rangle) = \widetilde{c}(\langle e_0^0, e_{30,32}^{9.5}\rangle) = \widetilde{c}(\langle e_0^0, e_{30,31,32}^{9.5}\rangle) = 0^3$

Then, the estimation is given as $Cap(MD\langle e_0^0, V^{9.5}\rangle) = 4\cdot 2^{-2\cdot 47.415} = 2^{-92.83}$. To verify the methodologies and results, we estimate $Cap(MD\langle e_0^0, V^r\rangle)$ for $r = 4.5$ and 5.5 to make a comparison with the experimental results. All the results are

---

[3] The bound $l\_bound = 6$ is so tight that the searching-and-estimating process returns zero. However, this does not prevent us from providing a lower bound.

listed in Table 4. They show that our estimation can (probably) give reliable lower bounds for the capacity. To illustrate more clearly, we describe how we obtain the 4.5-round MD distinguisher in Appendix A.

Table 4. MD distinguishers for CTC2. 1: Computed experimentally using 2^{16} plaintext pairs and averaged over 200 random key values

Rounds Covered	Input Difference	Output Subspace Basis	Capacity (theoretical)	Capacity (experimental[1])
4.5	e_0	$\{e_{30}, e_{31}, e_{32}\}$	$2^{-3.18}$	$2^{-1.50}$
5.5	e_0	$\{e_{30}, e_{31}, e_{32}\}$	$2^{-15.91}$	$2^{-5.85}$
9.5	e_0	$\{e_{30}, e_{31}, e_{32}\}$	$2^{-92.83}$	-

Attack against 11-round CTC2. We apply the 9.5-round MD distinguisher $MD\langle e_0^0, V^{9.5}\rangle$ between round 2 and the **D** operation of round 11 to attack the first 11 rounds. The attack proceed by guessing the subkey involved in the first round, partially encrypting one round, and then ranking the key guesses according to the non-randomness revealed by the ciphertexts. Since the 9.5-round MD distinguisher shares the same input difference (e_{32}) with the 8.5-round DL distinguisher used by Lu [15], we can reuse some of his techniques, including key guessing and plaintexts organizing. For simplicity, in the following discussions we denote by K^i the subkey involved during the i-th round encryption, and by M^i the intermediate encryption result produced by the i-th round encryption. As pointed out by [15], for the **D** operation of round 1, it holds that

$$e_{17,21,40,59,78,97,116,135,139,154,158,177,196,215,234,253} \xrightarrow{\mathbf{D}} e_0.$$

These 16 bits correspond to 16 S-boxes of round 1: S-boxes 5, 7, 13, 19, 26, 32, 38, 45, 46, 51, 52, 59, 65, 71, 78 and 84 (numbering the S-boxes from 0 to 84 from right to left). Let $\nabla^{0.5} = e_{17,21,40,59,78,97,116,135,139,154,158,177,196,215,234,253}$, Θ be the set of the 16 S-boxes, and K_Θ be the 48 bits of K^0 corresponding to the 16 S-boxes in Θ. We define the plaintext structure in the same way as [15]: a structure is defined to be a set of 2^{48} plaintexts $P_{i,j}$ with the 48 bits for the S-boxes in Θ taking all the possible values and the other 207 bits fixed,$(j = 0, 1, \ldots, 2^{48} - 1)$. Note that for two plaintexts $P_{i,1}$ and $P_{i,2}$ withdrawn from the same structure, the difference of their corresponding first round intermediate encryption results might be e_0. By this approach, we have to guess 48 bits subkey, i.e. K_Θ; then by Equation (4), we calculate that to attack 11-round CTC2, $2^{99.35} \approx 2^{100}$ samples are necessary to achieve the full advantage – 48 – and a success probability of 99.9%. Hence the data complexity is 2^{101}, and we need 2^{53} structures. The attack is described as follows:

1. Choose 2^{53} structures $S_i, (i = 0, 1, \ldots, 2^{53} - 1)$, each as described before. Obtain ciphertexts $C_{i,j}$ for all the plaintext $P_{i,j}$ in S_i (time complexity 2^{101}).
2. Initialize $2^{48} \times 2^3$ counters $c_{(j,k)}$, with j ranging from 0 to $2^{48} - 1$ and k ranging from 0 to 7.

3. For each guessed value of K_Θ (time complexity 2^{48}):

    (a) Partially encrypt every plaintext $P_{i,j}$ with K_Θ to get its intermediate value $M_{i,j}^{0.5} = \mathbf{S}(P_{i,j} \oplus K_\Theta)$, and then organize $P_{i,j}$ into a hash table T according to the 48 bits of $M_{i,j}^{0.5}$ corresponding to the 16 S-boxes in Θ (time complexity 2^{101}).

    (b) For each hash value pair $(M_i^{0.5}, M_j^{0.5})$ drawn from T where $M_j^{0.5} = M_i^{0.5} \oplus \nabla^{0.5}$:

      – For each plaintext $p_{i,k}$ in the plaintext set P_i corresponding to $M_i^{0.5}$ and each plaintext $p_{j,l}$ in the plaintext set P_j corresponding to $M_j^{0.5}$, compute $D^{-1}(c_{i,k} \oplus c_{j,l})[32, 31, 30]$ (time complexity 2^{100}).

      – Increase counter $c_{D^{-1}(c_{i,k} \oplus c_{j,l})[32,31,30], K_\Theta}$ by 1.

    (c) Calculate the empirical χ^2 statistics χ^{K_Θ} under key guess K_Θ as $\chi^{K_\Theta} = 2^{100} \sum_{\eta=0}^{7} \frac{(\frac{c_{\eta, K_\Theta}}{2^{100}} - 2^{-3})^2}{2^{-3}}$ (time complexity negligible).

4. For the guessed K_Θ corresponding to the largest χ^{K_Θ} value, exhaustively search for the remaining 207 key bits with one plaintext-ciphertext pair and output the final suggestion as the user key of CTC2 (time complexity 2^{207}).

The time complexity is $2^{101} + 2^{48} \cdot (2^{101} + 2^{100}) + 2^{207} \approx 2^{207}$ 11-round CTC2 encryptions. The memory requirement is approximately 2^{101} 255-bits words (cost by the hash table T) plus 2^{51} counters.

6   Conclusion

We investigate how to apply the closed theory of DL cryptanalysis in [5] in practice. As results, first, we propose a meet-in-the-middle style searching-and-estimating process; second, we give a new way to theoretically estimate the capacity of multiple differential distinguisher by showing that the capacity of a multiple differential distinguisher using χ^2 statistical test can be expressed as the summation of squared correlations of several DL distinguishers; finally, we give results on CTC2 with a 255-bit block size and key as the first application to concrete designs. Our attack against 11-round CTC2 is the best with respect to the number of attacked rounds to our knowledge.

Acknowledgements. This work is partially supported by National Key Basic Research Project of China (2011CB302400), National Science Foundation of China (61379139) and the "Strategic Priority Research Program" of the Chinese Academy of Sciences, Grant No. XDA06010701.

References

1. Biham, E., Dunkelman, O., Keller, N.: Enhancing differential-linear cryptanalysis. In: Zheng, Y. (ed.) ASIACRYPT 2002, Lecture Notes in Computer Science, vol. 2501, pp. 254–266. Springer Berlin Heidelberg (2002)

2. Biham, E., Shamir, A.: Differential cryptanalysis of des-like cryptosystems. Journal of Cryptology 4(1), 3–72 (1991)
3. Biham, E., Shamir, A.: Differential cryptanalysis of the full 16-round des. In: Brickell, E. (ed.) CRYPTO 1992, Lecture Notes in Computer Science, vol. 740, pp. 487–496. Springer Berlin Heidelberg (1993)
4. Blondeau, C., Gérard, B., Nyberg, K.: Multiple differential cryptanalysis using llr and χ^2 statistics. In: Visconti, I., Prisco, R. (eds.) Security and Cryptography for Networks, Lecture Notes in Computer Science, vol. 7485, pp. 343–360. Springer Berlin Heidelberg (2012)
5. Blondeau, C., Leander, G., Nyberg, K.: Differential-linear cryptanalysis revisited. In: Fast Software Encryption 2014. Lecture Notes in Computer Science, Springer Berlin Heidelberg (2014, to appear)
6. Blondeau, C., Nyberg, K.: New links between differential and linear cryptanalysis. In: Johansson, T., Nguyen, P. (eds.) EUROCRYPT 2013, Lecture Notes in Computer Science, vol. 7881, pp. 388–404. Springer Berlin Heidelberg (2013)
7. Blondeau, C., Nyberg, K.: Links between truncated differential and multidimensional linear properties of block ciphers and underlying attack complexities. In: EUROCRYPT 2014. Lecture Notes in Computer Science, Springer Berlin Heidelberg (2014, to appear)
8. Chabaud, F., Vaudenay, S.: Links between differential and linear cryptanalysis. In: EUROCRYPT'94. pp. 356–365. Springer (1995)
9. Cho, J.: Linear cryptanalysis of reduced-round present. In: Pieprzyk, J. (ed.) CT-RSA 2010, Lecture Notes in Computer Science, vol. 5985, pp. 302–317. Springer Berlin Heidelberg (2010)
10. Courtois, N.T.: Ctc2 and fast algebraic attacks on block ciphers revisisted. Tech. rep., Cryptology ePrint Archive, Report 2007/152, 2007. http://eprint.iacr.org
11. Dunkelman, O., Keller, N.: Cryptanalysis of ctc2. In: Fischlin, M. (ed.) CT-RSA 2009, Lecture Notes in Computer Science, vol. 5473, pp. 226–239. Springer Berlin Heidelberg (2009)
12. Lallemand, V., Naya-Plasencia, M.: Cryptanalysis of klein. In: Fast Software Encryption 2014 (2014, to appear)
13. Langford, S., Hellman, M.: Differential-linear cryptanalysis. In: Desmedt, Y. (ed.) CRYPTO 1994, Lecture Notes in Computer Science, vol. 839, pp. 17–25. Springer Berlin Heidelberg (1994)
14. Liu, Z., Gu, D., Zhang, J., Li, W.: Differential-multiple linear cryptanalysis. In: Bao, F., Yung, M., Lin, D., Jing, J. (eds.) Information Security and Cryptology, Lecture Notes in Computer Science, vol. 6151, pp. 35–49. Springer Berlin Heidelberg (2010)
15. Lu, J.: A methodology for differential-linear cryptanalysis and its applications. In: Canteaut, A. (ed.) Fast Software Encryption, Lecture Notes in Computer Science, vol. 7549, pp. 69–89. Springer Berlin Heidelberg (2012)
16. Lu, J.: A methodology for differential-linear cryptanalysis and its applications. Designs, Codes and Cryptography pp. 1–38 (2014)
17. Matsui, M.: Linear cryptanalysis method for des cipher. In: Helleseth, T. (ed.) EUROCRYPT 1993, Lecture Notes in Computer Science, vol. 765, pp. 386–397. Springer Berlin Heidelberg (1994)
18. Matsui, M., Yamagishi, A.: A new method for known plaintext attack of feal cipher. In: Rueppel, R. (ed.) EUROCRYPT 1992, Lecture Notes in Computer Science, vol. 658, pp. 81–91. Springer Berlin Heidelberg (1993)

A   On the 4.5-round MD Distinguisher

Besides $\widetilde{c}(DL\langle e_0^0, e_{32}^{4.5}\rangle) = 2^{-2.36}$ mentioned in Sect. 5, we set *meet_rnd* to 2, *d_bound* to 10, and *l_bound* to 6, and obtain the following results:

- $\widetilde{c}(DL\langle e_0^0, e_{30}^{4.5}\rangle) = 2^{-3.19}$
- $\widetilde{c}(DL\langle e_0^0, e_{31}^{4.5}\rangle) = 2^{-3.81}$
- $\widetilde{c}(DL\langle e_0^0, e_{30,31}^{4.5}\rangle) = 2^{-2.48}$
- $\widetilde{c}(DL\langle e_0^0, e_{30,32}^{4.5}\rangle) = 2^{-3.52}$
- $\widetilde{c}(DL\langle e_0^0, e_{31,32}^{4.5}\rangle) = 2^{-3.00}$
- $\widetilde{c}(DL\langle e_0^0, e_{30,31,32}^{4.5}\rangle) = 2^{-5.98}$

Therefore the capacity of the 4.5-round distinguisher is

$$Cap(MD < e_0, \{e_{30}, e_{31}, e_{32}\} >) = 2^{-2\cdot3.19} + 2^{-2\cdot3.81} + 2^{-2\cdot2.48} + 2^{-2\cdot2.36}$$
$$+ 2^{-2\cdot3.52} + 2^{-2\cdot3.00} + 2^{-2\cdot5.98}$$
$$= 2^{-3.18}$$

Combined Cache Timing Attacks and Template Attacks on Stream Cipher MUGI*

Shaoyu Du[1,4,**], Zhenqi Li[1], Bin Zhang[1,2], and Dongdai Lin[3]

[1] Trusted Computing and Information Assurance Laboratory,
Institute of Software, Chinese Academy of Sciences, Beijing, China
[2] State Key Laboratory of Computer Science, Institute of Software,
Chinese Academy of Sciences, Beijing, China
[3] State Key Laboratory of Information Security, Institute of Information Engineering,
Chinese Academy of Sciences, Beijing, China
[4] University of Chinese Academy of Sciences, Beijing, China
du_shaoyu@163.com

Abstract. The stream cipher MUGI was proposed by Hitachi, Ltd. in 2002 and it was specified as ISO/IEC 18033-4 for keystream generation. Assuming that noise-free cache timing measurements are possible, we give the cryptanalysis of MUGI under the cache attack model. Our simulation results show that we can reduce the computation complexity of recovering all the 1216-bits internal state of MUGI to about $O(2^{76})$ when it is implemented in processors with 64-byte cache line. The attack reveals some new inherent weaknesses of MUGI's structure. The weaknesses can also be used to conduct a noiseless template attack of $O(2^{60.51})$ computation complexity to restore the state of MUGI. And then combining these two attacks we can conduct a key-recovery attack on MUGI with about $O(2^{30})$ computation complexity. To the best of our knowledge, it is the first time that the analysis of cache timing attacks and template attacks are applied to full version of MUGI and that these two classes of attacks are combined to attack some cipher. Moreover, the combination can be used to improve the error-tolerance capability of each attack. If each measurement has one additional error, the key-recovery attack will take about $O(2^{50})$ computation complexity.

Keywords: Stream cihper, MUGI, analytical side-channel attacks, cache timing attacks, template attacks.

1 Introduction

Cache Timing attacks[2,3,4] and template attacks[16] are two classes of side-channel attacks. The cache timing attack assumes that the attacker can use

---

* This work was supported by the National Grand Fundamental Research 973 Programs of China(Grant No. 2013CB338002, 2011CB302400),the programs of the National Natural Science Foundation of China (Grant No. 61303258, 60833008, 60603018, 61173134, 91118006, 61272476).
** Corresponding author.

J. Lopez and Y. Wu (Eds.): ISPEC 2015, LNCS 9065, pp. 235–249, 2015.
DOI: 10.1007/978-3-319-17533-1_17

time measurements to learn something about the cache accesses of the legitimate party. Since 2005, it has drawn a lot of attention[5,6,7,8], most of which mainly focused on blocks ciphers. In SAC 2008, Erik Zenner[1] applied the cache timing attack to HC-256 and provided a cache timing attack model for stream cipher. Soon after that Gregor Leander[9] et al. applied the model to stream ciphers that use word-based LFSRs. And Goutam Paul et al.[15] extended the attack in [9] to HC-128 in 2012. The common template attack[17,19,20,21,22] model targets on cipher's S-boxes and collects hamming weight leakages of S-box's output. In Inscrypt 2009, [23] combined the template attacks' hamming weight leakage model with algebraic analysis. Then in 2010, [24] combined template attack with cube attack. And in 2014, [18] generalized these two attacks on the template attack model and analyzed its ability in the face of noise.

At FSE 2002[10], Hitachi, Ltd. proposed a new keystreamgenerator MUGI, which was designed for use as a streamcipher. MUGI has a 128-bit secret key and a 128-bit initial vector and generates 64-bit output words per round. It was specified as ISO/IEC 18033-4 for keystream generation. To our knowledge, the exiting cryptanalysis of MUGI mainly focuses on its linear[11] and nonlinear[12] part respectively or attacks its simplified version[13]. A fault analysis on MUGI[14] was proposed in 2011, which mainly uses the characteristics that MUGI's two kinds of update functions are mutually dependent. It was stated in [10] that the user can utilize the fast software implementation of AES to speed up the software implementation of MUGI, which is exactly the target of cache timing attacks. And also due to the usage of S-box, the cipher's microcontroller implementations are insecure under template attacks.

In this paper, we firstly present the cache timing analysis of MUGI under Erik Zenner's model. In the common processors whose cache line is 64 bytes, we only need 10 consecutive rounds' noise-free cache access measurements to recover the whole state with about $O(2^{76})$ computation complexity and $O(2^{71})$ memory complexity. Then we give a noise-free template attack analysis of MUGI with about $O(2^{60.51})$ computation complexity. These two attacks both guess the internal state of MUGI upon the side-channel leakage information and then filter out the wrong candidates through equations derived from MUGI's update function.

Then due to the characteristic of additive stream cipher that encryption and decryption have the same process of generating keystreams, we can combine these two attacks together. The combined side-channel attack takes advantage of the leakage information of cache accesses and hamming weights simultaneously. The increase of the information contributes to the decrease of the candidates' number and reduces the attack complexity to about $O(2^{30})$. Moreover, the combined attack can tolerate more noise, which makes the attack model more robust and closer to the practical situation. Assuming that each measurement has one additional error, the combined attack takes about $O(2^{50})$ computation complexity to retrieve the key. All the complexity results are computed by the simulation experiments.

The paper is organized as follows. In Section 2, we present the notations and a brief description of the MUGI cipher with its implementations. Section 3 specifies the cache timing attack model, the cache timing attack of MUGI and the experimental details. And we introduce the template attack, the combined attack and the attack under noise model in Section 4. Finally, conclusions and future works are given in Section 5.

2   Description of MUGI and Its Implementations

2.1   Notations in This Paper

In this paper, "word" is used to denote an 8-byte block and we use the following notations throughout this paper.

a_i^t: An 8-byte state in round t where $i = 0, \ldots, 2$

b_i^t: An 8-byte state in round t where $i = 0, \ldots, 15$

$(x)^{i, \cdots, j}$: The ith to jth bits of word x (0 denotes the most significant bit)

$x \oplus y$: Bitwise exclusive-OR operation

$\ggg_n$: Circular rotation of n bits to the right (in the 64-bit register)

$\lll_n$: Circular rotation of n bits to the left (in the 64-bit register)

$(x)_i$: The ith byte of an 8-byte word x

2.2   Structure of MUGI

The state of MUGI in round t can be divided into two parts: the linear words b_i^t ($i = 0, \ldots, 15$) and nonlinear words a_i^t ($i = 0, \ldots, 2$). There are two dependent update functions λ and ρ. The function λ updates the linear states as:

$$b_j^{t+1} = b_{j-1}^t (j \neq 0, 4, 10),$$
$$b_0^{t+1} = b_{15}^t \oplus a_0^t,$$
$$b_4^{t+1} = b_3^t \oplus b_7^t,$$
$$b_{10}^{t+1} = b_9^t \oplus (b_{13}^t \lll_{32}),$$

and the function ρ updates the nonlinear states as:

$$a_0^{t+1} = a_1^t,$$
$$a_1^{t+1} = a_2^t \oplus F(a_1^t, b_4^t) \oplus C_1,$$
$$a_2^{t+1} = a_0^t \oplus F(a_1^t, b_{10}^t \lll_{17}) \oplus C_2,$$

where C_1 and C_2 are known constants and F is the round function. The F function, whose structure is showed in the left part of Fig.1, consists of a key addition (the data addition from the buffer b_4^t or $b_{10}^t \lll_{17}$), a nonlinear transformation using the S-box, a linear transformation using the MDS matrix and a byte shuffle. The S-box and MDS matrix are the same as that of AES.

The output function of MUGI is simple which outflows a 64-bit nonlinear state word directly, i.e., $Output[t] = a_2^t$. Note that the output of round t is the state word in the beginning of round t. We ignore the initialization phase which has less correlation with the attack in this paper. For that and a more detailed description of MUGI, please refer to [10].

2.3 Target Implementations of MUGI

The fast software implementation of MUGI takes advantage of four tables: T_0, T_1, T_2 and T_3, where $T_i[x] = m_i \cdot S[x]$, $i = 0, \ldots, 3$. Here and hereafter $S[\cdot]$ stands for the S-box of AES and m_i stands for one column of AES's mix-column matrix. The right part of Fig. 1 displays F function's fast software implementation. Once MUGI outputs a word, the F function is called twice, i.e., $F(a_1^t, b_4^t)$ and

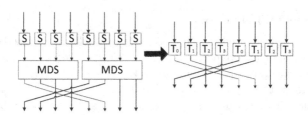

Fig. 1. Round function F (left) and its fast software implementation (right)

$F(a_1^t, b_{10}^t \lll_{17})$. It means that in order to output one word, the cipher needs 16 table-look-up operations. Each table T_i ($i = 0, \ldots, 3$) is accessed four times. For example, the indexes used for looking up table T_0 are $(a_1^t \oplus b_4^t)^{0,\ldots,7}$, $(a_1^t \oplus b_4^t)^{32,\ldots,39}$, $(a_1^t \oplus b_{10}^t \lll_{17})^{0,\ldots,7}$ and $(a_1^t \oplus b_{10}^t \lll_{17})^{32,\ldots,39}$.

On the other hand, MUGI's microcontroller implementation is more direct as described in [10]. And the F function's microcontroller implementation is displayed in the left part of Fig.1, which shows that every byte addition and S-box operation executes independently.

3 Cache Timing Attacks on MUGI

In this section, we firstly introduce the cache attack model we used. After that we give a cache attack on MUGI under a simplified condition, which is easy to analyze. Then based on the simplified attack, we give the regular cache attack analysis of MUGI. Moreover, the experiment result is presented in the end of this section.

3.1 The Attack Model and Information Available

In this paper, we use the model proposed by Zenner[1] to analyze MUGI. It assumes that the attacker has the following two oracles: **KEYSTREAM(i)** returns the i-th keystream block of the cipher; **SCA_KEYSTREAM(i)**[1] returns a noise-free list of all cache accesses made by KEYSTREAM(i) per round, which has no information about their order.

---

[1] Note that the SCA_KEYSTREAM(i) oracle assumes that the measurements are undisturbed by noise. The result obtained in this section is for an idealized setting.

And the leakage information depends on the cache line size of the target implementation platform. Assume that the cipher's table contains 2^c items, each item is d bytes and the cache line size is γ bytes. Then a single cache line stores γ/d items. Therefore, the attacker can get the $b = c - log_2(\gamma/d)$ most significant bits of the table's index from one cache access. In this paper we assume the size of the cache line is 64 bytes. Each item in the four tables occupies 4 bytes and there are 2^8 items per table. Then the attacker can derive the $8 - log_2 16 = 4$ most significant bits of the indexes. As to T_0, the bits are $(a_1^t \oplus b_4^t)^{0,\ldots,3}$, $(a_1^t \oplus b_4^t)^{32,\ldots,35}$, $(a_1^t \oplus b_{10}^t \lll 17)^{0,\ldots,3}$ and $(a_1^t \oplus b_{10}^t \lll 17)^{32,\ldots,35}$.

Note that MUGI uses four tables and each table is accessed four times per round, then the attacker can get four lists (or sets since there is no order) of cache accesses and each list corresponds to one table. The size of the list is between 1 and 4, as four random table indexes can just in the same cache line or in four cache lines different from each other. For example, the attacker can derive four sets at some round i from the output of SCA_KEYSTREAM(i):

$$T_0 : \{0xc, 0x7\}, T_1 : \{0x5, 0x9, 0xd, 0x8\}, T_2 : \{0xf, 0x2\}, T_3 : \{0x7, 0xd, 0xe\}.$$

3.2 Recover the Internal State of MUGI in A Simplified Condition

Firstly, we found that if the attacker knows the order of the elements in each list, he can conduct the key recovery attack as follows.

The attacker can use Eq. 1[2], which is deduced from the function ρ.

$$F(a_1^t, b_4^t) \oplus F(a_1^{t+2}, b_{10}^{t+2} \lll 17) = a_2^t \oplus a_2^{t+3} \oplus C_1 \oplus C_2. \qquad (1)$$

By inversing the two sides of Eq. 1 based on the linear operation of F, we can deduce eight equations:

$$S[(a_1^t \oplus b_4^t)_i] \oplus S[(a_1^{t+2} \oplus b_{10}^{t+2} \lll 17)_i] = F'(a_2^t \oplus a_2^{t+3} \oplus C_1 \oplus C_2)_i, \qquad (2)$$

where $i \in \{0, \ldots, 7\}$ and F' denotes the inverse of F function's linear part. The right side of Eq. 2 is known and the 4 most significant input bits of each S boxes, i.e., $(a_1^t \oplus b_4^t)_i^{0,\ldots,3}$ and $(a_1^t \oplus b_{10}^t \lll 17)_i^{0,\ldots,3}$ ($i \in \{0, \ldots, 7\}$), can be derived from the cache access information.

By exhausting the rest 8 bits of the input and filtering the candidates using Eq. 2, the attacker can determine the correct candidate. We have enumerated all the possibilities of the known 16-bit values , calculated the number of candidates that make Eq. 2 hold for each case. The result is summarized in Table 1. Under the assumption that the known values' order is correct, the complexity of solving Eq. 2 is $O(2^8)$ and the average number of the solutions is 1.54. Therefore, the complexity of solving Eq. 1 is $O(8 \cdot 2^8) = O(2^{11})$ and the number of candidates reserved is about $1.54^8 \approx 31.63$ on average.

After that, the attacker can recover the internal state according to STEP 1 to STEP 5 in this section. For simplicity, the words revealed in STEP i are denoted as "i" in Fig. 2[3].

---

[2] In this paper "the Eq. 1 of round $t + i$" denotes the Eq. 1 when $t = t + i$.

[3] Fig. 2 is similar to the Figure 2 in [14].

Table 1. Distribution of the solutions of Eq. 2 under cache timing attack model

number of the solutions	0	1	2	3	4	5	6	8	16
number of the equations	65536								
number of the equations	23014	24790	13595	3284	761	54	21	1	16
percentage	35.12%	37.83%	20.75%	5.01%	1.16%	0.08%	0.03%	≈0	0.02%
number of the equations	—	42522							
percentage	—	58.30%	31.97%	7.72%	1.79%	0.13%	0.05%	≈0	0.04%
expectation	—	1.54							

STEP 1. Solve Eq. 1 for six sequential rounds, and combine the update function $a_1^{t+1} = a_2^t \oplus F(a_1^t, b_4^t) \oplus C_1$ to reveal some words of the linear and nonlinear states. The equations used and the words retrieved are shown below and in Fig. 2 (denoted by "1").

$$t \ : \ F(a_1^t, b_4^t) \oplus F(a_1^{t+2}, b_{10}^{t+2} \lll_{17}) = a_2^t \oplus a_2^{t+3} \oplus C_1 \oplus C_2 \tag{3}$$
$$\Rightarrow a_1^t \oplus b_4^t, a_1^{t+2} \oplus b_{10}^{t+2} \lll_{17} \Rightarrow a_1^{t+1}$$

$$t+1 \ : \ F(a_1^{t+1}, b_4^{t+1}) \oplus F(a_1^{t+3}, b_{10}^{t+3} \lll_{17}) = a_2^{t+1} \oplus a_2^{t+4} \oplus C_1 \oplus C_2$$
$$\Rightarrow a_1^{t+1} \oplus b_4^{t+1}, a_1^{t+3} \oplus b_{10}^{t+3} \lll_{17} \Rightarrow a_1^{t+2}, b_{10}^{t+2}, b_4^{t+1}$$

$$t+2 \ : \ F(a_1^{t+2}, b_4^{t+2}) \oplus F(a_1^{t+4}, b_{10}^{t+4} \lll_{17}) = a_2^{t+2} \oplus a_2^{t+5} \oplus C_1 \oplus C_2$$
$$\Rightarrow a_1^{t+2} \oplus b_4^{t+2}, a_1^{t+4} \oplus b_{10}^{t+4} \lll_{17} \Rightarrow a_1^{t+3}, b_{10}^{t+3}, b_4^{t+2}$$

$$t+3 \ : \ F(a_1^{t+3}, b_4^{t+3}) \oplus F(a_1^{t+5}, b_{10}^{t+5} \lll_{17}) = a_2^{t+3} \oplus a_2^{t+6} \oplus C_1 \oplus C_2$$
$$\Rightarrow a_1^{t+3} \oplus b_4^{t+2}, a_1^{t+5} \oplus b_{10}^{t+5} \lll_{17} \Rightarrow a_1^{t+4}, b_{10}^{t+4}, b_4^{t+3}$$

$$t+4 \ : \ F(a_1^{t+4}, b_4^{t+4}) \oplus F(a_1^{t+6}, b_{10}^{t+6} \lll_{17}) = a_2^{t+4} \oplus a_2^{t+7} \oplus C_1 \oplus C_2$$
$$\Rightarrow a_1^{t+4} \oplus b_4^{t+4}, a_1^{t+6} \oplus b_{10}^{t+6} \lll_{17} \Rightarrow a_1^{t+5}, b_{10}^{t+5}, b_4^{t+4}$$

$$t+5 \ : \ F(a_1^{t+5}, b_4^{t+5}) \oplus F(a_1^{t+7}, b_{10}^{t+7} \lll_{17}) = a_2^{t+5} \oplus a_2^{t+8} \oplus C_1 \oplus C_2$$
$$\Rightarrow a_1^{t+5} \oplus b_{10}^{t+5}, a_1^{t+7} \oplus b_{10}^{t+7} \lll_{17} \Rightarrow a_1^{t+6}, b_{10}^{t+6}, b_4^{t+5}$$

STEP 2. Recover some state words as shown in Fig. 2 (denoted by "2") according to the LFSR's shift operation and the update function of nonlinear state.

STEP 3. Recover b_{10}^{t+7}, b_{10}^{t+8}, b_{10}^{t+9}, b_{10}^{t+10} and b_{10}^{t+11} according to $b_{10}^{t+1} = b_9^t \oplus (b_{13}^t \lll_{32})$ and some other words according to the shift operation of the LFSR.

STEP 4. Recover a_1^{t+7}, a_1^{t+8}, a_1^{t+9}, a_1^{t+10} and a_1^{t+11} according to $a_2^{t+1} = a_0^t \oplus F(a_1^t \oplus b_{10}^t \lll_{17}) \oplus C_2$ and then a_0^{t+i} (i=8..., 12) since $a_0^{t+1} = a_1^t$.

STEP 5. Recover b_4^{t+6}, b_4^{t+7}, b_4^{t+8}, b_4^{t+9} and b_4^{t+10} from $a_1^{t+1} = a_2^t \oplus F(a_1^t, b_4^t) \oplus C_1$. Then combine the shift operation of the LFSR and $b_{10}^{t+1} = b_9^t \oplus b_{13}^t \lll_{32}$ to get b_{10}^{t+12} and a_1^{t+12} (according to that $a_2^{t+1} = a_0^t \oplus F(a_1^t \oplus b_{10}^t \lll_{17})$). And then recover b_4^{t+11} through $a_1^{t+1} = a_2^t \oplus F(a_1^t, b_4^t) \oplus C_1$. Finally, backtrack the LFSR and get all the state words at round $t+7$.

Round	b_4	b_{10}	$a_0 a_1$
t			
t+1	1		1
t+2	1 2	1	2 1
t+3	1 2 2	1 2	2 1
t+4	1 2 2 2	1 2 2	2 1
t+5	1 2 2 2 2	1 2 2 2	2 1
t+6	5 5 5 5 5 2 2 2 2 2	1 2 2 2 2	2 1
t+7	5 5 5 5 5 5 2 2 2 2	3 2 2 2 2 2	2 4
t+8	5 5 5 5 5 5 2 2 2	3 3 2 2 2 2	4 4
t+9	5 5 5 5 5 5 2 2	3 3 3 2 2 2	4 4
t+10	5 5 5 5 5 5 2	3 3 3 3 2 2	4 4
t+11	5 5 5 5 5 5 5	3 3 3 3 3 2	4 4
t+12	5 5 5 5 5 5 5	3 3 3 3 3	4 5

Fig. 2. The procedure of recovering the states of MUGI

3.3 Recover the State of MUGI under Cache Attack Model

Recall that actually the order of the accesses is not given to the attacker in cache timing attack. He must firstly guess the order and then use the procedure in Section 3.2 to recover the internal state, which will make the complexity high. In order to reduce the complexity, we use the following two strategies.

Strategy 1. We guess the order of the cache accesses in two interleaved rounds and use their correlations to solve the equations. This will reduce the complexity, since the look-up operations to one table are dependent. For example, if one list has four elements then any two inputs must be different from each other.

In brief, the attacker can simultaneously get the solutions of the equations:

$$t : F(a_1^t, b_4^t) \oplus F(a_1^{t+2}, b_{10}^{t+2} \lll 17) = a_2^t \oplus a_2^{t+3} \oplus C_1 \oplus C_2, \qquad (4)$$
$$t + 2 : F(a_1^{t+2}, b_4^{t+2}) \oplus F(a_1^{t+4}, b_{10}^{t+4} \lll 17) = a_2^{t+2} \oplus a_2^{t+5} \oplus C_1 \oplus C_2.$$

For the four cache access sets of round $t + 2$, the attacker needs to guess all the orders of their elements. And he only needs to guess two elements and their order for each cache access set of round t and round $t + 4$, since only $F(a_1^t, b_4^t)$ and $F(a_1^{t+4}, b_{10}^{t+4} \lll 17)$ are used. Table 2 shows the number of possible orders when the size of the set is from 1 to 4.

According to Table 2, the number of possible inputs to the Equation Set. 4 is about $(36 \times 12 \times 12)^4 \approx 2^{49.32}$ (in the worst cases). Simulations (which are presented in Section 3.4) show that there will be about 2^{45} solutions reserved on average.

Table 2. Relations between the size of the set and the number of possible orders

size of the set	look up four times	look up two times
4	24	12
3	36	9
2	20	4
1	1	1

Strategy 2. We use the cache accesses after round $t + 7$ to filter out a large part of the wrong candidates. The relations used for filtering are the following equations deduced from the update function λ.

$$b_{10}^{t+7} = b_4^{t+1} \oplus (b_{10}^{t+3} \lll 32), \tag{5}$$

$$b_{10}^{t+8} = b_4^{t+2} \oplus (b_{10}^{t+4} \lll 32). \tag{6}$$

Note that both b_4^{t+1} and b_{10}^{t+3}, which are presented in Eq. 5, appear in

$$t + 1 : F(a_1^{t+1}, b_4^{t+1}) \oplus F(a_1^{t+3}, b_{10}^{t+3} \lll 17) = a_2^{t+1} \oplus a_2^{t+4} \oplus C_1 \oplus C_2. \tag{7}$$

If the solutions of Eq. 7 and the values of a_1^{t+1} and a_1^{t+3}, which can be derived from the solutions of Eq. 1s of round t and round $t + 2$ respectively, are known, then one can get the right side of Eq. 5, i.e. $b_4^{t+1} \oplus (b_{10}^{t+3} \lll 32)$. The analysis of the right side of Eq. 6 is similar.

For the left sides of Eq. 5 and Eq. 6, one needs to solve the Eq. 1s of round $t+5$, $t + 6$ and $t + 7$. Then one can use Eq. 5 and Eq. 6 to match the solutions of two sides. Under the assumption that the internal states of MUGI are independent and random, there will be about $2^{90+45+30}/2^{64+64} = 2^{37}$ solutions[4] reserved since both b_{10}^{t+7} and b_{10}^{t+8} are 64-bit.

Procedure. We can conduct an attack based on the above two strategies and hash table technique.

STEP 1. Guess the inputs of equations

$$t : F(a_1^t, b_4^t) \oplus F(a_1^{t+2}, b_{10}^{t+2} \lll 17) = a_2^t \oplus a_2^{t+3} \oplus C_1 \oplus C_2,$$
$$t + 1 : F(a_1^{t+1}, b_4^{t+1}) \oplus F(a_1^{t+3}, b_{10}^{t+3} \lll 17) = a_2^{t+1} \oplus a_2^{t+4} \oplus C_1 \oplus C_2,$$
$$t + 2 : F(a_1^{t+2}, b_4^{t+2}) \oplus F(a_1^{t+4}, b_{10}^{t+4} \lll 17) = a_2^{t+2} \oplus a_2^{t+5} \oplus C_1 \oplus C_2,$$

and solve them to get $b_4^{t+1} \oplus (b_{10}^{t+3} \lll 32)$. The number of solutions is about $2^{45+30} = 2^{75}$. At the same time guess the inputs of equations

$$t + 5 : F(a_1^{t+5}, b_4^{t+5}) \oplus F(a_1^{t+7}, b_{10}^{t+7} \lll 17) = a_2^{t+5} \oplus a_2^{t+8} \oplus C_1 \oplus C_2,$$
$$t + 6 : F(a_1^{t+6}, b_4^{t+6}) \oplus F(a_1^{t+8}, b_{10}^{t+8} \lll 17) = a_2^{t+6} \oplus a_2^{t+9} \oplus C_1 \oplus C_2,$$

---

[4] Simulation results also verify that there are about 2^{30} solutions reserved for a single equation such as the Eq. 1 of round $t + i$ under the cache timing attack model.

and solve them to get b_{10}^{t+7}. The number of solutions is about $2^{30+30} = 2^{60}$. Then use the hash table technique to find the matched solutions based on Eq. 5, which have size of $2^{60+75-64} = 2^{71}$. The computation complexity of this step is about $O(2^{75})$ with memory complexity of $O(2^{60})$.

STEP 2. Similarly, guess the inputs of equations

$$t+1 : F(a_1^{t+1}, b_4^{t+1}) \oplus F(a_1^{t+3}, b_{10}^{t+3} \lll 17) = a_2^{t+1} \oplus a_2^{t+4} \oplus C_1 \oplus C_2,$$
$$t+2 : F(a_1^{t+2}, b_4^{t+2}) \oplus F(a_1^{t+4}, b_{10}^{t+4} \lll 17) = a_2^{t+2} \oplus a_2^{t+5} \oplus C_1 \oplus C_2,$$
$$t+3 : F(a_1^{t+3}, b_4^{t+3}) \oplus F(a_1^{t+5}, b_{10}^{t+5} \lll 17) = a_2^{t+3} \oplus a_2^{t+6} \oplus C_1 \oplus C_2,$$

and solve them to get $b_4^{t+2} \oplus (b_{10}^{t+4} \lll 32)$. The number of solutions is about 2^{75}. At the same time guess the inputs of equations

$$t+6 : F(a_1^{t+6}, b_4^{t+6}) \oplus F(a_1^{t+8}, b_{10}^{t+8} \lll 17) = a_2^{t+6} \oplus a_2^{t+9} \oplus C_1 \oplus C_2,$$
$$t+7 : F(a_1^{t+7}, b_4^{t+7}) \oplus F(a_1^{t+9}, b_{10}^{t+9} \lll 17) = a_2^{t+7} \oplus a_2^{t+10} \oplus C_1 \oplus C_2,$$

and solve them to get b_{10}^{t+8}. Then find the matched solutions based on Eq. 6. The complexity of this step is the same as that of STEP 1 above.

STEP 3. Use the hash table technique to find the matched solutions of STEP. 1 and STEP. 2. This step costs about $O(2^{71})$ computation complexity and memory complexity. And based on the previous analysis in this section, the solutions matched has number of about 2^{37}.

STEP 4. Combine the solutions of equation $F(a_1^{t+4}, b_4^{t+4}) \oplus F(a_1^{t+6}, b_{10}^{t+6} \lll 17) = a_2^{t+4} \oplus a_2^{t+7} \oplus C_1 \oplus C_2$ to recover the internal state of MUGI based on the STEP 1-5 in section 3.2. The computation complexity in this step is about $O(2^{67})$.

Complexity. As mentioned above, STEP 1 and 2 in this section cost most time complexity, which means the computation complexity of the attack is $O(2^{76})$. The memory complexity is $O(2^{71})$ and the cache access information of 10 successive rounds (from round t to round $t+9$) is required. As an illustration, we show the experimental results of recovering the internal state of MUGI under some random key and IV in Section 3.4.

3.4 Simulation Results

For different states initialized by 100 random keys and nonces, we have recorded their initial 206 rounds' output and 202 rounds' cache access information. The cache access information is obtained by simulation, i.e., the 4 most significant bits of the indexes are extracted directly when implementing the cipher. From the output and cache access information, we can solve the Equation Set. 4.

We record three numbers each round. The first number denoted as "no. 1" in Table 4 (see Appendix A) stands for the number of solutions of Equation Set. 4. The third number is denoted as "no. 3". It records the number of solutions of a single equation $F(a_1^t, b_4^t) \oplus F(a_1^{t+2}, b_{10}^{t+2} \lll_{17}) = a_2^t \oplus a_2^{t+3} \oplus C_1 \oplus C_2$ from Equation Set. 4. And the second number is denoted as "no. 2", which records the number of solutions of the equation $F(a_1^t, b_4^t) \oplus F(a_1^{t+2}, b_{10}^{t+2} \lll_{17}) = a_2^t \oplus a_2^{t+3} \oplus C_1 \oplus C_2$ choosing from the solutions of the equation set:

$$t - 2 : F(a_1^{t-2}, b_4^{t-2}) \oplus F(a_1^t, b_{10}^t \lll_{17}) = a_2^{t-2} \oplus a_2^{t+1} \oplus C_1 \oplus C_2,$$
$$t : F(a_1^t, b_4^t) \oplus F(a_1^{t+2}, b_{10}^{t+2} \lll_{17}) = a_2^t \oplus a_2^{t+3} \oplus C_1 \oplus C_2.$$

Then we compute the number of solutions as mentioned in Step 1 and Step 2 of section 3.3 for each round (from round 0 to round 200). We choose the minimum values for two successive rounds as the computation complexity of the attack in this paper, which are statistically around 2^{75}. It means that if the attacker collects the initial 202 rounds' noise-free cache accesses, then from ten of them he will recover the internal state of MUGI with computation complexity around $O(2^{76})$. Considering the space limit, Table 4 only shows the first 108 rounds' results and the IV and key are:

$$IV:0xf0e0d0c0b0a090807060504030201000,$$
$$K :0x000102030405060708090a0b0c0d0e0f.$$

4   Template Attack and Combined Side-Channel Attacks

In this section, we firstly introduce the template attacks in brief and the information we can derived. The leakage information of the template attacks is a little different from that of the cache timing attacks. Then we present the template attack analysis on MUGI and propose the combined cache timing and template attack with its applied circumstance. Additionally, we give the error-tolerant combined attack of MUGI.

4.1   Template Attack Basis and Information Available

Template attacks use a profiling step to compute the parameters of a multivariate normal distribution from a training device and an attack step in which the parameters obtained during profiling are used to infer some secret value on a target device. As to the microcontroller devices, the target parameter in the profiling step is usually the hamming weight of some operations, such as the S-box operations.

In this paper, we use a template attack model that collects the hamming weight leakage of each output of the S-box operation in the attack step. Recall that MUGI executes the F function two times per round, which results in 16 S-box operations. Then the noiseless leakage information per round is a list of 16 hamming weights in order. For example, the values of one round is:

hamming weigh list : $\{1, 2, 8, 3, 0, 6, 8, 2, 7, 1, 4, 4, 8, 1, 2, 3\}$.

4.2   The Template Attack Analysis

The analytical procedure of template attack is similar as that in Section 3.2 except that when solving Eq. 2, the attacker knows the hamming weight of S-boxes' output in the left side of the equations. The attacker needs to exhaust all the candidates with the known hamming weight and then use Eq. 2 to filter the correct ones. We have enumerated all the known values (the hamming weights and the right side of the equation), calculated the number of the correct candidates. The result is summarized in Table 3[5].

Table 3. Distribution of the solutions of Eq. 2 under template attack model

0	1	2	3	4	5	6	7	8	10	12	15	16	20	21	24	28	30	35	36	40	56	70
	20736																					
14848	1020	112	448	560	448	504	64	4	448	112	672	280	112	64	280	4	560	64	70	56	4	2
71.6	4.92	0.54	2.16	2.70	2.16	2.43	0.31	0.02	2.16	0.54	3.24	1.35	0.54	0.31	1.35	0.02	2.70	0.31	0.34	0.27	0.02	0.01
—	5888																					
—	17.32	1.90	7.61	9.51	7.61	8.56	1.09	0.07	7.61	1.90	11.41	4.76	1.90	1.09	4.76	0.07	9.51	1.09	1.19	0.95	0.07	0.03
—	5.74																					

Under the noise-less model that the known values are correct, the complexity of solving Eq. 2 in template attack is about

$$O(2^{11.3}) = O((\frac{1^2 + 8^2 + 28^2 + 56^2 + 70^2 + 56^2 + 28^2 + 8^2 + 1^2}{256})^2).$$

And the average number of the solutions is 5.74. Therefore, the complexity of solving Eq. 1 is $O(8 \times 2^{11.3}) = O(2^{14.3})$ and the number of solutions reserved is about $5.74^8 = 2^{20.17}$ on average. Then we can use Strategy 2 in Section 3.3 to recover the correct internal states, which will cost about $O(2^{20.17 \times 3}) = O(2^{60.51})$ computation complexity and about $O(2^{20.17 \times 2}) = O(2^{40.34})$ memory complexity.

4.3   Combined Cache Timing and Template Attacks

Since the analyses of MUGI under cache timing attack model and template attack model both depend on guessing and determining the solutions of Eq. 2 and the Strategy 2, we can conduct a side-channel attack with the cache access leakage and hamming weight leakage together.

Assume the attacker has two devices which runs the fast software implementation and the microcontroller implementation of MUGI respectively. At the beginning of the attack step, he collects the noiseless leakage from these two devices independently. Then he combines the two types of information to filter the solutions of Eq. 2, which makes the number of candidates reserved decrease. We have simulated the leakage for 1000 random keys and IVs and calculated the number of remaining candidates after the whole attack (using Strategy 2). The calculating process is similar as that in Section 3.4. The experiment results in Fig. 3 show that the combined attack costs about $O(2^{30})$ computation complexity and $O(2^{18})$ memory complexity under the noiseless condition.

---

[5] The explanation of each row is the same as that in Table 1.

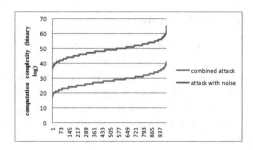

Fig. 3. Experiment results of combined attacks

Applied Circumstance. The combined attack needs two devices running MUGI with the same key and IV. It seems possible in the communication process which uses some stream ciphers to keep the information secure. As to additive stream ciphers, the encryption and decryption both use the same key and IV and generate the same keystreams. And in traditional cryptanalysis of additive stream cipher, the plaintext, ciphertext and keystreams are all known to the attacker.

In a word, if one can attack two devices which are communicating to each other using MUGI as the cryptographic algorithm, one of the devices runs MUGI's software implementation and the other is a microcontroller, then he can conduct the combined attack proposed in this section.

4.4   Error Tolerant Side-Channel Attack

The combination of these two attacks can also be effective when the measurements have some noise. The noise model we used is similar as that in [18], which assumes that the correct leakage value is always in the measurement sets. It is called additional error model in this paper. The oracles under the additional error model which is deduced from the practical measurements are as follows.

- **KEYSTREAM(i)**: Through this oracle, we can request the cipher to return the i-th keystream block to us.
- **CA_KEYSTREAM(i)**: This oracle returns four lists of cache access information per round corresponding to $T_0, ..., T_3$. Each list contains the correct cache accesses and one random error.
- **HM_KEYSTREAM(i)**: This oracle returns 16 hamming weight lists of the S-boxes' output. Each list contains two values, one correct hamming weight value and one error, whose value is just adjacent to the correct one. It means that, if the correct hamming weight is 0 (or 8), then the error is 1 (or 7). And in other cases, the error is randomly chosen from the correct value-1 and correct value$+1$.

Then we do experiments to simulate the additional error model and conduct the attack in Section 4.2. The results (in Fig. 3) of 1000 experiments with random keys and errors show that the computation complexity is $O(2^{50})$ medially, with memory complexity around $O(2^{32})$.

5   Conclusion and Future Works

In this paper, we present the cryptographic analysis of stream cipher MUGI under the cache timing attack model. The attack exploits some weaknesses of the MUGI cipher, which can also be used to conduct the template attacks. Then we present the template key-recovery attack of MUGI under the hamming weight leakage model. And due to the fact that the encryption and decryption of the stream cipher MUGI are almost the same except the keystream addition operation, we proposed a combined cache timing and template attack, which will reduce the computation complexity to practically $O(2^{30})$. Furthermore, the combined attack can tolerate errors. When there is one additional error in each measurement, the attack will cost about $O(2^{50})$ computation complexity on average. We also did experiments to verify these results.

To the best of our knowledge, it is the first time that cache attacks, template attacks and their combination are applied to the stream cipher MUGI. And the combination of these two attacks puts forward a new method of analyzing some complex stream ciphers. However, the complexity of the attack under noises is still high. We will employ more weaknesses of the MUGI cipher or other stream ciphers to improve the error tolerance of the combined and individual attacks in the further work.

References

1. Zenner, E.: A cache timing analysis of HC-256. In: Avanzi, R.M., Keliher, L., Sica, F. (eds.) SAC 2008. LNCS, vol. 5381, pp. 199–213. Springer, Heidelberg (2009)
2. Berstein, D.: Cache timing attacks on AES (2005), http://cr.yp.to/papaers.html#cachetiming
3. Osvik, D., Shmir, A., Tromer, E.: Cache attacks and countermeasures: The case of AES (2005), http://eprint.iacr.org/2005/271.pdf
4. Osvik, D.A., Shamir, A., Tromer, E.: Cache attacks and countermeasures: The case of AES. In: Pointcheval, D. (ed.) CT-RSA 2006. LNCS, vol. 3860, pp. 1–20. Springer, Heidelberg (2006)
5. Neve, M., Seifert, J., Wang, Z.: A refined look at Bersein's AES side-channel analysis. In: Proc. ASIACCS 2006, p. 369. ACM, New York (2006)
6. Bonneau, J., Mironov, I.: Cache-collision timing attacks against AES. In: Goubin, L., Matsui, M. (eds.) CHES 2006. LNCS, vol. 4249, pp. 201–215. Springer, Heidelberg (2006)
7. Bogdanov, A., Eisenbarth, T., Paar, C., Wienecke, M.: Differential cache-collision timing attacks on AES with applications to embedded CPUs. In: Pieprzyk, J. (ed.) CT-RSA 2010. LNCS, vol. 5985, pp. 235–251. Springer, Heidelberg (2010)
8. Blömer, J., Krummel, V.: Analysis of countermeasures against access driven cache attacks on AES. In: Adams, C., Miri, A., Wiener, M. (eds.) SAC 2007. LNCS, vol. 4876, pp. 96–109. Springer, Heidelberg (2007)
9. Gregor, L., Erik, Z., Philip, H.: Cache timing analysis of LFSR-Based stream ciphers. In: Parker, M.G. (ed.) Cryptography and Coding 2009. LNCS, vol. 5921, pp. 433–445. Springer, Heidelberg (2009)

10. Watanabe, D., Furuya, S., Yoshida, H., Takaragi, K., Preneel, B.: A new keystream generator MUGI. In: Daemen, J., Rijmen, V. (eds.) FSE 2002. LNCS, vol. 2365, pp. 179–194. Springer, Heidelberg (2002)

11. Golić, J.D.: A weakness of the linear part of stream cipher MUGI. In: Roy, B., Meier, W. (eds.) FSE 2004. LNCS, vol. 3017, pp. 178–192. Springer, Heidelberg (2004)

12. Biryukov, A., Shamir, A.: Analysis of the non-linear part of MUGI. In: Gilbert, H., Handschuh, H. (eds.) FSE 2005. LNCS, vol. 3557, pp. 320–329. Springer, Heidelberg (2005)

13. Matt, H., Ed, D.: Rekeying issues in the MUGI stream cipher. In: Preneel, B., Tavares, S. (eds.) SAC 2005. LNCS, vol. 3897, pp. 175–188. Springer, Heidelberg (2006)

14. Takahashi, J., Fukunaga, T., Sakiyama, K.: Fault analysis of stream cipher MUGI. In: Rhee, K.-H., Nyang, D. (eds.) ICISC 2010. LNCS, vol. 6829, pp. 420–434. Springer, Heidelberg (2011)

15. Paul, G., Raizada, S.: Impact of extending side channel attack on cihper variants: A case study with the HC series of stream ciphers. In: Bogdanov, A., Sanadhya, S. (eds.) SPACE 2012. LNCS, vol. 7644, pp. 32–44. Springer, Heidelberg (2012)

16. Suresh, C., Josyula, R., Pankaj, R.: Template attacks. In: Kaliski Jr., B.S., Koç, Ç.K., Paar, C. (eds.) CHES 2002. LNCS, vol. 2523, pp. 13–28. Springer, Heidelberg (2003)

17. Archambeau, C., Peeters, E., Standaert, F., Quisquater, J.: Template attacks in principal subspaces. In: Goubin, L., Matsui, M. (eds.) CHES 2006. LNCS, vol. 4249, pp. 1–14. Springer, Heidelberg (2006)

18. Shize, G., Xinjie, Z., Fan, Z., Tao, W., Shi, Z., Standaert, F., Chujiao, M.: Exploiting the incomplete diffusion feature: A specialized analytical side-channel attack against the AES and its application to microcontroller implementations. IEEE Transactions on Information Forensics and Security 9(6), 999–1014 (2014)

19. Standaert, F., Archambeau, C.: Using subspace-based template attacks to compare and combine power and electromagnetic information leakages. In: Oswald, E., Rohatgi, P. (eds.) CHES 2008. LNCS, vol. 5154, pp. 411–425. Springer, Heidelberg (2008)

20. Fouque, P.-A., Leurent, G., Réal, D., Valette, F.: Practical electromagnetic template attack on HMAC. In: Clavier, C., Gaj, K. (eds.) CHES 2009. LNCS, vol. 5747, pp. 66–80. Springer, Heidelberg (2009)

21. Brumley, B.B., Hakala, R.M.: Cache-timing template attacks. In: Matsui, M. (ed.) ASIACRYPT 2009. LNCS, vol. 5912, pp. 667–684. Springer, Heidelberg (2009)

22. Choudary, O., Kuhn, M.G.: Efficient template attacks. In: Francillon, A., Rohatgi, P. (eds.) CARDIS 2013. LNCS, vol. 8419, pp. 253–270. Springer, Heidelberg (2014)

23. Renauld, M., Standaert, F.-X.: Algebraic side-channel attacks. In: Bao, F., Yung, M., Lin, D., Jing, J. (eds.) Inscrypt 2009. LNCS, vol. 6151, pp. 393–410. Springer, Heidelberg (2010)

24. Itai, D.: Generic analysis of small cryptographic leaks. In: FDTC (2010)

A   The Specific Complexity by Experiments of Cache Timing Attack

Table 4. Experimental Results

t	no. 1	no. 2	no. 3	t	no. 1	no. 2	no. 3
0	47.3509	28.9981	27.0705	1	50.921	28.5945	27.1017
2	49.0643	27.5159	26.6423	3	46.6784	28.0786	29.0766
4	46.3759	28.0867	26.8686	5	48.1104	29.0766	25.1943
6	46.3867	27.4281	27.9698	7	43.903	25.7611	26.8602
8	47.4667	28.4552	27.6596	9	47.2052	27.474	26.996
10	47.1117	28.1901	27.4097	11	48.6334	28.0127	27.4727
12	47.5161	28.0257	27.6494	13	46.3224	28.5242	26.4111
14	45.9828	27.6494	28.9132	15	45.3336	27.148	28.5666
16	47.8531	28.9132	27.7978	17	47.7174	28.5666	27.7701
18	48.4237	27.7978	25.6582	19	48.7684	28.5961	29.3945
20	44.1097	28.4165	26.1636	21	48.9583	29.9915	29.3262
22	46.3717	26.1636	26.8518	23	46.492	29.3262	27.5033
24	47.5681	27.424	30.4981	25	45.839	27.5033	26.6708
26	47.5424	30.4981	27.2728	27	44.049	27.3004	25.5948
28	43.1314	27.2728	23.0602	29	44.9469	26.0465	26.0629
30	43.0833	24.2284	25.5057	31	46.7404	27.2685	26.3102
32	46.0621	26.0318	27.1015	33	44.9913	27.5132	26.3473
34	46.986	28.1879	27.2464	35	45.6894	26.965	27.4929
36	47.9547	27.5061	25.8861	37	46.1987	27.9346	26.9924
38	48.4645	27.2471	27.9855	39	45.0192	27.6628	27.5818
40	48.4359	28.938	26.4909	41	45.1961	27.5818	28.1108
42	46.514	27.589	29.1062	43	45.6971	28.1108	26.5453
44	47.7289	29.2933	27.1953	45	46.3846	27.1842	27.7792
46	46.2511	27.5173	27.0833	47	49.6913	28.4541	30.1637
48	46.9726	27.6683	26.28	49	46.0552	30.5658	25.8014
50	48.595	27.2579	28.0368	51	47.62	25.7425	26.88
52	48.1584	29.1577	29.068	53	44.6038	27.8254	25.8778
54	48.5889	29.068	26.3889	55	43.7939	26.4139	23.8476
56	48.118	27.4159	27.7111	57	43.8566	24.3902	25.7037
58	48.2903	28.9045	26.273	59	46.7458	26.2154	24.2089
60	46.2103	27.2178	27.9989	61	45.1311	26.2436	26.9673
62	48.2168	28.4936	26.6533	63	47.6924	28.4897	26.0603
64	46.0573	27.4558	27.199	65	44.1093	27.2203	27.4709
66	46.0927	27.6095	25.4505	67	48.4191	27.4709	27.8988
68	47.1719	26.4609	25.7727	69	47.9947	29.1981	27.3852
70	47.2365	27.5984	26.7361	71	47.0072	27.9096	24.4661
72	48.2017	27.9188	27.3486	73	43.571	26.0648	26.2677
74	45.4647	28.0821	25.9365	75	45.9542	26.8371	27.913
76	45.1819	26.4372	25.2186	77	44.0763	28.4774	26.1185
78	46.6937	25.8195	27.2227	79	46.6482	26.1185	27.7476
80	46.0952	27.8184	26.9143	81	48.4962	28.4385	27.0868
82	47.2031	27.6233	28.3754	83	46.2649	28.2392	24.9903
84	47.5988	28.8169	27.7597	85	46.1004	25.9355	28.0577
86	46.8197	28.1281	26.6183	87	46.5389	28.0577	27.1923
88	45.6531	26.6183	24.3084	89	46.7723	27.742	25.9333
90	45.6657	25.9939	27.0464	91	47.2544	26.9745	28.7895
92	44.6624	28.1701	26.7274	93	46.8608	29.3672	26.1112
94	46.8214	26.7274	25.017	95	45.6586	26.8116	27.5414
96	46.3832	26.7314	24.974	97	47.4925	28.0889	29.6201
98	47.6166	26.6652	27.583	99	47.2731	29.6201	28.1071
100	49.2612	28.696	27.5861	101	48.0282	28.1071	26.765
102	48.5664	28.5168	27.0791	103	47.8993	27.8778	28.7475
104	45.7113	28.0744	28.4403	105	48.801	29.3145	28.1192
106	43.0075	28.4403	23.4564	107	49.1241	28.5173	29.2333

Authentication

Half a Century of Practice:
Who Is Still Storing Plaintext Passwords?

Erick Bauman, Yafeng Lu, and Zhiqiang Lin

Department of Computer Science, The University of Texas at Dallas
800 W. Campbell RD, Richardson, TX 75080 USA
{firstname.lastname}@utdallas.edu

Abstract. Text-based passwords are probably the most common way to authenticate a user on the Internet today. To implement a password system, it is critical
to ensure the confidentiality of the stored password—if an attacker obtains a password, they get full access to that account. However, in the past several years, we
have witnessed several major password leakages in which all the passwords were
stored in plaintext. Considering the severity of these security breaches, we believe
that the website owners should have upgraded their systems to store password
hashes. Unfortunately, there are still many websites that store plaintext passwords.
Given the persistence of such bad practice, it is crucial to raise public awareness
about this issue, find these websites, and shed light on best practices. As such,
in this paper, we systematically analyze websites in both industry and academia
and check whether they are still storing plaintext passwords (or used to do so). In
industry, we find 11 such websites in Alexa's top 500 websites list. Also, we find
this is a universal problem, regardless of the profile of the websites according to
our analysis of almost 3,000 analyzed sites. Interestingly, we also find that even
though end users have reported websites that are storing plaintext passwords, significant amounts of website owners ignore this. On the academic side, our analysis
of 135 conference submission sites shows that the majority of them are also still
storing plaintext passwords despite the existence of patches that fix this problem.

1 Introduction

To access sensitive information (e.g., online financial accounts, social networks, and
email services) protected by a computer system, end users often need to provide a
password, which is a secret string of characters that is matched with a stored value
in a database to authenticate a user. While password based schemes are disliked by
users [16] and have many alternatives [18], they are still the de facto standard for
authentication, especially in today's Internet, due to their easier deployment (no need
of special hardware), low cost, and simplicity.

However, implementing a secure password system is still complicated, and many
things can go wrong. Among these password threats, some of them can be fixed easily.
For instance, we should always store passwords as hashes instead of as plaintext. Note
that the systems and security field began discussing password secrecy half a century
ago [32,37], and it was decided early on that using hashes provided needed security
and storing plaintext passwords was unwise. As a statement of fact, a website should

© Springer International Publishing Switzerland 2015
J. Lopez and Y. Wu (Eds.): ISPEC 2015, LNCS 9065, pp. 253–267, 2015.
DOI: 10.1007/978-3-319-17533-1_18

never store plaintext passwords, but this statement can be made even stronger by adding that sites should also not store passwords with reversible encryption. While encrypting passwords is stronger than nothing, the key in many cases may be on the same server that is compromised, thereby defeating its purpose. Therefore, regardless of the way a password is being stored on the server, the salient fact is that for proper security a website should never be able to retrieve a user's original password. This should preclude the fact that under no circumstances should a user's password be sent to them in plain text.

Unfortunately, in practice, website owners ignore these facts and continue to store and send passwords insecurely. Regardless of how the passwords are being stored on the server side, if a server sends a user's plaintext password back to them, it is following bad password practices. While some sites may consider sending a user's password to them a matter of convenience, we define a site following such practices as "insecure" regardless of motivations. Note that insecure here means "subject to password leakage".

In the past several years, we have witnessed a number of major password leakage incidents. More specifically, as illustrated in Table 1, we can notice that many of the leaked passwords were actually in plaintext, and in total more than 100,000,000 plaintext passwords have been leaked. Given that end users often tend to reuse their passwords for different websites [28,24,21], such leakage forces users to change their passwords or risk someone breaking into their accounts.

Do website owners learn lessons from the mistakes of others and quickly fix their websites in response to reports of millions of leaked plaintext passwords? Table 1 shows that is clearly not always the case. For instance, the massive password leakage of rockyou.com in 2009 [39] resulted in substantial media coverage, but

Table 1. Notable Examples of Recent Password Leakages.

Site Address	Amount	Year	Plaintext?	Source
myspace.com	34,000	2006	✔	[25]
rockyou.com	32,603,388	2009	✔	[39]
hotmail.com	8,931	2009	✔	[20]
gawker.com	1,300,000	2010	✗	[35]
csdn.net	6,428,632	2011	✔	[9]
tianya.cn	31,761,424	2011	✔	[9]
webo.com	4,765,895	2011	✔	[9]
7k7k.com	6,541,991	2011	✔	[9]
renren.com	4,768,600	2011	✔	[9]
17173.com	18,333,776	2011	✔	[9]
duowan.com	8,305,005	2011	✔	[9]
uuu9.com	5,577,553	2011	✔	[9]
ieee.org	100,000	2011	✔	[10]
rootkit.com	81,4501	2011	✗	[11]
youporn.com	1,566,156	2012	✔	[15]
voices.yahoo.com	453,000	2012	✔	[14]
militarysingles.com	163,792	2012	✗	[13]
linkedin.com	6,500,000	2012	✗	[12]
adobe.com	150,000,000	2013	✗	[43]

we still observe that over 70 million plaintext passwords were stolen in 2011 [9], which is a historic record. While the most recent password leakage was not plaintext (the leaked passwords from Adobe were encrypted), we can still find websites that store plaintext passwords. This is in fact true in both academia and industry. Specifically, we find many academic conference paper submission sites (especially those using HotCRP [29]) that store plaintext passwords, and we also find several websites from Alexa's top 500 websites list that store plaintext passwords as well.

Therefore, given the existence of such a bad practice, it is crucial to raise public awareness, find these websites, and shed light on best practices. As such, in this paper, we systematically analyze websites in both industry and academia, investigate whether they are insecure (or used to be insecure), and discuss why they are still insecure. In industry, we find 11 insecure websites in Alexa's top 500 websites list. Interestingly, we also find that even though end users have reported that a website is insecure, significant numbers of website owners appear to ignore this. On the academic side, we examine 135 academic conferences in security, systems, and networking from the past five years. Our results reveal that many conference paper submission sites remain insecure and store plaintext passwords, in spite of the existence of patches to fix this problem.

2 Background

Password security has been an important security issue for decades. Users trust service providers with valuable information that can be reached by anyone with the correct username and password; maintaining password secrecy is paramount. While the use of password hashing can be traced back to Multics and UNIX in the 1960s and 1970s[1], we focus on the web. We do not discuss password transmission, although we note that the client-server connection should be encrypted at the very least. We also do not discuss alternatives to password authentication, because we want to focus on the most popular authentication mechanism.

2.1 How to Store a Password

There are many ways to store a password. At a high level, there are three basic ways: (1) plaintext, (2) encrypted plaintext, (3) hashed plaintext. In the following, we review these approaches and discuss their pros and cons.

Plaintext. The most straightforward approach to implement a password system is to store the user's password in plaintext and perform a simple comparison to authenticate a user. While this approach is easy to implement, it creates a lot of security problems.

First, anyone with access to the database can view all users' passwords. Given that many Internet users tend to reuse their passwords [28,24,21], it may allow malicious owners of a site to login to user accounts on other sites. Second, even if we trust the website owners, if an attacker gains database access, all passwords will be leaked. This also makes password collection trivial, and is the reason that millions of plaintext passwords have been revealed.

The advantages of plaintext are appealing to an inexperienced developer. It is simple authentication without the need to use cryptography, and it gives an illusion of security. The disadvantages are obvious and serious enough that plaintext should never be used.

Encrypted Plaintext. A natural solution is to encrypt the user's password. One can either directly encrypt the password with a single key, or encrypt a constant with a user supplied password as the key.

For the first approach, the server must store the key so it can encrypt the password. Therefore, passwords are at risk of being revealed if the key is compromised. While one can separate the key from the data by putting the key in the code and the passwords in the database, this only slightly reduces the attack vectors. Also, if the key is ever

---

[1] An incident on the CTSS system in the mid-1960s, in which the contents of the password file were displayed on login, was inspiration for password hashing [32]. Such an algorithm was in use in Multics since at least the early 1970s [37] and in UNIX since Version 3 in 1973 [31].

revealed, all passwords encrypted with the key are compromised, and the owners will know the passwords since they have the key. Finally, an attacker with access to only ciphertext can still tell if users have the same password.

The second approach operates in a similar manner to hash functions. It produces a fixed-length ciphertext. It is better than the first approach but can reveal identical passwords like the first approach does. The strength of the password will rely on the encryption, which was not designed specifically for such use.

Hashed Plaintext. One-way cryptographic hash functions exist for the specific purpose of authentication. There is no need to decrypt a password; the server can compare the final hash with the value in its database. By default, we should use the hash function to transform user provided passwords and then store the hashes. Security then depends on which hash function is used. Some well-known hashing algorithms are MD5, SHA-1, SHA-2, and SHA-3. MD5 and SHA-1 are no longer recommended for cryptographic purposes. These functions can produce hashes relatively quickly.

Using a cryptographic hash function (with salts) has been proven to be the right approach for storing passwords, but it still remains susceptible to certain attacks (§2.2). The use of salts makes precomputing passwords for rainbow table attacks impractical, slows dictionary attacks, and hides the presence of identical passwords, and therefore it notably improves the process. Also, hashing costs can be increased with algorithms such as PBKDF2 or bcrypt.

2.2   Attacks against a Stored Password

Large password databases are tempting targets to hackers and crackers, and therefore server administrators must take care to secure their servers as best they can. Here are some ways that attackers can obtain and crack passwords:

Password Stealing. The first objective of an attacker is usually to gain access to the server or to user accounts. One client-side strategy that is near-impossible for a site to defend from is phishing attacks, in which an attacker sets up a fake version of the real site to fool users[2]. Other client-side attacks include keyloggers or other malware that steals a user's password.

An issue of greater concern to the owners of a site is maintaining the security of their database of passwords and user data. One significant attack vector for sites is SQL injection, which exploits mistakes made in sanitizing user data before passing it to the database. Other attacks include obtaining server dumps (as an inside job) or convincing the server to divulge its memory contents, which is what happened with the Heartbleed SSL vulnerability.

Password Cracking. If passwords are stored in plaintext, then once an attacker retrieves the contents of the database their job is done. Hashing forces an attacker to perform extremely difficult calculations in order to retrieve usable passwords, and in theory the calculations require a high enough time complexity to render them infeasible. Unfortunately, there are several strategies attackers can take to make cracking the hashes easier.

---

[2] While a site can hope that its SSL certificate will help a user distinguish an untrusted impostor from the real site, if a user is fooled, the real site may have no way of knowing the attack even happened.

Hashing algorithms are one-way functions; they are easy to calculate one way and extremely hard to calculate the other way. Therefore, the most straightforward attack on hashes is to simply attempt to compute hashes for every possible password by brute force instead of trying to derive passwords from the hashes, which is nearly impossible [32]. The disadvantage to this attack is that the password space is enormous and slower hashing algorithms make computing many hashes a very time-consuming process.

Instead of choosing every possible password combination, it is much faster if an attacker instead selects candidate passwords from a dictionary or database of common passwords or phrases. Since many users choose weak passwords, it is much more likely that an attacker will find a valid password sooner in their search than with simple brute forcing. In addition, attackers can make changes to the dictionary words to reflect common modifications that users perform on their passwords to make them more "secure." Again, one way to try to defend against this is by making it computationally expensive to calculate a large number of hashes, but an attacker would likely still be able to obtain the weakest passwords despite this.

3 Practice in Industry

Since storing plaintext passwords is a very bad practice, it is important to make sure website owners properly store users' passwords. However, from a client perspective, we cannot tell how the passwords are being stored in the server's database. However, there is a straightforward method to determine if the website is able to retrieve a user's original password. In particular, we can use the "forgot password" option, in which website owners mail the user a password reset link, a new (random) password, or the user's previous password. If it is the user's previous password, then the server must be storing user passwords in plaintext or reversible encryption with the server having access to the decryption key, and they are sending the plaintext password via an unencrypted channel (email). We therefore consider websites that send a user's password back to them as insecure.

Experiment Setup. Therefore, to determine whether a particular website is subject to password leakage or not, we must first register a user and then trigger the password mailing option. While we wish we could write a robot to automatically scan these websites and perform a large scale study, captchas and special verification such as using SMS require manual inspection, which limits the number of sites that can be collected.

Fortunately, we noticed that there is a website dedicated to reporting websites of this type called PLAINTEXTOFFENDERS [5], which allows Internet users to submit examples of websites that store user passwords. Therefore, those submitted websites could serve as first hand raw data and enable us to extract insights from industry practice. However, these insecure sites are submitted in an ad-hoc manner, and therefore the archive may be missing certain important websites. Given the fact that it is not feasible to register to a large number of sites, but it is still desirable to obtain a large sample, we decided to inspect the PLAINTEXTOFFENDERS archive first (§3.1), and then manually inspect the top 500 websites (§3.2). In the following, we present our findings.

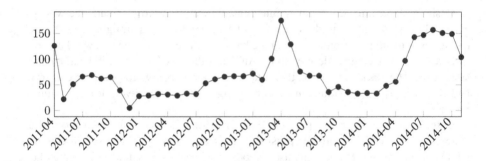

Fig. 1. Plain Text Offenders website reporting rate by year and month. Some posts had multiple URLs. The data shows no downward trend in the number of websites being reported.

3.1   Results from PLAINTEXTOFFENDERS

PLAINTEXTOFFENDERS [5] is a website that allows users to submit examples of websites that store user passwords. It has a substantial archive of sites with submissions that contain a URL for each insecure site, and an image of an email containing the user's password, demonstrating that the site is storing user passwords without hashing them. However, at the time of our original study, PLAINTEXTOFFENDERS did not provide any aggregated statistics or analysis of its submissions. Therefore, we developed a script to automatically scrape the entire site contents. We perform four types of studies that aim to understand (1) the trend of industry practice, (2) site rankings, (3) site classification, and (4) the properties of reformed sites.

The Trend. We first wanted to see whether industry practice has been improving. Since PLAINTEXTOFFENDERS's archives go back to 2011, we decided to obtain information on the reporting rate. We retrieved the date the site was posted, the URL, and the description of the site from PLAINTEXTOFFENDERS. In total, the site yielded 2,914 URLs. We calculated the number of websites reported per month over the lifetime of PLAINTEXTOFFENDERS; the results are shown in Figure 1. The number of submissions to the site shows no clear indication of a trend. Ideally,

Table 2. PLAINTEXTOFFENDERS websites grouped by their Alexa rankings. The majority of the sites are in the top million sites.

Ranking	Site Count
1-500	41
501-1000	41
1001-10000	297
10001-100000	747
100001-1000000	989
1000001-10000000	491
>10000000	88
UNKNOWN	224

the graph would show a downward trend to indicate less websites storing plain text passwords. However, due to external factors such as increases in the number of global websites and potential increasing popularity of PLAINTEXTOFFENDERS, it is difficult to accurately determine the change in percentage of such websites on the Internet.

Site Ranking. It is important to determine how popular the insecure sites are, because the problem is more significant if popular, high-traffic sites are also insecure. Therefore, we decided to rank the sites by using Alexa to determine the popularity of the listed insecure sites. By retrieving their Alexa rankings, we could group them to show the distribution of the sites by number of users. We show this result in Table 2. The UNKNOWN category consists of sites that did not rank in Alexa's system. Note that ranks in Alexa's ranking system are not considered statistically meaningful beyond 100,000, but there is still a substantial number of them in that range—over 1,000.

Observation 1. *Over 350 sites are in the top 10,000, 82 sites in the top 1,000, and 41 in the top 500. Some of the world's most popular sites are showing passwords in plaintext.*

It is important to note that Alexa rankings change frequently. While the rankings listed were accurate at the time of retrieval, the distribution will change over time, even if the underlying list of sites stays the same.

Site Classification. We then ran each URL through uClassify [8], a free API for text classification. We developed a script allow it to analyze the contents of the home page of each site. The contents were classified into one of thirty business categories. The UNKNOWN category consists of sites that did not respond when uClassify attempted to query them. The top categories are shown in Table 3. There are important sectors dealing with potentially sensitive data, and PLAINTEXTOFFENDERS offers hundreds of concrete examples of websites in these sectors. There are URLs for many online retailers, over ten banks, and sites dealing with tax forms, which shows that the risk to consumers in these sectors is real.

Table 3. PLAINTEXTOFFENDERS websites categorized by uClassify business categories, sorted by greatest to least. The bottom 15 categories are omitted.

Category	Site Count
Information Technology	494
UNKNOWN	282
Marketing and Advertising	281
Retail Trade	227
Telecommunications	192
Investing	157
Hospitality	147
Accounting	142
Consumer Goods and Services	122
Arts and Entertainment	107
Opportunities	97
Cooperatives	69
Food and Related Products	67
Business Services	65
International Business and Trade	65
Environment	62

Observation 2. *Password plaintext storage is common in industries working with sensitive data.*

Reformed Sites. One important consideration is whether sites that once stored passwords insecurely have improved. If they have, then this indicates growing awareness and willingness of site owners to change and improve their sites.

The sites that were reported on PLAINTEXTOFFENDERS in 2011 have had three years to improve their password storage systems. We decided that this set of sites was a good candidate for investigating to see if they have stopped storing plaintext passwords. We performed a manual investigation of the sites reported on PLAINTEXTOFFENDERS in 2011 to determine if they had fixed their password systems, and in total there are 483 sites. Among them, 293 (i.e., 60.7%) could be tested. There are several reasons why the sites could not be tested: some were no longer online, and some needed a phone number or other special information that could not be provided. Of the 293 sites that were tested, 205 had fixed the problem and 88 remain insecure, meaning that approximately 70% of the testable sites no longer store passwords in plain text.

PLAINTEXTOFFENDERS has a list of "Reformed Offenders," which consists of sites that have been confirmed to no longer send passwords in plaintext. Surprisingly, the list is extremely short; people may be less inclined to verify existing sites in the database than to add new ones. As indicated by our results, there may be a significant number of sites reported on PLAINTEXTOFFENDERS that are no longer insecure, and so the actual number of still-insecure sites may not be as serious as it first appears. We will submit the list of reformed sites that we found to PLAINTEXTOFFENDERS after publication.

We took the 205 fixed sites and grouped them by category like we did for the entire set of PLAINTEXTOFFENDERS sites. This way, we could compare the demographics of the reformed sites and the entirety of the PLAINTEXTOFFENDERS archives to determine if there are any specific kinds of sites that improved. . Interestingly, the sites fell into similar category groupings. While the order varied slightly, these sites had very similar distributions to the overall distribution of the PLAINTEXTOFFENDERS archives.

There was no specific type of site that indicated that the site would be more or less likely to be fixed. Less new sites may adhere to best practices than long-established sites, but many websites do eventually stop storing passwords in plaintext. Therefore, we can conclude that

Insight 1. *There is no specific website profile that can definitively indicate the probability of whether it is handling user passwords correctly, or its likelihood to fix the problem if it is not following best practices. However, a website is more likely to have fixed the problem the longer they have existed.*

This result corresponds well with previous studies; it has been found that longer-lived sites tend to follow better security practices [19].

3.2   Result of the Manual Analysis of Top 500

As discussed earlier, insecure sites are submitted to PLAINTEXTOFFENDERS in an ad-hoc manner, as the existence of a submission depends on a user knowing about PLAIN-TEXTOFFENDERS, using the insecure site, and choosing to report it. To have a better view, we decided to perform a manual analysis systematically on a given number of sites. We chose Alexa's top 500 sites as input, and manually analyzed whether there are any websites that still store plaintext passwords. Recall earlier we found 41 insecure sites on PLAINTEXTOFFENDERS in Alexa's top 500 sites (Observation 1), and this study would also allow us to confirm how many of these top 500 sites have fixed the problem.

We used the manual methodology discussed earlier to determine whether a given website is insecure by registering a user and checking the site's response to the "forgot password" option. For the current top 500 sites, we were able to manually inspect 393 (i.e., 78.6%) of them (the rest cannot be verified due to constraints such as requiring special verification, a special account, special utilities or

Table 4. The sites from our study of the top 500. None of these have been fixed yet. The countries were determined by Alexa based on popularity.

Site Address	Rank.	Category	Country
fc2.com	58	Business Services	Japan
lists.wikimedia.org	135	Cooperatives	United States
badoo.com	164	Cooperatives	Italy
espncricinfo.com	188	Arts & Entertainment	India
liveinternet.ru	192	Arts & Entertainment	Russia
rutracker.org	301	Arts & Entertainment	Russia
corriere.it	380	Arts & Entertainment	Italy
extratorrent.cc	415	Arts & Entertainment	India
jrj.com.cn	456	Investing	China
kooora.com	464	Arts & Entertainment	Saudi Arabia
xywy.com	484	Healthcare	China

services, a referee, an existing account number, or a safe code). Among them, we found at least 11 reported insecure sites have not been patched yet. Among the remaining 30 top 500 sites from PLAINTEXTOFFENDERS , they could either not be verified due to requiring personal information, or they were fixed or incorrectly reported. The sites found on PLAINTEXTOFFENDERS and manually verified by us are presented in Table 4.

Observation 3. *There are likely insecure sites that have not been reported, and there may be several more in the top 500 that we were unable to verify.*

However, the number we were able to confirm is a small percentage (2.2%) of the top 500 sites, and even the total number reported on PLAINTEXTOFFENDERS (8.2%) is not nearly as serious as it could be. This matches the pattern found in previous studies that more popular sites tend to have better password security [19].

4 Practice in Academia

We have observed the mistakes made by industry. Does academia perform better? Since academic researchers often need to set up conference websites to manage paper submissions and reviews, we investigated how conference submission sites manage user passwords. In this section, we present our findings regarding this.

Table 5. Conference Management Software Inspected in Our Study.

Software Name	Centralized	Checked #	Checked %	Plaintext #	Plaintext %
HotCRP (HC)	✗	106	78.5	103	97.2
EasyChair (EC)	✔	19	14.1	7	36.8
SoftConf (SC)	✔	4	3.0	3	75.0
EDAS (ED)	✔	5	3.7	3	60.0
CMT (CM)	✔	1	0.7	0	0

4.1 Experiment Setup

Conference paper submission and review is an important activity for academic researchers, especially in computer science. During a paper submission, an author/reviewer often needs to register on a submission site and choose a username (or email) and password for authentication. There are a number of frequently used examples of conference management software, such as HotCRP [29], EasyChair [1], Softconf [7], EDAS [2], and CMT [4], and they are hosted on web servers to provide this service.

As presented in Table 5, some of the conference management software is managed through a centralized service (e.g., EasyChair), some of them are hosted independently by individual conference submission sites (e.g., HotCRP), and some of them are mixed, with both centralized hosting and individual hosting (e.g., SoftConf). Centralized services host the conference software themselves and perform all setup and maintenance for a conference. However, many conference organizers choose to host their own paper submission sites, which gives them more control, but also puts the responsibility of patching and updating the conference software on each individual conference.

In our study, we selected these five conference management software packages for study, and observed how they managed their users' passwords. Except for CMT, a closed source service from Microsoft which we cannot confirm, all others have been identified as having been insecure in the past, but they have all been patched within the last few years. In total, we examined 135 conferences from security, systems, and networking, using the past five years as the time window. For each conference, we checked which conference software it used and whether it was insecure. If the website was still live, we used the same "forgot password" option as we did in the industry study to validate whether it was insecure. Otherwise, we checked our own email history as well as the email of our colleagues to confirm whether they were insecure.

4.2   Our Findings

The detailed inspection results for these conferences are presented in Table 6. Interestingly, we notice that the majority (78.4%) of them use HotCRP, especially in systems conference management, with the second being EasyChair, which accounts for 14.2%. Surprisingly we found 97.1% of HotCRP sites were insecure. We would have assumed the conference sites managed by security researchers should be more secure, but there was no exception for the security conferences.

Observation 4. *Surprisingly, website owners often do not follow best security practices, even when they are well-educated and understand the risks.*

Also, it is important to note that the trend is moving towards good practice, as we have seen Oakland, SIGCOMM, and MobiCOM in 2014 store hashes when they use HotCRP. However, why were so many conferences before 2014 insecure, especially those using HotCRP? Fortunately, HotCRP is open source, so we decided to inspect its source to determine how it handled passwords and when it started storing hashed passwords.

We examined the code and configurations on the git repository of the most recent release of HotCRP. Interestingly, we noticed that it contains a flag called "safePasswords", which enables the storage of password hashes instead of plaintext. This flag is enabled by default. However, work on this feature did not begin until August 2013, as documented in the changelog [3]. This explains why all conferences before 2013 that used HotCRP were insecure: HotCRP did not have the ability to store password hashes until late summer 2013. Then why are some conferences in 2014 still insecure? We suspect they are running an older version of HotCRP (such as all the conferences hosted by USENIX) or the administrators did not configure it correctly. If it is the latter case, our Observation 4 is further reinforced. We would like to emphasize that the confidentiality of research is considered important; if someone obtained the password to an account for a conference, they could view papers or modify reviews.

Finally, we noticed from our investigation that EasyChair and SoftConf fixed this problem in 2011, and EDAS fixed it in 2012. Also, we did find that one user submitted a report to PLAINTEXTOFFENDERS exposing EasyChair's plaintext practice in 2011.

5   Discussions and Implications

After analyzing insecure sites in both industry and academia, we must answer why websites are still storing plaintext passwords. To this end, we would like to ask the following questions:

Q1. Does the fact that a website is physically isolated make it more secure?

Table 6. Statistics on the Conference Submission Sites. Symbol ✔ denotes the corresponding site was plaintext, ✗ denotes not plaintext, and – denotes the conference was not held in that year.

Conference Name	2014		2013		2012		2011		2010	
	Software	Plaintext?	Software	Plaintext?	Software	Plaintext?	Software	Plaintext?	Software	Plaintext?
CCS	EC	✗	EC	✗	EC	✗	EC	✔	EC	✔
CSF	EC	✗	EC	✗	HC	✔	HC	✔	EC	✔
ESORICS	EC	✗	EC	✗	EC	✗	EC	✔	EC	✔
NDSS	HC	✔	EC	✗	EC	✗	HC	✔	SC	✔
Oakland	HC	✗	HC	✔	HC	✔	HC	✔	HC	✔
RAID	HC	✔	EC	✗	HC	✔	HC	✔	EC	✔
USENIX-Security	HC	✔	HC	✔	HC	✔	HC	✔	HC	✔
ASPLOS	HC	✔	EC	✗	SC	✗	SC	✔	SC	✔
EuroSys	HC	✔	HC	✔	HC	✔	HC	✔	HC	✔
FAST	HC	✔	HC	✔	HC	✔	HC	✔	HC	✔
HPCA	HC	✔	HC	✔	HC	✔	HC	✔	HC	✔
ISCA	HC	✔	HC	✔	HC	✔	HC	✔	HC	✔
LISA	HC	✔	HC	✔	HC	✔	HC	✔	HC	✔
MICRO	HC	✔	HC	✔	HC	✔	HC	✔	HC	✔
OSDI	HC	✔	-	-	HC	✔	-	-	HC	✔
PACT	HC	✔	HC	✔	HC	✔	HC	✔	HC	✔
SenSys	HC	✔	HC	✔	HC	✔	HC	✔	HC	✔
SoCC	HC	✔	HC	✔	HC	✔	HC	✔	CM	✗
SOSP	-	-	HC	✔	-	-	HC	✔	-	-
USENIX-ATC	HC	✔	HC	✔	HC	✔	HC	✔	HC	✔
VEE	HC	✔	HC	✔	HC	✔	EC	✔	HC	✔
CoNEXT	HC	✔	HC	✔	HC	✔	ED	✔	ED	✔
IMC	HC	✔	HC	✔	HC	✔	HC	✔	HC	✔
MobiCom	HC	✗	HC	✔	HC	✔	HC	✔	HC	✔
MobiHoc	ED	✗	ED	✗	HC	✔	HC	✔	ED	✔
MobiSys	HC	✔	HC	✔	HC	✔	HC	✔	HC	✔
NSDI	HC	✔	HC	✔	HC	✔	HC	✔	HC	✔
SIGCOMM	HC	✗	HC	✔	HC	✔	HC	✔	HC	✔

Insight 2. *Site owners may think that their sites are sufficiently secured or isolated from attackers that they do not need to worry about intruders. However, repeated security breaches of websites that considered themselves secure have proved this is unrealistic.*

Q2. Why have operating systems been hashing passwords for almost 50 years, as in Multics or UNIX, but some websites today do not?

Insight 3. *Such systems were designed by experts. They quickly discovered that they could not eliminate the threat of a breach and therefore came up with a provably secure solution. Unlike with the development of an OS, a website can be created by someone with no experience. Therefore, some websites are developed without following any best practices.*

Q3. Is a password a critical piece of private data that is as sensitive as bank accounts and SSNs?

Insight 4. *Some websites do not store any valuable personal data like addresses or credit card numbers. Therefore, owners of those sites may think that there is no need to protect passwords. However, due to password reuse, an attacker can use passwords retrieved from a breached site to retrieve valuable data from a more secure one. This opens up an attack vector that very secure websites cannot protect against. This threat is* *significant enough that even sites that do not store other sensitive data should consider passwords as highly sensitive. However, many of these sites do not.*

It is important to note that these insights are not revolutionary, and have been the subject of previous discussions of password security. However, we wish to very clearly emphasize these conclusions; it is crucial that both academia and industry unequivocally condemn plaintext password storage so as to provide correct guidance to website owners.

6   Mitigations and the Future

Getting websites to change their password practices is clearly difficult. Here are several mitigations for users and potential solutions for the future.

Password Generator and Manager. One solution is to use a password generator to create unique passwords for each website, and then use a password manager to store each password. However, this requires a master password or a key and (in the case of an online password manager), introduces the challenge of secure password transmission across the Internet. There are many password managers, however, and there are ones that do take security seriously [6]. Therefore, this is likely a significant security improvement for the average user if they can keep their master password safe.

Client-Side Hashing. With a client-side program or browser extension [36], a user can hash their password before sending it to a website, effectively making that hash their de facto password for that site. If the user adds a salt to their password based on the site in question (by, for example, using the site domain), the password's hash will be different for every site. From the site's perspective, the user is sending a long string of random characters, with no hint as to the original password and salt. Therefore, even if a site with poor security is compromised, the only user information revealed is the hash of their password, which is unique to—and only usable for—that specific site.

Single Sign-On and Related Technologies. Another alternative for securing login credentials is to trust them with a central authority and use a framework like OpenID, OAuth, or Facebook Connect. Such a system requires the user to log in to the central authority, which then authenticates the user to any third-party site integrated with the system. An advantage of this is that the user never has to give their credentials to any third-party site. However, these systems are not foolproof [40], and the user must trust that the central authority is storing their password securely.

Established Standards. Many aspects of password security lack an agreed-upon standard [19]. If a comprehensive standard were developed for password storage, it could provide a baseline to compare sites to. In addition, a reference implementation from a trusted authority could discourage developers from designing their own potentially flawed authentication, and provide developers with an authoritative, publicly audited starting point for making secure design decisions.

7   Related Work

There has been a substantial amount of research centered around password security. In general, the research mostly focuses on how to generate (e.g., [23,38,30]), transfer (e.g., [34,44]), store (e.g., [26]), manage (e.g., [45,24,17]), and attack and defend passwords from numerous attack vectors (e.g., [32,28,27,46]). In this section, we review related work on password storage attacks and defenses.

In 2010, Bonneau et al. performed a large-scale general analysis of how websites handle passwords. They covered many aspects of password security, including password storage. In their study of 150 sites, 29% emailed user passwords in plaintext [19]. To motivate websites to fix their bad password practices, PLAINTEXTOFFENDERS [5] was launched in April 2011. Our work is closely related to the site in that we both aim to raise public awareness. The difference is that we also perform a more systematic study of the problem and its solutions.

Since security experts advocate storing hashes, there has been a great amount of interest in efficiently cracking hashes and obtaining plaintext. The earliest attempts stem from brute forcing and evolved into dictionary attacks. Recently, there were also efforts to make dictionary attacks smarter by employing Markov models (e.g., [33]), probabilistic context free grammars (e.g., [42]), and history based guessing (e.g., [46]).

Interestingly, the large amounts of plaintext passwords revealed from recent password leakages have also enabled many valuable password studies. Dell'Amico et al. [22] analyzed the strength of passwords from leaked MySpace passwords and two other websites. Weir et al. [41] leveraged the 32M passwords leaked from RockYou to test the metrics (especially the entropy) for password creation policies. Das et al. [21] investigated several hundred thousand leaked passwords and conducted a password reuse survey, finding that about 43-51% users reuse their passwords for several websites. In addition, they have also developed a password guessing algorithm to guess cross-site passwords.

8 Conclusion

Despite almost 50 years of practice of storing and managing passwords, we still find many websites storing plaintext passwords. In this paper, we systematically analyzed the insecure sites from both industry and academia to investigate the reasons behind this issue. We found 11 of the most popular 500 websites and over 100 conference submission sites from the past five years that do not hash user passwords. Finally, we discuss how the illusion of security, lack of security experts, and lack of attention to secure passwords on sites not storing other sensitive data are likely the root causes of why today we are still storing plaintext passwords.

Acknowledgements. We thank the anonymous reviewers for their feedback. This research was supported in part by AFOSR grant FA9550-14-1-0119. Any opinions, findings, conclusions, or recommendations expressed are those of the authors and not necessarily of the AFOSR.

References

1. Easychair home page, http://www.easychair.org/
2. Edas, https://www.edas.info/index.php

3. Hotcrp begin work on safe password storage, https://github.com/kohler/hotcrp/commit/127613bfbee196c06b6e799bbc4705b7be37cc06

4. Microsoft's conference management toolkit, https://cmt.research.microsoft.com/

5. Plain text offenders, http://plaintextoffenders.com/

6. Security - keepass, http://keepass.info/help/base/security.html

7. Softconf start v2 conferencemanager, http://www.softconf.com/

8. uclassify, http://www.uclassify.com/

9. Hackers released the passwords of over 70 million chinese internet accounts (2011), https://dazzlepod.com/rootkit/

10. Ieee data breach: 100k passwords leak in plain text (2011), http://www.neowin.net/news/ieee-data-breach-100k-passwords-leak-in-plain-text

11. rootkit.com cleartext passwords (2011), https://dazzlepod.com/rootkit/

12. Linkedin password hack: Check to see if yours was one of the 6.5 million leaked (2012), http://www.huffingtonpost.com/2012/06/07/linkedin-password-hack-check_n_1577184.html

13. Militarysingles.com hack exposes over 160,000 users information (2012), http://www.databreaches.net/militarysingles-com-hack-exposes-over-160000-users-information/

14. Yahoo hack leaks 453,000 voice passwords. http://www.darkreading.com/attacks-and-breaches/yahoo-hack-leaks-453000-voice-passwords/d/d-id/1105289?, 2012.

15. Youporn passwords available for download, thousands of users exposed (2012), http://nakedsecurity.sophos.com/2012/02/22/youporn-password-download/

16. Adams, A., Sasse, M.A.: Users are not the enemy. Commun. ACM 42(12), 40–46 (1999)

17. Bojinov, H., Bursztein, E., Boyen, X., Boneh, D.: Kamouflage: Loss-resistant password management. In: Gritzalis, D., Preneel, B., Theoharidou, M. (eds.) ESORICS 2010. LNCS, vol. 6345, pp. 286–302. Springer, Heidelberg (2010)

18. Bonneau, J., Herley, C., Oorschot, P.C.V., Stajano, F.: v. Oorschot, and F. Stajano. The quest to replace passwords: A framework for comparative evaluation of web authentication schemes. In: SP 2012, pp. 553–567. IEEE Computer Society, Washington, DC (2012)

19. Bonneau, J., Preibusch, S.: The password thicket: Technical and market failures in human authentication on the web. In: WEIS (2010)

20. Calin, B.: Statistics from 10,000 leaked hotmail passwords (2009), http://www.acunetix.com/blog/news/statistics-from-10000-leaked-hotmail-passwords/

21. Das, A., Bonneau, J., Caesar, M., Borisov, N., Wang, X.: The Tangled Web of Password Reuse. In: NDSS (February 2014)

22. Dell'Amico, M., Michiardi, P., Roudier, Y.: Password strength: An empirical analysis. In: INFOCOM 2010, pp. 983–991. IEEE Press, Piscataway (2010)

23. Florencio, D., Herley, C.: A large-scale study of web password habits. In: WWW 2007, pp. 657–666. ACM, New York (2007)

24. Gaw, S., Felten, E.W.: Password management strategies for online accounts. In: SOUPS 2006, pp. 44–55. ACM, New York (2006)

25. Grimes, R.A.: Myspace password exploit: Crunching the numbers

26. Hart, J., Markantonakis, K., Mayes, K.: Website credential storage and two-factor web authentication with a java SIM. In: Samarati, P., Tunstall, M., Posegga, J., Markantonakis, K., Sauveron, D. (eds.) WISTP 2010. LNCS, vol. 6033, pp. 229–236. Springer, Heidelberg (2010)

27. Holz, T., Engelberth, M., Freiling, F.: Learning more about the underground economy: A case-study of keyloggers and dropzones. In: Backes, M., Ning, P. (eds.) ESORICS 2009. LNCS, vol. 5789, pp. 1–18. Springer, Heidelberg (2009)

28. Ives, B., Walsh, K.R., Schneider, H.: The domino effect of password reuse. Commun. ACM 47(4), 75–78 (2004)

29. Kohler, E.: Hotcrp conference management software (2014), http://read.seas.harvard.edu/~kohler/hotcrp/

30. Komanduri, S., Shay, R., Kelley, P.G., Mazurek, M.L., Bauer, L., Christin, N., Cranor, L.F., Egelman, S.: CHI 2011, pp. 2595–2604. ACM, New York (2011)

31. McIlroy, M.D.: A research unix reader: Annotated excerpts from the programmers manual (1971)

32. Morris, R., Thompson, K.: Password security: A case history. Communications of the ACM 22(11), 594–597 (1979)

33. Narayanan, A., Shmatikov, V.: Fast dictionary attacks on passwords using time-space tradeoff. In: CCS 2005, pp. 364–372. ACM, New York (2005)

34. Peyravian, M., Zunic, N.: Methods for protecting password transmission. Computers& Security 19(5), 466–469 (2000)

35. Raphael, J.: Gawker hack exposes ridiculous password habits (2010), http://www.pcworld.com/article/213679/Gawker_Hack_Exposes_Ridiculous_Password_Habits.html

36. Ross, B., Jackson, C., Miyake, N., Boneh, D., Mitchell, J.C.: Stronger password authentication using browser extensions. In: Proceedings of the 14th Usenix Security Symposium, vol. 31 (2005)

37. Saltzer, J.H.: Protection and the control of information sharing in multics. Commun. ACM 17(7), 388–402 (1974)

38. Shay, R., Komanduri, S., Kelley, P.G., Leon, P.G., Mazurek, M.L., Bauer, L., Christin, N., Cranor, L.F.: Encountering stronger password requirements: User attitudes and behaviors. In: SOUPS 2010, pp. 2:1–2:20. ACM, New York (2010)

39. Siegler, M.: One of the 32 million with a rockyou account? you may want to change all your passwords (2009), http://techcrunch.com/2009/12/14/rockyou-hacked/

40. Wang, R., Chen, S., Wang, X.: Signing me onto your accounts through facebook and google: A traffic-guided security study of commercially deployed single-sign-on web services. In: SP 2012, pp. 365–379. IEEE (2012)

41. Weir, M., Aggarwal, S., Collins, M., Stern, H.: Testing metrics for password creation policies by attacking large sets of revealed passwords. In: CCS 2010, pp. 162–175. ACM, New York (2010)

42. Weir, M., Aggarwal, S., de Medeiros, B., Glodek, B.: Password cracking using probabilistic context-free grammars. In: SP 2009, pp. 391–405. IEEE Computer Society, Washington, DC (2009)

43. White, C.: Adobe leaks 150 million passwords; facebook and others impacted (2013), http://www.neowin.net/news/adobe-leaks-150-million-passwords-facebook-and-others-impacted

44. Yang, C.-C., Chang, T.-Y., Hwang, M.-S.: Security of improvement on methods for protecting password transmission. Informatica 14(4), 551–558 (2003)

45. Yee, K.-P., Sitaker, K.: Passpet: Convenient password management and phishing protection. In: SOUPS 2006, pp. 32–43. ACM, New York (2006)

46. Zhang, Y., Monrose, F., Reiter, M.K.: The security of modern password expiration: An algorithmic framework and empirical analysis. In: CCS 2010, pp. 176–186. ACM, New York (2010)

User Identity Verification Based on Touchscreen Interaction Analysis in Web Contexts

Michael Velten[1], Peter Schneider[1], Sascha Wessel[1], and Claudia Eckert[2]

[1] Fraunhofer Research Institute for Applied and Integrated Security
Munich, Germany
{michael.velten,peter.schneider,sascha.wessel}@aisec.fraunhofer.de
[2] Technische Universität München,
Computer Science Department Munich, Germany
claudia.eckert@in.tum.de

Abstract. The ever-increasing popularity of smartphones amplifies the risk of loss or theft, thus increasing the threat of attackers hijacking critical user accounts. In this paper, we present a framework to secure accounts by continuously verifying user identities based on user interaction behavior with smartphone touchscreens. This enables us to protect user accounts by disabling critical functionality and enforcing a reauthentication in case of suspicious behavior. We take advantage of standard mobile web browser capabilities to remotely capture and analyze touchscreen interactions. This approach is completely transparent for the user and works on everyday smartphones without requiring any special software or privileges on the user's device. We show how to successfully classify users even on the basis of limited and imprecise touch interaction data as is prevalent in web contexts. We evaluate the performance of our framework and show that the user identification accuracy is higher than 99% after collecting about a dozen touch interactions.

1 Introduction

Modern touch devices like smartphones and tablets have become ubiquitous in everyday life. Consequently, they are used for an increasing number of security-sensitive tasks ranging from reading email to more critical tasks like online banking. The risk of loss or theft of such mobile devices is especially prevalent because users carry them around and use them in unprotected environments. Additionally, users often choose simple and weak secrets, increase the screen lock timeouts of their devices, or completely disable unlock [10]. This allows attackers to hijack accounts, sometimes even without having to enter a password or PIN because having physical access to the device, often entails direct access to several accounts where the user is still logged into. A technique to protect against such threats is continuous user authentication. This can be realized by continuously verifying the user identity based on individual interaction behavior with the touch device caused by physical differences between users, varying habits, and personal preferences. In case of suspicious user behavior, the user account may be

© Springer International Publishing Switzerland 2015
J. Lopez and Y. Wu (Eds.): ISPEC 2015, LNCS 9065, pp. 268–282, 2015.
DOI: 10.1007/978-3-319-17533-1_19

temporarily locked and a reauthentication enforced. This provides an additional protection layer which can be used in combination with existing, complementary techniques.

In contrast to other authentication mechanisms such as entering a PIN or fingerprint recognition, where it is possible for an attacker to enter the PIN himself or to trick the fingerprint sensor with a mold of the legitimate user's fingerprint, individual behavior patterns are difficult to imitate precisely [2]. This fact has been utilized to identify users in normal desktop computer scenarios based on their keystroke dynamics [14] and mouse movements [24,7]. Recent research advances these techniques by exploring ways to identify users based on their individual interaction patterns with touch devices. There exists diverse research ranging from identifying users based on their behavioral patterns when tapping on the touchscreens [12,23] to work that analyzes interactions like scroll gestures [10,2,25]. Other work tries to infer keystrokes based on touch events [5] or device sensor information [15]. Some research utilizes dedicated hardware, e.g., modified touch displays [9] or even specially prepared gloves [8].

However, all these approaches require dedicated software on the user's device. Furthermore, computationally intensive user identification algorithms executed on the smartphone can negatively affect user experience. A more generally applicable solution would be to verify user identities from remote servers, without the need to install and run any special software on the device itself. Continuous user identity verification is then performed by a remote entity, e.g., an online banking service. On the one hand, such a solution does not suffer from the above problems and users can use their unmodified everyday devices. On the other hand, users can still benefit from increased security by having their identities continuously verified.

In this paper, we show how to continuously verify a user's identity by remotely analyzing the user's touch behavior using machine learning analysis. Depending on a calculated confidence value indicating whether the active user is indeed the legitimate user, we either provide the full service functionality or disable critical functionality and enforce a reauthentication. In contrast to previous work [12,23,13,10,2,25], our proposed method only requires a web browser running on the user's device which is used by the user to access web pages of remote sites that utilize the techniques described in this paper. Our approach does not require any special privileges on the device and is completely transparent for the user. A major challenge is that in contrast to existing work, we do not have direct access to the API of the touch device's operating system. This means that touch interaction data, proven to be beneficial for user classification [17], has a lower degree of precision and some data cannot be obtained at all. We provide a selection of features that still allow for successful user classification under these conditions and implement a framework to continuously verify user identities. We evaluate the performance of our framework by analyzing touch interaction data sets of 45 users. The results indicate the feasibility of our approach with both False Acceptance Rate (FAR) and False Rejection Rate (FRR) potentially being as low as $< 1\%$ after collecting about 14 touch interactions.

The rest of this paper is organized as follows. Section 2 evaluates suitable touch interactions for user classification in web contexts. Section 3 explains the touch behavior model training of our framework and details the user identity verification strategy. Section 4 describes our framework implementation. Section 5 presents our performance evaluation results. Section 6 discusses related work. Section 7 concludes this paper.

2   Touch Interaction Selection in Web Contexts

In contrast to existing work [12,23,13,10,2,25], we do not have direct access to the API of the touch device's operating system. Instead, we capture touch interaction data from the user's web browser. As a consequence, this data has a lower degree of precision and some data, proven to be beneficial for user classification [17], cannot be obtained at all. Another difficulty arises from the fact that different users are likely to use various kinds of touch devices, all with potentially different properties. Hence, the touch interactions must have enough generality to allow for comparison of user behavior across devices. Furthermore, they must be sufficiently precise and available on all touch devices, operating systems, and web browsers. This requires us to carefully select suitable touch interactions that can be successfully used for user classification under these constraints.

In the following, we evaluate and select several touch interactions for user classification in web contexts and give the rationale for our choice. We distinguish two classes of information: details about gestures executed by the user on the touchscreen, and complementary device sensor data obtained from the device while executing those gestures.

2.1   Touchscreen Gestures

Scroll or *Swipe* (actions: press, move, lift) is one of the most common gestures used in web browser contexts as it constitutes the primary means of touch-based navigation on web pages. Scroll gestures between different users are quite distinctive, yet we discovered that scroll gestures of a single user are relatively similar and consistent (cf. Sect. 5.1). These properties make scroll gestures well suited for user classification in web contexts. However, as mentioned above, we have to deal with less precise data and only know a few, varying number of points along the scroll gesture's path. We will show how to solve this problem in Sect. 3.3.

Tap (actions: press, lift) is primarily used to follow hyperlinks on web pages. In general, behavioral tapping patterns can be used for user classification [12,23,13]. However, in web contexts, discriminative tap features like the point in time where the maximal pressure occurs or the area covered by the finger touching the screen cannot be obtained at all or only with low precision. Furthermore, in our experiments, tap gestures occurred about 90% less than scroll gestures. Therefore, we exclude tap gestures for user classification in this paper.

Zoom (e.g., pinch, double tapping, double touch drag) allows to increase or decrease the web page's content. Even though zooming may be recognized by

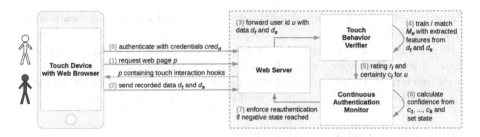

Fig. 1. System architecture

interpreting primitive touch events [21], we do not consider it for user classification as the (internal) coordinate resolution and page offsets of captured data changes, thus resulting in data that is difficult to compare.

Other gestures like *Drag* or *Rotate* normally do not occur in web contexts and will therefore not be considered in this paper.

2.2 Device Sensor Data

Acceleration data represents the acceleration force along the device's x, y, and z axes. We use it to evaluate the device's feedback to scroll gestures, thus increasing the classification accuracy. Capturing the acceleration data as done in this paper does not require any special privileges (as opposed to, for example, capturing GPS location data) and is completely transparent for the user.

Force indicates how much pressure the user applied to the touchscreen. According to [17], the finger pressure gives discriminative information for user classification. However, with current web browsers this data cannot be retrieved (see Sect. 4 for the list of tested browsers). We compensate for lack of this information by analyzing the device's acceleration feedback to touch interactions.

Gyroscope data gives the rate of rotation around the x-axis (compass direction), y-axis (front-to-back tilt), and z-axis (left-to-right tilt). We do not incorporate this information for classification as it caused overfitting in our experiments, for example, front-to-back tilt differed depending on whether the user was standing or sitting, thus hindering generalization.

3 System Overview

The system architecture is shown in Fig. 1. The smartphone on the left is used to access web pages hosted by the web server on the right. Our framework consists of the web server, the Touch Behavior Verifier (TBV), and the Continuous Authentication Monitor (CAM). The web server is responsible for authenticating users (e.g., password authentication) in order to provide access to user accounts. TBV trains and maintains touch behavior models in order to classify users based on their touch interactions. CAM continuously assesses whether the current user is the legitimate user and enforces a reauthentication on suspicious behavior.

In general, there exist two phases: *training* and *verification*. In the training phase, a touch behavior model of a specific user will be created based on the user's touch interactions and supplemental device sensor data. In the verification phase, this touch behavior model is used to verify the identity of the user.

3.1   Touch Behavior Model Training

A user u authenticates himself to the web server with credentials $cred_u$ (step 0), for example, by entering a combination of username and password on a page hosted by the web server. For each requested web page p (step 1), the web server provides a modified version of p containing *touch interaction hooks*. The hooks cause the user's web browser to record touch interaction data d_t along with supplemental device sensor data d_s. Both d_t and d_s will be periodically sent to the web server (step 2) which, in turn, forwards the data to the TBV (step 3). In step 4, the TBV parses the recorded (raw) touch interaction data d_t and identifies high-level gestures. The recognized gestures will be augmented with device sensor data d_s that occurred during the time the respective gesture was executed. The combined result is called an *observation*. The TBV extracts relevant features from an observation and uses them to train a touch behavior model $\mathcal{M}_u$. A detailed description of the features used by our framework is given in Sect. 3.3. Note that the just-described training phase inherently assumes that the recorded data indeed belongs to the legitimate user u and that no illegitimate user compromised the account during this time. The trained model $\mathcal{M}_u$ is eventually used in the verification phase (which additionally includes steps 5-7) to identify users.

Our utilized hooking technique (cf. Sect. 4) works out of the box with all common mobile operating systems and browsers and does not require any special permissions from the user (neither for recording touch interactions nor for recording sensor data) and there is no indication provided to the user that interactions are being recorded. This way it is completely transparent for the user.

3.2   User Identity Verification

After the model $\mathcal{M}_u$ has been trained, subsequently recorded interaction data of the active user u' (steps 0-3) will be used by the TBV to verify that u' is indeed the legitimate user u (as claimed by the credentials $cred_u$ of the currently active user u'). We use the touch behavior model $\mathcal{M}_u$ and utilize machine learning analysis to identify the user (step 4). In step 5, the TBV calculates for an observation o_i a *binary rating* r_i (*true* or *false*) indicating whether the framework considers the active user to be the legitimate user (*true*) or an illegitimate user (*false*). The TBV also calculates an associated *certainty score* c_i that represents the probability that the rating r_i is correct. Since the accuracy to identify a user based on a single observation is not very high (as shown in Sect. 5.2 as well as in [2]), we consider sequences of (consecutive) observations in order to improve the overall accuracy. This is achieved by aggregating the certainty scores of all observations of a sequence (as explained in Sect. 3.4) in order to calculate an aggregated certainty score called *confidence*. The CAM calculates and uses this confidence value to decide if the active user is still the legitimate user (step 6). The details will be explained in Sect. 3.4.

CAM distinguishes three states depending on the ratings and the confidence: *uncertain*, *positive*, and *negative*. The uncertain state is the initial state and is also entered if the ratings of consecutive observations are too inconsistent or the confidence is lower than a specified threshold θ. In this case, critical functionality may be temporarily disabled until the positive state is entered (again). The positive state is entered if the ratings are consistently true *and* the confidence exceeds θ. This state indicates that the framework deems the active user legitimate and the full functionality is provided. The negative state is entered if the ratings are consistently false *and* the confidence exceeds θ. In this case, the framework considers the active user to be an illegitimate user and enforces a reauthentication (step 7)—possibly combined with other actions, e.g., notifying the system administrator. Note that CAM's described behavior is optimized for security-critical applications where protecting against attackers is prioritized over the risk of (temporarily) restricting legitimate users.

Finally, the observations used for identity verification will also be used as training data to continuously improve the model $\mathcal{M}_u$. However, since illegitimate users may only be recognized after inspecting multiple observations, the inclusion is deferred until the TBV is sufficiently sure that the observations actually belong to the legitimate user.

3.3   Feature Extraction

For user identity verification, we extract various features from scroll gestures and the device's acceleration sensor data. A scroll gesture is composed of multiple touch events. A *touch event* t is a triplet $t = \langle t^\tau, t^x, t^y \rangle$ representing a touched point $\langle t^x, t^y \rangle$ at time t^τ on the two-dimensional Euclidean plane represented by a device's touch screen. Each touch event t is one of three *basic touch events*: t_s (*touch start*, i.e., finger pressed down), t_m (*touch move*, i.e., finger is moving while pressed down), or t_e (*touch end*, i.e., finger lifted), that is, $t \in \{t_s, t_m, t_e\}$. A *scroll gesture* S_k refers to a sequence of basic touch events starting with a *touch start* event, followed by one or more *touch move* events, and terminated with a *touch end* event. Consequently, a scroll gesture S_k is represented by an ordered list of touch events $S_k := \langle t_s, t_{m_1}, \ldots, t_{m_n}, t_e \rangle$ with $n \geq 1$.

The following features will be used for user identity verification by our framework.

Path Offsets. In web contexts, only a few unevenly distributed points along the path described by a scroll gesture are known (cf. Sect. 2). However, it is necessary to have the same number of points for all scroll gestures in order to make their feature sets comparable. We solve this by dividing the overall duration of a scroll gesture into a globally fixed number I of equal-sized time intervals (where the interval size is fixed w.r.t. a single scroll gesture). At each time interval boundary, we approximate the touch coordinates along the path. These touch coordinates are called *intermediate points* $t_1, \ldots, t_I$. The respective x-components of the intermediate points are enumerated with $t_1^x, \ldots, t_I^x$ (analogously, the following descriptions apply to the y-components). The x-component t_i^x of an intermediate point t_i is interpolated based on the x-components of the two (chronologically) adjacent touch events $t_i^{\leftarrow}, t_i^{\rightarrow} \in S_k$ of t_i. In order to facilitate the following calculations, we further define $t_0^x := t_s^x$ and $t_{I+1}^x := t_e^x$. Finally, *intermediate offsets* are defined by calculating the distance of each intermediate point to the touch start event $t_s \in S_k$, that is, $t_i^{\triangle x} := t_i^x - t_s^x$ where $0 \leq i \leq I+1$.

Bounding Box. A bounding box is constructed around a scroll gesture shape in order to obtain a coarse representation of the gesture. The bounding box's width and height reflect individual user behavior and scroll preferences on an abstract level (cf. Fig. 3). The width of a scroll gesture S_k is defined as $S_k^w := \max_{t \in S_k} \pi_2(t) - \min_{t \in S_k} \pi_2(t)$, where π_2 is the second projection t^x of a triplet $t = \langle t^\tau, t^x, t^y \rangle$. Similarly, the height of a scroll gesture S_k is defined as $S_k^h := \max_{t \in S_k} \pi_3(t) - \min_{t \in S_k} \pi_3(t)$.

Raster. A coarse grid is fit over a scroll gesture's bounding box to obtain an abstract scroll gesture representation. The intention is to allow for better recognition of gestures at different sizes as well as across different devices with varying screen sizes. If the path of a scroll gesture S_k crosses the cell $\langle i, j \rangle \in \{1, \ldots, R\}^2$ of an $R \times R$ raster, then $S_k^{r_i \times j} = 1$. Otherwise, $S_k^{r_i \times j} = 0$.

Velocity. The velocity of the finger's motion is analyzed at different times when executing a scroll gesture. The velocity varies for different users and different sections of a scroll gesture (cf. Fig. 4). We utilize intermediate offsets as defined above in order to calculate the velocity over the horizontal distance intervals $[t_{i-1}^x, t_i^x]$, where $1 \leq i \leq I+1$, and analogously over the vertical distance intervals. We define $t_i^{v_x} := \left(t_i^{\triangle x} - t_{i-1}^{\triangle x} \right) \cdot \frac{I+1}{t_e^\tau - t_s^\tau}$, where $1 \leq i \leq I+1$, and analogously $t_i^{v_y}$.

Curvature. The curvature of a scroll gesture is inspected at each intermediate offset in order to recognize the same gesture shape executed at different sizes. This approach is similar to the techniques used by gesture-recognition applications like easystroke [11]. We define $t_i^{\angle} := \arctan \left(\frac{t_i^{\triangle y}}{t_i^{\triangle x}} \right)$ where $1 \leq i \leq I+1$.

Acceleration. A scroll gesture's intrinsic features are augmented with the device's acceleration sensor data obtained at each intermediate point.[1] This allows

---

[1] To be precise, the device's acceleration will be recorded at the points in time when the touch events $t_1, \ldots, t_n$ of a scroll gesture S_k occurred and will then be used for the interpolated intermediate points calculated from these touch events.

us to evaluate the device's feedback to touch interactions and is similar to the approach used in [2]. For an intermediate point t_i, we combine the x, y, and z accelerations $t_i^{a_x}$, $t_i^{a_y}$, and $t_i^{a_z}$, respectively, and define $t_i^a := \sqrt{(t_i^{a_x})^2 + (t_i^{a_y})^2 + (t_i^{a_z})^2}$ where $0 \leq i \leq I + 1$.

Finally, for a scroll gesture S_k with intermediate points $t_0, \ldots, t_{I+1}$ the feature vector F_{S_k} is defined as $F_{S_k} := \langle T^{\triangle x}, T^{\triangle y}, S_k^w, S_k^h, S_k^r, T^{v_x}, T^{v_y}, T^{\triangleleft}, T^a \rangle$ where (for reasons of readability) T^X is an abbreviation for $t_0^X, \ldots, t_{I+1}^X$ and S_k^r for the raster $S_k^{r_1 \times 1}, \ldots, S_k^{r_R \times R}$.

3.4 Verification Strategy

We use the touch behavior model $\mathcal{M}_u$ and utilize a random forest [4] with one-vs-rest classification to verify the identity of a user u. Random forests have proven to be fast and effective classifiers [19] with good results in the context of touchscreen interaction classification [8,1] similar to our scenario. As explained above, the overall user identification accuracy is improved by considering subsequences $\langle o_i, \ldots, o_j \rangle$ of the sequence of all observations $\mathcal{O} := \{o_1, \ldots, o_n\}$, with $1 \leq i \leq j \leq n$, instead of only considering single observations. Such a subsequence is denoted w.l.o.g. with $\mathcal{O}_{1,k} := \langle o_1, \ldots, o_k \rangle$.

Subsequence Processing. For a subsequence $\mathcal{O}_{1,k}$, we calculate the corresponding binary ratings $R_{1,k} := \langle r_1, \ldots, r_k \rangle$ with each $r_i \in \{true, false\}$ indicating whether the features of the corresponding observation o_i match ($true$) or do not match ($false$) the model $\mathcal{M}_u$. All ratings of $\mathcal{O}_{1,k}$ are required to be consistent, i.e., $r_1 = \ldots = r_k = true$ or $r_1 = \ldots = r_k = false$, and we always consider the longest possible subsequences with consistent ratings. For binary ratings $R_{1,k}$, we derive associated certainty scores (probability values) $C_{1,k} := \langle c_1, \ldots, c_k \rangle$ based on the class probabilities calculated from the random forest. Finally, for certainty scores $C_{1,k}$, the confidence value $\mathfrak{C}_{1,k}$ is calculated as an aggregated certainty score.

Confidence Value Calculation. We identified three requirements for a reliable and accurate confidence value. First, a subsequence $\mathcal{O}_{1,k}$ should have a minimum length $\mathcal{L}$ in order to compensate for the impact of unusually high certainty scores of single observations. Otherwise, the framework might, for example, enforce a reauthentication solely based on one outlier. Second, the confidence should increase proportionally to the sequence length because, intuitively, the more consistent ratings exist the more likely it is that the rating value is correct. Third, the chronological order of observations is significant: more recent observations should be considered more important than older ones. This is achieved by assigning different weights $w_1 \leq \ldots \leq w_k$ to the certainty scores $C_{1,k}$.

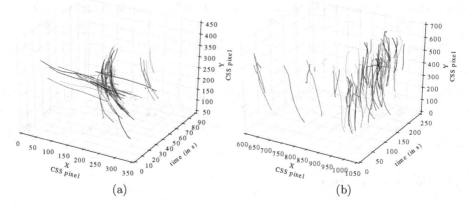

Fig. 2. Plotted scroll gestures of two users. In (a), the user utilizes both vertical and horizontal scroll gestures, where vertical gestures have pronounced curvatures. In (b), the vertical scroll gestures are rather straight and quite distinct from (a).

The following formula satisfies the above requirements and is used by CAM to calculate the confidence for a subsequence $\mathcal{O}_{1,k}$ with certainty scores $c_1, \ldots, c_k$:

$$\mathfrak{C}_{1,k} := \mathfrak{C}(c_1, \ldots, c_k) := f(k) \cdot \frac{1}{\sum_{i=1}^{k} w_i} \cdot \sum_{i=1}^{k} w_i c_i, \quad f(k) := \begin{cases} 0 & : k < \mathcal{L} \\ g(k) & : k \geq \mathcal{L} \end{cases}$$

The function g with $0 \leq g(k) \leq 1$ should be monotonically increasing in order to satisfy the second requirement. The actual definition of g as well as the values of the minimum length $\mathcal{L}$ and the weights $w_1, \ldots, w_k$ may be flexibly adjusted depending on the use case scenario and policy rules.

4   Framework Implementation

We have implemented our framework (as shown in Fig. 1) as a proof of concept. We run an Apache web server and utilize a Python script responsible for authentication and for injecting JavaScript code for the touch interaction hooks into all web pages hosted by the web server. The hooks will be executed on the client side within the user's web browser. To realize the hooking functionality, we take advantage of the JavaScript Touch Event API [18,20] in order to capture the required touch events. We add event listeners for the following events: *touchstart* (t_s), *touchmove* (t_m), and *touchend* (t_e) as well as the *devicemotion* acceleration data (t^a). Capturing the touch events and device sensor data does not require any special privileges and is completely transparent for the user—as tested on Android 4.4.4 with Android Browser 4.4.4, Chrome 39.0.2171.59, and Firefox 33.1 as well as on iOS 7.1 with Safari 7.0 and Chrome 39.0.2171.45. The browser periodically transmits the captured data in the background to the web server using AJAX. Both TBV and CAM are implemented in Python and run within the web server.

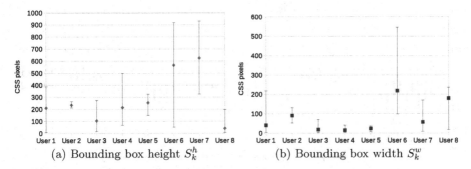

Fig. 3. Minimum, mean, and maximum values calculated (on a per-user basis) over all bounding boxes of the scroll gestures of eight random users

The TBV utilizes the *scikit-learn* open source machine learning library [16] to invoke Breiman's random forest algorithm [4] with one-vs-rest classification. The CAM continuously calculates the confidence value as explained in Sect. 3.4. If the ratings are consistently false and the confidence exceeds a certain threshold, CAM triggers a user reauthentication by the web server.

5   Performance Evaluation

We use the implementation described in Sect. 4 and adapt it within an experimental setup in order to evaluate the suitability of the extracted features (cf. Sect. 3.3) and to evaluate the overall user classification accuracy of our framework. The test web server hosts several hyperlinked web pages. We recorded and evaluated touch interaction data sets of 45 users. The users were intentionally not informed about the experiment's objective of identifying users based on their touch interaction patterns in order for them to be unbiased. To evaluate our framework under real-world conditions, the users used their normal everyday devices. This entails that the data sets were obtained from a heterogeneous group of devices, operating systems, and web browsers.

5.1   Feature Suitability

We demonstrate the suitability of scroll gestures for user classification as used by our framework and show the rationale for selecting certain classification features. Figure 2 depicts the scrolling behavior of two users. The visualization is based on the calculated intermediate points of each scroll gesture (cf. Sect. 3.3). Note that scroll gestures between these two users are quite distinctive (e.g., the curvature $t_i^{\angle}$), yet the scroll gestures of a single user are relatively consistent. This property makes scroll gestures well suited for user classification.

Figure 3 exemplarily shows that the bounding boxes vary between different users. In particular, different mean values are characteristic for different users. Note that in Fig. 3 very low minimum values for both S_k^h and S_k^w (e.g., user 3) may also be caused by accidental screen touches interpreted as scroll gestures.

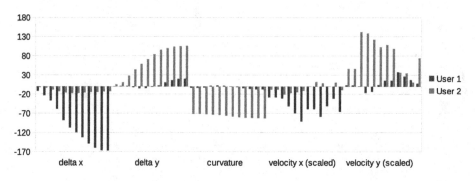

Fig. 4. Feature value comparison of scroll gestures by different users

Figure 4 shows various features of a horizontal scroll gesture from right to left (user 1) and of a vertical scroll gesture from the bottom up (user 2), respectively. We use $I := 12$ for the evaluation which results in twelve intermediate points for a scroll gesture (plus start and end points both of which are omitted in the diagram). The *delta x* bars represent the intermediate offsets $t_1^{\triangle x}, \ldots, t_{12}^{\triangle x}$ of the respective scroll gesture in CSS pixels (analogously for *delta y*). The *curvature* bars show the angles $t_1^{\angle}, \ldots, t_{12}^{\angle}$ in degrees for each section of the scroll gesture. The *velocity x* bars show the (scaled) velocities $t_1^{v_x}, \ldots, t_{12}^{v_x}$ for each section of the scroll gesture (analogously for *velocity y*). These features reflect subtle but distinct individual user behavior, for example, by indicating where the curvature's peak values are located or by representing the velocity fluctuations within scroll gestures.

5.2 Classification Accuracy

We evaluate the user classification accuracy of the framework. The scores are obtained by cross-validation with a 70% (training set) to 30% (validation set) partitioning of the gathered data. We inspect the False Acceptance Rate (FAR) and False Rejection Rate (FRR) based on different numbers of observations.

Single Gesture. We analyze the classification accuracy based on only a single scroll gesture. In this case, the FAR and FRR are 23% and 22%, respectively. Figure 5 shows how the FAR and FRR develop for different users over an increasing amount of training data. Each pair of blue and red bars represents a single user with the specified number of samples. The reason the FAR and FRR fluctuate is because some users may be classified more easily than others (e.g., some user's features may be rather unique among the set of users and thus classification works well even with fewer samples). Nonetheless, for 70 or more samples the FAR and FRR development, on average, stabilizes and starts to improve noticeably. These results indicate that it is advisable to trigger actions (e.g., a forced reauthentication) not before this minimum number of samples has been acquired. The above results indicate, however, that user classification on

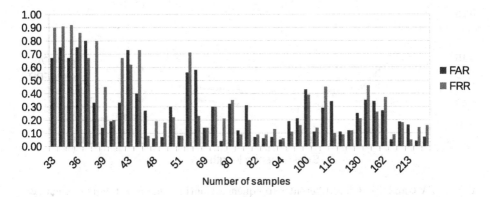

Fig. 5. FAR and FRR based on only a single scroll gesture for (different) users with increasing number of samples (non-linear x-axis). Each pair of blue and red bars represents a different user, thus FAR and FRR fluctuate.

the basis of only one gesture is not accurate enough to reliably identify users. This has even been shown to be the case when more precise interaction data can be gathered directly on the device [22,2]. Therefore, we consider sequences of consecutive scroll gestures (as explained in Sect. 3.4). This enables us to significantly improve the classification accuracy.

Multiple Gestures. We evaluate how the classification accuracy changes within our experimental setup if we increase the number of considered scroll gestures. The graph in Fig. 6 shows the FAR and FRR for different subsequence lengths. For subsequences containing just four scroll gestures, we are already able to achieve FAR and FRR of less than 10%. Further significant improvement requires more than ten scroll gestures, resulting in FAR and FRR of less than 5%. When increasing the subsequence length to 14 scroll gestures, both FAR and FRR can further be reduced to < 1% within the experimental setup. These results can be utilized to adjust the parameters (e.g., the minimum subsequence length) used for calculating the confidence values.

6   Related Work

The field of biometric authentication is usually divided into two categories: physiological and behavioral biometrics. Physiological biometrics consider static physical attributes like human fingerprints, facial features, or DNA. Behavioral biometrics distinguish user behavior such as speaking, walking, or typing. We focus on behavioral biometrics.

Early work considers how users interact with computer peripherals like mice and keyboards. In [14], Monrose et al. combine keyboard typing patterns with the user's password to generate a hardened password. Zheng et al. [24] and Feher et

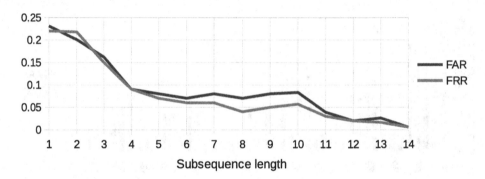

Fig. 6. FAR and FRR for different subsequence lengths. Significant improvement is achieved after only considering four scroll gestures with FAR and FRR < 10%. After ten scroll gestures, both FAR and FRR are < 5%, and after 14 scroll gestures < 1%.

al. [7] verify user identities according to characteristics of their interaction with a computer mouse.

The focus of recent research has shifted towards analyzing the interaction behavior with modern touch devices like smartphones and tablets. In [23], Zheng et al. build a user verification system based on tapping behaviors to increase the security when entering a PIN. Kolly et al. [12] programmed and published a quiz game to collect and analyze tap interaction data. De Luca et al. [6] and Angulo et al. [1] analyze how patterns are drawn on a device's touchscreen in order to enhance smartphone lock patterns. We do not include tap dynamics for classification as in web contexts discriminative tap features (e.g., finger pressure) cannot be obtained at all or only with low precision.

In addition to touchscreens, modern smartphones are equipped with a wide variety of sensors including accelerometers and gyroscopes. Owusu et al. [15] extract sequences of entered text on touchscreen keyboards, allowing them to break passwords. In [13], Miluzzo et al. identify tap locations on the screen to infer passwords based on accelerometer and gyroscope data. While those scenarios are different from ours, the same hooking technique used in our paper could be utilized by an attacker to capture accelerometer data over the web. In fact, in work developed parallel to ours, Bojinov et al. [3] exploit this technique in order to de-anonymize mobile devices as they connect to web sites.

The following work combines touch behavior with device sensor data to identify users and is closest to our research. Zhu et al. [25] construct a behavior model based on user gestures and device sensor data from accelerometers, gyroscopes, and magnetometers. Their prototype allows to identify smartphone owners and non-owners. In [10], Frank et al. examine basic navigation maneuvers such as scroll gestures and analyze the effectiveness of various features. Bo et al. [2] analyze user classification based on tap and scroll gestures along with the device's feedback (accelerometer and gyroscope) to these actions. Both [10] and [2] improve the classification accuracy by inspecting multiple, consecutive observations. This approach is similar to ours, however, we calculate a confidence value based on additional parameters like the minimum required length of observations and different weights for the certainty scores of individual gestures.

In this paper, and in contrast to previous work, we present a framework that does not require any special software or privileges on the user's smartphone. We rather take advantage of standard mobile web browser capabilities to remotely capture and analyze touchscreen interactions in order to continuously verify user identities.

7 Conclusion

We have presented a framework that allows to continuously verify user identities from remote servers by analyzing user interaction behavior with smartphone touchscreens. This enables us to protect user accounts by disabling critical functionality and enforcing a reauthentication in case of suspicious behavior. Our solution is widely applicable on everyday smartphones and does not require any special software or privileges on the device, and is completely transparent for the user. We have shown how to successfully classify users even on the basis of limited and imprecise touch interaction data. This is achieved by constructing a touch behavior model of the user and only selecting features that possess sufficient precision and are available on all touch devices, operating systems, and web browsers. For user classification based on only a single scroll gesture, we are able to achieve FAR and FRR of 23% and 22%, respectively. We show how to significantly improve the classification accuracy by considering sequences of observations instead of only single touch interactions. This technique is used in the calculation of a confidence value that allows for a more stable and reliable assessment of whether the current smartphone user is indeed the legitimate user. The final performance evaluation of our framework implementation shows that both FAR and FRR can be as low as < 1% after collecting a sequence of about 14 scroll gestures.

References

1. Angulo, J., Wästlund, E.: Exploring touch-screen biometrics for user identification on smart phones. In: Camenisch, J., Crispo, B., Fischer-Hübner, S., Leenes, R., Russello, G. (eds.) Privacy and Identity Management for Life. IFIP AICT, vol. 375, pp. 130–143. Springer, Heidelberg (2012)
2. Bo, C., Zhang, L., Li, X.-Y., Huang, Q., Wang, Y.: Silentsense: Silent user identification via touch and movement behavioral biometrics. In: International Conference on Mobile Computing & Networking, vol. 19, pp. 187–190 (2013)
3. Bojinov, H., Michalevsky, Y., Nakibly, G., Boneh, D.: Mobile device identification via sensor fingerprinting. arXiv preprint arXiv:1408.1416 (2014)
4. Breiman, L.: Random forests. Machine Learning 45(1), 5–32 (2001)
5. Damopoulos, D., Kambourakis, G., Gritzalis, S.: From keyloggers to touchloggers: Take the rough with the smooth. Computers & Security 32, 102–114 (2013)
6. Luca, A.D., Hang, A., Brudy, F., Lindner, C., Hussmann, H.: Touch me once and i know it's you!: implicit authentication based on touch screen patterns. In: SIGCHI Conference on Human Factors in Computing Systems, pp. 987–996 (2012)

7. Feher, C., Elovici, Y., Moskovitch, R., Rokach, L., Schclar, A.: User identity verification via mouse dynamics. Information Sciences 201, 19–36 (2012)
8. Feng, T., Liu, Z., Kwon, K.-A., Shi, W., Carbunar, B., Jiang, Y., Nguyen, N.: Continuous mobile authentication using touchscreen gestures. In: 2012 IEEE Conference on Technologies for Homeland Security (HST), pp. 451–456. IEEE (2012)
9. Feng, T., Prakash, V., Shi, W.: Touch panel with integrated fingerprint sensors based user identity management. In: 2013 IEEE International Conference on Technologies for Homeland Security (HST), pp. 154–160. IEEE (2013)
10. Frank, M., Biedert, R., Ma, E., Martinovic, I., Song, D.: Touchalytics: On the applicability of touchscreen input as a behavioral biometric for continuous authentication. IEEE Information Forensics and Security 8, 136–148 (2013)
11. Jaeger, T.: Easystroke (2013), https://sourceforge.net/projects/easystroke/
12. Kolly, S.M., Wattenhofer, R., Welten, S.: A personal touch: Recognizing users based on touch screen behavior. In: Proceedings of the Third International Workshop on Sensing Applications on Mobile Phones, p. 1. ACM (2012)
13. Miluzzo, E., Varshavsky, A., Balakrishnan, S., Choudhury, R.R.: Tapprints: your finger taps have fingerprints. In: Proceedings of the 10th International Conference on Mobile Systems, Applications, and Services, pp. 323–336. ACM (2012)
14. Monrose, F., Reiter, M.K., Wetzel, S.: Password hardening based on keystroke dynamics. International Journal of Information Security 1(2), 69–83 (2002)
15. Owusu, E., Han, J., Das, S., Perrig, A., Zhang, J.: Accessory: password inference using accelerometers on smartphones. In: Proceedings of the Twelfth Workshop on Mobile Computing Systems & Applications, p. 9. ACM (2012)
16. Pedregosa, F., et al.: Scikit-learn: Machine learning in python. Journal of Machine Learning Research 12, 2825–2830 (2011)
17. Saevanee, H., Bhatarakosol, P.: User authentication using combination of behavioral biometrics over the touchpad acting like touch screen of mobile device. In: Computer and Electrical Engineering, pp. 82–86. IEEE (2008)
18. Schepers, D., Brubeck, M., Barstow, A., Moon, S.: Touch events. W3c recommendation, W3C (2013), http://www.w3.org/TR/touch-events/
19. Shotton, J., Sharp, T., Kipman, A., Fitzgibbon, A., Finocchio, M., Blake, A., Cook, M., Moore, R.: Real-time human pose recognition in parts from single depth images. Communications of the ACM 56(1), 116–124 (2013)
20. Steve Block, A.P.: Device orientation event specification. W3c working draft, W3C (2011), http://www.w3.org/TR/orientation-event/
21. Tangelder, J.: hammer.js (2014), https://hammerjs.github.io/
22. Xu, H., Zhou, Y., Lyu, M.R.: Towards continuous and passive authentication via touch biometrics: An experimental study on smartphones. In: Symposium On Usable Privacy and Security (SOUPS 2014). USENIX Association (2014)
23. Zheng, N., Bai, K., Huang, H., Wang, H.: You are how you touch: User verification on smartphones via tapping behaviors. Technical report, WM-CS-2012-06 (2012)
24. Zheng, N., Paloski, A., Wang, H.: An efficient user verification system via mouse movements. In: Proceedings of the 18th ACM conference on Computer and communications security, pp. 139–150 (2011)
25. Zhu, J., Wu, P., Wang, X., Zhang, J.: Sensec: Mobile security through passive sensing. In: 2013 International Conference on Computing, Networking and Communications (ICNC), pp. 1128–1133. IEEE (2013)

Adaptive-ID Secure Revocable Identity-Based Encryption from Lattices via Subset Difference Method

Shantian Cheng* and Juanyang Zhang**

Division of Mathematical Sciences,
School of Physical and Mathematical Sciences,
Nanyang Technological University
SPMS-MAS-04-20, 21 Nanyang Link, 637371, Singapore
{scheng002,zh0078ng}@e.ntu.edu.sg

Abstract. In view of the expiration or reveal of user's private credential (or private key) in a realistic scenario, identity-based encryption (IBE) schemes with an efficient key revocation mechanism, or for short, revocable identity-based encryption (RIBE) schemes, become prominently significant. In this paper, we present an RIBE scheme from lattices by combining two Agrawal et al.'s IBE schemes with the subset difference (SD) method. Our scheme is secure against adaptive identity-time attacks in the standard model under the learning with errors (LWE) assumption. In particular, our scheme serves as one solution to the challenge posed by Chen et al. (ACISP '12).

Keywords: Revocable identity-based encryption, Lattices, Subset difference method, Adaptive security, Standard model.

1 Introduction

Since Shamir [25] proposed the concept of identity-based encryption (IBE), in which the sender may use the recipient's identity as a public key to encrypt a message, it was a longstanding open problem to construct a practical IBE scheme. Later, Boneh and Franklin [9] proposed the first practical IBE scheme using pairings. After then, IBE becomes extensively attractive from both theoretical and practical perspectives. As a result, there have been many IBE schemes proposed based on various tools and assumptions such as quadratic residue modulo a hard-to-factor integer [13,10], and lattices [15,1,3] as well as pairings [8,26,27].

In the practical use of IBE, a user's private key may be expired or revealed for various reasons. In such situations, an efficient key revocation mechanism is needed to keep the whole system stable and secure. To handle this issue, there have been various solutions presented based on pairings. The first revocable

---

* Supported by NTU Research Scholarship at Nanyang Technological University.
** Supported by the Singapore Ministry of Education under Research Grant MOE2013-T2-1-041.

J. Lopez and Y. Wu (Eds.): ISPEC 2015, LNCS 9065, pp. 283–297, 2015.
DOI: 10.1007/978-3-319-17533-1_20

IBE (RIBE) scheme was proposed by Boneh and Franklin [9], but their suggestion is inefficient in terms of the workload of the key authority. Later, Boldyreva et al. [7] presented the first selective-ID secure scalable RIBE scheme by combining a fuzzy IBE scheme [22] and the complete subtree (CS) method [20]. The first adaptive-ID secure scalable RIBE scheme was proposed by Libert and Vergnaud [17].

Subsequently, Seo and Emura [24] presented an enhanced security model of RIBE by considering one special realistic threat, which is called decryption key exposure attack, and provided a concrete construction based on pairings. Recently, Lee et al. [16] succeeded in constructing an adaptively secure RIBE scheme based on pairings using the subset difference (SD) method.

However, as a counterpart of pairings, lattices have not been extensively used to construct RIBE schemes. Lattice-based cryptography is widely believed to be resistant against quantum computers. In addition, lattice-based cryptography owns provable security under worst-case hardness assumptions [5,21,15]. Therefore, lattices have become a promising and powerful tool to construct a mass of cryptographic primitives. However, to the best of our knowledge, in terms of RIBE schemes, Chen et al. [11] solely offered a selective-ID secure RIBE scheme from lattices. Besides, they left the problem of constructing adaptive-ID secure RIBE schemes from lattices as a challenge.

1.1   Our Results

We present the first adaptive-ID secure RIBE scheme from lattices via the SD method in the standard model. To this end, we employ two adaptive-ID secure IBE schemes for an identity and a time, respectively, proposed by Agrawal et al. [1]. Then, we combine them with the SD method for the revocation and use a secret sharing scheme utilized in fuzzy IBE proposed by Agrawal et al. [4] to share one common random vector in the SD method.

Our construction achieves adaptive-ID security in the standard model under the LWE assumption. Our security proof follows the Libert and Vergnaud's security model [17] with a slight modification that uses a game that captures a strong privacy property, called *indistinguishable from random*, as in [1]. As a result, we provide one solution to the challenge posed by Chen et al. [11].

1.2   Our Techniques

Our new construction of RIBE from lattices consists of the following building blocks:

(i) adaptive-ID secure IBE proposed by Agrawal et al. [1];
(ii) the SD method proposed by [20];
(iii) Shamir's secret sharing scheme utilized in fuzzy IBE proposed by Agrawal et al. [4].

Agrawal et al.'s adaptive-ID secure IBE scheme is a lattice analog of Waters' fully secure IBE scheme [27]. Note that as the time space in RIBE is polynomial size in public parameters, we may just use Agrawal et al.'s selective-ID secure IBE scheme for time part. However, for simplicity and less clutter, we apply two instances of Agrawal et al.'s adaptive-ID secure IBE scheme regarding to users' identities and times, respectively. Our scheme does not just roughly combine the two adaptive-ID secure IBE instances to achieve the adaptive-ID security of RIBE. In contrast to single adaptive-ID secure IBE scheme, the adversary in our RIBE scheme may have already queried the private key for the challenge identity ID* and the update key for the challenge time T* before the challenge phase. So we can not easily adopt the non-abort probability as in [1]. Instead, to achieve the adaptive-ID security, we further investigate the abort-resistant hash functions used in [26,1] and provide more general analysis of the abort-resistant properties of Waters' hash families [26] with respect to our requirements. Then we carefully design the abort events in the series of security challenging games and prove that they are indistinguishable under the properties of the abort-resistant hash functions and the learning with errors (LWE) assumption. Note that the LWE problem is as hard as the worst-case approximation of the short vectors on arbitrary lattices [21].

For revocation, we adopt the SD scheme, an alternative subset cover framework to the well-known CS scheme. Both instantiations are binary tree based and introduced by Naor et al. [20]. However, the main advantage of the SD method is that for r revoked leaf nodes out of total N leaf nodes in one binary tree, the size of the covering set is at most $2r - 1$ (in the worst case, or $1.25r$ in the average case) and independent of N, whereas the covering set in the CS method has size $r \log \left(\dfrac{N}{r} \right)$, logarithmic complexity in N. The tradeoff is that the size of private sets is slightly increased from $O(\log N)$ to $O(\log^2 N)$. While the private key is a long-term key transferred only once via a secure channel and the update key is a short-term key that will be broadcast periodically via public channels, therefore, using the SD method can efficiently reduce the overheads of the key authority.

We require a random n-vector $\mathbf{u}$ to be part of the public parameters. It acts as the secret for sharing and the subsets in one binary tree formed by the same ancestor and same depth descendants act as sharing parties. Different from the CS framework used in prior works [11,24], the SD method requires a pair of certain subsets, instead of one common node, to determine the non-revocation and generate the decryption key. Thus we can not apply Chen et al.'s methods that directly and randomly split the vector $\mathbf{u}$ inside one node, which indeed is a 2-out-of-2 secret sharing scheme. Based on the SD framework, we have to share $\mathbf{u}$ inside families of subsets formed by the same ancestor and same depth descendants. The size of one such family is a power of 2. Thus it is necessary to consider 2-out-of-n secret sharing scheme. One natural candidate to solve this problem is Shamir's secret sharing scheme. However, to ensure the correctness of dual-Regev type encryption scheme in our scheme, we have to bound the size of vectors in the decryption key. Then we apply the "clear the denominators" of Lagrangian coefficients methods from [4] to revise the encryption and set proper parameters to ensure the correctness.

1.3 Comparison to Chen et al.'s Scheme

Chen et al.'s RIBE scheme [11] is a pioneering work on constructing RIBE schemes from lattices. In Table 1, we elucidate the pros and cons of our scheme in comparison with Chen et al.'s scheme.

Table 1. δ is a small constant such that $n^\delta > O(\log n)$, and ϵ is a small constant such that $\epsilon < 1/2$. r is the number of revoked users out of N users. When r is small compared with N, our scheme has shorter update key. Both schemes are secure under LWE assumption in the standard model. However, our scheme is based on the LWE assumption with sub-exponential parameters, in contrast to polynomial parameters in Chen et al.'s scheme.

	public key size	private key size	update key size	ct size	Security
Chen et al.'s	$\widetilde{O}\left(n^{2+\delta}\right)$	$O(\log N) \cdot \widetilde{O}\left(n^{1+\delta}\right)$	$r \log \dfrac{N}{r} \cdot \widetilde{O}\left(n^{1+\delta}\right)$	$\widetilde{O}\left(n^{1+\delta}\right)$	Selective
Ours	$\widetilde{O}\left(n^{2+\delta+\epsilon}\right)$	$O\left(\log^2 N\right) \cdot \widetilde{O}\left(n^{1+\delta}\right)$	$(2r-1) \cdot \widetilde{O}\left(n^{1+\delta}\right)$	$\widetilde{O}\left(n^{1+\delta+\epsilon}\right)$	Adaptive

2 Preliminaries

Notation. We say a function $d : \mathbb{N} \to \mathbb{R}$ is negligible, if for sufficient large λ, $|d(\lambda)|$ is smaller than reciprocal of any polynomial in λ.

2.1 Definition of RIBE Scheme

Definition 1 ([7,11,24]). *An identity-based encryption with efficient revocation or simply RIBE scheme has seven probabilistic polynomial-time (PPT) algorithms,* **Setup, PriKeyGen, UpdateKey, DecKeyGen, Encrypt, Decrypt,** *and* **Revoke** *with associated message space* $\mathcal{M}$, *ciphertext space* $\mathcal{C}$, *identity space* $\mathcal{I}$, *and time space* $\mathcal{T}$. *The size of* $\mathcal{T}$ *is polynomial in the security parameter. We treat time as discrete as opposed to continuous. Explicitly the RIBE scheme proceeds as follows:*

Setup$(1^\lambda, 1^N)$ *takes as input a security parameter* λ *and a maximal number of users* N. *It outputs public parameters* pp, *a master key* msk, *a revocation list* RL *(initially empty), and a state* st. *(This is stateful and run by the key authority.)*

PriKeyGen(pp, msk, id, st) *takes as input the public parameters* pp, *the master key* msk, *an identity* $id \in \mathcal{I}$, *and the state* st. *It outputs a private key* sk_{id} *and an updated state* st. *(This is stateful and run by the key authority.)*

UpdateKey(pp, msk, t, RL, st) *takes as input the public parameters* pp, *the master key* msk, *a key update time* $t \in \mathcal{T}$, *the revocation list* RL *at time* t, *and the state* st. *It outputs an update key* uk_t. *(This is run by the key authority.)*

DecKeyGen(pp, sk_{id}, uk_t) *takes as input the public parameters* pp, *a private key* sk_{id}, *and an update key* uk_t. *It outputs a decryption key* $dk_{id,t}$, *or* $\perp$ *if id has been revoked before t. (This is deterministic and run by the receiver.)*

Encrypt(pp, id, t, b) *takes as input the public parameters* pp, *an identity* $id \in \mathcal{I}$, *a time* $t \in \mathcal{T}$, *and a message* $b \in \mathcal{M}$. *It outputs a ciphertext* $ct_{id,t}$. *(This is run by the sender.)*

Decrypt($pp, dk_{id,t}, ct_{id,t}$) *takes as input the public parameters* pp, *a decryption key* $dk_{id,t}$, *and a ciphertext* $ct_{id,t}$. *It outputs a message* $b \in \mathcal{M}$ *or* $\bot$. *(This is deterministic and run by the receiver.)*

Revoke(id, t, RL, st) *takes as input an identity* $id \in \mathcal{I}$ *to be revoked, a revocation time* $t \in \mathcal{T}$, *the current revocation list* RL *and a state* st. *It outputs an updated revocation list* RL. *(This is stateful and run by the key authority.)*

The correctness condition requires that for any $\lambda \in \mathbb{N}$ and N, any $(pp, msk) \leftarrow$ **Setup**($1^{\lambda}, 1^N$), any $b \in \mathcal{M}$, all possible state st, and a revocation list RL, if $id \in \mathcal{I}$ is not revoked on a time $t \in \mathcal{T}$, and for $(sk_{id}, st) \leftarrow$ **PriKeyGen**(pp, msk, id, st), $uk_t \leftarrow$ **UpdatKey**(pp, msk, t, RL, st), $dk_{id,t} \leftarrow$ **DecKeyGen**(pp, sk_{id}, uk_t), then **Decrypt** ($pp, dk_{id,t}, $**Encrypt** ($pp, id, t, b$)) $= b$ always holds except for a negligible probability.

The security model of RIBE was introduced by Boldyreva et al. [7], where a selectively secure RIBE was given. Later Libert and Vergnaud [17] proposed a RIBE scheme satisfying adaptive security model. Recently, Seo and Emura [24] advanced the security model by considering the decryption key exposure attack.

In this paper, we follow Libert and Vergnaud's security model. The slight difference is that we formalize the RIBE adaptive security using a game that captures a strong privacy property called *indistinguishable from random*. Agrawal et al. [1] defined this kind of game for IBE. They also referred that indistinguishability from random implies both semantic security and recipient anonymity, and also ciphertext hides the public parameters (pp) used to create it. For RIBE, the game is designed as follows.

Setup: The challenger $\mathcal{B}$ runs **Setup**($1^{\lambda}, 1^N$) to generate public parameters pp, a master key msk, a revocation list RL (initially empty), and a state st. Then $\mathcal{B}$ gives pp to the adversary $\mathcal{A}$.

Query: $\mathcal{A}$ is allowed to adaptively make a polynomial number of queries of the following oracles (the oracles share the state) with some restrictions.

1. **PriKeyGen**($\cdot$): On input an identity id, return a private key sk_{id} by running **PriKeyGen**(pp, msk, id, st) $\rightarrow sk_{id}$.
2. **UpdateKey**($\cdot$): On input a time t, return an update key uk_t by running **UpdateKey**(pp, msk, t, RL, st) $\rightarrow uk_t$.
3. **Revoke**($\cdot, \cdot$): On input an identity id and a time t, update RL by running **Revoke**(id, t, RL, st).

Challenge: $\mathcal{A}$ outputs an identity id^*, a time t^*, and a plaintext $b^* \in \mathcal{M}$, on which it wishes to be challenged. $\mathcal{B}$ picks a random bit $r \in \{0, 1\}$ and a random ciphertext $C \in \mathcal{C}$. If $r = 1$, it sets the challenge ciphertext to $C^* := C$. If $r = 0$, it sets the challenge ciphertext to $C^* :=$ **Encrypt**(pp, id^*, t^*, b^*). It sends C^* as the challenge ciphertext to the adversary $\mathcal{A}$.

Guess: $\mathcal{A}$ may further make a polynomial number of queries of the oracles as in the query phase, then it outputs a bit r'. We say $\mathcal{A}$ succeeds if $r' = r$.

In the above game, the following restrictions must hold:

1. **UpdateKey**($\cdot$) and **Revoke**($\cdot, \cdot$) can only be queried on time that is greater than or equal to the time of all previous queries.

2. **Revoke**$(\cdot, \cdot)$ can not be queried on time t if **UpdateKey**$(\cdot)$ has already been queried on time t.

3. If **PriKeyGen**$(\cdot)$ was queried on id*, then **Rovoke**$(\cdot, \cdot)$ must be queried on (id^*, t) for some $t \leq t^*$.

We call such an adversary $\mathcal{A}$ as an INDr-RID-CPA PPT adversary. The advantage of $\mathcal{A}$ attacking a RIBE scheme $\mathcal{RIBE}$ is defined as

$$\text{Adv}^{\text{INDr-RID-CPA}}_{\mathcal{RIBE}, \mathcal{A}}(\lambda) = \left| \Pr\left[r' = r\right] - \frac{1}{2} \right|.$$

We say that a RIBE scheme $\mathcal{RIBE}$ is indistinguishable from random under adaptive identity-time attacks, if for all INDr-RID-CPA PPT adversary $\mathcal{A}$, we have that its advantage $\text{Adv}^{\text{INDr-RID-CPA}}_{\mathcal{RIBE}, \mathcal{A}}(\lambda)$ is a negligible function in λ.

2.2   Subset Difference Method

Let BT be a full binary tree with $N_{\max}$ leaf nodes. Label the nodes in BT by 1 to $2N_{\max} - 1$ in the way that root is labeled 1, if parent is labeled i, then the left child is labeled $2i$ and the right child is labeled $2i + 1$. One example of the labeling is in Figure 1. Let v_i denote the node labeled i for $i \in [2N_{\max} - 1]$. The depth of a node v_i is the length of the path from the root to v_i. For any $v_i \in$ BT, T_i is defined as a subtree that is rooted at v_i. For any $v_i, v_j \in$ BT, $T_{i,j}$ is defined as a subtree $T_i - T_j$. S_i, $S_{i,j}$ are the sets of leaf nodes of T_i, $T_{i,j}$, respectively.

For a binary tree BT and a subset R of nodes, $ST(R)$ is the Steiner tree induced by R and the root node, that is, the minimal subtree of BT that connects all the leaf nodes in R and the root node.

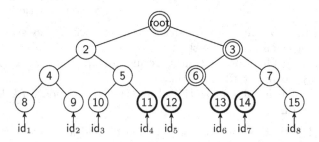

Fig. 1. $R = \{id_4, id_5, id_6, id_7\}$. Let v_i denote the node labeled i for $i \in [2N_{\max} - 1]$, while the root is labeled 1. First choose v_6 as lca of v_{12} and v_{13}. Get v_6 as a leaf; then v_3 is lca of v_{14} and v_6. Get v_3 as a leaf, $CV_R = \{S_{7,14}\}$; then the root is lca of v_{11} and v_3, $CV_R = \{S_{7,14}, S_{2,11}\}$. Get the root as a leaf. Then, $PV_{id_2} = \{S_{1,2}, S_{1,4}, S_{1,9}, S_{2,4}, S_{2,9}, S_{4,9}\}$ and SD.Match(CV_R, PV_{id_2}) outputs $(S_{2,11}, S_{2,9})$. Similarly, SD.Match(CV_R, PV_{id_8}) outputs $(S_{7,14}, S_{7,15})$. For $\nu \in R$, SD.Match(CV_R, PV_ν) outputs $\perp$.

The SD scheme is summarized as follows:

SD.Setup(N_{max}): This algorithm takes as input the maximum number of users N_{max} (for simplicity, $N_{max} = 2^d$). It sets a full binary tree BT of depth d. Every user is assigned to a different leaf node in BT. The collection S is the set of all subsets $S_{i,j}$ with $v_i, v_j \in$ BT where v_i is an ancestor of v_j. It outputs BT.

SD.Assign(BT, ν): This algorithm takes as input the full binary tree BT and a user ν. Let v_ν be the leaf node assigned to ν and $Path(v_\nu) = (v_{k_0}, v_{k_1}, ..., v_{k_n})$ be the path from the root node v_{k_0} to the leaf node $v_{k_n} = v_\nu$. For all $i, j \in \{k_0, k_1, ..., k_n\}$ such that v_j is a descendant of v_i, it adds $S_{i,j}$ defined by two nodes v_i and v_j in the path into a private set PV_ν. Finally, it outputs PV_ν.

SD.Cover(BT, R): This algorithm takes as input the binary tree BT and a revoked set R of users. Let T be the Steiner tree $ST(R)$, then it computes CV_R iteratively by removing nodes from T until T only has a single node as follows (an example is given in Figure 1):

1. Find two leaves v_i and v_j in T such that the least-common-ancestor (lca) v of v_i and v_j does not contain any other leaf node of T in its subtree. Let v_l and v_k be the two children of v such that v_i is a descendant of v_l, and v_j a descendant of v_k. (If there is only one leaf node, make $v_i = v_j$ the leaf, v the root of T and $v_l = v_k = v$.)
2. If $v_l \neq v_i$, $CV_R = CV_R \cup \{S_{l,i}\}$; if $v_k \neq v_j$, $CV_R = CV_R \cup \{S_{k,j}\}$.
3. Remove from T all the descendants of v and make it a leaf.

SD.Match(CV_R, PV_ν): This algorithm takes as input a covering set $CV_R = \{S_{i,j}\}$ and a private set $PV_\nu = \{S'_{i',j'}\}$. If it finds two subsets $S_{i,j} \in CV_R$ and $S'_{i',j'} \in PV_\nu$ with $(i = i') \wedge (d_j = d_{j'}) \wedge (j \neq j')$ where d_j is the depth of v_j, then it outputs $(S_{i,j}, S'_{i',j'})$. Otherwise, it outputs $\perp$.

The correctness of the SD scheme is defined as follows: for all $N = 2^d$, BT $\leftarrow$ SD.Setup(N), $PV_\nu \leftarrow$ SD.Assign(BT, ν), R a set of leaf nodes in BT, let $CV_R \leftarrow$ SD.Cover(BT, R), then

1. If $u \notin R$, then SD.Match(CV_R, PV_ν) = $(S_{i,j}, S'_{i',j'})$;
2. If $u \in R$, then SD.Match(CV_R, PV_ν) = $\perp$.

Lemma 1 ([20]). *Let N_{max} be the number of leaf nodes and r be the size of a revoked set. The size of a private set is $O(\log^2 N_{max})$ and the size of a covering set is at most $2r - 1$ in the SD scheme.*

2.3 Background on Lattices

In this subsection, we review the required knowledge of lattices.

Integer Lattices. Let $\mathbf{B} = \{\mathbf{b}_1, ..., \mathbf{b}_k\} \subseteq \mathbb{R}^m$ consist of k linearly independent vectors, where $k \leq m$. Define k-*dimensional lattice* Λ generated by $\mathbf{B}$ as $\Lambda = \mathcal{L}(\mathbf{B}) = \{\mathbf{Bc} = \sum_{i \in [k]} c_i \cdot \mathbf{b}_i : \mathbf{c} \in \mathbb{Z}^k\}$.

For a set of vectors $\mathbf{S} = \{\mathbf{s}_1, \cdots, \mathbf{s}_k\} \subseteq \mathbb{R}^m$, we call the norm of $\mathbf{S}$ as $\|\mathbf{S}\| = \max_{1 \leq i \leq k} \|\mathbf{s}_i\|$, where $\|\mathbf{s}\|$ denotes the ℓ_2-norm of the column vector $\mathbf{s}$. Moreover,

$\tilde{\mathbf{S}} := \{\tilde{\mathbf{s}}_1, \cdots, \tilde{\mathbf{s}}_k\} \subseteq \mathbb{R}^m$ represents the Gram-Schmidt orthogonalization of the vectors $\mathbf{s}_1, \cdots, \mathbf{s}_k$. Let $\|\tilde{\mathbf{S}}\|$ denote the Gram-Schmidt norm of $\mathbf{S}$.

In our case, we only consider integer lattices, that is, $\Lambda \subseteq \mathbb{Z}^m$. For a prime q, a matrix $\mathbf{A} \in \mathbb{Z}^{n \times m}$ and a vector $\mathbf{u} \in \mathbb{Z}_q^n$, define $\Lambda_q^\perp(\mathbf{A}) = \{\mathbf{e} \in \mathbb{Z}^m : \mathbf{A}\mathbf{e} = \mathbf{0} \mod q\}$, and $\Lambda_q^{\mathbf{u}}(\mathbf{A}) = \{\mathbf{e} \in \mathbb{Z}^m : \mathbf{A}\mathbf{e} = \mathbf{u} \mod q\}$.

Trapdoor for Lattices

Proposition 1 ([5,6,18]). *Let $q \geq 3$ be a prime and $m \geq 2n \log q$. Then there exists a probabilistic polynomial-time algorithm* TrapGen(q, n) *that outputs a pair $\mathbf{A} \in \mathbb{Z}_q^{n \times m}$, $\mathbf{T_A} \in \mathbb{Z}^{m \times m}$ such that $\mathbf{A}$ is statistically close to uniform and $\mathbf{T_A}$ is a basis for $\Lambda_q^\perp(\mathbf{A})$ with length $L = \|\widetilde{\mathbf{T_A}}\| \leq O(\sqrt{m})$ with all but $n^{-\omega(1)}$ probability.*

Discrete Gaussians. Let Λ be a lattice in $\mathbb{Z}^m$. For any vector $\mathbf{c} \in \mathbb{R}^m$ and any parameter $\sigma \in \mathbb{R}_{>0}$, define $\rho_{\sigma,\mathbf{c}}(\mathbf{x}) = \exp(-\pi \frac{\|\mathbf{x} - \mathbf{c}\|^2}{\sigma^2})$ and $\rho_{\sigma,\mathbf{c}}(\Lambda) = \sum_{\mathbf{x} \in \Lambda} \rho_{\sigma,\mathbf{c}}(\mathbf{x})$. The *discrete Gaussian distribution* over Λ with center $\mathbf{c}$ and parameter σ is $\mathcal{D}_{\Lambda,\sigma,\mathbf{c}}(\mathbf{y}) = \frac{\rho_{\sigma,\mathbf{c}}(\mathbf{y})}{\rho_{\sigma,\mathbf{c}}(\Lambda)}$, for $\forall \mathbf{y} \in \Lambda$. If $\mathbf{c} = \mathbf{0}$, we conveniently use ρ_σ and $\mathcal{D}_{\Lambda,\sigma}$.

Lemma 2 ([19,15]). *For any m-dimensional integer lattice Λ, any vector $\mathbf{c} \in \mathbb{Z}^m$, any real $\epsilon \in (0,1)$ and $\sigma \geq \omega(\sqrt{\log m})$, the following probability satisfies* $\Pr[\mathbf{x} \sim \mathcal{D}_{\Lambda,\sigma,\mathbf{c}} : \|\mathbf{x} - \mathbf{c}\| > \sqrt{m} \cdot \sigma] \leq \frac{1+\epsilon}{1-\epsilon} \cdot 2^{-m}$.

Sampling Algorithms. In [1,4], there have been two algorithms proposed to sample short vectors from lattices. We will employ these two algorithms, SampleLeft and SampleRight, for our construction and security analysis, respectively, in a black-box manner.

SampleLeft$(\mathbf{A}, \mathbf{M}, \mathbf{T_A}, \mathbf{u}, \sigma)$: On input a rank n matrix $\mathbf{A} \in \mathbb{Z}_q^{n \times m}$, a matrix $\mathbf{M} \in \mathbb{Z}_q^{n \times m_1}$, a short trapdoor basis $\mathbf{T_A}$ of $\Lambda_q^\perp(\mathbf{A})$, a vector $\mathbf{u} \in \mathbb{Z}_q^n$, and a Gaussian parameter $\sigma \geq \|\widetilde{\mathbf{T_A}}\| \cdot \omega(\sqrt{\log(m + m_1)})$, it outputs a vector $\mathbf{e} \in \mathbb{Z}^{m+m_1}$ sampled from a distribution statistically close to $\mathcal{D}_{\Lambda_q^{\mathbf{u}}(\mathbf{F}_1),\sigma}$, where $\mathbf{F}_1 = (\mathbf{A} \,|\, \mathbf{M})$. In particular, $\mathbf{e} \in \Lambda_q^{\mathbf{u}}(\mathbf{F}_1)$.

SampleRight$(\mathbf{A}, \mathbf{B}, \mathbf{R}, \mathbf{T_B}, \mathbf{u}, \sigma)$: On input a matrix $\mathbf{A} \in \mathbb{Z}_q^{n \times m}$, a rank n matrix $\mathbf{B} \in \mathbb{Z}_q^{n \times m}$, a uniform random matrix $\mathbf{R} \in \mathbb{Z}^{m \times m}$, a short trapdoor basis $\mathbf{T_B}$ of $\Lambda_q^\perp(\mathbf{B})$, a vector $\mathbf{u} \in \mathbb{Z}_q^n$, and a Gaussian parameter $\sigma \geq \|\widetilde{\mathbf{T_B}}\| \cdot s_\mathbf{R} \cdot \omega(\sqrt{\log m})$ (where $s_\mathbf{R} := \|\mathbf{R}\|_R = \sup_{\|\mathbf{x}\|=1} \|\mathbf{R}\mathbf{x}\|$), it outputs a vector $\mathbf{e} \in \mathbb{Z}^{2m}$ sampled from a distribution statistically close to $\mathcal{D}_{\Lambda_q^{\mathbf{u}}(\mathbf{F}_2),\sigma}$, where $\mathbf{F}_2 = (\mathbf{A} \,|\, \mathbf{A}\mathbf{R} + \mathbf{B})$. In particular, $\mathbf{e} \in \Lambda_q^{\mathbf{u}}(\mathbf{F}_2)$.

It is known that the distributions of the outputs given by the two algorithms are statistically indistinguishable under the appropriate parameters when $m_1 = m$. See [1,4] for further details of these algorithms.

The LWE Hardness Assumption. The learning with errors (LWE) problem, defined as follows, was first defined by Regev [21]. The security of our RIBE scheme is based on the hardness of this problem.

Definition 2 (LWE). *For a positive integer n, a prime $q = q(n)$ and a distribution χ over $\mathbb{Z}_q$, an $(\mathbb{Z}_q, n, \chi)$-LWE problem instance consists of access to an unspecified challenge oracle $\mathcal{O}$, being, either a noisy pseudo-random sampler $\mathcal{O}_s$ under some constant random secret key $s \in \mathbb{Z}_q^n$, or a truly random sampler $\mathcal{O}_\$$. The behaviors of the two samplers are as follows:*
$\mathcal{O}_s$: *outputs samples of the form $(\mathbf{u}_i, v_i) = (\mathbf{u}_i, \mathbf{u}_i^\top s + x_i) \in \mathbb{Z}_q^n \times \mathbb{Z}_q$, where $s \in \mathbb{Z}_q^n$ is a uniformly distributed vector which keeps persistent across invocations, $x_i \in \mathbb{Z}_q$ is a fresh sample form χ, and $\mathbf{u}_i$ is uniformly sampled from $\mathbb{Z}_q^n$.*
$\mathcal{O}_\$$: *outputs samples from $\mathbb{Z}_q^n \times \mathbb{Z}_q$ uniformly at random.*

We state that an algorithm $\mathcal{B}$ decides the $(\mathbb{Z}_q, n, \chi)$-LWE problem if

$$\mathsf{Adv}_{\mathcal{B}}^{(\mathbb{Z}_q, n, \chi)\text{-LWE}} = \left| \Pr\left[\mathcal{B}^{\mathcal{O}_s} = 1\right] - \Pr\left[\mathcal{B}^{\mathcal{O}_\$} = 1\right] \right|$$

is non-negligible for a random $s \in \mathbb{Z}_q^n$.

Definition 3. *For an $\alpha \in (0,1)$ and a prime q, let $\overline{\Psi}_\alpha$ denote the distribution over $\mathbb{Z}_q$ of the random variable $\lfloor qX \rceil \mod q$, where X is a normal distributed random variable with mean 0 and standard deviation $\alpha/\sqrt{2\pi}$, and $\lfloor x \rceil$ denotes the closest integer to x.*

Throughout the paper, $x \xleftarrow{\overline{\Psi}_\alpha} \mathbb{Z}_q$ (resp., $\mathbf{x} \xleftarrow{\overline{\Psi}_\alpha^m} \mathbb{Z}_q^m$) denotes that x (resp., $\mathbf{x}$) is selected from $\mathbb{Z}_q$ (resp., $\mathbb{Z}_q^m$) according to the distribution $\overline{\Psi}_\alpha$ (resp., $\overline{\Psi}_\alpha^m$).

Proposition 2 ([21]). *If there exists an efficient, possibly quantum, algorithm for deciding the $(\mathbb{Z}_q, n, \overline{\Psi}_\alpha)$-LWE problem for $\alpha \cdot q > 2\sqrt{n}$, then there exists a quantum with $q \cdot \mathrm{poly}(n)$-time algorithm for approximating the SIVP and GapSVP problems in the ℓ_2 norm, in the worst case, to within $\tilde{O}(n/\alpha)$ factors.*

As the best known algorithms for 2^k-approximations of gapSVP and SIVP run in time $2^{\tilde{O}(n/k)}$ [14,23], it derived from above that the LWE problem with noise ratio $\alpha = 2^{-n^\epsilon}$ is likely hard for some constant $\epsilon < 1$.

3 RIBE from Lattices via Subset Difference Method

In this section, we provide our RIBE scheme from lattices via SD. Then, we look into the proper parameter sizes for our construction.

3.1 Our Construction

We treat an identity id and a time t as a sequence of length ℓ in $\{-1, 1\}^\ell$, with possible redundancy, for some $\ell \in \mathbb{Z}$. The requirement is that any tuple $(\mathrm{id}, \mathrm{t}) \in \mathcal{I} \times \mathcal{T}$, as two $\{-1, 1\}$-vectors, are $\mathbb{Z}_q$-linearly independent. One possible technique to realize it is that if one sequence ends with 1, we put it in $\mathcal{T}$, otherwise in $\mathcal{I}$. Then for each sequence in $\mathcal{I} \cup \mathcal{T}$, we add extra 1 to the end. Thus, any id $\in \mathcal{I}$ ends with 01, while any t $\in \mathcal{T}$ ends with 11. As a result, the two vectors id, t are $\mathbb{Z}_q$-linearly independent.

Now, we describe our construction.

Setup$(1^\lambda, 1^N)$: On input a security parameter λ and the maximal number of users N, set the parameters $n, m, q, \sigma, \ell, \alpha$ as specified in Subsection 3.3 below. Then, it performs as follows:

1. Use the algorithm $\mathsf{TrapGen}(q, n)$ to generate a uniformly random matrix $\mathbf{A} \in \mathbb{Z}_q^{n \times m}$ together with a short basis $\mathbf{T_A}$ for $\Lambda_q^\perp(\mathbf{A})$.
2. Select $2\ell + 2$ uniformly random matrices $\mathbf{B}_1, \cdots, \mathbf{B}_\ell, \mathbf{C}; \mathbf{D}_1, \cdots, \mathbf{D}_\ell, \mathbf{G} \in \mathbb{Z}_q^{n \times m}$ and select a uniformly random vector $\mathbf{u} \in \mathbb{Z}_q^n$.
3. Let $\mathsf{UL}, \mathsf{RL}, \mathsf{FL}$ be three initially empty sets, which will be used to record the user list $\{(\mathsf{id}, \nu)\}$, revoked list $\{(\mathsf{id}, \mathsf{t})\}$, function list $\{(\mathsf{GL}_{d_j}^i, \mathsf{F}_{d_j}^i)\}$ respectively, where the domain of the parameters $\nu, \mathsf{GL}_{d_j}^i, \mathsf{F}_{d_j}^i$ will be specified in later steps.
4. Obtain a binary tree BT by running $\mathsf{SD.Setup}(N)$. Let $\mathcal{S}$ be the collection of all subsets $S_{i,j}$ of BT and $\mathsf{GL}_{d_j}^i$ be the subset of $\mathcal{S}$ consisting of $S_{i,j}$ such that the depth of node ν_j is d_j. Save $(\mathsf{GL}_{d_j}^i, \perp)$ to FL. Set the state to $\mathsf{st} = (\mathsf{BT}, \mathsf{UL})$.
5. Output the public parameters PP and master key MK given by

$$\mathsf{PP} = (\mathbf{A}, \{\mathbf{B}_1, \cdots, \mathbf{B}_\ell, \mathbf{C}\}, \{\mathbf{D}_1, \cdots, \mathbf{D}_\ell, \mathbf{G}\}, \mathbf{u}), \quad \mathsf{MK} = (\mathbf{T_A}, \mathsf{FL}).$$

PriKeyGen$(\mathsf{PP}, \mathsf{MK}, \mathsf{id}, \mathsf{st})$: On input the public parameters PP, the master key MK, an identity $\mathsf{id} = (b_1, \cdots, b_\ell) \in \{-1, 1\}^\ell$, and the state st, it works as follows:

1. Randomly choose an unassigned leaf node ν in BT and assign it to the identity id. Save (id, ν) to UL. Run $\mathsf{SD.Assign}(\mathsf{BT}, \nu)$ to obtain $PV_\nu = \{S_{i,j}\}$.
2. Let $\mathbf{A}_{\mathsf{id}} = \mathbf{C} + \sum_{i=1}^\ell b_i \mathbf{B}_i \in \mathbb{Z}_q^{n \times m}$.
3. For each $S_{i,j} \in PV_\nu$, perform the following:
   - Retrieve the record $(\mathsf{GL}_{d_j}^i, *)$ from FL. If the second coordinate $*$ is not $\perp$, go to next step. Else, randomly select $\mathsf{F}_{d_j}^i(x) \in (\mathbb{Z}_q[x])^n$ such that each coordinate of $\mathsf{F}_{d_j}^i$ is a polynomial of degree 1 and $\mathsf{F}_{d_j}^i(0) = \mathbf{u}$. Update $(\mathsf{GL}_{d_j}^i, \mathsf{F}_{d_j}^i)$ to FL.
   - Sample $\mathbf{e}_{i,j}^{\mathsf{id}} \leftarrow \mathsf{SampleLeft}\left(\mathbf{A}, \mathbf{A}_{\mathsf{id}}, \mathbf{T_A}, \mathsf{F}_{d_j}^i(j), \sigma\right)$.

   Note that for two sets $S_{i,j}, S_{i,j'} \in \mathsf{GL}_{d_j}^i$ with $j \neq j'$, we have $d_j = d_{j'}$. For given i and d_j, let $\mathsf{F} = \mathsf{F}_{d_j}^i$. We can compute fractional Lagrangian coefficients $L_j = j' \cdot (j' - j)^{-1}$ and $L_{j'} = j \cdot (j - j')^{-1}$ such that $\mathbf{u} = \mathsf{F}(0) = L_j \mathsf{F}(j) + L_{j'} \mathsf{F}(j')$ mod q. That is, as a fraction of integers, L_j can also be evaluated in $\mathbb{Z}_q$, then L_j can be regarded as an integer in $\{0\} \cup [q-1]$.
4. Output the updated state st and the private key $\mathsf{sk}_{\mathsf{id}} = \left(PV_\nu, \{\mathbf{e}_{i,j}^{\mathsf{id}}\}_{S_{i,j} \in PV_\nu}\right)$.

UpdateKey$(\mathsf{PP}, \mathsf{MK}, \mathsf{t}, \mathsf{RL}, \mathsf{st})$: On input the public parameters PP, the master key MK, a time $\mathsf{t} = (t_1, \cdots, t_\ell) \in \{-1, 1\}^\ell$, the revoked list RL, and the state st, it works as follows:

1. Take R as a set consisting of such id's that for some $t' \leq t$, $(id, t') \in RL$. By using UL, define RI as the set of index of leaf nodes corresponding the id's in R. That is, for any id $\in R$, if $(id, \nu) \in UL$, then put ν in RI.
2. Run SD.Cover(BT, RI) to obtain $CV_{RI} = \{S_{i,j}\}$.
3. Let $\mathbf{A}_t = \mathbf{G} + \sum_{i=1}^{\ell} t_i \mathbf{D}_i \in \mathbb{Z}_q^{n \times m}$.
4. For each $S_{i,j} \in CV_{RI}$, perform the following:
   - Retrieve the record $(GL_{d_j}^i, *)$ from FL. If the second coordinate $*$ is not $\perp$, go to next step. Else, randomly select $F_{d_j}^i(x) \in (\mathbb{Z}_q[x])^n$ such that each coordinate of $F_{d_j}^i$ is a polynomial of degree 1 and $F_{d_j}^i(0) = \mathbf{u}$. Update $(GL_{d_j}^i, F_{d_j}^i)$ to FL.
   - Sample $\mathbf{e}_{i,j}^t \leftarrow$ SampleLeft $\left(\mathbf{A}, \mathbf{A}_t, \mathbf{T_A}, F_{d_j}^i(j), \sigma \right)$.
5. Output the update key $uk_t = \left(CV_{RI}, \{\mathbf{e}_{i,j}^t\}_{S_{i,j} \in CV_{RI}} \right)$.

Encrypt(PP, id, t, b): On input the public parameters PP, an identity id, a current time t, and a message $b \in \{0, 1\}$, it performs as follows:

1. Let $D = (N-1)!$.
2. Choose a uniformly random vector $\mathbf{s} \in \mathbb{Z}_q^n$.
3. Choose 2ℓ uniformly random matrixes $\mathbf{R}_i \in \{-1, 1\}^{m \times m}$ for $i = 1, \cdots, 2\ell$ and define $\mathbf{R}_{id} = \sum_{i=1}^{\ell} b_i \mathbf{R}_i$, $\mathbf{R}_t = \sum_{i=1}^{\ell} t_i \mathbf{R}_{\ell+i} \in \{-\ell, \cdots, \ell\}^{m \times m}$.
4. Choose a noise value $x \xleftarrow{\overline{\Psi}_\alpha} \mathbb{Z}_q$ and a noise vector $\mathbf{y} \xleftarrow{\overline{\Psi}_\alpha^m} \mathbb{Z}_q^m$. Set $\mathbf{x}_{id} = \begin{pmatrix} \mathbf{y} \\ \mathbf{R}_{id}^\top \mathbf{y} \end{pmatrix}$ and $\mathbf{x}_t = \begin{pmatrix} \mathbf{y} \\ \mathbf{R}_t^\top \mathbf{y} \end{pmatrix}$.
5. Output the ciphertext $ct_{id,t} = (c_0, \mathbf{c}_1, \mathbf{c}_2)$, where $c_0 \leftarrow \mathbf{u}^\top \mathbf{s} + Dx + b \lfloor \frac{q}{2} \rfloor \in \mathbb{Z}_q$, $\mathbf{c}_1 \leftarrow (\mathbf{A} \mid \mathbf{A}_{id})^\top \mathbf{s} + D\mathbf{x}_{id} \in \mathbb{Z}_q^{2m}$, $\mathbf{c}_2 \leftarrow (\mathbf{A} \mid \mathbf{A}_t)^\top \mathbf{s} + D\mathbf{x}_t \in \mathbb{Z}_q^{2m}$.

DecKeyGen(PP, sk_{id}, uk_t): On input the public parameters PP, a private key sk_{id} and an update key uk_t given by $sk_{id} = \left(PV_\nu, \{\mathbf{e}_{i,j}^{id}\}_{S_{i,j} \in PV_\nu} \right)$ and $uk_t = \left(CV_{RI}, \{\mathbf{e}_{i,j}^t\}_{S_{i,j} \in CV_{RI}} \right)$, it performs as follows:

1. If id $\notin R$, run SD.Match(CV_{RI}, PV_ν) to obtain a set pair $(S_{i,j}, S_{i',j'})$ such that $S_{i,j} \in CV_{RI}$, $S_{i',j'} \in PV_\nu$, and $(i = i') \wedge (d_j = d_{j'}) \wedge (j \neq j')$. Else, output $\perp$.
2. Retrieve $\mathbf{e}_{i',j'}^{id}$ from sk_{id} and $\mathbf{e}_{i,j}^t$ from uk_t.
3. Compute the fractional Lagrangian coefficients L_j and $L_{j'}$ and evaluate them in $\mathbb{Z}_q$, that is, they can be interpreted as elements in $\mathbb{Z}_q$, i.e. integers in $\{0\} \cup [q-1]$.
4. Output the decryption key $dk_{id,t} = \left(L_{j'} \mathbf{e}_{i',j'}^{id}, L_j \mathbf{e}_{i,j}^t \right)$.

Decrypt(PP, $ct_{id,t}$, $dk_{id,t}$): On input the public parameters PP, a ciphertext $ct_{id,t}$, and a decryption key $dk_{id,t}$, it performs as follows:

1. Evaluate $dk_{id,t}$ in $\mathbb{Z}_q^{2m}$ as $(\mathbf{d}_1, \mathbf{d}_2)$, where $\mathbf{d}_1, \mathbf{d}_2 \in \mathbb{Z}_q^m$.
2. Compute $w \leftarrow c_0 - \mathbf{d}_1^\top \mathbf{c}_1 - \mathbf{d}_2^\top \mathbf{c}_2 \mod q$.
3. Compare w and $\lfloor \frac{q}{2} \rfloor$ regarding them as integers in $\mathbb{Z}$. If $|w - \lfloor \frac{q}{2} \rfloor| < \lfloor \frac{q}{4} \rfloor$ output 1. Else, output 0.

Revoke(id, t, RL, st): On input an identity id, a revocation time t, the revocation list RL, and the state st = (BT, UL): If (id, ∗) ∉ UL, then output ⊥ as the private key for id was not generated. Else, add (id, t) to RL. Then output the updated revocation list RL.

3.2   Correctness

Let $F = F_{d_j}^i$. If the ciphertext is generated by operating as described above, we can compute the error term in the decryption algorithm from the following:

$$w = c_0 - L_{j'} \left(e_{i',j'}^{\mathsf{id}} \right)^{\top} \mathbf{c}_1 - L_j \left(e_{i,j}^{\mathsf{t}} \right)^{\top} \mathbf{c}_2$$

$$= b \left\lfloor \frac{q}{2} \right\rfloor + \underbrace{Dx - DL_{j'} \left(e_{i',j'}^{\mathsf{id}} \right)^{\top} \mathbf{x}_{\mathsf{id}} - DL_j \left(e_{i,j}^{\mathsf{t}} \right)^{\top} \mathbf{x}_{\mathsf{t}}}_{\text{error term } \tau},$$

where all the equalities are in $\mathbb{Z}_q$.

Hence, for the correctness, it suffices to set the parameters such that the error term $\tau \leq (N!) \left(|x| + 2 \left| \left(e_{i',j'}^{\mathsf{id}} \right)^{\top} \mathbf{x}_{\mathsf{id}} \right| + 2 \left| \left(e_{i,j}^{\mathsf{t}} \right)^{\top} \mathbf{x}_{\mathsf{t}} \right| \right) \leq q/5$, except with negligible probability. For the first inequality, as j and j' have the same depth, we know $|j - j'| \leq N - 1$, and hence $j - j'$ divides D. Moreover, j, j' lie in the interval $[2N - 1]$, so $DL_j, DL_{j'}$ are integers not exceeding $(N - 1)! \times (2N - 1) < 2(N!)$. Therefore, if we set the parameters such that q is sufficiently larger than $N!$, then our construction satisfies the correctness.

3.3   Parameters

To bound the error term in the decryption algorithm of our construction, we first introduce the following lemma. The proof is similar as the case analyzed in Lemma 24 in [2]. We omit the details of the proof.

Lemma 3. *The norm of the error term in Subsection 3.2 is bounded by*

$$4q\sigma\ell m\alpha \cdot \omega(\sqrt{\log m}) \cdot (N!) + 4O(\sigma m^{1.5}) \cdot (N!)$$

except for a negligible probability.

Now we set the parameters to guarantee that the decryption is correct and the security reduction is meaningful. The parameters are set under the following requirements:

1. For the lattice trapdoor generation algorithm in Proposition 1, the parameters should satisfy $m \geq 2n \log q$. Under this selection of m, the output basis of TrapGen has Gram-Schmidt norm at most $O(\sqrt{m})$. The private key $\mathsf{sk}_{\mathsf{id}}$ and the update key uk_t are generated from the algorithm SampleLeft in real scheme and SampleRight in simulated games (see [12]), respectively. The two algorithms are presented in Subsection 2.3. By Lemma 2, if we set Gaussian parameter $\sigma \geq \ell m \log m$, then the vectors inside the two keys have length at most $\sigma\sqrt{2m} \leq 2\ell m^{1.5} \log m$ with high probability.

2. The noise distribution is set as $\chi = \overline{\Psi}_\alpha^m$, where $\alpha \geq 2\sqrt{m}/q$ in order to apply Regev's reduction (see Proposition 2). Any vector $\mathbf{y}$ sampled from this distribution has length satisfying $O(\alpha q \sqrt{m}) \leq 2m$ with high probability.

3. From Lemma 3, the norm of the error term is bounded by

$$(N!) \left(|x| + 2 \left| \left(\mathbf{e}_{i',j'}^{\mathsf{id}}\right)^\top \mathbf{x}_{\mathsf{id}} \right| + 2 \left| \left(\mathbf{e}_{i,j}^{\mathsf{t}}\right)^\top \mathbf{x}_{\mathsf{t}} \right| \right)$$
$$\leq 16\ell^2(N!) \cdot m^{2.5}(\log m)^{1.5} \leq 2^{N\log N}\ell^2 \cdot m^{2.5} \cdot (\log m)^{1.5}$$

where we used the fact that $N! \leq 2^{N\log N}$. The modulus q satisfying $q \geq 2^{N\log N}\ell^2 \cdot m^{2.5} \cdot (\log m)^{1.5}$ ensures the correctness of our construction.

4. The modulus q should satisfy $q \geq 2(Q^{\mathsf{id}} + |\mathcal{T}|)$, where Q^{id} is the number of identity queries from the adversary, $|\mathcal{T}|$ is the size of time space. This requirement ensures that our reduction in the security analysis applies.

5. The identity space $\mathcal{I}$ is sufficient for N users, so $2^\ell \geq N$.

To satisfy these requirements, given a constant $\epsilon \in (0,1)$, we set the parameters as follows, taking n to be the security parameter:

$$n = (N\log N)^{1/\epsilon}, \quad m = 2n^{1+\delta}, \quad q \geq \max\left\{2\left(Q^{\mathsf{id}} + |\mathcal{T}|\right), 2^{N\log N}\ell^2 \cdot n^5\right\}, \quad (1)$$
$$\sigma = \ell n^2 \log n, \qquad \ell = \log N, \quad \alpha = \left[2^{N\log N}\ell^2 \cdot n^4\right]^{-1}, \qquad (2)$$

where q is the nearest larger prime, and δ is selected such that $1 > \delta > \epsilon$.

Note that from Regev's reduction (see Proposition 2), the security of our scheme is finally based on the hardness of $2^{O(n^\epsilon)}$-approximating gapSVP or SIVP on n-dimension lattices using algorithms that run in time $q \cdot \mathsf{poly}(n) = 2^{O(n^\epsilon)}$. The same assumption has been used to construct fuzzy IBE by Agrawal et al. in [4]. The security holds for $\epsilon < 1/2$.

3.4 Security

Our RIBE scheme defined in Subsection 3.1 with parameters $(n, m, q, \sigma, \ell, \alpha)$ as in (1), (2), is indistinguishable from random under adaptive identity-time attacks provided that the $(\mathbb{Z}_q, n, \overline{\Psi}_\alpha)$-LWE assumption holds. In particular, we have the following theorem.

Theorem 1. *Under the condition that Q^{id} the number of private key queries and $|\mathcal{T}|$ the size of time space satisfy $2(Q^{\mathsf{id}} + |\mathcal{T}|) \leq q$, and both of them are polynomial size of n, if there exists a PPT adversary $\mathcal{A}$ that wins INDr-RID-CPA game with advantage ϵ, then there exists a PPT algorithm $\mathcal{B}$ that solves the $(\mathbb{Z}_q, n, \overline{\Psi}_\alpha)$-LWE problem in about the same time as $\mathcal{A}$ and with advantage $\epsilon' \geq \epsilon/(8q^2 Q^{\mathsf{id}} \cdot |\mathcal{T}|)$.*

The proof is obtained by further investigating the abort-resistant hash functions used in [26,1]. Due to space limit, we leave the details to the full version [12].

4   Conclusion and New Challenges

We have provided the first adaptive-ID secure revocable identity-based encryption scheme from lattices in the standard model under the LWE assumption. To realize identity revocation, our scheme employs the subset difference method.

However, unfortunately, our construction can not achieve to thwart the decryption key exposure attack, proposed by Seo and Emura [24], which considers not only exposure of a long-term private key and a short-term update key, but also exposure of a short-term decryption key. To directly apply Seo and Emura's approach which randomizes a short-term decryption key, we need a proper one-way function to randomize the short-term decryption key in our scheme, but we could not find such a proper one-way function and we leave it as a new challenge.

It would be also interesting to construct revocable identity-based signatures and revocable attribute-based encryption schemes from lattices.

Acknowledgments. The authors are particularly grateful to Khoa Nguyen and Hyung Tae Lee for the helpful discussions. Meanwhile, the authors would like to thank San Ling, Huaxiong Wang, Chaoping Xing for their support all along, and the anonymous referees for the valuable comments.

References

1. Agrawal, S., Boneh, D., Boyen, X.: Efficient Lattice (H)IBE in the Standard Model. In: Gilbert, H. (ed.) EUROCRYPT 2010. LNCS, vol. 6110, pp. 553–572. Springer, Heidelberg (2010)
2. Agrawal, S., Boneh, D., Boyen, X.: Efficient Lattice (H)IBE in the Standard Model. Full version of [1],
http://crypto.stanford.edu/~dabo/pubs/papers/latticebb.pdf
3. Agrawal, S., Boneh, D., Boyen, X.: Lattice Basis Delegation in Fixed Dimension and Shorter-Ciphertext Hierarchical IBE. In: Rabin, T. (ed.) CRYPTO 2010. LNCS, vol. 6223, pp. 98–115. Springer, Heidelberg (2010)
4. Agrawal, S., Boyen, X., Vaikuntanathan, V., Voulgaris, P., Wee, H.: Functional Encryption for Threshold Functions (or Fuzzy IBE) from Lattices. In: Fischlin, M., Buchmann, J., Manulis, M. (eds.) PKC 2012. LNCS, vol. 7293, pp. 280–297. Springer, Heidelberg (2012)
5. Ajtai, M.: Generating Hard Instances of the Short Basis Problem. In: Wiedermann, J., Van Emde Boas, P., Nielsen, M. (eds.) ICALP 1999. LNCS, vol. 1644, pp. 1–9. Springer, Heidelberg (1999)
6. Alwen, J., Peikert, C.: Generating Shorter Bases for Hard Random Lattices. Theory of Computing Systems 48(3), 535–553 (2011)
7. Boldyreva, A., Goyal, V., Kumar, V.: Identity-Based Encryption with Efficient Revocation. In: Ning, P., Syverson, P.F., Jha, S. (eds.) CCS 2008, pp. 417–426. ACM (2008)
8. Boneh, D., Boyen, X.: Efficient Selective-ID Secure Identity-Based Encryption Without Random Oracles. In: Cachin, C., Camenisch, J.L. (eds.) EUROCRYPT 2004. LNCS, vol. 3027, pp. 223–238. Springer, Heidelberg (2004)

9. Boneh, D., Franklin, M.: Identity-Based Encryption from the Weil Pairing. In: Kilian, J. (ed.) CRYPTO 2001. LNCS, vol. 2139, pp. 213–229. Springer, Heidelberg (2001)

10. Boneh, D., Gentry, C., Hamburg, M.: Space-Efficient Identity Based Encryption Without Pairings. In: FOCS 2007, pp. 647–657. IEEE (2007)

11. Chen, J., Lim, H.W., Ling, S., Wang, H., Nguyen, K.: Revocable Identity-Based Encryption from Lattices. In: Susilo, W., Mu, Y., Seberry, J. (eds.) ACISP 2012. LNCS, vol. 7372, pp. 390–403. Springer, Heidelberg (2012)

12. Cheng, S., Zhang, J.: Adaptive-ID Secure Revocable Identity-Based Encryption from Lattices via Subset Difference Method. Available on the first author's webpage (2015), http://eprint.iacr.org/2015/098

13. Cocks, C.: An Identity Based Encryption Scheme Based on Quadratic Residues. In: Honary, B. (ed.) Cryptography and Coding 2001. LNCS, vol. 2260, pp. 360–363. Springer, Heidelberg (2001)

14. Gama, N., Nguyen, P.Q.: Finding Short Lattice Vectors within Mordell's Inequality. In: Dwork, C. (ed.) STOC 2008, pp. 207–216. ACM (2008)

15. Gentry, C., Peikert, C., Vaikuntanathan, V.: Trapdoors for Hard Lattices and New Cryptographic Constructions. In: Dwork, C. (ed.) STOC 2008, pp. 197–206. ACM (2008)

16. Lee, K., Lee, D.H., Park, J.H.: Efficient Revocable Identity-Based Encryption via Subset Difference Methods. Cryptology ePrint Archive, Report 2014/132 (2014), http://eprint.iacr.org/2014/132

17. Libert, B., Vergnaud, D.: Adaptive-ID Secure Revocable Identity-Based Encryption. In: Fischlin, M. (ed.) CT-RSA 2009. LNCS, vol. 5473, pp. 1–15. Springer, Heidelberg (2009)

18. Micciancio, D., Peikert, C.: Trapdoors for Lattices: Simpler, Tighter, Faster, Smaller. In: Pointcheval, D., Johansson, T. (eds.) EUROCRYPT 2012. LNCS, vol. 7237, pp. 700–718. Springer, Heidelberg (2012)

19. Micciancio, D., Regev, O.: Worst-Case to Average-Case Reductions Based on Gaussian Measures. SIAM Journal on Computing 37(1), 267–302 (2007)

20. Naor, D., Naor, M., Lotspiech, J.: Revocation and Tracing Schemes for Stateless Receivers. In: Kilian, J. (ed.) CRYPTO 2001. LNCS, vol. 2139, pp. 41–62. Springer, Heidelberg (2001)

21. Regev, O.: On Lattices, Learning with Errors, Random Linear Codes, and Cryptography. In: Gabow, H.N., Fagin, R. (eds.) STOC 2005, pp. 84–93. ACM (2005)

22. Sahai, A., Waters, B.: Fuzzy Identity-Based Encryption. In: Cramer, R. (ed.) EUROCRYPT 2005. LNCS, vol. 3494, pp. 457–473. Springer, Heidelberg (2005)

23. Schnorr, C.: A Hierarchy of Polynomial Time Lattice Basis Reduction Algorithms. Theoretical Computer Science 53, 201–224 (1987)

24. Seo, J.H., Emura, K.: Revocable Identity-Based Cryptosystem Revisited: Security Models and Constructions. IEEE Transactions on Information Forensics and Security 9(7), 1193–1205 (2014)

25. Shamir, A.: Identity-Based Cryptosystems and Signature Schemes. In: Blakely, G.R., Chaum, D. (eds.) CRYPTO 1984. LNCS, vol. 196, pp. 47–53. Springer, Heidelberg (1985)

26. Waters, B.: Efficient Identity-Based Encryption Without Random Oracles. In: Cramer, R. (ed.) EUROCRYPT 2005. LNCS, vol. 3494, pp. 114–127. Springer, Heidelberg (2005)

27. Waters, B.: Dual System Encryption: Realizing Fully Secure IBE and HIBE under Simple Assumptions. In: Halevi, S. (ed.) CRYPTO 2009. LNCS, vol. 5677, pp. 619–636. Springer, Heidelberg (2009)

Attribute-Based Encryption

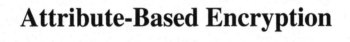

Outsourcing the Re-encryption Key Generation: Flexible Ciphertext-Policy Attribute-Based Proxy Re-encryption

Yutaka Kawai

Mitsubishi Electric, 5-1-1 Ofuna, Kamakura, Kanagawa 247-8501, Japan
Kawai.Yutaka@da.MitsubishiElectric.co.jp

Abstract. In this paper, we introduce a new proxy re-encryption (PRE) in that the re-encryption key generation can be outsourced, in attribute-based encryption. We call this new notion *flexible* ciphertext-policy attribute-based proxy re-encryption (flexible CP-AB-PRE). In ordinary PRE scheme, re-encryption keys are generated by using user's decryption key and an access structure. So, whenever the access structure is changed, a PRE user has to generate new different re-encryption keys. In order to overcome this disadvantage of the ordinary PRE, the re-encryption key generation of the proposed scheme is divided into the following two steps. First, a user generates *universal* re-encryption key urk_S which indicates delegator's attributes set S. Second, an authority who has re-encryption secret key rsk generates ordinary re-encryption key $\mathsf{rk}_{S \to \mathbb{M}'}$ by using urk_S, rsk, and an access structure $\mathbb{M}'$. The user has only to generate single urk_S for all re-encryption keys. By this "outsourcing", the task of re-encryption key generation for a user is reduced only to generate one urk_S. Furthermore, supposing a Private Key Generator (PKG) generates urk simultaneously at the time of decryption key generation, the load of re-encryption key generation for users almost vanishes.

1 Introduction

1.1 Background

Attribute-Based Encryption, ABE. *Attribute-based encryption* (ABE) was introduced by Sahai and Waters [23]. They constitute an advanced class of encryption, and provide more flexible and fine-grained functionalities in sharing and distributing sensitive data than traditional symmetric and public-key encryption as well as identity-based encryption (IBE) [3,5,6,11,21,22,26,27]. ABE system is one of the special systems of functional encryptions (FE). In FE, there is a relation $R(v, x)$, that determines whether a secret key associated with a parameter v can decrypt a ciphertext encrypted under another parameter x. We note $R(v, x) = 1$ if and only if there is a relation R between v and x. In ABE systems, either one of the parameters for encryption and secret key is a set of attributes, and the other is an access structure or (monotone) span program over a universe of attributes, e.g., a secret key for a user is associated with an access

© Springer International Publishing Switzerland 2015
J. Lopez and Y. Wu (Eds.): ISPEC 2015, LNCS 9065, pp. 301–315, 2015.
DOI: 10.1007/978-3-319-17533-1_21

policy $\mathbb{M}$ over a set of attributes S for encryption and a ciphertext is associated with a set of attributes, where a secret key can decrypt a ciphertext, iff the attribute set satisfies the policy, that is $R(S, \mathbb{M}) = 1$. If the access policy is for a secret key, it is called key-policy ABE (KP-ABE), and if the access policy is for encryption, it is ciphertext-policy ABE (CP-ABE).

Proxy Re-encryption, PRE. Proxy re-encryption (PRE) is an interesting extension of traditional public key encryption (PKE). In addition to the normal operations of PKE, with a dedicated *re-encryption key* (generated by receiver A), a proxy can turn (re-encrypt) a class of ciphertexts destined for user A into those for user B. A remarkable property of PRE is that the proxy carrying out the transformation being totally ignorant of the plaintext. PRE concept was first formalized and a bidirectional PRE was proposed by Blaze et al. [4]. After that there are many PRE scheme (based on PKE) with implementations have been presented; refer to [4,1,8,17,25,16,9] for some examples. Also, various types of PRE, other than the PKE based one, have been proposed. To implement PRE in the identity-based encryption setting, Green et al. introduced identity-based proxy re-encryption (IB-PRE) and proposed a specific scheme in the random oracle model. Later on, many IB-PRE schemes have been proposed [12,19,10]. And then, attribute-based encryption type PRE schemes were proposed. Liang et al. [16] defined ciphertext-policy attribute-based proxy re-encryption (CP-AB-PRE). After that several AB-PRE schemes were proposed [16,20,18,15,14].

1.2   Motivation

In this paper, we focus on CP-AB-PRE scheme. First, we show an example where CP-AB-PRE is applied to a file sharing service in a company. A user stores an encrypted data CT_X to a cloud server in order to share documents with "the Dept. X" by using CP-ABE. The manager of the Dept. X can decrypt CT_X by using his decryption key corresponding to his own attributes. Here, we consider the situations where personnel changes, integration, or abolition happen to the Dept. In these situations, access structures of some ciphertexts have to be changed since users belong to new affiliation, with new attributes. By using normal CP-ABE, plaintexts should be recovered from some ciphertexts and encrypted under new access structure. On the other hand, by using CP-AB-PRE, access structures which are included in ciphertexts can be changed without decrypting them. So, we believe that CP-AB-PRE is very useful to the file sharing service.

However, there are some problems applying CP-AB-PRE to the above application. One of the problems is the cost of generating many different re-encryption keys for users. For example, let us assume that several encrypted data, CT_X, $CT_{(X \wedge Y)}$, $CT_{(X \vee Y)}$, are stored in a cloud server for groups X and Y by using CP-AB-PRE. In this situation, if the group X splits into two groups $X1$ and $X2$, access structures of the above ciphertexts need to change to $CT_{X1}, CT_{X2}, CT_{X1 \wedge Y}, CT_{X2 \wedge Y}, CT_{X1 \vee Y}$ and $CT_{X2 \vee Y}$. In order to change the access structure by using CP-AB-PRE, six re-encryption keys have to be generated by the user. This might be undesirable in practice due to high computational and data complexity.

Second problem is the risk of increasing the leak of decryption keys or a master secret key. In ordinary AB-PRE system, there are two types of re-encryption key generation method. First method is that a user executes re-encryption key generation algorithm using own decryption key. Second method is that a PKG (Private Key Generator), who has master secret key, generates a decryption key by executing the key generation algorithm with a set of attributes. Then, it executes re-encryption key generation algorithm using its decryption key and generates a re-encryption key. In the former method, whenever access structures of ciphertexts are changed, the user has to generate different re-encryption keys repeatedly using own decryption key. In the latter method, the opportunity of accessing PKG online increases, leading to the risk of the disclosure of decryption keys/master secret key by various malfunction of the system.

Outsourcing the Re-encryption Key Generation. Our main motivations are to reduce a load of generating re-encryption key for users and to reduce the frequency of accessing to decryption keys and master secret key in generating re-encryption keys in order to reduce the risk of leaking them. For that purpose a new PRE concept, *flexible* ciphertext-policy attribute-based PRE (flexible CP-AB-PRE) is introduced. The framework of flexible CP-AB-PRE is shown in Fig.1. The difference with flexible CP-AB-PRE and ordinary CP-AB-PRE is that in the former the re-encryption key generation has two processes, instead of one. In the first process of generation, a user generates *universal* re-encryption key urk_S by using own decryption key corresponding to a set of attributes S. urk_S indicates only the attributes set S. In the second process, an authority who has a trapdoor (we call it *re-encryption secret key*, rsk) generates a re-encryption key $\mathsf{rk}_{S \to \mathbb{M}'}$ by using urk_S, rsk, and an access policy $\mathbb{M}'$. This authority is called *re-encryption key generator, RKG* in this paper.

Universal re-encryption keys are generated by decryption keys. So, the task of re-encryption key generation for a user is to generate urk_S only once. Moreover, as the method of another re-encryption key generation, when PKG generates a pair of sk_S and urk_S in the decryption key generation, the load of re-encryption key generation for users mostly vanishes. In flexible CP-AB-PRE, a decryption key or a master secret key is not used in re-encryption key generation. It is reduced that the number of accessing decryption keys and master secret key in re-encryption key generation. So, the risk of leaking the processing data, which is temporarily disposed on the memory, can be reduced.

Remark 1. By using a flexible CP-AB-PRE scheme, the task of re-encryption key generation for users is reduced. However, we have to pay attention that RKG has obtain the very high decryption ability. The adversary who has both urk and rsk can convert any ciphertext into re-encrypted ciphertexts under *any* access structure. Thus, if he has decryption keys, he obtains the decrypting ability against any ciphertext. So, he who has rsk should not obtain decryption

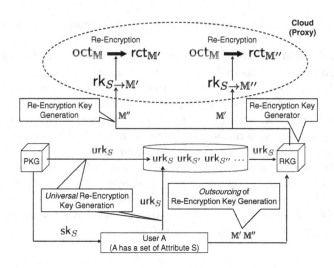

Fig. 1. Flexible Ciphertext-Policy Attribute-Based Proxy Re-Encryption

keys and master secret key and re-encryption secret key rsk should be managed safely and separately.

1.3   Key Techniques of Our Construction

In this section, we describe a methodology for constructing a flexible CP-AB-PRE scheme. Our scheme is constructed by combining *key randomized and encrypted methodology* and *adaptive attribute-based encryption* which was proposed in [13]. First, we explain these two concepts.

Key Randomized and Encrypted Methodology: Re-encryption key generation methodologies of many identity-based/attribute-based proxy re-encryption schemes are classified into this technique. We call it *key randomized and encrypted methodology* in this paper. We describe an overview of this methodology.

First, we introduce a randomized algorithm Rand and an algorithm which removes randomness algorithm Rem. That is, $X = \mathsf{Rem}(R, \mathsf{Rand}(R, X))$ where R is a randomness.

As a first attempt, in order to conceal a decryption key sk_S from a (malicious) proxy, in a re-encryption key generation algorithm (RKG) we encrypt it as $(\mathsf{Rand}(R, \mathsf{sk}_S), \mathsf{Enc}(\mathsf{pk}, R, \mathbb{M}'))$ in a re-encryption key $\mathsf{rk}_{S \to \mathbb{M}'}$, where Rand is a randomized algorithm for a decryption key sk_S with a secret randomness R, Enc is an encryption algorithm which outputs an original ciphertext with an access structure $\mathbb{M}'$ and pk is a public key.

$$\mathsf{rk}_{S \to \mathbb{M}'} := (S, \mathbb{M}', \widetilde{\mathsf{sk}}_S := \mathsf{Rand}(R, \mathsf{sk}_S), \mathsf{Enc}(\mathsf{pk}, R, \mathbb{M}'))$$

Then, if an adversary has no matching decryption key for $\mathbb{M}'$, he has no information of sk_S.

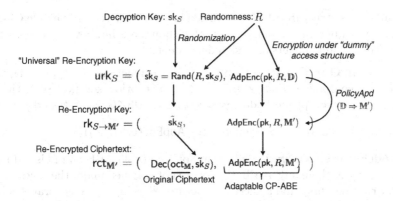

Fig. 2. Overview of Our Flexible CP-AB-PRE Construction

Next, in a re-encryption algorithm (REnc), a proxy executes a decryption procedure $\mathsf{Dec}(\mathsf{pk}, \tilde{\mathsf{sk}}_S, \mathsf{oct}_{\mathbb{M}})$ where $\mathsf{oct}_{\mathbb{M}} := \mathsf{Enc}(\mathsf{pk}, m, \mathbb{M})$. Here, it is assumed that a decryption procedure Dec has the following property.

$$\mathsf{Dec}(\mathsf{pk}, \tilde{\mathsf{sk}}_S = \mathsf{Rand}(R, \mathsf{sk}_S), \mathsf{oct}_{\mathbb{M}} = \mathsf{Enc}(\mathsf{pk}, m, \mathbb{M})) = \mathsf{Rand}(R, m)$$

The above property is very natural by using applicable Rand in several schemes. Then, $\tilde{m} := \mathsf{Rand}(R, m)$ is a randomized plaintext by the randomness R. A re-encrypted ciphertext $\mathsf{rct}_{\mathbb{M}'}$ is formed as shown below.

$$\mathsf{rct}_{\mathbb{M}'} := (\mathbb{M}', \tilde{m} := \mathsf{Dec}(\mathsf{pk}, \mathsf{Rand}(R, \mathsf{sk}_S), \mathsf{oct}_{\mathbb{M}}), \mathsf{Enc}(\mathsf{pk}, R, \mathbb{M}'))$$

A receiver who has a decryption key $\mathsf{sk}_{S'}$ obtains a secret randomness R by decrypting $\mathsf{oct}_{\mathbb{M}'}$. Finally, he can obtain m by computing $\mathsf{Rem}(\tilde{m}, R)$.

Adaptable Attribute-Based Encryption: Adaptable ABE [24,13][1] extends traditional ABE by allowing a semi-trusted third party to change a ciphertext under one access structure $\mathbb{M}$ into ciphertext under *any* other access structure $\mathbb{M}'$ by using an algorithm $\mathsf{PolicyAdp}$ and a trapdoor key tk. The property of $\mathsf{PolicyAdp}$ is very useful when the data owner uses the cloud service. The cloud is semi-trusted as the delegation party which is given the trapdoor for encrypted data transformation. The data owner asks that the cloud to re-encrypt the encrypted data by providing the new access structure. In [13], the proposed adaptable ABE is based on Waters ABE [27].

The major differences between adaptable CP-ABE and flexible CP-AB-PRE are summarized as follows. In adaptable ABE a procedure of re-encryption is very simple. However, since any ciphertext can be re-encrypted using only tk, a user cannot distinguish whether ciphertexts are re-encrypted or not. On the other hand, in flexible CP-AB-PRE, a ciphertext for an access structure $\mathbb{M}$ cannot be re-encrypted if a user does not publish urk_S where S satisfies $\mathbb{M}$. Also, when a trapdoor tk is leaked, an adversary who has tk can decrypt any ciphertext by transforming a ciphertext

---

[1] In [24], this type ABE scheme is called flexible ABE.

under an access structure which is satisfied his attribute sets. In flexible CP-AB-PRE, since an adversary cannot re-encrypt without urk, the above security risk can be reduced by managing urk and rsk independently[2].

Overview of Our Construction: In our construction, we apply adaptable ABE to the component $\mathsf{Enc}(\mathsf{pk}, R, \mathbb{M}')$ of re-encryption key $\mathsf{rk}_{S \to \mathbb{M}}$ in the key randomize and encrypt methodology (see Fig. 2). URKG generates urk_S as

$$\mathsf{urk}_S := (S, \mathsf{Rand}(R, \mathsf{sk}_S), \mathsf{AdpEnc}(\mathsf{pk}, R, \mathbb{D}))$$

where AdpEnc is an encryption algorithm of adaptable ABE and $\mathbb{D}$ is a dummy access structure where any attribute sets are not satisfied under the access structure $\mathbb{D}$. RKG takes urk_S and an access structure $\mathbb{M}'$ as input and generates $\mathsf{rk}_{S \to \mathbb{M}'}$ as follow by using rsk=tk.

$$\mathsf{rk}_{S \to \mathbb{M}'} := (S, \mathbb{M}', \mathsf{Rand}(R, \mathsf{sk}_S), \mathsf{PolicyAdp}(\mathsf{AdpEnc}(\mathsf{pk}, R, \mathbb{D}), \mathbb{M}', \mathsf{tk}))$$
$$= (S, \mathbb{M}', \mathsf{Rand}(R, \mathsf{sk}_S), \mathsf{AdpEnc}(\mathsf{pk}, R, \mathbb{M}'))$$

By the property of adaptable ABE, $\mathsf{PolicyAdp}(\mathsf{AdpEnc}(\mathsf{pk}, R, \mathbb{D}), \mathbb{M}', \mathsf{tk})$ outputs a ciphertext which contains an access structure $\mathbb{M}'$ and a secret randomness R, that is $\mathsf{PolicyAdp}(\mathsf{AdpEnc}_{\mathbb{D}}(R), \mathbb{M}', \mathsf{tk}) = \mathsf{AdpEnc}(\mathsf{pk}, R, \mathbb{M}')$. Thus, by combining the key randomize and encrypt methodology and adaptable ABE, we can construct a specific flexible CP-AB-PRE scheme.

2   Preliminaries

2.1   Notations

When A is a random variable or distribution, $y \xleftarrow{\mathsf{R}} A$ denotes that y is a randomly selected value from A according to its distribution. When A is a set, $y \xleftarrow{\mathsf{U}} A$ denotes that y is uniformly selected from A. $y := z$ denotes that y is set, defined or substituted by an expression z. When a is a fixed value, $A(x) \to a$ (e.g., $A(x) \to 1$) denotes the event that machine (algorithm) A outputs a on input x. $\boldsymbol{x}$ denotes $(x_1, \ldots, x_n) \in \mathbb{Z}_p$. When S is a set of attributes and $\mathbb{M}$ is an access structure, $R(S, \mathbb{M}) = 1$ and $R(S, \mathbb{M}) = 0$ denotes that S satisfies $\mathbb{M}$ and S does *not* satisfy $\mathbb{M}$, respectively.

2.2   Access Structures and Linear Secret Sharing Scheme

Definition 1 (Access Structure [2]). *Let* $P = \{P_1, \ldots, P_n\}$ *be a set of parties. A collection* $\mathbb{M} \subseteq 2^{\{P_1, \ldots, P_n\}}$ *is monotone if* $\forall B$ *and* C: *if* $B \in \mathbb{M}$ *and* $B \subseteq C$ *then* $C \in \mathbb{M}$. *An access structure (resp., monotonic access structure) is a collection (resp., monotone collection)* $\mathbb{M}$ *of non-empty subsets of* P, *it.,* $\mathbb{M} \subseteq 2^{\{P_1, \ldots, P_n\}} \setminus \{\emptyset\}$. *The sets in* $\mathbb{M}$ *are called the authorized sets, and the sets not in* $\mathbb{M}$ *are called the unauthorised sets.*

---

[2] In the case that all urk are public, this security risk is the same as the case which is applied adaptable CP-ABE.

In ABE, the role of parties P_i is taken by the attributes. Thus, the access structure $\mathbb{M}$ will contain the authorised sets of attributes. From now on, by an access structure we mean a monotone access structure. As shown in [2], any monotone access structure can be represented by a linear secret sharing scheme (LSSS).

Definition 2 (Linear Secret Sharing Scheme (LSSS)). *A secret-sharing scheme Π over a set of parties $\mathcal{P}$ is called linear over $\mathbb{Z}_p$ if (a) The shares for each party from a vector over $\mathbb{Z}_p$. (b) There exists a matrix M with ℓ rows and n columns called the share generating matrix for Π. For all $i = 1, \ldots, \ell$, the i-th row of M is labelled by a party $\rho(i)$ where ρ is a function from $\{1, \ldots, \ell\}$ to $\mathcal{P}$. When we consider the column vector $\boldsymbol{v} = (s, r_2, \ldots, r_n)$ where $s \in \mathbb{Z}_p$ is the secret to be shared, and $r_2, \ldots, r_n \in \mathbb{Z}_p$ are randomly chosen, then $M\boldsymbol{v}$ is the vector of ℓ shares of the secret a according to Π. The share $(M\boldsymbol{v})_i$ belongs to party $\rho(i)$.*

In [2], it is shown that every LSSS according to the above definition achieves the linear reconstruction property. Assume that Π be an LSSS for the access structure $\mathbb{M}$ and $S \in \mathbb{M}$, that is S satisfies $\mathbb{M}$ (we note that this case $R(S, \mathbb{M}) = 1$ in this paper), be any authorized set, and let $I \subset \{1, 2, \ldots, \ell\}$ be defined as $I = \{i : \rho(i) \in S\}$. There will constants $w_i \in \mathbb{Z}_p$ for $i \in I$ such that $\Sigma_{i \in I} w_i \cdot \lambda_i = s$ if λ_i is valid share of any secret s according to Π. In [2], it is shown that $\{w_i\}$ can be found in polynomial time in the size of the share-generating matrix M.

2.3   Computational Assumptions

In this section, we give a brief review of bilinear maps and the decisional q-parallel bilinear Diffie-Hellman exponent assumption [27] and decisional bilinear Diffie-Hellman assumption.

Definition 3 (Symmetric Bilinear Pairing Groups). *Symmetric bilinear pairing groups $(q, \mathbb{G}, \mathbb{G}_T, G, e)$ are a tuple of a prime q, cyclic multiplicative group $\mathbb{G}$ and multiplicative group $\mathbb{G}_T$ of order q, $g \neq 0 \in \mathbb{G}$, and a polynomial-time computable nondegenerate bilinear pairing $e : \mathbb{G} \times \mathbb{G} \to \mathbb{G}_T$ i.e., $e(g^s, g^t) = e(g, g)^{st}$ and $e(g, g) \neq 1$.*

Definition 4 (q-parallel Bilinear Diffie-Hellman Exponent Assumption). *First, we define q-parallel BDHE problem as follow: Chosen a group $\mathbb{G}$ of prime order p, g of a generator of $\mathbb{G}$, and $a, s, b_1, \ldots, b_q \in \mathbb{Z}_p$, If an adversary is given a tuple $\vec{y} = (g, g^s, g^a, \ldots, g^{a^q}, g^{a^{q+2}}, \ldots, g^{a^{2q}}, \forall 1 \leq j \leq q\ g^{s \cdot b_j}, g^{a/b_j} \ldots, g^{a^q/b_j},$ $g^{a^{q+2}/b_j}, \ldots, g^{a^{2q}/b_j}, \forall 1 \leq j, k \leq q, k \neq j\ g^{a \cdot s \cdot b_k/b_j}, \ldots, g^{a^q \cdot s \cdot b_k/b_j})$. it must remain hard to distinguish $T = e(g, g)^{a^{q+1}} \in \mathbb{G}_T$ from a random element $R \in \mathbb{G}_T$. An algorithm A that outputs $\mathbf{b} \in \{0, 1\}$ has advantage ϵ in solving the above problem in the group $\mathbb{G}$ if $|\Pr[\mathcal{A}(\vec{y}, T = e(g, g)^{a^{q+1}}) = 0] - \Pr[\mathcal{A}(\vec{y}, T = R) = 0]| \geq \epsilon$.*

We say that the q-parallel BDHE assumption holds if there is no polytime algorithm has a non-negligible advantage ϵ is solving the decisional q-parallel BDHE problem.

Definition 5 (Decisional Bilinear Diffie-Hellman Assumption). *We define DBDH problem as follow: Chosen a group $\mathbb{G}$ of prime order p, g of a generator of $\mathbb{G}$, and $a, b, c \in \mathbb{Z}_p$, If an adversary is given a tuple $\vec{y} = (g, g^a, g^b, g^c)$, it must remain hard to distinguish $T = e(g, g)^{abc} \in \mathbb{G}_T$ from a random element $R \in \mathbb{G}_T$. An algorithm A that outputs $\mathbf{b} \in \{0, 1\}$ has advantage ϵ in solving the above problem in the group $\mathbb{G}$ if $|\Pr[\mathcal{A}(\vec{y}, T = e(g,g)^{abc}) = 0] - \Pr[\mathcal{A}(\vec{y}, T = R) = 0]| \geq \epsilon$. We say that the DBDH assumption holds if there is no poly-time algorithm has a non-negligible advantage ϵ is solving the decisional DBDH problem.*

3   Flexible Ciphertext-Policy Attribute-Based Proxy Re-Encryption

In this section, we define a notion of flexible ciphertext-policy attribute-based proxy re-encryption (flexible CP-AB-PRE), and its securities.

3.1   Syntax

Definition 6 (Flexible CP-AB-PRE). *A flexible ciphertext-policy attribute-based proxy re-encryption scheme consists of the following eight algorithms*

Setup: *takes as input a security parameter 1^λ . It outputs public key pk, master secret key msk, and re-encryption secret key rsk.*

KG: *takes as input the public key pk, the master secret key msk, and a set of attribute S. It outputs a corresponding decryption key sk_S.*

URKG: *takes as input the public key pk, a decryption key sk_S. It outputs a universal re-encryption key urk_S*

RKG: *takes as input the public key pk, a universal re-encryption key urk_S, a re-encryption secret key rsk, and an access structure $\mathbb{M}'$. It outputs a re-encryption key $\mathsf{rk}_{S \to \mathbb{M}'}$.*

Enc: *takes as input the public key pk, an access structure $\mathbb{M}$, and a plaintext m in some associated plaintext space. It outputs an original ciphertext $\mathsf{oct}_\mathbb{M}$.*

REnc: *takes as input the public key pk, a re-encryption key $\mathsf{rk}_{S \to \mathbb{M}'}$, and an original ciphertext $\mathsf{oct}_\mathbb{M}$. It outputs a re-encrypted ciphertext $\mathsf{rct}_{\mathbb{M}'}$ or a special symbol $\bot$.*

$\mathsf{Dec}_{\mathsf{Enc}}$: *takes as input the public key pk, a decryption key sk_S, and an original ciphertext $\mathsf{oct}_\mathbb{M}$. It outputs either a plaintext m or $\bot$.*

$\mathsf{Dec}_{\mathsf{ReEnc}}$: *takes as input the public key pk, a decryption key $\mathsf{sk}_{S'}$, and a re-encrypted ciphertext $\mathsf{rct}_{\mathbb{M}'}$. It outputs either a plaintext m or $\bot$.*

Correctness. In this paper, $R(S, \mathbb{M}) = 1$ denotes that S satisfies $\mathbb{M}$. The correctness for a flexible ciphertext-policy attribute-based proxy re-encryption scheme is defined as: For any plaintext m, any $(\mathsf{pk}, \mathsf{msk}, \mathsf{rsk}) \xleftarrow{\mathsf{R}} \mathsf{Setup}(1^\lambda)$, any attribute set S, and access structure $\mathbb{M}$, we have $m = \mathsf{Dec}_{\mathsf{Enc}}(\mathsf{pk}, \mathsf{KG}(\mathsf{pk}, \mathsf{msk}, S), \mathsf{Enc}(\mathsf{pk}, \mathbb{M}, m))$ if $R(S, \mathbb{M}) = 1$, that is $\mathbb{M}$ satisfies S. Otherwise, it holds with negligible probability. For any plaintext m, any $(\mathsf{pk}, \mathsf{msk}, \mathsf{rsk}) \xleftarrow{\mathsf{R}}$

Setup(1^λ), any decryption key $\mathsf{sk}_{S_1} \xleftarrow{R} \mathsf{KG}(\mathsf{pk}, \mathsf{msk}, S_1)$, any re-encryption key $\mathsf{rk}_{S_1 \to \mathbb{M}_2} \xleftarrow{R} \mathsf{RKG}(\mathsf{pk}, \mathsf{URKG}(\mathsf{pk}, \mathsf{sk}_{S_1}), \mathsf{rsk}, \mathbb{M}_2)$, any original ciphertext $\mathsf{oct}_{\mathbb{M}_1} \xleftarrow{R} \mathsf{Enc}(\mathsf{pk}, \mathbb{M}_1, m)$, and re-encrypted ciphertext $\mathsf{rct}_{\mathbb{M}_2} \xleftarrow{R} \mathsf{REnc}(\mathsf{pk}, \mathsf{rk}_{S_1 \to \mathbb{M}_2}, \mathsf{oct}_{\mathbb{M}_1})$, we have $m = \mathsf{Dec}_{\mathsf{ReEnc}}(\mathsf{pk}, \mathsf{KG}(\mathsf{pk}, \mathsf{msk}, S_2), \mathsf{rct}_{\mathbb{M}_2})$ if $R(S_1, \mathbb{M}_1) = R(S_2, \mathbb{M}_2) = 1$, that is $\mathbb{M}_1$ satisfies S_1 and $\mathbb{M}_2$ satisfies S_2, respectively. Otherwise, it holds with negligible probability.

3.2 Security Definitions

We now give formal definitions of security for a flexible CP-AB-PRE scheme. Our security definitions are natural extensions of several CP-AB-PRE schemes [16,20,18,15]. In our security games, an adversary can obtain universal re-encryption key by using *universal re-encryption key generation query*. First, we describe a payload-hiding security for original ciphertexts game in flexible CP-AB-PRE.

Definition 7 (Payload-Hiding (PH) for Original Ciphertext Security).
The model for defining the payload-hiding for original ciphertext security of flexible attribute-based PRE against adversary $\mathcal{A}$ (under chosen plaintext attacks) is given by the following game. A flexible CP-AB-PRE scheme has payload-hiding for original ciphertext security if, for all PPT adversaries $\mathcal{A}$, the advantage of $\mathcal{A}$ in winning the above game is negligible in the security parameter λ.

Setup. The challenger runs the setup algorithm $(\mathsf{pk}, \mathsf{msk}, \mathsf{rsk}) \xleftarrow{R} \mathsf{Setup}(1^\lambda)$, and it gives the security parameter λ and the public key pk to the adversary $\mathcal{A}$.
Phase 1. The adversary $\mathcal{A}$ is allowed to adaptively issue a polynomial number of queries as follows.
    Decryption key query. For a decryption key query S, the challenger gives $\mathsf{sk}_S \xleftarrow{R} \mathsf{KG}(\mathsf{pk}, \mathsf{msk}, S)$ to $\mathcal{A}$.
    Universal re-encryption key query. For a universal re-encryption key query S, the challenger computes $\mathsf{urk}_S \xleftarrow{R} \mathsf{URKG}(\mathsf{pk}, \mathsf{sk}_S)$ where $\mathsf{sk}_S \xleftarrow{R} \mathsf{KG}(\mathsf{pk}, \mathsf{msk}, S)$. It gives urk_S to $\mathcal{A}$.
    Re-encryption key query. For a re-encryption key query $(S, \mathbb{M}')$, the challenger computes $\mathsf{rk}_{S \to \mathbb{M}'} \xleftarrow{R} \mathsf{RKG}(\mathsf{pk}, \mathsf{URKG}(\mathsf{pk}, \mathsf{sk}_S), \mathsf{rsk}, \mathbb{M}')$ where $\mathsf{sk}_S \xleftarrow{R} \mathsf{KG}(\mathsf{pk}, \mathsf{msk}, S)$. It gives $\mathsf{rk}_{S \to \mathbb{M}'}$ to $\mathcal{A}$.
    Re-encryption query. For a re-encryption query $(\mathsf{oct}_{\mathbb{M}}, \mathbb{M}')$, the challenger computes $\mathsf{rk}_{S \to \mathbb{M}'} \xleftarrow{R} \mathsf{RKG}(\mathsf{pk}, \mathsf{URKG}(\mathsf{pk}, \mathsf{KG}(\mathsf{pk}, \mathsf{msk}, S)), \mathsf{rsk}, \mathbb{M}')$ and $\mathsf{rct}_{\mathbb{M}'} \xleftarrow{R} \mathsf{REnc}(\mathsf{pk}, \mathsf{rk}_{S \to \mathbb{M}'}, \mathsf{oct}_{\mathbb{M}})$ where $R(S, \mathbb{M}) = 1$, that is $\mathbb{M}$ satisfies S. It gives $\mathsf{rct}_{\mathbb{M}'}$ to $\mathcal{A}$.
Challenge. For a challenge query $(m^{(0)}, m^{(1)}, \mathbb{M}^*)$ subjected to the following restrictions: (1)Any decryption key query S satisfies $R(S, \mathbb{M}^*) = 0$ that is S is not satisfied $\mathbb{M}^*$. (2)Any re-encryption key query $(S, \mathbb{M}')$ and decryption key query S' satisfies $R(S, \mathbb{M}^*) \cdot R(S', \mathbb{M}') = 1$. The challenger flips a random bit $b \xleftarrow{U} \{0, 1\}$ and computes $\mathsf{oct}_{\mathbb{M}^*} \xleftarrow{R} \mathsf{Enc}(\mathsf{pk}, \mathbb{M}^*, m^{(b)})$. It gives the challenge original ciphertext $\mathsf{oct}_{\mathbb{M}^*}$ to $\mathcal{A}$.

Phase 2. The adversary $\mathcal{A}$ may continue to issue decryption key queries, universal re-encryption key queries, re-encryption key queries and re-encryption queries, subjected to the restriction in challenge phase and the following additional restriction for re-encryption queries.

    Re-encryption query. For a re-encryption query $(\mathsf{oct}_M, \mathbb{M}')$, subject to the following restrictions: $R(S', \mathbb{M}') = 0$ for any decryption key query for S' if $\mathsf{oct}_M = \mathsf{oct}_M^*$ which is the challenge ciphertext.

Guess. $\mathcal{A}$ outputs its guess $b' \in \{0,1\}$ for b and wins the game if $b = b'$.

We define the advantage of $\mathcal{A}$ as $\mathsf{Adv}_{\mathcal{A}}^{\mathsf{PH\text{-}OC}}(\lambda) := \Pr[b = b'] - \frac{1}{2}$.

Next, we describe a payload-hiding security for re-encrypted ciphertexts game.

Definition 8 (Payload-Hiding (PH) for Re-Encrypted Ciphertext Security). *The model for defining the payload-hiding for re-encrypted ciphertext security of flexible attribute-based PRE against adversary $\mathcal{A}$ (under chosen plaintext attacks) is given by the following game. A flexible CP-AB-PRE scheme has payload-hiding for re-encrypted ciphertext security if, for all PPT adversaries $\mathcal{A}$, the advantage of $\mathcal{A}$ in winning the above game is negligible in the security parameter λ.*

Setup and Phase1. Setup and Phase1 are same as in setup and phase 1 in Definition 7.

Phase 1. The adversary $\mathcal{A}$ is allowed to adaptively issue a polynomial number of decryption key queries, re-encryption key queries, and re-encryption queries as in phase 1 in Definition 7.

Challenge. For a challenge query $(m^{(0)}, m^{(1)}, \mathbb{M}_1^*, S_1^*, \mathbb{M}_2^*)$ subjected to the following restrictions: (1)An access structure $\mathbb{M}_1^*$ and an attribute S_1^* are satisfied $R(S_1^*, \mathbb{M}_1^*) = 1$. (2)Any decryption key query S_2 satisfies $R(S_2, \mathbb{M}_2^*) = 0$ that is S_2 is not satisfied $\mathbb{M}_2$. The challenger flips a random bit $b \xleftarrow{U} \{0,1\}$ and computes $\mathsf{oct}_{\mathbb{M}_1^*} \xleftarrow{R} \mathsf{Enc}(\mathsf{pk}, \mathbb{M}_1^*, m^{(b)})$, $\mathsf{rk}_{S_1 \to \mathbb{M}_2} \xleftarrow{R} \mathsf{RKG}(\mathsf{pk}, \mathsf{URKG}(\mathsf{pk}, \mathsf{KG}(\mathsf{pk}, \mathsf{msk}, S_1)), \mathsf{rsk}, \mathbb{M}_2))$, $\mathsf{rct}_{\mathbb{M}_2^*} \xleftarrow{R} \mathsf{REnc}(\mathsf{pk}, \mathsf{rk}_{S_1 \to \mathbb{M}_2}, \mathsf{oct}_{\mathbb{M}_1^*})$. It gives the challenge re-encrypted ciphertext $\mathsf{rct}_{\mathbb{M}_2^*}$ to $\mathcal{A}$.

Phase 2. The adversary $\mathcal{A}$ may continue to issue decryption key queries, universal re-encryption key queries, re-encryption key queries and re-encryption queries, subjected to the restriction in challenge phase.

Guess. $\mathcal{A}$ outputs its guess $b' \in \{0,1\}$ for b and wins the game if $b = b'$.

We define the advantage of $\mathcal{A}$ as $\mathsf{Adv}_{\mathcal{A}}^{\mathsf{PH\text{-}RC}}(\lambda) := \Pr[b = b'] - \frac{1}{2}$.

Selective Security. We say that a scheme is *selectively* secure if we add an **Init** phase before setup where the adversary commits to the challenge access structure(s). Our construction will be proved secure in the selective security model.

    Next, we define a payload-hiding security against RKG, who has a re-encryption secret key(rsk). Since RKG has rsk, malicious RKG can decrypt any original ciphertext by re-encrypting original ciphertext using rsk. So, an adversary who has rsk cannot obtain decryption keys in the following security game. This security notion is similar to *Type2* security in [13].

Definition 9 (Payload-Hiding (PH) for Original Ciphertext Security against RKG). *The model for defining the payload-hiding for original ciphertext against RKG security of flexible attribute-based PRE against adversary $\mathcal{A}$ (under chosen plaintext attacks) is given by the following game. A flexible CP-AB-PRE scheme has payload-hiding for re-encrypted ciphertext security if, for all PPT adversaries $\mathcal{A}$, the advantage of $\mathcal{A}$ in winning the above game is negligible in the security parameter λ.*

Setup. The challenger runs the setup algorithm $(\mathsf{pk}, \mathsf{msk}, \mathsf{rsk}) \xleftarrow{R} \mathsf{Setup}(1^\lambda)$, and it gives the security parameter λ and the public key pk and rsk to the adversary $\mathcal{A}$.

Challenge. For a challenge query $(m^{(0)}, m^{(1)}, \mathbb{M}^*)$. The challenger flips a random bit $b \xleftarrow{U} \{0,1\}$ and computes $\mathsf{oct}_{\mathbb{M}^*} \xleftarrow{R} \mathsf{Enc}(\mathsf{pk}, \mathbb{M}^*, m^{(b)})$. It gives the challenge original ciphertext $\mathsf{oct}_{\mathbb{M}^*}$ to $\mathcal{A}$.

Guess. $\mathcal{A}$ outputs its guess $b' \in \{0,1\}$ for b and wins the game if $b = b'$.

We define the advantage of $\mathcal{A}$ as $\mathsf{Adv}_{\mathcal{A}}^{\mathsf{PH-OC-RKG}}(\lambda) := \Pr[b = b'] - \frac{1}{2}$.

Next, we describe a payload-hiding security for re-encrypted ciphertexts game against RKG.

Definition 10 (Payload-Hiding (PH) for Re-Encrypted Ciphertext Security against RKG). *The model for defining the payload-hiding for re-encrypted ciphertext against RKG security of flexible attribute-based PRE against adversary $\mathcal{A}$ (under chosen plaintext attacks) is given by the following game. A flexible CP-AB-PRE scheme has payload-hiding for re-encrypted ciphertext security if, for all PPT adversaries $\mathcal{A}$, the advantage of $\mathcal{A}$ in winning the above game is negligible in the security parameter λ.*

Setup. Setup is same as in setup and phase 1 in Definition 9.

Challenge. For a challenge query $(m^{(0)}, m^{(1)}, \mathbb{M}_1^*, S_1^*, \mathbb{M}_2^*)$. The challenger flips a random bit $b \xleftarrow{U} \{0,1\}$ and computes $\mathsf{oct}_{\mathbb{M}_1^*} \xleftarrow{R} \mathsf{Enc}(\mathsf{pk}, \mathbb{M}_1^*, m^{(b)})$, $\mathsf{rk}_{S_1 \to \mathbb{M}_2} \xleftarrow{R} \mathsf{RKG}(\mathsf{pk}, \mathsf{URKG}(\mathsf{KG}(\mathsf{pk}, \mathsf{msk}, S_1)), \mathsf{rsk}, \mathbb{M}_2)) \; \mathsf{rct}_{\mathbb{M}_2^*} \xleftarrow{R} \mathsf{REnc}(\mathsf{pk}, \mathsf{rk}_{S_1 \to \mathbb{M}_2}, \mathsf{oct}_{\mathbb{M}_1^*})$. It gives the challenge re-encrypted ciphertext $\mathsf{rct}_{\mathbb{M}_2^*}$ to $\mathcal{A}$.

Guess. $\mathcal{A}$ outputs its guess $b' \in \{0,1\}$ for b and wins the game if $b = b'$.

We define the advantage of $\mathcal{A}$ as $\mathsf{Adv}_{\mathcal{A}}^{\mathsf{PH-RC-RKG}}(\lambda) := \Pr[b = b'] - \frac{1}{2}$.

4   Proposed Construction

Specific Construction. We describe our specific construction of flexible CP-AB-PRE scheme based on adaptable CP-ABE [13].

Setup takes a security parameter λ and a small universe description $U = \{1, 2, \ldots, |U|\}$. It outputs a bilinear group $(p, \mathbb{G}, \mathbb{G}_T, e)$ where $\mathbb{G}$ and $\mathbb{G}_T$ are cyclic groups of prime order p. It picks $g, h_1, \ldots, h_{|U|}, \widehat{h}_1, \ldots, \widehat{h}_{|U|} \xleftarrow{U} \mathbb{G}$ and

$\alpha, \beta, \widehat{\alpha}, \widehat{\beta} \xleftarrow{\mathsf{U}} \mathbb{Z}_p$. Next, it chooses an (dummy) access structure $\widetilde{\mathbb{M}} = (\widetilde{M}, \tilde{\rho})$ where $\widetilde{M}$ is a $\tilde{\ell} \times \tilde{n}$ matrix[3]. And, let $\mathsf{E} : \mathbb{Z}_p \to \mathbb{G}_T$ be an encoding between $\mathbb{Z}_p$ and $\mathbb{G}_T$. It sets $\mathsf{pk} := (\mathbb{G}, \mathbb{G}_T, e, g, g^\beta, g^{\widehat{\beta}}, e(g,g)^\alpha, e(g,g)^{\widehat{\alpha}}, h_1, \ldots, h_{|U|}, \widehat{h}_1,$ $\ldots, \widehat{h}_{|U|}, \mathsf{E}, \widetilde{\mathbb{M}}), \mathsf{msk} := (\alpha, \beta, \widehat{\alpha}, \widehat{\beta})$, and $\mathsf{rsk} := \widehat{\beta}$. and returns $(\mathsf{pk}, \mathsf{msk}, \mathsf{rsk})$.

KG takes $(\mathsf{pk}, \mathsf{msk}, S)$ where S is a set of attributes as input, first if $R(S, \widetilde{\mathbb{M}}) = 1$ output $\perp$[3]. Otherwise, it generates $K_0 := g^\alpha g^{\beta t}$, $K_1 := g^t$, $\widehat{K}_0 := g^{\widehat{\alpha}} g^{\widehat{\beta} \widehat{t}}$, $\widehat{K}_1 := g^{\widehat{t}}$, $K_{2.i} := h_i^t$, $\widehat{K}_{2.i} := \widehat{h}_i^{\widehat{t}}$ where $t, \widehat{t} \xleftarrow{\mathsf{U}} \mathbb{Z}_p, \forall i \in S$, and returns $\mathsf{sk}_S := (S, K_0, K_1, \widehat{K}_0, \widehat{K}_1, \{K_{2.i}, \widehat{K}_{2.i}\}_{i \in S})$.

Enc takes $(\mathsf{pk}, m \in \mathbb{G}_T, \mathbb{M} := (M, \rho)))$ where M is an $\ell \times n$ matrix as input, and picks a random vector $\boldsymbol{v} := (s, v_2, \ldots, v_n) \in \mathbb{Z}_p^n$. These values will be used to share the encryption exponent s. It picks $r_i \in \mathbb{Z}_p$ for each row M_i of M to an attribute $\rho(i)$. Next, it generates $C_0 := m \cdot e(g,g)^{\alpha s}$, $C_1 := g^s$, $C_{2.i} := g^{\beta M_i \boldsymbol{v}} h_{\rho(i)}^{-r_i}$, $D_i := g^{r_i}$ where $\forall i \in \{1, 2, \ldots, \ell\}$ and returns $\mathsf{oct}_{\mathbb{M}} := (\mathbb{M}, C_0, C_1, \{C_{2.i}, D_i\}_{i \in \{1,2,\ldots,\ell\}})$.

URKG takes $(\mathsf{pk}, \mathsf{sk}_S)$ as input. First, it picks $d \xleftarrow{\mathsf{U}} \mathbb{Z}_p$ and generates $RK_0 := K_0^d = (g^\alpha g^{\beta t})^d$, $RK_1 := K_1^d = g^{td}$, $RK_{2.i} := K_{2.i}^d = h_i^{td}$. where $\forall i \in S$.

Next, it picks a random vector $\tilde{\boldsymbol{v}} := (\tilde{s}, \tilde{v}_2, \ldots, \tilde{v}_{\tilde{n}}) \in \mathbb{Z}_p^{\tilde{n}}$ and $\tilde{r}_i \in \mathbb{Z}_p$ for each row $\widetilde{M}_i$ of $\widetilde{M}$ to an attribute $\tilde{\rho}(i)$. It generates $\widehat{RC}_0 := \mathsf{E}(d) \cdot e(g,g)^{\widehat{\alpha} \tilde{s}}$, $\widehat{RC}_1 := g^{\tilde{s}}$ $\widehat{RC}_{2.i} := g^{\widehat{\beta} \widetilde{M}_i \tilde{\boldsymbol{v}}} \widehat{h}_{\tilde{\rho}(i)}^{-\tilde{r}_i}$, $\widehat{RD}_i := g^{\tilde{r}_i}$ where $\forall i \in \{1, \ldots, \tilde{\ell}\}$. Finally, it returns $\mathsf{urk}_S := (S, RK_0, RK_1, \{RK_{2.i}\}_{i \in S}, \widehat{RC}_0, \widehat{RC}_1, \{\widehat{RC}_{2.i}, \widehat{RD}_i\}_{i \in \{1,2,\ldots,\tilde{\ell}\}})$.

RKG takes $(\mathsf{pk}, \mathsf{urk}_S, \mathsf{rsk} = \widehat{\beta}, \mathbb{M}' = (M', \rho'))$ as input where M' is a $\ell' \times n'$ matrix. It picks a random vector $\boldsymbol{v}' := (s', \widehat{v}_2, \ldots, \widehat{v}_{n'}) \in \mathbb{Z}_p^{n'}$ and $r_i' \in \mathbb{Z}_p$ for each row M_i' of M' to an attribute $\rho'(i)$. Let $\widehat{\boldsymbol{v}} := (\widehat{s} = \tilde{s} + s', \widehat{v}_2, \ldots, \widehat{v}_{n'}) \in \mathbb{Z}_p^{n'}$. It generates $\widehat{RC}_0' := \widehat{RC}_0 \cdot (e(g,g)^{\widehat{\alpha}})^{s'}$, $\widehat{RC}_1' := \widehat{RC}_1 \cdot g^{s'} = g^{\widehat{s}}$ $\widehat{RC}_{2.i}' := g^{\widehat{\beta} M_i' \widehat{\boldsymbol{v}}} h_{\rho'(i)}^{-r_i'}$, $\widehat{RD}_i' := g^{r_i'}$ where $\forall i \in \{1, 2, \ldots, \ell'\}$ Note that, though the parameter s (or $\widehat{s}$) is not known, $g^{\widehat{\beta} M_i' \widehat{\boldsymbol{v}}}$ can be computed as follow by using $\mathsf{rsk} = \widehat{\beta}$ [4]. Finally, it returns $\mathsf{rk}_{S \to \mathbb{M}'} := (S, \mathbb{M}', RK_0, RK_1, \{RK_{2.i}\}_{i \in S}, \widehat{RC}_0', \widehat{RC}_1', \{\widehat{RC}_{2.i}', \widehat{RD}_i'\}_{i \in \{1,2,\ldots,\ell'\}})$.

REnc takes $(\mathsf{pk}, \mathsf{rk}_{S \to \mathbb{M}'}, \mathsf{oct}_{\mathbb{M}})$ as input where M (resp., M') is an $\ell \times n$ (resp., $\ell' \times n'$) matrix. If $R(S, \mathbb{M}) = 0$, it returns the special symbol $\perp$. Otherwise, let $I \subset \{1, 2, \ldots, \ell\}$ be defined as $I = \{i : \rho(i) \in S\}$. It computes constants

---

[3] This dummy access structure $\widetilde{\mathbb{M}}$ is used in URKG algorithm. If an adversary has a decryption key $\mathsf{sk}_{\tilde{S}}$ corresponding to a set of attributes $\tilde{S}$ where $R(\tilde{S}, \widetilde{\mathbb{M}}) = 1$, the adversary can obtain the secret key from a universal re-encryption keys urk, since $\mathsf{E}(d)$ is encrypted under $\widetilde{\mathbb{M}}$ in URKG. So, KG has not to generate a decryption key $\mathsf{sk}_{\tilde{S}}$.

[4] $g^{\widehat{\beta} M_i' \widehat{\boldsymbol{v}}} = g^{\widehat{\beta}(m_{i,1}' \widehat{s} + m_{i,2} \widehat{v}_2 + \ldots + m_{i,n}' \widehat{v}_{n'})} = g^{\widehat{\beta} m_{i,1}' \widehat{s}} \cdot g^{\widehat{\beta}(m_{i,2}' \widehat{v}_2 + \ldots + m_{i,n}' \widehat{v}_{n'})} = (\widehat{RC}_1')^{\widehat{\beta} m_{i,1}'} \cdot g^{\widehat{\beta}(m_{i,2}' \widehat{v}_2 + \ldots + m_{i,n}' \widehat{v}_{n'})}$ where $M_i' = (m_{i,1}', \ldots, m_{i,n'}')$.

$\omega_i \in \mathbb{Z}_p$ such that $\Sigma_{i \in I} \omega_i M_i = (1, 0, \ldots, 0)$ where M_i is i-th row of M. It generates as follow:

$$ReC_1 := \frac{e(C_1, RK_0)}{\prod_{i \in I}(e(C_{2.i}, RK_1) \cdot e(RK_{2.\rho(i)}, D_i))^{\omega_i}} = e(g, g)^{sad}$$

and sets $ReC_0 := C_0$. Finally, it returns $\mathsf{rct}_{\mathbb{M}'} := (\mathbb{M}', ReC_0, ReC_1, \widehat{RC}_0', \widehat{RC}_1', \{\widehat{RC}_{2.i}', \widehat{RD}_i'\}_{i \in \{1,2,\ldots,\ell'\}})$.

$\mathsf{Dec}_{\mathsf{Enc}}$ takes $(\mathsf{pk}, \mathsf{sk}_S := (S, K_0, K_1, \widehat{K}_0, \widehat{K}_1, \{K_{2.i}, \widehat{K}_{2.i}\}_{i \in S}), \mathsf{oct}_{\mathbb{M}} := (\mathbb{M} = (M, \rho), C_0, C_1, \{C_{2.i}, D_i\}_{i \in \{1,2,\ldots,\ell\}}))$ as input where M is a $\ell \times n$ matrix. If $R(S, \mathbb{M}) = 0$, it returns the special symbol $\perp$. Otherwise, let $I \subset \{1, 2, \ldots, \ell\}$ be defined as $I = \{i : \rho(i) \in S\}$. It computes constants $\omega_i \in \mathbb{Z}_p$ such that $\Sigma_{i \in I} \omega_i M_i = (1, 0, \ldots, 0)$ where M_i is i-th row of M. It computes

$$C_0 \cdot \frac{\prod_{i \in I}(e(C_{2.i}, K_1) \cdot e(K_{2.\rho(i)}, D_i))^{\omega_i}}{e(C_1, K_0)} = \frac{m \cdot e(g, g)^{\alpha s}}{e(g, g)^{s\alpha}} = m$$

and returns m.

$\mathsf{Dec}_{\mathsf{ReEnc}}$ takes $(\mathsf{pk}, \mathsf{sk}_{S'} := (S', K_0', K_1', \widehat{K}_0', \widehat{K}_1', \{K_{2.i}', \widehat{K}_{2.i}'\}_{i \in S'}), \mathsf{rct}_{\mathbb{M}'} := (\mathbb{M}'' = (M', \rho'), ReC_0, ReC_1, RC_0', RC_1', \{RC_{2.i}', RD_i'\}_{i \in \{1,2,\ldots,\ell'\}}))$ as input where M' is a $\ell' \times n'$ matrix. If $R(S', \mathbb{M}') = 0$, it returns the special symbol $\perp$. Otherwise, let $I' \subset \{1, 2, \ldots, \ell'\}$ be defined as $I' = \{i : \rho'(i) \in S'\}$. It computes constants $\omega_i' \in \mathbb{Z}_p$ such that $\Sigma_{i \in I'} \omega_i' M_i' = (1, 0, \ldots, 0)$ where M_i' is i-th row of M'. It computes

$$\widehat{RC}_0' \cdot \frac{\prod_{i \in I'}(e(\widehat{RC}_{2.i}', \widehat{K}_1') \cdot e(\widehat{K}_{2.\rho'(i)}', \widehat{RD}_i'))^{\omega_i'}}{e(\widehat{RC}_1', \widehat{K}_0')} = \mathsf{E}(d)$$

Next, it computes d by decoding $\mathsf{E}(d)$ and computes $ReC_0/ReC_1^{1/d} = m \cdot e(g, g)^{\alpha s}/(e(g, g)^{\alpha s d})^{1/d} = m$. Finally, it returns m.

Remark 2. In proposed construction, we use an encoding function E. Practically, d is encrypted using a symmetric key encryption and KEM-DEM framework.

Security. Our scheme is constructed based on the adaptable CP-ABE [13]. Since this adaptable CP-ABE is selectively secure, thus our proposed construction is also selectively secure. Our security proofs of Theorem 1 is similar to the proof of Waters CP-ABE [27] and proofs of Theorem 2 is similar to the proof of adaptable CP-ABE [13] (*Type2* adversary), respectively.

Theorem 1. *If decisional q-parallel BDHE assumption holds, proposed flexible CP-AB-PRE has payload-Hiding for original and re-encrypted ciphertexts security against any PPT adversary $\mathcal{A}$ in selective model.*

Theorem 2. *If decisional DBDH assumption holds, proposed flexible CP-AB-PRE has payload-Hiding for original and re-encrypted ciphertext against RKG security against any PPT adversary $\mathcal{A}$.*

4.1   Re-encryption Queries

In our security proof, an adversary $\mathcal{A}$ cannot be allowed to access *re-encryption* query. If $\mathcal{A}$ is allowed submitting re-encryption query, $\mathcal{A}$ can break PH-OC security by using the following steps. First, $\mathcal{A}$ modifies C_0^* which is the part of challenge ciphertext to $C_0'^* := X \cdot C_0^* = X \cdot m^{(\mathbf{b})} \cdot e(g, g)^{\alpha s}$ by choosing a randomness $X \in \mathbb{G}_T$. Next, $\mathcal{A}$ submits $(\mathsf{oct}'_{\mathbb{M}*}, \mathbb{M}'^*)$ where $\mathsf{oct}'_{\mathbb{M}*}$ which exchanged C_0^* to $C_0'^*$ in the challenge ciphertext $\mathsf{oct}_{\mathbb{M}*}$, and obtains the re-encrypted ciphertext $\mathsf{rct}_{\mathbb{M}'*}$. Here, since $\mathsf{oct}'_{\mathbb{M}*}$ is not equivalent to the challenge ciphertext, $\mathcal{A}$ can obtain the decryption key $\mathsf{sk}_{S'*}$ where $R(S'^*, \mathbb{M}'^*) = 1$ by using decryption key query. Thus, $\mathcal{A}$ decrypts $\mathsf{rct}_{\mathbb{M}'*}$ by using $\mathsf{sk}_{S'*}$ and can obtain $X \cdot m^{(\mathbf{b})}$ by decrypting $\mathsf{rct}_{\mathbb{M}'*}$ with $\mathsf{sk}_{S'*}$. Finally, $\mathcal{A}$ can compute $m^{(\mathbf{b})}$ by using X which is chosen by own. The reason that this attack works is that original ciphertext does not have non-malleability (chosen ciphertext security). So, our scheme can be modified by using the technique of Canetti, Hallevi, and Katz [7] in order to protect the above attacks.

References

1. Ateniese, G., Fu, K., Green, M., Hohenberger, S.: Improved Proxy Re-encryption Schemes with Applications to Secure Distributed Storage. ACM Trans. Inf. Syst. Secur. 9(1), 1–30 (2006)
2. Beimel, A.: Secure schemes for secret sharing and key distribution. PhD Thesis, Israel Institute of Technology, Technion, Haifa (1996)
3. Bethencourt, J., Sahai, A., Waters, B.: Ciphertext-policy attribute-based encryption. In: IEEE Symposium on Security and Privacy, pp. 321–334 (2007)
4. Blaze, M., Bleumer, G., Strauss, M.J.: Divertible Protocols and Atomic Proxy Cryptography. In: Nyberg, K. (ed.) EUROCRYPT 1998. LNCS, vol. 1403, pp. 127–144. Springer, Heidelberg (1998)
5. Boneh, D., Hamburg, M.: Generalized identity based and broadcast encryption schemes. In: Pieprzyk, J. (ed.) ASIACRYPT 2008. LNCS, vol. 5350, pp. 455–470. Springer, Heidelberg (2008)
6. Boneh, D., Waters, B.: Conjunctive, subset, and range queries on encrypted data. In: Vadhan, S.P. (ed.) TCC 2007. LNCS, vol. 4392, pp. 535–554. Springer, Heidelberg (2007)
7. Canetti, R., Halevi, S., Katz, J.: Chosen-ciphertext security from identity-based encryption. In: Cachin, C., Camenisch, J.L. (eds.) EUROCRYPT 2004. LNCS, vol. 3027, pp. 207–222. Springer, Heidelberg (2004)
8. Canetti, R., Hohenberger, S.: Chosen-Ciphertext Secure Proxy Re-encryption. In: Proceedings of the 14th ACM Conference on Computer and Communications Security - ACM CCS 2007, pp. 185–194 (2007)
9. Chow, S.S.M., Weng, J., Yang, Y., Deng, R.H.: Efficient Unidirectional Proxy Re-Encryption. In: Bernstein, D.J., Lange, T. (eds.) AFRICACRYPT 2010. LNCS, vol. 6055, pp. 316–332. Springer, Heidelberg (2010)
10. Emura, K., Miyaji, A., Omote, K.: An Identity-Based Proxy Re-Encryption Scheme with Source Hiding Property, and its Application to a Mailing-List System. In: Camenisch, J., Lambrinoudakis, C. (eds.) EuroPKI 2010. LNCS, vol. 6711, pp. 77–92. Springer, Heidelberg (2011)

11. Goyal, V., Pandey, O., Sahai, A., Waters, B.: Attribute-based encryption for fine-grained access control of encrypted data. In: Proceedings of the 13th ACM Conference on Computer and Communications Security - ACM CCS 2006, pp. 89–98 (2006)
12. Green, M., Ateniese, G.: Identity-Based Proxy Re-encryption. In: Katz, J., Yung, M. (eds.) ACNS 2007. LNCS, vol. 4521, pp. 288–306. Springer, Heidelberg (2007)
13. Lai, J., Deng, R.H., Yang, Y., Weng, J.: Adaptable Ciphertext-Policy Attribute-Based Encryption. In: Cao, Z., Zhang, F. (eds.) Pairing 2013. LNCS, vol. 8365, pp. 199–214. Springer, Heidelberg (2014)
14. Kawai, Y., Takashima, K.: Fully-Anonymous Functional Proxy-Re-Encryption. IACR Cryptology ePrint Archive, pp. 318, 201
15. Liang, K., Fang, L., Wong, D.S., Susilo, W.: A ciphertext-policy attribute-based proxy re-encryption with chosen-ciphertext security. IACR Cryptology ePrint Archive, 2013, 236 (2013)
16. Liang, X., Cao, Z., Lin, H., Shao, J.: Attribute based proxy re-encryption with delegating capabilities. In: Proceedings of the 4th International Symposium on Information, Computer, and Communications Security, ASIACCS 2009, pp. 276–286. ACM (2009)
17. Libert, B., Vergnaud, D.: Unidirectional Chosen-Ciphertext Secure Proxy Re-encryption. In: Cramer, R. (ed.) PKC 2008. LNCS, vol. 4939, pp. 360–379. Springer, Heidelberg (2008)
18. Luo, S., Hu, J., Chen, Z.: Ciphertext Policy Attribute-Based Proxy Re-encryption. In: Soriano, M., Qing, S., López, J. (eds.) ICICS 2010. LNCS, vol. 6476, pp. 401–415. Springer, Heidelberg (2010)
19. Matsuo, T.: Proxy re-encryption systems for identity-based encryption. In: Takagi, T., Okamoto, T., Okamoto, E., Okamoto, T. (eds.) Pairing 2007. LNCS, vol. 4575, pp. 247–267. Springer, Heidelberg (2007), http://dx.doi.org/10.1007/978-3-540-73489-5_13
20. Mizuno, T., Doi, H.: Hybrid proxy re-encryption scheme for attribute-based encryption. In: Bao, F., Yung, M., Lin, D., Jing, J. (eds.) Inscrypt 2009. LNCS, vol. 6151, pp. 288–302. Springer, Heidelberg (2010)
21. Ostrovsky, R., Sahai, A., Waters, B.: Attribute-based encryption with non-monotonic access structures. In: ACM CCS 2007, pp. 195–203 (2007)
22. Pirretti, M., Traynor, P., McDaniel, P., Waters, B.: Secure attribute-based systems. In: ACM CCS 2006, pp. 99–112 (2006)
23. Sahai, A., Waters, B.: Fuzzy identity-based encryption. In: Cramer, R. (ed.) EUROCRYPT 2005. LNCS, vol. 3494, pp. 457–473. Springer, Heidelberg (2005)
24. Arita, S.: Flexible Attribute-Based Encryption. In: Chim, T.W., Yuen, T.H. (eds.) ICICS 2012. LNCS, vol. 7618, pp. 471–478. Springer, Heidelberg (2012)
25. Shao, J., Cao, Z.: CCA-Secure Proxy Re-encryption without Pairings. In: Jarecki, S., Tsudik, G. (eds.) PKC 2009. LNCS, vol. 5443, pp. 357–376. Springer, Heidelberg (2009)
26. Shi, E., Waters, B.: Delegating capabilities in predicate encryption systems. In: Aceto, L., Damgård, I., Goldberg, L.A., Halldórsson, M.M., Ingólfsdóttir, A., Walukiewicz, I. (eds.) ICALP 2008, Part II. LNCS, vol. 5126, pp. 560–578. Springer, Heidelberg (2008)
27. Waters, B.: Ciphertext-policy attribute-based encryption: An expressive, efficient, and provably secure realization. In: Catalano, D., Fazio, N., Gennaro, R., Nicolosi, A. (eds.) PKC 2011. LNCS, vol. 6571, pp. 53–70. Springer, Heidelberg (2011)

Revocable Threshold Attribute-Based Signature against Signing Key Exposure

Jianghong Wei[1], Xinyi Huang[2], Xuexian Hu[1], and Wenfen Liu[1,*]

[1] State Key Laboratory of Mathematical Engineering and Advanced Computing,
Zhengzhou 450002, China
[2] School of Mathematics and Computer Science, Fujian Normal University,
Fuzhou 350007, China

Abstract. For a cryptosystem with a large number of users, it is necessary to provide an efficient revocation mechanism to preserve the security of whole system. In this paper, we aim to provide a scalable revocation mechanism for attribute-based signature (ABS). Specifically, we first formally define the syntax of revocable ABS (RABS), followed with a corresponding security model that considers a realistic threat called *signing key exposure*. Then, built on the ideas of an ABS scheme and binary data structure, we present a concrete construction of RABS with signing key exposure resistance. Finally, the proposed scheme is proved to be existentially unforgeable under adaptively chosen message attacks in the selective-predicate model, without random oracles. In addition to the necessary revocation functionality, the proposed scheme remains efficient in terms of storage cost and computation complexity.

Keywords: Attribute-based signature, revocation, signing key exposure.

1 Introduction

In order to defend the security of a cryptosystem with a large number of users, an efficient revocation mechanism is necessary to inform that a user's authorization is expired or a user's secret key is compromised. Once a user is revoked, the original secret key can no longer be used to access sensitive data or produce digital signatures. The revocation problem was initially studied in the setting of public key infrastructure (PKI), and several revocation means [5,11] have been proposed and implemented. To eliminate the mandatory need for PKI, Shamir [17] introduced the notion of identity-based encryption (IBE), which was first instantiated by Boneh and Franklin [3] with bilinear pairing over elliptic curves. Furthermore, Sahai and Waters [14] extended the notion of IBE to attribute-based encryption (ABE) to deal with fine-grained access control. Either in the context of IBE or ABE, a revocation mechanism is equally needed.

Based on an ABE scheme [14] and binary tree data structure, Boldyreva et al. [2] first proposed an IBE scheme with efficient revocation, in which the

---

* Corresponding author.

© Springer International Publishing Switzerland 2015
J. Lopez and Y. Wu (Eds.): ISPEC 2015, LNCS 9065, pp. 316–330, 2015.
DOI: 10.1007/978-3-319-17533-1_22

complexity of the authority performing key update is logarithmic in the number of non-revoked users. Subsequently, Libert and Vergnaud [9] constructed an adaptively secure revocable IBE, and Seo and Emura [15] further enhanced its security by allowing an adversary to obtain decryption key. Using the binary tree data structure in a similar manner, Attrapadung and Imai [1] introduced directly/indirectly revocable ABE schemes. Moreover, Sahai et al. [13] gave a generic construction of revocable ABE.

Besides public key encryption, the revocation problem in the setting of digital signature is also well studied. Particularly, Lian et al. [8] proposed a revocable attribute-based signature (RABS) scheme. In their scheme, each time period is regarded as an attribute, and the authority periodically distributes a new key component corresponding to the current time period for each non-revoked user. We note that this scheme does not scale well, and also cannot withstand a realistic threat named signing key exposure. Namely, an adversary can extract a signer's secret key from a compromised signing key, and then forges signatures by combining it with subsequent updated keys.

Related Work. The notion of ABS was formalized by Maji et al. [10], associated with three concrete ABS schemes for general signing predicates. However, the security of these schemes is proved secure in a generic group model. Shahandashti and Safavi-Naini [16], Li et al. [7] respectively proposed an ABS scheme supporting flexible threshold signing predicates under a standard assumption. Herranz et al. [6] noted that the signature size of all previous ABS schemes is linear in the number of attributes used to produce the signature, and thus constructed two threshold ABS schemes with constant signature size. Based on a fully secure ABE scheme, Okomato and Takashima [12] presented the first fully secure ABS scheme for non-monotone predicates.

Our Contribution. In this paper, we present a scalable RABS scheme with enhanced security. Specifically speaking, we first formally define the syntax of RABS, and present a security model for RABS against signing key exposure. Furthermore, based on Herranz et al.'s [6] ABS scheme and binary tree data structure, we give a concrete construction of RABS supporting flexible threshold predicates. Finally, we prove the security of the proposed scheme under ℓ-Diffie-Hellman Exponent (ℓ-DHE) assumption in the defined model without random oracles. The performance discussions show that our scheme still remains efficient in terms of computation complexity and storage cost, with the functionality of revocation.

1.1 Outline

The remainder of the paper is structured as follows: In Section 2, we review some preliminaries. Then we formally define RABS and present a security model in Section 3. A concrete construction of RABS scheme is provided in Section 4. We give the security proof and performance discussions of the proposed scheme in Section 5. Finally, we conclude this paper in Section 6.

2   Preliminaries

Lagrange Interpolation. Firstly, the Lagrange coefficient is defined as $\Delta_i^{\Upsilon}(x) = \prod_{j \in \Upsilon, j \neq i} \frac{x-j}{i-j}$, where $i \in \mathbb{Z}_p$, $\Upsilon \subseteq \mathbb{Z}_p$, and p is a prime number. Then, a polynomial $q(x)$ over $\mathbb{Z}_p$ with order $d-1$ can be evaluated by using Lagrange interpolation as $q(x) = \sum_{i \in \Upsilon} q(i) \Delta_i^{\Upsilon}(x)$, where $|\Upsilon| = d$.

Complexity Assumption. [4]. Let G_1 be a finite cyclic group with prime order p, and let g be a generator of G_1. Given an instance of ℓ-DHE problem in the form of $(G_1, p, g, g^a, \ldots, g^{a^{\ell}}, g^{a^{\ell+2}}, \ldots, g^{a^{2\ell}})$, where $a \in \mathbb{Z}_p$, denote $Adv_{G_1}^{\ell\text{-DHE}}(\mathcal{A})$ the probability of a probabilistic polynomial-time (PPT) adversary $\mathcal{A}$ successfully computing $g^{a^{\ell+1}}$.

Definition 1. *We say that ℓ-DHE assumption holds on a cyclic group G_1 if for any PPT adversary $\mathcal{A}$, its advantage $Adv_{G_1}^{\ell\text{-DHE}}(\mathcal{A})$ is negligible.*

KUNode Algorithm. In order to improve the key update efficiency, we mainly follow Boldyreva et al.'s [2] strategy that defines a KUNode algorithm by using binary tree data structure. For convenience, we first give several notations. Let $\mathcal{BT}$ be a binary tree with $N = 2^n$ leaf nodes, root be the root node. For each non-leaf node θ, denote by θ_l and θ_r its left and right child, respectively. Each user is assigned a leaf node η, and denote by $\mathsf{Path}(\eta)$ the set of all nodes over the path from root to η.

The KUNode algorithm takes as input a binary tree $\mathcal{BT}$, a revocation list RL comprised of two-tuples recorded in the form of (η_i, t_i) and a time period t. It outputs a minimal set Y of nodes of $\mathcal{BT}$ such that for any node $\eta \in RL$ it holds that $\mathsf{Path}(\eta) \cap \mathsf{Y} = \emptyset$. Below we give the details of this algorithm.

$$\mathsf{KUNode}(\mathcal{BT}, RL, t):$$
$$\mathsf{X}, \mathsf{Y} \leftarrow \emptyset$$
$$\forall (\eta_i, t_i) \in RL$$
$$\quad \text{if } t_i \leq t \text{ then add } \mathsf{Path}(\eta_i) \text{ to}$$
$$\qquad \mathsf{X}$$
$$\forall \theta \in \mathsf{X}$$
$$\quad \text{if } \theta_l \notin \mathsf{X} \text{ then add } \theta_l \text{ to } \mathsf{Y}$$
$$\quad \text{if } \theta_r \notin \mathsf{X} \text{ then add } \theta_r \text{ to } \mathsf{Y}$$
$$\text{If } \mathsf{Y} = \emptyset \text{ then add root to } \mathsf{Y}$$
$$\text{Return } \mathsf{Y}$$

3   Definition and Security Model of RABS

In this section, we give the formal definition of RABS and the corresponding security model. Since we focus on threshold signing policies in this paper, the following definition is specialized for such policies in form of $\Gamma_{k,W}(\cdot)$, where W is an attribute set and k is an integer satisfying $1 \leq k \leq |W|$. We say that an attribute set S satisfies the signing policy $\Gamma_{k,W}(\cdot)$ (i.e., $\Gamma_{k,W}(S)=1$) provided that $|W \cap S| \geq k$. Conversely, if $|W \cap S| < k$, we say that S does not satisfy $\Gamma_{k,W}(\cdot)$ (i.e., $\Gamma_{k,W}(S) = 0$).

3.1   Definition of RABS

Definition 2 (Revocable Attribute-based Signature). *A revocable attribute-based signature scheme supporting threshold signing predicates with respect to an attribute universe U, a message space $\mathcal{M}$, an identifier space $\mathcal{I}$ and a time bound T consists of the following algorithms:*

Setup(λ): The setup algorithm takes as input a security parameter λ, and then chooses an upper bound on the size of threshold predicates d and a maximum number of system users N. It outputs the public parameter PP, the master secret key MSK, the initial revocation list $RL = \emptyset$ and a state st.

Extract(PP, MSK, S, ID): The extraction algorithm takes as input PP, MSK, an attribute set S associated with a unique identifier $ID \in \mathcal{I}$, and outputs a secret key $SK_{S,ID}$ and an updated state st.

KeyUp(PP, MSK, RL, t, st): The key update algorithm takes as input PP, MSK, the current revocation list RL, the current time period $t \leq T$ and state st, and outputs an update key UK_t.

SKGen($PP, SK_{S,ID}, UK_t$): The signing key generation algorithm takes as input PP, $SK_{S,ID}$, UK_t, and outputs a signing key $SK_{S,ID}^t$ if ID is not revoked at time period t. Otherwise, it outputs an error symbol $\perp$.

Sign($PP, SK_{S,ID}^t, \Gamma_{k,W}(\cdot), t, m$): The signing algorithm takes as input PP, $SK_{S,ID}^t$, a signing policy $\Gamma_{k,W}(\cdot)$ satisfying $k \leq |W| \leq d$, the current time period t and a message $m \in \mathcal{M}$, and outputs a signature σ on m with respect to $\Gamma_{k,W}(\cdot)$ and t.

Verify($PP, \Gamma_{k,W}(\cdot), m, t, \sigma$): The verification algorithm takes as input PP, $\Gamma_{k,W}(\cdot)$ m, t and σ, and outputs 1 indicating that σ is valid and 0 otherwise.

Revoke(ID, RL, t, st): The revocation algorithm takes as input an identifier ID to be revoked, the current revocation list RL, a revocation time period t and a state st. It outputs an updated revocation list RL.

CORRECTNESS OF RABS. Given a threshold RABS scheme, for any

- $(PP, MSK, RL, st) \leftarrow$ Setup(λ), $(SK_{S,ID}, st) \leftarrow$ Extract(PP, MSK, S, ID),
- $UK_t \leftarrow$ KeyUp(PP, MSK, RL, t, st), $SK_{S,ID}^t \leftarrow$ SKGen($PP, SK_{S,ID}, UK_t$),

its correctness requires that

$$\text{Verify}\big(PP, \Gamma_{k,W}(\cdot), \text{Sign}(PP, SK_{S,ID}^t, \Gamma_{k,W}(\cdot), t, m)\big) = 1, \quad \text{if } \Gamma_{k,W}(S) = 1.$$

3.2   Security Model for RABS

An attribute-based signature scheme should satisfy two kinds of typical security requirements, i.e., unforgeability and attribute signer privacy.

Unforgeability. In this work, we consider a kind of relatively weak unforgeability for RABS, namely, *semi-static* selective-predicate unforgeability under chosen message attacks (sP-UF-CMA), which requires an adversary to submit a challenged signing predicate $\Gamma_{k^*,W^*}(\cdot)$ and a time period t^* associated with the corresponding revocation list RL^* before starting the security experiment. The sP-UF-CMA security for RABS that captures signing key exposure is formally defined according to the following experiment played between a challenger $\mathcal{C}$ and a PPT adversary $\mathcal{A}$:

Initialization. The adversary $\mathcal{A}$ chooses a signing predicate $\Gamma_{k^*,W^*}(\cdot)$ and a time period t^* associated with the corresponding revocation list RL^* to be challenged, and sends them to $\mathcal{C}$.

Setup. The challenger $\mathcal{C}$ runs the setup algorithm and gives the public parameter PP to the adversary $\mathcal{A}$.

Queries Phase. The adversary $\mathcal{A}$ can repeatedly make the following queries in an adaptive way:

- $\mathcal{O}_E(S, ID)$: The challenger $\mathcal{C}$ runs the extraction algorithm on the tuple (S, ID), and returns the corresponding output $SK_{S,ID}$ to the adversary $\mathcal{A}$.
- $\mathcal{O}_{KU}(RL, t)$: The challenger $\mathcal{C}$ performs the key update algorithm to obtain KU_t and forwards it to $\mathcal{A}$.
- $\mathcal{O}_{SKG}((S, ID), t)$: The challenger carries out the extraction and key update algorithms on (S, ID) and (RL, t) respectively, and subsequently performs the signing key generation algorithm to obtain $SKG_{S,ID}^t$ and sends it to $\mathcal{A}$.
- $\mathcal{O}_R(ID, t)$: The challenger $\mathcal{C}$ runs the revocation algorithm on (ID, t), and returns an updated revocation list RL.
- $\mathcal{O}_S(m, t, \Gamma_{k,W}(\cdot))$: The challenger $\mathcal{C}$ first makes a query $\mathcal{O}_{SKG}((S, ID), t)$ to get a signing key $SK_{S,ID}^t$ such that $\Gamma_{k,W}(S) = 1$, and then performs the signing algorithm on $(m, t, \Gamma_{k,W}(\cdot))$ and returns a signature σ to $\mathcal{A}$.

In addition, there are several restrictions placed on the process of $\mathcal{A}$ performing the above queries:

(1) $\mathcal{O}_{KU}(\cdot)$ and $\mathcal{O}_R(\cdot, \cdot)$ cannot be queried on a time period that is lower than the time periods of all previous queries.
(2) If $\mathcal{O}_{KU}(\cdot, \cdot)$ was queried on a time period t then $\mathcal{O}_R(\cdot, \cdot)$ cannot be queried on t.
(3) $\mathcal{O}_{SKG}((\cdot, \cdot), \cdot)$ cannot be queried on a time period t before a query $\mathcal{O}_{KU}(\cdot, t)$ was made.

Forge Phase. In this phase, the adversary $\mathcal{A}$ outputs a forged signature σ^* with respect to a message m^*, and the singing predicate $\Gamma_{k^*,W^*}(\cdot)$ and the time period t^*. We say that $\mathcal{A}$ wins the experiment provided that the following conditions hold:

(1) $\text{Verify}(PP, \Gamma_{k^*,W^*}(\cdot), m^*, t^*, \sigma^*) = 1$.
(2) $\mathcal{O}_R(ID, t)$ for $t \leq t^*$ must be queried if $\mathcal{O}_E(S, ID)$ was queried such that $\Gamma_{k^*,W^*}(S) = 1$.
(3) $\mathcal{O}_{SKG}((S, ID), t^*)$ satisfying $\Gamma_{k^*,W^*}(S) = 1$ has not been queried.
(4) $\mathcal{O}_S(m^*, t^*, \Gamma_{k^*,W^*}(\cdot))$ has not been queried.

Denote by Suc the probability that $\mathcal{A}$ wins the above experiment. Then, the probability of $\mathcal{A}$ breaking the sP-UF-CMA security is defined as

$$Adv_{RABS,\mathcal{A}}^{\text{sP-UF-CMA}}(\lambda) = \Pr[\text{Suc}].$$

Definition 3 (sP-UF-CMA). *A threshold RABS scheme is said to be selective-predicate adaptive-message unforgeable provided that* $Adv_{RABS,\mathcal{A}}^{sP\text{-}UF\text{-}CMA}(\lambda)$ *is negligible with respect to the security parameter* λ *for any PPT adversary* $\mathcal{A}$.

Attribute Signer Privacy. Informally, attribute signer privacy requires a signature must not reveal any information about the attributes and the identifier that are involved in the signature. In other words, an adversary cannot know which attributes and identifier are used to produce the signature. The formal definition is specified as follows:

Definition 4. *A RIBS scheme satisfies perfect attribute signer privacy provided that for any two attribute sets* S_1 *and* S_2, *a signature* σ *on a message* m *with respect to a time period* t *and a signing predicate* $\Gamma_{k,W}(\cdot)$ *satisfying* $\Gamma_{k,W}(S_1) = \Gamma_{k,W}(S_2) = 1$, *any adversary cannot identify which attribute set* $(S_1$ *or* $S_2)$ *was used to produce the signature better than random guessing.*

4 Our Construction

The detailed construction consists of the following algorithms.

Setup(λ): This algorithm takes as input a security parameter λ. Let d be an upper bound of the size of threshold predicates supported, N be the maximum number of users, U be the universe of attributes, and $T = 2^{l_1}$ be the total number of time periods. Then, the attribute authority runs this algorithm as follows:

(1) Choose a prime number p of size $\Theta(\lambda)$, and generate an efficient bilinear pairing $e : G_1 \times G_1 \to G_2$, where G_1 and G_2 are two cyclic groups of order p. Let g be a generator of G. Pick a binary tree $\mathcal{BT}$ with N leaves, and set $RL = \emptyset$ and $st = \mathcal{BT}$. In addition, let $\mathcal{N}$ be the set of all nodes of $\mathcal{BT}$, and for each node $\theta \in \mathcal{N}$, choose and store a random integer $r_\theta \in \mathbb{Z}_p$ in θ.

(2) Set each attribute in U as a different element of $\mathbb{Z}_p^*$. Define a default attribute set $\Omega = \{\phi_1, ..., \phi_d\}$ of d distinct elements that are chosen from $\mathbb{Z}_p$.

(3) Select a random integer $\alpha \in \mathbb{Z}_p$, and set $Z = e(g,g)^\alpha$. Further pick a random vector $(\gamma_0, \gamma_1, ..., \gamma_\ell) \in \mathbb{Z}_p^{\ell+1}$, where $\ell = 2d + 1$, and let $h_i = g^{\gamma_i}$ for $i = 0$ to ℓ. Choose random group elements $f_0, f_1, ..., f_{l_1}, m_0, m_1, ..., m_{l_2} \in G_1$. Here, l_2 is the length of a message to be signed. For subsequent convenience, given a time period t and a message m, we define the following two functions

$$F_1(t) = f_0 \prod_{j=1}^{l_1} f_j^{t[j]} \quad \text{and} \quad F_2(m) = m_0 \prod_{i=1}^{l_2} m_j^{m[j]},$$

where $t[i]$ and $m[j]$ indicate i-th and j-th bits of t and m, respectively.

(4) Let the master key $MSK = \alpha$, and publish the public parameter as:

$$PP = (G_1, G_2, e, p, g, Z, \boldsymbol{f}, \boldsymbol{m}, \boldsymbol{h}),$$

where $\boldsymbol{f} = (f_0, f_1, ..., f_{l_1})$, $\boldsymbol{m} = (m_0, m_1, ..., m_{l_2})$ and $\boldsymbol{h} = (h_0, h_1, ..., h_\ell)$.

Extract(PP, MSK, S, ID): To generate a secret key for a user with identifier ID and an attribute set S, the attribute authority carries out the following steps:

(1) Choose an unassigned leaf node η of $\mathcal{BT}$ and store (ID, S) in the node η.
(2) For each node $\theta \in \mathsf{Path}(\eta)$, select random integers $a_1, ..., a_{d-1} \in \mathbb{Z}_p$, and define a polynomial $q_\theta(x) = \sum_{i=1}^{d-1} a_i x^i + \alpha - r_\theta$. Then, for each attribute $w \in S \cup \Omega$, choose a random integer $r_w \in \mathbb{Z}_p$ and generate a key component $\boldsymbol{SK}_{\theta,w} = (D_{w,0}, D_{w,1}, K_{w,1}, ..., K_{w,\ell-1})$, where

$$D_{w,0} = g^{q_\theta(w)} \cdot h_0^{r_w}, \quad D_{w,1} = g^{r_w}, \quad K_{w,i} = (h_1^{-w^i} \cdot h_{i+1})^{r_w} \text{ for } 1 \le i \le \ell - 1.$$

(3) Return the secret key $SK_{S,ID} = \left\{ \left(\theta, \{\boldsymbol{SK}_{\theta,w}\}_{w \in S \cup \Omega} \right) \right\}_{\theta \in \mathsf{Path}(\eta)}$.

KeyUp(PP, MSK, RL, t, st): The attribute authority first parses the current state as $st = \mathcal{BT}$, and then performs as follows:

(1) For each node $\theta \in \mathsf{KUNode}(\mathcal{BT}, RL, t)$, retrieve r_θ stored in the node θ.
(2) Choose a random exponent $\tau_\theta \in \mathbb{Z}_p$, and compute

$$\boldsymbol{UK}_{t,\theta} = (UK_{\theta,0}, UK_{\theta,1}) = (g^{r_\theta} \cdot F_1(t)^{\tau_\theta}, g^{\tau_\theta}).$$

(3) Return the update key $UK_t = \{(\theta, \boldsymbol{UK}_{t,\theta})\}_{\theta \in \mathsf{KUNode}(\mathcal{BT}, RL, t)}$.

SKGen($PP, SK_{S,ID}, UK_t$): For a user with identifier ID that was not revoked on time period t, there must exist a node $\theta \in \mathsf{Path}(\eta) \cap \mathsf{KUNode}(\mathcal{BT}, RL, t)$, where the leaf node η was used to store ID. Then, the user generates a signing key according to the following steps:

(1) For each attribute $w \in S \cup \Omega$, choose a random exponent $v_w \in \mathbb{Z}_p$, and let

$$SK_{w,0} = D_{w,0} \cdot UK_{\theta,0} \cdot F_1(t)^{v_w}, \quad SK'_{w,0} = D_{w,1},$$
$$SK_{t,w} = UK_{\theta,1} \cdot F_1(t)^{v_w}, \quad SK_{w,i} = K_{w,i} \text{ for } 1 \le i \le \ell - 1.$$

(2) Return the signing key $SK_{S,ID}^t = \{(SK_{w,0}, SK'_{w,0}, SK_{t,w}, \boldsymbol{SK}_w)\}_{w \in S \cup \Omega}$, where $\boldsymbol{SK}_w = (SK_{w,1}, ..., SK_{w,\ell-1})$.

Sign($PP, SK_{S,ID}^t, \Gamma_{k,W}(\cdot), t, m$): To sign a message m with respect to a signing predicate $\Gamma_{k,W}(\cdot)$ on a time period t, a signer carries out the following steps:

(1) Choose an attribute subset $W' \subset W \cap S$ and a default attribute subset $\Omega' \subset \Omega$ such that $|W'| = k$ and $|\Omega'| = d - k$, and assign the set $\Upsilon = W' \cup \Omega'$. Define a coefficient vector $\boldsymbol{b} = (b_1, ..., b_\ell) \in \mathbb{Z}_p^\ell$ from the following polynomial:

$$\varphi(y) = \prod_{w \in W \cup \Omega'} (y - w) \triangleq \sum_{i=1}^{\ell} b_i y^{i-1} \qquad (a).$$

Particularly, we set $b_i = 0$ for $|W \cup \Omega'| + 2 \le i \le \ell$.

(2) For each attribute $w \in \Upsilon$, compute

$$SK_w = SK_{w,0} \cdot \prod_{i=1}^{\ell-1} SK_{w,i}^{b_{i+1}}, \quad SK_0 = \prod_{w \in \Upsilon} SK_w^{\Delta_w^\Upsilon(0)},$$

$$SK_0' = \prod_{w \in \Upsilon} SK_{w,0}'^{\Delta_w^\Upsilon(0)}, \quad SK_t = \prod_{w \in \Upsilon} SK_{t,w}^{\Delta_w^\Upsilon(0)}.$$

(3) Choose random integers $s_0, s_1, s_2 \in \mathbb{Z}_p$, and compute

$$\sigma_0 = SK_0 \cdot \left(h_0 \prod_{i=1}^{\ell} h_i^{b_i}\right)^{s_0} \cdot F_1(t)^{s_1} \cdot F_2(m)^{s_2},$$

$$\sigma_0' = SK_0' \cdot g^{s_0}, \quad \sigma_1 = SK_t \cdot g^{s_1}, \quad \sigma_2 = g^{s_2}.$$

(4) Return the signature $\sigma = (\sigma_0, \sigma_0', \sigma_1, \sigma_2)$.

Verify($PP, \Gamma_{k,W}(\cdot), m, t, \sigma$): A verifier checks the validity of σ as follows:

(1) Choose the default attribute subset Ω', and then get the vector $\boldsymbol{b} = (b_1, ..., b_\ell)$ from the polynomial $\varphi(y)$ as defined in equality (a).
(2) Verify the following equation:

$$\frac{e(g, \sigma_0)}{e(h_0 \prod_{i=1}^{\ell} h_i^{b_i}, \sigma_0') \cdot e(F_1(t), \sigma_1) \cdot e(F_2(m), \sigma_2)} \stackrel{?}{=} Z.$$

If the equality holds then output 1 indicating that the signature is considered to be valid. Otherwise output 0.

Revoke(ID, RL, t, st): Suppose that η be the node used to store the identifier ID. Update the revocations list RL by adding (η, t) to it, and return the updated revocation list.

CORRECTNESS. The correctness of our scheme is similar to Herranz et al.'s [6] scheme, and we omit the details here.

5   Security Analysis and Performance Discussions

5.1   Security Proof

Theorem 1. *The proposed RABS scheme provides sP-UF-CMA security if the $\ell-DHE$ assumption holds in the group G_1.*

Proof. We will show that if there exists a PPT adversary $\mathcal{A}$ that can break the sP-UF-CMA security of the proposed RABS scheme, then we can construct an algorithm $\mathcal{C}$ that can solve the $\ell-DHE$ problem with a non-negligible probability by simulating the security experiment.

Initialization. $\mathcal{A}$ is required to provide a signing predicate $\Gamma_{k^*, W^*}(\cdot)$ and a time period t^* associated with the revocation list RL^* on this time period. Denote by

$\mathcal{I}^*$ the set of such identifiers involved in RL^*. In addition, $\mathcal{C}$ is given an instance of $\ell-$DHE problem in the form of $(G_1, p, g, g^a, g^{a^2}, ..., g^{a^\ell}, g^{a^{\ell+2}}, ..., g^{a^{2\ell}})$. Let $g_i = g^{a^i}$ for $1 \leq i \leq 2\ell$, and the goal of $\mathcal{C}$ is to compute $g_{\ell+1}$.

Setup. $\mathcal{C}$ simulates the setup algorithm by carrying out the following steps:

(1) Generate a bilinear mapping $e : G_1 \times G_1 \to G_2$ and a binary tree $\mathcal{BT}$ with N leaves, and set $RL = \emptyset$ and $st = \mathcal{BT}$. Denote by $\mathcal{N}$ the set of all nodes of $\mathcal{BT}$. For each identifer $ID \in \mathcal{I}^*$, randomly choose a leaf node η of $\mathcal{BT}$ to store ID, and let $\mathcal{L}^*$ be the set of such leaf nodes and $\mathcal{N}^* = \{\theta \in \mathsf{Path}(\eta) | \eta \in \mathcal{L}^*\}$. For each node $\theta \in \mathcal{N}$, select and store a random integer $r'_\theta \in \mathbb{Z}_p$ in θ. Moreover, pick a random integer $\alpha' \in \mathbb{Z}_p$, and for each node $\theta \in \mathcal{N}^*$ set $r_\theta = \alpha' a^{\ell+1} - r'_\theta$, and for each node $\theta \in \mathcal{N} \setminus \mathcal{N}^*$ let $r_\theta = r'_\theta$.

(2) Define the attribute universe U and default attribute set Ω as in the original scheme. In addition, choose a default attribute subset $\Omega^* = \{\phi_1, ..., \phi_{d-k^*}\}$. Furthermore, according to the polynomial $\varphi^*(y)$ as defined in (a), compute a coefficient vector $\boldsymbol{b}^* = (b_1^*, b_2^*, ..., b_\ell^*)$ by using the attribute set $W^* \cup \Omega^*$.

(3) Let $Z = e(g_1, g_\ell)^{\alpha'}$, which implicitly defines $\alpha = \alpha' a^{\ell+1}$, an unknown value for $\mathcal{C}$. Choose a random vector $(\gamma_0, \gamma_1, ..., \gamma_\ell) \in \mathbb{Z}_p^{\ell+1}$, and let $h_i = g_i \cdot g^{\gamma_i}$ for $1 \leq i \leq \ell$ and $h_0 = g^{\gamma_0} \prod_{i=1}^\ell h_i^{-b_i^*}$. Choose another random vector $(\delta_0, \delta_1, ..., \delta_{l_1}) \in \mathbb{Z}_p^{l_1+1}$, and assign $f_j = g^{\delta_j} g_{\ell-j+1}$ for $1 \leq j \leq l_1$[^1] and $f_0 = g^{\delta_0} \prod_{j=1}^{l_1} g_{\ell-j+1}^{-t^*[j]}$. Furthermore, randomly pick an integer $\rho \in \{0, 1, ..., l_2\}$, integers $x_0, ..., x_{l_2} \in \mathbb{Z}_{2q_s-1}$ and $y_0, ..., y_{l_2} \in \mathbb{Z}_p$, where q_s is the number of signing queries made by the adversary. Subsequently, let $m_0 = g_1^{x_0-2\rho q_s} g^{y_0}$ and $m_j = g_1^{x_j} g^{y_j}$ for $1 \leq j \leq l_2$.

(4) Set the master secret key $MSK = \alpha$, and publish the public parameter as $PP = (G_1, G_2, e, p, g, Z, \boldsymbol{f}, \boldsymbol{m}, \boldsymbol{h})$, where $\boldsymbol{f} = (f_0, f_1, ..., f_{l_1})$, $\boldsymbol{m} = (m_0, m_1, ..., m_{l_2})$ and $\boldsymbol{h} = (h_0, h_1, ..., h_\ell)$.

For convenience, we define the following two functions:

$$J(m) = x_0 + \sum_{j=1}^{l_2} x_j m[j] - 2\rho q_s, \quad K(m) = y_0 + \sum_{j=1}^{l_2} y_j m[j],$$

which implies that $F_2(m) = g_1^{J(m)} g^{K(m)}$.

Queries phase. In this phase, $\mathcal{C}$ answers $\mathcal{A}$'s queries as follows.

$-\mathcal{O}_E(S, ID)$: If $ID \notin \mathcal{I}^*$, we first randomly choose a leaf node η of $\mathcal{BT}$ to store ID. Then, depending on the choice of S, we discuss the following subcases.

▶ *Case 1*: $\Gamma_{k^*,W^*}(S) = 0$. As in Herranz et al.'s [6] proof, there exits a vector $\boldsymbol{u} = (u_0 = -1, u_1, ..., u_{d-1})$ such that for each attribute $w \in \Lambda \triangleq (S \cap W^*) \cup \Omega^*$, it holds that $\sum_{j=1}^d u_j w^{j-1} = 0$. Moreover, we utilize $\boldsymbol{u}$ to define a polynomial $q_u(x) = \sum_{j=1}^d u_{j-1} x^{j-1}$. Obviously, for any $w \in \Lambda$ we have that $q_u(w) = 0$.

[^1]: Here, we suppose that $l_1 \leq \ell$. Otherwise, we can reduce the security of the scheme to l_1-DHE assumption in a similar way.

To generate a secret key for the attribute set S, we first need to define a polynomial $q_\theta(x)$ satisfying $q_\theta(0) = \alpha - r_\theta$ for each node $\theta \in \mathsf{Path}(\eta)$. According to the fact that $\theta \in \mathcal{N}^*$ or not, we further divide this case into two subcases:

•*Case* 1.1: $\theta \in \mathsf{Path}(\eta) \cap \mathcal{N}^*$. In this case, note that $\alpha - r_\theta = r'_\theta$, which is available for $\mathcal{C}$. Thus, $\mathcal{C}$ can randomly choose integers $a_1, \ldots, a_{d-1} \in \mathbb{Z}_p$, and then define a computable polynomial $q_\theta(x) = \sum_{j=1}^{d-1} a_j x^j + r'_\theta$. Consequently, $\mathcal{C}$ can produce a key component $\{SK_{\theta,w}\}_{w \in S \cup \Omega}$ as in the original construction.

•*Case* 1.2: $\theta \in \mathsf{Path}(\eta) \setminus \mathcal{N}^*$. In this case, observe that $\alpha - r_\theta = \alpha - r'_\theta$. To define the polynomial, we choose random integers $a_1, \ldots, a_{d-1}$ and first define an auxiliary polynomial $q'_\theta(x) = \sum_{j=1}^{d-1} a_j x^j - r'_\theta$, and then let the polynomial $q_\theta(x) = q'_\theta(x) - \alpha q_u(x)$. It is easy to verify that $q_\theta(0) = \alpha - r'_\theta$.

Now, for each attribute $w \in S \cup \Omega$, we intend to compute a key component $SK_{\theta,w} = (D_{w,0}, D_{w,1}, K_{w,1}, ..., K_{w,\ell-1})$. To this end, we separate $S \cup \Omega$ into two subsets Λ and $(S \cup \Omega) \setminus \Lambda$, and respectively generate the key components.

(1) For each attribute $w \in \Lambda$, choose a random integer $r_w \in \mathbb{Z}_p$, and compute

$$D_{w,0} = g^{q_\theta(w)} \cdot h_0^{r_w}, \ D_{w,1} = g^{r_w}, \ K_{w,i} = (h_1^{-w^i} \cdot h_{i+1})^{r_w} \text{ for } 1 \le i \le \ell - 1.$$

(2) For each attribute $w \in (S \cup \Omega) \setminus \Lambda$, we have that $w \notin W^* \cup \Omega^*$, which also means that $\varphi^*(w) \neq 0$. Choose a random integer $r'_w \in \mathbb{Z}_p$, and let $r_w = r'_w - \alpha' q_u(w) \frac{\sum_{j=1}^{\ell} w^{j-1} a^{\ell-j+1}}{\varphi^*(w)}$. Then, firstly compute

$$D_{w,0} = g^{q_\theta(w)} h_0^{r_w}$$

$$= g^{q'_\theta(w)} h_0^{r'_w} \left(\prod_{j=1}^{\ell} g_{\ell-j+1}^{w^{j-1}} \right)^{-\frac{\alpha' q_u(w)(\gamma_0 - \sum_{i=1}^{\ell} b_i^* \gamma_i)}{\varphi^*(w)}}$$

$$\cdot \left(\prod_{i=2, i \neq \ell+1}^{2\ell} g_i^{\sum_{j=1}^{i-1} b_j^* w^{\ell-i+j}} \right)^{\frac{\alpha' q_u(w)}{\varphi^*(w)}}.$$

Secondly, let

$$D_{w,1} = g^{r_w} = g^{r'_w} \cdot g^{-\alpha' q_u(w) \frac{\sum_{j=1}^{\ell} w^{j-1} a^{\ell-j+1}}{\varphi^*(w)}} = g^{r'_w} \cdot \left(\prod_{j=1}^{\ell} g_{\ell-j+1}^{w^{j-1}} \right)^{-\frac{\alpha' q_u(w)}{\varphi^*(w)}}.$$

Finally, for $1 \le i \le \ell - 1$, set

$$K_{w,i} = (h_1^{-w^i} \cdot h_{i+1})^{r_w}$$

$$= (h_1^{-w^i} h_{i+1})^{r'_w} \left(\prod_{j=1}^{\ell} g_{\ell-j+1}^{w^{j-1}} \right)^{\frac{\alpha' q_u(w)(w^i \gamma_1 - \gamma_{i+1})}{\varphi^*(w)}}$$

$$\cdot \left(\prod_{j=2}^{\ell} g_{\ell-j+2}^{w^{j+i-1}} \prod_{j=1, j \neq i+1}^{\ell} g_{\ell-j+i+2}^{w^{j-1}} \right)^{\frac{-\alpha' q_u(w)}{\varphi^*(w)}}.$$

▶ *Case* 2: $\Gamma_{k^*,W^*}(S) = 1$. In this case, it must be that $ID \in \mathcal{I}^*$, which also implies that $\alpha - r_\theta = r'_\theta$ for each $\theta \in \mathsf{Path}(\eta)$. Therefore, $\mathcal{C}$ can generate a key component $\{\boldsymbol{SK}_{\theta,w}\}_{w \in S \cup \Omega}$ in the same manner as in the *Case* 1.1.

$-\mathcal{O}_{KU}(RL, t)$: For such a query, $\mathcal{C}$ runs the key update algorithm as follows:

▶ *Case* 1: $t = t^*$. In this case, for each node $\theta \in \mathsf{KUNode}(\mathcal{BT}, RL, t)$, we have that $\theta \notin \mathcal{N}^*$, which indicates that $r_\theta = r'_\theta$. Thus, $\mathcal{C}$ can compute a key component $\boldsymbol{UK}_{t,\theta}$ as in the original scheme, since it knows r'_θ.

▶ *Case* 2: $t \neq t^*$. For each node $\theta \in \mathsf{KUNode}(\mathcal{BT}, RL, t) \setminus \mathcal{N}^*$, $\mathcal{C}$ performs the same as in the *Case* $t = t^*$, since $r_\theta = r'_\theta$. However, for each node $\theta \in \mathcal{N}^* \cap \mathsf{KUNode}(\mathcal{BT}, RL, t)$, we have that $r_\theta = \alpha - r'_\theta$. Thus, the algorithm $\mathcal{C}$ needs to adopt a different strategy to compute the key component

$$\boldsymbol{UK}_{t,\theta} = (UK_{\theta,0}, UK_{\theta,1}) = (g^{r_\theta} \cdot F_1(t)^{\tau_\theta}, g^{\tau_\theta}).$$

Since $t \neq t^*$, there exists an index $1 \leq j' \leq l_1$ such that $t[j'] \neq t^*[j']$. Then, $\mathcal{C}$ selects a random integer $\tau'_\theta \in \mathbb{Z}_p$, lets $\tau_\theta = \tau'_\theta - \alpha' \frac{a^{j'}}{t[j']-t^*[j']}$, and then computes

$$UK_{\theta,0} = g^{r_\theta} \cdot F_1(t)^{\tau_\theta} = g^{\alpha - r'_\theta} \cdot F_1(t)^{\tau'_\theta} \cdot \left(f_0 \prod_{j=1}^{l_1} f_j^{t[j]}\right)^{-\alpha' \frac{a^{j'}}{t[j']-t^*[j']}}$$

$$= g^{-r'_\theta} \cdot F_1(t)^{\tau'_\theta} \cdot \left(g_{j'}^{-\alpha'}\right)^{\frac{\gamma_0 + \sum_{j=1}^{l_1} \gamma_j t[j]}{t[j']-t^*[j']}} \cdot \left(\prod_{j=1, j \neq j'}^{l_1} g_{\ell-j+j'+1}^{t[j]-t^*[j]}\right)^{\frac{-\alpha'}{t[j']-t^*[j']}}.$$

Furthermore, $\mathcal{C}$ computes

$$UK_{\theta,0} = g^{\tau_\theta} = g^{\tau'_\theta} \cdot g^{-\alpha' \frac{a^{j'}}{t[j']-t^*[j']}} = g^{\tau'_\theta} \cdot \left(g_{j'}^{-1}\right)^{\frac{\alpha'}{t[j']-t^*[j']}}.$$

$-\mathcal{O}_{SKG}((S, ID), t)$: For this kind of query, $\mathcal{C}$ first makes queries $\mathcal{O}_E(S, ID)$ and $\mathcal{O}_{KU}(RL, t)$ to obtain a secret key $SK_{S,ID}$ and an update key UK_t, respectively. Then, $\mathcal{C}$ runs the algorithm $\mathbf{SKGen}(PP, SK_{ID,S}, UK_t)$ to get the signing key $SK_{S,ID}^t$. It is easy to verify that the signing key $SK_{S,ID}^t$, which is directly derived from key the components $\{\boldsymbol{SK}_{\theta,w}\}_{w \in S \cup \Omega}$ and $\boldsymbol{UK}_{t,\theta}$ for some node $\theta \in \mathsf{Path}(\eta) \cap \mathsf{KUNode}(\mathcal{BT}, RL, t)$, is valid.

$-\mathcal{O}_R(ID, t)$: $\mathcal{C}$ answers this query in the same way as in the real scheme.

$-\mathcal{O}_S(m, t, \Gamma_{k,W}(\cdot))$: Note that a valid signature σ with respect to $(m, t, \Gamma_{k,W}(\cdot))$ owns the following form:

$$\sigma = (\sigma_0, \sigma'_0, \sigma_1, \sigma_2) = \left(g^\alpha \cdot \left(h_0 \prod_{i=1}^{\ell} h_i^{b_i}\right)^{s_0} \cdot F_1(t)^{s_1} \cdot F_2(m)^{s_2}, g^{s_0}, g^{s_1}, g^{s_2}\right),$$

where s_0, s_1, s_2 are random integers in $\mathbb{Z}_p$, and $F_2(m) = g_1^{J(m)} g^{K(m)}$.

$\mathcal{C}$ first evaluates the value of $J(m)$. If $J(m) = 0$ then $\mathcal{C}$ aborts the simulation. Otherwise, $\mathcal{C}$ gets the coefficients $b_1, \ldots, b_\ell$ by the equality (a), chooses random integers $s_0, s_1, s'_2 \in \mathbb{Z}_p$ and lets $s_2 = s'_2 - \frac{\alpha' a^\ell}{J(M)}$, and then computes

$$\sigma = \left(\left(h_0 \prod_{i=1}^{\ell} h_i^{b_i}\right)^{s_0} \cdot F_1(t)^{s_1} \cdot F_2(m)^{s'_2} g_\ell^{\frac{-\alpha' K(m)}{J(m)}}, g^{s_0}, g^{s_1}, g^{s'_2} g_\ell^{\frac{-\alpha' K(m)}{J(m)}}\right).$$

Forge Phase. $\mathcal{A}$ eventually forges a signature $\sigma^* = (\sigma_0^*, \sigma_0'^*, \sigma_1^*, \sigma_2^*)$ with respect to $(m^*, t^*, \Gamma_{k^*, W^*}(\cdot))$. If σ is valid, we say that $\mathcal{A}$ wins the experiment. In this case, if $J(m^*) \neq 0$, $\mathcal{C}$ aborts the simulation. Otherwise, $\mathcal{C}$ can solve the $\ell-$DHE problem in the following way.

Firstly, observe that

$$
\sigma_0^* = g^\alpha \Big(h_0 \prod_{i=1}^\ell h_i^{b_i^*} \Big)^{s_0} F_1(t^*)^{s_1} F_2(m^*)^{s_2} = g^\alpha g^{\gamma_0 s_0} g^{s_1 (\delta_0 + \sum_{j=1}^{l_1} \delta_j t^*[j])} g^{s_2 K(m^*)}
$$

$$
= g^\alpha (\sigma_0'^*)^{\gamma_0} (\sigma_1^*)^{(\delta_0 + \sum_{j=1}^{l_1} \delta_j t^*[j])} (\sigma_2^*)^{K(m^*)}.
$$

Then, $\mathcal{C}$ can trivially get that

$$
g_{\ell+1} = g^{a^{\ell+1}} = \Big(\frac{\sigma_0^*}{(\sigma_0'^*)^{\gamma_0} \cdot (\sigma_1^*)^{(\delta_0 + \sum_{j=1}^{l_1} \delta_j t^*[j])} \cdot (\sigma_2^*)^{K(m^*)}} \Big)^{\frac{1}{\alpha'}}.
$$

Probability Analysis. Viewed from $\mathcal{C}$'s perspective, to completely simulate the experiment without aborting, the following conditions must be fulfilled:

(1) For $1 \leq i \leq q_s$, the i-th signing query $\mathcal{O}_S(m, t, \Gamma_{k,W}(\cdot))$ satisfies the restriction $J(m) \neq 0$;
(2) In the forge phase, the involved message m^* has $J(m^*) = 0$.

As explained in [18], the probability that the above events do not appear is at leat $\frac{1}{4q_s(l_2+1)}$. We can thus conclude with

$$
Adv_{G_1}^{\ell\text{-DHE}}(\mathcal{C}) \geq \frac{1}{4q_s(l_2+1)} \cdot Adv_{\text{RABS}, \mathcal{A}}^{\text{sP-UF-CMA}}(\lambda).
$$

$\square$

Theorem 2. *The proposed RABS scheme achieves perfect attribute signer privacy.*

Proof (sketch). Note that a valid signature σ with respect to $(m, t, \Gamma_{k,W}(\cdot))$ is structured in the following way:

$$
\sigma = (\sigma_0, \sigma_0', \sigma_1, \sigma_2) = \Big(g^\alpha \cdot \Big(h_0 \prod_{i=1}^\ell h_i^{b_i} \Big)^{s_0} \cdot F_1(t)^{s_1} \cdot F_2(m)^{s_2}, g^{s_0}, g^{s_1}, g^{s_2} \Big),
$$

where s_0, s_1, s_2 are random integers in $\mathbb{Z}_p$. Suppose that σ is produced by using a signing key corresponding to some attribute set S that has $\Gamma_{k,W}(S) = 1$.

Obviously, $\sigma_0', \sigma_1, \sigma_2$ are independent of the choice of S. Furthermore, by the definition of b_i $(1 \leq i \leq \ell)$, we know that these values also do not depend on the choice of S, and hence σ_1 also reveal no information about S. In other words, σ has a uniform distribution over G_1^4. Thus, the proposed RABS scheme can provide perfect attribute signer privacy. $\square$

5.2 Performance Discussions

In this section, we discuss the performance of our RABS scheme in terms of storage cost, time complexity and functionality.

As shown in Table 1, compared with other ABS schemes, the public key size of Okamoto and Takashima's [12] scheme is linear in the size of attribute universe, and hence their scheme only supports small universe (v.s. large universe). However, their scheme is proved fully secure, and can implement more general signing predicate. Further more, we can see that the secret key sizes of the schemes of Okamoto and Takashima [12], Li et al. [7] and Lian et al. [8] only depend on the cardinality of a user's attribute set. On the other hand, although Herranz et al.'s [6] scheme and our construction have larger secret key size, the two schemes achieve constant signature size, instead of growing linearly in the number of attributes involved in a signature. In the aspect of update key size, unlike Lian et al.'s [8] scheme, our scheme provides a kind of scalable revocation manner. Namely, the authority does not need to separately generate an update key for each unrevoked user.

Table 1. Comparisons of storage cost with previous works

Schemes	Public parameter	Secret key	Signature	Update key ($r \leq N/2$)
[12]	$\Theta(\vartheta)$	$\Theta(\omega)$	$\Theta(\kappa)$	0
[7]	$\Theta(1)$	$\Theta(\omega + d)$	$\Theta(\kappa + d)$	0
[6]	$\Theta(d + l_2)$	$\Theta(d \cdot \omega + d^2)$	$\Theta(1)$	0
[8]	$\Theta(r_{\max})$	$\Theta(\omega)$	$\Theta(r_{\max} + \kappa)$	$\Theta(N - r)$
Ours	$\Theta(l_1 + l_2 + d)$	$\Theta(nd \cdot (\omega + d))$	$\Theta(1)$	$\Theta(r \log(N/r))$

* ϑ = size of attribute universe. ω = size of a user's attribute set. κ = size of attributes involved in a signature. $r_{\max}$ = maximum number of columns of LSSS matrix. d = upper bound of the size of threshold predicates. N = number of users in the system. Particularly, $N = 2^n$ in our scheme. r = number of users to be revoked. l_1 and l_2 are lengths of a time period and a message, respectively.

Table 2 shows that the size of attributes used to produce a signature has no effect on the time complexities of signing and verifying algorithms in Herranz et al.'s [6] scheme and our scheme, although they can only deal with simpler signing predicates. In addition, Lian et al.'s scheme and our scheme additionally have a key update algorithm since they provide revocation functionality. A user in Lian et al.'s scheme does not update his/her available secret key, and just needs to receive a key component corresponding to the current time period. Consequently, their scheme cannot withstand signing key exposure. However, our scheme re-randomizes the signing key in each update process to conquer this kind of attack, which also brings in extra but acceptable computation cost.

Table 2. Comparisons of time complexity and functionality with previous works

Schemes	Sign	Verify	Predicate	Revocation	Signing key exposure
[12]	$\Theta(\kappa)e$	$\Theta(\kappa)p$	LSSS	✗	✗
[7]	$(\kappa+d)e$	$(\kappa+d)p$	Threshold	✗	✗
[6]	$\Theta(d)e$	$\Theta(d)e+\Theta(1)p$	Threshold	✗	✗
[8]	$\Theta(\kappa r_{max})e$	$\Theta(\kappa r_{max})p$	LSSS	✓	✗
Ours	$\Theta(d)e$	$\Theta(d)e+\Theta(1)p$	Threshold	✓	✓

* e and p indicate one exponentiation operation and one pairing operation, respectively.

6 Conclusions

In this paper, we studied the revocation problem in the setting of ABS, and presented a concrete revocable attribute-based signature scheme. By using binary data structure, the key update of the proposed scheme is more efficient than previous work. In addition, the proposed scheme is secure against signing key exposure, a kind of rather realistic threat. We proved the security of the proposed scheme in the selective-predicate and adaptive-messages model under ℓ-DHE assumption. We also demonstrated that the proposed scheme enjoys attribute signer privacy. Compared with regular ABS schemes, the proposed scheme is also efficient in terms of storage and computation costs.

Acknowledgements. Jianghong Wei, Xuexian Hu and Wenfen Liu are supported by the National Basic Research Program of China (2012CB315905) and National Natural Science Foundation of China (61379150). Xinyi Huang is supported by National Natural Science Foundation of China (61472083, U1405255) and Program for New Century Excellent Talents in Fujian University (JA14067).

References

1. Attrapadung, N., Imai, H.: Attribute-based encryption supporting direct/Indirect revocation modes. In: Parker, M.G. (ed.) Cryptography and Coding 2009. LNCS, vol. 5921, pp. 278–300. Springer, Heidelberg (2009)
2. Boldyreva, A., Goyal, V., Kumar, V.: Id-based encryption with efficient revocation. In: Proceedings of the 15th ACM Conference on Computer and Communications Security, pp. 417–426 (2008)
3. Boneh, D., Franklin, M.: Identity-based encryption from the weil pairing. In: Kilian, J. (ed.) CRYPTO 2001. LNCS, vol. 2139, pp. 213–229. Springer, Heidelberg (2001)
4. Boneh, D., Gentry, C., Waters, B.: Collusion resistant broadcast encryption with short ciphertexts and private keys. In: Shoup, V. (ed.) CRYPTO 2005. LNCS, vol. 3621, pp. 258–275. Springer, Heidelberg (2005)

5. Gentry, C.: Certificate-based encryption and the certificate revocation problem. In: Biham, E. (ed.) EUROCRYPT 2003. LNCS, vol. 2656, pp. 272–293. Springer, Heidelberg (2003)
6. Herranz, J., Laguillaumie, F., Libert, B., Ràfols, C.: Short attribute-based signatures for threshold predicates. In: Dunkelman, O. (ed.) CT-RSA 2012. LNCS, vol. 7178, pp. 51–67. Springer, Heidelberg (2012)
7. Li, J., Au, M.H., Susilo, W., Xie, D., Ren, K.: Attribute-based signature and its applications. In: Proceedings of the 5th ACM Symposium on Information, Computer and Communications Security, pp. 60–69. ACM (2010)
8. Lian, Y., Xu, L., Huang, X.: Attribute-based signatures with efficient revocation. In: 5th International Conference on Intelligent Networking and Collaborative Systems (INCoS), pp. 573–577. IEEE (2013)
9. Libert, B., Vergnaud, D.: Adaptive-ID secure revocable identity-based encryption. In: Fischlin, M. (ed.) CT-RSA 2009. LNCS, vol. 5473, pp. 1–15. Springer, Heidelberg (2009)
10. Maji, H.K., Prabhakaran, M., Rosulek, M.: Attribute-based signatures. In: Kiayias, A. (ed.) CT-RSA 2011. LNCS, vol. 6558, pp. 376–392. Springer, Heidelberg (2011)
11. Naor, M., Nissim, K.: Certificate revocation and certificate update. IEEE Journal on Selected Areas in Communications 18(4), 561–570 (2000)
12. Okamoto, T., Takashima, K.: Efficient attribute-based signatures for non-monotone predicates in the standard model. In: Catalano, D., Fazio, N., Gennaro, R., Nicolosi, A. (eds.) PKC 2011. LNCS, vol. 6571, pp. 35–52. Springer, Heidelberg (2011)
13. Sahai, A., Seyalioglu, H., Waters, B.: Dynamic credentials and ciphertext delegation for attribute-based encryption. In: Safavi-Naini, R., Canetti, R. (eds.) CRYPTO 2012. LNCS, vol. 7417, pp. 199–217. Springer, Heidelberg (2012)
14. Sahai, A., Waters, B.: Fuzzy identity-based encryption. In: Cramer, R. (ed.) EUROCRYPT 2005. LNCS, vol. 3494, pp. 457–473. Springer, Heidelberg (2005)
15. Seo, J.H., Emura, K.: Revocable identity-based encryption revisited: Security model and construction. In: Kurosawa, K., Hanaoka, G. (eds.) PKC 2013. LNCS, vol. 7778, pp. 216–234. Springer, Heidelberg (2013)
16. Shahandashti, S.F., Safavi-Naini, R.: Threshold attribute-based signatures and their application to anonymous credential systems. In: Preneel, B. (ed.) AFRICACRYPT 2009. LNCS, vol. 5580, pp. 198–216. Springer, Heidelberg (2009)
17. Shamir, A.: Identity-based cryptosystems and signature schemes. In: Blakely, G.R., Chaum, D. (eds.) CRYPTO 1984. LNCS, vol. 196, pp. 47–53. Springer, Heidelberg (1985)
18. Waters, B.: Efficient identity-based encryption without random oracles. In: Cramer, R. (ed.) EUROCRYPT 2005. LNCS, vol. 3494, pp. 114–127. Springer, Heidelberg (2005)

Fully Secure Online/Offline Predicate and Attribute-Based Encryption

Pratish Datta, Ratna Dutta, and Sourav Mukhopadhyay

Department of Mathematics
Indian Institute of Technology Kharagpur
Kharagpur-721302, India
{pratishdatta,ratna,sourav}@maths.iitkgp.ernet.in

Abstract. This paper presents the *first fully secure online/offline predicate encryption* (PE) and *attribute-based encryption* (ABE) schemes that split the computation required for encryption into two phases: A preparation phase that does the vast majority of the work to encrypt a message before knowing the actual message and the attributes or access control policy that will be used. A second phase can then rapidly assemble a ciphertext when the specifications become known. Our PE schemes *support generalized inner-product predicates*, while, our ABE scheme supports *non-monotone access structures*. All the proposed schemes are *unbounded* in the sense that the size of the public parameters is constant. The security of all the schemes are based on the *Decisional Linear* assumption. The best part of our constructions is that they exhibit *better online performance* despite of providing stronger security guarantees compared to the existing work.

Keywords: Predicate encryption, attribute based encryption, online/offline encryption, generalized inner-product, dual pairing vector spaces.

1 Introduction

The notion of *predicate encryption* (PE) and *attribute-based encryption* (ABE), introduced by Katz et al. [2] and Sahai et al. [10] respectively, constitute an advanced class of encryption primitives known as *functional encryption* (FE) that provides more flexible and fine-grained functionalities in sharing and distributing sensitive data compared to traditional symmetric and public-key encryption, as well as, identity-based encryption (IBE). In FE, there is a relation $R(v, x)$, that determines whether a private key associated with a parameter v can decrypt a ciphertext encrypted under another parameter x. The parameters for PE with *inner-product predicates* are vectors $\vec{x}$ for encryption and $\vec{v}$ for private key, where $R(\vec{v}, \vec{x})$ hold, if and only if $\vec{v} \cdot \vec{x} = 0$, where $\vec{v} \cdot \vec{x}$ is the standard inner-product. In ABE systems, either one of the parameters for encryption and private key is a set of attributes, and the other is an access policy over a universe of attributes. If the access policy is for a secret key, it is called *key-policy* ABE (KP-ABE), where a private key can decrypt a ciphertext if and only if the attribute

© Springer International Publishing Switzerland 2015
J. Lopez and Y. Wu (Eds.): ISPEC 2015, LNCS 9065, pp. 331–345, 2015.
DOI: 10.1007/978-3-319-17533-1_23

set satisfies the policy. On the other hand, if the access policy is for encryption, it is *ciphertext-policy* ABE (CP-ABE).

One principle drawback of these richer encryption primitives is that the computation cost of encryption scales with the length of the vector for PE supporting inner-product predicates, and the complexity of the access policy or number of attributes for ABE. The situation is more severe when the PE or ABE constructions aim to provide *adaptive security* [3], [4], [6], [5], [7], which is more realistic compared to selective notion of security, given the increasing amount of security breaches that are taking place now a days. This cost could impact several applications. For instance, if the encryption algorithm is executed on a mobile device, encryption time and battery consumption are of large importance. Specially, an exacerbating factor is that the cost for operations may vary widely between each ciphertext; thus, forcing a system to provision for a load that matches a worst case scenario.

Recently, Hohenberger et al. [1] took a step forward to mitigate the above bottleneck by introducing methods for *online/offline* encryption in ABE setting. One motivating application for splitting the work in the online/offline phases is that a mobile device could be programmed to automatically do some preparatory work whenever it is plugged into a power source, and then when it is unplugged, ciphertexts could be rapidly formed with significantly less battery consumption.

Our Contribution: In this paper, we develop *first fully attribute-hiding online/offline* PE schemes, denoted by PKEM-I and PKEM-II, for *generalized inner-product predicates* [8]. Our PE schemes are *unbounded* in the sense that the size of the public parameters is constant. The proposed PE constructions are built on the PE schemes of Okamoto et al. [8] that has the desired algebraic structure to support online/offline encryption. Note that among the few *fully attribute-hiding* PE constructions, identifying one *amenable to online/offline mechanism* is a *non-trivial* task since such schemes are even *fewer*. In order to avoid wasteful computation during offline phases, we adopt a "pooling" technique. In such a system, an encrypter will continuously create offline ciphertext pieces and add those to a ciphertext pool. When the encrypter later needs to encrypt to a vector $\vec{x}$ with index set $I_{\vec{x}}$ it grabs $\sharp I_{\vec{x}}$ many pieces from the pool connecting each one to a single attribute within $\vec{x}$, where $\sharp I_{\vec{x}}$ denotes the number of elements in $I_{\vec{x}}$. The security of our PE schemes are reduced directly to the security of the PE schemes of Okamoto et al. [8] which is proven secure under the *Decisional Linear* (DLIN) assumption.

Further, we propose the *first adaptive payload-hiding unbounded online/offline* (key-policy) ABE, denoted by KP-ABKEM, for *non-monotone access structure* by extending the ABE scheme of Okamoto et al. [8]. Here also we employ the pooling method and reduce the security to that of the underlying ABE scheme of Okamoto et al. [8].

In view of the fact that the most common instantiation of bilinear groups of prime order use elliptic curves where a group operation is equivalent to 2–3 multiplications in $\mathbb{F}_q$ together with at least 2 inversions in $\mathbb{F}_q$ that again involve some

Table 1. Online Computation Comparison

Schemes	Security	Complexity Assumptions	Online Computation
KP-ABKEM of [1]	Selective Payload-Hiding	Q-RW1	$\sharp\Gamma\, m, \sharp\Gamma\, gr$
Our KP-ABKEM	Adaptive Payload-Hiding	DLIN	$3\sharp\Gamma\, m$
Our PKEM-I	Adaptive Attribute-Hiding	DLIN	$2\sharp I_{\vec{x}}\, m$
Our PKEM-II	Adaptive Attribute-hiding	DLIN	$2\sharp I_{\vec{x}}\, m$

Here Q-RW1, DLIN respectively denote the Q type assumption defined by Rouselakis and Waters [9], and the Decisional Linear assumption.

In this table, $m, gr, \sharp\Gamma$, and $\sharp I_{\vec{x}}$ respectively represents number of multiplications in finite field $\mathbb{F}_q$, number of group operations, the size of the attribute set for encryption (for KP-ABKEM), and the size of the index set of the vector $\vec{x}$ used in encryption (for PKEM).

additional multiplications in $\mathbb{F}_q$, we can see from Table 1 that our online/offline KP-ABE and PE constructions have much better online performance despite of providing stronger security guarantees compared to that of the ABE of [1] which, to the best of our knowledge, is the only work done in this direction so far.

2   Preliminaries

• **Notations**: We will use the following notations throughout this paper.

$\sharp S$: the number of elements in set S.

$y \xleftarrow{\$} A$: y is randomly selected from A according to its distribution, when A is a random variable, and y is uniformly selected from A, when A is a set.

$\vec{x}$: a vector $(x_1, \ldots, x_n) \in \mathbb{F}_q^n$ of length n for some $n \in \mathbb{N}$.

$\boldsymbol{x}$: an element of vector space $\mathbb{V} \neq \mathbb{F}_q^n$ over $\mathbb{F}_q$.

$\text{span}\langle \boldsymbol{b}_1, \ldots, \boldsymbol{b}_m \rangle \subseteq \mathbb{V}$: the subspace of $\mathbb{V}$ generated by $\{\boldsymbol{b}_1, \ldots, \boldsymbol{b}_m\} \subseteq \mathbb{V}$.

$\text{span}\langle \vec{x}_1, \ldots, \vec{x}_m \rangle \subseteq \mathbb{F}_q^n$: the subspace of $\mathbb{F}_q^n$ spanned by $\{\vec{x}_1, \ldots, \vec{x}_m\} \subseteq \mathbb{F}_q^n$.

$(x_1, \ldots, x_m)_{\mathbb{B}}$: $\sum_{i=1}^{m} x_i \boldsymbol{b}_i$, i.e., a linear combination of vectors in $\mathbb{B} = \{\boldsymbol{b}_1, \ldots, \boldsymbol{b}_m\} \subseteq$ $\mathbb{V}$ with scalars $x_1, \ldots, x_m \in \mathbb{F}_q$.

$\text{GL}(m, \mathbb{F}_q)$: The general linear group of degree m over $\mathbb{F}_q$.

2.1   Dual Pairing Vector Spaces by Direct Product of Symmetric Pairing Groups

Definition 1 (Symmetric Bilinear Pairing Groups). *A symmetric bilinear pairing group* $(q, \mathbb{G}, \mathbb{G}_T, G, e)$ *is a tuple of a prime* q, *cyclic additive group* $\mathbb{G}$ *and multiplicative group* $\mathbb{G}_T$ *of order* q *each,* $G \neq 0 \in \mathbb{G}$, *and a polynomial time computable non-degenerate bilinear pairing* $e : \mathbb{G} \times \mathbb{G} \to \mathbb{G}_T$, *i.e.,* $e(sG, tG) = e(G, G)^{st}$ *for all* $s, t \in \mathbb{F}_q$ *(bilinearity) and* $e(G, G) \neq 1$ *(non-degeneracy). Let* $\mathcal{G}_{\text{bpg}}$ *be an algorithm that takes input* 1^λ *and outputs a description of bilinear pairing group* $(q, \mathbb{G}, \mathbb{G}_T, G, e)$ *with security parameter* λ.

Definition 2 (Dual Pairing Vector Spaces (DPVS)). *As introduced in* [6], *a dual pairing vector space* (DPVS) $(q, \mathbb{V}, \mathbb{G}_T, \mathbb{A}, E)$ *by a direct product of symmetric pairing groups* $(q, \mathbb{G}, \mathbb{G}_T, G, e)$ *is a tuple of prime* q, *n dimensional vector space* $\mathbb{V} = \mathbb{G}^n = \overbrace{\mathbb{G} \times \ldots \times \mathbb{G}}^{n}$ *over* $\mathbb{F}_q$, *cyclic group* $\mathbb{G}_T$ *of order* q, *canonical basis* $\mathbb{A} = \{\boldsymbol{a}_1, \ldots, \boldsymbol{a}_n\}$ *of* $\mathbb{V}$, *where* $\boldsymbol{a}_i = (\overbrace{0, \ldots, 0}^{i-1}, G, \overbrace{0, \ldots, 0}^{n-i})$, *and pairing* $E : \mathbb{V} \times \mathbb{V} \to \mathbb{G}_T$. *The pairing* E *is defined by* $E(\boldsymbol{x}, \boldsymbol{y}) = \prod_{i=1}^{n} e(G_i, H_i) \in \mathbb{G}_T$ *where* $\boldsymbol{x} = (G_1, \ldots, G_n) \in \mathbb{V}$ *and* $\boldsymbol{y} = (H_1, \ldots, H_n) \in \mathbb{V}$. *The map* E *is non-degenerate bilinear, i.e.,* $E(s\boldsymbol{x}, t\boldsymbol{y}) = E(\boldsymbol{x}, \boldsymbol{y})^{st}$ *for* $s, t \in \mathbb{F}_q, \boldsymbol{x}, \boldsymbol{y} \in \mathbb{V}$, *and if* $E(\boldsymbol{x}, \boldsymbol{y}) = 1$ *for all* $\boldsymbol{y} \in \mathbb{V}$, *then* $\boldsymbol{x} = 0$. *For all* i *and* j, $E(\boldsymbol{a}_i, \boldsymbol{a}_j) = e(G, G)^{\delta_{i,j}}$ *where* $\delta_{i,j} = 1$ *if* $i = j$, *and 0 otherwise, and* $e(G, G) \neq 1 \in \mathbb{G}_T$. DPVS *generation algorithm* $\mathcal{G}_{\mathsf{dpvs}}$ *takes input* 1^λ $(\lambda \in \mathbb{N})$, $n \in \mathbb{N}$ *together with* $\mathsf{param}_\mathbb{G} = (q, \mathbb{G}, \mathbb{G}_T, G, e)$, *and outputs a description of* $\mathsf{param}_\mathbb{V} = (q, \mathbb{V}, \mathbb{G}_T, \mathbb{A}, E)$ *with security parameter* λ *and* n-*dimensional* $\mathbb{V}$. *It can be constructed by using* $\mathcal{G}_{\mathsf{bpg}}$ *as a subroutine.*

In Figure 1, we describe *random dual orthogonal basis generator* $\mathcal{G}_{\mathsf{ob}}$, which is used as a subroutine in our **PE** and **ABE** schemes.

Henceforth, for simplicity, we denote $n = n_1$, $\mathbb{V} = \mathbb{V}_1$, $\mathbb{A} = \mathbb{A}_1$, $\mathbb{B} = \mathbb{B}_1 = \{\boldsymbol{b}_1, \ldots, \boldsymbol{b}_{n_1}\}$ and $\mathbb{B}^* = \mathbb{B}_1^* = \{\boldsymbol{b}_1^*, \ldots, \boldsymbol{b}_{n_1}^*\}$ for variables with $t = 1$.

2.2 Definition of Online/Offline Predicate Encryption

This subsection presents the notion of online/offline predicate encryption (**PE**) for generalized inner-product relations together with the associated security model.

The parameters of generalized inner-product predicates are expressed as a vector $\overrightarrow{x} = \{(t, x_t) | t \in I_{\overrightarrow{x}}, x_t \in \mathbb{F}_q\} \backslash \{\overrightarrow{0}\}$ with finite index set $I_{\overrightarrow{x}} \subset \mathbb{N}$ for encryption and a vector $\overrightarrow{v} = \{(t, v_t) | t \in I_{\overrightarrow{v}}, v_t \in \mathbb{F}_q\} \backslash \{\overrightarrow{0}\}$ with finite index set $I_{\overrightarrow{v}} \subset \mathbb{N}$ for a decryption policy embedded in a private key. There are two types of online/offline predicate encryption supporting inner-product predicates R with respect to the decryption conditions:

Type I Predicate: $R(\overrightarrow{v}, \overrightarrow{x}) = 1 \iff I_{\overrightarrow{v}} \subseteq I_{\overrightarrow{x}}$ and $\sum_{t \in I_{\overrightarrow{v}}} v_t x_t = 0$.

Type II Predicate: $R(\overrightarrow{v}, \overrightarrow{x}) = 1 \iff I_{\overrightarrow{v}} \supseteq I_{\overrightarrow{x}}$ and $\sum_{t \in I_{\overrightarrow{x}}} v_t x_t = 0$.

A third type of decryption condition, which is essentially a particular case of the above two types, is considered in [8] for conventional prefix type vectors $\overrightarrow{v} = (v_1, \ldots, v_n)$ and $\overrightarrow{x} = (x_1, \ldots, x_{n'})$, namely, Type 0 inner-product predicate defined by $R(\overrightarrow{v}, \overrightarrow{x}) = 1 \iff n = n'$ and $\overrightarrow{v} \cdot \overrightarrow{x} = \sum_{t=1}^{n} v_t x_t = 0$.

As in [1], we work in the key encapsulation mechanism (**KEM**) setting, where the **PE** ciphertext hides a symmetric session key that can then be used to symmetrically encrypt data of arbitrary length.

$\mathcal{G}_{ob}(1^\lambda, (n_t)_{t=0,1})$: This algorithm performs the following operations:

- Generate $(\mathsf{param}_{\mathbb{G}} = (q, \mathbb{G}, \mathbb{G}_T, G, e) \xleftarrow{\$} \mathcal{G}_{bpg}(1^\lambda)$, $\psi \xleftarrow{\$} \mathbb{F}_q^\times$, where $\mathbb{F}_q^\times = \mathbb{F}_q \backslash \{0\}$.
- For $t = 0, 1$ execute the following:
  - Obtain $\mathsf{param}_{\mathbb{V}_t} = (q, \mathbb{V}_t, \mathbb{G}_T, \mathbb{A}_t, E) \xleftarrow{\$} \mathcal{G}_{dpvs}(1^\lambda, n_t, \mathsf{param}_{\mathbb{G}})$ such that $\mathbb{V}_t = \overbrace{\mathbb{G} \times \ldots \times \mathbb{G}}^{n_t}$ and $\mathbb{A}_t = \{a_{t,1}, \ldots, a_{t,n_t}\}$ is canonical basis of $\mathbb{V}_t$, where $a_{t,i} = (\overbrace{0, \ldots, 0}^{i-1}, G, \overbrace{0, \ldots, 0}^{n_t-i})$.
  - Choose $X_t = (\chi_{t,i,j})_{i,j=1,\ldots,n_t} \xleftarrow{\$} \mathsf{GL}(n_t, \mathbb{F}_q)$.
  - Compute $X_t^* = (\vartheta_{t,i,j})_{i,j=1,\ldots,n_t} = \psi(X_t^\mathsf{T})^{-1}$, where Y^T denotes transpose of the matrix Y. Hereafter, $\vec{\chi}_{t,i}$ and $\vec{\vartheta}_{t,i}$ represent the i-th rows of X_t and X_t^* respectively, for $i = 1, \ldots, n_t$. Note that, for $i, i' = 1, \ldots, n_t$, $\vec{\chi}_{t,i} \cdot \vec{\vartheta}_{t,i'} = \sum_{j=1}^{n_t} \chi_{t,i,j} \vartheta_{t,i',j} = \psi$, if $i = i'$, and 0, otherwise.
  - For $i = 1, \ldots, n_t$, set $b_{t,i} = (\vec{\chi}_{t,i})_{\mathbb{A}_t} = \sum_{j=1}^{n_t} \chi_{t,i,j} a_{t,j} = (\chi_{t,i,1} G, \ldots, \chi_{t,i,n_t} G)$,

    $b_{t,i}^* = (\vec{\vartheta}_{t,i})_{\mathbb{A}_t} = \sum_{j=1}^{n_t} \vartheta_{t,i,j} a_{t,j} = (\vartheta_{t,i,1} G, \ldots, \vartheta_{t,i,n_t} G)$, and define $\mathbb{B}_t = \{b_{t,1}, \ldots, b_{t,n_t}\}$, $\mathbb{B}_t^* = \{b_{t,1}^*, \ldots, b_{t,n_t}^*\}$.
- Compute $g_T = e(G, G)^\psi$ and set $\mathsf{param} = (\{\mathsf{param}_{\mathbb{V}_t}\}_{t=0,1}, g_T)$.
- Return $(\mathsf{param}, \{\mathbb{B}_t, \mathbb{B}_t^*\}_{t=0,1})$.

Observe that for $t = 0, 1; i, i' = 1, \ldots, n_t$,

$$\begin{aligned} E(b_{t,i}, b_{t,i'}^*) &= E((\vec{\chi}_{t,i})_{\mathbb{A}_t}, (\vec{\vartheta}_{t,i'})_{\mathbb{A}_t}) \\ &= E((\chi_{t,i,1} G, \ldots, \chi_{t,i,n_t} G), (\vartheta_{t,i',1} G, \ldots, \vartheta_{t,i',n_t} G)) \\ &= \prod_{j=1}^{n_t} e(G, G)^{\chi_{t,i,j} \vartheta_{t,i',j}} = e(G, G)^{\vec{\chi}_{t,i} \cdot \vec{\vartheta}_{t,i'}} \\ &= e(G, G)^\psi = g_T, \text{ if } i = i', \text{ and 0 otherwise.} \end{aligned}$$

Fig. 1. Dual orthogonal basis generator $\mathcal{G}_{ob}(1^\lambda, (n_t)_{t=0,1})$

• Syntax of Online/Offline Predicate Key Encapsulation Mechanism:
An online/offline predicate key encapsulation mechanism (PKEM) for generalized inner-product relations R consists of the following probabilistic polynomial-time algorithms:

OOPKEM.Setup(1^λ): The trusted key-generation center takes as input a security parameter 1^λ and publishes public parameters PK while keeps the master secret key MK to itself.

OOPKEM.Extract(PK, MK, $\vec{v}$): Taking input public parameters PK, master secret key MK and a vector $\vec{v}$ from a user, the key generation center provides a corresponding private key SK$_{\vec{v}}$ to the user.

OOPKEM.OfflineEncrypt(PK): In the offline phases, the encrypter takes as input the public parameters PK and prepares an intermediate ciphertext pool IT.

OOPKEM.OnlineEncrypt(PK, IT, $\vec{x}$): In the online phase, on input the public parameters PK, intermediate ciphertext pool IT, and a vector $\vec{x}$, the encrypter outputs a ciphertext $CT_{\vec{x}}$ while generates the session key key to be kept to itself.

OOPKEM.Decrypt(PK, SK$_{\vec{v}}$, CT$_{\vec{x}}$): A user takes as input the public parameters PK, its private key SK$_{\vec{v}}$ for $\vec{v}$, and a ciphertext CT$_{\vec{x}}$ associated with vector $\vec{x}$ and decapsulates ciphertext CT$_{\vec{x}}$ to recover a session key key or outputs the distinguished symbol $\perp$.

• **Correctness:** An online/offline PKEM scheme for generalized inner-product predicates must satisfy the following correctness property: For all PK, MK generated by OOPKEM.Setup(1^λ), all vectors $\vec{v}$, $\vec{x}$, all private keys SK$_{\vec{v}}$ output by OOPKEM.Extract(PK, MK, $\vec{v}$), if OOPKEM.OnlineEncrypt(PK, IT, $\vec{x}$) generates key, CT$_{\vec{x}}$, where IT is output by OOPKEM.OfflineEncrypt(PK), and if $R(\vec{v}, \vec{x}) = 1$, then OOPKEM.Decrypt(PK, SK$_{\vec{v}}$, CT$_{\vec{x}}$) outputs key. Otherwise, it holds with negligible probability.

• **Security Model for Online/Offline PKEM Scheme:** The model for defining the adaptively fully-attribute-hiding security of online/offline PKEM against probabilistic adversary $\mathcal{A}$ under chosen plaintext attack (CPA) is defined by the following game between the adversary $\mathcal{A}$ and a probabilistic challenger $\mathcal{B}$:

Setup: $\mathcal{B}$ runs OOPKEM.Setup(1^λ) and gives the public parameters PK to $\mathcal{A}$.

Phase 1: $\mathcal{A}$ may adaptively make a polynomial number of key queries for vectors, $\vec{v}$, to $\mathcal{B}$. In response, $\mathcal{B}$ gives the corresponding private key SK$_{\vec{v}}$ to $\mathcal{A}$ by executing OOPKEM.Extract(PK, MK, $\vec{v}$).

Challenge: $\mathcal{A}$ submits challenge vectors $\vec{x}^{(0)}$, $\vec{x}^{(1)}$ with the same index set $I_{\vec{x}^{(0)}} = I_{\vec{x}^{(1)}}$ subject to the following restriction: Any key query $\vec{v}$ in **Phase 1** satisfies $R(\vec{v}, \vec{x}^{(0)}) = R(\vec{v}, \vec{x}^{(1)})$.

$\mathcal{B}$ flips a coin $b \xleftarrow{\$} \{0, 1\}$ and performs the following:

(a) If for all key queries $\vec{v}$ in **Phase 1**, $R(\vec{v}, \vec{x}^{(0)}) = R(\vec{v}, \vec{x}^{(1)}) = 0$, then $\mathcal{B}$ runs OOPKEM.OnlineEncrypt(PK, OOPKEM.OfflineEncrypt(PK), $\vec{x}^{(b)}$) to obtain a challenge ciphertext CT^* and the corresponding encapsulated key key*. In case $b = 0$, $\mathcal{B}$ gives CT^* and key* to $\mathcal{A}$. Otherwise, $\mathcal{B}$ gives CT^* and a random session key to $\mathcal{A}$.

(b) If $R(\vec{v}, \vec{x}^{(0)}) = R(\vec{v}, \vec{x}^{(1)}) = 1$ for some key query $\vec{v}$ in **Phase 1**, $\mathcal{B}$ runs OOPKEM.OnlineEncrypt(PK, OOPKEM.OfflineEncrypt(PK), $\vec{x}^{(b)}$) to obtain the challenge ciphertext CT^* and an encapsulated key key*. $\mathcal{B}$ gives CT^*, key* to $\mathcal{A}$.

Phase 2: Phase 1 is repeated under the above restriction for key queries $\vec{v}$ and challenge $\vec{x}^{(0)}$, $\vec{x}^{(1)}$ together with the following additional constraint: If $R(\vec{v}, \vec{x}^{(0)}) = R(\vec{v}, \vec{x}^{(1)}) = 0$ for all queries $\vec{v}$ in Phase 1 then the same should also hold for all key queries $\vec{v}$ in this phase.

Guess: $\mathcal{A}$ eventually outputs a bit b', and wins the game if $b' = b$.

An online/offline PKEM scheme is adaptively fully-attribute hiding (AH) against chosen plaintext attacks (CPA) if for all probabilistic polynomial-time adversaries $\mathcal{A}$ and for all security parameters λ, the probability of $\mathcal{A}$ of winning the above game is at most negligible.

2.3 Definition of Online/Offline Attribute-Based Encryption with Non-Monotone Access Structure

Definition 3 (Span Program). *Let $\{p_1, \ldots, p_N\}$ be a set of variables. A span program over $\mathbb{F}_q$ is a labeled matrix $\widehat{M} = (M, \rho)$ where M is an $\ell \times r$ matrix over $\mathbb{F}_q$ and ρ is a labeling of the rows of M by literals from $\{p_1, \ldots, p_N, \neg p_1, \ldots, \neg p_N\}$, i.e., $\rho : \{1, \ldots, \ell\} \to \{p_1, \ldots, p_N, \neg p_1, \ldots, \neg p_N\}$. A span program accepts or rejects an input according to the following criterion: For every input sequence $\varsigma \in \{0, 1\}^N$ consider the submatrix M_ς of M consisting of those rows whose labels are set to 1 by the input ς, i.e., either rows labeled by some p_i such that $\varsigma_i = 1$ or rows labeled by some $\neg p_i$ such that $\varsigma_i = 0$.*

The span program $\widehat{M}$ accepts ς if and only if $\overrightarrow{1} \in \mathsf{span}\langle M_\varsigma \rangle$, i.e., some linear combination of the rows of M_ς gives the all one vector $\overrightarrow{1}$.

A span program computes a Boolean function f if it accepts exactly those inputs ς where $f(\varsigma) = 1$.

Definition 4 (Access Structure ([8])). *Let for each $t \in \{1, \ldots, d\} \subset \mathbb{N}$, $\mathbb{U}_t \subset \{0, 1\}^*$ be a sub-universe, a set of attributes, each of which is expressed by a pair of sub-universe id and value of attribute, i.e., (t, v), where $t \in \{1, \ldots, d\}$ and $v \in \mathbb{F}_q$.*

We now define such an attribute to be a variable p of a span program $\widehat{M} = (M, \rho)$, i.e., $p = (t, v)$. An access structure $\mathbb{S}$ is a span program $\widehat{M} = (M, \rho)$ along with variables $p = (t, v), p' = (t', v'), \ldots$, i.e., $\mathbb{S} = (M, \rho)$ such that M is an $\ell \times r$ matrix and $\rho : \{1, \ldots, \ell\} \to \{(t, v), (t', v'), \ldots, \neg(t, v), \neg(t', v'), \ldots\}$.

Let Γ be a set of attributes, i.e., $\Gamma = \{(t, x_t) | t \in \{1, \ldots, d\}, x_t \in \mathbb{F}_q\}$.

The access structure $\mathbb{S} = (M, \rho)$ accepts Γ if and only if $\overrightarrow{1} \in \mathsf{span}\langle M_i | [(\rho(i) = (t, v_i)) \wedge ((t, x_t) \in \Gamma) \wedge (v_i = x_t)] \vee [(\rho(i) = \neg(t, v_i)) \wedge ((t, x_t) \in \Gamma) \wedge (v_i \neq x_t)] \rangle$.

Definition 5 (Secret-Sharing Scheme for Non-Monotone Access Structure ([8])). *A secret-sharing scheme for span program $\widehat{M} = (M, \rho)$ is defined as follows:*

1. *Let M be a $\ell \times r$ matrix. Let column vector $\overrightarrow{f}^{\mathsf{T}} = (f_1, \ldots, f_r)^{\mathsf{T}} \xleftarrow{\$} \mathbb{F}_q^r$. We define $s_0 = \overrightarrow{1} \cdot \overrightarrow{f}^{\mathsf{T}} = \sum_{k=1}^{r} f_k$ is the secret to be shared and $\overrightarrow{s}^{\mathsf{T}} = (s_1, \ldots, s_\ell)^{\mathsf{T}} = M \cdot \overrightarrow{f}^{\mathsf{T}}$ is the vector of ℓ shares of the secret s_0 and the share s_i belongs to $\rho(i)$.*

2. *If span program $\widehat{M} = (M, \rho)$ accepts ς, or access structure $\mathbb{S} = (M, \rho)$ accepts Γ, then there exists constants $\{\alpha_i \in \mathbb{F}_q | i \in I\}$ such that $I \subseteq \{i \in \{1, \ldots, \ell\} | [(\rho(i) = (t, v_i)) \wedge ((t, x_t) \in \Gamma) \wedge (v_i = x_t)] \vee [((\rho(i) = \neg(t, v_i)) \wedge$*

$((t, x_t) \in \Gamma) \wedge (v_i \neq x_t)]\}$ and $\sum_{i \in I} \alpha_i s_i = s_0$. Furthermore, these constants $\{\alpha_i | i \in I\}$ can be computed in time polynomial in the size of matrix $\boldsymbol{M}$.

We now define an online/offline key-policy ABE. The ciphertext-policy version can be defined analogously by moving the access structure to the encryption side and the set of attributes to the key generation side. As described earlier, here also we will operate in the key encapsulation mode.

● **Syntax of Online/Offline Key-Policy Attribute-Based Key Encapsulation Mechanism**: An online/offline key-policy attribute-based key encapsulation mechanism (KP-ABKEM) consists of the following probabilistic polynomial-time algorithms:

OOKP-ABKEM.Setup(1^λ): The trusted key generation center takes as input a security parameter 1^λ. It publishes the public parameters PK and generates the master secret key MK for itself.

OOKP-ABKEM.Extract(PK, MK, $\mathbb{S}$): Taking as input the public parameters PK, master secret key MK, and an access structure $\mathbb{S} = (\boldsymbol{M}, \rho)$ from a user, the key generation center provides a corresponding private key SK$_\mathbb{S}$ to the user.

OOKP-ABKEM.OfflineEncrypt(PK): During the offline phases, the encrypter takes as input the public parameters PK only and generates and stores an intermediate ciphertext pool IT.

OOKP-ABKEM.OnlineEncrypt(PK, IT, Γ): In the online phase, on input the public parameters PK, an intermediate ciphertext pool IT, and a set of attributes Γ, the encrypter outputs a ciphertext CT$_\Gamma$ and generates a session key key to be kept to itself.

OOKP-ABKEM.Decrypt(PK, SK$_\mathbb{S}$, CT$_\Gamma$): A user takes as input the public parameters PK, its private key SK$_\mathbb{S}$ for access structure $\mathbb{S}$, and a ciphertext CT$_\Gamma$ associated with an attribute set Γ. It decapsulates ciphertext CT$_\Gamma$ to recover a session key key or outputs the distinguished symbol $\perp$.

The correctness condition as well as the model for defining the adaptive payload-hiding security against CPA for online/offline KP-ABKEM are provided in [1] and are omitted here due to space constraint.

3 Our PKEM Schemes with Online/Offline Encryption

3.1 PKEM-I: Type I **Online/Offline** PKEM **Construction**

OOPKEM.Setup(1^λ): The trusted key generation center takes as input a security parameter 1^λ. It proceeds as follows:

1. It runs $\mathcal{G}_{ob}(1^\lambda, (n_0 = 5, n = 15))$, described in Figure 1, to obtain (param = (param$_{\mathbb{V}_0}$, param$_\mathbb{V}$, $g_T = e(G, G)^\psi$), $\{\mathbb{B}_0 = \{b_{0,1}, \ldots, b_{0,5}\}, \mathbb{B}_0^* = \{b_{0,1}^*, \ldots, b_{0,5}^*\}\}, \{\mathbb{B} = \{b_1, \ldots, b_{15}\}, \mathbb{B}^* = \{b_1^*, \ldots, b_{15}^*\}\}$).

2. It defines $\widehat{\mathbb{B}}_0 = \{b_{0,1}, b_{0,3}, b_{0,5}\}, \widehat{\mathbb{B}} = \{b_1, \ldots, b_4, b_{14}, b_{15}\}, \widehat{\mathbb{B}}_0^* = \{b_{0,1}^*, b_{0,3}^*, b_{0,4}^*\}, \widehat{\mathbb{B}}^* = \{b_1^*, \ldots, b_4^*, b_{12}^*, b_{13}^*\}$.

3. It publishes the public parameters $\mathsf{PK} = (\mathsf{param}, \widehat{\mathbb{B}}_0, \widehat{\mathbb{B}})$ and stores master secret key $\mathsf{MK} = (\widehat{\mathbb{B}}_0^*, \widehat{\mathbb{B}}^*)$.

OOPKEM.Extract($\mathsf{PK}, \mathsf{MK}, \vec{v}$): Taking as input the public parameters PK, master secret key MK, and a vector $\vec{v} = \{(t, v_t)|t \in I_{\vec{v}} \subset \mathbb{N}\}$ from a user, the key generation center performs the following steps:

1. It selects $\delta, \eta_0 \xleftarrow{\$} \mathbb{F}_q$, together with $s_t \xleftarrow{\$} \mathbb{F}_q$ for each $t \in I_{\vec{v}}$, and sets $s_0 = \sum_{t \in I_{\vec{v}}} s_t$. It computes $\boldsymbol{k}_0^* = (-s_0, 1, \eta_0)_{\widehat{\mathbb{B}}_0^*} = (-s_0, 0, 1, \eta_0, 0)_{\mathbb{B}_0^*}$ using $\widehat{\mathbb{B}}_0^*$ extracted from MK.

2. For each $t \in I_{\vec{v}}$, it chooses $\mu_t, \eta_{t,1}, \eta_{t,2} \xleftarrow{\$} \mathbb{F}_q$ and computes

$$\boldsymbol{k}_t^* = (\mu_t(t, -1), \delta v_t, s_t, \eta_{t,1}, \eta_{t,2})_{\widehat{\mathbb{B}}^*} = (\mu_t(t, -1), \delta v_t, s_t, 0^7, \eta_{t,1}, \eta_{t,2}, 0^2)_{\mathbb{B}^*}$$

using $\widehat{\mathbb{B}}^*$ extracted from MK.

3. It provides the private key $\mathsf{SK}_{\vec{v}} = (I_{\vec{v}}, \boldsymbol{k}_0^*, \{\boldsymbol{k}_t^*\}_{t \in I_{\vec{v}}})$ to the user.

Note that we have represented $\boldsymbol{k}_0^*$ and $\boldsymbol{k}_t^*$ as linear combinations of vectors in $\mathbb{B}_0^*$ and $\mathbb{B}^*$ respectively taking the coefficients of vectors in $\mathbb{B}_0^* \backslash \widehat{\mathbb{B}}_0^*$ and $\mathbb{B}^* \backslash \widehat{\mathbb{B}}^*$ as zeroes for ease of explanation. Here after a similar notation will be followed for representing linear combinations in $\mathbb{V}_0$ and $\mathbb{V}$.

OOPKEM.OfflineEncrypt(PK): During the offline phases the encrypter takes as input the public parameters PK only. It prepares the intermediate ciphertext pool IT that will be comprised of two logical type of objects– main module and component module.

(a) The main module is computed as follows: The encrypter selects $\widetilde{\omega}, \zeta, \varphi_0 \xleftarrow{\$} \mathbb{F}_q$ and computes $\boldsymbol{c}_0 = (\widetilde{\omega}, 0, \zeta, 0, \varphi_0)_{\mathbb{B}_0}$, $\mathsf{key} = g_T^{\zeta}$. It sets $\mathsf{IT}_{\mathsf{main}} = (\boldsymbol{c}_0, \mathsf{key}, \widetilde{\omega})$.

(b) The component module is computed as follows: The encrypter picks $\sigma, t', \pi, \xi, \varphi_1, \varphi_2 \xleftarrow{\$} \mathbb{F}_q$ and computes $\boldsymbol{c}' = (\sigma(1, t'), \pi, \xi, 0^7, 0^2, \varphi_1, \varphi_2)_{\mathbb{B}}$. It sets $\mathsf{IT}_{\mathsf{comp}} = (\boldsymbol{c}', \sigma, t', \pi, \xi)$.

OOPKEM.OnlineEncrypt($\mathsf{PK}, \mathsf{IT}, \vec{x}$): In the online phase, on input the public parameters PK, the offline ciphertext pool IT, and a vector $\vec{x} = \{(t_\iota, x_{t_\iota})|t_\iota \in I_{\vec{x}} \subset \mathbb{N}\}$, the encrypter computes the ciphertext as follows:

1. It pricks any main module $\mathsf{IT}_{\mathsf{main}} = (\boldsymbol{c}_0, \mathsf{key}, \widetilde{\omega})$ together with any $\sharp I_{\vec{x}}$ component modules $\mathsf{IT}_{\mathsf{comp}_\iota} = (\boldsymbol{c}'_\iota, \sigma_\iota, t'_\iota, \pi_\iota, \xi_\iota)$, for $\iota = 1, \ldots, \sharp I_{\vec{x}}$, available in the offline ciphertext pool IT and removes those elements from IT.

2. It outputs the ciphertext $\mathsf{CT}_{\vec{x}} = (I_{\vec{x}}, \boldsymbol{c}_0, \{\boldsymbol{c}_{t_\iota}^{(1)} = \boldsymbol{c}'_\iota, c_{t_\iota}^{(2)} = \sigma_\iota(t_\iota - t'_\iota), c_{t_\iota}^{(3)} = \omega x_{t_\iota} - \pi_\iota, c_{t_\iota}^{(4)} = \widetilde{\omega} - \xi_\iota\}_{t_\iota \in I_{\vec{x}}})$, where $\omega \xleftarrow{\$} \mathbb{F}_q$ is chosen by the encrypter during the online phase. The encapsulated key is key.

OOPKEM.Decrypt($\mathsf{PK}, \mathsf{SK}_{\vec{v}}, \mathsf{CT}_{\vec{x}}$): A user takes as input the public parameters PK, its private key $\mathsf{SK}_{\vec{v}} = (I_{\vec{v}}, \boldsymbol{k}_0^*, \{\boldsymbol{k}_t^*\}_{t \in I_{\vec{v}}})$ and a ciphertext $\mathsf{CT}_{\vec{x}} = (I_{\vec{x}}, \boldsymbol{c}_0, \{\boldsymbol{c}_t^{(1)}, c_t^{(2)}, c_t^{(3)}, c_t^{(4)}\}_{t \in I_{\vec{x}}})$.

(a) If $I_{\vec{v}} \subseteq I_{\vec{x}}$, it retrieves the encapsulated key as

$$\mathsf{key}' = E(\boldsymbol{c}_0, \boldsymbol{k}_0^*) \cdot \prod_{t \in I_{\vec{v}}} E(\boldsymbol{c}_t^{(1)} + c_t^{(2)}\boldsymbol{b}_2 + c_t^{(3)}\boldsymbol{b}_3 + c_t^{(4)}\boldsymbol{b}_4, \boldsymbol{k}_t^*). \quad (1)$$

(b) Otherwise, it outputs $\perp$.

Remark 1. Observe that during offline phases, an arbitrary number of main and component modules are independently created and all those values are stored as the offline ciphertext pool IT. Furthermore, note that the main modules and the component modules are created such that any component module can be attached to any main module. The online phase uses exactly what it needs and modules left in the pool can be used on subsequent ciphertexts. Note that a ciphertext associated with a vector $\vec{x}$ would consume one main module along with at most L many component modules where L is the maximum size of $\sharp I_{\vec{x}}$ supported by the system. It is obvious from the construction that we need to create less main modules and more component modules during the offline phase. Finally, observe that in order to support a *polynomial* number of online encryption, which is a reasonable supposition since low power devices are usually charged at regular intervals, the size of the offline ciphertext pool IT would only be *polynomial.*

The correctness of the above scheme follows from the fact that

$$E(\boldsymbol{c}_0, \boldsymbol{k}_0^*) \cdot \prod_{t \in I_{\vec{v}}} E(c_t^{(1)} + c_t^{(2)} \boldsymbol{b}_2 + c_t^{(3)} \boldsymbol{b}_3 + c_t^{(4)} \boldsymbol{b}_4, \boldsymbol{k}_t^*) = g_T^{\zeta},$$

provided $I_{\vec{v}} \subseteq I_{\vec{x}}$ and $\sum_{t \in I_{\vec{v}}} v_t x_t = 0$.

Theorem 1. *The online/offline* Type I PKEM, *described in Section 3.1, is adaptively attribute-hiding against* CPA, *as per the security model, described in Section 2.2, under the assumption that the scheme of Okamoto et al.* [8] *is an adaptively attribute-hiding-*CPA*-secure* Type I PE *system.*

Proof. To prove Theorem 1, we show that any probabilistic polynomial-time attacker $\mathcal{A}$ with a non-negligible advantage against the online/offline PKEM scheme given in Section 3.1, denoted by $\Pi_{\mathsf{OOPKEM\text{-}I}} = $ (OOPKEM.Setup, OOPKEM.Extract, OOPKEM.OfflineEncrypt, OOPKEM.OnlineEncrypt, OOPKEM.Decrypt), can be employed to break the adaptive CPA-security of the Okamoto et al. scheme [8], denoted by $\Pi_{\mathsf{OTPE\text{-}I}} = $ (Setup$_{\mathsf{OTPE\text{-}I}}$, Extract$_{\mathsf{OTPE\text{-}I}}$, Encrypt$_{\mathsf{OTPE\text{-}I}}$, Decrypt$_{\mathsf{OTPE\text{-}I}}$), with a probabilistic polynomial-time simulator $\mathcal{B}$.

$\mathcal{B}$ plays the role of the challenger and interacts with $\mathcal{A}$ in the online/offline PKEM security game, defined in Section 2.2 with security parameter λ.

Setup: $\mathcal{B}$ receives the public parameters PK $= (\mathsf{param}, \widehat{\mathbb{B}}_0, \widehat{\mathbb{B}})$ from the OTPE challenger and passes them to $\mathcal{A}$ unchanged.

Phase 1: The private keys are the same in both schemes, so any key generation request from $\mathcal{A}$ is passed to the OTPE challenger by $\mathcal{B}$ and the answer received from the OTPE challenger is passed to $\mathcal{A}$.

Challenge: $\mathcal{B}$ receives two challenge vectors $\vec{x}^{(0)}, \vec{x}^{(1)}$ with $I_{\vec{x}^{(0)}} = I_{\vec{x}^{(1)}} = I$ (say) from $\mathcal{A}$. $\mathcal{B}$ proceeds as follows:

1. If it is found that $R(\vec{v}, \vec{x}^{(0)}) = R(\vec{v}, \vec{x}^{(1)}) = 0$ for all key queries $\vec{v}$ in **Phase 1**, then $\mathcal{B}$ selects two distinct random messages M_0, M_1 in the OTPE-I message space. On the other hand, if it is found that $R(\vec{v}, \vec{x}^{(0)}) = R(\vec{v}, \vec{x}^{(1)}) = 1$ for some key query $\vec{v}$ in **Phase 1**, then $\mathcal{B}$ chooses random message $M_0 = M_1$ in the OTPE-I message space.

2. $\mathcal{B}$ sends M_0, M_1 together with $\vec{x}^{(0)}, \vec{x}^{(1)}$ to its OTPE challenger and receives back a challenge ciphertext $\mathsf{CT}^*_{\mathsf{OTPE}} = (I, c_0, \{c_t\}_{t \in I}, c_T)$ generated following $\mathsf{Encrypt}_{\mathsf{OTPE\text{-}I}}$ of $\Pi_{\mathsf{OTPE\text{-}I}}$ [8]. Here, $c_T = g_T^\zeta M_b, c_0 = (\widetilde{\omega}, 0, \zeta, 0, \varphi_0)_{\mathbb{B}_0}$, and $c_t = (\sigma_t(1, t), \omega x_t^{(b)}, \widetilde{\omega}, 0^7, 0^2, \varphi_{t,1}, \varphi_{t,2})_{\mathbb{B}}$, for each $t \in I$, where $\widetilde{\omega}, \zeta, \varphi_0, \omega, \sigma_t, \varphi_{t,1}, \varphi_{t,2} \xleftarrow{\$} \mathbb{F}_q$, and $b \xleftarrow{\$} \{0, 1\}$ has been selected by the OTPE challenger and is unknown to $\mathcal{B}$.

3. $\mathcal{B}$ selects $u_t, y_t, z_t \xleftarrow{\$} \mathbb{F}_q$ and sets the challenge ciphertext as $\mathsf{CT}^* = (I, c_0^*, \{c_t^{*(1)}, c_t^{*(2)}, c_t^{*(3)}, c_t^{*(4)}\}_{t \in I})$, where $c_0^* = c_0, c_t^{*(1)} = c_t - u_t b_2 - y_t b_3 - z_t b_4, c_t^{*(2)} = u_t, c_t^{*(3)} = y_t, c_t^{*(4)} = z_t$. One can easily check that this is a correctly formed ciphertext for our Type I online/offline PKEM $\Pi_{\mathsf{OOPKEM\text{-}I}}$ by computing the second set of pairings of equation (1), namely, $E(c_t^{(1)} + c_t^{(2)} b_2 + c_t^{(3)} b_3 + c_t^{(4)} b_4, k_t^*)$. Also, observe that the ciphertext is randomized to have the proper distribution.

4. $\mathcal{B}$ computes the encapsulated key $\mathsf{key}^* = c_T / M_0$.

5. Finally $\mathcal{B}$ sends to $\mathcal{A}$ the tuple $(\mathsf{CT}^*, \mathsf{key}^*)$.

Phase 2: $\mathcal{B}$ proceeds exactly as in **Phase 1**.

Guess: Eventually, $\mathcal{A}$ outputs a bit b'. $\mathcal{B}$ also outputs b'.

In case when $R(\vec{v}, \vec{x}^{(0)}) = R(\vec{v}, \vec{x}^{(1)}) = 0$ for all key queries $\vec{v}$ in **Phase 1** and **Phase 2** and challenge vectors $\vec{x}^{(0)}, \vec{x}^{(1)}$, from $\mathcal{B}$'s simulation it follows that if $b = 0$, then CT^* encodes $\vec{x}^{(0)}$ and key^* is a proper session key, whereas, if $b = 1$, then CT^* encodes $\vec{x}^{(1)}$ and key^* is a random session key. On the other hand, in case $R(\vec{v}, \vec{x}^{(0)}) = R(\vec{v}, \vec{x}^{(1)}) = 1$ for some key query $\vec{v}$, from $\mathcal{B}$'s simulation it follows that CT^* encodes $\vec{x}^{(0)}$ or $\vec{x}^{(1)}$ according as $b = 0$ or 1 and in both cases key^* is a proper encapsulated key. Thus the distribution of $\mathcal{A}$ is perfect. Hence, if $\mathcal{A}$ has advantage ϵ in the online/offline PKEM security game against $\Pi_{\mathsf{OOPKEM\text{-}I}}$, then $\mathcal{B}$ breaks $\Pi_{\mathsf{OTPE\text{-}I}}$ with advantage ϵ. $\qquad\square$

3.2 PKEM-II: Type II **Online/Offline PKEM Construction**

OOPKEM.Setup(1^λ): Same as the Type I construction of Section 3.1.

OOPKEM.Extract(PK, MK, $\vec{v}$): The key generation center takes as input the public parameters PK, master secret key MK, and a vector $\vec{v} = \{(t, v_t) | t \in I_{\vec{v}} \subset \mathbb{N}\}$ from a user. It performs the following steps:

1. It selects $\omega, \widetilde{\omega}, \eta_0 \xleftarrow{\$} \mathbb{F}_q$ and computes $k_0^* = (\widetilde{\omega}, 0, 1, \eta_0, 0)_{\mathbb{B}_0^*}$.

2. For each $t \in I_{\vec{v}}$, it picks $\mu_t, \eta_{t,1}, \eta_{t,2} \xleftarrow{\$} \mathbb{F}_q$ and computes $k_t^* = (\mu_t(t, -1), \omega v_t, \widetilde{\omega}, 0^7, \eta_{t,1}, \eta_{t,2}, 0^2)_{\mathbb{B}^*}$.

3. It provides the private key $\mathsf{SK}_{\vec{v}} = (I_{\vec{v}}, k_0^*, \{k_t^*\}_{t \in I_{\vec{v}}})$ to the user.

OOPKEM.OfflineEncrypt(PK): During the offline phases, on input the public parameters PK, the encrypter computes the intermediate ciphertext pool IT comprised of main modules and component modules as follows:

(a) For a main module, it picks $s_0', \zeta, \varphi_0 \xleftarrow{\$} \mathbb{F}_q$, obtains $c_0' = (-s_0', 0, \zeta, 0, \varphi_0)_{\mathbb{B}_0}$, key $= g_T^\zeta$, and sets $\mathsf{IT}_{\mathsf{main}} = (c_0', \mathsf{key}, s_0')$.

(b) For a component module, it selects $\sigma, t', \pi, s, \varphi_1, \varphi_2 \xleftarrow{\$} \mathbb{F}_q$, computes $c' = (\sigma(1, t'), \pi, s, 0^7, 0^2, \varphi_1, \varphi_2)_{\mathbb{B}}$, and it sets $\mathsf{IT}_{\mathsf{comp}} = (c', \sigma, t', \pi, s)$.

OOPKEM.OnlineEncrypt(PK, IT, $\vec{x}$): In the online phase, the encrypter takes as input the public parameters PK, the offline ciphertext pool IT, and a vector $\vec{x} = \{(t_\iota, x_{t_\iota}) | t_\iota \in I_{\vec{x}} \subset \mathbb{N}\}$ and prepares the ciphertext as follows:

1. It selects any one main module $\mathsf{IT}_{\mathsf{main}} = (c_0', \mathsf{key}, s_0')$ and $\sharp I_{\vec{x}}$ many component modules $\mathsf{IT}_{\mathsf{comp}_\iota} = (c_\iota', \sigma_\iota, t_\iota', \pi_\iota, s_\iota)$, for $\iota = 1, \ldots, \sharp I_{\vec{x}}$, from the pool IT and removes them from IT.

2. It chooses $\delta \xleftarrow{\$} \mathbb{F}_q$, sets $s_0 = \sum_{t_\iota \in I_{\vec{x}}} s_\iota$ and outputs the ciphertext $\mathsf{CT}_{\vec{x}} =$
$(I_{\vec{x}}, c_0^{(1)} = c_0', c_0^{(2)} = -s_0 + s_0', \{c_{t_\iota}^{(1)} = c_\iota', c_{t_\iota}^{(2)} = \sigma_\iota(t_\iota - t_\iota'), c_{t_\iota}^{(3)} = \delta x_{t_\iota} - \pi_\iota\}_{t_\iota \in I_{\vec{x}}})$. The encapsulated key is key.

OOPKEM.Decrypt(PK, $\mathsf{SK}_{\vec{v}}$, $\mathsf{CT}_{\vec{x}}$): A user takes as input the public parameters PK, its private key $\mathsf{SK}_{\vec{v}} = (I_{\vec{v}}, k_0^*, \{k_t^*\}_{t \in I_{\vec{v}}})$, and a ciphertext $\mathsf{CT}_{\vec{x}} = (I_{\vec{x}}, c_0^{(1)}, c_0^{(2)}, \{c_t^{(1)}, c_t^{(2)}, c_t^{(3)}\}_{t \in I_{\vec{x}}})$.

(a) If $I_{\vec{v}} \supseteq I_{\vec{x}}$, it retrieves the encapsulated key as

$$\mathsf{key}' = E(c_0^{(1)} + c_0^{(2)} \boldsymbol{b}_{0,1}, k_0^*) \cdot \prod_{t \in I_{\vec{x}}} E(c_t^{(1)} + c_t^{(2)} \boldsymbol{b}_2 + c_t^{(3)} \boldsymbol{b}_3, k_t^*).$$

(b) Otherwise, it outputs $\perp$.

The correctness of the above scheme can be easily verified. The formal security statement of the above scheme is given below, the proof of which is analogous to that of Theorem 1.

Theorem 2. *The online/offline* Type II PKEM *scheme, described in Section 3.2, is adaptively attribute-hiding against* CPA *as per the security model of Section 2.2 under the assumption that the scheme of Okamoto et al. [8] is a adaptive attribute-hiding-*CPA*-secure* PE *system of* Type II.

4   KP-ABKEM: Our KP-ABKEM System with Online/Offline Encryption

Let d be the total number of attribute sub-universe supported by the system. For an access structure $\mathbb{S} = (M, \rho)$, M being an $\ell \times r$ matrix, we define $\widetilde{\rho} : \{1, \ldots, \ell\} \to \{1, \ldots, d\}$ by $\widetilde{\rho}(i) = t$ if $\rho(i) = (t, v_i)$ or $\rho(i) = \neg(t, v_i)$. In the proposed scheme $\widetilde{\rho}$ is assumed to be injective for all access structures $\mathbb{S}$. This restriction, however, can be relaxed following the technique of [8].

OOKP-ABKEM.Setup(1^λ): The trusted key generation center takes input a security parameter 1^λ and proceeds as follows:

1. It runs $\mathcal{G}_{ob}(1^\lambda, (n_0 = 5, n = 14))$, described in Figure 1 to obtain (param $=$ (param$_{\mathbb{V}_0}$, param$_{\mathbb{V}}, g_T$), $\{\mathbb{B}_0, \mathbb{B}_0^*\}, \{\mathbb{B}, \mathbb{B}^*\}$).

2. It defines $\widehat{\mathbb{B}}_0 = \{\boldsymbol{b}_{0,1}, \boldsymbol{b}_{0,3}, \boldsymbol{b}_{0,5}\}, \widehat{\mathbb{B}} = \{\boldsymbol{b}_1, \ldots, \boldsymbol{b}_4, \boldsymbol{b}_{13}, \boldsymbol{b}_{14}\}, \widehat{\mathbb{B}}_0^* = \{\boldsymbol{b}_{0,1}^*, \boldsymbol{b}_{0,3}^*, \boldsymbol{b}_{0,4}^*\}, \widehat{\mathbb{B}}^* = \{\boldsymbol{b}_1^*, \ldots, \boldsymbol{b}_4^*, \boldsymbol{b}_{11}^*, \boldsymbol{b}_{12}^*\}$.

3. It publishes the public parameters PK $= (\text{param}, \widehat{\mathbb{B}}_0, \widehat{\mathbb{B}})$ and stores the master secret key MK $= (\widehat{\mathbb{B}}_0^*, \widehat{\mathbb{B}}^*)$.

OOKP-ABKEM.Extract(PK, MK, $\mathbb{S}$): On input the public parameters PK, master secret key MK, and an access structure $\mathbb{S} = (\boldsymbol{M}, \rho)$ from a user where $\boldsymbol{M}$ is an $\ell \times r$ matrix and ρ is a labeling of the rows of $\boldsymbol{M}$, the key generation center performs the following steps:

1. It selects $\overrightarrow{f} \xleftarrow{\$} \mathbb{F}_q^r$ and computes $s_0 = \overrightarrow{1} \cdot \overrightarrow{f}^\mathsf{T}, \overrightarrow{s}^\mathsf{T} = (s_1, \ldots, s_\ell)^\mathsf{T} = \boldsymbol{M} \cdot \overrightarrow{f}^\mathsf{T}$. It picks $\eta_0 \xleftarrow{\$} \mathbb{F}_q$ and computes $\boldsymbol{k}_0^* = (-s_0, 0, 1, \eta_0, 0)_{\mathbb{B}_0^*}$.

2. For $i = 1, \ldots, \ell$, it chooses $\mu_i, \theta_i, \eta_{i,1}, \eta_{i,2} \xleftarrow{\$} \mathbb{F}_q$ and computes $\boldsymbol{k}_i^*$ as follows:
   (a) If $\rho(i) = (t, v_i)$, $\boldsymbol{k}_i^* = (\mu_i(t, -1), s_i + \theta_i v_i, -\theta_i, 0^6, \eta_{i,1}, \eta_{i,2}, 0^2)_{\mathbb{B}^*}$.
   (b) If $\rho(i) = \neg(t, v_i)$, $\boldsymbol{k}_i^* = (\mu_i(t, -1), s_i(v_i, -1), 0^6, \eta_{i,1}, \eta_{i,2}, 0^2)_{\mathbb{B}^*}$.

3. It provides the private key SK$_{\mathbb{S}} = (\mathbb{S}, \boldsymbol{k}_0^*, \{\boldsymbol{k}_i^*\}_{i=1,\ldots,\ell})$ to the user.

OOKP-ABKEM.OfflineEncrypt(PK): During the offline phases, the encrypter takes as input the public parameters PK only. It prepares the intermediate ciphertext pool IT comprised of main modules and attribute modules as follows:

(a) The encrypter chooses $\omega, \zeta, \varphi_0 \xleftarrow{\$} \mathbb{F}_q$, obtains $\boldsymbol{c}_0 = (\omega, 0, \zeta, 0, \varphi_0)_{\mathbb{B}_0}$, key $= g_T^\zeta$, and sets a main module as IT$_{\text{main}} = (\boldsymbol{c}_0, \text{key}, \omega)$.

(b) The encrypter $\sigma, t', \omega', x', \varphi_1, \varphi_2 \xleftarrow{\$} \mathbb{F}_q$, computes $\boldsymbol{c}' = (\sigma(1, t'), \omega'(1, x'), 0^6, 0^2, \varphi_1, \varphi_2)_{\mathbb{B}}$, and sets an attribute module as IT$_{\text{attr}} = (\boldsymbol{c}', \sigma, t', x', \omega')$.

OOKP-ABKEM.OnlineEncrypt(PK, IT, Γ): in the online phase, taking as input the public parameters PK, the offline ciphertext pool IT, and a set of attributes $\Gamma = \{(t_\iota, x_{t_\iota}) | 1 \leq t_\iota \leq d\}$, the encrypter computes the ciphertext as follows:

1. It selects any main module IT$_{\text{main}} = (\boldsymbol{c}_0, \text{key}, \omega)$ together with $\sharp\Gamma$ many attribute modules IT$_{\text{attr}_\iota} = (\boldsymbol{c}_\iota', \sigma_\iota, t_\iota', x_\iota', \omega_\iota')$, for $\iota = 1, \ldots, \sharp\Gamma$, from the pool IT and removes them from IT.

2. It outputs the ciphertext CT$_\Gamma = (\Gamma, \boldsymbol{c}_0, \{\boldsymbol{c}_{t_\iota}^{(1)} = \boldsymbol{c}_\iota', \boldsymbol{c}_{t_\iota}^{(2)} = \sigma_\iota(t_\iota - t_\iota'), \boldsymbol{c}_{t_\iota}^{(3)} = \omega - \omega_\iota', \boldsymbol{c}_{t_\iota}^{(4)} = \omega x_{t_\iota} - \omega_\iota' x_\iota'\}_{(t_\iota, x_{t_\iota}) \in \Gamma})$. The encapsulated key is key.

OOKP-ABKEM.Decrypt(PK, SK$_{\mathbb{S}}$, CT$_\Gamma$): A user takes as input the public parameters PK, its private key SK$_{\mathbb{S}} = (\mathbb{S}, \boldsymbol{k}_0^*, \{\boldsymbol{k}_i^*\}_{i=1,\ldots,\ell})$ for its access structure $\mathbb{S} = (\boldsymbol{M}, \rho)$, and a ciphertext CT$_\Gamma = (\Gamma, \boldsymbol{c}_0, \{\boldsymbol{c}_t^{(1)}, \boldsymbol{c}_t^{(2)}, \boldsymbol{c}_t^{(3)}, \boldsymbol{c}_t^{(4)}\}_{(t,x_t) \in \Gamma})$ associated with an attribute set Γ.

1. If $\mathbb{S} = (\boldsymbol{M}, \rho)$ accepts $\Gamma = \{(t, x_t) | 1 \leq t \leq d\}$, then it obtains I and $\{\alpha_i\}_{i \in I}$ such that $\overrightarrow{1} = \sum_{i \in I} \alpha_i \boldsymbol{M}_i$, where $\boldsymbol{M}_i$ is the i-th row of $\boldsymbol{M}$, and

$I \subseteq \{i \in \{1, \ldots, \ell\} | [(\rho(i) = (t, v_i)) \wedge ((t, v_i) \in \Gamma)] \vee [(\rho(i) = \neg(t, v_i)) \wedge ((t, x_t) \in \Gamma) \wedge (v_i \neq x_t)]\}$. Otherwise, it outputs $\bot$.

2. It retrieves the encapsulated key as

$$\mathsf{key}' = E(c_0, \boldsymbol{k}_0^*) \cdot \prod_{\substack{i \in I \\ \rho(i)=(t,v_i)}} E(\boldsymbol{c}_t^{(1)} + c_t^{(2)}\boldsymbol{b}_2 + c_t^{(3)}\boldsymbol{b}_3 + c_t^{(4)}\boldsymbol{b}_4, \boldsymbol{k}_i^*)^{\alpha_i} \cdot$$

$$\prod_{\substack{i \in I \\ \rho(i)=\neg(t,v_i)}} E(\boldsymbol{c}_t^{(1)} + c_t^{(2)}\boldsymbol{b}_2 + c_t^{(3)}\boldsymbol{b}_3 + c_t^{(4)}\boldsymbol{b}_4, \boldsymbol{k}_i^*)^{\frac{\alpha_i}{v_i-x_t}}. \qquad (2)$$

It is easy to prove the correctness, defined in [1], for the above scheme.

Theorem 3. *The online/offline KP-ABKEM scheme, described in Section 4, is adaptively payload-hiding against CPA as per the security model, described in [1], under the assumption that the KP-ABE scheme of Okamoto et al. [8] is an adaptively payload-hiding secure scheme against CPA.*

Proof. To prove Theorem 3, we show that any probabilistic polynomial-time attacker $\mathcal{A}$ with a non-negligible advantage against the KP-ABKEM scheme of Section 4 can be used to break the full payload-hiding CPA-security of the scheme of Okamoto et al. [8], denoted by OTABE, with a probabilistic polynomial-time simulator $\mathcal{B}$.

$\mathcal{B}$ plays the role of the challenger and interacts with $\mathcal{A}$ in the online/offline KP-ABKEM security game, described in [1] with security parameter λ.

Setup: $\mathcal{B}$ receives the public parameters $\mathsf{PK} = (\mathsf{param}, \widehat{\mathbb{B}}_0, \widehat{\mathbb{B}})$ from the OTABE challenger and passes them to $\mathcal{A}$ unchanged.

Phase 1: The secret keys are the same in both schemes, so any key generation request from $\mathcal{A}$ for access structure $\mathbb{S}$ is passed to the OTABE challenger by $\mathcal{B}$ and the answer received from the OTABE challenger is passed to $\mathcal{A}$.

Challenge: $\mathcal{B}$ receives a challenge attribute set $\Gamma^* = \{(t, x_t) | 1 \leq t \leq d\}$ from $\mathcal{A}$ subject to the restriction that no key query $\mathbb{S}$ in **Phase 1** accepts Γ^*. $\mathcal{B}$ proceeds as follows:

1. $\mathcal{B}$ selects two distinct random messages M_0, M_1 in the OTABE message space.

2. $\mathcal{B}$ sends M_0, M_1 together with Γ^* to its OTABE challenger and receives back a challenge ciphertext $\mathsf{CT}^*_{\mathsf{OTABE}} = (\Gamma^*, \boldsymbol{c}_0, \{\boldsymbol{c}_t\}_{(t,x_t)\in\Gamma^*}, c_{d+1})$ generated by following the encryption algorithm of OTABE [8]. Here c_{d+1} is the message, selected by the OTABE challenger, times g_T^ζ, $\boldsymbol{c}_0 = (\omega, 0, \zeta, 0, \varphi_0)_{\mathbb{B}_0}$ and $\boldsymbol{c}_t = (\sigma_t(1, t), \omega(1, x_t), 0^6, 0^2, \varphi_{t,1}, \varphi_{t,2})_{\mathbb{B}}$, for each $(t, x_t) \in \Gamma^*$, where $\omega, \zeta, \varphi_0, \sigma_t, \varphi_{t,1}, \varphi_{t,2} \overset{\$}{\leftarrow} \mathbb{F}_q$.

3. $\mathcal{B}$ picks $u_t, y_t, z_t \overset{\$}{\leftarrow} \mathbb{F}_q$ and sets the challenge ciphertext as $\mathsf{CT}^* = (\Gamma^*, \boldsymbol{c}_0^*, \{\boldsymbol{c}_t^{*(1)}, c_t^{*(2)}, c_t^{*(3)}, c_t^{*(4)}\}_{(t,x_t)\in\Gamma^*})$ where $\boldsymbol{c}_0^* = \boldsymbol{c}_0, \boldsymbol{c}_t^{*(1)} = \boldsymbol{c}_t - u_t\boldsymbol{b}_2 - y_t\boldsymbol{b}_3 - z_t\boldsymbol{b}_4, c_t^{*(2)} = u_t, c_t^{*(3)} = y_t, c_t^{*(4)} = z_t$. One can easily verify that this is a correctly formed ciphertext by computing the second and

third set of pairings of equation (2), namely, $E(c_t^{(1)} + c_t^{(2)}b_2 + c_t^{(3)}b_3 + c_t^{(4)}b_4, k_i^*)$. Also, observe that the ciphertext is randomized to have the proper distribution.

4. Next $\mathcal{B}$ guesses a bit $b_{\mathcal{B}} \in \{0,1\}$, i.e., it guesses which message was encrypted by OTABE challenger in $\mathsf{CT}^*_{\mathsf{OTABE}}$, and computes the encapsulated key $\mathsf{key}^* = c_{d+1}/M_{b_{\mathcal{B}}}$.

5. Finally, $\mathcal{B}$ sends to $\mathcal{A}$ the tuple $(\mathsf{CT}^*, \mathsf{key}^*)$.

Phase 2: $\mathcal{B}$ proceeds as in **Phase 1**.

Guess: Eventually, $\mathcal{A}$ outputs a bit $b_{\mathcal{A}}$. If $b_{\mathcal{A}} = 0$ (meaning that $\mathcal{A}$ guesses that key^* is the key encapsulated by CT^*), then $\mathcal{B}$ outputs $b_{\mathcal{B}}$. If $b_{\mathcal{A}} = 1$ (meaning that $\mathcal{A}$ guesses that key^* is a random session key), then $\mathcal{B}$ outputs $1 - b_{\mathcal{B}}$.

The distribution of $\mathcal{A}$ is perfect. Thus, if $\mathcal{A}$ has advantage ϵ in the online/offline KP-ABKEM security game, then $\mathcal{B}$ breaks the OTABE system with the same advantage ϵ. □

References

1. Hohenberger, S., Waters, B.: Online/Offline attribute-based encryption. In: Krawczyk, H. (ed.) PKC 2014. LNCS, vol. 8383, pp. 293–310. Springer, Heidelberg (2014)

2. Katz, J., Sahai, A., Waters, B.: Predicate encryption supporting disjunctions, polynomial equations, and inner products. In: Smart, N.P. (ed.) EUROCRYPT 2008. LNCS, vol. 4965, pp. 146–162. Springer, Heidelberg (2008)

3. Lewko, A., Okamoto, T., Sahai, A., Takashima, K., Waters, B.: Fully secure functional encryption: Attribute-based encryption and (Hierarchical) inner product encryption. In: Gilbert, H. (ed.) EUROCRYPT 2010. LNCS, vol. 6110, pp. 62–91. Springer, Heidelberg (2010)

4. Lewko, A., Waters, B.: Unbounded HIBE and attribute-based encryption. In: Paterson, K.G. (ed.) EUROCRYPT 2011. LNCS, vol. 6632, pp. 547–567. Springer, Heidelberg (2011)

5. Okamoto, T., Takashima, K.: Hierarchical predicate encryption for inner-products. In: Matsui, M. (ed.) ASIACRYPT 2009. LNCS, vol. 5912, pp. 214–231. Springer, Heidelberg (2009)

6. Okamoto, T., Takashima, K.: Fully secure functional encryption with general relations from the decisional linear assumption. In: Rabin, T. (ed.) CRYPTO 2010. LNCS, vol. 6223, pp. 191–208. Springer, Heidelberg (2010)

7. Okamoto, T., Takashima, K.: Adaptively attribute-hiding (Hierarchical) inner product encryption. In: Pointcheval, D., Johansson, T. (eds.) EUROCRYPT 2012. LNCS, vol. 7237, pp. 591–608. Springer, Heidelberg (2012)

8. Okamoto, T., Takashima, K.: Fully secure unbounded inner-product and attribute-based encryption. In: Wang, X., Sako, K. (eds.) ASIACRYPT 2012. LNCS, vol. 7658, pp. 349–366. Springer, Heidelberg (2012)

9. Rouselakis, Y., Waters, B.: Practical constructions and new proof methods for large universe attribute-based encryption. In: Proceedings of the 2013 ACM SIGSAC Conference on Computer & Communications Security, pp. 463–474. ACM (2013)

10. Sahai, A., Waters, B.: Fuzzy identity-based encryption. In: Cramer, R. (ed.) EUROCRYPT 2005. LNCS, vol. 3494, pp. 457–473. Springer, Heidelberg (2005)

Mobile Security

A Rapid and Scalable Method for Android Application Repackaging Detection

Sibei Jiao, Yao Cheng, Lingyun Ying, Purui Su, and Dengguo Feng

Trusted Computing and Information Assurance Laboratory
Institute of Software, Chinese Academy of Sciences
{jiaosibei,chengyao,yly,supurui,feng}@tca.iscas.ac.cn

Abstract. Nowadays the security issues of Android applications (apps) are more and more serious. One of the main security threats come from repackaged apps. There already are some researches detecting repackaged apps using similarity measurement. However, so far, all the existing techniques for repackaging detection are based on code similarity or feature (e.g., permission set) similarity evaluation. In this paper, we propose a novel approach called ImageStruct that applies image similarity technique to locate and detect the changes coming from repackaging effectively. ImageStruct performs a quick repackaging detection by considering the similarity of images in target apps. The intuition behind our approach is that the repackaged apps still need to maintain the "look and feel" of the original apps by including the original images, even they might have their additional code included or some of the original code removed. To prove the effectiveness and evaluate the reliability of our approach, we carry out the compare experiments between ImageStruct and the code based similarity scores of AndroGuard. The results demonstrate that ImageStruct is not only with good performance and scalability, but also able to resistant to code obfuscation.

Keywords: Android Malware, Repackaged Application Detection, Image Similarity

1 Introduction

Android is privileging in recent years. Data shows that Android has shared 85% of the global smartphone market in Q2 2014 [1]. Normally, users purchase or download apps to their mobile phones from centralized application markets. For Android phones, Google hosts the official Android market Google Play, while all the other markets that provide application downloading is called third party markets, such as Amazon Appstore for Android. Android apps are emerging nowadays. There have been more than 1,400,000 apps in Google Play only [3]. From the huge amount of apps, there come the security threats, despite Android's security system based on permission and sandbox, and Google Play's bouncer mechanism [16]. As a matter of fact, the Android ecosystem suffers from malicious apps seriously, among which repackaging is one of the major security threats [13].

© Springer International Publishing Switzerland 2015
J. Lopez and Y. Wu (Eds.): ISPEC 2015, LNCS 9065, pp. 349–364, 2015.
DOI: 10.1007/978-3-319-17533-1_24

There are mainly two motivations for app repackaging. Firstly, dishonest developers embed the advertisements related to their own benefit accounts to other developers' apps and repackage the apps using their own signatures. After republishing the repackaged apps to the Android market, the apps are able to earn monetary profit when the embedded advertisements displayed or clicked on users' phones. Secondly, malware writers modify popular apps by inserting some malicious payload into the originals. The malicious payload is to take over mobile devices, steal user's private information, send premium SMS messages stealthily, or purchase apps without user's awareness, which all lead to the user privacy leakage or financial loss. Malware writers leverage the popularity of the original apps to increase the propagation of the repackaged malicious ones. The repackaging not only violates the copyright of original app developers, but also brings disorder factors along with severe threats to the Android markets. It has been found that about 5% to 13% of apps in the third party Android markets are the plagiarism of apps in the official Android market with no consideration of code obfuscation [22]. Besides, according to a recent study[13], it shows that 1083 of the analyzed 1260 malware samples (86.0%) are repackaged versions of legitimate apps with malicious payloads, indicating that repackaging is a favorable channel for mobile malware propagation. Moreover, since users can choose to download apps from both official market and third party markets that from different countries (e.g., Anzhi, one of the biggest Android market in China), the repackaging problem appears in both inter- and intra- market, which increases the scale and challenge for repackaging detection.

Currently, the problem of app repackaging is widely explored and several solutions have been proposed to identify plagiarized apps [5][19][8][15]. Most of these solutions are based on features extracted from the apps' code which is often impacted by the repackaging process, as the added functionality, i.e. new advertisement libraries and/or malware code, requires modification of apps' code. Of great importance, code obfuscation techniques are widely adopted to evade detection. However, the existing systems comparing similarity based on bytecode or statistical patterns of control-flow or API are *not* able to deal with the obfuscated repackaged apps [10]. In this paper, we focus on dealing with the code obfuscation problem in repackaging detection.

The intuition behind our work is that when an illegitimate author repackages an app to include malicous functions or create a pirated copy, the repackaged apps still need to maintain the "look and feel" of the original one by including the original images and other resource files, even though they might have additional code included or original code removed. Based on above observations, we explore similarity analysis on the apps' resource files especially image files to detect repackaged apps.

We propose ImageStruct which takes advantage of our novel approach and can be served as a complementary to existing repackaging systems. ImageStruct measures the similarity between two apps, based on which repackaged apps can be further detected. Specifically, giving each app from a third party Android marketplace, we measure its similarity with those apps from the official Google

Play. In order to handle the large number of apps in the marketplaces, we extract distinguishing features from apps and generate app-specific fingerprints which are based on apps' images to locate and detect the similar apps. When the similarity of two apps with differen signatures exceeds certain threshold, one of the app is considered repackaged. We construct large scale real-world experiments and run ImageStruct on apps from four third-party Android marketplaces (two from China and the other two from America) and one malware set against 39,492 apps from the official Google Play. In summary, we make four main contributions in this paper:

- We propose a novel technique to detect repackaged Android applications based on apps' image resources, which is able to resilient to code obfuscation.
- A fast algorithm to detect repackaged apps is proposed based on image fingerprint generation. It manages to compare on average 1 app every 10 second on our dataset using a commodity hardware. The data shows that our approach runs faster than existing system, e.g. DNADroid, AndroGuard.
- We implement ImageStruct that carries the image similarity measurement and evaluate the practicality of our approach. By comparing the resource-based similarity score produced by ImageStruct with the code-based similarity score computed by the open-source AndroGuard [2], the results show that the ImageStruct similarity score is strongly correlated with the Andro-Guard code similarity score.
- We evaluate the effectiveness of the ImageStruct on a dataset with more than 48,000 apps crawled from Google play and 4 alternative markets. The experiments shows that repackaging rates of alternative markets ranging from 6.7% to 14.5%, which is relatively high for a healthy mobile ecosystem.

In the following section, we describe the background and related work. In section 3, we detail our methodology and its implementation. Then in section 4, we present empirical results from two experiments. In section 5, we discuss the problem of false positives and evasion. The last section includes our conclusion and future work.

2   Background and Related Work

In this section, we introduce the structure of Android application and the existing work for repackaging detection.

2.1   Background

Android apps on the devices exist in the form of Android packages (apk files). The package contains executable code, manifest file, libraries and resource files, all compressed in a zip archive with signature from developer (Fig.1 is an unzipped FruitNinja apk [18]). Nowadays, smartphones have powerful processors, advanced video and audio systems, meaning that smartphones are able to support screens with high resolutions and to produce sounds of good quality.

```
Archive:  com.halfbrick.fruitninjafree_19199200_0.apk
  Length      Date   Time   Name
---------  ---------- -----  ----
   187151  08-20-2012 10:25  META-INF/MANIFEST.MF
   187272  08-20-2012 10:25  META-INF/IDREAMSK.SF
      949  08-20-2012 10:25  META-INF/IDREAMSK.RSA

     7975  04-19-2012 13:21  assets/sound/bonus-banana-x2.ogg
     4035  04-19-2012 13:21  assets/sound/bonus-count-up.ogg
    16062  04-19-2012 13:21  assets/sound/bonus-drum-roll.ogg
     5976  04-19-2012 13:21  assets/sound/bonus-explosion-1.ogg
     6032  04-19-2012 13:21  assets/sound/bonus-explosion-3.ogg
     6253  04-19-2012 13:21  assets/sound/bonus-explosion-5.ogg

   194807  08-15-2012 10:15  res/drawable/wood2.png
     3578  08-15-2012 10:15  res/drawable/yourall.png
     3422  08-15-2012 10:15  res/drawable/yourfriend.png
     2592  08-15-2012 10:15  res/layout/achievementdesc.xml
     1168  08-15-2012 10:15  res/layout/admob.xml
```

Fig. 1. Files inside FruitNinja

Fig. 2. User interfaces of official (left) and repackaged (right) FruitNinja

The apps are not only the composition of code any more. The multimedia factors are essential for apps to fully utilizing the power of smartphones and attracting users. These resource files become an inseparable part of modern mobile apps. The large portion of resource files in Android packages is also confirmed by our dataset that consists of 49,000 apps. The rescouses are delivered to the device packaged together with logical code. To deceive or mislead users, the repackaged apps usually maintain the original functionality and appearance. Fig.2 shows the user interfaces of an official FruitNinja and a repackaged FruitNinja which are hard to distinguish. The observation that apps with different functionality typically have different images, and similar apps (e.g. different versions of the same app) have similar images is the basis our approach relies on.

2.2 Related Work

There have been much work related to repackaging apps. The analysis performed in [22] shows that 5-13% apps hosted in alternative markets are repackeged. Jiang et. al. [22] search repackaged applications in third-party markets using Google Play as baseline. Another tool called DroidMOSS uses fuzzy hashing of code to calculate fingerprint of the app and then computes the edit distance between two fingerprints to score the similarity. Grace et. al. [21] further investigate the problem of repackaged apps and concentrate on detection of piggybacked apps (repackaged apps that carry a malicious payload). They decouple code into primary and non-primary modules, and then generate fingerprint for each primary module, which contains the main functionality. While iterating over the fingerprints, the linearithmic algorithm detects similar primary modules that are considered as piggybacked candidates. Finally, piggybacked apps are detected by comparing the sets of non-primary modules of these similar apps. The experiments show the presence of 1.3% piggybacked apps in the dataset. DNADroid [5] detects cloned (plagiarized) apps using semantic similarity. It extracts PFG (Program Flow Graph) of each method in target apps, based on which the subgraph isomorphism problem serves as final criteria. DNADroid managed to detect 191 cloned pairs (0% false positives was reported). The authors also compared their tool with AndroGuard [2]. In the total of 191 pairs, AndroGuard failed for 24 pairs and with very low similarity score for 10 pairs, meaning that it missed 18% of the pairs found by DNADroid. Based on the work on DNADroid, Crussell et al. developed AnDarwin which extracts features from app code and compares in non-pairwise way, allowing performing large-scale analysis apps. On a dataset of 265,359 third-party apps collected from 17 markets DNADroid detected 4,295 cloned and 36,106 rebranded apps. Juxtapp [8] presents another approach to detect code reuse among Android apps. To discover the similarity between the code, they use k-grams of Dalvik opcode sequences as features. To obtain app representation, they apply hashing to the extracted features. The Juxtapp can detect (a) buggy and vulnerable code reuse, (b) known malware instances and (c) pirated apps. To assess the Juxtapp efficiency, the authors ran the experiment of pairwise comparison on a set of 95,000 Android apps (an Amazon EC2 cluster with 25 slave nodes was used), which costed about 200 minutes. As for effectiveness, 174 and 239 samples containing vulnerable patterns were identified in the in-app billing code and the code using Licence Verification Library respectively. Moreover, they identified 34 new instances of known malware in the alternative Anzhi market. MIGDroid [9] is able to detect repackaged malwares based on method invocation graph. The method invocation graph reflects the "interaction" connections between different methods. MIGDroid constructs method invocation graph on the smali code level, which will be divided into weakly connected sub-graphs further. The thread score of each sub-graph is calculated based on the invoked sensitive APIs. The sub-graphs with higher scores will be more likely to be malicious. Experiment results based on 1,260 Android malware samples demonstrate the specialty of MIGDroid in detecting repackaged malwares.

Recently, a framework for evaluating Android app repackaging detection algorithms has been proposed [10]. The paper classifies currently available approaches for detection of repackaged apps and presents a framework that can assess the effectiveness of such algorithms. The framework translates Dalvik bytecode into Java code, applies obfuscation techniques and packs back the code back to the Dalvik. The effectiveness assessment is to run over real and converted apps modified by the framework. It assesses repackaging detection algorithms by broadness (i.e., how an algorithm can stand to obfuscation techniques applied separately) and by depth (i.e., if an algorithm is resilient to techniques applied sequentially). As the case study, the authors applied the framework to Andro-Guard - the only publicly available tool for repackaging detection. The results show that AndroGuard can successfully combat with different obfuscation techniques and, thus, can be widely used to detect repackaged apps. It is worth noticed that ImageStruct will successfully pass the tests as it does not rely on code similarity.

Much of the existing work on similarity analysis is focused on program code, which faces a number of domain specific considerations when performing code similarity analysis: the source code is not available for most apps so a preprocessing step is needed; each app includes common libraries that it uses, which leads to significant code copying that can undermine code similarity scores; Android developers often obfuscate code to make the reverse engineering more difficult at the same time misbehaving authors obfuscate code to evade detection. These problems motivate an alternative approach for determining the similarity between apps. Li et al. [15] proposed a system called DStruct , which detects similar apps based on their directory structures. The files inside the APPs are typically organized into directories. They construct a tree to represent the directory structure, and compute the edit distances among them. However, DStruct is very time consuming and Android app's directory structures can be easy obfuscate.

We propose ImageStruct which is a scalable and rapid tool to determine the repackaged apps based on the images in apps' archives. This approach avoids all the problems that are associated with the code and provides another metric for determining app similarity. Even though, we do not consider ImageStruct as a replacement for existing system, since the latter performs quite effectively and has the capability to detect vulnerable code reuse. Instead, we develop ImageStruct so that we could use it in conjunction with existing systems to eliminate false positives and negatives and to reaffirm results of each other.

3   Design

There are three design goals for repackaging detection: accuracy, rapid speed, and scalability. Accuracy is a natural requirement to effectively identify apprepackaging behavior in current marketplaces. However, challenges arise from the fact that the repackaging process might dramatically use code obfuscation technique in the repackaged app, which renders app bytecode similar schemes ineffective. Meanwhile, due to the large number of apps in various marketplaces, our approach needs to be rapid and scalable. Our current data set for app similarity measurement has 49,000 apps, which makes the expensive semantic-aware full app analysis not feasible. In our design, we use images in app packages for app fingerprint generation. The generated fingerprints need to be robust in order to accommodate possible changes from app-repackaging behavior.

In this paper, we aim to uncover repackaged apps and understand the overall repackaging situation in current marketplaces. We focus on images inside Android apps instead of bytecode. Observation shows repackaged app always has similar "look and feel" with original app. And at meantime, our dataset shows that all the apps contain images with no exception. There are two assumptions our approach based on. First, we assume that the apps from the Google Play are more authentic and assumed to be trusted and not repackaged. In real-world situation, there may be exceptions when bouncer fails (which has happened before), but still ImageStruct is helpful to distinguish app pairs with repackaging relationship. Second, we assume that the signing keys of app developers are not leaked (which is the identical certificate that developers should have enough security awareness of) so that there is no possibility for a repackaged app shares the same signature with the original one.

3.1 Overview

As illustrated in previous sections, repackaged apps share two common characteristics. First, the one who clones the application, seeks to resemble the original one as much as possible to increase the installation probability of cloned one. Second, the original app and the repackaged app are signed by different developer keys. By leverages these two insights, ImageStruct extracts related features from apps and then discerns whether one app is repackaged from the other one.

Fig.3 illustrates the overview of our approach. In essence, ImageStruct has three key steps. The first step is to extract two kinds of features from each app, i.e., image fingerprints and author information. These two features are used to uniquely identify each app. After that, the second step is to store these features efficiently. As there are tens of millions of apps in the market, full pairwise comparison is not a good choice. We design a better way to store app features for similarity measurement. Finally, based on app features, the third step discerns the source of apps, i.e., either from the Google play or from the third-party marketplaces, and measures their similarity scores to detect repackaged apps. In the following subsections, we demonstrate each step in detail.

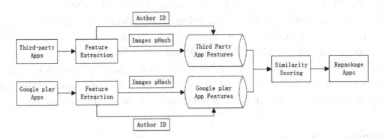

Fig. 3. The ImageStruct work flow

3.2 Feature Extraction

An Android app is essentially a compressed archive file including image files, META-INF subdirectory and other necessary files (executables, libraries and multimedia resource files). The images determine the app's appearance while the META-INF subdirectory contains the author information.

There are many image feature calculation methods, such as color histogram [20], SIFT [14], pHash [7] and etc. PHash using discrete cosine transform to remove the useless high frequency characteristics, and retain the low-frequency characteristics of the image. It is able to detect similarity within 25% changes to original image which often happens when repackage (e.g. image cropping and resolution adjusting). This characteristic of PHash distinctly differs from the other calculation methods. Based on efficiency and accuracy consideration, pHash is used as ImageStruct's feature extraction algorithms.

For the author information, the META-INF subdirectory includes the full developer certificate. The certificate provides information of developer name, contact, organization, as well as the public key fingerprints. In ImageStruct, we map each developer certificate into a unique 32-bit identifier (authorID). This unique identifier is then integrated into the feature for comparison.

3.3   Feature Storage

After feature extraction, we need to apply a appropriate way to store feature information. The easiest way is store in the form of {application, features}. It is a simple and intuitive way, which however increase the time consuming of similarity detection. Suppose there are n apps already in the original database, then there come m new apps for similarity detection, the time complexity is $n * m$. Nowadays, there are thousands of apps are newly published every day. Accordingly, the time complexity of similarity detection will grow rapidly. To deal with the problem, we utilize a new storage method in the form of {features, applications}. In practice, the number of images in one Android app is ranging from 10 to 10000, and the average number is around 2000. With the improvement of storage structure, the time complexity is $2000 * m$ which is of constant and much better to satisfy the purpose of rapid and scalable.

As shown in Fig.4, apps' feature is stored in two databases, redis[17] and MySQL[12]. Redis is an advanced key-value cache and store database. It is often referred to as data structure server, since keys can contain strings, lists and sets. The redis database stores app hash indexed by image fingerprint. Each fingerprint corresponds to a set of apps' hash values. MySQL is the world's most popular open source database. The MySQL database stores apps' information, including app name, signature and source indexed by app's hash value.

3.4   Similarity Scoring

After features extraction, we got two databases which store the necessary information to calculate app's similarity. The above first two steps are applied to each app regardless of its source. In the third step, we treat apps differently according to where it comes from, Google Play or alternative marketplaces. The similarity scores based on the derived fingerprints are calculated against the Google Play apps. Our image features is deterministic, as the same fingerprints will be generated if two images are identical. In addition, PHash, the algorithm we adopt, can also effectively locate the image changes possibly made in repackaged apps.

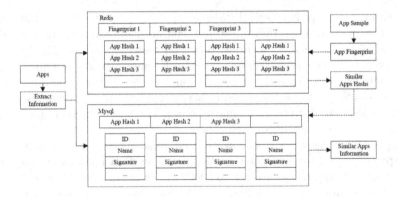

Fig. 4. Implementation framework

We also perform containment analysis on the fingerprint sets to determine the similarity percentage of images in both apps. Containment is defined as the percentage of features in app A that also exist within app B. This value $C(A|B)$ is computed by dividing the number of features existing in both apps by the number of images in A.

$$C(A|B) = \frac{|A \cap B|}{A}$$

The app similar formula is as follows.

$$similarityScore(app_1, app_2) = \frac{|app_1 images \cap app_2 images|}{app_1 images}$$

If the similarity score between two apps exceeds certain threshold and the two apps are signed with different developer keys, ImageStruct reports the one that is not from the Google Play as repackaged. The threshold is very important as it affects both false positives and false negatives of our system. Specifically, a high threshold would likely lead to low false positives but high false negatives, while a low threshold would introduce high false positives but low false negatives. In our experiments, we empirically find the threshold 0.6 is a good balance between the two metrics.

Once the similarity percentage computation is completed, we sort (e.g. quick sort) the results so that the pairs of more significant similarity appear first. More information of these apps can be retrieved from the MySQL database by apps' hash value.

4 Evaluation Experiments and Results Analysis

To conduct an overall evaluation of our approach, we implement ImageStruct on Linux system. Specifically, we use pHash [7] which is a image fingerprint generation tool to extract image feature in application package. For the apps' author information, we adopt keytool[11] which is already a part of Android SDK. After the features are extracted, they are stored separately in redis and mysql database as we explained in previous sections. Based on these features, similarity scoring is carried out. The similarity scoring takes both image features and author information into account. Apps that share the same author information are excluded from repackaging detection process. Otherwise, ImageStruct calculates the edit distance and hence derives the similarity score. The larger the score is, the more similar the pair of apps are to each other.

Images are pervasive existence in Android apps. We analyze top 100 popular free apps of every category in Google Play. The data shows that the image number in each app ranges from 1 to 5000. The average value of image number is 422. This number gives ImageStruct confidence that using image as a universal feature can be applicable to almost all apps.

To demontrate the repackaging detection ability, we crawl apps from four popular third-party Android marketplaces, two of which are from US and two of which are from China. Our study is based on the apps collected in the November 2014. Meanwhile, we also collect nearly 40,000 apps from the Google Play as benchmark database between July 2014 and November 2014. Besides, we also analyse the malware set from Android Malware Genome Project [23]. The dataset details in Table 1.

Table 1. App number in experiment datasets from Google Play, third-party markets and Genome

App source	# of Apps
Android Drawer (US)	985
Freeware Lovers (US)	1,438
eoeMarket (CN)	3,347
Anzhi (CN)	3,009
Malware Genome	1,246
Google Play	39,492

4.1 Repackaged Applications in Alternative Marketplaces and Malware Set

To perform a concrete study on the repackaged apps in markets and measure the effectiveness of ImageStruct, we detect the apps from four third-party marketplaces and Android Malware Genome Project against Google Play dataset to find out whether there is any repackaged app. Specifically, for each app, ImageStruct scores the similarity score between the app and each of the 39,492 Google Play apps. In practice, we apply 0.6 as the threshold due to the balance of false positive and false negative. Thus, if the similar score of a pair of apps is higher than 0.6, we consider they are in a repackaging relationship.

The results are shown in Table 2. The second column indicates the number of repackaged apps in each market dataset detected by ImageStruct. We can see that ImageStruct reports 6% to 14% of apps came from 4 alternative markets are repackaged, which is relatively high for a healthy app market and further can seriously affect the security of entire smartphone ecosystem. We manually verify 20 apps randomly out of the repackaged apps in each market reported by ImageStruct. For each marketplace, only one or two false positives are found, which validate the effectiveness of ImageStruct. As for the false negative cases, the main contributing factor is the completeness of original app set. If the original app is not in the benchmark dataset (Google Play dataset), the similarity could never be detected. ImageStruct can be improved as the accumulation of original data from Google Play.

Table 2. Repackaging detection results for 5 dataset

App source	Repackaged #	Repackaging %
Android Drawer (US)	122	12.4%
Freeware Lovers (US)	121	8.4%
eoeMarket (CN)	225	6.7%
Anzhi (CN)	438	14.5%
Malware Genome	178	14.3%

4.2 Comparison with AndroGuard

AndroGuard have the capability to analyze similarity of Dalvik code [6]. The difference between two apps, such as newly-added or deleted methods could be detected. AndroGuard performs it in 3 steps; a) generates signature for each Dalvik method in apps, b) identifies the identical methods in both apps, c) discovers all methods that are similar. The signature of Dalvik method is generated based on the control flow information, API calls and exceptions inside the method. Methods are considered identical if they have the same signature hashes. Normalized Compression Distance (NCD) [4] is used to measure the similarity between methods.

A random selection of 250 pairs with the same certificate and 250 pairs with different certificates are used to perform AndroGuard similarity metrics, which averages out the similarity score with no predominance of score range. This two groups are different by nature which is reinforced by our experiment data. Fig.5 presents a scatterplot of the similarity values from AndroGuard (Y-axis) and ImageStruct (X-axis). It shows that the difference between AndroGuard and ImageStruct is within a certain range highly correlated with each other, which confirms that ImageStruct can effectively detect repackaged applications. However, there are some points with high AndroGuard similarity scores, but with ImageStruct similarity scores varying. After manually inspecting these pairs, we manage to find the reason causing the problem. One of the most common observed cases is that the same logical code is used for displaying different content. For instance, we find several reading apps, which can load digital books. For every different book, a individual application is been developed. All these

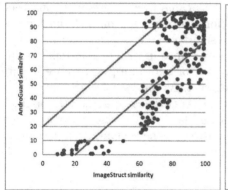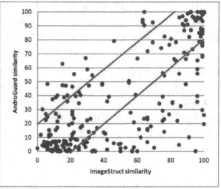

Fig. 5. Scatterplots of similarity scores from ImageStruct (X-axis) vs. AndroGuard (Y-axis) for app pairs signed with different certificates (left) and same certificates (right)

applications use the same code, but the images (e.g. the book cover or chapter cover) are different. We also inspect some pairs with low AndroGuard similarity scores and high ImageStruct scores. One of the case is that the same images are used in different apps, e.g. the apps developed by same author share many same images. Besides, for the random pairs expected to have low similarity.

ImageStruct does not deviate from AndroGuard a lot on average. We can see that for the app pairs not marked as similar by ImageStruct, AndroGuard does not output significant code similarity score either. 60% of the times, the difference between results of ImageStruct and AndroGuard is within 20% (within red line in Fig.5). It means that if developers include little images in apps similar with another app, they are also likely not to reuse the code, which is often the case for apps intensively produced by companies.

During the experiment we find that AndroGuard takes significantly more time than ImageStruct. The time of comparison depends on the complexity and similarity of target app pair. It takes much less time to compare more similar apps than totally different ones. Average time for one pair is approximately 85 seconds using AndroGuard. Hence, measurement of similarity metrics for the whole app corpus we have crawled is not feasible.

4.3   Performance Evaluation

ImageStruct runs on Ubuntu 12.04 with Intel Core CPU (4 cores) and 32GB of RAM, which is a regular or a little weaker hardware configuration for most of the repackaging detection systems. The time consuming ranges from 1 seconds to 2 minutes for ImageStruct to compare one app against all the other apps in the benchmark dataset. The time depends on the number of images included in the target app. The lower boundary of time occurs when target app has less than 10 images, and the upper boundary of time occurs when the app has over 2000 images. Fig.6 shows the feature extraction time cost changing with the number of images per-app. The time cost is proportional to the number of images. ImageStruct takes about 1 minute to deal with 1409 images, which is efficient enough for large dataset and could be accelerated in distributed way.

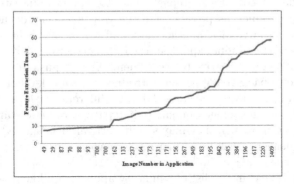

Fig. 6. Feature extraction time cost (Y-axis) is proportional to the number of images inside the Android app (X-axis)

We use parallel program to divide the tasks up to improve performance greatly when dealing with large dataset. Each processor works on the fingerprints extraction and distance calculation in parallel. Table 3 shows the time cost for ImageStruct running different datasets under 8 threads, which indicates the good scalability of ImageStruct.

Table 3. Performance of repackaging detection under 8 threads

Source	App#	Feature extraction(s)	Repackaging detection(s)
Android Drawer (US)	985	10,976	60
Freeware Lovers (US)	1,438	12,064	48
eoeMarket (CN)	3,347	34,233	113
Anzhi (CN)	3,009	29,431	101
Malware Genome	1,246	1,623	28
Total	10,025	88,327	350

4.4 Discussion

False positives can arise due to multiple facts as we use feature extracted from images. Different apps may appear similar if their image resources are similar. For example, the image similarity of different apps published by same company are higher than 80%. In fact, this case will not affect the repackaging judgement as the apps are with the same signature. False positives mainly result from the apps that differ in functionality but reuse images. Usually, developers download image materials from Internet and then use them in their own apps. This pattern leads to the situation that the images among different apps appear similar, which further results in ImageStruct's false positives.

Currently, the false positives and false negatives are both significant, as authors mainly focus on modifying code to add their components or advertisements instead of the resources of apps when repackaging. As there are already many techniques to detect code reuse, repackagers attempt to obfuscate the code to avoid detection as much as possible. On the contrary, they do not pay much attention to the resource files, another reason of which is they have to maintain the appearance of the original app. We test ImageStruct on different versions of one app and find high similarity between them. This means our approach could effectively detect repackaged apps that introduce the same level of modifications to the images as that occurs when evolving to different versions. Since our approach depends on the image similarity, if repackagers understand the detail mechanism of our approach, they may significantly alter images when repackaging as countermeasure, such as adding futile images or modifying the contents, which will lower the image similarity score reported by ImageStruct. But still, these apps will appear in the list of similarity apps with a low percentage similarity, as the repackaged apps still need some similarities with the original app, such as interfaces and icons. Besides, we could adopt other valid image similarity detection algorithm that are more complex and powerful, such as SIFT which considers approximate match to improve the performance.

5   Conclusion

In this paper, we propose an novel approach to detect Android application repackaging based on the image resources and implement ImageStruct which is capable of effective and fast repackage detection. ImageStruct scores the similarity for target apps and classifies them as similar if substantial number of images in packages are with same feature. We have evaluated the practicality of ImageStruct in two aspects to determine whether it shows correlated results with the code based repackaging detection techniques, and whether it is scalable and fast enough to handle significant large number of apps. Our results are encouraging. The ImageStruct similarity score is strongly correlated with the AndroGuard code-based similarity score, especially for the apps signed with different certificates, i.e. potentially plagiarized. ImageStruct also has good performance. It is able to extract features for a dataset of more than 39,000 apps in less than 48 hours, and only takes 24 hours to check 10,000 apps if they are repackaged or not. At the meantime, the approach can be easily parallelized using different parallelization algorithms to further enhance the performance.

The methodology in ImageStruct inspires new feature in application plagiarism detection algorithms not only for Android but also for other systems, such as iOS and Windows Phone. Useful patterns and meaningful findings can be inferred from the results output by ImageStruct to find out more repackaging characteristics and further improve the feature extraction and threshold configuration, which could be an interesting future work. Moreover, ImageStruct can be used to improve the on-market plagiarism detection algorithms by complementing the code similarity-based approaches to provide a healthy mobile ecosystem.

Acknowledgments. This work is supported by National Basic Research Program (Grant No.2012CB315804), National Natural Science Foundation of China (Grant No.91118006), and Beijing Natural Science Foundation (Grant No.4154089).

References

1. Strategy Analytics. Strategy analytics: 85% of phones shipped last quarter run android (2014),
   http://bgr.com/2014/07/31/
   android-vs-ios-vs-windows-phone-vs-blackberry/
2. anthony.desnos@gmail.com. Androguard: Reverse engineering, malware and goodware analysis of android applications (2013),
   https://code.google.com/p/androguard/
3. AppBrain. Number of android applications (2014),
   http://www.appbrain.com/stats/number-of-android-apps
4. Cilibrasi, R., Vitanyi, P.M.B.: Clustering by compression. IEEE Transactions on Information Theory 51(4), 1523–1545 (2005)
5. Crussell, J., Gibler, C., Chen, H.: Attack of the clones: Detecting cloned applications on android markets. In: Foresti, S., Yung, M., Martinelli, F. (eds.) ESORICS 2012. LNCS, vol. 7459, pp. 37–54. Springer, Heidelberg (2012),
   http://dx.doi.org/10.1007/978-3-642-33167-1_3
6. Desnos, A.: Android: Static analysis using similarity distance. In: 2012 45th Hawaii International Conference on System Science (HICSS), pp. 5394–5403 (January 2012)
7. Evan, K., David, S.: Phash (2014), http://www.phash.org/
8. Hanna, S., Huang, L., Wu, E., Li, S., Chen, C., Song, D.: Juxtapp: A scalable system for detecting code reuse among android applications. In: Flegel, U., Markatos, E., Robertson, W. (eds.) DIMVA 2012. LNCS, vol. 7591, pp. 62–81. Springer, Heidelberg (2013), http://dx.doi.org/10.1007/978-3-642-37300-8_4
9. Hu, W., Tao, J., Ma, X., Zhou, W., Zhao, S., Han, T.: Migdroid: Detecting app-repackaging android malware via method invocation graph. In: 2014 23rd International Conference on Computer Communication and Networks (ICCCN), pp. 1–7 (August 2014)
10. Huang, H., Zhu, S., Liu, P., Wu, D.: A framework for evaluating mobile app repackaging detection algorithms. In: Huth, M., Asokan, N., Čapkun, S., Flechais, I., Coles-Kemp, L. (eds.) TRUST 2013. LNCS, vol. 7904, pp. 169–186. Springer, Heidelberg (2013)
11. Google Inc. Android dvelopment guide: Signing your applications (2014),
   http://developer.android.com/guide/publishing/app-signing.html
12. Oracle Inc. Mysql (2014), http://www.mysql.com/
13. Symantec Inc. Android threats getting steamy (May 7 (2011),
   http://www.symantec.com/connect/blogs/android-threats-getting-steamy
14. J. Craig Venter Institute. Sift (2014), http://sift.jcvi.org/
15. Li, S.: Juxtapp and DStruct: Detection of Similarity Among Android Applications. PhD thesis, EECS Department, University of California, Berkeley (2012)
16. Oberheide, J.: Dissecting the android bouncer (2012),
   https://jon.oberheide.org/files/summercon12-bouncer.pdf
17. Sanfilippo, S.: Redis (2014), http://redis.io/topics/sponsors

18. Studios, H.: Fruit ninja (2013), `http://halfbrick.com/`
19. Ulrich, B., Paolo, M.C., Clemens, H., Christopher, K., Engin, K.: Scalable, behavior-based malware clustering. In: Proceedings of Network and Distributed System Security Symposium 2009. Citeseer (2009)
20. Wikipedia. Color histogram (2014), `http://en.wikipedia.org/wiki/Color_histogram`
21. Zhou, W., Zhou, Y., Grace, M., Jiang, X., Zou, S.: Fast, scalable detection of "piggybacked" mobile applications. In: Proceedings of the Third ACM Conference on Data and Application Security and Privacy, pp. 185–196. ACM (2013)
22. Zhou, W., Zhou, Y., Jiang, X., Ning, P.: Detecting repackaged smartphone applications in third-party android marketplaces. In: Proceedings of the 2nd ACM Conference on Data and Application Security and Privacy, pp. 317–326. ACM (2012)
23. Zhou, Y., Jiang, X.: Dissecting android malware: Characterization and evolution. In: 2012 IEEE Symposium on Security and Privacy (SP), pp. 95–109 (May 2012)

Comprehensive Analysis of the Android Google Play's Auto-update Policy

Craig Sanders, Ayush Shah, and Shengzhi Zhang

Department of Computer Sciences and Cybersecurity,
Florida Institute of Technology, USA
{csanders2013,ashah2014}@my.fit.edu, zhangs@fit.edu

Abstract. Google Play provides a large Android application repository and the companion service application handles the initial installation and update processes. For the ease of management effort, a recent policy change by Google allows users to configure auto-update for installed applications based on permission groups, rather than individual permission. By analyzing the effects of the new auto-update policy on Android permission system with an emphasis on permission groups and protection levels, we find a new privilege escalation attack vector. Then 1200 Android applications are evaluated to identify potential privilege escalation candidates, and 1260 malware samples are investigated to study how the new attack vector could be utilized by the malware to increase the chance of distribution without users' attention. Based on the evaluation results, we confirm that such new policy can be easily manipulated by malicious developers to gain high privileged permissions without users' consent. It is highly recommended that users of the new auto-update feature carefully review permissions obtained after each update via global setting, or simply turn off the feature.

Keywords: Android permission system, privilege escalation, Google Play's auto-update.

1 Introduction

Recently, the number of smartphone users has been increasing tremendously. According to eMarkerter, the smartphone users worldwide will total 1.75 billion in 2014 [1], simply because they can access a rich and sometimes diverse ecosystem of applications. For instance, as of July 2014, there are 1.3 million applications available in Google Play and 1.2 million applications available in Apple store [2]. Users are now able to conduct much of their computing needs via these mobile devices, including document processing, social media, financial management and many more. As the capabilities of these devices continue to grow, so do the security requirements necessary to protect the users' sensitive information on these devices.

One of the security solutions that Android—the most popular mobile OS—uses to accomplish these goals is application sandboxing [3]. The OS separates

© Springer International Publishing Switzerland 2015
J. Lopez and Y. Wu (Eds.): ISPEC 2015, LNCS 9065, pp. 365–377, 2015.
DOI: 10.1007/978-3-319-17533-1_25

running applications into their own execution environments and controls their access to system resources as well as their interaction with other applications. Android exposes sensitive API calls to applications to access system resources and invoking them is controlled by permission system. Applications must explicitly declare permissions they need, and display them to the users at installation time in order to gain users' approval. If the users do not wish to grant all the permissions to the application, the application will not be installed. The model, therefore, offers a "take-it or leave-it" approach to the users' decision regarding permissions.

However, the system varies this process slightly depending on the application installation method being utilized, e.g., via Google Play, other third-party application repositories, or side-loading directly. When an application is installed via Google Play, not all of the application's permissions are disclosed to the user. In an effort to reduce the burden on users, Google Play relies on permission protection level defined by Android to present only the high-privilege permissions to the user prior to installation. Additionally, Google recently revised its auto-update policy to push out and install updates based on permission groups, not individual permissions themselves. Although this revision reduces the amount of annoying approval requests, it also severely degrades the granularity of access control.

There is a vast amount of research in regards to Android permission system. Stowaway [4] detects over-privileged Android applications by comparing the permissions declared in the manifest to the permissions required by the API calls made by the application. VetDroid [5] that effectively identifies how the applications utilize the permissions to access system resources and [6] uses Self-Organizing Maps (SOM) to provide empirical analysis of permission-based security models. PScout [7] applies static analysis on Android OS source code to extract the permission specification, and etc. However, none of the research focuses on Google Play's mechanisms of the application installation and auto-update.

In this paper, we analyze the impacts of the Google Play's new auto-update policy with respect to user security. First, we mapped the 78 Android permissions available to third-party applications into each of the 28 permission groups. We then identified six "at risk" permission groups that mix permissions of both *normal* and *dangerous* protection levels. These groups are particularly susceptible to privilege escalation attack under the new auto-update policy. Second, we statically analyzed 1200 popular Android applications to evaluate the security impact introduced by the new auto-update policy. Among them, we found 926 applications request *normal* level permissions in at least one of the six "at risk" groups. Thus, their updates could obtain *dangerous* level permissions in those groups without users' consent. Last, we evaluated 1260 malware samples and found 496 of them are multiple versions of 152 different malware packages. Further study shows that 221 updates (Two malware samples with unique package name but adjacent version code) can escalate privilege by declaring *normal* level permission in a previous version but obtaining *dangerous* level permission of the same group in a later version.

The rest of this paper is organized as follows. The next section overviews the background of the Android security model, Android permission system, Google Play auto-update policy, and the problem statement of this paper. Section 3 discusses the privilege escalation attack vector introduced by the new auto-update policy in detail. In Section 4, we provide the evaluation results of popular applications on Google Play as well as malware samples to show the potential risks imposed by the attack vector. Finally, we present related works in Section 5 and conclude in Section 6.

2   Background and Problem Statement

2.1   Android Security Overview

The Android system is designed with multi-layered security to protect user data and system resources. First, it employs a customized Linux kernel as the base layer of the security model. The android framework and binder middleware are running on top of the kernel. Each application is assigned a unique user identification (UID) by Linux kernel, which is used to enforce conventional Linux discretionary access control (DAC) policy over applications accessing different resources (files). One exception to this rule occurs when applications are signed with the same developer's certificate. This allows a developer to run multiple applications under the same UID, thereby allowing the direct sharing of resources.

Second, the applications are also sandboxed from interacting with each other or the other resource providers unless through a controlled inter-process communication (IPC) mechanism implemented by binder. Android offers a set of defined permissions that refines application's access to sensitive application programming interfaces (API), which are used to interact with protected system resources such as location information, SMS message send/receive, phone call, etc. Although Android does not publish full documentation regarding which APIs require which permissions, research ([4] and [7]) has been done to map the permissions needed per API. Any permissions that an application requires in order to function must be declared in the packaged manifest file. Note that applications can also define permissions to protect their own assets. Recently, researchers tried to implant Security Enhanced Linux (SELinux) into Android kernel for mandatory access control (MAC), e.g., [11] and [12]. Starting from Android 4.3, SEAndroid is run with permissive mode, in which permission denials are logged but not enforced. In the recent release of Android 5.0 (L), SEAndroid moves to enforcement mode, in which denials are both logged and enforced. Android 4.4 compromises with partial enforcement mode [13].

2.2   Android Permission Model

For sensitive APIs that correspond to critical resources on Android, permissions are defined as specific capability to access them. Applications must declare necessary permissions in the manifest file to function. Note that when a permission is declared in the manifest, it does not necessarily mean that the application contains any API calls that require the permission. This may occur if the application developer makes a mistake, possibly due to incomplete documentation, which is particularly true for Android. This may also happen if a developer plans to later distribute an update that accesses API calls which need the permission. Each permission definition contains a number of attributes, and noteworthy ones are the protection Level and the permission Group.

Permission Protection Level. Each permission is associated with a protection level, which is defined as to characterize the potential risk implied in the permission. It is used to determine which approval procedure that Android application installer needs to follow to determine whether or not to grant the permission to the application requesting it [8]. Android documents four protection levels: *normal, dangerous, signature,* and *signatureOrsystem.* Of the four, the former three are available to third-party developers. According to Android documentation, *normal* is used to classify permissions that provide minimal risk to other applications and, therefore, does not require the users' explicit approval during the installation of the application. The *dangerous* protection level is reserved for higher-risk permissions and requires users' approval at installation time. The *signature* level permission will be granted to the application signed by the same certificate as the application that defines the permission. However, *signatureOrsystem* is typically reserved for Android system services, not available to third-party developers.

Permission Group. The other important attribute of an Android permission is the permission group. It is used to logically group related permissions for easy presentation to the user at installation time. Note it is not mandatory for an individual permission to be assigned to a group. A summary of all permission groups can be found at [9].

2.3   Google Play

For the scope of this paper, Google Play is the repository for Android applications and media, comparable to Apple's Application Store. A user can access Google Play through any web browser or on an Android device itself via an application that is preinstalled by the device manufacturer. The preinstalled application provides a user the capability to browse and download hundreds of thousands of applications, both paid and free, from Google's repository. Additionally, Android device manufacturers preinstall an application called Google Play service, which links the device to a user account, provides authentication and synchronization services, and keeps applications from Google Play updated as newer versions are released.

The Google Play service periodically checks for new versions of applications that are currently installed on the device. When it locates a newer version, Google Play service has two options. If the auto-update option is not selected, it will alert the user of the update via the notification window. However, if the auto-update option is selected, Google Play service must check the permissions declared in the new manifest file and compare them to the permissions granted to the currently installed version. Requesting for *dangerous* level permissions that haven't been granted in current version will result in a pop-up asking user's explicit approval. Otherwise, the application will be automatically updated without users' interaction. Based on the most recent change to the Google Play service, auto-update policy allows the application to be updated to the new version even if new *dangerous* level permissions are declared in the manifest as long as they belong to the same permission group as a previously approved permission [10].

2.4 Problem Statement

Allowing auto-update to occur based on permission groups effectively eases users' effort of maintaining the applications they installed, but severely reduces the granularity achieved by many individual permissions. Google also advocates that "users who wish to have full control over new individual permissions being added to an app can review individual permissions for an app at any time, or may consider turning off auto-updates for one or more apps" [10]. However, such auto-update policy may incur another more severe problem, privilege escalation. As described in the previous section, permissions available for third party applications include both *normal* and *dangerous* protection levels. But the classification of permissions into different groups failed to consider the permission level, which is critical to determine if users' consent is needed or not. An application can be published with a minimal set of permissions mostly at the *normal* level without requesting users' approval. Once it has achieved large market penetration, an update can be published requesting *dangerous* level permissions in the same group. Thus, its privileges can be escalated without users' consent.

This new attack vector for privilege escalation is the focus of this paper. The problem introduced by Google Play's new auto-update policy is that the approval-free feature of *normal* level permission within a permission group essentially brings in every permission (both *normal* and *dangerous* levels) within the same group after auto-update without users' approval. Given this new auto-update policy, it is necessary to study the map all of the *normal* and *dangerous* Android permissions to the permission groups they are assigned, to examine if any group contains mixed levels of permissions, which is vulnerable to the privilege escalation. Additionally, if such group exists, it is highly desired to evaluate popular applications on Google Play to learn how this new policy could be misused, as well as those known malware to determine if the new policy opens up new attack vectors for them.

3   Feasibility Analysis of the Privilege Escalation

To fully understand the implications of the new auto-update policy, we first determine into which groups the individual permissions are assigned. Thus, we

Table 1. Permission Groups Mixed with Different Levels of Permissions

Permission Group	Normal	Dangerous
STORAGE	READ_EXTERNAL_STORAGE	WRITE_EXTERNAL_STORAGE
ACCOUNTS	GET_ACCOUNTS	AUTHENTICATE_ACCOUNTS USE_CREDENTIALS MANAGE_ACCOUNTS
NETWORK	ACCESS_NETWORK_STATE ACCESS_WIFI_STATE CHANGE_NETWORK_STATE ACCESS_WIMAX_STATE	CHANGE_WIFI_STATE CHANGE_WIMAX_STATE INTERNET, NFC
APP_INFO	REORDER_TASKS KILL_BACKGROUND_PROCESSES RECEIVE_BOOT_COMPLETED	GET_TASKS
AFFECT BATTERY	VIBRATE, WAKE_LOCK FLASHLIGHT, TRANSMIT_IR	CHANGE_WIFI _MULTICAST_STATE
SYSTEM TOOLS	ACCESS_LOCATION_EXTRA _COMMANDS, WRITE_SETTINGS BROADCAST_STICKY SUBSCRIBED_FEEDS_READ GET_PACKAGE_SIZE	ACCESS_MOCK_LOCATION INSTALL_SHORTCUT UNINSTALL_SHORTCUT SUBSCRIBED_FEEDS_WRITE CLEAR_APP_CACHE

can easily identify any groups that contain at least one *normal* level permission *AND* at least one *dangerous* level permission, which will be labelled an "at-risk" group. Then, we develop a sample application taking advantage of the privilege escalation to obtain *dangerous* level permissions via auto-update without users' explicit approval.

3.1   Mapping Permissions to Groups

We locate the Android manifest file for Android 4.4.2 from the Android Open Source Project (*/frameworks/base/core/res/AndroidManifest.xml*), which defines all available permissions as well as their assigned groups. To validate the permission to group mapping results above, we developed a basic Android application that declares every *normal* and *dangerous* permission in the manifest file and initiated the installation procedure on two test devices, a HTC One M7 and a Nexus 5 both running Android 4.4.2. Conducting the permission analysis of the Android manifest file, we identified a total of 30 *normal* and 48 *dangerous* level permissions assigned into 28 permission groups. Table 1 shows that 6 out of the 28 groups contain at least one *normal* and one *dangerous* permissions. They are referred to as "at risk" groups, since auto-update policy for those groups clearly violates the definition of protection level.

3.2   Other Findings

First, we noticed a number of discrepancies between the documentation on the Android developers' network and the implementation of permissions within Android. For instance, three permissions are included in the system manifest file but not mentioned in the developers' documentation, i.e., *ACCESS_WIMAX_STATE*, *CHANGE_WIMAX_STATE*, and *READ_CELL_BROADCASTS*. Furthermore,

(a) Installation of Demo Application   (b) Update of Demo Application

Fig. 1. Installation and Update of Demo Application on Nexus 5

the developers' network documents the permission $BODY\_SENSORS$ which is not defined in Android 4.4.2 manifest file. However, it is defined in Android 5.0 recently released, which makes it susceptible to Pileup Flaws [14].

Second, it is observed that there are some permission groups defined in the Android manifest file, yet no permissions assigned to the group. For example, the Android manifest file defines a $CALENDAR$ permission group, but the two permissions associated with the calendar ($READ\_CALENDAR$ and $WRITE\_CALENDAR$) are assigned to the $PERSONAL\_INFO$ permission group. These oversights simply add to manufacturer and developer confusion.

Finally, we also noticed the use of the "costsmoney" permission flag, indicating those permissions that could result in direct financial charge to the device owner. There are only two permissions that are associated with this flag, i.e., $CALL\_PHONE$ and $SEND\_SMS$, which belong to the permission groups ($PHONE\_CALLS$ and $MESSAGES$ respectively) that only contain dangerous level permissions. However, other permissions in those groups are not associated with "costsmoney" flag. It is unclear how Google Play handles these two permissions with respect to the auto-update policy and is left for our future work.

3.3   Demo Application Release and Auto-update

We developed a demo application taking advantage of the above mentioned privilege escalation attack vector. The application itself is quite simple, requesting one *normal* level permission in all the groups in TABLE 1 except for *APP_INFO*, which differs and deserves a separate experiment as explained later. Those *normal* level permissions are *READ_EXTERNAL_STORAGE, GET_ACCOUNTS, ACCESS_NETWORK_STATE, VIBRATE,* and *GET_PACKAGE_SIZE.* We successfully published it in Google Play and downloaded it to our Nexus 5 smartphone. During the installation, we noticed that permission approval is still requested from users for *GET_ACCOUNTS* and *READ_EXTERNAL_STORAGE,* even if they are only *normal* level permissions as shown in Fig. 1(a). Here it conflicts with Android's definition of *normal* level permission, which does not need users' consent.

Then we configured auto-update for all installed applications on Google Play and released our update requesting one *dangerous* level permissions in each of the above groups. The permissions requested by the update include *WRITE_EXTERNAL_STORAGE, AUTHENTICATE_ACCOUNTS, INTERNET, CHANGE_WIFI_MULTICAST_STATE,* and *CLEAR_APP_CACHE.* The smartphone was connected to Internet via WIFI and the demo application got automatic update. The end of update, we did not receive any alert or approval request regarding additional *dangerous* level permissions as shown in Fig. 1(b). By browsing the global setting of the demo application, we indeed find that it now holds all the permissions requested during installation and update .

However, Google Play auto-update policy seems not appliable to the *APP_INFO* group. We developed another sample application named "Get Task Demo AutoUpdate", which requests only the *RECEIVE_BOOT_COMPLETED normal* level

(a) Installation of Demo Application   (b) Update of Demo Application

Fig. 2. Installation and Update of Demo Application Requesting Permissions in *APP_INFO* Group

permission. The installation required users to approve the *Device & app history* usage as shown in Fig. 2(a). Then the update requests the *dangerous* level permission *GET_TASKS* in *APP_INFO* group. In this instance, Google Play auto-update did require users' approval for the update as shown in Fig. 2(b). It is not clear if Android has a separate policy to control the permissions in *APP_INFO* group. Still, we can confirm any malicious developer can fully take advantage of the new auto-update policy to first release a look-like-benign application without special permission request, and then simply wait for auto-update configuration to gain privilege escalation. Note that we immediately removed our demo applications from Google Play once the update completed on our phone, to avoid impacting other legitimate users.

3.4 Survey on Auto-update

We designed a straightforward survey with three questions targeting students in different majors at our university. The sample questions are quite simple, but effective for our purpose: (Q1) Do you use Android smartphone? (Q2) Are you familiar with Google Play? and (Q3) Do you use Google Play auto-update? At the time when this paper was written, we received 369 feedbacks with 244 positive answers to the first question, 217 positive answers to the second and 207 positive answers to the last. Though our dataset is limited and biased (all participants are well-educated), it is sufficient to demonstrate that Google Play auto-update is a well-known service and even widely used by well-educated Android users, which makes the new privilege escalation attack more severe.

4 Evaluation Results

4.1 Popular Applications from Google Play

In order to illustrate the potential risk of the new auto-update policy, we also downloaded 1200 top free applications in different categories from Google Play. We used Android apktool [23] to disassemble the APK files and extracted the permission declaration from the manifest files. By analyzing the declared permissions over all applications as well as their corresponding permission groups, we can easily identify all applications that would be candidates for privilege escalation under the new auto-update policy. We find that 926 applications request *normal* level permissions in at least one of the six "at risk" groups. For instance, we find a number of applications that declared *VIBRATE* permission (the *normal* protection level) within the *AFFECTS_BATTERY* permission group. The new policy will allow these applications to auto-update even if its new manifest includes the permission declaration of *CHANGE_WIFI_MULTICAST_STATE*, a *dangerous* level permission. Hence, the update of those applications could look more "benign" by utilizing auto-update policy to eliminate the permission request as long as the permission falls into the granted permission group in previous version.

Table 2. Sample Malware Packages with Multiple Version Codes and Groups of Requested Permissions

Package Name	Version Code	Permission Groups
com.mogo.katongllk	9	SYSTEM_TOOLS, DEVELOPMENT_TOOLS, STORAGE, PHONE_CALLS, LOCATION, NETWORK, MESSAGE, UNCLASSIFIED
	12	SYSTEM_TOOLS, DEVELOPMENT_TOOLS, STORAGE, PHONE_CALLS, LOCATION, NETWORK, MESSAGE, UNCLASSIFIED
	13	SYSTEM_TOOLS, DEVELOPMENT_TOOLS, STORAGE, PHONE_CALLS, LOCATION, NETWORK, APP_INFO
de.mobinauten.smsspy	1	LOCATION, MESSAGES
	4	LOCATION, MESSAGES
	5	LOCATION, MESSAGES
	6	LOCATION, MESSAGES
	7	LOCATION, MESSAGES, SOCIAL_INFO, PHONE_CALLS
	9	LOCATION, MESSAGES, SOCIAL_INFO, PHONE_CALLS

4.2 Malware Evaluation

We obtained 1260 malware samples from GENOME project [15], and would like to determine if the new attack vector can be leveraged by the well known Android malware. Again using the apktool, we disassembled all the malware packages and extracted the version code from application manifest files. Since the version code of the application is used to check an upgrade or downgrade relationship, we removed the malware samples without indicating version code in their manifest files, which left us 1022 malware samples. Then we gathered the remaining malware samples into different categories based on their package names, which should be unique in any specific Android marketplace. Afterwards, we got 152 categories (each with one unique package name), each of which contains multiple versions of instances, with the total number of 496 instances. For example, Table 2 shows two malware categories, each with the same package name, *com.mogo.katongllk* with three different versions (*9*, *12*, and *13*) of instances and *de.mobinauten.smsspy* with six different versions (*1*, *4*, *5*, *6* and *9*) of instances.

Within each category, we paired two instances with adjacent version code together, e.g., Version *9* and Version *12* of *com.mogo.katongllk* or Version *7* and Version *9* of *de.mobinauten.smsspy*, and analyzed the permission declaration and the corresponding groups of each pair. If any pair shares at least one of the six "at risk" groups identified in Table 1, we marked those pairs as *risky* for the privilege escalation attack vector introduced by Google Play's auto-update policy. For example, Version *9* and Version *12* or Version *12* and Version *13* of *com.mogo.katongllk* are *risky*, since they share *SYSTEM_TOOLS* permission group, which is one of the "at risk" groups. We identified 221 such pairs and those malware can automatically benefit from Google Play's new auto-update policy to obtain additional high privileged permissions without users' consent.

5   Related Work

Permission Model Analysis. Due to the incomplete documentation of Android permission system, Stowaway [4] and PScout [7] independently performed a comprehensive analysis of Android API calls and permissions, and constructed a mapping between them for better understanding of Android permission model. VetDroid [5] proposed a dynamic analysis platform that studies how permissions are used to access sensitive system resources and how these resources are further handled by Android applications. SORNET [16] formally analyzed Android permission systems against several proposed security properties, and presented enforcement to overcome the shortcomings of existing Android permission model. [16] applied static analysis approach to study permission gaps of applications, e.g., not use all permissions they declare. In this paper, we focus on the analysis of different attributes of permissions, e.g., protection level and permission group, and study how they can lead to both confusion and possible attacks.

Privilege Escalation. IPC inspection [18] first discussed the permission re-delegation problem on smartphone systems and browsers. Lots of surveyed Android applications are found to offer public interfaces, through which their obtained permissions could be leveraged by attackers. XManDroid [19] comprehensively analyzed the privilege escalation attacks on Android, and proposed a systematic runtime monitoring approach at multiple layers, Android middleware layer and kernel layer to defeat both confused deputy and collusion attacks. Woodpecker [20] successfully identified a number of privileged permissions explicitly leaked on different brands of Android phones, which could be maliciously leveraged by third-party developers to gain unnecessary privileges. Our paper studies the side effects of the Google Play's auto-update policy, which could be misused by attackers to gain higher privilege than what users have granted.

Malware Analysis. [22] studied 46 pieces of iOS, Android, and Symbian malware samples, and summarized their common incentives behind. Existing mitigation techniques used by different application markets are also evaluated for effectiveness. In contrast, [21] analyzed the Android permission model and discussed its potential weakness. A seminal work [15] collected more than 1200 malware samples, and systematically studied different characteristics of them, including installation methods, activation methods, malicious payload and permission usage. Evolution of the malware is also given based on existing characteristics, and some widely used mobile anti-virus software are evaluated for effectiveness of the malware detection.

6   Conclusion

In this paper, we identified a new privilege escalation attack vector based on Google Play's new auto-update policy. In particular, we mapped the Android permissions available to third-party developers into their respective permission groups. We then analyzed the protection level of each permission within each group and identified six permission groups susceptible to the privilege escalation attack. Thousands of Android applications from Google Play and malware samples are studied to evaluate the potential damage that could be caused by the privilege escalation attack. It is highly recommended that Google redesign the auto-update policy and consider the separation of *dangerous* and *normal* level permissions into different groups to eliminate the attack vector.

References

1. Smartphone Users Worldwide Will Total 1.75 Billion in 2014 in Emarkerter, http://www.emarketer.com/Article/Smartphone-Users-Worldwide-Will-Total-175-Billion-2014/1010536
2. Number of apps available in leading app stores as of July 2014 in Statista, http://www.statista.com/statistics/276623/number-of-apps-available-in-leading-app-stores/
3. Prevelakis, V., Spinellis, D.: Sandboxing Applications. In: Proceedings of USENIX Annual Technical Conference, FREENIX Track (2001)
4. Felt, A.P., Chin, E., Hanna, S., Song, D., Wagner, D.: Android Permissions Demystified. In: Proceedings of the 18th ACM Conference on Computer and Communications Security (2011)
5. Zhang, Y., Yang, M., Xu, B., Yang, Z., Gu, G., Ning, P.: Vetting Undesirable Behaviors in Android Apps with Permission Use Analysis. In: Proceedings of the 20th ACM Conference on Computer and Communications Security (2013)
6. David Barrera, H., Kayacik, G., van Oorschot, P.C., Somayaji, A.: A Methodology for Empiracal Analysis of Permission-based Security Models and its Application to Android. In: Proceedings of the 17th ACM Conference on Computer and Communications Security (2010)
7. Au, K.W.Y., Zhou, Y.F., Huang, Z., Lie, D.: PScout: Analyzing the Android Permission Specification. In: Proceedings of the 19th ACM Conference on Computer and Communications Security (2012)
8. Android permission, http://developer.android.com/guide/topics/manifest/permission-element.html
9. Manifest.permission_group, http://developer.android.com/reference/android/Manifest.permission_group.html
10. Review App Permissions, https://support.google.com/googleplay/answer/6014972?hl=en
11. Shabtai, A., Fledel, Y., Elovici, Y.: Securing Android-Powered Mobile Devices Using SELinux. IEEE Security & Privacy 8(3), 36–44 (2010)
12. Smalley, S., Craig, R.: Security Enhanced (SE) Android: Bringing Flexible MAC to Android. In: 20th Annual Network & Distributed System Security Symposium, NDSS (2013)
13. Security-Enhanced Linux in Android, https://source.android.com/devices/tech/security/selinux/index.html

14. Xing, L., Pan, X., Wang, R., Yuan, K., Wang, X.: Upgrading Your Android, Elevating My Malware: Privilege Escalation Through Mobile OS Updating. In: Proceeding of IEEE Symposium on Security and Privacy (2014)
15. Zhou, Y., Jiang, X.: Dissecting Android Malware: Characterization and Evolution. In: Proceedings of the 33rd IEEE Symposium on Security and Privacy (Oakland 2012), San Francisco, CA (May 2012)
16. Fragkaki, E., Bauer, L., Jia, L., Swasey, D.: Modeling and Enhancing Android's Permission System. In: Proceeding of the 17th European Symposium on Research in Computer Security (2012)
17. Bartel, A., Klein, J., Traon, Y.L., Monperrus, M.: Automatically securing permission-based software by reducing the attack surface: an application to Android. In: Proceedings of the 27th IEEE/ACM International Conference on Automated Software Engineering (2012)
18. Felt, A.P., Wang, H.J., Moshchuk, A., Hanna, S., Chin, E.: Permission Re-Delegation: Attacks and Defenses. In: USENIX Security Symposium (2011)
19. Bugiel, S., Davi, L., Dmitrienko, A., Fischer, T., Sadeghi, A.-R., Shastry, B.: Towards Taming Privilege-Escalation Attacks on Android. In: Proceedings of the 19th Annual Network and Distributed System Security Symposium (2012)
20. Grace, M., Zhou, Y., Wang, Z., Jiang, X.: Systematic Detection of Capability Leaks in Stock Android Smartphones. In: Proceedings of the 19th Annual Network and Distributed System Security Symposium (2012)
21. Vidas, T., Votipka, D., Christin, N.: All your droid are belong to us: a survey of current android attacks. In: Proceeding of the 5th USENIX conference on Offensive technologies (2011)
22. Felt, A.P., Finifter, M., Chin, E., Hanna, S., Wagner, D.: A Survey of Mobile Malware in the Wild. Proceedings of the 1st ACM workshop on Security and privacy in smartphones and mobile devices
23. android-apktool - A tool for reverse engineering Android apk files, https://code.google.com/p/android-apktool/

IVDroid: Static Detection for Input Validation Vulnerability in Android Inter-component Communication*

Zhejun Fang, Qixu Liu, Yuqing Zhang, Kai Wang, and Zhiqiang Wang

National Computer Network Intrusion Protection Center,
University of Chinese Academy of Sciences, Beijing, China
{fangzj,wangk,wangzq}@nipc.org.cn,
{liuqixu,zhangyq}@ucas.ac.cn

Abstract. Input validation vulnerability in Android inter-component communication is a kind of severe vulnerabilities in Android apps. Malicious attacks can exploit the vulnerability to bypass Android security mechanism and compromise the integrity, confidentiality and availability of Android devices. However, so far there is not a sound approach at source code level designed for app developers to detect such vulnerabilities. In this paper we propose a novel approach aiming at detecting input validation flaws in Android apps and implement a prototype named IVDroid, which provides practical static analysis of Java source code. IVDroid leverages backward program slicing to abstract application logic from Java source code. On slice level, IVDroid detects flaws of known pattern by security rule matching and detects flaws of unknown pattern by duplicate validation behavior mining. Then IVDroid semi-automatically confirms the suspicious rule violations and report the confirmed ones as vulnerabilities. We evaluate IVDroid on 3 versions of Android spanning from version 2.2 to 4.4.2 and it detects 37 vulnerabilities including confused deputy and denial of service attack. Our results prove that IVDroid can provide a practical defence solution for app developers.

Keywords: Input Validation Vulnerability, Static Analysis, Program Slicing, Vulnerability Detection, Android Security

1 Introduction

Android security mechanism based on permission and sandbox has improved app security effectively. However, Android inter-component communication(ICC) mechanism brings in some new threat. In some cases if app developers didn't validate the input in Android inter-component communication, malicious Intent(the carrier of ICC data) would be injected and perform security-sensitive behaviors. It is so-called input validation vulnerability [1]. In this paper we talk about

---

* This research is supported in part by National Information Security Special Projects of National Development and Reform Commission of China under grant (2012)1424, National Natural Science Foundation of China under grants 61272481 and 61303239.

J. Lopez and Y. Wu (Eds.): ISPEC 2015, LNCS 9065, pp. 378–392, 2015.
DOI: 10.1007/978-3-319-17533-1_26

the detection of such vulnerability in the context of Android inter-component communication mechanism, which can lead to various attacks such as confused deputy, deny of service, etc. The former includes capability leaks [2], permission re-delegation [3], content leaks and pollution [4], component hijacking [5][6], etc. The latter includes null point dereference [7], array index exception, illegal state exception, etc.

Prior work primarily focuses on automatic detection of confused deputy attack. Most approaches [2][4][5][6] predefine a certain kind of vulnerability pattern based on expert knowledge and identify confused deputy attack through pattern matching on the reachable execution path. Their approaches are all designed in the perspective of online market and detect vulnerabilities in thousands of executable apps (in form of .APK files). However, there should be a tool designed for app developers to detect confused deputy attack at source code level for two reasons: (1)Analyzing the source code prior to compilation provides a scalable method of security code review[8]. Besides, evolving techniques of anti-tamper and anti-decompiler greatly increase the difficulty of bytecode analysis. (2) App developers are the first battle line defending against vulnerabilities but have little security training. Unfortunately, there is no free and sound tool designed for app developers to secure their development lifecycle.

Detection of DoS attack and other input validation vulnerabilities is not given enough attention to. That's because app crashes are supposed as trivial flaws, and these vulnerabilities are application-specific and hard to be extracted into general vulnerability pattern. To better detect these vulnerabilities relevant to application logic, some researchers extract security policy from source code[11][12] and binary code[13], and check whether the implementation is inconsistent with the stated policy. However, there is so far no sound work focusing on these vulnerabilities in Android inter-component communication.

In this paper we propose a novel approach aiming at detecting input validation vulnerability in Android ICC mechanism and implement a plugin named IVDroid, which provides practical static analysis of Java source code in Eclipse. We employ backward program slicing on the control flow graph (CFG) to precisely capture application logic at slice level. Then we leverage predefined security rules to detect input validation vulnerability in known patterns. Besides, we extract the repeated validation behaviors as implicit and undocumented security rules to detect flaws in unknown pattern. Finally, we infer the inputs of suspicious flaws and confirm them semi-automatically on a running virtual machine.

The contributions of this paper are as follows:

- We propose a detecting technique to defeat input validation vulnerability in Android ICC mechanism, which could be used by app developers to avoid serious threats before app submission.
- We develop a practical plugin of Eclipse called IVDroid in 37 thousand lines of Java code, which is precise for known vulnerabilities and flexible to be expanded for new ones.
- We evaluate IVDroid on original apps in Android 2.2 ,4.0.3 and 4.4.2 and have detected 37 input validation vulnerabilities (16 confused deputy

vulnerabilities and 21 denial of service errors), among which 23 vulnerabilities are undisclosed. The vulnerability report to Android Open Source
Project(AOSP) is in progress.

The rest of this paper is structured as below: Section 2 presents an illustrative
example and the goal of this paper. In section 3 we give an overview and detail
of our approach; Section 4 evaluates the performance of IVDroid together with
case studies of discovered vulnerabilities; Section 5 discusses the limitation of
IVDroid; Related work is presented in Section 6. Section 7 is a brief conclusion.

2   Motivating Example and Problem Statement

2.1   Running Example of Input Validation Vulnerability

Here is an example of capability leak vulnerabilities(a typical and severe kind of
input validation vulnerabilities) existing in *Settings* app [10], an original Android
app providing a GUI to configure system settings and user preferences. The Class
com.android.settings.ChooseLockGeneric lacks necessary security check and in
consequence some running malicious app could exploit the flaw to remove existing device lock and unlock the device. The affected platforms range from Android
4.0 to 4.3.

In Android security model, the device has to ask the user for confirmation
of the previous lock for modification or removal in password settings. However,
the activity ChooseLockGeneric, which has the capability of remove device lock
without any confirmation, is exported unexpectedly without any protection. Fig
1 is a code snippet of ChooseLockGeneric.java in Android 4.0. Line 93, 178, 359,
360 are an execution path leading to the function in charge of clearing screen
lock. The malicious Intent has to be crafted well to satisfy the path branch
conditions(line 85, 167, 309, 318, 338, 355, 358). Ironically, app developer wrote
the annotation(line 308) about password confirmation and do the check(line 309)
which could be easily bypassed. The exploit is available in [10]. The vulnerability
is fixed in 4.4 by setting ChooseLockGeneric activity *unexported* in manifest.xml
of Settings app.

In summary, two factors must be met for the formation of input validation
vulnerability as above. Firstly, there exists a reachable path from the entry
of component to the call site of sensitive API. Secondly, the input validations
are not designed properly. The two factors can lead to many security-sensitive
behaviors. As [1] says, "this is a recipe for disaster".

2.2   Problem Statement

If we want to detect an input validation vulnerability, we should find the reachable paths and check the validation behaviors carefully. In this paper, we extract
the reachable path on the control flow graph(CFG) and take all the branch conditions on the path as validation behaviors. The vetting of validation behaviors
is a challenge we need to solve.

```
69   public void onCreate(Bundle savedInstanceState) {        307  void updateUnlockMethodAndFinish(int quality, boolean disabled) {
77      final boolean confirmCredentials = getActivity().getIntent()  308     // Sanity check. We should never get here without
            .getBooleanExtra(CONFIRM _CREDENTIALS, true);            confirming user's existing password.
71      mPasswordConfirmed = ! confirmCredentials;               309     if (!mPasswordConfirmed)
85      if (mPasswordConfirmed) {                                310        throw new IllegalStateException();
93          updatePreferencesOrFinish();                         316     quality = upgradeQuality(quality, null);
...                                                               318     if (quality >= PASSWORD_QUALITY_NUMERIC) {...}
164   private void updatePreferencesOrFinish() {                 338     else if (quality == PASSWORD_QUALITY_SOMETHING) {...}
165     Intent intent = getActivity().getIntent();               355     else if (quality == PASSWORD_QUALITY_BIOMETRIC_WEAK) {...}
166     int quality = intent.getIntExtra(                        358     else if (quality == PASSWORD_QUALITY_UNSPECIFIED) {
            LockPatternUtils.PASSWORD_TYPE_KEY, -1);             359        mChooseLockSettingsHelper.utils().clearLock(false);
167     if (quality == -1) {...}                                 360        mChooseLockSettingsHelper.utils().setLockScreenDisabled(disabled);
177     else
178        updateUnlockMethodAndFinish(quality, false);
```

Fig. 1. Code snippet of class "ChooseLockGeneric" of Settings app

We anticipate our proposed technique to be leveraged as a vetting plugin of Android IDE and achieve the following goals:

- **Security Development.** During the development of a new app, developers can run our plugin to detect input validation vulnerabilities, even when the app may not be runnable at that check point.
- **Minimal demand on users.** Even if developers do not have enough security knowledge, we hope our plugin would be helpful in most cases and be able to guide them about how to confirm and patch.
- **Extensible for future flaws.** The tool should be extensible for unknow vulnerabilities.

3 Approach Overview

Fig 2 depicts the workflow of our proposed technique. It works in the following steps:

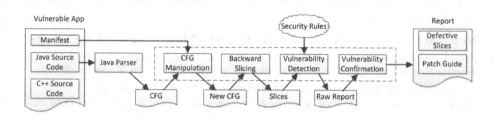

Fig. 2. The architecture of IVDroid

(1) **Java Parser.** The source code of an Android app consists of Java, C++ (native code) and xml (manifest.xml etc.) code, and We focus on Java source code and manifest.xml file. We leverage JavaParser, an open-source parser written by

jgsser, to parse Java code and generate the Abstract Syntax Tree(AST), Control Flow Graph(CFG) and System Dependence Graph(SDG) automatically.

(2) CFG Manipulation. The main task of this step is to modify the CFG according to Android features and remove unnecessary control flow for the next slicing step.

(3) Backward Slicing. At this step, we perform *flow-sensitive context-sensitive inter-procedural backward slicing* [14] to extract *transaction slices* and *constraint slices*. *Transaction slice* contains a statement of sensitive system API invocation as slicing criterion and its minimal set of data-dependent statements. *Constraint slice* is similar to transaction slice but its slicing criterion is an "if" statement.

(4) Vulnerability Detection. At slice level, the problem of detecting input validation vulnerability is transformed into how to detect pattern violation. The core of this step is to detect known flaws by security rule matching and detect unknown flaws by frequent validation behavior mining.

(5) Vulnerability Confirmation. We implement a semi-automatic vulnerability confirming module to validate the raw report. We can infer the inputs of simple suspicious flaws and confirm them on a running Android virtual machine dynamically. The complex suspicious flaws will be left for manual validation. Then the final report is generated with defective slices and patch guides.

3.1   CFG Manipulation

We gain basic CFGs of an app by leveraging JavaParser, and modify them according to Android features and remove unnecessary control flow. The new modified CFG only has basic blocks and conditional jumps, and does not have any loops, or throw statements.

Special Considerations for Android. Some access control policy are saved in the manifest file in the form of XML attribute *"exported"* or *"permission"*. To collect them in the program slicing, we transform these access control policy to the form of "if" statement and add them to the entry point of corresponding components.

Remove Unnecessary or Uncertain Control Flow. Java Assert statements would test assumption and throws an exception if the test fails. Android *checkPermission(perm)* API family is similar to them and checks if the permission *perm* has been granted to the calling application and throws a security exception when the check fails. To avoid such unexpected control flow transfer, IVDroid extracts the condition expressions of them and enforce them as implicit constraints for the following statements. For the similar reason, to "loop" statements we take the inverse expression of its condition as constraints for the following statements.

3.2   Backward Slicing

With the modified CFG, we now leverage backward program slicing to extract transaction and constraint slices. The basic algorithm is fairly standard and similar to other work such as [14]. In comparison, our slicing works in the context of Android platform and thus needs to be somewhere different.

Basic Algorithm. The algorithm begins from the last statement of a function (often is "return" statement) and searches all invocations of security-sensitive system API as slicing criterions backward on the control flow. From each slicing criterion, we compute all data-dependent statements via backward slicing until we get to the start point of the input. Then we get a transaction slice, which consists of a slicing criterion and all its dependent statements. In the same way, we extract constraint slices for each transaction slice by starting slicing from each "if" statement of the transaction.

Special Considerations for Android Apps. To leverage the above algorithm in Android platform, we have several special considerations for Android environment.

System API. We choose the security-sensitive system APIs as slice criterions especially when the API accesses Internet or mobile communication, or manipulates database or file system. The work of Pscout[16] about API calls mappings helps us construct the API list. In addition, the list also includes inter-component communication API such as *startActivity(), sendBroadcast()*.

Handle. A Handler(android.os.Handler) allows developers to send and process Message and Runnable objects associated with a thread's MessageQueue. It is an asynchronous message handling mechanism. To deal with such implicit method invocation, in the CFG we add a link between *Handle.sendMessage()* and *Handle.handleMessage()*.

Slice Example. Fig. 3 is a transaction and constraint slice example of Fig. 1. The last statement of transaction slice is the slicing criterion *clearLock(false)*, which is a security-sensitive function and maps the permission WRITE_SETTINGS. Also, we present the constraint slices of this transaction. It consists of seven security checks, one from a Throw statement (line 10) and six from "if" statements (line 8,9,11-14). These constraints check some property of variable *quality* and *mPasswordConfirmed*, whose values are both assigned from the input. Due to space limitations, we do not detail the constraint slices.

3.3   Vulnerability Detection

With transaction and constraint slices in hand, we can perform vulnerability detection at the slice level. We firstly leverage the predefined security rules to detect known-pattern vulnerabilities. Then we extract the duplicated constraints as implicit security rules from the slices and verify them to detect vulnerabilities with unknown pattern. Finally we generate the suspicious violations as raw report, which will be confirmed in the next step.

(1) Detecting Vulnerabilities of Known Pattern

In this section we validate each transaction slice according to predefined security rules. Prior work has undisclosed a lot of vulnerability patterns for input validation flaws, especially for confused deputy. We leverage Pscout [16] to write rules

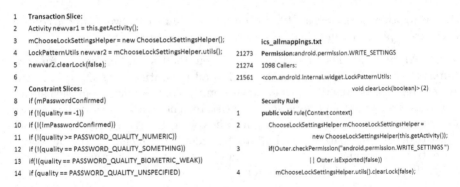

```
1    Transaction Slice:
2    Activity newvar1 = this.getActivity();
3    mChooseLockSettingsHelper = new ChooseLockSettingsHelper();
4    LockPatternUtils newvar2 = mChooseLockSettingsHelper.utils();
5    newvar2.clearLock(false);
6
7    Constraint Slices:
8    if (mPasswordConfirmed)
9    if (!(quality == -1))
10   if (!(!mPasswordConfirmed))
11   if (!(quality >= PASSWORD_QUALITY_NUMERIC))
12   if (!(quality == PASSWORD_QUALITY_SOMETHING))
13   if(!(quality == PASSWORD_QUALITY_BIOMETRIC_WEAK))
14   if (quality == PASSWORD_QUALITY_UNSPECIFIED)
```

```
         ics_allmappings.txt
21273    Permission:android.permission.WRITE_SETTINGS
21274    1098 Callers:
21561    <com.android.internal.widget.LockPatternUtils:
                            void clearLock(boolean)> (2)

         Security Rule
1        public void rule(Context context)
2          ChooseLockSettingsHelper mChooseLockSettingsHelper =
                  new ChooseLockSettingsHelper(this.getActivity());
3          if(Outer.checkPermission("android.permission.WRITE_SETTINGS")
                  || Outer.isExported(false))
4          mChooseLockSettingsHelper.utils().clearLock(false);
```

Fig. 3. Transaction and constraint slices from class "ChooseLockGeneric" of Settings app

Fig. 4. An example of security rules

for detection and the final rule list contains 33,624 items. To make reading and writing rules as readily as possible, the rules are designed to be written in Java language. They are just similar to a transaction slice of Java code invocating critical system API but with necessary permission validation. Fig. 4 is an example to illustrate how we write a security rule to detect the flaw in Section 2.1. The first three lines are from the result of Pscout(ics_allmappings.txt). First, We analyse it and map the permission *WRITE_SETTINGS* with the API *clearLock()*. Second, we extract all the data-dependent statements from the source code of *com.android. settings.ChooseLockGeneric* manually to fill minimal execution context of the rule. After these steps a rule is constructed completely, which checks whether the permission WRITE_SETTINGS is validated and whether the component is exported.

The rule matching procedure is as follows: IVDroid first leverage JavaParser to parse the security rules and compare them with all extracted transaction slices. If a transaction slice and a security rule have the same slicing criterion, we demand that slice should perform the same permission checks. If not, the violation would be reported as suspicious flaw. Given slicing criterions of two transactions as $o_1.fun_1(p_1, p_2, ..., p_n)$ and $o_2.fun_2(q_1, q_2, ..., q_n)$, they are equal only if the classes of o_1 and o_2 are the same or inherit from the same parent class, function names of fun_1 and fun_2 are equal and parameter types are equal. Suppose O_1 is o_1's class, O_2 is o_2's class, the symbol "$<$" stands for the relationship of inheritance, P_x is p_x's class and Q_x is q_x's class, then $o_1.fun_1(p_1, p_2, ..., p_n) = o_2.fun_2(q_1, q_2, ..., q_n)$ if and only if $(O_1 = O_2 \vee \exists Class\ O, (O_1 < O) \wedge (O_2 < O)) \wedge fun_1.name = fun_2.name \wedge (\forall x \in [1, n], (P_x = Q_x \vee \exists Class\ R, (P_x < R) \wedge (Q_x < R)))$.

(2) Detecting Vulnerabilities of Unknown Pattern

Input validation vulnerability, particularly DoS flaw, is very relevant to application logic and it is hard to extract application-specific validation behaviors in general vulnerability patterns. To enhance the capability of IVDroid, we propose an algorithm to extract duplicated validation behaviors as implicit security rules by frequent pattern mining and detect violations at slice level.

Firstly, IVDroid divides the transactions into different categories by equality of slicing criterion. Then IVDroid traverses all constraints in the category, and take the constraints appearing frequently as implicit security rules. Second, we verify all extracted rules and record suspicious violations. The details are described as below.

Extracting Implicit Security Rules. In this step, we classify transactions according to the equality of their slicing criterions. That's because the slicing criterion is the core statement of a transaction and stands for its functionality. Specially, inter-component communication APIs such as *startActivity(), start-Service() and sendBroadcast()* are treated as equal slicing criterions because their functionalities are just the same.

Secondly, we infer the security specifications for each transaction category. We traverse all constraints from each transaction in a category and only treat the constraints appearing more than once in different transactions as implicit security rules we need. The equality of two constraints is similar to the equality of two transactions.

Verification of Implicit Rules. After obtaining these implicit security rules, we apply them as mandatory property to the original transaction category and record the suspicious violation. One challenge is how to judge the relevance of specific transaction and implicit security rules. The judging criterion is: for any extracted security rule SR_x from a transaction category, only when the dependent variable set of a transaction contains the dependent variable set of SR_x, the transaction should contain a constraint which is equal to SR_x. When we infer the relationship of dependent variable sets, we actually use variables' type instead of variables themselves and ignore primitive types. For example, if the dependent variable set of a transaction is *Intent, Message, SmsMessage, Context* and the dependent variable set of security rule is *Context, Intent, String, int*, we can tell that the security rule is necessary for and relevant to the transaction.

3.4   Vulnerability Confirmation

In this part, we confirm the above suspicious violations semi-automatically. Through data flow dependence analysis, we can collect all the constraints the input should satisfy. Then the work divides into two parts: (1)if the constraints only contain boolean expressions of string or integer, IVDroid generates exploit code and validates them automatically. (2)if the constraints are too complex to resolve, IVDroid leaves them for manual validation.

As Fig.5 shows, we implement a very simple resolver to infer the value of input automatically, such as *Extra* property. Then IVDroid generates the exploit code and send it to Android virtual machine (VM). The VM has bee deployed a modified system, in which *ActivityManagerService* is reprogrammed to monitor API calls[9]. IVDroid also leverages *logcat* to monitor app crash. If either of the above two situations is monitored, the vulnerability is recorded as confirmed

Fig. 5. Automatically Validate Exploitable Vulnerabilities

Fig. 6. An example of report of IVDroid

one, or it would be recorded as false alarm. The vulnerability would be recorded as unconfirmed one if the input can not be resolved, or there is no executable app(.apk).

After all these steps, a final report is generated, in which suspicious vulnerabilities are listed with the defective slices and possible patch guide.

4   Evaluation

We evaluate the performance of IVDroid on different Android distributions including 2.2, 4.0 and 4.4. We choose original apps in the folder *packages/apps* as test cases because they are available in almost every version of Android ROMs. In total, there are 27 apps in 2.2_r1.1, 34 in 4.0.3_r1 and 45 in 4.4.2_r1.

4.1   Results Overview

IVDroid running on each distribution produces a lot of suspicious input validation vulnerability reports. We then manually verify the reports by checking the corresponding source code.[1]. The results are shown in Table 1. Column "Apps" indicates the name of app which contains at least one input validation vulnerability. The dot mark means we do not find any vulnerability of that category in target app. The cross mark means the app doesn't exist in that version(NFC is available since Android 2.3). Column "Vulnerable Component" indicates the name of component which contains the vulnerabilities.

In total, IVDroid finds 37 input validation vulnerabilities, 23 of which are undisclosed. Among them, there are 16 confused deputy attacks(2 are undisclosed) and 21 null pointer dereferences(all are undisclosed). The experiment results provide encouraging evidence proving the effectiveness of IVDroid.

The results also tell that the code quality of Android is improved while the number of confused deputy is decreasing. However, null dereference vulnerabilities are still not taken seriously and are not patched in all systems. In next section we'll give out an example to demonstrate that null dereference can lead to severe DoS (Denial of Service) attack. There is another interesting fact that some vulnerabilities only exist in the version 4.x not 2.2.

---

[1] The vulnerability details are available on http://ivdroid.sinaapp.com

Table 1. Detected Input Validation Vulnerabilities (C: confused deputy; N: null dereference)

ID	Apps	2.2_r1.1		4.0.3_r1		4.4.2_r1		Vulnerable Component
		C	N	C	N	C	N	
1	com.android.mms	1	1	1	1	·	1	.transaction.SmsReceiverService
2	com.android.bluetooth	·	1	·	1	·	1	.pbap.BluetoothPbapService
3	com.android.deskclock	1	1	·	1	·	1	AlarmInitReceiver
4	com.android.music	1	·	·	·	·	·	MediaPlaybackService
5	com.android.phone	2	1	2	1	2	1	PhoneAppBroadcastReceiver
6	com.android.settings	5	1	1	·	·	·	.widget.SettingsAppWidgetProvider&ChooseLockGeneric
7	com.android.stk	·	2	·	2	·	2	StkCmdReceiver&BootCompletedReceiver
8	com.android.nfc	×	×	·	1	·	1	.handover.HandoverManager
	vulnerabilities in total	10	7	4	7	2	7	

4.2   Detail analysis

Vulnerabilities Detected by Security Rule Matching. The security rule database is effective to detect confused deputy attacks. In detail, confused deputy vulnerabilities in App 3, 4, 5, 6(.widget.SettingsAppWidgetProvider) are simple. Intent only containing "action" field and simple "extra" field would trigger the vulnerability. So IVDroid could confirmed these flaws automatically. In comparison, confused deputy vulnerabilities in App 1 and 6(ChooseLockGeneric) are much more complex. The content of Intent should be constructed manually to reach the sensitive API and manipulate privacy information.

In Fig.3, we depict the DeskLock capability leak vulnerability in App 7(ChooseLockGeneric). Fig.4 is the security rule to detect that vulnerability. Fig. 6 is a snippet of the final report, containing defective slice and patch guide. As the report says, capability leak vulnerability can be mitigated by adding access restriction in manifest.xml file. In fact, many capability leaks are simply patched in higher version by setting "*exported*" property *false*.

Vulnerabilities Detected by Duplicate Validation Behavior Mining. Vulnerabilities of unknown patterns can be detected by duplicate validation behavior mining. This method is effective to detect deny of service attacks, which are particularly dangerous when an adversary leverage them to stop critical service [7], i.e. anti-virus and security enhancement software.

In detail, DoS attacks in App 1, 2, 3, 5, 6, 7 are null dereference vulnerabilities missing necessary vetting for the input. In App 8 there is an array bound error, which we could only validate it manually. The rest of vulnerabilities are simple enough to be confirmed automatically. In our observation, null pointer dereference appears frequently but there are not many null point dereference flaws reported because of two reasons: one is that null dereferences in activity components have minimal impact [7]; the other is that some potential null dereferences can't be triggered actually because the vulnerable components may be not exported or the pointer is checked somewhere else.

In Fig. 7, we depict a null pointer dereference in app 7 *com.android.stk*, which are undisclosed before. App com.android.stk is a STK (short for SIM Application

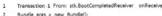

```
1    Transaction 1 From: stk.BootCompletedReceiver  onReceive
2    Bundle args = new Bundle();
3    args.putInt(StkAppService.OPCODE, StkAppService.OP_BOOT_COMPLETED);
4    context.startService(new Intent(context, StkAppService.class).putExtras(args));
5    Constraint Slices:
6    if(action.equals(Intent.ACTION_BOOT_COMPLETED))

7    Transaction 2 From: phone.InCallScreen onNewintent
8    startActivity(intent.setClassName(this, EmergencyCallHandler.class.getName()));
9    Constraint Slices:
10   if(intent == null || intent.getAction() == null)
11   if(!(action.equals(ACTION_SHOW_ACTIVATION))
12   if(!(action.equals(Intent.ACTION_ANSWER))
13   if(action.equals(Intent.ACTION_CALL)||action.equals(Intent.ACTION_CALL_EMERGENCY))
14   if(okToCallStatus != InCallInitStatus.SUCCESS)
15   if(isEmergencyNumber && (okToCallStatus == InCallInitStatus.POWER_OFF))
```

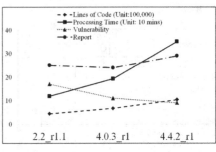

Fig. 7. Null pointer dereference vulnerability of STK app

Fig. 8. Performance of IVDroid

Toolkit) app in charge of value-added services based on GSM communication. If STK app crashes, the mobile communication of the phone will be cut off.

The flaw exists in the *onReceive()* function of *BootCompletedReceiver* component, as shown in Fig. 7. Transaction 1 is extracted from *onReceive()* and neither of its constraint slices check whether the Intent's *"Action"* property is null. If the incoming Intent's *"Action"* property is set null on purpose, the application will crash when it is dereferenced, which, in consequence, leads to the crash of Phone app. A persistent attack would prevent mobile communication totally, neither in nor out. IVDroid gets the needed security rule from transaction 2, which is extracted in another application(com.android.phone) and supplies the validation behavior we need. Transaction 1 & 2 are divided into the same category because *startService()* and *startActivity()* are treat equally. This kind of situation is not rare especially when the programmer has weak security concepts.

Null pointer dereference can be mitigated by adding content checking statements in source code. For example, the content of Intent needs null check, and the index of Array needs bound check.

4.3   Performance Measurement

In this section we evaluate the performance of IVDroid. The results are shown in Table 2. Column "Apps" indicates the number of apps and providers in certain Android version. Column "LoC" indicates the sum-up of lines of code of apps and providers in certain Android version. Column "Time" indicates the running time it takes to process a version of Android distribution. Column "Report" indicates the number of reported suspicious violations. Column "Vul" indicates the number of vulnerabilities IVDroid has detected. Column "Confirmed Vul" indicates the number of vulnerabilities IVDroid has confirmed automatically. Column "False Alarm" indicates the number of false alarm IVDroid has confirmed automatically. Column "Unconfirmed Alarm" indicates the number of unconfirmed alarms, in which the first number indicates the number of vulnerabilities we have confirmed manually.

Table 2. Performance of IVDroid

Version	Apps	LoC	Time	Report	Vul	Confirmed Vul	False Alarm	Unconfirmed Alarm
2.2_r1.1	27	445,836	119min	25	17	16	7	1/2
4.0.3_r1	34	674,156	193min	24	11	9	11	2/4
4.4.2_r1	45	1,040,688	351min	29	9	9	16	0/4

We measure the processing time by running IVDroid on an Intel Core i7 2.93GHz machine with 8GB of memory and Windows 7 SP1 OS. We believe the average processing time (about 6 minutes per app) is reasonable for offline detection. From Fig 8 we can tell that the processing time is increasing faster than the speed of lines of code because the implicit validation mining is applied in all transaction categories. The larger the category is, the more time it takes for IVDroid to collect constraint set and calculate the relevance of transaction and constraint.

We can also tell that the vulnerability confirmation module of IVDroid is effective to decrease false positive rate. Most of the suspicious vulnerabilities IVDroid reported are simple enough to be confirmed automatically. Specially, DoS vulnerabilities' input is easy to generate and app crashes information can always be monitored by logcat. Unconfirmed vulnerabilities are complex ones detailed in 4.2. The analysis of complex vulnerabilities can also benefit from the vulnerability confirmation module.

We do not measure false negatives because we don't have enough ground truth in the target apps. Here are two reasons which may lead to false negatives. First, dynamic vulnerability confirmation would raise false negatives if some system behavior is not monitored or the resolved input is wrong. Second, since the implicit security specifications are inferred from the extracted transactions, we can't get enough specifications for flaw detection if the programmer didn't make any security-sensitive check.

5 Discussion

IVDroid has so far uncovered a lot of input validation vulnerabilities in three Android distributions. It is important to give a further discussion about its own advantages and disadvantages.

Advantages of IVDroid. IVDroid has meet the goals we proposed in Section 2.2. IVDroid is a practical framework of input validation vulnerability detection for app developers. With predefined security rules and semi-automatic vulnerability confirmation module, we have lowered knowledge demand of IVDroid impressively. In addition, we leverage duplicate validation behavior mining to detect vulnerabilities of unknow pattern.

Limitation of IVDroid. IVDroid is only our first step for input validation vulnerability detection. Although it has identified several serious vulnerabilities in current Android version, it's still neither sound nor complete. IVDroid can not handle the complex situation when several system API call co-work together to accomplish a transaction. The vulnerability confirmation module is very simple so far and it can be enhanced by leveraging current constraint resolve technique in the future. Meanwhile, IVDroid can not handle the situation when apps use Java reflection techniques.

Detection for Other Vulnerabilities. Logic vulnerability is another common kind of vulnerabilities in Android apps, which misleads the legitimate processing flow of an application into unexpected negative consequence. IVDroid can detect some certain kinds of logic vulnerabilities. Application logic can be extracted by backward slicing and the validation behavior mining can help us understand undocumented application logic.

6   Related Work

Automatic Detection of Vulnerabilities in Android Inter-component Communication. When researchers turn to Android platform, they focus on a subset of input validation flaws, such as permission re-delegation [3], capability leak [2], and denial of service [7]. Felt etc. [3] firstly discover the permission re-delegation problem in the Android IPC mechanism and propose defence mechanism. Stowaway [17] detects overprivilege in compiled Android applications by comparing the required and requested permissions. To our best knowledge, there is no approach addressing static analysis of input validation vulnerabilities on source code level comprehensively in Android apps before.

Woodpecker [2] employs inter-procedural data flow analysis to systematically expose possible capability leaks. Our approach tries to detect capability leaks in a different way and focus on the execution path with necessary checks. Another difference is that IVDroid aims at the source code and Woodpecker operates on binary code. This leads to different scenarios. IVDroid tries to provide defence for app developers but Woodpecker are designed for automatic vetting in online app market. In comparison, IVDroid covers all the vulnerabilities Woodpecker detects and IVDroid can detect more types of input validation vulnerabilities than Woodpecker. Additionally, IVDroid can extract application-specific rules and Woodpecker does not have that capability.

Appsealer [6] focuses on the component hijacking attacks in Android applications and proposes a patch automatic generation technique. Appsealer injects minimal required code in vulnerable apps and provides a runtime defence for component hijacking attacks. Both IVDroid and Appsealer leverage static backward program slicing to extract application logic. The main difference between IVDroid and Appsealer is, however, that IVDroid can extract new vulnerability patterns from the code automatically. Similarly to Woodpecker, another difference is that Appsealer takes binary code as input.

Automatic Infering and Understanding of Security Specifications of Android Applications. SCanDroid [11] and Kirin [13] validate manifest files containing the access control policy of an application. Mustafa et al. [12]

extracts the implemented access control policy existing in the form of check-Permission APIs from Android system services with the help of program slicing. They admit that their approach would miss some security checks. Compared with their approach, IVDroid focus on Android ICC mechanism and gets more but smaller slices. We argue that IVDroid extracts more kinds of constraints and more fine-grained application logic, and cover all the policy Mustafa gains. Some vulnerabilities detected by IVDroid cannot be identified by Mustafa, as Mustafa doesn't analyse the specifications in manifest and "if" statements. All of the approaches before can not extract the whole implemented security specifications of Android apps and IVDroid is the first approach that extracts all security policies including manifest, checkPermission() APIs and "if" statements.

To describe access control policies formally, Kirin [13], Mustafa [12] and Sohr [18] use auxiliary language such as Java Modeling Language (JML), Kirin Security Language (KSL) and Object Constraint Language (OCL). It needs extra effort to understand the grammar of these languages and create new policy. IVDroid overcomes that disadvantage by directly using Java language to describe security rules.

Comprehensive Study on Android Vulnerabilities. Enck etc. [7] propose a study of Android application security based on static analysis of 21 million lines of recovered codes. Their approach uncovers different kinds of pervasive vulnerabilities and bugs, such as misuse of personal information and null pointer dereference. They think that many application-specific errors are often ignored, which inspired us a lot.

Dynamic Testing on Android. Yang etc.[9] detect capability leaks of Android apps by dynamic fuzzing the Intent. We are inspired by their work and implement our own dynamic vulnerability confirmation module.

7   Conclusions

This paper proposes a static approach to detect input validation vulnerabilities in Android inter-component communication. We employ program slicing to extract application logic. Then we detect vulnerabilities of known patterns through predefined security rules and detect vulnerabilities of unknown patterns through implicit validation mining. The suspicious flaws are validated by dynamic testing to lower the false positives. We implement a prototype plugin named IVDroid and evaluate it on Android 2.2, 4.0.3 and 4.4.2. The results prove that IVDroid has good precision. In the future work we will leverage more accuracy analysis such as symbolic execution and improve the dynamic vulnerability confirmation module.

References

1. Category:input validation on owasp,
   https://www.owasp.org/index.php/Category:Input_Validation

2. Grace, M., Zhou, Y., Wang, Z., et al.: Systematic detection of capability leaks in stock Android smartphones. In: NDSS (2012)
3. Felt, A.P., Wang, H.J., Moshchuk, A., et al.: Permission Re-Delegation: Attacks and Defenses. USENIX Security Symposium (2011)
4. Zhou, Y., Jiang, X.: Detecting Passive Content Leaks and Pollution in Android Applications. In: NDSS (2013)
5. Lu, L., Li, Z., Wu, Z., et al.: Chex: statically vetting android apps for component hijacking vulnerabilities. In: Proceedings of the 2012 ACM Conference on Computer and Communications Security, pp. 229–240 (2012)
6. Zhang, M., Yin, H.: AppSealer: Automatic Generation of Vulnerability-Specific Patches for Preventing Component Hijacking Attacks in Android Applications. In: Proceedings of the 21th Annual Network and Distributed System Security Symposium, NDSS 2014 (2014)
7. Enck, W., Octeau, D., McDaniel, P., et al.: A Study of Android Application Security. In: USENIX security symposium (2011)
8. SDL Process: Implementation, http://www.microsoft.com/security/sdl/process/implementation.aspx
9. Yang, K., Zhuge, J., Wang, Y., et al.: IntentFuzzer: detecting capability leaks of android applications. In: Proceedings of the 9th ACM Symposium on Information, Computer and Communications Security, pp. 531–536. ACM (2014)
10. CVE-2013-6271: Security Advisory Curesec Research Team, http://dl.packetstormsecurity.net/1311-advisories/CURE-2013-1011.txt
11. Fuchs, A.P., Chaudhuri, A., Foster, J.S.: SCanDroid: Automated security certification of Android applications Manuscript, Univ. of Maryland. Citeseer (2009), http://www.cs.umd.edu/avik/projects/scandroidasca
12. Mustafa, T., Sohr, K.: Understanding the Implemented Access Control Policy of Android System Services with Slicing and Extended Static Checking. Technical report, University of Bremen (2012)
13. Enck, W., Ongtang, M., McDaniel, P.: On lightweight mobile phone application certification. In: Proceedings of the 16th ACM Conference on Computer and Communications Security, pp. 235–245 (2009)
14. Fang, Z., Zhang, Y., Kong, Y., et al.: Static detection of logic vulnerabilities in Java web applications Security and Communication Networks. Security and Communication Networks 7(3), 519–531 (2014)
15. Enck, W., Ongtang, M., McDaniel, P.: Understanding android security. IEEE Security & Privacy 7, 50–57 (2009)
16. Au, K.W.Y., Zhou, Y.F., Huang, Z., et al.: Pscout: analyzing the android permission specification. In: Proceedings of the 2012 ACM Conference on Computer and Communications Security, pp. 217–228 (2012)
17. Felt, A.P., Chin, E., Hanna, S., et al.: Android permissions demystified. In: Proceedings of the 18th ACM Conference on Computer and Communications Security, pp. 627–638 (2011)
18. Berger, B.J., Sohr, K., Koschke, R.: Extracting and Analyzing the Implemented Security Architecture of Business Applications. In: 17th European Conference on Software Maintenance and Reengineering (CSMR), pp. 285–294 (2013)

Theory

New Constructions of T-function

Dibyendu Roy, Ankita Chaturvedi, and Sourav Mukhopadhyay

Department of Mathematics,
Indian Institute of Technology Kharagpur,
Kharagpur-721302, India
{dibyendu.roy,ankita,sourav}@maths.iitkgp.ernet.in

Abstract. T-function is a mapping from a Boolean matrix to a Boolean matrix with the property that i-th column of the output matrix depends on the first i columns of the input matrix. In 2003, Klimov and Shamir first introduced the concept of T-function. Using T-function we can construct some invertible functions which can be used to construct block cipher. Some invertible and full cycle T-functions can be used to construct stream cipher. Inversion procedure of these functions are different from the normal invertible functions and which is also hard. In 2005, Hong et al. constructed new class of full cycle T-function. In their construction the i-th column of the output matrix actually depends only on the i-th column of the input matrix. Our construction is more general than Hong et al's construction with good cryptographic properties. In this paper, we present a new construction of T-function. We study the invertibility, cycle length and nonlinearity of this T-function. Furthermore, we construct a new full cycle T-function. Invertible and highly nonlinear functions can be used to design block cipher. Full cycle functions can be used in LFSR based stream cipher to get the full period of the stream cipher in place of linear state update function.

Keywords: T-function, Boolean function, cycle length, nonlinearity, permutations.

1 Introduction

A function from a Boolean matrix to a Boolean matrix is called T-function if the i-th column of the output matrix depends on the first i columns of the input matrix. If the i-th column of the output matrix depends on the first $i - 1$ columns of the input matrix then T-function known as parameter. The concept of T-function was first introduced by Klimov and Shamir [4]. Now we discuss the main concept behind the invention of T-function. Suppose we have a matrix, now we will do some operations on the rows of the matrix. If the operators are not invertible then it is difficult to get the pre-image of the output matrix. To get the inverse of this mapping, we will see the changes in the columns of the matrix after doing operations in the rows. From there we will try to find the mapping between the columns of the input and output matrix to get the inverse mapping. i.e., we will try to find the relations between the columns of the input

© Springer International Publishing Switzerland 2015
J. Lopez and Y. Wu (Eds.): ISPEC 2015, LNCS 9065, pp. 395–405, 2015.
DOI: 10.1007/978-3-319-17533-1_27

matrix and the output matrix after doing some operations on the rows. From this idea, in 2003, Klimov and Shamir [4] tried to construct some invertible mapping whose forward mapping is fast but to get the inverse one needs to follow some other method which is hard. To construct this type of mapping in 2003 they introduced this new class of function known as T-function.

Invertible mappings have great importance in cryptography. In block cipher, it is necessary that the round functions should be invertible. As, to decrypt the ciphertext we need to use the inverse of the round functions. In case of stream cipher, the functions should be bijective to avoid the collision but, we do not need to invert the functions for decrypting the ciphertext. In case of LFSR based stream cipher we can get full period by using a primitive connection polynomial. But because of the linear state update function many attacks are possible. So if we can construct a nonlinear function which can give full period then it will be very effective in place of linear state update function used in LFSR based stream cipher. In 2003, Klimov and Shamir[4] constructed new invertible function using T-function they found a new class of functions which are invertible but inversion process is different from normal invertible functions. The software implementation of this class of function is also very fast. They also showed the general algebraic normal form of an (n, n) T-function. In 2004, Klimov and Shamir [5] discussed some cryptographic applications of this new class of functions. In 2005, Klimov and Shamir [6] found some applications of the T-functions in block cipher and hash function. They constructed MDS(maximum distance separable) mapping by using T-functions.

In 2005, Hong et al. [3] constructed a new class of T-function using a S-box and a parameter. They constructed a full cycle T-function by imposing some conditions on the S-box and the parameter. They also showed the application of their function in stream cipher and constructed two new stream ciphers which are known as TSC-1 and TSC-2.

In 2006, Zhang and Wu [7] demonstrated the general algebraic normal form of an (n, n) full cycle T-function. They also found the total number of such T-functions and studied the linear complexity of single cycle (n, n) T-functions.

Motivation and Objectives. In 2003 Klimov and Shamir [4] first introduced the concept of T-function. After that some constructions and applications of T-functions and their properties has been studied in some literatures [5], [7]. In 2005 Hong et al. [3] introduced a new full cycle T-function. In Hong et al's [3] construction the i-th column of the output of the T-function is actually a function of only the i-th column of the input matrix which is a particular type of T-function. They have also used only one full cycle S-box which is fixed for all clockings. Our aim is to construct a general T-function with good cryptographic properties.

Our Contribution. In this paper, we have constructed a new T-function based on two permutations and a parameter. We have demonstrated that this T-function does not have any fixed point under some conditions. This type of T-function is also invertible under some conditions. We have also found the cycle length of our T-function. Further, we have also discussed the nonlinearity of this T-function in a particular case. Finally, we have also constructed a more general full cycle T-function. Our constructions are more general than the Hong et al's [3] construction with better cryptographic properties.

Organization of the Article. The rest of this article is organised as follows: In Section 2, some basic definitions and properties of previously constructed T-functions are discussed. The new construction of T-function is proposed in Section 3. Some properties of this new construction is also demonstrated in Section 3. Construction of full cycle T-function is described in Section 4. Finally, the paper is concluded in Section 5.

2   Preliminaries

In this section, we will discuss some basic definitions, notations and some properties of previously constructed T-functions for better understanding of our construction.

2.1   Definitions and Notations

Definition 1. *Boolean Function*
A Boolean function f on n variables is a mapping from $\{0,1\}^n$ to $\{0,1\}$.

Definition 2. *Algebraic Normal Form of Boolean Function*
Every Boolean function f can be expressed as a multivariate polynomial over $\mathbb{F}_2$. This polynomial is known as algebraic normal form of the Boolean function f. The general form of the algebraic normal form of f is given by,

$$f(x_1, ..., x_n) = a_0 \oplus \bigoplus_{1 \leq i \leq n} a_i x_i \oplus \bigoplus_{1 \leq i < j \leq n} a_{ij} x_i x_j \oplus ..... \oplus a_{12...n} x_1 x_2 .... x_n.,$$

where the coefficients are either 0 or 1.

Definition 3. *Degree of a Boolean Function*
The degree of a Boolean function f is defined as $\deg(f) =$number of variables in the highest order product term in the algebraic normal form of f. Functions of degree at most one are called affine functions. An affine function with constant term equal to zero is called linear function. The set of all affine functions of n variables is denoted by $\mathcal{A}(n)$.

Definition 4. *Distance between two Boolean Functions*
Distance between two Boolean functions is defined by the number of positions where they are not equal and it is denoted by $d(f,g)$, where f, g are two Boolean functions of same variables.

Definition 5. *Non-linearity of a Boolean Function*
Non-linearity of a Boolean function f is defined by the minimum distance between f and the set of all affine functions. i.e., $nl(f) = \min\{d(f,g)|\ g \in \mathcal{A}(n)\}$. The functions with highest nonlinearity are known as bent functions.

Definition 6. *M-M Bent Function*
Let $\pi : \{0,1\}^n \to \{0,1\}^n$ is a permutation and $g : \{0,1\}^n \to \{0,1\}$ is a Boolean function then the function $f : \{0,1\}^{2n} \to \{0,1\}$ of the form $f(x,y) = x \cdot \pi(y) \oplus g(y)$, $\forall x \in \{0,1\}^n$, $y \in \{0,1\}^n$ is a M-M bent function. The nonlinearity of this function is $2^{2n-1} - 2^{n-1}$.

Definition 7. *Nonlinearity of a S-box*
Let $S : \{0,1\}^n \to \{0,1\}^m$ is a S-box with the coordinate functions f_i; $i = 1, 2, ..., m$. Then the nonlinearity of the S-box will be
$$nl(S) = \min_g \{nl(g \circ S)| \ g : \{0,1\}^m \to \{0,1\} \text{ is a linear function}\}. \ i.e., \ minimum$$
nonlinearity of all possible linear combinations of the coordinate functions f_i.

Definition 8. *T-function*
A function T from $\{0,1\}^{m \times n}$ to $\{0,1\}^{l \times n}$ is called T-function if the i-th column of the output matrix is a function of first i columns of the input matrix.

Definition 9. *(n,n)-T function*
A function $T : \{0,1\}^n \to \{0,1\}^n$ is a (n,n)-T function if the i-th bit of $T(x)$ depends on first i bits of x.

Definition 10. *Parameter*
A function α from $\{0,1\}^{m \times k}$ to $\{0,1\}^m$ is called parameter if the i-th bit of the output depends only on the first $i - 1$ columns of the input matrix.

Definition 11. *Parametric Invertible Function*
The functions whose arguments are separated by a semicolon into inputs and parameters are known as parametric functions. If the parametric function is invertible for any fixed value of the parameter then the parametric function is known as parametric invertible function. i.e., $\forall \alpha$ and $\forall x, y \ : g(x; \alpha) = g(y; \alpha) \Leftrightarrow x = y$, where x, y are the inputs and α is the parameter of the function g.

2.2   Examples of Some Existing T-functions and Their Properties

In this section, we will discuss some examples of previous constructions of T-function. The concept of T-function was first introduced by Klimov and Shamir [4] in 2003. In the very next year they showed the cryptographic applications of T-functions. Using the concept of T-function, they constructed some invertible, full cycle, MDS mappings. These T-functions are very useful to construct latin squares. Now we will discuss some existing constructions of T-functions. Consider a small example of T-function discussed in [4], the addition function: $x + y = z \ (mod \ 2^n)$. The least significant bit of z will be $[z]_0 = [x]_0 \oplus [y]_0$. The second bit of z depends on the first and second bits as $[z]_1 = [x]_1 \oplus [y]_1 \oplus \alpha_1$, where α_1 is the carry into the second bit from first bit. Similarly the third bit of z will be $[z]_2 = [x]_2 \oplus [y]_2 \oplus \alpha_2$, where α_2 is the carry into third bit from second bit. As second bit depends on the first bit then α_2 depends on the first bit also. i.e., the third bit is the function of first three bits of x, y. Clearly this is a T-function as the i-th bit of z depends on the first i bits of x, y . Klimov and Shamir [4] illustrated the concept of parametric invertible T-function by some examples. One example of parametric invertible function given in [4] is $x' = x + 2(x \wedge y)$ and $y' = (y + 3x^3) \oplus x$. If we write the previous mapping in terms of the i-th bit and parameter it will be of the form $[x']_i = [x]_i \oplus \theta$ and $[y']_i = [y]_i \oplus \beta[x]_i \oplus \tau$ where θ, β, τ all are parameters and clearly the function is parametric invertible function. Consider another example $x \to x \oplus x^2$. Its i-th bit slice mapping for $i > 0$ is invertible $[x']_i = [x]_i \oplus \alpha$, but for $i = 0$, we get $[x']_0 = [x]_0 \oplus [x]_0 = 0$. Clearly the first bit slice mapping is not invertible. To solve this problem, Klimov and Shamir [4] modified the mapping $x \to x \oplus (x^2 \vee 1)$, which is invertible. By observing the above result they proved the following result

Theorem 1. *[4] The mapping $f(x) = x + (x^2 \vee C)$ over n-bit words is invertible if and only if the least significant bit of C is 1. For $n \geq 3$ it is a permutation with a single cycle if and only if both the least significant bit and the third least significant bit of C are 1.*

In 2004, Klimov and Shamir [5] proved the algebraic normal form of (n, n) invertible T-function. The statement of the result is as follows,

Theorem 2. *[5] An (n, n) T-function is invertible iff its algebraic normal is of the form*

$$\pi(x) = (\phi_1(x), \phi_2(x), \ldots, \phi_n(x))$$
$$= (x_1 + a, x_2 + f_2(x_1), x_3 + f_3(x_1, x_2), \ldots, x_n + f_n(x_1, x_2, \ldots, x_{n-1}))$$

where $a = 0$ or 1; $f_i, i = 2, \ldots, n$ are Boolean functions.

In 2005, Hong et al. [3] constructed a new class of full cycle T-function. Their construction is based on one full cycle S-box. From a full cycle S-box $S : \{0, 1\}^m \mapsto \{0, 1\}^m$ they defined a new mapping, $\mathbf{S} : (\{0, 1\}^n)^m \mapsto (\{0, 1\}^n)^m$ by the setting $[\mathbf{S}(\mathbf{x})]_i = S([\mathbf{x}]_i)$. i.e., i-th column of the output matrix$=S(i$-th column of the input matrix). They defined some operations like as, let $\mathbf{x} = (x_k)_{k=0}^{m-1}$ and $\mathbf{y} = (y_k)_{k=0}^{m-1}$ be two vectors of size m then $\mathbf{x} \oplus \mathbf{y} = (x_k \oplus y_k)_{k=0}^{m-1}$, and for a single word α, $\alpha \cdot \mathbf{x} = (\alpha \wedge x_k)_{k=0}^{m-1}$. Bitwise complement of a vector $\mathbf{x}$ is denoted by $\sim \mathbf{x}$. Using these definitions Hong et al. [3] proved the following results,

Theorem 3. *[3] Let S be a single cycle S-box and let α be an odd parameter. If S^o is a an odd power of S and S^e is an even power of S, the mapping*

$$\mathbf{T}(\mathbf{x}) = (\alpha(\mathbf{x}) \cdot \mathbf{S^o}(\mathbf{x})) \oplus (\sim \alpha(\mathbf{x}) \cdot \mathbf{S^e}(\mathbf{x}))$$

defines a single cycle T-function.

From the above theorem they proved the following corollary,

Corollary 1. *[3] Given a single cycle S-box S and an odd parameter α, the following mapping defines a single cycle T-function.*

$$\mathbf{x} \mapsto \mathbf{x} \oplus (\alpha(\mathbf{x}) \cdot (\mathbf{x} \oplus \mathbf{S}(\mathbf{x})))$$

In 2006, Zhang and Wu [7] studied some properties of T-function. They found the algebraic normal form of the invertible and full cycle T-functions. The statement of the result is as follows,

Theorem 4. *[7] Let $\pi = (\phi_1, \ldots, \phi_n)$ be an invertible T-function over $GF^n(2)$. Then π is a single-cycle T-function if and only if its algebraic normal form has the following form*

$$\pi(x) = (\phi_1, \ldots, \phi_n)$$
$$= (x_1 + 1, x_2 + x_1 + \psi_2, x_3 + x_1 x_2 + \psi_3, x_4 + x_1 x_2 x_3 + \psi_4, \ldots,$$
$$x_n + x_1 x_2 \ldots x_{n-1} + \psi_n(x_1, x_2, \ldots, x_{n-1}))$$

where $\phi_i = x_i + x_1 \ldots x_{i-1} + \psi_i(x_1, \ldots, x_{i-1})$, $\deg(\psi_i) \leq i - 2$, $i \geq 2$.

3   New Construction of T-function

In this section, we propose a new construction of T-function. Let us consider a permutation $\pi : \{0,1\}^m \to \{0,1\}^m$ and the co-ordinate functions of this permutation are f_i, $i = 1, 2, \ldots, m$. Suppose a S-box $S : \{0,1\}^m \to \{0,1\}^m$ whose co-ordinate functions are denoted by g_i, $i = 1, 2, \ldots, m$. Now define some operations on two multi-words. Let $\mathbf{x} = (x_k)_{k=0}^{m-1}$ and $\mathbf{y} = (y_k)_{k=0}^{m-1}$ are two multi-words. Define $\mathbf{x} \oplus \mathbf{y} = (x_k \oplus y_k)_{k=0}^{m-1}$ and $\mathbf{x} \cdot \mathbf{y} = \oplus_{k=0}^{m-1} x_k \cdot y_k$. For a single bit c, $c \oplus \mathbf{x} = (c \oplus x_k)_{k=0}^{m-1}$. We will take $B = \{0,1\}$ through out the paper. Now define a function α, $\alpha : B^{m \times k} \to B^m$. The output of the parameter $\alpha(X_1, X_2, \ldots, X_k) = (\alpha_1, \alpha_2, \ldots, \alpha_m)$. Let c_i's are the coordinate functions of $\alpha(\cdot)$. Now we define our T-function,

$$T : B^{m \times n} \to B^{m \times n}$$

where

$$[T(\mathbf{X})]_i = \alpha(\mathbf{Y}) \cdot \pi([\mathbf{X}]_i) \oplus S([\mathbf{X}]_i) \tag{1}$$

where $\mathbf{Y}$ is the previous columns of the input matrix and $[\mathbf{X}]_i$ is the i-th column of the input matrix. The i-th column of the output matrix of this T-function is $\alpha(previous\ columns) \cdot \pi(i^{th}\ column) \oplus S(i^{th}\ column)$. It is clear that the function T is a T-function.

3.1   Properties of Newly Constructed T-function

In this section, we will demonstrate some properties of the newly constructed T-function. In the following theorem we prove that this T-function does not have any fixed point under some conditions.

Theorem 5. *If the following properties hold for the S-box then T-function defined in (1) does not have any fixed point.*

1. $S(X) \neq X, \forall X$
2. $S(X) \neq\sim X, \forall X.$

Proof. First, we write the expression of the i-th bit of any column of the output matrix of T-function. The expression of the i-th bit of any column is $\sum_j c_j f_j(X) \oplus$ $g_i(X)$. Now if this T-function has any fixed point then $\sum_j c_j f_j(X) \oplus g_i(X) = x_i$ should hold for all i and for atleast one X, where $X = (x_0, x_1, ..., x_m)$. But $\sum_j c_j f_j(X) = 0$ or 1. If $\sum_j c_j f_j(X) = 0$ then it implies $g_i(X) = x_i$ $\forall i$ i.e., $S(X) = X$ which contradicts our assumption. Now if $\sum_j c_j f_j(X) = 1$ then it implies $g_i(X) = 1 \oplus x_i$ $\forall i$ i.e., $S(X) =\sim X$ which also contradicts our assumption. Hence if our assumptions for S-box hold then our defined T-function does not have any fixed point.

From the above result we can see that by imposing some conditions on the S-box we can construct a T-function which does not have any fixed point. Now we will see a practical example of this kind of S-box.

Example 1. Here we discuss a practical example of such S-box. Consider a S-box $S : \{0,1\}^3 \to \{0,1\}^3$. The cycle expression of the S-box is

$$(0,0,0) \to (0,0,1) \to (0,1,0) \to (1,0,0) \to (1,1,1) \to (1,1,0) \to (1,0,1)$$
$$\to (0,1,1).$$

From the above description of the S-box we can see that the S-box is satisfying

1. $S(X) \neq X, \forall X$
2. $S(X) \neq\sim X, \forall X.$

Next we will discuss the invertibility of newly constructed T-function.

Theorem 6. *If f_i's are coordinate functions of the permutation π and the S-box and the coordinate functions of $\alpha(\cdot)$ satisfies the following property*

$$c_0 = c_1 \oplus c_2 \oplus \ldots \oplus c_{m-1}$$

then the T-function as in (1) is invertible.

Proof. We have $[T(\mathbf{X})]_i = \alpha(\mathbf{Y}) \cdot \pi([\mathbf{X}]_i) \oplus S([\mathbf{X}]_i)$. From our assumption the expression of the i-th bit of any column is $C_i = \sum_{j=0}^{m-1} c_j f_j \oplus f_i$. Let $C_i = (y_0, y_1, ..., y_{m-1})$. If we write the column in a matrix form then the form will be

$$\begin{bmatrix} y_0 \\ y_1 \\ y_2 \\ \vdots \\ y_{m-1} \end{bmatrix} = \begin{bmatrix} c_0+1 & c_1 & \cdots & c_{m-1} \\ & c_0 & c_1+1 & \cdots & c_{m-1} \\ \vdots & \vdots & \ddots & \vdots \\ & c_0 & c_1 & \cdots & c_{m-1}+1 \end{bmatrix} \times \begin{bmatrix} f_0 \\ f_1 \\ f_2 \\ \vdots \\ f_{m-1} \end{bmatrix} \qquad (2)$$

Let

$$A = \begin{bmatrix} c_0 + 1 & c_1 & \cdots & c_{m-1} \\ c_0 & c_1 + 1 & \cdots & c_{m-1} \\ \vdots & \vdots & \ddots & \vdots \\ c_0 & c_1 & \cdots & c_{m-1} + 1 \end{bmatrix}$$

now XOR 1st row with all rows we will get

$$A' = \begin{bmatrix} c_0 + 1 & c_1 & \cdots & c_{m-1} \\ 1 & 1 & \cdots & 0 \\ \vdots & \vdots & \ddots & \vdots \\ 1 & 0 & \cdots & 1 \end{bmatrix}$$

To get 1's in the first column, we need to XOR all other columns but from our assumption $c_0 \oplus 1 \neq c_1 \oplus c_2 \oplus \ldots \oplus c_{m-1}$. So, the columns of A' are linearly independent hence $rank(A) = rank(A') = m$. Hence, the matrix A is invertible. The functions of each columns of the T-function are invertible. Hence, the T-function with the given property is invertible.

Next we will show the cycle length of the above described T-function under some assumptions. From the equation (2) we are getting if f_i's are the coordinate functions of the S-box and the permutation $\pi(\cdot)$ then the expression of any column of the output of T-function is $Y = A \cdot S(X)$, where A is the coefficient matrix.

Theorem 7. *Let k_1 is the smallest number such that $A^{k_1} = I_m$ and the cycle length of the S-box is k_2 and the S-box is linear. Then the cycle length of the T-function $Y = A \cdot S(\cdot)$ is $lcm(k_1, k_2)$, where Y is any column of the output matrix of the T-function.*

Proof. Let X be i-th column of the input matrix. Then the expression of the i-th column of the output matrix is $Y_1 = A \cdot S(X)$, where A is the coefficient matrix which depends on the previous $i - 1$ columns of the input matrix. Let $Y_2 = A \cdot S(Y_1)$

$$\begin{aligned} Y_2 &= A \cdot S(Y_1) \\ &= A \cdot S(A \cdot S(X)) \\ &= A \cdot A \cdot S(S(X)), \quad \text{as } S \text{ is linear} \\ &= A^2 \cdot S^2(X) \end{aligned}$$

Similarly $Y_k = A^k \cdot S^k(X)$ for any integer k. It is given that k_1 is the smallest integer such that $A^{k_1} = I$ and k_2 is the smallest integer such that $S^{k_2}(X) = X$. Let $l = lcm(k_1, k_2)$ then $l = p_1 \cdot k_1$ and $l = p_2 \cdot k_2$ for integer p_1 and p_2. Now we calculate Y_l which is basically equal to $A^l \cdot S^l(X)$.

$$Y_l = A^l \cdot S^l(X)$$
$$= A^{k_1 p_1} \cdot S^{k_2 p_2}(X)$$
$$= (A^{k_1})^{p_1} \cdot (S^{k_2}(X))^{p_2}, \quad as \ A^{k_1} = I \ and \ S^{k_2} \ is \ identity \ permutation$$
$$= I_m \cdot X$$
$$= X$$

Now we can say that the cycle length of $A \cdot S(X)$ must divide l. Let p is the cycle length of $A \cdot S(X)$. Then $p|l$. Let $d = gcd(k_1, k_2)$ i.e., $k_1 = m_1 d$, $k_2 = m_2 d$ and $l = m_1 m_2 d$. We have $Y_p = X = A^p \cdot S^p(X)$, from this we can say that $A^{pk_2} = I_m$. As k_1 was the least positive integer such that $A^{k_1} = I_m$ then $k_1|pk_2$ i.e., $m_1 d|pk_2$ i.e., $l|p(m_2 k_2)$ as $l \nmid m_2$, $l \nmid k_2$. Hence $l|p$ i.e., $p = l$. Hence the cycle length of $A \cdot S(X)$ is $lcm(k_1, k_2)$.

The general form of our T-function is

$$[T(\mathbf{X})]_i = \alpha(\mathbf{Y}) \cdot \pi([\mathbf{X}]_i) \oplus S([\mathbf{X}]_i) \tag{3}$$

where $[\mathbf{X}]_i$ is the i-th column of the input matrix and $\mathbf{Y}$ is the previous columns of the input matrix. It is clear that if $\alpha(\cdot)$ is a function of only one column among previous $i-1$ columns of input matrix then each bit of one column of the output matrix of the T-function is in the form of M-M bent function. From the above observation we have the following result.

Lemma 1. *If $\alpha(\cdot)$ is a function of only one column among $i - 1$ columns of the input matrix then the nonlinearity of i-th column of output matrix of the T-function as in (3) is $2^{2m-1} - 2^{m-1}$, where $i \neq 1$.*

Proof. Clearly the each column of the output matrix of the T-function is an output of a S-box. So the nonlinearity of each column is the minimum nonlinearity of all possible linear combinations of the functions of each column. Let $[T(\cdot)]_i = (F_1, F_2, ..., F_m)$. Now the nonlinearity of each column except the first column will be $\min_g \{nl(g \circ [T(\cdot)]_i)\} = \min_g \{nl(\sum_i c_i F_i)\}$.

Now

$$\sum_i c_i F_i = \sum_i c_i [\alpha(\cdot) \cdot \pi(X) \oplus g_i(X)]$$
$$= \sum_i [c_i \alpha(\cdot) \cdot \pi(X) \oplus c_i g_i(X)]$$
$$= c_1[\alpha_1.f_1 + \alpha_2 f_2 + ... + \alpha_m f_m] + c_2[\alpha_1.f_1 + \alpha_2 f_2 + ... + \alpha_m f_m] + ..$$
$$.......... + c_m[\alpha_1.f_1 + \alpha_2 f_2 + ... + \alpha_m f_m] + \sum_i c_i g_i(X)$$
$$= \alpha_1[c_1 f_1 + c_2 f_1 + ... + c_m f_1] + \alpha_2[c_1 f_2 + c_2 f_2 + ... + c_m f_2] + ...$$
$$....... + \alpha_m[c_1 f_m + c_2 f_m + ... + c_m f_m] + \sum_i c_i g_i(X)$$

$$= \alpha(\cdot) \cdot \pi'(X) + \sum_i c_i g_i(X)$$

$$= \alpha(\cdot) \cdot \pi'(X) \oplus G(X)$$

where π' is a permutation with the coordinate functions $\sum_j c_j f_i, i = 1, 2, \ldots, m$ and $G(X) = \sum_i c_i g_i(X)$ is a Boolean function. Now $\sum_i c_i F_i$ is of the form $\alpha(\cdot) \cdot \pi'(X) \oplus G(X)$ which is also a M-M bent function. So all possible linear combinations of each column except the first column of the output of the T function is bent function of $2m$ variables which always achieves the nonlinearity $2^{2m-1} - 2^{m-1}$.

4   Construction of Full Cycle T-function

In this Section, we propose a new construction of full cycle T-function. Let $S : \{0, 1\}^m \to \{0, 1\}^m$ be a non-full cycle S-box. Let $A_k : \{0, 1\}^{m \times k} \to \{0, 1\}^{m \times m}$ be a mapping. Now we define

$$T : B^{m \times n} \to B^{m \times n}$$

such that

$$[T(X)]_i = A_k(Y) \times S([X]_i) \tag{4}$$

where Y is the previous columns of i-th column of input matrix. Clearly it is a T-function, as the i-th column of the output matrix is depending on the first i columns of the input matrix. [Here $\times$ is original matrix multiplication.]

Consider two any permutations π_1 and π_2 on 2^m numbers ($D = [0\ 1\ 2 \ldots\ 2^m - 1]$). Then we can write these permutations in terms of the permutation matrix, where $\pi_1(\cdot) = P_1 \times D$ and $\pi_2(\cdot) = P_2 \times D$. These permutation matrices are related by the multiplication of an elementary matrix i.e., $P_1 = E \times P_2$ where E is an elementary matrix.

Let $S : \{0, 1\}^m \to \{0, 1\}^m$ be a non-full cycle S-box. Let P_s denotes the permutation matrix corresponding to the S-box S. Let M be a set which contains all possible elementary matrix such that if $E_i \in M$ then $E_i \times P_s$ will be a permutation matrix of a full cycle S-box on $\{0, 1\}^m$.

Now we will define the $A_k(\cdot)$ in such a way that for any Y, $A_k(Y) \in M$.

Theorem 8. *If $A_k(Y) \in M$ for any Y then the T-function defined in (4) is a full cycle T-function.*

Proof. If for any Y, $A_k(Y) \in M$ then we will prove that T-function defined in (4) is a full cycle T-function. For the first column of the input matrix the image will be $T(C_1) = A_1(\cdot) \times S(C_1)$. Now $S(\cdot)$ is not a full cycle S-box but as $A_1(\cdot) \in M$ then $A_1(\cdot) \times S(\cdot)$ is a full cycle S-box. So the period of the first column will be 2^m. Now by induction hypothesis, assume that the cycle length of the T-function upto i-th column is 2^{mi}. We have to prove that the cycle length of the T-function upto $(i+1)$-th column will be $2^{m(i+1)}$. For the fixed previous columns the form of the $(i+1)$-th column is $A_{i+1}(\cdot) \cdot S(C_{i+1})$ as $A_{i+1}(\cdot) \in M$ then $A_{i+1}(\cdot) \cdot S(\cdot)$ is a full cycle S-box on $\{0, 1\}^m$. For one fixed previous i columns, the cycle length of $(i + 1)$-th column of the T-function will be 2^m. Therefore, the cycle length upto the $(i + 1)$-th column will be $2^{m(i+1)}$. Hence above defined T-function is a full cycle T-function.

Note. In the construction defined in (4) different possible full cycle S-boxes are operating on the each column of the input matrix which is determined by previous columns.

5   Conclusion

We have proposed a new construction of T-function in which the i-th column of the output matrix of T-function directly depends on the previous columns and i-th column of the input matrix. Our proposed T-function is more general T-function than Hong et al.'s construction with good cryptographic properties. Our constructed T-function does not have any fixed point under some certain conditions. In some cases this T-function is also invertible which is useful for block cipher and stream cipher. We have found the cycle length of the T-function for a particular case. Also, we have observed that this T-function is achieving a good nonlinearity in a particular case. Moreover, we have constructed a full cycle T-function. These T-functions can be used for designing block cipher and stream cipher to prevent many attacks like linear cryptanalysis, differential cryptanalysis. Full cycle T-function can be used for designing full periodic stream cipher.

References

1. Carlet, C.: Boolean Functions for Cryptography and Error Correcting codes, Boolean Models and Methods in Mathematics. In: Crama, Y., Hammer, P. (eds.) Computer Science and Engineering, pp. 257–397. Cambridge University Press, Cambridge (2010)
2. Cusick, T.W., Stanica, P.: Cryptographic Boolean functions and applications. Access Online via Elsevier (2009)
3. Hong, J., Lee, D.H., Yeom, Y., Han, D.: A new class of single cycle T-functions. In: Gilbert, H., Handschuh, H. (eds.) FSE 2005. LNCS, vol. 3557, pp. 68–82. Springer, Heidelberg (2005)
4. Klimov, A., Shamir, A.: A new class of invertible mappings. In: Kaliski Jr., B.S., Koç, Ç.K., Paar, C. (eds.) CHES 2002. LNCS, vol. 2523, pp. 470–483. Springer, Heidelberg (2003)
5. Klimov, A., Shamir, A.: Cryptographic applications of T-functions. In: Matsui, M., Zuccherato, R.J. (eds.) SAC 2003. LNCS, vol. 3006, pp. 248–261. Springer, Heidelberg (2004)
6. Klimov, A., Shamir, A.: New applications of T-functions in block ciphers and hash functions. In: Gilbert, H., Handschuh, H. (eds.) FSE 2005. LNCS, vol. 3557, pp. 18–31. Springer, Heidelberg (2005)
7. Zhang, W., Wu, C.K.: The algebraic normal form, linear complexity and k-error linear complexity of single-cycle T-function. In: Gong, G., Helleseth, T., Song, H.-Y., Yang, K. (eds.) SETA 2006. LNCS, vol. 4086, pp. 391–401. Springer, Heidelberg (2006)

A New Lattice-Based Threshold Attribute-Based Signature Scheme

Qingbin Wang, Shaozhen Chen, and Aijun Ge

State Key Laboratory of Mathematical Engineering and Advanced Computing,
Zhengzhou Information Science and Technology Institute, Zhengzhou 450001, China
qingbinwang2008@163.com

Abstract. In this paper, we present a new construction of attribute-based signature (ABS) scheme supporting flexible threshold predicates from lattices. The new construction is proved to be selective-predicate and adaptive-message unforgeable under chosen message attacks in random oracle model if the small integer solution (SIS) assumption holds. In addition, this scheme can also achieve privacy, which means the signature reveals nothing about the attributes or identity information about the real signer. Compared with existing lattice-based threshold ABS scheme, the new construction provides better efficiency.

Keywords: attribute-based signature, threshold, lattice, random oracle model.

1 Introduction

Attribute-based cryptography offers a powerful alternative for fine-grained access control with respect to security policies. In the case of attribute-based signature (ABS), each user receives from a master entity a secret key which depends on the attributes that he possesses. With the secret key, a signer can compute a signature on a message for any predicate satisfied by his attributes. Everybody can convince that someone whose set of attributes satisfies the signing predicate has endorsed the message without learning any information about the actual attributes or the identity of the real signer. Unforgeability is also the essential security property of ABS schemes, which requires that a signature cannot be computed by a signer whose attributes don't satisfy a given predicate, even through colluding with other users. The ABS schemes have a wide range of applications such as anonymous authentication, attribute-based messaging systems and trust-negotiation.

The past few years have seen much progress in constructing ABS schemes. Maji et al. [1] proposed the notion of ABS and provided a scheme that supported very expressive signing predicates with a proof in the generic group model. Schemes supporting flexible threshold signing predicates have been designed in [2,3,4]. Okamoto et al. [5] designed a full-secure ABS scheme which can support non-monotone predicates in the standard model. Very recently, Okamoto et al. [6] and El Kaafarani et al. [7] presented the first decentralized multi-authority ABS schemes, which has

© Springer International Publishing Switzerland 2015
J. Lopez and Y. Wu (Eds.): ISPEC 2015, LNCS 9065, pp. 406–420, 2015.
DOI: 10.1007/978-3-319-17533-1_28

no central authority and no trusted setup. Unfortunately, most of existing ABS schemes are dependent on the hardness of discrete logarithm problem, which leaves them vulnerable to quantum cryptanalysis. Lattice-based cryptography is widely believed to be secure against attacks using quantum computers, a property not achievable by cryptographic primitives based on hard number theory problems. Moreover, it enjoys provable security under worst-case hardness assumption. An intriguing challenge for the research community is how to design secure and efficient lattice-based ABS schemes. Recently, Wang et al. [8] proposed a lattice-based ABS construction that can support flexible threshold signing predicates and can achieve selective security in the standard model. However, their constructions have long private key size. This is a noticeable disadvantage since long private key increases the hardware cost of secure storage.

1.1 Our Contributions

Inspired by the work of [9] and [13], we propose in this paper a new lattice-based ABS scheme supporting flexible threshold signing predicates, which departs from the approach of [8] at the very core of the construction. The main building block of this new scheme is a proof of knowledge protocol, which is converted to a signature scheme via Fiat-Shamir heuristic [10] with random oracle. Our scheme is proved to be selective-predicate and adaptive-message unforgeable under chosen message attacks in the random oracle model if the small integer solution (SIS) assumption holds. This scheme is also equipped with privacy property. When compared with [8], our scheme enjoys significantly better efficiency in terms of the private key storage cost, while the public key size and signature size remain comparable. Although it is believed that random oracle model is not as secure as standard model theoretically, it still achieves an acceptable level of security. In some special scenarios which put efficiency as the most important factor, our scheme maybe a better choice.

1.2 Organization

Some preliminaries used in this paper, including the formal definition of ABS and its security model, and lattice problems are reviewed in section 2. An interactive protocol is proposed in section 3. The main construction is given in section 4. The security analysis is given in section 5. The parameters are instantiated in section 6. Finally, this paper is concluded in section 7.

2 Preliminaries

2.1 Notation

We denote the real numbers and integers by $\mathbb{R}$ and $\mathbb{Z}$ respectively. For a positive integer k, $[k]$ denotes the set $\{1, ..., k\}$. If S is a set then $|S|$ denotes its size. For $\mathbf{X} \in \mathbb{R}^{n \times m}$ and $\mathbf{Y} \in \mathbb{R}^{n \times m'}$, $[\mathbf{X} \parallel \mathbf{Y}] \in \mathbb{R}^{n \times (m+m')}$ denotes the concatenation of the rows of $\mathbf{X}$ followed by the rows of $\mathbf{Y}$. For any $p \geq 1$, the ℓ_p norm of a vector $\mathbf{x} = (x_1, ..., x_n) \in \mathbb{R}^n$, denoted by $\|\mathbf{x}\|_p$, is $(\sum_{i \in [n]} (x_i^p))^{1/p}$. For simplicity, denote ℓ_2 norm by $\|\cdot\|$. The ℓ_∞ norm is defined as $\|\mathbf{x}\|_\infty = \max_{i \in [n]} |x_i|$. The standard notations O and ω was used to classify the growth of functions. If $f(n) = O(g(n) \cdot \log^c n)$ for some constant c, we denote $f(n) = \tilde{O}(g(n))$. A function $f(n)$ is negligible if for every $c > 0$, there exists a N such that $f(n) < 1/n^c$ for all $n > N$. Let $negl(n)$ denote a negligible function of n.

The statistical distance between two probability distributions $\mathbf{X}, \mathbf{Y}$ over a finite or countable domain $\mathcal{D}$ is defined as $\Delta(\mathbf{X}, \mathbf{Y}) = \frac{1}{2} \sum_{\alpha \in \mathcal{D}} |\mathbf{X}(\alpha) - \mathbf{Y}(\alpha)|$. We say that two ensembles of probability distributions $\{\mathbf{X}_n\}_{n \in \mathbb{N}}$ and $\{\mathbf{Y}_n\}_{n \in \mathbb{N}}$ are statistically close if $\Delta(\mathbf{X}_n, \mathbf{Y}_n)$ is a negligible function in n.

2.2   Syntax of ABS

A threshold ABS scheme consists of four polynomial time algorithms: **Setup**, **KeyGen**, **Sign** and **Verify** described as follows:

Setup(n): This Setup algorithm is a probabilistic algorithm takes as inputs a security parameter n, and outputs a master secret key MSK and public parameters PP. We assume that the universe of attributes $\mathbf{U}$ is also contained in the public parameters PP.

KeyGen(MSK,PP,W): This KeyGen algorithm is a probabilistic algorithm takes as inputs the public parameters PP, the master secret key MSK and a user's attribute set $W \subset \mathbf{U}$, and outputs the corresponding private key SK_W.

Sign(PP,M,SK_W,Γ): This Sign algorithm is a probabilistic algorithm takes as inputs the public parameters PP, a message M, a threshold signing predicate $\Gamma = (t, S)$ where $S \subset \mathbf{U}$ and $1 \leq t \leq |S|$, and a user's private key SK_W with the attribute set W satisfying $|W \cap S| \geq t$, and outputs a signature e.

Verify(PP,M,Γ,e): This Verify algorithm is a deterministic algorithm takes as inputs the public parameters PP, the message M, the signing predicate $\Gamma = (t, S)$ and the corresponding signature e, and outputs "accept" or "reject".

For correctness, it is required that a signature for a threshold predicate $\Gamma = (t, S)$ that is computed by using SK_W such that $|W \cap S| \geq t$ must pass the verification test.

2.3   Security Model for ABS

An ABS scheme must satisfy two security requirements: privacy and unforgeability.

Privacy. The property of privacy requires that a signature reveals nothing about the actual attribute set or the identity of the signer beyond the fact that his attribute set satisfies the specified signing predicate. The formal security definition is defined in the following game between an adversary $\mathcal{D}$ and its challenger $\mathcal{C}$:

SetUp: The challenger $\mathcal{C}$ chooses a sufficiently large security parameter n, runs **Setup** algorithm to obtain the public parameters PP and a master secret key MSK, and sends PP to the adversary $\mathcal{D}$.

Phase 1: $\mathcal{D}$ can issue a polynomially bounded number of **private key** queries and **signature** queries, and $\mathcal{C}$ answers these queries with *MSK*.

Private Key Queries: $\mathcal{D}$ adaptively requests a private key SK_W for any attribute set W.   **Signature Queries:** $\mathcal{D}$ requests a signature for a message M' and a signing predicate $\Gamma' = (t', S')$, where $S' \subset \mathbf{U}$ and $1 \le t' \le \left| S' \right|$.

Challenge: $\mathcal{D}$ outputs a tuple (Γ, M, W_0, W_1) where $\Gamma = (t, S)$ is a threshold predicate such that $1 \le t \le |S|$ and W_0, W_1 are attribute sets satisfying $|W_i \cap S| \ge t$ for each $i \in \{0, 1\}$. $\mathcal{C}$ randomly chooses a bit $b \in \{0, 1\}$, computes $SK_{W_b} := \mathbf{Keygen}(PP, MSK, W_b)$ and $e := \mathbf{Sign}(PP, SK_{W_b}, \Gamma, M)$. It sends e as the challenge to $\mathcal{D}$.

Phase 2: The same as Phase 1.

Guess: $\mathcal{C}$ outputs a guess $b' \in \{0, 1\}$, and wins the game if $b = b'$.

The advantage of adversary $\mathcal{D}$ in this game is defined as

$$Adv_{\mathcal{D}}(n) = \left| \Pr[b = b'] - \frac{1}{2} \right|.$$

Definition 1. *A threshold ABS scheme satisfies the privacy property if there exists no adversary having a non-negligible advantage in this game.*

Unforgeability. The property of unforgeability requires that an adversary, even additionally colluding with a group users that put their private keys together, still cannot forge a valid signature with any signing predicate which his attribute set does not satisfy. In this work, we consider the security model of ABS scheme as selective-predicate and adaptive-message unforgeability under chosen message attacks (sP-UF-CMA), which is weaker than the fully chosen predicate attacks. The difference is that the selective-predicate adversary has to select the signing predicate that he wants to attack at the beginning of the game. The formal security definition is defined in the following game between an adversary $\mathcal{F}$ and its challenger $\mathcal{C}$:

Initial Phase: $\mathcal{F}$ outputs a challenge threshold predicate $\Gamma^* = (t, S^*)$ where $S^* \subset \mathbf{U}$ and $1 \le t \le |S^*|$.

Setup Phase: $\mathcal{C}$ chooses a sufficiently large security parameter n and runs **Setup** algorithm. It retains the master key *MSK* and sends the public parameters *PP* to $\mathcal{F}$.

Query Phase: $\mathcal{F}$ can issue a polynomially bounded number of **private key** queries and **signature** queries, and $\mathcal{C}$ answers these queries with *MSK*.

Private Key Queries. $\mathcal{F}$ adaptively requests a private key SK_W for any attribute set W under the restriction that $|W \cap S^*| \le t - 1$.

Signature Queries. $\mathcal{F}$ requests a signature for a message M_i and a signing predicate $\Gamma = (t', S)$, where $S \subset \mathbf{U}$ and $1 \le t' \le |S|$.

Forgery: At the end of the game, $\mathcal{F}$ outputs a tuple (Γ^*, M^*, e^*). We say that $\mathcal{F}$ wins the game if the following hold true:

(1) **Verify**$(PP, \Gamma^*, M^*, e^*) = 1$.

(2) $\mathcal{F}$ has not made any signature query for the pair (M^*, Γ^*).

The adversary's advantage in breaking the *sP-UF-CMA* security of the ABS scheme is defined as $Adv_{\mathcal{F}}^{sP-UF-CMA}(n) = \Pr[\mathcal{F} \text{ wins}]$.

Definition 2. *A threshold ABS is selective-predicate and adaptive-message unforgeable under chosen message attacks (sP-UF-CMA) if $Adv_{\mathcal{F}}^{sP-UF-CMA}(n)$ is negligible with respect to the security parameter n, for any polynomial time adversary $\mathcal{F}$.*

2.4   Lattices

Let $\mathbf{B} = [b_1, ..., b_m] \in \mathbb{R}^{m \times m}$ be an $m \times m$ matrix whose columns are linear independent vectors $b_1, ..., b_m \in \mathbb{R}^m$. The $m-$dimensional full-rank lattice Λ generated by $\mathbf{B}$ is the set

$$\Lambda = \mathcal{L}(\mathbf{B}) = \left\{ y \in \mathbb{R}^m \text{ s.t. } \exists s \in \mathbb{Z}^m, \; y = \mathbf{B}s = \sum_{i=1}^{m} s_i b_i \right\}.$$

Definition 3. *For a prime q, $\mathbf{A} \in \mathbb{Z}_q^{n \times m}$ and $\mathbf{u} \in \mathbb{Z}_q^n$, we define:*

$$\Lambda_q^{\perp}(\mathbf{A}) = \{ \mathbf{e} \in \mathbb{Z}^m \text{ s.t. } \mathbf{Ae} = \mathbf{0} \,(\mathbf{mod}q) \}$$
$$\Lambda_q^{\mathbf{u}}(\mathbf{A}) = \{ \mathbf{e} \in \mathbb{Z}^m \text{ s.t. } \mathbf{Ae} = \mathbf{u} \,(\mathbf{mod}q) \}$$

Let S be a set of vectors $S = \{\mathbf{s}_1, ..., \mathbf{s}_k\} \in \mathbb{R}^m$, we denote as follows:
(1) $\|S\|$ denotes the Euclidean norm of the longest vector in S, i.e.,

$$\|S\| = \max_{1 \le i \le k} \sqrt{s_{i,1}^2 + ... + s_{i,m}^2}, \text{where } \mathbf{s}_i = (s_{i,1}, ..., s_{i,m}).$$

(2) $\tilde{S} = \{\tilde{\mathbf{s}}_1, ..., \tilde{\mathbf{s}}_k\} \in \mathbb{R}^m$ denotes the Gram-Schmidt orthogonalization of the vectors $\mathbf{s}_1, ..., \mathbf{s}_k$ in that order. $\left\|\tilde{S}\right\|$ denotes the Gram-Schmidt norm of S.

Definition 4. *Let L be a subset of $\mathbb{Z}^m$. For any vector $c \in \mathbb{R}^m$ and any positive parameter $\sigma \in \mathbb{R}_{>0}$, define the Gaussian function $\rho_{\sigma,c}(x)$ on $\mathbb{R}^m$ with center c and parameter σ :*

$$\rho_{\sigma,c}(x) = \exp\left(-\pi \frac{\|x - c\|^2}{\sigma^2}\right).$$

Let $\rho_{\sigma,c}(L) = \sum_{x \in L} \rho_{\sigma,c}(x)$. Denote the discrete Gaussian distribution over L with parameter σ and center c as

$$\forall y \in L, \; \mathcal{D}_{L,\sigma,c}(y) = \frac{\rho_{\sigma,c}(y)}{\rho_{\sigma,c}(L)}.$$

For notational convenience, $\rho_{\sigma,0}$ and $\mathcal{D}_{L,\sigma,0}$ are abbreviated as ρ_σ and $\mathcal{D}_{L,\sigma}$ respectively.

Theorem 1. ([11]) *Let $q \geq 3$ be odd and $m \geq 6n \log q$. There exists a probabilistic polynomial-time (PPT) algorithm TrapGen(q,n) that outputs a pair $\left(\mathbf{A} \in \mathbb{Z}_q^{n \times m}, \mathbf{T} \in \mathbb{Z}^{m \times m}\right)$ such that $\mathbf{A}$ is statistically close to uniform in $\mathbb{Z}_q^{n \times m}$ and $\mathbf{T}$ is a basis for $\Lambda_q^{\perp}(\mathbf{A})$, satisfying $\left\|\widetilde{\mathbf{T}}\right\| \leq O(\sqrt{n \log q})$ and $\|\mathbf{T}\| \leq O(n \log q)$ with overwhelming probability in n.*

Lemma 1. ([12,13]) *Let $q \geq 2$ and let $\mathbf{A} \in \mathbb{Z}_q^{n \times m}$ be a matrix with $m > n$. Let $\mathbf{T_A}$ be a basis for the lattice $\Lambda_q^{\perp}(\mathbf{A})$ and $\sigma \geq \left\|\widetilde{\mathbf{T_A}}\right\| \cdot \omega(\sqrt{\log m})$. Then for any vector $c \in \mathbb{R}^m$ and $u \in \mathbb{Z}_q^n$:*

(1). There exists a PPT algorithm SampleGaussian$(\mathbf{A}, \mathbf{T_A}, \sigma, c)$ that outputs a vector $x \in \mathbb{Z}^m$ distributed statistically close to $\mathcal{D}_{\Lambda_q^{\perp}(\mathbf{A}),\sigma,c}$

(2). There exists a PPT algorithm SamplePre$(\mathbf{A}, \mathbf{T_A}, u, \sigma)$ that outputs a vector $x \in \mathbb{Z}^m$ distributed statistically close to $\mathcal{D}_{\Lambda_q^u(\mathbf{A}),\sigma}$.

(3). If the vector x is sampled from the distribution $\mathcal{D}_{\Lambda_q^{\perp}(\mathbf{A}),\sigma}$ then the probability $\Pr[\|x\| \geq \sqrt{m}\sigma]$ is negligible in m.

Lemma 2. ([12]) *Let n and q be integers, and let $m \geq 2n \log q, \sigma \geq \left\|\widetilde{\mathbf{T_A}}\right\| \cdot \omega(\sqrt{\log m})$. Then for all but a $2q^{-n}$ fraction of all $\mathbf{A} \in \mathbb{Z}_q^{n \times m}$, the distribution of the syndrome $u = \mathbf{A}e(mod q)$ is statistically close to uniform over $\mathbb{Z}_q^n$, where e is chosen from the distribution $\mathcal{D}_{\mathbb{Z}^m,\sigma}$.*

Definition 5. (SIS_{q,n,m,β_0}^p)([12],[14]) *The small integer solution problem in ℓ_p norm is defined as follows: given an integer q, a matrix $\mathbf{A} \in \mathbb{Z}_q^{n \times m}$, a real β_0, find a non-zero integer vector $x \in \mathbb{Z}^m$ such that $\mathbf{A}x=0(mod q)$ and $\|x\|_p \leq \beta_0$.*

Proposition 1. ([12]) *For any parameters $m = m(n)$, $\beta_0 = \beta_0(n)$ and for any prime $q \geq \beta_0 \omega(\sqrt{n \log n})$, the average-case problem SIS_{q,n,m,β_0}^2 is as hard as approximating the shortest independent vector problem (SIVP) in the ℓ_2 norm in the worst case with certain $\beta_0 \widehat{O}(\sqrt{n})$ factors. It then follows from the relationship between the ℓ_2 and ℓ_∞ norms (i.e., for any vector $\mathbf{x} \in \mathbb{R}^n$, we have $\|\mathbf{x}\|_\infty \leq \|\mathbf{x}\|_2 \leq \sqrt{n}\|\mathbf{x}\|_\infty$) that the average-case problem $SIS_{q,n,m,\beta_0}^\infty$ is at least as hard as approximating SIVP problem, to within $\beta_0 \widehat{O}(n)$ factors in the ℓ_2 norm, in the worst case.*

According to [15,16], the state-of-the-art algorithms for SIVP problem run in time nearly exponential in the dimension n. It is believed to be hard for 2^{n^θ}−approximating SIVP on n−dimensional lattices for some constant $\theta \in (0, \frac{1}{2})$.

Definition 6. *A statistically hiding, computational binding string commitment scheme $COM(\mu, \rho)$ is a PPT algorithm, such that :*
(1) For any message $\mu_1, \mu_2 \in \{0,1\}^*$, there exists no adversary can distinguish between $COM(\mu_1, \cdot)$ and $COM(\mu_2, \cdot)$;

(2) *For all PPT algorithm $\mathcal{A}$ returning (μ_1, ρ_1) and (μ_2, ρ_2), where $\mu_1 \neq \mu_2$, it follows that* $\Pr[COM(\mu_1, \rho_1) = COM(\mu_2, \rho_2)] = negl(n)$.

Kawachi et al. [17] proposed a lattice-based string commitment scheme COM: $\{0,1\}^* \times \{0,1\}^{\frac{m'}{2}} \to \mathbb{Z}_q^n$. If $m' > 2n(1 + \delta)\log q$ and the $\text{SIS}^\infty_{n,m',q,1}$ problem is hard, then the commitment scheme of [17] satisfies both statistically hiding and computational binding.

Lemma 3. ([18]) *Let $l \in \mathbb{Z}$ and $D = ((2l)!)^2$. Given $l+1$ numbers $I_1, ..., I_{l+1} \in [2l]$, set the Lagrangian coefficients $L_j = \prod_{i \neq j} \frac{-I_i}{(I_j - I_i)}$. For each $j \in [l+1]$, DL_j is an integer and $|DL_j| \leq D^2 \leq ((2l)!)^4$.*

3   The Interactive Protocol

Ling et al. [19] proposed a Stern [20] zero-knowledge proof of knowledge, which was three-pass interactive protocol: the prover computes three commitments and sends them to the verifier; the verifier sends a uniformly random challenge to the prover; prover reveals two commitments according to the challenge. A variant later was proposed in [9], which was used to construct a group signature scheme. By adapting the protocol of [9], we present a proof of knowledge protocol, which allows a prover to convince the verifier that he possesses a valid secret signing key. In section 4, the protocol is repeated $\omega(\log n)$ times to make the soundness error negligibly small, and then is transformed to a signature scheme via Fiat-Shamir heuristic.

3.1   Some Specific Sets

As in [9], we define some specific sets of vectors and permutations that will be used in this protocol as follows:

(1) $\mathbf{C}_{3m}$:The set of all vectors in $\{-1, 0, 1\}^{3m}$ having exactly m coordinates -1; m coordinates 1; m coordinates 0.

(2) Let $\overline{S} = \{i_1, ..., i_{k_1}\}$, $S_0 \in \overline{S}$ and $|S_0| = l + 1$. Define two sets of vectors as follows:

$\mathbf{C}_{m,\beta}(\overline{S}, l+1, S_0)$:The set of all vectors $\mathbf{X} = (x_{i_1}, ..., x_{i_{k_1}}) \in \mathbb{Z}^{k_1 m}$ consisting of k_1 blocks of size m, where $\|\mathbf{X}\|_\infty \leq \beta$ and for all $i_j \in \overline{S} - S_0$, x_{i_j} is a zero-block 0^m.

$\mathbf{C}_{3m}(\overline{S}, l+1, S_0)$:The set of all vectors $\mathbf{X} = (x_{i_1}, ..., x_{i_{k_1}}) \in \{-1, 0, 1\}^{k_1 3m}$ consisting of k_1 blocks of size $3m$, such that for each $i_j \in S_0$, x_{i_j} is an element of $\mathbf{C}_{3m}$, and the remaining blocks are zero-blocks 0^{3m}.

(3) Let $\overline{S} = \{i_1, ..., i_{k_1}\}$ and $\mathbf{X} = (x_{i_1}, ..., x_{i_{k_1}}) \in \mathbb{Z}^{k_1 3m}$. Define some sets of permutations as follows:

φ: The set of all permutations that keep the arrangement of the blocks. If $\pi \in \varphi$, then $\pi(\mathbf{X}) = (\tau_1(x_{i_1}), ..., \tau_{k_1}(x_{i_{k_1}}))$, where $\tau_1, ..., \tau_{k_1}$ are certain permutations of $3m$ elements..

F : The set of all permutations that rearrange the blocks. If $f_\phi \in F$, then $f_\phi(\mathbf{X}) = (x_{\phi(i_1)}, ..., x_{\phi(i_{k_1})})$ where ϕ is a certain permutation of k_1 elements in $\overline{S}$.

3.2 Some Techniques

We construct the following procedures by adapting the Decomposition-Extension technique of [9,19].

Extension: Given a vector $\mathbf{w}' \in \{-1, 0, 1\}^m$, extend $\mathbf{w}'$ to a vector $\mathbf{w} \in \mathbf{C}_{3m}$ as follows: Denote the number of coordinates $-1, 0$ and 1 in $\mathbf{w}'$ are λ^{-1}, λ^0, λ^1 respectively, then choose a random vector $\mathbf{w}'' \in \{-1, 0, 1\}^{2m}$ that has exactly $(m - \lambda^{-1})$ coordinates -1, $(m - \lambda^0)$ coordinates 0 and $(m - \lambda^1)$ coordinates 1. Output $\mathbf{w} = (\mathbf{w}', \mathbf{w}'') \in \mathbf{C}_{3m}$.

Matrix Extension: On input a matrix $\mathbf{Z} = (\mathbf{Z}_1 \parallel ... \parallel \mathbf{Z}_{k_1}) \in \mathbb{Z}_q^{n \times k_1 m}$. For each $i \in [k_1]$, append $2m$ zero-columns to the component-matrix $\mathbf{Z}_i$ and denote the resulting new component-matrix by $\mathbf{Z}_i' \in \mathbb{Z}_q^{3m}$. Output the the extended matrix $\mathbf{Z}' = (\mathbf{Z}_1' \parallel ... \parallel \mathbf{Z}_{k_1}') \in \mathbb{Z}_q^{n \times k_1 3m}$.

Decomposition: Given a vector $\mathbf{V} = (\mathbf{v}_1, \mathbf{v}_2, ..., \mathbf{v}_m) \in \mathbb{Z}^m$ which satisfying $\|\mathbf{v}\|_\infty \leq \beta$. This procedure proceeds as follows: (1) Let $p = \lfloor \log \beta \rfloor + 1, \beta_1 = \lceil \frac{\beta}{2} \rceil, \beta_2 = \lceil \frac{\beta - \beta_1}{2} \rceil, \beta_3 = \lceil \frac{\beta - \beta_1 - \beta_2}{2} \rceil, ..., \beta_p = 1$.
(2) For each $i \in [m]$, express $\mathbf{v}_i = \beta_1 v_{i,1} + \beta_2 v_{i,2} + ... + \beta_p v_{i,p}$ where $v_{i,j} \in \{-1, 0, 1\}$ for all $i \in [m], j \in [p]$.
(3) For each $i \in [p]$, let $\mathbf{w}_i = (v_{1,i}, v_{2,i}, ..., v_{m,i}) \in \{-1, 0, 1\}^m$. Output $\mathbf{w}_1, \mathbf{w}_2, ..., \mathbf{w}_p$, which satisfying $\mathbf{V} = \sum_{i=1}^{p} \beta_i \mathbf{w}_i$.

Witness Decomposition and Extension. Let $\overline{S} = \{i_1, ..., i_{k_1}\}, S_0 \in \overline{S}$ and $|S_0| = l + 1$. On input a vector $\mathbf{X} = (x_{i_1}, ..., x_{i_{k_1}}) \in \mathbf{C}_{m,\beta}(\overline{S}, l+1, S_0)$, do as follows:
(1) For each $j \in [k_1]$, use algorithm Decomposition on each block $\mathbf{x}_{i_j}$ to obtain p decomposed vectors. Then use algorithm Extension on the decomposed vectors to obtain $k_1 p$ vectors in $\mathbf{C}_{3m}$, denoted respectively by $\{\mathbf{w}_{i_1, j}\}_{j=1}^{p}, ...,$ $\{\mathbf{w}_{i_{k_1}, j}\}_{j=1}^{p}$.
(2) For each $j \in [p]$, let $\mathbf{z}_j = (\mathbf{w}_{i_1, j}, ..., \mathbf{w}_{i_{k_1}, j})$.
Output $\mathbf{z}_1, ..., \mathbf{z}_p \in \mathbf{C}_{3m}(\overline{S}, l+1, S_0)$.

3.3 The Protocol

The public parameters are a set $\overline{S} = \{i_1, ..., i_{k_1}\}$, a matrix $\mathbf{A} = (\mathbf{A}_{i_1} \parallel ... \parallel \mathbf{A}_{i_{k_1}}) \in \mathbb{Z}_q^{n \times k_1 m}$, a vector $\mathbf{u} \in \mathbb{Z}_q^n$ and a positive integer l. The prover holds a witness $\mathbf{X} = (x_{i_1}, ..., x_{i_{k_1}}) \in \mathbf{C}_{m,\beta}(\overline{S}, l+1, S_0)(S_0 \in \overline{S}$ and $|S_0| = l+1)$. The prover's goal is to convince the verifier in that $\mathbf{AX} = \mathbf{u}(mod q)$ and $\mathbf{X} \in \mathbf{C}_{m,\beta}(\overline{S}, l+1, S_0)$ while keeping S_0 secret.

Let COM be the KTX commitment scheme [17]. For simplicity, we will omit the randomness ρ of the commitment scheme COM. Let $p = \lfloor \log \beta \rfloor +$

$1, \beta_1 = \lceil \frac{\beta}{2} \rceil, \beta_2 = \lceil \frac{\beta - \beta_1}{2} \rceil, \beta_3 = \lceil \frac{\beta - \beta_1 - \beta_2}{2} \rceil, ..., \beta_p = 1$. The prover runs algorithm Witness Decomposition and Extension on the vector $\mathbf{X}$ to obtain $z_1, ..., z_p \in \mathbf{C}_{3m}(\overline{S}, l+1, S_0)$, and runs algorithm MatrixExtension on the matrix $\mathbf{A}$ to obtain $\mathbf{A}' \in \mathbb{Z}_q^{n \times k_1 3m}$.

The interactive protocol is described as follows:

1. Commitment: The prover randomly chooses p vectors $r_1, ..., r_p \in \mathbb{Z}_q^{k_1 3m}$, p permutations $\pi_1, ..., \pi_p \in \varphi$ and a permutation $f_\phi \in F(\phi$ is a certain permutation of k_1 elements in $\overline{S}$). It sends the commitment $CMT = (\mathbf{c}_1, \mathbf{c}_2, \mathbf{c}_3) \in (\mathbb{Z}_q^n)^3$, where

$$\begin{cases} \mathbf{c}_1 = COM(\phi, \pi_1, ..., \pi_p, \mathbf{A}'(\sum_{i=1}^{p} \beta_i r_i)(mod q)); \\ \mathbf{c}_2 = COM(f_\phi \circ (\pi_1(r_1)), ..., f_\phi \circ (\pi_p(r_p))); \\ \mathbf{c}_3 = COM(f_\phi \circ (\pi_1(z_1 + r_1)), ..., f_\phi \circ (\pi_p(z_p + r_p))). \end{cases}$$

2. Challenge: Receiving CMT, the verifier randomly chooses a challenge $Ch \in \{1, 2, 3\}$ and sends it to prover.

3. Response: The prover replies as follows:

If $Ch = 1$, let $v_i = f_\phi \circ (\pi_i(z_i)), w_i = f_\phi \circ (\pi_i(r_i))$ for all $i \in [p]$ and $S_1 = \phi(S_0)$. Send $RSP = \{S_1, v_1, ..., v_p, w_1, ..., w_p\}$.

If $Ch = 2$, let $\Phi_i = \pi_i, s_i = z_i + r_i$ for all $i \in [p]$ and $\phi_2 = \phi$. Send $RSP = \{\phi_2, \Phi_1, ..., \Phi_p, s_1, ..., s_p\}$.

If $Ch = 3$, let $\Psi_i = \pi_i, h_i = r_i$ for all $i \in [p]$ and $\phi_3 = \phi$. Send $RSP = \{\phi_3, \Psi_1, ..., \Psi_p, h_1, ..., h_p\}$.

4. Verification: Receiving the response RSP, the verifier performs the following checks:

If $Ch = 1$, check that $v_i \in \mathbf{C}_{3m}(\overline{S}, l+1, S_1)$ for each $i \in [p]$, and that:

$$\begin{cases} \mathbf{c}_2 = COM(w_1, ..., w_p); \\ \mathbf{c}_3 = COM(v_1 + w_1, ..., v_p + w_p). \end{cases}$$

If $Ch = 2$, check that:

$$\begin{cases} \mathbf{c}_1 = COM(\phi_2, \Phi_1, ..., \Phi_p, \mathbf{A}'(\sum_{i=1}^{p} \beta_i s_i) - \mathbf{u}(mod q)); \\ \mathbf{c}_3 = COM(f_{\phi_2} \circ (\Phi_1(s_1)), ..., f_{\phi_2} \circ (\Phi_p(s_p))). \end{cases}$$

If $Ch = 3$, check that:

$$\begin{cases} \mathbf{c}_1 = COM(\phi_3, \Psi_1, ..., \Psi_p, \mathbf{A}'(\sum_{j=1}^{p} \beta_i h_i)(mod q)); \\ \mathbf{c}_2 = COM(f_{\phi_3} \circ (\Psi_1(h_1)), ..., f_{\phi_3} \circ \Psi_p(h_p)). \end{cases}$$

The verifier outputs 1(accept) if all the verification conditions hold, otherwise outputs 0(reject).

Theorem 2. *Given 3 valid responses RSP_1, RSP_2, RSP_3 with respect to all 3 different values of the challenge Ch for the same commitment CMT. If COM is computationally binding, then we can efficiently extract a vector $\mathbf{Y}_0$, which* satisfying $\mathbf{AY}_0 = \mathbf{u}(mod q)$, $\mathbf{Y}_0 \in \mathbf{C}_{m,\beta}(\overline{S}, l+1, S')$ for some $S' \in \overline{S}$ and $|S'| = l+1$.

Proof. Because the space is limited, the proof is present in the full version.

4   Our ABS Scheme

In this section, we describe our core constructions of threshold ABS scheme from lattices. As in [21], we use the method of adding "default attributes" to achieve a flexible threshold. Besides this normal universe of attributes $\mathbf{U}$, the default attributes $\mathbf{U}^*$ are also publicly known. Note that the default attributes $\mathbf{U}^*$ are possessed by every user in this system. The threshold predicate is associated with an attribute set (S, t) where $S \subset \mathbf{U}$ is an attribute set and integer t is a threshold. Let n be the security parameter and $k = \omega(\log n)$. The other parameters m, q, σ, β will be instantiated later in section 6.

Setup: On input a security parameter n, do:

(1) Define the universe set of attributes $\mathbf{U} = \{1, 2, .., l\}$ and the default attributes $\mathbf{U}^* = \{l+1, l+2, .., 2l\}$.

(2) For each attribute $i \in \mathbf{U} \cup \mathbf{U}^*$, use algorithm TrapGen$(q, n)$ to obtain a random matrix $\mathbf{A}_i \in \mathbb{Z}_q^{n \times m}$ together with a basis $\mathbf{T}_{\mathbf{A}_i} \in \mathbb{Z}^{m \times m}$ for $\Lambda_q^{\perp}(\mathbf{A}_i)$ such that $\left\| \widetilde{\mathbf{T}_{\mathbf{A}_i}} \right\| \leq O(\sqrt{n \log q})$.

(3) Choose a random vector $\mathbf{u}_x \in \mathbb{Z}_q^n$.

(4) Set $D = ((2l)!)^2$ and $\mathbf{u} = D\mathbf{u}_x(mod q)$.

(5) Let $H : \{0,1\}^* \to \{1, 2, 3\}^k$ be a hash function.

Output the public parameters $PP = (\{\mathbf{A}_i\}_{i \in [2l]}, \mathbf{u}, H)$ and the master secret key $MSK = (\{\mathbf{T}_{\mathbf{A}_i}\}_{i \in [2l]})$.

Keygen: On input the public parameters PP, the master secret key MSK and an attribute set $W \subset \mathbf{U}$, do:

(1) Parse $\mathbf{u}_x = (a_1, ..., a_n) \in \mathbb{Z}_q^n$. Choose a random l degree polynomial $f_i(x) \in \mathbb{Z}_q[x]$ such that $f_i(0) = a_i$ for each $i \in [n]$.

(2) For each $i \in W \cup \mathbf{U}^*$, set $\mathbf{u}_i = (f_1(i), ..., f_n(i)) \in \mathbb{Z}_q^n$ and use algorithm SamplePre$(\mathbf{A}_i, \mathbf{T}_{\mathbf{A}_i}, \mathbf{u}_i, \sigma)$ to obtain a vector $x_i \in \mathbb{Z}^m$ such that $\|x_i\| \leq \sigma\sqrt{m}$.

Output the private key $SK_W = (\{x_i\}_{i \in W \cup \mathbf{U}^*})$.

Sign: On input the public parameters PP, a private key $SK_W = (\{x_i\}_{i \in W \cup \mathbf{U}^*})$, a message $M = \{0,1\}^*$ and a threshold predicate $\Gamma = (S, t)$ such that $S \subset \mathbf{U}$ and $1 \leq t \leq d(|S| = d)$. Without loss of generality, suppose $S = \{1, ..., d\}$. The signer performs as follows:

(1) Select a random t-element subset $W' \subseteq S \cap W$. W.l.o.g, suppose $W' = \{1, ..., t\}$.

(2) Define the default attribute subset $W^* = \{l+1, .., 2l+1-t\}$.

(3) Set $\mathbf{A} = [\mathbf{A}_1 \| ... \| \mathbf{A}_i \| ... \| \mathbf{A}_{2l+1-t}]_{i \in S \cup W^*} \in \mathbb{Z}_q^{n \times (l+|S|+1-t)m}$, $\overline{S} = S \cup W^*$ and $S_0 = W' \cup W^*$.

(4) Use the private key SK_W to compute a vector $\mathbf{Y}$ such that $\mathbf{AY} = \mathbf{u}(mod q)$ and $\mathbf{Y} \in \mathbf{C}_{m,\beta}(\overline{S}, l+1, S_0)$ as follows:

(a) For $j \in W' \cup W^*$, let the Lagrangian coefficient $L_j = \prod_{i \in W' \cup W^*, i \neq j} \frac{-i}{j-i}$.

(b) Note that $D = ((2l)!)^2$. By lemma 3, it follows that DL_j is an integer and $|DL_j| \leq ((2l)!)^4$ for each $j \in W' \cup W^*$.

(c) Set $\mathbf{Y} = (\mathbf{y}_1, ..., \mathbf{y}_i, ..., \mathbf{y}_{2l+1-t})_{i \in S \cup W^*} \in \mathbb{Z}^{(l+|S|+1-t)m}$ where $\mathbf{y}_i = DL_i x_i$ for each $i \in W' \cup W^*$ and the remaining blocks are zero-blocks 0^m. Moreover, we have that $\|\mathbf{Y}\|_\infty \leq ((2l)!)^4 \sigma \sqrt{m}$.

(5) Generate a proof that the user owning at least t attributes among S. This can be achieved by repeating k times the protocol from section 3.3 with public parameters $(\mathbf{A}, \mathbf{u})$ and prover's witness $\mathbf{Y}$, and then making it resulting protocol non-interactive via the Fiat-Shamir heuristic as follows:

(a) For each $i \in [k]$, compute the value $CMT^{(i)}$ using $(\mathbf{A}, \mathbf{u}, \mathbf{Y})$ according to the protocol from section 3.3.

(b) Set $\{Ch^{(i)}\}_{i=1,...,k} = H(M, \{CMT^{(i)}\}_{i=1,...,k})$.

(c) For each $i \in [k]$, compute the value $RSP^{(i)}$ using $Ch^{(i)}$ according to the protocol from section 3.3.

Output the signature $e = (M, \{CMT^{(i)}\}_{i=1,...,k}, \{RSP^{(i)}\}_{i=1,...,k})$.

Verify: On input a signature e of a message M for predicate $\Gamma = (t, S)$, the verifier proceeds as follows:

(1) Set $\{Ch^{(i)}\}_{i=1,...,k} = H(M, \{CMT^{(i)}\}_{i=1,...,k}) \in \{1, 2, 3\}^k$.

(2) For each $i \in [k]$, run the verification of the protocol as in section 3.3 to check the validity of $RSP^{(i)}$ with respect to $\{CMT^{(i)}\}$ and $\{Ch^{(i)}\}$.

Output 1(accept) if all the verification conditions hold, otherwise output 0(reject).

Theorem 3. *The proposed scheme is correct with overwhelming probability.*

Proof. Because the space is limited, the proof is present in the full version.

5   Security Analysis

Theorem 4. *If COM is a statistically hiding scheme, then the proposed ABS scheme satisfies the privacy property in the random oracle model.*

Proof. Because the space is limited, the proof is present in the full version.

Theorem 5. *If there exists a $(T, \varepsilon)-$sP-UF-CMA adversary $\mathcal{F}$ against the proposed ABS scheme in the random oracle model, asking at most Q_H, Q_K and Q_S times queries to the random oracle $H : \{0,1\}^* \to \{1,2,3\}^k$, private key queries and signature queries respectively, then there exists a algorithm $\mathcal{C}$ that solves the $SIS^\infty_{n,2lm,q,2\beta}$ problem in time $T' \leq (32Q_H T)/(\epsilon - 3^{-k}) + (Q_K + Q_S)poly(n)$ and with probability $\varepsilon' \geq \frac{1}{2}(1 - (7/9)^k)\epsilon$.*

Proof. Suppose that there exists such a forger $\mathcal{F}$. If $\mathcal{F}$ can break the computational binding property of the commitment scheme COM with non-negligible probability, we can use $\mathcal{F}$ to solve the solves the $SIS^\infty_{n,2lm,q,2\beta}$ problem (see section 2.4). Therefore, it is assumed that COM is computationally binding.

We can build an algorithm $\mathcal{C}$ that uses $\mathcal{F}$ to solve the $SIS_{n,2lm,q,2\beta}^{\infty}$ problem. Algorithm $\mathcal{C}$ is given a uniformly random matrix $\bar{\mathbf{A}} \in \mathbb{Z}_q^{n \times 2lm}$, parsing $\bar{\mathbf{A}} = [\mathbf{W}_1 \| \ldots \| \mathbf{W}_i \| \ldots \| \mathbf{W}_{2l}]_{i \in [2l]}$ for matrices $\mathbf{W}_i \in \mathbb{Z}_q^{n \times m}$. Define the universe set of attributes $\mathbf{U} = \{1, 2, .., l\}$ and the default attributes $\mathbf{U}^* = \{l+1, l+2, .., 2l\}$.

Initial Phase: $\mathcal{F}$ outpus a challenge threshold predicate $\Gamma^* = (t, S^*)$ where $S^* \subset \mathbf{U}$ and $1 \leq t \leq |S^*|$.

Setup Phase: $\mathcal{C}$ constructs the system's public parameters PP as follows:

(1) Define the $(l + 1 - t)$ default attribute subset $W^* = \{l+1, .., 2l+1-t\}$.

(2) For each attribute $i \in S^* \cup W^*$, define $\mathbf{A}_i = \mathbf{W}_i$; and for each attribute $i \in (\mathbf{U}/S^*) \cup (\mathbf{U}^*/W^*)$, use algorithm TrapGen$(q, n)$ to obtain a random matrix $\mathbf{A}_i \in \mathbb{Z}_q^{n \times m}$ together with a basis $\mathbf{T}_{\mathbf{A}_i} \in \mathbb{Z}^{m \times m}$ for $\Lambda_q^{\perp}(\mathbf{A}_i)$ such that $\left\| \widetilde{\mathbf{T}_{\mathbf{A}_i}} \right\| \leq O(\sqrt{n \log q})$.

(3) Choose a vector $\mathbf{Z}_0$ from $\mathcal{D}_{\mathbb{Z}^{2lm}, \sigma}$ and compute $\mathbf{u}_x = \bar{\mathbf{A}} \mathbf{Z}_0 \in \mathbb{Z}_q^n$.

(4) Let $D = ((2l)!)^2$ and $\mathbf{u} = D\mathbf{u}_x (mod q)$

(5) Let $H : \{0, 1\}^* \rightarrow \{1, 2, 3\}^k$ be a hash function.

Output the public parameters $PP = (\{\mathbf{A}_i\}_{i \in [2l]}, \mathbf{u}, H)$.

Query Phase: $\mathcal{F}$ issues a series of queries as follows:

Hash Queries. $\mathcal{C}$ maintains a table L to simulate hash oracle H. For a tuple $(M, \{CMT^{(i)}\}_{i=1,...,k})$, $\mathcal{C}$ checks if the value of $H(M, \{CMT^{(i)}\}_{i=1,...,k})$ was already defined. If it was, the same answer as before is simply returned. Otherwise, $\mathcal{C}$ returns a uniformly random value in $\{1, 2, 3\}^k$ as the answer and then inserts the tuple $(M, \{CMT^{(i)}\}_{i=1,...,k})$ into L.

Private Key Queries. $\mathcal{F}$ adaptively chooses a set of attributes $W \subset \mathbf{U}$ under the restriction that $|W \cap S^*| \leq t - 1$. $\mathcal{C}$ generates the corresponding private key as follows:

(1) Let $t' = |W \cap S^*|$ and a $(l - t')$-element default attribute subset $W_1 = \{l+1, .., 2l - t'\} \subset \mathbf{U}^*$.

(2) For each $i \in (W \cap S^*) \cup W_1$, choose a random vector x_i from $\mathcal{D}_{\mathbb{Z}^m, \sigma}$ and compute $\mathbf{u}'_i = \mathbf{A}_i x_i (mod q)$.

(3) Using the Lagrange interpolation formula, we can get l-degree polynomials $f_1(x), ..., f_n(x) \in \mathbb{Z}_q[x]$ such that $\mathbf{u} = D(f_1(0), ..., f_n(0))$ and $\mathbf{u}'_i = (f_1(i), ..., f_n(i))$ for each $i \in (W \cap S^*) \cup W_1$.

(4) For each $i \in (W/(W \cap S^*)) \cup ((\mathbf{U}^*/W_1))$, compute $\mathbf{u}'_i = (f_1(i), ..., f_n(i)) \in \mathbb{Z}_q^n$, and use algorithm SamplePre$\left(\mathbf{A}_i, \mathbf{T}_{\mathbf{A}_i}, \mathbf{u}'_i, \sigma\right)$ to obtain a vector $x_i \in \mathbb{Z}_q^m$.

Finally, $\mathcal{C}$ sends the corresponding private key $SK_W = (\{x_i\}_{i \in W \cup \mathbf{U}^*})$ to $\mathcal{F}$.

Signature Queries. $\mathcal{F}$ chooses a message M', an attribute set W' and a threshold predicate $\Gamma' = \left(t'', S'\right)$. $\mathcal{C}$ constructs the signature as follows:

(1) If $\left| S^* \cap W' \right| \leq t - 1$, $\mathcal{C}$ can generated a simulated private key SK_W as in the private key simulation, and uses SK_W to generate a signature e on message M' with respect to the predicate Γ'.

(2) If $\left| S^* \cap W' \right| \geq t$, $\mathcal{C}$ can generate a simulated signature by programming the random oracle.

Forgery. $\mathcal{F}$ gives a forged signature $e^* = (M^*, \{CMT^{(i)}\}_{i=1,\ldots,k}, \{RSP^{(i)}\}_{i=1,\ldots,k})$ and a message M^* with respect to the predicate Γ^*, which satisfying

(1) **Verify**$(PP, M^*, \Gamma^*, e^*) = 1$.

(2) $\mathcal{F}$ has not made any signature query for the pair (M^*, Γ^*).

The forgery is exploited as follows: In the unlikely case where $\mathcal{F}$ has not queried H on input $(M^*, \{CMT^{(i)}\}_{i=1,\ldots,k})$, as otherwise, the probability that $H(M^*, \{CMT^{(i)}\}_{i=1,\ldots,k}) = \{Ch^{(i)}\}_{i=1,\ldots,k}$ is at most 3^{-k}. Thus there exists certain $i^* \leq Q_H$ such that the i^*th hash query involves the tuple $(M^*, \{CMT^{(i)}\}_{i=1,\ldots,k})$. At this stage, $\mathcal{C}$ set i^* as the target forking point and replays $\mathcal{F}$ many executions with the same random tape and input as in the original execution. Since $\mathcal{C}$ has recorded the transcript in the original execution, $\mathcal{C}$ can give exactly the same answers to the first $i^* - 1$ queries in each execution. From the i^*th query onwards, $\mathcal{C}$ chooses a new fresh random values in $\{1, 2, 3\}^k$ as the answer. By applying the Improved Forking Lemma [22], with probability $\geq \frac{1}{2}$, $\mathcal{C}$ can obtain a 3-fork involving the tuple $(M^*, \{CMT^{(i)}\}_{i=1,\ldots,k})$ after at most $32Q_H/(\epsilon - 3^{-k})$ executions. Now let the answers of $\mathcal{F}$ corrsponding to the 3-fork branches be

$$r_{i^*}^1 = (Ch_1^{(1)}, \ldots, Ch_k^{(1)}); r_{i^*}^2 = (Ch_1^{(2)}, \ldots, Ch_k^{(2)}); r_{i^*}^3 = (Ch_1^{(3)}, \ldots, Ch_k^{(3)}).$$

There exists an index $i \in [k]$ such that $\{Ch_i^{(1)}, Ch_i^{(2)}, Ch_i^{(3)}\} = \{1, 2, 3\}$ with probability $1 - (7/9)^k$. Parse the 3 forgeries corresponding to the fork branches to obtain $(RSP_i^{(1)}, RSP_i^{(2)}, RSP_i^{(3)})$. Namely, they are three valid responses corresponding to three different challenges for the same commitment $CMT^{(i)}$. By theorem 2, we can obtain a vector $\mathbf{Z}_1 \in \mathbf{C}_{m,\beta}(\overline{S}, l+1, S')(\overline{S} = S^* \cup W^*)$ for some $S' \in \overline{S}$ and $\left|S'\right| = l+1$, which satisfying $\mathbf{A}\mathbf{Z}_1 = \mathbf{u}(mod q)$. By inserting zeros into $\mathbf{Z}_1$, we can get a vector $\mathbf{Z}' \in \mathbb{Z}^{2lm}$, which satisfying $\overline{\mathbf{A}}\mathbf{Z}' = \mathbf{u}(mod q)$.

Note that $\mathbf{Z}_0$ is unknown to the adversary. With the min-entropy property, we have that $\mathbf{Z}_0 \neq \mathbf{Z}'$ with overwhelming probability. Let $\overline{\mathbf{Z}} = \mathbf{Z}_0 - \mathbf{Z}' \in \mathbb{Z}^{2lm}$ s.t. $\overline{\mathbf{A}}\overline{\mathbf{Z}} = 0(mod q)$ and $\left\|\overline{\mathbf{Z}}\right\|_\infty \leq 2((2l)!)^4\sigma\sqrt{m}$. At last, $\mathcal{C}$ outputs the vector $\overline{\mathbf{Z}}$, which is a valid solution to the given problem $\text{SIS}_{n,2lm,q,2\beta}^\infty$. (An instantiation of β is present in section 6.) Therefore, the advantage of $\mathcal{C}$ is bounded by $\epsilon' \geq \frac{1}{2}(1 - (7/9)^k)\epsilon$ and the running time is bounded by $T' \leq (32Q_HT)/(\epsilon - 3^{-k}) + (Q_K + Q_S)poly(n)$.

6   Parameters

In order to ensure that the proposed ABS scheme works right and the security reductions are meaningful, our parameters are defined under the following constraints: For the TrapGen algorithm can operate, we need $q \geq 3, m \geq 6n\log q$. For the SampleGaussian algorithm and SamplePre algorithm can operate, we need to set $\sigma \geq O(\sqrt{n\log q})\omega(\sqrt{\log m})$. For the signatures of our scheme are difficult $\text{SIS}_{n,(2l+1)m,q,2\beta}^\infty$ solutions, we need $\beta \geq ((2l)!)^4\sigma\sqrt{m}$. To ensure that the $\text{SIS}_{n,(2l+1)m,q,2\beta}^\infty$ problem should have a worst case lattice reduction, we set $q \geq 2\beta\omega(\sqrt{n\log n})$.

Let n be the security parameter and δ be a constant such that $n^\delta \geq 6 \log q$. Set the parameters $m = n^{1+\delta}, \sigma = \sqrt{m}\omega(\sqrt{\log m}), \beta = ((2l)!)^4 m\omega(\sqrt{\log m})$, and $q = (2l)!)^4 m\omega(\sqrt{m \log m})$ to be prime.

Since $((2l)!)^4 \leq (2l)^{2l} = O(2^{2l \log 2l})$, we have $\beta = 2^{2l \log 2l} poly(n)$. Set $2^{2l \log 2l}$ up to 2^{n^θ} for some constant $\theta \in (0, 1/2)$. Thus the security of our ABS scheme is based on the hardness of 2^{n^θ}−approximating SIVP on n−dimensional lattices.

7 Conclusion

In this paper, a new attribute-based signature (ABS) scheme from lattices is given, which supports flexible threshold signing predicates. The security of the proposed scheme is proved in the random oracle model under the SIS assumption. When compared to previous scheme, the scheme provides significant improvement in efficiency. It remains an open problem to construct a lattice-based ABS scheme that can support more general signing predicates.

References

1. Maji, H.K., Prabhakaran, M., Rosulek, M.: Attribute-based signatures: Achieving attribute-privacy and collusion-resistance. IACR Cryptology ePrint Archive 2008, 328 (2008)
2. Shahandashti, S.F., Safavi-Naini, R.: Threshold attribute-based signatures and their application to anonymous credential systems. In: Preneel, B. (ed.) AFRICACRYPT 2009. LNCS, vol. 5580, pp. 198–216. Springer, Heidelberg (2009)
3. Li, J., Au, M.H., Susilo, W., Xie, D., Ren, K.: Attribute-based signature and its applications. In: ASIACCS 2010, pp. 60–69. ACM Press (2010)
4. Ge, A., Ma, C., Zhang, Z.: Attribute-based signature scheme with constant size signature in the standard model. IET Information Security 6(2), 47–54 (2012)
5. Okamoto, T., Takashima, K.: Efficient attribute-based signatures for non-monotone predicates in the standard model. In: Catalano, D., Fazio, N., Gennaro, R., Nicolosi, A. (eds.) PKC 2011. LNCS, vol. 6571, pp. 35–52. Springer, Heidelberg (2011)
6. Okamoto, T., Takashima, K.: Decentralized attribute-based signatures. In: Kurosawa, K., Hanaoka, G. (eds.) PKC 2013. LNCS, vol. 7778, pp. 125–142. Springer, Heidelberg (2013)
7. El Kaafarani, A., Ghadafi, E., Khader, D.: Decentralized traceable attribute-based signatures. In: Benaloh, J. (ed.) CT-RSA 2014. LNCS, vol. 8366, pp. 327–348. Springer, Heidelberg (2014)
8. Wang, Q., Chen, S.: Attribute-based signature for threshold predicates from lattices. Security and Communication Networks (2014) (in press)
9. Langlois, A., Ling, S., Nguyen, K., Wang, H.: Lattice-based group signature scheme with verifier-local revocation. In: Krawczyk, H. (ed.) PKC 2014. LNCS, vol. 8383, pp. 345–361. Springer, Heidelberg (2014)
10. Fiat, A., Shamir, A.: How to Prove Yourself: Practical Solutions to Identification and Signature Problems. In: Odlyzko, A.M. (ed.) CRYPTO 1986. LNCS, vol. 263, pp. 186–194. Springer, Heidelberg (1987)

11. Alwen, J., Peikert, C.: Generating shorter bases for hard random lattices. In: STACS, pp. 75–86 (2009)
12. Micciancio, D., Regev, O.: Worst-case to average-case reductions based on Gaussian measures. SIAM Journal of Computing 37(1), 267–302 (2007)
13. Gentry, C., Peikert, C., Vaikuntanathan, V.: Trapdoors for Hard Lattices and New Cryptographic Constructions. In: STOC, pp. 197–206. ACM (2008)
14. Ajtai, M.: Generating Hard Instances of Lattice Problems (Extended Abstract). In: STOC, pp. 99–108. ACM (1996)
15. Gama, N., Nguyen, P.Q.: Finding short lattice vectors within Mordell's inequality. In: STOC 2008 – Proc. 40th ACM Symposium on the Theory of Computing, ACM (2008)
16. Micciancio, D., Voulgaris, P.: A deterministic single exponential time algorithm for most lattice problems based on voronoi cell computations. In: Proceedings of the 42nd ACM Symposium on Theory of Computing, STOC 2010, pp. 351–358. ACM, New York (2010)
17. Kawachi, A., Tanaka, K., Xagawa, K.: Concurrently Secure Identification Schemes Based on the Worst-Case Hardness of Lattice Problems. In: Pieprzyk, J. (ed.) ASIACRYPT 2008. LNCS, vol. 5350, pp. 372–389. Springer, Heidelberg (2008)
18. Agrawal, S., Boyen, X., Vaikuntanathan, V., Voulgaris, P., Wee, H.: Functional encryption for threshold functions (or fuzzy IBE) from lattices. In: Fischlin, M., Buchmann, J., Manulis, M. (eds.) PKC 2012. LNCS, vol. 7293, pp. 280–297. Springer, Heidelberg (2012)
19. Ling, S., Nguyen, K., Stehlé, D., Wang, H.: Improved Zero-Knowledge Proofs of Knowledge for the ISIS Problem, and Applications. In: Kurosawa, K., Hanaoka, G. (eds.) PKC 2013. LNCS, vol. 7778, pp. 107–124. Springer, Heidelberg (2013)
20. Stern, J.: A New Paradigm for Public Key Identification. IEEE Transactions on Information Theory 42(6), 1757–1768 (1996)
21. Sahai, A., Waters, B.: Fuzzy Identity-Based Encryption. In: Cramer, R. (ed.) EUROCRYPT 2005. LNCS, vol. 3494, pp. 457–473. Springer, Heidelberg (2005)
22. Pointcheval, D., Vaudenay, S.: On Provable Security for Digital Signature Algorithms. Technical Report LIENS-96-17, LIENS (October 1996)

Hard Invalidation of Electronic Signatures

Lucjan Hanzlik[1,*], Mirosław Kutyłowski[1], and Moti Yung[2]

[1] Faculty of Fundamental Problems of Technology,
Wrocław University of Technology, Poland
`lucjan.hanzlik@pwr.edu.pl`
[2] Google Inc. and Columbia University, USA

Abstract. We present a new concept for invalidating electronic signatures which, in many situations, seem to be better suited for real business and society applications. We do not rely on an administrative invalidation process executed separately for each single signing key and based on certificate revocation lists. Instead, all signatures created with a certain group are invalidated by a certain event.

We propose a hard invalidation via releasing of the inherent cryptographic proof value – instead of soft invalidation via revoking certificates which leaves intact the cryptographic strength of signatures (even if legal validity is partially lost).

We present concrete efficient realizations of our ideas based on verifiable encryption, trapdoor discrete logarithm groups and ring signatures.

Keywords: electronic signature, revocation, deniability, verifiable encryption, trapdoor discrete logarithm, ring signature.

1 Introduction

1.1 Shortcomings of Electronic Signature Model

Business failure of electronic signatures has essential reasons and is not due to lack of good cryptographic algorithms. The real reason is the model of electronic signatures that does not really fit into business and societal needs. Below we discuss such issues.

Validity of Electronic Authentication. So far, the development of electronic authentication techniques has been focused on two extremes: volatile zero-knowledge proofs and non-volatile electronic signatures. Signature revocation is treated as a necessary evil for handling situations of security breach nature, such as losing control over a cryptographic device used for signing. Revocation methods such as CRL lists and OCSP protocols are purely administrative/organizational means – the signatures preserve their cryptographic strength and can be used after revocation – and this, in fact, is usually the case for the web applications that tend to ignore checking CRL lists. Furthermore, certificate revocation (as for CRL and OCSP) changes only the legal status of an electronic signature (but not its perceived validity). Moreover, from the point of view of *continental law* it only revokes the status of so-called *written form*.

---

* Corresponding author.

© Springer International Publishing Switzerland 2015
J. Lopez and Y. Wu (Eds.): ISPEC 2015, LNCS 9065, pp. 421–436, 2015.
DOI: 10.1007/978-3-319-17533-1_29

On the other hand, the advances of cryptanalysis and technical attacks are hard to be predicted in advance (this advances have been termed catacrypt (catastrophe in cryptography), recently). Therefore, we really do not know when a signature will lose its cryptographic strength. Even worse, the public might be unaware of effective attacks for a long time. For many applications it would be convenient to know in advance when a signature loses its cryptographic proof value. This may have purely practical reasons: in many areas of business and legal processes a document has to be used within a limited time only. Therefore, according to the security principle of keeping only necessary information, the electronic signatures should be somehow "erased" after the period when the document was intended to be used (a prime example is negotiation of a contract, in which drafts are signed, but at the end there should not be a record of versions and the deal signed has to be oblivious to the history of negotiation).

PKI Issues. Within the traditional PKI framework each pair of keys has to be handled separately. So in case of a general problem, such as revealing a critical flaw in cryptographic smart cards, all corresponding certificates must be revoked. This may mean millions of certificates to be invalidated. Even worse, this would also mean the necessity of downloading huge CRL lists by the end users, which is practically infeasible.

Legal Issues. The standard legal model of electronic signatures is that a signature remains valid after revocation of the certificate for a public key used for signature verification, provided that the signature has been created before the revocation. In order to enable automatic verification of the signing time we need to extend the model and demand attaching timestamps (and timestamping service) to the signatures. However, the timestamps are again nothing else but signed confirmations and the same problem as above occurs for the timestamps. Moreover, what happens if the timestamping system turns out to be compromised? This cascading effect may have profound consequences due to undermining trust in the whole system of electronic signatures.

Note that all problems are due to the attempts to mimic exactly the framework of handwritten signatures. We feel that this is a major mistake and the legal model of electronic signatures should be related directly to what can be easily achieved with technology (hand signed documents have a limited number of copies and can be burned at any time; and these do not apply in electronic modes!). One solution is to introduce the legal institution of signatures that "vanish" at a stated situation.

Cloud Systems. Processing data in a cloud may also be connected with authentication services – confirming validity of data. Remote services such as implementation of private signing keys has been recognized even in regulatory documents such as eIDAS Regulation [17]. So despite of all concerns, the users will perform their signing activities in a cloud. In this situation the user may gradually loose control over the signing activities performed on his behalf. Therefore, at least some countermeasures are necessary for reducing the risks. For instance, unlike for the traditional electronic signature model we may need to revoke past signatures if the cloud service provider turns out to be untrustworthy. We may need also nonstandard solutions such as delegating the right to create a limited number of signatures only and for a limited validity period.

1.2 Previous Work

Key Exposure for Signatures with Unlimited Validity Period. Possibility of exposure of secret keys is one of the major real problems of applied cryptography. This issue is critical for digital signatures that are supposed to last forever according to the legal framework of qualified signatures. Unfortunately, despite provable security of cryptographic schemes, they eventually fail due to either insufficient protection offered by so-called secure storage for cryptographic keys or by advances in cryptanalytic methods (either classical ones, or depending for instance on side-channels). There have been a lot of efforts to mitigate this situation with cryptographic means.

The first step would be to detect that some signatures have been forged [9]: Given two signatures, it will be possible to say whether one of them was generated by a forger. Stronger consequences are proposed in [2]: if a signature becomes forged, then with a certain probability the secret keys become known to the public and thereby forging a valid signature becomes useless despite knowledge of all secrets. All the adversary can do is to invalidate all signatures created with these keys. Many authors propose methods reducing the effects of a key exposure by distributing the cryptographic material – a good example of this approach is intrusion resilience with a home base [10] or strong key-insulated signature schemes [5], where a compromise of a weaker device creates problems only for signatures from a certain time period. Limiting the consequences of key exposure is the basic motivation for the seminal forward secure signatures introduced by Anderson and followed by Bellare and Miner [1].

While the above mentioned methods are focused mainly on hardware problems and insufficient key protection, the fail-stop signatures [14] deal with successful cryptanalysis. Even if a very strong adversary can derive the secret key(s), she cannot use them to forge the signatures, as easily an undeniable proof of forgery can be created.

Signatures with Limited Time Validity. The signatures created according to the scheme from [11] start to exist effectively after a certain event generated by the third party occurs. However, in this paper we consider a dual situation: we aim to create time limits for validity of electronic signatures created with and bound to them, and we mean here "hard limits." The approaches such as expiration of a validity period of a qualified certificate is not much effective. We still have a strong cryptographic evidence that a certain signature has been created with a certain private key.

Finally, we note that already at the very beginning of the history of electronic signatures it has been observed that signatures may be invalidated undeniable via revealing signing keys [16]. However, implementations and, in particular, the so called *secure signature creation devices* have been explicitly designed to prevent this. No framework for controlled private key exposure has been proposed so far despite the fact that all private keys for asymmetric schemes are expected to be eventually exposed.

Electronic Signatures and the Right-to-be-Forgotten. One of the new trends in personal data management is the right-to-be-forgotten adopted by European Union in a General Data Protection Regulation proposal [6] and by some national laws.

The legal concept creates a number of technical problems. Physical erasure is never fully effective. For instance, for data stored in data archives in an encrypted form erasing the decryption key might be considered as a method of forgetting. However, even if the key was in a black box and the black box has been destroyed, we are never sure whether there is a copy elsewhere available to an adversary.

Our idea is to implement forgetting on a different level: not as document erasure but deprivation of their authenticity proofs. Namely, electronic signatures create a challenge for the right-to-be-forgotten – cryptography persists even if we do not wish it to!

Our Goals. In order to solve the problems mentioned above we have to rethink the model of electronic signatures. Below we list the main features of our approach:

Hard Revocation: revocation should be indisputable on cryptographic level.

Event Driven: revocation must occur via an event initiated by a third party and not by the signer himself (as proposed in [16]), revocation events must be public.

Scalability: it should be possible to revoke a group of signatures or a group of users at once. Revocation conditions should be stated explicitly in a signature, thereby a verifier knows in advance under what circumstances the signature will expire.

1.3   Application Scenarios

Documents with Limited Time Horizon. In some areas documents are valid only for a limited time period. E.g. business offers are binding only within the stated time (explicitly or implicitly by default legal rules). The same holds for invoices and other tax documents. In this case "forgetting" cryptographic validation at a stated time would be convenient due to obligations of data protection. Once a document has expired in some sense, it is better to rip off its authenticity guarantees automatic (in particular without access to the document). This would be particularly useful in complex distributed systems with no central control over the flow of documents.

Destroying Electronic Documents. Cryptographers have been focused on how to secure electronic documents. In practice, not a less important question is how to destroy them! Even if we erase completely electronic storage medium, we cannot be sure that all copies of a document have been stored there. Therefore, we need effective tools to "kill" such documents wherever they are. E.g., if a system creating signatures have been penetrated by an adversary, then it is reasonable to "kill" all signatures originating from this system and reconstruct the data under a strict control.

Archives. There is a growing number of systems where we can easily insert data records, but where removing data is a complicated process requiring special rights. If the data are authenticated by the author, then the situation is even worse as the data have strong authenticity guarantees. In this case a good solution would be to "kill" the signatures without any interaction with a digital archive storing the data.

Note that revealing the private keys to "kill" the cryptographic proof value may be used to "hide in a crowd". If the system provider has difficulties to remove a signed document with a certain statement, he may add other documents on the same topic with a modified or contradictory statement. As in this moment the signatures can be forged, it will become impossible to distinguish which document has been signed by the user.

Chameleon Hashing. Some stated above goals can be achieved with chameleon hash [12]. Let α and β be such that $\log_\beta \alpha$ is known only for a Revocation Authority. Instead of signing a regular hash of a document M, the signer chooses u at random, computes $h := \alpha^{\mathrm{Hash}(M)} \beta^u$ and applies the signing algorithm for h. The result of this computation together with u is a signature of M. In order to invalidate such a signature it suffices to disclose $\log_\beta \alpha$. The crucial point is that u has not been signed, so one can obtain the same h for $M' \neq M$ and $u' = u + (\mathrm{Hash}(M) - \mathrm{Hash}(M')) \cdot \log_\beta \alpha$.

The main problem with this solution is that the main signature remains valid. For the user it will be impossible to deny the fact of creating the signatures and their number.

Paper Contribution. The main goal of the paper is to indicate a new pragmatic model for a system of electronic signatures (Sect 2). In the second part we sketch constructions that implement this model: one based on verifiable encryption (Sect. 3), one based on trapdoor discrete logarithm (Sect. 4) and one based on ring signatures (Sect. 5).

2 Model

Definition 1. *A* **Signature with Hard-Revocation** *(SHR) is a system consisting of the following procedures:*

System Setup: *on a security parameter (size of keys) and the number of revocation authorities k, it specifies a key space $\mathcal{K}$ for signatures, and a pair of keys $(Pub_{RA_i}, Priv_{RA_i})$ for each revocation authority RA_i, $i = 1, \ldots, k$.*
A Revocation Group List RGL and Revocation Event List REL are initialized as empty lists.

Setup of a User: *given a user U, a random pair of keys (k_U, K_U) is chosen at random from the key space $\mathcal{K}$. The public key K_U is appended to the Users' Public Key List (UPKL).*

Creation of Revocation Group: *given a revocation condition $Cond_j$ and authority R_i, the procedure creates a group parameter $Par_{Cond_j,i}$ and a trapdoor $Trap_{Cond_j,i}$. The following triple is appended to the list RGL:*

$$(i, Cond_j, Par_{Cond_j,i}) \ .$$

Signature Creation: *given a private key k_U, and a message M, user U creates a signature*

$$\sigma := Sign(k_U, Par_{Cond_j}, M)$$

related to Revocation Condition $Cond_j$ managed by revocation authority RA_i.

Revoking a Group: *for a triple $(i, Cond_j, Par_{Cond_j,i}) \in RGL$, the trapdoor $Trap_{Cond_j,i}$ and the private key $Priv_{RA_i}$, the procedure executed by RA_i generates $RevTok(i, Cond_j)$, a reveal token for the group with parameter $Par_{Cond_j,i}$.*
The tuple $(i, Cond_j, RevTok(i, Cond_j))$ is appended to the list REL.

Group revocation procedure for condition $Cond_j$ should be executed immediately after the condition $Cond_j$ becomes fulfilled.

Signature Verification: *it returns* valid *or* invalid *according to the standard signature verification.*

Forging Signatures in a Revoked Group: given a message M, condition $Cond_j$, the public key K_U of user U, and the revocation token $RevTok(i, Cond_j)$, the procedure outputs a forged signature of M allegedly created by the user U for condition $Cond_j$:

$$\sigma' := FSign(K_U, RevTok(i, Cond_j), Par_{Cond_j}, M)$$

The model, as above, is analogous to the usual signature model, where key generation and signature creation are run by the signer, and verification run by anyone. However, the signatures are grouped into "bunches" called a Revocation Group (a group can be a singleton), via a generation of the group parameters $Par_{Cond_j,i}$.

Each revocation group is associated with a condition $Cond_j$ that triggers revocation of all signatures in the group. The revocation has to be executed by a revocation authority responsible for $Cond_j$ and requires a trapdoor for $Par_{Cond_j,i}$ as well as the private key of the revocation authority.

The crucial points are the following properties:

Definition 2 (Correctness). *Given a signature $Sign(U, i, Cond_j, M)$ corresponding to $Cond_j$ and revocation authority RA_i, message M, generated with Signature Creation procedure by employing the private key k_U, then with overwhelming probability the verification result is* valid.

Definition 3 (Unforgeability). *We say that SHR is* **unforgeable***, if an attacker is unable to win the following game.*

The game is initialized with a set of n_U users and n_{RA} revocation authorities, both given as oracles. In the first phase the attacker interacts adaptive with arbitrary users and revocation authorities. This phase consists of polynomial many steps, meaning that the number of queries the attacker is allowed to issue to the user oracle is bound by q_U and to the revocation authority by q_{RA}. The attacker may ask revocation authorities to create or revoke revocation groups. The attacker may also ask users to sign arbitrary messages for arbitrary revocation groups and corrupt users and revocation authorities by requesting their signing keys.

Finally, the attacker outputs a signature S of an arbitrary user U and message M corresponding to a condition $Cond_j$ managed by a revocation authority RA_i. He wins the game if

- *S has not been created during the first phase,*
- *S passes positively the verification procedure,*
- *the attacker has access neither to the key k_U nor to the private key of RA_i,*
- *there is no entry starting with $i, Cond_j$ on the REL list, i.e., the group of the signature S has not been revoked.*

Informally, we say that SHR possesses the **Hard Revocation Property**, if no PPT adversary can distinguish between signatures generated by the user and those created by third parties after publishing revocation tokens with a non-negligible advantage.

Definition 4 (Hard Revocation Property). *SHR fulfills Hard Revocation Property, if there is no PPT adversary $\mathcal{A}$ such that it has a non-negligible advantage over $\frac{1}{2}$ to win the following Forgery Detection Game.*

The first part of the game is just as for the unforgeability property. In particular, the challenger can ask for the token $RevTok(i, Cond_j)$.

At some point the adversary queries a tuple consisting of: user identifier U, message M and a revoked group with parameters Par_{Cond_j}, to the challenger.

This starts the second phase in which the challenger chooses bit $b \xleftarrow{\$} \{0, 1\}$ and computes signatures $\sigma_b := Sign(k_U, Par_{Cond_j}, M)$ and $\sigma_{1-b} := FSign(K_U, RevTok(i, Cond_j), Par_{Cond_j}, M)$. Then the challenger returns σ_0, σ_1 to the adversary.

In the next phase, the adversary may interact with the oracles in a similar way as in the first phase. Finally, the adversary returns bit $\hat{b}$ and wins the game if $\hat{b} = b$.

Our revocation conditions $Cond_j$ and revocation token $RevTok(i, Cond_j)$ are associated typically with a well defined window of time, but can model other physical variations on the signature generation e.g., each signature can be its own group, or splitting the signature capability among servers and revoking a server (in the space domain) are possible variations. Note that verification, besides checking the validity of the signature also makes sure it is revocable by the information carried by the signature itself (which is important to allow any granularity of signature groups).

3 Solution Based on Verifiable Encryption

In order to focus our attention we assume that the revocation is based on the expiration time, that is, the RA authority enables to create signatures that will be "killed" at a certain time. The ideas are generic but we concentrate here on a specific design suitable for smart card implementations. The general idea is:

- For each expiration time T the RA creates parameters a_T, S_T to be used by the signatories as parameters for the public key encryption (a_T plays the role a generator in a group and S_T is the public encryption key).
- If a signer intends to create signatures with expiration time T, then he generates an ephemeral key pair (e_T, E_T), creates a certificate of E_T signed with his long-term private key, encrypts e_T using a_T, S_T, and then signs everything together with the message using the ephemeral signing key e_T. The ciphertext of e_T must enable checking that the plaintext is the discrete logarithm of the public key E_T.
- The first part of the verification process is standard: the certificate of E_T as well as the signature created with e_T are checked. Additionally, the verifier may check that the ciphertext contains the discrete logarithm of E_T.
- The revocation process is signing the message *"the time T has passed"*. At the same time the signature created in this way will reveal the discrete logarithm $\log_{a_T} S_T$ and thereby it will enable to decrypt the ciphertext of the ephemeral key e_T.

An important part of the scheme described above is that a verifier may convince himself that the signature will expire at time T. Note that in some applications this is unnecessary – as the signer has incentive to create the ciphertext correctly. In the other case we apply a *verifiable encryption* scheme. Recall that a verifiable encryption scheme enables the verifier of a ciphertext to check that the plaintext fulfills some property without revealing the plaintext [4]. The definition refers to an arbitrary property, but in our case the verifier should be able to check whether the ciphertext encrypts the discrete logarithm of a given public key.

From the legal point of view this is a nice feature that in order to revoke the signatures with expiration time T the RA has to sign a message stating that time T has passed. Our RA will do exactly that. How robust is this setting? Of course, it may happen that RA creates this signature in advance in order to learn the ephemeral keys. However, creating the signature in advance is not only breaking the contract, but also falsifying a document. While in the first case the involved parties may sue the RA in a civil court, in the second case the criminal law applies and there are severe consequences for the RA. For example, according to the German criminal law, the punishment for this offense is from six months up to 10 years imprisonment [7, §267].

3.1 Solution Details

Revocation Group Setup. The following parameters have to determined:

- a group G for ElGamal signatures, and a generator γ of G (of order ρ),
- a randomly chosen private signing key x_{RA}, and the public key $y_{\mathrm{RA}} = \gamma^{x_{\mathrm{RA}}}$,
- a keyed pseudorandom function PRNG P, and a randomly chosen key R for P.

The values $G, \gamma, y_{\mathrm{RA}}$ are published. Keys x_{RA}, R are kept secret by RA.

Creating a Commitment for Time T. (A Technique Borrowed from [11]) RA creates the following data necessary to create signatures with expiration time T.

$$k_T := \mathrm{PRNG}_R(T), \quad a_T := \gamma^{k_T},$$
$$S_T := \gamma^{\mathrm{Hash}(M(T))}/y_{\mathrm{RA}}^{a_T}, \text{ where } M(T) \text{ is the message } \textit{``the time } T \textit{ has passed''}.$$

The values (a_T, S_T) are published.

Note that the ElGamal signature for $M(T)$ with the first component a_T has the second component

$$b_T = k_T^{-1}(\mathrm{Hash}(M(T)) - x_{\mathrm{RA}} \cdot a_T) \bmod \rho \ .$$

So

$$(a_T)^{b_T} = \gamma^{k_T \cdot b_T} = \gamma^{\mathrm{Hash}(M(T)) - x_{\mathrm{RA}} \cdot a_T} = \gamma^{\mathrm{Hash}(M(T))}/y_{\mathrm{RA}}^{a_T} = S_T \ .$$

Creating a Signature by a User. We assume that a user U has a pair of keys (x_U, y_U) for a signature scheme Sign, and the public key y_U is authenticated (e.g. via a certificate in a traditional PKI system). The following initial steps are executed by U in order to create signatures with expiration time T:

- U generates a pair of ephemeral keys: a random private key $e_{U,T}$ and the corresponding public key $E_{U,T} = \gamma^{e_{U,T}}$ (these parameters come from an arbitrary group suited for creating signatures),
- U issues a certificate Cert of $E_{U,T}$ signed with its long-term key x_U,
- U creates a verifiable ciphertext C of $e_{U,T}$ using the public key (a_T, S_T).

The values Cert and C can be published at this moment. Alternatively, they can be attached to each signed document.

In order to sign a message W, the user U creates a signature with the ephemeral signing key $e_{U,T}$ over a data consisting of Cert, C and W. The user delivers the resulting signature together with Cert, C and W.

Signature Verification. The verifier should check the signature against the public key $E_{U,T}$ and the certificate Cert with the public key y_U. Additionally, the verifier may check that C encrypts the discrete logarithm of $E_{U,T}$.

Expiring Signatures at Time T. RA signs the message $M(T)$ stating that the time T has passed:

$$k_T := \mathrm{PRNG}_R(T), \quad a_T := \gamma^{k_T},$$
$$b_T := k_T^{-1}(\mathrm{Hash}(M(T)) - x_{\mathrm{RA}} \cdot a_T) \bmod \rho.$$

Then it publishes b_T. (There is no need to publish a_T, as it has been published before.)

Forging a Signature after Expiration Time. With b_T one can decrypt the ciphertext C of the private key $e_{U,T}$ and then create the signatures in the regular way. This is possible, if at least one signature of U is available or the certificate Cert has been published.

Verifiable Encryption. In order to see the difference with the scheme of the next section we recall a few details about verifiable encryption from [4]. It enables to encrypt $\log_\gamma \delta$, where γ is an element of order ρ (ρ must be not too big with respect to the parameters used for encryption). Otherwise, the group generated by γ is arbitrary.

The basic construction is a combination of Paillier encryption [13] and ElGamal encryption: it uses the group $\mathbb{Z}_{n^2}^*$, where $n = pq$, $p = 2p' + 1$, $q = 2q' + 1$, and p, q, p', q' are appropriate primes. Let $g' \in \mathbb{Z}_{n^2}^*$, x_1, x_2, x_3 be chosen at random. Let $g = (g')^{2n}$, $y_1 = g^{x_1}$, $y_2 = g^{x_2}$, $y_3 = g^{x_3}$, and hk be a key for a hash function. Then hk, n, g, y_1, y_2, y_3 is the public part, and x_1, x_2, x_3 are the secrets. Let $h = (1 + n) \bmod n^2$. Encryption starts with choosing at random $r \in [0, \ldots, \lfloor n/4 \rfloor]$. Then the ciphertext (u, e, v) of m with label L is computed as follows:

$$u := g^r, \quad e := y_1^r h^m, \quad v := abs((y_2 y_3^{\mathrm{Hash}_{\mathrm{hk}}(u,e,L)})^r)$$

($abs(a) = a \bmod n^2$ for $a \leq n^2/2$, otherwise $n^2 - a \bmod n^2$). To decrypt one first check that $abs(v) = v$, $u^{2(x_2 + \mathrm{Hash}_{\mathrm{hk}}(u,e,L)x_3)} = v^2$ and halt if it does not hold. Finally, one outputs $m = (e/u^{x_1})^{2t}$, where $t = 2^{-1} \bmod n$. Note that only x_1 is used to recover plaintext m, while x_2 and x_3 are used to verify integrity of the ciphertext.

The verifiable version of the protocol executes a short interactive protocol – and it can be converted into an non-interactive proof with Fiat-Shamir heuristic. The main point is to create an analogous ciphertext (u', e', v') of a random m' corresponding to $\delta' = \gamma^{m'}$. Then for a challenge c of the verifier, the prover has to find in $\mathbb{Z}$ exponents $\tilde{r}, \tilde{s}, \tilde{m}$ that create a relationship between u and u', e and e', v and v', σ and σ'.

In our setting, we use a_T instead of g and $y_1 = S_T$ (so $x_1 = b_T$). The values x_2 and x_3 are chosen at random. The value n must be different for each T.

Security of the Proposed Solution. The scheme's proof relies on a hybrid argument involving the Camenisch-Shoup Encryption, the ElGamal signature scheme, the pseudorandom function being secure and the random oracle assumption (ROM) about the hash function used (in the authenticated encryption; note that already the ElGamal signing security relies on the ROM). This can be summarized by the following theorem:

Theorem 1. *Assuming a strong pseudorandom function, the existential unforgeability under adaptive chosen message attacks (EUF-CMA) of the ElGamal signature scheme, the EUF-CMA security of the signature scheme used for users certificates and the security of the Camenisch-Shoup verifiable encryption, the above construction is a correct, secure SHR with hard revocation in the Random Oracle Model (ROM).*

Proof. To prove the security of the construction we have to show that it is correct, unforgeable and has the hard revocation property. We omit correctness as it is obvious.

Lemma 1 (Unforgeability). *Assuming the EUF-CMA security of the ElGamal signature scheme, the EUF-CMA security of the signature scheme used for users certificates and the security of the Camenisch-Shoup verifiable encryption, the above construction is unforgeable, as per Definition 3, in the ROM.*

Proof (Sketch). Without loss of generality we distinguish two types of adversaries. Type 1 adversary wins the unforgeability game by generating a certificate under a different ephemeral public key. On the other hand, a type 2 forger wins the game by forging a signature verifiable with an existing ephemeral public key. We now show that each of those two adversaries has negligible chances to win the unforgeability game.

For type 1 adversary the results is obvious - as it would mean forging a signature in a certificate (note that the certificates are independent from the rest of the scheme.)

For type 2 adversary, we also show that there exists a reduction algorithm R that, using a adversary that wins the SHR unforgeability game, wins the EUF-CMA game of the ElGamal signature scheme. At first, algorithm R tries to guess the revocation group for which the returned signature S will be created. With probability at least $1/q_{RA}$, the algorithm R guesses correct (it guesses the right group creation query made to the revocation authority oracle). Next, R tries to guess the user for which the returned signature S will be created. Similar, to the type 1 adversary it guesses correct with probability $1/n_U$. For this specific user, revocation group combination, the algorithm R uses the EUF-CMA game public key as the users ephemeral key. Algorithm R can generate a valid certificate Cert for this ephemeral key since it knows the users long term secret key. To process signature queries for this ephemeral key, algorithm R uses the EUF-CMA game oracle, encrypts the value 0 (instead of the ephemeral private key) and simulates the proof for the verifiable encryption scheme in the ROM. Finally, the adversary outputs signature S that can be used by R to win the EUF-CMA game.   □

Now we show that the construction has the hard revocation property.

Lemma 2 (Hard Revocation). *Assuming the soundness of the Camenisch-Shoup verifiable encryption, the above construction has the hard revocation property, as per Definition 4, in the ROM.*

Proof. A signature on M is valid only if the ephemeral public key $E_{U,T}$ is certified by the users long-term key K_U, the message M is signed using the ephemeral private key $e_{U,T}$ and the ciphertext C passes the Camenisch-Shoup verifiable encryption verification for the public key $E_{U,T}$. By the soundness property of verifiable encryption, the ciphertext C *must* encrypt the discrete logarithm of $E_{U,T}$ (which is the private key $e_{U,T}$). Note that everyone that has access to the revocations group trapdoor and a signature of a user, can decrypt the ephemeral private key $e_{U,T}$ and generate signatures that are unconditionally indistinguishable from the ones computed by the user. It follows that signatures σ_0 and σ_1 are unconditionally indistinguishable and the adversary can only guess the bit b. □

4 Solution Based on Trapdoor DLP

4.1 General Idea

A trapdoor discrete logarithm group is a group G created in such a way that there is a trapdoor t such that computing discrete logarithms in G is easy if t is known. Otherwise, computing discrete logarithms in G is hard. Our main idea is the following:

1. For each revocation event R_i, RA chooses a trapdoor DLP group G_i. The trapdoor, say t_{R_i}, is kept secret. RA publishes (G_i, g_i, R_i), where g_i is a generator of G_i.
2. A signer U chooses at random a pair $(e_{U,i}, E_{U,i})$ of keys for G, $E_{U,i} = g^{e_{U,i}}$, and issues a certificate for the public key $E_{U,i}$ signed with its long-term key k_U.
3. U generates signatures based on G and the key $e_{U,i}$.
4. If the event R_i occurs, then RA publishes the trapdoor t_{R_i}.

Note that in case of trapdoor DLP scheme no ciphertexts of the ephemeral private keys are needed to supplement the signature.

The trapdoor information must be unknown to the signer before the revocation event. Therefore, there are technical problems to apply the idea directly. For instance, if the order of G is unknown and itself is a trapdoor, we cannot apply a signatures scheme such as ElGamal. The idea is to use signatures based on the discrete logarithm problem, where the second signature element is computed as an integer without modular computations relying on the trapdoor information. The first step in this direction has been made by Stern and Poupard [15] where they avoid reducing the second component of a Schnorr signature modulo the order of the group. However, they still use the component (called S in the original description) which is unique for the group chosen. This parameter is in fact a trapdoor information as well.

The other related construction is GPS identification scheme [8], re-using the basic idea from [15] but allowing the user to choose arbitrarily a secret exponent. Thereby, a group of users can share the same revocation group. The last step is to enable efficient computation of discrete logarithm with a trapdoor information. Here we use the mechanism of decryption from the Paillier encryption [13]. We use the scheme to generate the public signing key as a Paillier ciphertext of the exponent (which should be small).

4.2   Solution Details

Setup. Extending the description in [8], we take a group $\mathbb{Z}_{n^2}^*$ used in [13]:

- randomly chosen two safe primes: $p = 2p' + 1$ and $q = 2q' + 1$, $n = p \cdot q$, and a generator g of $\mathbb{Z}_{n^2}^*$,
- trapdoor: (λ, μ), where $\lambda = \operatorname{lcm}(p-1, q-1) = 2p'q'$, $\mu = (L(g^\lambda \bmod n^2))^{-1} \bmod n$ for $L(x) = \lfloor \frac{x-1}{n} \rfloor$.

Moreover, we have parameters typical for the GPS scheme: integers A, B and S that are relatively small compared to n^2, but at the same time large enough to get a negligible probability of forging a signature.

User Key Generation.

- choose at random an odd number $s \in [0, S - 1]$,
- $g_I := gu^n \bmod n^2$, for u chosen at random, $I := g_I^s \bmod n^2$,
- (g_I, I) is the public key, s is the corresponding signing key (note that when publishing the public key, there are zero-knowledge techniques (range proofs) to assure the right range for s was employed [3]).

Signature Creation.

- choose $k \in [0, A - 1]$ at random, $r := g_I^k$,
- $c := \operatorname{Hash}(M, r)$,
- $s := k + c \cdot s$ (note that this computation is performed without modular reduction),
- output (c, s).

Signature Verification.

- if $c \notin [0, B - 1]$ or $s \notin [0, A + (B - 1) \cdot (S - 1) - 1]$, then output invalid,
- compute $r' := g_I^s/I^c$ and $c' := \operatorname{Hash}(M, r')$,
- if $c' \neq c$, then output invalid, else output valid.

Revocation. RA publishes the parameters λ, μ corresponding to the revocation event.

Forging a Signature After Revocation. For the parameters λ, μ published via revocation, and the public key (g_I, I) of a user, the Paillier decryption algorithm is executed:

$$s' := L(I^\lambda \bmod n^2) \cdot \mu \bmod n .$$

The number s' should be the secret s of the user with the public key (g_I, I). It can be used then to create fake signatures according to the original scheme.

4.3   Assumptions and Discussion

The GPS signature requires Discrete Logarithm with Short Exponent Assumption [8, page 472]. It states that the Discrete Logarithm Problem is hard even for the case that we know in advance that the discrete logarithm is in the interval $[0, S - 1]$, where S is substantially smaller than the cyclic group order. For our scheme we assume that the Short Exponent Assumption holds for the group $\mathbb{Z}_{n^2}^*$ used by our construction.

The public key of the user is itself a Paillier ciphertext of the secret key. The original description of Paillier would use $I := g^s \cdot v^n \bmod n^2$, with v randomly distributed, while we use $I = g^s \cdot (u^s)^n \bmod n^2$, with u chosen at random. However, if u is not of a small order (which happens with overwhelming probability), and s is coprime with p, q, p', q', then u^s is distributed exactly as v. Note that if $S \ll \sqrt{n}$, then s is automatically coprime with p, q, p', q' as these prime numbers are close to $\sqrt{n}$.

The results on semantic security of Paillier ciphertexts do no apply here as for signatures we must show the base g_I for the discrete logarithm problem. Therefore, given a candidate secret key z, we can always check if this is the right key by simply computing g_I^z. There is no way to avoid this situation unless we design completely new paradigms for creating digital signatures based on hardness of the Discrete Logarithm Problem.

To summarize:

Theorem 2. *Assuming the Short Exponent DLOG Assumption holds for the group $\mathbb{Z}_{n^2}^*$, the GPS signature scheme is EUF-CMA secure for the group $\mathbb{Z}_{n^2}^*$, the EUF-CMA security of the signature scheme used for users certificates, the scheme above is correct and secure SHR with hard revocation in the ROM.*

Proof (Sketch). To prove the security of the construction we have to show that it is correct, unforgeable and has the hard revocation property. Again, we omit correctness as it obvious from the construction.

First, we consider unforgeability. We reuse the idea from the proof of Lemma 1. Namely, we distinguish two types of adversaries. Type 1 adversary wins the game by generating a certificate under a different ephemeral public key and type 2 wins the game by forging a signature verifiable with an existing ephemeral public key.

The same reasoning for the type 1 adversary as in the proof of Lemma 1 can be applied. Moreover, we can also apply the same reasoning for type 2 adversary but instead of playing the EUF-CMA game of the ElGamal signature scheme, the reduction algorithm R plays the EUF-CMA game of the modified GPS signature scheme.

Now we show that the construction has the hard revocation property. First note that the user must use the group modulus n^2 in order to create his public key. Moreover, during revocation of a group, the revocation authority publishes the trapdoor (λ, μ) that can be used to decrypt the users ephemeral private key s. Once s is available, everyone that has access to this trapdoor and a signature of the user, can generate signatures that are unconditionally indistinguishable from the ones computed by the user. It follows that signatures σ_0 and σ_1 are unconditionally indistinguishable and the adversary can only guess the bit b. □

5   Solution Based on Ring Signatures

Our main idea is the following. A user creates a ring signature such that:

1. there are two ring members: the user himself and a virtual user related to a revocation event, the user creates the ring signature with his own private key,
2. the private key of the virtual user is uknown,
3. when the revocation event occurs, the RA creates a signature that at the same time leaks the private key of the virtual user.

After revocation event, the knowledge of the private key of the virtual user enables forging signatures.

Lemma 3. *Signatures with Hard-Revocation constructed using the above generic approach are unforgeable and possess the hard revocation property assuming, that the used ring signature scheme is unforgeable and anonymous.*

We leave this lemma without a proof, since it follows from the definitions of unforgeability, hard revocation and anonymity.

Below we describe an instantiation for this generic approach. We use a slightly customized Schnorr ring signatures. For now we omit the security proof (unforgeability and anonymity) of this customized scheme.

Revocation Group Setup. The RA is created exactly as described in Sect. 3.

Creating a Commitment for Revocation Event T. Just as described in Sect. 3, for revocation event T the values (a_T, S_T) are published, where

$$a_T := g^{k_T},$$
$$S_T := g^{\text{Hash}(M(T))}/y_{\text{RA}}^{a_T}, \text{ where } M(T) \text{ is the message } \textit{"the event } T \textit{ has occurred"}.$$

As observed before, the ElGamal signature for $M(T)$ with the first component a_T has the second component $b_T = k_T^{-1}(\text{Hash}(M(T))) - x_{\text{RA}} \cdot a_T)$ and $(a_T)^{b_T} = S_T$. The user has merely to fetch the pair (a_T, S_T).

Creating a Signature by a User. A signature of user U for revocation event T is a ring signature corresponding to the key pairs (x_U, y_U) (for the generator g), and (b_T, S_T) (for the generator a_T). Namely, U performs the following steps in order to sign M:

1. choose k_1 at random, $r_1 := g^{k_1}$,
2. $e_2 := \text{Hash}(M, r_1)$,   choose s_2 at random, $r_2 := a_T^{s_2} \cdot S_T^{e_2}$,
3. $e_1 := \text{Hash}(M, r_2)$, $s_1 := k_1 - e_1 x_U$,
4. output the signature (r_1, s_1, r_2, s_2).

Signature Verification. The test is: $g^{s_1} \cdot y_U^{\text{Hash}(M, r_2)} \overset{?}{=} r_1$, $a_T^{s_2} \cdot S_T^{\text{Hash}(M, r_1)} \overset{?}{=} r_2$.

Revoking Signatures for the Event T. As described in Sect. 3, the RA signs the message $M(T)$ stating that T has occurred and thereby discloses b_T such that $S_T = a_T^{b_T}$.

Forging a Signature after Revocation. Given the discrete logarithm b_T, one can generate the signatures without x_U in the same way as described above, but switching the roles of g, x_U and a_T, b_T.

Acknowledgments. This work has been initiated during the second author's visit in Google Inc. The visit was supported within a project funded by the European Social Fund. Work done by the first author was supported by project S40012/K1102 at Wrocław University of Technology.

HUMAN CAPITAL
NATIONAL COHESION STRATEGY

References

1. Bellare, M., Miner, S.K.: A forward-secure digital signature scheme. In: Wiener, M. (ed.) CRYPTO 1999. LNCS, vol. 1666, pp. 431–448. Springer, Heidelberg (1999)
2. Błaśkiewicz, P., Kubiak, P., Kutyłowski, M.: Two-Head Dragon Protocol: Preventing Cloning of Signature Keys. In: Chen, L., Yung, M. (eds.) INTRUST 2010. LNCS, vol. 6802, pp. 173–188. Springer, Heidelberg (2011)
3. Camenisch, J.L., Chaabouni, R., Shelat, A.: Efficient protocols for set membership and range proofs. In: Pieprzyk, J. (ed.) ASIACRYPT 2008. LNCS, vol. 5350, pp. 234–252. Springer, Heidelberg (2008)
4. Camenisch, J., Shoup, V.: Practical verifiable encryption and decryption of discrete logarithms. In: Boneh, D. (ed.) CRYPTO 2003. LNCS, vol. 2729, pp. 126–144. Springer, Heidelberg (2003)
5. Dodis, Y., Katz, J., Xu, S., Yung, M.: Strong key-insulated signature schemes. In: Desmedt, Y.G. (ed.) PKC 2003. LNCS, vol. 2567, pp. 130–144. Springer, Heidelberg (2002)
6. European Commission: Proposal for a regulation of the European Parliament and of the council on the protection of individuals with regard to the processing of personal data and on the free movement of such data (general data protection regulation). COM, 11 (2012)
7. Federal Republic of Germany: Bundesstrafbuch. BGBl. I S. 3322 (1998)
8. Girault, M., Poupard, G., Stern, J.: On the fly authentication and signature schemes based on groups of unknown order. J. Cryptology 19(4), 463–487 (2006)
9. Itkis, G.: Cryptographic tamper evidence. IACR Cryptology ePrint Archive 31 (2003)
10. Itkis, G., Reyzin, L.: SiBIR: Signer-Base Intrusion-Resilient Signatures. In: Yung, M. (ed.) CRYPTO 2002. LNCS, vol. 2442, pp. 499–514. Springer, Heidelberg (2002)
11. Klonowski, M., Kutyłowski, M., Lauks, A., Zagórski, F.: Conditional Digital Signatures. In: Katsikas, S.K., López, J., Pernul, G. (eds.) TrustBus 2005. LNCS, vol. 3592, pp. 206–215. Springer, Heidelberg (2005)
12. Krawczyk, H., Rabin, T.: Chameleon signatures. In: Network and Distributed System Security Symposium, NDSS 2000. The Internet Society (2000)
13. Paillier, P.: Public-key cryptosystems based on composite degree residuosity classes. In: Stern, J. (ed.) EUROCRYPT 1999. LNCS, vol. 1592, pp. 223–238. Springer, Heidelberg (1999)
14. Pfitzmann, B.: Digital Signature Schemes. LNCS, vol. 1100. Springer, Heidelberg (1996)

15. Poupard, G., Stern, J.: On the fly signatures based on factoring. In: Motiwalla, J., Tsudik, G. (eds.) 6th ACM Conference on Computer and Communications Security, CCS 1999, pp. 37–45. ACM (1999)
16. Saltzer, J.H.: On digital signatures. Operating Systems Review 12(2), 12–14 (1978)
17. The European Parliament and European Council: Regulation (EU) no 910/2014 of the European Parliamnt and of the Council on electronic identification and trust services for electronic transactions in the internal market and repealing Directive 1999/93/EC. Official Journal of the European Union L 257/73 (2014)

Implementation

Lightweight Function Pointer Analysis

Wei Zhang and Yu Zhang

School of Computer Science and Technology
University of Science and Technology of China, Hefei 230027, P.R. China
xtxwy@mail.ustc.edu.cn, yuzhang@ustc.edu.cn

Abstract. How to detect and classify the huge malware samples received every day is a major challenge of security area. In recent years, using function call graph to detect and classify malicious software has become a feasible method. As the basic technology of call graph construction, function pointer analysis becomes more noticeable. Previous works often use the result of pointer analysis to determine the possible targets of function pointer calls. However, the inherent complexity and efficiency problem of the pointer analysis often leads to unsatisfactory results when applied to practical programs. This paper presents a strong connected component (SCC) level flow-sensitive and context-sensitive function pointer analysis algorithm (referred as *FP algorithm*). This algorithm not only makes up for the speed deficiency of pointer analysis, but also obtains higher precision. Measurements for 8 practical C programs show that FP algorithm advances 42.6 times on average compared with DSA algorithm and the precision is also improved.

Keywords: Function pointer analysis algorithm, Function pointer reference graph, SCC-level flow-sensitive, Context-sensitive, LLVM.

1 Introduction

With the advent of automated malware development toolkits, creating new variants of existing malware has become relatively easy. According to the latest Symantec Internet Threat Report [1], the number of new malware families increased slowly as malware authors preferred to work on existing malware. When security companies receive a malicious sample, they need to detect and classify the sample to determine whether it is a variant of the already existing malware. In recent years, using function call graph for malware detection [9,10] and classification [11,13] has become an important technique. How to construct call graph efficiently and accurately has become an urgent problem for security tools. In fact, the call graph construction problem is equivalent to an inter-procedural pointer analysis problem [6], and its bottleneck mainly comes from the efficiency of function pointer analysis.

The mechanism of function pointer allows procedural invocation by means of pointer variables. Because of this, for many static analysis techniques, the targets of function pointers cannot be uniquely determined. Previous algorithms [4, 8, 12, 18] perform pointer analysis first, and then obtain the targets of a function

© Springer International Publishing Switzerland 2015
J. Lopez and Y. Wu (Eds.): ISPEC 2015, LNCS 9065, pp. 439–453, 2015.
DOI: 10.1007/978-3-319-17533-1_30

pointer from its results. We use another strategy which distinguishes function pointers from other pointers and analyses them independently at the beginning.

The goal of our work is to develop a lightweight function pointer analysis algorithm that can both meet the requirements of speed and precision in practical program analysis. In this paper, we propose a strongly connected component (SCC) level flow-sensitive and context-sensitive function pointer analysis algorithm (referred as *FP algorithm*). It can be applied to practical C program analysis, including type-unsafe code and incomplete program. Measurements show that the speed and accuracy of *FP* algorithm are quite competitive and the algorithm has great practical value. The major contributions of this paper are as follows:

1) Compared with pointer analysis algorithms, in the intra-procedural analysis phase *FP* algorithm only analyses instructions related with function pointers which are a small part of the whole instructions. And *FP* algorithm only merges context information whose parameters and return values contain function pointers in the inter-procedural analysis phase, which avoids more repeated analysis. The optimization in the intra- and inter-procedural analysis phase of *FP* algorithm greatly improves its efficiency and ensures its lightweight character.

2) *FP* algorithm introduces the concept of function pointer reference graph (referred as *FPG*), and separates all the function pointers into two categories by usage: *analytic objects* (consisting of the function pointer callsites and function pointer return values) and *reference objects* (consisting the remaining function pointers). *FPG* defines the relationship between function pointers and it can be tailored by combining with SCC dominance relationship. Besides, *FPG* can help to merge context information more accurately, which improves the precision of *FP* algorithm.

2   The Source Language and Types

The analysis target of *FP* algorithm is a subset of LLVM (Low-Level Virtual Machine) intermediate representation(referred as *LLVM IR*) [15,21], whose abstract grammar and non-standard abstract type are shown in Fig. 1.

$$t ::= t * \mid [s \times t] \mid \{\overline{t_j}^j\} \mid t\ \overline{t_j}^j$$

$$L ::=\ r\ =\ load\ t * v$$

$$\mid\ store\ t_1\ v_1\ t_2 * v_2$$

$$\mid\ r\ =\ bitcast\ t_1\ v\ to\ t_2$$

$$\mid\ r\ =\ call\ t\ v(\overline{t_j\ v_j}^j)$$

$$\mid\ r\ =\ getelementptr\ t * v\ \overline{t_j\ v_j}^j$$

$$\mid\ ret\ t\ v$$

$$\rho ::=\ \tau \mid \lambda$$

$$\tau ::= [s \times t], t = \lambda$$

$$\mid \{\overline{t_j}^j\}, \exists t \in t_j, t = \lambda$$

$$\lambda ::= t\ \overline{t_j}^j$$

Fig. 1. Abstract grammar and non-standard abstract type of the target language

LLVM IR is denoted as the form of static single assignment (SSA), and contains two kinds of objects: the register object and the memory object. In Fig. 1, r represents a register object and v represents a register object or a memory object. t represents a type, which could be a pointer type ($t*$), an array type ($[s \times t]$) of s elements, an anonymous structure type ($\{\overline{t_j}^j\}$) containing a list of fields with specified types, or a function type ($t \ \overline{t_j}^j$) with a specified return type and a given list of parameter types. Here, $\overline{t_j}^j$ is a sequence of types which can represent field types of a structure type or parameter types of a function type. Array types and structure types belong to the aggregate types.

The instructions appearing in Fig. 1 include the memory access instructions (*load* and *store*), the type conversion instruction (*bitcast*), the function call instruction (*call*), the getting address of sub-element of an aggregate data structure instruction (*getelementptr*) and the function return instruction (*ret*).

LLVM IR is a typed language which contains almost all the common types. But *FP* algorithm only deals with a small subset of these types, that is, the function pointer type and the aggregate type with function pointer member. In Fig. 1, ρ is the target type of *FP* algorithm. The type may be a function type (defined as λ) or an aggregate type (defined as τ) including array type and structure type. And we use Φ to represent the set of types satisfying the definition of Fig. 1.

Considering the assignment statement, x=y, assume that the type of x and y is t, x and y can be treated as aliases to an object, namely, x and y are equivalent. The corresponding LLVM IR is: %0=load t* %y;store t %0, t* %x, where x and y are corresponding to %x and %y respectively. The %0 is an intermediate value generated by LLVM. In order to obtain the equivalent semantic of source code and highlight the target type concerned by *FP* algorithm, we introduce an equivalence relation (represented by $\bowtie$) as the analysis rule of LLVM IR. The $\bowtie$ is described as follow:

Definition 1: Suppose V denotes the set of values and $\bowtie$ is the equivalence relation on V, $\exists v_1, v_2 \in V$, such that $v_1 \bowtie v_2$ where:

$$\frac{v_1 : t_1 \quad v_2 : t_2 \quad t_1, t_2 \in \Phi \quad t_1 \sim t_2}{v_1 \bowtie v_2} \ (P_1)$$

$$\frac{v_1 : [s_1 \times t_1] \quad v_2 : [s_2 \times t_2] \quad t_1, t_2 \in \Phi \quad t_1 \sim t_2}{v_1 \bowtie v_2} \ (P_2)$$

$$\frac{v_1 : t_1 \quad v_2 : [s \times t_2] \quad t_1, t_2 \in \Phi \quad t_1 \sim t_2}{v_1 \bowtie v_2} \ (P_3)$$

$$\frac{v_1 : \{\overline{t_i}^i\} \quad v_2 : \{\overline{t_j}^j\} \quad t_i, t_j \in \Phi \quad t_i \sim t_j}{v_1 \bowtie v_2} \ (P_4)$$

$$\frac{v_1 : t \quad v_2 : \{\overline{t_i}^i\} \quad t, t_i \in \Phi \quad t \sim t_i}{v_1 \bowtie v_2} \ (P_5)$$

$$\frac{v_1 : [s \times t] \quad v_2 : \{\overline{t_i}^i\} \quad t, t_i \in \Phi \quad t \sim t_i}{v_1 \bowtie v_2} \ (P_6)$$

From rules P1 to P6, $t_1 \sim t_2$ represents that type t_1 and type t_2 are compatible. In rule P2, v_1 and v_2 both represent a specific object of an array type. In rule P4, v_1 and v_2 both represent a specific object of an structure type. In LLVM IR, $v_1 \bowtie v_2$ stands for the reference or dereference relationship.

3   A Simple Example

```
1 typedef void (*OP)(int*);
2 typedef struct _Node {
3    int data;
4    OP op;
5    struct _Node *next;
6 }Node;
7 Node* init(int num,OP op,Node *n) {
8    Node *temp = malloc(sizeof(Node));
9    temp->data = num;
10   temp->op = op;
11   temp->next = n;
12   return temp;
13 }
14 void add(int *Num) { *Num += 10; }
15 void opOnList(Node *head) {
16   do { head->op(&head->data);
17       head = head->next;
18   } while(head);
19 }
20 void freeList(Node *head) {...}
21 void main() {
22   Node *X = init(2, add, NULL);
23   Node *Y = init(4, add, X);
24   opOnList(Y);
25   freeList(Y);
26 }
```

(a)

```
1 %struct._Node = type { i32, void (i32*)*, %struct._Node* }
2 define %struct._Node* @init(...) {...}
3 declare i8* @malloc(i64)
4 define void @add(i32* %Num) {...}
5 define void @opOnList(%struct._Node* %head) {
6 entry:
7    %head.addr = alloca %struct._Node*
8    store %struct._Node* %head, %struct._Node** %head.addr
9    br label %do.body
10 do.body:
11   %0 = load %struct._Node** %head.addr
12   %op = getelementptr %struct._Node* %0,i32 0,i32 1
13   %1 = load void (i32*)** %op
14   %2 = load %struct._Node** %head.addr
15   %data = getelementptr %struct._Node* %2,i32 0,i32 0
16   call void %1(i32* %data)
17   %3 = load %struct._Node** %head.addr
18   %next = getelementptr %struct._Node* %3,i32 0,i32 2
19   %4 = load %struct._Node** %next
20   store %struct._Node* %4, %struct._Node** %head.addr
21   br label %do.cond
22 do.cond:
23   %5 = load %struct._Node** %head.addr
24   %tobool = icmp ne %struct._Node* %5, null
25   br i1 %tobool, label %do.body, label %do.end
26 do.end:
27   ret void
28 }
29 define void @freeList(%struct._Node* %head) {...}
30 define void @main() {...}
```

(b)

```
EC:<set1>
set1:<%head,%head.addr,
    %0,%op,%1,%2,%data,
    %3,%next,%4,%5
    >
```

(c)

(d)

Fig. 2. C,LLVM sample code fragment and partial results

Fig. 2 is an example to explain some details of *FP* algorithm. Fig. 2(a) shows a simple C program implementing the creation and modification of a single linked list. Fig. 2(b) shows the LLVM IR generated by *Clang* compiler frontend. Fig. 2(c) and Fig. 2(d) show partial results of intra-procedural analysis of *FP* algorithm.

In Fig. 2(b), we give the LLVM IR of the opOnlist function and others are ignored. In LLVM IR, global variables begin with identifier @ and register variables with identifier %. The fifth line in Fig. 2(b) is corresponding to the fifteenth line in Fig. 2(a) which gives the declaration of opOnList function. In the lines 7-8 of Fig. 2(b), LLVM allocates a local memory unit and assigns it to %head.addr, then stores the address of parameter %head in it. Line 9 is an unconditional jump into the loop body. Lines 10-20 are the loop body corresponding to lines 16-17 of Fig. 2(a). In the loop body of Fig. 2(b), lines 11-13 store op of head to %1. Lines 14-15 gets data. Line 16 is a function pointer call. Lines 17-20 store next to head. Lines 22-25 are the loop condition judgement corresponding to line 18 of Fig. 2(a).

The EC in Fig. 2(c) is the equivalence class analysis results of opOnList function. The rules of equivalence class analysis are shown in **Definition 1**. The EC contains only one member set1 which means that opOnList function only has one equivalence class. The set1 has a function pointer callsite %1 (is an *analytic object*) and *FP* algorithm can get the possible targets of %1.

Fig. 2(d) illustrates the *FPG* built based on equivalence classes in Fig. 2(c). Fig. 2(d) means that the @opOnList function has an *analytic object* %1. And getting %1's targets need, firstly, to obtain the targets of @opOnList's parameter.

4   Implementation of FP Algorithm

FP algorithm has three analysis stages: the global analysis phase, the intra-procedural analysis phase and the inter-procedural analysis phase. The global analysis phase obtains global variables whose types meet the definition in Fig. 1. The intra-procedural analysis phase is divided into equivalence class analysis and *FPG* construction. Equivalence class analysis traverses the instructions and then generates the equivalence classes. *FPG* construction is based on equivalence classes and it can be tailored by combining with SCC's dominance relationship. Due to the missing context information, the *FPG* constructed in intra-procedural analysis phase is not complete. In inter-procedural analysis phase, context information is merged and the *FPG* is then finally constructed completely.

4.1   Global Variable Analysis Phase

The global variable analysis traverses all the global instructions to collect variables whose type t meets the definition of Fig. 1 (i.e. $t \in \Phi$). Each member in the global analysis result is a 2-tuple: $< g,F >$, where g denotes a global variable and F denotes its referred functions. If g is not initialized, F is null.

4.2   SCC-Level Flow-Sensitive Intra-Procedural Analysis Phase

As mentioned above, the intra-procedural analysis phase is divided into two steps: equivalence class analysis and *FPG* construction. In Fig. 3, intraProcess(M) function describes the process of intra-procedural analysis. M is a function in LLVM IR. Firstly, intraProcess creates an empty function summary S. Secondly, the ECAnalysis function traverses all the instructions of M to get equivalence

444   W. Zhang and Y. Zhang

```
intraProcess(M)
  new S
  ECAnalysis(M,S)
  buildFPG(EC,S)

ECAnalysis(M,S)
  foreach instruction c in M:
    switch(c):
      r = load t* v:
        if t ∈ Φ
          join(r,v)
      store t₁ v₁ t₂* v₂:
        if t₁ ∈ Φ ∧ t₂ ∈ Φ
          join(v₁, v₂)
      r = bitcast t₁ v to t₂:
        if t₂ ∈ Φ
          join(r,v)
      r = call t v(t̄ⱼ v̄ⱼʲ):
        if t ∈ Φ ∨ ∃tⱼ ∈ Φ
          record(v,S)
      r = getelementptr t* v t̄ⱼ v̄ⱼʲ:
        if t ∈ Φ
          join(r,v)
      ret t v:
        if t ∈ Φ
          record(v,S)
```

```
join(val₁, val₂)
  set₁ = ecr(val₁)
  set₂ = ecr(val₂)
  if set₁ ≠ set₂
    merge(set₁, set₂)

record(val, S)
  info = val extraction
  insert info into S

buildFPG(EC,S)
  foreach cr = c_f or r_f in S
    o₁:=newObject(cr)
    N_f = N_f ∪ {o₁}
    E_f = E_f ∪ {< m, o₁ >}
    foreach ec in ecr(cr)
      if ec is reference object:
        o₂:=newObject(ec)
        N_o = N_o ∪ {o₂}
        E_d = E_d ∪ {< o₁, o₂ >}
  foreach n_f in N_f and < n_f, n_o > in E_d
    if scc_dom(n_f, n_o)
      unique(< n_f, n_o >, E_d)
```

Fig. 3. Intra-procedural analysis algorithm

classes. Finally, the buildFPG function constructs the *FPG* based on the obtained equivalence classes.

Definition 2: Suppose $\mathbb{M}$ is a LLVM IR module of a given C program. All the function pointers are divided into two categories: *analytic objects* (consisting of the function pointer callsites and function pointer return values) and *reference objects* (consisting of the remaining function pointers).

Definition 3: Suppose M is a function in LLVM IR. The *FPG* of M is a directed graph, denoted as G=$(m \cup N_f \cup N_o, E_f \cup E_d)$ where:

- Graph node set $N = m \cup N_f \cup N_o$, where m represents M, N_f is the set of *analytic objects* whose members may be function pointer callsites or function pointer return values, and N_o is the set of *reference objects* whose members may be function parameters, return value of callees, global or local variables.
- Graph edge set $E = E_f \cup E_d$, where E_f represents the set of edges from m to *analytic objects*, and E_d represents the set of the edges from *analytic objects* to *reference objects*. For example, in Fig. 2(d), the left edge belongs to E_f, and the right edge belongs to E_d.

Definition 4: Suppose M is a function in LLVM IR. The function summary S of M is a 5-tuple: $<C,R,P,\mu,G>$. C represents function call information, including the library function call, normal function call and the function pointer call. R represents return value with type t ($t \in \Phi$). P stands for the parameter information of M. μ ($\mu \in \{\mu_n, \mu_p, \mu_c\}$) represents the analysis status of S. μ_n means that S is not analysed. μ_p means that S has been analysed partly and μ_n means that S has been analysed completely. G represents the *FPG* of M.

Equivalence Class Analysis. In Fig. 3, ECAnalysis function describes the equivalence class analysis algorithm. Each value object in LLVM IR is initialized with a disjoint set. Traversing the instructions in M sequentially, when a value object is identified as equivalent to another value object, the join function merges the related two sets into one set. Take the *load* instruction for example, if the value object v has the same type as another value object r, their sets will be merged.

In Fig. 3, the join function merges two sets. The ecr(val) returns the equivalence class representation of val. The merge function performs the merging operation. The record(val,S) function inserts val information into function summary S. For example, if val is a callsite, the recorded information consists of the callsite name, the arguments and the return value of the callsite. The extraction of val is performed by LLVM.

As the Clang compiler frontend does semantic checking strictly before generating LLVM IR, the operands' types in a LLVM instruction are compatible, accordingly the judgement of $\sim$ relation in Fig. 3 is ignored.

***FPG* Construction and SCC-Level Flow-Sensitive Analysis.** Notice that the equivalence class analysis is flow-insensitive, which can get high speed but sacrifice precision. In order to make up for the defect, *FPG* is tailored by combining with SCC dominance relationship which is defined as follows:

Definition 5: Suppose object A is in SCC S_a and object B is in SCC S_b. We say A is SCC-level flow-sensitive to B, iff, S_a dominates S_b as well as A and B are in the same equivalence class.

In Fig. 3, buildFPG shows the *FPG* construction algorithm. Firstly, the algorithm traverses all the *analytic objects* (including function pointer call c_f and function pointer return value r_f) in S, then it creates *analytic object* cr's graph node o_1, inserts it to N_f, and records the edge (from m to o_1) to E_f. Secondly, the algorithm traverses the equivalence class of cr. If equivalence class member ec is a *reference object*, the algorithm creates a new graph node o_2, inserts it to set N_o, and then records the edge (from o_1 to o_2) to E_d. Finally, the algorithm traverses all the *analytic objects* and gets tuple $< n_f, n_o >$. If n_f is SCC-level flow-sensitive to n_o, the *FPG* can be tailored. SCC construction is provided by LLVM, and $scc\_dom(n_f, n_o)$ is used to judge whether n_f is

SCC-level flow-sensitive to n_o. Function unique only retains the edge from n_f to n_o by deleting other edges starting from n_f. In order to ensure the accuracy of dominance relationship analysis between SCCs, the analysis order for scc_dom is from intra-basic block to inter-basic block. For example, if n_f and n_o are in the same basic block with use-def relation, the use-def relations of n_f from other basic blocks will be ignored. If n_f and n_o are in the different basic blocks, we need to judge the SCC dominance relationship based on **Definition 5**.

4.3   Inter-procedural Analysis Phase

interProcess($\mathbb{S}$)
    foreach S in $\mathbb{S}$ and $S.status == \mu_n$
        process(S)

process(S)
    set S is being visited
    foreach c in $S.C$ and c is unresolved
        if c is normal function:
            $s_1 = getS(c)$
            if $s_1.status == \mu_n$ or μ_p:
                $s_2 = doCall(c)$
                if s_2 is not being visited: process(s_2)
        if c is function pointer:
            $n_o = S.G.c$
            switch(n_o):
                case $global$ or $local$:
                    $s_1 = doFPGL(c, n_o)$
                case $function\ parameter$:
                    $S.status = \mu_p$
                    $s_1 = doFPFA(c, S.P)$
                case $callee\ c_1's\ return\ value$:
                    $s_2 = getS(c_1)$
                    if s_2 is not being visited:
                        process(s_2)
                    $s_1 = doFPCD(c, s_2)$
                if s_1 is not being visited: process(s_1)
    if $S.status \neq \mu_p$: $S.status = \mu_c$
    set S is not being visited

doCall(c)
    $s = getS(c)$
    $s.P =$ referred functions of
           c'parameter
    ret s

doFPGL(c,n)
    $s = getS(c)$
    $s.C = s.C \cup$ referred functions of n
    ret s

doFPFA(c,p)
    $s = getS(c)$
    $s.C = s.C \cup p$
    ret s

doFPCD(c,s)
    $s_1 = getS(c)$
    $s_1.C = s_1.C \cup s.R$
    ret s_1

Fig. 4. Inter-procedural analysis algorithm

In Fig. 4, interProcess function shows the inter-procedural analysis algorithm. The parameter of interProcess is the function summary set $\mathbb{S}$. The algorithm traverses $\mathbb{S}$ to get the unresolved member S whose status is μ_n (μ_n represents S is not analysed), and then invokes the process function to deal with S. The process(S) function marks S with being visited first. And it traverses S to get each unresolved callsite c, and then processes c according to its categories:

- If c is a normal function call (normal function calls refer to the calls excluding library function calls and function pointer calls), the algorithm invokes getS to get c's function summary s_1 first. And if s_1 is not analysed ($s_1.status$ is μ_n) or analysed partly ($s_1.status$ is μ_p), it invokes doCall to merge the argument information and return the function summary s_2, and then processes s_2 recursively. The if judgment on s_2 can avoid a infinite loop caused by recursive invocation. Function doCall invokes getS to get c's function summary s, then stores the arguments of callsite c in $s.P$.
- If c is a function pointer, the algorithm gets the *reference object* n_o from *FPG*, and processes n_o according to its categories:
  1) If n_o is a global variable or a local variable, the algorithm invokes doFPGL to process c. doFPGL(c,n) invokes getS to get c's function summary s, and stores functions referenced by n in s's callsite information C.
  2) If n_o is a function parameter, the algorithm sets $S.status$ into μ_p first (μ_p means that S need to merge context information every time), and invokes doFPFA to process c. The doFPFA(c,p) function invokes getS to get c's function summary s, and stores the parameter's referred functions P in s's callsite information C.
  3) If n_o is another callee c_1's return value, the algorithm invokes getS to get c_1's function summary s_2 and then processes s_2 recursively. Then the algorithm invokes doFPCD to process c. The doFPCD function invokes getS to get c's function summary s_1, and stores the referred functions of s's return value in s_1's callsite information C.

After getting c's function summary s_1, the algorithm processes s_1 recursively. And in the end, it sets $S.status$ as μ_c or μ_p and marks S as non-visited.

The algorithm shown in Fig. 4 uses depth-first traversal to do the bottom-up analysis. As function summary S's context information is merged every time when $S.status$ is μ_p, the propagation of function pointer information is sensitive to context. Thus the *FP* algorithm is ensured to be context-sensitive.

5   Experiment Results

The *FP* algorithm described in this paper has been implemented on LLVM3.3. In order to evaluate its performance, we select eight practical programs and libraries of C language as shown in Table 1. All the test programs run on the computer with Intel i7-3770 CPU @ 3.40GHz × 4, 15.4G memory, and the OS is Ubuntu 14.04.

For each test program, Table 1 gives the name, the number of code line (LOC), the number of function pointer calls (ind.call), the total number of the function calls(total.call) and the percentage of function pointer calls in the total function calls (ind.call/total.call*100%).

Table 1. Characteristics of benchmark programs

Benchmark	LOC	ind.call	total.call	ind.call/total.call
diction-1.10	2448	5	199	2.51%
gdbm-1.8.3	3468	1	330	0.30%
gzip-1.6	4861	4	613	0.65%
less-444	18032	5	1143	0.44%
minicom-2.7	22658	5	2433	0.21%
bash-4.3	50883	46	8365	0.55%
dgesvd.c	12521	64	1408	4.55%
clapack	545501	231	71088	0.32%

From Table 1, we can see that: (1) The use of function pointers is very common in practical programs. (2) The function pointer calls have a low proportion in the total number of function calls. Therefore, for some applications (e.g., the call graph construction), the function pointers analysis is essential, but it is not efficient to get the targets of function pointer by pointer analysis. After all, the use of function pointers only accounts for a small part of the total function calls.

5.1   Comparison of the Analysis Time and Accuracy

Table 2 shows the efficiency comparison results between *DSA* (Data Structure Analysis) algorithm [17] and *FP* algorithm on function pointer analysis. *DSA* algorithm is a context-sensitive pointer analysis algorithm developed on LLVM by Chris Lattner. It can reach the product level analysis efficiency and is used as the basic algorithm in some sub-projects on LLVM [7,16].

The *Time(s)* column and the *Precision* column of Table 2 separately show the time analysis results and the accuracy analysis results of *DSA* algorithm and *FP* algorithm.

For the *Time(s)* column, taking the diction-1.10 program as an example, the analysis time of *DSA* algorithm is 0.038s. For the same command to run the program, the analysis time of *FP* algorithm is 0.001s, advanced 38 times than *DSA* algorithm. From Table 2, we can conclude that the analysis speed of *FP*

Table 2. Comparison of the analysis time and accuracy between DSA and FP algorithm

Benchmark	Time(s)			Precision								
					DSA				FP			
	DSA	FP	DSA/FP	ind.	refs	refs/ind.	min.	max.	refs	refs/ind.	min.	max.
diction-1.10	0.038	0.001	38.0	5	5	1	1	1	5	1	1	1
gdbm-1.8.3	0.101	0.006	16.8	1	0	0	0	0	0	0	0	0
gzip-1.6	0.163	0.003	54.3	4	16	4	1	7	14	3.50	1	6
less-444	0.573	0.014	40.9	5	73	14.60	0	20	60	12	0	15
minicom-2.7	0.332	0.007	47.4	5	75	15	15	15	10	2	2	2
bash-4.3	9.254	0.135	68.5	46	3505	76.19	0	167	73	1.59	0	22
dgesvd.c	0.297	0.006	49.5	64	66	1.03	1	2	64	1	1	1
clapack	66.274	2.578	25.7	231	8196	35.48	0	36	360	2.42	0	7

algorithm is very efficient. With respect to the *DSA* algorithm, the minimum speedup is 16.8× and the maximum is 68.5×. When dealing with the clapack library with more than 500,000 lines of source code, *FP* algorithm takes only about 2.5 seconds. For other test programs, the cost time is all less than one second.

For the *Precision* column, taking the minicom-2.7 program as an example, the "ind." has the value of 5 which means that the number of function pointers is 5 in the source code. The "refs" of *DSA* has the value of 75 and it represents that the number of possible referred functions of the five function pointers determined by the *DSA* algorithm is 75 and the average number of the referred functions is 15 (represented by "refs/ind."). Among them, the minimum value of the referred functions (represented by "min.") is 15 and so is the maximum value (represented by "max."). For the results of *FP* algorithm, the value of "refs" is 10, indicating that the total number of possible functions that may be referenced by the five function pointers is 10. The average number of functions referenced by each function pointer is 2. The minimum and maximum number of referred functions is both 2. We can see that for the minicom-2.7 program *FP* algorithm performs better than *DSA* algorithm in precision. With further analysis, we find that the referred functions of the five pointer functions in minicom-2.7 are the same both for the *DSA* algorithm and *FP* algorithm. The analysis result for *DSA* algorithm shows that the referred function set of each pointer contains: {dopath, do_output, kb_handler,namecmpr, timecmpr, udcatch, doproto, doserial, domodem, donamsave, vdodflsave, get_alrm, shjump, change_size, hangup}. Each string in the set represents a function. For the *FP* algorithm, the set of the referred functions contains: {do_output, kb_handler}.

Combined with the results of the *DSA* algorithm and *FP* algorithm, we resolve the source code of minicom-2.7 program by hand and obtain that the minicom-2.7 program use the function pointers all in "vt100.c", distributed in the function of vt_init, v_termout, state1 and dec_mode. In the source code of "vt100.c", there are two global function pointers, vt_keyb and termout, and these two function pointers are used for 10 times. We can see from the source code that, the referred function of the vt_keyb function pointer at runtime in "vt100.c" is kb_handler, and the referred function of the termout is do_output. It can be seen that, although the *FP* algorithm does not achieved the accurate results, it still improves a lot with respect to the *DSA* algorithm.

In Table 2, some benchmarks (e.g. gdbm-1.8.3) have 0 value in "min.", indicating that the minimum number of referred functions of the function pointer is 0. This occurrence is because the source code does not have enough context to analyse this function pointer or in the source code the function pointer is always assigned to NULL. Combining the results in Table 2 with resolving source code by hand, we can conclude that the *DSA* algorithm analyses two test programs with accuracy, the diction-1.10 and the gdbm-1.8.3, and the *FP* algorithm has three, the diction-1.10, the gdbm-1.8.3 and the dgesvd.c. For other benchmarks, analysis results of the *FP* algorithm are much better compared with *DSA* algorithm.

5.2 Complexity Analysis

We further analyse the complexity of the two algorithms in this section. The *DSA* algorithm is divided into three analysis processes, the intra-procedural process, the bottom-up and top-down analysis processes. The time complexity of intra-procedural process is $O(n * a(n))$. n represents the instruction number of LLVM IR. $a(n)$ is the average time for analysis of each instruction. The *DSA* analysis algorithm will traverse instructions in the intra-procedural process and gradually build a map called DS. The inter-procedural process is to replicate and merge DS maps based on the call relations. The time complexity of the bottom-up process of *DSA* algorithm analysis is $O(fcl + ls^2)$, where f stands for the number of function, c represents the number of callees, s denotes the SCC number in functions and l represents the replication and merger time of DS maps. The top-down analysis process has the same time complexity as the bottom-up analysis.

FP analysis algorithm is also divided into three parts: global variable analysis, intra-procedural analysis and inter-procedural analysis. The time complexity of the global variable analysis is $O(ga(g))$, where g represents the number of the global instructions in LLVM IR and $a(g)$ denotes the average analysis time for each instruction. The time complexity of intra-procedural analysis is $O(n_f a(n_f))$, which is related with the instruction number of the LLVM IR. n_f stands for the number of instructions that satisfy definitions defined in Fig 1 and $a(n_f)$ represents the average analysis time for each instruction. Known from Table 1, in almost all practical applications, the function pointer calls occupy only a small part of the total calls, so the number of instructions associated with it also occupies a very small proportion of the total instructions. Based on this, though the intra-procedural analysis of *FP* analysis algorithm and the *DSA* analysis both have linear time complexity, the number of instructions handled in this stage by *FP* analysis algorithm is much smaller than the *DSA* algorithm. The inter-procedural analysis of *FP* algorithm only contains the bottom-up analysis. It has the time complexity of $O(fct_c)$. f and c shares the same meaning consistent with symbols in *DSA* algorithm. t_c represents the combined time with contextual information when performing function summary analysis. In addition, from the inter-procedural analysis in Fig 4, we know that the function summary analysis of a function should be carried out again only when it is a callee and its summary state is μ_p. The condition for a μ_p function summary is that its corresponding function has function pointer type parameters. Thus *FP* algorithm can get context sensitivity only by dealing with function summaries with the μ_p state. The optimization also improves the analysis speed of *FP* algorithm.

6 Related Work

The construction and application of the function call graph has been hot for a long time. In addition to its significance in security area, it also plays an important role in the software understanding and optimization. Hung [20] constructed function call graph for the embedded client code of the dynamic web applications to help programmers have a better understanding of the code. Murali [2] used the function call graph to prefetch instructions to improve the efficiency of database application. Thorsten [14] introduced function call graph to help programmers better understand and edit the unknown code. Bohnet [5] used the function call graph to locate featured codes in the software.

Associated with the call graph construction, the analysis of function pointers also has a long research history. Cheng [6] performed case studies on SPECint92 and SPECint95 benchmarks. Results show that the construction of the function call graph is an inter-procedural pointer analysis problem. Antoniol [3] and Milanova [18] did comprehensive study about the impact of function pointer on the call graph construction for C program. Results show that the use of function pointer will greatly influence the structure of function call graph. In addition, when constructing inter-procedural data flow diagram, we should also consider the influence brought by the impact of the function pointer [19].

7   Conclusion

This paper proposes an algorithm called *FP* algorithm to analyse function pointer. It can help to improve the analysis speed by reducing the range of pointers (i.e. limit to function pointers) and optimizing the analysis process. In order to maintain the balance of the speed and the accuracy of the analysis, it introduces the SCC-level flow-sensitive and context-sensitive techniques. Experiments show that *FP* algorithm is very efficient when applied in practical C program analysis. We conclude that *FP* algorithm can be used in function pointer related applications to accelerate the speed and improve the accuracy. Compared with costly methods, *FP* algorithm has more practical value.

Acknowledgments. This work was supported in part by the National Natural Science Foundation of China under Grant No. 61170018, the National High Technology Research and Development 863 Program of China under Grant No. 2012AA010901. Also, special thanks to Wei Shi for her valuable comments in preliminary versions of this work.

References

1. Symantec Corp.: 2014 internet security threat report. Technical Report, Volume 19 (April 2014), www.symantec.com
2. Annavaram, M., Patel, J.M., Davidson, E.S.: Call graph prefetching for database applications. ACM Trans. Comput. Syst. 21(4), 412–444 (2003)
3. Antoniol, G., Calzolari, F., Tonella, P.: Impact of function pointers on the call graph. In: 3rd CSMR European Conference on Software Maintenance and Reengineering, CSMR 1999, p. 51. IEEE Computer Society, Washington, DC (1999)
4. Atkinson, D.C.: Accurate call graph extraction of programs with function pointers using type signatures. In: 11th APSEC Asia-Pacific Software Engineering Conference, pp. 326–335. IEEE Computer Society, Washington, DC (2004)

5. Bohnet, J., Döllner, J.: Visual exploration of function call graphs for feature location in complex software systems. In: 2006 ACM Symposium on Software Visualization, SoftVis 2006, pp. 95–104. ACM, New York (2006)

6. Cheng, B.-C., Hwu, W.-m.: An empirical study of function pointers using spec benchmarks. In: Carter, L., Ferrante, J. (eds.) LCPC 1999. LNCS, vol. 1863, pp. 490–493. Springer, Heidelberg (2000)

7. Dhurjati, D., Kowshik, S., Adve, V.: SAFECode: Enforcing alias analysis for weakly typed languages. In: ACM SIGPLAN Conference on Programming Language Design and Implementation, PLDI 2006, pp. 144–157. ACM, New York (2006)

8. Endre, H., Istvn, F., kos, K., Judit, J., Tibor, G.: General flow-sensitive pointer analysis and call graph construction. In: Proceedings of the Estonian, vol. 11(4), Academy of Sciences (December 2005)

9. Faruki, P., Laxmi, V., Gaur, M.S., Vinod, P.: Mining control flow graph as api call-grams to detect portable executable malware. In: Proceedings of the Fifth International Conference on Security of Information and Networks, SIN 2012, pp. 130–137. ACM, New York (2012)

10. Gascon, H., Yamaguchi, F., Arp, D., Rieck, K.: Structural detection of android malware using embedded call graphs. In: Proceedings of the 2013 ACM Workshop on Artificial Intelligence and Security, AISec 2013, pp. 45–54. ACM, New York (2013)

11. Hu, X., Chiueh, T.-c., Shin, K.G.: Large-scale malware indexing using function-call graphs. In: 16th CCS ACM Conference on Computer and Communications Security, pp. 611–620. ACM, New York (2009)

12. Huang, B., Ling, X., Wu, G.: Field-sensitive function pointer analysis using field propagation for state graph extraction. JSW 8(7), 1592–1603 (2013)

13. Jang, J.-W., Woo, J., Yun, J., Kim, H.K.: Mal-netminer:malware classification based on social network analysis of call graph. In: 23rd WWW Companion International Conference on World Wide Web Companion, pp. 731–734. Republic and Canton of Geneva, Switzerland (2014); International World Wide Web Conferences Steering Committee

14. Karrer, T., Krämer, J.-P., Diehl, J., et al.: Stacksplorer:call graph navigation helps increasing code maintenance efficiency. In: 24th UIST Annual ACM Symposium on User Interface Software and Technology, pp. 217–224. ACM, New York (2011)

15. Lattner, C., Adve, V.: LLVM: A compilation framework for lifelong program analysis & transformation. In: International Symposium on Code Generation and Optimization: Feedback-directed and Runtime Optimization, CGO 2004, p. 75. IEEE Computer Society, Washington, DC (2004)

16. Lattner, C., Adve, V.: Automatic pool allocation: Improving performance by controlling data structure layout in the heap. SIGPLAN Not. 40(6), 129–142 (2005)

17. Lattner, C., Lenharth, A., Adve, V.: Making context-sensitive points-to analysis with heap cloning practical for the real world. In: ACM SIGPLAN Conference on Programming Language Design and Implementation, PLDI 2007, pp. 278–289. ACM, New York (2007)

18. Milanova, A., Rountev, A., Ryder, B.G.: Precise call graph construction in the presence of function pointers. In: 2nd SCAM IEEE International Workshop on Source Code Analysis and Manipulation, SCAM 2002, p. 155. IEEE Computer Society, Washington, DC (2002)

19. Robert Muth and Saumya Debray. On the complexity of function pointer may-alias analysis. Technical report, Tucson, AZ, USA (1996)

20. Nguyen, H.V., Kästner, C., Nguyen, T.N.: Building call graphs for embedded client-side code in dynamic web applications. In: Proceedings of the 22Nd ACM SIGSOFT International Symposium on Foundations of Software Engineering, FSE 2014, pp. 518–529. ACM, New York (2014)
21. Zhao, J., Nagarakatte, S., Milo, M.K., Zdancewic, S.: Formalizing the LLVM intermediate representation for verified program transformations. In: 39th POPL ACM SIGPLAN-SIGACT Symposium on Principles of Programming Languages, pp. 427–440. ACM, New York (2012)

Accelerating RSA with Fine-Grained Parallelism Using GPU

Yang Yang[1,2,3], Zhi Guan[1,2,3,*], Huiping Sun[2,3,4], and Zhong Chen[1,2,3]

[1] Institute of Software, School of EECS, Peking University, China
[2] MoE Key Lab of High Confidence Software Technologies (PKU)
[3] MoE Key Lab of Network and Software Security Assurance (PKU)
[4] School of Software and Microelectronics, Peking University, China
{yangyang,guanzhi,chen}@infosec.pku.edu.cn
sunhp@ss.pku.edu.cn

Abstract. RSA is a public key cryptography widely used for end-to-end authentication and key exchange in various Internet protocols, such as SSL and TLS. Compared with symmetric cryptography, the cryptographic operations in RSA is much more time consuming. This brings pressure on performance to service providers using secure protocols, and hinders these protocols from being more widely used. Graphics Processing Units (GPUs) are increasingly used for intensive data parallelism general purpose computing. GPUs often provide better throughput than CPUs at the same cost. In this paper, we propose a new approach to parallelize Montgomery multiplication under the Single Instruction Multiple Thread (SIMT) threading model of GPUs, and construct a parallel RSA implementation based on this approach, combining with other optimization techniques both in the algorithmic level and implementation level. The performance evaluation shows our RSA implementation achieves a record-breaking latency for RSA decryption implementations on GPUs: 2.6 ms for RSA-1024 and 6.5 ms for RSA-2048. The peak throughtput of decryptions per second of our implementation reaches 5,244 for RSA-2048 and 34,981 for RSA-1024 respectively, which is much faster than existing integer-based implementations. The peak throughput of our implementation is slightly slower than the fastest floating-point based implementation, while the latency of our implementation is 3 times faster.

Keywords: RSA, GPGPU, CUDA, Montgomery Multiplication, CRT.

1 Introduction

Public key cryptography provides fundamental cryptographic functions for secure protocols and cryptosystems, including authentication, encryption, digital signature generation, etc. The RSA algorithm[17] is a well-known public-key cryptography widely used in various Internet protocols, including SSL (Security Socket Layer) and TLS (Transport Layer Security) which are de-facto standard

---

* Corresponding author.

© Springer International Publishing Switzerland 2015
J. Lopez and Y. Wu (Eds.): ISPEC 2015, LNCS 9065, pp. 454–468, 2015.
DOI: 10.1007/978-3-319-17533-1_31

protocols for transport layer communication. In these protocols, RSA is used to perform end-to-end authentication and key exchange when establishing the connection. Unlike symmetric cryptography, public key cryptographic operations are much more time consuming, over 90% of the time in cryptographic operations was spent on the RSA key exchange according to the study[21]. At the meantime, the RSA key length required to secure internet domains has increased from 1024 bits to 2048 bits since 2013 according to NIST recommendations[4]. This brings much more impact on performance of internet servers that need to handle thousands of connections per second, as it is only possible to perform about 1000 RSA-2048 decryptions per second on a state-of-the-art CPU core. This is a key reason that only a small fraction of internet services involving critical user information employ SSL and TLS to protect their internet transmission, such as online banking, mail, user authentication, etc, leaving other services which also manage various user private information unprotected[2]. In this case, finding a way to accelerate RSA computations may facilitates the employment of secure protocols to a wider range of internet services.

Graphics Processing Unit (GPU) has been proved as a viable choice for high data parallelism computations. GPU provides a much greater throughput than that provides by CPU of the same level [1]. GPU was designed to deal with graphics processing as it name suggests at first, and researchers found it to be appropriate for intensive parallel computing before long. The presence of Compute Unified Device Architecture (CUDA)[3] and OpenCL [2] finally made developers be able to exploit the great power of GPU on general purpose computing[3]. Lots of algorithms have been ported to GPU platform and achieve a much higher throughput when running on GPUs[11]. Lots of researches have been done on accelerating various cryptography on GPU, including AES[12][19], RSA[8][15], ECC[5], etc. It is straightforward to parallelize RSA coarsely by performing a modular exponentiation serially in each thread. This method is easy to implement, while hard to make full use of computation resources of GPU: a) A GPU thread runs tens of times slower than a CPU thread, therefore a serial program often has a much larger latency running on a GPU than running on a CPU of the same level. For example, a fully optimized serial RSA implementation takes about 70 ms to complete an RSA-1024 decryption on a single thread[15]. b) It is necessary to allocate tens of words of registers and shared memory for intermediate result in a thread for a serial RSA program. Since the number of threads allowed to run concurrently in a SM is limited by the resources allocated to each thread, such as the amount of registers and shared memory, etc, it is difficult to assign the serial program to sufficient number of GPU threads to make full use of the processors. As a result, it is important to exploit the fine-grained parallelism within the algorithm for an RSA implementation on GPUs.

In this paper, we propose a parallel Montgomery multiplication implementation that exploits the fine-grained parallelism of the algorithm, and a high performance parallel RSA implementation for GPU is constructed based on

---

[1] http://en.wikipedia.org/wiki/List_of_Nvidia_graphics_processing_units
[2] https://www.khronos.org/registry/cl/

it, combined with various optimization techniques on both algorithmic level and implementation level, including Chinese Remainder Theorem (CRT), constant length non-zero window (CLNW) method, and the warp shuffle functions recently proposed in CUDA Kepler architecture, etc. Because of these improvements and optimizations, the performance of our implementation has a significant increase compared to existing works. The performance evaluation is conducted on a mid-end GT 750m GPU for the mobile platform. Our implementation achieves a record-breaking latency of 2.6 ms for a single RSA-1024 decryption, and 6.5 ms for a single 2048-bit RSA decryption, which are both much faster than the fastest existing RSA implementations on GPUs. The throughput of our implementation reaches about 34,981 RSA-1024 decryptions per second and 5,244 RSA-2048 decryptions per second, which are both faster than the fastest existing integer-based RSA implementation, and comparable with the fastest floating-point-based RSA implementation.

The rest of the paper is organized as follows. In section 2, we introduce related works on accelerating RSA on GPUs. In section 3, we give a brief introduction to the background of CUDA and RSA algorithm. In section 4, we explain how we parallelize the Montgomery multiplication at a fine-grained level under SIMT threading model. In section 5, we give details of our proposed RSA implementation. In section 6, we evaluate the performance of our RSA implementation and compared the result with that of other works. Finally, we conclude the paper in section 7.

2   Related Works

Lots of existing researches have demonstrated the viability to use GPU to accelerate asymmetric cryptography. Moss et al. presented the first parallel RSA implementation on an NVIDIA 7800 GTX GPU[14]. They used residue number system (RNS) to represent big integers and implemented 1024-bit modular exponentiation with OpenGL. Their implementation has a long latency and is only relatively efficient when computing a large number of modular exponentiations concurrently. Szerwinski et al presented an RSA implementation with CUDA framework on an NVIDIA 8800 GTS GPU[18]. They implemented both Montgomery and RNS methods version modular exponentiation. The performance of their implementation is up to 813 1024-bit decryptions per second, while the latency is longer than 6 seconds. Harrison et al. improved both throughput and latency of existing work using both Montgomery Coarsely Integrated Operand Scanning (CIOS) method and parallel RNS method[7]. Their parallel implementation had a shorter latency while their CIOS serial method had a higher throughput when the number of decryptions performed concurrently is large. Neves et al. used a single GPU thread to perform a modular exponentiation using different serial Montgomery multiplication methods[15]. They achieved a throughput of 41,426 modular exponentiations per second and a latency of 70ms on an NVIDIA GTX 260 GPU. They also reported that serial Finely Integrated Operand Scanning(FIOS) method performed slightly better in their experiment.

Jang et al. proposed a parallel Separated Operand Scanning (SOS) method and combined it with CRT method[8]. They achieved a latency of 3.8 ms for 1024-bit RSA and 13.83 ms for 2048-bit RSA decryption, and a throughput of 74,732 op/s for 1024-bit RSA and 12,044 op/s for 2048-bit RSA, on a NVIDIA GTX 580 GPU. Recently, Zheng et al. proposed a double precision floating point based multi-limbs parallel Montgomery multiplication[22]. They exploited the floating point computing power of GPU and achieved a throughput at 38,975 operations per second. However, their implementation is much more complex than integer based implementations and hard to be generalized.

3 Background

3.1 CUDA Architecture

CUDA is a general purpose parallel computing platform and programming model invented by NVIDIA[3] for GPUs. In an abstract view, CUDA defines the threading model, calling conventions and memory hierarchy for CUDA programmers. CUDA applications following the model scale automatically on different CUDA GPUs. In a physical view, CUDA defines the architecture of Streaming Multiprocessors(SMs), amount of memories in each level of hierarchy, and other implementation details. Compared with CPU, GPU spend more transistors on data processing rather than data caching and flow control. This makes GPU be well suited for intensive, highly data-parallel computations, and also makes a single thread on GPU runs serial code much slower than that on CPU.

CUDA GPU follows a Single Instruction Multiple Thread (SIMT) threading model. In this model, thread is the basic computation and resource allocation unit that executes the kernel program, which is the code runs on GPU. Threads are grouped into blocks, and blocks are grouped into a grid. All threads within a grid execute the same code of the kernel until finish. Block is also a computation and resource allocation unit, as all threads in the same block share a block of shared memory, and their running status can be synchronized with synchronization instructions. The amount of registers, shared memory and threads are limited in a block, and the limitation varies according to the CUDA version code. Threads in a block are partitioned into warps by the number of 32. All threads within a warp run concurrently, and each path of the divergence is executed in serial. Threads in a block can communicate with shared memory and synchronization mechanism, and threads within a warp can also access registers of others directly with shuffle instructions since CUDA 3.x[1]. The number of blocks in a grid and the number of threads in a block, along with the amount of shared memory and the stream used to launch the kernel are configured by programmers during the kernel invocation. A stream is a sequence of commands that execute in order. Cuda applications manage concurrency through streams, and the execution of different streams may overlap.

The memory hierarchy of CUDA includes registers, shared memory, caches, global memory and host memory. Registers are on-chip transistors having the best latency and throughput. Shared memory and L1 Cache are also on-chip and fast, while the bank conflicts should be avoided[3]. L2 cache is also used to cache accesses to local and global memory and shared by all multiprocessors. Local memory and global memory are much slower while has a much larger amount. Constant memory and texture memory are read-only memories optimized for different usages. The leverage of memory hierarchy should be fully considered to maximize the performance.

3.2   RSA and Modular Exponentiation

RSA[17] is a widely used asymmetric cryptography which is constructed upon the practical difficulty of factoring the product of two large prime numbers. The generation of an RSA key pair requires the generation of two distinct large prime numbers p and q randomly. Let $n = pq$ and $\phi(n) = \phi(p)\phi(q) = (p-1)(q-1)$, where ϕ is Euler's totient function[3]. The public key exponent e is chosen as a small integer which is co-prime with $\phi(n)$ and has a small Hamming weight. The private key exponent d is computed as $d = e^{-1} \mod \phi(n)$. The public key consists of n and e, which can be sent to others for encryptions. The private key consists of n and d, which should be kept secret for decryptions. To encrypt a message M, it should be first mapped into a integer m, then the ciphertext c is calculated as

$$c = m^e \mod n$$

After receiving the ciphertext, the plaintext can be recovered by computing m as

$$m = c^d \mod n$$

and mapping m to M in a reverse way. The bit length of n should be large enough to achieve a sufficient secure level, such as 1024 bits or 2048 bits.

Modular multiplication $c = ab \mod n$ is the basic operation of modular exponentiations. A school book method that performs a trial division after a naïve multiplication is expensive for both software and hardware implementations and hard to be parallelized. Instead, Montgomery multiplication is often used in high performance implementations of large modular exponentiations since it allows modular multiplications without trial division[13]. Let $\bar{a} = aR \mod n$ be the montgomeritized form, where n is the modulus and R is co-prime with n, then $\bar{c} = \overline{ab} = \overline{ab}R^{-1} \mod n$ can be computed as Algorithm 1 shows. Since $n = pq$ where p and q are large primes, we can choose R as 2^{sw} where w is the bit size of the word and s is the number of words required to hold n. In this case, R is co-prime with n, and the last division can be performed as a words shifting efficiently. Let $\text{MonPro}(\bar{a}, \bar{b})$ be the Montgomery multiplication between $\bar{a}$ and $\bar{b}$, then the montgomeritized form of a is computed as

$$\bar{a} = \text{MonPro}(a, R^2)$$

and converting from the montgomeritized form is computed as

$$a = \text{MonPro}(\bar{a}, 1)$$

---

[3] http://en.wikipedia.org/wiki/Euler%27s_totient_function

Because of the conversion needed between the montgomeritized form and the normal form, the Montgomery multiplication is efficient for a large number of modular multiplications performed successively, such as a modular exponentiation, rather than a single modular multiplication.

Algorithm 1. Montgomery Multiplication Algorithm

Input: $\bar{a}, \bar{b}, n, R, n' = -R^{-1} \mod n$
Output: $\bar{a} \cdot \bar{b} \cdot R^{-1} \mod n$
  1. $T \leftarrow \bar{a} \cdot \bar{b}$
  2. $M \leftarrow T \cdot n' \mod R$
  3. $T \leftarrow (T + M \cdot n)/R$
  4. **if** $T \geq n$ **then**
  5.   **return** $T - n$
  6. **else**
  7.   **return** T
  8. **end if**

The asymptotic time complexity of Montgomery multiplication based modular exponentiation is $O(n^3)$, which means doubling the size of the input takes about 8 times running time. On the other hand, reducing the size of the input to half also reduces the running time to about $\frac{1}{8}$. Based on this observation, Chinese Remainder Theorem (CRT) is often used to speed up the computation[16]. For each modular exponentiation $m = c^d \mod n$, it can be divided into 2 separate modular exponentiations with CRT as

$$m_1 = c^{d \mod (p-1)} \mod p$$

$$m_2 = c^{d \mod (q-1)} \mod q$$

then the two part of results can be combined using the mixed-radix conversion (MRC) algorithm as

$$m = m_1 + [(m_2 - m_1) \cdot (p^{-1} \mod q) \mod q] \cdot p$$

It can be estimated that the CRT based algorithm will be about 8 times faster if the two separate modular exponentiations can be computed in parallel[9].

4 Montgomery Multiplication Parallelization

In this work, we represent integers in the positional number system with radix 2^w, where w is the number of bits in a word. For an integer m, denoting k to be the number of bits required to represent m, namely that $k \leftarrow \lceil \log_2^n \rceil$. Then it requires at least s words to represent m, where $s \leftarrow \lceil \frac{k}{w} \rceil$. It is common to hold the s words of the integer m in an array in the memory in any architecture. Words of m are referred as **limbs**, and the jth limb is denoted as m_j. For a parallel

---

Algorithm 2. Integrated Montgomery Multiplication Algorithm

Input: $\bar{a}, \bar{b}, n, R, n' = -R^{-1} \mod n, n'_0 \leftarrow n' \mod 2^{w'}, w' = lw, 0 < l \leq s$
Output: $\bar{a} \cdot \bar{b} \cdot R^{-1} \mod n$

1. $T \leftarrow 0$
2. **for** $i \leftarrow 1$ to s **do**
3. $T \leftarrow T + \bar{a} \cdot \bar{b}_i$
4. $m \leftarrow T_0 \cdot n'_0 \mod 2^{w'}$
5. $T \leftarrow (T + m \cdot n)/2^{w'}$
6. **end for**
7. **if** $T \geq n$ **then**
8.   **return** $T - n$
9. **else**
10.   **return** T
11. **end if**

GPU program, it could also be placed in registers of consecutive d threads, with every thread deals with $\lceil \frac{s}{d} \rceil$ limbs.

The Separate Operand Scanning (SOS) method requires $2s + 1$ words of temporary space. Improvements can be made by integrating the multiplication and reduction steps iteratively once for one or multiple limbs, as shown in Algorithm 2[6], where $w' = lw$ and $l, 0 < l \leq s$ is a positive integer. When $l = s$, Algorithm 2 degenerates to Algorithm 1. CIOS (Coarsely Integrated Operand Scanning) method, FIOS (Finely Integrated Operand Scanning) method, and FIPS (Finely Integrated Product Scanning) method all derives from this algorithm[10]. The time complexity of Algorithm 2 and Algorithm 1 are both $O(s^2)$, while the former requires only $s+3$ words of temporary space and the structure is more tight. We employ the following strategies to parallelize the Algorithm 2:

1. Computes one or consecutive multiple limbs of multi-precision multiplications and additions in every threads in parallel.
2. Postpones and merges the carry processing to minimize the inter-threads communication.
3. Computes redundantly if necessary to reduce the divergence between threads.

Suppose d threads are allocated to process one decryption, the parallelized algorithm executed in the jth threads is listed in Algorithm 3, and l limbs are processed in every thread. The pseudo function used in the algorithm is defined as follows:

mul.lo(a, b): Return $a \cdot b \mod 2^w$, where a and b are both non-negative integers less than $2^{w'}$.
mad.lo(a, b, c): Return $(a \cdot b) \mod 2^w + c$, where a, b and c are all non-negative integers less than $2^{w'}$.
mad.hi(a, b, c): Return $(a \cdot b)/2^w + c$, where a, b and c are all non-negative integers less than $2^{w'}$.
any(pred): Return **true** if the value of **pred** in any limb is true.

Every **mul.lo**, **mad.lo** and **mad.hi** operation working on $2^{w'}$ operands consists l^2 basic multiplication operations working on 2^w operands. The time complexity of Algorithm 3 is $O(dl^2) = O(\frac{s}{l} \cdot l^2) = O(sl)$. It is obvious that the algorithm degenerates to a serial algorithm When $l = s$.

Algorithm 3. Parallel Montgomery multiplication algorithm for limb j.

Input: $\bar{a}, \bar{b}, n, d, R = 2^{dw'}, n_0' = (R^{-1} \bmod n) \bmod 2^{w'}, j \in \{0, \ldots, d-1\}, w' = lw, 0 < l \le s$

Output: $\bar{a} \cdot \bar{b} \cdot R^{-1} \bmod n$

1. $u_j \leftarrow 0$
2. $v_j \leftarrow 0$
3. **for** $i = 0$ to $d - 1$ **do**
4. $\quad (u_j', v_j) \leftarrow \mathrm{mad.lo.cc}(a_j, b_i, v_j)$
5. $\quad u_j \leftarrow u_j + u_j'$
6. $\quad m_j \leftarrow \mathrm{mul.lo}(u_j, n_0')$
7. $\quad m_j \leftarrow m_0$
8. $\quad (u_j', v_j) \leftarrow \mathrm{mad.lo.cc}(n_i, m_j, v_j)$
9. $\quad u_j \leftarrow u_j + u_j'$
10. $\quad v_j \leftarrow v_{j+1 \bmod d}$
11. $\quad (u_j, v_j) \leftarrow u_j + v_j$
12. $\quad (u_j', v_j) \leftarrow \mathrm{mad.hi.cc}(a_j, b_i, v_j)$
13. $\quad u_j \leftarrow u_j + u_j'$
14. $\quad (u_j', v_j) \leftarrow \mathrm{mad.hi.cc}(n_i, m_j, v_j)$
15. $\quad u_j \leftarrow u_j + u_j'$
16. **end for**
17. $c_j \leftarrow u_j$
18. **while** any(u_j) **do**
19. $\quad u_j \leftarrow u_{j-1 \bmod d}$
20. $\quad$ **if** i = 0 **then**
21. $\quad\quad u_j \leftarrow 0$
22. $\quad$ **end if**
23. $\quad (u_j, v_j) \leftarrow v_j + u_j$
24. $\quad c_j \leftarrow c_j + u_j$
25. **end while**
26. $t_j \leftarrow v_j$
27. $c_j \leftarrow c_{d-1}$
28. **if** c_j **then**
29. $\quad T \leftarrow T - n$
30. **else**
31. $\quad$ **return** T
32. **end if**

A brief explanation to Algorithm 3 is given as follows: two variables v_j and u_j are used in each thread. The former is used as an accumulator, and the latter is used to hold the carry. Both variables could be allocated in registers for fast access. Their values are initialized to 0. Each iteration begins with accumulating the lower word of $a_j \cdot b_i$ to v_j in line 4. Then the value of m_j is calculated. However, only the m_0 in thread 0 is needed, so it is broadcasted to all threads in line 7. Then the lower word of $n_j \cdot m_j$ is accumulated on v_j in line 8. At this time the least significant limb of $T + m \cdot n$ as shown in Algorithm 2 is produced and stored in v_0 in thread 0, and its value must be 0[6]. Then it is safe to shift the accumulator value to the thread with a lower index and set v_{d-1} to 0 in line 10. Meanwhile, the shifting makes the carry values be shifted to the right place, so we add the accumulator and the carry together in each thread and generate the new carry value in line 11. Then the iteration is finished by accumulating the higher word of $a_j \cdot b_i$ and $n_j \cdot m$ on v_j, without propagating the carries. The integrated multiplications and reductions are completed after the loop ends. Then we finally process carries by calculating $(u_j, v_j) \leftarrow v_j + u_{j-1}$ iteratively until the carry u_j in all threads equals to zero. This process takes $s-1$ iterations in the worst situation, while in practice it takes 1 or 2 iterations at most. c_j counts the number of carries generated in the jth thread when merging the accumulators and the carries between line 17–25. The final subtraction is performed if $c_{d-1} > 0$. We use incomplete reduction[20] here to avoid the word-by-word comparisons and simplify the algorithm.

5   RSA Implementation

In this section, we first give a overview of the design of the RSA implementation, then present the implementation details and optimizations target at CUDA 3.x platform and above.

5.1   Design Overview

The target application scenario of our implementation is to decrypt multiple messages with a single private key. This scenario is common such as an Internet domain handles thousands of SSL connections or generates digital signatures in parallel. Under this condition, the divergence handling is simplified during modular exponentiations. The input for the k-bit RSA decryption procedure is a message represented as a k-bit multi-precision integer $c, c < n$, where n is the modulus in key pair. $c_1 \leftarrow c \bmod p$ and $c_2 \leftarrow c \bmod q$ are first calculated in the CRT method, namely that transforms c into residue number system whose base is p and q. Then $m_1 \leftarrow c_1^{d \bmod p}$ and $m_2 \leftarrow c_2^{d \bmod q}$ are computed using our proposed parallel Montgomery multiplication method. Finally, m is computed by combining m_1 and m_2 by MRC algorithm The overview of the computation procedure is shown in Equation 1.

$$c \Rightarrow \left\{ \begin{array}{l} c_1 \leftarrow c \bmod p \Rightarrow m_1 \leftarrow c_1^{d \bmod p} \\ \\ c_2 \leftarrow c \bmod q \Rightarrow m_2 \leftarrow c_2^{d \bmod q} \end{array} \right\}$$
$$\Rightarrow m_1 + [(m_2 - m_1) \cdot (p^{-1} \bmod q) \bmod q] \cdot p$$
$$\Rightarrow m \tag{1}$$

5.2   Implementation and Optimizations

Montgomery Multiplication. We implement the parallel Montgomery multiplication algorithm following Algorithm 3. The values of a, b, n and t are all held in the shared memory during the multiplication. The value of a_j and n_j are preloaded into registers before the loop begins for a better access latency. The values of u and v are held in registers until the loop finishes and the carries are processed. The pseudo function shuffle is implemented using the `shuffle` functions introduced in CUDA 3.x. In this way, few accesses to the shared memory are needed and the register files are intensively used, which leads to faster accesses and fewer bank conflicts.

Adaptive Limbs Selection. It is possible to handle either a single limb or multiple limbs in a thread in the implementation following Algorithm 3. A single-limb implementation fully exploits the fine-grained inner parallelism of Montgomery multiplication. On the other hand, a l-limbs implementation processes l words in each thread and performs a Montgomery multiplication with $d = s/l$ threads. It has been proved that the time complexity of our algorithm is $O(sl)$ running on d threads concurrently. As a result, a single-limb implementation has the lowest time complexity and often leads to a better latency. However, the lower time complexity does not reduce the total number of operations need to be performed, while introduces more communication and synchronization overheads and resource consumptions. As a result, a multiple-limbs implementation often leads to a better throughput when the GPU is fully utilized to perform multiple decryptions in parallel.

To optimize the implementation for both latency and throughput, the single-limb and the two-limbs Montgomery multiplication methods are both implemented and be used to compute modular exponentiations. The implementation employs the single-limb implementation when the batch size is less than a threshold, and the two-limbs implementation is used on the other hand. The threshold is selected through a simple benchmark automatically as the batch size at which the two-limbs implementation outperforms the single-limb implementation. The benchmark is only required to be performed once for a certain platform to select the threshold. We have also tried to handle more than two limbs in a single thread, while the result shows the extra limbs handled in a thread have minor contribution to the performance and make the implementation more complex. This optimization makes the implementation runs fast at various batch sizes.

CLNW. The expected number of modular multiplications for a k-bit modular multiplication is $3k/2$ with the binary square-and-multiply method[9]. The number can be reduced with m-ary or sliding window methods by scanning multiple bits instead of individual bits of the exponent. We employ the constant length non-zero window(CLNW) method in our implementation with the window size 6, which caches 32 intermediate products temporarily and reduces the number of multiplications by 28% approximately for a modular exponentiation instance.

Modular Operation. As shown in Equation 1, there are still 3 time consuming modular operations involved. The Montgomery method is not commonly used for a single modular operation, as it requires the transformation between the normal form and montgomeritized form. However, as the time complexity of our parallel Montgomery multiplication is reduced from $O(s^2)$ of serial version to $O(sl)$, a single modular operation still benefits from Montgomery method compared to the trial division method. As a result, we implement the 3 single modular operations as sequences of Montgomery multiplications.

CRT. The CRT computation is also implemented on GPU in our implementation, as it not only can be paralleled on the task level for a better throughput, but also benefits from our parallel Montgomery multiplication method in a fine-grained level for a shorter latency.

6   Performance Evaluation

In this section, we first conduct experiments to evaluate the performance of our implementation, considering both latency and throughput at various batch size. Then we compare the performance of our implementation with the result from related works. The hardware and software configuration of the experiment platform is listed in Table 1

Table 1. The hardware and software configuration of the experiment platform

CPU	Intel Core i5 3230m at 2.6 GHz
GPU	NVIDIA GT 750m at 967 MHz
OS	Windows 8.1
Tool chain	Visual Studio 2013, CUDA 6.5
OpenSSL	1.0.1f

6.1   Performance Result

Although our RSA implementation supports various key sizes, the performance of RSA-1024 and RSA-2048 decryptions are measured in the experiments respectively. Because these key lengths are most commonly used at the moment, and it's easy to compare the performance with that of related works. The evaluation works as decrypting messages at various batch size and record the latency and the throughput. Table 2 shows the value of the latency at the batch size of 1, and the throughput at the batch size of 1024. Figure 1 shows the variation trend of latency and throughput when the batch size increases.

Table 2. The value of latency at batch size of 1 and throughput at batch size of 1024 of our RSA implementation

Key Size	GPU		CPU	
	Latency(ms)	Throughput(op/s)	Latency(ms)	Throughput(op/s)
RSA-1024	2.6	34,981	0,18 ms	5,556
RSA-2048	6.5	5,244	1.4	714

As shown in Figure 1, the latency of GPU implementation is about an order of magnitude higher than the CPU version when performing only one decryption at a time. However, the throughput of GPU implementation grows as the batch size increases, and the latency stays low until the GPU is fully utilized, while the throughput of CPU implementation stays almost the same. The GPU implementation outperforms the CPU implementation when the batch size is greater than 16 for RSA-1024, and when the batch size is greater than 8 for RSA-2048.

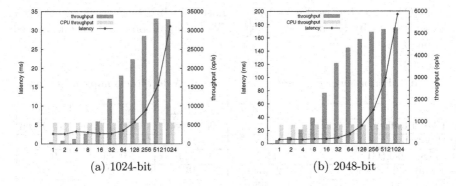

Fig. 1. The performance of our RSA decryption implementation on GT 750m, compared with OpenSSL implementation on i7-2600

The peak throughput of the GPU implementation is over 6 times faster than the throughput of the CPU implementation.

The evaluation result consists with our expectation. First, when performing a single decryption, the CPU implementation is much first than the GPU implementation, since a GPU thread runs much slower than a CPU thread. Second, the throughput of the GPU implementation increases as the batch size increases, while the throughput of the CPU implementation stays almost the same. This is because the GPU implementation is able to utilize the hundreds of computation units in GPU concurrently to perform multiple decryptions in parallel. Third, it is interesting to see that the latency gap to perform a single decryption on GPU and on CPU decreases as the key length increases. This is because RSA-1024 is parallelly computed in $2 \times \frac{512}{32}$ threads, while RSA-2048 is parallelly computed in $2 \times \frac{1024}{32}$ threads. The degree of parallelism of the latter is twice as that of the former.

6.2   Performance Comparison and Discussion

The performance of our implementation is compared with the performance reported from the existing fastest works[15] [8] [22] in this section. The performance results of these works are scaled into our GPU hardware for a fair comparison based on the processing power. Both the latency of a single decryption and the throughput when the GPU is fully utilized are compared. For the latency of a single decryption, the GPU is not fully utilized, therefore we estimate the scale factor as the ratio between the shader frequency of different GPUs, as it is reasonable to assume each implementation spends same instruction count on different GPU platforms. For the throughput when GPU is fully utilized, we estimate the scale factor as the ratio between the overall integer multiplications per second of different GPUs, which is the product of shader clock frequency, integer multiplications per clock on a single SM, and the number of SMs. As only 24-bit multiplication instructions are supported on GPUs supporting CUDA 1.x only, such as GTX 260[15], we follow the estimation in [22] by further adjust their processing capacity by multiplying $(\frac{24}{32})^2$. The comparison result is summarized in Table 3.

Table 3. Performance comparison of different RSA decryption implementation

	Neves et al.[15]	Jang et al.[8]	Zheng et al.[22]	Ours
CUDA Platform	GTX 260	GTX 580	GTX Titan	GT 750m
SM Number	24	14	14	2
Shader Clock(GHz)	1.242	1.544	0.836	0.967
Int Mul/SM (/Clock)	8(24-bit)	16	32	32
Int Mul (G/s)	134(238)	395	375	62
Latency Scaling Factor	1.28	1.60	0.86	1
Throughput Scaling Factor	2.16	6.37	6.04	1
RSA-1024 (ms)	70	3.8	-	2.6
RSA-2048 (ms)	-	13.83	22.47	6.5
RSA-1024(scaled) (ms)	89.6	6.08	-	2.6
RSA-2048(scaled) (ms)	-	22.13	19.32	6.5
RSA-1024 (op/s)	41,426	74,732	-	34,981
RSA-2048 (op/s)	-	12,044	38,975	5,244
RSA-1024(scaled) (op/s)	19,178	11,732	-	34,981
RSA-2048(scaled) (op/s)	-	1,891	6,453	5,244

As shown in Table 3, our implementation has the best latency for both 1024-bit and 2048-bit RSA decryptions. The latency of ours is better then the next fastest implementation by a factor of 134% and 240% after scaled for 1024-bit and 2048-bit RSA respectively. The throughput of our implementation is faster than the existing fastest integer-based implementation by a factor of 82% and 177% after scaled for 1024-bit and 2048-bit RSA respectively. Although our throughput is slower than the fastest floating-point-based implementation by a factor of 27%, our latency is about three times faster.

Compared with existing works, the improvements of performance in our implementation result mainly from our parallelized Montgomery multiplication optimized for SIMT threading model. It enables us to give a tight and efficient implementation of Montgomery multiplication algorithm to utilize the great parallel power of GPU. The use of warp shuffle functions also contributes to the performance improvements a lot, because it speeds up the inter-threads communication, and reduce the usage of the shared memory. The throughput advantage of the floating-point-based implementation mainly results from the combination of the floating-point and the integer processing power together, and the multiple-limbs scheme. In fact, it would be more powerful to combine their work with ours together to make full use of both the integer and floating-point process capability.

7   Conclusion

In this paper, we propose a new approach to parallelize Montgomery multiplication on the CUDA SIMT threading model platform. We elaborate the parallelized Montgomery multiplication algorithm, and implement an RSA cryptosystem on GPU based on it. The performance evaluation on a GT 750m GPU shows our approach achieves a record-breaking latency, which is much better than any existing RSA implementation on GPUs: 2.6 ms for an RSA-1024 decryption and 6.5 ms for an RSA-2048 decryption. The throughput of our approach reaches 34,981 RSA-1024 decryptions per second and 5,244 RSA-2048 decryptions per second, which outperforms the existing fastest integer-based RSA implementation by a factor of 82% and 177% respectively.

SIMD platforms may also benefit from the approach proposed in this paper and achieve a better performance. One of our future works is to adapt this approach to these platforms, including AVX2 instruction set of Intel X86 CPUs, and the upcoming AVX-512 instruction set.

Acknowledgements. This work is supported by National High Technology Research and Development Program of China under Grant No. 2014AA123001.

References

1. NVIDIA kepler-GK110-architecture whitepaper,
   http://www.nvidia.com/object/nvidia-kepler.html
2. Netcrafts SSL survey. Tech. rep. (2013), http://news.netcraft.com/SSL-survey
3. CUDA c programming guide 6.5 (August 2014),
   http://docs.nvidia.com/cuda/cuda-c-programming-guide/
4. Barker, E., Roginsky, A.: Transitions: Recommendation for transitioning the use of cryptographic algorithms and key lengths. NIST Special Publication 800, 131 (2011), http://www.gocs.eu/pages/fachberichte/archiv/075-sp800-131A.pdf
5. Cui, S., Großschädl, J., Liu, Z., Xu, Q.: High-speed elliptic curve cryptography on the NVIDIA GT200 graphics processing unit. In: Huang, X., Zhou, J. (eds.) ISPEC 2014. LNCS, vol. 8434, pp. 202–216. Springer, Heidelberg (2014)
6. Dussé, S.R., Kaliski Jr., B.S.: A cryptographic library for the motorola DSP 56000. In: Damgård, I.B. (ed.) EUROCRYPT 1990. LNCS, vol. 473, pp. 230–244. Springer, Heidelberg (1991)
7. Harrison, O., Waldron, J.: Efficient acceleration of asymmetric cryptography on graphics hardware. In: Preneel, B. (ed.) AFRICACRYPT 2009. LNCS, vol. 5580, pp. 350–367. Springer, Heidelberg (2009)
8. Jang, K., Han, S., Han, S., Moon, S.B., Park, K.: SSLShader: Cheap SSL acceleration with commodity processors. In: NSDI (2011)
9. Koc, C.K.: High-speed RSA implementation. Tech. rep., Technical Report, RSA Laboratories (1994)
10. Koc, E.K., Acar, T.: Analyzing and comparing montgomery multiplication algorithms. IEEE Micro 16, 26–33 (1996)

11. Lee, V.W., Kim, C., Chhugani, J., Deisher, M., Kim, D., Nguyen, A.D., Satish, N., Smelyanskiy, M., Chennupaty, S., Hammarlund, P., Singhal, R., Dubey, P.: Debunking the 100x GPU vs. CPU myth: An evaluation of throughput computing on CPU and GPU. In: Proceedings of the 37th Annual International Symposium on Computer Architecture, ISCA 2010, pp. 451–460. ACM, New York (2010)

12. Manavski, S.A.: CUDA compatible GPU as an efficient hardware accelerator for AES cryptography. In: IEEE International Conference on Signal Processing and Communications, ICSPC 2007, pp. 65–68 (November 2007)

13. Montgomery, P.L.: Modular multiplication without trial division. Mathematics of Computation 44(170), 519–521 (1985)

14. Moss, A., Page, D., Smart, N.P.: Toward acceleration of RSA using 3D graphics hardware. In: Galbraith, S.D. (ed.) Cryptography and Coding 2007. LNCS, vol. 4887, pp. 364–383. Springer, Heidelberg (2007)

15. Neves, S., Araujo, F.: On the performance of GPU public-key cryptography. In: 2011 IEEE International Conference on Application-Specific Systems, Architectures and Processors (ASAP), pp. 133–140 (September 2011)

16. Quisquater, J.-J., Couvreur, C.: Fast decipherment algorithm for RSA public-key cryptosystem. Electronics Letters 18(21), 905–907 (1982)

17. Rivest, R.L., Shamir, A., Adleman, L.: A method for obtaining digital signatures and public-key cryptosystems. Commun. ACM 21(2), 120–126 (1978)

18. Szerwinski, R., Güneysu, T.: Exploiting the power of gPUs for asymmetric cryptography. In: Oswald, E., Rohatgi, P. (eds.) CHES 2008. LNCS, vol. 5154, pp. 79–99. Springer, Heidelberg (2008)

19. Yang, Y., Guan, Z., Zhu, J., Dong, Q., Chen, Z.: Accelerating AES in javaScript with webGL. In: Qing, S., Zhou, J., Liu, D. (eds.) ICICS 2013. LNCS, vol. 8233, pp. 275–287. Springer, Heidelberg (2013)

20. Yanik, T., Savas, E., Koc, C.K.: Incomplete reduction in modular arithmetic. IEE Proceedings Computers and Digital Techniques 149(2), 46–52 (2002)

21. Zhao, L., Iyer, R., Makineni, S., Bhuyan, L.: Anatomy and performance of SSL processing. In: IEEE International Symposium on Performance Analysis of Systems and Software, ISPASS 2005, pp. 197–206 (2005)

22. Zheng, F., Pan, W., Lin, J., Jing, J., Zhao, Y.: Exploiting the floating-point computing power of gPUs for RSA. In: Chow, S.S.M., Camenisch, J., Hui, L.C.K., Yiu, S.M. (eds.) ISC 2014. LNCS, vol. 8783, pp. 198–215. Springer, Heidelberg (2014)

On the Impacts of Mathematical Realization over Practical Security of Leakage Resilient Cryptographic Schemes

Guangjun Fan[1], Yongbin Zhou[2], François-Xavier Standaert[3], and Dengguo Feng[1]

[1] State Key Laboratory of Computer Science, Institute of Software,
Chinese Academy of Sciences, Beijing, China
`guangjunfan@163.com, feng@tca.iscas.ac.cn`
[2] State Key Laboratory of Information Security, Institute of Information Engineering,
Chinese Academy of Sciences, Beijing, China
`zhouyongbin@iie.ac.cn`
[3] ICTEAM/ELEN/Crypto Group, Université catholique de Louvain,
Louvain-la-Neuve, Belgium
`fstandae@uclouvain.be`

Abstract. In real world, in order to transform an abstract and generic cryptographic scheme into actual physical implementation, one usually undergoes two processes: mathematical realization at algorithmic level and physical realization at implementation level. In black-box model (i.e. leakage-free setting), a cryptographic scheme can be mathematically realized without affecting its theoretical security as long as the mathematical components meet the required cryptographic properties. However, up to now, no previous work formally show that whether one can mathematically realize a leakage resilient cryptographic scheme in existent ways without affecting its practical security. Our results give a negative answer to this important question by introducing attacks against several kinds of mathematical realization of a practical leakage resilient cryptographic scheme. To be specific, there may exist a big gap between the theoretical tolerance leakage bits number and the practical tolerance leakage bits number of the same leakage resilient cryptographic scheme if the mathematical components in the mathematical realization are not provably secure in leakage setting.

Keywords: Physical Attacks, Leakage Resilient Cryptography, Mathematical Realization, Physical Realization.

1 Introduction

Countermeasures for protecting against physical attacks (such as the most studied side-channel attacks) are taken on three levels: the software level, the hardware level, and the combination of the above two levels. However, these countermeasures have many issues [2]. In order to solve these pressing issues from the area of practical

© Springer International Publishing Switzerland 2015
J. Lopez and Y. Wu (Eds.): ISPEC 2015, LNCS 9065, pp. 469–484, 2015.
DOI: 10.1007/978-3-319-17533-1_32

security about implementation, Dziembowski et al. firstly proposed one general and theoretical methodology called Leakage Resilient Cryptography (LRC) [2].

In real world, in order to transform an abstract and generic cryptographic scheme into actual physical implementation, one usually undergoes two processes: mathematical realization at algorithmic level and physical realization at implementation level. *Mathematical realization* refers to a process in which an abstract and generic cryptographic scheme is transformed into an exact and specific mathematical scheme (After this process, we say the cryptographic scheme is mathematically realized.). This means that *all* the cryptographic components utilized by the cryptographic scheme are instantiated with exact and specific mathematical components. For example, for a public key encryption scheme based on cycle groups with prime order, the implementor chooses specific mathematical representation of the group elements in this process. Another example is that the implementor chooses AES-128 or 3DES to mathematically realize a cryptographic scheme which uses block ciphers as a building block. *Physical realization* refers to a subsequent process in which any exact and specific mathematical scheme (the output of mathematical realization) is transformed into a physical cryptographic module that runs as a piece of software, or hardware, or combination of both.

For both cryptographic schemes in black-box model and leakage resilient cryptographic schemes, it has turned out that practical security highly depends on the details of the physical realization. For example, the physical cryptanalysis results of the leakage resilient cryptographic scheme in paper [18] do not contradict its theoretical security proof and show that whether the theoretical tolerance leakage bits number can be guaranteed depends on the details of the physical realization.

Motivations. In recent years, in the field of LRC, many leakage models have been proposed. These leakage models are mainly based on two different leakage properties.

"*Only Computation Leaks Information*" There are some leakage models that follow the "*Only Computation Leaks Information*" axiom, which states that memory contents that are not accessed during computation, do not leak [3]. This axiom is regarded as the most representative axiom according to side-channel attacks. Leakage resilient stream cipher [2], practical leakage resilient PRNG [20], and leakage resilient ElGamal encryption scheme [1] follow this axiom are given out.

"*Memory Leakage*" Inspired by [4], Akavia et al. [6] introduced the leakage model of "*security against memory attacks*" where one requires that the scheme remains secure even if the adversary obtains bounded memory leakages about the secret key. Public key encryption schemes under this leakage property were introduced in [7]. *Continuous Memory Leakage* [10,11] extends *Memory Leakage*.

There are some other leakage models, such as *Bounded Retrieval Model* [8,9] and *Auxiliary Input Model* [21,22]. Theoretical security of a leakage resilient cryptographic scheme in these leakage models holds only for physical attacks which *rigorously* fit the claimed leakage model. In this paper, we concentrate on mathematical realization. In black-box model (i.e. leakage-free setting), a cryptographic scheme can be mathematically realized without affecting its theoretical security as long as all the mathematical components in the mathematical realization meet the required cryptographic properties. In leakage setting, we say a leakage resilient cryptographic scheme is practically secure after it is mathematically realized if the practical tolerance leakage bits number equals to the theoretical tolerance leakage bits number even if the adversary knows all the details of the mathematical realization[1] and can obtain leakage bits from any position of all the mathematical components in the mathematical realization by exploiting efficient computable leakage functions (if possible according to the leakage property, e.g. *"Only Computation Leaks Information"* or *"Memory Leakage"*). If a kind of mathematical realization of the leakage resilient cryptographic scheme can guarantee the practical security of the leakage resilient cryptographic scheme, we call this kind of mathematical realization is practically secure for simplicity. However, up to now, no previous work formally show that whether one can mathematically realize a leakage resilient cryptographic scheme in existent ways without affecting its practical security.

In order to answer this important question, we will take the leakage resilient ElGamal encryption scheme instantiated over arbitrary groups of prime order p (where $p - 1$ is not smooth) in the paper [1][2] (i.e. scheme EG*) as an example. The scheme EG* is constructed in a leakage model that follow the *"Only Computation Leaks Information"* axiom. For simplicity, we only concentrate on how to mathematically realize the process of generating random numbers r_i for scheme EG* and ignore other abstract cryptographic components which also need to be mathematically realized. We will introduce four different kinds of mathematical realization of scheme EG*. In each mathematical realization, we use generic Random Number Generator (RNG) or Pseudorandom Number Generator (PRNG) to mathematically realize the process of generating random numbers r_i (Note that, PRNG is used widely for generating random numbers in practice.). We want to see whether or not the four kinds of mathematical realization are practically secure by attacks against them. Note that, in this paper, we only consider mathematical realization, not physical realization. That is to say, our work is regardless of any specific physical attack against physical realization.

Our Contributions. Main contributions of this paper are two-fold as follows. First, by some counterexamples, our research gives a negative answer to the important question that whether one can mathematically realize a leakage resilient cryptographic scheme in existent ways without affecting its practical security.

---

[1] According to Kerckhoffs' principle, this assumption is reasonable.

[2] The same leakage resilient ElGamal scheme instantiated over bilinear groups of prime order p (where $p - 1$ is not smooth) is leakage resilient in the generic-group model (i.e. scheme BEG*). However, it is very hard to implement the generic-group model in practice. This drawback of the generic-group model goes against our recommendation to at least provide mathematical realization for a cryptographic scheme. Therefore, in this paper, we consider the scheme EG* which can be implemented in practice easily.

There may exist a big gap between the theoretical tolerance leakage bits number and the practical tolerance leakage bits number of the same leakage resilient cryptographic scheme if the mathematical components in the mathematical realization are not provably secure in leakage setting.

Second, for any leakage resilient cryptographic scheme, tolerance leakage rate reflects its expected security. Therefore, (accurate or rough) estimation of tolerance leakage rate of any leakage resilient cryptographic scheme does make very good sense. For each of the four kinds of mathematical realization of scheme EG^*, this paper specifies an upper bound of the practical tolerance leakage rate that scheme EG^* can tolerate *by-product*. These upper bounds are the best known so far, even thought it might not be the tightest one.

Organization of This Paper. The rest of this paper is organized as follows. In Section 2, we first present some basic symbols, notations, and concepts. Then, we briefly review the scheme EG^*. Section 3 introduces the four kinds of mathematical realization of scheme EG^* and their practical tolerance leakage bits number. Section 4 concludes the whole paper.

2   Preliminaries

In this section, we first present some symbols, notations, and concepts used throughout this paper. Then, we briefly review the scheme EG^*.

2.1   Symbols, Notations, and Concepts

If S is a binary bit string, we denote the most significant a bits of S by $S^{[a]}$ and denote the least significant b bits of S by $S_{[b]}$. We denote the length of S by $|S|$ and assume that the binary bit string representation of all the elements in $\mathbb{Z}_p$ has the same length. We denote the least significant bit of S is the 1st bit of S and the most significant bit of S is the $|S|^{th}$ bit of S. We use the symbol $[S]_{(i)}$ to denote the ith bit of S.

2.2   Brief Description of Scheme EG^*

We describe the scheme $EG^* = (KG^*_{EG}, Enc^*_{EG}, Dec1^*_{EG}, Dec2^*_{EG})$ and the corresponding security definition in the same way as that in the paper [1]. Let the security parameter of scheme EG^* is κ. Let Gen denote a probabilistic algorithm that outputs a cyclic group $\mathbb{G}$ of order p, where p is a strong prime and $|p| = \kappa$. The scheme EG^* is described as a Key Encapsulation Mechanism (KEM) and is shown as follows:

$KG^*_{EG}(\kappa)$: Compute $(\mathbb{G}, p) \xleftarrow{*} Gen(n)$, $g \xleftarrow{*} \mathbb{G}$, $x \xleftarrow{*} \mathbb{Z}_p$, $h = g^x$. Choose random $\sigma_0 \xleftarrow{*} \mathbb{Z}_p^*$ and set $\sigma_0' = x\sigma_0^{-1} \bmod (p)$. The public key is $pk = (\mathbb{G}, p, h)$ and the secret key is $sk = x$. Two secret states are σ_0 and σ_0'.

$Enc^*_{EG}(pk)$: Choose random $r \xleftarrow{*} \mathbb{Z}_p$. Let $C \leftarrow g^r \in \mathbb{G}$ and $K \leftarrow h^r \in \mathbb{G}$. The ciphertext is C and the symmetric key is K.

$\mathsf{Dec1}^*_{\mathsf{EG}}(\sigma_{i-1}, C)$: Choose random $r_i \xleftarrow{\ *\ } \mathbb{Z}_p^*$, $\sigma_i = \sigma_{i-1} r_i \bmod (p)$, $K' = C^{\sigma_i}$, return(r_i, K').

$\mathsf{Dec2}^*_{\mathsf{EG}}(\sigma'_{i-1}, (r_i, K'))$: Set $\sigma'_i = \sigma'_{i-1} r_i^{-1} \bmod (p)$, and $K = K'^{\sigma'_i}$. The symmetric key is K and the updated states are σ_i and σ'_i.

The theoretical security definition of scheme EG* is CCLA1 which was introduced in the paper [1]. In CCLA1, the two leakage functions f_i and g_i are efficient computable functions *adaptively* chosen by the adversary and get as inputs only the secret states that are *actually* accessed during computation. The leakage functions can simulate any computation with the inputs and output any kind of leakages that might occur. The only restriction about the leakage functions is that the ranges of the leakage functions are bounded by leakage parameter λ. For scheme EG*, the leakage functions f_i and g_i are as follows:

$$\Lambda_i \leftarrow f_i(\sigma_{i-1}, r_i),\ \Lambda'_i \leftarrow g_i(\sigma'_{i-1}, (r_i, K'), r_i^{-1}),\ \text{and } |\Lambda_i| \leq \lambda, |\Lambda'_i| \leq \lambda.$$

Note that, when the theoretical security is considered, only $\{\sigma_{i-1}, r_i\}$ and $\{\sigma'_{i-1}, (r_i, K'), r_i^{-1}\}$ are the inputs of the leakage functions. However, when the practical security is considered, according to the "*Only Computation Leaks Information*" axiom, the information in any position of all the mathematical components in the mathematical realization could be the inputs of the leakage functions as long as the position is actually accessed during computation.

Although the authors of the paper [1] didn't prove the theoretical security of scheme EG* and only presented the following conjecture, the crucial technique of scheme EG* (i.e. multiplicative secret sharing) is used widely in the context of LRC [24,25] and scheme EG* is more practical than other leakage resilient cryptographic schemes. Therefore, we take the scheme EG* as an example.

Conjecture 1. *The scheme EG* is CCLA1 secure if $p - 1$ has a large prime factor (say, $p - 1 = 2q$ for a prime q).*

In [1], the authors conjectured that roughly λ equals to $0.25|p|$ bits in [17] (i.e. the theoretical tolerance leakage rate $\lambda/|p| = 0.25$). Thus total theoretical tolerance leakage bits number in one decapsulation query equals to $2\lambda = 0.5|p|$ bits. We use $\lambda/|p|$ to denote tolerance leakage rate of scheme EG* and define $\rho = (|f_i| + |g_i|)/|p|$. Any implementation of scheme EG* will be secure against every side-channel attack that rigorously fits the leakage model, i.e. as long as the amount of information that is leaked during each invocation is sufficiently bounded, and moreover the cryptographic device adheres the "*Only Computation Leaks Information*" axiom. However, the authors said *nothing* about how to mathematically realize the process of generating random numbers r_i for scheme EG*. Therefore, the implementors may use True Random Number Generator (TRNG) or PRNG to mathematically realize this process in practice.

3   Mathematical Realizations of Scheme EG*

It is well known that one can use TRNG or PRNG to generate random numbers. Although there exist some TRNGs, PRNG is used more widely than TRNG in practice. The reasons of this fact are in the following. First, TRNG requires a naturally occurring source of randomness. Designing a hardware device or software program to exploit this randomness and produce a bit sequence that is free of biases and correlations is a difficult task. Second, for most cryptographic applications, the random number generator must not be subject to observation or manipulation by an adversary. However, TRNG is subject to influence by external factors, and also to malfunction. Third, the generation of true random number is an inefficient procedure in most practical environments. Finally, it may be impractical to securely store and transmit a large number of true random bits if these are required in applications. Therefore, we mainly consider the case of utilizing PRNG to mathematically realize the process of generating random numbers in this paper.

In this section, we will introduce four kinds of mathematical realization of scheme EG^*. In each mathematical realization, the process of generating random numbers r_i is mathematically realized by a generic RNG or a specific PRNG. We want to see whether the four kinds of mathematical realization are practically secure by presenting specific attacks against them. The goal of all our attacks is to recover the secret key x. To achieve this goal, our attacks need to obtain all the bits of the random number r_i for each invocation of the decapsulation query of scheme EG^*. The adversary can recover all the bits of σ_i and σ_i' ($i = 0, 1, \ldots$) and obtain a candidate value x' of the correct secret key x. The adversary can verify the correctness of x' by a correct pair (C, K).

In the first kind of mathematical realization, we assume the process of generating random numbers r_i is mathematically realized by a generic RNG and the adversary does not know the internal mathematical structure of the generic RNG. The attack against this kind of mathematical realization (denoted by ATTACK I) can also be viewed as an attack against the theoretical security of scheme EG^*. ATTACK I satisfies the leakage model of scheme EG^* defined in [1] except that it requires a large number of leakage bits. Hence, ATTACK I poses no threat on the theoretical security of scheme EG^*. In the rest three kinds of mathematical realization, we assume the process of generating random numbers r_i is mathematically realized by three specific PRNGs. For convenience, the attacks against the three kinds of mathematical realization are denoted by ATTACK II. ATTACK II have the same basic principle as ATTACK I. However, it is amazing that the results of ATTACK II show that the practical tolerance leakage bits number of scheme EG^* will decrease dramatically when some specific PRNGs are used. *The decrease of the practical tolerance leakage bits number shows the impacts of mathematical realization over practical security of leakage resilient cryptographic schemes.* In the following, we will introduce the four kinds of mathematical realization and the attacks against them. Finally, we will show some discussions and results of the attacks. For both ATTACK I and ATTACK II, we assume the random number r_i is generated by Algorithm 1.

Algorithm 1. The Algorithm of Generating Random Numbers r_i

Input: no input
Output: a random number r_i
Step 1 Invoke generic RNG or PRNG to generate a new random number t and $|t| = |r_i|$.
Step 2 If $t = 0$ then return to Step 1 else go to Step 3.
Step 3 If $t < p$ then go to Step 4 else go to Step 5.
Step 4 Let $r_i := t$ and return r_i.
Step 5 Let $r_i := t \bmod p$ and return r_i.

3.1 Mathematical Realization Using Generic RNG

If the process of generating random numbers r_i is mathematically realized by generic RNG, we can attack this kind of mathematical realization as follows (ATTACK I):

In the 1st invocation of decapsulation query of scheme EG^*, the adversary chooses the leakage functions as follows:

$$f_1(\sigma_0, r_1) = \langle [\sigma_0]_{(1)}, r_1^{[|p|/2]} \rangle, \quad g_1(\sigma_0', (r_1, K'), r_1^{-1}) = \langle [\sigma_0']_{(1)}, r_{1[|p|/2]} \rangle.$$

Now, the adversary knows r_1 ($r_1 := r_1^{[|p|/2]} \parallel r_{1[|p|/2]}$), r_1^{-1} (Note that, the prime number p is public.), $\sigma_{0[1]}$, and $\sigma_{0[1]}'$. In the 2nd invocation of decapsulation query, the adversary chooses the leakage functions as follows:

$$f_2(\sigma_1, r_2) = \langle [\sigma_1 r_1^{-1} \bmod p]_{(2)}, r_2^{[|p|/2]} \rangle = \langle [\sigma_0]_{(2)}, r_2^{[|p|/2]} \rangle,$$

$$g_2(\sigma_1', (r_2, K'), r_2^{-1}) = \langle [\sigma_1' r_1 \bmod p]_{(2)}, r_{2[|p|/2]} \rangle = \langle [\sigma_0']_{(2)}, r_{2[|p|/2]} \rangle.$$

After the 2nd invocation of decapsulation query, the adversary knows $r_1, r_1^{-1}, r_2,$ $r_2^{-1}, \sigma_{0[2]},$ and $\sigma_{0[2]}'$. Let $R_{\{a,b\}} := \prod_{s=a}^{b} r_s \bmod p$ and $R_{\{a,b\}}^{-1} := \prod_{s=a}^{b} r_s^{-1} \bmod p$. In the ith ($i = 2, \ldots, |p| - 1$) invocation of decapsulation query, the adversary chooses the leakage functions as follows:

$$f_i(\sigma_{i-1}, r_i) = \langle [\sigma_{i-1} R_{\{1,i-1\}}^{-1} \bmod p]_{(i)}, r_i^{[|p|/2]} \rangle = \langle [\sigma_0]_{(i)}, r_i^{[|p|/2]} \rangle,$$

$$g_i(\sigma_{i-1}', (r_i, K'), r_i^{-1}) = \langle [\sigma_{i-1}' R_{\{1,i-1\}} \bmod p]_{(i)}, r_{i[|p|/2]} \rangle = \langle [\sigma_0']_{(i)}, r_{i[|p|/2]} \rangle.$$

In the $|p|^{th}$ invocation of decapsulation query, the adversary chooses the leakage functions as follows:

$$f_{|p|}(\sigma_{|p|-1}, r_{|p|}) = \langle [\sigma_{|p|-1} R_{\{1,|p|-1\}}^{-1} \bmod p]_{(|p|)} \rangle = \langle [\sigma_0]_{(|p|)} \rangle,$$

$$g_{|p|}(\sigma_{|p|-1}', (r_{|p|}, K'), r_{|p|}^{-1}) = \langle [\sigma_{|p|-1}' R_{\{1,|p|-1\}} \bmod p]_{(|p|)} \rangle = \langle [\sigma_0']_{(|p|)} \rangle.$$

In this way, after invoking the decapsulation query $|p|$ times, the adversary knows all the bits of σ_0 and σ_0'. Then, he can recover a candidate value

$x' = \sigma_0 \sigma_0' \bmod p$ of the correct secret key x. Then, the adversary can verify the correctness of x' by a correct pair (C, K).

To successfully execute ATTACK I, the leakage parameter λ should achieve $0.5|p| + 1$ bits, which is larger than $0.25|p|$. Therefore, ATTACK I poses no threat on the theoretical security of scheme EG^*. Note that, ATTACK I can also be executed after the ith decapsulation query similarly. After the adversary obtaining σ_i and σ_i', he can recover a candidate value $x' = \sigma_i \sigma_i' \bmod p$ of the correct secret key x.

3.2   Mathematical Realization Using Specific PRNG

Now, we assume that the process of generating random numbers r_i is mathematically realized by specific PRNGs. According to Kerckhoffs' principle, the adversary knows the concrete mathematical structure of the specific PRNG used by the mathematical realization. When the PRNG is invoked to generate a random number r_i in the decapsulation query, all the internal secret states of the PRNG which are actually accessed during computation can be leaked to the adversary due to the "Only Computation Leaks Information" axiom.

We know that if the adversary obtains all the bits of all the secret states (such as the seed) of any PRNG, he can totally recover the output of the PRNG trivially. Therefore, for ATTACK II, we *do not* allow the adversary to *directly* obtain all bits of all the secret states of the PRNG from leakages *in one invocation*. Specifically speaking, what the adversary can obtain from leakage functions in one invocation of the decapsulation query of scheme EG^* includes only *part* of bits about the internal secret states of the PRNG and *part* of bits about the output of the PRNG. But the amount of leakages is bounded by λ bits (the leakage parameter). The central idea of ATTACK II is that the adversary tries to recover all bits of the seed of the PRNG (not from direct leakages) by using the specific mathematical structure of the PRNG with at most λ bits from leakages. In this manner, we show the impacts of mathematical realization over the practical security for the leakage resilient scheme EG^*.

We surprisingly find that practical tolerance leakage bits number of scheme EG^* will reduce to a value less than $0.25|p|$ bits when three specific PRNGs are used to mathematically realize the process of generating random numbers r_i. Therefore, the corresponding three kinds of mathematical realization are not practically secure. The three specific PRNGs are ANSI X9.17 PRNG, ANSI X9.31 PRNG, and FIPS 186 PRNG for DSA per-message secrets. We also assume that the seed of the specific PRNG is refreshed in each invocation of the decapsulation query.

3.2.1   Case 1: ANSI X9.17 PRNG and ANSI X9.31 PRNG

The ANSI X9.17 PRNG [12] has been used as a general purpose PRNG in many applications. Let E_{key} (resp. D_{key}) denotes DES E-D-E two-key triple-encryption (resp. decryption) under a key key, which is generated somehow at initialization time and must be reserved exclusively used only for this generator. The key is a internal secret state of the PRNG which is never changed for every invocation of the PRNG. ANSI X9.17 PRNG is shown in Algorithm 2.

Algorithm 2. ANSI X9.17 PRNG

Input: a random (and secret) 64-bit seed $seed[1]$, integer v, and E_{key}.
Output: v pseudorandom 64-bit strings (denoted by $output[1], \ldots, output[v]$).
Step 1 For l from 1 to v do the following:
      1.1 Compute $I_l = E_{key}(input[l])$, where $input[l]$ is a 64-bit representation of
the system date/time.
      1.2 $output[l] = E_{key}(I_l \oplus seed[l])$
      1.3 $seed[l + 1] = E_{key}(I_l \oplus output[l])$
Step 2 Return $(output[1], output[2], \ldots, output[v])$

Suppose that each $input[l]$ ($l = 1, 2, \ldots, v$) has 10 bits that the adversary does not know (We assume these 10 bits are the least significant 10 bits of each $input[l]$.). This is a reasonable assumption for many systems[1] [16]. Before doing our attack, due to the fact that key is never changed for every invocation of the PRNG (*stateless*), the adversary can completely obtain key from leakage function f_i by invoking the decapsulation query repeatedly. In each invocation, the leakage function f_i leaks only part of bits about key (not all the bits of key). After knowing key completely, the adversary continually invoke the decapsulation query for $|p|$ times. Let

$$state_{i+u} := \{output[1]_{i+u}, input[1]_{i+u[10]}, \ldots, input[v]_{i+u[10]}\}$$

and the leakage functions are defined as follows. For $u = 1$,

$$f_{i+u}(\sigma_{i+u-1}, r_{i+u}) = \langle [\sigma_i]_{(1)}, state_{i+u} \rangle,$$

$$g_{i+u}(\sigma'_{i+u-1}, (r_{i+u}, K'), r_{i+u}^{-1}) = \langle [\sigma'_i]_{(1)} \rangle.$$

For $u = 2, \ldots, |p| - 1$,

$$f_{i+u}(\sigma_{i+u-1}, r_{i+u}) = \langle [\sigma_{i+u-1} R_{\{i+1, i+u-1\}}^{-1} \bmod p]_{(u)}, state_{i+u} \rangle,$$

$$g_{i+u}(\sigma'_{i+u-1}, (r_{i+u}, K'), r_{i+u}^{-1}) = \langle [\sigma'_{i+u-1} R_{\{i+1, i+u-1\}} \bmod p]_{(u)} \rangle.$$

For $u = |p|$,

$$f_{i+u}(\sigma_{i+u-1}, r_{i+u}) = \langle [\sigma_{i+u-1} R_{\{i+1, i+u-1\}}^{-1} \bmod p]_{(|p|)} \rangle = \langle [\sigma_i]_{(|p|)} \rangle$$

$$g_{i+u}(\sigma'_{i+u-1}, (r_{i+u}, K'), r_{i+u}^{-1}) = \langle [\sigma'_{i+u-1} R_{\{i+1, i+u-1\}} \bmod p]_{(|p|)} \rangle = \langle [\sigma'_i]_{(|p|)} \rangle.$$

Now, the adversary obtains

$$\{output[1]_{i+u}, input[1]_{i+u}, \ldots, input[v]_{i+u}\}, \ (u = 1, \ldots, |p| - 1)$$

and he can further compute

---

[1] For example, consider a millisecond timer, and an adversary who knows the nearest second when an output was generated.

$$seed[1]_{i+u} := D_{key}(output[1]_{i+u}) \oplus E_{key}(input[1]_{i+u}).$$

Then the adversary can easily get

$$seed[s]_{i+u} := E_{key}(E_{key}(input[s-1]_{i+u}) \oplus output[s-1]_{i+u})$$

as well as

$$output[s]_{i+u} := E_{key}(E_{key}(input[s]_{i+u}) \oplus seed[s]_{i+u}), \ (s = 2, 3, \ldots, v).$$

Thus the adversary obtain all the bits of r_i for every decapsulation query. Figure 1 and Figure 2 show that the mathematical realization of scheme EG^* is not practically secure any more, if it uses ANSI X9.17 PRNG for strong prime p with size larger than 700 bits.

Note that ANSI X9.31-1998 Appendix A 2.4 in [15] introduces PRNGs using 3-key triple DES or AES. In 3-key triple DES case, due to the fact that $input[l]$, $seed[l]$ and $output[l]$ have the same length as that of ANSI X9.17 PRNG, we can obtain the same attack results as those of the attack against ANSI X9.17 PRNG. Our attack is still valid for this PRNG using AES-128 similarly. Therefore, we do not introduce the attack against this PRNG for AES-128 case here. Figure 1 and Figure 2 show that the mathematical realization of scheme EG^* is not practically secure any more, if it uses ANSI X9.31 PRNG Using AES-128 for strong prime p with size larger than 756 bits.

Analysis. Although these PRNGs are not secure even in leakage-free setting if the adversary knows the *key*, what we want to emphasize here is the drawbacks of the mathematical structures of these PRNGs, which make these PRNGs become insecure in leakage setting. The designers of these PRNGs exploit block ciphers (such as DES, 3DES, and AES-128) to mathematically realize an abstract One-Way Permutation (OWP). These PRNGs themselves can compute the output of the OWP because they know the keys of the block ciphers. In leakage-free setting, if the adversary does not know the keys, he can not recover the inputs of the block ciphers (i.e. the seeds of the PRNGs) and the "One-Way" property holds. However, in leakage setting, the adversary can obtain the keys completely from leakages because they are *stateless*. This means that the One-Way Permutation is replaced by a "One-Way Trapdoor Permutation" and the adversary obtains the trapdoor (i.e. the stateless keys) from leakages. Therefore, the "One-Way" property does not hold any more.

3.2.2   Case 2: FIPS 186 PRNG for DSA Pre-message Secrets

The Digital Signature Standard (DSS) specification (FIPS 186) [13] also describes a fairly simple PRNG based on SHA or DES, which is used for generating DSA per-message secrets. This PRNG is shown in Algorithm 3.

For general purpose PRNG, *mod q* operation in this PRNG could be omitted. It is necessary only for DSS where all arithmetic is done *mod q*. In this paper, we only consider the DES version of this PRNG, where the G function is based on DES. Therefore, the seed (as well as the output) of this PRNG is 160 bits long. We show the attack against this PRNG when $|p| = 964$ bits as an example. To generate a 964 bits long random number, one needs to invoke this PRNG 7 times ($v = 7$) iteratively to obtain a 1120 bits long random number and discards $output[v]_{[156]}$. Let $state_i = \{output[1]_i^{[40]}, output[2]_i^{[30]}, output[3]_i^{[20]}, output[4]_i^{[10]}, output[5]_i^{[10]}, output[6]_i^{[6]}, output[7]_i^{[4]}\}$. The leakage functions are as follows.

For $i = 1$,

$$f_i(\sigma_{i-1}, r_i) = \langle[\sigma_0]_{(1)}, seed[1]_i^{[120]}, state_i\rangle, \quad g_i(\sigma'_{i-1}, (r_i, K'), r_i^{-1}) = \langle[\sigma'_0]_{(1)}\rangle.$$

For $i = 2, \ldots, |p| - 1$,

$$f_i(\sigma_{i-1}, r_i) = \langle[\sigma_{i-1}R_{\{1,i-1\}}^{-1} \bmod p]_{(i)}, seed[1]_i^{[120]}, state_i\rangle,$$

$$g_i(\sigma'_{i-1}, (r_i, K'), r_i^{-1}) = \langle[\sigma'_{i-1}R_{\{1,i-1\}} \bmod p]_{(i)}\rangle.$$

For $i = |p|$,

$$f_i(\sigma_{i-1}, r_i) = \langle[\sigma_{i-1}R_{\{1,i-1\}}^{-1} \bmod p]_{(i)}\rangle = \langle[\sigma_0]_{(|p|)}\rangle,$$

$$g_i(\sigma'_{i-1}, (r_i, K'), r_i^{-1}) = \langle[\sigma'_{i-1}R_{\{1,i-1\}} \bmod p]_{(i)}\rangle = \langle[\sigma'_0]_{(|p|)}\rangle.$$

Algorithm 3. FIPS 186 PRNG for DSA pre-message secrets

Input: an integer v and a 160-bit prime number q.
Output: v pseudorandom numbers $output[1], \ldots, output[v]$ in the interval $[0, q-1]$, which may be used as the per-message secret numbers in the DSA.
Step 1 If the SHA based G function is to be used in step 4.1 then select an integer $160 \le b \le 512$. If the DES based G function is to be used in step 4.1 then set $b \leftarrow 160$.
Step 2 Generate a random (and secret) b-bit seed $seed[1]$.
Step 3 Define the 160-bit string $str = efcdab89\ 98badcfe\ 10325476\ c3d2e1f0\ 67452301$ (in hexadecimal).
Step 4 For l from 1 to v do the following:
   4.1 $output[l] \leftarrow G(str, seed[l]) \bmod (q)$.
   4.2 $seed[l + 1] \leftarrow (1 + seed[l] + output[l]) \bmod (2^b)$.
Step 5 Return $(output[1], output[2], \ldots, output[v])$.

After the adversary getting the most significant 120 bits of the seed (i.e. $seed[1]_i^{[120]}$ ($i = 1, 2, \ldots, |p|-1$)) from leakages, he could compute all the possible values of the least significant 40 bits of $seed[1]_i$ (i.e. $seed[1]_{i[40]}$) and gets 2^{40} candidate values of $seed[1]_i$. Denote a candidate value by $seed[1]'_i$. For each $seed[1]'_i$, the adversary computes

$$state'_i = \{output[1]_i'^{[40]}, output[2]_i'^{[30]}, output[3]_i'^{[20]},$$

$$output[4]_i'^{[10]}, output[5]_i'^{[10]}, output[6]_i'^{[6]}, output[7]_i'^{[4]}\}.$$

using $seed[1]'_i$ and tests the correctness of this candidate value $seed[1]'_i$ using $state_i$ obtained from leakages. For the correct candidate value $seed[1]'_i$ (i.e. $seed[1]_i$), $state'_i$ must equal to $state_i$. This test fails with extremely low probability. For larger size p, the adversary also obtain $seed[1]^{[120]}_i$ from leakages. The number of total leakage bits about the output of the PRNG should keep 120 bits unchanged but the distribution of the leakage bits is changed. For every output block $output[l]$ ($l = 1, 2, \ldots, v$), the adversary must obtain some bits about it from leakages (In other words, there does not exist one block of the output blocks of the PRNG ($output[l], l \in \{1, 2, \ldots, v\}$) where no leakage occurs.).

We verified our attack by experiments for different size p. The results of experiments verified that our attack against this PRNG is valid. Giving out theoretical success rate of our attack would be interesting but is beyond the scope of this paper. Figure 1 and Figure 2 show that the mathematical realization of scheme EG* is not practically secure any more, if it uses this PRNG for strong prime p with size larger than 964 bits.

Analysis. It is well known that one bit difference in the input of G function will cause many bits difference in the output of G function. Moreover, this PRNG is invoked *iteratively* to generate random numbers. These drawbacks make our attack become valid.

3.3   The Results of Our Attacks and Discussions

Figure 1. shows the minimum ρ required to successfully recover x for different kinds of mathematical realization. Figure 2. shows the minimum $\lambda/|p|$ required to successfully recover x for different kinds of mathematical realization. According to [23], for long-term security, 1024-bit or larger modulus should be used. Therefore, we can see that if the implementor uses the above-mentioned four PRNGs to mathematically realize the process of generating random numbers r_i for scheme EG*, the corresponding mathematical realization will not be practically secure any more. From Figure 1 and Figure 2, we find that if the process of

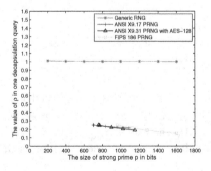 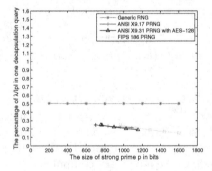

Fig. 1. Minimum ρ required to successfully recover x for different kinds of mathematical realization

Fig. 2. Minimum $\lambda/|p|$ required to successfully recover x for different kinds of mathematical realization

generating random numbers r_i is leakage-free, our attacks will become invalid. However, assuming the process of generating random numbers r_i is leakage-free contradicts with the *"Only Computation Leaks Information"* axiom. Therefore, we must notice the impacts of mathematical realization over practical security for leakage resilient cryptographic schemes.

The process of generating random numbers r_i for scheme EG^* can also be mathematically realized by TRNGs or other PRNGs. However, it is very difficult to rule out all the attacks against TRNGs or other PRNGs, which can make the corresponding mathematical realizations become practically insecure in leakage setting. The reason is that the security of these specific mathematical algorithms (TRNGs or PRNGs) in leakage setting is usually based on cryptanalysis but is not based on rigorous proof (i.e. in provable security way).

Although practical tolerance leakage rate can be made arbitrarily small for Case 2 with the increase of the size of p, the success of *all* our attacks against these PRNGs is not depend on the size of p but is depend on the drawbacks about the mathematical structures of these PRNGs. The authors of the paper [1] conjectured that the theoretical tolerance leakage rate $\lambda/|p|$ of scheme EG^* equals to 0.25. If the actual value of $\lambda/|p| > 0.25$, all our attacks are valid. Otherwise, if the actual value of $\lambda/|p| < 0.25$, some attacks against these PRNGs *may* become invalid. However, there still exist some kinds of mathematical realization which are not practically secure. For example, for large size p, our attack against FIPS 168 PRNG is still valid.

In paper [20], a practical leakage resilient PRNG in the standard model was introduced. This leakage resilient PRNG is based on $(\epsilon, s, n/\epsilon)-$secure weak Pseudorandom Function (wPRF) $F(k, pr) : \{0,1\}^\kappa \times \{0,1\}^n \to \{0,1\}^m$. The symbol pr denotes public randomness. The initial state of this PRNG is (pr_0, pr_1, k_0) for public randomness $(pr_0, pr_1) \xleftarrow{*} (\{0,1\}^n)^2$ and the random seed $k_0 \xleftarrow{*} \{0,1\}^\kappa$. This leakage resilient PRNG can be instantiated with any length-expanding wPRF $(m > \kappa)$, which in turn can be mathematically realized from any secure block cipher $BC : \{0,1\}^\kappa \times \{0,1\}^n \to \{0,1\}^\kappa$. That is, if BC is an $(\epsilon, s, 2q)-$secure wPRF, then $F(k, pr_l \parallel pr_r) = BC_k(pr_l) \parallel BC_k(pr_r)$ is an $(\epsilon, s, q)-$secure wPRF. Note that, the amount of leakages this PRNG can tolerate (denoted by λ_{prng}) equals to $log(\epsilon^{-1})/6$ and depends on the hardness of the underlying wPRF F [14]. Thus, if F is secure against adversaries of super-polynomial size (i.e. $\epsilon = 2^{\omega(log\kappa)}$), then the amount of leakages λ_{prng} equals to $\omega(log\kappa)$, which is quite small. If $\lambda = 0.25|p| \leq \lambda_{prng}$, the size of the seed k_0 (i.e. κ) should be much larger than $|p|$. Even if the wPRF F is exponentially hard (i.e. $\epsilon = 2^{-\Omega(\kappa)}$), $\epsilon = 2^{-a\kappa}$ ($a \in (0,1]$) and $\lambda_{prng} = a\kappa/6$. This PRNG is leakage resilient if and only if $\kappa \geq 1.5|p|$ ($\lambda = 0.25|p| \leq \lambda_{prng}$). For large size p, to find a secure block cipher with $1.5|p|$ bits long key size is unrealistic. Therefore, this leakage resilient PRNG is not suitable to mathematically realize the process of generating random numbers r_i for scheme EG^*.

The secret key x can also be recovered by exploiting the Hidden Number Problem [17,19] with lower theoretical tolerance leakage bits number (i.e. $\frac{3}{8}|p| + o(|p|)$) than that of ATTACK I. However, practical tolerance leakage bits number of this attack method (also equals to $\frac{3}{8}|p|+o(|p|)$) is higher than that of ATTACK II when only the process of generating random numbers r_i is mathematically realized with the above PRNGs.

4   Conclusion and Future Work

There may exist a big gap between the theoretical tolerance leakage bits number and the practical tolerance leakage bits number of the same leakage resilient cryptographic scheme if the mathematical components in the mathematical realization are not provably secure in leakage setting even if the theoretical security of the leakage resilient cryptographic scheme still holds. We note that the security of the mathematical components in leakage setting is usually based on cryptanalysis. Moreover, based on the state-of-the-art approach of cryptography, to rigorously prove the security of the mathematical components in leakage setting is rather difficult. Due to the goal of LRC is to theoretically solve the pressing issues from the area of practical security about implementation, we anticipate this great difficulty will hinder the application of leakage resilient cryptographic schemes.

It is well known that specifying all details of implementation in a leakage model is tedious. The paper further [5] shows that it is very difficult to state assumptions at logic gate level. Moreover, it is not clear if it is feasible at all to prove the security with assuming some kind of bounded leakages at higher abstraction level (like mathematical realization at algorithmic level). So, even from the practical point of view, working at mathematical realization in algorithmic level seems appealing. Therefore, we suggest that all (practical) leakage resilient cryptographic schemes should at least come with a kind of mathematical realization. Using this kind of mathematical realization, the practical security of the leakage resilient cryptographic scheme can be guaranteed. Our discoveries also inspire cryptographers to design advanced leakage resilient cryptographic schemes whose practical security is independent of the specific details of mathematical realization.

Whether mathematical realization of other cryptographic components would affect the practical security of a leakage resilient cryptographic scheme is still not known. Furthermore, whether similar problems for other leakage resilient cryptographic schemes in different leakage models are also existent is till unclear. These questions are worthy of research in the future.

Acknowledgments. This work was supported by the National Basic Research Program of China (No. 2013CB338003), National Natural Science Foundation of China (Nos. 61472416, 61272478), and National Key Scientific and Technological Project (No. 2014ZX01032401-001).

References

1.   Kiltz, E., Pietrzak, K.: Leakage Resilient ElGamal Encryption. In: Abe, M. (ed.) ASIACRYPT 2010. LNCS, vol. 6477, pp. 595–612. Springer, Heidelberg (2010)

2. Dziembowski, S., Pietrzak, K.: Leakage-Resilient Cryptography, FOCS 2008, pp. 293–302 (2008)
3. Micali, S., Reyzin, L.: Physically Observable Cryptography. In: Naor, M. (ed.) TCC 2004. LNCS, vol. 2951, pp. 278–296. Springer, Heidelberg (2004)
4. Halderman, J.A., Schoen, S.D., Heninger, N., Clarkson, W., Paul, W., Calandrino, J.A., Feldman, A.J., Appelbaum, J., Felten, E.W.: Lest we remember: cold-boot attacks on encryption keys. Communications of the ACM - Security in the Browser 52(5), 91–98 (2009)
5. Mangard, S., Popp, T., Gammel, B.M.: Side-Channel Leakage of Masked CMOS Gates. In: Menezes, A. (ed.) CT-RSA 2005. LNCS, vol. 3376, pp. 351–365. Springer, Heidelberg (2005)
6. Akavia, A., Goldwasser, S., Vaikuntanathan, V.: Simultaneous Hardcore Bits and Cryptography against Memory Attacks. In: Reingold, O. (ed.) TCC 2009. LNCS, vol. 5444, pp. 474–495. Springer, Heidelberg (2009)
7. Naor, M., Segev, G.: Public-Key Cryptosystems Resilient to Key Leakage. In: Halevi, S. (ed.) CRYPTO 2009. LNCS, vol. 5677, pp. 18–35. Springer, Heidelberg (2009)
8. Cash, D.M., Ding, Y.Z., Dodis, Y., Lee, W., Lipton, R.J., Walfish, S.: Intrusion-Resilient Key Exchange in the Bounded Retrieval Model. In: Vadhan, S.P. (ed.) TCC 2007. LNCS, vol. 4392, pp. 479–498. Springer, Heidelberg (2007)
9. Alwen, J., Dodis, Y., Wichs, D.: Leakage-Resilient Public-Key Cryptography in the Bounded-Retrieval Model. In: Halevi, S. (ed.) CRYPTO 2009. LNCS, vol. 5677, pp. 36–54. Springer, Heidelberg (2009)
10. Dodis, Y., Haralambiev, K., López-Alt, A., Wichs, D.: Cryptography against Continuous Memory Attacks. In: FOCS 2010, pp. 511–520 (2010)
11. Lewko, A., Lewko, M., Waters, B.: How to Leak on Key Updates. In: STOC 2011, pp. 725–734 (2011)
12. ANSI X 9.17 (Revised), American National Standard for Financial Institution Key Management (Wholesale). American Bankers Association (1985)
13. National Institute for Standards and Technology, Digital Signature Standard. NIST FIPS PUB 186, U.S. Department of Commerce (1994)
14. Pietrzak, K.: A Leakage-Resilient Mode of Operation. In: Joux, A. (ed.) EUROCRYPT 2009. LNCS, vol. 5479, pp. 462–482. Springer, Heidelberg (2009)
15. Keller, S.S.: NIST-Recommended Random Number Generator Based on ANSI X9.31 Appendix A.2.4 Using the 3-Key Triple DES and AES Algorithms
16. Kelsey, J., Schneier, B., Wagner, D., Hall, C.: Cryptanalytic attacks on pseudorandom number generators. In: Vaudenay, S. (ed.) FSE 1998. LNCS, vol. 1372, p. 168. Springer, Heidelberg (1998)
17. http://www.spms.ntu.edu.sg/Asiacrypt2010/AsiaCrypt_slides/pietrzakAC11.pdf
18. Standaert, F.-X.: How Leaky Is an Extractor? In: Abdalla, M., Barreto, P.S.L.M. (eds.) LATINCRYPT 2010. LNCS, vol. 6212, pp. 294–304. Springer, Heidelberg (2010)
19. Galindo, D., Vivek, S.: Limits of a conjecture on a leakage-resilient cryptogystem. Information Processing Letters 114(4), 192–196 (2014)
20. Yu, Y., Standaert, F.-X., Pereira, O., Yung, M.: Practical Leakage-Resilient Pseudorandom Generators. In: CCS 2010 (2010)
21. Dodis, Y., Goldwasser, S., Tauman Kalai, Y., Peikert, C., Vaikuntanathan, V.: Public-Key Encryption Schemes with Auxiliary Inputs. In: Micciancio, D. (ed.) TCC 2010. LNCS, vol. 5978, pp. 361–381. Springer, Heidelberg (2010)

22. Dodis, Y., Kalai, Y.T., Lovett, S.: On Cryptography With Auxiliary Input, STOC2009
23. Menezes, A., van Oorschot, P., Vanstone, S.: Handbook of Applied Cryptography, Ch. 8, p. 296. CRC Press (1996)
24. Clavier, C., Joye, M.: Universal exponentiation algorithm. In: Koç, Ç.K., Naccache, D., Paar, C. (eds.) CHES 2001. LNCS, vol. 2162, pp. 300–308. Springer, Heidelberg (2001)
25. Kocher, P.C.: Timing Attacks on Implementations of Diffie-Hellman, RSA, DSS, and Other Systems. In: Koblitz, N. (ed.) CRYPTO 1996. LNCS, vol. 1109, pp. 104–113. Springer, Heidelberg (1996)

Non-interactive Revocable Identity-Based Access Control over e-Healthcare Records

Yunya Zhou[1,2,3], Jianwei Liu[4,1], Hua Deng[5], Bo Qin[2,6], and Lei Zhang[7]

[1] School of Electronic and Information Engineering, Beihang University, Beijing, China
maomaozyy@163.com, liujianwei@buaa.edu.cn
[2] State Key Laboratory of Integrated Services Networks, Xidian University, Xi'an, China
[3] State Key Laboratory of Information Security, Institute of Information Engineering,
Chinese Academy of Sciences, Beijing, China
[4] The Academy of Satellite Application, Beijing, China
[5] School of Computer, Wuhan University, Wuhan, China
denghua@whu.edu.cn
[6] Knowledge Engineering (Renmin University of China) Ministry of Education,
School of Information, Renmin University of China, Beijing, China
bo.qin@ruc.edu.cn
[7] Software Engineering Institute, East China Normal University, Shanghai, China
leizhang@sei.ecnu.edu.cn

Abstract. Revocation of access control on private e-healthcare records (EHRs) allows to revoke the access rights of valid users. Most existing solutions rely on a trusted third party too much to generate and update decryption keys, or require the computations of non-revoked users during the revocation, which make them impractical for some more complicated scenarios. In this paper, we propose a new revocation model, referred to as non-interactive revocable identity-based access control (NRIBAC) on EHRs. In NRIBAC, a trusted third party only needs to generate secret keys for group authorities and each group authority can generate decryption keys for the users in its domain. The NRIBAC distinguishes itself from other revocation schemes by the advantageous feature that it does not require any participation of non-revoked users in the revocation. We construct an NRIBAC scheme with short ciphertexts and decryption keys by leveraging hierarchical identity-based encryption and introducing the version information. We formally prove the security of the NRIBAC scheme and conduct thorough theoretical analysis to evaluate the performance. The results reveal that the scheme provides favorable revocation procedure without disturbing non-revoked users.

Keywords: E-healthcare records, Identity-based access control, Revocation, Non-interaction.

1 Introduction

Advances in information and communication techniques have brought great forces for the migration of healthcare systems from paper-based records to electronic healthcare records, which leads to improved efficiency in human operations, reduced storage spaces, enhanced scalability of healthcare records and so on. The electronic healthcare

© Springer International Publishing Switzerland 2015
J. Lopez and Y. Wu (Eds.): ISPEC 2015, LNCS 9065, pp. 485–498, 2015.
DOI: 10.1007/978-3-319-17533-1_33

record (EHR) systems [20] allow patients to create, manage and control their healthcare records stored in a storage server through internet or wireless communications, which makes the storage and sharing of healthcare records more efficient.

The primary concerns about the EHR systems may be the data security. In particular, the patients have great trepidations about the security of their healthcare records stored in the storage server, since they lose physical control over the records once outsourcing them to the server. A feasible and promising approach to protect the security of the e-healthcare records is to let the patients to encrypt the records before outsourcing. There are many cryptographic encryption techniques leveraged to achieve efficient access control over private e-healthcare records, such as wireless access control [1], semantic access control [21], fine-grained access control [10], etc.

Revocation is another important requirement in EHR systems since it can prevent a user from accessing sensitive e-healthcare records by revoking the user whose private key is leaked or expired. The revocation mechanism in identity-based setting proposed by Boldyreva *et al.* [2] allows a trusted authority to revoke users by requiring non-revoked users to update their keys with update keys. In this identity-based revocation system, the public keys of users can be any recognizable strings (e.g., telephone numbers or IP addresses), which eliminates the need for a certificate authority that publishes public keys for all users. Although this feature is attractive for EHR systems, the revocation mechanism [2] and other identity-based revocation schemes ([12,18,9]) requires all non-revoked users to wait for receiving the update keys and then compute the updated decryption keys by themselves, which may not be practicable in EHR systems.

We consider the following scenario. In an EHR system, there are many hospitals and clinics signing contracts to employ a storage server to store and share e-healthcare records of their patients. To protect the security of e-healthcare records, a patient can specify an access policy on the records, saying that which doctor in which hospital or clinic can access the records. Then only the matching doctor can access the e-healthcare records using the decryption key issued by a trusted authority. To revoke the doctors whose decryption keys are leaked or expired, the trusted authority initializes the revocation procedure to update the decryption keys for non-revoked doctors. However, due to the complicated computation of decryption key update, the doctors may be unwilling to compute the keys by themselves for every revocation; even worse, due to the network delay or accidental loss of the update keys, the decryption keys of non-revoked doctors may not be updated in time or even unable to be updated.

Most existing revocation schemes [2,12,18,9,19,15] seem hard to be employed in this scenario since they require the non-revoked users to interact with other parties to fulfill the revocation. Besides, in these schemes, the decryption keys and the updated keys are increased in the number of users, which costs a significant computing and communication overheads of the trusted authority to distribute users' keys.

1.1 Our Contributions

In this paper, we revisit the identity-based revocation and propose a non-interactive revocable identity-based access control (NRIBAC) over private e-healthcare records. The NRIBAC allows arbitrary strings to serve as public keys, so that there is no need for the trusted authority to publish public-key certificates for users. Moreover, the NRIBAC provides an efficient revocation mechanism different from existing ones in that the revocation does not need any participation of non-revoked users. Therefore, the non-revoked users do not need to perform any computation to update their decryption keys, nor worry about any error that would lead to the failure of key updates. Our contributions include the following aspects.

We present a non-interactive revocable identity-based access control (NRIBAC) framework to revoke decryption keys from accessing encrypted e-healthcare records. In an NRIBAC system, users are partitioned into distinct groups, which corresponds to the organization where doctors are often involved in distinct hospitals or clinics. A trusted third party (TTP) is employed to distribute secret keys for group managers and with the group secret key, a group manage is able to generate secret keys for its members. As an advantageous feature, the NRIBAC does not require the participant of any non-revoked user since all the tasks of key update are done by the TTP and group managers.

We instantiate an NRIBAC scheme by adopting the hierarchical identity-based encryption (HIBE) [3] and introducing the version number. We employ the HIBE scheme with a maximum two depth to achieve the key generation from group managers to users. That is, with the group secret key like the first-level key in the HIBE, the group manager can create the second-level keys just as in the delegation of the HIBE scheme. The version number is embedded into the secret keys and the ciphertexts so that a secret key is able to decrypt a ciphertext if both have the same version number. The version number also helps to realize the revocation in the sense that when there are users revoked from the system, the secret keys of non-revoked users are updated by a new version number. Due to the key generation pattern and the introduced version number, all non-revoked users will not be disturbed during the whole revocation.

We formally prove the security of the NRIBAC scheme assuming the security of the HIBE scheme [3] and the hardness of the decisional q-BDHE problem. We also conduct theoretic analysis to evaluate the performance of the NRIBAC scheme. The results show that our NRIBAC scheme provides efficient key distribution and outsourcing/access procedures. Further, the revocation procedure takes manageable costs for the TTP and the group managers when the number of users in a group and the number of groups are reasonably set. These feature render our NRIBAC scheme a practicable solution to revoke access control on e-healthcare records.

1.2 Related Work

Data privacy is a major concern in the usage of e-healthcare records (EHR) systems. To enable patient-centric access control on the sensitive e-healthcare records stored in a third party, a unified access control scheme [8] is proposed so that patients can selectively share their virtual composite EHRs using different level of granularity. Sun et al. [21] utilized the role-based access control model and semantic web technologies to achieve semantic access control for cloud computing based on e-healthcare. Li et al. [10] employed the attribute-based encryption to achieve the fine-grained access control on outsourced personal health records. Deng et al. [6] elaborated attribute-based encryption and proposed hierarchical attribute-based encryption which can resolve the problem of key management in EHRs systems. Mashima and Ahamad [13] enabled information accountability in EHR systems so that patients know how their records reached certain consumers and who were involved in the records' sharing. To resist inside attacks, Yi et al. [22] proposed a multi-party framework in which an encrypted EHR can be decrypted by the cooperation of all parties. Deng et al. [7] introduced a tracing mechanism into attribute-based encryption systems so that at least one of the leaked access credential to sensitive data can be found.

Revocation is a crucial task in EHR systems since it can revoke the access rights of users who leaked their secret keys or violated some regulations. Li et al. [10] introduced the revocable attribute-based encryption into the EHR systems to revoke one's access rights to sensitive records. Perumal et al. [16] used a refined attribute-based encryption, called hierarchical attribute-set-based encryption to achieve scalability and flexibility of access control on health records and proposed a revocation mechanism to revoke users' attributes. Compared to attribute-based encryption, identity-based encryption is a more efficient cryptographic tool allowing fast encryption and decryption. Boneh and Franklin [4] proposed the first functional IBE scheme that allows one to encrypt to any ID string and only the one has the secret key for the ID string can decrypt. This IBE scheme also achieves the revocation by representing a user's identity as $ID\|T$ and a user periodically receives his secret key on time T from the key generation authority. This method is impractical for a large number of users since the authority would be exhausted for generating numerous secret keys.

To improve the efficiency of revocable IBE (RIBE), Boldyreva et al. [2] used the revocation encryption of Naor et al. [14] to construct a new RIBE scheme where a trusted authority broadcasts an update key for each revocation and non-revoked users compute new secret keys by using the broadcasted update key. The security of Boldyreva et al.'s RIBE scheme is proved in the selective-ID setting where an adversary needs to declare the identity to be attacked before seeing the public key. Libert and Vergnaud [12] enhanced the RIBE scheme [2] to achieve a stronger security, i.e., adaptive-ID security. Seo and Emura [18] identified the decryption key exposure threat in RIBE schemes following Boldyreva et al.'s method and proposed a simple RIBE scheme with decryption key exposure resistance. Seo and Emura [19] also provides an method to delegate key generation and revocation functionalities in IBE systems, which allows reduction of excessive workload for a single key generation authority. Recently, Sahai et al. [17] proposed a revocable-storage ABE scheme for outsourced data environments by extending the idea of RIBE. Lee et al. [9] improved the Sahai et al.'s scheme and proposed a revocable-storage predicate encryption scheme. Park et al. [15] constructed a RIBE scheme from multilinear maps to reduce the complexity of key update in [2]. In cloud computing environments, Liang et al. [11], Yu et al. [23] and Deng et al. [5] utilized some ciphertext transformation techniques to revoke the access rights of users who do not have updated keys, although these techniques would be low efficient for a large number of ciphertexts.

The aforementioned schemes achieve the revocation of access rights by requiring the authority to generate secret keys for all users in each revocation, or all the non-revoked users to interact with the authority and take costs to generate updated keys by themselves. Our proposed NRIBAC scheme allows the authority to distribute its key generation tasks to group managers, which alleviates the authority's burden of key generation and update. Further, the scheme does not require the non-revoked users to take any cost in the revocation. These features make the NRIBAC scheme a prominent solution to protect data security and revoke access rights in the motivating scenario.

1.3 Organization

The rest of this paper is organized as follows. Section 2 presents our system model and security model. Then we provides detailed description of our scheme in Section 3. The security proof is given in Section 4. In Section 5, we evaluate the system's performance theoretically. Section 6 concludes the paper.

2   System Architecture and Security Model

We consider the non-interactive revocable identity-based access control (NRIBAC) over private e-healthcare records. In reality, there may be many groups of users with accesses to the records. We organize all users in different groups and associate each group with a group manager to authorize users with access rights to e-healthcare records. To revoke users from the system, we are mainly interested in the revocation that does not require the non-revoked users to interact with any party, which has been rarely achieved in previous work.

2.1   System Architecture

As shown in Fig. 1, an NRIBAC system consists of the following entities:

- Trusted third party (TTP), a party trusted by other entities to publish system public parameters and issue/update secret keys for group managers.
- Group managers (GMs), the parties responsible for issuing/updating secret keys for the users in their own groups.
- Storage services provider (SSP), a party that provides services for the file owners to store their encrypted files and returns the files requested by the file consumers.
- File owners, users who encrypt their sensitive files and outsource the encrypted files to SSP.
- File consumers, users who can access the content of the files stored in SSP with the secret keys generated by the GMs.

In the NRIBAC system, the file consumers are partitioned into distinct groups managed by group managers; thus a file consumer is associated with a user identity UID and the identity GID of the group that the consumer belongs to. A file owner can encrypt the file with identities (GID, UID) before outsourcing to the SSP so that only the file consumer UID in group GID can access. For example, we consider an EHR system that involves many hospital and clinics. Each hospital or clinic is like a group in the NRIBAC system and the file consumers are the doctors. When a file owner (i.e., a patient) outsources his e-healthcare records to the storage server, i.e., SSP, he can specify an access policy saying that which doctor in which hospital or clinic can access the records. The TTP publishes the system public parameters for encryption and issues

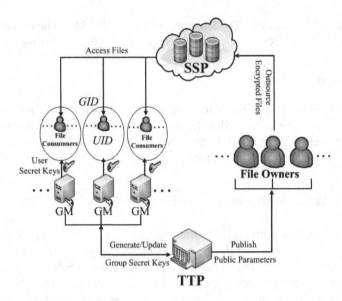

Fig. 1. System Model

group secret keys for group managers (e.g, IT centers of hospitals). With the group secret keys, the group managers are able to generate user secret keys for their member file consumers. To revoke users from accessing any newly outsourced files, the TTP first updates the public parameters and then interacts with the group managers to renew the group secret keys. With the updated group secret keys, the group managers can update secret keys for the non-revoked users (file consumers) in their groups. During the whole revocation, all non-revoked file consumers will not be disturbed since all the tasks are done by the TTP and the group managers.

2.2 Security Model and Assumptions

As previous work [4,6,18], we assume that the TTP is fully trusted. The SSP is assumed to be curious-but-honest in the sense that it may be curious about the content of the stored files, but still be honest to perform the tasks assigned to it. The group managers and the file consumers may collude to access the files stored in SSP without any authorization.

To capture realistic attacks, we model an adversary which is able to access the public parameter and compromise the group managers and the file consumers by having their secret keys. We then require that for such an adversary, it cannot obtain any useful information about the content of the target file, provided that it does not have the authorized user secret key or the group secret key able to generate the authorized key. We note that this is a strong security notion since it resists attacks from collusion of both unauthorized group managers and unauthorized file consumers. The formal security definition will be given in Section 4.

3 Construction

In this section, we present a concrete NRIBAC scheme. Before describing the scheme, we first introduce the basic idea of the construction.

3.1 Basic Idea

In an NRIBAC system, file consumers are organized in many groups and associated with their own identities and the identities of their groups. For instance, in an EHR system, all doctors are organized in their hospitals and will be labeled by their identities (e.g, names, professions) and the identities (e.g., names) of their hospitals. Hence a file consumer in the NRIBAC scheme is associated with a pair of identities, i.e., (GID, UID). The trusted third party (TTP) generates group secret keys for group managers (e.g, IT centers of hospitals) and given the secret keys, the group managers can generate user secret keys for the file consumers in their domains.

We exploit the hierarchical identity-based encryption (HIBE) scheme [3] with a maximum two depth to realize the generation of users' secret keys. That is, the TTP generates secret keys of HIBE in the first level for the group managers and the group managers uses the delegation mechanism of HIBE to generate HIBE secret keys in the second level for the users. This corresponds to the practical scenario where each hospital is responsible for authorizing its doctors and the TTP only need to authorize each hospital. This key generation technique allows the TTP to share its key generation burden with multiple group managers; further, with this hierarchical key distribution, we can update the secret keys of non-revoked users in the revocation without requiring any help of the users.

We adopt the version number in the NRIBAC scheme to realize the revocation of access rights. In the system parameters, the TTP publishes the version information so that a user can use the latest parameters to encrypt his file. The encrypted file will contain the version information and only the secret key that also involves the same version information can decrypt the file. To revoke a set S of users from accessing any newly generated encrypted files, the TTP first updates the system parameters and then interacts with the group managers to update the group secret keys. Given the updated group secret keys, the group managers are able to generate new secret keys that involve the updated version information for the users not in S. During the whole revocation, the non-revoked users are not required to take any responsibility since the key update tasks have been done by the TTP and the group managers. The users' secret keys is combinations of the version information and the HIBE keys of depth two. We employ different values to randomize the version information and the HIBE keys to resist conclusion attacks from unauthorized accesses.

3.2 NRIBAC Scheme

Our NRIBAC scheme is built on a bilinear group. For completeness, we briefly review the definition of bilinear groups. Let $G(1^\lambda)$ be a generator of bilinear groups and λ be the security parameter. The generator outputs two cyclic groups $\mathbb{G}$ and $\mathbb{G}_T$. We say that $\mathbb{G}$ is a bilinear group if there exists an efficient map $e : \mathbb{G} \times \mathbb{G} \rightarrow \mathbb{G}_T$ that satisfies the following features: i) $\hat{e}(g^a, h^b) = \hat{e}(g, h)^{ab}$ for all $g, h \in \mathbb{G}$ and all $a, b \in \mathbb{Z}_p$; and ii) $\hat{e}(g, h) \neq 1$.

The NRIBAC scheme consisting of the six procedures is described as follows.

System Setup. The trusted third party (TTP) calls the **Setup** algorithm to create system public parameters PP and master secret key MSK, where PP will be made public to other parties and MSK will be kept secret.

$(PP, MSK) \leftarrow$ **Setup**(1^λ): The algorithm chooses groups $\mathbb{G}, \mathbb{G}_T$ of order p and a bilinear map $e : \mathbb{G} \times \mathbb{G} \to \mathbb{G}_T$. It chooses a random $\alpha \in \mathbb{Z}_p$ and sets $g_1 = g^\alpha$. Next, select random elements $g_2, g_3, u_1, u_2, f \in \mathbb{G}$. For the current version v, choose v random elements $h_1, h_2, ..., h_v \in \mathbb{G}$. The public parameters and the master secret key are

$$PP = (g, g_1, g_2, g_3, u_1, u_2, f, h_1, ..., h_v, e(g_1, g_2)), \quad MSK = g_2^\alpha.$$

In the system public parameters PP, the version information is in the parameters $(h_1, ..., h_v)$. These parameters will increase when the TTP needs to update PP for revocation.

GM Grant: A group manager (GM) is associated with a unique group identity GID. When a new GM asks for joining the system, the TTP first verifies whether it is a valid group manager. If so, the TTP runs the group key generation algorithm **GMKeyGen** to generate a group secret key for GM.

$GSK_{GID} \leftarrow$ **GMKeyGen**(PP, MSK, GID). The algorithm picks two random values $r, t \in \mathbb{Z}_p$ and computes

$$d_0 = g_2^\alpha (h_1 \cdots h_v f)^r (u_1^{GID} g_3)^t$$

and

$$d_1 = g^r, \quad d_2 = g^t, \quad d_3 = u_2^t.$$

Then, output $GSK_{GID} = (d_0, d_1, d_2, d_3)$.

User Admission: When a new user associated with identity UID in group GID asks for joining the system, the domain group manager first checks whether this user is valid. If yes, the GM generates a secret key SK for the user by calling the user key generation algorithm **KeyGen**.

$SK_{UID} \leftarrow$ **KeyGen**(PP, GSK_{GID}, UID): The algorithm takes as inputs the group secret key $GSK_{GID} = (d_0, d_1, d_2, d_3)$, the user identity UID and public parameters PP. It chooses two random elements $r'', t'' \in \mathbb{Z}_p$ and computes

$$K_0 = d_0 (h_1 \cdots h_v f)^{r''} \cdot d_3^{UID} \cdot (u_1^{GID} u_2^{UID} g_3)^{t''}$$
$$= g_2^\alpha (h_1 \cdots h_v f)^{r'} (u_1^{GID} u_2^{UID} g_3)^{t'}$$

and

$$K_1 = d_1 \cdot g^{r''} = g^{r'}, \quad K_2 = d_2 \cdot g^{t''} = g^{t'}.$$

Then outputs $SK_{UID} = (K_0, K_1, K_2)$.

In the generation of user secret key, assuming that r and t are the random exponents used in generating the group secret key GSK_{GID}, then we have $r' = r + r''$ and $t' = t + t''$, which properly randomize the user secret key.

File Encryption: To securely share a file with the user UID in group GID, the file owner first encrypts the file with a random symmetric encryption key $M \in \mathbb{G}_T$ and then encrypts M by calling the following asymmetric encryption algorithm **Encrypt**. The file owner then outsources the file ciphertext generated with M together with the ciphertext for M to the SSP.

$CT \leftarrow$ **Encrypt**(PP, M, UID, GID): To encrypt the symmetric encryption key M under UID and GID, pick a random $s \in \mathbb{Z}_p$ and compute

$$C_0 = Me(g_1, g_2)^s, C_1 = g^s, C_2 = (h_1 \cdots h_v f)^s, C_3 = \left(u_1^{GID} u_2^{UID} g_3\right)^s.$$

Then, output $CT = (C_0, C_1, C_2, C_3)$.

File Decryption: When a user UID in group GID receives an encrypted file, he decrypts the file by first calling the asymmetric decryption algorithm **Decrypt** to obtain the symmetric encryption key M and then recovers the file by calling the symmetric decryption algorithm with M.

$M \leftarrow$ **Decrypt**(CT, SK_{UID}): To decrypt a ciphertext $CT = (C_0, C_1, C_2, C_3)$, use the secret key $SK_{UID} = (K_0, K_1, K_2, K_3)$ to compute

$$M' = \frac{e(K_0, C_1)}{e(K_1, C_2) \cdot e(K_2, C_3)}$$

and output $M = C_0/M'$.

Indeed, for a valid ciphertext, we have that

$$M' = \frac{e\left(g_2^\alpha, g^s\right) \cdot e\left((h_1 \cdots h_v f)^r, g^s\right) \cdot e\left(\left(u_1^{GID} u_2^{UID} g_3\right)^t, g^s\right)}{e\left(g^r, (h_1 \cdots h_v f)^s\right) \cdot e\left(g^t, \left(u_1^{GID} u_2^{UID} g_3\right)^t\right)}$$

$$= e\left(g_2^\alpha, g^s\right) = e\left(g_1, g_2\right)^s.$$

It then follows that $M = C_0/M' = Me\left(g_1, g_2\right)^s / e\left(g_1, g_2\right)^s$.

Revocation: Suppose that there are some users leaving the system or leaking their secret keys. Then the secret keys of these users should be revoked from the system. Let $S = \{UID_i\}$ denote the set of the identities of the secret keys to be revoked. To revoke the secret keys with identities in S, the TTP first increases the version number by one and update the system public parameters. Then the TTP interacts with each group manager to update the group secret key. Given a new group secret key, the group manage is able to generate new user secret keys for the users with identities not involved in revocation set S. Assume that the current version number is v'. The TTP sets the new version number $v = v' + 1$ and calls the following algorithm to update public parameters.

$(PP, MSK) \leftarrow$ **SysUpdate**(PP', MSK'): The algorithm chooses a random exponent $\gamma_v \in \mathbb{Z}_p$ and computes $h_v = g^{\gamma_v}$. Then, publish the updated public parameters PP that is identical to PP' except that PP involves an additional component h_v and the current version is set as $v = v' + 1$. The updated master secret key is $MSK = (MSK', \gamma_v)$, where the random value γ_v will not be abandoned until the group secret keys are updated.

When the public parameters have been updated, the TTP interacts with each group manager to update the group secret key by running the following procedure.

$GSK_{GID} \leftarrow$ **GMKeyUpdate**(PP, MSK, GSK'_{GID}): For a group manager which has the group secret key $GSK'_{GID} = (d'_0, d'_1, d'_2, d'_3)$, it sends the component $d'_1 = g^r$ to the TTP. Then the TTP uses the random value γ_v and d'_1 to compute

$$a_v = (d'_1)^{\gamma_v} = h_v^r.$$

Given a_v, the GM updates its group secret key by replacing d'_0 with

$$d_0 = d'_0 \cdot a_v = g_2^\alpha (h_1 \cdots h_{v'} h_v f)^r \left(u_1^{GID} g_3 \right)^t$$

and keeping rest components unchanged.

Having the updated group secret key GSK_{GID}, the group manager is able to update the secret keys of the users not involved in the revocation set S. To update the secret key for user UID in group GID, the group manager calls the following algorithm.

$SK_{UID} \leftarrow$ **KeyUpdate**(PP, GSK_{GID}, UID, S): For a user $UID \notin S$, the algorithm uses the updated group secret key $GSK_{GID} = (d_0, d_1, d_2, d_3)$ to generate a new user secret key $SK_{UID} = (K_0, K_1, K_2)$ by performing the same computations described in algorithm **KeyGen**.

We note that in SK_{UID}, the updated version information with regard to h_v has been embedded since the group key component d_0 resulting K_0 has already contained the version information. This guarantees that all non-revoked users can obtain functional secret keys to decrypt the ciphertexts generated on the updated version.

4   Security Analysis

In this section, we formally analyze the security of our NRIBAC scheme. At a high level, we show that the NRIBAC scheme is secure against any number of unauthorized users. Further, we show that the NRIBAC scheme can protect data security against collusion of group managers. We also demonstrate that our NRIBAC scheme can completely deprive the access rights of revoked users so that they cannot decrypt any ciphertext generated on an updated version. The security of an NRIBAC system is defined by the following security game.

Security Game: To capture realistic attacks from collusion of unauthorized users and group managers, we define an adversary which is able to access the public parameters, collude with users and group managers by having the user secret keys and group secret keys, and access the encrypted files stored on SSP. In this formal game, we require this adversary to declare an identity UID^* of a user in group GID^* and a version number

v^* to be attacked. In the system of version v^*, the adversary can query the secret keys of any user except the user UID^* in group GID^*, as well as any group secret key except that for GID^*. The adversary also can query the revoked secret keys for any user and any group manager, i.e., the secret keys with version $v < v^*$. We require that even such an adversary cannot distinguish the ciphertexts of two messages under (GID^*, UID^*) and v^*. The security game is defined as follows between an adversary $\mathcal{A}$ and the challenger.

Init. The adversary $\mathcal{A}$ outputs an identity UID^* of a user in group GID^*, as well as a version number v^*.

Setup. The challenger runs **Setup** to obtain (PP, MSK) of version v^* and gives PP to $\mathcal{A}$.

Phase 1. The adversary $\mathcal{A}$ adaptively makes any of types of the following queries.

- **Reveal**(GID, v): $\mathcal{A}$ queries the secret key for a group manager GID on version v. In response, the challenger runs the algorithm **GMKeyGen** to output a group secret key GSK_{GID} and returns this key to $\mathcal{A}$.
- **Reveal**(GID, UID, v): $\mathcal{A}$ queries the secret key for a user UID in group GID on version v. In response, the challenger runs algorithm **KeyGen** to output a user secret key SK_{UID} and returns this key to $\mathcal{A}$.

Challenge. The adversary $\mathcal{A}$ outputs two equal-length messages M_0 and M_1 with the restriction that the group secret key for GID^* and the user secret key for UID^* have never been queried for $v = v^*$. In response, the challenger chooses a random $\beta \in \{0, 1\}$ and encrypts M_β under (GID^*, UID^*) and v^*, returning the ciphertext CT^* to $\mathcal{A}$.

Phase 2. Phase 1 is repeated with the added restriction that $\mathcal{A}$ cannot query group secret key for GID^* or user secret key for (GID^*, UID^*) on the version v^*.

Guess. The adversary $\mathcal{A}$ outputs a guess $\beta' \in \{0, 1\}$ and wins the game if $\beta' = \beta$.

The advantage of such an adversary $\mathcal{A}$ in this game is defined as $Adv_{\mathcal{A}} = |\Pr[\beta' = \beta] - 1/2|$.

Definition 1. *Our NRIBAC system is semantically secure against chosen-plaintext and chosen-version attack if for all probabilistic polynomial-time adversary $\mathcal{A}$ we have that $Adv_{\mathcal{A}}$ is negligible in the above game.*

The security of NRIBAC stands from two aspects. First, if the adversary queries secret keys of version $v < v^*$, then it obtains revoked secret keys. In this notion, the adversary is allowed to query the secret keys for GID^* and UID^*. The security states that this adversary cannot distinguish the ciphertexts of two messages using revoked secret keys. Second, when the adversary queries secret keys for $v = v^*$, the security guarantees that the adversary still cannot distinguish the ciphertexts of two messages, provided that it did not query the secret key for the challenge group identity GID^* or the challenge user identity UID^*.

To prove the security of NRIBAC, we first review the decisional q-BDHE assumption [3].

Decisional q-BDHE Assumption. Let $\mathbb{G}$ and $\mathbb{G}_T$ be two cyclic groups of prime p and $\mathbb{G}$ is a bilinear group with a map $e : \mathbb{G} \times \mathbb{G} \to \mathbb{G}_T$. Let g be a generator of $\mathbb{G}$. Choose random elements $\alpha, s \in \mathbb{Z}_p$. Compute g^{α^i} for each i from 1 to q and from $q + 1$ to $2q$. For a tuple $\boldsymbol{y} = (g, g^{\alpha}, ..., g^{\alpha^q}, g^{\alpha^{q+1}}, ..., g^{\alpha^{2q}}, g^s)$, the decisional q-BDHE assumption says that there is no polynomial-time adversary that can distinguish $T = e(g, g)^{\alpha^{q+1}s}$ from a random element in $\mathbb{G}_T$.

The following theorem shows the semantic security of our NRIBAC. The proof of this theorem is given in the full version.

Theorem 1. *Our NRIBAC system is semantically secure in the standard model if the HIBE scheme [3] is semantically secure and the decisional q-BDHE assumption holds.*

Since the HIBE scheme [3] has been proved to be semantically secure in the standard model and the q-BDHE assumption has been shown hard to be solved, then our NRIBAC is also secure.

5   Theoretical Analysis

In this section, we evaluate the performance of the NRIBAC theoretically. We analyze the computation complexity of each procedure of the NRIBAC scheme. In the analysis, since the NRIBAC scheme is built in bilinear groups, we evaluate the time consumed by the basic group operations, i.e., exponentiation and bilinear map operation, denoted by t_e and t_p respectively. We do not consider the time cost by the symmetric encryption and decryption, since they are only related to the file size and independent of the revocation and identity-based access control of the proposed scheme.

Table 1 summarizes the time consumed by each procedure of the NRIBAC system. It can be seen that the time cost by the GM Grant is very closed to that of User Admission, which means that the groups managers share the burden of the TTP to distribute secret keys for users. The file encryption and file decryption consume a few exponentiations and bilinear pairings respectively, which allows users to take less time to outsource and access the e-healthcare records. When the revocation mechanism is called, the TTP first updates the system public parameters, which costs just one exponentiation, and

Table 1. Computation Complexity

Operation	Computation Complexity
System Setup	$2t_e + t_p$
GM Grant	$6 \cdot t_e$
User Admission	$7 \cdot t_e$
File Encryption	$6 \cdot t_e$
File Decryption	$3 \cdot t_p$
Revocation	$\mathbf{Sys} : t_e;\ \mathbf{GMKey} : t_e;\ \mathbf{UserKey} : 7t_e$

then updates the secret keys of group managers. For each group manager, the TTP takes only one exponentiation to renew the group manager's secret key. Later, for each user that is not involved in the revocation set, the group manager generates a new user secret key by calling the user key generation algorithm. Hence this sub-procedure is as efficient as the user admission procedure. These features make our NRIBAC a practicable solution to enforce a revocation mechanism for access control over sensitive user data.

6 Conclusion

This paper investigated the issues of revocation of access control in EHR systems. The proposed NRIBAC system can not only reduce the key distribution burden of a trusted third party by hierarchically organizing users, but also revoke access rights of users without disturbing any non-revoked one. The NRIBAC scheme is proven to be semantically secure assuming the security of the underlying HIBE scheme and the hardness of decisional q-BDHE problem. The theoretical analysis shows that the scheme has reasonable performance after introduced into the hierarchical key distribution and revocation mechanisms.

Acknowledgments. We appreciate the anonymous reviewers for their valuable suggestions. This paper was supported by the National Key Basic Research Program (973 program) under project 2012CB315905, the Natural Science Foundation of China through projects 61272501, 61321064, 61202465, 61370190, 61173154, 61472429, 61402029 and 61003214, the Shanghai NSF under Grant No. 12ZR1443500, the Shanghai Chen Guang Program (12CG24), the Science and Technology Commission of Shanghai Municipality under grant 13JC1403500, the Research Funds(No. 14XNLF02) of Renmin University of China, the Open Research Fund of The Academy of Satellite Application, and the Open Research Fund of Beijing Key Laboratory of Trusted Computing.

References

1. Belsis, P., Vassis, D., Gritzalis, S., Skourlas, C.: W-ehr: a wireless distributed framework for secure dissemination of electronic healthcare records. In: IWSSIP 2009, pp. 1–4. IEEE (2009)
2. Boldyreva, A., Goyal, V., Kumar, V.: Identity-based encrytion with efficient revocation. In: ACM CCS 2008, pp. 417–426. ACM (2008)
3. Boneh, D., Boyen, X., Goh, E.-J.: Hierarchical identity based encryption with constant size ciphertext. In: Cramer, R. (ed.) EUROCRYPT 2005. LNCS, vol. 3494, pp. 440–456. Springer, Heidelberg (2005)
4. Boneh, D., Franklin, M.: Identity-based encryption from the weil pairing. In: Kilian, J. (ed.) CRYPTO 2001. LNCS, vol. 2139, pp. 213–229. Springer, Heidelberg (2001)
5. Deng, H., Wu, Q., Qin, B., Chow, S.S.M., Domingo-Ferrer, J., Shi, W.: Tracing and revoking leaked credentials: accountability in leaking sensitive outsourced data. In: ASIACCS 2014, pp. 425–434. ACM (2014)
6. Deng, H., Wu, Q., Qin, B., Domingo-Ferrer, J., Zhang, L., Liu, J., Shi, W.: Ciphertext-policy hierarchical attribute-based encryption with short ciphertexts. Information Sciences 275, 370–384 (2014)

7. Deng, H., Wu, Q., Qin, B., Mao, J., Liu, X., Zhang, L., Shi, W.: Who is touching my cloud. In: Kutyłowski, M., Vaidya, J. (eds.) ESORICS 2014, Part I. LNCS, vol. 8712, pp. 362–379. Springer, Heidelberg (2014)

8. Jin, J., Ahn, G.-J., Hu, H., Covington, M.J., Zhang, X.: Patient-centric authorization framework for sharing electronic health records. In: SACMAT 2009, pp. 125–134. ACM (2009)

9. Lee, K., Choi, S.G., Lee, D.H., Park, J.H., Yung, M.: Self-updatable encryption: Time constrained access control with hidden attributes and better efficiency. In: Sako, K., Sarkar, P. (eds.) ASIACRYPT 2013, Part I. LNCS, vol. 8269, pp. 235–254. Springer, Heidelberg (2013)

10. Li, M., Yu, S., Zheng, Y., Ren, K., Lou, W.: Scalable and secure sharing of personal health records in cloud computing using attribute-based encryption. IEEE Trans. Parallel and Distributed Systems 24(1), 131–143 (2013)

11. Liang, K., Liu, J.K., Wong, D.S., Susilo, W.: An efficient cloud-based revocable identity-based proxy re-encryption scheme for public clouds data sharing. In: Kutyłowski, M., Vaidya, J. (eds.) ESORICS 2014, Part I. LNCS, vol. 8712, pp. 257–272. Springer, Heidelberg (2014)

12. Libert, B., Vergnaud, D.: Adaptive-ID secure revocable identity-based encryption. In: Fischlin, M. (ed.) CT-RSA 2009. LNCS, vol. 5473, pp. 1–15. Springer, Heidelberg (2009)

13. Mashima, D., Ahamad, M.: Enabling robust information accountability in e-healthcare systems. In: 3rd USENIX Workshop on Health Security and Privacy (2012)

14. Naor, D., Naor, M., Lotspiech, J.: Revocation and tracing schemes for stateless receivers. In: Kilian, J. (ed.) CRYPTO 2001. LNCS, vol. 2139, pp. 41–62. Springer, Heidelberg (2001)

15. Park, S., Lee, K., Lee, D.H.: New constructions of revocable identity-based encryption from multilinear maps. In: Cryptology ePrint Archive, Report 2013/880 (2013), http://eprint.iacr.org/2013/880

16. Perumal, B., Rajasekaran, M.P., Duraiyarasan, S.: An efficient hierarchical attribute set based encryption scheme with revocation for outsourcing personal health records in cloud computing. In: ICACCS 2013, pp. 1–5. IEEE (2013)

17. Sahai, A., Seyalioglu, H., Waters, B.: Dynamic credentials and ciphertext delegation for attribute-based encryption. In: Safavi-Naini, R., Canetti, R. (eds.) CRYPTO 2012. LNCS, vol. 7417, pp. 199–217. Springer, Heidelberg (2012)

18. Seo, J.H., Emura, K.: Revocable identity-based encryption revisited: Security model and construction. In: Kurosawa, K., Hanaoka, G. (eds.) PKC 2013. LNCS, vol. 7778, pp. 216–234. Springer, Heidelberg (2013)

19. Seo, J.H., Emura, K.: Efficient delegation of key generation and revocation functionalities in identity-based encryption. In: Dawson, E. (ed.) CT-RSA 2013. LNCS, vol. 7779, pp. 343–358. Springer, Heidelberg (2013)

20. Shoniregun, C.A., Dube, K., Mtenzi, F.: Secure e-healthcare information systems. In: Electronic Healthcare Information Security, pp. 101–121. Springer US (2010)

21. Sun, L., Wang, H., Yong, J., Wu, G.: Semantic access control for cloud computing based on e-Healthcare. In: CSCWD 2012, pp. 512–518. IEEE (2012)

22. Yi, X., Miao, Y., Bertino, E., Willemson, J.: Multiparty privacy protection for electronic health records. In: GLOBECOM 2013, pp. 2730–2735. IEEE (2013)

23. Yu, S., Wang, C., Ren, K., Lou, W.: Attribute based data sharing with attribute revocation. In: ASIACCS 2010, pp. 261–270. ACM (2010)

Efficient File Sharing in Electronic Health Records[*]

Clémentine Gritti, Willy Susilo, and Thomas Plantard

Centre for Computer and Information Security Research
School of Computer Science and Software Engineering
University of Wollongong, Australia
cjpg967@uowmail.edu.au, {wsusilo,thomaspl}@uow.edu.au

Abstract. The issue of handling electronic health records have become paramount interest to the practitioners and security community, due to their sensitivity. In this paper, we propose a framework that enables medical practitioners to securely communicate among themselves to discuss health matters, and the patients can be rest assured that the information will only be made available to eligible medical practitioners. Specifically, we construct a new cryptographic primitive to enable File Sharing in Electronic Health Records (**FSEHR**). This primitive enables doctors to read the information sent by the hospital, or by any other individuals (such as patients' health records), when the doctors have their 'license' validated by that given hospital. We construct such a cryptographic primitive and capture its security requirements in a set of security models. Subsequently, we present a concrete scheme, which is proven selectively chosen-ciphertext security (CCA-1) secure under the Decisional Bilinear Diffie-Hellman Exponent (DBDHE) assumption and fully collusion resistant.

Keywords: File Sharing, Electronic Health Records, Broadcast Encryption, Certificate-Based Encryption, Bilinear map, Chosen-Ciphertext Security.

1   Introduction

Electronic Health Records (EHR) have become of paramount interest to practitioners and security community, due to their data size as well as their security issues and sensitivity. In the existing literature, there have been a number of papers [9,12,13,2] that discuss the way to secure this type of data. In this work, we take a new direction by proposing a framework that enables secure communication among medical practitioners. The communication channel enabled here will allow medical practitioners, i.e. medical doctors, to communicate among themselves as well as to review the patients' EHRs. Additionally, it also allows the hospital to broadcast any important information to the doctors who are working in that hospital, and this information will only be made available to them.

---

[*] This work is partially supported by the Australian Linkage Project LP120200052.

J. Lopez and Y. Wu (Eds.): ISPEC 2015, LNCS 9065, pp. 499–513, 2015.
DOI: 10.1007/978-3-319-17533-1_34

The issue is the fact that the doctors have their own rights in a hospital, delivered by the government or the medical legislators. Therefore, our framework should be able to specify which are the doctors that have access to the data by updating their license as authorized in that hospital. To generalize this scenario, we decouple several entities involved in this scenario, namely the hospital (as the data owner), the government and the other medical legislators, who grant the license for the doctors to work in that hospital. This scenario is depicted in Figure 1. We note that the hospital would be the entity that generates the encrypted data for the doctors, which includes all important information that the doctors need to know. Additionally, any other members (such as the nurse or any other entities outside the doctors) should also be able to send any information to the group of doctors in that hospital. This is to represent a case for instance when a patient provides his/her X-ray or blood test results to the hospital.

Our Work. Based on the above scenario, we present a new cryptographic notion called File Sharing in Electronic Health Records (FSEHR). In this system, there are four entities, namely the Group Manager (GM), a group of Certificate Authorities (CA), or simply of Certifiers, a set of doctors and the rest of the universe. The GM represents an entity such as the hospital in this scenario. A CA represents the government, the medical institute or other medical legislator who grants the rights to some doctors to work in a given hospital. The set of doctors is denoted as a set of users, U_i, who are the main players in this setting. The rest of the universe includes the patients, nurses, and any other players who are not captured in the above set of entities. The scenario of the FSEHR primitive is depicted in Figure 1. In this work, we provide a sound security model to capture this scenario.

One may think that FSEHR could be achieved easily by combining the two cryptographic primitives, namely certificate-based encryption and broadcast encryption schemes. Unfortunately this is false. The primary difficulty of achieving such a scheme is due to the need to achieve a shorter ciphertext, in comparison to merely combining the ciphertexts into one to achieve a linear size. Furthermore, the notion of certificate-based encryption usually allows a sender to interact with only a single receiver, with the help of a CA. Hence, it is clear that by a simple combination of the existing certificate-based encryption scheme and a broadcast encryption will lead a construction with a linear size of ciphertext (in number of both users and certifiers), which is undesirable (otherwise, it would be better for the broadcaster to just simply encrypt each ciphertext individually for each user). Moreover, we require that a FSEHR scheme to be fully collusion resistant, which follows the original notion of broadcast encryption schemes. Hence, even if all the users in the system collude, only the users in the selected subset with valid certificates can recover the plaintext.

Related Work. Modelling and securing authorization and access control to EHR has become a challenge. In [9], such a model, called Role-Based Access Control (RBAC), is proposed to inscrease the patient privacy and confidentiality of his data but it remains flexible to allow specific situations (for instance, emergency cases). A literature review about security and privacy in EHR can be found in [2].

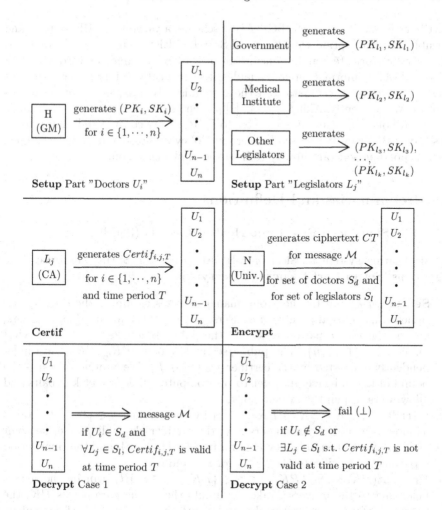

Fig. 1. A hospital H (GM) generates and sends the public/secret key pairs (PK_i, SK_i) for doctor U_i, where $i = 1, \cdots, n$. The government, the medical institute and the other medical legislators L_j (CAs) create their public/secret key pairs $(PK_{l_1}, SK_{l_1}), (PK_{l_2}, SK_{l_2}), (PK_{l_3}, SK_{l_3}), \cdots, (PK_{l_k}, SK_{l_k})$ respectively. The legislators then compute and give the certificates $Certif_{i,j,l}$ for doctor U_i, where $i = 1, \cdots, n$, $j = 1, \cdots, k$, and time period T. Finally, a hospital staff member (Universe), for instance a nurse N, selects a subgroup of doctors $S_d = \{U_{i_1}, \cdots, U_{i_{|S_d|}}\}$ and a subgroup of legislators S_l, encrypts a message $\mathcal{M}$ for doctors in S_d, legislators in S_l and time period T, and sends the resulting ciphertext CT. Only a doctor $U_{i_{i'}}$ in S_d, with certificate $Certif_{i,j,l}$ valid at time period T and where $L_j \in S_l$, can recover $\mathcal{M}$.

Benaloh et al. [3] combined a Hierarchical Identity-Based Encryption (HIBE) and a searchable encryption to obtain a privacy-preserving and patient-centered EHR system. However, the patients have to create and manage manifold keys and check the credentials of the healthcare providers (doctors, nurses, ...). Narayan et al. [10] proposed an EHR system using a broadcast Ciphertext-Policy

Attribute-Based Encryption (bCP-ABE) scheme, a variant of ABE system, and a Public key Encryption with Keyword Search (PEKS) scheme. Their system is secure, allows private search on health records by performing keyword matching without leaking information, and enable direct revocation of user access without having to re-encrypt the data. But the system is only designed for online access control. More recently, Akinyele et al. [1] presented a system along with a mobile app for iPhone for secure offline access to EHRs. They constructed their scheme based on ABE (Key-Policy and Ciphertext-Policy versions) and they developped a corresponding software library to help the implementation.

2   Preliminaries and Definitions

2.1   File Sharing in Electronic Health Records (FSEHR)

A File Sharing system in Electronic Health Records (FSEHR) comprises four algorithms (**Setup, Certif, Encrypt, Decrypt**):

1. **Setup**(λ, n, k) run by the group manager, takes as inputs the security parameter λ, the total number n of users, and the total number k of cerfitiers, output the public parameters PK, the public/secret key pair (PK_i, SK_i) for user $i \in \{1, \cdots, n\}$. The public/secret key pair (PK_{c_j}, SK_{c_j}) are independently generated by the certifier $j \in \{1, \cdots, k\}$. We assume that n is the bound of the universe, in order to pre-compute public/secret key pairs and allow users to join the system later.

2. **Certif**$(PK, (PK_{c_j}, SK_{c_j}), PK_i, l)$ run by the certifier $j \in \{1, \cdots, k\}$, takes as inputs the public parameters PK, the certifier j's public/secret key pair (PK_{c_j}, SK_{c_j}), the public key PK_i for user $i \in \{1, \cdots, n\}$, and the time period l, output the certificate $Certif_{i,j,l}$ for i, j and l.

3. **Encrypt**$(PK, S_u, S_c, \{PK_i : i \in S_u\}, \{PK_{c_j} : j \in S_c\}, l)$, run by the sender belonging to the universe, takes as inputs the public parameters PK, the subset S_u of users selected by the sender such that $S_u \subseteq \{1, \cdots, n\}$, the subset S_c of certifiers selected by the sender such that $S_c \subseteq \{1, \cdots, k\}$, the public keys PK_i for users $i \in S_u$, the certifier's public key PK_{c_j} for certifers $j \in S_c$, and the time period l, output the header Hdr and the session key K.

4. **Decrypt**$(PK, S_u, S_c, l, (PK_i, SK_i), \{Certif_{i,j,l} : j \in S_c\}, Hdr)$ run by user i, takes as inputs the public parameters PK, the subset S_u of users selected by the sender, the subset S_c of certifiers selected by the sender, the time period l, the public/secret key pair (PK_i, SK_i) and the certificates $Certif_{i,j,l}$ for user i and certifier $j \in S_c$, and the header Hdr, output the session key K if $i \in S_u$ and $Certif_{i,j,l}$ is valid for time period l; otherwise $\perp$.

We require that for user $i \in \{1, \cdots, n\}$ and certifier $j \in \{1, \cdots, k\}$ such that $(PK, (PK_i, SK_i), (PK_{c_j}, SK_{c_j})) \leftarrow$ **Setup**(λ, n, k), and subsets $S_u \in \{1, \cdots, n\}$ and $S_c \in \{1, \cdots, k\}$: if user $i \in S_u$, certifier $j \in S_c$ and $Certif_{i,j,l}$ is valid for time period l, then $K \leftarrow$ **Decrypt**$(PK, S_u, S_c, l, (PK_i, SK_i), \{Certif_{i,j,l} : j \in S_c\},$ **Encrypt**$(PK, S_u, S_c, \{PK_i : i \in S_u\}, \{PK_{c_j} : j \in S_c\}, l))$; otherwise $\perp$

$\leftarrow$ **De- crypt**$(PK, S_u, S_c, l, (PK_i, SK_i), \{Certif_{i,j,l} : j \in S_c\},$ **Encrypt**$(PK, S_u, S_c, \{PK_i : i \in S_u\}, \{PK_{c_j} : j \in S_c\}, l)).$

We call the *header*, Hdr, as the encryption of the session key K. We call the *full header* as the header Hdr along with the descriptions of the set S_u of users and the set S_c of certifiers selected by the sender. Without losing generalization, we only consider the header Hdr when discussing the size of the scheme.

2.2 Security Requirements

We first present the definitions for chosen-plaintext attack (CPA) and chosen-ciphertext attack (CCA) securities. We adopt the security definitions from the certificate-based encryption [7]. There are two basic attacks which may be launced by an uncertified user or by the certifier. These are captured in the following two distinct games. In Game 1, the adversary plays the role of an uncertified user: it first proves that it knows the secret key of the uncertified user and then, it can make Decryption and Certification queries. In Game 2, the adversary plays the role of a trusted certifier: it first proves that it knows the secret key of the certifier and then, it can make Decryption queries. Eventually, we say that the FSEHR system is secure if no adversary can win either game.

Game 1. Setup. The challenger runs the algorithm **Setup**(λ, n, k) to obtain the public parameters PK, the public keys PK_i for users $i \in \{1, \cdots, n\}$, and the public keys PK_{c_j} for certifiers $j \in \{1, \cdots, k\}$, and gives them to $\mathcal{A}_1$.

Certification Query Phase. For time period l, for user $i \in \{1, \cdots, n\}$, and for $j \in \{1, \cdots, k\}$, the challenger first checks that SK_i is the secret key corresponding to the public key PK_i. If so, it runs **Certif** and returns $Certif_{i,j,l}$ to the adversary $\mathcal{A}_1$; otherwise, it returns $\perp$.

Decryption Query Phase. For time period l, for user $i \in \{1, \cdots, n\}$, and for certifier $j \in \{1, \cdots, k\}$, the challenger first checks that SK_i is the secret key corresponding to the public key PK_i. If so, it returns **Decrypt**$(PK, S_u, S_c, l, (PK_i, SK_i), \{Certif_{i,j,l} : j \in S_c\}, Hdr)$ to the adversary $\mathcal{A}_1$; otherwise, it returns $\perp$.

Challenge. For time period l^*, $\mathcal{A}_1$ outputs a challenge set $S_u^* \subseteq \{1, \cdots, n\}$. For user $i \in S_u^*$, the challenger first checks that SK_i^* is the secret key corresponding to the public key PK_i^*. If so, it chooses a set $S_c^* \subseteq \{1, \cdots, k\}$ and a random bit $b \in_R \{0, 1\}$, and runs $(Hdr^*, K^*) \leftarrow$ **Encrypt**$(PK^*, S_u^*, S_c^*, \{PK_i^* : i \in S_u^*\}, \{PK_{c_j}^* : j \in S_c^*\}, l^*)$. It then sets $K_b^* = K^*$, picks at random K_{1-b}^* in the key space, and gives $(Hdr^*, K_b^*, K_{1-b}^*)$ to the adversary $\mathcal{A}_1$. Otherwise, it gives $\perp$.

Guess. The adversary $\mathcal{A}_1$ outputs its guess $b' \in_R \{0, 1\}$ for b and wins the game if $b = b'$, (l^*, S_u^*, Hdr^*) was not the subject of a valid Decryption query after the Challenge, and (l^*, S_u^*) was not subject of any valid Certification query.

We define $\mathcal{A}_1$'s advantage in attacking the File Sharing system in Electronic Health Records for Game 1 with parameters (λ, n, k) as $Adv\mathsf{FSEHR}_{\mathcal{A}_1, n, k}^{Game1}(\lambda) = |Pr[b = b'] - \frac{1}{2}|$.

Game 2. Setup. The challenger runs the algorithm **Setup**(λ, n, k) to obtain the public parameters PK, the public keys PK_i for users $i \in \{1, \cdots, n\}$, and the public keys PK_{c_j} for certifiers $j \in \{1, \cdots, k\}$, and gives them to $\mathcal{A}_2$.

Decryption Query Phase. For time period l and for certifier $j \in \{1, \cdots, k\}$, the challenger first checks that SK_{c_j} is the secret key corresponding to the public key PK_{c_j}. If so, it returns **Decrypt**$(PK, S_u, S_c, l, (PK_i, SK_i), \{Certif_{i,j,l} : j \in S_c\}, Hdr)$ to the adversary $\mathcal{A}_2$; otherwise, it returns $\perp$.

Challenge. For time period l^*, $\mathcal{A}_2$ outputs a challenge set $S_u^* \subseteq \{1, \cdots, n\}$. The challenger first checks that $SK_{c_j}^*$ is the secret key corresponding to the public key $PK_{c_j}^*$. If so, it chooses a set $S_c^* \subseteq \{1, \cdots, k\}$ such that $j \in S_c^*$ and a random bit $b \in_R \{0, 1\}$, and runs $(Hdr^*, K^*) \leftarrow$ **Encrypt**$(PK, S_u^*, S_c^*, \{PK_i^* : i \in S^*\}, \{PK_{c_j}^* : j \in S_c^*\}, l^*)$. It then sets $K_b^* = K^*$, picks at random K_{1-b}^* in the key space, and gives $(Hdr^*, K_b^*, K_{1-b}^*)$ to the adversary $\mathcal{A}_2$. Otherwise, it gives $\perp$.

Guess. The adversary $\mathcal{A}_2$ outputs its guess $b' \in_R \{0, 1\}$ for b and wins the game if $b = b'$ and $(l^*, PK_{c_j}^*, Hdr^*)$ was not the subject of a valid Decryption query after the Challenge.

We define $\mathcal{A}_2$'s advantage in attacking the File Sharing system in Electronic Health Records for Game 2 with parameters (λ, n, k) as $Adv\mathsf{FSEHR}_{\mathcal{A}_2, n, k}^{Game2}(\lambda) = |Pr[b = b'] - \frac{1}{2}|$.

Definition 1. *We say that a File Sharing system in Electronic Health Records is adaptively $(t, \varepsilon, n, k, q_C, q_D)$-secure if no t-time algorithm $\mathcal{A}$ that makes at most q_C Certification queries (in Game 1) and $q_D = q_{D1} + q_{D2}$ Decryption queries (in the Game 1 and Game 2 respectively), has non-negligible advantage in either Game 1 or Game 2, i.e. $Adv\mathsf{FSEHR}_{\mathcal{A}, n, k}^{Game1}(\lambda) + Adv\mathsf{FSEHR}_{\mathcal{A}, n, k}^{Game2}(\lambda) \leq \varepsilon$.*

We also mention the selective CCA security: a selective adversary $\mathcal{A}$ provides the set $S_u^* \subseteq \{1, \cdots, n\}$ that it wishes to be challenged on at the beginning of the security game.

We then define the Fully Collusion Resistance security, in order to capture the notion of encryption against arbitrary collusion of users. Let the number of users n, the number of certifiers k and the security parameter λ be given to the adversary $\mathcal{A}$ and the challenger. The game between the two entities proceeds as follows:

Game Fully Collusion Resistant

1. The adversary $\mathcal{A}$ outputs a set $S_{u,n'} = \{u_1, \cdots, u_{n'}\} \subseteq \{1, \cdots, n\}$ of colluding users.
2. The challenger runs the algorithm **Setup**(λ, n, k) to obtain the public parameters PK, the keys pairs (PK_i, SK_i) for users $i \in S_{u,n'}$, and the keys pair (PK_{c_j}, SK_{c_j}) for the certifier $j \in \{1, \cdots, k\}$. It gives $(PK, \{PK_i, SK_i : i \in S_{u,n'}\}, \{PK_{c_j} : j \in \{1, \cdots, k\}\})$ to the adversary $\mathcal{A}$ and keeps SK_{c_j} to itself. It also runs the algorithm **Certif**$(PK, (PK_{c_j}, SK_{c_j}), PK_i, l)$ to obtain the certificates $Certif_{i,j,l}$ for user $i \in S_{u,n'}$, $j \in \{1, \cdots, k\}$, and time period l, and gives them to the adversary $\mathcal{A}$.

3. The challenger runs the algorithm **Encrypt**$(PK, S_u, S_c, \{PK_i : i \in S_u\}, \{PK_j : j \in S_c\}, l')$ for a subset $S_u \subseteq \{1, \cdots, n\}$ such that $S_u \cap S_{u,n'} = \emptyset$ and $l' \neq l$, and for a subset $S_c \subseteq \{1, \cdots, k\}$, and gives the resulting header Hdr to the adversary $\mathcal{A}$ and keeps the associated session key K to itself.

4. The adversary $\mathcal{A}$ outputs $K^* \leftarrow$ **Decrypt**$(PK, S_u, S_c, l', (f(\{PK_i : i \in S' \subseteq S_{u,n'}\}), f(\{SK_i : i \in S' \subseteq S_{u,n'}\})), \{f(\{Certif_{i,l} : i \in S' \subseteq S_{u,n'}\}) : j \in S_c\}, Hdr^*)$ where f is a function that takes as input public keys, secret keys or certificates, and outputs a new public key, a new secret key or a new certificate as a combination of public keys, secret keys or certificates, respectively.

5. The adversary $\mathcal{A}$ wins the game if $K^* = K$.

Definition 2. *We say that a File Sharing system in Electronic Health Records is fully collusion resistant if no t-time algorithm $\mathcal{A}$ has non-negligible advantage in the above game.*

2.3 Broadcast Encryption

A Broadcast Encryption (BE) system [6,5,4,8] is made up of three randomized algorithms (**Setup**$_{\mathsf{BE}}$, **Encrypt**$_{\mathsf{BE}}$, **Decrypt**$_{\mathsf{BE}}$) such that:

1. **Setup**$_{\mathsf{BE}}(n)$ takes as input the number of receivers n. It outputs n secret keys $d_1, \cdots, d_n$ and a public key PK.

2. **Encrypt**$_{\mathsf{BE}}(S, PK)$ takes as inputs a subset $S \subseteq \{1, \cdots, n\}$ and a public key PK. It outputs a pair (Hdr, K) where Hdr is called the header and $K \in \mathcal{K}$ is a message encryption key chosen from a finite key set $\mathcal{K}$. We will often refer to Hdr as the broadcast ciphertext.
   Let M be a message to be broadcast that should be decipherable precisely by the receivers in S. Let C_M be the encryption of M under the symmetric key K. The broadcast consists of (S, Hdr, C_M). The pair (S, Hdr) is often called the *full header* and C_M is often called the *broadcast body*.

3. **Decrypt**$_{\mathsf{BE}}(S, i, d_i, Hdr, PK)$ takes as inputs a subset $S \subseteq \{1, \cdots, n\}$, a user identity $i \in \{1, \cdots, n\}$ and the secret key d_i for user i, a header Hdr, and the public key PK. If $i \in S$, then the algorithm outputs a message encryption key $K \in \mathcal{K}$. Intuitively, user i can then use K to decrypt the broadcast body C_M and obtain the message body M.

We require that for all subset $S \subseteq \{1, \cdots, n\}$ and all $i \in S$, if $(PK, (d_1, \cdots, d_n)) \leftarrow$ **Setup**$_{\mathsf{BE}}(n)$ and $(Hdr, K) \leftarrow$ **Encrypt**$_{\mathsf{BE}}(S, PK)$, then **Decrypt**$_{\mathsf{BE}}(S, i, d_i, Hdr, PK) = K$.

2.4 Certificate-Based Encryption

A certificate-updating Certificate-Based Encryption (CBE) system is made up of six randomized algorithms (**Gen**$_{\mathsf{IBE}}$, **Gen**$_{\mathsf{PKE}}$, **Upd1**, **Upd2**, **Encrypt**$_{\mathsf{CBE}}$, **De-crypt**$_{\mathsf{CBE}}$) such that:

1. **Gen**$_{\mathsf{IBE}}(\lambda_1,t)$ takes as inputs a security parameter λ_1 and (optionally) the total number of time periods t. It outputs SK_{IBE} (the certifier's master secret key) and public parameters $params$ that include a public key PK_{IBE} and the description of a string space $\mathcal{S}$.

2. **Gen**$_{\mathsf{PKE}}(\lambda_2,t)$ takes as inputs a security parameter λ_2 and (optionally) the total number of time periods t. It outputs SK_{PKE} and public key PK_{PKE} (the client's secret and public keys).

3. **Upd1**$(SK_{\mathsf{IBE}}, params, l, s, PK_{\mathsf{PKE}})$ takes as inputs SK_{IBE}, $params$, l, string $s \in \mathcal{S}$ and PK_{PKE}, at the start of time period l. It outputs $Cert'_l$, which is sent to the client.

4. **Upd2**$(params, l, Cert'_l, Cert_{l-1})$ takes as inputs $params$, l, $Cert'_l$ and (optionally) $Cert_{l-1}$, at the start of time period l. It outputs $Cert_l$.

5. **Encrypt**$_{\mathsf{CBE}}(params, l, s, PK_{\mathsf{PKE}}, M)$ takes as inputs $(params, l, s, PK_{\mathsf{PKE}}, M)$, where M is a message. It outputs a ciphertext C on message M intended for the client to decrypt using $Cert_l$ and SK_{PKE} (and possibly s).

6. **Decrypt**$_{\mathsf{CBE}}(params, Cert_l, SK_{\mathsf{PKE}}, C, l)$ takes as inputs $(params, Cert_l, SK_{\mathsf{PKE}}, C)$ in time period l. It outputs either M or the special case $\perp$ indicating failure.

We require that **Decrypt**$(params, Cert_l, SK_{\mathsf{PKE}},$ **Encrypt**$(params, l, s, PK_{\mathsf{PKE}}, M), l) = M$ for the given $params \leftarrow$ **Gen**$_{\mathsf{IBE}}(\lambda_1, t)$, $PK \leftarrow$ **Gen**$_{\mathsf{PKE}}(\lambda_2, t)$, $Cert_l \leftarrow$ **Upd2**$(params, l, $**Upd1**$(SK_{\mathsf{IBE}}, params, l, s, PK_{\mathsf{PKE}}), Cert_{l-1})$.

3   An Efficient Construction

Our construction FSEHR is an effective combination of the BGW Broadcast Encryption (BE) scheme [4] and the Gentry's Certificate-Based Encryption (CBE) scheme [7]. Notice that the Gentry's CBE scheme is designed for a communication between one sender and one receiver. Therefore, applying the Gentry's CBE scheme directly to the BGW, will lead to the linear size of the headers in the number of users and of certifiers in the two respective subsets designed by the sender, which is impractical. However, we managed to overcome this issue and achieve constant size for header, secret keys and certificates. Moreover, our scheme FSEHR is proved selective CCA secure using the standard transformation from the REACT scheme proposed by Okamoto and Pointcheval [11].

Setup(λ, n, k). On input the security parameter λ, the total number n of users, and the total number k of certifiers, run $(p, \mathbb{G}, \mathbb{G}_T, e) \leftarrow$ **GroupGen**(λ, n, k). Pick at random $g \in_R \mathbb{G}$ and $\alpha \in_R \mathbb{Z}_p$, compute $g_i = g^{(\alpha^i)}$ for $i = 1, \cdots, n, n+2, \cdots, 2n$. Pick at random $\gamma \in_R \mathbb{Z}_p$ and compute $v = g^\gamma$. Choose three hash functions $H_1 : \mathbb{G} \times \{0,1\}^* \to \mathbb{G}$, $H_2 : \mathbb{G} \times \mathbb{G} \to \mathbb{G}$, and $H_3 : \mathbb{G}_T \times \mathbb{G} \times \mathbb{G} \times \mathbb{G} \times \mathbb{G} \to \{0,1\}^\lambda$. For user $i \in \{1, \cdots, n\}$, compute the user's secret key as $d_i = g_i^\gamma (= v^{(\alpha^i)})$.

Independently, for $j \in \{1, \cdots, k\}$, certifier j computes its own public/secret key pair as follows: choose at random an exponent $\sigma_j \in_R \mathbb{Z}_p$ and then compute the public key $w_j = g^{\sigma_j}$. Set the secret key as $d_{c_j} = \sigma_j$.

Set the public parameters as $PK = (p, \mathbb{G}, \mathbb{G}_T, g, g_1, \cdots, g_n, g_{n+2}, \cdots, g_{2n}, v, w_1, \cdots, w_k, H_1, H_2, H_3)$.

Certif(PK, d_{c_j}, i, l). On input the public parameters PK, the certifier j's secret key d_{c_j}, the user i, and the time period l represented as a string in $\{0,1\}^*$, pick at random $r_{i,j,l} \in_R \mathbb{Z}_p$ and compute the user's certificate $e_{i,j,l} = (e_{i,j,l,1}, e_{i,j,l,2})$ as follows:

$$e_{i,j,l,1} = g_i^{\sigma_j} \cdot H_1(w_j, l)^{\sigma_j \cdot r_{i,j,l}} (= w_j^{(\alpha^i)} \cdot H_1(w_j, l)^{\sigma_j \cdot r_{i,j,l}})$$

$$e_{i,j,l,2} = g^{\sigma_j \cdot r_{i,j,l}} (= w_j^{r_{i,j,l}})$$

Encrypt(PK, S_u, S_c, l). On input the public parameters PK, a set $S_u \subseteq \{1, \cdots, n\}$ of users, a set $S_c \subseteq \{1, \cdots, k\}$ of certifiers, and the time period l, pick at random an exponent $t \in_R \mathbb{Z}_p$, compute the session key $K = e(g_{n+1}, g)^t$, and set the header $Hdr = (C_1, C_2, C_3, C_4, C_5)$ as follows:

$$(g^t, \prod_{j \in S_c} H_1(w_j, l)^t, (v \cdot \prod_{j \in S_c} w_j \cdot \prod_{i' \in S_u} g_{n+1-i'})^t, H_2(C_1, C_3)^t, H_3(K, C_1, C_2, C_3, C_4))$$

Decrypt$(PK, S_u, S_c, l, i, d_i, e_{i,j,l}, Hdr)$. On input the public parameters PK, a set $S_u \subseteq \{1, \cdots, n\}$ of users, a set $S_c \subseteq \{1, \cdots, k\}$ of certifiers, the time period l, the user i with its secret key d_i and its certificates $e_{i,j,l}$ for $j \in S_c$, parsed as $(e_{i,j,l,1}, e_{i,j,l,2})$, and the header Hdr parsed as $(C_1, C_2, C_3, C_4, C_5)$, check whether $e(C_1, H_2(C_1, C_3)) \stackrel{?}{=} e(g, C_4)$, and output

$$K = \frac{e(g_i, C_3) \cdot e(\prod_{j \in S_c} e_{i,j,l,2}, C_2)}{e(d_i \cdot \prod_{j \in S_c} e_{i,j,l,1} \cdot \prod_{i' \in S_u \setminus \{i\}} g_{n+1-i'+i}, C_1)} = e(g_{n+1}, g)^t$$

Then, compute $C_5' = H_3(K, C_1, C_2, C_3, C_4)$. If $C_5' = C_5$, then return K; otherwise return $\bot$.

Correctness. Notice that $g_i^{(\alpha^{i'})} = g_{i+i'}$ for any i, i'. At time period l, user $i \in S_u \subseteq \{1, \cdots, n\}$ with secret key d_i and certificate $e_{i,l,j}$ for $j \in S_c \subseteq \{1, \cdots, k\}$ decrypts as follows:

$$K = \frac{e(g_i, C_3) \cdot e(\prod_{j \in S_c} e_{i,j,l,2}, C_2)}{e(d_i \cdot \prod_{j \in S_c} e_{i,j,l,1} \cdot \prod_{i' \in S_u \setminus \{i\}} g_{n+1-i'+i}, C_1)}$$

$$= \frac{e(g^{(\alpha^i)}, (v \cdot \prod_{j \in S_c} w_j \cdot \prod_{i' \in S_u} g_{n+1-i'})^t) \cdot e(\prod_{j \in S_c} g^{\sigma_j \cdot r_{i,j,l}}, \prod_{j \in S_c} H_1(w_j, l)^t)}{e(v^{(\alpha^i)} \cdot \prod_{j \in S_c} w_j^{(\alpha^i)} \cdot H_1(w_j, l)^{\sigma_j \cdot r_{i,j,l}} \cdot \prod_{i' \in S_u \setminus \{i\}} g_{n+1-i'+i}, g^t)}$$

$$= e(g_{n+1}, g)^t$$

Performance. In the following table, we evaluate the efficiency of our scheme FSEHR. We use results of cryptographic operation implementations (exponentiations and pairings) using the MIRACL library, provided by Certivox for the MIRACL Authentication Server Project Wiki. All the following experiments are based on Borland C/C++ Compiler/Assembler and tested on a processor 2.4 GHz Intel i5 520M.

For our symmetric pairing-based systems, AES with a 80-bit key and a Super Singular curve over $\mathbb{GF}_p$, for a 512-bit modulus p and an embedding degree equal to 2, are used. We assume that there are $n = 100$ users and $k = 20$ certifiers.

		Exponentiation in $\mathbb{G}$	Exponentiation in $\mathbb{G}_T$	Pairings
Time/computation		1.49	0.36	3.34
Algorithms	**Setup**	546,80		
	Certif	89,40		
	Encrypt	5,96	0,36	3,34
	Decrypt			16,70

Fig. 2. Timings for our symmetric pairing-based system FSEHR. Times are in milliseconds

We note that the total time in the algorithm **Setup** is substantial, but we recall that this algorithm should be run only once to generate the public parameters and the static secret keys for both users and certifiers. In the algorithm **Certif**, it requires 89,40 milliseconds because $k = 20$ certificates are created. Finally, in the algorithms **Encrypt** and **Decrypt**, it takes 9,66 and 16,70 milliseconds respectively, mainly due to the cost of pairing computations.

4   Security Proofs

Assumption. We prove the security of our scheme FSEHR using the Decisional n-Bilinear Diffie-Hellman Exponent (DBDHE) assumption, which is as follows.

Definition 3. *The (t,n,ε)-BDHE assumption says that for any t-time adversary $\mathcal{B}$ that is given $(g,h,g^a,g^{a^2},\cdots,g^{a^n},g^{a^{n+2}},\cdots,g^{a^{2n}}) \in \mathbb{G}^{2n+1}$, and a candidate to Decisional n-BDHE problem, that is either $e(g,h)^{a^{n+1}} \in \mathbb{G}_T$ or a random value T, cannot distinguish the two cases with advantage greater than ε:*

$$AdvBDHE_{\mathcal{B},n} = |Pr[\mathcal{B}(g,h,g^a,g^{a^2},\cdots,g^{a^n},g^{a^{n+2}},\cdots,g^{a^{2n}},e(g,h)^{a^{n+1}}) = 1]$$
$$-Pr[\mathcal{B}(g,h,g^a,g^{a^2},\cdots,g^{a^n},g^{a^{n+2}},\cdots,g^{a^{2n}},T) = 1]| \le \varepsilon$$

Selective CCA Security Proof

Theorem 1. *The File Sharing scheme in Electronic Health Records FSEHR achieves Selective CCA Security under the Decision n-BDHE assumption, in the random oracle model.*

Proof. We assume there exists an adversary $\mathcal{A}$ that breaks the semantic security of the FSEHR scheme with probability greater than ε within time t, making q_{H_1}, q_{H_2} and q_{H_3} random oracle queries, q_{cf} certification queries and q_d decryption queries. Using this adversary $\mathcal{A}$, we build an attacker $\mathcal{B}$ for the Decisional n-BDHE problem in $\mathbb{G}$. $\mathcal{B}$ proceeds as follows.

For simplicity, we write $g_i = g^{(\alpha^i)}$ for an implicitly defined α. $\mathcal{B}$ first takes as input a Decisional n-BDHE intance $(g, h, g_1, \cdots, g_n, g_{n+2}, \cdots, g_{2n}, Z)$ where $Z = e(g_{n+1}, h)$ or $Z \in_R \mathbb{G}_T$. $\mathcal{B}$ makes use of three random oracles H_1, H_2 and H_3, and three respective hash lists L_1, L_2 and L_3, initially set empty, to store all the query-answers.

Init. $\mathcal{A}$ outputs a set $S_u^* \subseteq \{1, \cdots, n\}$ of users that it wishes to be challenged on.

Setup. $\mathcal{B}$ needs to generate the public parameters PK, the secret keys d_i for $i \notin S_u^*$, and the secret keys d_{c_j} for the certifier $j \in \{1, \cdots, k\}$. It chooses random elements $x, y_1 \cdots, y_k \in_R \mathbb{Z}_p$, and sets $v = g^x / \prod_{i' \in S_u^*} g_{n+1-i'}$, $w_j = g^{y_j}$ and $d_{c_j} = y_j$ for $j \in \{1, \cdots, k\}$. It then computes

$$d_i = g_i^x / \prod_{i' \in S_u^*} g_{n+1-i'+i} = g^{x \cdot (\alpha^i)} \cdot \left(\prod_{i' \in S_u^*} g_{n+1-i'} \right)^{-(\alpha^i)} = v^{(\alpha^i)}.$$

Eventually, $\mathcal{B}$ gives $\mathcal{A}$ the public parameters $PK = (p, \mathbb{G}, \mathbb{G}_T, e, g, g_1, \cdots, g_n, g_{n+2}, \cdots, g_{2n}, v, w_1, \cdots, w_k, H_1, H_2, H_3)$, where H_1, H_2 and H_3 are controlled by $\mathcal{B}$ as follows:

- Upon receiving a query (w_j, l_j) to the random oracle H_1 for some $j \in [1, q_{H_1}]$:
  - If $((w_j, l_j), u_j, U_j)$ exists in L_1, return U_j.
  - Otherwise, choose $u_j \in_R \mathbb{Z}_p$ at random and compute $U_j = g^{u_j}$. Put $((w_j, l_j), u_j, U_j)$ in L_1 and return U_j as answer.
- Upon receiving a query (W_{1j}, W_{2j}) to the random oracle H_2 for some $j \in [1, q_{H_2}]$:
  - If $((W_{1j}, W_{2j}), X_j)$ exists in L_2, return X_j.
  - Otherwise, choose $X_j \in_R \mathbb{G}$ at random. Put $((W_{1j}, W_{2j}), X_j)$ in L_2 and return X_j as answer.
- Upon receiving a query $(K_j, C_{1j}, C_{2j}, C_{3j}, C_{4j})$ to the random oracle H_3 for some $j \in [1, q_{H_3}]$:
  - If $((K_j, C_{1j}, C_{2j}, C_{3j}, C_{4j}), C_{5j})$ exists in L_3, return C_{5j}.
  - Otherwise, choose $C_{5j} \in_R \{0, 1\}^\lambda$ at random. Put $(K_j, C_{1j}, C_{2j}, C_{3j}, C_{4j})$, $C_{5j})$ in L_3 and return C_{5j} as answer.

Phase 1. $\mathcal{B}$ answers $\mathcal{A}$'s queries as follows.

1. Upon receiving a Certification query $(PK_{i'}, d_i, l_{i'})$ for some $i \in \{1, \cdots, n\}$ and $i' \in [1, q_{cf}]$:
   - If $((w_{i',j}, l_{i'}), u_{i',j}, U_{i',j})$ exists in L_1, return the pair $(u_{i',j}, U_{i',j})$ for $j \in \{1, \cdots, k\}$.
   - Otherwise, choose $u_{i',j} \in_R \mathbb{Z}_p$ at random, compute $U_{i',j} = g^{u_{i',j}}$, and put $((w_{i',j}, l_{i'}), u_{i',j}, U_{i',j})$ in L_1.

Then, pick at random $r_{i,j,l_{i'}} \in_R \mathbb{Z}_p$ and return the certificate $e_{i,j,l_{i'}}$ where

$$e_{i,j,l_{i'},1} = g_i^{y_j} \cdot (U_{i',j}^{y_j})^{r_{i,j,l_{i'}}} = g^{y_j \cdot (\alpha^i)} \cdot (g^{u_{i',j}})^{r_{i,j,l_{i'}} \cdot y_j}$$

$$= g^{y_j \cdot (\alpha^i)} \cdot H_1(w_{i',j}, l_{i'})^{r_{i,j,l_{i'}} \cdot y_j} = w_{i',j}^{(\alpha^i)} \cdot w_{i',j}^{r_{i,j,l_{i'}} \cdot u_{i',j}}$$

$$e_{i,j,l_{i'},2} = w_{i',j}^{r_{i,j,l_{i'}}}$$

2. Upon receiving a Decryption query $(S_{u,i'}, Hdr_{i'}, i, l_{i'})$ for some $i \in \{1, \cdots, n\}$ and $i' \in [1, q_d]$, where $Hdr_{i'} = (C_{1i'}, C_{2i'}, C_{3i'}, C_{4i'}, C_{5i'})$:
   - If $((K_{i'}, C_{1i'}, C_{2i'}, C_{3i'}, C_{4i'}), C_{5i'})$ exists in L_3, do the following:
     - Compute $H_1(w_{i',j}, l_{i'})$ using the simulation of H_1 as above and check whether $e(C_{2i'}, g) \overset{?}{=} e(C_{1i'}, \prod_{j \in S_c} H_1(w_{i',j}, l_{i'}))$ for $j \in S_c \subseteq \{1, \cdots, k\}$. If not, return $\perp$. Otherwise, compute $H_2(C_{1i'}, C_{3i'})$ using the simulation of H_2 as above and check whether $e(C_{1i'}, H_2(C_{1i'}, C_{3i'})) \overset{?}{=} e(g, C_{4i'})$. If not, return $\perp$. Otherwise, check whether $K_{i'}$ is equal or not to

$$\frac{e(g_i, C_{3i'}) \cdot e(g, C_{2i'})}{e(g_i^{x+sum_{j \in S_c} y} \cdot \prod_{j \in S_c} H_1(w_{i',j}, l_{i'}), C_{1i'})}.$$

       If the above equation holds, return $K_{i'}$. Otherwise, return $\perp$.
   - Else, return $\perp$.

Challenge. $\mathcal{B}$ generates the challenge on the challenge set S_u^* as follows. First, $\mathcal{B}$ sets $C_1^* = h$ and searchs in L_1 to get u that corresponds to (w_j, l) such that $j \in S_c \subseteq \{1, \cdots, k\}$. Then, it computes $C_2^* = h^u$. It also computes $C_3^* = h^{x + \sum_{j \in S_c} y}$. Informally, we write $h = g^t$ for an unknown $t \in \mathbb{Z}_p$. Then, it randomly chooses an exponent $z \in_R \mathbb{Z}_p$, and sets $C_4^* = h^z = H_2(C_1^*, C_3^*)^t$. Second, it randomly chooses a bit $b \in_R \{0, 1\}$ and sets $K_b = Z$ and picks a random K_{b-1} in $\mathbb{G}_T$. It also picks $C_5^* \in_R \{0, 1\}^*$ at random, and sets $C_5^* = H_3(K_b, C_1^*, C_2^*, C_3^*, C_4^*)$. Finally, it returns $(Hdr^* = (C_1^*, C_2^*, C_3^*, C_4^*, C_5^*), K_0, K_1)$ as the challenge to $\mathcal{A}$.

When $Z = e(g_{n+1}, h)$, then (Hdr^*, K_0, K_1) is a valid challenge for $\mathcal{A}$'s point of view, as in the real attack. Indeed, if we write $h = g^t$ for an unknown $t \in \mathbb{Z}_p$, then

$$h^{x + \sum_{j \in S_c} y} = h^x \cdot \prod_{j \in S_c} h^{y_j} \cdot \left(\frac{\prod_{i' \in S_u^*} g_{n+1-i'}}{\prod_{j \in S_u^*} g_{n+1-i'}} \right)^t = g^{t \cdot x} \cdot \prod_{j \in S_c} g^{t \cdot y_j} \cdot \left(\frac{\prod_{i' \in S_u^*} g_{n+1-i'}}{\prod_{j \in S_u^*} g_{n+1-i'}} \right)^t$$

$$= \left(\frac{g^x}{\prod_{i' \in S_u^*} g_{n+1-i'}} \cdot \prod_{j \in S_c} g^{y_j} \cdot \prod_{i' \in S_u^*} g_{n+1-i'} \right)^t = C_3^*$$

Therefore, by definition, Hdr^* is a valid encryption of the session key $e(g_{n+1}, g)^t$. Moreover, $e(g_{n+1}, g)^t = e(g_{n+1}, h) = Z = K_b$, and thus (Hdr^*, K_0, K_1) is a valid challenge to $\mathcal{A}$. When $Z \in_R \mathbb{G}_T$, then K_0 and K_1 are random independent elements in $\mathbb{G}_T$.

Phase 2. $\mathcal{B}$ responds to the Certification and Decryption queries as in **Phase 1**. We note that if $(K_b^*, C_1^*, C_2^*, C_3^*, C_4^*)$ is asked to the random oracle H_3, the value C_5^* created in the simulation of the Challenge is returned.

Guess. The adversary $\mathcal{A}$ outputs its guess $b' \in_R \{0, 1\}$ for b.

Analysis. In the simulations of the secret key generation and the certificate generation, the responses to $\mathcal{A}$ are perfect.

The simulation of the random oracle H_1 is not entirely perfect. Let **Query**H_1 be the event that $\mathcal{A}$ has queried before the **Challenge** phase (w_j^*, l^*) to H_1 for $j \in \{1, \cdots, k\}$. Except for the case above, the simulation of H_1 is perfect. This event happens with probability k/p.

The simulation of the random oracles H_2 and H_3 are not entirely perfect. Let **Query**H_2 and **Query**H_3 be the events that $\mathcal{A}$ has queried before the **Challenge** phase (C_1^*, C_3^*) to H_2 and $(K_b^*, C_1^*, C_2^*, C_3^*, C_4^*)$ to H_3. Except for the cases above, the simulations of H_2 and H_3 are perfect. These two events happen with probability $1/p$ and $1/2^\lambda$ respectively.

The simulation of the Decryption oracle is nearly perfect, but a valid header can be rejected sometimes. Indeed, in the simulation of the Decryption oracle, if (K, C_1, C_2, C_3, C_4) has not been queried to H_3, then the header is rejected. This leads to two cases:

1. $\mathcal{A}$ uses the value C_5^*, which is part of the challenge, as a part of its Decryption query.
2. $\mathcal{A}$ has guessed a right value for the output of H_3 without querying it.

However, in the first case, since $(C_1^*, C_2^*, C_3^*, C_4^*)$ and K_b are provided as input to H_3, the Decryption query that $\mathcal{A}$ would ask is the same as the challenge, which is not allowed to query. The second case may happen but with negligible probability $1/2^k$. Let **DecO** denote the event that $\mathcal{A}$ correctly guesses the output of H_3. Therefore, if $\mathcal{B}$ does not correctly guess the output of H_3, $\mathcal{A}$'s point of view in the simulation is identical to the one in the real attack.

Thus, we have $Pr[\mathcal{B}(g, g_1, \cdots, g_n, g_{n+2}, \cdots, g_{2n}, h) = e(g_{n+1}, h)] = |Pr[b' = b| \neg$ **Query**$H_1 \wedge \neg$**Query**$H_2 \wedge \neg$**Query**$H_3 \wedge \neg$**DecO**$] - \frac{1}{2}|$ By definition of $\mathcal{A}$, we have $|Pr[b' = b] - \frac{1}{2}| > \varepsilon - Pr[$**Query**$H_1] - Pr[$**Query**$H_2] - Pr[$**Query**$H_3] - Pr[$**DecO**$]$. Hence, we have

$$|Pr[b' = b|\neg\mathbf{Query}H_1 \wedge \neg\mathbf{Query}H_2 \wedge \neg\mathbf{Query}H_3 \wedge \neg\mathbf{DecO}] - \frac{1}{2}|$$

$$> |Pr[b' = b] - Pr[\mathbf{Query}H_1] - Pr[\mathbf{Query}H_2] - Pr[\mathbf{Query}H_3] - Pr[\mathbf{DecO}] - \frac{1}{2}|$$

$$> \varepsilon - Pr[\mathbf{Query}H_1] - Pr[\mathbf{Query}H_2] - Pr[\mathbf{Query}H_3] - Pr[\mathbf{DecO}]$$

Since $\mathcal{A}$ makes q_{H_1}, q_{H_2} and q_{H_3} random oracle queries during the attack, $Pr[\mathbf{Query}H_1] \leq kq_{H_1}/p$, $Pr[\mathbf{Query}H_2] \leq q_{H_2}/p$ and $Pr[\mathbf{Query}H_3] \leq q_{H_3}/2^\lambda$. In the same way, since $\mathcal{A}$ makes q_d Decryption queries during the attack, $Pr[\mathbf{DecO}] \leq q_d/2^\lambda$. Therefore, we have $\mathcal{B}$'s winning probability $\varepsilon' > \varepsilon - \frac{k \cdot q_{H_1} + q_{H_2}}{p} - \frac{q_d + q_{H_3}}{2^\lambda}$.

Fully Collusion Resistance Proof

Theorem 2. *The File Sharing scheme in Electronic Health Records* FSEHR *is fully secure against any number of colluders, in the random oracle model.*

Proof. We assume there exists an adversary $\mathcal{A}$ that breaks the semantic security of the FSEHR scheme with probability greater than ε when interacting with an algorithm $\mathcal{B}$.

$\mathcal{A}$ chooses a subset $S_{u,n'} = \{u_1, \cdots, u_{n'}\} \subseteq \{1, \cdots, n\}$ of colluding users. $\mathcal{B}$ then runs $\mathbf{Setup}(\lambda, n, k)$, provides the public parameters $PK = (p, \mathbb{G}, \mathbb{G}_T, g, g_1, \cdots, g_n, g_{n+2}, \cdots, g_{2n}, v, w_1, \cdots, w_k, H_1, H_2, H_3)$, the secret keys $d_i = v^{(\alpha^i)}$ for user $i \in S_{u,n'}$ to $\mathcal{A}$, and keeps secret the certifier's secret keys $d_{c_j} = \sigma_j$ for $j \in \{1, \cdots, k\}$. It also runs $\mathbf{Certif}(PK, d_{c_j}, i, l)$ and gives the certificate $e_{i,j,l} = (e_{i,j,l,1} = w_j^{(\alpha^i)} \cdot H_1(w_j, l)^{\sigma_j \cdot r_{i,j,l}}, e_{i,j,l,2} = w_j^{r_{i,j,l}})$ to $\mathcal{A}$ for user $i \in S_{u,n'}$, $j \in \{1, \cdots, k\}$, and time period l.

Afterwards, $\mathcal{B}$ chooses a subset $S \subseteq \{1, \cdots, n\}$ of users such that $S \cap S_{u,n'} = \emptyset$, time period $l' \neq l$, and set $S_c \subseteq \{1, \cdots, k\}$. It outputs $(Hdr, K) \leftarrow \mathbf{Encrypt}(PK, S, S_c, l)$, gives $Hdr = (C_1 = g^t, C_2 = \prod_{j \in S_c} H_1(w_j, l)^t, C_3 = (v \cdot \prod_{j \in S_c} w_j \cdot \prod_{i' \in S} g_{n+1-i'})^t, C_4 = H_2(C_1, C_3)^t, C_5 = H_3(K, C_1, C_2, C_3, C_4))$ to $\mathcal{A}$ and keeps secret the session key $K = e(g_{n+1}, g)^t$.

$\mathcal{A}$ computes new secret key d_χ and certificate $e_{\chi,j,l}$ from the secret keys and certificates of users in $S_{u,n'}$ that it previously obtained as follows. First, $\mathcal{A}$ defines a subset $S_{u,\bar{n}} \subseteq S_{u,n'}$, and sets

$$d_\chi = \prod_{i' \in S_{u,\bar{n}}} d_{i'} = v^{\sum_{i' \in S_{u,\bar{n}}} \alpha^{i'}} = v^{f_\chi(\alpha)}$$

$$e_{\chi,j,l,1} = \prod_{i' \in S_{u,\bar{n}}} e_{i',j,l,1} = w_j^{\sum_{i' \in S_{u,\bar{n}}} \alpha^{i'}} \cdot H_1(w_j, l)^{\sigma_j \cdot \sum_{i' \in S_{u,\bar{n}}} r_{i',j,l}}$$

$$= w_j^{f_\chi(\alpha)} \cdot H_1(w_j, l)^{\sigma_j \cdot r_{\chi,j,l}}$$

$$e_{\chi,j,l,2} = w_j^{\sum_{i' \in S_{u,\bar{n}}} r_{i',j,l}} = w_j^{r_{\chi,j,l}}$$

where $f_\chi(\alpha) = \sum_{i' \in S_{u,\bar{n}}} \alpha^{i'}$. For a user i belonging to S, it has to cancel out the following terms

$$\frac{e(g, (v^{(\alpha^i)} \cdot \prod_{j \in S_c} w_j^{(\alpha^i)} \cdot \prod_{i' \in S \setminus \{i\}} g_{n+1-i'+i})^t)}{e(v^{f_\chi(\alpha)} \cdot \prod_{j \in S_c} w_j^{f_\chi(\alpha)} \cdot \prod_{i' \in S \setminus \{i\}} g_{n+1-i'+i}, g^t)} = \frac{e(g, v^{(\alpha^i)} \cdot \prod_{j \in S_c} w_j^{(\alpha^i)})}{e(v^{f_\chi(\alpha)} \cdot \prod_{j \in S_c} w_j^{f_\chi(\alpha)}, g)}$$

$$\frac{\prod_{j \in S_c} e(g^{\sigma_j \cdot r_{\chi,j,l}}, \prod_{j \in S_c} H_1(w_j, l')^t)}{\prod_{j \in S_c} e(H_1(w_j, l)^{\sigma \cdot r_{\chi,j,l}}, g^t)} = \frac{e(g, \prod_{j \in S_c} H_1(w_j, l'))}{e(\prod_{j \in S_c} H_1(w_j, l), g)}$$

In the first equality, the two terms $v^{\alpha^i - f_\chi(\alpha)}$ and $w_j^{\alpha^i - f_\chi(\alpha)}$ should be wiped out. Thus, one wants to have $f_\chi(\alpha) = \sum_{i' \in S_{u,\bar{n}}} \alpha^{i'} = \alpha^i \bmod p$. In other words, α is one root of the polynomial $P(x) = \sum_{i' \in S_{u,\bar{n}} \cup \{i\}} x^{i'}$ of degree $\bar{n} + 1$. This happens with probability $Pr[f_\chi(\alpha) = \alpha^i \bmod p] \leq (\bar{n} + 1)/p$. In the second equality, if we suppose that $l \neq l'$, $j, j' \in \{1, \cdots, k\}$, and the hash function H_1 is a random oracle, then the probability that the two outputs are equal $Pr[H_1(w_{j'}, l') = H_1(w_j, l)] \leq 1/p$. Finally, $\mathcal{A}$ has negligible advantage $Adv\mathsf{FSEHR}_{\mathcal{A}, n, k} \leq (\bar{n} + 2)/p$ to retrieve the session key K.

References

1. Akinyele, J.A., Pagano, M.W., Green, M.D., Lehmann, C.U., Peterson, Z.N., Rubin, A.D.: Securing electronic medical records using attribute-based encryption on mobile devices. In: SPSM 2011, pp. 75–86. ACM (2011)
2. Alemán, J.L.F., Señor, I.C., Lozoya, P.A.O., Toval, A.: Security and privacy in electronic health records: A systematic literature review. Journal of Biomedical Informatics 46(3), 541–562 (2013)
3. Benaloh, J., Chase, M., Horvitz, E., Lauter, K.: Patient controlled encryption: Ensuring privacy of electronic medical records. In: CCSW 2009, pp. 103–114. ACM (2009)
4. Boneh, D., Gentry, C., Waters, B.: Collusion resistant broadcast encryption with short ciphertexts and private keys. In: Shoup, V. (ed.) CRYPTO 2005. LNCS, vol. 3621, pp. 258–275. Springer, Heidelberg (2005)
5. Dodis, Y., Fazio, N.: Public key broadcast encryption for stateless receivers. In: Feigenbaum, J. (ed.) DRM 2002. LNCS, vol. 2696, pp. 61–80. Springer, Heidelberg (2003)
6. Fiat, A., Naor, M.: Broadcast encryption. In: Stinson, D.R. (ed.) CRYPTO 1993. LNCS, vol. 773, pp. 480–491. Springer, Heidelberg (1994)
7. Gentry, C.: Certificate-based encryption and the certificate revocation problem. In: Biham, E. (ed.) EUROCRYPT 2003. LNCS, vol. 2656, pp. 272–293. Springer, Heidelberg (2003)
8. Gentry, C., Waters, B.: Adaptive security in broadcast encryption systems (with short ciphertexts). In: Joux, A. (ed.) EUROCRYPT 2009. LNCS, vol. 5479, pp. 171–188. Springer, Heidelberg (2009)
9. Motta, G.H.M.B.: A contextual role-based access control authorization model for electronic patient record. IEEE Transactions on Information Technology in Biomedicine 7(3), 202–207 (2003)
10. Narayan, S., Gagné, M., Safavi-Naini, R.: Privacy preserving ehr system using attribute-based infrastructure. In: CCSW 2010, pp. 47–52. ACM (2010)
11. Okamoto, T., Pointcheval, D.: REACT: Rapid enhanced-security asymmetric cryptosystem transform. In: Naccache, D. (ed.) CT-RSA 2001. LNCS, vol. 2020, pp. 159–174. Springer, Heidelberg (2001)
12. Peleg, M., Beimel, D., Dori, D., Denekamp, Y.: Situation-based access control: Privacy management via modeling of patient data access scenarios. J. of Biomedical Informatics 41(6), 1028–1040 (2008)
13. Wang, H., Wu, Q., Qin, B., Domingo-Ferrer, J.: Frr: Fair remote retrieval of outsourced private medical records in electronic health networks. J. Biomed. Inform. (2014)

A Framework for Analyzing Verifiability in Traditional and Electronic Exams

Jannik Dreier[1], Rosario Giustolisi[2], Ali Kassem[3]
Pascal Lafourcade[4], and Gabriele Lenzini[2]

[1] Institute of Information Security, ETH Zurich
[2] SnT/University of Luxembourg
[3] Université Grenoble Alpes, CNRS, VERIMAG, Grenoble, France
[4] Université d'Auvergne, LIMOS

Abstract. The main concern for institutions that organize exams is to detect when students cheat. Actually more frauds are possible and even authorities can be dishonest. If institutions wish to keep exams a trustworthy business, anyone and not only the authorities should be allowed to look into an exam's records and verify the presence or the absence of frauds. In short, exams should be *verifiable*. However, what verifiability means for exams is unclear and no tool to analyze an exam's verifiability is available. In this paper we address both issues: we formalize several *individual* and *universal verifiability properties* for traditional and electronic exams, so proposing a set of verifiability properties and clarifying their meaning, then we implement our framework in ProVerif, so making it a tool to analyze exam verifiability. We validate our framework by analyzing the verifiability of two existing exam systems – an electronic and a paper-and-pencil system.

1 Introduction

Not a long time ago, the only way for a student to take an exam was by sitting in a classroom with other students. Today, students can take exams using computers in test centers or even from home and can be graded remotely. This change is possible thanks to computer-aided or computer-based exams, generally called electronic exams (e-exams). E-exams are integrated in Massive Open Online Courses (MOOC), platforms to open a worldwide access to university lectures. E-exams are also trialled at university exams: at the University Joseph Fourier, exams in pharmacy have been organized electronically in 2014 using tablet computers, and all French medicine exams are planned to be managed electronically by 2016 [13].

All such diverse exam and e-exam protocols should provide a comparable guarantee of security and not only against students that cheat, the main concern of exam authorities, but also against other frauds and the frauds perpetrated by the authorities themselves. More or less effective mitigations exist but to really address the matter exams must be *verifiable*. Verifiable exams can be checked for the presence or the absence of irregularities and provide evidence about the fairness and the correctness of their grading procedures. And they should be welcome by authorities since exam verifiability is also about to be transparent about an exam's being compliance with regulations as well

J. Lopez and Y. Wu (Eds.): ISPEC 2015, LNCS 9065, pp. 514–529, 2015.
DOI: 10.1007/978-3-319-17533-1_35

as being able to inspire public trust. Specially, some recent scandals [14, 17] show that frauds do not come only from students, but also from exam authorities.

Ensuring verifiability is generally hard and for exams and e-exams one part of the problem lays in the lack of clarity about what verifiability properties they should offer. Another part comes from the absence of a framework to check exams for verifiability. This paper proposes a solution for both.

Contributions. We provide a clear understanding of verifiability for exam protocols and propose a methodology to analyze their verifiability: we define a formal framework where we model traditional paper-and-pencil and electronic exams. We formalize eleven verifiability properties relevant for exams and, for each property, we state the conditions that a sound and complete verifiability test has to satisfy. Following a practice already explored in other domains [2,3,7,20], we classify our verifiability properties into individual and universal, and we formalize them within our framework. Finally, we implement the verifiability tests in the applied π-calculus and we use ProVerif [5] to run an automated analysis. We validate the effectiveness and the flexibility of our framework by modelling and analyzing two different exam protocols: a paper-and-pencil exam currently used by the University of Grenoble, and an internet-based exam protocol called Remark! [16]. We check whether they admit sound and complete verifiabile tests and discuss what exam roles are required to be honest.

Outline. The next section comments the related work. Section 3 provides definitions and models for exam protocols. Section 4 describes and formalizes eleven verifiability properties, and develops a framework of analysis for them. Section 5 validates the framework. Section 6 draws the conclusions and outlines the future work.

2   Related Work

To the best of our knowledge, there is almost no research done on verifiability for exams. A handful number of papers list informally a few security properties for e-exams [6,15,21]. Only one offers a formalization [11]. We comment them shortly.

Castella-Roca *et al.* [6] discuss a secure exam management system which is claimed to provide authentication, privacy, correction and receipt fullness, properties that are described informally. Huszti & Pethő [21] refine these notions as security requirements and propose a cryptographic protocol that is claimed to fulfil the requirements, but the claims are only sustained informally. Bella *et al.* [15] comment a list of requirements which are desirable for electronic and traditional exams, and similar to the previous works, they do not formalize the properties they propose. Instead, Dreier *et al.* [11] propose a model for several authentication and secrecy properties in the formal framework of the Applied π-Calculus [1]. No paper outlined above addresses verifiability.

However, verifiability has been studied in other domains than exams, specially in voting and in auctions. In these domains formal models and definitions of security properties exist stably [12,22,23]. In voting, *individual verifiability* ensures that a voter can verify her vote has been handled correctly, that is, cast as intended, recorded as cast, and counted as recorded [3, 20]. The concept of *universal verifiability* has been introduced to express that voters and non-voters can verify the correctness of the tally using only public information [2, 3, 7]. Kremer *et al.* [22] formalize both individual and universal verifiability in the Applied π-Calculus [1]. They also consider *eligibility verifiability*, a specific universal property assuring that any observer can verify that the set of votes from which the result is determined originates only from eligible voters, and that each eligible voter has cast at most one vote. Smyth *et al.* [25] use ProVerif to check different verifiability notions that they express as reachability properties, which ProVerif processes natively. In this paper, we also use ProVerif for the analysis, but the model and the definitions here proposed are more general and constrained neither to the Applied π-Calculus nor to ProVerif.

Verifiability for e-auction is studied in Dreier *et al.* [12]. The manner in which they express sound and complete tests for their verifiability properties has been a source of inspiration for what we present here.

Notable notions related to verifiability are *accountability* and *auditability*. Küsters *et al.* [23] study accountability ensuring that, when verifiability fails, one can identify the participant responsible for the failure. They also give symbolic and computational definitions of verifiability, which they recognize as a weaker variant of accountability. However, their framework needs to be instantiated for each application by identifying relevant verifiability goals. Guts *et al.* [18] define auditability as the quality of a protocol that stores sufficient evidence to convince an honest judge that specific properties are satisfied. Auditability revisits the universal verifiability defined in this paper: anyone, even an outsider without knowledge of the protocol execution, can verify the system relying only on the available pieces of evidence.

3   Exam Model

Any exam, paper-and-pencil or electronic, involves at least two roles: the *candidate* and the *exam authority*. The exam authority can have several sub-roles: the *registrar* registers candidates; the *question committee* prepares the questions; the *invigilator* supervises the exam, collects the answers, and dispatches them for marking; the *examiner* corrects the answers and marks them; the *notification committee* delivers the marking.

Exams run generally in phases, commonly four of them: *Registration*, where the exam is set up and candidates enroll; *Examination*, where candidates answer the questions, give them to the authority, and have them accepted officially; *Marking*, where the exam-tests are marked; and *Notification*, where the grades are notified. Usually, each phase ends before the next one begins, an assumption we embrace.

Assuming such roles and such phases, our model of exam consists of four sets — a set of candidates, a set of questions, a set of answers (questions and answers together are called *exam-tests*) and a set of marks. Three relations link candidates, exam-tests, and marks along the four phases: Accepted, Marked, and Assigned. They are assumed to be recorded during the exam or build from data logs such as registers or repositories.

Definition 1 (Exam). *An exam E is a tuple (I, Q, A, M, α) where I of type $\mathcal{I}$ is a set of candidate identities, Q of type $\mathcal{Q}$ is a set of questions, A of type $\mathcal{A}$ is a set of answers, M of type $\mathcal{M}$ is a set of marks, and α is the set of the following relations:*

- Accepted $\subseteq I \times (Q \times A)$: *the candidates' exam-tests accepted by the authority;*

- Marked $\subseteq I \times (Q \times A) \times M$: *the marks delivered on the exam-tests;*
- Assigned $\subseteq I \times M$: *the marks assigned (i.e., officially linked) to the candidates;*
- Correct : $(Q \times A) \rightarrow M$: *the function used to mark an exam-test;*

Definition 1 is simple but expressive. It can model electronic as well as paper-and-pencil exams, and exams executed honestly as well as exams with frauds. It is the goal of verifiability to test for the absence of anomalies. For this aim we recognize two specific subsets: (a) $I_r \subseteq I$ as the set of candidates who registered for the exam (thus, $I \setminus I_r$ are the identities of the unregistered candidates who have taken the exam), and (b) $Q_g \subseteq Q$ as the questions that the question committee has prepared (thus, $Q \setminus Q_g$ are the additional and illegitimate questions that appear in the exam).

The function Correct models any objective mapping that assigns a mark to an answer. This works well for single-choice and with multiple-choice questions, but it is inappropriate for long open questions. Marking an open question is hardly objective: the ambiguities of natural language can lead to subjective interpretations by the examiner. Thus, independently of the model, we cannot hope to verify the marking in such a context. Since in our framework the function Correct is used to verify the correctness of the marking, exams that do not allow a definition of such a function cannot be checked for that property; however, all other properties can still be checked.

4   Verifiability Properties

To be verifiable with respect to specific properties, an exam protocol needs to provide tests to verify these properties. A test t is a function from $\mathcal{E} \rightarrow$ bool, where $\mathcal{E}$ is the set of data used to run the test. Abstractly, a verifiable property has the format $t(e) \Leftrightarrow c$, where t is a test, e is the data used, and c is a predicate that expresses the property the test is expected to check. Direction $\Rightarrow$ says that the test's success is a sufficient condition for c to hold (soundness); direction $\Leftarrow$ says that the test's success is a necessary condition for c to hold (completeness).

Definition 2. *An exam for which it exists a test for a property is* testable *for that property. An exam is* verifiable *for that property when it is testable and when the test is* sound *and* complete.

To work, a test needs pieces of data from the exam's execution. A verifier, which is the entity who runs the test, may complementarity use personal knowledge about the exam's run if he has any. We assume data to be taken after the exam has ended, that is, when they are stable and not subject to further changes.

To be useful, tests have to be sound even in the presence of an attacker or of dishonest participants: this ensures that when the test succeeds the property holds despite any attempt by the attacker or the participants to falsify it. However, many sound tests are not complete in such conditions: a misbehaving participant can submit incorrect data and, in so doing, causing the test to fail although the property holds. Unless said differently, we check for soundness in presence of some dishonest participants (indeed we seek for the maximal set of dishonest participants that preserve the soundness of the test), but we check for completeness only with honest participants.

A verifiability test can be run by the exam participants or by outsiders. This brings to two distinct notions of verifiability properties: *individual* and *universal*. In exams, individual verifiability means verifiability from the point of view of a candidate. She can feed the test with the knowledge she has about the exam, namely her personal data (identity, exam-test, mark) and the messages she exchanged with the other participants during the exam. Universal verifiability means verifiability from the point of view of an external observer. In practical applications this might be an auditor who has no knowledge of the exam: he has no candidate ID, he has not seen the exam's questions and answered any of them, and he did not receive any mark. Besides, he has not interacted with any of the exam participants. In short, he runs the test only using the exam's public pieces of data available to him.

In Table 1 we select six individual (left) and five universal (right) relevant verifiability properties. These properties cover the verifiability of all phases of a typical exam. We define one property about registration verifiability, one about the validity of questions, two about the integrity of exam-test, two about the process of marking, and one about the integrity of notification. More details are given in the reminder of the section.

Generally speaking, an exam is fully (individual or universal) verifiable when it satisfies all the properties. Of course, on an exam each property can be verified separately to clearly assess its strengths and weaknesses.

Individual Verifiability Properties (I.V.): Here is the candidate that verifies the exam. She knows her identity i, her submitted exam-test q and a, and her mark m. She also knows her perspective p of the exam run, that is, the messages she has sent and received. Her data is a tuple (i, q, a, m, p). Note that the candidate's perspective p is not necessary to define the properties, that's why it does not appear in the right-hand-side of the equivalent (see Table 1). However, it might be necessary to implement the test depending on the case study.

There is no individual verifiability property about registration as a candidate knows whether she has registered, and she might even have a receipt of it. Instead, what a candidate does not know, but wishes to verify, is whether she got the correct questions, and whether she got her test correctly marked. To verify the validity of her question, we propose the property *Question Validity* which ensures that the candidate receives questions actually generated by the question committee. This is modeled by a test which returns true, if and only if, the questions q received by the candidate belong to the set of the valid questions Q_g generated by the question committee. To verify that her mark is correct, the candidate can check the property *Marking Correctness* which ensures that the mark received by the candidate is correctly computed on her exam-test. Verifying *Marking Correctness* could e.g. be realized by giving access to the marking algorithm, so the candidate can compute again the mark that corresponds to her exam-test and compare it to the mark she received. As discussed in Section 3, this is feasible with multiple-choice questions or short open-questions, but rather difficult in other cases such as the case of long and open questions. In this case, a candidate may wish to verify more properties about her exam test, and precisely that the integrity of the candidate's exam-test is preserved till marking, and that the integrity of the candidate's mark is preserved from delivery till reception. Preserving the integrity of the exam-test and that

Table 1. Individual and Universal Verifiability

	Individual Verifiability	Universal Verifiability
Registration		$R_{UV}(e) \Leftrightarrow$ $I_r \supseteq \{i : (i, x) \in \text{Accepted}\}$
Question Validity	$QV_{IV}(i, q, a, m, p) \Leftrightarrow$ $(q \in Q_g)$	
Marking Correctness	$MC_{IV}(i, q, a, m, p) \Leftrightarrow$ $(\text{Correct}(q, a) = m)$	$MC_{UV}(e) \Leftrightarrow$ $(\forall (i, x, m) \in \text{Marked},$ $\text{Correct}(x) = m$
Exam-Test Integrity	$ETI_{IV}(i, q, a, m, p) \Leftrightarrow$ $((i, (q, a)) \in \text{Accepted}$ $\wedge \exists m' : (i, (q, a), m') \in \text{Marked})$	$ETI_{UV}(e) \Leftrightarrow$ $\text{Accepted} =$ $\{(i, x) : (i, x, m) \in \text{Marked}\}$
Exam-Test Markedness	$ETM_{IV}(i, q, a, m, p) \Leftrightarrow$ $(\exists m' : (i, (q, a), m') \in \text{Marked}))$	$ETM_{UV}(e) \Leftrightarrow$ $\text{Accepted} \subseteq$ $\{(i, x) : (i, x, m) \in \text{Marked}\}$
Marking Integrity	$MI_{IV}(i, q, a, m, p) \Leftrightarrow$ $\exists m' : ((i, (q, a), m') \in \text{Marked}$ $\wedge (i, m') \in \text{Assigned})$	$MI_{UV}(e) \Leftrightarrow$ $\text{Assigned} =$ $\{(i, m) : (i, x, m) \in \text{Marked}\}$
Marking Notification Integrity	$MNI_{IV}(i, q, a, m, p) \Leftrightarrow$ $(i, m) \in \text{Assigned}$	

of the mark is sufficient for the candidate to be convinced that she got the correct mark, provided the examiner follows the marking algorithm correctly.

Each of the remaining four individual properties covers a different step from exam-test submission till mark reception. This allows to identify in which step the error happened in case of failure. The first property, *Exam-Test Integrity*, is to ensure that the candidate's exam-test is accepted and marked as she submitted it without any modification. Running the *Exam-Test Integrity* test after the end of the exam does not invalidate the property since if an exam-test is lost or modified before being marked, it remains modified also after the exam is over. But the event consisting of an exam-test that is first changed before the marking, and then restored correctly after marking, is not captured by *Exam-Test Integrity*. However, such an event can still be detected by verifying *Marking Correctness*. Another property that also concerns the integrity of the exam-test is *Exam-Test Markedness* which ensures that the exam-test submitted by a candidate is marked without modification. Note that if *Exam-Test Integrity* (*i.e.*, the test ETI_{IV}) succeeds, then *Exam-Test Markedness* (*i.e.*, the test ETM_{IV}) also succeeds, namely $ETI_{IV}(i, q, a, m, p) \Rightarrow ETM_{IV}(i, q, a, m, p)$. However, if the test ETI_{IV} fails, but the test ETM_{IV} succeeds, this would mean that the candidate's exam-test is modified upon acceptance by the authority, but then restored to its correct version before marking. The latter case could be not relevant to the candidate as her exam-test was unmodified when marked; however such an error can be reported to the responsible authority to investigate the problem and see where the error comes from. Moreover, we might have a protocol that does not provide a test for ETI_{IV}, but a test for ETM_{IV}, this could depend on the available data at the end of the exam execution. The remaining two properties ensure that the integrity of the mark attributed to a candidate's exam-test by the examiner is preserved. The property *Mark Integrity* ensures that the mark attributed to a candidate's exam-test is assigned to that candidate by the responsible authority without any modification; and the property *Mark Notification Integrity* ensures that the candidate receives the mark assigned to her by the authority.

Universal Verifiability Properties (U.V.): These properties are designed from the viewpoint of a generic observer. In contrast to the individual viewpoint, the observer does not have an identity and does not know an exam-test or a mark, because he does not have an official exam role. The observer runs the test on the public data available after a protocol run. Hence, we simply have a general variable e containing the data.

In the universal perspective, properties such as Question Validity and Mark Notification Integrity are not relevant because the external observer has no knowledge of the questions nor of the markings received by the candidates. However, an observer may want to verify other properties revealing whether the exam has been carried out correctly, or he may want to check that the exam authorities and examiners have played by the rules. Precisely, an observer would be interested in verifying that only eligible candidates can submit an exam-test, and this is guaranteed by *Registration*, which ensures that all accepted exam-tests are submitted by registered candidates. An observer may wish to test that all the marks attributed by the examiners to the exam-tests are computed correctly. This property, *Marking Correctness*, raises the same practical questions as the individual case and therefore the same discussion applies here. However, even in case of open questions, to increase their trustworthiness, universities should allow auditors to access their log for an inspection to the marking process. It may be also interested in checking that no exam-test is modified, added, or deleted till the end of the marking phase: this *Exam-Test Integrity*, which ensures that all and only accepted exam-tests are marked without any modification. Another property that could be useful for an observer is *Exam-Test Markedness*. This ensures that all the accepted exam-tests are marked without modification. Thus, if *Exam-Test Integrity* fails but *Exam-Test Markedness* succeeds, then there is at least one extra marked exam-test which is not included in the set of accepted exam-test by the exam authority. Finally, the observer may wish to check that all and only the marks assigned to exam-tests are assigned to the corresponding candidates with no modifications. This is guaranteed by *Mark Integrity*.

5 Validation

We validate our framework and show its flexibility with two different use cases: a paper-and-pencil exam procedure and an internet-based exam protocol. We analyze their verifiability fully. The modeling and the analysis is done in ProVerif. For the full treatment of the case studies, we refer the reader to our technical report [10]. The ProVerif code is available on line[1]. We consider the Dolev-Yao [9] intruder model that is used in ProVerif. Dishonest roles, when needed, are processes controlled by the intruder.

---

[1] `apsia.uni.lu/stast/codes/exams/proverif_ispec15.tar.gz`

5.1   Use Case # 1: The Grenoble Exam

The first exam that we analyze is the paper-and-pencil procedure used to evaluate undergraduate students at the University of Grenoble. It involves candidates (C), an examiner (E), a question committee (QC), and an exam authority (EA). It has four phases:

Registration: All the students of the course are automatically registered as candidates for the exam; they are informed about the exam's date, time and location. EA assigns a fresh pseudonym to each C. The QC, the course's lecturer(s), prepares the questions and hands them to EA.

Examination: After EA authenticates all Cs, EA lets them take a seat. There, each C finds a special exam paper: the top-right corner is glued and can be folded. Each C signs it, and writes down her name and student number in such a way that the corner, when folded, hides them. Each C also writes down visibly their pseudonyms. Then, EA distributes the questions, and the exam begins. At the end, EA collects the exam-tests, checks that all copies have been returned, that all corners are correctly glued, and gives the exam-tests to E.

Marking: E evaluates the exam-tests: each pseudonym is given a mark. E returns them, along with the marks, to EA.

Notification: EA checks that the corner is still glued and maps the pseudonyms to real identities (names and student numbers) without opening the glued part. Then, EA stores the pairs student numbers / marks and publishes them. C can review her exam-test in presence of E to check the integrity of her exam-test and verify the mark. If, for instance, C denies that the exam-test containing her pseudonym belongs to her, the glued part is opened.

Formal Model. We model the Grenoble protocol in ProVerif. EA, QC, E and the Cs are modeled as communicating processes that exchange messages over public or private channels. They can behave honestly or dishonestly. We detail later when we need private vs. public channels and honest vs. dishonest participants.

Data sets I, Q, A and M are as in Definition 1. Each set is composed by a selection of messages taken from the data generated by the processes, possibly manipulated by the attacker. For example, Q are all the messages that represent a question. Q_g, subset of Q, are all the messages representing a question that are generated by the QC. The exam's relations are also as in Definition 1. Accepted contains all the messages $(i, (q, a))$ (*i.e.,* identity and exam-test) that EA has collected. If the EA is honest, it accepts only the exam-tests submitted by registered candidates. Marked contains all the messages $(i, (q, a), m)$ (*i.e.,* identity, exam-test, and mark) that the E has generated after having marked the exam-tests. If E is honest, he marks only exam-tests authenticated by EA. Assigned contains all the messages (i, m) originating from the EA when it assigns mark m to candidate i. If EA is honest, it assigns a mark to C only if E notifies that it is the mark delivered on C's exam-test. Correct is a deterministic function that outputs a mark for a given exam-test.

We made a few choices when modeling the Grenoble exam's "visual channels". These are face-to-face channels that all the participants use to exchange data (exam-sheets, student pseudonyms, marks). Intrinsically, all such communications are mutually authenticated. To model visual channels in ProVerif, we could have used private channels, but this would have made the channels too strong, preventing the attacker even from knowing if a communication has happened at all. More appropriately, visual channels are authenticated channels, where authentication is expressed by an equational theory similar to the one commonly used for cryptographic signatures, but with the assumption that the verification key is only known to the intended receiver, namely: $\texttt{openauth}(\texttt{auth}(m, s)) = m$, and $\texttt{authcheck}(\texttt{auth}(m, s), \texttt{generate}(s)) = m$. Function $\texttt{auth}$ takes as input a message m and a secret s that only the sender knows, and outputs an authenticated value. The verification key that corresponds to this secret, $\texttt{generate}(s)$, is possessed only by the receiver/verifier. Anyone can get the message, m, but only the owner of $\texttt{generate}(s)$ can verify its origin.

Analysis of Individual Verifiability. We model individual verifiability tests as processes in ProVerif, guided by the   properties defined in Table 1. Each test emits two events: the event OK, when the test succeeds, and the event KO, when the test fails. We use correspondence assertions, *i.e.,* *"if an event e is executed the event e' has been previously executed"* [24], to prove soundness, and resort to unreachability of KO to prove completeness. We also use unreachability to prove soundness for Marking Correctness.

A sound test receives its input via public channels. This allows an attacker to mess with the test's inputs. Participants can be dishonest too. Thus, we check that the event OK is always preceded by the event emitted in the part of the code where the predicate becomes satisfied. Below, we describe how this works for Question Validity.

A complete test receives its input via private channels and by honest participants. The intruder cannot change the test's input this time. Then, we check that the test does not fail, that is, the event KO is unreachable.

Figure 1 reports the result of the analysis. All properties hold ($\checkmark$) despite the intruder, but often they hold only assuming some roles to be honest : there are attacks otherwise. All properties but Marking Correctness have sound tests (Figure 1, middle column) only if we assume at least the honesty of the exam authority (EA), or of the examiner (E), or of

Property	Sound	Complete
Question Validity	$\checkmark$(EA)	$\checkmark$(all)
Exam-Test Integrity	$\checkmark$(EA, E)	$\checkmark$(all)
Exam-Test Markedness	$\checkmark$(E)	$\checkmark$(all)
Marking Correctness	$\checkmark$	$\checkmark$(all)
Mark Integrity	$\checkmark$(EA, E)	$\checkmark$(all)
Mark Notification Integrity	$\checkmark$(EA)	$\checkmark$(all)

Fig. 1. I.V. properties for the Grenoble exam

both. This in addition to the honesty of candidate, who must be necessarily honest because he is the verifier. The minimal assumptions for all the properties are reported in brackets. All properties have complete tests (Figure, right columns) but all roles except the intruder have to be honest for them to hold.

Due to the limited space, we only comment in detail on how we tested one verifiability property: Question Validity. It must be said that, in reality, the Grenoble exam does not provide any means for a candidate to verify question validity. The questions she receives from the EA comes without any proof that they actually were generated by the QC: there is no QC's signature or stamp. But, if we assume an honest EA, a simple test exists: the candidate can authenticate EA when it distributes the questions.

The QV test inputs the verification value ver_AC, which is used to authenticate the exam authority. On channel chTest, the test inputs the authenticated question auth_q, which it checks for origin-authenticity. The test succeeds if the question is authenticated by the EA, it fails otherwise. The test emits the event OK when it succeeds, otherwise emits the event KO. Namely,

```
let test(chTest, ver_AC) =
 in(chTest, (auth_q)); let question = openauth(auth_q)
 in if authcheck(auth_q, Ver_AC) = question
 then event OK else event KO.
```

In the proof for soundness, we modified the ProVerif code for EA in such way to emit an event valid just after the process receives the question from QC and checks its origin-authenticity, and just before EA sends the question to the C. ProVerif shows, in case of honest EA, that any OK is preceded by valid: the test outputs true only if the question is generated by QC. Note that any tampering that QC can perform on the questions (for example, generating dummy questions or by trashing them after having generated them) does not violate question validity *per se*: according to this property the questions that C received are still those generated, honestly or dishonestly, by the QC: the origin of the question is not compromised.

In the proof for completeness, ProVerif shows that the event KO is unreachable. All participants are assumed to be honest in this case.

Analysis of Universal Verifiability. Universal verifiable tests should use some public data. But, since the Grenoble exam is a paper-and-pencil based exam, in general, there is no publicly available data. Thus, originally Grenoble exam does not satisfy any of the universal verifiability properties. To be universally testable, an auditor has to be given access to the following data: (1) for Registration verifiability, he can read the list of registered candidates and the set of accepted exam-tests. Thus, he can check whether all accepted exam-tests are submitted by registered candidates; (2) for Exam-Test Markedness, in addition to the accepted exam-tests, he knows the set of marked exam-tests. Then, he can check whether all the accepted exam-tests are marked; (3) for Exam-Test Integrity, he knows the same data as in Exam-Test Markedness. The auditor has to check that all and only the accepted exam-tests are marked; (4) for Marking Correctness, he knows the correction algorithm and the marked exam-tests together with the delivered marks. The test is to run the correction algorithm again on each exam-test and check if the obtained mark is the same as the delivered one; finally, for (5) Mark Integrity, in addition to the delivered marks, he can access the assigned marks. The auditor can check whether the assigned marks are exactly the ones delivered and whether they are assigned to the correct candidates. Having access to such significant data mentioned above could break candidate's privacy (for instance identities, answers, and marks can be disclosed to the auditor); that noticed, discussing the compatibility between the universal verifiability and privacy is not in the scope of this paper.

Similar to what we did for the individual verifiability tests, we use correspondence assertions to prove soundness and unreachability of a KO event to prove completeness.

Figure 2 depicts the result of the analysis. We must report that in our testing universal verifiability, not for all tests we were able to run a fully automatically

Property	Sound	Complete
Registration	✓(EA)	✓(all)
Exam-Test Integrity	✓(EA, E)	✓(all)
Exam-Test Markedness	✓(EA, E)	✓(all)
Marking Correctness	✓(E)	✓(all)
Mark Integrity	✓(EA, E)	✓(all)

Fig. 2. U.V. properties for the Grenoble exam

analysis in the general case requiring any number of participants. This is because ProVerif does not support loops and to prove the general case we would have needed to iterate over all candidates. For these tests we ran ProVerif only for the base case, that where we have only one accepted exam-test or one assigned mark; then we completed a manual induction proof that generalizes this result to the general case with an arbitrary number of candidates.

5.2 Use Case #2: Remark!

The second exam system that we analyze is an internet-based cryptographic exam protocol called Remark! [16]. It aims to guarantee several authentication, privacy, and verifiability properties. Remark! has been only proved formally in [11] to ensure authentication and privacy properties, without discussing the protocol's verifiability properties.

Remark! engages the typical exam roles: the candidate (C), the examiner (E), and the exam authority (EA) (called *manager* in the original paper). The protocol uses two particular building blocks: an *exponential mixnet* (NET) [19] and an *append-only bulletin board* (BB) [8]. The protocol's only trust assumption is that there is at least one honest server in NET. We briefly describe the four phases of Remark! below. For the full description we refer to [16].

Registration: The NET generates pseudonyms for C and E using their public keys. The pseudonyms also serve as public encryption and verification keys, and allow C and E to communicate anonymously still guaranteeing some form of authentication. The NET publishes the pseudonyms on the BB. Only C and E can identify their pseudonyms.

Examination: The EA encrypts the question with C's pseudonym, and publishes them on the BB. C retrieves the question, answers it, signs the pair "question and answer" (*i.e.,* the exam-test) using the private key that corresponds to her pseudonym, and submits anonymously the exam-test. Once the EA receives the signed exam-test, it publishes a hashed version of the exam-test on the BB (a *receipt*). The receipt is signed by the EA and can only be verified by C because it is encrypted with C's pseudonym. Then, the EA signs the exam-test and publishes a new post on the BB encrypted with E's pseudonym, which is meant to mark the exam-test.

Marking: E retrieves the exam-test, marks, signs, and sends it back to the EA. The EA encrypts the marked exam-test with the C's pseudonym, and publishes it on the BB.

Notification: When all the marked exam-tests have been posted on the BB, the NET de-anonymizes C's pseudonyms, while E's pseudonyms remain anonymous. To do so, each server of the NET reveals the secret exponents used to generate C's pseudonyms. Finally, the EA can register the mark for the corresponding C.

Formal Model. All roles are modelled as communicating processes, except the BB which is a public channel; the equational theory is the following:

$$\text{checkpseudo}(\text{pseudo\_pub}(\text{pk}(k), rce), \text{pseudo\_priv}(k, \exp(rce))) = \text{true}$$
$$\text{decrypt}(\text{encrypt}(m, \text{pk}(k), r), k) = m$$
$$\text{decrypt}(\text{encrypt}(m, \text{pseudo\_pub}(\text{pk}(k), rce), r), \text{pseudo\_priv}(k, \exp(rce))) = m$$
$$\text{getmess}(\text{sign}(m, k)) = m$$
$$\text{checksign}(\text{sign}(m, k), \text{pk}(k)) = m$$
$$\text{checksign}(\text{sign}(m, \text{pseudo\_priv}(k, \exp(rce))), \text{pseudo\_pub}(\text{pk}(k), rce)) = m$$

Data sets I, Q, A and M are as in Definition 1. Set I contains the C's pseudonyms rather than their identities. This replacement is sound because any candidate is uniquely identified by her pseudonym and the equational theory preserves this bijection. The sets Q, A, and M are the messages that correspond to questions, answers, and marks generated during the protocol's run. The relations are built from the posts that appear on the BB. Precisely, the tuple $(i, (q, a))$ of Accepted is built from the receipts that EA publishes at Examination. The tuples $(i, (q, a), m)$ and (i, m) of Marked and Assigned respectively consist of the posts that EA publishes at Marking. Precisely, the tuple $(i, (q, a), m)$ is built from the marked exam-test signed by E, while the tuple (i, m) is built from the encryption of the marked exam-test that EA generates. In fact, the encryption requires a pseudonym, and officially links C with their identities. This replacement is sound because C is uniquely identified by her key and the marked exam-test. Correct is the algorithm used to mark the exam-tests and is modeled using a table.

Analysis of Individual Verifiability. Similarly to what we did in the previous analysis we use assertions to prove soundness and unreachability of the event KO to prove completeness. In checking the soundness of a test, we assumed an honest C (the verifier), in addition to the honest NET. The roles of E and co-candidates (*i.e.*, candidates other than the verifier) are dishonest for all tests. The input of a test consists of the data sent via private channel from C, the data sent via public channel from EA, and the data posted on BB. To check the completeness of a test, we model all roles as honest. They send their data via private channel to the test, whose input also includes data posted on BB.

Remark! originally mandates only two individual verifiability properties: Mark Notification Integrity and a weaker version of Exam-Test Integrity. However, we checked which assumptions Remark! needs in order to ensure all our properties. For the sake of space, we only report Question Validity here. Remark! assumes that EA both generates the questions and sends them to the candidates. EA has to be honest to avoid that it sends to C questions that are different from the ones generated.

```
let testQV(pkA,pch, bb)=
 in (bb, eques);
 in (pch, (ques, priv_C:skey));
 let(ques', sques)=decrypt(eques, priv_C)
 in let (ques'', pseudoC)=checksign(sques, pkA)
 in if ques'=ques && ques''=ques' then event OK else event KO.
```

The test receives the question published on the BB (eques), C's question and her private key (ques, priv_C) on a private channel. The test checks whether C actually received the question published on BB from EA. To model soundness in ProVerif, we insert the event generated(ques) where the EA process generates the question, and

Property	Sound	Complete
Question Validity	✓ (EA)	✓ (all)
Exam-Test Integrity	✓	✓ (all)
Exam-Test Markedness	✓	✓ (all)
Marking Correctness	✓ (EA)	✓ (all)
Mark Integrity	✓	✓ (all)
Mark Notification Integrity	✓	✓ (all)

Fig. 3. I.V. properties for Remark!

the event accepted(ques) into the test process, exactly inside the if branch where the test succeeds. The test is sound if each occurrence of the event accepted(ques) is preceded by the event generated(ques). ProVerif confirms the test is sound and complete, so Remark! is question validity verifiable.

Figure 3 summarizes the result of our analysis. In the column about the soundness of the verifiability properties the minimal trust requirements to ensure the properties are in brackets. The honesty of the verifier, that is, the candidate, is assumed implicitly. In the column reporting the completeness results all roles are assumed to be honest.

Analysis of Universal verifiability. We verify most universal verifiability tests using a different approach compared to the individual ones. This is needed because C can be dishonest, in contrast to the case of individual verifiability, thus no sufficient events can be insert in any process to model correspondence assertions. In general, the idea of this approach is that every time the test succeeds, which means that it emits the event OK, we check if the decryption of the concerned ciphertext gives the expected plaintext. If not, the event KO is emitted, and we check soundness of the tests using unreachability of the event KO. We can still model soundness using correspondence assertions for Registration, because the NET is honestly emitting events when registration concludes.

Since all the bulletin board posts are encrypted with C's or E's pseudonyms, no public data can be used as it is. Moreover, the encryption algorithm is a probabilistic encryption, thus the random value used to encrypt a message is usually needed. So, like Grenoble exam, Remark! does not originally provide universal verifiability. Remark! can be universally testable if EA gives an auditor access to some data after the exam concludes. Again, this might affect candidate's privacy. Here we assume the auditor is given the following data: (1) for Registration, the EA reveals the signatures inside the receipts posted on BB and the random values used to encrypt the receipts. By looking at the bulletin board, the auditor can check that EA only accepted tests signed with pseudonyms posted by the NET during registration; (2) for Exam-Test Integrity, the EA reveals the marked exam-test and the random values used to encrypt them in addition to the data given for Registration. In so doing, the auditor can check if pseudonyms, questions, and answers access the same data outlined above for Exam-Test Integrity. However, since Remark! is exam-test integrity universally verifiable, it is easy to show that the protocol is exam-test markedness universally verifiable too; (4) for Marking Correctness, the EA reveals the marked exam-test, the random values used to encrypt the marked exam-test, and a table that maps a mark to each answer, after the exam concludes. The auditor can thus check if the mark of each exam-test corresponds to the mark of the given table provided the answer; finally, for (5) Mark Integrity, the EA reveals the examiners' signatures on the marked exam-test and the random values that EA used to encrypt them before posting on the BB. In so doing, the auditor can check that each mark notified to the candidate has a correct signature.

Property	Sound	Complete
Registration	✓	✓ (all)
Exam-Test Integrity	✓	✓ (all)
Exam-Test Markedness	✓	✓ (all)
Marking Correctness	✓ (EA)	✓ (all)
Mark Integrity	✓	✓ (all)

Fig. 4. U.V. properties for Remark!

Figure 4 summarizes the results of our analysis. Marking Correctness is sound only if EA is honest. ProVerif shows an attack if EA is dishonest because it can change the table that the auditor uses to check the correctness of the marks.

Similar to the analysis outlined for the Grenoble exam, ProVerif is unable to handle the general case for the universal verifiability properties also for Remark!. We thus prove in ProVerif the case with one candidate, and also rely on manual induction proofs for the general case.

6 Conclusion

This paper studies verifiability for exam protocols, a security feature that has been studied for voting and auctions but not for exams. In this domain, verifiability properties revealed to be peculiar and required novel definitions. We defined several properties which we organized in individual and universal verifiability properties; moreover, we developed a formal framework to analyze them. As far as we know, we are the first to have developed a framework for verifiability of exam protocols.

Our properties and our methodology work for both to electronic (*e.g.*, cryptographic) exam protocols and to traditional (*e.g.*, paper-and-pencil) exams. Thus, in addition to cryptographic protocols, our methodology is applicable to systems that handle physical security measures, such as a face-to-face authentication. In ProVerif, where we implement our framework, such communications are tricky and we developed ad-hoc equational theories to capture their properties.

We have validated our framework by analyzing the verifiability of two existing exams, one paper-and-pencil-based and the other Internet-based. We run most of the tests automatically; but where ProVerif could not handle the verification of the general case for some universal verifiability properties, we proved manually the tests by induction.

The paper-and-pencil exam has been proved to satisfy all the verifiability properties under the assumption that authorities and examiner are honest. This seems to be peculiar to paper-and-pencil exams, where log-books and registers are managed by the authorities that can tamper with them. Only *Marking Correctness* holds even in presence of dishonest authorities and examiner: here, a candidate can consult her exam-test after marking, thus verifying herself whether her mark has been computed correctly.

The result of the analysis of the Internet-based protocol are somehow complementary. All properties but three are sound without assuming that the exam's roles are honest. But *Marking Correctness*, which worked without assumption in the paper-and-pencil case, holds only assuming an honest exam authority. In fact, a student can check her mark by using the exam table, but this is posted on the bulletin board by the exam authority who can nullify the verification of correctness by tampering with the table.

Since the interest in exam protocols is growing, as future work we plan to analyze more protocols and corroborate more extensively the validity of our framework. Another future work regards the use of tools. Since ProVerif's equational theories, used to model cryptographic primitives, introduce an abstraction which may bring the analyst to miss attacks, we intend to trail CryptoVerif [4] and achieve stronger proofs. In a framework extended with the new tool, we plan to show how to set up an analysis based on the computational model.

Acknowledgements. This research was conducted with the support of the "Digital trust" Chair from the University of Auvergne Foundation.

References

1. Abadi, M., Fournet, C.: Mobile values, new names, and secure communication. In: POPL 2001, pp. 104–115. ACM, New York (2001)
2. Benaloh, J.: Verifiable Secret-Ballot Elections. Ph.D. thesis, Yale University (December 1996)
3. Benaloh, J., Tuinstra, D.: Receipt-free secret-ballot elections (extended abstract). In: STOC 1994, pp. 544–553. ACM, New York (1994)
4. Blanchet, B.: A Computationally Sound Mechanized Prover for Security Protocols. In: Proc. of the IEEE Symposium on Security and Privacy, Oakland, pp. 140–154 (May 2006)
5. Blanchet, B.: An Efficient Cryptographic Protocol Verifier Based on Prolog Rules. In: CSFW, pp. 82–96. IEEE Computer Society, Cape Breton (2001)
6. Castellà-Roca, J., Herrera-Joancomartí, J., Dorca-Josa, A.: A Secure E-Exam Management System. In: ARES, pp. 864–871. IEEE Computer Society (2006)
7. Cohen, J., Fischer, M.: A robust and verifiable cryptographically secure election scheme (extended abstract). In: FOCS 1985, pp. 372–382. IEEE Computer Society (October 1985)
8. Culnane, C., Schneider, S.: A peered bulletin board for robust use in verifiable voting systems. In: CSF (2014)
9. Dolev, D., Yao, A.C.: On the security of public key protocols. IEEE Transactions on Information Theory 29(2), 198–208 (1983)
10. Dreier, J., Giustolisi, R., Kassem, A., Lafourcade, P., Lenzini, G.: On the verifiability of (electronic) exams. Tech. Rep. TR-2014-2, Verimag (April 2014)
11. Dreier, J., Giustolisi, R., Kassem, A., Lafourcade, P., Lenzini, G., Ryan, P.Y.A.: Formal analysis of electronic exams. In: SECRYPT 2014. SciTePress (2014)
12. Dreier, J., Jonker, H., Lafourcade, P.: Defining verifiability in e-auction protocols. In: ASI-ACCS 2013, pp. 547–552. ACM (2013)
13. Figaro, L.: Etudiants: les examens sur tablettes numériques appellés a se multiplier. Press release (January 2015), goo.gl/ahxQJD
14. Flock, E.: Aps (atlanta public schools) embroiled in cheating scandal. (November 2011), http://goo.gl/fqzBBR (retrieved)

15. Giustolisi, R., Lenzini, G., Bella, G.: What security for electronic exams? In: CRiSIS 2013, pp. 1–5. IEEE (2013)
16. Giustolisi, R., Lenzini, G., Ryan, P.Y.A.: Remark!: A secure protocol for remote exams. In: Christianson, B., Malcolm, J., Matyáš, V., Švenda, P., Stajano, F., Anderson, J. (eds.) Security Protocols 2014. LNCS, vol. 8809, pp. 38–48. Springer, Heidelberg (2014)
17. Guénard, F.: La Fabrique des Tricheurs: La fraude aux examens expliquée au ministre, aux parents et aux professeurs. Jean-Claude Gawsewitch (2012)
18. Guts, N., Fournet, C., Zappa Nardelli, F.: Reliable evidence: Auditability by typing. In: Backes, M., Ning, P. (eds.) ESORICS 2009. LNCS, vol. 5789, pp. 168–183. Springer, Heidelberg (2009)
19. Haenni, R., Spycher, O.: Secure internet voting on limited devices with anonymized dsa public keys. In: EVT/WOTE 2011. USENIX (2011)
20. Hirt, M., Sako, K.: Efficient receipt-free voting based on homomorphic encryption. In: Preneel, B. (ed.) EUROCRYPT 2000. LNCS, vol. 1807, pp. 539–556. Springer, Heidelberg (2000)
21. Huszti, A., Pethő, A.: A secure electronic exam system. Publicationes Mathematicae Debrecen 77, 299–312 (2010)
22. Kremer, S., Ryan, M., Smyth, B.: Election verifiability in electronic voting protocols. In: Gritzalis, D., Preneel, B., Theoharidou, M. (eds.) ESORICS 2010. LNCS, vol. 6345, pp. 389–404. Springer, Heidelberg (2010)
23. Küsters, R., Truderung, T., Vogt, A.: Accountability: definition and relationship to verifiability. In: CCS 2010, pp. 526–535. ACM (2010)
24. Ryan, P.Y.A., Schneider, S.A., Goldsmith, M., Lowe, G., Roscoe, A.W.: The Modelling and Analysis of Security Protocols: The CSP Approach. Addison-Wesley Professional (2000)
25. Smyth, B., Ryan, M., Kremer, S., Kourjieh, M.: Towards automatic analysis of election verifiability properties. In: Armando, A., Lowe, G. (eds.) ARSPA-WITS 2010. LNCS, vol. 6186, pp. 146–163. Springer, Heidelberg (2010)

Privacy and Indistinguishability

ADKAM: A-Diversity K-Anonymity Model via Microaggregation

Liang Cheng, Shaoyin Cheng, and Fan Jiang

School of Computer Science and Technology,
University of Science and Technology of China, Hefei, 230037, China

Abstract. A great challenge in privacy preservation is to trade off two important issues: data utility and privacy preservation, in publication of dataset which usually contains sensitive information. Anonymization is a well-represent approach to achieve this, and there exist several anonymity models. Most of those models mainly focuses on protecting privacy exerting identical protection for the whole table with pre-defined parameters. As a result, it could not meet the diverse requirements of protection degrees varied with different sensitive values. Motivated by this, this paper firstly introduces an a-diversity k-anonymity model (ADKAM) to satisfy the diversity deassociation for sensitive values, ant then designs a framework based on an improved microaggregation algorithm, as an alternative to generalization/suppression to achieve anonymization. By using this framework, we improve the data utility and disclosure risk of privacy disclosure. We conduct several experiments to validate our schemes.

Keywords: Data publishing, k-anonymity, privacy preservation, microaggregation

1 Introduction

With the advent of the era of big data and rapid development of information techniques, enormous data have been collected and stored by kinds of organizations which we called *dataholders*, like governments or medical institutions. For the purpose of researches or information sharing, *dataholders* often need to publish datasets (e.g., census information,health care records) to the public. These released datasets, also called *microdata*, can be often utilized in several fields, e.g., e-commerce, e-health. Meanwhile, datasets may contain confidential information about individual.

While the public could benefit a lot from released datasets, it is also vulnerable to privacy disclosure over individuals in the dataset. The basic task in publication of datasets is to prevent the sensitive information of individuals from being disclosed. Initially, the solution was simply removing explicit identities (e.g. names) of data before publishing, which could not guarantee the security. A real case happened to AOL. AOL published randomly selected user search data by replacing names or user IDs with identification numbers, which lead to heavily privacy leakage that a part of users among the released data can easily be identified based on the searches each individual conducted.

For example, assume a released hospital dataset shown in Table 1(a) which does not contain explicit identity attribute. While the dataset is seemingly secure, that is not true.

© Springer International Publishing Switzerland 2015
J. Lopez and Y. Wu (Eds.): ISPEC 2015, LNCS 9065, pp. 533–547, 2015.
DOI: 10.1007/978-3-319-17533-1_36

Table 1. Microdata and a Voter Registration List

<table>
<tr><td colspan="5" align="center">(a) Microdata</td><td colspan="4" align="center">(b) A Voter Registration List</td></tr>
<tr><th>Name</th><th>Age</th><th>Gender</th><th>Zipcode</th><th>Disease</th><th>Age</th><th>Gender</th><th>Zipcode</th><th>Disease</th></tr>
<tr><td>Allen</td><td>12</td><td>Female</td><td>0001</td><td>flue</td><td>12</td><td>Female</td><td>0001</td><td>flue</td></tr>
<tr><td>Alice</td><td>16</td><td>Female</td><td>0002</td><td>flue</td><td>16</td><td>Female</td><td>0002</td><td>flue</td></tr>
<tr><td>Bob</td><td>24</td><td>Male</td><td>0011</td><td>flue</td><td>24</td><td>Male</td><td>0011</td><td>flue</td></tr>
<tr><td>Tom</td><td>26</td><td>Male</td><td>0012</td><td>lung cancer</td><td>26</td><td>Male</td><td>0012</td><td>lung cancer</td></tr>
<tr><td>Jenny</td><td>30</td><td>Female</td><td>0021</td><td>bronchitis</td><td>30</td><td>Female</td><td>0021</td><td>bronchitis</td></tr>
<tr><td>Eric</td><td>34</td><td>Male</td><td>0022</td><td>gastritis</td><td>34</td><td>Male</td><td>0022</td><td>gastritis</td></tr>
</table>

There usually exist other microdatas outward to the pubic, e.g., a voter registration shown in Table 1(b) and member information of a specified website, etc. If an adversary has access to Table 1(b), he/she can easily discover the identities of all individuals by linking the two datasets on {Age, Gender, Zipcode}.

Anonymous method is an advisable approach to tackle the privacy problem, which requires that dataset must be anonymized before publishing. Samarati and Sweendy [17] firstly introduced the concept of k-anonymity that each record is indistinguishable with at least k-1 other records. Machanavajjhala et al. [10] introduced l-diversity, which requires that the distribution of a sensitive attribute has at least l values. Li et al. [9] proposed a framework of t-closeness, which requires that the distribution of a sensitive attribute in each group is close to the distribution of the attribute in the original data set. Wong et al. [19] presented a (a, k)-anonymity model to realize k-anonymity by restricting confidential attribute's frequency.

However, two limitations exist in pre-mentioned schemes. Firstly, most of related k-anonymity models provide the same privacy protection degree for the whole table from a global point of view. Thus, those methods do not take the differences of individuals' privacy protection requirements into consideration. In addition, most of these models adopted generalization/suppression technique, which transforms attribute values to be more less-specific, as the way to achieve anonymity. However, an optimal generalization/suppression is proven to be NP-hard [11], and this method could lead to a higher information loss and time complexity. Domingo-Ferrer [3,4,5] presented a method of micro-aggregation, a widely used SDC technique to substitute generalization/suppression. Compared with generalization/suppression, this method is a unified approach that does not complicate data analysis by adding new categories to the original scale. However, it is generally lack of flexibility for adapting different models.

In this paper, we present a privacy preservation model (ADKAM) to meet the different requirements of each sensitive value. Our contribution is as follows:

- We propose a a-diversity deassociation which consider divers protection degrees of attributes-oriented , and then we put forward a ADKAM model based on a-diversity deassociation by extending the (a, k)-anonymity model. This model is more favorable to provide personalized privacy preservation.
- To achieve this model, we design a framework based on an improved Maximum Distance to Average Vector method (MDAV) algorithm of microaggregation.

By this framework, groups can be shaped with more records satisfying constraints under the limitation of k.

The rest of the paper is organized as follows. Section 2 introduces some related works, including attack models, anonymous models and techniques. Section 3 gives some basic definitions of microdata publishing and then introduces the ADKAM model. In section 4, we describe an overview and detailed steps of the framework. Section 5 experimentally evaluates the effectiveness of our schemes in comparison with k-anonymity and (a, k)-anonymity. In Section 6, we conclude the paper together with future works.

2 Related Work

2.1 Attack Models

There are many attack models to re-identify individuals.

- Linking attack. An intruder usually foreign keys to link two datasets together. This attack is often combined with other attacks.
- Homogeneous attack. Assuming a group contains records with the same sensitive value, for each individual in this group, an intruder can re-identify individuals with the probability of 100%.
- Background attack. If an intruder already gets some background knowledge on an individual, he/she can infer the sensitive attribute of the individual with high confidence.
- Similarity attack. When the sensitive attribute values in a group are distinct but semantically similar, an intruder can learn important information.

2.2 Anonymous Models

While k-anonymity model reduces the probability of re-identifying records, it does not provide sufficient protection against attribute disclosure [8,10,18,20]. Machanavajjhala et al. [10] introduced two attack models on k-anonymous dataset, namely homogeneity attack and background knowledge attack. Moreover, the author proposed a notion of l-diversity, which requires that the distribution of a sensitive attribute in each equivalence class has at least l "well-represented" values. l-diversity principle made up the drawbacks of k-anonymity, however, it also has several deficiencies [9]. The one is that l-diversity makes an assumption of adversarial knowledge. In addition, l-diversity model is not suitable for dataset which has data skew. We use a example to illustrate this. Suppose that the original dataset contains 10000 records, there is a sensitive attribute for a disease taking two values : yes (1%) and no (99%). To satisfy 2-diversity, there can be at most 10000 *1% = 100 equivalence classes. Meanwhile, this presents a serious privacy risk. If a group has an equal number of yes records and no records, that anyone in this group would be considered to suffer from the disease with 50% possibility ,compared with the 1% of the overall population.

Based on this, Li et al. [9] proposed a novel privacy notion of t-closeness, which requires the distribution of sensitive attribute in each group is close to the original distribution in the table. This effectively limits the amount of individual-specific information that an intruder can learn. Wong [19] proposed a privacy model called (a, k)-anonymity. Differ from l-diversity, (a, k)-anonymity maintains the diversity of groups by limiting the occurrence frequency of records with the same sensitive attribute value. Therefore, the intruder can not make sure whether an individual links to certain sensitive value. One major drawback of (a, k)-anonymity is setting the same a-deassociation for all values of sensitive attribute [20].

Xiao and Tao [20] firstly proposed concept of personalized anonymity, and developed a new generalization framework that considers customized privacy requirements. This framework allow individuals to specify the degree of privacy protection according to his/her own preference. Such a preference is formulated through a "guarding node" in a taxonomy. Gedik et al. described a personalized k-anonymity in [6,7] for protecting location privacy against various privacy threats through location information sharing. Yuan et al. design a privacy protection framework for labeled social networks [22]. In this framework users are allowed to set personalized privacy requirements based on their own assumptions about adversary's background knowledge. Therewith, Xu et al. [21] presented a scalable way for users to automatically build rich user profiles.

2.3 Anonymous Techniques

A common approach to achieve k-anonymity is generalization/suppression, which attribute values are replaced with values less-specific. However, optimal generalization/-suppression is NP-hard [11], and even effectively combined together, this method may cause a higher information loss and time complexity.

For the reasons sketched before, Domingo-Ferrer [2] presented microaggregation, a SDC technique as an alternative to generalization/suppression to achieve anonymity. It has been pointed out that microaggregation can achieve the same goal of generalization/suppression without resulting in partially suppressed or coarser data [5]. There are several works focus on microaggregation in [2,13,14,15,16], and the process of microaggregation can be divided into the following two steps.

- Partition: i.e. k-partition. In this step, the original dataset is partitioned into several clusters which each of them satisfy k-anonymity property. In other words, records have the same values on the projection of quasi-identifier attributes in each group which contains at least k records.
- Aggregation: After the step of partitioning, aggregation operators which varies with different type of QI attributes(e.g., the mean for continuous data or the median for categorical data), are used to compute the centroid for each group. Then the original records are replaced with the centroid of belonged cluster.

Table 2(a) and Table 2(b) are two anonymous tables by using techniques of microaggregation and generalization/suppression, respectively. As shown in the tables, these two ways to achieve anonymity are distinctive.

While an optimal microaggregation is NP-hard as illustrated above, near-optimal heuristics exist [12]. The Maximum Distance to Average Vector method (MDAV) was proposed in [2] as part of a heuristic multivariate microaggregation method, which proceed the clustering process with the Nearest Neighbor (NN) [1,2,15]. The process of

Table 2. Anonymous Tables

(a) Generalization/Suppression

Age	Gender	Zipcode	Disease	
[10,20]	Female	000*	flue	Group
[10,20]	Female	000*	flue	A
[20,30]	Male	001*	flue	Group
[20,30]	Male	001*	lung cancer	B
[30,40]	*	002*	bronchitis	Group
[30,40]	*	002*	gastritis	C

(b) Microaggregation

Age	Gender	Zipcode	Disease	
14	Female	0001	flue	Group
14	Female	0001	flue	A
25	Male	0011	flue	Group
25	Male	0011	lung cancer	B
32	Female	0022	bronchitis	Group
32	Female	0022	gastritis	C

MDAV iteratively chooses a unlabelled record x_r farthest to the centroid of dataset to shape a cluster, then adds k-1 unsigned records nearest to x_r into the cluster. The method generates groups of fixed size k, thus, it lacks flexibility for adapting the group size to the distribution of the records in the dataset.

3   Problem Definition

In this section then give several basic definitions of microdata publishing in Section 3.1 and propose the ADKAM model in Section 3.2.

3.1   Basic Definitions

Let D be a micro-data set storing information about a set of individuals. The attributes in D can be classified into 4 categories:

- Identifier attribute, which can definitely identifies an individual and must be removed from T before releasing. Examples are name, ID number, etc.
- Quasi-identifier attributes (QI). Quasi-identifier attributes are a set of attributes that can be used to re-identify an individual in D, when linking to an external database. Examples are gender, age, Zipcode, etc.
- Sensitive attribute (SA), which usually contain some sensitive information about an individual. Examples are salary, job, disease, etc.
- No-sensitive attributes, which can be directly published without any disclosure risks.

Definition 1 (Microdata Publishing). *For a microdata D with n records, a microdata publishing problem on D is to compute a aggregated dataset D* by some transformation $T : D \rightarrow D^*$ and publish D* instead of D. Such transformation T should satisfy some specify privacy constraint F.*

We give the definition QI-group and k-anonymity below.

Definition 2 (QI-group). *After QI-aggregation, a QI-group (i.e., equivalence class) consist of tuples with identical values on all QI attributes. The ith QI-value of the QI-group equals $t.A_i^{qi}$, where t is an arbitrary tuple in the QI-group.*

Definition 3 (*k*-**anonymity**). *Given a microdata D^*, D^* satisfies k-anonymity if each QI-group in D^* satisfies k-anonymity. That is, an arbitrary QI group in D^* contains at least k records.*

Wong et.al. [19] presented (a, k)-anonymity model based on a-deassociation which satisfy k-anonymity by restricting the frequency(in fraction) of confidential attribute in an QI-group. We give the definition of a-deassociation as follows.

Definition 4 (*a*-**deassociation**). *Given a data set D, a equivalence class set G and a sensitive attribute set S with For an equivalence class G_i in G and a sensitive value s in S, let (G_i, s) be the set of tuples in G_i with the sensitive value s and a be a user-specified threshold with $0< a <1$. Data set D is a-deassociation if the frequency of s in each equivalence class is no more than a. That is, $| (G_i, s) | / | G_i | \leq a$ for any G_i in G.*

Definition 5 ((a, k)-**anonymity**). *Given a data set D, a equvillalence class set G and confidential attributes set S with Dom(S)=$\{s_1, s_2, \dots\}$. For any G_i in G, if G_i satisfies both k-anonymity and a-deassociation, that we can say the anonymous table D satisfies (a, k)-anonymity with respect to the QI-group.*

Actually, most of existing transformation methods offer such a global consistent privacy constraint $\mathcal{F}$ overall QI-groups.

3.2   ADKAM Model

Inspired by the idea of deassociation in which the paremeter a is defined within the whole dataset, we extend the notion of a-deassociation from the whole dataset to each group, by which the frequency of each sensitive value should be limited to a a-diversity deassociation.

It is worthful to mention that, privacy protection degrees are different for different sensitive value. The degrees can be divided into two categories:attributes-oriented and individual-oriented. The former one is set by data holder that can provide privacy protection from a global view, the latter one is set by respondents that individuals can decide the protection degree based on their personal requirements. In our work, we take the protection degrees into consideration from the perspective of individual-oriented on the real dataset.

We use one parameters: RES_{ij}, to represents the protection degrees set by and respondents. For a set of records with an arbitrary value s_i of sensitive attribute, each value of RES_{ij} represents the protection degree of jth individual, and the value varies with different individual. Then we formalize the unified definition of PD_{s_i} in Equation 1 for each sensitive individual value s_i.

$$PD_{s_i} = \frac{\sum_{j=1}^{n_i} RES_{ij}}{n_i} \tag{1}$$

where n_i is the number of records with the value s_i.

To achieve privacy protection by different protection degrees, we establish the transformation of protection degrees to a-diversity deassociation for each sensitive value s_i. The conversion is shown in Equation 2.

$$a_{s_i} = 1 - PD_{s_i} \tag{2}$$

Now, we give the formal descriptions of a-diversity deassociation as follow.

Definition 6 (a-**diversity deassociation**). *Given a Data set D, a QI-group set G and a sensitive attribute set S with DOM(S)=$\{s_1, s_2, ...\}$. For each s_i in S, we define a-diversity deassociation as a 2-tuple set (α_{s_i}, s_i). That means the frequency of records with the sensitive value s_i in each group is no more than α_{s_i}.*

a-diversity deassociation requires each individual to specify their personal requirements, during the phase of data collection, for any sensitive values to be protected according to their preference. Considering two extreme cases with the value of a_{si} as follows:

- $a_{si}=1$, which means that the association between records with value s_i and s_i is no more than 1. In this case, the sensitive value s_i is not sensitive to those individuals, because the condition is always satisfied.
- $a_{si}=0$, which means that individuals with value s_i does not want to have any relations with s_i.

Table 3. A Personalized deasscociation table with protection degrees

Name	Age	Gender	Zipcode	Disease	Protection degrees
Allen	12	Female	0001	flue	0.2
Alice	16	Female	0002	flue	null
Bob	24	Male	0011	flue	0.3
Tom	26	Male	0012	lung cancer	0.7
Jenny	30	Female	0021	bronchitis	0.7
Eric	34	Male	0022	gastritis	0.6

(a, k)-anonymity is a particular case of our proposed model if its deassociation requirements are the same for each record. Table 3 is a collected microdata containing the column of protection degrees, which the value is assigned by individuals in accordance with their personal preferences. This table demonstrates the diverse protection requirements varies with individuals. For example, Allen defines her protection degree as 0.2 for the sensitive value $flue$, and Thomas defines the protection degree as 0.7 for the sensitive value $lung\ cancer$, while Allen defines the protection degree as null for the sensitive value $flue$. The table shows us a-diversity deassociation by two comparisons: Alice and Tom, Alice and Allen. The former comparison illustrates that different protection degrees with different sensitive value, while the latter one illustrate that protection degree value also maybe different even with the same sensitive value.

4   Our Framework

As mentioned before, the traditional MDAV algorithm is not suitable for our proposed model. Motivated by this, we present an improved MDAV algorithm to achieve it. In this algorithm, the process of partition is divided into two steps: k-partition and Extending k-partition. In the former step, the original dataset is partitioned into groups with at most k records, specially, we make an stipulation that the cardinality of each group is

k when judging a candidate record whether satisfies the a-diversity deassociation. The benefit is that a group can be shaped with more correct records under the limitation of k. Therewith, we re-cluster those unlabelled records into adequate shaped clusters as possible in the latter step.

In this section, we design a framework based on the improved MDAV algorithm described before. We first give an overview of the framework in Section 4.1, and then describe each step of the framework from Section4.2 to Section4.4 in details.

4.1   Overview

The overview of the framework is illustrated below:

- **Minimum k-partition.** In this step, the original dataset D is partitioned into groups satisfying minimum k-constraint, that each group contains at most k records.
- **Extending k-partition.** In this step, we re-cluster unlabelled records into adequate shaped clusters.
- **Aggregation.** We retain a set of groups which contain at least k records, and aggregate each group by replacing QI values of each record with the centroid of belonged cluster. Then publish it as the final dataset D^*.

4.2   Minimum k-partition

Distance Measurement. Unlike classification criterion of operating principle, data can be divided into three categories: continuous, ordinal, and nominal. The latter two categories are known as categorical. Computing methods of centroid and distance between records vary with the data types, and are described below [5].

- Continuous. The average operator used is the arithmetical mean, and the squared Euclidean distance is generally used to measure the distances between continuous attributes. The distance measure is defined in Equation 3.

$$Dist_{CON}(X,Y) = \| X - Y \|^2 = \sum_{i=1}^{p} (x(i) - y(i))^2 \tag{3}$$

where $x(i), y(i)$ denote as the ith dimension attribute values of record X, Y.
- Ordinal. The distance between two values a and b $(a < b)$ of an ordinal attribute A_i is below.

$$Dist_{ORD}(a,b) = \frac{|\{i|a \leq i < b\}|}{|D(A_i)|} \tag{4}$$

where $|D(A_i)|$ denotes as the cardinality of the range of attribute A_i.
The average operators we used for ordinal attributes are median and the convex median.
- Nominal. Distance for nominal attributes is defined using the equality predicate. The definition of distance between two values a and b of a nominal attribute is described as follows.

$$Dist_{NOM}(a,b) = \begin{cases} 0, & a = b \\ 1, & a \neq b \end{cases} \tag{5}$$

Meanwhile, the mode rule is used as the average operator. This is, for a set S = $\{a_1, a_2, \ldots, a_n\}$, the value with the most frequency is selected as the average.

Therewith, we give a formal definition of distance between two records as follows.

Definition 7. *Let* $Q = \{C_1, \ldots C_r, O_1, \ldots, O_s, N_1, \ldots, N_t\}$ *be the QI attributes of table T, where* $C_i(i = 1, \ldots, r), O_i(i = 1, \ldots, s)$ *and* $N_i(i = 1, \ldots, t)$ *denote as continuous, ordinal and nominal attribute, respectively. The distance between X and Y is*

$$Dist(X, Y) = \sum_{i=1}^{i=r} \mu_i Dist_{CON}(X[C_i], Y[C_i]) + \sum_{i=1}^{i=s} \nu_i Dist_{ORD}(X[O_i], Y[O_i])$$
$$+ \sum_{i=1}^{i=t} \omega_i Dist_{NOM}(X[C_i], Y[C_i]) \tag{6}$$

where $\mu_i(\nu_i/\omega_i)$ *denotes as the dissimilarity weights of attribute* $C_i(O_i/N_i)$.

Clustering Process. We define some relevant parameters in advance. For an original dataset D with n records, C denotes as the centroid of D, a_{sa} is a set of a-deassociataion for sensitive value s_i, and $dist_{max}$ denotes the preset distance threshold between two records in a group.

Algorithm 1 shows the process of shaping a cluster. Line 1 chooses a record x_r which is unlabelled and farthest to C, as the centroid of G_i. Then Line 3 to Line 9 describe the process of selecting candidate records. For a record x nearest to c_i, it can be added to G_i if the constraints (Line 3, 5, 6) are satisfied. Then we extend it to the process over D in Algorithm 2, and returns a set of clusters $G = \{G_1, G_2, \ldots\}$ and another set of un-clustered records T^*.

Input: $T \leftarrow D$
1 $x_r \leftarrow MaxDistance(C);$
2 $G_i \leftarrow \{x_r\};$
3 **while** $Cardinality(G_i) < k$ **do**
4      $x \leftarrow MinDistance(C_i);$ /* choose a record nearest to C_i */
5   **if** $(dist(x, C_i) < dist_{max})$ **then**   /* distance constraint */
6   **if** $(|(G_i \cup x, x.sa)| \le k * a_{x.sa})$ **then**   /* satisfy personalized association */
7              $G_i.append(x);$ /* append record to G_i */
8              $T \leftarrow T \setminus \{x\};$ /* eliminate candidate record from T */
9              $C_i \leftarrow Centroid(G_i);$ /* update the centroid C_i of G_i */
10   **else**   /* choose another record */
11   **continue;**
12   **else**   /* terminal */
13   **break;**
14 **return** $G_i;$

Algorithm 1. Clustering process $ShapeCluster$ of a cluster

Input: $G, T^* \leftarrow \emptyset; T \leftarrow D$;
Output: G, T^*;
1 $i = 0$;   /* the iteration counter */
2 **while** $Cardinality(T) >= k$ **do**
3 | $G_i \leftarrow ShapeCluster(T)$;   /* call the function of $ShapeCluster$ */
4 | $G.append\{G_i\}$;
5 | $i + +$;   /* shape the next cluster */
6 $T^* = T$;
7 **return** G, T^*;

Algorithm 2. Clustering process of overall table

4.3 Extending k-partition

T^* contains many un-clustered records, which could be reallocated. In this section, we extend the minimum k-partition by re-clustering these records into adequate clusters. The process of extending algorithm is shown in Algorithm 3.

Input: T^*, G
1 **while** $Cardinality(T) \geq 0$ **do**
2 | **foreach** $x_j \in T$ **do**   /* unlabelled records in T */
3 | | $C_i \leftarrow MinDistance(x_j)$;   /* choose a cluster nearest to x_j */
4 | | **if** $dist(C_i, x_j) \leq dist_{max}$ **then**   /* distance constraint */
5 | | | **if** $(|(G_i \cup \{x_j\}, x_j.sa)| \leq k * a_{x_j.sa})$ **then** /* personalized association */
6 | | | | $G_i.append\{x_j\}$;
7 | | **else**
8 | | | $T^* \leftarrow T^* \setminus x_j$;
9 **return** G;

Algorithm 3. Extending k-partition process

4.4 Aggregation and Data Publishing

After the step of k-partition, the original dataset is divided into several groups. However, there still exist some records unlabelled and groups contain less than k records, both of them are called noisy data. In this step, we first eliminate those noisy data (Lines 2 - 3), and then aggregate survival groups by replacing QI values with the centroid of belonged group (Lines 5-6). The returned clusters set G can be used to publish, and the detail of aggregation process is shown in Algorithm 4.

5 Evaluation

5.1 Dataset

In this section, we evaluate the performance of our model on a particular dataset—The Basic Insurance settlement data (BISD), registered by the local hospital for one year, from September 2013 to September 2014. To reflect personalized requirements,

---

Input: $G = \{G_1, G_2, ...\}$; $C_i \leftarrow$ the centroid of ith cluster;
1 **foreach** $G_i \in G$ **do**
2   **if** *Cardinality*$(G_i) < k$ **then**
3 | $G \leftarrow G \setminus G_i$;   /* eliminate clusters with$<k$ records */
4   **else**
5   **foreach** *record* $x_j \in G_i$ **do**
6 | *Replace*$(x_j(QI), C_i)$;   /* replace QI values with centroid */
7 **return** G;

Algorithm 4. Aggregation

respondents, i.e., insureds in our dataset, are allowed to set the value of protection degree according to their own preferences. Before experiments started, we firstly eliminate records with missing values. The dataset contains a relation with nearly 40k tuples, each storing information of a hospitalization record. The relation has 8 columns: *Age, Gender, Edu, Address, Insucategory, Hospdays, Hosprank, Majordiscode*. The first two columns are continuous and the others are categorical. *Majordiscode* is the single sensitive attribute; all of the others are the QI attributes.

5.2 Experimental Environment

All of the experiments are performed using a desktop running the Windows 7 professional operating system with Inter(R) Core(TM) i5-3450 CPU at 3.10GHz, and the memory is 8.00GB. During experiments, many well-behaved softwares are used, including Microsoft Visual Studio 2008, Weka and MATLAB 7.0.

5.3 Evaluation Results

We evaluate the effectiveness and utility of our schemes compared with two non-personalized version, k-anonymity and (a, k)-anonymity model, from data quality, disclosure risk and execution time aspects respectively. We pre-define the value $a = 0.5$ as a-deassociation for (a, k)-anonymity and k-values $=\{5, 10, 15, 20\}$ respectively.

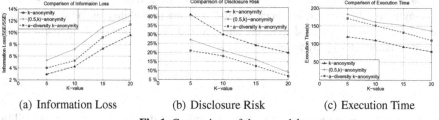

(a) Information Loss   (b) Disclosure Risk   (c) Execution Time

Fig. 1. Comparison of three models

Data Utility. In this section, we compare the performance of three models for the data utility of BISD. In order to minimize the information loss caused by microaggregation, groups should be formed with maximum the within-group homogeneity. The most common homogeneity measure is $IL=SSE/SST$, where SSE denotes as the total sum of the within-group squared errors and SST denotes as the total sum of square errors.

A lower IL value performs higher data utility of released dataset. We give the definitions of GSE, SSE, and SST as follows:

$$GSE(G_i) = \sum_{j=1}^{n_i} Dist(x_{ij}, \overline{x_i}) \tag{7}$$

where $n_i(n_i \geq k)$ is the number of records in G_i, x_{ij} denotes as the jth element in G_i and $\overline{x_i}$ signifies the centroid of G_i.

$$SSE = \sum_{i=1}^{g} GSE(G_i) = \sum_{i=1}^{g}\sum_{j=1}^{n_i} Dist(x_{ij}, \overline{x_i}) \tag{8}$$

$$SST = \sum_{i=1}^{g} GSE(G_i) = \sum_{i=1}^{g}\sum_{j=1}^{n_i} Dist(x_{ij}, \overline{x}) \tag{9}$$

$$IL = \frac{SSE}{SST} \tag{10}$$

where g is the number of groups. n_i denotes as the number records in G_i. $\overline{x_i}$ and $\overline{x}$ respectively signify the centroid of G_i and the dataset.

Fig.1(a) plot the performance curves of information loss over three models. As shown in the figure, the information loss increase with the k-value increasing. The reason is that the k-value increases, the value of IL decreases accordingly, which will lead to higher information loss. Moreover, our model incurs a higher IL ratio than k-anonymity and lower than $(0.5, k)$-anonymity, due to the different clustering criteria. That is, k-anonymity simply considers the distance as the only clustering criterion, and a-deassociation provided by $(0.5, k)$-anonymity for the whole table could result in higher information loss without considering a-diversity requirements.

Disclosure Risk. Disclosure risk is usually used as the criterion to assess the security of anonymous table, which has been evaluated as the probability of the original data that can be correctly matched from the anonymized dataset, that is, the percentage of Record Linkages (RL) [15] defined as follow:

$$RL = 100 * \frac{\sum_{x_j \in X} Pr(x_j')}{n} \tag{11}$$

where n denotes as the number of original records and the record linkage probability for an anonymized record ($Pr(x_j')$) is calculated as:

$$Pr(x_j') = \begin{cases} 0, & x_j \notin G' \\ \frac{1}{|G'|}, & x_j \in G' \end{cases} \tag{12}$$

where G' is the set of original records that are at minimum distance from x'_j. If the original record x_j is in G, the $Pr(x'_j)$ is computed as the probability of guessing x_j in G', that is, $1/|G'|$. Otherwise, $Pr(x'_j) = 0$.

As curves shown in Fig.1(b), the RL values are decreasing with the k-value increases. The reason is that, the information loss will gain more with increasing k-value. As a result, the probability of linked successfully will be much lower. Fig.1(b) also shows that for the same k-value, the RL value of our model is lower than the others. The reason is that we provide privacy preservation by taking different privacy requirements which will effectively decrease the privacy disclosure risk. That we can say our schemes outperform others from the view of resisting attacks.

Execution Time. Fig.1(c) plots the execution time curves over various k-value. The results are obtained from the average values of 5 experiments. As shown in the figure, the execution time of three models decrease with k-value increasing for all three models. That is because, the bigger the value of k, the fewer of clustering times. Meanwhile, for the same k-value, k-anonymity method outperforms all other models, while the difference between $(0.5, k)$-anonymity and our model is similar. The explanation is that, distance is the only criterion for clustering records in the process of k-anonymity, while deassociation must be satisfied in the latter two methods. The similarity of performances between $(0.5, k)$-anonymity and our model is related to the predefined value of a-association.

6 Conclusion and Future Works

A primary principle of privacy preservation is that individuals have the right to decide protection degrees according to their homogeneous requirements. In this paper, we propose a framework to protect privacy by considering the attributes-oriented protection degrees for microdata to be released. Each individual in the dataset is allowed to set privacy protection degree value according to his/her personal preferences. Meanwhile, we use an improved microaggregation method to achieve the framework. We validate the effectiveness of our schemes through extensive experiments on real dataset.

Although, this framework outperforms other models, it still exists some deficiencies. In our framework, we make some assumptions that the sensitive attribute is unidimensional and categorical, and records have the same priority when adding into groups. To enhance its applicability, future works will focus on applying this model to satisfy multidimensional, different types of sensitive attributes and records of different priority.

Acknowledgement. This research was supported in part by the Fundamental Research Funds for the Central Universities of China (WK2101020004), the Specialized Research Fund for the Doctoral Program of Higher Education of China (20113402120026) and OATF, USTC.

References

1. Domingo-Ferrer, J., Martínez-Ballesté, A., Mateo-Sanz, J.M., Sebé, F.: Efficient multivariate data-oriented microaggregation. The VLDB Journal 15(4), 355–369 (2006)
2. Domingo-Ferrer, J., Mateo-Sanz, J.M.: Practical data-oriented microaggregation for statistical disclosure control. IEEE Transactions on Knowledge and Data Engineering 14(1), 189–201 (2002)
3. Domingo-Ferrer, J., Sebé, F., Solanas, A.: A polynomial-time approximation to optimal multivariate microaggregation. Computers & Mathematics with Applications 55(4), 714–732 (2008)
4. Domingo-Ferrer, J., Solanas, A., Martinez-Balleste, A.: Privacy in statistical databases: k-anonymity through microaggregation. In: GrC, pp. 774–777 (2006)
5. Domingo-Ferrer, J., Torra, V.: Ordinal, continuous and heterogeneous k-anonymity through microaggregation. Data Mining and Knowledge Discovery 11(2), 195–212 (2005)
6. Gedik, B., Liu, L.: Location privacy in mobile systems: A personalized anonymization model. In: Proceedings of 25th IEEE International Conference on Distributed Computing Systems, ICDCS 2005, pp. 620–629. IEEE (2005)
7. Gedik, B., Liu, L.: Protecting location privacy with personalized k-anonymity: Architecture and algorithms. IEEE Transactions on Mobile Computing 7(1), 1–18 (2008)
8. Lambert, D.: Measures of disclosure risk and harm. Journal of Official Statistics-Stockholm 9, 313–313 (1993)
9. Li, N., Li, T., Venkatasubramanian, S.: t-closeness: Privacy beyond k-anonymity and l-diversity. In: ICDE, vol. 7, pp. 106–115 (2007)
10. Machanavajjhala, A., Kifer, D., Gehrke, J., Venkitasubramaniam, M.: l-diversity: Privacy beyond k-anonymity. ACM Transactions on Knowledge Discovery from Data (TKDD) 1(1), 3 (2007)
11. Meyerson, A., Williams, R.: On the complexity of optimal k-anonymity. In: Proceedings of the Twenty-third ACM SIGMOD-SIGACT-SIGART Symposium on Principles of Database Systems, PODS 2004, pp. 223–228. ACM, New York (2004)
12. Oganian, A., Domingo-Ferrer, J.: On the complexity of optimal microaggregation for statistical disclosure control. Statistical Journal of the United Nations Economic Commission for Europe 18(4), 345–353 (2001)
13. Panagiotakis, C., Tziritas, G.: Successive group selection for microaggregation. IEEE Transactions on Knowledge and Data Engineering 25(5), 1191–1195 (2013)
14. Solanas, A., Martinez-Balleste, A., Domingo-Ferrer, J.: V-mdav: a multivariate microaggregation with variable group size. In: 17th COMPSTAT Symposium of the IASC, Rome (2006)
15. Soria-Comas, J., Domingo-Ferrer, J.: Probabilistic k-anonymity through microaggregation and data swapping. In: 2012 IEEE International Conference on Fuzzy Systems (FUZZ-IEEE), pp. 1–8 (2012)
16. Soria-Comas, J., Domingo-Ferrer, J., Sánchez, D., Martínez, S.: Enhancing data utility in differential privacy via microaggregation-based k-anonymity. The VLDB Journal, 1–24 (2014)
17. Sweeney, L.: k-anonymity: A model for protecting privacy. International Journal of Uncertainty, Fuzziness and Knowledge-Based Systems 10(05), 557–570 (2002)
18. Truta, T.M., Vinay, B.: Privacy protection: p-sensitive k-anonymity property. In: ICDE Workshops, p. 94 (2006)
19. Wong, R.C.-W., Li, J., Fu, A.W.-C., Wang, K.: (α, k)-anonymity: an enhanced k-anonymity model for privacy preserving data publishing. In: Proceedings of the 12th ACM SIGKDD International Conference on Knowledge Discovery and Data Mining, pp. 754–759. ACM (2006)

20. Xiao, X., Tao, Y.: Personalized privacy preservation. In: Proceedings of the 2006 ACM SIG-MOD International Conference on Management of Data, pp. 229–240. ACM (2006)
21. Xu, Y., Wang, K., Zhang, B., Chen, Z.: Privacy-enhancing personalized web search. In: Proceedings of the 16th International Conference on World Wide Web, pp. 591–600. ACM (2007)
22. Yuan, M., Chen, L., Yu, P.S.: Personalized privacy protection in social networks. Proceedings of the VLDB Endowment 4(2), 141–150 (2010)

Visualizing Privacy Risks of Mobile Applications through a Privacy Meter

Jina Kang[1], Hyoungshick Kim[1], Yun Gyung Cheong[1], and Jun Ho Huh[2]

[1] Department of Computer Science and Engineering, Sungkyunkwan University, Korea
[2] Honeywell ACS Labs, USA

Abstract. When it comes to installing mobile applications on Android devices, users tend to ignore privacy warning messages about permissions being requested. Warning messages are often shown too late and are hard to interpret for normal users. To improve users' awareness of potential privacy implications of installing an application, we designed a "privacy meter" that visualizes the risks (in a slider bar format) imposed by the types of permissions being requested. Interpreting and understanding privacy risks become quick and easy.

Our lab study shows that the privacy meter is the most effective solution compared to Google's existing permission screens and privacy fact feature. With the privacy meter in place, only about 26% of participants recommended applications that have high privacy risks to their friends and family members. That is a significant improvement from the 61% of participants who recommended high risk applications when Google's permission screens were used. The time taken to make recommendation decisions, on average, also dropped from 72 seconds to 26 seconds when the privacy meter was used.

Index Terms: Permission, Android, Mobile, Decision-making.

1 Introduction

When a user tries to install a mobile application (app) from Google Play (the official marketplace for Android apps), the user is asked to grant a set of *permissions* for the app to access information or use features from the user's smartphone. However, recent studies [7, 10, 11] have shown that the majority of users tend to ignore any warning messages shown on those permission requesting displays. For example, Felt et al. [7] showed that about 83% of their study participants did not pay attention to the permission information screens, and only about 3% of users correctly understood the meaning of given permissions. This is mainly because warning messages are shown when users have already decided to install an app; at that stage, most users just want to continue with installation without being interrupted [3]. Moreover, many users found it difficult to understand the terms and words used to describe permissions [11].

Although designing an effective warning message system for permissions seems challenging, Kelley et al. [10] proposed a warning display about permissions called *privacy facts* and showed that the use of privacy-focused warning messages do affect users' app selection behavior. This indicates that there is still room for improvement in

© Springer International Publishing Switzerland 2015
J. Lopez and Y. Wu (Eds.): ISPEC 2015, LNCS 9065, pp. 548–558, 2015.
DOI: 10.1007/978-3-319-17533-1_37

designing a warning display system for apps to highlight their privacy risks. A type of meter may be a reasonable candidate for providing provide warning to the users. Meter is a popular form of user interface for warning systems. In particular, password strength meter was intensively studied before (e.g., [15]). Since users are already familiar with such meter designs for warning systems, an app's privacy risks related to permissions might also be effectively visualized.

This paper proposes a new warning display mechanism called the *'privacy meter'* to warn users about potentially dangerous permissions (requested by an app). The privacy meter evaluates the risks associated with the permissions requested by an app, and visualizes the computed risk scores. In designing a prototype of the meter, we considered how many dangerous permissions (e.g., INTERNET and READ_PHONE_STATE) are included in the collection of permissions requested by an app. To evaluate the effectiveness of our prototype implementation, we conducted a user study involving 36 participants, asking participants to recommend apps to their friends or family members in a simulated role playing scenario. Each participant was assigned to one of the four experiment conditions: (1) our new privacy meter display, (2) the privacy facts display [10], (3) the current Google Play store permissions display, or (4) the previous Google Play store permissions display (before version 4.8.20). We compared the numbers of times a high risk app (an app that requests a high number of potentially dangerous permissions) was recommended under each condition, demonstrating that our privacy meter significantly outperforms all other mechanisms in affecting participants' recommendation decisions.

In summary, our contributions can be briefly described as follows: First, the proposed interface for app's permissions (*privacy meter*) is more effective than the existing methods in warning users before installing apps. Second, we found that the new Google Play store interface based on permission groups is significantly better than the previous Google one.

2 Related Work

We focus on Android permissions display due to its historically more detailed permissions system and its large user base. Prior work suggests that users tend to ignore the permission display on Android, mainly because the messages appear after users have already decided to download an app [11]. Furthermore, users who pay attention to permissions lists have trouble using them because the screens are jargon-filled, provide confusing explanations, and lack explanations for why the data is collected [7]. There were several different studies on user expectations about Android access control system (e.g., [11,12]). In particular, Felt and her colleagues have published a series of papers on the Android permission model, and how users understand it. They found that most users (83%) do not pay attention to the permission screens during installation. Also, only 3% of their surveyed users had a good understanding of what the permissions were actually asking in terms of accessing data on the phone [7].

Those studies showed the problems of Google permission lists. To solve those problems, some researchers developed automated tools to detect overprivileged and malicious apps. Stowaway [5] was created to detect overprivileged Android apps by checking whether an app requests for excessive permissions. Taintdroid [4] developed a mechanism for inspecting whether a running app requires the user information it has access to. Papamartzivanos et al. [13] proposed a cloud-based system that runs on a crowdsourcing logic, providing a privacy-flow tracking service in real-time. Felt et al. [6] found that about one third of 940 Android apps they experimented were considered overprivileged.

The problem is that users often ignore the permission lists and warnings messages. To improve users' awareness of privacy implications of permissions being requested by apps, Felt et al. [10] suggested a new warning display interface called *privacy facts* that shows a checklist of permissions requested by an app. Privacy facts display eight different types of information an app can collect: personal information, contacts, location, calendars, credit card or financial, diet or nutrition, health or medical, and photos. These items are displayed with a checkbox next to it, indicating whether each information type is being requested by that app. Privacy facts help users avoid apps that suspiciously require unnecessary permissions.

To help users make more privacy-conscious decisions, Harbach et al. [9] proposed to leverage many personal data available on smartphones by providing customized examples. Providing private information examples can help users pay more attention to the relevant, important information and make better decisions. Our goals are inline with their research goals. We want users to be able to decide for themselves the risks associated with an app they are about to install. The key difference, however, is that they use images to visualize the meaning of permissions. On the other hand, our privacy meter visualizes the privacy risk information through an one-dimension slider bar.

Some researchers have tried grading apps. PrivacyGrade [12, 14] aims to improve users' awareness of app behaviors that may compromise users' privacy. PrivacyGrade provides detailed information about an app's privacy-sensitive behaviors. Such behaviors are summarized as grades, ranging from "A+" (being the most privacy sensitive) to "D" (being the least privacy sensitive). Gates et al. [8] proposed a scoring system that assigns a risk score to each app and displays summary of the risk scores to users. Again, the key difference between their scoring system and our meter is the way the risks are visualized. Recently, Biswas et al. [2] proposed metrics to quantify privacy risks associated with an app accessing user data. There are some similarities between privacy panel and our privacy meter, but their primary focus is to track privacy-flows. Moreover, user study is missing from their work.

3 Privacy Meter Design

This section presents the design of a *privacy meter* that measures the risks associated with permissions requested by an app by counting the number of privacy-sensitive, potentially dangerous permissions. Our privacy meter was designed and prototyped with a simple focus on visualizing the safety (privacy risks) of apps. With the initial work presented in this paper, our goal was not to develop very accurate risk scoring functions, but to first demonstrate the effectiveness of visualizing privacy risks through a meter type display. Once we can show the effectiveness of a simple meter design, we will then focus on building more precise risk scoring functions as part of future work. We used a circular slider thumb to indicate where the privacy risks for an app lie on

Table 1. Top 10 popularly requested permissions for Android malware [1]

Rank	Permission name	Description
1	INTERNET	Full network access
2	READ_PHONE_STATE	Allows read only access to phone state
3	SEND_SMS	Allows an application to send SMS messages
4	WRITE_EXTERNAL_STORAGE	Allows an application to read from external storage
5	RECEIVE_SMS	Allows an application to receive SMS messages
6	READ_SMS	Allows an application to read SMS messages
7	ACCESS_COARSE_LOCATION	Allows an app to access approximate location derived from network location sources
8	READ_CONTACTS	Allows an application to read the user's call log
9	ACCESS_FINE_LOCATION	Allows an app to access precise location from location sources such as GPS, cell towers, and Wi-Fi
10	WRITE_SMS	Allows an application to write SMS messages

the slider bar (see Fig. 1), which is the default slider design available in Android SDK. The next three sections explain the meter features we carefully considered in the meter design.

3.1 Counting the Number of Dangerous Permissions

Most importantly, the meter was designed to reflect on how many privacy-sensitive, potentially dangerous permissions are being requested by an app. We simply counted the number of privacy-sensitive permissions in the requested permission set based on an existing list of dangerous permissions available in [1], and computed the privacy risk score by dividing that counter value by the maximum number of dangerous permissions. Table 1 shows the top 10 of the most popularly requested permissions by Android malware. For more intuitive visualization, the number of dangerous permissions were scaled and normalized to values ranging from 0 to 1.

3.2 Computing the Privacy Risk Score

Since we used the list of 30 most popularly used dangerous permissions by malware samples [1], the maximum number of dangerous permissions in an app would always be 30 in our design. However, previous research has shown that for top 234 popular apps, the number of dangerous permissions requested by the apps is much smaller than 30 (95% confidence interval, 3.059 to 3.540) [reference removed for anonymous submission]. Therefore, given a set of dangerous permissions p, we calculated the privacy score S_p as follows: $S_p = \min(|p|, 4)/4$ where $|p|$ is the number of permissions in p. Based on the observed confidence interval, we assumed that an app can be dangerous if the number of requested dangerous permissions is greater than or equal to 4. For example, if an app requests two dangerous permissions such as INTERNET and

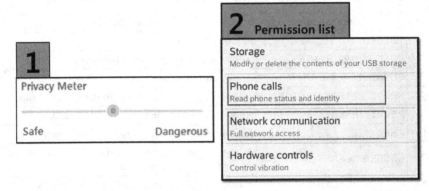

Fig. 1. Our prototype implementation of *privacy meter*. "1" is privacy meter; and "2" is the requested permission list (dangerous permissions are highlighted in red box) which can additionally be shown when the slider bar is clicked.

READ_PHONE_STATE, S_p would be 0.5, and the slider thumb would be located at the half way of the slider bar (see Fig. 1).

3.3 Display Style

As indicated above, we simply used the default interactive slider available on Android SDK to minimize any visualization bias that could be introduced by designing our own proprietary slider design. Our prototype, shown in Fig. 1, is based on an Android interactive slider with a height of 90 pixels and a width that stretches the full width of a given Android phone. The circular slider thumb visualizes the level of privacy risks associated with an app. By clicking on the slider bar, users can see the details of the requested permissions.

4 Methodology

This section describes our hypotheses and describes the user study, which was designed based on the hypotheses to help evaluate the effectiveness of the proposed privacy meter.

4.1 Hypotheses

The primary goal of this work is to design a highly effective visualization mechanisms for privacy risks that can effectively protect users from installing (potentially) privacy-compromising apps. Based on that goal, the following hypotheses were defined.

1. The privacy meter interface is more effective than existing warning displays such as the privacy facts interface [10] in visualizing the privacy risks associated with an app.
2. Current Google design is more effective than previous Google design in presenting the privacy risks associated with an app.

(a) Google (previous)   (b) Google (current)   (c) Privacy facts   (d) Privacy meter

Fig. 2. The warning displays used for user study

4.2   Existing Warning Displays about Permissions

We compared the effectiveness of the privacy meter with the following two representative warning displays.

- *Google permission displays.* A warning display is currently used in the official app store in Google. When a user tries to install an app through the store, it shows a list of permissions required to use the app. We used two different interfaces: Fig. 2(a) and (b) show the warning displays before and after version 4.8.20, respectively. After version 4.8.20, permissions have been organized into groups.
- *Privacy facts.* A warning display was proposed by Kelley et al. [10] to help users become more aware about privacy risks upon installing apps; their warning display shows personal information that can be accessed by an app. Their study results show that privacy facts are more effective in influencing users' app selection behavior than Google's existing permission lists [10].

4.3   User Study Design

We used a mixed-method design, an experiment and a follow-up questionnaire, to study participants' behaviors in understanding the the the privacy risks of requested permissions, and test our two hypotheses. To test the hypotheses, we designed a between-subject study in which each participant was given only one of the four warning display mechanisms (the previous Google warning display, the current Google warning display, the *privacy facts* checklist, and the *privacy meter* warning display). The participants were sequentially allocated to one of the four warning displays (See Fig. 2) in the order in which they were recruited.

4.4   Procedure

We advertised and conducted the user study as a *application recommendation* role playing experience. The study was carried out in an on-campus lab.

For each participant, we provided an Android smartphone with a pre-installed app that we developed for simulating a "custom Android market" and explained a brief overview of the experiment (without mention of the privacy or security issues associated with the app). Before performing the app selection tasks, each participant was asked to complete a short pre-survey about demographic information, which allowed us to find out whether that a participant currently uses an Android phone. After the pre-survey, through the pre-installed app, we asked the participant to (1) select one between two similar apps but each requiring a totally different permission set, and (2) recommend that app to his or her friends. We repeated this exercise six times with different six app pairs that belong to the six different categories (word game, documents scanning, Facebook, nutrition, review movie, travel apps) that we carefully selected. Once the participant finished the app recommendation tasks, he or she was interviewed to explain his or her decisions; the interviews were audio-recorded. On average, the participants spent about 15 minutes to complete the entire process and received a two-dollar cafe voucher for completing it.

4.5   Tested Apps

For the app selection task, we carefully chose 2 apps for each of six representative categories ('document', 'social networks', 'movie', 'health', 'travel', and 'word game') in Google Play where one app (*safe* app) requested less access to permissions compared with the other app (*dangerous* app). All of the apps we used were real apps which can be found in Google Play, but those apps were chosen in a manner that they are similar in terms of functionality and popularity (e.g., with 100 to 1,000 download range); we made our best efforts to eliminate bias occurring in the app selection task.

We implemented an Android app for the user study, which simulated a "custom Android market" to achieve a reasonable amount of ecological validity. That app sequentially asked a participant to select one app in each of the six app pairs that we defined. The order of the six categories presented to a participant and the two apps selected for each category were randomly defined.

5   Results

This section presents the data collected through the user study and the statistical analysis results.

5.1   Demographics

We recruited a total of 36 Android phone users. 10 participants (27.78%) were female and 26 participants (72.22%) were male. All participants were aged between 23 and 32 and had a computer science bachelors degree. We wanted to find out the security knowledge and awareness levels of participants when it comes to using Android phones. Therefore we asked the participants whether they are currently using a security lock (e.g., PINs, patterns, etc.) to protect their mobile phones. Most participants (77.78%) did not use any security lock because they found entering patterns or passwords annoying.

Table 2. Proportion of participants who decided to recommend potentially dangerous applications to their friends and family members, and average time take to make recommendation decisions

Design	# recommended	Time
Google (previous)	41/54 (75.92%)	70.67 sec
Google (current)	33/54 (61.11%)	71.50 sec
Privacy facts	24/54 (44.44%)	53.54 sec
Privacy meter	14/54 (25.92%)	26.11 sec

5.2 Recommending Potentially Dangerous Applications

First, we look at the proportion of participants who decided to recommend to their friends potentially dangerous applications that contain 3 or more privacy-compromising permissions. As shown in Table 2, with the privacy meter being present, only 14 participants (25.92%) decided to recommend potentially dangerous applications to their friends. In contrast, 33 participants (61.11%) decided to recommend potentially dangerous applications when Google's current permission lists were used, which is a huge jump.

The Fisher's Exact Tests (FET) were used to compare the proportion of participants in a statistically significant manner. Post-hoc comparisons were corrected for multiple-testing using the Benjamini-Hochberg method. The test results of all the warning displays appeared to be significantly different (corrected FET, all $p < 0.05$).

Most importantly, there is a statistically significant difference between the proportions of participants recommending potentially dangerous applications when the privacy meter was present and when the privacy facts were used (corrected FET, $p < 0.05$). It is also interesting to note that Google's current permission screens are more effective than the previous screens (corrected FET, $p < 0.05$), showing that the newer permission screens have indeed improved users' experience in making more informed decisions. From those observations, we confidently conclude that the privacy meter is more effective than privacy facts in visualizing the privacy risks associated with the permissions requested by an app. We also conclude that current Google privacy display design is better than the previous Google privacy display design.

5.3 Decision Time

We now look at the average time taken to make recommendation decisions. As Table 2 shows, the participants who were given the privacy meter took the shortest time on average to make decisions. We used unpaired t-test to show statistical significance. Google's current and pervious permission screens did not show any statistical significant difference in the average decision times (corrected unpairwise t-test, $p = 0.773$). The average decision time for privacy meter (26.11 sec) did show statistically significant improvement over privacy facts (53.54 sec) though (corrected unpairwise t-test, $p < 0.05$). From those results, we confidently conclude that the privacy meter can help users become more efficient in making privacy-conscious decisions. The participants' decision time for the privacy meter was much shorter than that of the privacy facts.

5.4 Interview Results

This section presents the interview results. We asked the following two questions.

Q1. When you are installing mobile applications, are you concerned about permission lists? Only 3 participants said that they are concerned about permission lists and make decisions based on them (8.33%). This result is similar to the results presented in Felt et al [7]. For those who are not concerned with permission lists, they provided several reasons. 14 of those participants (38.89%) believe that most applications request similar list of permissions anyway. 10 of those participants (27.78%) trust Google to inspect applications for privacy and security. 5 of those participants (13.89%) ignored the list due to long descriptions. 4 of those participants (11.11%) ignore permission lists because by that stage they would have already made decisions to install an application. 5 of those participants (13.89%) mentioned that these interfaces cannot be trusted since Android system can be compromised — Interestingly, all of them are using a security lock, which implies that they are more concerned with the security of their mobile phones.

Q2. Why did you not recommend a mobile application? 6 participants (16.67%) said that they did not recommend an application that contains version information in its name (e.g., FreeTravel ver.2) because it looks suspicious. 5 participants (13.89%) did not recommend an app that has a name of an unusual manufacturing company. Some participants wanted to know the relation between the requested permissions and their privacy impact, which are lacking in the privacy facts. In comparison, our privacy meter is capable of visualizing the privacy impact. The interview results also indicate that 11 participants pay attention to video files and images (31%), and popularity ratings (31%) when making decisions. 8 participants (22%) said that they read the application descriptions before downloading an application.

6 Limitations

This study was limited in several ways. First, all of our participants are from a single pool of users who major in Computer Science and Engineering. This may make it difficult to generalize the findings to all Android users with various backgrounds. Second, the main task (*application recommendation* task) in the user study was artificially designed through a simulation of the app installation process. Inherently, using such a simulation model might lower the ecological validity of the experiment compared with conducting real empirical studies.

7 Conclusions and Future Work

To improve users' awareness of privacy risks associated with installing mobile applications, we proposed a novel privacy measuring mechanism called the privacy meter. The privacy meter looks at different types of permissions requested by a mobile application to gauge the level of privacy risks associated with it. The outcomes are visualized through a slider bar, making it quick and easy for users to interpret the associated risks and make decisions.

Our user study and statistical analysis show that the privacy meter outperforms other existing warning systems like Google's permission screens and the privacy facts. When only Google's permission screens were used, about 61% of the participants recommended mobile applications that have high privacy risks to their friends and family members. In comparison, that proportion went down dramatically to 26% when our privacy meter was present.

As part of future work, we will conduct more user studies to optimize the privacy meter design in terms of its visualization effects and accuracy in measuring risks.

Acknowledgements. This work was partly supported by the ICT R&D program (2014-044-072-003 , 'Development of Cyber Quarantine System using SDN Techniques') of MSIP/IITP and was also supported by the National Research Foundation of Korea (NRF) grant funded by the Korea government (No. 2014R1A1A1003707).

References

1. AV-Comparatives. Mobile security review. Technical report (2012)
2. Biswas, D., Aad, I., Perrucci, G.P.: Privacy Panel: Usable and Quantifiable Mobile Privacy. In: Proceedings of the 8th IEEE International Conference on Availability, Reliability and Security (2013)
3. Egelman, S., Tsai, J., Cranor, L.F., Acquisti, A.: Timing is Everything?: the Effects of Timing and Placement of Online Privacy Indicators. In: Proceedings of the 27th SIGCHI Conference on Human Factors in Computing Systems (2009)
4. Enck, W., Gilbert, P., Han, S., Tendulkar, V., Chun, B.-G., Cox, L.P., Jung, J., McDaniel, P., Sheth, A.N.: TaintDroid: an Information-Flow Tracking System for Realtime Privacy Monitoring on Smartphones. In: Proceedings of the 9th USENIX Conference on Operating Systems Design and Implementation (2014)
5. Felt, A.P., Chin, E., Hanna, S., Song, D., Wagner, D.: Android Permissions Demystified. In: Proceedings of the 18th ACM Conference on Computer and Communications Security (2011)
6. Felt, A.P., Greenwood, K., Wagner, D.: The Effectiveness of Application Permissions. In: Proceedings of the 2nd USENIX Conference on Web Application Development (2011)
7. Felt, A.P., Ha, E., Egelman, S., Haney, A., Chin, E., Wagner, D.: Android Permissions: User Attention, Comprehension, and Behavior. In: Proceedings of the 8th Symposium on Usable Privacy and Security (2012)
8. Gates, C.S., Chen, J., Li, N., Proctor, R.W.: Effective Risk Communication for Android Apps. IEEE Transactions on Dependable and Secure Computing 11(3), 252–265 (2014)
9. Harbach, M., Hettig, M., Weber, S., Smith, M.: Using Personal Examples to Improve Risk Communication for Security & Privacy Decisions. In: Proceedings of the 32nd SIGCHI Conference on Human Factors in Computing Systems (2014)
10. Kelley, P.G., Cranor, L.F., Sadeh, N.: Privacy as Part of the App Decision-Making Process. In: Proceedings of the 31st SIGCHI Conference on Human Factors in Computing Systems (2013)

11. Kelley, P.G., Consolvo, S., Cranor, L.F., Jung, J., Sadeh, N., Wetherall, D.: A Conundrum of Permissions: Installing Applications on an Android Smartphone. In: Blyth, J., Dietrich, S., Camp, L.J. (eds.) FC 2012. LNCS, vol. 7398, pp. 68–79. Springer, Heidelberg (2012)
12. Lin, J., Amini, S., Hong, J.I., Sadeh, N., Lindqvist, J., Zhang, J.: Expectation and Purpose: Understanding Users' Mental Models of Mobile App Privacy through Crowdsourcing. In: Proceedings of the 2012 ACM Conference on Ubiquitous Computing (2012)
13. Papamartzivanos, D., Damopoulos, D., Kambourakis, G.: A Cloud-Based Architecture to Crowdsource Mobile App Privacy Leaks. In: Proceedings of the 18th Panhellenic Conference on Informatics (2014)
14. Lin, J., Sadeh, B.L.N., Hong, J.I.: Modeling users Mobile App Privacy Preferences: Restoring Usability in a Sea of Permission settings. In: Proceedings of the 10th Symposium on Usable Privacy and Security (2014)
15. Ur, B., Kelley, P.G., Komanduri, S., Lee, J., Maass, M., Mazurek, M.L., Passaro, T., Shay, R., Vidas, T., Bauer, L., et al.: How Does Your Password Measure Up? The Effect of Strength Meters on Password Creation. In: Proceedings of the 21st USENIX Conference on Security Symposium (2012)

One-Round Witness Indistinguishability from Indistinguishability Obfuscation*

Qihua Niu[1,2], Hongda Li[1], Guifang Huang[1], Bei Liang[1], and Fei Tang[1]

[1] State Key Lab of Information Security, Institute of Information Engineering
Chinese Academy of Sciences, Beijing 100093
[2] School of Science, China University of Petroleum, Qingdao 266580
niuqihua@163.com, {lihongda,huangguifang,liangbei,tangfei}@iie.ac.cn

Abstract. In this work, we build up the relationship between witness indistinguishability (WI) and indistinguishability obfuscation ($i\mathcal{O}$) by constructing a one-round witness indistinguishable argument system for all languages in **NP** based on the existence of indistinguishability obfuscator for general circuit class and a number-theoretic assumption. The key tool in our construction is witness encryption scheme with unique decryption which is also proposed and constructed in this work. Our construction of witness encryption scheme with unique decryption is based on a general witness encryption scheme and a weak auxiliary input multi-bit output point obfuscation.

Keywords: Witness indistinguishability, indistinguishability obfuscation, weak auxiliary input multi-bit output point obfuscation, witness encryption scheme with unique decryption.

1 Introduction

The concept of zero-knowledge (ZK) is introduced by Golewasser, Micali and Rackoff in their seminal paper [18]. ZK maintains the most comprehensive privacy of the prover. Goldreich, Micali and Wigderson [19] showed that any **NP** has ZK proof system.

A useful and meaningful relaxation of zero-knowledge is witness indistinguishability (WI) which was proposed by Feige and Shamir [11]. A protocol is WI if any two proofs for the same statement that use different witnesses are indistinguishable. Sometimes, WI is enough for many cryptographic applications and WI protocols play important roles in the design of ZK protocols.

It has been proved that the number of round of ZK protocol must be greater than 2 [14], but the number of WI protocol has no limit. The first two-round WI (Zap) is given by Dwork and Naor [10] under the existence assumption of trapdoor permutations. Subsequently, by derandomizing the Zaps of Dwork and Naor [10], Barak, Ong and Vadhan [3] constructed the first one-round WI

---

* This work is supported by the National Natural Science Foundation of China (Grant No. 60970139,61003276).

J. Lopez and Y. Wu (Eds.): ISPEC 2015, LNCS 9065, pp. 559–574, 2015.
DOI: 10.1007/978-3-319-17533-1_38

and they posed the issue: *Either constructions (of one-round WI) for specific problems based on specific assumptions or general constructions for all of **NP** based on alternative assumptions would be interesting.* The second one-round WI is constructed by Groth, Ostrovsky and Sahai [17]. Their construction is based on a specific assumption on bilinear groups.

In this work, we give another construction of one-round WI based on two kinds of obfuscation. One is indistinguishability obfuscation, the other is a weak auxiliary input multi-bit output point obfuscation. In fact, indistinguishability obfuscation and point obfuscation are the only research fields of program obfuscation in which positive results have so far been reached.

Program Obfuscation. Program obfuscation is formally initiated by Barak et al. [1,2] in 2001. Program obfuscation aims to make computer program "unintelligible" while preserving their functionality. The compiler that takes programs and makes them difficult to understand is called obfuscator. Ideally, an obfuscated program should be a "virtual black box (VBB)", in the sense that anything one can compute from it could also be computed from the input-output behavior of the program. Unfortunately, Barak et al. [1,2] showed that general-purpose obfuscation in the sense of VBB is impossible.

(1) Indistinguishability Obfuscation ($i\mathcal{O}$). Just like that WI is a relaxation of ZK, $i\mathcal{O}$ is a relaxation of VBB-sense obfuscation. $i\mathcal{O}$ requires only that obfuscation of any two distinct programs with the same functionality is computationally indistinguishable from each other. $i\mathcal{O}$ is initialized by Barak et al. [1,2]. In a recent breakthrough, Garg et al. [12] proposed the first candidate construction of an efficient indistinguishability obfuscator (for the sake of simplicity of notation, which is also denoted by $i\mathcal{O}$) for general programs and also showed how to apply $i\mathcal{O}$ to achieve powerful new functional encryption schemes for general circuits.

(2) Point Obfuscation. Point obfuscation is the obfuscation of point circuit class $\{I_m : m \in \{0,1\}^\lambda\}_{\lambda \in \mathbb{N}}$ where I_s outputs 1 on input s and outputs 0 on any other input. Canetti [8] and Wee [24] constructed two VBB-sense point obfuscators respectively in 1997 and 2005 based on different assumptions.

Canetti also considered auxiliary input point obfuscation in the sense that given invertible a-priori information $f(m)$, any PPT adversary cannot distinguish the obfuscation of I_m from the obfuscation of I_u for a random u with length $|m|$. In contrast to VBB-sense obfuscation, such kind of obfuscation is also called distributional version obfuscation. Canetti proved that his construction of point obfuscation is also distributional version auxiliary input point obfuscation under a number-theoretic assumption.

For obfuscation for multi-bit output circuit class $\{I_{m \to r} : m \in \{0,1\}^n, r \in \{0,1\}^{poly(n)}\}_{n \in \mathbb{N}}$ ($I_{m \to r}$ outputs r on input m and 0 otherwise), Canetti et al. [9] gave such a construction and Bitansky and Canetti [4] proved that under a strong variant of DDH assumption such construction is VBB-sense multibit output point obfuscator, while such construction cannot be shown to be auxiliary input VBB-sense obfuscator. But very recently Brzuska et al. [7] pointed out that neither VBB-sense nor distributional version of auxiliary input multi-bit output point obfuscator exists if $i\mathcal{O}$ exists.

In this work, we just need a weaker version of auxiliary input multi-bit output point obfuscator. This version is weak in the sense that we just require that if it is hard to get the point address m of $I_{m \to r}$ from the auxiliary input z it is also hard to get m from z together with $\mathcal{MO}(I_{m \to r})$ (the obfuscation of $I_{m \to r}$). We prove that the construction in [9] just satisfies the weaker definition under a rational number-theoretic assumption which is implied by a variant DDH assumption [8] and this kind of obfuscation is enough for our applications.

1.1 Our Results

Theorem (informal). *One-round witness indistinguishability argument system for all **NP** language exists if the indistinguishability obfuscator for general circuit class and the weak auxiliary input multi-bit output point obfuscator exist.*

1.2 An Overview of Our Approach

The common indistinguishability in "witness indistinguishability" and "indistinguishability obfuscation" motivates us to build the connection between them. The idea of getting one-round witness indistinguishability from indistinguishability obfuscation is to indistinguishably obfuscate the decryption algorithm of a witness encryption scheme which is implied by the existence of indistinguishability obfuscation. The only message exchanged is the obfuscated decryption circuit.

Concretely, suppose L is an **NP** language, R_L is the corresponding witness relation. $(Enc(1^\lambda, x, \cdot), Dec(\cdot, w))$ is a witness encryption scheme for L. The only message exchanged in the one-round WI protocol is an indistinguishably obfuscated circuit $T_w = i\mathcal{O}(D_{x,w}(\cdot))$ of the decryption circuit $D_{x,w}$ such that $D_{x,w}(c) = Dec(c, w)$. The verifier samples a random string $m \leftarrow \{0,1\}^\lambda$ and encrypts it using the encryption algorithm $Enc(1^\lambda, x, \cdot)$, then it feeds $CT = Enc(1^\lambda, x, m)$ to T_w. If T_w returns m, the verifier accepts and rejects otherwise. When $x \notin L$, by the soundness security of witness encryption scheme, T_w returns m on input $CT = Enc(1^\lambda, x, m)$ with negligible probability, so the verifier rejects with overwhelming probability. Therefore the soundness of the protocol holds.

If for any w, w' such that $(x, w), (x, w') \in R_L$ and any (possibly invalid) ciphertext CT^*, the decryption circuits $D_{x,w}$ and $D_{x,w'}$ have the same output, the indistinguishability of $i\mathcal{O}$ guarantees the witness indistinguishability of the protocol. Unfortunately, there exists witness encryption scheme such that $D_{x,w}$ and $D_{x,w'}$ may have different functionality if the ciphertext is not validly generated. This results in the premise of applying $i\mathcal{O}$ disappears and thus the protocol is not witness indistinguishable.

We therefore propose the concept of witness encryption with unique decryption which satisfies that for any ciphertext, no matter which decryption key is used, the decryption is unique. The construction of such scheme $(Enc'(1^\lambda, x, \cdot), Dec'(\cdot, w))$

is based on a general witness encryption scheme $(Enc(1^\lambda, x, \cdot), Dec(\cdot, w))$. The ciphertext of the new scheme consists of $C = Enc(1^\lambda, x, m)$ as a part and we want the decryption algorithm $D'_{x,w} = Dec'(\cdot, w))$ returns a non$-\perp$ value only when it makes sure that the ciphertext submitted by the verifier is valid. Thus, the decryption of C is unique no matter which decryption key is used (this is guaranteed by the correctness of the witness encryption scheme $(Enc(1^\lambda, x, \cdot), Dec(\cdot, w)))$. To get such a witness encryption scheme, our idea is that the ciphertext of a message m consists of in addition to $C = Enc(1^\lambda, x, m; r)$ an value MO that "locks" the randomness r used in the encryption algorithm. The key of MO is the plaintext of C. After getting the ciphertext (C, MO), $Dec'(\cdot, w)$ invokes $Dec(\cdot, w)$ on input C and get the plaintext m, if $m =\perp$, it returns $\perp$; otherwise, if $m \neq\perp$, it opens MO using m, if it get $\perp$ or get r but $C \neq Enc(1^\lambda, x, m; r)$ it returns $\perp$. Otherwise, it returns m. Now suppose w, w' are witnesses of x, if $Dec'((C, MO), w)$ returns a string m, then $Dec(C, w) = m$ and $C = Enc(1^\lambda, x, m; r)$ for $r = MO(m)$. It implies that C is a valid encryption of m. By the correctness of $(Enc(1^\lambda, x, \cdot), Dec(\cdot, w))$, $Dec(C, w') = m$ and $Dec'((C, MO), w')$ can also open MO and complete the verification of the validity of C. Thus $Dec'((C, MO), w')$ also returns m. It implies that $Dec'(\cdot, w')$ and $Dec'(\cdot, w')$ have the same functionality and $i\mathcal{O}$ works.

However, the soundness security of $(Enc'(1^\lambda, x, \cdot), Dec'(\cdot, w))$ may be damaged (this results in the soundness of the one-round WI unsatisfied). Because what $Dec'(\cdot, w)$ gets are a ciphertext C of a random m and MO which contains information about both m and the randomness r in C. We need to guarantee that when $x \notin L$, $Dec'((C, MO), w)$ return m only with negligible probability. We wish MO does not help $Dec'(\cdot, w)$ to decrypt. That is, $Dec'(\cdot, w)$ cannot get more benefit when given input (C, MO) than given only C.

Our another key observation is that a weak auxiliary input multi-bit output point obfuscation for unpredictable distribution satisfies the required property. Such obfuscation satisfies that if it is hard to get the point address m of $I_{m \to r}$ from the auxiliary input z it is also hard to get m from z together with $\mathcal{MO}(I_{m \to r})$ (the obfuscation of $I_{m \to r}$). The soundness of our protocol follows.

1.3 Other Related Work

In light of the impossibility results of Barak et al [1,2], several followup works studied notions of obfuscation with relaxed security [20,21,22,4]. There are also impossibility results with respect to auxiliary inputs [15,16,5]. An interesting phenomenon is that the possibility results of obfuscation drive the impossibility results. For example, the impossibility result in [16,5] are that: the existence of $i\mathcal{O}$ implies that all functions with sufficient pseudo-entropy cannot be obfuscated w.r.t (in)dependent auxiliary input.

1.4 Outline

We start with reviewing the definitions of known cryptography primitives in section2. Later in section 3, We recall the concept of auxiliary input point obfuscation and present the concept of weak auxiliary input multi-bit output point obfuscation and show that the previous construction given by Canetti et al. satisfies our definition. We present the concept of witness encryption scheme with unique decryption and constructs such a scheme in section 4. Section 5 is devoted to constructing a one-round WI protocol.

2   Definitions and Tools

In this paper, we use the following standard definitions and tools.

2.1   Distributions and Indistinguishability

Let $\mathcal{X} = \{X_n\}$ be a distribution ensemble, $x \leftarrow X_n$ means sampling x from the distribution X_n. $x \leftarrow U_n$ or $x \leftarrow \{0,1\}^n$ means sampling x from $\{0,1\}^n$ uniformly. Suppose $\mathcal{A}$ is an algorithm, $\mathcal{A}(X_n)$ denotes the distribution induced by running (the probabilistic) $\mathcal{A}$ on an input sampled from X_n. We say that a function $negl(\cdot)$ is negligible if $negl(n) = n^{-\omega(1)}$ (i.e. it decays faster than any polynomial).

Given two distribution ensembles $\mathcal{X} = \{X_n\}_{n \in \mathbb{N}}$ and $\mathcal{Y} = \{Y_n\}_{n \in \mathbb{N}}$, where $Supp(X) \cup Supp(Y) \subseteq \{0,1\}^{poly(n)}$, we say that $\mathcal{X}$ is computationally indistinguishable from $\mathcal{Y}$, if for any polynomial-time adversary $\mathcal{A}$ there exists a negligible $negl(\cdot)$ such that for all sufficiently large n: $|Pr_{x \leftarrow X_n}[\mathcal{A}(x) = 1] - Pr_{y \leftarrow Y_n}[\mathcal{A}(y) = 1]| \leq negl(n)$. We denote it by $\mathcal{X} \approx_c \mathcal{Y}$.

2.2   Argument System

If $R_L = \{(x,y)\} \in \{0,1\}^* \times \{0,1\}^*$ is polynomial-time-recognizable and L is defined as $\{x : \exists\, y \ s.t. \ (x,y) \in R_L \ and \ |y| \leq poly(|x|)\}$, we say that L is an **NP** language and R_L is the corresponding witness relation. An interactive argument [18] is an interactive protocol in which the soundness condition is only required to hold against PPT prover strategy.

Definition 1 (interactive argument system). *A pair of PPT Turing machines* (P, V) *is called an interactive argument system for a language L if the following conditions holds:*

1. **Completeness.** *If $x \in L$, then $Pr[(P, V)(x) = 1] \geq 1 - negl(|x|)$.*

2. **Soundness.** *If $x \notin L$, then for any PPT P^*, $Pr[(P^*, V)(x) = 1] \leq negl(|x|)$.*

The number of rounds in an interactive proof is the total number of messages exchanged in the interaction. An argument system with one round is called noninteractive.

A *view* of a party in a protocol contains the public input, the party's private input and random tape, and the list of message that this party received during the protocol.

2.3   Witness Indistinguishable Protocol

The concept of *witness indistinguishability* was proposed by Feige and Shamir [11] as a relaxation of zero-knowledge.

Definition 2 (witness indistinguishability [11,3]). *Let L be an* **NP** *language with witness relation R_L. Let (P, V) be an argument system for L. We say that (P, V) is witness indistinguishable if for any polynomial-time verifier V^*, and every two sequences $W^1 = \{w_x^1\}_{x \in L}$ and $W^2 = \{w_x^2\}_{x \in L}$ such that (x, w_x^1), $(x, w_x^2) \in R_L$, $\{view_{V^*}\langle P(x, w_x^1), V^*(x)\rangle\}_{x \in L}$ and $\{view_{V^*}\langle P(x, w_x^2), V^*(x)\rangle\}_{x \in L}$ are computationally indistinguishable.*

Theorem 1 ([11]). *Every zero-knowledge protocol is witness indistinguishable. Witness indistinguishable is preserved under parallel and concurrent composition of protocols.*

ZAPs. A *zap* [10] is a 2-round public-coin interactive proof system that is witness indistinguishable.

Theorem 2. *If trapdoor permutations (secure against polynomial-size circuits) exist, then every language in* **NP** *has a ZAP.*

2.4   Indistinguishability Obfuscation

Indistinguishability obfuscation is the weak version of program obfuscation. Informally, an indistinguishability obfuscator for a class of circuits $\mathcal{C}$ guarantees that for any two circuits C_0 and C_1 which are "functionally equivalent" (i.e., for all inputs x in the domain, $C_0(x) = C_1(x)$), the obfuscation of C_0 must be computationally indistinguishable from the obfuscation of C_1. Below we present the formal definition following the syntax of [12].

Definition 3 (indistinguishability obfuscation [12]). *A uniform PPT machine $i\mathcal{O}$ is called an indistinguishability obfuscator for a circuit class $\{\mathcal{C}_\lambda\}$ if the following conditions are satisfied:*

1. **Preserving Functionality.** *For all security parameters $\lambda \in \mathbb{N}$, for all $C \in \mathcal{C}_\lambda$, for all inputs x, we have that*

$$Pr[C'(x) = C(x) : C' \leftarrow i\mathcal{O}(\lambda, C)] = 1.$$

2. **Indistinguishability.** *For any (not necessarily uniform) PPT distinguisher D, there exists a negligible function $negl(\cdot)$ such that the following holds: For all security parameters $\lambda \in \mathbb{N}$, for all pairs of circuits $C_0, C_1 \in \mathcal{C}_\lambda$, we have that if $C_0(x) = C_1(x)$ for all inputs x, then*

$$|Pr[D(i\mathcal{O}(\lambda, C_0)) = 1] - Pr[D(i\mathcal{O}(\lambda, C_1)) = 1]| \leq negl(\lambda).$$

Garg et al. [12], based upon a variant of the multilinear maps framework, gave the first candidate construction for a general-purpose indistinguishability obfuscator(i.e. the indistinguishability obfuscator for general poly-sized circuit class) satisfying this notion.

3 Weak Auxiliary Input Multi-bit Output Point Obfuscation (Weak AI-MBPO)

Point circuit I_m is the circuit that outputs 1 on a point $m \in \{0,1\}^\lambda$ and 0 otherwise. Multi-bit output point circuit $I_{m\to r}$ is the circuit which outputs a string $r \in \{0,1\}^{poly(\lambda)}$ instead of a bit $b \in \{0,1\}$ on input $m \in \{0,1\}^\lambda$ and $0^{|r|}$ otherwise.

In this section, we propose a weak version of auxiliary input multi-bit output point obfuscation which is weaker than the concept in [6,8,23,7]. It only requires that if it is hard to predict m from z with (z, m, r) sampled from a unpredictable distribution D_n, it is still hard to predict m from z together with $\mathcal{MO}(I_{m\to r})$.

Definition 4 (unpredictable distribution [6,8]). *A distribution ensemble $\mathcal{D} = \{D_\lambda = (Z_\lambda, M_\lambda, R_\lambda)\}_{\lambda \in \mathbb{N}}$, on triple of strings is unpredictable if no poly-size circuit family can predict M_λ from Z_λ. That is, for every poly-size circuit family $\{C_\lambda\}_{\lambda \in \mathbb{N}}$ and for all large enough λ:*

$$Pr_{(z,m,r) \leftarrow D_\lambda}[C_\lambda(z) = m] \leq negl(\lambda).$$

Suppose $(\mathcal{G}, \mathcal{E}, \mathcal{D})$ is a semantic secure encryption scheme and the message space is $\{0,1\}^\lambda$ when the security parameter is λ, then the distribution $\{(z, m, r) : m \leftarrow U_\lambda, r \leftarrow U_{poly(\lambda)}, K \leftarrow \mathcal{G}(1^\lambda), z = \mathcal{E}(K, m; r)\}_{\lambda \in \mathbb{N}}$ is an unpredictable distribution where r is the randomness in $\mathcal{E}$.

Definition 5 (weak auxiliary input multi-bit output point obfuscation for unpredictable distribution). *A PPT algorithm $\mathcal{MO}$ is a weak auxiliary input multi-bit output point obfuscator of the circuit class $\mathcal{C} = \{\mathcal{C}_\lambda = \{I_{m\to r} | m \in \{0,1\}^\lambda, r \in \{0,1\}^{poly(\lambda)}\}\}_{\lambda \in \mathbb{N}}$ for unpredictable distributions if it satisfies:*

1. **Functionality.** *For any $\lambda \in \mathbb{N}$, any $I_{m\to r} \in \mathcal{C}_\lambda$ and any $x \neq m$, $\mathcal{MO}(I_{m\to r})(x) = I_{m\to r}(x)$ and $Pr[\mathcal{MO}(I_{m\to r})(m) \neq r] \leq negl(\lambda)$ where the probability is taken over the randomness of $\mathcal{MO}$.*
2. **Polynomial Slowdown.** *For any $\lambda \in \mathbb{N}$, $I_{m\to r} \in \mathcal{C}_\lambda$, $|\mathcal{MO}(I_{m\to r})| \leq poly(|I_{m\to r}|)$.*
3. **Secrecy.** *For any unpredictable distribution $\mathcal{D} = \{D_\lambda = (Z_\lambda, M_\lambda, R_\lambda)\}_{\lambda \in \mathbb{N}}$ over $\{0,1\}^{poly(\lambda)} \times \{0,1\}^\lambda \times \{0,1\}^{poly(\lambda)}$, it holds that: for any PPT algorithm $\mathcal{A}$*

$$Pr_{(z,m,r) \leftarrow D_\lambda}[\mathcal{A}(1^\lambda, z, \mathcal{MO}(I_{m\to r})) = m] \leq negl(\lambda)$$

Note: There are several secrecy requirements in different definitions of AI-MBPO. Here we show one of them and the others are similar.

For any unpredictable distribution $\mathcal{D} = \{D_\lambda = (Z_\lambda, M_\lambda, R_\lambda)\}_{\lambda \in \mathbb{N}}$ over $\{0,1\}^{poly(\lambda)} \times \{0,1\}^\lambda \times \{0,1\}^{poly(\lambda)}$, it holds that: for any PPT algorithm $\mathcal{A}$

$$\{(z, \mathcal{MO}(I_{m\to r})) : (z, m, r) \leftarrow D_\lambda\}_{\lambda \in \mathbb{N}}$$
$$\approx_c \{(z, \mathcal{MO}(I_{m'\to r'})) : (z, m, r) \leftarrow D_\lambda, m' \leftarrow U_\lambda, r' \leftarrow U_{poly(\lambda)}\}_{\lambda \in \mathbb{N}}.$$

Brzuska and Mittelbach [7] showed AI-MBPOs do not exist if indistinguishability obfuscation exists for general circuit class. But their result does not rule out the existence of weak AI-MBPO. In what follows, we show that under a rational assumption, the construction of Canetti and Dakdouk [9] satisfies the required properties of definition 5.

Assumption 3.1: *There exists an ensemble of prime order groups* $\mathcal{G} = \{\mathbb{G}_\lambda : |\mathbb{G}_\lambda| = p_\lambda, |p_\lambda| = \lambda + 1\}$ *such that for any unpredictable distribution* $\mathcal{D} = \{D_\lambda = (Z_\lambda, M_\lambda, R_\lambda)\}_{\lambda \in \mathbb{N}}$ *with support* $\{0,1\}^{poly(\lambda)} \times \{0,1\}^\lambda \times \{0,1\}^{poly(\lambda)}$, *the distribution* $\mathcal{D}' = \{(z' = (z, g, g^m), m, r) : (z, m, r) \leftarrow D_\lambda, g \leftarrow \mathbb{G}_\lambda^*\}_{\lambda \in \mathbb{N}}$ *is also unpredictable, where* $\mathbb{G}_\lambda^* = \mathbb{G}_\lambda \backslash \{e\}$ *is the set of all generators of* $\mathbb{G}_\lambda$.

Note: Canetti's strong DDH assumption [8] requires that

$$\{(z, g, g^m) : (z, m, r) \leftarrow D_\lambda, g \leftarrow \mathbb{G}_\lambda^*\}_{\lambda \in \mathbb{N}}$$
$$\approx_c \{(z, g, g^u) : (z, m, r) \leftarrow D_\lambda, u \leftarrow M_\lambda, g \leftarrow \mathbb{G}_\lambda^*\}_{\lambda \in \mathbb{N}}$$

Under such an assumption, Canetti [8] gave a construction of auxiliary input point obfuscator. In fact, this assumption implies Assumption 3.1 because the indistinguishability of the two distributions means the distribution $\mathcal{D}'$ in assumption 3.1 is unpredictable.

The following construction is given by Canetti and Dakdouk [9].

Construction 3.1 $(C_n, (g_0, g_0^m), (g_1, g_1^{a_1}), ..., (g_t, g_t^{a_t}))$ **obfuscator** $\mathcal{MO}$.

Let $\mathcal{G} = \{\mathbb{G}_\lambda\}_{\lambda \in \mathbb{N}}$ *be a group ensemble whose existence is guaranteed by assumption 3.1. For multi-bit output point circuit* $I_{m \to r}$ *with* $m \in \{0,1\}^\lambda$ *and* $r = r_1 r_2 ... r_t \in \{0,1\}^t$ *with* $t = poly(\lambda)$, $\mathcal{MO}$ *independently samples* $u_1, ..., u_t$ *from* U_λ *and* $g_1, ..., g_t$ *from* $\mathbb{G}_\lambda^*$ *and let* $a = (a_1, ..., a_t)$ *where* $a_i = m$ *if* $r_i = 1$ *and* $a_i = u_i$ *otherwise. The obfuscator* $\mathcal{MO}$ *is defined as:*

$$\mathcal{MO}(I_{m \to r}) = (C_\lambda, (g_0, g_0^m), (g_1, g_1^{a_1}), ..., (g_t, g_t^{a_t})),$$

where C_λ *is a circuit with functionality* $C_\lambda(g, \alpha) = g^\alpha$. *That is* $\mathcal{MO}(I_{m \to r})$ *is the circuit with* C_λ *and* $g_0, g_0^m ... g_t, g_t^{a_t}$ *hardwired into it and its functionality is as follows:*

On input α *of length* λ, $\mathcal{MO}(I_{m \to r})$ *firstly runs* C_λ *on* (g_0, α), *if* $C_\lambda(g_0, \alpha) \neq g_0^m$, *it outputs* 0^t. *Otherwise, it runs* C_λ *on* (g_i, α) *to find all other coordinates such that* $a_i = \alpha = m$ *and outputs* $y = y_1 y_2 ... y_t$ *where* $y_i = 1$ *if* $C_\lambda(g_i, \alpha) = g_i^{a_i}$ *and 0 otherwise.*

Now we prove that construction 3.1 is a weak auxiliary input multi-bit output point obfuscation for unpredictable distribution in the sense that it is still hard to recover m from $\mathcal{MO}(I_{m \to r})$ together with an invertible auxiliary $z = z(m, r)$.

Theorem 3. *The obfuscator* $\mathcal{MO}$ *in construction 3.1 is a weak auxiliary input multi-bit output point obfuscator of the circuit class* $\mathcal{C} = \{\mathcal{C}_\lambda = \{I_{m \to r} | m \in \{0,1\}^\lambda, r \in \{0,1\}^{poly(\lambda)}\}\}_{\lambda \in \mathbb{N}}$ *for unpredictable distribution under the assumption 3.1.*

Proof. From the construction 3.1,

$$\mathcal{MO}(I_{m \to r}) = (C_\lambda, (g_0, g_0^m), (g_1, g_1^{a_1}), ..., (g_t, g_t^{a_t})).$$

It is clear that $\mathcal{MO}(I_{m \to r})(x)$ always outputs $0^{|r|}$ when $x \neq m$, and it is negligible that there exists some u_i such that $u_i = m$, so

$$Pr[\mathcal{MO}(I_{m \to r})(m) \neq r] \leq negl(\lambda).$$

It is also clear that the polynomial slowdown property holds.

Now, suppose $\mathcal{D} = \{\mathcal{D}_\lambda = (Z_\lambda, M_\lambda, R_\lambda)\}_{\lambda \in \mathbb{N}}$ is any given unpredictable distribution, we need to prove that for any PPT algorithm $\mathcal{A}$

$$Pr_{(z,m,r) \leftarrow D_\lambda}[\mathcal{A}(1^\lambda, z, \mathcal{MO}(I_{m \to r})) = m] \leq negl(\lambda)$$

From assumption 3.1 we know that the distribution

$$\mathcal{D}' = \{(z' = (z, g, g^m), m, r) : (z, m, r) \leftarrow D_\lambda, g \leftarrow \mathbb{G}_\lambda^*\}_{\lambda \in \mathbb{N}}$$

is unpredictable, So is

$$\mathcal{D}^0 = \{\mathcal{D}_\lambda^0\}_{\lambda \in \mathbb{N}} = \{(z^0 = (z, C_\lambda, g_0, g_0^m), m, r) : (z, m, r) \leftarrow D_\lambda, g_0 \leftarrow \mathbb{G}_\lambda^*\}_{\lambda \in \mathbb{N}}$$

because C_λ is just the computation circuit in the construction of $\mathcal{MO}$.

Now, let's define the distribution $\mathcal{D}^1$ as follows:

$$\mathcal{D}^1 = \{(z^1 = (z, C_\lambda, g_0, g_0^m, g_1, g_1^{a_1}), m, r) : (z, m, r) \leftarrow D_\lambda, g_0, g_1 \leftarrow \mathbb{G}_\lambda^*\}_{\lambda \in \mathbb{N}}$$
$$= \{((z^0, g_1, g_1^{a_1}), m, r) : (z^0, m, r) \leftarrow D_\lambda^0, g_1 \leftarrow \mathbb{G}_\lambda^*\}_{\lambda \in \mathbb{N}},$$

where $a_1 = m$ if $r_1 = 1$ and u_1 otherwise, where u_1 is uniformly sampled from $\{0, 1\}^\lambda$.

If $r_1 = 1$ with probability 1, then $a_1 = m$, by the assumption 3.1, $\mathcal{D}^1$ is unpredictable because $\mathcal{D}^0$ is unpredictable. Otherwise if $r_1 = 0$ and $a_1 = u_1$ for a uniformly random u_1 in $\{0, 1\}^\lambda$ with probability 1, $\mathcal{D}^1$ is also unpredictable because u_1 is unrelated to m. So $\mathcal{D}^1$ is always unpredictable no matter what is the value of $Pr_{(z,m,r) \leftarrow D_\lambda}[r_1 = 1]$.

Similarly, $\mathcal{D}^t$ is also unpredictable for $t = poly(\lambda)$, where

$$\mathcal{D}^t = \{(z^t = (z, C_\lambda, g_0, g_0^m, g_1, g_1^{a_1}, ..., g_t, g_t^{a_t}), m, r) : (z, m, r) \leftarrow D_\lambda, g_0, ..., g_t \leftarrow \mathbb{G}_\lambda^*\}_{\lambda \in \mathbb{N}},$$

for each $i \in [t]$, $a_i = m$ when $r_i = 1$ and u_i otherwise, where each u_i is uniformly and independently sampled from $\{0, 1\}^\lambda$.

That is $\{((z, \mathcal{MO}(I_{m \to r})), m, r) : (z, m, r) \leftarrow D_\lambda, g_0, ..., g_t \leftarrow \mathbb{G}_\lambda^*\}_{\lambda \in \mathbb{N}}$ is unpredictable. The secrecy requirement of $\mathcal{MO}$ follows.□

4   Witness Encryption with Unique Decryption

In this section we propose the concept and give a construction for witness encryption with unique decryption for **NP** which is the key tool when we construct our one-round WI in the next section.

Witness Encryption for **NP** was introduced by Garg et al. [13] recently. A witness encryption scheme is defined for an **NP** language L (with corresponding witness relation R_L). In such a scheme, a user can encrypt a message M to a particular problem instance x (which acts as encryption key) to produce a ciphertext. A recipient of such ciphertext is able to decrypt the message if x is in the language and the recipient knows a witness w (the decryption key) of x (i.e. $(x, w) \in R_L$). However, if x is not in the language, no polynomial-time attacker can distinguish between encryptions of any two messages of equal length. The encrypter himself may have no idea whether x is actually in the language.

In our setting, we need a stronger witness encryption scheme which is a witness encryption scheme and have the following additional property: the decryption of a (possibly invalid) ciphertext is unique no matter which decryption key w is used in the decryption algorithm. We call such scheme as witness encryption scheme with unique decryption.

Definition 6 (witness encryption scheme (with unique decryption)). *A witness encryption scheme for an **NP** language L (with corresponding witness relation R_L) consists of the following two polynomial-time algorithms:*

- **Encryption.** *The algorithm $Encrypt(1^\lambda, x, m)$ take as input a security parameter 1^λ, a string x, and a message $m \in \mathcal{M}$ for some message space $\mathcal{M}$, and outputs a ciphertext CT.*
- **Decryption.** *The algorithm $Decrypt(1^\lambda, CT, w)$ takes as inputs a ciphertext CT and a string w, and outputs m' or the symbol $\perp$.*

The algorithms satisfy the following two conditions:

- **Correctness.** *For any security parameter λ, for any $m \in \mathcal{M}$, and for any x and w such that $(x, w) \in R_L$, we have that*

$$Pr[Decrypt(1^\lambda, Encrypt(1^\lambda, x, m), w) \neq m] \leq negl(\lambda).$$

- **Soundness Security.** *For any $x \notin L$, any PPT adversary $\mathcal{A}$ and any messages $m_0, m_1 \in \mathcal{M}$ with equal length:*

$$|Pr[\mathcal{A}(Encrypt(1^\lambda, x, m_0)) = 1] - Pr[\mathcal{A}(Encrypt(1^\lambda, x, m_1)) = 1]| \leq negl(\lambda).$$

We say that witness encryption scheme has unique decryption if it has additional property: if w_1, w_2 satisfies $(x, w_1), (x, w_2) \in R_L$, then for any (possibly invalid) ciphertext CT, $Decrypt(1^\lambda, CT, w_1) = Decrypt(1^\lambda, CT, w_2)$.

From the definition of witness encryption scheme, the encryption algorithm is polynomial-time, so when the security parameter is λ, the length of encryption key x and the message m must be polynomial in λ. In our setting, we restrict the message space to $\mathcal{M}_\lambda = \{0, 1\}^\lambda$ and $|x| = \lambda$ when the security parameter is λ.

In what follows, due to the clearness of the randomness in the encryption algorithm, we denote this algorithm as $Encrypt(1^\lambda, x, \cdot; \cdot)$ instead of $Encrypt(1^\lambda, x, \cdot)$.

4.1   The Witness Encryption Scheme of Garg et al.

Garg et al. [12] gave a construction of witness encryption scheme for all language in **NP** based on $i\mathcal{O}$. Now, let's recall their construction. Let L be an **NP** language with corresponding relation R_L.

Construction 4.1: *Witness encryption scheme (Encrypt$(1^\lambda, x, \cdot; \cdot)$, Decrypt $(1^\lambda, \cdot, w)$) for **NP** language L (with corresponding relation R_L) of Garg et al. [12].*

Encrypt$(1^\lambda, x, \cdot; \cdot)$: On input a message m of length λ, it constructs a circuit $F_{x,m}$ with functionality $F_{x,m}(w) = \begin{cases} m, & \text{if } (x, w) \in R_L \text{ ;} \\ \bot, & \text{otherwise.} \end{cases}$ Then it samples $r \in_R \{0,1\}^{poly(\lambda)}$ and computes $i\mathcal{O}(F_{x,m}(\cdot); r)$, where $i\mathcal{O}$ is an indistinguishable obfuscator of the encryption circuit class $\mathcal{E} = \{\mathcal{E}_\lambda\}$, $\mathcal{E}_\lambda$ consists of the circuits $F_{x,m}$ with $|x| = |m| = \lambda$, r is the randomness of the encryption algorithm that is used in $i\mathcal{O}$. At last, it returns $CT = Encrypt(1^\lambda, x, m; r) = i\mathcal{O}(F_{x,m}(\cdot); r)$.

Decrypt$(1^\lambda, \cdot, w)$: On input a ciphertext CT, it runs CT on w and returns $m = CT(w)$.

Assume there exists general-purpose indistinguishability obfuscator, the witness encryption scheme in construction 4.1 is well-defined.

The correctness of the scheme is obvious. Now suppose that $x \notin L$ with $|x| = \lambda$, and m_0, m_1 are strings in $\{0,1\}^\lambda$, then $F_{x,m_0}(\cdot)$ and $F_{x,m_1}(\cdot)$ are constant functions that always output $\bot$, which means $F_{x,m_0}(\cdot)$ and $F_{x,m_1}(\cdot)$ have the same functionality, thus the ciphertext $i\mathcal{O}(F_{x,m_0}(\cdot))$ and $i\mathcal{O}(F_{x,m_1}(\cdot))$ are computationally indistinguishable and the soundness security follows.

4.2   Construction of Witness Encryption Scheme with Unique Decryption

When the decryption keys vary, the decryption of an invalid ciphertext may vary. Let's take a look at the witness encryption scheme in section 4.1, the decryption procedure is just running the ciphertext on decryption key w. If an invalid ciphetext CT^* has functionality $CT^*(t) = t$ for any input t, the decryption of CT^* is w when the decryption key is w.

In our setting, we want to construct a one-round witness indistinguishable protocol. The only message exchanged is the obfuscated decryption algorithm T_w (with w hardwired into it) which is sent by the prover to the verifier. On input the verifier's ciphertext, the decryption algorithm returns the decryption of the ciphertext. If the ciphertext is designed such that the decryption is different when the decryption keys are different, the protocol cannot be witness indistinguishable. In order to avoid such situation, we need the encryption scheme to have unique decryption. Fortunately, such scheme is not hard to get given any witness encryption scheme.

In our construction of witness encryption scheme with unique decryption, we need to invoke a witness encryption scheme $(Encrypt(1^\lambda, x, \cdot), Decrypt(1^\lambda, \cdot, w))$ for **NP** language L (with corresponding relation R_L) and a weak auxiliary input multi-bit output point obfuscator $\mathcal{MO}$ for unpredictable distribution which is given in construction 3.1. Assume that the length of the random string used in the encryption algorithm $Encrypt(1^\lambda, x, \cdot; \cdot)$ is $poly(\lambda)$, we denote our witness encryption scheme with unique decryption as $(Enc(1^\lambda, x, \cdot), Dec(1^\lambda, \cdot, w))$. The message space is $\mathcal{M}_\lambda = \{0,1\}^\lambda$ when the security parameter is λ.

Construction 4.2: *Witness encryption scheme with unique decryption $(Enc(1^\lambda, x, \cdot; \cdot), Dec(1^\lambda, \cdot, w))$ for **NP** language L (with corresponding relation R_L):*

$Enc(1^\lambda, x, \cdot)$: *On input a message $m \in \{0,1\}^\lambda$, the algorithm samples a random $r \in \{0,1\}^{poly(\lambda)}$ and invokes the algorithm $Encrypt(1^\lambda, x, \cdot; \cdot)$ to compute $C = Encrypt(1^\lambda, x, m; r)$, then it computes $MO = \mathcal{MO}(I_{m \to r})$. At last, it returns $CT = (C, MO)$.*

$Dec(1^\lambda, \cdot, w)$: *On input a ciphertext $CT = (C, MO)$, if CT is not well formed, the algorithm returns $\perp$; otherwise it invokes the algorithm $Decrypt(1^\lambda, \cdot, w)$ to compute $m = Decrypt(1^\lambda, C, w)$, if $m = \perp$ it returns $\perp$; otherwise, it computes $r = MO(m)$, if $r = \perp$ or $C \neq Encrypt(1^\lambda, x, m; r)$, it returns $\perp$, otherwise it returns m.*

Theorem 4. *Under the assumption 3.1, $(Enc(1^\lambda, x, \cdot), Dec(1^\lambda, \cdot, w))$ in construction 4.2 is a witness encryption scheme with unique decryption for **NP** language L (with corresponding relation R_L) if $(Encrypt(1^\lambda, x, \cdot; \cdot), Decrypt(1^\lambda, \cdot, w))$ is a witness encryption scheme for the same **NP** language L (with the same corresponding relation R_L).*

Proof. Firstly, Assumption 3.1 guarantees the validity of the weak auxiliary input multi-bit output point obfuscator $\mathcal{MO}$ for unpredictable distribution and by the construction of algorithms $Enc(1^\lambda, x, \cdot)$ and $Dec(1^\lambda, \cdot, w)$, they are both polynomial-time.

Secondly, suppose $(x, w) \in R_L$ and $|x| = |m| = \lambda$. Let $CT = (C, MO)$ with $C = Encrypt(1^\lambda, x, m; r)$ and $MO = \mathcal{MO}(I_{m \to r})$. On input $CT = (C, MO)$, $Dec(1^\lambda, \cdot, w)$ firstly invokes the algorithm $Decrypt(1^\lambda, \cdot, w)$ and computes $m' = Decrypt(1^\lambda, C, w)$, by the correctness of $(Encrypt(1^\lambda, x, \cdot; \cdot), Decrypt(1^\lambda, \cdot, w))$, m' equals m with overwhelming probability. Then $Dec(1^\lambda, \cdot, w)$ runs MO on $m' = m$ and gets $r' = MO(m) = \mathcal{MO}(I_{m \to r})(m)$. By the functionality of the weak AI-MBPO, r' equals r with overwhelming probability. Thus, $Dec(1^\lambda, \cdot, w)$ returns m with overwhelming probability and the correctness of $(Enc(1^\lambda, x, \cdot), Dec(1^\lambda, \cdot, w))$ follows.

Thirdly, let $\mathcal{A}$ be a PPT algorithm. By the soundness security of the witness encryption scheme $(Encrypt(1^\lambda, x, \cdot; \cdot), Decrypt(1^\lambda, \cdot, w))$, the distribution

$$\tilde{\mathcal{D}} = \{\tilde{D}_x\}_{x \notin L} = \{(Encrypt(1^{|x|}, x, m; r), m, r) : m \leftarrow U_{|x|}, r \leftarrow U_{poly(|x|)}\}_{x \notin L}$$

is unpredictable. Here, the distribution $\tilde{D}$ is indexed by $x \notin L$ instead of $\lambda \in \mathbb{N}$ because here we only consider the case of $x \notin L$. That is if $x \notin L$,

$$Pr[\mathcal{A}(Encrypt(1^{|x|})) = m : (Encrypt(1^{|x|}, x, m; r), m, r) \leftarrow \tilde{D}_x] \leq negl(|x|).$$

Then from the secrecy property of the weak AI-MBPO $\mathcal{MO}$, the distribution

$$\{((Encrypt(1^{|x|}, x, m; r), \mathcal{MO}(I_{m \rightarrow r})), m, r) : m \leftarrow U_{|x|}, r \leftarrow U_{poly(|x|)}\}_{x \notin L}$$

is also unpredictable.

That is, for $x \notin L$ with length λ (recall that the lengths of the message m and the encryption key x are both λ when the security parameter is λ), we have

$$Pr[\mathcal{A}(Encrypt(1^{\lambda}, x, m; r), \mathcal{MO}(I_{m \rightarrow r})) = m] \leq negl(\lambda).$$

This inequality is equivalent to the form defined in soundness security of $(Enc(1^{\lambda}, x, \cdot), Dec(1^{\lambda}, \cdot, w))$.

At last, suppose that $(x, w), (x, w') \in R_L$ and $CT^* = (C^*, MO^*)$ is a (possible invalid) ciphertext, then by the construction of $(Enc(1^{\lambda}, x, \cdot), Dec(1^{\lambda}, \cdot, w))$, on input $CT^* = (C^*, MO^*)$, either both $Dec(1^{\lambda}, CT^*, w)$ and $Dec(1^{\lambda}, CT^*, w')$ are $\perp$, or one of them is m. In the second case, without loss of generality, suppose $Dec(1^{\lambda}, CT^*, w) = m$, then there must exists r such that

$$C^* = Encrypt(1^{\lambda}, x, m; r) \text{ and } r = MO^*(m).$$

By the correctness property of $(Encrypt(1^{\lambda}, x, \cdot; \cdot), Decrypt(1^{\lambda}, \cdot, w)), Decrypt(1^{\lambda}, C^*, w')$ also equals to m and $r = MO^*(m)$. So $Dec(1^{\lambda}, CT^*, w') = m$. □

Remark. The technique we use in construction 4.2 can be generalized to transform a semantic secure encryption scheme $(Encrypt(\cdot), Decrypt(\cdot))$ to a semantic secure encryption scheme $(Enc(\cdot), Dec(\cdot))$ that has verification functionality. That is, the ciphertext $CT = (C, MO)$ of the encryption scheme $(Enc(\cdot), Dec(\cdot))$ contains also a weak AI-MBPO MO in addition to an encryption C of a message m. The decryption algorithm returns the decryption only when CT passes the verification: CT is well-formed, $Decrypt(C) = m$ lies in the message space, $MO(m) = r$ is a polynomial long string and C is really equal to $Encrypt_K(m; r)$.

5   One-Round Witness Indistinguishable from Indistinguishability Obfuscation

Witness indistinguishability means that the prover proves the validity of a statement with some witness, but the verifier cannot distinguish which witness the prover uses. Indistinguishability obfuscator of a circuit class is a program that takes as input a circuit $C \in \mathcal{C}_{\lambda}$ of a circuit class $\mathcal{C} = \{\mathcal{C}_{\lambda}\}$ such that when the input circuits have the same functionality, it is hard to distinguish which input $i\mathcal{O}$ has taken. The same meaning of indistinguishability in the two concepts motivates us to explore the relation between "witness indistinguishability" and "indistinguishability obfuscation". In this section we build up the relation between WI and $i\mathcal{O}$ by constructing a one-round witness indistinguishable argument system for **NP** based on the existence assumption of $i\mathcal{O}$.

In the following one-round witness indistinguishable protocol for **NP** language L, the main cryptographic tools we use are witness encryption scheme with unique decryption $(Enc(1^\lambda, x, \cdot), Dec(1^\lambda, \cdot, w))$ for L (with the corresponding witness relation R_L) which is constructed in section 4 and a indistinguishability obfuscator $i\mathcal{O}$ for the decryption circuit class $\mathcal{D} = \{\mathcal{D}_\lambda\}$, where $\mathcal{D}_\lambda$ consists of circuits $D_{x,w}$ with the functionality $D_{x,w}(\cdot) = Dec(1^\lambda, \cdot, w)$. The completeness and soundness properties of our one-round WI are from the correctness and soundness security of $(Enc(1^\lambda, x, \cdot), Dec(1^\lambda, \cdot, w))$ respectively. The WI is from the unique decryption property of our witness encryption scheme $(Enc(1^\lambda, x, \cdot), Dec(1^\lambda, \cdot, w))$ and the indistinguishability property of $i\mathcal{O}$. The assumptions we need are the existence of indistinguishability obfuscator for general circuit class and the number-theoretic assumption 3.1.

Now, we present our one-round witness indistinguishable protocol.

One-Round WI Proof for $L \in$ NP. On common input $x \in \{0,1\}^\lambda$ and auxiliary input w for the prover, such that $(x, w) \in R_L$, do the following.

Prover's Message
1. Construct the circuit $D_{x,w}(\cdot)$ with the functionality $D_{x,w}(\cdot) = Dec(1^\lambda, \cdot, w)$.
2. Compile the circuit $D_{x,w}$ by the indistinguishability obfuscator $i\mathcal{O}$ of $\{\mathcal{D}_\lambda\}$ and get
   $$T_w = i\mathcal{O}(D_{x,w}).$$
3. Send to the verifier T_w.

Verifier's Test
1. Choose randomly the strings $m \in \{0,1\}^\lambda$, and compute $CT = Enc(1^\lambda, x, m)$.
2. Feed CT to T_w and get the output $T_w(CT)$. Accept if $T_w(CT) = m$ and reject otherwise.

Theorem 5. *The above protocol is a one-round witness indistinguishable argument system for all languages in **NP** under the assumption 3.1 and the existence assumption of indistinguishability obfuscator for general circuit class.*

Proof. The existence assumption of indistinguishability obfuscator for general circuit class implies the existence of indistinguishability obfuscator $i\mathcal{O}$ of the decryption circuit class $\mathcal{D} = \{\mathcal{D}_\lambda\}$ and the existence of witness encryption scheme. The existence of witness encryption scheme together with the assumption 3.1 means the existence of witness encryption scheme with unique decryption $(Enc(1^\lambda, x, \cdot), Dec(1^\lambda, \cdot, w))$.

In what follows, we need to prove that the protocol is (1) complete, (2) sound, and (3) witness indistinguishable.

Firstly, if the prover and the verifier are both honest, by the correctness of the scheme $(Enc(1^\lambda, x, \cdot), Dec(1^\lambda, \cdot, w))$ and the functionality of $i\mathcal{O}$, for any ciphertext $CT = Enc(1^\lambda, x, m)$, the verifier can get the exact decryption of CT with overwhelming probability. Thus the protocol is complete.

Secondly, assume $x \notin L$ with length λ and T^* is the message exchanged, because T^* is constructed by the polynomial-time sender, it is also a polynomial-time algorithm. By the soundness security of the witness encryption scheme with unique decryption $(Enc(1^\lambda, x, \cdot), Dec(1^\lambda, \cdot, w))$, for random strings $m \in \{0,1\}^\lambda$, $T^*(Enc(1^\lambda, x, m))$ returns m with only negligible probability. The soundness follows.

The witness indistinguishability is direct from the unique decryption property of the witness encryption scheme $(Enc(1^\lambda, x, \cdot), Dec(1^\lambda, \cdot, w))$ and the indistinguishability of iO.   ☐

Concluding Remarks. The main aim of this work is to build up the relationship between indistinguishability obfuscation and witness indistinguishability. Indeed, we construct a one-round witness indistinguishable argument system based on the existence assumption of indistinguishability obfuscation for general circuit class and a number-theoretic assumption.

The construction of our one-round WI protocol is different from that of Barak et al. [3] and that of Groth et al. [17] in that our results are based on different assumptions. Barak et al. [3] obtained their one-round WI by derandomizing the Zap of Dwork et al. [10] and the assumption needed is that trapdoor permutations and an efficient 1/2-HSG against co-nondeterministic exist where HSG is hitting set generator. The construction of one-round WI of Groth et al. [17] is based on a specific assumption on bilinear groups, that is, Decisional Linear Assumption.

References

1. Barak, B., Goldreich, O., Impagliazzo, R., Rudich, S., Sahai, A., Vadhan, S.P., Yang, K.: On the (Im)possibility of Obfuscating Programs. In: Kilian, J. (ed.) CRYPTO 2001. LNCS, vol. 2139, pp. 1–18. Springer, Heidelberg (2001)
2. Barak, B., Goldreich, O., Impagliazzo, R., Rudich, S., Sahai, A., Vadhan, S.P., Yang, K.: On the (im)possibility of obfuscating programs. J.ACM 59(2), 6 (2012)
3. Barak, B., Ong, S.J., Vadhan, S.: Derandomization in Cryptography. In: Boneh, D. (ed.) CRYPTO 2003. LNCS, vol. 2729, pp. 299–315. Springer, Heidelberg (2003)
4. Bitansky, N., Canetti, R.: On strong simulation and composable point obfuscation. In: Rabin, T. (ed.) CRYPTO 2010. LNCS, vol. 6223, pp. 520–537. Springer, Heidelberg (2010)
5. Bitansky, N., Canetti, R., Paneth, O., Rosen, A.: More on the impossibility of VBB obfuscation with auxiliary input. IACR Cryptology ePrint Archive, 2013:701 (2013)
6. Bitansky, N., Paneth, O.: Point obfuscation and 3-round zero-knowledge. In: Cramer, R. (ed.) TCC 2012. LNCS, vol. 7194, pp. 190–208. Springer, Heidelberg (2012)
7. Brzuska, C., Mittelbach, A.: Indistinguishability obfuscation versus point obfuscation with auxiliary input. IACR Cryptology ePrint Archive, 2014:405 (2014)

8. Canetti, R.: Towards realizing random oracles: Hash functions that hide all partial information. In: Kaliski Jr., B.S. (ed.) CRYPTO 1997. LNCS, vol. 1294, pp. 455–469. Springer, Heidelberg (1997)
9. Canetti, R., Dakdouk, R.R.: Obfuscating point functions with multibit output. In: Smart, N.P. (ed.) EUROCRYPT 2008. LNCS, vol. 4965, pp. 489–508. Springer, Heidelberg (2008)
10. Dwork, C., Naor, M.: Zaps and their applications. In: proceedings of the 41th Annual Symposium on Foundations of Computer Science, pp. 283–293. ACM (2000)
11. Feige, U., Shamir, A.: Witness Indistinguishable and Witness Hiding Protocols. In: Proc. 22nd ACM Symposium on the Theory of Computing, pp. 416–426 (1990)
12. Garg, S., Gentry, C., Halevi, S., Raykova, M., Sahai, A., Waters, B.: Candidate indistinguishability obfuscation and functional encryption for all circuits. In: FOCS, pp. 40–49 (2013)
13. Garg, S., Gentry, C., Sahai, A., Waters, B.: Witness encryption and its applications. In: STOC, pp. 467–476 (2013)
14. Goldreich, O., Oren, Y.: Definitions and properties of zero-knowledge proof systems. Journal of Cryptology 7(1), 1–32 (1994)
15. Goldwasser, S., Kalai, Y.T.: On the impossibility of obfuscation with auxiliary input. In: FOCS, pp. 553–562 (2005)
16. Goldwasser, S., Kalai, Y.T.: A Note on the Impossibility of Obfuscation with Auxiliary Inputs. IACR Cryptology ePrint Archive, 2013:665 (2013)
17. Groth, J., Ostrovsky, R., Sahai, A.: New techniques for noninteractive zero-knowledge. J.ACM 59(3), 11 (2012)
18. Goldwasser, S., Micali, S., Rackoff, C.: The knowledge complexity of interactive proof systems. SIAM Journal on Computing 18(16), 186–208 (1989)
19. Goldreich, O., Micali, S., Wigderson, A.: Proofs that yield nothing but their validity or all languages in NP have zero-knowledge proof systems. J. of the ACM 38(3), 691–729 (1991)
20. Goldwasser, S., Rothblum, G.N.: On best-possible obfuscation. In: Vadhan, S.P. (ed.) TCC 2007. LNCS, vol. 4392, pp. 194–213. Springer, Heidelberg (2007)
21. Hofheinz, D., Malone-Lee, J., Stam, M.: Obfuscation for cryptographic purposes. In: Vadhan, S.P. (ed.) TCC 2007. LNCS, vol. 4392, pp. 214–232. Springer, Heidelberg (2007)
22. Hohenberger, S., Rothblum, G.N., Shelat, A., Vaikuntanathan, V.: Securely obfuscating re-encryption. In: Vadhan, S.P. (ed.) TCC 2007. LNCS, vol. 4392, pp. 233–252. Springer, Heidelberg (2007)
23. Matsuda, T., Hanaoka, G.: Chosen ciphertext security via point obfuscation. In: Lindell, Y. (ed.) TCC 2014. LNCS, vol. 8349, pp. 95–120. Springer, Heidelberg (2014)
24. Wee, H.: On obfuscating point functions. In: STOC, pp. 523–532 (2005)

Author Index

Printed in the United States
By Bookmasters